Enhanced Photoshop 4

David Xenakis
Sherry London

VENTANA

Enhanced Photoshop 4

Library of Congress Cataloging-in-Publication Data

London, Sherry.

Enhanced Photoshop 4 / Sherry London and David Xenakis. – 1st ed.

p. cm.

Includes index.

ISBN 1-56604-692-0

1. Computer graphics. 2. Adobe Photoshop. I. Xenakis, David. II. Title

T385.L648 1997

006.6'869—dc21 97-30087

CIP

First Edition 9 8 7 6 5 4 3 2 1

Printed in the United States of America

Ventana Communications Group

P.O. Box 13964

Research Triangle Park, NC 27709-3964

919.544.9404

FAX 919.544.9472

http://www.vmedia.com

Ventana Communications Group is a division of International Thomson Publishing.

Limits of Liability & Disclaimer of Warranty

Trademarks

President
Michael E. Moran

Associate Publisher
Robert Kern

Editorial Operations Manager
Kerry L. B. Foster

Production Manager
Jaimie Livingston

Brand Manager
Jamie Jaeger Fiocco

Art Director
Marcia Webb

Creative Services Manager
Diane Lennox

Outstanding Performance Employee for September 1997
R. Allen Wyke,
Multimedia Manager

Acquisitions Editor
Christopher D. Grams

Project Editor
Ellen Fussell

Development Editor
Martin V. Minner

Copy Editor
Suzanne Rose

CD-ROM Specialist
Shadrack Frazier

Technical Reviewers
Kate Binder
Mark Johnston

Desktop Publishers
Patrick Berry
Scott Hosa
Lance Kozlowski
Kristin Miller
Manny Rosa

Proofreader
Jessica Ryan

Indexer
Tim Griffin

Interior Designer
Patrick Berry

Cover Illustrator
Lisa Gill

About the Authors

David Xenakis is president of XRX, Inc., a corporation that produces *Knitters* magazine, *Weavers* magazine, Stitches Fair and Consumer Show, and operates Xenakis Design Services (specializing in corporate consulting, high-end color print preparation, and training for users of digital prepress systems). The publications of XRX, Inc. first used digital technology in 1987 with the purchase of Macintosh computers and then little-known software packages such as QuarkXPress and Adobe Illustrator. *Knitters* magazine was the first nationally distributed publication to be done entirely in QuarkXPress. With the advent of the second XRX, Inc. publication, *Knitters* magazine, David became the driving force which steered the publications toward digital methods. With his experience in real-world situations, David was increasingly called upon as a consultant to companies making the transition to digital methods.

David is recognized as a superb teacher and communicator who is readily able to make the most sophisticated concepts accessible to everyone. He has conducted his two-day seminar *Navigating Photoshop* in 35 cities across the nation with great success and with critical acclaim. More recently, he has added to his seminar activities with two additional classes, *Navigating Illustrator* and *Preparing Graphics for the World Wide Web.*

Sherry London is an artist, a writer, and a teacher, which is exactly what a going-into-college aptitude test predicted. Sherry is the author of a number of books including *Photoshop 4.0: An Interactive Course, Photoshop Textures Magic, Painter 5 f/x* (with Rhoda Grossman and Sharron Evans), and *Photoshop 3.0 Special Effects How-To.* She teaches Photoshop and PrePress in the Continuing Education Department at Moore College of Art and Design in Philadelphia and has spoken at a number of conferences, including the Thunder Lizard Photoshop Conference and the Professional Photographers of America convention.

Sherry has worked as a social studies teacher, an instructional systems designer, a programmer, a fiber artist, and a graphic designer. She is the principal of London Computing: PhotoFX, a full-service design studio. She has designed needlework for the Philadelphia Museum of Art gift store and the Horchow catalog. Her fiber art has been exhibited in many group shows including shows at the Delaware Museum of Art, Ormond Memorial Art Museum, and the Brevard Art Center. She was a contributing editor for *Computer Artist* magazine and has written for *Pre, MacWeek, MacUser, Digital Vision*, and the combined *MacWorld/MacUser* magazine.

Acknowledgments

Despite the hours spent alone, looking at a computer screen, a book about a piece of software as large and as complex as Adobe's Photoshop is not written in a vacuum. I offer my gratitude to those who have helped me as I worked on this project.

My partners Elaine Rowley and Alexis Xenakis took away the pressure of other duties so that I could concentrate on the task.

My son Benjamin is a genius at running interference, and at helping with the thousands of small tasks that seem to get in the way of the work to be done.

My co-author Sherry London, who has proved to be a mine of esoteric knowledge as well as the possessor of one of the most interesting minds I've ever encountered, gave me the opportunity to collaborate on this book.

To the staff at Ventana Communications Group and other collaborators—Chris Grams, Martin V. Minner, Ellen Fussell, Kate Binder, Jaimie Livingston, Patrick Berry, Suzanne Rose, Jessica Ryan—I would like to say: I'll never be able to adequately thank you for the kindness, helpfulness, and encouraging words that have made this writer's first book a wonderful experience.

Finally, thanks to Samantha and Christopher whose innocent, blue-eyed smiles can charm me out of thinking about the intricacies of the Apply Image command!

—David Xenakis
Sioux Falls, South Dakota
September 15, 1997

I need to add a few additional notes of thanks.

Margot Malley, my agent, was instrumental in the birth of this book. It was she who introduced me to Chris Grams—one of the most capable acquisitions editors with whom I have worked.

I also want to thank the vendors who have contributed their products to this CD-ROM. You have helped to make the CD-ROM an even more useful part of the entire package, and you have enriched the Photoshop community with the creativity of your software.

Words are inadequate to thank my co-author, David Xenakis. His breadth of knowledge about Photoshop is astounding. Finding a kindred spirit has been an amazing experience.

Finally, I need to thank my husband, Norm, for putting up with the phone ringing every time we sat down to dinner, and for being willing to eat whatever managed to get put on the table (even if it was only take-out).

—Sherry London
Cherry Hill, New Jersey
September 15, 1997

Dedications

To Elaine and Alexis who have contributed nearly as much to this book as I have.

—David Xenakis

To my husband Norm—as always!

—Sherry London

Contents

Introduction

Hello!

We haven't met yet but perhaps we will become acquainted within the pages of this book.

You are probably a current user of Photoshop, or perhaps you would like to become one. (Otherwise, there would be little reason for you to have picked up this very heavy book to see whether this might be the one—out of all the competing titles—that you need.) Is this the book you need? We would like to think so. We have spent a good deal of time putting concepts and ideas into words and figures. But how we have spent our time isn't your problem: your problem is to decide if this book will give you the essentials of what you need to know about Enhanced Photoshop 4. Because of that, it falls on us to tell you what we've done, and what we've assumed that you will want in a book of this sort. After that, you can flip through the pages, look at the example illustrations, read some of the explanations, check to see what topics are included, and decide if we've done our job well enough to justify your investment and your time.

What's "Enhanced" About This Book?

We have written this volume for the advanced user of Photoshop—or for an intermediate-level user who would like to *become* a power user of this application. We assume that you are familiar with the program and that you need a book that shows you the range of possibilities inherent in expert use of Photoshop. While our explanations are clear, they do assume a prior general knowledge of the program. For this reason, we feel that we have written a book that enhances your knowledge of Photoshop and builds on your previous accomplishments. If you are at this level, you don't need a book that explains how to save a file. You already know that! By starting at a higher level, we can talk about the more critical and advanced skills. We've had fun writing this book; we hope you profit from reading it.

What's in the Book

This book is divided into twelve chapters. The order of the chapters is progressive. You'll learn the basics in the first few chapters, and then go on to explore increasingly advanced material. The following are short synopses of what you'll find in each of the chapters.

- Chapter 1, "Optimizing Photoshop." We begin with one of the most important topics, that of making the program perform at its best in your computer environment. You need to know about the important issues of RAM and drive space, environment settings, and the all-important Photoshop Preferences which make the program perform at its best. You'll learn to set up your system so that running Photoshop becomes a pleasure. System and configuration issues can then recede in importance as you concentrate on using the program.
- Chapter 2, "Acquiring Images." Since many people use Photoshop mainly as an editing program—where pre-existing data is manipulated and changed—rather than as a program in which new digital artwork is created, the next topic on your list of subjects to be mastered is that of acquiring images. You'll be introduced to the pixel—really introduced!—and will learn the basics of scanning. We'll take a thorough look at what scanning software can do to eliminate some of the tedious aspects of acquiring your picture files, and how you can arrive at the best quality your scanner can give you. You'll also learn how to clean up your scans, to remove dust, scratches, and other artifacts that interfere with the eventual use of the image. Finally, we'll take a close look at Photo CD and explain how you can make use of this inexpensive source of digital images.
- Chapter 3, "Toolbox Techniques." Perhaps you have already experimented with Photoshop's superb collection of tools. If you have, we think this chapter will open your eyes to possibilities that you might not have suspected. This chapter, one of the largest in the book, will show you each tool in action (except for the Pen tool which is so important that it merits a chapter of its own), look at all of the options associated with it, and suggest fast ways of choosing the tools and their options from the keyboard. This chapter also introduces a selection method called Quick Mask. You're going to love Quick Mask for the simple way it allows you to mask an image using both the Paint tools and the Selection tools. Two lovely photographs are furnished to give you an enjoyable, step-by-step look at some very different aspects of Quick Mask.
- Chapter 4, "Paths & the Pen Tool." This chapter is really the conclusion of Chapter 3 since its topic is the Pen tool (and the associated Paths palette). Having said that, this tool will carry you into areas of special effects that you'll find easy to master and thrilling as possibilities for your own work. We're also going to sidestep Photoshop temporarily—as we do in many places in this book—to take a look at Adobe Illustrator's handling of paths, and at how you can use these two amazing programs in tandem. As in Chapter 3, more practice files are provided so that you can get into doing useful things at once.

- Chapter 5, "Using Channels." You may have heard of the word *channel* connected with Photoshop and thought of it as a technical term. It certainly is technical, but it is far more than just a word. Channels, as you'll see in this chapter, are a way of displaying different kinds of information. Channels can be masks or selections, representations of color strength, an analog for transparency information, even a visual way of representing a way of controlling the effects of a command. Once you begin to understand channels, you'll have a behind-the-scenes look at some of Photoshop's most sophisticated inner mechanisms. Not only that, you'll have a foundation for some of Photoshop's most powerful editing functions. We'll show you how to use the channels that are native to all Photoshop files, make new channels, and produce other channels that are the result of adding two channels together or subtracting one or more from another. The process will sound complex, at first, but under your own hands, you'll find that it is effortless and a good deal less challenging than rocket science.
- Chapter 6, "Using Layers." Everyone who uses Photoshop is amazed by layers. These really are Photoshop's most wonderful gift to the world of digital art. They are powerful and flexible and so easy to use! Once you get past the surface delights of layers, you are going to find surprisingly interesting things that go beyond simply stacking up groups of pixels and playing with blends modes and changes in opacity. We'll show you how to use layer masks, clipping groups, and options that will allow you to make parts of your layer invisible based on its brightness or color or on the brightness or color of the pixels beneath it. This chapter includes a look at transformations of the pixels on a layer. You will learn how to subtly change the orientation of objects on a layer so that they seem to belong to the same reality as pixels on other layers. What else can we say about layers? If you like working in Photoshop—or think that you might—layers are just about the most fun you can have without laughing aloud.
- Chapter 7, "Calculations." This chapter deals with just two menu commands: Apply Image and Calculations. You've probably seen examples of the wild and wonderful photographic montages that are dominating the world of the graphic arts. If so, you've probably seen examples of images that flow together in ways that seem nearly impossible. High-level users of Photoshop make use of these two commands—as well as many other powerful Photoshop capabilities—to achieve such complex effects. To show you how these commands can be used in several situations, the Companion CD-ROM provides files on which you will apply our step-by-step instructions. Once you've been through the basics and have seen how many possibilities you have at your disposal, you'll be in good shape to strike out on your own. Who knows? In a few months, maybe it will be *your* awesome photo montage that is furnishing amazement to the world of the graphic arts.

- Chapter 8, "Filter Frolics." No Photoshop book is complete without a look at filters. You'll see examples in use as they are applied to a photograph of a beautiful cat named Marmalade. Our hero the cat, as you will see, survives his encounters with altered reality in fine style. He, of course, remembers that removing the effects of an applied filter is as simple as the Undo command.

- Chapter 9, "Photoshop Prepress." This is the first of two large-scale chapters that deal with the subject of Photoshop and prepress. If you need to prepare digital images for any kind of reproduction, we think you'll appreciate both of these chapters as they cover just about every topic that you'll need to know about. Chapter 9 begins with a short course on press conditions and what you need to know when you are processing files. We then provide precise information for preparing halftones and duotones so they appear clean, clear, and beautifully balanced when they come from the press. Next, you'll learn about preparing line art and handling spot color. This chapter includes, among other topics, how-to-do-it information for using touch and bump plates—additional inks to augment black and process-color printing—that you'll find difficult to locate anywhere else.
- Chapter 10, "Calibration & Color Reproduction." Here is the second of our comprehensive chapters on using Photoshop to prepare images for printing. This chapter tackles calibration, color management, and making color separations. What have you read about color management? Or calibration? Did much of what you've read seem as if it were being driven by marketing hype? We agree. Color management is simply a matter of understanding how what you see on the monitor relates to what you will get from the press. We employ a number of strategies to take away the mystery. If knowledge is power, then this chapter is going to make you a powerful producer of colored printing.
- Chapter 11, "Manipulating Images." In the two prepress chapters, you will have learned a good deal about editing your Photoshop files so that you end up with clear and pleasing images. Chapter 11 continues that process by showing you how to make corrections that can be revised as you go. This chapter also will show you how to use Photoshop's new layout features. We will get to show you some clever ways to position your image layers with great precision.
- Chapter 12, "Photoshop & the Web." Since Photoshop was first introduced by Adobe Systems, it has become the best-selling image-editing software in the world. It has been used for many purposes but none of such far-reaching importance as the preparation of photographic material for the World Wide Web. We bring you a comprehensive look at what you can do to make your images look good, and how you can make sure that your digital files move from server to client as fast as possible. You'll hear about file formats for the Web, how to deal with Web color, and even a bit about what's involved with HTML code. If you are involved in Web or multimedia development work, this chapter will serve you well.

The CD-ROM

What else about the book should you find interesting? The CD-ROM disk. Many books of this type come with CD-ROMs, and many announce that they contain a selection of high-quality stock photos. How does ours differ from others? Read the fine print accompanying most CD-ROM stock images and you'll see that most of them are actually small, low-resolution demos/samples from stock photo companies and that you can't actually *use* the images unless you pay a licensing fee. This book does not do that. The files that accompany this book—many of which are used as practice files—are good-looking, high-resolution images of a size that you can use for many purposes. They are absolutely royalty-free files. If you decide that you want to use any or all for a purpose of your own, go ahead and do it. Period. (If you come up with a good-looking photo presentation that uses one of this book's photos, we'd be happy to get an e-mail telling us where we might see it. It's a lot of fun for us to feel that we may have helped you in some small way!)

What else is on the CD-ROM? The usual stuff—demos, shareware, freeware. Check these things out. Some of the shareware and freeware filters are great! The demo software will give you a good idea whether the product is going to work in the way that you expect and for the purpose that you expect. What better way to evaluate an interesting software title than to try it at no cost?

Ventana's Online Community of Photoshop Professionals

Probably the most fun you'll have—beyond learning to use what is arguably the finest piece of microcomputer software ever published—is with Ventana's *Online Community of Photoshop Professionals*. The software is included on the Companion CD-ROM. With it you can:

- Chat in real time with other Photoshop users.
- Exchange information, ideas, and your own solutions on the bulletin board.
- Link to online updates and helpful resources.
- Participate in live discussions hosted by the authors.

For further information, read the following section, "Welcome to Ventana's Online Community of Photoshop Professionals."

Other Resources

Some other useful resources are available to you simply because you have purchased the book. E-mail addresses, for example. Make a note of these two: slondon@earthlink.com and xenakis.david@xrx-inc.com. If you have a problem with anything that you find in the book, let us know. You will *not* get an automated response promising that we'll get back to you within the next 6-8 weeks. You may have to wait a day or two (sometimes we're not home), but we will respond with reasonable promptness with whatever help we can give you.

How to Use This Book

The simplest thing for us to tell you is this: turn to page one and start reading. We know, this is a *software* book and hardly the sort of thing you'll want to read for entertainment. If this were a large paper on particle physics, or on the symbolism of ancient Norse religious figures, perhaps we would be a little more hesitant about telling you to just get started. But this is Photoshop we're talking about. You're already interested in Photoshop, so you might as well just jump in. You can easily follow what's going on, even at the beginning stages. Just don't try to read in bed: the thing's too heavy.

If you know the basics, go ahead and jump around. But be aware that we've built up a sequence where one idea leads to the next. If you get lost, try backing up a few pages—or maybe to the previous chapter—and then move forward from there.

We have used very few conventions in the book that distinguish between the two platforms—Windows and Macintosh—on which Photoshop is most commonly used. If a piece of information is relevant to one platform over the other, we usually make that clear. Where key commands are used, we provide the Macintosh command first followed by the Windows command. (For example: "...hold Command or Ctrl and press e." The Macintosh will always be the first modifier key listed, with the Windows modifier second.) Beyond these small cautions, you can read this material without worrying that you are in the midst of information that might not apply to your platform.

We recommend keeping the CD-ROM disk handy so that you can get at the practice files whenever you need them. As we mentioned above, nearly all of those files are high-resolution images. If you find that memory problems occur because of the sizes of the images, simply choose Image | Image Size, and change the resolution from 300 ppi down to 72–100 ppi. That should give you the same image but with far less data with which to saddle your machine's memory.

Above all, have fun with this book. If an interesting idea comes to you as you work with the practice files, take a break and pursue it. It might come to nothing, it might turn out to be wonderful. Either way, you'll have learned something useful. And we'll always be waiting, ready to continue whenever you return from your side exploration.

Welcome to the Ventana Photoshop Community

The Companion CD-ROM disk accompanying this book is your gateway to a valuable online resource called the Ventana Photoshop Community. We would like to welcome you as a member of this community. That's right, you are already a member. When you purchased this book, you also purchased entry into a unique online environment that will allow you to have close contact with hundreds of your fellow Photoshop users. We hope you will get involved and become an active member. Your contributions will begin the growth of a dynamic online community. So get busy! Share your Photoshop ideas and experiences, chat live with other members, offer your own solutions to Photoshop questions from other users, and contribute to live discussions hosted by Photoshop notables. Look for regular tips from Ventana's multimedia team and check our up-to-date calendar of Photoshop-related events. Web Chat? Forget it! Newsgroups? Too much spam! This community offers an accessible, unique alternative designed especially for the Photoshop user.

Insert the CD-ROM Disk Into Your Computer...

After connecting to the Internet, all you need to do is:

- Macintosh users: double-click the LAUNCHME icon from the desktop;
- Windows 95 or NT users: double-click the RUNME_32.EXE icon from your Windows Explorer window.

That's it. No configuration work, no hassles. Just double-click to get started.

When your application has loaded, you will be met with a screen similar to the one shown in Figure 1. This screen is divided into four parts. For first-time users, click on the *Preferences* button. Since this is your first appearance in the Community, you'll need to tell us a little about yourself and set up a Password.

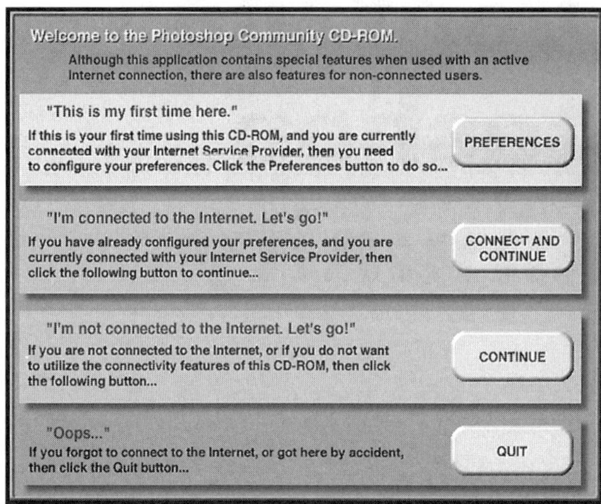

Figure 1: The Online Photoshop Community Welcome screen.

Don't worry about filling out a lengthy questionnaire—there are just a few simple questions (Figure 2). A few moments after the Registration screen in Figure 2 appears, a small dialog box will appear. It will ask you to assign for yourself a log-in name (your User Name) and a Password. Go ahead and enter a name that you would like to be called while you are active in this Community. It can be your real name, or it can be something fanciful such as *Photoshop Jock*. Enter what you wish to use as a Password—be sure to write your Password down so that you don't forget it when you want to log in again—and then type the Password again to confirm it. Now, proceed with the questionnaire. Once you're finished, you'll never have to repeat it. You are now a full-fledged member!

Once you've taken care of your registration, you can enter the Community directly from the Welcome screen by pressing the button *Connect & Continue*. After entering your Password, you'll be taken to the Main screen (Figure 3), from which you can connect to all of the Community's activities. You can even use some of the features of this CD-ROM without being connected to the Internet. When you click on the Continue button, you'll also be taken to the Main screen where you can click on any of the buttons except the top one.

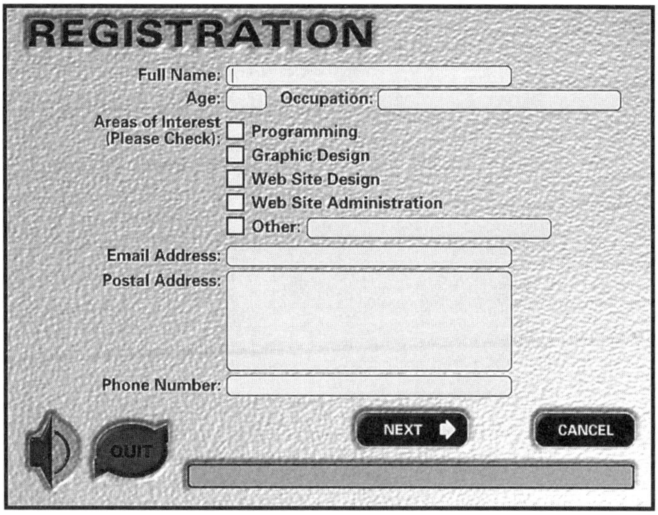

REGISTRATION

Full Name:

Age: Occupation:

Areas of Interest (Please Check):

- Programming
- Graphic Design
- Web Site Design
- Web Site Administration
- Other:

Email Address:

Postal Address:

Phone Number:

QUIT NEXT CANCEL

Figure 2: The Registration window.

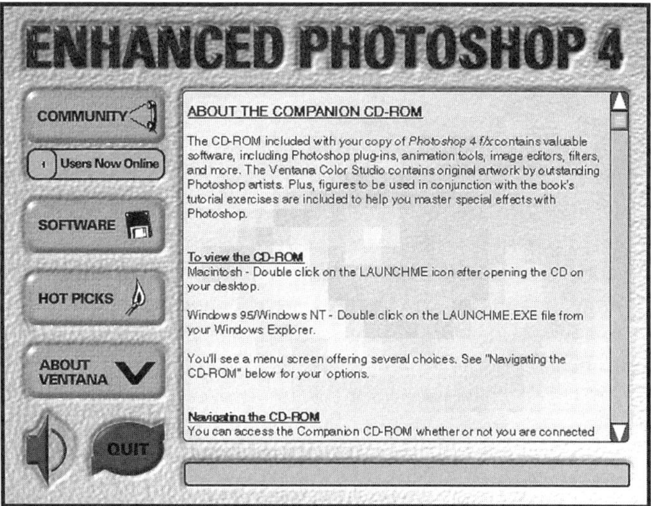

Figure 3: The Online Photoshop Community Main screen.

The Community

When you arrive at the Community's main window (Figure 4), you can steer yourself to any of the activities listed. Chat, Message Board, Events & Schedule.

Figure 4: The Community screen.

The Chat Room

Never visited a Chat room before? Take a look at Figure 5. When you join the Chat room, an ongoing discussion of the members, your user name will appear in the *Who's Here* list along with the names of everyone else present. You can jump right into the discussion, or linger and get an idea about what's being discussed. When it's time for you to join in, just type your words in the small entry field above the *Back* button. Click on the *Send* button, and your type will appear as part of the larger text field where the dialog is taking place. Got a private comment for a colleague you know is present? Just type your message, click on the *Whisper to* button, and direct your words only to your friend.

The Message Board

The Message Board (Figure 6) has a much different feel than the Chat Room. First, you need not be present to interact with the other members. Second, you can make your message as long as you wish. Finally, the Message Board has several boards from which to choose—*Effects, Plug-Ins,* & *General Photoshop*. That allows you to concentrate on the area of Photoshop that you enjoy the most, and to share your knowledge and experiences with other members who have similar interests.

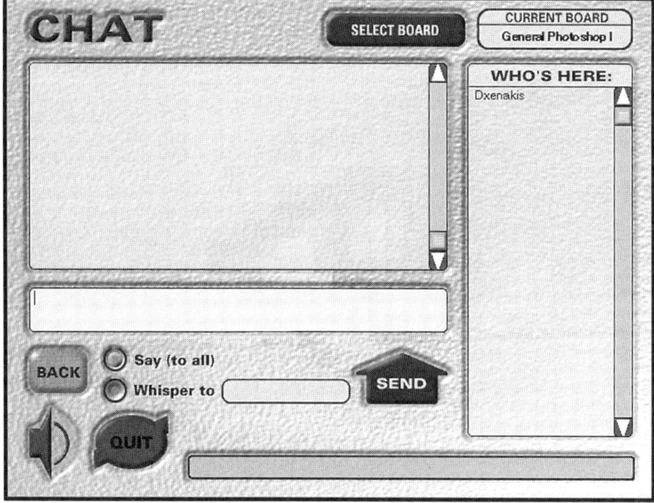

Figure 5: The Chat Room screen.

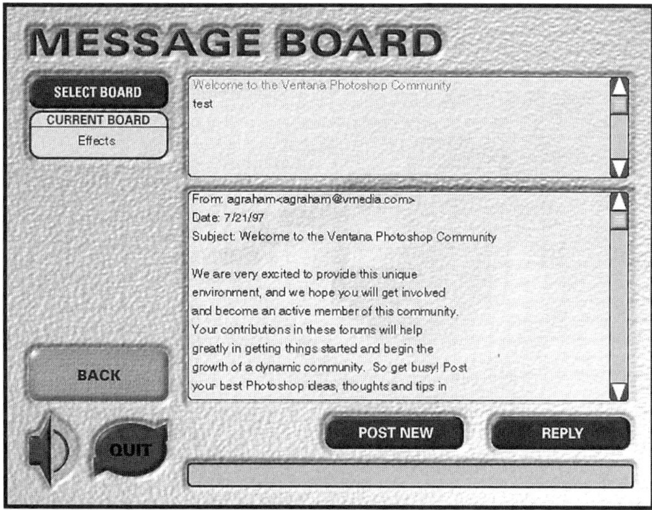

Figure 6: The Message Board screen.

Events & Schedule

Don't forget to check out the *Events & Schedule* area to find out what's going on in the world of Photoshop. This is the place to find out when famous Photoshop users—writers, lecturers, teachers, artists—will visit the Community for an informal conversation. This is your opportunity to ask questions from high-voltage people who can give you a definitive answer. This is also the area where Ventana's Photoshop authors will post their schedules for attendance. If you've found something in one of Ventana's Photoshop books that's giving you some puzzling moments, what better way to resolve the problem than by directly questioning the author?

Software

The second button on the Main screen is *Software* (Figure 7). Even if you decide not to join in the online activities, you can still go to the software area and try out one of the products listed. All of the listed items are demonstration packages. In other words, you can install them onto your system and try them out. If you decide that you want to keep them, you can purchase them from the publishers. Otherwise, you'll have had the benefit of knowing how they work and whether they will suit what you do with Photoshop.

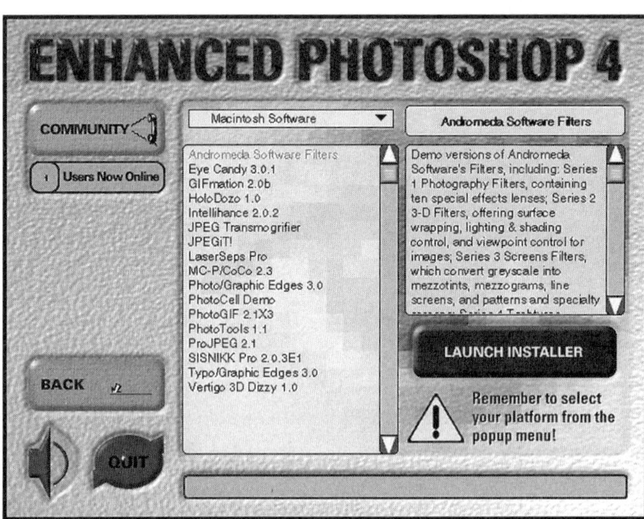

Figure 7: The Software screen.

Hot Picks

Hot Picks is the third Main screen button (Figure 8). Here you can take a look at what's available among the newest of Ventana's Photoshop titles. Besides *Enhanced Photoshop 4*, there are other terrific Photoshop books that you might enjoy owning. Visiting Hot Picks is not like visiting a bookstore, but it will give you some good ideas. You can even print an Order Form from Hot Picks—very useful for leaving casually around along with a lot of broad hints about birthday and holiday presents.

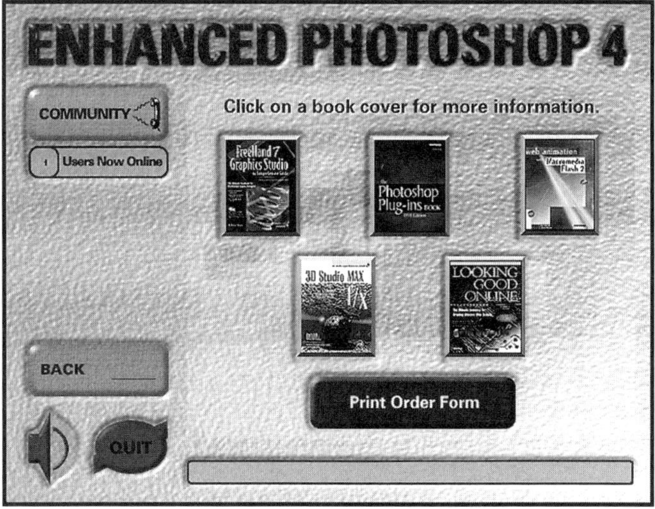

Figure 8: Hot Picks, a screen with Ventana's newest Photoshop titles.

About Ventana

Curious about Ventana Communications Group? Here is the screen (Figure 9) that appears when you press the last button on the Main screen.

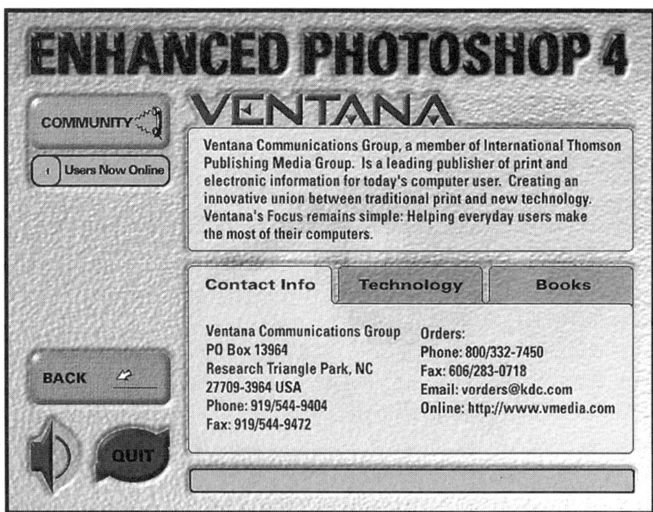

Figure 9: About Ventana.

See You There!

We hope you'll give your community software a try. There are other Photoshop forums available to you, but very few of them are this focused or exclusive. When you've stopped in, why not pause at the Main menu on your way and send us a message—click on the *Feedback* button—telling us how you like the Online Community and ways we can make it better.

chapter 1

Optimizing Photoshop

If you are going to work with Photoshop, it always helps to have the right equipment and the right configuration. Photoshop is the most powerful raster graphics program available on Macintosh or Windows, but it can also be ornery and recalcitrant if you do not know how to set it up correctly. It is also the program that stresses your computer more than almost any other application.

Photoshop is like the canary in the coal mine (a canary is very sensitive to atmospheric changes and to gases that are undetectable to most humans; they were used—at least in tales—as an early warning system for miners). If there is a problem in your system configuration or in your hardware, Photoshop is more likely to find it before you notice it on any other program.

In this chapter, you will learn about setting up preferences, configuring your system, troubleshooting, and working faster with Actions—a new feature in Photoshop 4.0.

Windows or Mac?

One of the most common questions asked about Photoshop performance is whether it is better on a Macintosh or Intel machine. While this is a simple question, there is really not a simple answer—unless you are happy to accept "it doesn't matter" as an answer.

The program is identical in function on both platforms. The interface—except for some preferences and the physical appearance of the windows—is also identical. If you are looking for raw speed, the 604 chip in the Mac usually slightly surpasses the Pentium chip, but that is not the entire story.

The raw performance that you see in test suites is not always indicative of the performance that you will see when you work at *your* normal tasks. There are many other factors that are involved as well—file size, the specific operation being performed, your disk speed, the amount of RAM, your hardware drivers, the operating system version, and sometimes, it seems, the phase of the moon!

If you are thinking of changing platforms, try out the competing system carefully. Your final decision needs to be based on two things—cost and feel. Either platform can produce exceptional speed, and if one platform is ahead now, the other will soon catch up. Therefore, you need to select the system that feels "best" to you at the cost that you are able to spend. There is a difference in the physical sensation of working on Mac or Windows that makes you enjoy one platform over the other. It can be very subtle—sometimes the issue of menus staying down or flying back up on their own is the only thing that makes someone prefer Mac or Windows.

There are more options for third-party filters on the Mac, but this gap is narrowing more every day. All of the major filter manufacturers such as Extensis, MetaCreations, and Alien Skin have versions for both platforms.

Color management software and controls are not as readily available on Windows as of yet, and Microsoft does not have an embedded color management system such as Color Sync for the Mac. If that is vital to you, then you need to look carefully at your options before switching platforms.

Except for these issues, however, you can be quite happy on either platform. If you work with a top-notch service bureau, either platform can produce excellent output.

Built for Speed

Production users of Photoshop are on a constant search for speed. In this section, we will look at some of the things that you can do to speed up Photoshop's performance. Some of them are easy—and others (also easy) only require large infusions of cash.

Photoshop & RAM

There was a line attributed to the Duchess of Windsor that went "You can never be too rich or too thin." We could paraphrase that for Photoshop users and categorically state that you can never have too much RAM. RAM—or random access memory—is the single most important thing that you can have which helps Photoshop to work faster.

The ideal scenario is to have enough RAM so that Photoshop can edit your file entirely in memory without needing to store much into temporary files on your hard drive (it always opens a temp file, regardless of whether it needs to use it a lot). Adobe has told us, over the years, that you need 3–5 times your file size in order to be able to edit images entirely in RAM.

If you edit files that are around 100MB in size (not uncommon if you prepare photographs for output to a film recorder), you need between 300–500MB RAM. This is a hefty financial investment, so it's also good to know whether you need to be closer to three times your file size or five times your file size (since at this writing the cost of a 32MB DIMM is approximately $150, and a 200MB difference translates into about $750—not a trivial amount of money for most users). The answer to how much RAM you need depends on what you do inside of Photoshop.

If you generally scan an image, color correct it, convert it to CMYK, and then save it for output from a page layout program, you will probably only need about twice the file size in RAM. This assumes that you are editing the image as a flat layer. If you tend to do a lot of image compositing and heavily use layers—or if you perform a number of actions that create *floating* selections (less of a problem in Photoshop 4.0 than it was in Photoshop 3.0), then you will need much closer to the maximum of five times the file size.

When you create a floating selection (via a transformation command or by moving an image area within the same layer), Photoshop must write the prior state of the image (for the Undo buffer), the current state of the image, the selection itself, a mask for the selection area, and a prior version of the selected area. Using layers is a bit more sparing of your RAM, but not much. Layers that are mostly empty take up relatively little RAM, but the more data you place on them, the more memory they consume.

This is not to imply that you should not user layers. On the contrary, layers are one of the best features in Photoshop, as they allow you to make compositing changes very easily and to edit those changes multiple times. You *should* use layers—but you will also need to purchase enough RAM to make working with Photoshop a pleasure rather than a penance. Few things are as discouraging as watching the Mac Watch or the Windows hourglass cursor drain away minutes and hours that could be put to more profitable use.

Unless you are only using Photoshop to prepare small Web graphics, you really need a minimum of 32MB RAM on either platform in order to work reasonably well in the program using medium-sized files.

Two Are Better Than One

Your operating system and the speed of your hardware also play a large part in the speed with which the program works. If adding RAM does not give you enough speed, make sure that you have:

- the most current version of Photoshop.
- the most current version of the operating system for your computer.

If you are still seeing pokey performance, it might be time to purchase a new machine. On both the Macintosh and Wintel platforms, the new chips are running at 200 MHz and up. You can even purchase multiple processor cards. These cards give you more than one computer chip with which to process your image. Photoshop on the Mac or under NT can take advantage of these cards. They can almost double your speed on many of the accelerated functions. Quadruple processor cards can shorten the time even more.

Multiple processor cards work by handing off part of the processing task to each chip. This is similar to dumping your groceries on two check-out counters so that you finish almost twice as fast. Of course, not every graphics task can be divided up (nor can every task in real life—the "classic" example in computer literature is that fact that it takes one woman nine months to give birth to a baby, and that time cannot be shortened to one month by employing nine women). Therefore, you only see an increase in speed when Photoshop can use all of the available chips.

While we are not yet sure what speed improvements will be found under the forthcoming releases of Windows or NT or Rhapsody, as of this writing, you will get the fastest speed from using Macintosh System 8 (with many system calls now written in native Power PC code) or from NT.

The MMX chips on the Wintel platform are good investments for those of you already using a Windows machine. They add speed and help Photoshop to perform many of the calculations needed to move large numbers of pixels. In tests conducted by *MacUser* magazine (www.zdnet.com/macuser/mu_0797/features/mmx.html), the MMX chip was found to be somewhat slower at most operations than a 200 MHz 604e chip. The differences are not massively significant (and the tests done on the beta of IBM's new "long trail" machines seem faster than the Mac). *MacUser* magazine is not the most neutral of testing grounds, but at the time of the tests, it was owned by Ziff-Davis, and the data regarding PC performance was obtained from the ZD testing labs—so the results cannot be dismissed as "Mac hype." However, the MMX chip, while possibly not a reason to switch platforms, is certainly a reason to upgrade from one Wintel machine to another.

Conserving RAM

You can work "smarter" in Photoshop to help conserve the RAM that you do have. The best way to help Photoshop use less RAM is to keep the clipboard buffer as free of data as possible. This means that you should use the Copy and Paste commands as infrequently as you possibly can.

How can you avoid Copy and Paste? It's actually fairly simple. Use the drag-and-drop capabilities of Photoshop to transfer images from one file to another. You can use the Move tool to drag entire layers from one document to another. You can use the Move tool to transfer selected areas from one image to another (the transferred area will appear as a new layer if you are using Photoshop 4.0).

If you need to duplicate part of a layer within a file, select the area and use the (Layer | New) New Layer via Copy or New layer via Cut commands (Mac: Command+J or Shift+Command+J; Windows: Ctrl+J or Shift+Ctrl+J). If you need to duplicate the entire layer, just drag the thumbnail for that layer onto the New Layer icon at the bottom of the Layers palette. None of these commands use the clipboard.

You can also use the Apply Image or Calculations commands in the Image menu. This is the best way to get image data into a channel without using the clipboard. Chapter 5, "Using Channels," discusses these commands. If you are not familiar with them, read the chapter, as these commands add greatly to Photoshop's power.

The ability to take a snapshot of your image at a specific point in time is very useful, but is costly in RAM. You can take a snapshot of either a single layer or of a merged version of the image. You can also take snapshots of multiple open images, and you will not lose one snapshot in order to capture the other. (However, snapshots only restore to their own images.) If you have multiple open images and like to use snapshots, you can easily tie up a large chunk of RAM. Sometimes, instead of creating a snapshot, it is less costly in RAM usage if you place a single layer into a new layer (by dragging it to the New Layer icon) and hide its visibility icon so that you have it there to restore when needed. You can easily do this with a merged layer copy as well. Create a new layer and press Mac: Shift+Option+Command+E or Windows: Shift+Alt+Ctrl+E. This takes the contents of the image (merged) and places them in the active layer (which, since you just created it, is empty). If you want to do this using the menus, you need to hold down the Option key (Mac) or Alt key (Windows) as you select Layer | Merge Visible.

You can purge the Clipboard, Undo, Snapshot, and Pattern buffers when you need to free up RAM and scratch disk. This is a very handy feature that is new to version 4.0. Select Edit | Purge as shown in Figure 1-1 and then select the extra storage area that you want to purge.

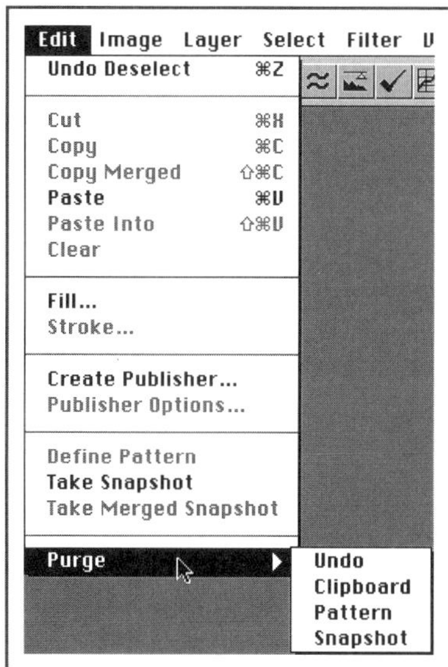

Figure 1-1: Purging Photoshop buffers to free up RAM.

TIP *If you allow the clipboard to be exported from Photoshop, you should purge the clipboard buffer before you transfer to another program if you do not need to use its contents. This allows your system to switch applications more quickly—and especially if there is a large image in the clipboard.*

Filters, RAM & Speed

Filters are not supposed to take up much RAM when they aren't running. However, we have discovered that loading every third-party filter known to man causes Photoshop to work more slowly—even with a lot of RAM. If there are filters that you don't need very often, you might want to leave them in a folder/directory outside of Photoshop and only put them into the Plug-Ins folder when you need them. Alternately, you can organize your filters into "sets" and select a specific set as your Plug-Ins folder.

Scratch Disks

Photoshop always opens up a *scratch disk* for your image. This is a temporary file that stores your work in progress. Unfortunately for those of you who experience crashes, this Temp file—which is left on your disk in the event of a crash—is not salvageable. You cannot open it and continue editing. All you can do is move it to the trash and weep (so save early and often).

In order to open a file in Photoshop, you must have free disk space that is *at least as large as the file size*. If you don't have that amount available, you'll get an error message—but it won't always tell you what the real problem is. The usual error message that you see in this situation is "Unable to open file. Scratch disk is full." If you cannot load a file, always check to see if you have enough free space on the hard drive(s) that you have selected for your scratch disks.

You can select up to two volumes to use as scratch disk. If one fills up, then Photoshop will use the other one. Even if you have enough RAM to edit a file in memory, Photoshop will still write some data to disk. Obviously, the more RAM you have, the less Photoshop needs to use the hard drive, and the faster the program performs edits. However, if you do not have enough RAM, Photoshop will run more slowly, but it will edit the file.

For those occasions when your file is too large to fit in RAM, it is helpful to have a disk that contains a large amount of contiguous storage. The best strategy is to devote an entire disk (or disk partition) to Photoshop to be used as scratch disk. Resist the urge to use the disk for anything else! Defragment your hard disks (to put files in order) by using Norton Utilities or Central Point on either the Mac or Windows. This makes the disk access faster.

You can tell how well Photoshop is performing by reading the status windows. There is an arrow that hides the four types of status readings. Clicking on the arrow (located on the image windows itself on the Mac as shown in Figure 1-2a and at the bottom of the application window in Windows as shown in Figure 1-2b) reveals the choices of Document Sizes, Scratch Sizes, Efficiency, or Timing.

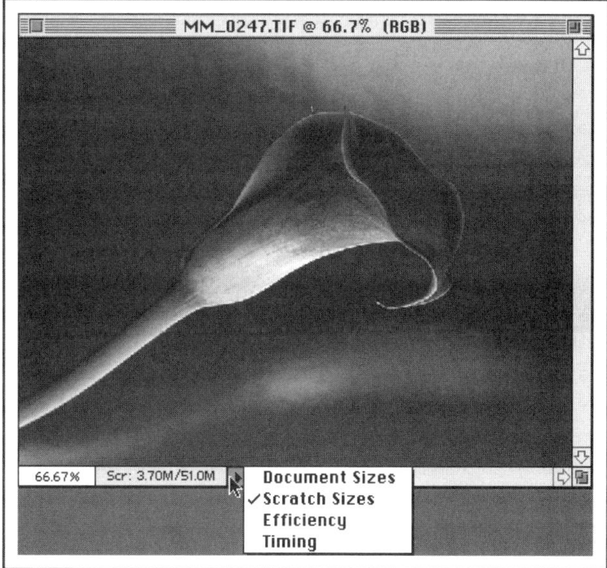

Figure 1-2a: Macintosh Status menu.

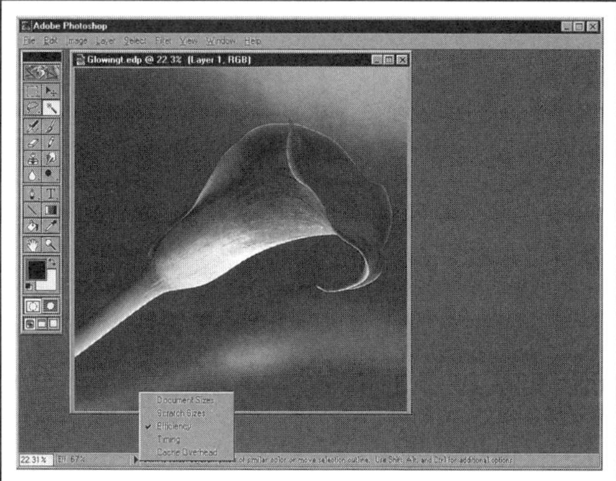

Figure 1-2b: Windows Status menu.

The Scratch Sizes show the RAM used by all open windows. The second number shows the amount of RAM available to the program. If the first number is larger than the second, then Photoshop has had to use the scratch disk to edit the image. When this happens, if you switch to the Efficiency indicator, you will notice that it falls below 100%. This also shows that Photoshop has had to make use of your scratch disks.

Other Hardware Goodies

If possible, invest in a fast hard drive. A fast and wide SCSI hard drive is a good solution. If you can afford it, a RAID disk array can also speed up access to your files. Both solutions are available in either platform flavor.

While you can designate a removable as your scratch disk, that is usually not a wonderful idea. Removable media is not usually as fast as fixed hard drives, though this may change in the future.

However, a Zip or Jaz drive (or MO or other removable) is certainly a plus when you need to exchange files with someone or take your images to a service bureau. They are not cost-effective methods, however, for backup (or for archiving).

To work efficiently in Photoshop, you also need to keep current backups. Get the largest, fastest backup tape unit that you can afford and use it frequently. Keep at least three complete sets of backup tapes and store one of them off-site (at home, if you work in an office; at a friend's house; in a bank vault). If your data is critical to you, consider what would happen if a fire, flood, or other catastrophe destroyed your computer. Make certain that you have a recent backup somewhere else to get you started again. One backup plan that works well is to create a complete backup at the end of each week and then backup incrementally each day. At the end of the week, backup completely over your *oldest* set of backup tapes.

The most cost-effective method of archiving your data (keeping old projects, finished assignments, completed images, etc.) is a CDR unit. This is a CD-ROM burner (a recordable CD-ROM). Each CD-ROM costs between $4–$9 and can store 650MB of data. Do not use this for backup (at least, not until technology lets you re-use them). However, we have found that a CDR unit is the best "luxury/necessity" that you can buy your computer.

If you want to purchase other enhancements for Photoshop, get a large monitor. If you need to create accurate prepress color, consider one of the Radius PressView monitors. They are available in 17-inch and 21-inch sizes. If your budget is really unlimited, look at a Barco monitor (which is all we've been able to do with one—i.e., look!). These monitors are very expensive but they contain excellent facilities for producing accurate color.

The Colortron or other colorimeter is also a good investment. It helps to calibrate your monitor and to create profiles that help you match your scanner or printer colors to the colors displayed on your monitor.

What's Your Preference?

Another factor in working efficiently with Photoshop is setting your Preferences to reflect the way that you work. Figure 1-3 shows the File | Preferences menu on the Mac (the menu is the same on Windows except for the Image Cache setting which is called Memory and Image Cache under Windows). Let's take a look at the Preferences settings that make a difference.

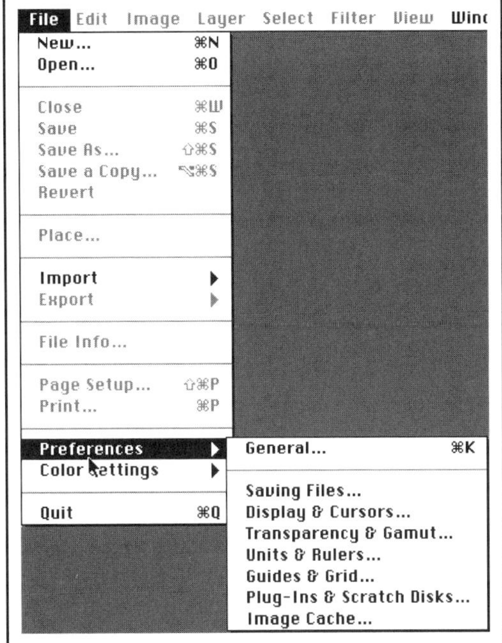

Figure 1-3: Preferences menu.

General Preferences

General Preferences is the first Preferences dialog. You can access it by pressing Command+K (Mac) or Ctrl+K (Windows). Figure 1-4 shows the General Preferences dialog.

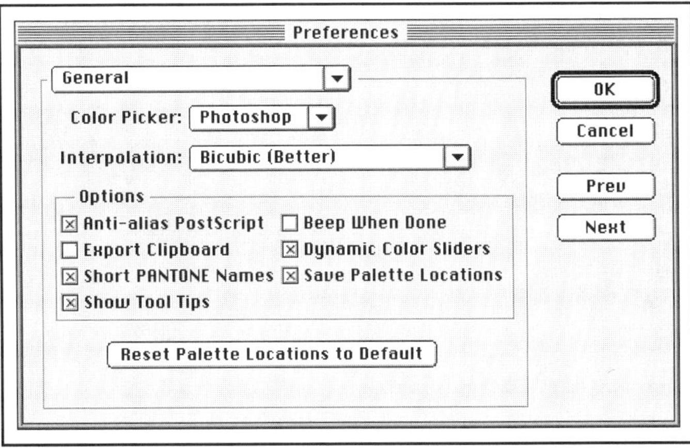

Figure 1-4: General Preferences dialog box.

Use the Photoshop Color Picker unless you have a good reason for not using it. A good reason might be to access one of the special Color Picker items on the Macintosh, such as the Pantone Web color set, or if you need values from the system Color Picker. The Mac System Color Picker, for example, returns different RGB numbers than Photoshop because it uses a scale of 1–100 rather than a scale of 1–255. The Windows RGB picker produces the same values as Photoshop.

You should always leave your Interpolation method set to Bicubic unless there is a compelling reason not to. The Interpolation method controls the way in which Photoshop calculates new pixels when it increases or decreases the number of pixels in an image or selection. The Preferences setting determines the method used by the Transform commands and sets the default in the Image Size dialog box as well. There is no reason to ever use bilinear interpolation, but you will want to use Nearest Neighbor whenever you need to scale a selection or file without creating any anti-aliased (fuzzy) edges. Nearest Neighbor produces a very "blocky" resizing that works best in whole increments (200%, 300%, etc.) or in 50% and 25% reductions. It can get very ugly if you do not follow these guidelines. When you resize an image, Photoshop 4.0 lets you choose the Interpolation method to be used. This is a wonderfully useful new feature because it allows you to leave the preference set to Bicubic but lets you resize using Nearest Neighbor when you need to. If you should change the Preferences setting, remember to *change it back* as soon as you are done.

You normally want to check the Anti-alias PostScript box. The only exception is during the probably infrequent times when you need to print at high resolution and want to import text or objects so that their edges do not blend toward transparent. Usually you are better off placing your image into a page layout program and setting type in that rather than doing it in Photoshop—especially if the type is small. However, you may have to import objects from Illustrator and keep them sharp. In any case, you usually have the option to turn anti-alias on or off except when you drag Paths in from Illustrator. That's the one circumstance when you are not given a chance to switch the status of the Preferences setting.

Unless you need to paste a part of an image in another program, you might consider unchecking the Export Clipboard preference. You will switch applications much faster with it off.

You do not need Short PANTONE Names turned on unless you are trying to place a Duotone or Platemaker image into an old copy of QuarkXPress. Otherwise, most programs use the same standard of naming that is used by Photoshop.

Show Tool Tips slows down the computer a bit. Use them or lose them as you prefer. Some folks like them; they drive other folks up a wall.

We usually keep Beep When Done off. The sounds of silence are quite welcome, and co-workers do not really need to know when you have finished something. However, if you like noise....

The Dynamic Color Sliders is a feature worth enabling. It shows you a preview of the colors that occurs if you move the sliders in the Color palette. Figure 1-5 shows the Color palette. If you were seeing it in color, you would see that the chosen color is a burgundy. If you move the red slider to the right, you obtain a stronger red. Moving the blue slider to the right gives a shade of purple. It is easier to mix your colors if you leave Dynamic Color Sliders turned on.

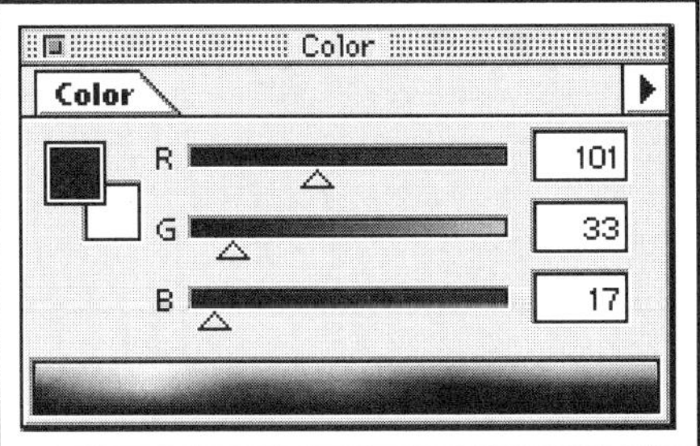

Figure 1-5: Color palette showing effect of Dynamic Color Sliders preference.

Unless you like to use the default settings for palette locations, keep the Save Palette Locations turned on. It saves a lot of time if you prefer your own arrangements. You can always return to the "factory" settings by clicking on the Reset Palette Locations to Default button. This is helpful if your Toolbox ever gets "stuck" under the menu bar at the top of the screen (an annoyance that seems limited to the Mac).

TIP *Make sure that you can see the Toolbox when you quit from Photoshop—especially on the Mac. That seems to be one of the things that causes the Toolbox to hide under the menu. If you have used the Tab key to hide the palettes, press it again to reveal all before leaving the application.*

Saving Files

The Saving Files preference is a bit different on the Mac and Windows. Figure 1-6a shows the Mac version and Figure 1-6b shows the Windows version.

The major difference in platforms is that the Mac is able to save small preview icons that the PC cannot. The icons are cute—and convenient—but are also capable of getting very scrambled on your hard disk. While the latest versions of the Mac operating system seem less subject to icon scramble, there have been times when every icon of the hard drive displayed the wrong picture (rebuilding the desktop usually fixes this, however). We recommend the Ask When Saving option for this preference—even on the PC. The Ask When Saving dialog allows you to decide on a case-by-case basis whether to create a preview or, on the Mac, a thumbnail icon.

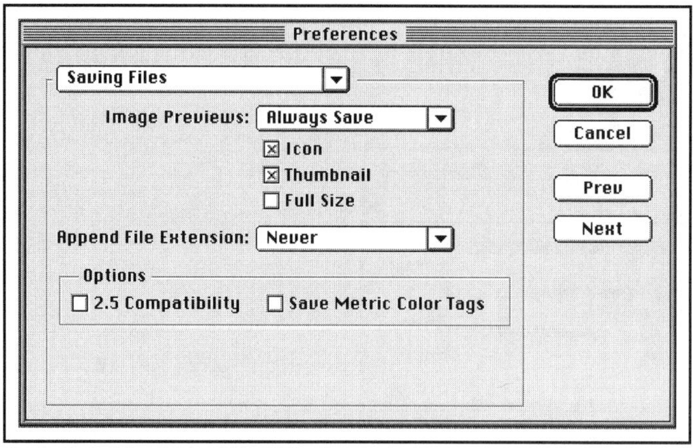

Figure 1-6a: Mac Saving Files dialog box.

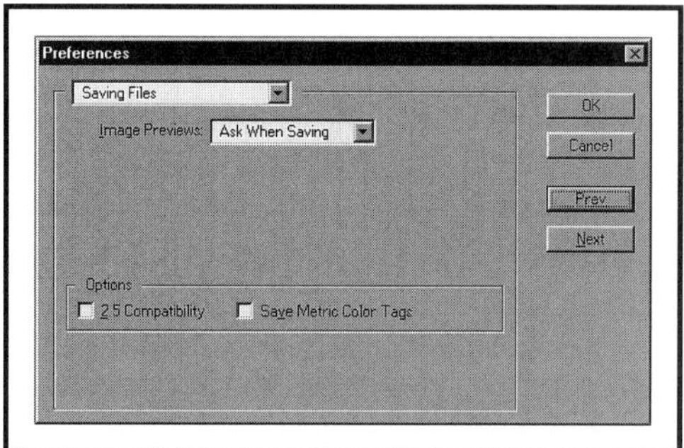

Figure 1-6b: Windows Saving Files dialog box.

When you create an image preview, especially of a large file, it can take a very long time to save the image. Saving a full-size preview also adds to the time and disk space occupied by the file (although you do not have the option to save a full-size preview in Windows). The advantage to saving a preview full size is that you get a better display in a page layout program, but this is not a necessity.

The Mac also gives you the option of saving a file extension automatically with the Append File. The jury is out on this one—it totally depends upon the way that you work and where your files end up when you are done with them. The Macintosh opens PC files if there is an extension (Windows always has a file extension). Win/Photoshop only opens a file *without* an extension if you use the Open As command. If you want to be able to use the Open command, you must attach the appropriate extension for the file to even appear in the file list.

TIP *The Mac does not have an "Open As" command. If you need to open a file that came from Windows but has no extension, you need to check the Show All Files box at the bottom of the Open dialog box.*

If you need to move files back and forth between platforms, it is usually safest to use "standard" DOS naming conventions of eight characters followed by a period and the correct file extension. It is really nice that you don't need to fuss with changing the Mac Type and Creator of a file imported from Windows as long as it has the correct extension. This is a welcome relief from the behavior of many Macintosh programs that do not read Windows files at all.

The Saving Files dialog box also allows you to save your images to allow for Photoshop 2.5 compatibility. Unless you need to place a flattened file into a program that doesn't read the Photoshop 3.0 specification (but does accept 2.5), turn off this preference. Using this option is a major waste of disk space. In order to save a file in 2.5 compatibility mode, Photoshop writes another (invisible) layer to the file; it then saves a flattened copy of the file that it can use when something asks for the 2.5 version. This can add a lot to the space used to save your file if you normally use layers in an image. Figure 1-7 shows two Info windows on the Mac. The files saved are identical but one was saved with Photoshop 2.5 compatibility turned on and the other one was not. Photoshop 2.5 compatibility changed the saved file size from 2.4MB to 3.2MB. The image contains a background layer, a copy of the background layer in Overlay mode, and two selections floated in the image—one layer in Multiply mode and the other in Screen mode.

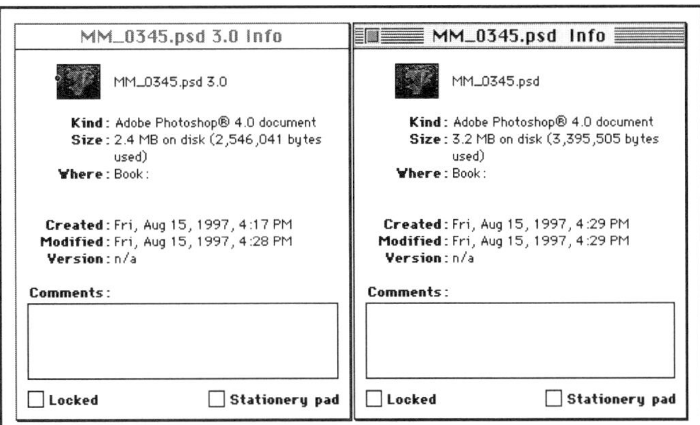

Figure 1-7: Files saved with and without Photoshop 2.5 compatibility.

Enable the Save Metric Color Tags option only if you use the EFI color option in QuarkXPress. This allows Quark to use the current EFI profile with your image. Otherwise, you really don't need this option.

Display & Cursors

This preference, shown in Figure 1-8, allows you to set up the display characteristics of your system. It contains a number of options.

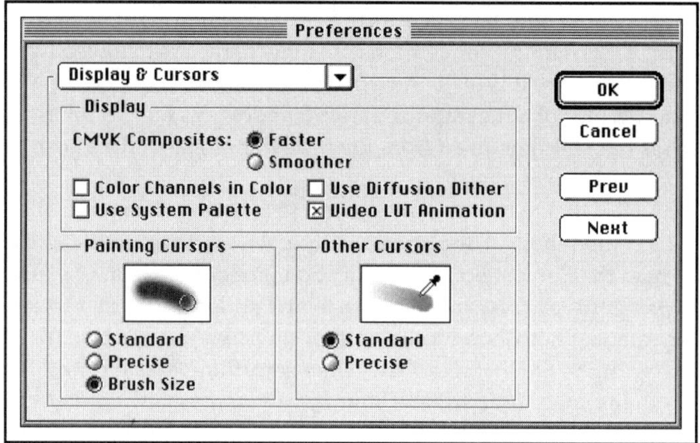

Figure 1-8: Display and Cursors option.

You can choose between Faster or Smoother CMYK Composites. This preference is used when you work in CMYK color space. The Faster option is, by definition, faster than the Smoother option, and also, by inference, less smooth. Actually, it is less accurate as well. You may see banding (hard lines and abrupt color breaks in areas of smooth gradations) that won't actually appear in your image. This is because the Faster option uses a lookup table to convert CMYK values into RGB values for display. The Smoother option gives you a more accurate preview of your final image (although you need to read more about calibrating your system in Chapter 10, "Calibration & Color Reproduction," if you want your preview to even closely resemble the printed final image). You should probably work in Faster mode until you are almost finished with your image and then switch into Smoother so that you can evaluate the final result.

Do not select the Color Channels in Color option. While nothing dire will result selecting it, you need to train yourself to think of each color as simply the grayscale values in that channel. Chapter 5, "Using Channels," has an in-depth discussion of the relationship between the color channels and the grayscale values that they contain. Since you really need to think "value and density" when you look at the contents of a specific channel, seeing the actual colors gets in the way.

If you own a decent color card (one that allows you to work in 24-bit color), then you don't need either of the next two options (and should not select them): Use System Palette or Use Diffusion Dither. If you don't own a 24-bit color card and work with Photoshop for anything other than Web or multi-media, you need to get one.

However, you *do* want to select Use Video LUT Animation (assuming, once again, that you have a color card that supports it—and you should, if you have one that allows 24-bit color).Video LUT animation gives you some additional options—especially when you are using the Levels dialog box. The option uses your color card to do a "quick and dirty" calculation of the changes that you make in the dialog box. This allows you to work with Preview off in the dialog box and see a fast "before" version of your image by clicking the title bar of the image window while you are in the Levels or Curves dialog box. With Preview off, you do not see a totally accurate preview, but it is usually good enough until you have the correct settings. Then, you can click the Preview button to make sure that you like your changes. However, it's really handy to be able to see a before and after image very quickly.

The other thing that Video LUT Animation allows you to do in the Levels dialog box is to find the lightest and darkest areas of the image very quickly. If you press the Option key (Mac) or Alt key (Windows) as you drag the White or Black point sliders (with Preview turned off in the dialog box), you can see where the black or white values will be clipped. If you have not used this feature before, try it. It can save a lot of "poking about" with the Info palette to find the darkest or lightest areas in an image that need to color correct.

Always select the Brush Size painting cursors (unless, of course, you like to be surprised about the size of the brush with which you are painting). This is one of Photoshop's best productivity features. It does have a price, however. It can slow down your drawing if you use a large brush—but that's probably when you also need to see your brush size the most.

TIP *If you should need to remove the Direct Cursors plug-in (because your cursor disappears when you place it over an image—see the Troubleshooting section later in this chapter), you will not be able to see any brush size over 16 pixels.*

It is your choice whether to use Standard or Precise cursors for the other tools such as the Marquee and the Eyedropper. Since you can change one type of cursor into the other by pressing the Caps Lock key, you can easily leave this option set to Standard.

Transparency & Gamut

The Transparency & Gamut settings allow you to pick the size of the grids that shows through transparent areas of your image and to set the colors of both the transparency and gamut warnings. Figure 1-9 shows the dialog box.

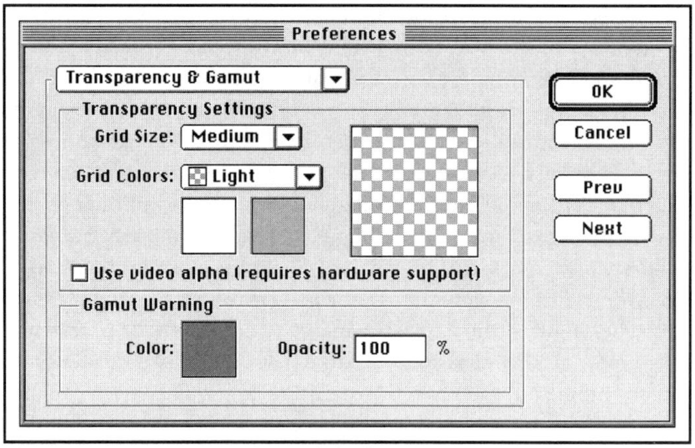

Figure 1-9: Transparency & Gamut dialog box.

The Gamut warning is an option that you can turn on under the View menu to show you the out-of-gamut colors in an image (out-of-gamut colors are colors that cannot be printed using the standard CMYK inks). You can also change the Opacity of the color displayed for the warning so that it does not totally obscure the out-of-gamut colors.

There are no particular suggestions for these settings. The defaults usually work without problem. You might want to change the color of the Gamut warning indicator if you are using an image on which the warning is not visible.

Units & Rulers

The Units & Rulers preferences box, shown in Figure 1-10, allows you to pick the measuring system for the Rulers and to specify default column widths for setting text.

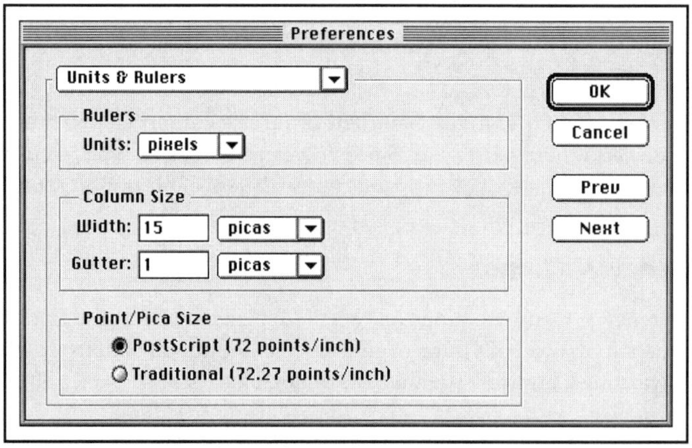

Figure 1-10: Units & Rulers Preferences box.

Select pixels as your default unit measure unless you have a really good reason not to. This setting controls the default unit when you choose File | New. Pixels are unambiguous. A pixel is a pixel is a pixel. A document that is 800 pixels X 800 pixels remains that size whether it is set to 10 pixels per inch or 5,000 pixels per inch—it still contains 800 X 800 pixels. If you create files of any other measurement, you need to know the output dimensions (resolution) or else your file will not be the "correct" size. Of course, you need to set physical dimensions (ppi) if you are going to print your image, but it is much easier to think and work in pixels. We usually leave the settings at pixels all the time—even if later we change the units on a new image to pick picas or inches.

TIP *You can change the Units preference quickly when you use Rulers by double-clicking on a ruler. This opens the Units & Rulers preference so that you can select a different ruler scale.*

Since the authors do not recommend setting text in Photoshop, we leave the column settings alone since we never use them anyway. However, since we work in a digital world, we typically leave Point/Pica Size set at 72 points/inch.

Guides & Grids

This preference allows you to set the color and style for guides and grids and to set the grid dimensions. This preference dialog box is shown in Figure 1-11.

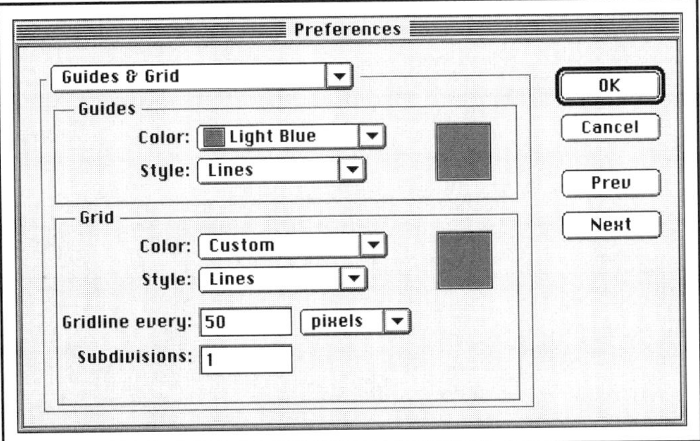

Figure 1-11: Guides & Grid preference.

You can easily leave the default values for this preference. This is a preference that you will probably change fairly often, but the changes are specific to the needs of the image that you are editing rather than a general purpose setting.

In most cases, there is little reason to view either guides or grids as dashed lines or dots, but you might need to change the color so that it stands out against your image.

Both authors are involved in the textile arts and would like to see the ability to use different grid settings for the width and height, but Photoshop only permits you one dimension. However, you can subdivide your image into major and minor divisions, and this is a useful feature to have.

Plug-Ins & Scratch Disk

The Plug-Ins & Scratch Disk Preferences settings allow you to select the Plug-Ins folder to use and to specify two locations where Photoshop can store it in temporary files. Figure 1-12 shows this dialog box.

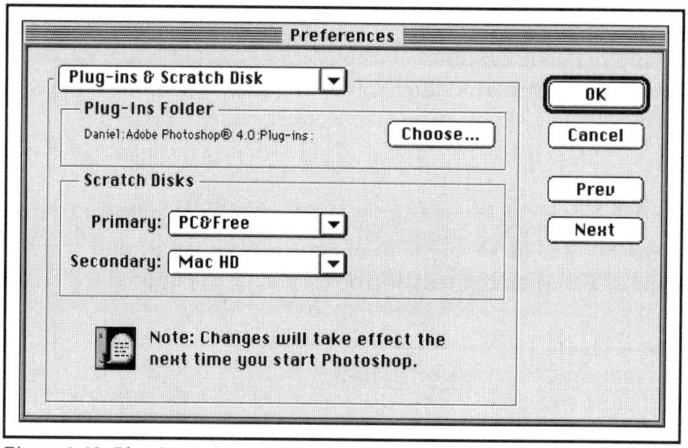

Figure 1-12: Plug-ins & Scratch Disk preference box.

Plug-ins are pieces of code that are optional for the program (Photoshop does not need them in order to run). They are also pieces of code that add functionality to the original program. There are two "flavors" of plug-ins, and several places on the menu where they can appear.

Plug-ins are either from Adobe or from a third-party. They can appear on the Filter menu or on the File menu (as Import or Export options). They can also appear as file type options when you open or save a file, and some correction options, such as Variations (Image | Adjust | Variations), are also plug-ins.

You can have only one plug-in folder/directory active at a time. However, on the Mac, you can place aliases of plug-ins into the folder so that the actual plug-ins can be kept elsewhere.

In versions of Photoshop earlier than 3.0, all of the plug-ins needed to be "loose" inside of the main folder/directory. You could not have subdirectories or embedded folders. In version 3.0, that changed. You may now nest folders and subdirectories, and we urge you to do that. It makes life much easier when you are able to organize your plug-ins, especially if you tend to collect a lot of third-party filters. The subfolders that are created when you install Photoshop are just for organization. Any filter may be placed in any subfolder or subdirectory.

TIP *Keep all of your third-party filters in a separate folder/directory. You can nest them with that folder as well. This makes applying upgrades or reinstalling the program much easier as you do not need to remember what came with the program and what pieces you need to re-install.*

There is a filter from CSI (Cytopia Software) that allows you to create different plug-in sets. It is only available on the Mac, but it is very useful. There had also been a plug-in manager from BeInfinite (also only for the Mac), but this company is now defunct and it is unlikely that you will be able to locate the plug-in.

If you have plug-ins that you don't want to keep loaded at all times, remove them not only from the Plug-Ins folder, but from the Photoshop directory as well. Photoshop sometimes loads any plug-in that it sees anywhere in its directory, even if the plug-in is not in the Plug-Ins folder.

To add a new plug-in to the Plug-Ins folder, *make sure that Photoshop is not open.* Then, either copy the file into the folder or run the Install program, if there is one for the plug-in. When you start Photoshop again, your new plug-in will be available.

If you need to change the Plug-Ins folder (or locate it), select the option in the Plug-Ins & Scratch Disk preference and locate the correct folder or directory on your disk (the Windows plug-ins folder is named Plugins, on the Mac, it is hyphenated to Plug-Ins).

You may also set up two scratch disks. As we mentioned above, leave plenty of free disk space and if possible, devote an entire disk or disk partition to Photoshop. Keep the scratch disk defragmented.

Memory & Image Cache

The final preference setting is slightly different on the PC and on the Mac. It sets the Image Cache on both platforms, but controls the amount of RAM usage on Windows. Figure 1-13a shows the Mac dialog box, and Figure 1-13b shows the Windows dialog box.

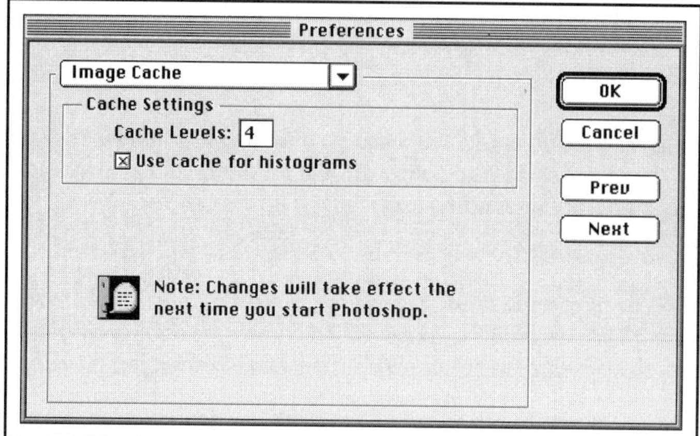

Figure 1-13a: Image Cache preference on the Mac.

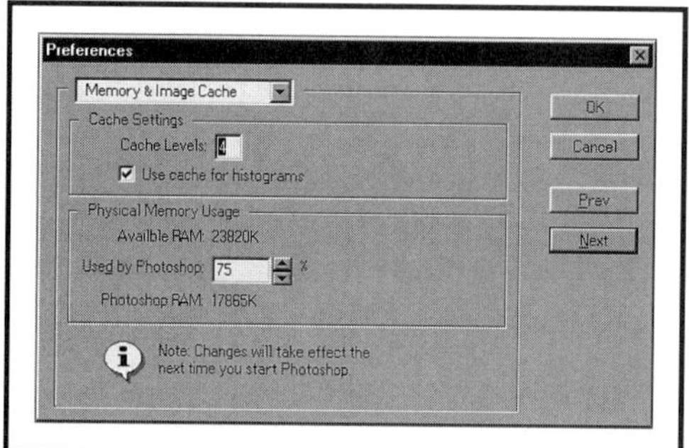

Figure 1-13b: Memory & Image Cache setting on Windows.

Let's look at the Memory setting first. In the discussion above, we already mentioned that Photoshop likes RAM. (You do know that it has an insatiable appetite for it, don't you?) The way that you satisfy Photoshop's appetite for RAM differs between the PC and the Mac. On the Mac, you need to offer Photoshop the specific amount of RAM for its meal by selecting the Photoshop program icon and pressing Command-I. This displays the Get Info dialog box shown in Figure 1-14. To change the Preferred amount of RAM for the program, enter the new amount in that field. It is rarely necessary to change the Minimum amount of RAM needed (a few third-party plug-ins, such as the ones from Human Software, require this in order to work properly). *Do not ever give Photoshop all of your available RAM, or you will cause the system to crash.* Leave at least 1–5MB RAM free beyond the amount used by the System file.

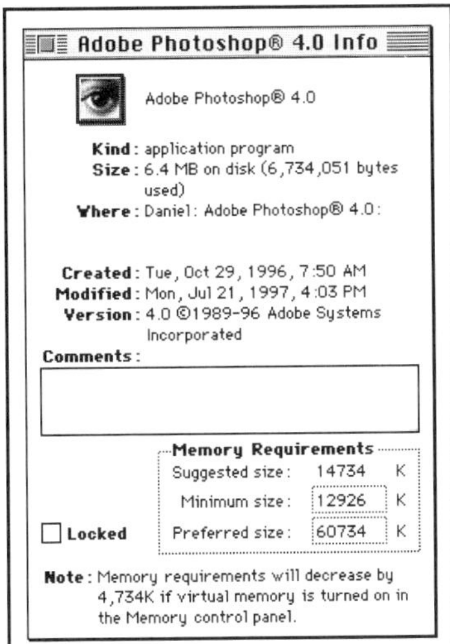

Figure 1-14: Setting Macintosh Memory requirements for Photoshop.

If you are working on the Windows platform (or on NT), you restrict Photoshop's appetite for RAM to a maximum percentage of RAM available. Just as on the Mac, it is wrong to allow Photoshop to get greedy and grab it all. While giving Photoshop all of your RAM will not cause as much trouble on Windows, it is still a bad idea. It is more reasonable to keep Photoshop "lean and mean" at 75% of available RAM.

The Image Cache is a feature that is new to Photoshop 4.0. It is the magic that is responsible for the very fast screen redraws that you see. When you open an image, Photoshop now creates a screen resolution preview of the image at a variety of zoom levels (using a pyramid scheme of cached redraws). When you need to zoom in or out on your image, Photoshop then pulls the new calculation from the cached views instead of reading the file or portion of the file from your hard drive. This makes the screen updates remarkably faster than they were in Photoshop 3.0 or earlier. It also allows Photoshop to anti-alias the edges more rapidly on the previews.

This wonderful speed increase also has a downside—of course. It is slower to open a file and takes more RAM. Therefore, you can set the optimum size of the Image Cache in the Image Cache preference. A setting of 1 disables the cache completely. Unless you always work at 100% magnification, you should not use a setting of 1. You almost always benefit from the use of the Image Cache even if it uses a bit more RAM. The additional RAM needed is not proportional to the cache setting selected.

For example, changing the cache setting from 1 to 2 adds about one-third more RAM to an image while changing the setting from 4 to 8 costs very little more. A setting of 8 caches all of the preview sizes from 6.25 to 100% and is only needed if your file is very large. For most users, a setting of 4 is a good compromise between speed and RAM. If your images are small enough to open at 50% size, then you might be okay with a cache setting of 2. You should choose your cache setting based on the largest image that normally edits. If Photoshop seems too slow or uses too much RAM, lower the cache setting. You can experiment until you find the setting that works best for you.

Special Issues

There are several topics that do not fit into troubleshooting as they are not problems, but they are important issues to consider. One is the topic of installing the program and applying upgrades; the other is the new Photoshop feature called "Big Data."

Installation & Upgrades

Many years ago, before CD-ROM drives became popular and Photoshop grew large enough to need one, the Photoshop application arrived with a number of installation disks. The directions stated that the program was to be installed with all extensions on the MAC or TSRs on the PC turned off. Now that the program ships with its installation code on CD-ROM, the warning is no longer given, in part, because you need to load the CD-ROM drivers in order to install Photoshop from the CD-ROM.

Photoshop should still be installed into a system that has as few other programs, extensions, and TSRs open as possible. Many problems that folks have with Photoshop stem from code that was corrupted by some other program that was in memory at the time that Photoshop was installed. Usually Photoshop's installation is not all that sensitive, but these corruption problems have occurred often enough that you need to be aware of the possibility. For safety's sake, if you can remove all unneeded memory-resident programs (especially on the Mac) when you install Photoshop, do so. The only extensions that should be running on the Mac when Photoshop is installed are the CD-ROM drivers and QuickTime. After you have checked the media for viruses (if you are so inclined), remove the virus software temporarily on either platform.

On Win95, you can start the machine in "safe mode." Here's how: when you turn on your machine, it will do a memory check. Right before Windows starts up, there is a message that appears at the bottom of the screen that says "Starting Win95". At that point, you have 2 or 3 seconds to press F8 to bring up a menu that has seven or eight options on it (depending upon your machine). The third option is Safe Mode. That is the option that you should choose. A faster way to do this is to press F4 at the "Starting Win95" message. That will take you directly to safe mode.

On Windows NT there is no such thing as safe mode.

Windows does a better job of installing a Photoshop version upgrade over an existing copy of Photoshop than the Mac does. On Windows, you can usually allow the install program to do what it wants if you are moving from Photoshop 3 to 4, for example. On the Mac, a Photoshop 3–4 upgrade will *not* replace the earlier version. Adobe Tech support recommends that you remove the entire Photoshop 3.0 install before placing 4.0 on your machine (back up first) as they have sometimes seen a tangled 3–4 hybrid that is very ugly if you leave both programs on the machine.

It is sometimes necessary to re-install the program if you are having problems with it. In that case, Windows users should be able to install the program directly over the original install, but if this does not fix the problem, then you need to run the Uninstall program. *Mac users should not try to install one copy of the program over the other.* Drag the

Photoshop program icon to the trash and also drag the Preferences file (from the System folder) to the trash. Your install may not work properly if you do not trash the Preferences file before you reinstall the software.

Sometimes, Adobe releases interim upgrades. For example, at press time, version 4.0.1 is the current version. This is a bug fix upgrade with a few additional refinements in it for both Mac and Windows. On Windows, it also allows the program to use the new MMX machines. Adobe releases upgrades either by making a patch available online or by releasing a new CD-ROM of the program—depending upon how large the changes are.

Sometimes, they release a patch and also make available a CD-ROM version for a nominal fee. We urge you to pay the additional fee (usually just a shipping and handling charge) whenever a new version is available on CD-ROM. Simply because it is larger, there are often unpublicized "goodies" on the CD-ROM that can add value to the program. If there is room, Adobe might also include the full version of the program on the CD-ROM instead of just the patch (it obviously cannot make available the full program code online where it could be downloaded by folks who do not own the original). It is always better to have a full version of the program than a patch (if you need to reinstall the program, you only need one process rather than two—one to replace the old version and the other to update it). Version 4.0.1 actually is available in two versions—a dual platform patcher CD-ROM and a full version CD-ROM. Get the full version.

If you download a patch with which to upgrade your copy of Photoshop, here are some suggestions:

- Back up your machine before you install anything new.
- If you have created custom gradients or Actions or you are fond of a custom Swatches palette, save these to disk before you upgrade.
- On the Mac, start the Mac without any extensions, trash your Photoshop Preferences file, and remove your Photoshop 4.0 installation (if you have third-party plug-ins, remember to get them out of the Plug-Ins folder before you trash the installation). Install a clean copy of Photoshop 4.0. Finally, install the patch updater.
- On Windows it is usually unnecessary to operate in safe mode and not possible if you are using Windows NT. Disable any virus-checking programs before running the upgrade. Unless the instructions say otherwise, just run the Installer and let it take over.

Big Data

In version 3.0 and earlier in Photoshop, when you pasted data into your image that was larger than your document, the extra image area was removed and only the parts of the pasted data that could fit in your image were saved. Photoshop 4.0 has a new data model called "Big Data." It can hold image data that does not fit inside of the document—almost like the pasteboard in PageMaker or QuarkXPress. This is a wonderful new convenience because you can paste large images and recover the data that did not fit in the image. Let's play with this (after all, you have done a lot of reading with no computer time yet!).

Working With Big Data

In this exercise, you will place some flowers inside of the knothole in a tree. The flowers image is larger than the tree image.

1. Open the files KNOTHOLE.PSD and BOUQUET.PSD from the Enhanced Photoshop CD-ROM. Figure 1-15 shows the knothole image and Figure 1-16 shows the bouquet image.

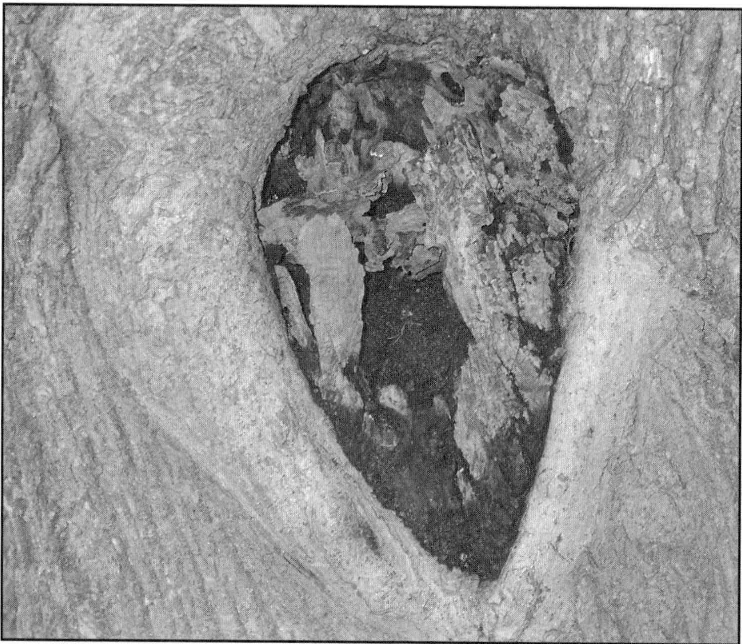

Figure 1-15: KNOTHOLE.PSD.

2. Click on the flower image to make it active. Press the modifier key (Mac: Command, Windows: Ctrl) and the Shift key, and drag the flower image on top of the tree image. Figure 1-17 shows the result. You can see by comparing that figure to Figure 1-16 how much larger the flower image really is.

Figure 1-16: BOUQUET.PSD

Figure 1-17: BOUQUET.PSD dragged onto KNOTHOLE.PSD and partially cut off.

3. The tree image contains a channel that selects the knothole. Load Channel 4 (Mac: Command+Option+4, Windows: Ctrl+Alt+4). Then create a layer mask by clicking on the Layer Mask icon at the bottom left of the Layers palette. Your mask automatically uses the selection, and the only area of the bouquet that is visible is in the knothole. Figure 1-18 shows this image.

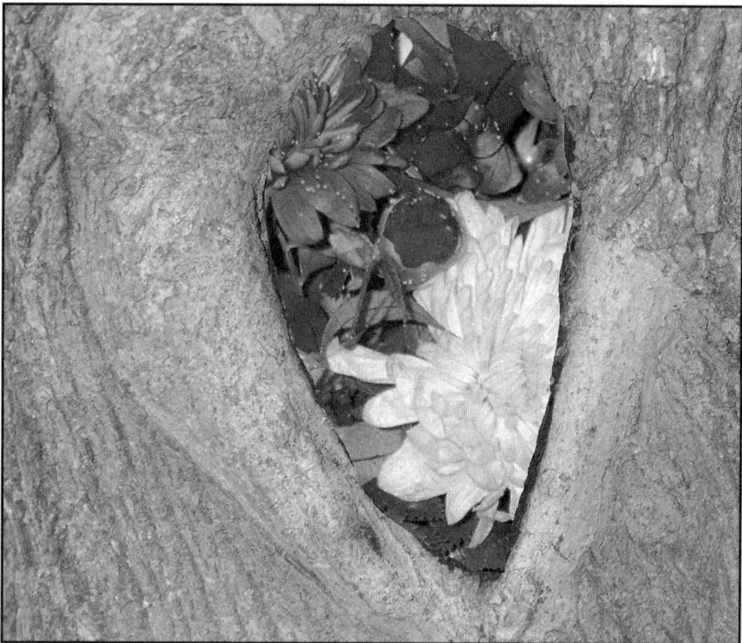

Figure 1-18: Flowers in the center of the knothole.

4. Click on the link icon between the thumbnail of the flowers and the flower layer mask on the Layers palette to unlink the layer and the layer mask. This allows you to move the layer while the masked area remains stationary.
5. Click on the layer thumbnail to select it. Figure 1-19 shows the Layers palette as it should look—notice that you have a Paintbrush icon in the second column next to the flower layer. Select the Move tool (or press the Mac: Command or Windows: Ctrl key) and move the flower image around. You can even move it so that the side edge of the original image is visible as you can see in Figure 1-20.
6. Use the Free Transform command (Mac: Command+T, Windows: Ctrl+T) to scale the flower image. The transform marquee appears inside of the document window even though the data is larger than the document. Press the Shift key to constrain the aspect ratio and at the same time, press the Option key (Mac) or Alt key (Windows) to scale from the center of the image as you drag the upper left corner of the transform marquee toward the center of the image. Figure 1-21

shows amount by which we scaled the image. Double-click inside of the marquee to complete the scaling operation.

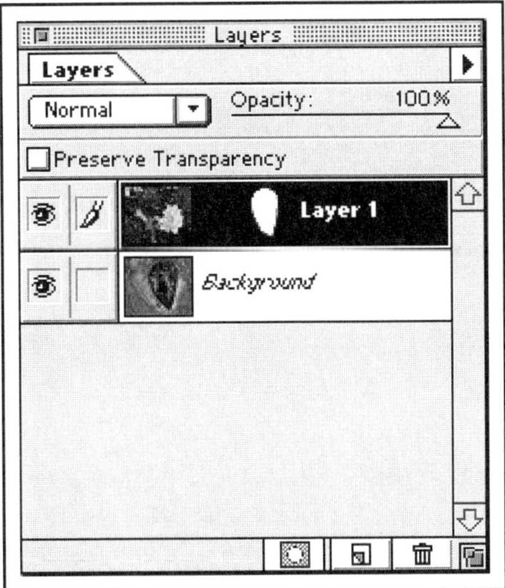

Figure 1-19: Layers palette with Paintbrush icon indicating that the layer rather than the layer mask is active.

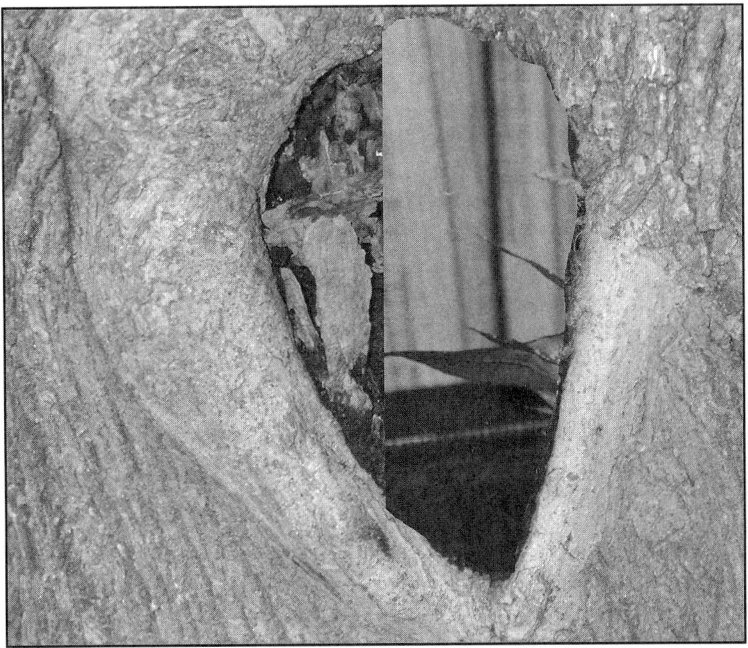

Figure 1-20: Big Data keeps the image area larger than that which will fit into the image.

Figure 1-21: Scaling the flower image.

7. Move the flower image inside of the layer mask until you like the view. Notice as you move the image that the edges of the original flower image are still in the file and have not been removed by the scaling that you did. You still have the entire original layer, even if it's now a bit smaller.

The flowers do not look as if they are inside of the knothole at all—which is a bit silly. So, even though it has nothing to do with Big Data, let's create some shadows to make the flowers look better.

8. Change the layer Opacity to 70%. This reduces the overall brightness of the flowers.
9. Make a new layer (click on the New Layer icon at the bottom of the Layers palette). Load Channel 4 as you did in Step 3. Create a Layer Mask (click on the Add Layer Mask icon—the bottom left icon on the Layers palette).
10. Click on the layer thumbnail to make the layer active. Load Channel 4 again. Reverse the selection (Select -> Inverse or Mac: Shift+Command+I, Windows: Shift+Ctrl+I). Press D to set the colors back to the default of black and white. Fill the area (Mac: Option-Delete, Windows: Alt-Delete). Your image still looks blank because you filled the area that is *masked*.
11. Deselect (Mac: Command-D, Windows: Ctrl-D).
12. Click on the link icon between the layer and the layer mask to turn it off. If you do not, the Gaussian Blur filter softens both the image and mask. Apply a Gaussian Blur (Filter | Blur | Gaussian Blur) of 20.

13. The softness of the blurred edge creates a general shadow around the edges of the knothole. It is not quite dark enough, however. Drag the icon for the shadow layer to the New Layer icon (the center icon at the bottom of the Layers palette). This duplicates the shadow layer. Change the Apply mode to Multiply.
14. Duplicate the new second shadow layer by dragging it to the New Layer icon. This is too dark. Set the opacity back to about 30% or to the setting that looks good on your monitor. Figure 1-22 shows the finished image.
15. Now that the image looks okay, what has happened to the data that was too large to fit? Nothing. It is still there and makes a very large file. There are several ways to get rid of the extra image area. You can apply the mask. Make the layer mask active and click on the trash-can icon at the bottom of the Layers palette. The dialog asks if you want to Apply or Discard the layer mask. Click Apply. Notice that the Document Size status window shows a greatly decreased amount.
16. Select Undo (Mac: Command+Z, Windows: Ctrl+Z).
17. Here is the other way to remove all of the extra image in the document. Select the entire image (Mac: Command-A, Windows: Ctrl-A). Choose Image | Crop. Once again, the Document Size decreases. Flattening the image also removes the pasteboard area.

Figure 1-22: Finished knothole image.

Now you should have a good idea of how best to work with the Big Data feature. Remember, as long as you save your image in Photoshop format, you will keep the pasteboard data unless you crop your image to the document size first. It is possible to perform transformations that keep the large data but orphan it as well, so it is important that you trim your document to size once you know you no longer need the extra material.

Troubleshooting

Photoshop is actually one of the most stable graphics applications. However, computers and operating systems have gotten very complex and problems can and do occur. This section discusses some of the issues that have surfaced most often on the CompuServe Adobe Photoshop Forum and reflects the advice given there. Although CompuServe is more expensive than many online services, the Adobe Forum is worth the price. It provides some of the fastest, and most complete, Photoshop advice available. It also attracts some of the best Photoshop users on the planet.

You can also obtain access to "pre-recorded" technical advice on Adobe's Web site (http://www.adobe.com). There is a large technical database that provides detailed information on a number of problem areas. When you encounter trouble with Photoshop that you cannot solve by yourself or with the advice given here, check the FAQ documents on Adobe's Web site. If all else fails, call Adobe Technical Support. You can either purchase a yearly service contract, pay a fixed fee for a call using a credit card, or use a 900 number at $2.00 per minute (including waiting time).

Common Concerns

Troubleshooting Photoshop is usually quite platform-specific. However, there are several issues that seem to be common across platforms. Let's look at these first.

TRAP

Here is the part where we need to include some legalese to tell you that neither Adobe, nor Ventana Communications Group, nor the authors take responsibility for any damage that might occur from following the troubleshooting advice. We strive to be accurate, but computers are quite complex and configurations (as well as user expertise) differ so much that what works on one machine might not behave the same way on another. So . . . proceed at your own risk.

Preference File Corruption

Have you ever looked at several-day-old food in your refrigerator and wondered if it was still good? Did you then hear a little voice say "When in doubt, throw it out?" Photoshop's preference file is like that. It turns bad in sneaky little ways that leave you wondering, "Is it or isn't it?"

It never hurts the application to toss out the preference file. On the Mac, the preference file is called Adobe Photoshop 4.0 Prefs and is located in the System folder Preferences subfolder. There are three preferences files for Win/Photoshop. They are PHOTOS40.PSP, PHOTOS40.INI, and CCOLORSD and they live in the PREFS subdirectory in the Photoshop directory.

PHOTOS40.PSP is the main preferences file for Windows. PHOTOS40.INI contains the initialization information and CCOLSD has the color calibration and printing inks setup preferences. All of these files are re-created the next time you launch Photoshop if you have removed them.

This is your first line of defense against program oddities. If something does not work correctly that used to, or you just get a "bad feeling" about something that is happening in the program, toss the prefs files. It is astonishing how much that simple action can help.

Just remember that you need to save your Actions, Gradients, and Swatches palette before you remove the prefs files, or else you will lose all of your custom settings.

Since the preferences file is so touchy, you might want to save a copy of it onto another of your hard drives when you have one that is configured to your liking (with all of the palettes where you want them to be, and all of your color settings in place). Do not use this copy of the file, and keep it in a safe place. Then, the next time that you need a "clean" copy, you can simply duplicate your "spare" and replace the old, worn-out file with it.

Do not try to reuse a prefs file from an earlier version. That is not a safe thing to try. However, if your work group uses the same version of Photoshop and you are all on the same platform, you can give your preferences file to other users so that all of your systems are set up the same way.

Just remember to ditch the prefs file at the first sign of trouble.

Old Filters

Another area of potential problem and conflict is with filters and plug-ins. They can sometimes cause the same havoc with one another that Mac extensions have been known to create. If you suspect a filter conflict, here's how to find it:

1. Remove all of the third-party plug-ins from the Photoshop directory (remember, we told you to keep them in a separate subdirectory for easy removal).
2. Open Photoshop and see if the problem disappears (of course, it might disappear because the filter has also disappeared). However, if the problem situation can be re-created and the problem is not there, then you know that a filter conflict caused it.
3. Put back one-half of your third-party filters and try again. If the problem comes back, then one of the filters in the group is the culprit.

4. Remove half of the set that you just put back. Does the problem go away? If it does not, remove half of what's left. If it does, then you have a smaller set of culprits.

Continue to add or remove filters by half until you locate the problem filter. If you want to try a technique that is not quite as random, *remove your oldest filters first*. They make the most likely suspects. Many filters were not updated for Photoshop 3.0 and they are quite likely to be the first ones to cause trouble. If they are valuable (and many of them are), then keep them outside of the Photoshop directory and load them (with as few other filters as possible) when needed. Also, check with the manufacturers to see if newer versions are available. As much as it is possible, you should keep your third-party filters up to date.

Known problem filters are Alien Skin Black Box 2.0, which does not run on Photoshop 4.0 on either platform (upgrade to 2.1 or Eye Candy 3.0) and, on the PC, early versions of Aldus Gallery Effects (you no longer need these since updated versions are included with version 4.0 of Photoshop). Version 3.0 of Kai's Power Tools needs to be updated to version 3.01 or later.

Scanner Noise

Another problem that we see fairly often on the Adobe Forum is noise along the bottom edge of a scan or across an entire scanned image. We have seen reports of lines appearing randomly in images. *This is not a Photoshop problem.*

It is not Photoshop that causes this noise, even if you have used Photoshop as your scanning application; the noise is coming from the SCSI chain on your computer. All scanners on Macs and most scanners on Windows systems are attached to a SCSI adapter in the computer. SCSI devices are chained together on the computer. The first device in the chain is connected to the SCSI adapter using a SCSI cable. The second device in the chain connects to the first and so on. Scanner noise is caused by a SCSI cable that is not in good condition, and it can take a lot of work to figure out which one is bad. Please believe us. Even if Photoshop is the only program in which you see the problem, it is not Photoshop that is at fault. We have never seen a case of this that was not caused by a defective SCSI cable.

Check all of your connections; the cable to the scanner might not be the one that is bad. Keep your SCSI cables very short. Buy the best cables that you can find from the most reputable manufacturer. Even if you end up spending a lot of money on SCSI cables, it is worth it in time saved.

Pixellated Proportional Scaling

This is the one major bug that was discovered in Photoshop 4.0—which is pretty good for a complex piece of software like Photoshop. Sometimes, when you press the Shift key and use the Free Transform command to scale an object, it becomes very pixellated and looks like it was done in low resolution. The fix: upgrade to version 4.0.1.

Corrupt Fonts

This is not the symptom of a problem so much as it can be the cause of a number of problems that are hard to solve on either Mac or Windows. On the Mac, you might get an "Unable to initialize" message. On Windows systems, a corrupt TrueType font is thought to be the cause of problems importing Adobe Illustrator files. If you have trouble, you need to test each font to see which one is causing the system to reject it.

General Troubleshooting Strategies

Some of the specifics to check are different on Mac and Windows, but what follows is an all-purpose "Before-I-throw-out-the-computer" guide to helping you figure out what could be bugging a system and program that had previously been working just fine. If you suddenly notice a problem with Photoshop, here's a general list of things to try (from simple to drastic):

1. Toss out the prefs file and restart Photoshop.
2. Did you install any new software on your computer? If you did, see if you can figure out what it replaced or what changes it made to your system files (the Control Panels or Extensions on the Mac or WIN.INI on Windows). Did it update any utilities such as ATM or QuickTime? If possible, revert back to the time before the changes. There are programs available on the Windows platform such as Uninstaller, Quarterdeck Clean Sweep, and others that can monitor software installations and allow you to easily see what has changed, or temporarily back out the programs to see if it makes your problem go away.
3. Have you changed anything in your system? Deleted any files? Moved anything? Had any children playing with your system? If so, check to see if anything significant was inadvertently deleted. Restore your system to the way it was and see if that works.
4. Try running without extensions on the Mac.
5. If you are still having problems, check your RAM allocation and make sure that it is enough on the Mac (and not too much on Windows). Check to make sure that the *computer* thinks you have as much RAM as is actually installed in the computer. On a MAC, choose About this Macintosh in the Finder on the Apple Menu. On Windows systems, open the Explorer and choose Help About Windows.
6. Test your RAM with a diagnostic program—especially if you are getting random crashes.
7. Reinstall Photoshop.
8. If nothing helps after you have gotten to Step 7, call Adobe Tech Support and then call your hardware vendor. You should not perform Steps 9 or 10 unless requested to by Tech Support.

9. Reinstall your operating system. Do NOT perform this step unless you know exactly what you are doing. Depending on your operating system, you may need to reinstall every existing application following this step.
10. Reformat your hard drive and restore from backup tape—then reinstall your system software and the application software. This is a major hassle. Try everything else first!

Mac Troubleshooting

Troubleshooting the Mac is a topic all to itself. It's not that the Mac is unstable, but it is delicate. It is usually "plug and play"—much more so than the Wintel platform—but when things don't work, they can be even harder to fix because the Mac tries to be user-friendly and to protect you from technical matters. Therefore, when something goes wrong, it often takes a professional technician to fix what a technically savvy PC user could do without a technician. Luckily, things don't usually go that wrong.

There are a number of issues that pertain only to the Macintosh (just as Windows has its own set of "gotchas").

Making the Mac Run Fast

When folks complain that their Mac runs Photoshop much too slowly, here is the standard CompuServe Adobe Photoshop Forum response:

1. Turn off Virtual Memory. Even on a Power Mac, where Adobe says that you can use a small amount of Virtual Memory, don't. Photoshop uses its own memory scheme when it writes to temporary files on your scratch disks. Unless RAM is critically short for you, do not turn on VM. It only gets in the way.
2. Do not set your cache higher than 96K. Most graphics programs do not require a high cache setting. You should be able to get away with a cache setting of 32K, which is the minimum.
3. Although they are very useful, turn off the Layer palette and Channel palette thumbnails. They slow down the screen redrawing. *Do not do this unless you are having a problem.* Better yet, get more RAM.
4. Make sure that you have a large area of free disk space for your scratch disk and keep it defragmented.
5. Get more RAM.
6. Consider a multi-processor card or a faster Mac.
7. Get more RAM.
8. Purchase a RAID disk array.
9. Get more RAM. (It's true, you can never have too much.)

Type 11 & Other System Errors

The dreaded Type 11 error message has plagued the Mac since the introduction of the Power Mac. It is not a very specific error—even though it indicates a memory error, all it really means is "You lose . . . system going down." You can get a Type 11 error from a buggy piece of software or from bad RAM or from a variety of other causes. The trick is to determine which it is. If you are getting constant Type 11 errors on a new computer, there are two very likely causes: you have noisy SCSI cables or bad RAM. Take the computer back to the vendor and have it checked out. Keep taking the machine back to the vendor until it is fixed.

It is not uncommon to get a Type 11 error several times a month; several times a day is too much. If you get Type 11 errors that are totally random and not repeatable, then your RAM is the first thing that you should suspect. We have found the Mac to be quite temperamental, in general, about the quality of the RAM that it wishes to consume. It only wants the "good stuff." Newer Technology makes an excellent RAM for the Mac. It is more expensive than "no name" brands, but it always seems to work. Sometimes, the Mac's RAM gets bored with its location and just wants to be rearranged. You might be able to recover from Type 11 errors by changing the placement of the RAM in your machine. Do not use composite RAM SIMMs. Make sure that all of your RAM is the same speed. In some rare instances, you might also need to replace the computer's motherboard.

TIP *O/S 8 seems to be much more successful at avoiding constant Type 11 errors, so you might want to upgrade your operating system.*

If RAM is not the problem and your SCSI cables seem to be working just fine, here are some other steps that you can take in addition to the general troubleshooting steps already mentioned:

1. Check your RAM, Cache, VM settings.
2. Start up the machine without extensions (usually by pressing the Shift key after you see the Welcome to Macintosh message, though non-Apple keyboards might have different methods).
3. Remove the Fonts folder from the System folder. Sometimes a corrupt font can cause the problem and the System will create a new folder with the minimum fonts that it needs. You can then put the fonts back a few at a time or get one of the new font checker programs that verify the integrity of the fonts.
4. If that does not help, remove the Extensions, Control Panels, and Preferences folders from the System folder. They, too, will be re-created with the minimum need to run. Don't trash the original folders—just drag them out of the System folder.

5. Make sure that you are using the latest disk drivers and that they are compatible with the System version that you are using. Check your disk for bad media using Disk First Aid or Norton or Central Point Utilities.
6. Remove the Enable Asynch I/O plug-in folder from the Photoshop Plug-Ins/Extensions folder.
7. Change your scratch disk so that it uses an internal hard drive (ideally your boot drive) and locate Photoshop on the internal drive as well.

Type 1 or Type 10 errors can be treated the same way, but they are neither as severe or prevalent as the Type 11 errors.

Extension Conflicts & the Usual Suspects

Mac extension conflicts are notorious and annoying. They can be hard to spot and there can also be conflicts between certain extensions and Mac plug-ins. While we do not want to make disparaging remarks about specific pieces of software, what follows is a list of "suspect" extensions—extensions that are known to *sometimes* cause trouble. They work flawlessly for most users and cause other users major headaches. If you use one of the suspects and have no problems, then consider yourself fortunate. If you begin to have flakies occur in Photoshop, these are the extensions that you should immediately remove to see if the problems go away:

1. Norton Directory Assistance. This program is bad news. Do not use it. Norton has discontinued it in Version 3. Its work-alikes such as Super Boomerang from NOW Utilities are also troublesome, though not as buggy.
2. RAM Doubler. This works for most users, but if there is a problem it should be one of the first programs disabled. If you use it, do not assign Photoshop any more RAM than the machine physically contains. If you have a 16MB machine, do not give Photoshop a RAM partition larger than 16MB.
3. QuickKeys. Usually okay, but disable if there is a problem. The CE Toolbox needed to run QuickKeys seems to cause the most trouble.
4. Any form of disk compression is asking for trouble. You are better off buying more hard drive.
5. The True Finder Integration feature that comes with Stuffit Deluxe can be another candidate for trouble.
6. Older versions of ATM and ATR (Adobe Type Reunion) in conjunction with older versions of Suitcase. This is a dangerous mix. Update them all. Tread warily with the new versions as well, although these are necessary extension categories.
7. The clock that appears in the top menu bar has been found to cause problems on some systems.
8. Any version of OneClick. This is a very badly behaved extension, which is a shame because it gives AutoF/X Power Pac most of its power (and you cannot run Power Pac without it).

9. Norton File Saver. This can cause Photoshop to crash or quit. If you are crashing whenever you leave Photoshop, then you are either running File Saver (or a similar program) or an old version of MetaCreations KPT 3.0. If KPT is the problem, there is an update available.
10. DOS Mounter Plus and DOS Mounter 95 seem to make the system a bit more crash-inclined. Don't stop using them, just be aware of the number of times that you crash and when the crashes happen. If they usually occur when you are opening or accessing files, try removing these Control Panels.
11. Don't run the Gamma Control Panel if you are using another Calibration program such as Color Synergy.
12. Master Juggler and some of the filters in Cytopia PhotoOptics do not get along with one another. The system crashes.

Memory Leaks

One of the most troublesome and difficult to remove problems in Photoshop is the memory leak. It seems to affect users with a lot of RAM. The symptoms are that you get a message "Unable to . . . because of insufficient RAM." This usually occurs after you have been working for a long time and have opened and closed a large number of windows. The message can appear when you have a tiny 1MB file open or even a 100K file. You look at your generous RAM allocation and wonder if Photoshop has lost its mind.

The problem seems to be caught somewhere between Photoshop and the Macintosh operating system. All systems perform an operation called "garbage collection" in which unused memory locations are reclaimed and recycled to give programs more space. Sometimes, the garbage collectors seem to go on strike. When this happens, you get a memory leak—and a message that tells you you are out of RAM, even though you know that it should not be possible.

Although the problem is hard to cure, it is easy to fix—quit Photoshop and restart it. The problem will disappear, at least for a while. Learn to anticipate this. Don't run Photoshop for three days without quitting from it. If new windows seem to appear very slowly, restart the program. Since you might not be able to save your image if there isn't enough RAM, it's better to quit Photoshop before you get into trouble. By the way, save early and often.

Lost Cursor

Another common problem that occurs for no reason that we can pin-point, is the "lost cursor" error. The symptoms are clear. When you drag your cursor over your image, you no longer can see it. That makes editing and painting very tricky!

The fix is easy. Remove the Direct Cursors plug-in from the Extensions folder inside of the Photoshop Plug-Ins folder. Unfortunately, you will no longer be able to see any painting tool that is larger than 16 pixels, but you *will* be able to see the cursor—which is more important in the scheme of things.

Cannot Initialize Because of a Disk Error

This error message is usually lying to you. Only very rarely is something actually wrong with your hard drive. The three most common causes of this message are a corrupt font, corrupted Preferences file, or the presence or absence of the Macintosh Easy Open Control Panel.

Trash your Prefs file. Remove the Fonts folder from the System folder. Check to see if Easy Open is loaded. If it is, remove it; if it is not; load it. One of these actions should fix the problem.

If a font is the problem, move your fonts back in one at a time until you locate the problem child.

In one case, this error message appeared after a system crash left the Prefs file both corrupt and open. The System thought that the file was open, so it could not replace the Prefs file. When we moved the Prefs file to the trash and emptied it, it was not really removed and the new file still could not be created. Unfortunately, with the file gone, there was no way to close it either. We needed to restore the Prefs file from a backup tape and then trash the restored copy in order to get the system up and running again. Bottom line: *Do not empty the trash until you are able to re-open Photoshop.*

Preview Icons Are Scrambled in the Finder or Do Not Launch Photoshop

Sometimes the cute preview icons that Photoshop creates are not worth the trouble. System 7.5 seemed to mangle them frequently, although the problem seems much better under System 7.5.3 and later. However, if you look at the preview icon and it does not match the name of the file, you know that you've been hit. You are more likely to find this occurring on a removable drive than on a fixed disk.

This is unrelated to the problem of not being able to launch a file by double-clicking it, but the fix is the same (and we will get to it in a moment): sometimes a program causes Photoshop's file creator to be incorrectly specified. Installing version 6.0 of Adobe Illustrator with the Gallery Effects filters turned all Photoshop documents into documents created by Gallery Effects. Double-clicking an icon does not invoke Photoshop when the file creator is incorrectly set.

When this happens, you need to rebuild your desktop (or every so often even when it doesn't). To rebuild the desktop, hold down the Option and Command keys after your extensions have loaded but before the hard drives are mounted. You then have the chance to rebuild all of desktop files for hard drives (or to skip those volumes that you prefer), but you might lose the Get Info comments when you rebuild the desktop (depending upon your operating system version).

For good measure, you might also want to reset your Parameter RAM. Reset the Parameter RAM (PRAM) by holding down the Command+Option+P+R keys when you restart the computer. Hold the keys until you hear two beeps, then release the keys. This resets the system preferences to the default.

Magnifier Keyboard Command Does Not Work

If you press the Command+Spacebar keys and do not see the Zoom tool icon, then you are probably not looking at an English language keyboard layout. Unfortunately, it is easy to accidentally change your language definition. Remove the WorldScript extension and the extra keyboard definitions and the problem will go away.

Windows Troubleshooting

Windows troubleshooting can get technical very quickly. Advice can differ depending on whether you're using Windows 95 or Windows NT. Unless we specify, advice applies to all Windows flavors. Adobe provides FAXBACK and online support via the World Wide Web. They have many FAQs available that give detailed advice on configuring Windows. You should check the Web site (http://www.adobe.com) first to see if there are any documents dealing with your problem. CompuServe's Adobe Forum is still the best way to ask specific questions and get customized advice.

Making Windows Run Fast

Here are some tips to make Photoshop run as fast as possible on a Windows machine. (Yes, much of the advice is similar to that for the Mac.)

1. Set up your Windows Swap file so that it is as large as the maximum amount of RAM that you have available for Photoshop. (To find out how much that is, select File | Preferences | Memory & Cache and temporarily set the amount available to Photoshop to 100%. Your permanent Windows swap file should be set to that size.) There is no benefit to creating a larger swap file than this. If this number is smaller than the amount suggested by your Windows installation, use the larger amount.
2. Leave at least 3–5 times the size of your largest file in free disk space on the disk that you specify as your scratch disk. If you can devote an entire disk partition to Photoshop for its scratch files, that is even better. Keep your scratch disk defragmented and optimized.
3. Although they are very useful, turn off the Layer palette and Channel palette thumbnails. They slow down the screen redrawing. *Do not do this unless you are having a problem.* Better yet, get more RAM.
4. Run the latest version of the operating system and the most current version of Photoshop. Run Windows 95 in preference to Windows 3.1 or Windows NT in preference to Windows 95.
5. Get more RAM.
6. Consider a multi-processor system or a faster machine. Photoshop should run faster under NT than under Windows 95, especially if you have more than one processor or are running a Pentium Pro processor.

7. Get more RAM.
8. Purchase a RAID disk array running on a Fast-Wide SCSI 3 adapter.
9. Get more RAM. (It's true, you can never have too much.)
10. If you choose to upgrade to a new, faster machine, look for a machine that allows you to exceed 256MB of RAM. (High-end PCs typically allow less RAM expansion than high-end Macs.)

Testing to Find Windows 95 Errors

You have already been shown how to start your computer in Safe Mode. However, when you do, you are not able to access all of the drivers and features that you need, and you cannot run Photoshop from Safe Mode because it typically loads the standard VGA driver (16 colors) which is not sufficient for Photoshop. You can create a test configuration for Photoshop, however, that allows you to selectively add and remove drivers, or whatever you need to help you determine the problem. It requires that you start the computer in Step by Step Confirmation mode. You can get more detail by reading the Adobe document "Minimizing Windows 95 to Troubleshoot Errors in Photoshop 3.0.5 and Later." Follow this procedure ONLY if you are using 16-bit drivers in Config.Sys. If you can't tell, don't bother (and if you do not understand this paragraph, *definitely* don't bother unless an Adobe Technical Support person walks you through it). Briefly, you need to:

1. Press F8 after you see the Starting Windows message.
2. Enable HIMEM.SYS, IFSHLP.SYS, all Windows drivers, and the Windows GUI. Also say "yes" to any devices that contain the word "double" in them. If you are using Doublespace to compress your disk, you need to have it running.
3. Once all of the Windows drivers are loaded, Windows will start.

If this doesn't fix the problem, you can set up a test configuration that will allow you to turn off one device at a time until you discover the driver or device that is causing the problem.

Windows NT Troubleshooting

Here is a sequence of items for you to check if you have trouble with your Photoshop installation under Windows NT. Many of these items are also applicable to Windows. For details of how to do the specifics, you need to consult your Windows manuals or to call Adobe Technical support. In the meantime, here's what you should be looking for if you have trouble with your Photoshop installation under Windows NT:

1. Make sure you have the minimum amount of random access memory (RAM) that Photoshop requires to run (at least 16MB for Photoshop 4.0). In Windows NT 4.0 choose Start > Settings > Control Panel > System. On the General tab, look

under the Computer section. This will tell you the amount of physical RAM on the system. If you are using any RAM-doubling software, turn it off and try to re-create the error.

2. Update to the latest Windows NT 4.0 Service Pack. Contact Microsoft for further information.
3. Trash and re-create Photoshop's Preferences files.
4. Specify a different default printer. You might try to install Microsoft's PostScript printer driver as the default. Even if you have no PostScript printer (or any printer), you should specify a default printer. If that helps, and you have a different PostScript printer, then contact your printer manufacturer to see if there is an updated driver.
5. Remove Photoshop and then reinstall it from the installation disks or CD-ROM while in VGA mode. (Make sure that you have moved your third-party plug-ins to a different location before you do this. Otherwise, you will lose them all and have to reinstall them from the original disks.
6. Ensure there's adequate free space on the hard disk to which Windows temporary (.tmp) variables are set. Exit all applications.
7. Ensure there's adequate free space on the hard disk to which Photoshop's scratch disks are set.
8. Change the location of and/or resize the Windows Virtual memory Paging File. If there is not enough free space on the drive, consider changing the drive on which the Paging file is located. Set the Initial Size to the amount of physical RAM on your system plus 12MB. The Maximum size should be not less than the amount set for the Initial Size; preferably it should be twice the amount of physical RAM on the computer.
9. If you have a dual-boot system, optimize and defragment your hard disk(s) using the ScanDisk and Disk Defragmenter utilities included with Windows 95. If you only use Windows NT 4.0, use an NT 4.0-compatible third-party utility to run disk scanning and defragging programs. Read the documentation before you do this!
10. Verify that all your device drivers are Windows NT 4.0 compatible and working correctly. Device drivers are software that runs things like your scanner, video card, SCSI card, mouse, keyboard, and so on. Contact the hardware manufacturer for the latest Windows NT 4.0 drivers. Adobe cannot keep track of all of the drivers and does not supply them.
11. Change the number of colors and resolution of the video display adapter. If your machine is set to 256 colors, try the millions of colors options; if it is set to millions, try setting it to 256 to see if the problem goes away. If it does, your drivers may be having trouble with Windows NT 4.0. If changing the video display driver fixes the problem, contact your video card manufacturer to see if updated drivers are available.

12. Disable hard drive compression or move the temporary files location and Photoshop's scratch disk to a non-compressed drive.
13. Use Event Manager to check for reports of damaged files or stopped drivers. These reports can sometimes give you valuable hints as to what system component is causing the problem. However, the messages tend to be cryptic.
14. Turn off Application Performance Boosting. To do this, go to Start | Settings | Control Panels | System | Performance. Under Application Performance, move the slider from Maximum to None.
15. Make sure that all of your hardware drivers are compatible with Windows NT 4.0 and are the most recent versions. SCSI adapters, video display adapters, sound cards, scanners, CD-ROMs, removable hard drives, removable media such as Syquest, Jaz, Zip drives all need to have updated and compatible Windows NT 4.0 drivers.
16. Check to make certain that your SCSI chain is terminated properly. When you check this, also make sure that your cables are connected properly and that they are in good condition.
17. Check the status of the SCSI Adapters. You can find this by going to Start > Settings > Control Panel > SCSI Adapters. Click on each adapter listed on the Devices tab, and then, for each, click on the Properties button. The Card info tab's Device Status section will tell you if the SCSI adapter is working correctly or not. You can find out what drivers are used by clicking on the Driver tab. If you suspect there's a problem with this device or driver, contact the manufacturer for updated drivers or further help.
18. Always shut down Windows NT 4.0 properly. Do not simply flick the switch to Off—no matter how annoyed you get with the computer!
19. Reinstall Windows NT 4.0. *WARNING:* This is a drastic step. Do not do this unless you have been instructed to do so and you know what you are doing!

MMX

If you are using Windows NT 4.0 and an MMX-enhanced Pentium processor, Photoshop may return the Access violation error if the MMX plug-ins are out of date (i.e., not from version 4.0.1 of Photoshop). The FastCore plug-in included with Photoshop 4.0 can cause Photoshop to return an error when running on a computer with an MMX-enhanced Pentium processor. The updated FastCore and MMXCore plug-ins replace the FastCore plug-in included with Photoshop 4.0.

To solve this problem, disable the FastCore plug-in, then install the updated FastCore and MMXCore plug-ins as follows:

1. Make sure that Photoshop is not running.
2. In Windows Explorer, rename the FASTCORE.8BX file in the Adobe\Photoshp\Plugins\Extensns folder to FASTCORE.OLD.

3. You can download the FastCore and MMXCore plug-ins file (FAST.EXE) from Adobe's Web site (http://www.adobe.com), but we recommend that you purchase the Photoshop 4.0.1 Update CD-ROM from Adobe Customer Services (800-833-6687).

MMX technology adds major performance boosts to Intel processors. The FastCore plug-in included with Photoshop 4.0 and the updated FastCore and MMXCore plug-ins let Photoshop take advantage of MMX technology. Photoshop can run without these plug-ins, though some of the functions will be slower.

Color

You must install a video driver with at least 256 colors in order for Photoshop to be able to operate.

Page Fault Errors in Windows 95

If you get a message that you cannot open Photoshop because of a page Fault error in module <unknown>, check your video drivers. This error is usually caused by a damaged or incorrect video driver. Install your video driver again using the original driver file either from the manufacturer or from the list in Windows. Sometimes, when Windows detects new hardware, it "helps" by loading a generic driver, even when the "real" thing is available. Generic drivers are rarely as good or as reliable as the driver that is supposed to be working.

Problems With Deluxe Tutorial

There have been a number of trouble reports when users have installed the Deluxe Tutorial. The most common problem is that games that used to work, no longer do. You might want to do a custom installation of Photoshop and not install the tutorial. The problem is that the installation program places a copy of QuickTime on your machine that might not be the one needed to run other applications. QuickTime and Windows are still trying to work together peaceably but they are not quite there yet, and the results can sometimes be unpredictable with different versions of QuickTime.

Mouse Problems

This is another well-known area of problems. The symptoms are GROWSTUB errors in Module POINTER.DLL or mouse freezes. You need to check to make sure that you have only one MOUSE.DRV file installed. You also need to use a Microsoft mouse driver. This issue has been tricky because, while you need to make sure that your mouse driver is not corrupt, sometimes you need to replace the driver with an *earlier* one. If you cannot get your mouse to work properly, you might need to call Adobe Tech support and have them work through this one with you.

Double-clicking an Icon Starts the Wrong Program

Windows systems use the file extension to determine what program to launch. When an application is installed, it tells Windows what to do when an icon with that extension is double-clicked. Most applications don't bother looking to see if a different program already claims that extension. If you install two applications that register the same extension (e.g., Photoshop and Corel Draw both register .TIF files), the last program installed is the one that launches when the icon is double-clicked.

If a newly installed application has grabbed an extension that you want processed by Photoshop, you have three choices:

1. Re-install Photoshop over your existing installation. This will do no harm as long as you are installing the same version and will take back the vagrant extension.
2. Live with it and open the files by first opening Photoshop and using the File Open dialog box.
3. Modify the Registry to change the extension's owner. If you do not know how to do this, don't even try. If you don't know what the Registry is, don't even *think* about trying this.

Using Actions

In Photoshop 4.0, Adobe has replaced the Commands palette with an Actions palette. While this is not a universally beloved change (the Commands palette allowed for quick access to frequently executed commands in a way that occupied much less screen real estate), the Actions facility adds a much-needed scripting environment to Photoshop and can be a real productivity-assist.

Actions allows you to save a series of steps and execute them again by clicking on the location where the steps are stored. This is very useful if you perform repetitive sequences of commands in Photoshop. If, for example, you scan a roll of film into the computer and discover that you need to add the same Curves correction to each image, you can create an action that applies the Curves setting, resizes the image to a specific size and resolution, and changes the image to CMYK. You can then drag all of the images for that roll of film into one folder and run your saved Action on all of the images at one time (using the Batch command on the Actions palette). Many of the grayscale images in this book were prepared in batch mode using an action to change the original color images into grayscale images by changing the RGB mode to LAB color and then removing channels a and b, and finally, setting the color space to grayscale.

Let's look at the Actions palette. Figure 1-23 shows the Actions palette with the default actions and the Actions palette menu visible. As you can see, you can do all of the "usual" things to an action—make a New Action, Save an Action, Delete an Action, and so forth. You can also Duplicate an Action, and, of course, Play an Action. The menu items are very straightforward, and selecting them does exactly what you would expect (for example, Replace Actions takes the current actions in your palette and deletes them and loads another set of actions).

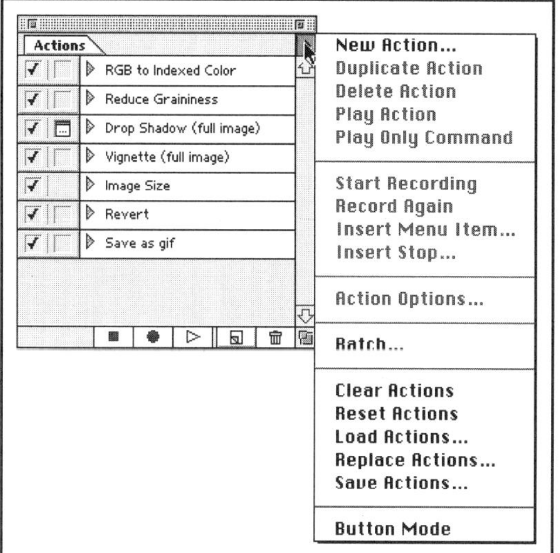

Figure 1-23: Actions palette and menu.

However, this only tells part of the story. There are two other tales to tell: what Actions *can't* do, and what Actions *can* do that you probably didn't think about.

Limitations of Actions

In order to create an action, you choose New Action and then simply perform the task that you want to record. The Actions palette "watches" what you do and writes a script that allows you to repeat that sequence of commands any time that you want. If this sounds too good to be true, it is. In this implementation of actions, there are only certain activities that can be recorded.

You can record most—but not all—of the commands found on the main menu and its submenus. On the File menu, for example, you cannot record File Info or Page Setup. You can record many of the activities that you perform on the Layers and Channels palettes, but you cannot record the Opacity or Apply mode changes. You can, however, capture the changes made to the Opacity and Apply mode settings if you create a new layer by using the modifier key (Mac: Option, Windows: Alt) when you click on the New Layer icon at the bottom of the Layers palette. (Creating a New Layer with the modifier key shows a dialog box that allows you to change the settings to the ones that you want.)

You can record the specific settings of most of Photoshop's built-in filters (with the exception of the Lighting Effects filter which is just too complex). Most of the third-party filters, however, are not recordable. The action will show that a specific third-party filter was used, but not the settings for the filter. All filters need to be updated to 4.0 standards for them to be recordable. The only major filter set that has been so updated is Kai's Power Tools using the KPT Actions pack.

You cannot record mouse actions at all. This means that the Paint tools on the menu are not recordable. You cannot capture brush strokes nor can you capture selecting and moving of areas of the image. This means that you cannot use the Actions palette to design a low-resolution version of your image and play it back at higher resolution to save time (as you can in Painter, for example). Perhaps the next version of Photoshop will permit this. Certainly, the Actions feature has not yet reached its full potential.

Recording an Action

Now that you've heard what Actions cannot do, there is still a lot that it can do. Let's create two fairly simple actions, just to give you an idea of how this is done. The two actions we'll create are changing an RGB image to grayscale using Lab mode (this usually produces a better grayscale image) and creating a simple emboss without using the Emboss filter (which will turn out to be not-so-simple after all).

Converting RGB to Grayscale

1. Open the image MONKEY2.PSD from the Enhanced Photoshop CD-ROM. Choose Image | Duplicate and click OK. You will use this duplicate image to record the action.
2. Click on the New Action icon at the bottom of the Actions palette (it looks just like the icons for New Layer, New Channel, etc.). Figure 1-24 shows the resulting dialog box. Name the Action RGB to Gray.

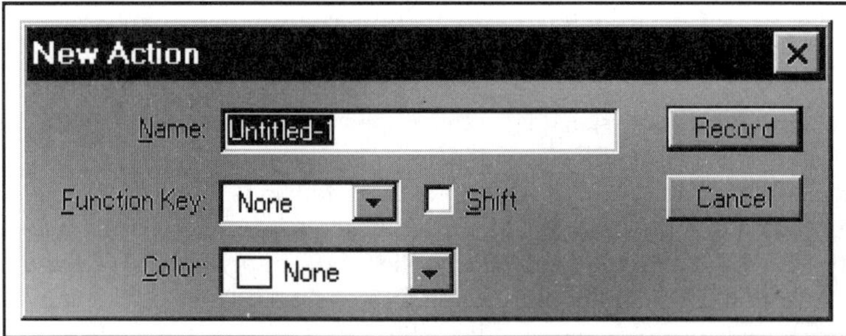

Figure 1-24: New Action dialog box.

3. Select Image | Mode | Lab. The Actions palette records "Convert Mode."
4. Click on the Channels tab to view the Channels palette (this step is not recorded, but it does not need to be). Figure 1-25 shows the Channels palette.

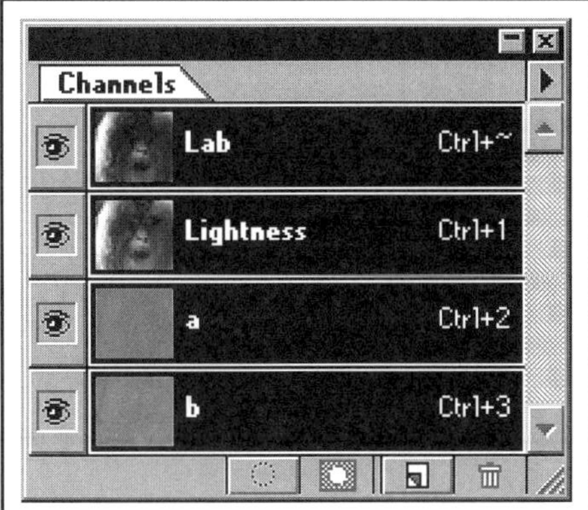

Figure 1-25: Channels palette in Lab mode.

5. Drag the b channel to the Trash icon at the bottom-right of the Channels palette. The Actions palette records "Delete."
6. Drag the a channel (now called #2) to the Trash icon at the lower right of the Channels palette. Again, you will see "Delete" appear in the Actions list.
7. Finally, choose Image | Mode | Grayscale to convert the image, which has become Multichannel once you removed the b channel, into a grayscale image.
8. Click on the Stop button to the left of the Record button in the Actions palette. Figure 1-26 shows the completed action expanded so that you can see exactly what was recorded.
9. Close the image that you used for the action without saving it. There is no way to undo the entire action, and, since the image was a duplicate and not saved, there is no way to revert it either.
10. Make the original image active again by clicking on it (actually, it becomes active again as soon as you close the copy, if it is the only other open image). Choose Image | Duplicate and click OK.
11. Click on the Play button on the Actions palette (it is the right-most button in the left group of buttons and looks like a right-pointing unfilled triangle). This tests your action to make sure that it does what you *want* it to do (as well as what you *told* it to do—which is a common problem with any kind of programming).

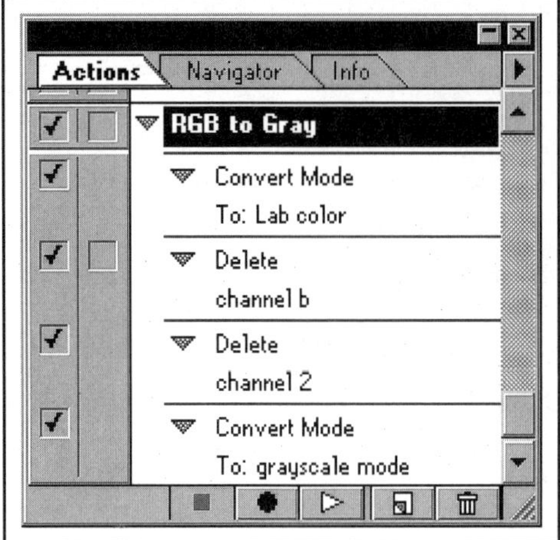

Figure 1-26: Completed action showing all recorded commands.

This action is typical of the type of action that you would want to record so that you could batch process a group of files at one time. The action that you just created does not save your file. Therefore, if you were to batch a folder full of RGB images to convert, you have to think about what you want done to the file after it has been converted. We will discuss several different possibilities.

Figure 1-27 shows the dialog box that results from selecting the Batch option on the Actions palette menu. You can see that it allows you to select your input method, the Action to run, and the output destination.

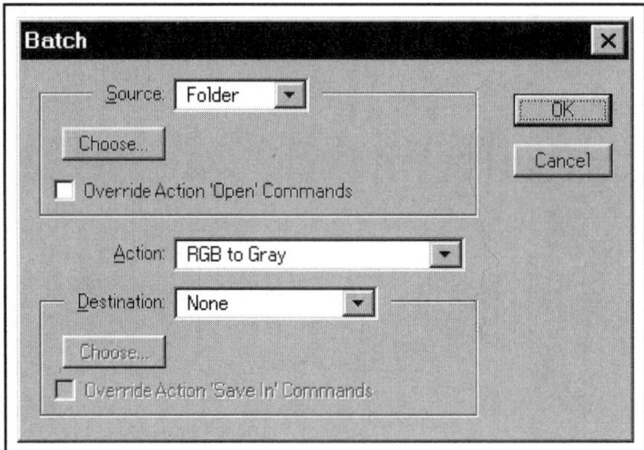

Figure 1-27: Expanded RGB to Gray Action showing all steps and options.

For input, you can select Folder or Import. Folder produces the standard File Open dialog box and allows you to select the folder or subdirectory that you want to process. The command is not recursive—it will not open folders nested within the selected folder. The Import option allows you to process successive input from QuickEdit, a TWAIN source, or your attached scanner.

There are three output options. When the Action is finished, you can do Nothing, Save and Close, or write the changed file to a specified folder. If you select Nothing as the option, the batch process ignores the file once the Action is completed. In the Action that you just created, this would leave all of the files open in Photoshop—which could lead you to run out of RAM if there are enough of them, and then, you would still have to save them if you wanted to keep the results (and if you didn't want to keep the results, why bother batching the files in the first place). "Nothing" is a good option when you have built into your Action the total number of steps needed to fully complete and save the file.

The Save and Close option does just what its name suggests. It saves the changes that the Action has made onto the original file in its original location. By doing so, it updates your original copy, and then closes it. This sounds like a wonderful option, but think for a moment about its implications. What happens if you accidentally run the wrong Action on it and walk away? Or if the Action does not quite do what you thought it would? You would lose all of your original images. This is a very dangerous option. If you want to use this option, *duplicate the folder and its contents before you run the batch process* and let Photoshop work with the copy.

The third option, Folder, allows you to select the location to which Photoshop will write the completed Action. It gives you a standard File dialog box and allows you to pick a folder or subdirectory. Usually, this is the best option. Create your subdirectory before you invoke the Batch command. Then your changes are written to a new location and your originals are safe. Maybe.

There is one major "gotcha" when you use this scenario. If you are preparing grayscale images for placement in a page-layout program, as the Action that you have created seems to indicate, then you might want to change the file type to .TIF to make it easier to place the files. The only way to change a file type when a file is saved is to use the Save As command. This writes the file to the location specified in the Action—not the location specified by the Folder choice in the Batch command. Unless you really understand what is happening, you will get unintended results:

1. If "Save As" is placed in Action on the Mac with "Never" as the Add file extension option in the Saving Files Preference and you select the same folder, then you are likely to select Replace as the Save option. When this happens, your batch will replace all of your original files with the grayscale ones and write the file again to the specified Folder location. This leaves you with two grayscale versions and no RGB originals.

2. If you are working on the PC or if the Mac is set to append a file extension, then you will not be writing over your original file. However, you will end up leaving a copy in the location specified in the Action and another copy in the batch folder. Now you have three versions—two grayscales and an RGB.

So, what's the solution? There are two, equally valid. You can re-record your Action and specify the new "Save As" folder for your grayscale files before you run each new batch. If you want to use this option, then add a Close command into the original Action as well. Choose Nothing as your option for the destination.

You can check the box that says Override Actions Save In Command. This then places the Save As file in the folder that you specify in the Batch command. Either way works.

Because there is no way to undo a completed Action and there is real potential for damage, you must test any action on a non-critical file. Remember, you are really writing a small computer program when you create an Action, and like any other computer program, it can have bugs (unfortunately). So an ounce of prevention....

There is another command that can also cause your Action to go haywire in Batch mode. This is the Image Size command. A very common way to use this in batch mode is to prepare files for printing by setting their resolution to 300 ppi.

We like to create images by specifying their pixel dimensions and are not always careful about setting the resolution to 300 ppi when the file is first created (if you know the accurate pixel sizes, then the resolution does not matter until the file needs to be printed). However, before we print the files, we need to make sure that they are all set to 300 ppi—with no resampling occurring.

When you insert an Image Size command, there is no way to record the status of the Resample Image flag. If you accidentally play the Action again with the Resample Image flag on (because you needed to enlarge or reduce an image and forgot to set the flag back), your file grows huge as it is resampled up to 300 ppi. Don't even ask how many times this has happened! The fix for this is to be very careful or to click on the second column of the Action to allow you to respond to the Image Size dialog box when the Action is played.

"To click on the second column of the Action . . . "—what does that mean? Follow along and let's try it. At the same time, you will learn how to add steps to an Action.

Editing an Action

1. Open the image file Monkey2.Psd on the companion CD-ROM. Choose Image | Duplicate | OK to make a copy.
2. Click on the twirly arrow next to the RGB to Gray Action to expand it (if it is closed). Then click to select the last step that says Convert Mode as shown in Figure 1-28.

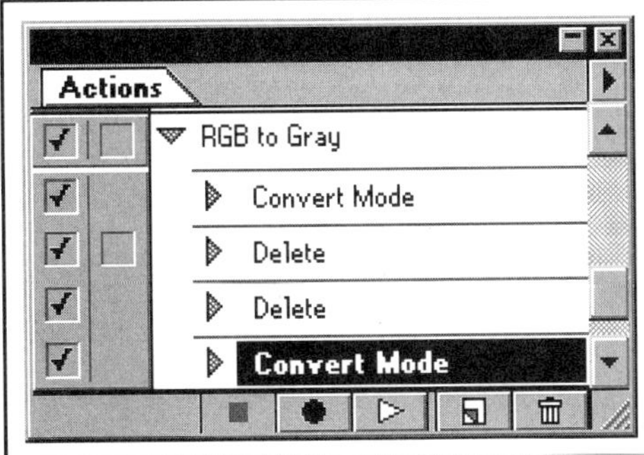

Figure 1-28: Expanded Action with last step selected.

3. Click the Record button of the Actions palette. You can add commands from the bottom of the list now.
4. Choose Image | Image Size. Make sure that Resample Image is not checked, and then change the image Resolution to 300 ppi.
5. Select File | Save As and select .TIF as the file type. If you are using the Mac, select a different directory so that you don't have to replace the original. Otherwise, you can save the TIFF file to any location that you want (including the current directory). Figure 1-29 shows the two new steps that you have recorded.

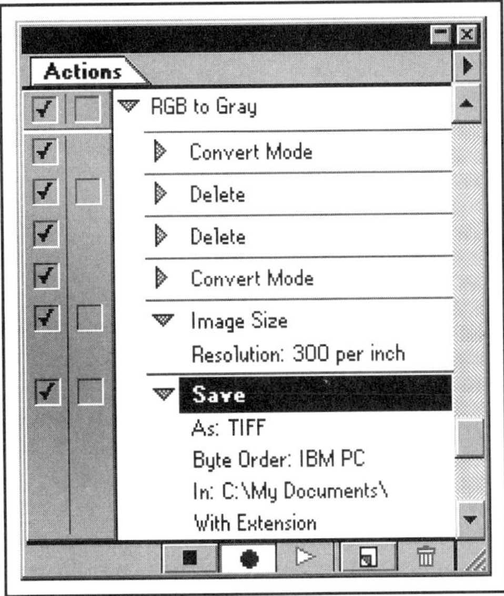

Figure 1-29: Additional steps added to RGB to Gray Action.

6. Click the Stop button.
7. Now you need to test the Action. Make another duplicate of the original image (Image | Duplicate | OK). Place your cursor on the RGB to Gray Action and press the Play button. Everything should work properly. Close the image that you just converted to grayscale.
8. Make another duplicate of the original image. Choose Image | Image Size. Click on the Resample Image box to place a checkmark there. Leave the resolution as it was and click OK.
9. Now, select the RGB to Gray Action and click on Play. Whoops! This time, the image resizes to over 4MB. By the time it is saved, it is too late to rescue it! Oh well . . . .
10. Examine Figure 1-30 very carefully. You should be able to see what looks like three little dots placed next to the Action title and next to the Image Size command in the second column. Click on the second column next to the Image Size command in the RGB to Gray Action on your Actions palette. You have just inserted a break point at that command.

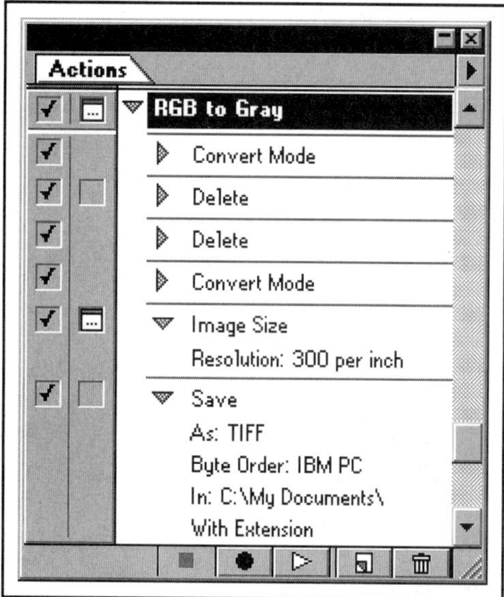

Figure 1-30: Inserting a Break Point into an Action.

11. Make another duplicate of the original file. Play the RGB to Gray Action again. This time, you actually have the opportunity to respond to the Image Size dialog box, and you can deselect the Resample Image box and change the Resolution to 300 ppi.

12. You can also change the order in which commands are performed. If, for some reason, you wanted the image resizing done first, all you need to do is to place the cursor on that command. It turns into a hand. Press the mouse and drag the command entry up until it is under the RGB to Gray title. Figure 1-31 shows the new order of the commands.

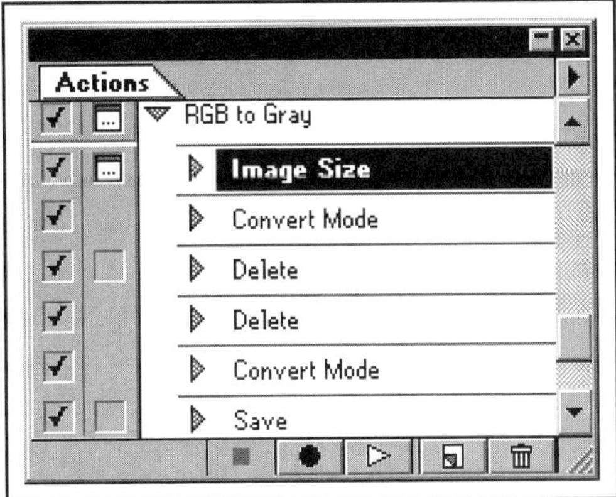

Figure 1-31: New order for RGB to Gray Action.

If you ever want to run the RGB to Gray Action in batch, you can make certain that the Image Size command is already set to not resample the image. You can then remove the break point and set the Batch command to override the Save option in the Action.

Action Workarounds

The Action that you just recorded had some tricky moments, but it was fairly straightforward and recorded just as you would normally perform those commands. However, in some cases, you might need to do some very creative thinking to develop an Action, or you will discover that you cannot record what you want at all (or at least not all of what you want). Here's an example of an embossing trick based on a tip posted a few years ago by Kai Krause (of MetaCreations).

You can emboss an image without using the Emboss filter by performing the steps below. Try it, and then we will see how you can create an Action to do the same thing.

Kai's Embossing Trick

1. Open the image TABLE1.PSD from the Enhanced Photoshop CD-ROM. Duplicate the image (Image | Duplicate | OK).
2. Drag the icon for the Background layer to the New Layer icon (the center icon at the bottom of the Layers palette).
3. Invert the image (Mac: Command-I, Windows: Ctrl-I).

4. Press 5 to change the Layer Opacity to 50%. (If it does not work, select the Marquee tool and try again.) The image turns solid gray. Why? Because every pixel on the top layer is the inverse of the pixel on the bottom, and when you add the two values together and divide by 2 (which is what happens at 50% Opacity), you always get 128—which is middle gray.
5. Press the modifier key (Mac: Command, Windows: Ctrl) and while holding the key, press the Left arrow key two times and the Down arrow key two times. Figure 1-32 shows the embossed image.

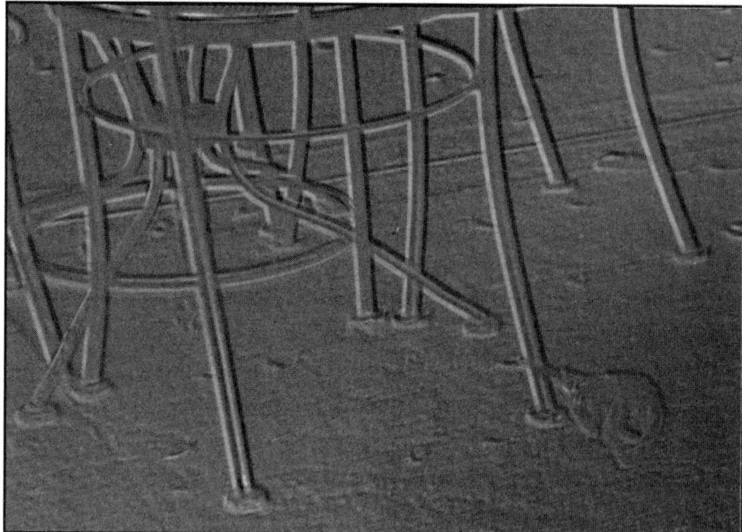

Figure 1-32: Embossed image created without the Emboss filter.

This is a very easy effect, but it is devilish to script because of the limitations of the current Actions implementation. However, the fact that you *can* create a script for it shows that Actions are also more powerful than they might first appear. Let's pull this effect apart and see where it has a problem.

The key trick to this effect is to invert a duplicate of the bottom layer and set its Opacity to 50%. Using Actions, you have a choice: you can either create a *new* layer that is 50% opaque, or you can duplicate the bottom layer. You cannot do both because the Actions palette will not record a *change* of opacity. It looks almost as if our attempt to script this is doomed.

What other ways are possible to get the data from the bottom layer to the top one? You could copy and paste the data, but that would create a layer of 100% Opacity. You could use the Apply Image command to place the image onto a layer that is 50% transparent, but Actions does not record the Apply Image command—not even the fact that it was used (although, if you wanted to "baby-sit" the Action each time it was run, you could insert the Apply Image menu item into the Action). What is left?

An embossed image really only needs gray values because color pixels just get in the way and cause flashes of spurious color in the final image. Therefore, you can desaturate an image as the first step in this procedure (and the Desaturate command is recordable). Once the image has been desaturated, all three of the RGB channels are (or should be) the same. You can script the creation of a new channel from an existing one. You can record the loading of that channel. What happens when you load a channel that is a grayscale picture and then fill the resulting selection with black? You get the inverse of the original image. Hmmm… That's just what we were trying to do. Let's script this new sequence.

Scripting Kai's Emboss

1. Open the image Table1.PSD from the Enhanced Photoshop CD-ROM. Duplicate the image (Image | Duplicate | OK).
2. Click on the New Action icon at the right of the Actions palette. Name the action Kai's Emboss Trick.
3. Select Image | Adjust | Desaturate (Mac: Shift+Command+U, Windows: Shift+Ctrl+U).
4. Click on the Channels palette and drag the Blue channel to the New Channels icon at the bottom of the Channels palette.
5. Click on the RGB channel to select it.
6. Return to the Layers palette. (This is not recorded.)
7. Make a new layer (press the Option key for the Mac or the Alt key on Windows and click on the New Layer icon at the bottom of the Layers Palette). In the dialog that appears, set the Opacity to 50% and the Mode to Normal.
8. Press D to set the colors back to the default of black and white.
9. Choose Edit | Fill and fill with Background color (white) or use the keyboard shortcut (Mac: Command+Delete or Windows: Ctrl+Backspace). This step makes the entire layer white, so that there are no transparent areas on it.
10. Load Channel 4 (Select | Load Selection; Channel 4 or Mac: Command+Option+4; Windows: Ctrl+Option+4). This turns Channel 4—a grayscale version of the image—into a selection.
11. Fill the selection with the foreground color (Mac: Option-Delete; Windows: Alt-Backspace). This step adds black in varying amounts to the lightest portions of the grayscale image. Thus, it effectively inverses (or creates a negative) of the original image. When you finish this step, which is analogous to Step 4 in the previous exercise, your image looks solid gray.
12. Deselect (Mac: Command-D, Windows: Ctrl-D).

13. Offset the image (Filter -> Other -> Offset, –2 pixels right, 2 pixels down, Wrap around). This makes the image look as if it is three-dimensional. Since you cannot script keystrokes such as arrow keys, the Offset filter accomplishes the same thing.
14. Click the Stop button. Your image looks exactly the same as if you had used the previous set of instructions. Figure 1-33 shows the expanded Action.

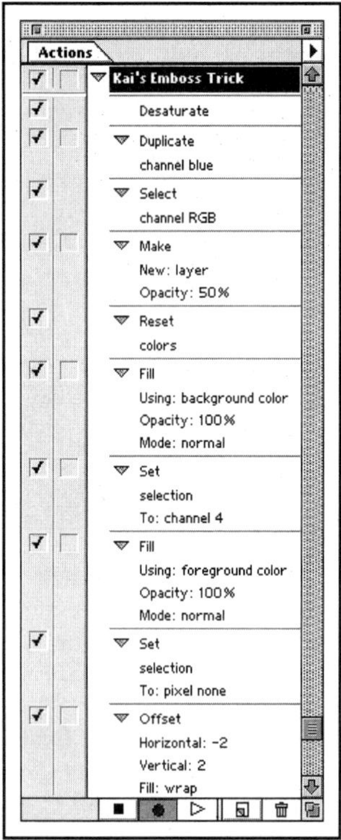

Figure 1-33: Kai's Emboss Trick script.

You might notice that Figure 1-32, which shows the embossed image, looks sharper than the one on your screen. We changed the Levels to accentuate the white and black in the image after the image was desaturated. If you want to add this feature to your Action, you should know how to do it (click on the last step in the Action, click Record, click on the Levels command and set your Levels as desired, click Stop, and then drag the step up just after the Desaturate command). Since you will choose a different Levels setting for each image that you process with this Action, place a checkmark in the Break Point column so that you get a dialog box. While you are creating Break Points, you might also want to place one on the Offset filter so that you can change the amount of the offset.

Getting Complex

You might have thought that the last Action was complicated enough. You can create even more complex steps using Actions. The next one that you will try is a special effect that uses the Clouds filter to create a repeating pattern. In this Action, you will see how to handle situations where the user must perform some activities that cannot be scripted, or even referred to, in the Actions list.

TIP *You can refer to any command found in the menus, even if you cannot script its options, by choosing the Insert Menu Item command on the Actions palette menu. This lets you insert a reference to the command so that when the Action is played, the command is chosen for the user to select the desired options. You can add the Apply Image command or the File Info command to your Actions in this manner, but it means that you cannot run a batch Action and simply walk away from the computer—user interaction is always required.*

Repeating Clouds Pattern

This Action creates a new document, runs the Clouds and Difference Clouds filter on it, Posterizes, Blurs, and finds a Threshold, Offsets the image, and then lets you edit the image using the Pencil tool. It then reduces the image to a "reasonable" pattern tile size and blurs it, selects the image and defines it as a pattern. The Action continues by creating a new document and allowing you to select a background color. It fills the background layer with the new color and creates a new layer which is set to Hard Light mode. It then fills the top layer with the previously defined pattern, and embosses and blurs it. That is quite a lot to happen almost automatically.

1. Click on the New Action icon on the Actions palette and name the Action "Cloud Repeat." Just follow the steps and let the Action record them.
2. Create a new document (Mac: Command+N, Windows: Ctrl+N), 400 X 400 pixels.
3. Press D to set the colors back to the default of black and white.
4. Select Filter | Render | Clouds. Figure 1-34 shows the image at this point.

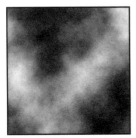

Figure 1-34: Image filled with Clouds filter.

5. Select Filter | Render | Difference Clouds. The Difference Clouds filter begins to build up complexity in the clouds structure. It is the basis for a number of wonderful special effects that do not belong in this book or in this chapter. However, the more times you apply this filter (within reason), the more interesting the structure is when you posterize it later or use the Find Edges filter on it. Figure 1-35 shows the clouds image with Difference Clouds applied once.
6. Select Filter | Clouds | Difference Clouds five more times (you will apply it a total of six times). Figure 1-36 shows the image after the Difference Clouds filter has been applied the sixth time.

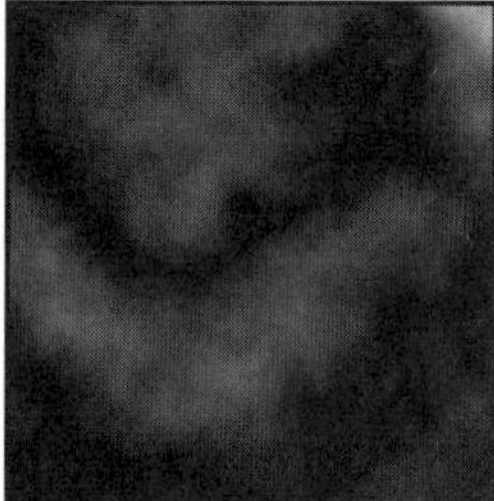

Figure 1-35: Difference Clouds filter applied one time.

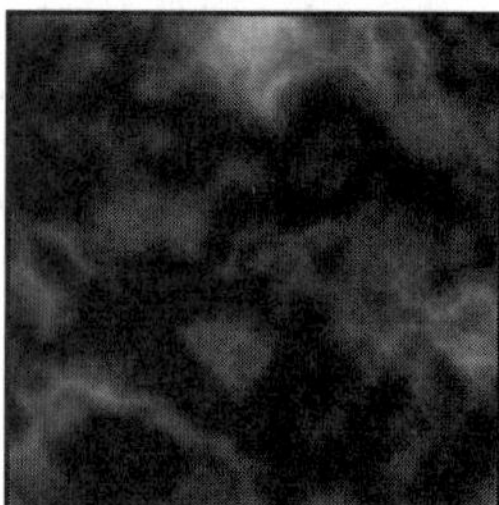

Figure 1-36: Difference Clouds filter applied six times.

7. Choose Image | Adjust | Posterize and select four levels in the dialog box. This begins to give you islands as shown in Figure 1-37.

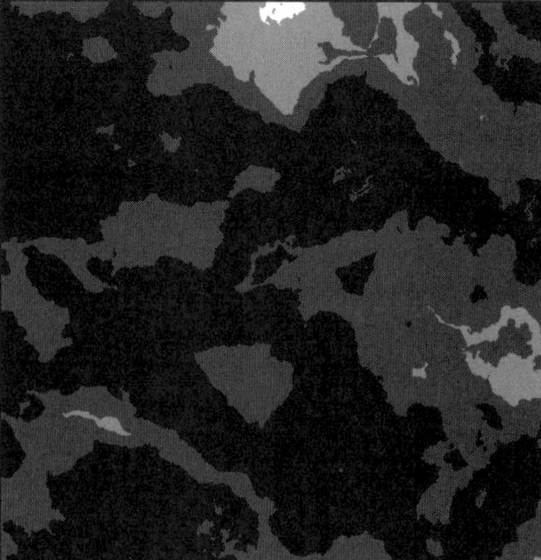

Figure 1-37: Difference Clouds posterized.

8. Choose Filter | Blur | Gaussian Blur; Radius 6.6.
9. Select Image | Adjust | Threshold and select a Threshold of 84. Figure 1-38 shows the pattern-to-be at this point.
10. Select Filter | Other | Offset; 200 pixels right, 200 pixels down, Wrap around. This divides the image in half so that you can see what the pattern seams will do. There will always be hard lines as shown in Figure 1-39.

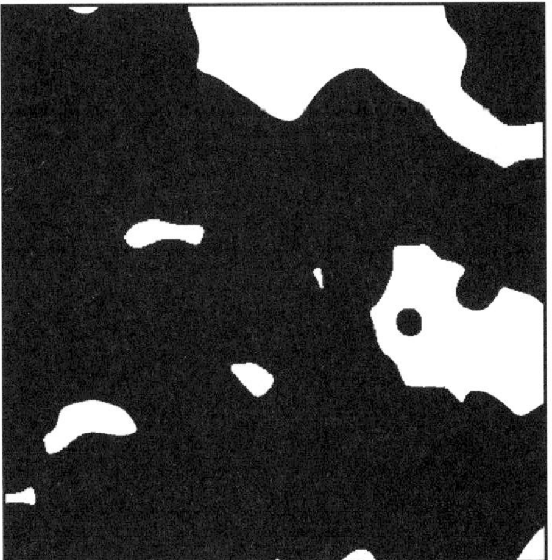

Figure 1-38: Image with Threshold command applied.

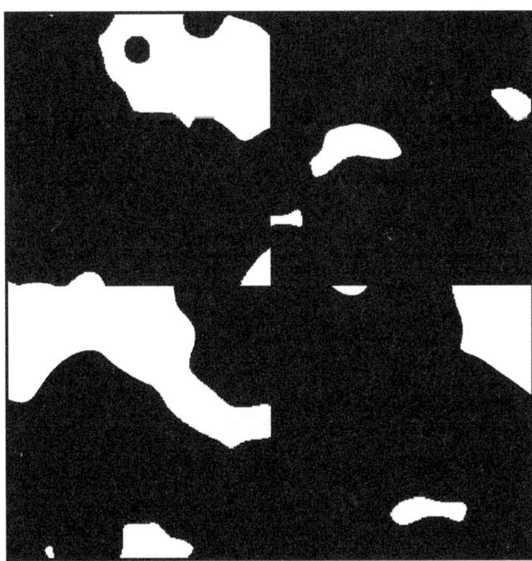

Figure 1-39: Image offset by half in each direction.

11. The next step is for the user to use the Pencil tool to color away the hard edges by adding black or white as desired to soften the edges along the seam line. This is the point at which the script gets very interesting. There is no way to create a script that shows the results of using the Paintbrush, and even if there were, the strokes need to be different for each image. So, how to do this? Let's try the following:

    Choose Insert Stop from the Actions palette and enter the message shown in Figure 1-40. This will stop the Action from playing but will not reset the "play from" to the top of the Action. It allows the Action to be continued from the next instruction in the list. You may click on the "Allow Continue" box if you feel that a hard-edged pattern is acceptable or should at least be an option. That box is very good for optional steps because it allows the user to click Continue to ignore whatever action they were supposed to take. Do not place a Continue option into an Action unless you do not care if the user follows the steps that they are supposed to do.

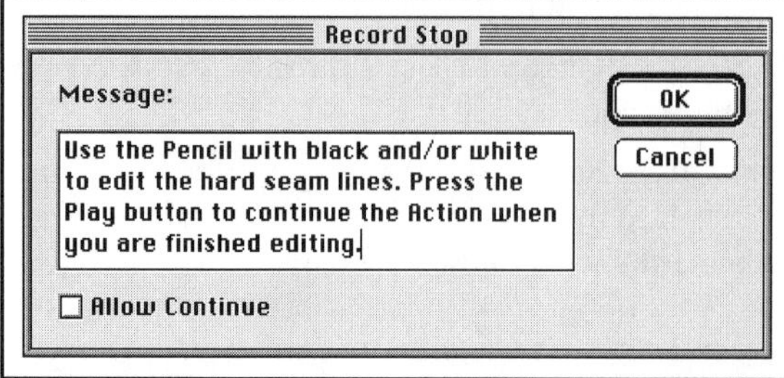

Figure 1-40: Enter this message to tell the user to stop the Action from playing.

When the script is executed, the message will be shown and the Action will stop playing. To finish performing the Action, the user needs to click on the Play button again. Figure 1-41 shows the result of making the tile seamless.

Figure 1-41: The seamless tile.

12. Choose Image | Image Size and set Resample Image on, Constrain Proportions On, and set the new dimensions to 100 pixels X 100 pixels. This is a fairly common size for a repeat pattern. At 300 ppi, each repeat is one-third of an inch, which is large enough to see.
13. Select the entire image (Mac: Command-A, Windows: Ctrl-A). Define this as a pattern (Edit ->Define Pattern).
14. You now need to create a new image for the pattern. Select File | New and create an image 1000 X 1000 pixels square.

15. You need to have the user pick a new color for the background of the image (the main color for the repeat pattern). Choose Insert Stop from the Action palette menu and enter the message "Pick a new Foreground color and click on Play to resume the Action." Do not allow Continue.
16. Fill the area (Mac: Option-Delete, Windows: Alt-Backspace).
17. Make a new layer (press the Option key for the Mac or the Alt key on Windows and click on the New Layer icon at the bottom of the Layers Palette). In the dialog box that appears, set the Opacity to 100% and the Mode to Hard Light.
18. Fill the new layer with the pattern (Shift-Delete | Pattern, 100 percent Opacity, Normal).
19. Choose Filter | Stylize | Emboss (Angle: 129°, Height: 3 pixels, Amount: 100).
20. Select Filter | Blur | Gaussian Blur; Radius 2.5. Figure 1-42 shows the final pattern.

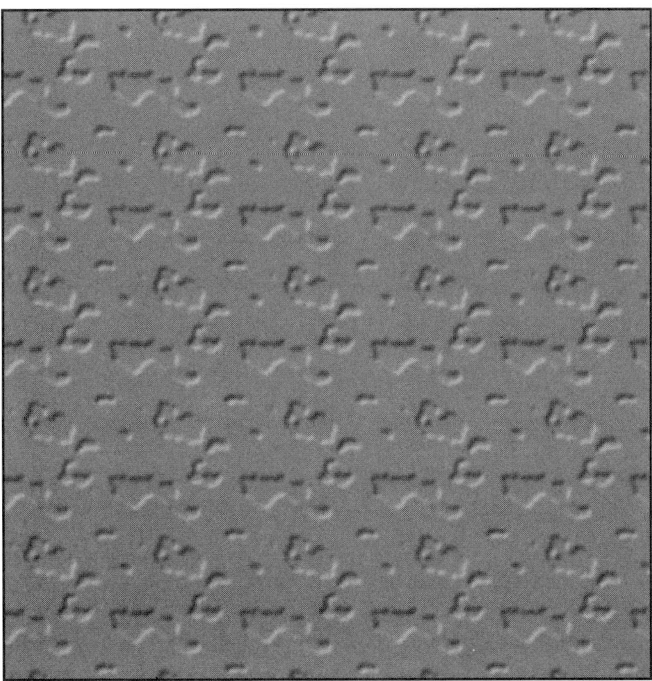

Figure 1-42: Pattern created from Clouds filter using an Action.

21. Click the Stop button on the Actions palette. Believe it or not, you are actually finished creating the Action.
22. Close all of your open documents and play the Action to make sure that it works correctly. Figures 1-43a through 1-43c show the expanded steps in the Action.

a

Actions

Clouds Repeat

Make
New: document
Mode: RGB color mode
Width: 5.555 inches
Height: 5.555 inches
Resolution: 72.001 per inch
Fill: white

Reset
colors

Clouds

Difference Clouds

Difference Clouds

Difference Clouds

Difference Clouds

Difference Clouds

Difference Clouds

Posterize
Levels: 4

Gaussian Blur
Radius: 6.6

Threshold
Level: 84

Offset
Horizontal: 200
Vertical: 200
Fill: wrap

Stop
Message: "Use the Pencil with black and/or white to edit the hard seam lines. Press the Play button to continue the Action when you are finished editing."

b

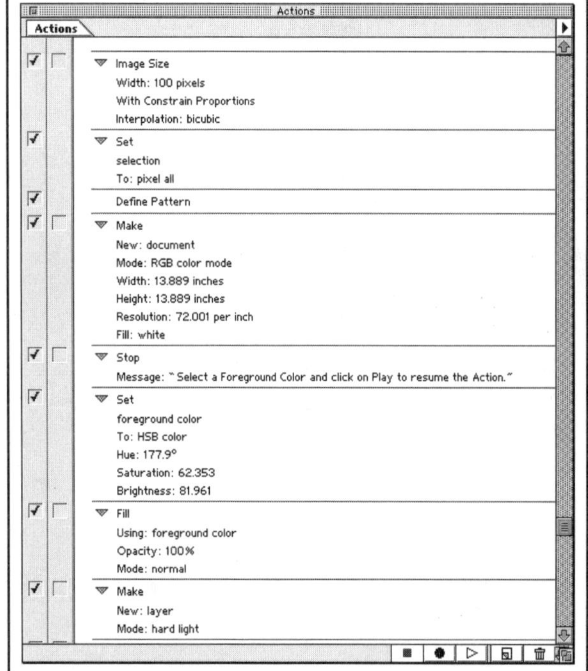

c

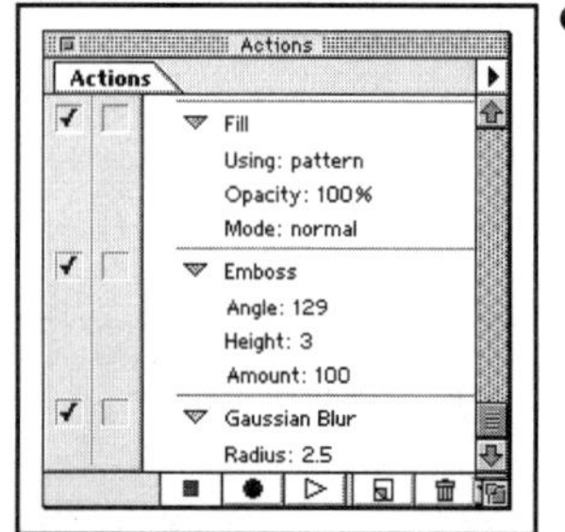

Figure 1-43 (a-c): Steps in Clouds Repeat Action.

Should you decide that you want to change any of the steps in the Action, double-clicking on them, if they have an attached dialog box, will allow you to edit the Action step. This is the same as selecting the Action step and choosing Record Again from the menu. If you use the menu, you must be careful that you are only re-recording that one step (which should be the default if you click to select the step first). For example, if you want to change the command that creates the 1,000 pixel square image so that it creates an image of a different size, first click on the statement and then look at the menu as shown in Figure 1-44.

Figure 1-44: Editing options for recorded Action.

It is interesting to see what other options are also available. You can duplicate the single statement within the Action, delete it (of course), play only that step or play the rest of Action starting with that step. In addition, you can also add additional steps after Make by selecting Start Recording, or you can insert a Stop or a Menu Item.

The ability to edit and fine-tune your Action after it has been recorded is one of the less obvious abilities of the Actions subsystem. However, it is a very powerful one. Another not-quite-obvious feature is that the checkmarks next to each step can be turned on or off. When the command is not checked, it is not executed—which gives you a very easy way to run an Action that is almost what you want, or to run part of an Action.

Saving & Recalling Actions

Actions can be saved and loaded. They are only saved in the Preferences file unless you specifically save the Actions palette to another location (which you ought to do whenever you create Actions that you do not want to lose). Although it is not possible to save an Action individually, you can do that if it is the *only* Action in the palette. Save your Actions, and then delete all of the Actions except for the one that you want to save by itself. Then Replace the Action with the Actions that you saved that contained the entire set. This gives you the ability to load in one specific Action if you need to.

Commands Palette R.I.P.

Some of the more agonizing yelps heard when Photoshop 4.0 first shipped were the cries of "Where did the Commands palette go?" Many users really miss it, although Adobe insists that Actions will do everything that the Commands palette did and more. Adobe does ship an Action set that replaces the Commands palette. If you created a custom Commands palette, you can record the items that it contained as "Insert Menu Item" commands.

You can change the Actions palette into Buttons if you want. This gives you the ability to play an Action simply by clicking on it. The disadvantage is that you cannot create columns of Actions, and the Actions palette is fairly wide—which wastes a lot of space in Button mode. If you really miss the Command palette for simple things like one-click access to Image Size, Convert to grayscale, Define Pattern, and so forth, consider purchasing Extensis PhotoTools. Figure 1-45 shows the button bar that one of the authors created to replace the Commands palette. From left to right, the icons provide access to the following commands:

Figure 1-45: Extensis PhotoTools button bar.

- File Info
- Page Setup
- Convert to Grayscale
- Image Size
- Save As
- Save
- Save a Copy
- Canvas Size
- Duplicate
- Define Pattern
- Select Similar (useful since its key command vanished in 4.0)
- Apply Image

- Levels
- AutoLevels
- Threshold
- Select | Inverse
- Feather
- Multi-channel
- Gaussian Blur
- Add Noise
- High Pass
- Unsharp Mask
- Offset
- Find Edges
- Emboss
- Layer Mask with Hide All
- Merge Visible
- Color Table
- Flip Horizontal
- Flip Vertical
- Layer | Transform menu (pops down all of the options on that menu)
- Crop
- Flatten

As you can see, a button bar that takes a minimum of space at the top of the screen can add a wealth of access. It is a waste of the features of the Actions palette to try to make it duplicate single one-click commands. PhotoTools is a wonderful filter set with many more filters in it, and the button bar is only a small part of it (even though the set would be worth the price for many users even if the only thing the set did was to create the button bar).

TIP

Have you ever produced a very complex image and then tried to re-create it? And you cannot remember what you did to produce those results? It has happened to us many times. Turn on Actions then "play" and, even if you do not get a usable Action from it, you should be able to reconstruct your steps when you are done.

Moving On

This chapter covered a lot of ground. We have discussed many ways to optimize your Photoshop system and to configure it. We have also looked at many of the ways to troubleshoot the most common problems. You have learned the Preferences settings that the authors consider to be the best for professional Photoshop users. Finally, you have learned—possibly more than you ever wanted to know—about Actions. Do master the Actions feature, though. It can prove very useful!

In the next chapter, you will learn about acquiring images. You will also learn how to make good scans, what to do if you are scanning a previously screened image, and how to work with PhotoCD.

chapter 2

Acquiring Images

A cartoon from a ten-year-old digital graphics publication has proved to be prescient. Picture a prepress technician, his computer loaded into a child's toy wagon trailing a long extension cord, holding up his flatbed scanner to record an outdoor scene. The caption reads, "The trick is to hold it steady for four minutes."

Hand-held miniature scanners in the form of digital cameras are now commonplace. However, the technology of the digital camera has not progressed very far past that shown in the cartoon. Digital cameras exhibit a number of deficiencies:

- They share the problem detailed by the cartoon: exposure times, when compared to traditional cameras, are lengthy.
- Because of the way the sensing mechanism must operate, the more inexpensive models can capture only a small number of pixels. The captured image is suitable only for placement on the World Wide Web, or as an offset reproduction at a small size.
- Though they range in price from a few hundred dollars to many thousands of dollars, only the most expensive units produce superior results.
- The most expensive units are nothing more than replacements for the film-cartridge back of a large-format camera and are most useful in studio environments for shooting static displays. That means an additional expense, the purchase of the large-format camera, the back of which is not required.

Another device which has its origins in the camera principle is the *video frame grabber*. A fairly inexpensive circuit board mounted in a computer allows the machine to receive and display *streaming video*. (Streaming video is a video signal that begins displaying on the monitor as soon as it reaches the processor. *Non-streaming video* must be received as a file that is then read into memory and displayed.) Through software, the individual frames of the video can be slowed and single frames extracted for processing as still images.

Digital cameras and video frame grabbers are two of the three principal *digitizing* (converting images to digital form) devices in widespread use. The third is the scanner, which, while it suffers some limitations, is still the most easily configured and easily used device. It also produces the most high-quality results.

Scanners are manufactured in two flavors: *charged coupled device* (*CCD*) and *drum*. The differences between the two are mainly in the sensing mechanisms. Flatbed scanners use CCD sensors, while drum scanners rely on photomultiplier vacuum tubes. CCD devices include digital cameras and the inexpensive desktop scanners in widespread use. The general scan quality of CCD devices is not as high, nor is the optical resolution as great as that achieved by a drum scanner. This difference is reflected in the average prices of the devices. Drum scanner prices range from about $15,000 on the low end of the scale, to as high as $200,000. The equivalent range for CCD devices is from less than $200 up to $25,000 (the latter are exceptionally well-engineered transparency scanners used mostly by separation houses). Drum scanners, although they are now more widely used than in the past, are still marketed for the professional user. Such a user might be a publication house wishing to reduce commercial scanning costs, or a professional scanning house furnishing high-quality digital files for the prepress world.

Another scanning device, albeit one which is not available to the average consumer, is the Photo CD scanner, developed by Kodak. Photo CD scanners are operated as a film-processing service. They place reasonably good-quality scans into the hands of the consumer at a modest per-image cost, as low as $.65 per image from some vendors. Photo CD purchasers receive their scans on CD-ROM disks or floppy disks. Each scanned image is saved at six resolutions which can be read from disk and processed with a program such as Photoshop. Typical Photo CD images are scans of 35mm films. A more advanced scanner is now available—called Photo CD Pro—which is able to scan large-format material. Photo CD Pro has not proven to be as successful as its predecessor due to the relatively high cost of the individual images: large format Photo CD scans are not cost-competitive with commercial service bureau drum scans.

With the advent of high-speed microcomputers, digital images have become increasingly important. This has lead to an increasingly important role for Adobe Photoshop as the most widely used image-manipulation software. The program now plays a pivotal role in the development of image material for the World Wide Web, for the multi-faceted world of print reproduction, and for the increasingly important multimedia industry. With Photoshop's strategic growth, scanners have also become vital equipment. To help you get the most from your scanner, this chapter is devoted to giving you a complete understanding of concepts such as pixels and resolution, how to operate your scanner effectively, what you can do to repair images that are less than perfect, and how to get the most from Photo CD.

Resolution, Pixels & Sampling Frequency

The terms *resolution* and *pixel* are difficult to understand but important.

Resolution, by itself, is simply a way of assigning an arbitrary two-dimensional value—width and height—to that chimerical beast, the *pixel*. The pixel, believe it or not, has no intrinsic real-world size: it is simply a collection of three or four numbers tied to a location within a raster coordinate system. A pixel begins to have a life of its own when you assign it a real-world size. In every way you can understand it, a pixel is however big *you* choose to make it.

The pixel receives its initial size at the time photographic material is digitized (scanned), or when other kinds of artwork are brought into Photoshop and converted to raster format. (Note: we will discuss rasterizing other kinds of information later in this book. Our discussion here will deal with the digitizing of information by means of a scanner.) The size of a pixel is part of an instruction to the scanning software which determines at what size an image is to be scanned and at what resolution you wish the final file to be. The scanner then reads the object to be scanned at its native *sampling rate* and gives you the number of pixels you need based on its sampling.

The terms *sampling rate* and *sampling frequency* mean exactly what they seem to mean. The scanner aims a light at the scanned object. As the light passes through transparent objects or is reflected from opaque objects, its color is analyzed and stored as a single component of the scan. Every analysis of a single spot on the scanned material is called a *sample*.

Scanners vary in the precision with which they can take samples. Some scanners may be able to analyze the color of the scanned material only 300 times in every inch. Other scanners may be able to analyze the color 6,000–10,000 times in every inch! The number of samples a scanner can take from the scanned material is a function of its optical assembly and its sensing hardware. In general, very high resolution is possible only with more expensive scanning equipment. Figure 2-1 shows how the increase of the sampling rate results in ever greater precision when the image is scanned. The original (a) is in the upper left-hand corner. The sections marked *b–f* show a range of sampling rates from coarse to fine. By studying this figure, it is easy to see why a scanned image loses some of its clarity in the digitizing process.

Interpolated Sampling

The optical precision of the scanner is sometimes augmented by what is called *interpolated* resolution. Interpolated resolution is used to amplify the scanner's sensing mechanism. It does its job by taking the scanner's individual samples and making an educated guess about what samples the scanner *might have taken* if its sensing system were capable of more precision. In short, the scanner's software invents new values for what it could *not* see based on what it *could* see.

Interpolated samples are sometimes useful, but not universally so. When scanning for line art (see Chapter 9, "Photoshop Prepress"), interpolated samples help to give smooth edges to simple shapes such as display type and logos. When used for other purposes—halftones, duotones, color separations—interpolated samples are not a good idea. Even though the scanning software might make extremely sophisticated guesses about the samples it invents, these samples are nothing more than mathematical fiction. An image containing interpolated samples will always contain detail information that has been softened and blurred.

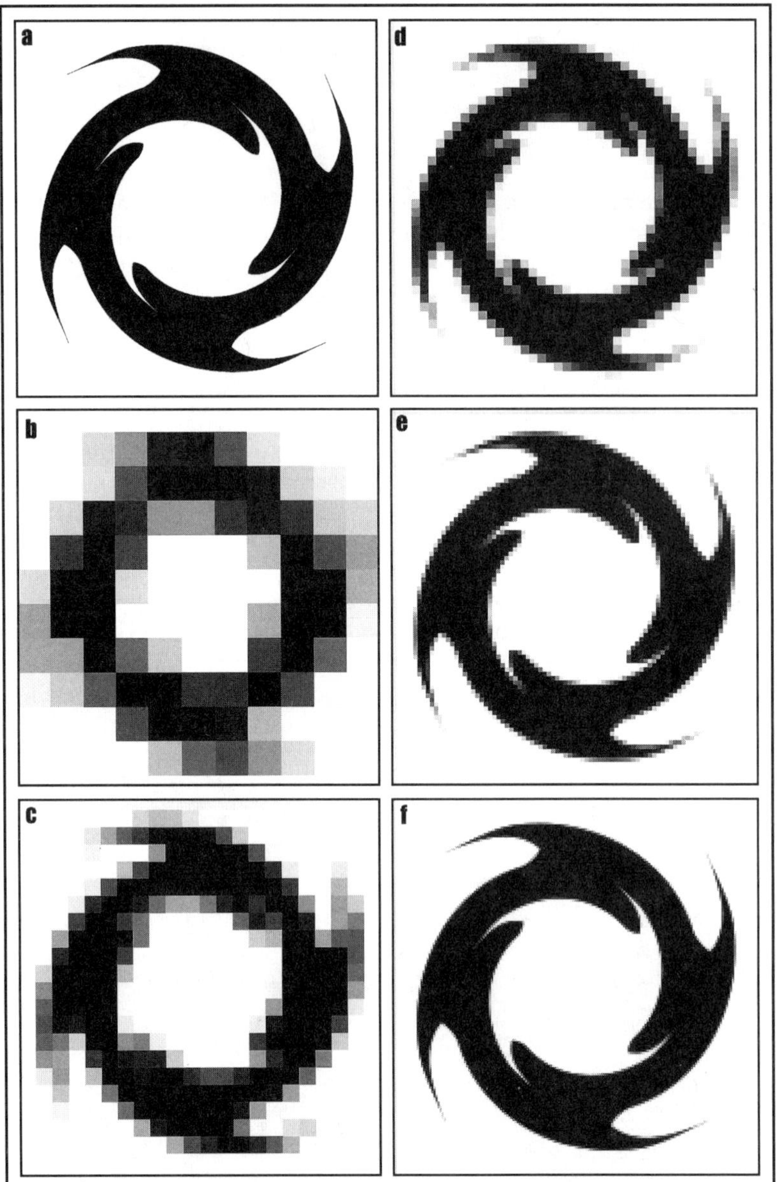

Figure 2-1: Increased sampling rates increase the precision of the scan.

Every sample—or group of samples—represents a value that eventually becomes a pixel. When your file is opened in Photoshop, you see a file which contains the requested physical dimensions and pixel density. It is important to recognize, however, that pixels and the sampling rate are not the same thing.

Your scans need not contain the largest number of pixels that your scanner can deliver. Your file's pixel frequency can vary. A scan intended for the World Wide Web or for a multimedia presentation would require just 72 ppi. For images intended to be reproduced on an offset press at 150 line-screen, a file of 300 ppi would be appropriate.

TIP *For offset reproduction, best results are achieved when the input file's ppi value is twice that of the line-screen value.*

As we discussed above, the scanner's software furnishes you with controls which allow you to specify two input values: the pixel frequency you desire, and the physical dimensions of the file. To arrive at the file you desire, your scanner's software is going to do some behind-the-scenes calculations.

Let's assume that your scanner has an optical resolution of 600 samples per inch. If you request a scan of 300 ppi at 100% of the size of the original material, your scanner will do the scan sampling at 600/inch, its native frequency. It then combines groups of pixels—2 wide and 2 tall, averaging the values—to make one pixel that is 1/300 inches on a side. (Think about it: 2/600 x 2/600 = 1/300 x 1/300.)

If you desire to scan so that your file is 200% of the size of the original material, the scanner still samples at 600 samples per inch. When you open the file, all of the pixels will be twice the size—1/300 inches—of the sampling frequency. This doubles the linear dimensions of the original material and gives you the 200% size.

The idea of pixels changing their sizes may be a little confusing. However, as we stated at the beginning of the chapter: the pixel is an abstraction. It can be any size you wish it to be as is illustrated in Figure 2-2. This figure is in six parts, labeled a-f. The upper part of the figure, *a*, shows a square which represents a pixel. Since this is a grayscale image, we can describe this pixel's file value as equal to one byte. A group of similar pixels is shown at *b*. There are 16 pixels in the group, making their combined file value equal to 16 bytes. In *c*, we can stipulate that we wish the group of sixteen to occupy an area twice as large in each dimension. The arbitrary size of each pixel enlarges, but each pixel remains equal to one byte. The *d* portion of the figure shows how pixels of the original size can be interpolated (see sidebar). The pixels retain their original size, but new pixels need to be added to cover the area. Notice that the original pixels are outnumbered by the invented pixels by three to one. In *e*, the pixels are made to occupy half the original space. The pixels are smaller but there are still sixteen of them. The file size for this group remains 16 bytes. Finally, in *f*, the pixels of the original group are made to occupy half the area but retain the original resolution, or pixel size. For this to happen, 75% of the pixels need to be discarded, which makes the file size 25% of the original. Note that discarding information also requires that pixels be interpolated. The difference between *d* and *f* is this: *d* contains invented values, while *f* contains only original information. Even though *f* contains less information, what it does contain is accurate.

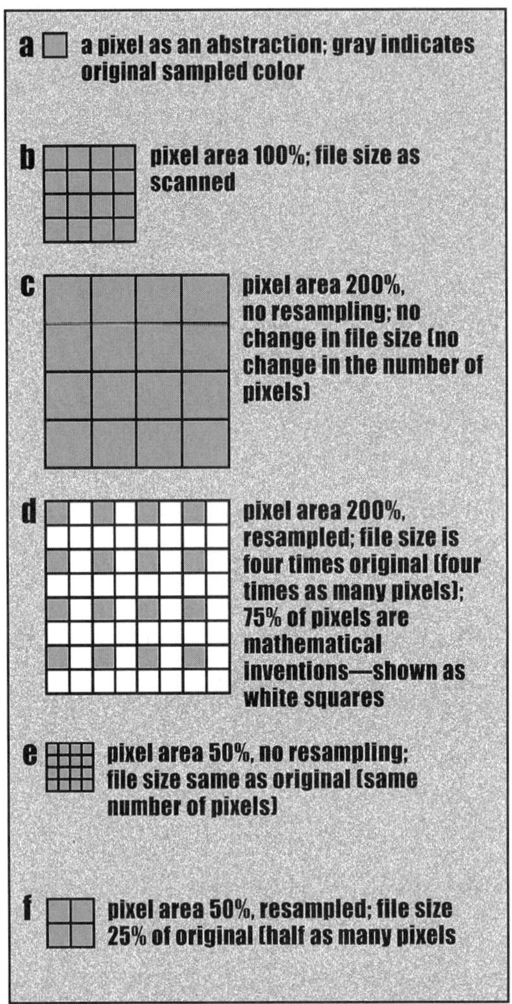

Figure 2-2: Pixel size and pixel interpolation are two commonly misunderstood concepts.

This whole system of scanning to size and causing the pixels to accommodate themselves seems wonderfully flexible. There are, however, some limitations which involve the sampling frequency of the scanner. Imagine that your scanner is capable of a sampling frequency of 600/inch. Now, suppose you wish to scan so that your final file is 300% of the original material's size, and that the resolution needs to be 300 ppi. If you'll recall that the scanner can only sample 600 places in the linear inch, you see that this would deliver a maximum enlargement of only 200% at 300 ppi. Unless you wish the scanning software to make use of interpolation, this scanner's sampling rate can deliver a 300% size only if the pixel density is changed to 200 ppi. To give 300% at 300 ppi, the scanner's sampling frequency would have to be 900/inch.

TIP *You can easily calculate your scanner's capabilities. If you divide the maximum optical sampling frequency of the scanner by the resize percentage you desire, you'll have the largest possible pixel density. In the case above, 600/300%=200 ppi. Alternately, you can use this formula: 100 (sampling frequency/desired ppi)=largest percentage of enlargement. For the case above, 100(600/300 ppi)=200%.*

The same kind of calculation takes place when you use Photoshop's Image | Image Size dialog box (Figure 2-3).

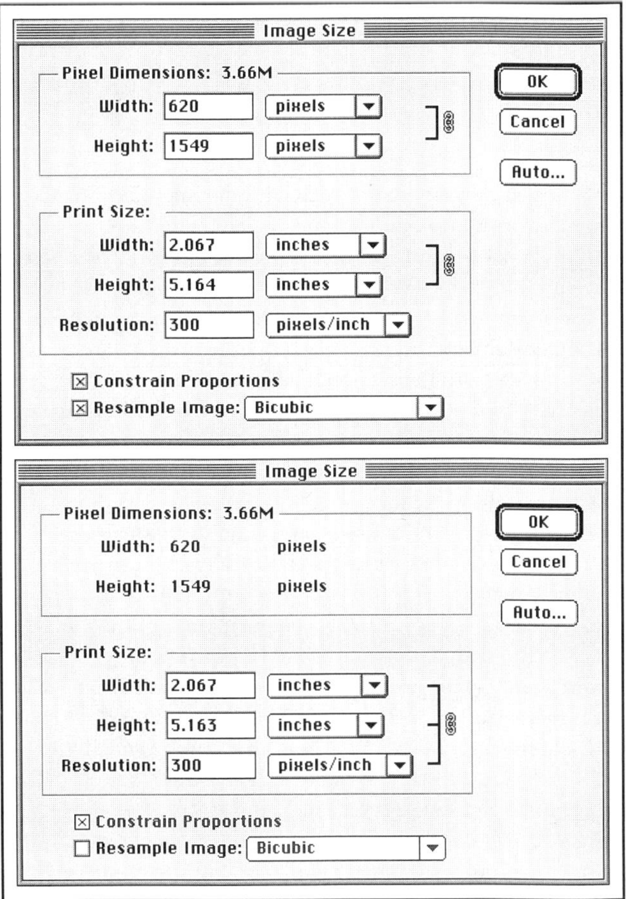

Figure 2-3: Photoshop's Image Size dialog box illustrates the difference between resampling (top) and resizing (bottom).

In the upper part of the figure, the Resample Image check box is turned on. When the dialog box is in this state, numerical information in any one of the five data entry fields can be changed. Changing the number of pixels—increasing or decreasing—does not affect the values for Print Size or Resolution. Changing the Print Size values does not affect the Resolution but will change the number of pixels. In either case, the Image Size will be changed using Interpolation. In the lower part of the figure, the Resample Image check box has been turned off. Note that the Pixel Dimensions can no longer be altered, nor can the file size be changed. A change in any one of the three data entry fields will immediately alter the other two. (The pop-up menu at the bottom of the dialog box tells Photoshop which method—Bicubic, Bilinear, or Nearest Neighbor—it should use to interpolate the image. The merits of these three are not relevant to a discussion of the change in an image's size. For best results when changing the size of a Photoshop file, leave this setting at its default.)

Basic Scanning

The technical parts of scanning an image vary with the intended purpose of the image. In general, a scanner's controls should be adjusted so that after you scan, you can work in Photoshop with the most accurate set of sampled pixels it is possible to obtain. Scanning isn't difficult, but it does require that you become adept at evaluating the original material for potential problems. You must also train yourself to accurately assess what the scanner delivers.

Scanner software varies with the scanner. Some scanning software contains controls of great sophistication, while other software can only be described—charitably—as adequate. The ultimate purpose of the scanner is to digitize the image so that you can alter it to suit the purpose for which it is intended. The difference in software is usually one of your convenience and assistance with your workflow.

Very expensive scanners generally use stand-alone software in which a variety of production tasks can be automated. Since the sensitivity of these scanners is usually more than adequate for general-purpose scanning, automating such tasks as removing screens and noise, correcting the tonal range, balancing the color, sharpening the image, and converting the scan to CMYK format (when files are changed to CMYK format, they contain channels for each of the four-color process inks—Cyan, Magenta, Yellow, and Black), are features which can greatly enhance a production environment. In fact, these production features—with the overall scanning sensitivity—are a significant part of a high-end scanner's cost. Whenever these kinds of automatic capabilities are available, they should be used to their fullest potential.

Low-end scanners are an iffy proposition. It would be nice to believe that cost alone would be sufficient to evaluate a scanner's ability to capture data. Unfortunately, cost seems to be only an approximate guide: in some cases, cost as a guide to a scanner's quality is totally unreliable. For example, one major manufacturer of imaging equipment markets CCD scanners with a cost range of $600–$12,000. It is true that the less expensive units are smaller and are bundled with less sophisticated software. However, it is also true that the overall quality of scans from the most expensive units does not greatly differ from the least expensive. The difference in quality is certainly not great enough to compensate for the difference in cost, nor is that cost difference sufficiently offset by powerful scanning software.

Evaluating a scanner is made difficult by the fact that scanners need to capture data for many different purposes. If a scanner is going to be used for digitizing images to be placed on the Internet, it may be that a low-cost CCD scanner—no matter the manufacturer—will serve the need. For more demanding jobs such as scanning for offset printing, a better quality scanner will be required. Typical parameters for offset work require that large-scale editorial images—and images for high-quality, four-color ads—be scanned by high-end machines. For this reason, much of the prepress industry makes use of service bureaus which specialize in custom scanning on drum machines.

Smaller images in the prepress world can usually be scanned in-house on less expensive equipment. These smaller images are probably the most demanding of performance in low-end machines because they must end up looking nearly as good as the high-end scans with which they are associated. These images also tend to be the most problem-laden. They are the ones that are reproduced at a small size because the original material is less than perfect. You can imagine the situation in the production room: "OK, we've got this wretched Polaroid which is too dark but we've got to use it anyway. Let's scan it here, rather than wasting $75 on a scan that won't improve it that much anyway."

The Scanner's Controls

If your scanner does not have a stand-alone scanning program, the chances are good that you have been furnished with a plug-in which allows you to do your scanning from within Photoshop. You may be using a scanner which follows the TWAIN (or "Technology Without An Interesting Name") standard, or you may be using hardware-specific software. In either case, your scanner controls are selected from the File | Import submenu.

When the scanner controls open, you see an interface window that differs only in detail from that shown in Figure 2-4. Your scanner software, unless it is a package shipped with a high-end model, will probably not have as many features as you see here, but its features will be similar to those we will discuss.

The window shown in the figure is that of a third-party scanning software package, ArtScan Pro by Jetsoft Development Software. We have used it here because it is fairly generic, and because it is a package with nearly all the features you are likely to encounter. It is also an excellent way to give new life to an older scanner that is no longer supported by the manufacturer. For example, the bundled software for the scanner

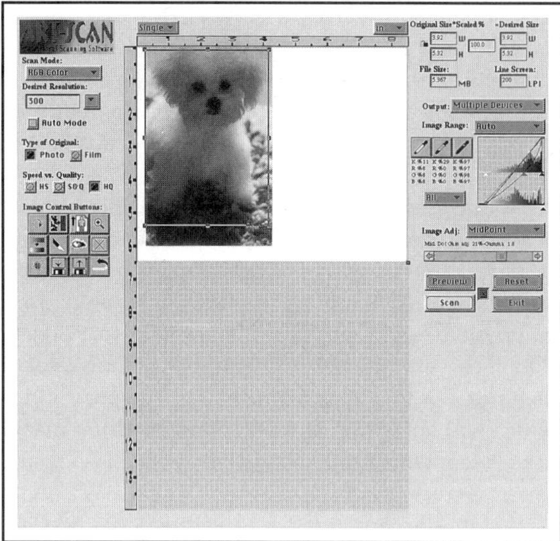

Figure 2-4: The interface window for the ArtScan Pro scanning software.

which generated the figure, is old enough that it does not operate under Macintosh system software version 7.5 or higher. The company which sold the machine has no interest in continuing to write update software for a machine which, while perfectly serviceable, has been superseded by about a gazillion newer models. The scanner is now functioning perfectly and will continue to do so for at least several more years. (By the way, ArtScan is able to drive a great many older scanners made by such companies as Agfa, Avec, Canon, Epson, Hewlett-Packard, Microtek, Nikon, PixelCraft, Relisys, Ricoh, Sharp, Tamarack, and UMAX. It is available for Windows, Macintosh, and Power Macintosh, and the cost is under $90. If you own such a scanner, you would be well-advised to investigate ArtScan. The URL of the Jetsoft web site is http://www.dpi-scanner-authority.com.)

Having placed the material to be scanned on the bed of the scanner, click on the Preview button. The scanner makes a preliminary, low-resolution scan of the entire bed area which allows you to draw a cropping rectangle so that, on the final scan, you acquire only the pixels within the crop and not the entire area.

The image to be scanned is shown in the central area of the figure. This software has a shape-recognition feature which assigns a crop rectangle automatically. In the figure, this rectangle has been drawn up manually along the bottom edge to eliminate part of the image. (ArtScan is intelligent enough to place the crop rectangle and then, if the image is not quite straight on the bed, to counter-rotate the scan to straighten it out while it is scanning.) ArtScan also allows you to zoom in to the area you have cropped. Click on the magnifying glass icon on the tool palette at the lower left. Another preview scan will take place automatically.

Figure 2-5 shows an expanded view of the interface window and several pop-up windows.

Figure 2-5: Expanded view of the ArtScan Pro dialog box.

Original Size, Scaled Size, File Size & Line Screen

Beginning at the top on the right-hand side, a series of data entry fields allow you to see the physical size of the crop rectangle, to change the post-scan dimensions, to see the size of the file at the dimensions you've requested, and to assign a Line Screen value. Any number assigned to the Line Screen automatically changes the Resolution value (left-hand side) to 150% of the Line Screen value. The reverse is also true: any change to the Resolution value changes the Line Screen to 66% of the Resolution. Since you want your scan to have a resolution that is twice your line-screen value, it is better for you to assign your values in the Resolution field. (Note that when Photoshop files are output, the pixel information is converted to lithographic dots. This is called *screening*. The size of the dots in an output image is based on the number of *lines of dots* in some unit of measurement. We could, for example, say that an image has been screened at 133 lpi, which means that there are 133 lines of screen dots in an inch. You may sometimes see measurements expressed as *lpc*—lines per centimeter. The *line screen*—another way of referring to the number of dot lines—is specified at the time of output.)

Output

The Output pop-up menu gives you a choice of output devices. Using the choice made here, the scanner will attempt to optimize the scan for the target. If you can find a profile that is reasonably close to the output device you wish to use, the scanner will do a fairly good job on the material for you so that your post-scan adjustments are minimal.

Image Range

The Auto Image Range setting is a choice which enables ArtScan to do much of your image adjustment work automatically. This option takes information from the prescan which tells what data is actually present in the original material—the range between dark and light values—and applies automatic adjustments. When you use the Auto Image Range setting, ArtScan attempts to give you the best possible scanned image by using its own analysis of the image to be scanned. As with most automation routines, you need to evaluate the results you get. While the scanner software may be very intelligent about the choices it makes, your scanner may not have the full-tone-range sensitivity to make the Auto adjustments worthwhile. In such cases, one of the other settings might be a better choice since you can then make use of Photoshop's capabilities to perform the same task. The choices here are Auto, Full, Medium, Small, and Set.

Auto Auto, as the name implies, does a complete analysis of the image and offers what it considers the best possible choices.

Full The Full setting allows you to see the raw scan just as the scanner sees it. There are no enhancements or modifications. Full is the setting to use when you wish to make all of your adjustments after the scan.

Medium The Medium setting allows the software to take a medium percentage of both the highlight and shadow areas and eliminate them. This gives a scan that looks better, but does not take into account the broad tonal range of the image. For images that are very dark, this setting lightens the image but it does not adjust for deep shadow areas. The resulting image does not have the desirable contrast that the Auto setting gives.

Small The Small setting is similar to Medium. It takes a larger percentage of both highlight and shadow values and discards them. This is a good setting for original material which lacks clearly defined highlights and shadows because it gives better contrast.

Set The Set option allows you to use the Eyedropper tools to manually set the highlight, midtone, and shadow values of the image. To set the shadow, click on the right-hand Eyedropper and move the cursor into the Preview window. As the cursor moves, the set of values directly below the Eyedropper tools will change. Keep an eye on these values and move to a very dark area of the image. Locate the darkest point you can find, and click. To set the highlight, click on the left-hand Eyedropper tool. Move your cursor into the image and locate the lightest point you can find. Click. Set the midtone value by finding, if you can, a neutral area which gives a K value of about 50%. Click. For a more complete understanding of how Eyedropper tools function when you select the endpoints and midpoints of the tonal range, please see the sections "Understanding and Customizing Curves" and "Understanding and Customizing Levels" in Chapter 9, "Photoshop Prepress."

Histograms, Curves & Input/Output Scales

Figure 2-6 shows an enlargement of the Histogram/Curves grid. The contents of this small grid are governed by the pop-up menu to the left. The choices are Histogram, Curves, Scroll Bar, and All.

The setting of the grid in the left-hand part of the figure (All) shows an overlay of the tone curves on top of two histograms (for a complete explanation of histograms and curves, please see below). Both of the histograms, displayed without the curves in the upper right-hand side of the figure, have slider arrows which can be used for manual adjustments. The curves are shown by themselves on the lower right-hand side. The curves in this grid cannot be moved the way they can in Photoshop: movement is limited to a slider which drags the curve to the left or to the right. This grid is linked to the pop-up menu to its left. The grid can display one of four configurations—Histograms, Curves, Scroll Bar, and All. The grid is also linked to the pop-up menu directly below it which governs what is to be adjusted—Midpoint, Cyan to Red range, Magenta to Green range, Yellow to Blue range, Shadows, Highlights, and Saturation—using either the grid controls or the scroll bar beneath the pop-up. Note that the scroll bar functions as a slider scale with the thumb button (the sliding rectangle on the horizontal scroll bar) used in place of a triangular slider.

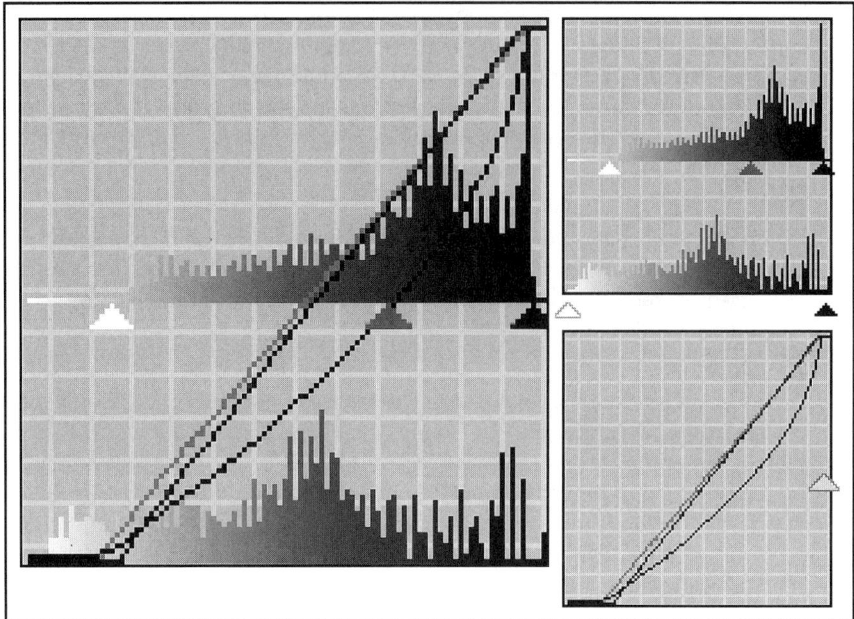

Figure 2-6: Enlarged detail—Curves and Histograms—of the ArtScan Pro scanning window.

Histogram A *histogram* is a very small bar chart showing all of the values present in the image. The light values are on the left, dark on the right. The layout of the histograms is similar to that of the Levels controls in Photoshop. In Photoshop's Levels dialog box, the dark values are on the left and the light values on the right.

The histogram at the top is a summary of the values found during the Preview scan. As you can see, the image is more dark than light. There are no values lighter than about 25%. There are no very dark values either: very few pixels are present with a darkness greater than about 95%. ArtScan has determined the end points of the values that are actually present and has moved the sliders at each end of the upper scale to reflect the real range. The program has also moved the center slider—the midtone values—to the right. This decreases the overall darkness of the image by forcing darker values to the left of the midpoint, or more accurately, to the lighter side of the 50% marker.

When the endpoint sliders of the upper scale are moved in this way, the sliders are made to point to real values. This is a graphic way of instructing the scanner software to take all of the values between the white slider and the midtone slider and to redistribute them from 0–50%. In the same way, the values from the midtone slider to the black slider become redistributed from 50–100%. After the final scan is done, the new histogram looks like the histogram shown at the bottom of the grid window. Note: the two histograms are described by the terms Input (upper) and Output (lower), an indication of the image's original values and the redistributed values of the finished scan.

The method behind this corrective part of the histogram controls lies in its ability to take a relatively narrow range of tones—in this case, color values weighted toward the dark end of the tone range—and to spread them over the entire visual range (with the additional shifting of the midtone values adding lightness to the image). The resulting scan has a much better contrast, is lighter, and its details show more clearly.

Sometimes it is necessary to make more drastic corrections. This can be done with the histogram grid by moving the sliders manually to accomplish some specific purpose. For example, the midtone slider could be moved even farther to the right in order to make the image even lighter. If your scanner has a good range of color sensitivity, this does not usually cause any harm unless the move is extreme. If the scanner has an average color sensitivity, an extreme move is injurious to the values in the range of 65–85%. Posterization effects—sharp lines of color delineation where there should be smooth, imperceptible color gradations—can cause the three-quarter tone range to look granular, irregular, and pretty ugly.

Another kind of manual correction that is possible on the histogram display is to reduce the range of values shown on the bottom set by moving either of the two sliders in from the edge. If the light-end slider is moved, the brightest values are discarded. This is useful for offset printing when the smallest printable value might be 5%. By moving the slider in, the brightest possible value can be made to match the brightest value that can be printed. In the same way, moving the dark-end slider causes a cutoff of the darkest values. To compensate for *dot gain* on press, it is useful to limit the values of the darkest areas of the scan to values that reproduce as individual tones. If the darker areas are not limited, a range of percentages lose their individual values and grow into a dark, featureless mass. (Please see Chapter 9, "Photoshop Prepress" for a complete discussion of dot gain.)

Curves & Scroll Bar The Curves controls as they are used in this software are more useful as a way of seeing what the automatic adjustment features have accomplished. Using these curves controls for fine-tuning is not possible, but large-scale corrections can be made. The movement of the single slider in the center of the curves grid is equivalent to moving the thumb button on the scroll bar beneath the grid. In fact, the scroll bar is probably a more satisfactory adjustment mechanism—despite the fact that it is an atypical use of the interface—than the Curves controls. When using the scroll bar, a continuous set of readings is shown onscreen just above the bar. This allows you to see, using precise numeric values, exactly how much adjustment you have made.

With the Curves or the Scroll Bar controls, you can also make adjustments to the image beyond the overall tone range. Specifically, you can tweak the colors of the image before it is scanned. The cyan-red, magenta-green, and yellow-blue adjustments are similar to the Color Balance controls of Photoshop. The highlight, shadows, and saturation adjustments are similar to the Hue/Saturation controls of Photoshop. Color Balance and Hue/Saturation are both more powerful than the limited controls given with this software. It would probably be wise to do your color adjustments after the scan using Photoshop's tools.

Units of Measurement

At the top left of the preview image is a pop-up menu which lets you choose the units of measurement you wish to use. Your setting of this pop-up affects the units of the rulers at the top and left of the preview, and the numeric fields in the upper right corner of the window.

Single, Multiple, Batch

Scanning is a repetitive task that requires a fair amount of patience. Getting a good scan is an accomplishment that is satisfying, but the scanning process is not one of those things that spring to mind when you think of fun. The items in this pop-up menu (upper left-hand side of the preview area) take some of the more tedious details and automate them.

Single Single is the generic method for most scans. You place the material to be scanned on the scanner, acquire the scanning software, request a preview, crop, adjust, and scan. To do another image, follow exactly the same procedure. When only a single scanned image is needed, this is a perfectly satisfactory way to do your scanning.

Multiple The Multiple setting is very handy for scanning more than one item which requires the same basic scan settings and the same area of the flatbed. When this option is selected, you follow the same set of steps through the completion of the first scan. When the scan is complete, the software asks if you wish to continue with another scan. If you answer yes, all you need to do is re-load the scanner bed and click OK. For example, you might wish to scan in four or five pages of a text document to be analyzed by OCR—Optical Character Recognition—software. Or you might wish to scan one area on a number of originals which differ only within the area you wish to scan. Using the Multiple setting allows you to continue scanning without relinquishing the scanner controls until you are finished.

Batch For those who are used to the Single method, batch capability is, as the Betty White saying goes, as slick as Pam on a banister.

First, you need to load the scanner with as many images as will fit the scanning area. Acquire the ArtScan software from the File menu, and click on the Preview button. When the preview is complete, choose the Batch option. A set of controls (shown in Figure 2-7) will appear at the top of the preview area.

Figure 2-7: Batch scan controls from ArtScan Pro.

The center of the Batch controls has an open area containing some numbers. The first time you use the batch feature, it will read *1 of 1*. Click on the button with the plus symbol (+) until the right-hand number is the same as the number of individual images in the preview window. Now, click on the left-hand button (<<) until the reading says *1 of xx*, with *xx* reflecting the number of images.

At the left of the preview window is a small tool palette (discussed later in this chapter). Click on the far right-hand tool of the center row. With this tool, draw a crop rectangle on the first of the images in your batch. Once you've drawn the crop, make whatever setting changes you wish—size, resolution, color range adjustments, and so forth. You can even select from the pop-up menu at the upper right of the window whether the designated image is to be scanned as color, grayscale, or line art. When you've completed your settings for the first image, click on the right-hand button (>>). Draw a new crop rectangle on the second image, and make selections for the scan. Continue in this way until all of your images have been selected and settings specific to each have been chosen.

As you cycle backwards through the batch controls (<<), you'll see each crop rectangle and see that the settings shift with the image. You may have set some images to be grayscale, some to be in color, some to be enlarged, some reduced, some at a low resolution, some at a high resolution, and some to be scanned as line art. When you have approved all of your choices, click the Scan button, and find something else to do for a little while. ArtScan scans your images one by one using the settings you've chosen for each. When the batch scan is complete, you will find each of the scans in an open window in Photoshop, ready for use. It isn't quite magic, but it's awfully close. As a production tool, having this feature on a relatively low-end scanner—most high-end scanners have been able to do batch scanning for years—is invaluable.

Scan Mode

The pop-up menu in the upper left corner of the ArtScan window gives the choice of scanning in RGB Color, Gray Scale, Line Art, or Vector Line Art. Under most circumstances, you will be scanning in color or grayscale modes. For very fast I-don't-care-if-it's-not-perfect line art scans, use the option from this pop-up. For line art that will need to be of higher quality, scan in grayscale. Complete details on scanning for line art can be found in Chapter 9, "Photoshop Prepress."

The fourth option, Vector Line Art, is a spectacular bonus from an already impressive software package. When this option is selected, line art scans are auto-traced, and then saved as EPS files. These files can then be edited in programs such as Adobe Illustrator or Macromedia FreeHand.

The impressive part of this option is the quality of the finished trace file, given that there is only a single tolerance setting available. It does not compare to a full-featured program such as Adobe Streamline which gives the ability to precisely tweak the settings which control the autotrace. But for very fast work, this option does a very good job. Figure 2-8 displays an example of the quality of this ArtScan feature. On the left is a 300 ppi printout of a Photoshop file. On the left, the printout was scanned and auto-traced using the software's default settings.

Figure 2-8: Original image (left), and an ArtScan Pro Vector Line Art autotraced image (right).

Resolution

The resolution pop-up menu is linked to the line-screen data entry field. If you enter your requested resolution, the line-screen field is updated. The numerical relationship between the two is 1.5:1. We recommend that your scan resolution be twice that of the line-screen value. Since the line-screen value in this software has no impact on the scan, you should enter your resolution as the pixel density you require and ignore the line-screen data field.

Although the scanner on which this software was operating for Figure 2-5 has an optical resolution of 600 samples/inch, the software has the ability to interpolate up to 9,600 ppi. When scanning a line art original which contains delicate lines, such high resolution numbers might be useful. You would never want to scan in color at maximum resolution: a CMYK file to bleed a standard letter-sized page would be over 37 gigabytes in size. To put that into perspective: 37 gigabytes would be about 58 times the size of the entire United States phone directory!

Auto Mode

This check box puts the ArtScan software into its default mode. When it is checked, all of the other controls disappear, and you are left with only the Scan and Exit buttons. When you check the auto button, you are saying to the scanner, "OK, you choose. Give me the best scan of whatever is on the flatbed." There must be a reason why someone would want to do something like that: we cannot imagine what that might be. It might be interesting to test this feature. Our opinion is that scanning is far too important for it to be done with no intervention in the process.

Type of Original

The two check boxes here inform the scanner whether to scan reflective material or transparency. If your scanner does not contain a transparency-scanning module, you won't be able to check the film option. The default is Photo (reflective).

Speed vs. Quality

There are three choices you can make: HS (High Speed), S&Q (Speed and Quality), and HQ (High Quality). We can't think of any circumstance where you would want your scan to be anything other than the best it could be. However, you do have a choice if you should require it.

Image Control Buttons

When you are using ArtScan, it is not necessary that you remember what each of the small button icons indicates. Small pop-up tags become visible as you move your cursor over each. All you need to do is to remember that you have these options at your disposal. Since we cannot show the pop-ups for the figure, we have included a labeled set of rectangles below which label the functions of each button. The buttons at the lower left do not exist in ArtScan. They were added to make the figure more understandable.

Arbitrary Rotate Although ArtScan will rotate-to-straighten original material, you might wish to rotate the material to be scanned for some other purpose. For example, the subject of the photograph might not be squared with the sides. If you would like the subject to be aligned so that it is straight, even if the edges of the photo are at an angle, you can use this button to rotate the rectangular crop.

Descreen If necessity forces you to scan original material that has been reproduced by a printing press, you will find that your scan is perfectly dreadful. Moiré patterns—interference patterns between the sampling of the scan and the screens used to reproduce the original—will make the image unusable.

There are a number of methods you can use to eliminate screen artifacts after scanning (we'll discuss one method that works really well later in this chapter). However, ArtScan will attempt to remove the screens for you. You should try this function and evaluate for yourself how well you think it works. If you find it satisfactory, it will prove to be a time-saving feature. If you do not like the results you get, please look at the method discussed later in this chapter as an alternative.

Rotate 90° If you need to scan from source material that doesn't fit the scanner bed in the correct orientation, you may need to scan at 90° from the way you eventually want the image to be positioned. This button counter-rotates the material during the scanning, eliminating the need to rotate in Photoshop.

Zoom Preview When you decide to use the Eyedropper tools to set your own tone-range endpoints, it is very helpful to be able to see a larger version of the image. After you have done your preview and drawn the crop rectangle, click on this button. ArtScan will do a new preview and enlarge the image to fit the preview area.

Calibrate Image This button is a component in your overall color fidelity system, which is discussed in considerable detail in Chapter 10, "Calibration & Color Reproduction." This button, when clicked, prompts you to choose a calibration file for the scanner. ArtScan uses this file to correct both the brightness and hue of what it sees so that your scans are accurate for your monitor and output devices.

A default scanner calibration file for every supported scanner model ships with the software. However, a file is also included that can be imaged and then rescanned. Using the data it gathers from the new scan, the program can construct a new calibration file for specific conditions.

Sharpen In a normal production situation, an image is sharpened slightly during the scan. The scan is then corrected, resized, and sharpened again at the last stage of preparation. Use this button to perform a modest amount of sharpening on the image while it is being scanned.

Invert If you wish, you can use this button to give you the color-inverse version on the original material. You would use this feature if you are scanning a transparency that would normally be used to produce a color print. This kind of transparency is called a *color negative*. It is the inverse of a transparency such as a 35mm slide.

Draw New Selection When you click on this button, the crop rectangle drawn by the scanner during the preview disappears. You can then draw a new rectangle to take its place.

Line, Noise, Artifact Removal This button directs the program to attempt to remove lines, noise, and other artifacts from the shadow areas of the scanned image.

Save Settings, Load Settings If you find that your scanning tasks divide themselves into groups of similar scan types, it will be useful for you to use the Save Settings command for each group. For example, your color scans might all be intended for use in multimedia. Or your grayscale scans might all be reproduced at 120 line-screen. You can then use the Load Settings command and bypass making all of the scanning choices every time you need to do a scan.

Flip Image Clicking on this button is equivalent to taking a transparency you have previewed, and turning it over so that it is scanned from the flip side. You would use this option if your scanner requires that you scan with the emulsion side of the transparency up, but you wish to have the image scanned as if the emulsion side was down.

A Few Points About Scanning Software

We have discussed in detail the features of a single multi-faceted scanning software package. We don't intend to suggest that you need to use this software in order to get good scans (although it does a very good job). Instead, we want you to realize that the software which shipped with your scanner may be of the type we would describe as barely adequate. If you do only a small amount of scanning, your software may be all that you need—particularly since you have Photoshop to remedy many of the deficiencies of your scanning software. However, if you do a large amount of scanning, you should investigate a scanning package—this one or any other which does the same tasks—to make your scanning faster and more efficient.

Another point, and one which has nothing much to do with your own scanning, has to do with the large numbers of older scanners which are sitting in corporate storage rooms all over the country simply because the driver software is out of date. There are also large numbers of graphic arts students who would be thrilled to have a scanner of their own. When a software package is as inexpensive as ArtScan, these older scanners might be usable to students, or as gifts to a local artist center, a library multimedia center, or a rural school where operating budgets are notoriously small. Why not consider it?

Evaluating Images for Scanning

Your scanner is simply a digitizing instrument. It may have a wide-ranging sensitivity to the tone values present in the material to be scanned, or it may be relatively insensitive. You also have Photoshop, which can accomplish miracles on fairly poor material. Even with these powerful tools, it is vital that you look at every image that you intend to scan. Try to assess how successful the scan will be based on the quality of the original. The better the quality of your input images, the better the quality of your scans.

You can tell a lot from just looking at the image. Does it seem to be a good exposure? Can you see details in the very light areas and in the very dark areas? Does the overall image look too light? Too dark? Does it have poor overall contrast? Your eyes, your common sense, and your increasing experience will be able to tell you a great deal. You can tell even more by doing a preliminary, low-resolution scan of the image, and looking at its histogram within Photoshop. By evaluating the histogram, you'll be able to tell what information the original image contains, and whether it can be sufficiently improved to be usable.

The image on the left in Figure 2-9 shows one kind of problem. The image is generally too light, overall, and has highlight areas where no detail remains. The wide spike at the highlight end of the histogram indicates a concentration of highlight values that have little to differentiate them. The lack of values showing above 70% on the histogram indicates that the image was probably underexposed.

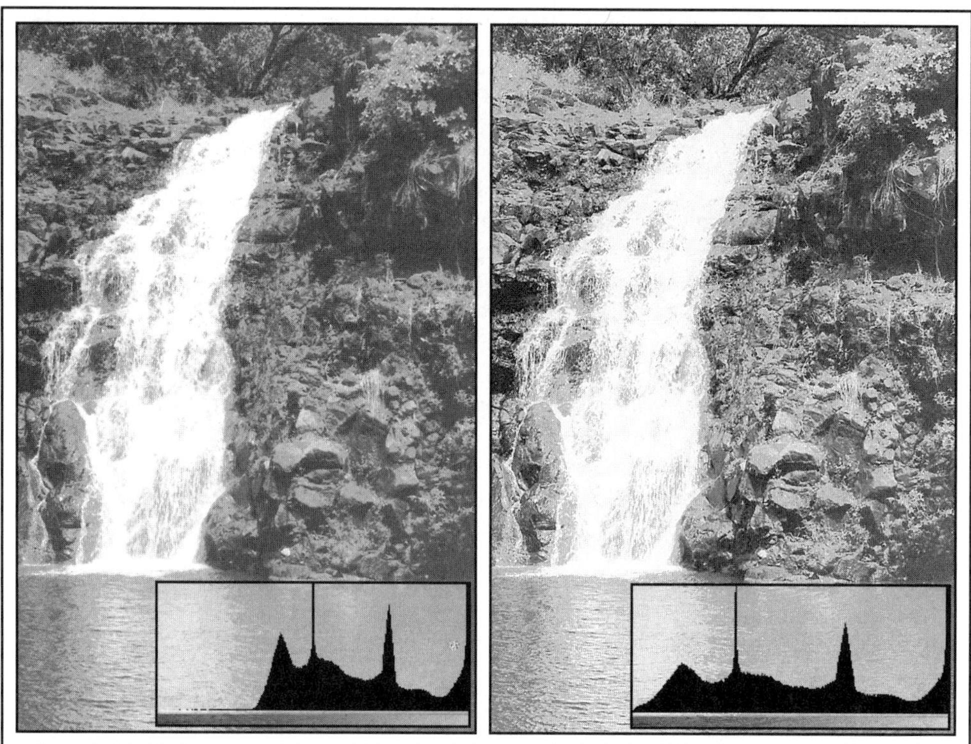

Figure 2-9: The preliminary histogram (left) shows image values clustered on the light end of the tone range. The redistributed histogram (right) is more satisfactorily arranged. Even with the better distribution, the highlight values are still blown out.

Using the methods discussed in the sections titled "Processing a Grayscale Image" in Chapter 9, "Photoshop Prepress" and "Processing an RGB File Intended for Color Separation" in Chapter 10, "Calibration & Color Reproduction," the scan can be made to look much better. The values present in the original have been redistributed over the entire range. There is better contrast in all of the areas of the image except for the falling water. With respect to the highlights, there is really no way to redistribute image data when it does not exist. As powerful as the Photoshop correction tools are, detail cannot be put back into the highlights. Consequently, even though the image does look better, its usability is open to question.

The image in the upper part of Figure 2-10 illustrates a problem that is the inverse of that shown in Figure 2-9. This image contains no values lighter than about 55%. There is a large spike containing slightly-darker-than-midtone values which are probably the range of tones within the sky and the medium tones within the shingle texture. The recognizable shadow values in this image contain very little detail. This is not always a weakness: the high-contrast look of certain parts of the image can be graphically effective. It simply depends upon whether that effect is what is desired.

Figure 2-10: The preliminary histogram (upper image) shows image values clustered on the dark end of the tone range. The redistributed histogram (lower) shows a better arrangement. The new arrangement has increased the overall contrast of the image.

The lower part of this figure has the value range redistributed. As you can see, the histogram maintains its overall configuration. It has simply been stretched to fit nearly all of the available range. Had it been stretched further, the sky tones would have ended as highlights and made the high-contrast effects much more pronounced.

The upper image in Figure 2-11 is much the same as the image in Figure 2-9. The histogram clearly shows the result of an aimed exposure of a shadowed area which has included very brightly lit areas as well. The picture divides itself into three general zones: the upper right-hand quadrant containing the very bright values, the upper left-hand quadrant containing most of the tones in the middle range, and the lower half containing most of the shadow values. Any attempt to lighten the lower part of the picture results in too much brightening of the upper half.

Figure 2-11: A difficult image showing clearly defined areas of bright values, medium values, and shadow values (upper image). The difficulty lies in lightening the shadows without bleaching out the medium and light tones (lower image).

There are a number of ways to make an image with these kinds of problems look even better than the corrected version in the lower part of Figure 2-11. Take a look at Chapter 11, "Manipulating Images."

The left-hand image in Figure 2-12 shows a histogram that is fairly satisfactory. There is a fairly uniform distribution of values across the entire range. The single spike at the highlight end comes from the bright sky and the foaming water at the bottom. Corrective measures taken, and the image on the right shows good contrast and good detail information in the highlights and the shadows.

Figure 2-12: The preliminary histogram (left) shows a wide distribution of values. Very little adjustment is required to make the image as open and clear as the one on the right.

A very good histogram is shown by the upper image in Figure 2-13. As you can see, there is a complete range of values with no prominent spikes other than that on the highlight end of the scale. This spike is specular since it is the result of sunlight flashing from very shiny leaves. The corrective work shown in the lower part of the figure has produced a picture that is clear, easy for the eye to grasp, and easy to reproduce.

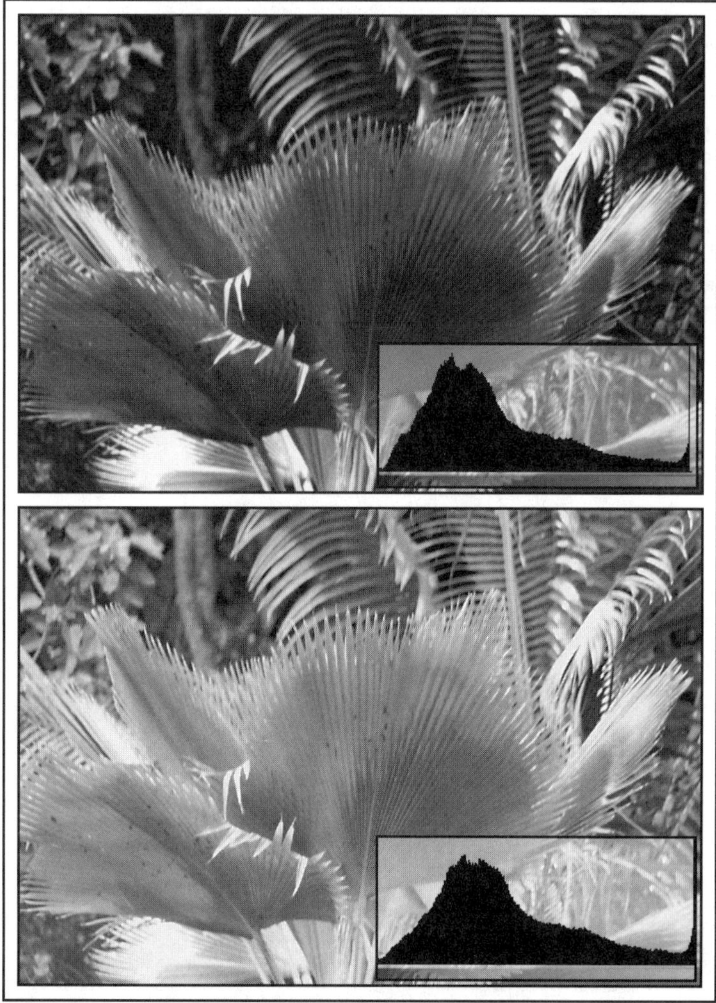

Figure 2-13: A good initial histogram (upper image) which requires almost no change and which flattens out only slightly in the adjustment process (lower).

Other Scanning Considerations

Beyond the mechanics of the scanner and the software which controls the hardware, there are a few other points which need to be made that deal with the material you intend to scan. These are simple housekeeping points, advice about cleaning the scanner and the material it will digitize.

Cleaning the Original Material

Considering that a flatbed scanner is a low-end digitizer, its sensitivity is good enough to pick up dust and fingerprints on the material to be scanned. They are easily visible as blemishes in the picture image. Removing the traces of surface dirt from the digital file is a waste of time since it is so easy to clean the image beforehand.

Handled with reasonable care—and properly stored—photographic prints and transparencies accumulate only small amounts of dust. You can purchase small aerosol cans with a plastic tube nozzle which focuses bursts of inert gas for blowing away the dust. If the material is too contaminated for the aerosol, you can purchase solvents made especially for cleaning photographic transparencies and prints. You must also purchase the special wiping cloths used with these solvents. Never use tissues or paper towels, particularly on the emulsion side of a transparency. Common paper products are very abrasive—tissues included, and some of them contain skin-softener lotions which can make the whole problem worse—and will damage the surface of the transparency. Even the ultra-soft wipes used with the solvent must be used totally saturated and with the lightest pressure you can manage.

The scanner bed must also be kept clean. This may mean that you have to disassemble the cover so that you can clean it inside and out with streakless cleaning solution and lint-free pads. While the scanner is open, you can use your inert-gas aerosol to blow away any dust that has accumulated on the inner surfaces.

Removing Artifacts From the Scanned File

No matter how carefully you treat your own photographic originals, at some time it will probably fall to you to scan material which is scratched and on which cleaning solvents have no effect. When there is no alternative, you need to go ahead and do the scan in the hope that Photoshop's powerful tools will help you to get rid of the artifacts without a lot of work.

Mounting With Oil

Oil-mount fluid can be purchased from any photo-supply or prepress supply retailer. It is a clear, light, volatile, oil-like substance which can be easily removed after scanning. It is very simple to use and does an amazingly good job on scratched transparencies. Place a few drops of the fluid onto the scan bed glass and push the transparency into the oil so that it is spread out to cover under the surface. Place a few more drops on top of the transparency. Cover the transparency with a larger piece of clear-base (or any kind of thin, transparent plastic or acetate). Push the clear-base onto the transparency to spread the oil. Tape the edges of the clear-base so that it is held tightly against the transparency. Scan as usual. When finished, remove the oil with photo-cleaning pads. You will find that the oil fills in the scratches and minimizes their visibility in the digital file.

Correction Filters

Four of Photoshop's bundled filters use blur methods which help to eliminate scratches and dust spots. Depending upon the kind of artifacts to be removed and the subject matter of the image, these filters can only be termed as partially successful. None of them work perfectly—some better than others—and all have the effect of eliminating some of the detail from the image. You have, then, a trade-off: eliminate dust/scratch artifacts and loose picture detail or leave the artifacts to disfigure the image while retaining whatever detail can be captured by the scanner. The choice is always difficult and needs to be made on a case-by-case basis. It does not usually take a lot of time to try each of the four filters on a problem image. If they give good results, then a good deal of manual work can be saved.

To illustrate how each of the four filters affects a blemished image, we have applied them to the photo shown in Figure 2-14. At the top is the complete photo, and at the bottom an enlargement of a section of the upper photo. The image contains dust speckling overall, as well as some serious scratches.

Figure 2-14: Every scanner operator's dream come true, a dusty image with scratches. The lower image is an enlargement of a section of the upper photo.

Despeckle The Despeckle filter is found under the Filter | Noise submenu. The filter has no parameters which can be set, it simply functions with built-in tolerances. As you can see in the two photos in Figure 2-15, the filter has a small effect on the scratch marks but does very little to eliminate the dust spots. This filter is very effective when used on images in which emulsion graininess is a problem; it smoothes out grainy textures without doing much harm to the image's detail. In short, Despeckle is a filter best used on images where noise artifacts are very small. The dust spots in the figure are far too large for it to affect a change.

Figure 2-15: The Despeckle filter has almost no effect on this problem image.

Gaussian Blur The Gaussian Blur (Filter | Blur | Gaussian Blur) is not usually considered to be a corrective filter. However, it can be used as such in some cases. The two photos in Figure 2-16 show the result of the filter at a Radius setting of 1. Although the resulting blur nearly eliminates all of the dust marks, the large scratch is still visible. The clarity of the image has also been reduced.

Figure 2-16: The Gaussian Blur filter eliminates the dust but not the scratches. It also reduces the clarity of the image.

Sometimes, a very small setting of the blur Radius will do the job. For example, a setting of .5 might be used. When small radius values are successful, some of the image details can be restored by using the Unsharp Mask filter (Filter | Sharpen | Unsharp Mask). Sharpening helps but it is not a perfect solution: you can never have the image as sharp and clear as it would have been without the Blur filter.

Median The Median filter (examples shown in Figure 2-17) works by taking an average of pixel values for the distance of the Radius value. As the Radius value increases, so does the amount of blurriness in the image. The Median filter, as you can see from the figure, is more successful than Gaussian Blur or Despeckle at eliminating the scratches and all but the largest dust marks. It also retains more image detail if used at small Radius values. Because this filter generates small areas of average or similar tones, there is an all-over posterization. Sharpening tends to accentuate the posterization rather than to restore image detail.

Figure 2-17: The Median filter works moderately well to remove surface blemishes, but does not lend itself to resharpening to increase the photo's clarity.

Dust & Scratches The Dust & Scratches filter works in much the same way as the Median filter, but with the additional Threshold control (Figure 2-18). The latter allows you to assign a value to the difference in pixel values below which the filter does not function. For example, with the Threshold set to 20 levels, two pixels might have values of 128 and 147. Because the difference between these two numeric values is less than 20, the filter will not touch them. Where the difference is greater than 20, the filter will function using the Radius value in precisely the same way the Median filter does.

Figure 2-18: The Dust & Scratches filter is the most successful of the four artifact-removal filters.

The Dust & Scratches filter is the most successful of the four correction filters. However, it also decreases the amount of image detail. With the Threshold control setting parameters over the pixels that will be affected, there is a less pronounced posterization effect. Unsharp Mask can be used more effectively after executing this filter.

The Rubber Stamp tool The Rubber Stamp tool is not a filter but it will be, if none of the filters are satisfactory, your best friend. You should learn to love this tool: if a photo is bad enough, you'll spend a lot of time with it! With the Rubber Stamp tool, you are able to clone pixels from one part of the image so that they cover up defective pixels in a different part of the image. A complete look at this tool will be found in Chapter 3, "Toolbox Techniques."

Descreening

Scanning photographic material that has been reproduced on a printing press is one of the least rewarding scanning tasks. If the reproduction was in color, you will only be able to capture the limited color range offered by four-color printing, as opposed to the broader range of colors present in a continuous-tone photographic image. For both color and halftone scans, you will be capturing an image from which much of the detail has been eliminated by the output screening process. Still, scanning screened material—they are often called *rescreens*—is sometimes necessary.

Almost every Photoshop user has a pet method for eliminating screens from a scan. Some users like the Median filter. Others go to elaborate lengths to place the rescreen originals on the scanner bed at 15°. We have a method that we think works very well, and we hope you'll try it out. It is a method that is based on the inverse of the process which originally produced the screens.

You need a small piece of equipment to do this job correctly, unless you have eyes that are good enough—or experienced enough—to be able to look at the material to be scanned and to tell the screen frequency used to produce it. Your extra equipment (shown in Figure 2-19) is a Gaebel Half-Tone Screen Determiner. You can purchase one of these from almost any prepress-supply retailer at a cost of less than $5. The Screen Determiner is simply a piece of positive film or a thin sheet of clear plastic with some not-quite-parallel lines drawn upon it. The lines are very close together at one end and diverge slightly toward the other end. Along the sides of the lines group are a set of numbers. To use the screen determiner, put it down on top of the screened material. Begin to rotate the plastic sheet until you see a four-pointed interference star begin to form within the area of the lines. Continue to rotate the sheet until the points of the star reach to the outer edges of the lines. The outer edge of the star will point to one of the numbers along the edge. The number it points to is the screen frequency used to produce the piece. Simple, huh? This thing is really clever!

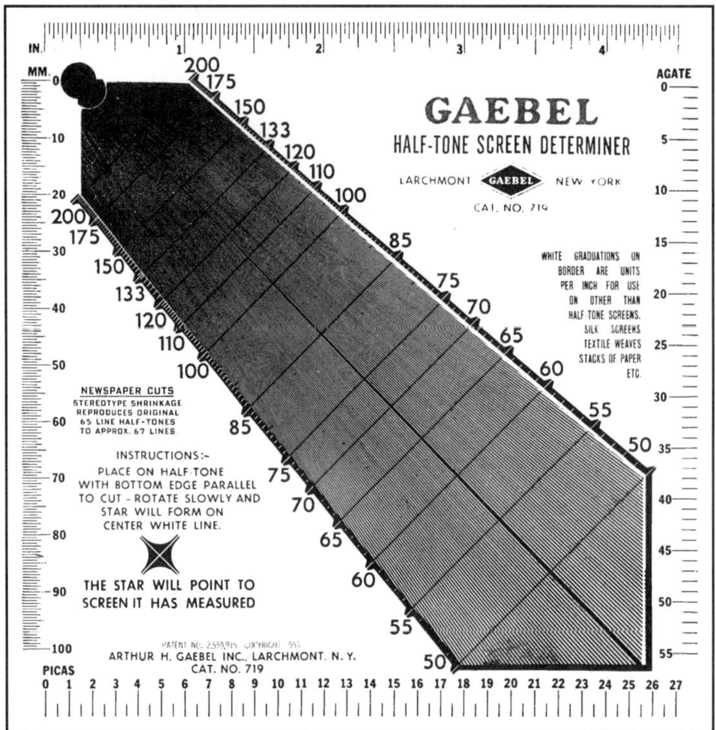

Figure 2-19: The Gaebel Half-Tone Screen Determiner, a remarkable and inexpensive gadget. No scanner user should be without one!

Once you've determined the line-screen which produced the piece, place the original on the scan bed, perform the preview scan, and crop the portion of the image you intend to use. Set the scan percentage to be 100% of the original size and the pixel density to twice the measured line-screen. These two values are crucial to the process. If, for example, the line-screen was determined to be 133, set the requested ppi to be 266 (2 X 133 = 266). Press the Scan button.

When the scan is complete, your image shows a screen interference pattern similar to that in Figure 2-20. From the Filter menu, choose Blur | Gaussian Blur. Set the Radius value to 1.5. With just this blur, your image loses all of its surface noise and appears as shown in Figure 2-21. Once the blur has been done, the scan can then be treated as any other scan.

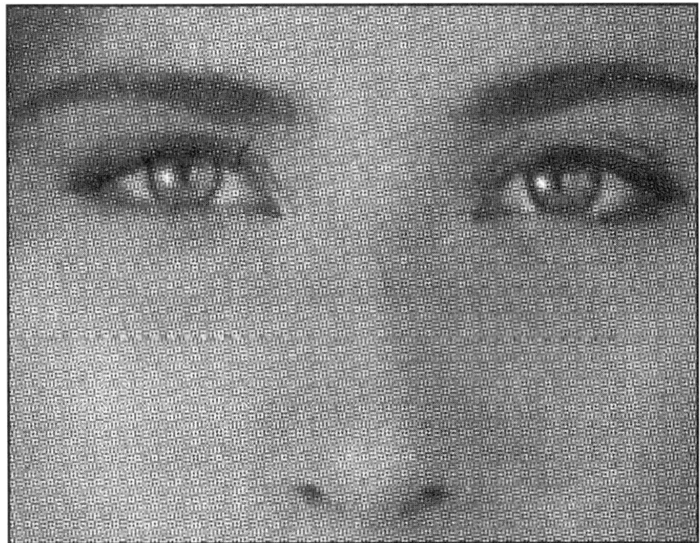

Figure 2-20: Untouched scan of a screened image.

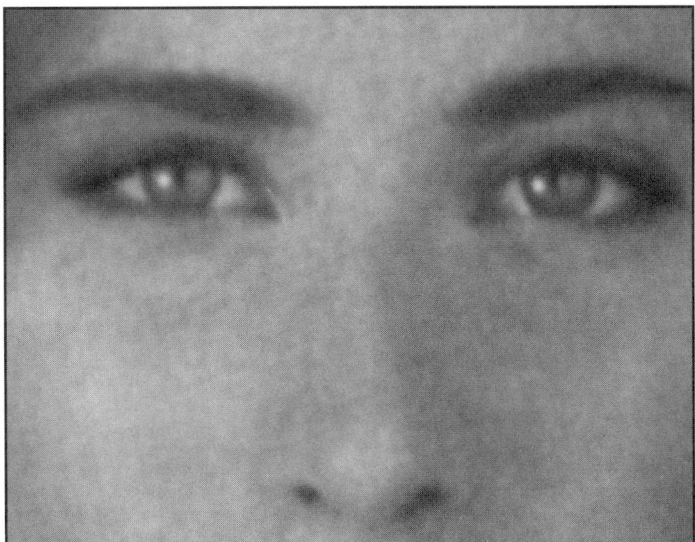

Figure 2-21: If the size and resolution of the scan are in the correct relationship to the line-screen of the original, one application of the Gaussian Blur filter removes the screen artifacts.

The image in Figure 2-22 (Figures 2-20 and 2-21 are enlarged details of this photo) was determined to have been printed at a 150 line-screen. It was scanned full size at 300 ppi and then subjected, on the right-hand side, to the Gaussian Blur filter. The right-hand part of the image was then processed in the usual way, the image was resized, and then the right-hand side was subjected to the Unsharp Mask filter. As you can see, this technique works very well indeed.

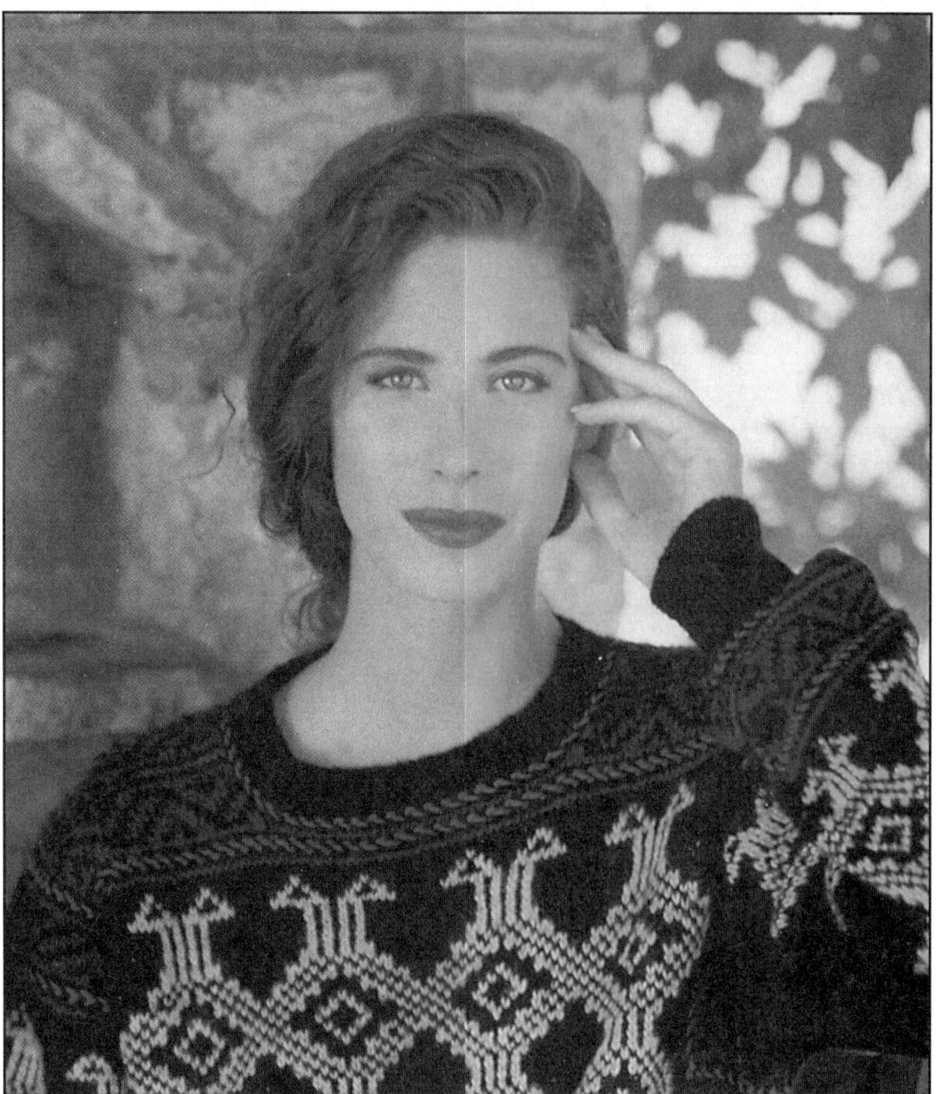

Figure 2-22: It's difficult to imagine how the before (left) could result in the after (right). It is a very simple procedure.

For other perspectives—and different kinds of solutions—on scanning material that has been screened, please see the sections titled "Reducing a Moiré Pattern" in Chapter 8, "Filter Frolics" and the section titled "Processing Line Art Scans" in Chapter 9, "Photoshop Prepress."

More-than-8-bit Digital Files Photoshop is internally geared to process digital files containing 8 bits of information in each channel. For example, every pixel in an RGB file can be described with 8 bits (one byte) for each of the channels—Red, Green, and Blue. Each RGB pixel, then, contains one of 256 possible values for each channel. The total number of colors this makes possible is 256^3, or 16,777,216. Many scanners have a sampling sensitivity that is able to describe each of a channel's pixel components with more than 8 bits. Some scanners use 10 bits, some 12, and some 16. With more bits come more values: a sixteen-bit scan, for example, represents a color range containing 2,858,455,254,310,656 values. That is a number that easily exceeds the human visual range.

Why scan with that many values? The explanation is really more theoretical than real, but to understand how such enormous numbers can affect your scan, you must first understand that all scanners have difficulty differentiating very dark values *and* very light values. (As a matter of fact, human eyes have much the same difficulty.) If you think about it, all of the problems that we typically associate with an imperfect scan have to do with shadows and highlights. Shadows become so dark that they merge into a single value and loose their details. Highlights wash out and leave us with only uniform areas of white. Perhaps you thought that these problems originated with the original photo material. Sometimes that is the case, but more often, the fault is with the scanner. There is less light reflected from a dark area of a scan—or transmitted by a dark area on a transparency—and simple rounding errors occur. When a larger bit depth is used, there is a more precise differentiation simply because sampling areas can be very close to each other and can still be discerned by the scanner as different from each other.

After the scanner has sampled an area, the extra bits can be discarded. However, having those extra bits means that the scanner software can make an intelligent choice with respect to the real value of a pixel. Reading the extra bits eliminates most of the rounding errors and makes the scan much more accurate than it would have been with only 8 bits. You also end up with a much larger tonal range which gives you much more latitude when making corrections, especially drastic corrections.

Some scanners allow Photoshop to retain a higher number of bits after the scan. The scanner delivers the information as an 8-bit file but a larger number of bits is still present. From the Image menu, choose Mode | 16 Bits/Channel. Photoshop can display only eight bits per channel, but it allows you to proceed with some functions even though you cannot see all of the values you have under your control. Adjustments on a 16-bit file are limited to whatever you are able to do using only the Levels or the Curves controls. Nearly all of Photoshop's normal tools and commands cannot be used.

If you have a normal 8-bit scan which, after scanner-software adjustment, still looks to be too dark (Figure 2-23), you might wish to use the Levels or the Curves controls to try to lighten it (Figure 2-24).

Figure 2-23: Scanner-adjusted scan is still too dark.

Figure 2-24: Gamma/midtone shift lightens the scan but damages the image by leaving too few values to represent the dark tones.

Using the Levels controls, the lightening would probably be accomplished by moving the midtone slider of the Input scale to the left. This move, with the cutoff of the shadow tones, results in too few values in the range between 50%–95%. Figure 2-25 shows an enlarged detail from Figure 2-24 in which the missing values result in severe posterization in the areas where dark tones are present. There are simply too few values present to represent a continuous range of tones. (This figure's posterization has been slightly exaggerated—with the Unsharp Mask filter—in order to make it easier to see.) The problem is fairly serious. If this image is to be reproduced on an offset press, some of the posterization will disappear because of the blurring which occurs due to dot gain. But enough of the posterization will remain as a visible defect in the image.

With a 16-bit image, you have considerably more latitude in your adjustments—in fact, you have a tonal range that is roughly 170,000,000 times as large as an equivalent 8-bit image. That gives you a lot of space in which to maneuver.

Adjustments on 16-bit images bend all the rules you might have heard about a series of small adjustments being injurious to the data in the image. With a normal 8-bit scan, these rules should be taken seriously: every adjustment which changes the image (Levels, Curves, Hue/Saturation, Color Balance, Selective Color, etc.) is destructive.

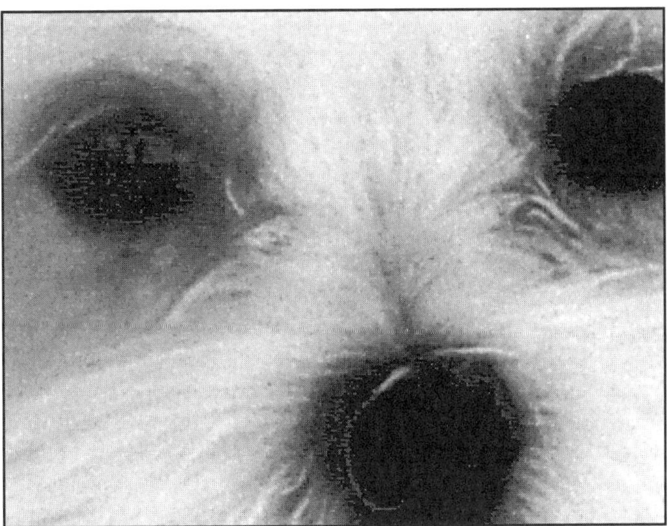

Figure 2-25: Enlarged detail shows the posterization of dark tones.

Each adjustment, although it probably improves the appearance of the image, leaves you with less data than you had before the adjustment. That is the reason why the images in Figures 2-23 and 2-24 suffered: after a serious adjustment by the scanner software, further adjustments forfeited enough data to cause visible harm to the continuous tone range.

With 16-bit scans, a series of three or four smaller adjustments actually works better than one large-scale move. Small adjustments help to distribute the values present in the image so that they are placed where they are needed. Figures 2-26, 2-27, 2-28, and 2-29 illustrate how this might work.

Figure 2-26 shows an image which seems so dark that it would normally be considered unusable. The initial histogram shows that the entire range of values is above 50%, with most of the tones concentrated above 70%.

In Figure 2-27, the first—and largest—set of changes was made to the image with the Levels controls. All three channels' Highlight sliders were moved over to the left to point to the first real values present in the image. The Midtone slider was shifted to read 1.30. After this set of adjustments, the histogram at the upper right shows a much more satisfactory—though still far from perfect—distribution of values.

Figure 2-28 shows the Shadow slider on the Levels' Input scale moved to 22, and the Midtone slider moved to read 1.24. The resulting histogram (upper left) now displays an even better distribution of tones.

In the last figure, 2-29, there is a small nudge of the Midtone slider to read 1.08. This further lightens the image and results in the final histogram, shown at the upper left. Notice that there is now a full range of values in the image. Notice, also, that despite making drastic moves with the Levels controls, there is still no degradation of the histogram as there would have been had this image been adjusted in the same way in 8-bit mode.

Figure 2-26: Very dark 16-bit image seems too dark to be usable.

Figure 2-27: Drastic shifts of the highlight sliders in all three channels as well as a shift of the midtone slider considerably lighten the image.

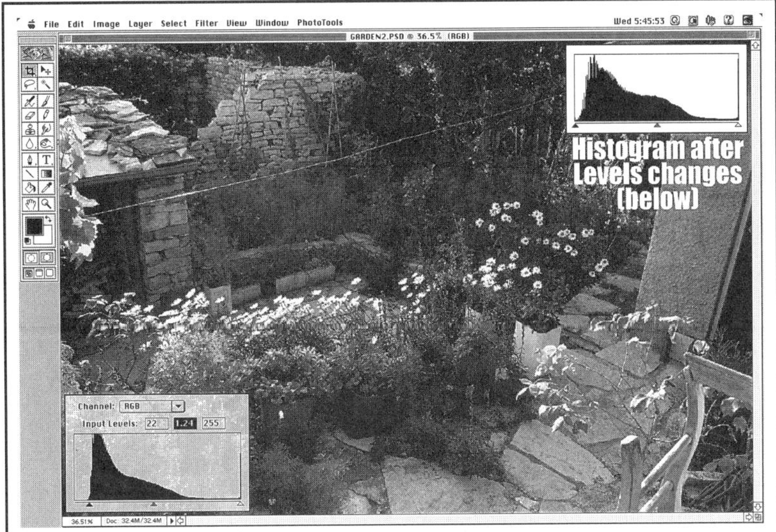

Figure 2-28: Another, smaller, tweak of the midtone slider makes the image better yet.

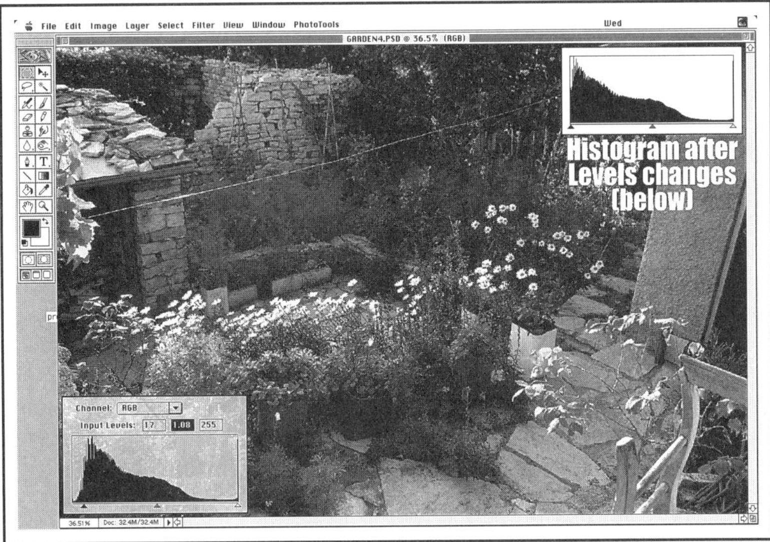

Figure 2-29: One more midtone adjustment gives an image that is not merely usable, but is quite good. There is no degradation of the histogram because the image was a 16-bit file.

The four stages of the photo shown in these figures can be seen in color in the color section of this book. The amount of change from first to last illustrates how vast is the amount of data you have at your disposal when working with a 16-bit scan. It also indicates how much corrective power you have! You can also, if you wish, perform these corrections on a copy of the file used in these figures. The file is titled GARDEN.PSD. It is located in the Chapter Two Practice Files folder on the Companion CD-ROM.

CD-ROM

After making tonal corrections in 16-bit mode, you will need to return to 8-bit mode (Image | Mode | 8 Bits/Channel) in order to do any further work on the image. Please note that your scanner may not scan in 16-bit color and may only have 10-bit or 12-bit capability. The extra data will still give you a tremendous amount of flexibility when it comes to problem images. You can still make use of the extra data using Photoshop's 16-bit mode if your scanner's software will allow it. A 10-bit or 12-bit file will work in 16-bit mode. You will not have the astronomical range of tones present in a true 16-bit file. But even a 10-bit file has 64 times as much data as an equivalent 8-bit file!

Photo CD

When Photo CD was introduced by the Eastman Kodak Company in 1993, it was marketed as an alternative to lab prints and slides. The basic idea was that consumers would purchase a home-television-compatible CD-ROM player. They would then, after having their film processed on a Kodak Photo CD scanner, be able to view snapshots and slides on the television screen. Despite formidable amounts of money thrown at the marketing of this system, consumers, as the saying goes, stayed away in droves.

Graphics professionals saw the potential for Photo CD very early. At a time when professional digital scans of questionable quality were being sold at three to five times the cost of the same scan today, Photo CD seemed a good alternative for many graphics purposes. The key to the desirability of Photo CD scans was, and still is, cost. Today, an average cost for a Photo CD scan is about $3.00. However, some vendors have pricing structures that bring the cost down as low as 65¢ with a quantity order. Even at the highest average cost, Photo CD scans are inexpensive. The fact that the scan quality is not as high as equivalent work done on a high-end drum scanner does not seem to be a deterring factor. The quality, in the opinion of many Photo CD consumers, is good enough for their purpose, and consumers include developers and technicians in multimedia, the Internet, CD-ROM authoring, and prepress. (Note: Photo CD costs include a fee that averages about $10 for the media. Once purchased, the media can be used repeatedly until it is filled to capacity—about 100 images.)

Photo CD scanners use CCD sensors in what is called a trilinear array. In common with most CCD scanners, Photo CD scanners are not as sensitive in very dark areas of the scanned material. This has been a conspicuous failing in many Photo CD scans. Figure 2-30 shows a typical example of a bright-light shot with deep shadows. All of the very dark areas in the figure have been clipped to the same digital value (in the lower half of the figure, all non-clipped pixels have been screened back to show how extensive the clipping problem really is). While problems with dark tones can be partially addressed by the Photo CD scanner operator, the dark tone clipping limit can be expanded only at the expense of highlight values. Recent changes in the scanner software has made an attempt to remedy the problem, but it remains one of Photo CD's most conspicuous drawbacks.

Figure 2-30: Photo CD scans often exhibit dark tones which clip to the same value.

Photo CD scans are stored in a Kodak-proprietary color model called YCC. YCC is somewhat analogous to the Lab color model in Photoshop. The Y channel of a YCC document carries luminance information while the two C channels carry color. The

YCC model is also associated with data compression, which makes it a good format for storing large-scale color scans. Programs such as Photoshop access the YCC data through plug-ins which function as converters. Photo CD data is read by the plug-in and then translated from YCC to Photoshop's RGB, Lab, or Grayscale modes. The bundled Kodak CMS plug-in that ships with Photoshop is one example of a converter. Kodak also furnishes an Acquire module (chosen, if available, from the File | Import submenu) that furnishes more functionality than the bundled Photoshop plug-in. This plug-in can be downloaded without cost from the Kodak Web site. The URL is ftp://ftp.Kodak.com/pub/photo-cd/drivers/dd0253.hqx. Since Kodak's plug-in has more features than the built-in converter, we recommend that you download and use it.

Beyond these two easily available utilities for opening Photo CD scans, Kodak also sells a modestly priced software package called Kodak Access. Access includes a set of generic profiles for output devices which are used when converting Photo CD files to CMYK mode. Kodak also sells custom profiles for color printers and proofing systems.

Photo CD scans are stored on a CD-ROM disk in Image Pack format, an amalgam of six related files all containing the same image but at different resolutions. The typical Image Pack file has six files. (The more recent Photo CD Pro format has seven.) When a Photo CD scan is to be loaded, the plug-in gives you the choice of loading any one of the six Base Values (Photo CD's term for the six available resolutions you can open). The chart in Figure 2-31 shows the size of each of the six, the number of pixels in each dimension, and the real-world size of each at both 72 ppi and 300 ppi. Because loading the larger sizes takes more time, having the smaller versions of the same file allows you to open the size that is appropriate for your purpose. (Note: the Base/64 file size is the one used by the Photo CD scanning station to print the small dye-sub thumbnail of each image which appears on the printed cover insert of the disk.)

Photo CD Source Size	Pixels (1.5:1)	Dimensions @ 72 ppi	Dimensions @ 300 ppi
Base/64	96 x 64	1.333" x .889"	.32" x .213"
Base/16	192 x 128	2.667" x 1.778"	.64" x .427"
Base/4	384 x 256	5.333" x 3.556"	1.28" x .853"
Base	768 x 512	10.667" x 7.111"	2.56" x 1.707"
4 Base	1536 x 1024	21.333" x 14.222"	5.12" x 3.413"
16 Base	3072 x 2048	42.667" x 28.444"	10.240" x 6.827"

Figure 2-31: Table of Photo CD Base values, pixel dimensions, and actual sizes at two common file resolutions.

Despite whatever market hype you've been exposed to, Photo CD is a valuable and useful way of acquiring reasonably good quality digital images. It is not, however, a poor man's answer to a drum scan. In fact, if you plan to use Photo CD, be prepared for the fact that, once you have the image loaded into Photoshop, you have to treat it as a raw scan. Automated translation software can be purchased for quantity users of Photo CD, but average users will have to make use of one of the plug-in modules. Neither of the easily available plug-in modules can do very much in the way of correction beyond simple lightening, darkening, or a primitive variety of sharpening of the CD file as it is translated. The loaded image should be processed using basic corrective methods described in Chapter 10, "Calibration & Color Reproduction," and Chapter 11, "Manipulating Images."

Loading a Photo CD Image

For best results, we recommend that you use version 3.0 of the Photo CD Acquire module. Once you have downloaded this Photoshop add-on from the Kodak Web site (the URL is given above) and mounted a Photo CD disk in your computer, choose the module from the Photoshop File | Import submenu.

Figure 2-32 shows the initial file-locator window. Having selected the Photo CD disk, you will find that it contains three directories titled CDI, Photos, and Photo_CD. Choose the last of these. Within this directory/folder are two files—Overview and Startup—as well as another directory/folder titled Images. The Photo CD Image pack files are within this folder. From within this folder, locate the image you wish to open: use the number given on the cover thumbnail printout and then locate the file using the 2 or 3 digits to the left of the part of the title that reads .PCD;1. Click on the Open button.

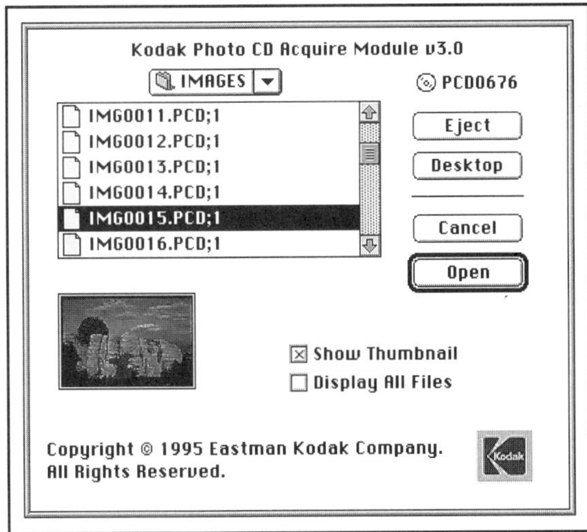

Figure 2-32: The first Photo CD image acquisition window.

Another window then appears. An expanded view of this window is shown in Figure 2-33.

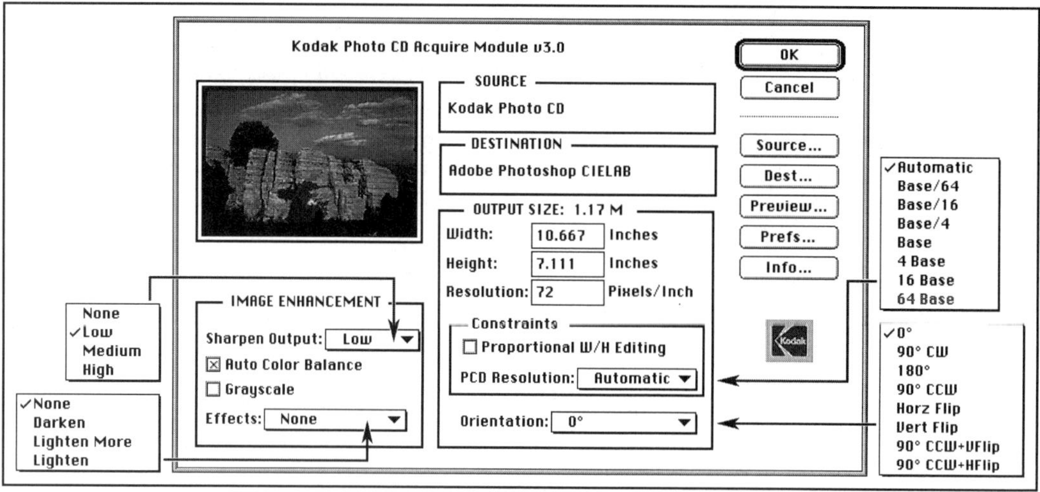

Figure 2-33: Expanded view of the main Photo CD image acquisition window.

Thumbnail

In the upper left-hand corner of the new window is a thumbnail of the image. If you move your cursor into the thumbnail, you can click and drag a crop marquee which will open only the part of the image within the selection. To eliminate the crop marquee, click once anywhere in the thumbnail window.

Image Enhancement

Directly below the thumbnail are two pop-up menus and two check boxes in a rectangular area devoted to Image Enhancement features.

Sharpening The first pop-up allows you to sharpen the image as you open it. The sharpening method is inferior to the Unsharp Mask filter of Photoshop and is probably not worth using.

Auto Color Balance The Auto Color Balance check box is a problematical choice. It does have a very noticeable effect on the image, but whether this change is something you will find desirable is something you have to decide for yourself. If you are opening an out-of-doors photo, the Auto check box will really jazz up the blues of the sky and the greens of the foliage. This will give a cool quality to everything else in the image. You might want to test this option by opening up two Base/16 versions of the file—one with Auto checked, and one without—and make your choice based on the comparison. Our guess is that you will find the checked version almost surreal in the way its color enhancement affects the image.

Grayscale The grayscale check box allows you to open the colored image directly into Grayscale mode. It doesn't work very well. If you need to use grayscale, you're better off translating the color image into Photoshop Lab mode and then retaining only the L channel for your grayscale file. To do this once the image is open in Photoshop, press Command+1 or Ctrl+1 to view the L channel. From the Image menu, choose Mode | Grayscale. Click OK when you are asked if you wish to discard the other channels. A comparison of the Acquire module's grayscale file and using the L channel of a Lab file will convince you of the superiority of the latter.

Effects The last pop-up lets you darken or lighten the image. This is another choice that you will have to judge based on comparisons between small versions of the file with and without these options selected. Some images benefit from these effects and some do not.

Source

The Source rectangle displays choices made in the dialog window (Figure 2-34) which opens when you click the Source button below the cancel button. The scrolling window will show you what kind of original was scanned to the CD. The pop-up menu gives three choices which are shown at the bottom of the window. You should probably use the default, Kodak Photo CD.

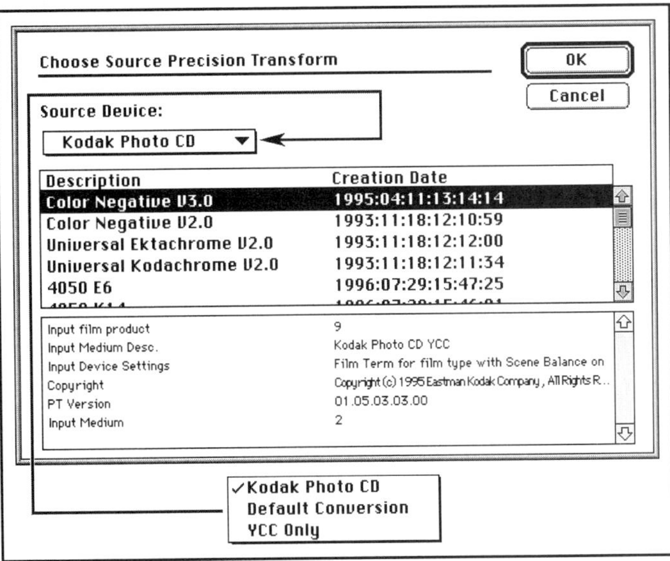

Figure 2-34: Photo CD Source window.

Destination

The Destination rectangle displays choices made in the dialog window (Figure 2-35) which opens when you click the Destination button below the Source button. The pop-up gives the choices. For color work, you should probably use the Adobe Photoshop RGB since it allows you to use many of the corrective techniques discussed throughout this book.

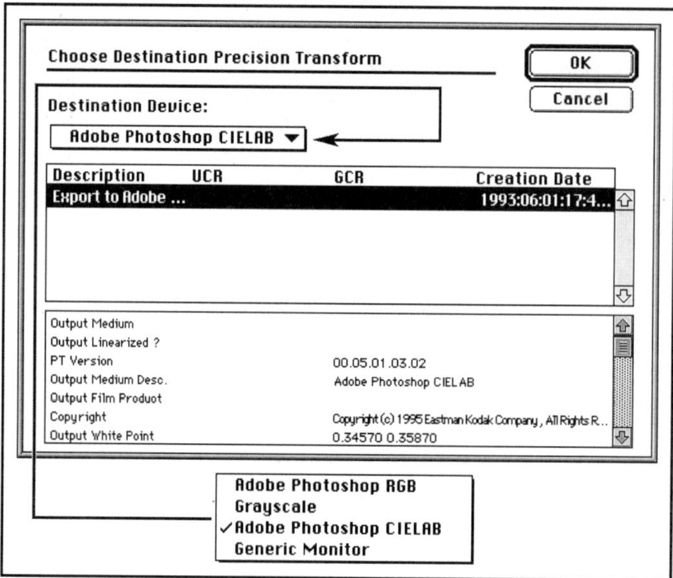

Figure 2-35: Photo CD Destination window.

Output Size

The first important choice to be made in this area of the dialog box is the resolution you wish to have for the translated file. Enter your choice in the Resolution data entry field. Next, make a selection from the PCD Resolution pop-up. The choices are shown at the side with Automatic as the default. The Base choices are explained in the chart in Figure 2-31. When you have made your choice, you'll find that the width and height have been entered for you. If you draw a crop marquee in the thumbnail window, the size of your crop will be shown as updated figures for both the Width and Height values.

At the bottom of this window, an Orientation pop-up lets you choose a variety of flip and rotate options. Since Photo CD scans are always done with the short axis of the image as vertical, an image taken with the long axis vertical will appear in the thumbnail window as sideways. You could, of course, rotate the image in Photoshop. The Orientation selections allow you to open the image already rotated the way you wish it to be.

Preview Button

Click on the Preview button to open a window with a larger thumbnail of the image (Figure 2-36). You can, if you wish, draw your selection crop within this window.

Figure 2-36: Photo CD Preview window.

Prefs Button

The Prefs dialog box (Figure 2-37) gives you some choices for measurement units and resolution. Another button within this window opens the window shown in Figure 2-38 which gives you the ability to choose a specific display. Unless you have purchased monitor profiles for use with this Acquire module, your choice will be limited to the selected Generic Display shown in the scrolling window.

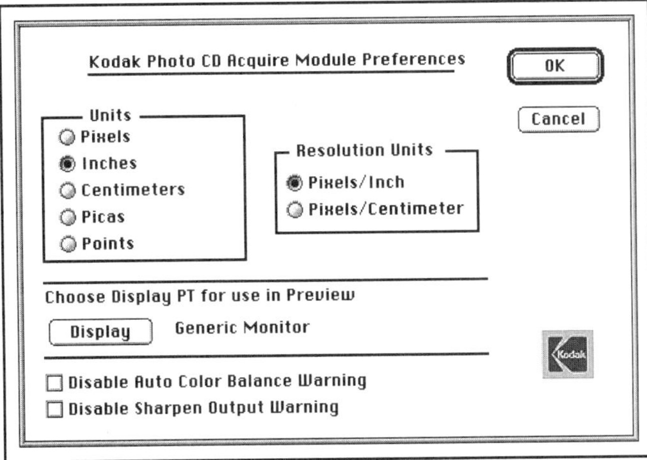

Figure 2-37: Photo CD Preferences dialog box.

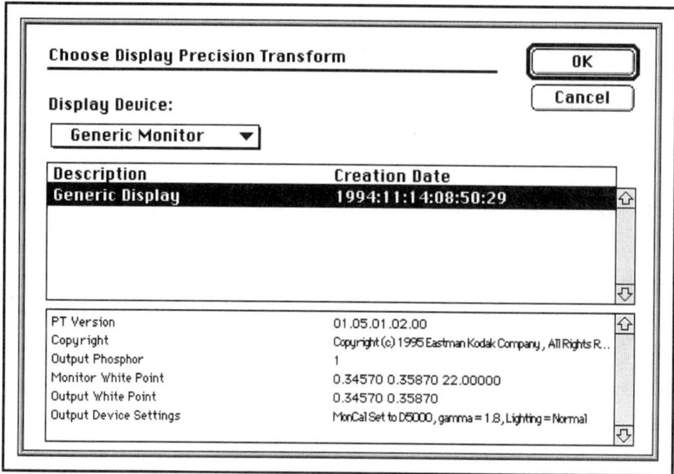

Figure 2-38: Photo CD Display Device window.

Info Button

Clicking on the Info button opens the screen shown in Figure 2-39. In this window are details of the film from which the Photo CD file was made, the scanner, the disk name, and the file name.

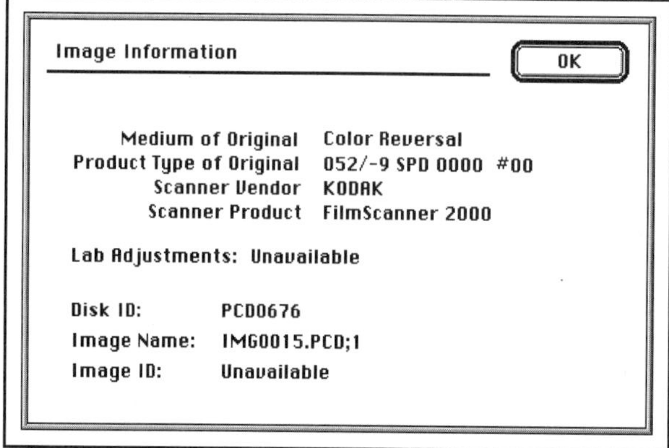

Figure 2-39: Photo CD Info window.

Correcting the Photo CD Image

After you have loaded the image from the Companion CD-ROM, you'll probably find that your image requires some modification before it can be used. What kinds of modifications you make depend upon the purpose for which you intend the picture. Please refer to the sections titled "Processing a Grayscale Image" in Chapter 9, "Photoshop Prepress" and "Processing an RGB File Intended for Color Separation" in Chapter 10, "Calibration & Color Reproduction." Other correction information is available in Chapter 11, "Manipulating Images."

Figures 2-40 and 2-41 show *before* and *after* versions of an image acquired by Photo CD. As you can see, the larger final image is very satisfactory although it was cropped to eliminate most of the problem shadow values noted in Figure 2-30. After cropping, we used the Rubber stamp tool to eliminate all traces of the shadows from the bottom of the picture. The resulting file is clear and shows very good fidelity of detail and tonal range. These same files are shown in the color plate section.

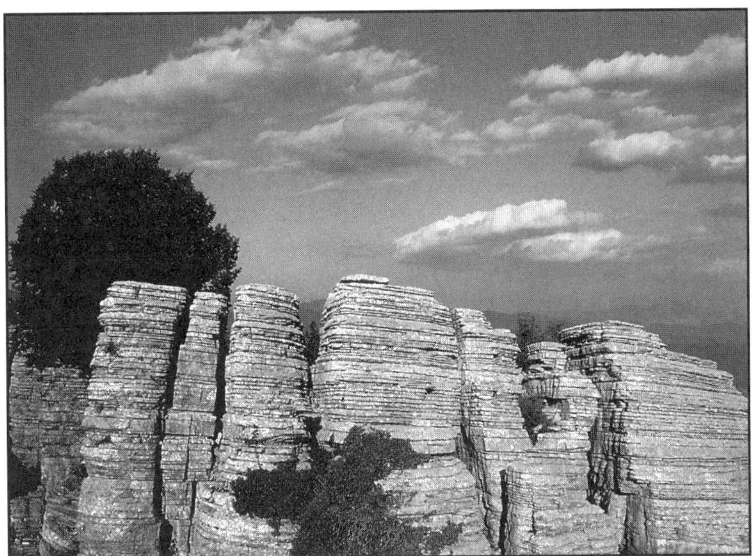

Figure 2-40: Image acquired from Photo CD. The photo looks fairly good but will require correction.

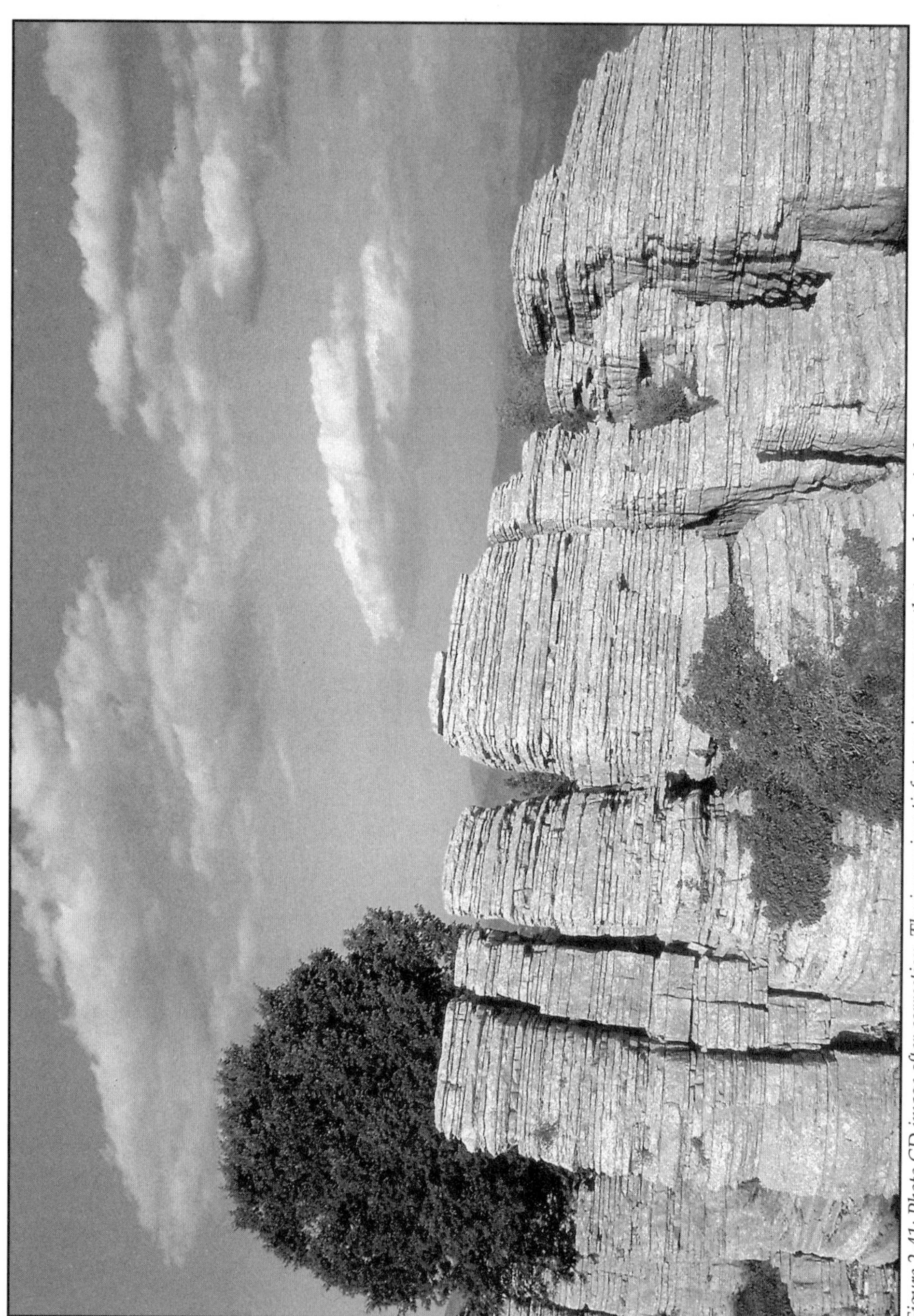

Figure 2-41: Photo CD image after correction. The image is satisfactory in every way that can be imagined.

Moving On

In this chapter, we've discussed the sometimes confusing terms: *resolution, pixels,* and *scanning frequency*. You've also seen how a well-constructed scanning program can help you with the task of acquiring images. Finally, you've had an extensive look at Kodak's Photo CD, a service technology that puts reasonably good-quality scans into the hands of Photoshop users at an affordable price.

Our discussion of scanning is not complete without a look at the eventual use of the scan. Once you have acquired an image, you'll probably want to work with it, edit it, or apply special procedures such as silhouetting, removing unwanted image details, and enhancing parts of the photo to show it to better advantage. For these tasks, you need a familiarity with Photoshop's tools. In Chapter 3, "Toolbox Techniques," we'll highlight a number of ways to make your image editing faster and more efficient.

chapter 3

Toolbox Techniques

Whenever you open a file in Photoshop, chances are good that you'll be working on specific areas of the file rather than on the file as a single object. Certainly global edits—manipulations of the entire file—are one kind of Photoshop work; in many cases, however, you will need to resort to local edits—changing just part of the file. Perfect pictures are, after all, the exception rather than the rule. For local editing, you can make use of Photoshop's powerful set of paint and selection tools. The palette for these tools usually opens, by default, in the upper left-hand corner of your computer screen.

The Toolbox is deceptively compact. It contains 33 separate tools (several of them variations of a single concept), two color selectors, controls for entering and exiting a fast masking mode called Quick Mask, and three buttons that control the way Photoshop displays your document. Most of the tools have additional flexibility in the form of options which allow you to control their behavior. Even if you are somewhat acquainted with the tools, you may be surprised at how powerful they really are.

In this chapter, you'll be learning about the tools in detail. You'll see several uses for each of the tools and have the opportunity to follow along with several small projects. These projects will give you knowledge of the tools, insight into the way Photoshop works, and provide tips on which tools to use for specific situations. You'll also be shown a number of techniques that will help you to become a more efficient user of Photoshop.

The tutorial information in this chapter will refer to several files contained on the Companion CD-ROM. Before starting this chapter, you may find it useful to copy the Chapter 3 Practice Files from the Companion CD-ROM onto your hard drive so that you have quick and easy access to them.

The Mouse *With* the Keyboard

Users of programs such as Photoshop often slow themselves down by relying too much on the mouse. Studies have shown that up to 40 percent of a user's time is spent moving the cursor from one place on the screen to another—cursor to menu, cursor to image, cursor to Toolbox, cursor back to image, cursor back to Toolbox, and so on. An efficient user with one hand on the keyboard and the other on the mouse can work circles around one who uses only the mouse.

Many of the Photoshop menu commands have keyboard equivalents. You can assign those that do not to the Actions palette (see Chapter 1). You can also assign keyboard commands with third-party macro/hot-key software such as CE Software's QuicKeys. Photoshop possesses another refinement that goes well beyond the capabilities of any other program—the ability to choose most of the tools and many editing options using the keyboard. While you are working, you can select tools and discard them without moving the cursor from the working area. In like manner, you can select brush sizes, change opacity and pressure settings, switch around the foreground/background colors, change the magnification of the image within the window, and make use of a wide variety of options that can be performed without moving the cursor from its working position. These features give a fluency to the program that make it one of the most efficient working environments of any graphics program.

Such fluency has a cost: there is a good deal of memorizing to do. Learning all of the keyboard commands might seem an impossible task—especially because most users are pretty busy using the program—but the extra work will really pay off. One way to make the task seem less intimidating is to divide the commands into logical groups. Menu commands could be one group, tool commands another, palette commands a third, and useful commands noted throughout this book might be a fourth. Once you begin to see what spectacular efficiency the program can bring you, it will be hard for you to be satisfied with old, slow work habits. For now, the Toolbox commands are a good place to begin.

Go on, Type a Tool...

Photoshop makes it easy to use the Toolbox. Simply press one of the alphabetical tool key commands and your tool is instantly selected. Most of the letter commands that select the tools are logical: *g* is for *gradient*, *b* is for *brush*, and so on. The illogical ones are not easy to remember simply because they don't make mnemonic sense: *y* for *pencil*, *o* for *dodge*, *burn*, or *sponge*. Some of the key commands fall into a unique category; they are the ones which use one of the inner consonants of the tool name or—in one case—a bad pun: *v* for *move tool*, *k* for *paint bucket*, and *i* for *eyedropper* (get it?). The complete chart is shown here in Figure 3-1.

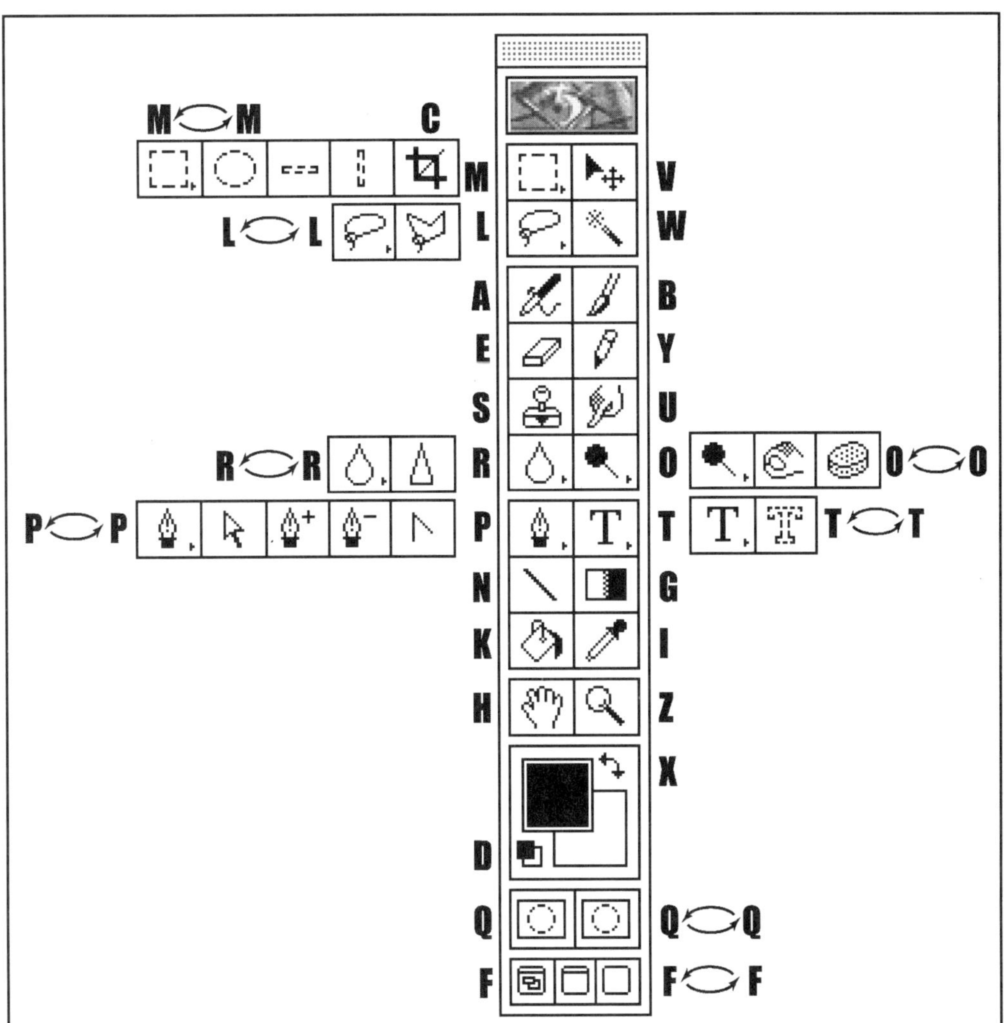

Figure 3-1: Expanded view of Photoshop's Toolbox with the keyboard commands for each tool.

Six of the tool rectangles contain small triangles in the lower right-hand corner. These indicate a pop-up menu with other tool choices. Click and drag on the pop-up tool icon if you wish to select a tool with the mouse cursor. An alternative is to hold down Option or Alt and click repeatedly on a tool icon containing a pop-up triangle. This cycles through all the tools the pop-up has available. In most cases, pressing the tool's letter command will cycle through the available choices. Press the letter p, for example, and the Pen tool is selected. Press p again and the arrow cursor (or the Direct Selection tool) is selected. More keystrokes of the same letter choose the Add Point, Delete Point, and Convert Anchor Point tools in turn. Pressing m repeatedly toggles back and forth between the rectangular and elliptical Marquee tools. Two of the tools that accompany the Marquee and Crop tools have no letter command and you must select them directly from the Toolbox. Single Row Marquee and Single Column Marquee are variations of the rectangular Marquee tool and have no key command because they are rarely used.

TIP *While trying to memorize the letters for each tool, you'll find it helpful to use the tiny balloon help windows that Photoshop has furnished. When you position the cursor over a tool, its name and command letter appear for a few moments within a small window. Eventually you can turn off the small balloons by selecting File | Preferences | General (press Command+k or Ctrl+k) and removing the checkmark from the Show Tool Tips option.*

Other Key Commands for the Toolbox

Located below the tools section of the palette you'll find three areas which are not really tool selectors but which control some important display and environment capabilities.

Foreground & Background Colors

The Foreground/Background colors are shown as two overlapping squares as seen in Figure 3-2. The Foreground color is uppermost. There is no logical reason why these two active colors should use position names; they could as easily be called color A and color B, upper and lower colors, and so on. I suspect that the names are a holdover from one of those Bronze Age programs such as MacPaint. In any case, the names are irrelevant as long as you understand how the two colors are acquired and used.

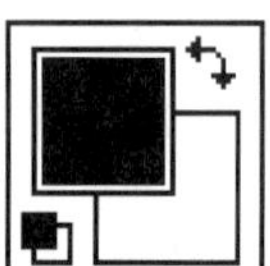

Figure 3-2: The Foreground/Background color squares.

- Click on either square to open the Photoshop Color Picker. From the Color Picker, select a new color. You can also select colors from the Color palette or the Swatches palette.
- The Eyedropper tool can be used to assign colors taken directly from an image window. A simple click makes the sampled color the Foreground color. Hold down the Option or Alt key and click in the image window to sample a new Background color. (The Eyedropper tool is also available while using six of the painting tools: Airbrush, Paintbrush, Pencil, Line, Gradient, and Paint. When you have any of these tools selected, press the Option or Alt key to temporarily access the Eyedropper tool.)

- The paint tools paint with the *Foreground* color.
- The Eraser tool paints with the *Background* color.
- When a selection is active on the Background layer, the selection can be filled with the Background color by pressing the Delete/Backspace key.
- Selections can be filled with the Foreground color by holding Option or Alt and pressing the Delete/Backspace key. Use Command+Delete or Ctrl+Delete to fill a selection with the Background color.

The default colors for Foreground and Background are black and white, respectively, unless you're working on a layer mask or in a channel, in which case the defaults are white and black. Even in extensive color work, these two are the most frequently used colors. The default colors can be restored by pressing the letter d (for default). The position of the two colors are switched by pressing the letter x.

Quick Mask

Located below the Foreground/Background colors on the Toolbox is the pair of icons which you use to enter (click on the right icon) and exit (click on the left icon) Quick Mask mode. A faster way to enter and exit Quick Mask is to press q.

You'll find Quick Mask is a superbly useful way of constructing masks using an overlay metaphor. The default color is a translucent red which is reminiscent of that Dark Ages artifact known as rubylith. Rubylith consists of a two transparent sheets of plastic—one red, one without color—lightly bonded to each other. To use it, a sheet of rubylith is taped over the material to be masked, red layer up. Then, with a very sharp blade, the area to be masked is traced with a cutting pressure that penetrates the red layer but does not cut entirely through the colorless layer. When the cut is complete, the red plastic is peeled away from the sheet in the non-masked areas. Quick Mask works in much the same way as rubylith did: red areas are masked while non-red, clear areas are not masked. To put it into Photoshop terms, any part of the image that is *not* painted red while in Quick Mask mode becomes selected after leaving Quick Mask. (See Figures 3-3 and 3-4.)

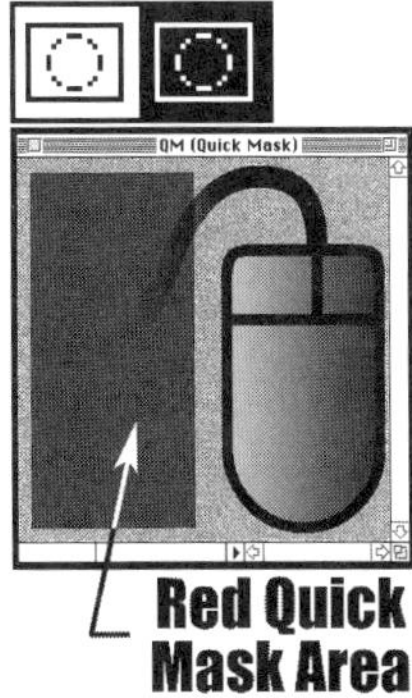

Figure 3-3: Red mask area in Quick Mask mode.

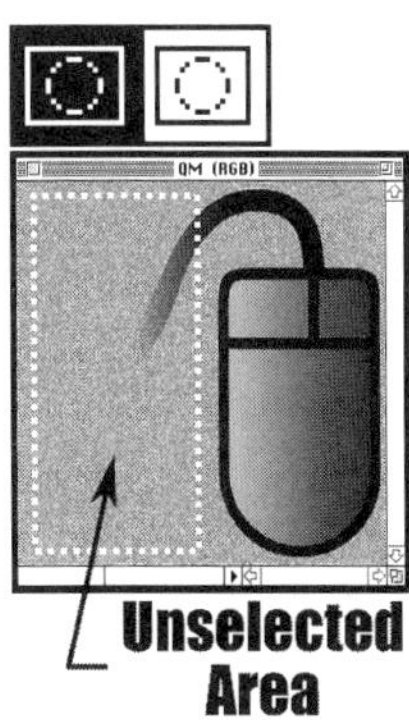

Figure 3-4: Selection outlining red masked area after leaving Quick Mask mode.

Sometimes the red of the Quick Mask may not be appropriate for the image but it's easy to change the color. Simply double-click on either icon. In the resulting dialog box, click once on the Color rectangle. The Color Picker then appears and allows you to choose a new mask color (see Figure 3-5).

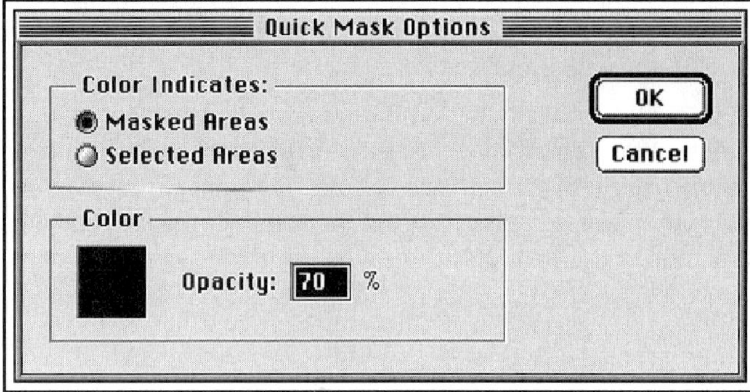

Figure 3-5: Color, selection, and transparency options for Quick Mask.

The Quick Mask dialog box shown in Figure 3-5 also has several other features that allow for adjustments:

- **Opacity.** Allows you to set how much of the image is visible through the masking color.
- **Color Indicates.** The default is Masked Areas. If, for some reason, you wish to reverse the color/non-color relationship, click on the other button, Selected Areas. Using this option is not as perverse as it may sound. There will be situations when it is easier to eliminate areas from all-over color than to add color to all-over non-color. To drastically understate the case, it is really important to remember which settings are in use. Switching these two settings can lead to a good deal of confusion.

You can also transpose the masked and unmasked areas by pressing Command+i or Ctrl+i. The mask/non-mask areas are instantly reversed as shown in Figures 3-6 and 3-7.

Figure 3-6: Shaded Quick Mask area, non-masked areas are white.

Figure 3-7: Quick Mask area inverted, non-masked areas are white.

Quick Mask is used for a surprising number of tasks, some of which seem unrelated to each other. As you use Quick Mask, you'll think of more and more interesting possibilities. In the following section, you'll discover how Quick Mask works and learn a few useful tricks as well.

Quick Mask Tryout

For a tour of Quick Mask, first open the file QM_01.PSD, Chapter 3 Practice Files on the Companion CD-ROM disk. Please note that the tryout file is of fairly high resolution (300 ppi). Some of the following instructions give specific numbers which are based on this file's resolution. If you wish to use a different tryout file, please make allowance for your file's resolution. For example, if your file is at a resolution of about 100 ppi, decrease the numbers given below by about two-thirds.

To enter Quick Mask mode:

1. Press q.
2. Then set your Foreground/Background colors to the default by (pressing d).
3. Next, choose the rectangular Marquee tool by pressing m and make a rectangular selection in the shape of the darkened area as shown in Figure 3-8. Hold down Option or Alt and press Delete.
4. Finally, press Command+d or Ctrl+d to Deselect Quick Mask. The image should look similar to Figure 3-8.

Figure 3-8: Add a rectangular area of Quick Mask.

Try inverting the mask by pressing Command+i or Ctrl+i. The clear areas become red and the red areas clear (Figure 3-9).

Figure 3-9: Invert the Quick Mask.

Next, let's invert the mask again so that the inner rectangular area is again darkened. Exit Quick Mask by pressing q. You now have two selection marquees—one around the outer edges of the window and one around the inner rectangle as shown in Figure 3-10.

Figure 3-10: A selection marquee outlines your mask when you exit Quick Mask.

The selection you now see is the area outside the rectangle you first drew. Press Delete to fill the selection with the Background color (Figure 3-11).

Figure 3-11: Fill the selection with the background color.

Now let's try painting two edges of the mask with a soft Paintbrush. To do that:

1. Press Command+z or Ctrl+z to undo the fill.
2. Press q again to re-enter Quick Mask mode.
3. Press b to choose the Paintbrush tool and select the 200-pixel brush. If you do not have a brush of that size, choose New Brush from the Brushes palette pop-up menu. Make the Size 200 pixels and the Hardness 0.
4. On the Options palette, set the Opacity to 100% by pressing 0 (zero) and the mode to Normal. Be certain that your Foreground/Background colors are set to the default because the colors can change when you move in and out of Quick Mask.
5. To actually paint two edges of the rectangle, center the brush over the upper left corner and click once.
6. Now, center the brush over the upper right corner, hold the Shift key and click again. Photoshop connects the two clicks with the Brush tool.
7. Continue to hold down the Shift key, center the brush over the lower right corner, and click again.

Your image should resemble that shown in Figure 3-12.

Figure 3-12: Paint two edges of the mask with a soft Paintbrush.

To see the difference in the selection edges, fill the new selection with white. Press q to exit Quick Mask, and then press Delete. The results are shown in Figure 3-13. Notice the difference in the edges between the painted and unpainted sides. Press Command+z or Ctrl+z to Undo the fill and re-enter Quick Mask mode.

Figure 3-13: Fill the new selection with white to see the difference in the selection edges.

Now let's paint the other two sides of the rectangle. Change the brush to 40% Opacity. This can be done on the Options palette or you can press 4. Notice that the Opacity and Pressure settings on the Options palettes and the Layers palette can be changed in 10% increments by using any of the number keys: 1 for 10%, 2 for 20%, 0 for 100%.

Paint the area outside the rectangle with the 40% opaque brush as shown in Figure 3-14.

Figure 3-14: Paint in the area around the rectangle with the Paintbrush set to 40% Opacity.

Next, let's fill the new selection with white to see how a semi-opaque brush affects the selection. First, exit Quick Mask and press the Delete Key. Notice that in Figure 3-15 the edges of the image are screened back while the inner portion of the image is left untouched.

Figure 3-15: Fill the new selection with white to see how a semi-opaque brush affects the selection.

Let's see what happens when the Quick Mask window is filled with black. Undo the fill and return to Quick Mask mode. Hold the Option or Alt key and press Delete. Your image fills with the masking color as seen in Figure 3-16.

Figure 3-16: Fill the Quick Mask window with black. The window appears to be filled with a translucent red.

To eliminate part of the Quick Mask covering the image, press x to make your Foreground color white. Choose the 100-pixel soft-edged brush and then set the Opacity of the brush to 80% by pressing 8. Paint the area on the right side of the image as shown in Figure 3-17.

Figure 3-17: Paint with 80% white to eliminate part of the Quick Mask covering the image.

To eliminate part of the Quick Mask in a different area of the image, divide the area into three parts: upper, lower, and underarm. As you paint each area, continue to hold the mouse button. What you are doing here is removing part of the mask by painting it with 80% white. As long as the mouse button is depressed, you are able to paint over the same area without removing more of the mask. If you release the mouse button, more of the mask is removed and results in a blotchy, uneven painted area.

Next, change the Opacity of the brush to 40% by pressing 4. Paint the other side of the image as seen in Figure 3-18. Be certain to paint the entire area without releasing the mouse button. When finished, the model should be untouched while the areas on each side are masked with lesser densities.

Figure 3-18: Paint with 40% white to eliminate part of the Quick Mask in a different area of the image.

Let's fill the selection with white to screen back the areas around the model. First exit Quick Mask by pressing q and then press the Delete key. The model is now shown (Figure 3-19) to be untouched while the areas on either side are screened back by 60% (right) and 20% (left). The two percentages are the reciprocals of the Paintbrush Opacity settings.

Figure 3-19: Outside of Quick Mask, fill the selection with white to screen back the areas around the model.

Quick Mask offers an easy way to edit portions of an image. In cases where unusual editing effects are to be applied, it is very helpful to use one of the large, soft-edged brushes so that there is a free and natural transition along the edges of the affected areas. The following set of directions show how a somewhat romanticized background can be added to the Quick Mask Tryout image. When you see how easy and quick some of these effects are, you'll want to experiment with your own combinations.

Let's return to Quick Mask mode and fill the image with the mask color. You can do this by returning the Foreground/Background colors to their defaults by pressing either d or x, then Option+Delete or Alt+Delete. Or you can fill the image with the background color—black—by pressing Command+Delete or Ctrl+Delete. Choose the 200-pixel brush and set its Opacity to 80%. Paint the area to the upper left of the model to partially remove its mask. The area to be painted is shown in Figure 3-20.

Figure 3-20: Paint out part of the Quick Mask with a white Paintbrush set to 80% Opacity.

Now let's try the Watercolor filter on the selected area. To do that, exit Quick Mask. Then from the Filter menu, choose Artistic | Watercolor. Experiment, if you wish, with the settings for this filter. When you find one you like, allow the filter to execute. The result is shown in Figure 3-21.

The Watercolor filter can also be applied to a completely unmasked area as well as an area which has been masked at 20%. But this will usually result in an overall darkening of the pixels to which it is applied. By using the partial mask, the darkening effect of the filter can be mitigated.

Figure 3-21: Use the Watercolor filter on the selected area.

Let's return to Quick Mask mode and eliminate a different area of the Quick Mask with a white Paintbrush. First, fill the entire window with the mask color. Then, using the same 200-pixel brush—this time with 60% Opacity—paint the lower left part of the image, as shown in Figure 3-22. Don't spend time trying to get the edges painted perfectly; the final image will probably be more successful if you paint out the mask in a fairly casual manner. It doesn't really matter that the filter to be applied next slightly overlaps the central figure.

Figure 3-22: Eliminate a different area of the Quick Mask with a white Paintbrush set to 60% Opacity.

Next, let's try the Pointillize filter on the new selection. With the mask complete, exit Quick Mask mode. From the Filter menu, choose Pixelate | Pointillize. Choose a cell size of 10 pixels and click OK. The effect of the filter is shown in Figure 3-23.

Figure 3-23: Use the Pointillize filter on the new selection.

Now let's enter Quick Mask mode and fill the entire image with the mask color using a white Paintbrush. Use the same brush size but set the Opacity to 20%. Paint out the entire right-hand side of the image as shown in Figure 3-24.

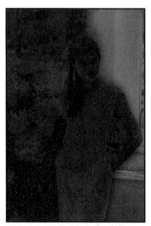

Figure 3-24: Paint out a different section of the Quick Mask with a white Paintbrush set to 20% Opacity.

Exit Quick Mask mode. Because of the low Opacity setting for the Paintbrush, you may receive a message that reads, "Warning: No pixels are more than 50% selected. The selection edges will not be visible." Don't worry about the message. Simply click OK and try to remember for the next few minutes that a selection is active even though you cannot see its edges.

Let's try the Retroscan filter on the selection to fill it with translucent horizontal lines. To do this, choose Deep Devices | Retroscan from the Filter menu. Experiment with the settings if you wish, or accept the defaults. When the Retroscan filter has executed, the selected area is filled with a set of narrow horizontal lines as shown in Figure 3-25. The Retroscan filter can be found on the Companion CD-ROM.

Figure 3-25: Use the Retroscan filter on the selection to fill it with translucent horizontal lines.

For another interesting effect, try using the Ripple filter on top of the Retroscan filter. Choose Distort | Ripple from the Filter menu. Experiment with the settings of the filter until the small preview window shows you a result you find pleasing. Allow the filter to execute. The results of the two filters are seen in Figure 3-26.

Figure 3-26: The Ripple filter used on top of the Retroscan filter gives a fill with attractive waving lines.

Let's try a more complex mask and make the sides of the unmasked area hard-edged while leaving the top soft-edged as shown in Figure 3-27. To do this, use the same brush with the Opacity set to 80%. Paint out the area of the model's slacks. Press x to reverse the Foreground/Background colors. Change the Opacity of the brush to about 20%. Then paint over the upper area of the slacks working downward. Finally, lay new color over old color to build up the gradual change from dark to light shown in the figure.

Figure 3-27: Make a more complex unmasked area with the Paintbrush: the sides of the unmasked area are hard-edged while the top is soft-edged.

To look at the final figure, exit Quick Mask. Choose Pixelate/Mosaic from the Filter menu. Use a cell size of 30 pixels. Click OK to execute the filter. Press Command+d or Ctrl+d to deselect, and take a look at the final image (see Figure 3-28).

Figure 3-28: The final figure is realistically centered amid romantic special effects.

Quick Mask can also be used to create a variety of textured edges for your images. Try these fast effects using an untouched copy of the file Quick Mask Tryout.

Let's create a Quick Mask rectangle subjected to 15-pixel Gaussian Blur. To do that, enter Quick Mask mode. Now draw a rectangular selection similar in size to that shown in Figure 3-29. Next, fill the rectangle with the mask color. Deselect by pressing Command+d or Ctrl+d. Then choose Blur | Gaussian Blur from the Filter menu using a pixel radius of 15. With the blur, the preparation for the edge effect is complete. In order to try a number of different effects, use the Image menu's Duplicate command to create a new image window. Perform the following steps on the duplicate of the image. If you wish to try more than one of these effects, continue to duplicate the original image and work from the copies.

Figure 3-29: Quick Mask rectangle subjected to 15-pixel Gaussian Blur.

The simplest edge effect, the vignette edge, can be accomplished at once. Simply exit Quick Mask mode after blurring the mask. With the Background color set to white, press the Delete key.

More interesting edges are made by applying filters of various kinds while in Quick Mask mode. Figure 3-30, for example, shows the Filter | Distort | Ripple effect—with settings of Large and 800—after it has been applied to the blurred rectangular mask area. To obtain another interesting border effect, simply exit Quick Mask and press Delete to fill the selection with white as shown in Figure 3-31.

Figure 3-30: The Ripple filter applied to the blur-edged Quick Mask.

Figure 3-31: Outside of Quick Mask, fill the selection with white for an interesting border effect.

Figures 3-32 and 3-33 were made in the same way. Figure 3-32 makes use of the Mosaic filter with a pixel value of 35. To get the edge effect shown in Figure 3-33, use the Filter | Pixelate | Color Halftone filter. Then set the Maximum Pixel Radius value to 20 and the value of Channel One to 45°.

Figure 3-32: A different edge effect uses the Mosaic filter.

Figure 3-33: Another edge effect can be made with the Color Halftone filter.

TIP

CD-ROM

Here's a useful tip for working with Quick Mask: By filling the Quick Mask window with a percentage of the masking color and then exiting Quick Mask, you have a tool for modifying—or masking—the results of a command or a filter. One example of this is seen in the application of the Watercolor filter to the upper left-hand part of the Tryout image. For another possibility, open the Companion CD-ROM file titled QM_02.PSD.

This CMYK image lost some color intensity from the translation from RGB mode to CMYK. There are a number of ways these colors can be brightened, but here is a very fast method:

1. *Press* q *to enter Quick Mask mode. Note that the Color palette switches to Grayscale mode.*
2. *Move the slider until the Foreground color value is 30%.*
3. *Fill the window with this value by pressing either Option+Delete or Alt+Delete.*
4. *Press* q *to exit Quick Mask.*
5. *Next, from the Filter menu, choose Sharpen | KPT Sharpen Intensity 2.1.*
6. *After the filter has executed, press Command+z or Ctrl+z a couple of times to undo and redo the effects of the masked filter.*
7. *If you wish, press Command+f or Ctrl+f to execute the filter again. Please note: this filter is part of a commercial filter package and has not been included with the Companion CD-ROM.*

There is no control offered for this filter; when you choose the filter, it simply executes without asking you for parameters. This nearly always results in a strengthening of color intensity that would be unusable for any purpose other than as a special effect. By filling the Quick Mask window with 30% of the masking color, the filter executes at 70% strength. You may wish to experiment with the percentages in order to achieve a stronger or a weaker effect.

Although the KPT filters of version 3.0 possess a built-in set of controls to modify the effects of the same filter (KPT Intensity f/x 3.0), it is still useful to understand that nearly all commands and filters can be modified using this Quick Mask technique.

Figure 3-34 uses Filter | Pixelate | Pointillize with a cellsize value of 15. After executing this filter, you need to fill in the pixellated areas within the central figure. Use a Paintbrush with the Foreground color set to black. If you don't fill in the speckled areas within the figure, you will eliminate parts of the model when, after you exit Quick Mask, you fill the selection with white.

Figure 3-34: This edge effect is made using the Pixelate/Pointillize filter.

Screen Mode Selectors

At the bottom of the Photoshop Toolbox are three icons which control the screen display. You can switch between the modes by clicking on the icons, or you can cycle through them by pressing f.

The first mode is the standard for Windows or Macintosh programs; in this mode, the desktop and other open windows are visible behind the active window (see Figure 3-35).

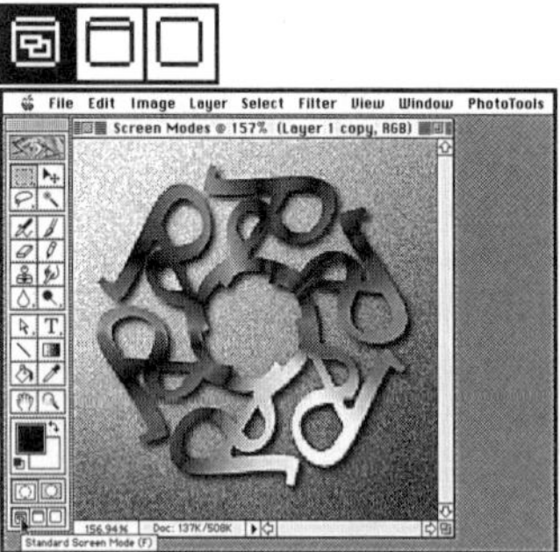

Figure 3-35: Photoshop's Standard window mode.

The second mode expands the image window to cover the desktop and all other open windows with a neutral gray. This mode is particularly handy in several situations. First, desktop patterns may be an enjoyable way of personalizing your computer, but they can sometimes interfere with your color perception as you make adjustments to an image. Covering the desktop with neutral gray is a good temporary solution. Second, when making selections—particularly on the far left edge of the active window—it is sometimes difficult to avoid clicking outside the window. The operating system interprets a click outside the window as a command to go back to the desktop. With the second screen mode active, you may paint or select past the boundaries of the image (Figure 3-36).

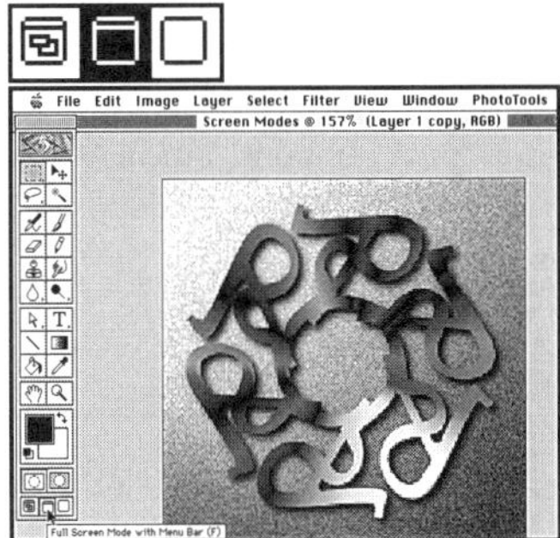

Figure 3-36: Photoshop's neutral gray background mode.

The third screen mode hides the menu bar, scroll bars, and all other open windows and replaces them with black. In this mode, it is possible to concentrate completely on the image. You may, if you wish, hide the open palettes in a two ways. First, press Shift+Tab which hides all of the palettes except the Toolbox. Press Tab to hide all of the palettes including the Toolbox. (You can make all of the palettes appear again simply by pressing the Tab key again.) To take a good look at your image without any distractions, do this: press f, f, Tab, and then Command+0 (zero) or Ctrl+0 (zero). Your image, and only your image, fills the screen from edge to edge as shown in Figure 3-37.

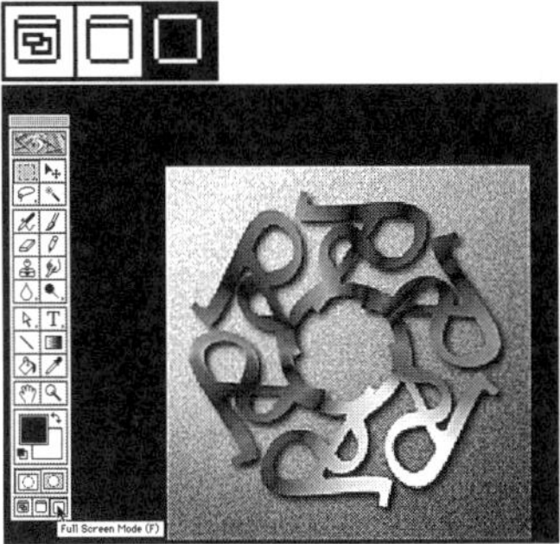

Figure 3-37: Photoshop's black background mode.

Tools

All of the Photoshop tools—with the exception of the Type tool—are governed by one or more variations or choices. These are set by means of the Options palette. If the Options palette is not visible, choose Show Options from the Window menu. The Options palette can also be summoned by double-clicking any of the tools on the Toolbox. The Options palette also contains a provision, except for the Type tool, for resetting a tool to its defaults or for resetting all tools to their defaults. Click and hold on the triangle at the upper right corner of the palette and choose either command from the palette menu.

All of Photoshop's tools have additional capabilities which can enable a power user to work quickly. These tool enhancements are accessed directly from within the working window and without having to move the cursor from its position. On the Macintosh, hold down the Ctrl key, click, and hold the mouse button. In Windows, press the right-hand mouse button. A contextual menu of commands relevant to the tool will appear as a pop-up menu at the cursor location. We will discuss these menus as we look at the individual tools in more detail.

About Selections

The selection tools include the Marquee tools, the Lasso, the Magic Wand, and the Pen tool. Of these, the Pen tool is sufficiently different from the others that will be discussed separately in Chapter 4, "Paths & the Pen Tool."

A selection in Photoshop is distinguished by the short black and white lines which dance clockwise around the edges of the selected area. Whether it is called one or not, a selection is really a mask. Commands that are issued execute only within the boundaries of the selection and tools function only within that area as well. The unselected part of the image is masked from all change.

The selection boundary, unless the Move tool is selected, is independent of the pixels which comprise the selection. When you place any of the selection tools into the selection area, the cursor changes to a Selection cursor. The selection boundary can be moved around within the window without disturbing the enclosed pixels. It can also be dragged from window to window. Using this capability, a selection made in one window can become a mask in another.

When you use the Move tool, dragging a selection boundary also drags the pixels. The selected pixels become what is called a *floating* selection. Floating selections are equivalent to a temporary layer; most of the capabilities of the Layers palette can be applied to floating selections. The disadvantage to a floating selection is that when the selection is dropped, the pixels are dropped back onto the image and replace the pixels behind them. With the Move tool, selections can also be cloned as they are moved. Simply hold Option or Alt while dragging the selection and the floating selection becomes a copy of the originally selected pixels.

The Select Menu

A variety of options that pertain to selections is found under the Select menu shown in Figure 3-38. Please note that this figure displays a Macintosh menu which uses the clover-shaped Command key. Windows users substitute the Ctrl key for the command key.

Select All, Select None & Select Inverse Select All of an image or a layer, and Select None, which deselects all selected pixels, are self-explanatory. When you use Select Inverse, selected pixels become deselected while all unselected pixels become selected. This command is the equivalent of using the Invert command while in Quick Mask mode.

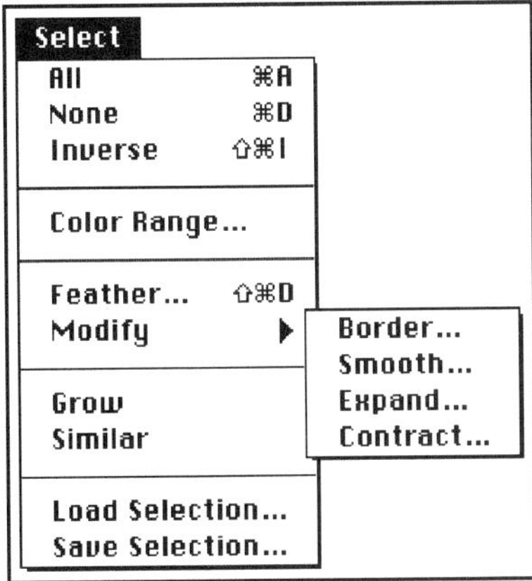

Figure 3-38: Photoshop's Select menu.

TIP *Select Inverse is a good candidate for assignment to a QuicKey or to the Actions palette. (There is a key command assigned to Select Inverse but it's one of those awkward, two-handed ones.) When you use any of the paint tools, it is often necessary to maintain a contour or a line of contrast between two adjoining areas. By making a selection along the line, you can place painting effects precisely along the line within the selection. Inverting the selection allows the same precision painting along the other side of the selection marquee. It is often useful to zoom into the line in question and to estimate the hardness of the line. If the line is soft, add a feather radius (see below) appropriate to the edge before using the paint tools as shown in Figure 3-39. Our task in this figure is to remove the gray circle from atop the black shape (1). Zooming in shows the soft edge of the black shape (2). By using one of the selection tools with a feather radius, the black area is painted, the selection inversed, and the light gray area is painted (3). A close-up of the finished edit is shown next (4), and finally, the completed image (5).*

Figure 3-39: Feathered selections let you edit pixels along a soft edge.

Select Color Range, Grow & Similar The Select Color Range, Grow, and Similar commands will be discussed later in the section on the Magic Wand tool.

Feather *Feathering* can be added to the edge of a selection while the selection is being drawn, or it can be applied afterward using this menu command. Feathering takes the normally hard edges of a selection and softens them. In effect, the edge of the selection disappears using a transition that fades from opaque to transparent. Feathering is measured in pixels and occurs both inside and outside the selection outlines.

Modify The Modify section of the Select menu allows you to make a modification of a selection in four different ways.

- **Border** The Border command makes a selection of the zone of pixels around the original selection marquee (1 and 2 in Figure 3-40). The size of this border zone depends upon the number entered which can range from 1–16. The border area is calculated inside and outside from the original selection perimeter and always has a feathered edge both inside and outside. See 3 in Figure 3-40 in which the border has been filled with black.

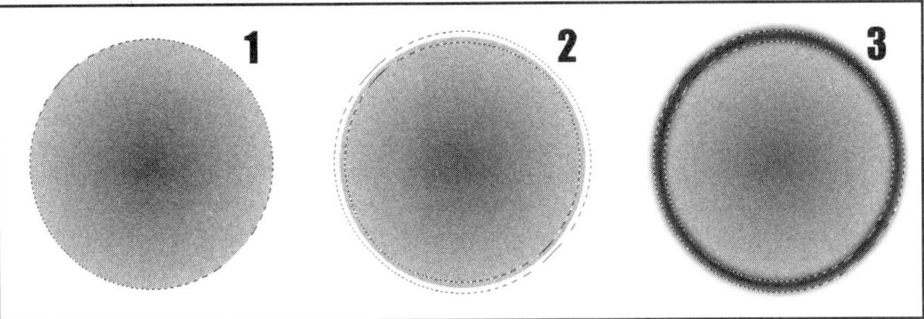

Figure 3-40: The Border command makes a selection enclosing the edges of the first selection.

- **Smooth** The Smooth command rounds off any corners in the selection marquee. In addition, it deselects any small selected areas outside of the main selection marquee and selects any stray unselected areas within that marquee. The input value is a radius in pixels which is used to calculate the amount of rounding and the minimum size of stray selected and deselected areas that will be affected. You can see the rounding effect in Figure 3-41 where 1 is the original selection and 2 the smoothed selection.

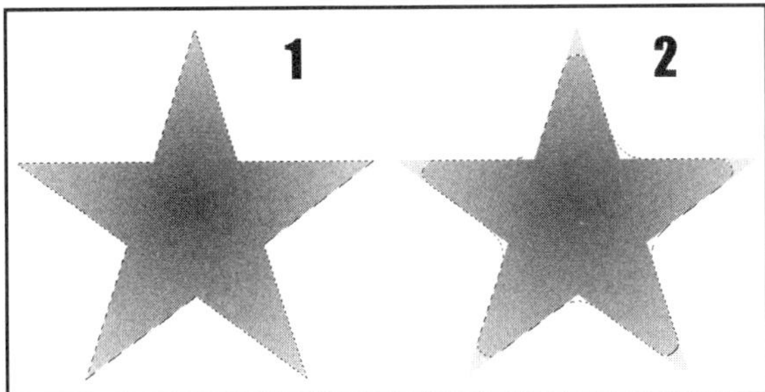

Figure 3-41: The Smooth command rounds off any corners on a selection.

- **Expand, Contract** Expand and Contract allow you to increase and decrease the area of a selection by moving the selection marquee out or in by some number of pixels. The effect is shown in Figure 3-42 where 1 is the original selection, 2 the expanded selection, and 3 the contracted selection.

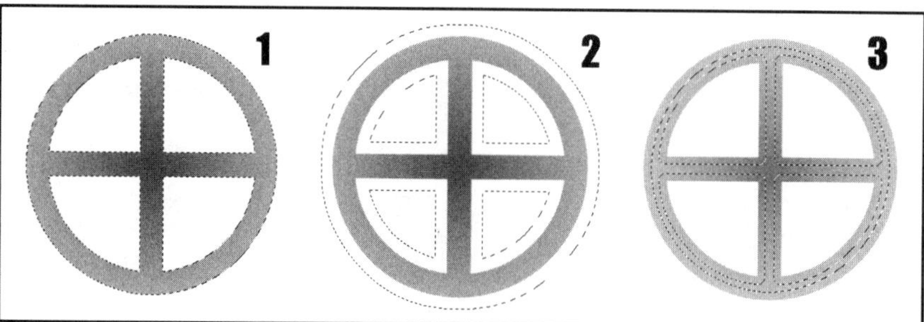

Figure 3-42: Expand pushes a selection's edges outward. Contract pulls the selection's edges inward.

Load Selection, Save Selection We'll discuss Load Selection and Save Selection later in Chapter 5, "Using Channels."

Other Ways to Modify Selections

Drawing selections is a straightforward task. After the selection has been completed, it is often necessary to alter its shape in some way. The selection might need to be larger in some portion, smaller in another. There are three useful keyboard combinations you can use with the selection tools to make such alterations:

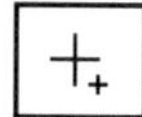

- When adding to a selection, any one of the selection tools may be used with the Shift key held down. You'll notice that the cursor adds a small plus shape to help remember which operation is being performed (see above). The area being added to the selection may adjoin the original area or it may be in another part of the image.

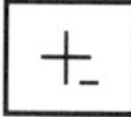

- Subtracting from an existing selection is done by holding the Option or Alt key while using one of the selection tools. The cursor will add a small minus shape. The area subtracted can be from the edges of the existing selection or even from entirely within the area.

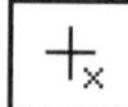

- The third method for altering the shape of a selection is to draw with any of the selection tools a shape that intersects the existing selection. While drawing, hold Shift+Option or Shift+Alt. The cursor will exhibit a small x shape. The resulting selection will be whatever parts of the original selection area were enclosed by the newly drawn selection. This method is the inverse of subtracting from an existing selection.

The Selection, Move & Crop Tools

The tools clustered at the top of the Toolbox allow you to isolate groups of pixels based upon a drawn shape. Once selected, the contents of the shape can be moved around within the window, moved to another window, painted, darkened, or lightened. Any operation you wish to perform on them happens to them alone. The rest of the image is left untouched.

The simple selection tools are the Marquee tools. The Lasso tool adds a free form capability. Both are so simple that you can use them within the first few minutes of your first experience with Photoshop. Once you have made your selection, use the Move tool to drag the selected pixels from one place to another.

Selecting and moving seem to be simple concepts. Keep your eyes open: you'll find that there are a lot of possibilities with just these simple tools.

Marquee Tools (pressing m toggles between Rectangular & Elliptical)

Rectangular, Elliptical, Single Row, and Single Column Marquee tools make simple, geometric shapes. The shapes for the two main tools, Rectangular & Elliptical, are customarily drawn from one corner to the opposite corner. They can be drawn from the center outward by holding down Option or Alt. Press the Shift key after the click and drag begins to constrain the vertical and horizontal proportions of the shapes to be equal (square and circle). A rectangular selection, provided that it is not feathered, also makes the Image | Crop command available.

The other two Marquee choices simply select a vertical or horizontal row of pixels as tall or as wide as the image. The options for the Marquee tools are shown in Figure 3-43.

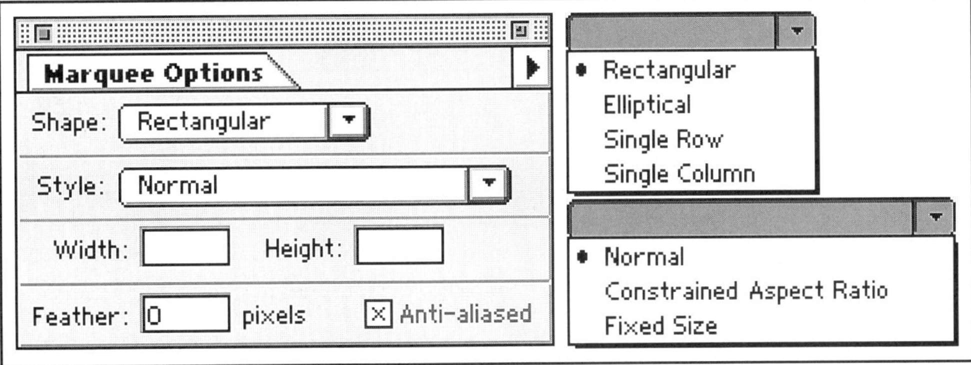

Figure 3-43: Options for the Marquee tools.

Normal The Normal option is the option most often used with the two principle tools. With Normal, freely drawn shapes enclose an area by approximate measurement.

Constrained Aspect Ratio Constrained Aspect Ratio (CAR) offers an easy way to draw perfect squares and circles if the numbers in the width and height box are equal. This gives the same effect as holding Shift when using the tools. Constrained Aspect Ratios can be integers or decimal fractions. Proportions might be, for example, 3:5.75. Or they could be as abstract as 247:355. CAR is also useful for making a variety of selections which have common proportions without being the same size. Simply enter the vertical and horizontal pixel numbers of one image as the proportions. With these numbers, you can make selections in other images that are larger or smaller than the original but which have the same proportional shape.

Fixed Size Fixed Size gives the possibility of making a selection based on an arbitrary number of pixels. This is very useful when making clips of a variety of pictures that must all be exactly the same size. Photoshop furnishes a convenient way to obtain information about an image file (including its size): hold Option or Alt. Then click and hold in the lower left-hand corner of the window in the area which gives the memory size of the document (Figure 3-44).

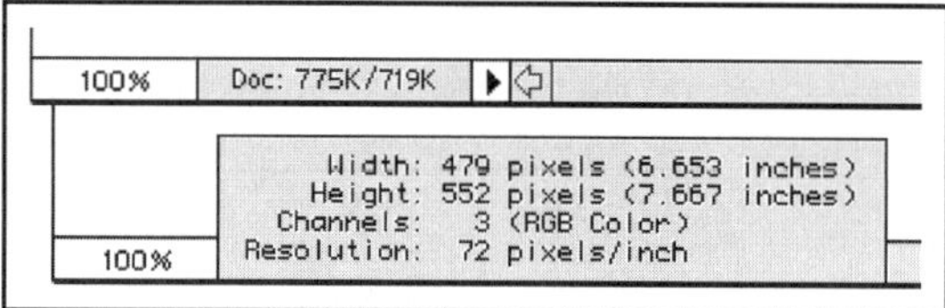

Figure 3-44: Information pop-up in the lower left-hand corner of a Photoshop document window.

TIP

The Single Column and Single Row Marquee tools come in very handy at times, especially if you have set up hot keys for Select Inverse and Image | Crop. When a scan has been cropped imprecisely and a single row of black or white pixels is visible along one edge, select the tool, click in the window, and run the cursor as far as it will go toward the faulty edge. Select Inverse, Crop, done!

Single Row can be used—this is admittedly a very exotic use for the tool—to emulate the coarse effect of file interlacing. Use this tool on a file that is not too large and that has been cropped so that the vertical pixel number is a multiple of eight or ten. Click in the image and run the cursor to the top of the window. Follow this procedure: hold Command+Option or Ctrl+Alt and click the Down arrow 79 times. Release the command keys. Press Command+e or Ctrl+e. Click the Down arrow once. Repeat the entire procedure to the bottom of the image. Figure 3-45 shows the effect using sets of fifteen pixels, sets of eight, and the original image.

Figure 3-45: Three emulations of the display of an interlaced file.

There are other ways this interesting visual effect can be accomplished. Because of the tedious nature of the following method, the effect could be made a sequence of commands and placed on the Actions palette. Here is the general method:

1. Work at fairly high magnification.
2. Select the Single Row tool, click in the window, and run the cursor to the top.
3. Choose Edit | Define Pattern. Change to the rectangular Marquee tool and choose Fixed Size from the Style pop-up menu on the Marquee Options palette.
4. Enter the width of the image in the Width field and a number such as 12 in the Height field.
5. Click again in the image and run the cursor to the top of the window. Choose Edit | Fill, and Fill with Pattern. Repeat this procedure on each set of 12 rows down the image. The same effect can be done using Single Columns.

The contextual menus which are available for the Marquee tools are shown in Figures 3-46 and 3-47. These menus pop up on the screen, springing from the position of the cursor in the image window. On the Macintosh, hold the Control key, and then press and hold the mouse button. In Windows, use the right-hand mouse button. Figure 3-46 is the menu which results when there is no active selection. Figure 3-47 is the menu when there is an active selection.

Figure 3-46: Contextual menu for Marquee tools when no selection is active.

Select None
Select Inverse
Layer Via Copy
Layer Via Cut
Feather...
Last Filter
Free Transform
Numeric Transform
Fill...
Stroke...
Make Work Path...
Save Selection...

Figure 3-47: Contextual menu for Marquee tools when a selection is active.

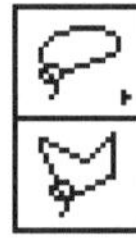

Lasso Tools (typing l toggles between Normal and Polygon)

The Lasso tools are the freehand selection tools. There are two choices, the original curved-line, click-and-drag selector, and the new Polygon Lasso. The Options for these tools are shown in Figure 3-48. The contextual menus are the same as for the Marquee tools (Figures 3-46 and 3-47).

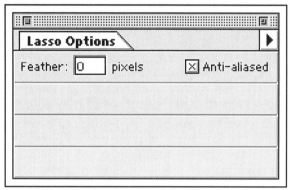

Figure 3-48: Options for the Lasso tools.

With the normal Lasso tool, selections are imprecise and fairly fast. The mouse is not an easy tool with which to draw along delicate edges. However, by holding Option or Alt, the normal Lasso is converted to polygon mode. The mouse clicks in one place. As the cursor is moved away from that point, a rubberband line follows the cursor. It is anchored with another click. By working at relatively high magnification, it is possible to lay small, straight-line segments against an edge and to make a very precise selection. The cursor, even with Option or Alt held, can still be dragged in the normal freehand manner. Notice that all selections in Photoshop are ultimately composed of straight-line segments since selections are based on the inclusion of tiny, square pixels.

The Polygon Lasso tool works in the same way the normal tool works with the modifier key (Option or Alt); straight lines rubberband from click-point to click-point. With Option or Alt held down, the tool can be dragged in freehand fashion.

When making a selection with the Polygon Lasso, the cursor has to move within a pixel or two of the starting click-point. A small circle appears next to the cursor to indicate that the next click will close the shape. The selection can be completed in another way: hold command or Ctrl. The next click makes a selection which connects the last click to the first.

To select an object with the Lasso tool for the purpose of dropping out the background, the procedure involves working at a high zoom level, selecting a small portion of the object, and using the Shift key to add to the selection. After working entirely around the edge of the object, zoom back. With the Shift key, add the interior of the object.

A simpler way to do the job is to work around the edges in Quick Mask mode. Press q to enter Quick Mask mode. Set the Background color to black. Work around the edges in the same manner as described above. As each area is drawn, press Delete to fill it with the mask color. Deselect, and move to the next area. The following set of instructions give complete details on how to do this, as well as some tips for making the silhouette edges look good without spending a lot of time on them:

1. Open the file QM_02.PSD, Chapter 3 Practice Files on the Companion CD-ROM (seen in Figure 3-49). Note that the file on disk is in color even though the examples pictured here are in black and white. That means you'll have more fun working through this tutorial than if you simply read through the material!

Figure 3-49: The tutorial image from which the background pixels are to be eliminated.

2. Zoom up to the image so that the magnification is approximately the same as shown in Figure 3-50.
3. Press q to enter Quick Mask mode.
4. Set the Foreground/Background colors to their defaults (press d).
5. Choose the Polygon Lasso tool. Draw carefully around an area along the figure.
6. When a small area is completed, press Option+Delete or Alt+Delete to fill the area with the mask color.
7. Deselect, and move to the next area. Do the same procedure again (Figure 3-51).
8. When you come to the hair, don't try to outline the soft edge with the Lasso tool. Select an area fairly close to the hair edge and fill it with the mask color.

Figure 3-50: Work at high magnification. Outline an area, fill it with the mask color, and Deselect.

Figure 3-51: Another area along the edge filled and masked.

TIP

Until you've practiced this and become fast at it, you might need to do this exercise over a period of time. Here is an easy way to preserve your place in the work so that you can come back to it at a later time:

- *Make certain the Channels palette is open. At the bottom of the list of channels, you can see the Quick Mask channel. The letters are in italic type to indicate that the channel is temporary.*
- *Click on this channel and drag it onto the page-shaped icon at the bottom of the palette (just to the left of the Trash icon). A new channel is then created. It will probably be called Channel 4.*
- *Now, let's exit Quick Mask, Deselect All, and save your file. When you come back to the work later, Command+click or Ctrl+click the extra channel's thumbnail at the bottom of the channels list.*
- *As soon as you have done that, press* q *to enter Quick Mask mode, and you are exactly where you left off. Be sure to discard the extra channel: as soon as you add new areas to your Quick Mask, the old channel is obsolete.*

9. Choose a brush—in this case a 15-pixel brush—set the brush to Normal mode and set the Opacity to 100%. Brush the edge of the hair with strokes which follow the grain of the hair (Figures 3-52 and 3-53). If you do not have a brush of that size, choose New Brush from the Brushes palette pop-up menu. Make the Size 15 pixels and the Hardness 0.

Figure 3-52: Select the area close to the hairline with the Lasso tool.

Figure 3-53: Use the Paintbrush tool, brushing with the grain of the hair, to mask the soft-edged hairline.

10. Continue working around the figure. When the entire edge has been masked, zoom back.
11. Use the Polygon Lasso tool to select the interior of the figure (Figure 3-54).
12. Fill the interior with the mask color (Figure 3-55).

Figure 3-54: The entire edge of the figure has been masked.

Figure 3-55: Use the Polygon Lasso tool to select the interior of the figure. Fill the interior selection with the mask color.

13. Since the purpose of this exercise is to silhouette the figure, the mask must now be inverted. Press Command+i or Ctrl+i. The image now appears as it does in Figure 3-56.

Figure 3-56: Invert the mask.

14. Press q to exit Quick Mask (the figure will be selected).

You could, if you wished, simply invert the selection and fill the background with white. However, it is good to keep your options open. Instead of deleting the background, try this as an alternative:

15. Press Command+j or Ctrl+j to turn the selected pixels into a layer.
16. On the Layers palette, click on the Background layer, and then click on the page-shaped icon at the bottom of the palette to create a new, blank layer between the background and the silhouetted figure's layer.
17. Fill this new layer with white. (The image will look the way it does in Figure 3-57.)

With the file in this three-layer form, you now have a range of other possibilities. You could, for example, change the Opacity of the center layer to 60% which would give the effect of screening back the area around the central figure. Or you could add another image, pattern, or color. You need not commit to the white background until you are certain that's what you want.

Zoom up to the figure (Figure 3-58) so that you can take a look at the edges of the silhouette shape. Do they look too much as though they don't belong to the image but to the hidden background? Do they look harsh and dark? Try the following procedure to make the edges look perfect.

Figure 3-57: The model's shape is now on a separate layer with a plain white layer behind. The original background is still intact below the white layer.

Figure 3-58: Zoom up to the image to see if the edges are perfect. Until you practice doing this, they probably won't be. If they're not, don't worry. Silhouette edges are easy to fix.

1. Click on the top layer of the Layers palette to select it.
2. Command+click or Ctrl+click the top layer's thumbnail. The figure is now selected.
3. From the Select menu, choose Modify | Border. Enter a value of 4 (Figure 3-59).
4. From the Edit menu, choose Fill.
5. Choose White from the Fill pop-up menu, and set the Opacity to 50%. The effect is shown in Figure 3-60.

Figure 3-59: Select the figure, then make a border selection along the edge.

Figure 3-60: Fill the border selection with 50% white.

6. After filling the border, choose Filter | Blur | Gaussian Blur. Set the radius to .5 pixels. The new edges now look as they do in 3-61.

Figure 3-61: Use a .5-pixel-radius Gaussian Blur on the border selection.

Use a glass, if you wish, to look at the larger image shown in Figure 3-62. The edges look clean, smooth, and absolutely natural.

Figure 3-62: The final silhouetted figure. The edges are perfect!

TIP *Here's something to keep in mind. With the exception of the hair, all of the selections in this image were along fairly hard edges. There are times, however, when a selection involves various kinds of edges. While working in Quick Mask mode, you can experiment with the Feather settings of the Lasso tools to arrive at an edge around a selection that will possess differing degrees of hardness.*

Magic Wand Tool (press w)

The Magic Wand tool makes selections based on a tolerance value. Click anywhere within an image. Pixels to the right, left, top, and bottom are examined to see if their color values fall within the tolerance range—above or below—of the original pixel. If they fall within that range, they are included in the selection. If not, they are not selected. This examination process proceeds outward from the original pixel until all contiguous pixels that fall within the range have been selected. With low tolerance values, the selection is usually small; often it is too small. With a higher tolerance value, the selection is larger; sometimes it is too large. Experimenting with tolerance values is a fact of life for users of the Magic Wand tool.

The Options for the Magic Wand tool are shown in Figure 3-63. The contextual menu with no active selection is shown in Figure 3-64. With a selection, the contextual menu is as seen in Figure 3-65. Please note that the latter figure is available only if it is summoned by clicking in an area *outside* of the current selection.

Magic Wand Options
Tolerance: 32
Anti-aliased
Sample Merged

Figure 3-63: Options for the Magic Wand tool.

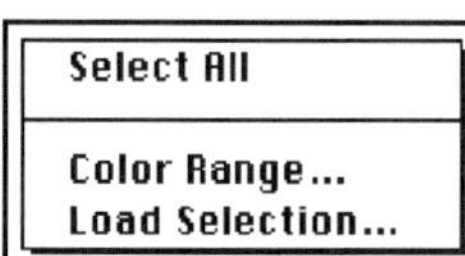

Figure 3-64: Contextual menu for the Magic Wand tool when clicked without an active selection.

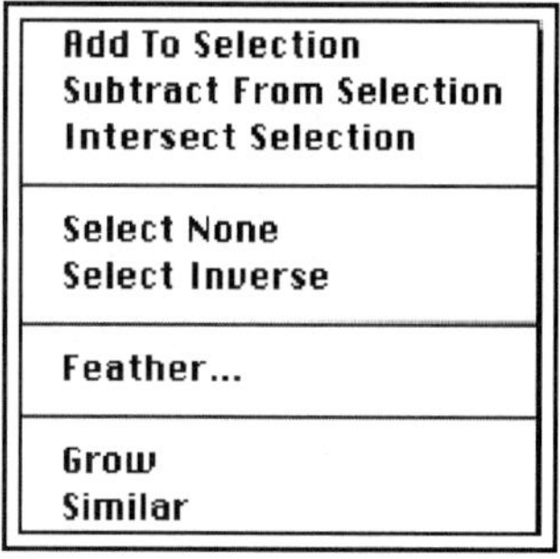

Figure 3-65: Contextual menu for the Magic Wand tool when clicked outside a selection area.

Of the choices in the contextual menu, two are particularly relevant to the Magic Wand tool (both are also available from the Select menu). Grow is a command to extend the current selection by adding to it. The added pixels are selected based on an enlargement of the original tolerance value. Similar is the command to select all of the pixels in the image which fall within the range of those already selected. For example, when selecting the sky in an outdoor photograph, these two commands might be used in this way: first, the wand would click somewhere in the sky of the image. Since the sky is multi-toned, one or two applications of the Grow command might be needed for all of the sky in a contiguous area to be selected. It might even be necessary to hold the Shift key and click in several places. After the main part of the sky has been selected, an application of the Similar command would add to the selection all of the parts of the sky not contiguous to the first selection. Such pixels might be those where the sky is glimpsed through the spaces between tree branches. Similar could also be used to select water reflections of sky-colored pixels.

Select Color Range (From the Select menu)

The Magic Wand tool is sometimes useful but often unpredictable. Fortunately, Photoshop has a really desirable alternative in the form of the Color Range command, found under the Select menu. Try this alternative, and you may never use the Magic Wand tool again!

Figure 3-66 shows a representation of an image with the Color Range dialog box. This dialog box shows the real power of Color Range: you are able to see the extent of your selection—and make adjustments to it—before you ever commit to it. The bottom pop-up menu gives several choices for how the preview is to be displayed. In this example, Black Matte has been chosen. The actual image window is filled with opaque black and only the areas to be selected show up to contrast with it. The image preview in the dialog box has been set to show the image. The top pop-up menu is set to Sampled Colors. Other choices for the top menu include specific color ranges—Reds, Yellows, Greens, Cyans, Blues, Magentas—as well as an automatic selection of all highlight values, midtones, or shadows.

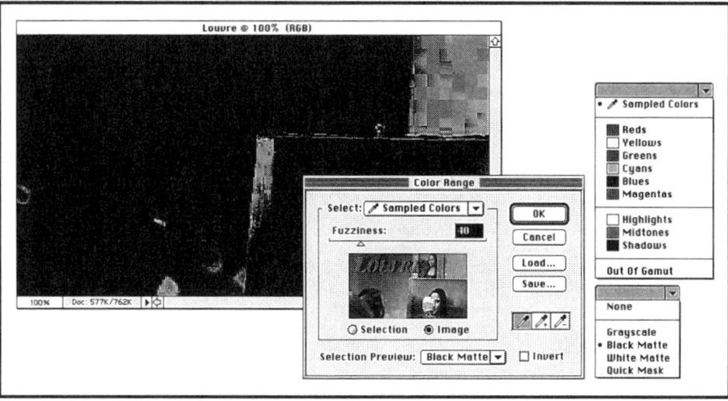

Figure 3-66: Expanded view of the Select Color Range dialog box.

When the dialog box opens, the cursor changes to an Eyedropper tool. Click anywhere in the preview image, and all of the related values are immediately displayed in the image window to contrast with the Black Matte. You may, if you wish, also click in the document window. There are three cursor choices in the window, the default Eyedropper, the same tool with a small plus, and the tool with a small minus. You may choose your cursor from this Toolbox, or you may choose them using the keyboard. Hold the Shift key to change to the Eyedropper with the plus, hold Option or Alt to change to the minus.

After making a preliminary selection, the Eyedropper-plus lets you extend the selection by adding more values. With these preview settings, clicking on a still-dark area in the image window adds more pixels from the same general tone range. Eyedropper-minus excludes values from the eventual selection.

The Fuzziness slider is generally analogous to the Tolerance setting of the Magic Wand tool. The main difference is that a change to the fuzziness value is instantly shown on the screen. With this slider, it is possible to fine-tune a selection and to know instantly how a change in value will affect the selection. When using Select Color Range, make a selection with the Eyedropper tool. Then, experiment with the Fuzziness slider before adding to or subtracting from the visible values.

The Color Selection dialog box contains another sophisticated setting. It is the Invert check box. With this box activated, you may choose your values from specific places in the image, and the dialog box will instantly convert your selection to its inverse.

Cropping Tool (press c)

The Cropping tool draws a rectangle within the boundaries of an image window. When the crop command is executed, all of the area outside the rectangle is discarded. To execute the crop command, press Return or Enter, or double-click inside the rectangle boundaries. The Options for the Cropping tool are shown in Figure 3-67. There is also a contextual menu available (Figure 3-68) but it is usable only before the crop rectangle is drawn.

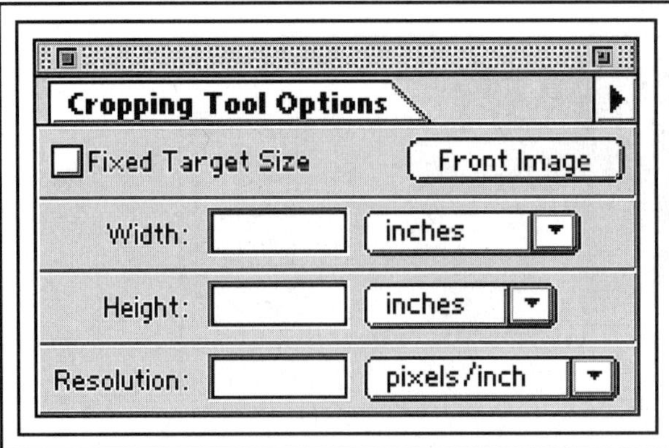

Figure 3-67: Options for the Cropping tool.

Figure 3-68: Contextual menu for the Cropping tool (available only if a crop rectangle is not active).

The drawn rectangle for this tool is resizable: click and drag on any of its eight live points. The entire rectangle is movable. Click and drag within its boundaries. It can also be rotated: click and drag outside the rectangle's edges. The latter feature is excellent for cropping and straightening images which have been scanned at a slight angle. The following figures show how this is done. The tilted scan is seen in Figure 3-69. Draw a small crop rectangle and orient it to an edge (Figure 3-70). Expand the rectangle to cover as much of the image as possible (Figure 3-71). Execute the Cropping command. The image is cropped and straightened (Figure 3-72).

Figure 3-69: The image has been scanned at an angle.

Figure 3-70: Draw a small rectangle and align its angle to a straight edge on the scan.

Figure 3-71: Increase the size of the rectangle to include as much of the image as possible.

Figure 3-72: After cropping, the image is straight, and the corner areas have been removed.

By using the Fixed Size option, the Cropping tool can enlarge or reduce as the image is cropped. Enlarging is rarely a good idea because even with the sophisticated interpolation scheme used by Photoshop to calculate the new size, increasing the physical size of an image always results in a softening of image detail. A good rule to follow: if the image needs to be enlarged, it should be rescanned to a larger size.

Width and height (expressed in pixels, inches, centimeters, points, picas, or columns) can be entered along with a desired resolution whenever Fixed Target Size is checked. If a number of images are open and you wish to crop them all to the same size, bring to the front the image which is the size to which all the others are to be cropped. Click on the Front Image button to load that image's dimensions into the data entry boxes. You may also leave Width, Height, or Resolution without a number. By doing so, you'll be able to crop a number of images which share one dimension but which are of different shapes.

Fixed Target size is most often useful when a project contains a number of large images which need to be reduced to thumbnails for indexing or contents purposes. If the amount of reduction in size is greater than 25% or 30%, it is a good idea to apply the Unsharp Mask filter to the image after it is used (see Chapter 2, "Aquiring Images").

It is often necessary to use high magnification to adjust the corners of a crop. Such a situation might occur when cropping the screen captures seen in this book. When you are cropping, it is difficult to see whether the one-pixel black line around a dialog box or palette has been included in the crop. Here's a fast way to handle the task:

1. Draw the crop rectangle while the entire image can be seen in its entirety within the window (press Command+0 or Ctrl+0).
2. To zoom in without resizing the window, press Command+ = or Ctrl+ = enough times so that the individual pixels are easily visible.
3. Press the Home key, which immediately scrolls the image so that the upper left-hand corner of the image is visible. Adjust this corner of the Cropping rectangle.
4. Now, press the End key. This scrolls the image to the lower right-hand corner.
5. Adjust the corner of the Cropping rectangle and press Return to crop the image.

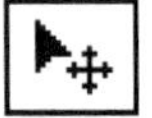

Move Tool (press m)

The Move tool does exactly as its name suggests: it shifts the contents of selections or layers within the image window—even outside of the boundaries of the window—or from one window to another. When the Move tool is selected, selections, or layers can be moved in one-pixel increments by using the arrow keys. Hold the Shift key when pressing the arrow keys to cause movement in 10-pixel increments. The Options for the Move tool are shown in Figure 3-73. There are no contextual menus for this tool.

The Pixel Doubling option on the Options palette causes Photoshop to display a half-resolution proxy of an object or layer while it is being moved. Prior versions of the program showed the status of a move by displaying a wireframe shape or, if the mouse button was depressed for a moment before the dragging movement began, a representation of the pixels being moved. Pixel Doubling eliminates the need to hold the mouse button before the move begins since its display generation is nearly instantaneous.

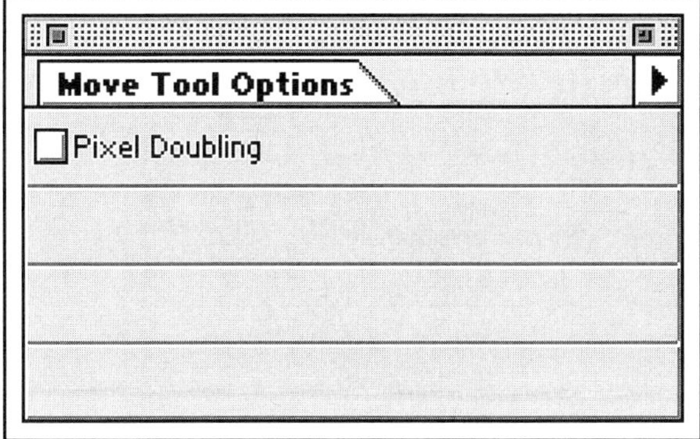

Figure 3-73: Options for the Move tool.

The Move tool need not be chosen from the Toolbox. It is instantly available, no matter which tool is in use, by holding Command or Ctrl.

The Airbrush, Paintbrush, Pencil & Eraser Tools

The four tools discussed here are grouped together because they all perform the same basic function: they apply color to the existing image. The first three paint with the Foreground color; the Eraser tool applies the Background color in some situations and erases using the behavior of the other brushes in other situations.

The Painting cursor for each brush is governed by the choice made in the lower left-hand corner of the dialog box which appears by choosing File | Preferences | Display & Cursors (Figure 3-74). Three choices are given; the first is Standard, which displays a cursor that is the same as the icon for the tool. When using Standard, be aware that each cursor has its own hot spot. The second is Precise. The Precise cursor is a plus-shaped cursor with a dot in the center; this center dot is the hot spot. When using this cursor, very exact placement is possible. The drawback to the Precise cursor is that it can be difficult to see at times. All cursors—no matter the setting in this preference box—can be changed to Precise cursors by pressing the Caps Lock key. The third choice is Brush Size. When this setting is used, Photoshop displays a wireframe outline of the brush which allows a high degree of accuracy as to where the paint is to be applied. The wireframe brush outline is visible for all brushes with a diameter of 600 pixels or less.

Each of these tools applies paint from a variably sized applicator tip chosen from the Brushes palette. Brushes are usually round but can be of any shape. They range in size from 1–999 pixels wide. The brushes used by the Paintbrush and the Airbrush are essentially the same. The brushes used by the Pencil tool are chosen from the same palette; however, when the Pencil tool is selected, all brushes become hard-edged. The brushes used by the Eraser tool depend upon which of the Eraser modes is used.

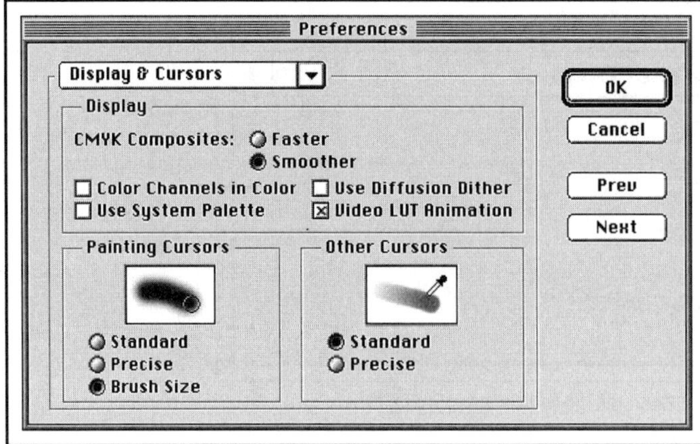

Figure 3-74: Photoshop's Display & Cursors Preferences.

New brushes are created by using the pop-up menu on the upper right-hand corner of the Brushes palette or by clicking in the blank area below the existing brushes. When a new brush is requested, or when a brush is double-clicked in order to be modified, the dialog box shown in Figure 3-75 appears.

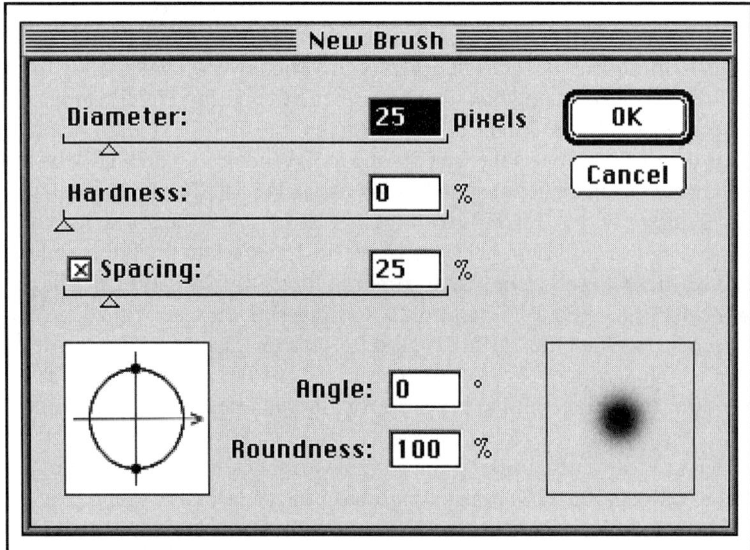

Figure 3-75: New Brush dialog box.

In this dialog box, the Roundness of the brush can be varied from a severely flattened oval to the default circle. Oval shapes can be angled to produce flattened, calligraphic-style brush strokes. The Diameter of the brush can be changed here, as well as the Hardness and the Spacing. Hardness can be varied between 0–100% as shown in Figure 3-76. Spacing controls the way the color is laid down by the brush; the default is 25%. The number, which is a percentage of the brush's diameter, indicates the distance the brush needs to be moved before a new iteration of the brush is laid down. Three percentages are shown in Figure 3-77 but the spacing can range between 1–999%. As the percentage rises above 100%, the iterations of the brush become detached from each other.

Figure 3-76: The range of Hardness values for a Brush tool is from 0 –100%.

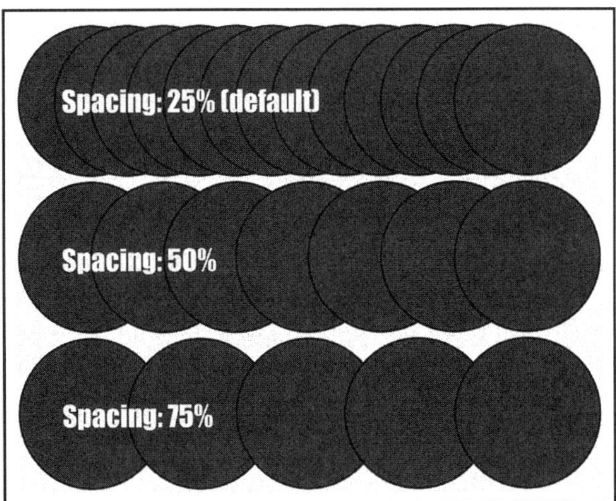

Figure 3-77: The range of Spacing values for a Brush tool is from 1–999%.

A rectangular selection can be defined as a brush. The command is located on the Brush palette menu. An example shape is shown in Figure 3-78. When the new brush stroke is applied, it produces the stroke shown in Figure 3-79. Double-click the brush to change its spacing. In this case (Figure 3-80), the spacing is changed to 112% (a figure arrived at by trial and error). With the new spacing, the stroke produced by the brush is shown in Figure 3-81.

Figure 3-78: Any rectangular selection can be defined as a brush.

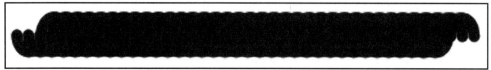

Figure 3-79: Painting with the new brush produces this result.

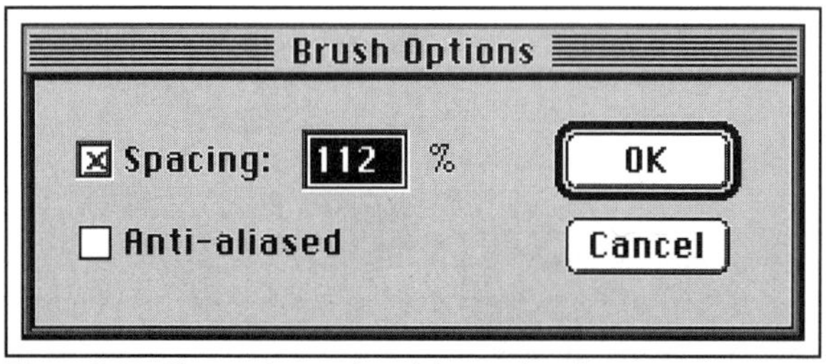

Brush Options

Spacing: 112 %

OK

Anti-aliased

Cancel

Figure 3-80: Change the spacing of the new brush.

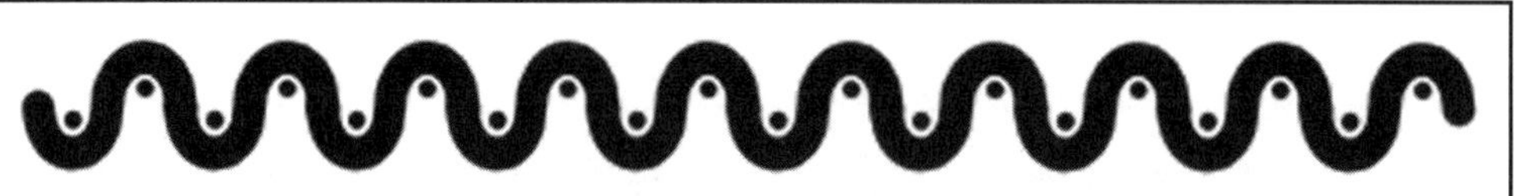

Figure 3-81: Painting with the new brush after the spacing adjustment produces a more interesting effect.

Brushes are usually used in freehand fashion. However, they can be made to draw straight lines in two ways. As the stroke begins, hold the Shift key to constrain the brush to follow a vertical or a horizontal line. You can also click in one place on the image, hold the Shift key, and click in another place. The brush stroke is drawn in a straight line between the two clicks. This is a useful technique for placing brushed borders around an image as seen in Figure 3-82. In this image, the star shape is defined as a brush with spacing set to 110%. The top, horizontal line was drawn first. The vertical lines made use of the Fade function found on the Airbrush, Paintbrush, and Pencil Options palettes.

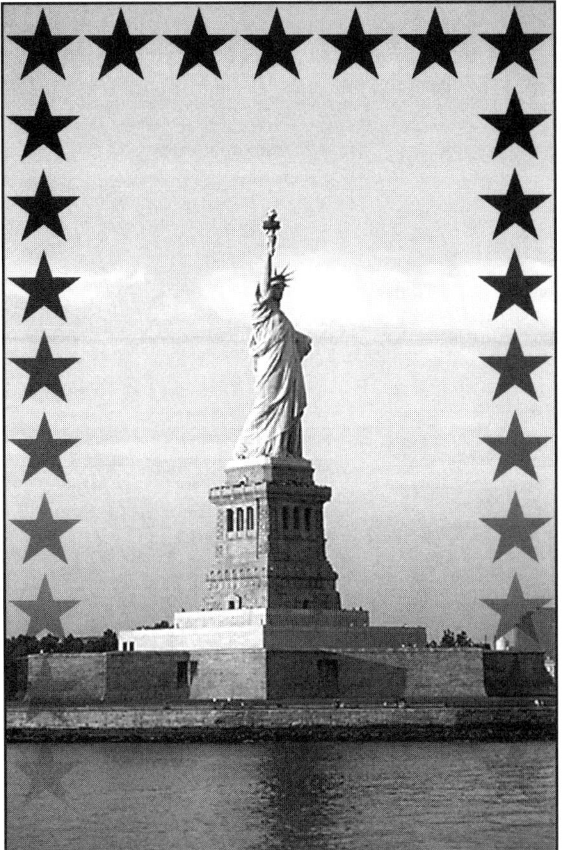

Figure 3-82: Straight-line brush strokes make adding borders to an image a simple task.

These borders use a spacing adjustment and the Fade option. When Fade is checked, the brush changes its color over the specified number of steps. The change can be to Transparent or to the Background color. In the figure, the Fade is set to 9 steps and to Transparent. Notice that the number of fade steps is the number of iterations of the brush as it is applied. The fade number is, consequently, tied to the Spacing setting. The length of the fade is tied to the size of the brush. With the spacing set to its default, a 100-pixel brush set to fade in 10 steps fades over the space of 250 pixels. A 40-pixel brush set to the same number of steps fades over the space of 100 pixels.

Another way to apply brush strokes is to use the Stroke function associated with the Paths palette. The Paths palette is covered in detail in Chapter 4, "Paths & the Pen Tool."

All four of these tools—and a number of the other tools as well—can paint in a variety of blending modes, which are covered later in the book. The blending modes are chosen from the Options palette menu for each. The default is Normal, with a variety of other settings available; complete definitions for these modes are found in Chapter 6, "Using Layers."

TIP

Besides the contextual menus used for the Paint tools, you can select brushes from the palette without moving the cursor. The two bracket keys, [and], move the brush selection, respectively, to the left and up or to the right and down. The movement is one brush for each push of the key. If the Shift key is held when the bracket keys are pressed, the selection jumps to the top left or bottom right—the first brush and the last brush.

Airbrush Tool (press a)

The Airbrush tool lays down a diffused stroke that is distinguished by its softness and ability to blend easily with whatever is painted. The Options for this tool are seen in Figure 3-83. The contextual menu is seen in Figure 3-84.

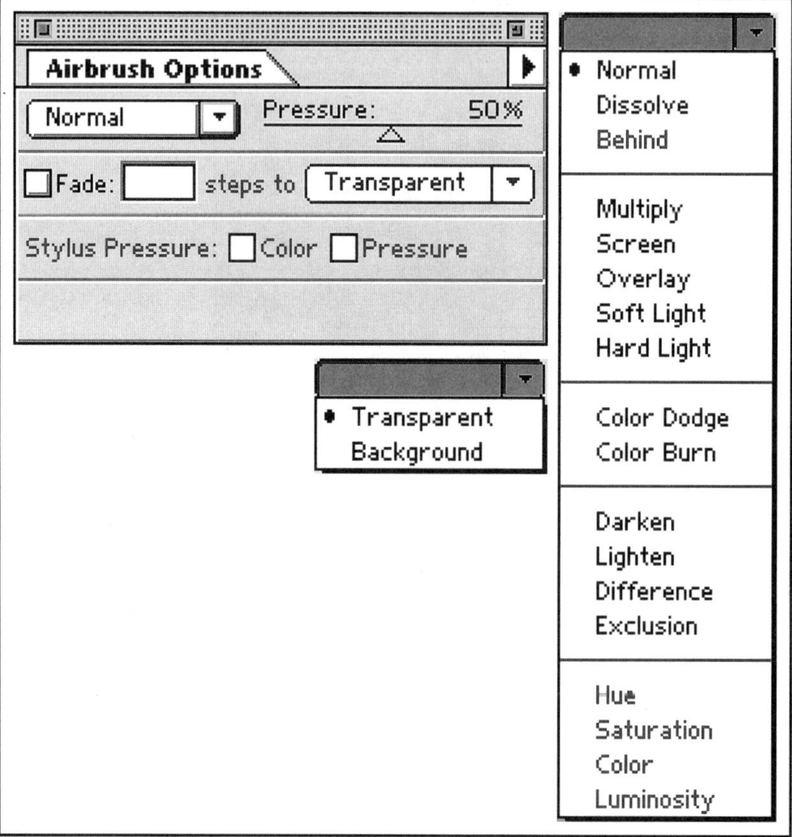

Figure 3-83: Expanded view of the Airbrush Options.

Figure 3-84: Contextual menu for the Airbrush tool.

The Airbrush differs from the Paintbrush and Pencil tools in that its main control setting is one of Pressure. This contrasts with the others which use an Opacity slider. The default Pressure setting is 50%. If this setting is moved up to 100% and compared to a stroke of the Paintbrush with an Opacity setting of 100%, there is almost no difference between the two. The Pressure setting, however, does work differently from Opacity. With the Airbrush, color can be applied again and again without releasing the mouse button. The painted area becomes increasingly covered with the paint color. In fact, when the brush can be held in one place while holding the mouse button, the paint continues to flow, making an ever-widening paint area which you can see in Figure 3-85. On the left, a 250-pixel brush leaves the light imprint when the mouse is clicked a single time. To the right, the mouse button was depressed for a length of time sufficient to give ten iterations of the brush. The actual size of the brush is shown by the dotted lines.

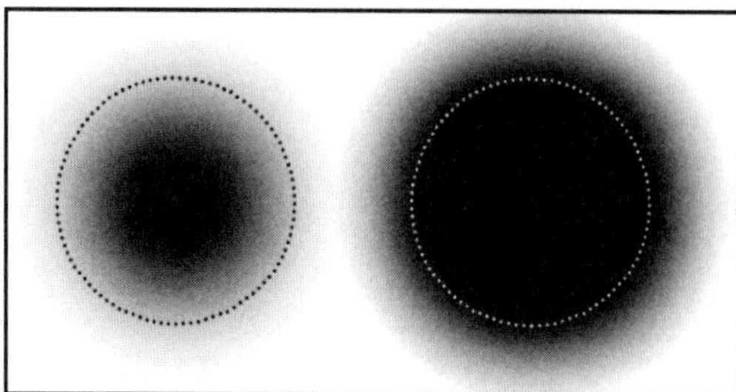

Figure 3-85: If the mouse button is held, paint continues to flow from the Airbrush.

TIP

It is easy to change the Pressure setting of the Airbrush or the Opacity settings of the other tools. Press any of the number keys to give a percentage multiplied by 10. Touch 1, for example, to change the setting to 10%, while 9 gives 90%, 0 gives 100%, and so on. These ten keyboard settings work remarkably well in nearly all situations.

The Airbrush tool is very well suited to brushing in shadows or glow effects (Figure 3-86), although learning to control it, to make the strokes look evenly applied, is fairly difficult. For further information about ways to use this brush with skill, please see Chapter 4, *"Paths & the Pen Tool."*

Figure 3-86: Use the Airbrush to paint with a light color to give a glow effect (left) or with a dark color to produce a shadow effect (right).

Paintbrush Tool (press b)

The Paintbrush tool is the most pliant and easily controlled of the three main paint tools. The Options for this tool are shown in Figure 3-87. The contextual menu for the Paintbrush is the same as for the Airbrush.

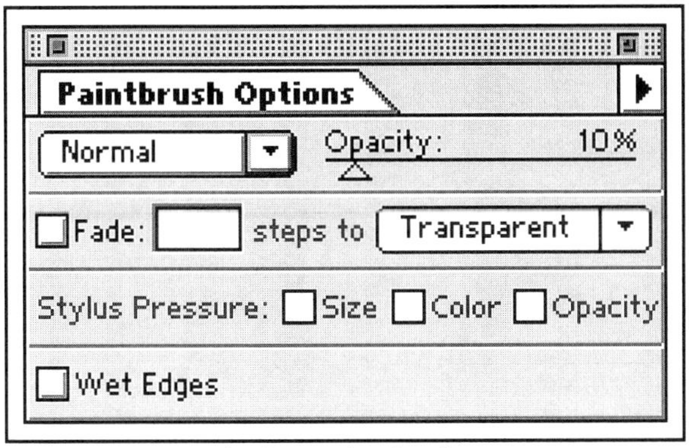

Figure 3-87: Options for the Paintbrush tool.

When using the Paintbrush, areas of color can be filled in with uniformity of tone by brushing over the same area several times without releasing the mouse button. As soon as the mouse button is released, the additional application of color is applied to the previous application. Because of this behavior, the Paintbrush is ideal for editing masks while in Quick Mask mode.

The Paintbrush has a Wet Edges option which appears to emulate the not-always-desirable effect sometimes seen in watercolor work in which pigment pools along the edge of a paint stroke. With this tool, the effect is controllable and useful for some effects. Figure 3-88 gives an idea of the appearance of the paint strokes at 100% and 50% Opacity with the Wet Edges option alternately turned off and on. Figure 3-89 shows the effect applied to the edges of the letterforms and the rectangular border.

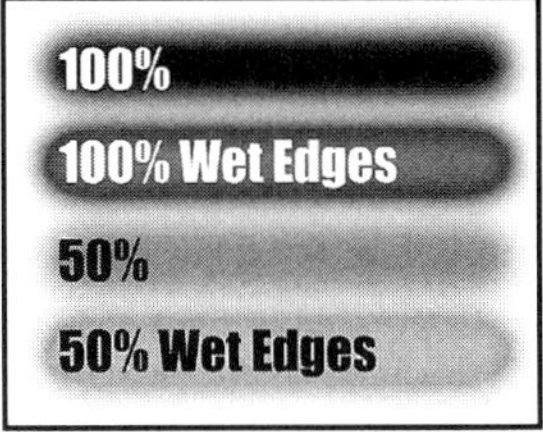

Figure 3-88: Examples of how the Wet Edges option varies with the Opacity of the brush stroke.

Figure 3-89: A Paintbrush with Wet Edges turned on produces a convincing neon effect.

Pencil Tool (press y)

The Pencil tool is unlike the Paintbrush or Airbrush in that it draws hard-edged lines. When the Pencil tool is selected, all of the brushes on the Brush palette become completely black. The tool's Options are shown in Figure 3-90. The contextual menu is the same as for the Paintbrush and Airbrush.

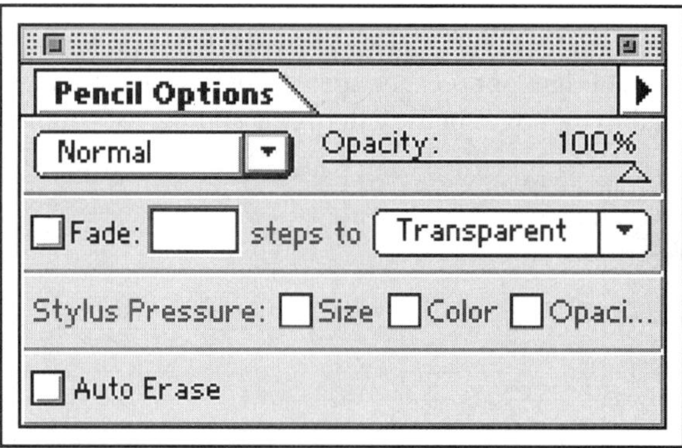

Figure 3-90: Options for the Pencil tool.

The Pencil tool has an Auto Erase function. With this function checked, the tool will paint with the Background color instead of the Foreground color if the cursor clicks on a pixel containing the Foreground color. This is a feature that has been used in many other paint applications. It has its uses if the Background color is the same as the background of the image since it seems to erase areas of Foreground color. The illusion of erasing is not quite so convincing on a layer where background color added to an area of transparency may not be desired.

Eraser Tool (press e)

The Eraser tool is an awfully useful tool: it can be itself or a block brush shape, as well as three other tools—the Pencil, Paintbrush, or Airbrush. In all guises, the Eraser tool paints with the Background color in two situations: first, when the tool is used on the Background layer of a document; second, when the tool is used on a layer with the Preserve Transparency option checked. Otherwise, its function is simply to erase. The Options for the tool and the contextual menu are shown in Figures 3-91 and 3-92.

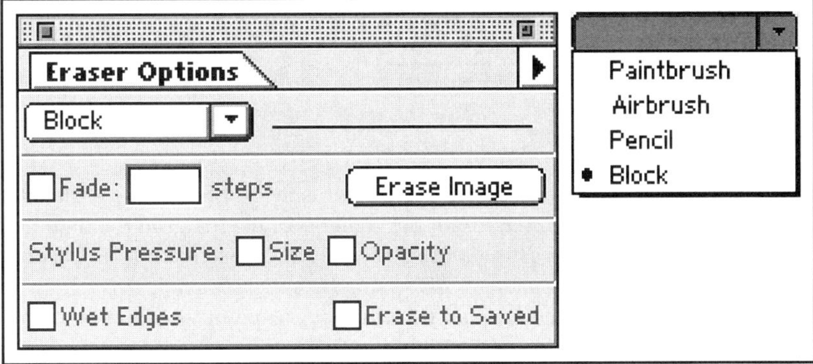

Figure 3-91: Options for the Eraser tool.

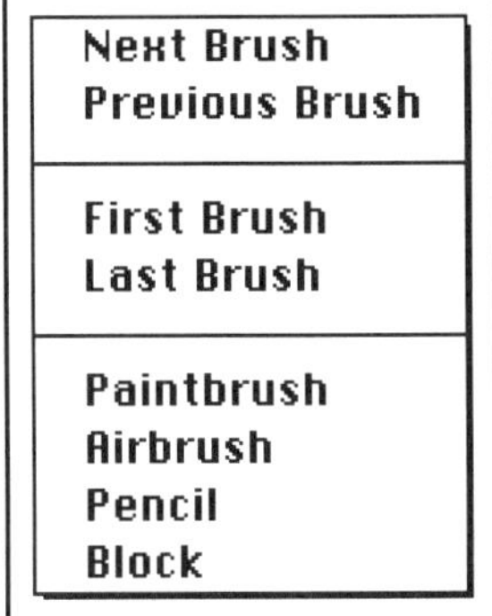

Figure 3-92: Contextual menu for the Eraser tool.

The Eraser tool is really an eraser in only one situation—when it is applied to the pixels of a layer which does not have the Preserve Transparency option checked. In that case, it removes the pixels, leaving behind complete or partial transparency in the area to which the tool was applied. The partial transparency is an effect possible when the tool is used as one of the paint tools—Airbrush, Paintbrush, Pencil—and the Opacity of the stroke is set to something less than 100%.

The Block option of the Eraser tool is one of the most curious features of Photoshop: it erases an area that is inversely proportional to the zoom factor of the image. In simpler terms, the Eraser's Block doesn't change size relative to the monitor display (although it does change size relative to the image). Because of this, it can be made to erase ever smaller areas by zooming in closer and closer to the image. The illustration in Figure 3-93 shows how this works. In the black area at the top of the figure, the Eraser block was clicked once. The number below indicates the degree of magnification at the time of the click.

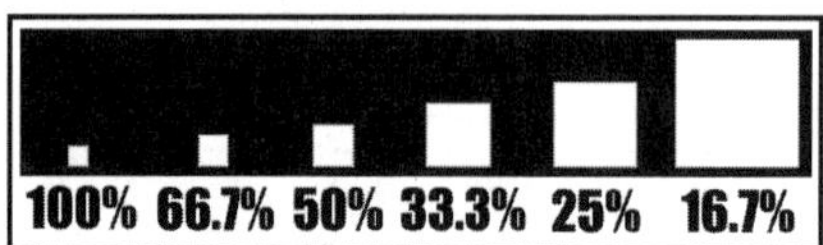

Figure 3-93: The Eraser tool's block erases pixel areas that are inversely proportional to the zoom factor of the image window.

The Eraser is one of two tools—the other is the Rubber Stamp—that allows you to paint in an area of the image with the contents of the image at the time the document was last saved to disk. This feature can be used to selectively work backward within the image, eliminating changes made since it was last saved. This feature is curiously powerful since it can be coupled with the various paint tools and their ability to paint with less than 100% Opacity or Pressure. To use this feature, turn on the Erase to Saved check box on the Options palette. An alternative is to hold Option or Alt while using the Eraser tool.

The Smudge, Focus, Toning & Rubber Stamp Tools

What these four sets of tools have in common is that they paint with the brushes of the Brush palette. Beyond that, they are not very much alike. They do not really *paint* in the sense that the Paintbrush or Airbrush paints. They all are effects tools: pixels across which these tools brush—or paint—are changed in some way. The change can be a darkening of values, a lightening of values, an increase in contrast values, an increase or decrease in color saturation, or a replacement of the pixels by other pixels in the same image.

The effects supplied by these tools are extremely powerful. With them, you have the power to correct problems in an image or to use your own creativity to alter the image so that it exactly matches your ideas.

Smudge Tool (press u)

The Smudge tool seems to push the pixels in the direction of the stroke. The effect is similar to a smudge stick rubbed over chalk or pastels or a dry brush pressed through wet oil paints. The number of pixels that get pushed depends upon the size of the brush chosen. The amount of push depends upon the Pressure setting. The Options and the contextual menu are shown in Figures 3-94 and 3-95.

Figure 3-94: Options for the Smudge tool.

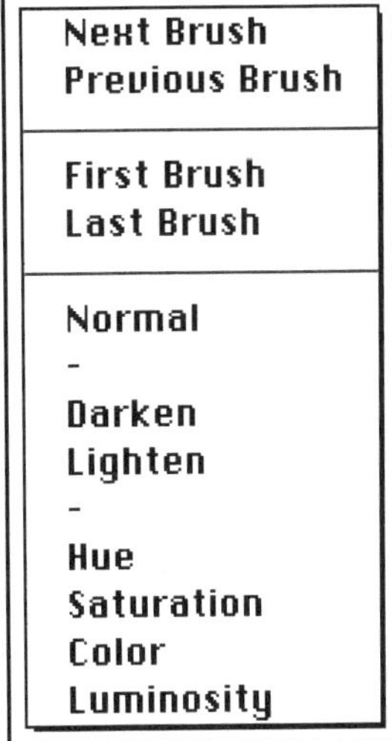

Figure 3-95: The contextual menu for the Smudge tool.

Beyond the Pressure setting, the other important setting on the Options palette for this tool is the Sample Merged check box. This setting is applicable only to layered documents. With the check box turned off, the Smudge tool only pushes around the pixels of the selected layer. Turned on, the tool is able to move the pixels of all the visible layers. Figure 3-96 shows the difference between the two settings.

Figure 3-96: When Sample Merged is turned off, only the active layer, which contains the type but not the background, is affected by the Smudge tool (upper streak). When the option is turned on, both layers are affected (lower streak).

This figure contains a Background and a layer on which reside the letters. With the layer selected, the Smudge tool has been drawn across the letters with the Sample Merged setting turned off. The pixels of the background are undisturbed. The lower smudge line has the Sample Merged box checked. As you can see, the smudge pushes the pixels of both the layer and the background.

The Smudge tool is useful for straightening out edges, for distorting edges to cause a camera jitter effect, and to provide an all-over texture. Figures 3-97, 3-98, and 3-99 show how this can be done. The first figure (Figure 3-97) is the original image. Quick Mask was used to mask the central figures (shown in Figure 3-98). After leaving Quick Mask mode, the Smudge tool, with a fairly large brush size, distorted the background of the image. All of the strokes for this background texture were made using a short v-shaped motion and were random in direction. There is, actually, a sinfully easy way to get Photoshop to do all the work for you; see Chapter 4, "Paths & the Pen Tool," for more information.

Figure 3-97: The original image to be changed by smudging the background.

Figure 3-98: Use Quick Mask to isolate the main Figures.

Figure 3-99: After exiting Quick Mask, the Smudge tool pushes the pixels in the background to provide an interesting texture.

The Finger Painting setting on the Options palette introduces extra color to the area being smudged. The Foreground color is added to the stroke and mixed with the other pixels over which the brush drags. The effect produced is similar to the Fade option for the Paint tools.

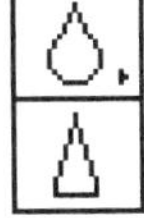

Focus Tools (press r repeatedly to cycle back and forth between the two tools)

There are two Focus tools, Blur and Sharpen. As their names suggest, they are able to *brush on* blurring or sharpening. The Options and contextual menus for these tools are shown in Figures 3-100 and 3-101. The Sample Merged check box works in the same way as it does for the Smudge tool.

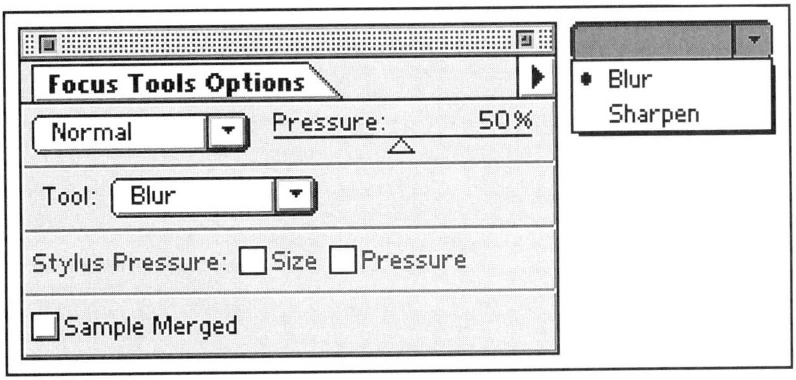

Focus Tools Options
Normal
Pressure: 50%
Tool: Blur
Stylus Pressure: Size Pressure
Sample Merged

• Blur
Sharpen

Figure 3-100: Options for the Focus tools.

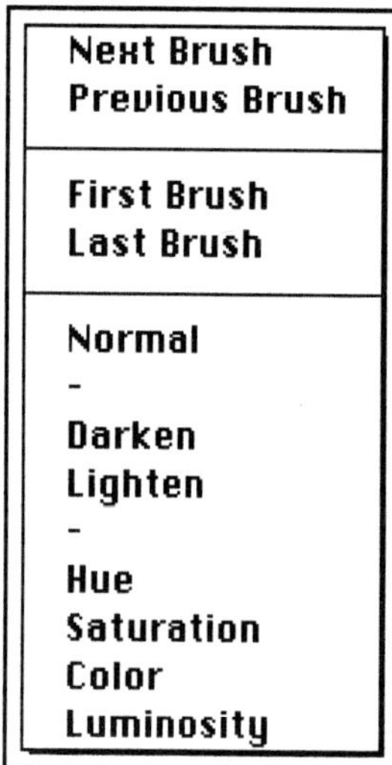

Figure 3-101: Contextual menu for the Focus tools.

Of the two tools, the Blur tool is the easiest to understand and to control. The default Pressure setting of 50% smoothly moves the brushed area out of focus. The Sharpen tool requires more finesse. The default, 50%, is often too high. A good trial setting is about 10%. When using this tool, brush over an area and avoid brushing it again until you are certain that you have not gone too far with it. It's nearly always a good idea to lay on a number of smaller strokes until the desired degree of sharpening is reached. Always pay attention when using this tool; too much brushing will produce an effect that is remarkably unattractive.

Used together, these tools can dramatically alter an image. The photo shown in Figure 3-102 is an example of an image which, betraying its 35mm origins, is fairly interesting but lacks the impact a professional photographer and more expensive lens system could have given it. Its principle problem is not one of composition but of too many clearly visible elements. The eye has no trouble deciphering the content, but there is really no single element in the image that draws the attention.

Figure 3-102: A pleasant image with too much detail and too many places to draw the eye.

With a fairly large brush—large enough so that the whole of this process takes no longer than a few seconds—the table top, the plants atop the table, and the pillow are sharpened. Using an even larger brush with a Pressure setting of 80%, everything else in the image is blurred (see Figures 3-103 and 3-104). A lot! The resulting image, shown with a more satisfactory crop, is seen in Figure 3-105. With this change in focus, the eye is led to the most important part of the image and not distracted by the peripheral information.

Figure 3-103: Use a large brush to quickly sharpen the important foreground parts of the image.

Figure 3-104: Use another large brush to quickly blur the areas around the foreground.

Figure 3-105: The final image—enlarged and with a better crop—and a clear center of visual interest.

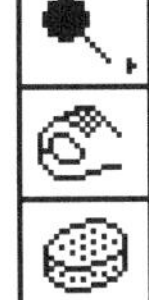

Toning Tools (press o repeatedly to cycle through the three tools)

There are three Toning tools: the Dodge tool, the Burn tool, and the Sponge tool. Using a brush metaphor (the effects are brushed onto the image incrementally the way paint can be brushed on), these tools alter the lightness, darkness, and saturation of an image. The Options and contextual menu for these tools are shown in Figures 3-106, 3-107 (Dodge tool and Burn tool), and 3-108 (Sponge tool).

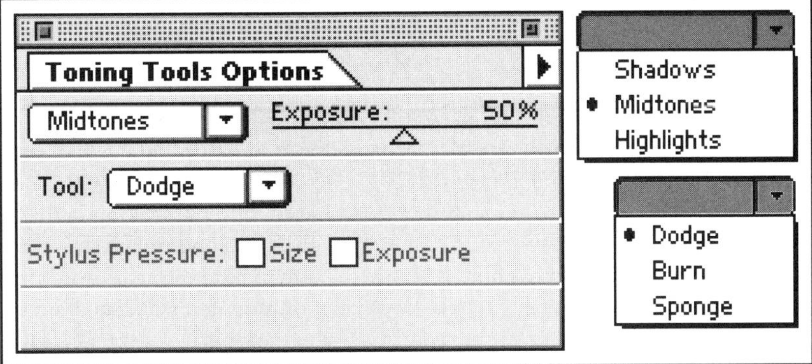

Figure 3-106: Options for the Toning tools.

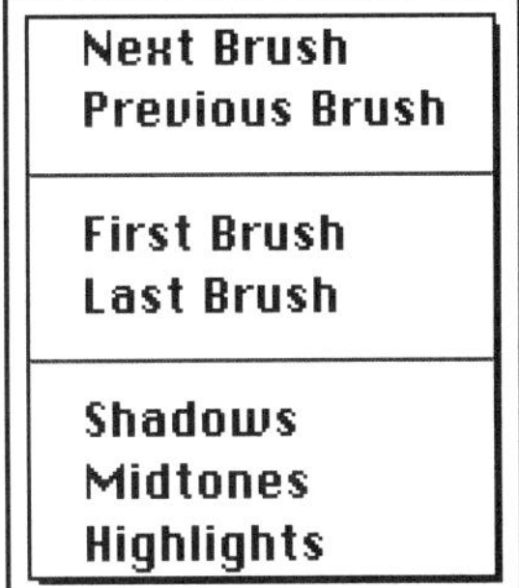

Figure 3-107: Contextual menu for the Burn and Dodge tools.

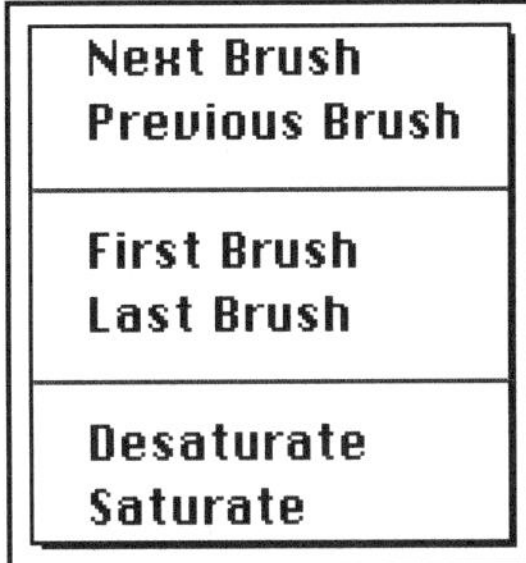

Figure 3-108: Contextual menu for the Sponge tool.

The terms *dodge* and *burn* are names derived from photo developing where image exposures are corrected mechanically. Areas of the film can be lightened or darkened in order to improve exposure problems or to enhance the original exposure. To *dodge*, in the photo darkroom context, is to lighten all or parts of the secondary image. To *burn* is to darken all or parts of the image. Photoshop's Dodge and Burn tools perform the same functions as the mechanical processes but with a power and flexibility beyond the dreams of photographic technicians.

When using either of these tools, the Options palette allows the choice of concentrating on specific tone ranges. The tools can function on Shadows, Midtones, or Highlights. When one tone range is chosen, the other two are more or less excluded from the effects of the tool but not completely. Because of this, brush applications of either have their greatest effects on the selected range but will operate in a lesser way on contiguous areas of either of the other two ranges. By this means, smooth transitions are maintained.

The Dodge and Burn tools are most often used to alter glaring errors in the image. For example, the Burn tool set to operate on highlights might be used to tone down blown-out highlight areas. Or the Dodge tool might be used to tone up a too-dark shadow.

The two tools can be used to completely change the original lighting of an image. When applied in this way, the change is editorial in nature rather than corrective. The three examples shown in Figures 3-109, 3-110, and 3-111 show how this can work. The first image is the original image, superficially pleasing but lacking in the drama that a more creative light source could have given it. The second image shows applications—to both Highlights and Midtones—of the Dodge tool on the shadowed parts of the flower. The flower now appears to have been illuminated from several light sources and provides a more interesting contrast to the dark background. The third image shows applications of both the Dodge and Burn tools. The Dodge tool has lightened the inside of the flower and the Burn tool has darkened the outside. The result is a concentration of the illumination source on the inside of the flower. The outside vanishes into the darkness of the background. Neither of these two can be considered better than the other. They are both more interesting than the original and either might be appropriate.

Figure 3-109: The original image ready for applications of the Dodge and Burn tools.

Figure 3-110: The Dodge tool applied to midtones and highlights gives a better contrast between the subject and the background.

Figure 3-111: The Dodge tool applied to the inside of the flower and the Burn tool applied to the outside concentrate the illumination for a more dramatic image.

The Dodge and Burn tools are also effective for color toning. Working directly on the image, it is obvious that colors over which these tools brush will either become lighter or darker. A more subtle way of influencing the color is shown in Figures 3-112, 3-113, and 3-114. The first photo is the original image. Although it does not show here, the image is of an Autumn forest taken on an overcast day (the original and altered images are seen in the color plate section). The sky is a light gray. The Photoshop image is in CMYK mode; the second photo is a representation of the Cyan channel. (For further information on channels, please see Chapter 5, "Using Channels.") This channel was altered in the third photo by application of the Burn tool to the highlights in the sky area. The sky is the lightest part of the Cyan channel. If the tool is set to highlights and simply brushed over the sky, only the sky is affected. There might be some slight darkening of the leaves and branches which adjoin the sky but the effect is minimal. The result of darkening the sky in the Cyan channel is to change the sky from a light, neutral gray to a pleasing blue. Notice that the painting done by the tool was deliberately not uniform; this gives the sky a mottled, more realistic appearance than a uniform tone would have given.

Figure 3-112: CMYK mode image with gray sky tones.

Figure 3-113: A view of this file's Cyan channel.

The third of the Toning tools is the Sponge, which can be set to Saturate or Desaturate colors. The Sponge tool was used on the image shown in Figure 3-112 which is seen in color, before and after adjustment, in the color plate section. Desaturation, carried to extremes, reduces the image to grayscale. The effect of the tool is to reduce the *Hue* while retaining the light and dark values. *Saturation* is the opposite. It boosts the amount and intensity of the colors over which the tool paints. Saturation is exactly the kind of correction needed for the drab yellows, browns, and reds in

Figure 3-114: The Dodge tool, set to darken the highlight tones, darkens the sky in the Cyan channel to produce a blue sky in the composite image.

the sample image. Once the color of the sky has been changed from the dim and deadening gray, the colors of the fall foliage need to be boosted so that they match the new tone of the light source. As you can see, the tool was used selectively so that some of the foliage continues to look dull and some very bright. This, again, is in the pursuit of realism: a realistic scene would not show consistent saturation of color but rather a variety of saturation levels.

When using any of the Toning tools, it is wise to begin with percentages of exposure well below the 50% default. The Burn tool, in particular, is used most successfully when its exposure is set to below 5%. Experiment with the settings to find the one most appropriate for the job at hand.

Rubber Stamp Tool (press s; while the tool is in use, pressing s repeatedly cycles through the seven options)

The Rubber Stamp tool often inspires the remark, "That's my favorite tool!" It is also the tool—along with its predecessors on high-end workstations—which should cause grave misgivings to anyone having to consider photographic material as evidential. Used in its default mode, this tool does not paint with a single tone but paints with areas of contiguous pixels. Often these pixels are from the same image, but pixels from another open image can also be used. With care, blemishes and unwanted material can be covered over so smoothly that there is no way to determine that the image was ever altered. This cloning of pixels combined with soft-edged brushes and a couple of the other available options make this tool one of the most versatile of Photoshop's tools. The Options for the tool and the contextual menu are shown in Figures 3-115 and 3-116.

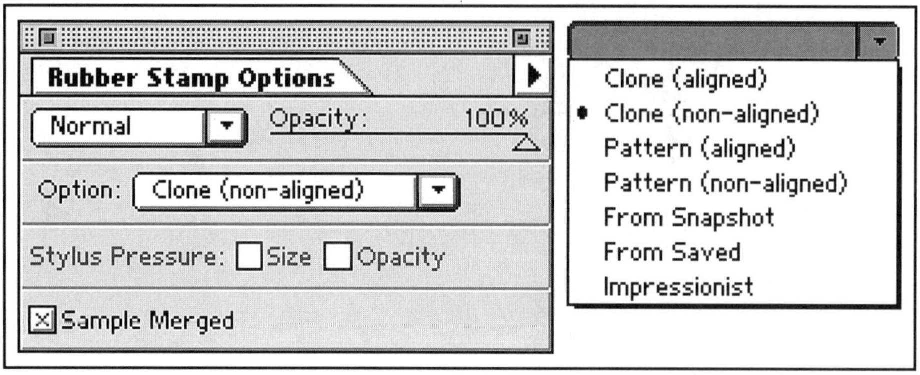

Figure 3-115: Options for the Rubber Stamp tool.

Figure 3-116: Contextual menu for the Rubber Stamp tool.

Clone Aligned Of the seven options, the one used most often is Clone Aligned. To paint with this option, position the cursor on an area of texture which you wish to copy onto another area. This area may be in the same image window or may be in another window. Hold Option or Alt and click the mouse. This click tells Photoshop the source of the cloned pixels. Move the cursor away from that spot to the area to be altered. Begin painting. With the first click, Photoshop establishes an alignment relationship that continues until a new source area is chosen. There will be two cursors, the one doing the painting—the cloning cursor—and a secondary cursor which marks the source pixels. The secondary cursor follows the first in parallel motion. As the painting proceeds, the position of the two relative to each other never changes until the Option or Alt key is held and another mouse click defines a new source area.

Clone Non-Aligned Clone Non-Aligned differs from the first in that the cursor relationship, once established, does not remain parallel. After the source location is identified with an Option/Alt mouse click, the cloning cursor begins to paint with the mouse button held down. As soon as the mouse button is released, the secondary cursor snaps back to its original position and the cloning cursor, even if it moves to another area, repeats the cloning of the original source pixels.

Clone Pattern Aligned Pattern Aligned is an option which paints with a pattern. Defining a pattern requires that a rectangular area of pixels be selected. With the selection operating, choose Edit | Define Pattern. The new pattern is placed on a special Clipboard or buffer where it can be used by the Edit | Fill command or painted using the Rubber Stamp tool. As the brush paints, the rectangular iterations of the pattern are laid down on the image. The patterns appear as if the entire image were sitting atop an array of the pattern tiles, and the brush simply uncovers them wherever it paints.

Clone Pattern Non-Aligned Pattern Non-Aligned is the pattern equivalent of Clone Non-Aligned.

TIP *Patterns may be constructed in such a way that there is no obvious seam as they repeat. The Rubber Stamp is excellent at making the edges of the pattern disappear. First, make the selection, copy it, choose File | New. Make a note of the pixel dimensions of the new window. Click on the OK button, and Paste (see Figure 3-135). Flatten the image. An example is shown in Figure 3-117.*

From the Filter menu, choose Other | Offset. In the two data entry fields, enter one-half the vertical and horizontal pixel dimensions of the image. Choose also the Wrap Around option. After clicking OK, the new image window resembles that shown in Figure 3-118.

Use the Rubber Stamp tool to obliterate the horizontal and vertical joins (Figure 3-119).

Select All and choose Edit | Define Pattern. Make a new window at least 3-5 times the size of the pattern tile. In this window, select All and choose Edit | Fill. Fill the window with the newly created pattern to see how the tiles will join each other. If you've been careful, there is obvious repetition but there should be no obvious seam from tile to tile (Figure 3-120).

Figure 3-117: Rectangular rock texture to be changed into a seamless repeating pattern.

Figure 3-118: Rock texture after applying the Offset filter with Wrap Around.

Figure 3-119: The Rubber Stamp obliterates the interior seams.

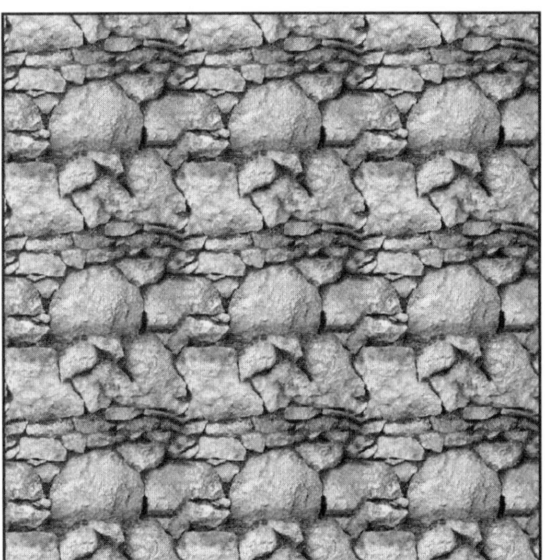

Figure 3-120: Three repeats vertically and horizontally of the patterns show how effectively textures can be made to overlap without an obvious join.

Clone From Snapshot Clone From Snapshot is an option that should be better known and much more extensively used. Most Photoshop users are familiar with the Revert to Saved command and the Erase to Saved option of the Eraser tool; Snapshot works in much the same way. From the Edit menu, either the Take Snapshot or Take Merged Snapshot command is chosen. The new Snapshot exists on a special kind of clipboard or buffer which stores the image as it is when the command is executed. After working on the image, it may be that the actions following the taking of the Snapshot need to be undone. Using either the Edit | Fill command or the Rubber Stamp tool, the image can be filled with the Snapshot or partially painted with the contents of the Snapshot. It is a kind of intermediary state that allows the image to be taken back to a certain point but not all the way back to the last saved version. There can be only one Snapshot at a time, and each new Snapshot obliterates the previous Snapshot. This is an exceptionally useful way of preserving the state of your work from time to time without using the Save command. Snapshots are not saved with the file and are wiped out when you quit Photoshop.

Clone From Saved Clone From Saved acts just the way the Eraser tool acts when it is in Erase to Saved mode. Pixels from the last saved version of your file are painted into the areas where your brush passes.

Clone Impressionist The Impressionist option smudges together pixels from the last saved version of the file. An example of the effect of this option is shown in Figures 3-121 and 3-122. What better subject for an Impressionist effect than water lilies? The Impressionist option is not easily mastered. As a matter of fact, finding a result with this tool that is acceptable—let alone beautiful—is a challenge for even the most skilled and patient of graphic designers. Fortunately, there is a workaround which is not only easy, but produces good results. It is also very fast. The pictured example took exactly 24 seconds. This technique is discussed in Chapter 4, "Paths & the Pen Tool." Notice that the two images are also shown in the color plate section. The original file has been prepared for you with paths included if you wish to make use of the technique shown here. It is found on the Companion CD-Rom as file RS_01.PSD, Chapter 3 Practice Files.

For convincing proof of the power of the Cloning tool (with a few assists from some other Photoshop capabilities), please look at the two photographs in Figures 3-123 and 3-124. In the first photo, a charming, turn-of-the-century home but with all of the visible artifacts of late 20th-century technology and suburban living: basketball hoop and back board, phone line, power lines, window air-conditioner, intruder lights, and even—above the left-hand gable—a distant microwave relay tower. The second photo turns back the clock by 100 years. All obvious traces of modern life are gone thanks to the Rubber Stamp tool. If you wish to practice on this image, it is included on the Companion CD-ROM as file RS_02.PSD, Chapter 3 Practice Files. The two images, before and after, are also seen in the color plate section.

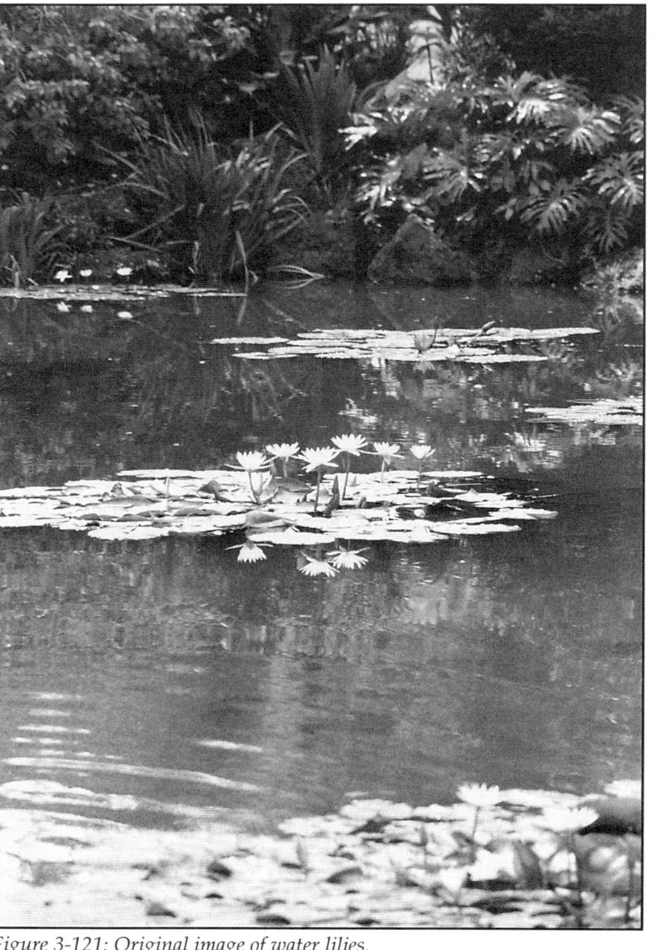

Figure 3-121: Original image of water lilies.

Figure 3-122: The Clone Impressionist option of the Rubber Stamp tool produces Monet on the cheap.

Figure 3-123: Image to which cloning tool is to be applied to remove the artifacts of 20th-century civilization.

Here's how to remove the signs of modern life:

1. Removing the power and phone lines requires a fairly high magnification with a constant modification of the size of the brush. Remember to leave the brush in position and use the bracket keys to move up or down in the Brushes palette. While working, pretend that you are not in a hurry and remember that this task *can* end with perfection.
2. The two parts of the image changed without using the Rubber Stamp tool were the window with the air-conditioner and the shadow area below that window. Use the Lasso tool to select the top half of the window. Make the selection into a Layer. Flip this layer vertically, tilt it slightly, and move it down to the bottom of the window. It will fit perfectly into position. Merge the layers and use the Rubber Stamp to get rid of extra bars in the center of the window and eliminate the faintly seen valence (at the top of the window) from the bottom copy.
3. The shadow area below? Looks like a lot of work. But do you see that bush on the left-hand side of the steps? Draw a selection line around that bush, make it into a layer, flip the layer horizontally, move the layer into position, and then

merge the layers. Now, using the From Saved option, carefully paint the shrubbery to the left of the new bush *back on top* of the new bush so that they overlap as shown. Use the From Saved option to get rid of unwanted bits from around the edges of your quick selection. Use the Clone Aligned option to slightly change the indentations in the bottom of the new bush so that it is not obviously a flipped copy of the other.

Figure 3-124: The Rubber Stamp tool has turned back the clock to a pre-electric time.

A more difficult cloning task is shown in Figures 3-125 and 3-126. The first photo, the original, is almost satisfactory but there are a couple of problems. First, there is a car far ahead that is too small to be interesting. Eliminating it will be a simple matter. Second, the shot was taken from inside an automobile and there is a distinct glare spot in the center right-hand side. At first glance, removing this would seem to be simple since the glare is entirely within the area of the sky. This, however, turns out to be the most difficult kind of cloning that Photoshop users encounter. If you wish to practice on this image, it can be located on the Companion CD-ROM as file RS_03.PSD, Chapter 3 Practice Files.

Figure 3-125: A good image except for the car on the road ahead and the glass reflection in the sky (center right).

Figure 3-126: The Rubber Stamp tool removes the unwanted parts of the photo and replaces them with natural textures.

If you zoom in to the sky, you can see that it is not a simple area of consistent blue. There are many blue tones in zones that are contoured shapes. The sky is also textured. This will be the case for many sky shots, particularly if the image was scanned from medium to fast 35mm film. As you begin to clone the sky, you'll immediately notice that great care needs to be taken to replace the defective areas with pixels which are very close by. Take care also that the cloning follows the *grain* of the sky.

Even after using your very considerable skills at eliminating the glare, you will probably find a strangely flat-looking and very visible area where the glare has been replaced. To eliminate this textureless look and to restore the sky to a more natural appearance, choose the Lasso tool. Set its feather radius to 10 pixels. Draw a line around the flat-looking area. Choose Filter | Noise | Add Noise and use a setting of about 8–15 for the Amount. For the other settings, choose Uniform and do not check the Monochromatic check box. When the filter has executed, you'll find that your cloning is invisible. This is a good thing to know: very small amounts of Noise added to an area within a diffused or feather-edged selection often adds a finishing touch to a pixel-cloned area that absolutely defeats detection!

One of the most-used capabilities of the Rubber Stamp tool is its ability to correct skin imperfections. Skin is just about as tricky to work on as sky. Small discolorations in skin offer no problems. The real challenges when working on a human face are wrinkles. There is, however, a very easy way to deal with wrinkles: don't get rid of them at all. Wrinkles are a natural part of the way skin wraps and folds over the musculature of the body. If they are eliminated completely, the result is not at all natural-looking. What is needed is a way of lightening the shadows which cause the wrinkles to look conspicuous. Use the Clone Aligned option of the Rubber Stamp tool with Opacity set to about 50%. Option+click or Alt+click fairly close to the wrinkle and simply paint through the deepest tones of the wrinkle. The skin magically smoothes out; the wrinkle does not disappear, it simply becomes one more detail in the topology of the skin. Figures 3-127 and 3-128 show examples of the way this cloning technique works and how it does not result in unnatural facial tones.

Figure 3-127: With wrinkles…

Figure 3-128: The wrinkles are still there, they simply look smoother because the deeper shadow tones that make them look conspicuous have been lightened.

Type in Photoshop

Type in Photoshop is unlike type in other programs. The reason for this is that type in other programs is usually made up of a set of vector shapes—tiny, individual graphic objects of the sort that might be drawn in a vector-based program such as Adobe Illustrator—which have been placed into a special file structure called a font. Using the font and the type-handling capability of programs which allow typing, you can simply use your keyboard to place these small pictures one after another and to deal with them not as tiny pictures, but as sets of symbols which combine into words and sentences. These shapes are based on vector outlines which allow the type to be scaled up or down in size. Attributes such as bolding and obliquing can also be applied. Under most circumstances, the type remains as a set of vector shapes until an output device translates them into raster shapes. Until their conversion to raster shapes, type is endlessly editable. Typographical errors can be corrected and new words substituted for older ones. In short, all of the operations we associate with word processing and typesetting are possible.

If you think of type as a set of vector shapes, then Photoshop can be considered as an output device. Its treatment of type is exactly the same as a printer's treatment of type. The outline shapes are converted to sets of tiny dots in a process called *rasterization*. Once the letter shape is rasterized, it no longer has the flexibility that allows it to be edited. In fact, once Photoshop has rasterized a character, it is merely a collection of pixels in the shape of a letter. Mistyped words cannot be fixed except by discarding them and re-rasterizing them. Type can be scaled up or down in size after it has been rasterized. Scaling up in size is not a very good idea for the same reasons cited in the discussion of the Cropping tool.

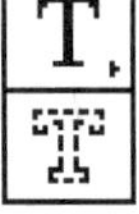

The Type Tools (press t repeatedly to alternate between the two type tools)

The Type tool, for all its importance, isn't Photoshop's weakest tool, but it's close. In fact, if the Type tool were the only way to get letter shapes into Photoshop, this section of the book would be devoted to a large number of *kludges*. Do you know that word? Kludge is defined as an unsatisfactory solution to a problem that shouldn't exist in the first place. There have been many kludges over the years where Photoshop type is concerned. Fortunately, there are a couple of other programs that make working with type in Photoshop very simple. Let's look at each and show how you can make use of their typographic strengths.

Photoshop does not allow you to type directly on the image window. If you think about the rasterization process, you'll see that this is done so that at some later stage in the creation of the letter shapes, you will have some control.

Now, let's check out the Type tool:

1. Press t to select the first Type tool. (The first tool, the one with the solid icon, is really the Type tool. The other tool is called the Type Mask tool.)
2. Click with this tool in the window to which you wish to add type. (If you are using the Type tool for the first time in your Photoshop session, you are notified of a wait while Photoshop builds the Font menu.) The dialog box seen in Figure 3-129 appears. Within this dialog box, you may choose your Font, the Size—in

points or pixels—that you want the characters to appear, Leading, Spacing, a variety of Style choices, and the kind of Alignment you wish.

3. Next, in the scrolling window, enter the set of characters.
4. When finished, click on the OK button, or press the Enter key (the Return key does not work in this dialog box; it places hard returns in the text).

Photoshop takes a moment to rasterize the type shapes at the resolution of your document and places the letter shapes in the window on a new layer. The new layer is created with Preserve Transparency turned on.

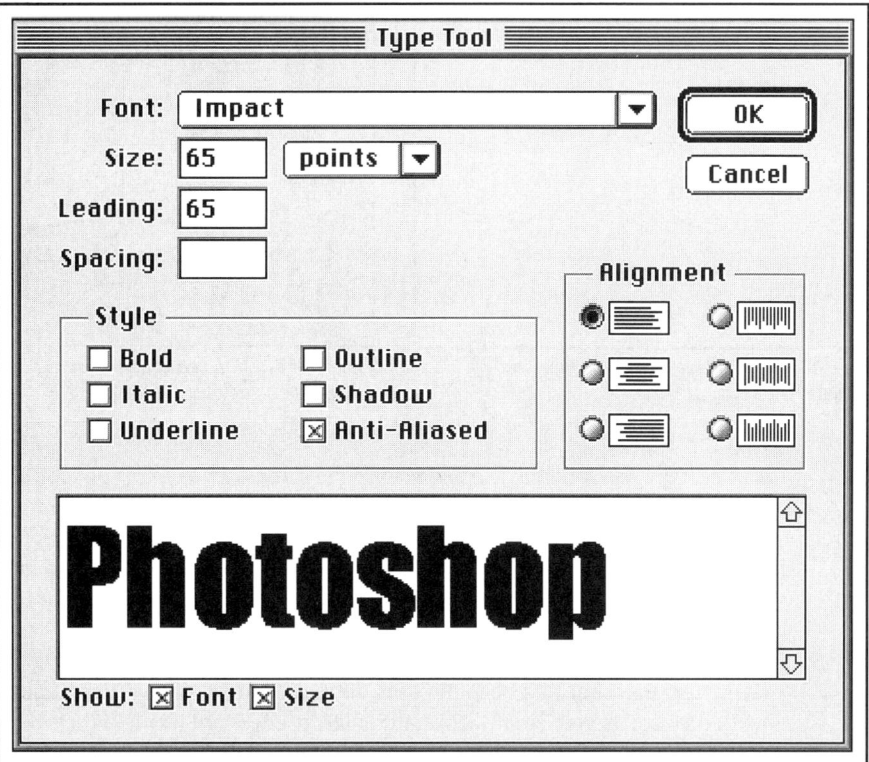

Figure 3-129: The Type Tool dialog box.

The text appears in one of two ways. If you choose an Alignment option from the three choices in the left-hand column of the dialog box, your text appears as shown at the top of Figure 3-130. If you choose your Alignment from the three right-hand choices, the text appears as shown at the left of Figure 3-130. Please note that the leading for the vertical alignment can be a little confusing. Changing the leading does not draw the characters closer together vertically; it draws vertical lines of characters together horizontally. This is shown in Figure 3-131. Use the Spacing setting to draw vertically aligned characters closer together vertically.

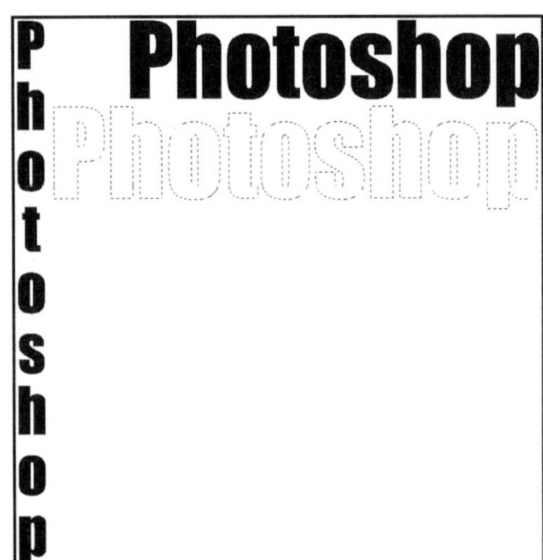

Figure 3-130: Vertical type, horizontal type, and type-shaped selections.

40-pt letters, 40-pt leading
1 1
2 2
3 3
4 4
5 5

40-pt letters, 20-pt leading
11
22
33
44
55

Figure 3-131: With vertical type, leading changes move the columns of type closer together or farther apart.

The Type Mask tool is used in exactly the same way as the Type tool. The difference is in what you have when Photoshop rasterizes the characters you've entered. Your document window is unchanged, but rather than a new layer with visible type on it, you have a selection on the current layer based on the text you entered in the dialog box. Such a selection is shown within Figure 3-130. The uses for each of these tools is discussed below.

The drawbacks to the Photoshop dialog box are apparent with a single use. The characters used must all be in the same font, they must all be the same size, and the text-entry box is very small, especially if large letters are wanted. If more than one font size or more than one font face is required, you will need to make more than one excursion to this dialog box.

Extensis PhotoTools

Yes! The Extensis Corporation of Portland, Oregon, offers a set of plug-in tools for Photoshop called PhotoTools. These tools include a variety of useful effects with an easy-to-master interface. Most of the special effects these tools offer can be achieved in other ways. The sparkling gem of PhotoTools, and the part of the set which is, by itself, worth the cost, is PhotoText.

A likeness of the PhotoText dialog box is shown in Figure 3-132.

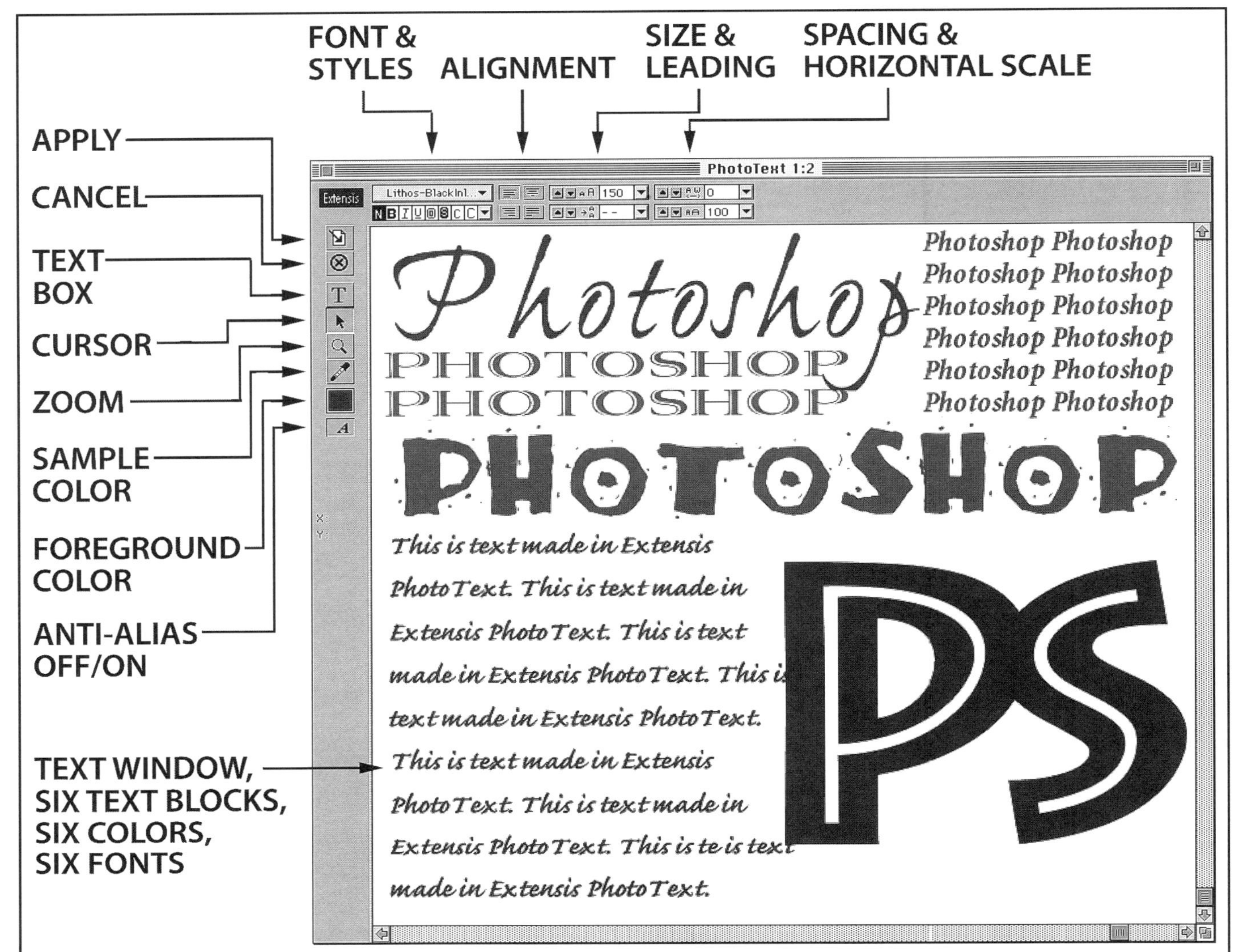

Figure 3-132: The Extensis PhotoText dialog box.

Because the figure is small and its features difficult to see, they are all labeled. What is very clear from this figure is that the PhotoText add-on to Photoshop furnishes a good deal of flexibility and power that Photoshop's own Type tool is lacking. Compare the text specimens in Figure 3-133. The two sets of letters from Figure 3-130 are now accompanied by the complex set of characters in the lower part of the figure, and all of those characters were placed at the same time.

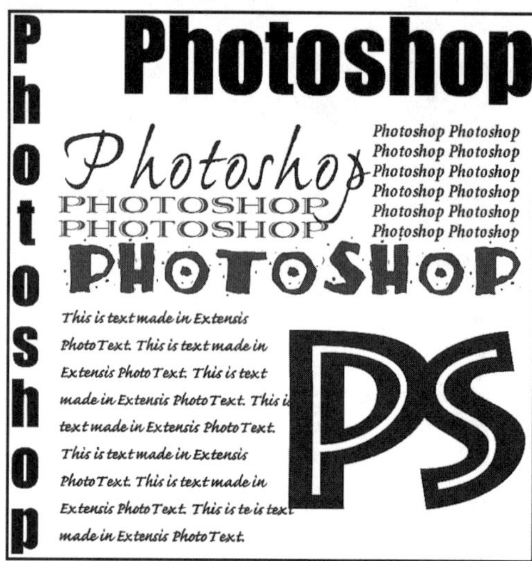

Figure 3-133: A variety of type faces, styles, and sizes rasterized into Photoshop in one operation.

Text From Adobe Illustrator

As excellent as the PhotoText tool is, there is another—and even better—way of getting text into Photoshop: use Adobe's own program, Illustrator. Working with type in Illustrator is not the same as working with type in a word-processing program. The possibilities Illustrator offers are far beyond any mere text cruncher. Rightfully so: Illustrator is an art program and must furnish the tools with which artists can transform type into attention-getting illustration. However, that means that the tools must be learned. The ability to type just won't get you very far in Illustrator. If you have never had a reason to learn the program, you have one now. Illustrator and Photoshop can work together almost as if they were two parts of one large program. With both programs working together, there is literally nothing which cannot be accomplished.

The type that follows a spiral path in Figure 3-134 is a good example of what Illustrator can do that even PhotoText cannot. To make your type in Illustrator, it is a good idea to set up the Illustrator document so that you are always aware of the boundaries of your Photoshop document. In Photoshop, Select All. From the Paths palette, choose Make Work Path from the palette menu. Choose the Direct Selection cursor from the Toolbox (type p twice). While holding Option or Alt, click on the new path to select it.

From the Edit menu, choose Copy. While the path around the edge of the window is active, delete it; you won't be needing it again. Switch to Illustrator and paste the path into a new Illustrator document. While the path is still selected, convert it to a guide. Your document now shows a non-printing dotted line that is the exact dimension of your Photoshop document.

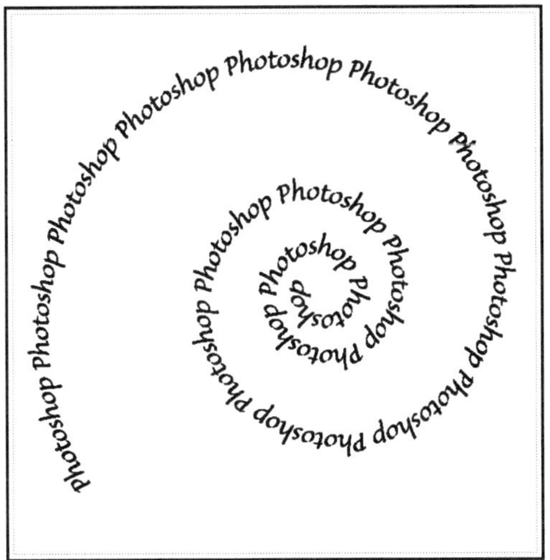

Figure 3-134: Set up very complex type configurations in Adobe Illustrator.

Use the Illustrator Type tools to make your type in any configuration you wish. When finished, select the type and convert it to outlines. While it is selected, copy it. Switch back to Photoshop and use the Paste command. A small dialog box appears (Figure 3-135) which gives you the choice of rasterizing the type (Paste As Pixels or Paste As Paths). (You may, if you wish, choose the former, but the second choice is a lot faster.) When you have pasted the paths, your screen appears as shown in Figure 3-136.

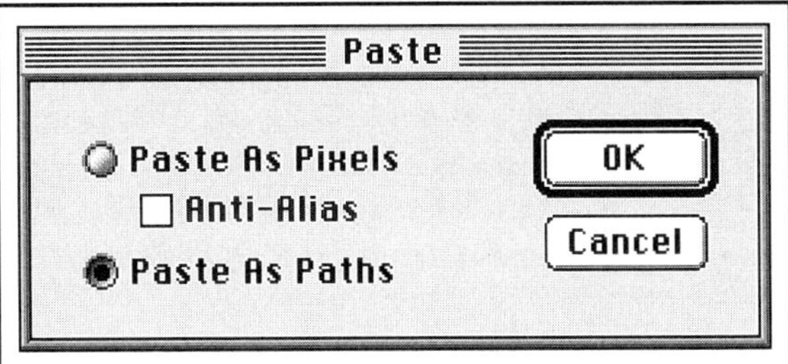

Figure 3-135: The dialog box which appears when you wish to Paste from Illustrator into Photoshop.

Figure 3-136: Illustrator paths pasted into Photoshop.

Paths in Photoshop give endless flexibility, and they may be saved for later use. Figures 3-137 and 3-138 show typical uses to which paths may be put. After pasting the paths, create a new layer (click once on the small icon which resembles a dog-eared page at the bottom of the Layers palette). With the paths of the type still visible (Figure 3-137), click once on the icon at the bottom of the Paths palette which contains a small circular shape filled with gray. Your paths are immediately filled with the foreground color. Turn the Preserve Transparency option for this layer on. Duplicate this layer by dragging it down onto the New Layer icon at the bottom of the Layers palette. Your new layer is now the top layer. In the example in Figure 3-138, a gradient was drawn from lower left to upper right. Because Preserve Transparency is on, the gradient fills only the letter forms. Switch to the middle layer, select the Move tool, and press the Down arrow key three times and the right arrow key three times. Switch to the Background layer and draw the same gradient but this time from upper right to lower left. The procedure is very simple, very fast, and visually effective.

Figure 3-137: More Illustrator paths pasted into Photoshop.

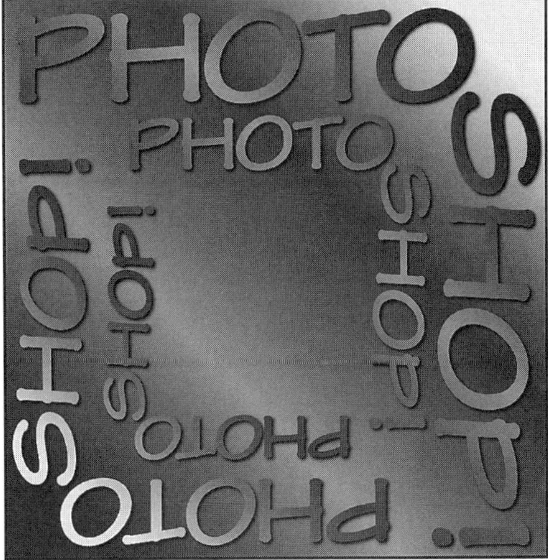

Figure 3-138: From the pasted paths, solid letter shapes and drop shadows can be generated.

Four examples are included in the following figures (Figures 3-139, 3-140, 3-141, and 3-142) to demonstrate a range of uses for type within Photoshop. Despite the complexity of appearance of these figures, all were done with layering techniques of unbelievable simplicity. Please consult Chapter 6, "Using Layers," for additional Information.

A Few Thoughts on Type in Photoshop

When type is used as it is in the pictorial figures on the following pages, the quality of the character edge is not as important as it would be if the type were not used as a container for picture information. When the type is used as a text element, the quality of the character edge becomes much more important. In many cases, particularly when type is to be used at a relatively small size and when the type is delicate in nature—lightweight character strokes, pointed serifs, and so on—it may not be a good idea to incorporate the type as part of the Photoshop file. A better look can be had by exporting the Photoshop file in a format that is usable by the program to be used for the type. Once imported into the type source program, the Photoshop file can serve as the backdrop for the type. For example, the Photoshop document might be saved in the TIFF file format and then *placed* in Adobe Illustrator. The type, in such an Illustrator file, would lie on top of the Photoshop file and would retain its vector edges.

Figure 3-139: Text.

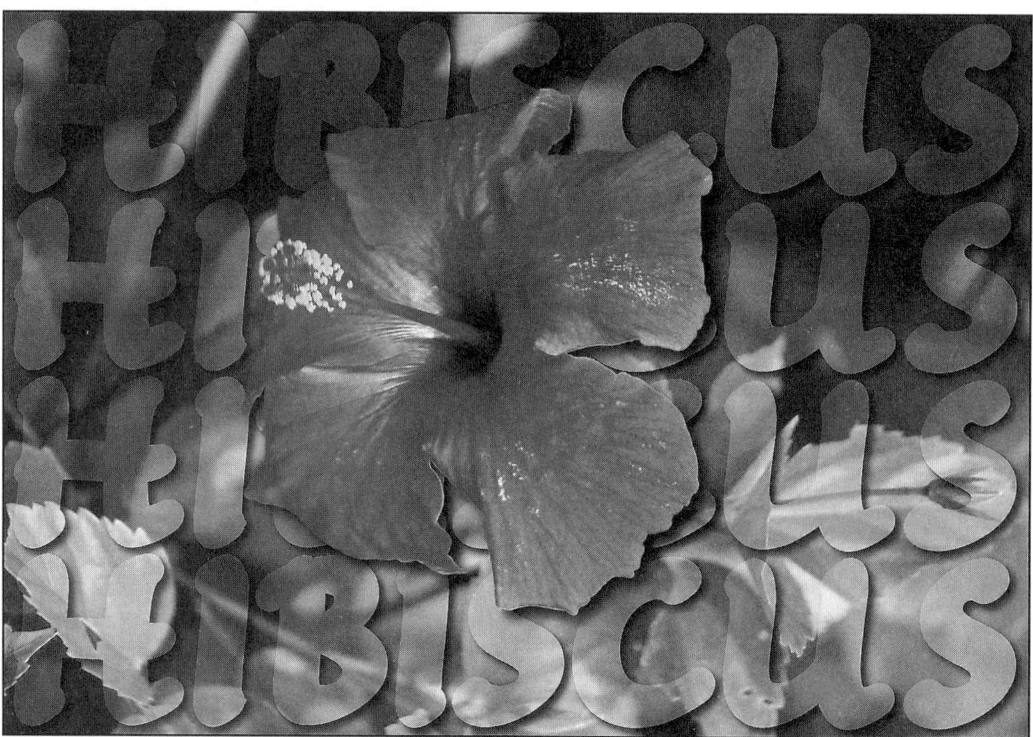

Figure 3-140: Type used to enhance an unremarkable background.

Figure 3-141: Type used as a way to merge images.

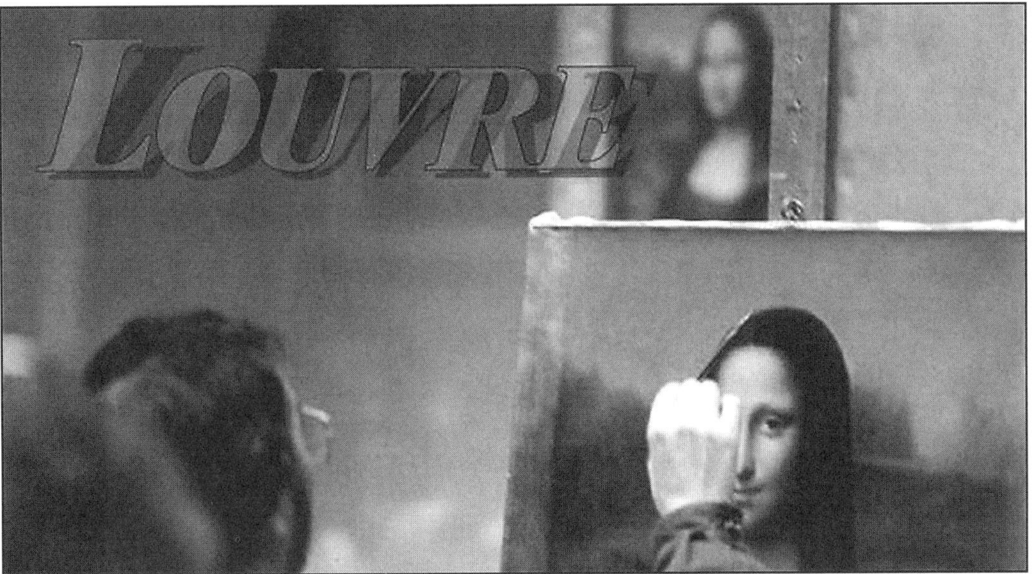

Figure 3-142: Type used as a mysterious headline.

There are two problems inherent with type rasterized into Photoshop. The first is *anti-aliasing*, a small blurring of the edge which deceives the eye into seeing a smooth line. The second is the resolution used in everyday work in Photoshop. When working with photographic material intended for use on the World Wide Web, a resolution of 72 ppi is appropriate. Grayscale photos intended to be reproduced as halftones in a newspaper might require a resolution of 170 ppi. So-called *hi-res* color separation files intended to be reproduced at 150 line-screen would need a resolution of 300 ppi. The three specimens in Figure 3-143 illustrate how the resolution has a strong effect on the edges of the characters. By contrast, when type is rasterized by a typical output device, its edges are not anti-aliased and the type is rasterized at the maximum resolution of the device. The edges of type characters produced by, say, a 2400 dpi device are razor sharp since they are composed of steps that are incredibly small.

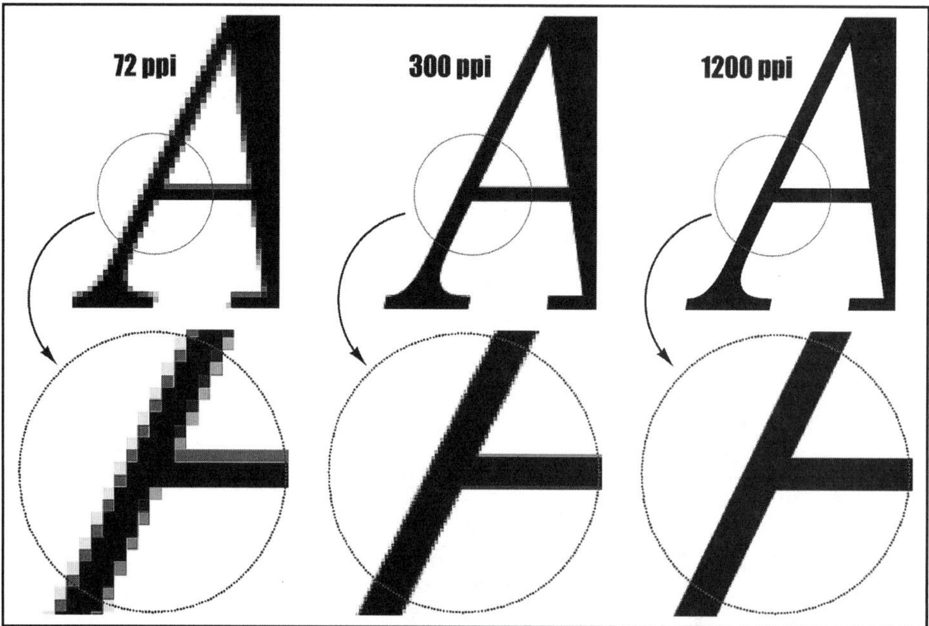

Figure 3-143: Resolution plays a vital role in the sharpness of the rasterized type's edges.

The Line, Paint Bucket & Gradient Tools

Unlike some of the other tool sets, the three that comprise this section have very little in common. They perform very different tasks and have drastically different merits. One, the Gradient tool, provides smooth gradations across a surface which make it invaluable when simulating realistic lighting. The second, the Line tool, is sometimes useful when linear effects or arrows are needed and time is short. The third, the Paint Bucket, is as close to redundant as any feature of Photoshop is likely to be. It provides no service that cannot be done in several other ways, all of which are superior to it. It is, in short, an orphan, the lonely child of the long-vanished MacPaint. Kindness is indicated here (even though we cannot remember the last time we used this tool for any other reason than to show someone else what it is; useless tools must have feelings too). Sigh. I know, I know. I was also mesmerized when I first saw MacPaint (even if I was convinced that no human hand had painted the Japanese lady).

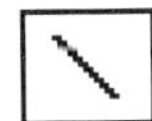

Line Tool (press n)

The Line tool provides a quick way to place straight lines and arrows on an image. The lines are drawn in the Foreground color. The Options for the Line tool and the contextual menu are shown in Figures 3-144 and 3-145.

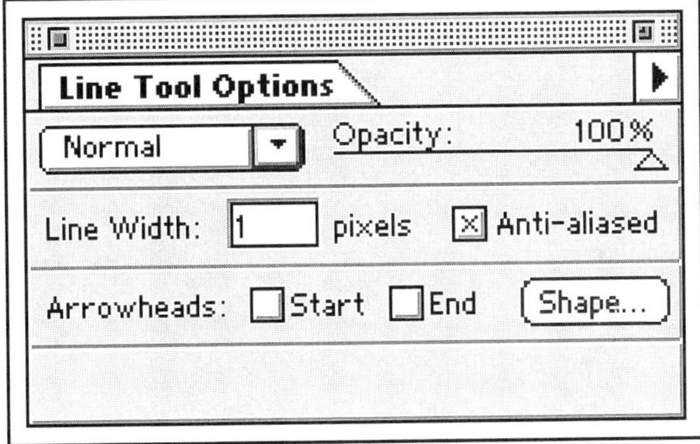

Figure 3-144: Options for the Line tool.

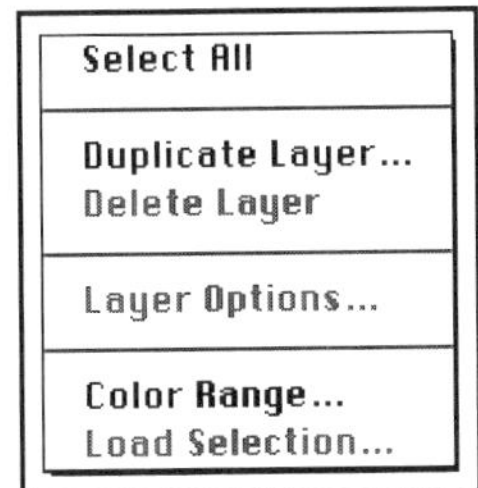

Figure 3-145: The contextual menu for the Line tool.

Line widths are specified in pixels. If a specific width is needed, a calculation must be made and that number entered. Calculating in points, for example, is done by dividing the ppi of the image by 72, multiplying that number by the number of points, and rounding the result to the nearest integer.

Lines can have arrowheads at one or both ends. The shape of the arrowhead is set in the small dialog box (Figure 3-146) which appears after clicking the Shape button. The default proportions work well in most cases. The Concavity setting changes the arrowhead by changing the angle of the base. A negative value angles the lines away from the point, a value of zero makes the base of the arrow straight across, and a positive value angles the baselines toward the point. Examples of all three—using values of 25%, 0%, and 25%—are seen in Figure 3-147.

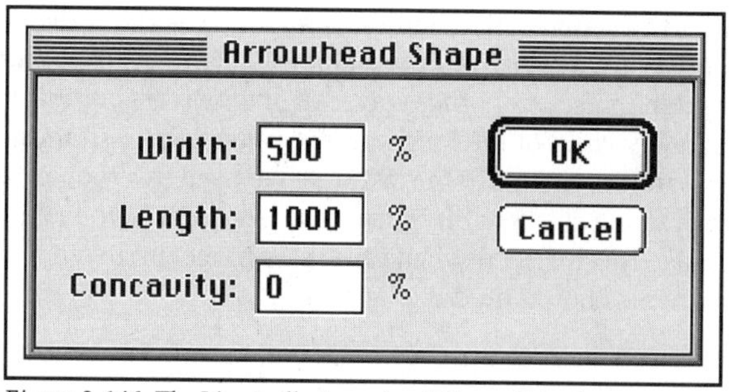

Arrowhead Shape
Width: 500 %
Length: 1000 %
Concavity: 0 %
OK
Cancel

Figure 3-146: The Line tool's Arrowhead Shape dialog box.

Figure 3-147: A selection of arrows.

When using lines and arrows within Photoshop, it is a good idea to draw the lines on a separate layer and to keep a copy of this layered file in case the lines need to be changed in the future. The alternative is to export the Photoshop file, import it into some other program, and lay the lines atop the Photoshop file there. There is a drawback to externally applied arrows: they cannot be made to do the wondrous transparency effects that are possible in Photoshop.

Paint Bucket Tool (press k)

What can we say? This tool works much the way the Magic Wand tool does except that it *fills*—with the Foreground color or with a Pattern—instead of *selects*. It can fill with any of the available blending modes operating as well as with a variable opacity.

Sorry. That's it. That's all the little guy does. Perhaps you're thinking: "But wait. If I were going to fill something, wouldn't I want it to be on a separate layer so that I could change my mind? Wouldn't I just use the Magic Wand tool to select the area, make the selection a layer, and then use the blending modes and opacity capabilities of the Layers palette? Couldn't I then fill the layer—Preserve Opacity turned on—with a color or a pattern? And couldn't I, if I wished, simply get rid of the layer if I didn't like the effect? With the Paint Bucket tool, I couldn't change my mind beyond one undo, could I?" If these are your thoughts, then you have seen the nature of the Paint Bucket tool's problem: even though it does what it is supposed to do, there isn't really a good reason for doing it. The options for the Paint Bucket are shown in Figure 3-148.

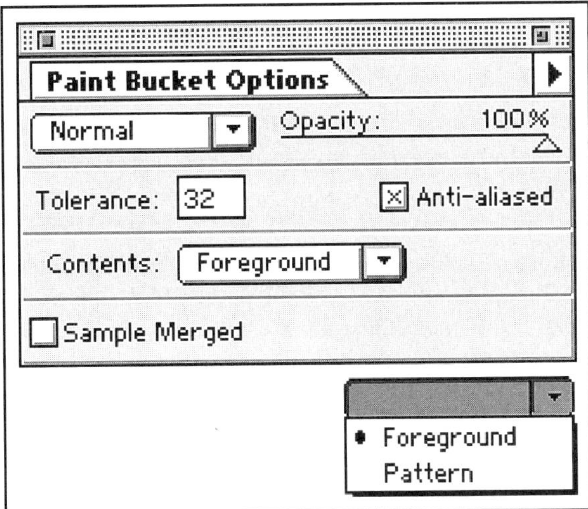

Figure 3-148: Options for the Paint Bucket tool.

Gradient Tool (press g)

Previous versions of Photoshop furnished a Gradient tool that served a few purposes but seemed a wimpy alternative when compared to the Gradient Designer module of Kai's Power Tools published by Metatools. The latest version of Photoshop offers a far more vigorous tool complete with blends containing up to 32 colors and segmented transparency. The options for the Gradient tool and its contextual menu are shown in Figures 3-149 and 3-150.

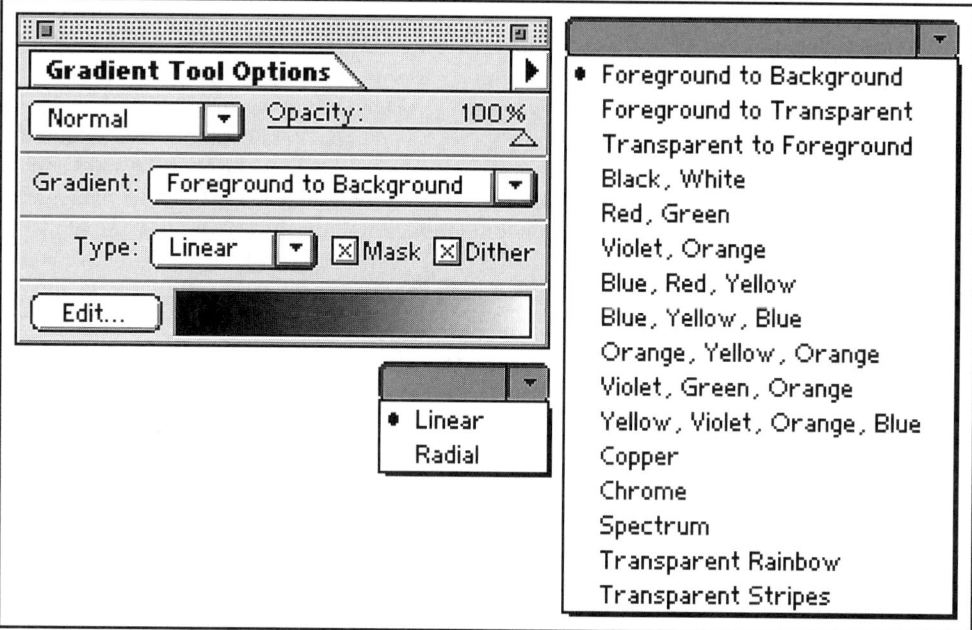

Figure 3-149: Options for the Gradient tool.

Photoshop's gradients come in two flavors, linear and radial. These would seem to be somewhat limited compared to the Baskin-Robbins-like 12 flavors available in the KPT Gradient Designer. However, amazing things can be done with just two gradient configurations.

To use the Gradient tool, place the cursor in the window and click and drag. The place where the operation begins is one of the endpoints for the gradient. The place where the mouse button is released is the other endpoint.

There are two check boxes on the Gradient Options palette which need some clarification. The first of these is Mask. With Mask enabled, the transparency function of the tool is also enabled. This allows the same gradient to be used in two ways: with transparency and without. The second is the Dither option. *Dither* is a strategy where colors are mixed in such a way that pixels opposite the vector direction of the gradient do not have the same values. Here's another way of putting it: if, say, a linear gradient is not dithered, rows of pixels at right angles to the direction of the gradient all have the same tone value. If the gradient is dithered, the pixels are scrambled. There is little visual difference between a dithered and non-dithered gradient. The benefit of dithering is that it goes a long way toward preventing the banding which often occurs in print reproduction. Banding has long been one of the banes of the prepress world. Often it can be partially overcome with the addition of small amounts of noise in the gradient. Dithering, which is really very like Noise, builds the solution to the problem into the Gradient tool.

Figure 3-150: The contextual menu for the Gradient tool.

Defining a Gradient To define a new gradient, click the Edit button on the Gradient Options palette. The dialog box which appears is shown in Figure 3-151.

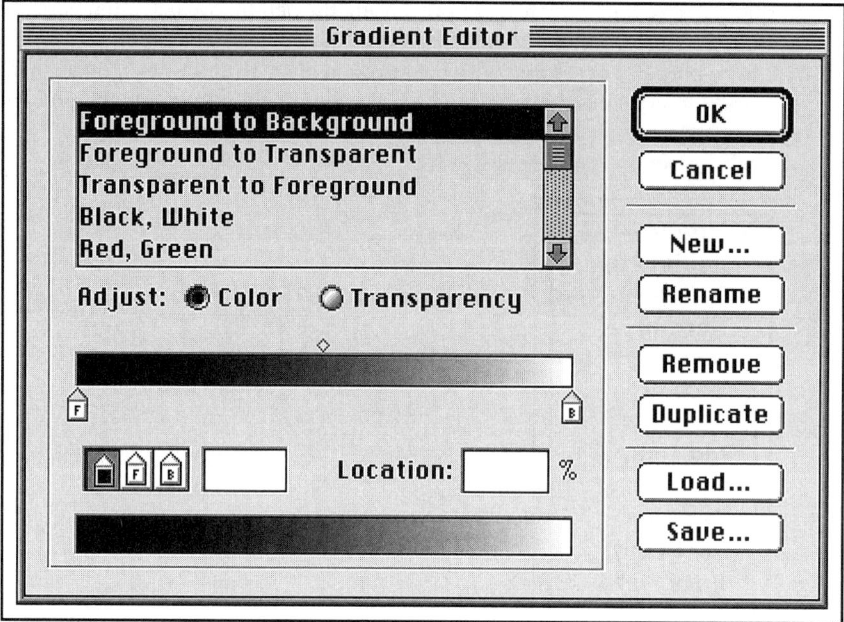

Figure 3-151: The Gradient Editor.

The box looks a little intimidating, doesn't it? Let's take it one step at a time. For the moment, ignore the already defined gradients. Ignore all of the buttons and the band, boxes, and oddly shaped icons at the bottom of the dialog box. Concentrate, instead, on the single band with the house-shaped icons below it. This band contains the definition of the gradient.

Let's go ahead and make a new gradient:

1. First, click on the New button and accept the title Gradient 1. Since you don't know yet what the gradient will look like, you may as well wait and use the Rename button after you're finished designing it.
2. Next, choose the colors. If the Color radio button is not checked, click on it now. Click first on the small icon to the lower left of the band which contains a small F. The F stands for Foreground color, but you're going to use a different color. About an inch to the left of the Location entry field is a color box. Click on it once. The Photoshop Color Picker appears. Choose the RGB value 0, 0, 255 (bright blue). Click OK. Now, click on the icon at the other end of the band. The B on this icon stands for Background color. Click again in the color box and select the RGB color 255, 0, 0 (bright red). Click OK. Take a look at the gradient now. You will see a smooth blend between blue and red. You control the weight, or predominance, of each color within the gradient by moving the diamond-shaped slider above the bar back and forth. Try it out so that you can see how it works.

3. Let's add another color to the gradient. Click just below the gradient bar. Another house-shaped icon appears. Make the color for this icon 255, 255, 0 (bright yellow). Click OK. Your gradient now blends from blue to yellow to red. If you are really on a roll with a gradient, you can design something that has 30 little icons between the endpoints.
4. Click on the Transparency radio button. Here's our strategy: we're going to keep intact the strong, bright primary colors and have the gradient fade to about 50% between them. Click below the gradient bar. A new icon appears. Move this icon so that it is about a quarter of the distance across from the left. What was the color box is now an Opacity box. Enter **50** in this box. Make another icon and move it about three-quarters of the way across and enter **50%** for this one as well. There is a representation of the gradient at the bottom of the dialog box. As you can see, the central yellow color is no longer opaque. You'll fix this by adding another icon directly below the yellow and setting its Opacity to 100%.
5. Now is a good time to rename your gradient. Something like *Blue, Yellow, Red* might be appropriate. Close the dialog box and try out your new gradient. Make a new window and fill it with black. Draw from side to side with the Gradient tool. Undo, change the gradient to Radial, and draw from the center of the window to one side. Bullseye, huh?

Digital Artists Need Gradients If you look around, you'll see that the surfaces of the world are not uniformly lit. A white-painted wall, for example, is not all-over white but a blend of tones depending upon the intensity of the light which falls upon it. Unless you make an attempt to match the variety of tones, you can never make the wall look realistic.

We use the gradient tool, among other things, to simulate realistic surfaces. The four examples which follow show how the use of the default Foreground/Background colors coupled with the Foreground to Background and Foreground to Transparent gradients can be used to simulate solid objects. The files are included on the Companion CD-ROM. They are titled GS_01.PSD, GS_02.PSD, GS_03.PSD, and GS_04.PSD Chapter 3 Gradient Solids.

Each of these four begins with a set of paths drawn in Illustrator, then copied and pasted into Photoshop. If one or two of the paths are used to make a selection, use the Pen's Direct Selection cursor (the arrow) and click on the needed path or paths while holding Option or Alt. Press the Enter key to change the selected paths into selections.

The examples show black arrows pointing in various directions. These arrows indicate the course of the click-and-drag for the Gradient tool. The angle and the start/stop places for these arrows are significant. If you wish to make your work look like the pictured examples, make your gradients follow the arrows carefully.

Sphere Shape To create a sphere shape:

1. Click on the Work Path so that the path is visible as shown in Figure 3-152. Select the path and press the Enter key so that the circle is now a selection.

Figure 3-152: Change this circular path into a selection.

2. Set the gradient to Foreground to Background, the Foreground/Background colors to defaults, and then reverse them. Set the Gradient tool type to Radial. Enter **5** to change the Opacity of the gradient to 50%. Make the gradient as shown in Figure 3-153.

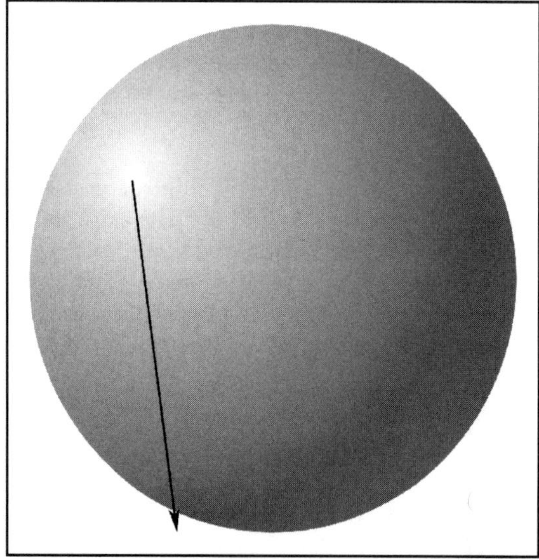

Figure 3-153: Draw a black-to-white gradient at 50% Opacity in the same direction as the arrow.

3. Draw another gradient as shown in Figure 3-154. Note that the three gradients used for this exercise are all drawn on top of each other and the start points are not in the same place.
4. Change the Opacity of the Gradient to 30% and draw the third gradient as shown in Figure 3-155. The final shape is shown in Figure 3-156.

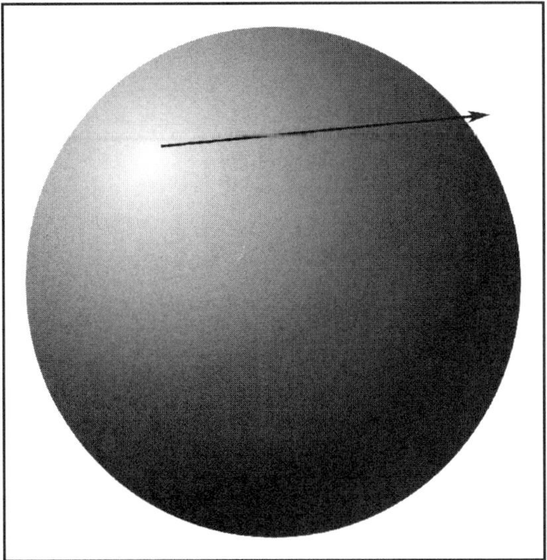

Figure 3-154: Draw another gradient on top of the first.

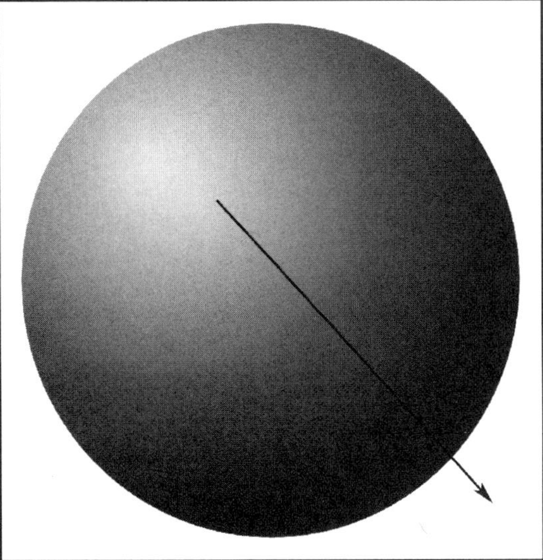

Figure 3-155: Draw a third gradient at 30% Opacity.

Figure 3-156: The final realistic-looking spherical shape.

Cube Shape To create a cube shape:

1. Click on the Work Path so that the paths are visible as shown in Figure 3-157. Select the upper path and press the Enter key so that the shape is now a selection.

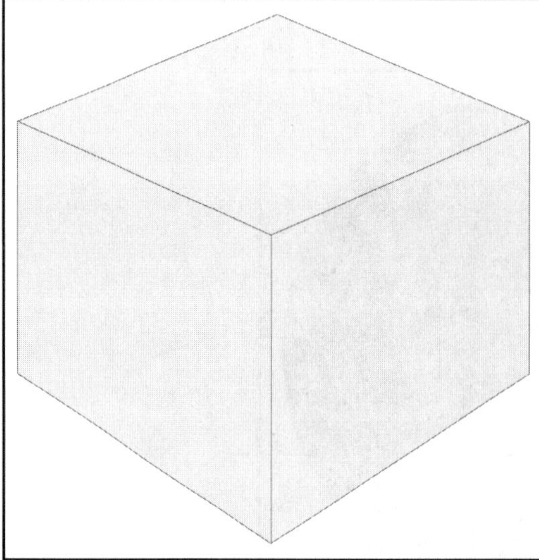

Figure 3-157: Three four-sided paths.

2. Set the gradient to Foreground to Transparent and the Gradient type to Linear. Enter **2** to change the Opacity of the Gradient tool to 20%. Draw the gradient as shown in Figure 3-158.

3. Deselect all. Choose the right-hand path shape and make it into a selection. Change the Gradient tool Opacity to 80%. Draw the gradient as shown in Figure 3-159.

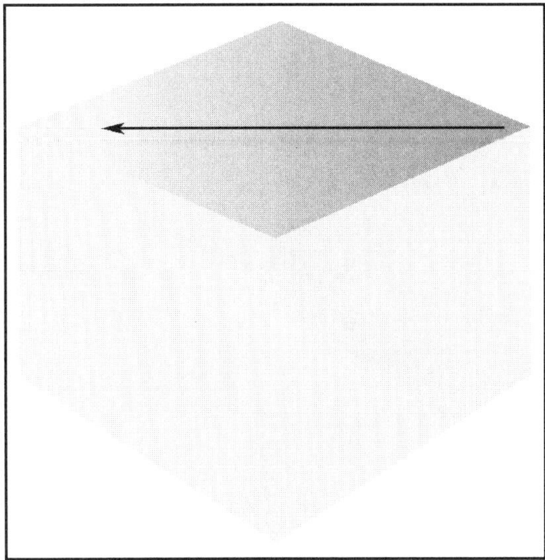

Figure 3-158: Make the top path into a selection. Draw a black-to-white gradient at 20% Opacity.

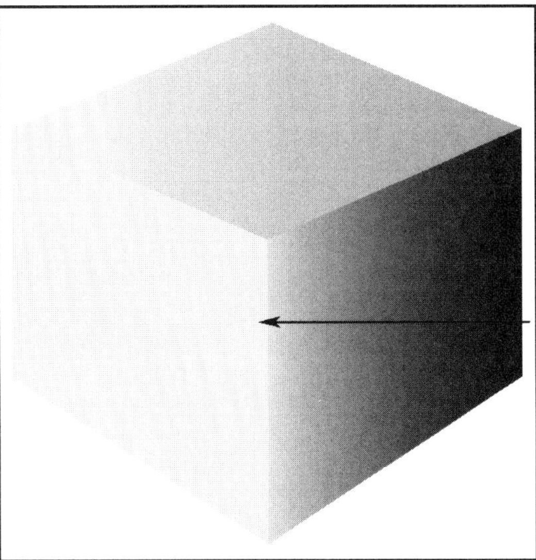

Figure 3-159: Make the right-hand path into a selection. Draw a black-to-white gradient at 80% Opacity.

4. Deselect all. Choose the left-hand path shape and make it into a selection. Change the Gradient tool Opacity to 40%. Draw the gradient as shown in Figure 3-160. The final shape is shown in Figure 3-161.

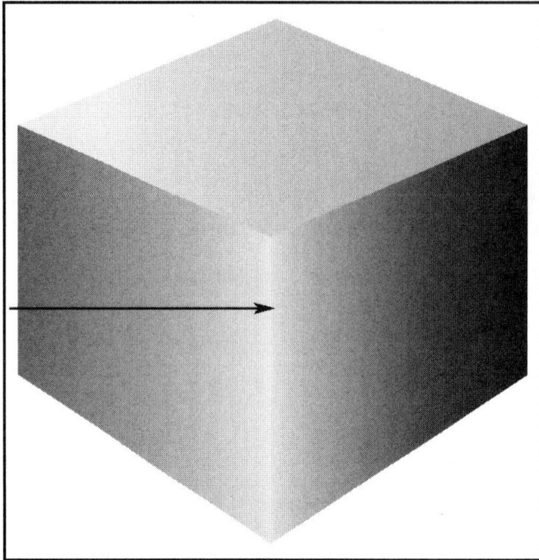

Figure 3-160: Make the left-hand path into a selection. Draw a black-to-white gradient at 40% Opacity.

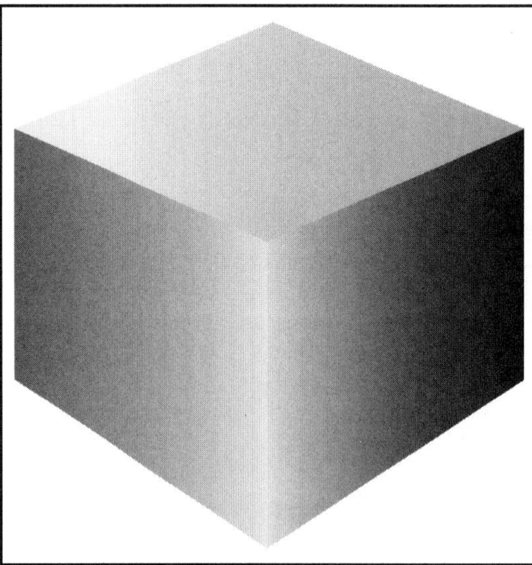

Figure 3-161: The completed cubic shape.

Concentric Shapes To create concentric shapes:

1. Click on the Work Path so that the paths are visible as shown in Figure 3-162. Select the two outer paths and press the Enter key so that the outer ring shape is now a selection.

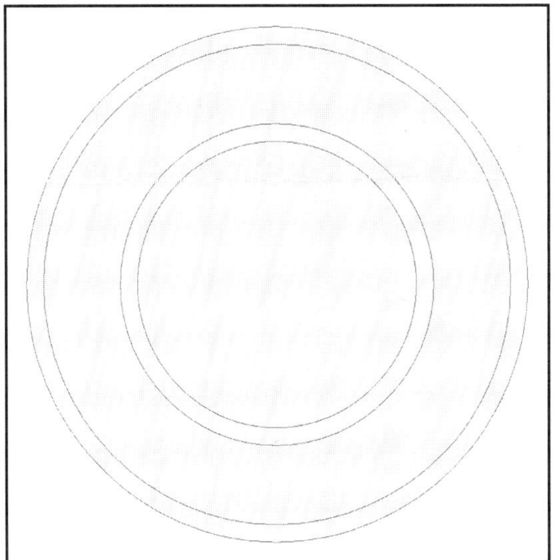

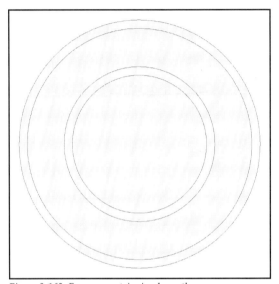

Figure 3-162: Four concentric circular paths.

2. Set the Foreground/Background colors to their defaults. Set the gradient to Foreground to Background and the Gradient type to Linear. Enter **8** to change the Opacity of the Gradient tool to 80%. Draw the gradient as shown in Figure 3-163.

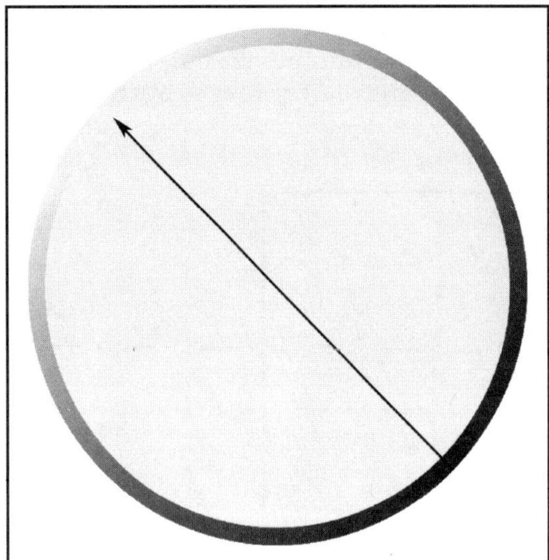

Figure 3-163: Select the two outer paths, make them into a selection, and draw the gradient.

3. Deselect all. Select the two paths between the inner and outer paths. Make them into a selection. Set the gradient Opacity to 60% and make the next gradient as shown in Figure 3-164.

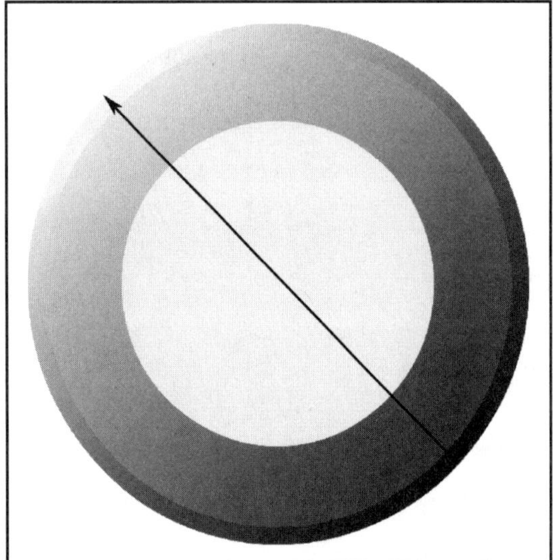

Figure 3-164: Select the next two inner paths, make them into a selection, and draw the gradient.

4. Deselect all. Select the two inner paths. Make them into a selection. Set the gradient Opacity to 70% and make the next gradient as shown in Figure 3-165.
5. Deselect all. Select the inner path. Make it into a selection. Set the gradient Opacity to 60% and make the next gradient as shown in Figure 3-166. The final shape is shown in Figure 3-167.

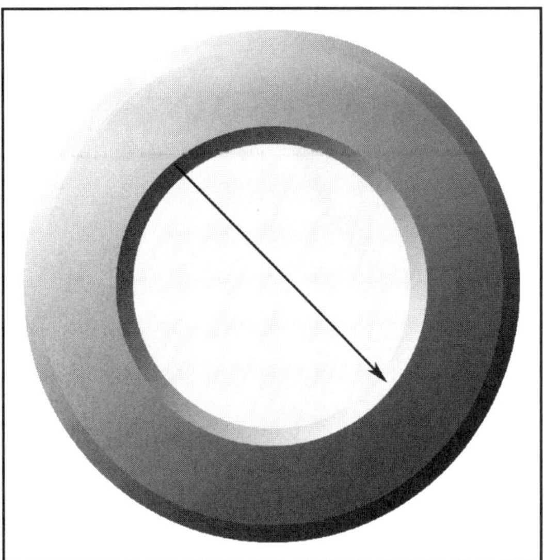

Figure 3-165: Select the two inner paths, make them into a selection, and draw the gradient as shown.

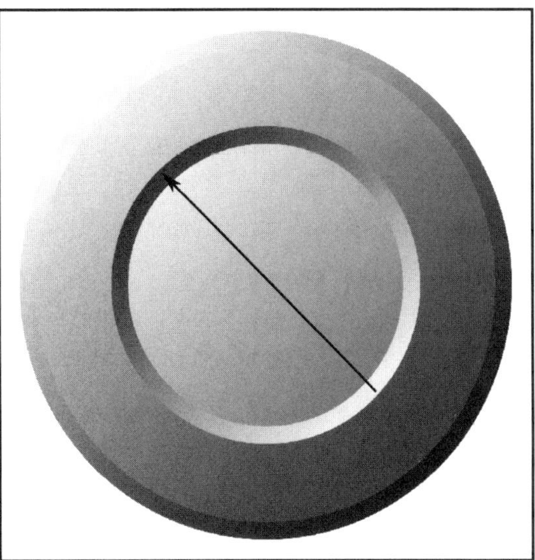

Figure 3-166: Select the inner path, make it into a selection, and draw the last gradient.

Figure 3-167: The completed shaded shape.

Cylinder Shape To create a cylinder shape:

1. Click on the Work Path so that the paths are visible as shown in Figure 3-168. Select the lower path and press the Enter key so that it becomes a selection.

Figure 3-168: Two closed path shapes.

2. Set the Foreground/Background colors to their defaults. Set the gradient to Foreground to Transparent and the type to Linear. Make the first gradient (Figure 3-169) with the gradient Opacity set to 80%. Make the second gradient (Figure 3-170) with the gradient set to 100%.

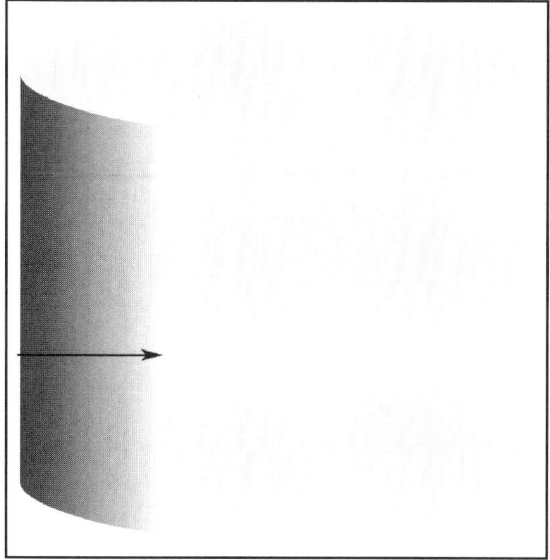

Figure 3-169: With the lower path changed to a selection, draw the first gradient.

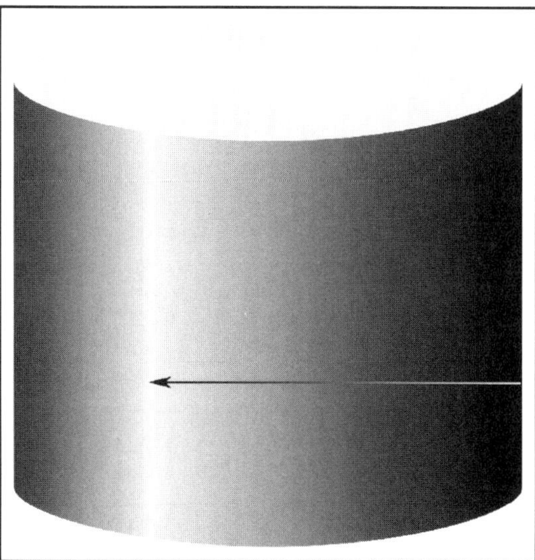

Figure 3-170: Draw the second gradient.

3. Deselect all. Select the upper (oval-shaped) path and make it into a selection. Set the Opacity to 60% and draw the gradient as shown in Figure 3-171. Change the Opacity to 40% and draw the gradient as shown in Figure 3-172. The final shape is shown in Figure 3-173.

Figure 3-171: With the upper path changed to a selection, draw the first gradient.

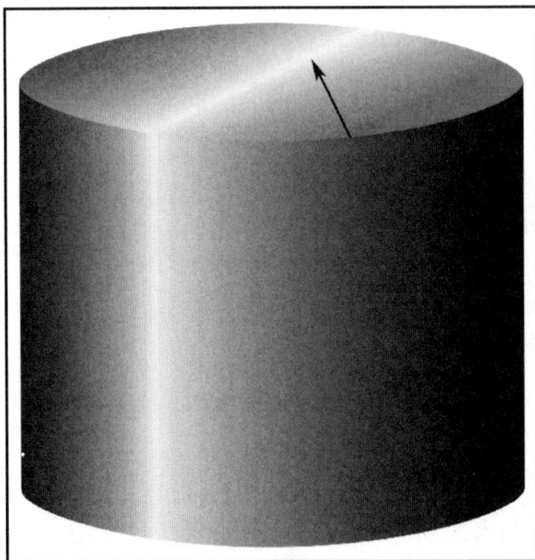

Figure 3-172: Draw the second gradient.

Figure 3-173: The completed cylindrical solid.

For the graphically untrained, this peek at one of the mechanical tasks of artwork might prove to be very instructive. For those with more training and experience, it is useful to note that even these primitive black-and-white shapes can have image information seemingly mapped onto them. An example is shown in Figure 3-174.

Figure 3-174: Pictorial information seemingly mapped onto the three-dimensional surface with the Overlay mode.

The water lily pond image, on a separate layer from the black-and-white shape, has been set to the Overlay mode. The mapping looks a little more sharp and clean if the grayscale concentric shape is subjected to the Image | Adjust | Auto Levels command.

The Eyedropper, Hand & Zoom Tools

Two navigation tools and a color sampler round out our examination of the tools. All three of these tools have keyboard shortcuts which makes it unlikely that you'll ever use them by selecting them from the Toolbox. However, all three have useful modification from their respective Options palettes which can tailor them to fit perfectly with the way you work in Photoshop.

Eyedropper Tool (press i)

The Eyedropper tool picks up color from an image. Simply click with the tool selected, and the color is taken up. Used with no modifier keys, the picked-up color becomes the new Foreground color. If Option or Alt is depressed at the time of the mouse click, the taken-up color becomes the new Background color. The default for this tool is for the values of a single pixel to be sampled. Single pixels are, however, unreliable guides to the general color of an area. Because of this, the tool can be set so that a 3 x 3-pixel or a 5 x 5-pixel area is averaged to become the sampled color. The options and contextual menu for this tool are shown in Figures 3-175 and 3-176.

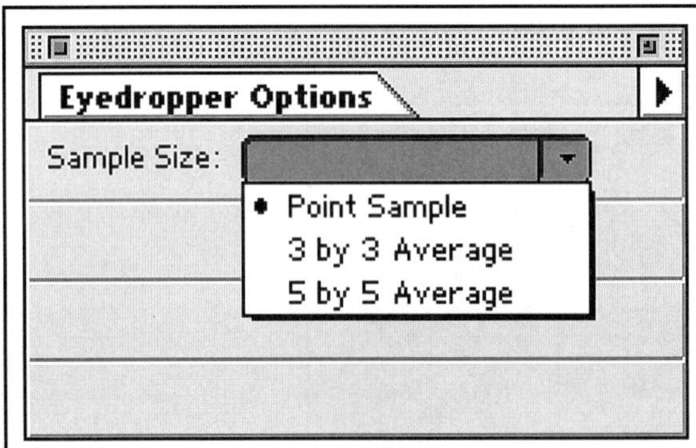

Figure 3-175: Options for the Eyedropper tool.

Point Sample
3 by 3 Average
5 by 5 Average

Figure 3-176: The contextual menu for the Eyedropper tool.

As we mentioned earlier in this chapter when discussing Foreground/Background colors, the Eyedropper tool is also available while using six of the painting tools: Airbrush, Paintbrush, Pencil, Line, Gradient, and Paint. When any of these tools is in use, depress the Option or Alt key to temporarily access the Eyedropper tool.

TIP

The selection of a color with the Eyedropper tool can be an iffy thing. You may want to try this strategy for locating the color which seems to be the best match for the area you are sampling. Set the tool to 5 by 5 Average. Locate the cursor in the area to be sampled, depress the mouse button, and move the cursor around slowly—do not let up on the mouse button—while watching the Foreground color box. When the color seems right, release the mouse button.

Hand Tool (press h)

The new Photoshop Navigator palette makes getting around inside a window so simple that there almost seems no need for the Hand tool. The Navigator palette has, however, a single drawback: to use it, you must move your cursor out of the window. No matter how quick you are, moving your cursor away from the area where you are working slows you down and interrupts your concentration. With the Hand tool, you can simply move the material in the window into a new position and continue working. The Options and contextual menu for the Hand tool are shown in Figures 3-177 and 3-178.

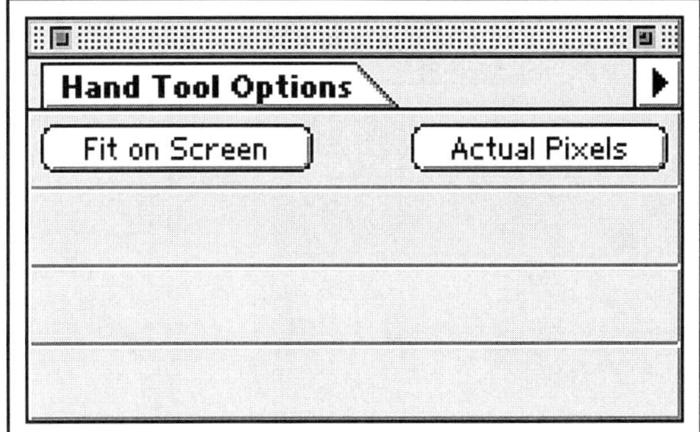

Figure 3-177: Options for the Hand tool.

Fit on Screen
Actual Pixels
Print Size

Figure 3-178: The contextual menu for the Hand tool.

To use the Hand tool, click and drag on an image window which is at sufficient magnification that not all of the pixels can be viewed at once. The result is the same as if you moved the scroll bars. The scroll bars, however, only move in one dimension and the Hand can move in two at the same time. Rather than pressing h to select the tool, it is easier to simply depress the spacebar whenever the Hand tool is needed. It doesn't matter which other tool you are using, the spacebar changes your cursor to that of the Hand.

It's interesting that the two command buttons on the Hand Tool Options palette are zoom commands. In fact, they are the same two buttons to be found on the Zoom tool's Options palette. The Hand's icon on the Toolbox has a zoom function associated with it: double-click it for your document window to fit onscreen. This would be very cool if it could be done by pressing h twice very quickly, but that doesn't work. It should because if pressing h is the same as clicking once on the tool icon, then pressing h twice should be like.... Anyway, there is already a keyboard command for the Fit onscreen command. It is Command+0 (zero) or Ctrl+0.

Zoom Tool (press z)

With the Zoom tool, the image is brought to higher or lower magnification. Choose the tool and the cursor becomes a small magnifier glass with a plus in the center. The plus indicates that a click will take you closer to the image. Hold Option or Alt and the plus changes to a minus. The Options and contextual menu for this tool are shown in Figures 3-179 and 3-180.

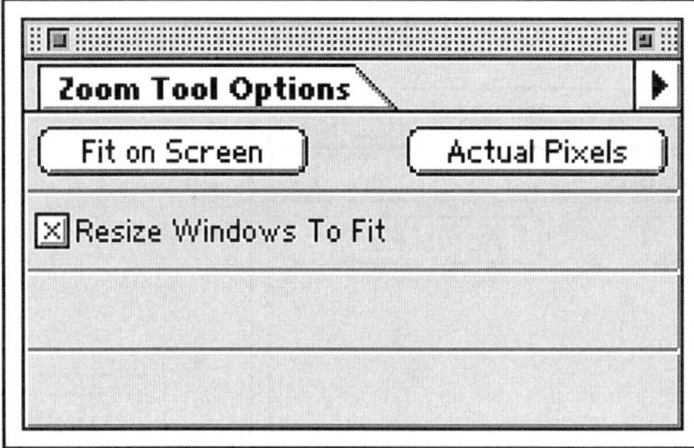

Figure 3-179: Options for the Zoom tool.

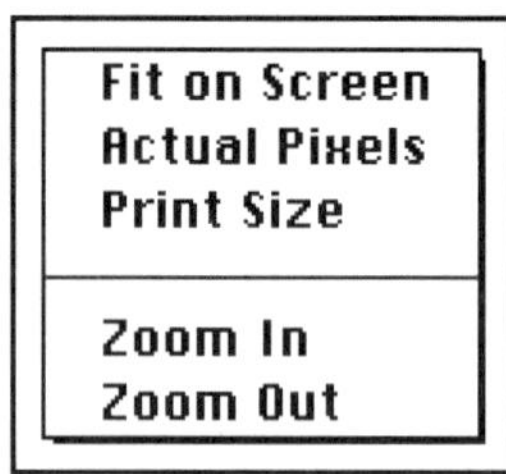

Figure 3-180: The contextual menu for the Zoom tool.

To use the Zoom tool, click in the window on the area you wish to magnify or reduce. Photoshop attempts to place the pixels on which you clicked in the center of the screen. The zoom performed will be, click by click, at a set of predefined percentages. Click and drag a selection marquee. Photoshop calculates the amount of magnification necessary to enlarge the marquee area and then centers it in your screen.

When using the Zoom tool, you have a choice about whether your windows will expand or become smaller as you zoom in and out. The Resize Windows to Fit check box on the Options palette determines the window's behavior.

The Zoom tool can be used at any time even without selecting it from the Tools palette. Hold Command+spacebar or Ctrl+spacebar for the zoom-in cursor. Add Option or Alt to the other two and the zoom-out cursor appears.

Double-click on the Zoom tool icon to zoom the document window to 100%.

Other Photoshop Zoom Commands

The View menu contains five Zoom commands. All but one of these, Print Size, have keyboard equivalents.

Zoom In and Zoom Out are commands issued by typing Command++ (plus) or Ctrl++ and Command+– (minus) or Ctrl+–. If the Resize Window to Fit option on the Zoom palette is checked, these two commands zoom up or down with the windows resizing appropriate to the amount of zoom. Holding Option or Alt as well as the command or Ctrl key when typing + or – will prevent the windows from resizing.

Command+0 (zero) or Ctrl+0 causes the image window to fit itself to the widest dimensions of the screen. With this command, the entire image is visible at whatever magnification is required. Using Option or Alt along with Command+0 (zero) or Ctrl 0 causes the image to display at what Photoshop calls Actual Size. This simply means that the pixels of the image and the pixels of the monitor are in a one-to-one ratio.

View | Print Size is useful only in that it gives you a real-world glimpse of your file's physical size. When working at low resolutions, this is probably useful. With higher resolutions you are given a view of the file that has little to recommend it. The decrease in magnification for a 300 ppi file viewed at Print Size is so extreme that little meaningful information can be derived from looking at the image.

Photoshop also furnishes a small box in the lower left-hand corner of the viewing window into which percentages can be entered. Double-click in this box, enter a new percentage, and press Return or Enter. The screen changes to the new amount of magnification without resizing the image window. This small box has a tryout feature. Hold the Shift key when you press the Return key. The number in the percentage box stays selected. If the amount of magnification is sufficient, press the Return key again. If the amount of magnification is not to your liking, go ahead and enter a new number without having to return the cursor to the box.

When you've magnified the image without changing the size of the window, there are two fast options for increasing the amount of the image that can be seen. Click in the Grow or Maximize box in the upper right corner of the window. The window expands to fit the image or the screen. You may also make use of the screen mode which moves the boundaries of the window out to the edges of the screen. To do this, click on the center icon at the bottom of the Toolbox, or press f.

Six other keyboard commands are also of use when working at high magnification:

- **Page Up key.** Moves the image slightly less than a full screen up.
- **Shift+Page Up key.** Moves the image up about one-tenth of a screen.
- **Page Down key.** Moves the image slightly less than a full screen down.
- **Shift+Page Down key.** Moves the image down about one-tenth of a screen.
- **Home key.** Displays the upper left-hand corner of the image.
- **End key.** Displays the lower right-hand corner of the image.

The Navigator Palette

The Navigator palette really isn't a part of the Toolbox but while we're on the subject of zooming....

This gadget is pure magic. A labeled representation of the palette is shown in Figure 3-181. The main part of the palette is composed of a thumbnail of the entire image. Within the thumbnail is the View Box. The default color of the View Box is red but it can be changed by using the palette menu at the upper right. Click and drag in the thumbnail window and the View Box moves around. Your screen is instantly updated to show the area of the View Box. Hold the command key or the Ctrl key and the cursor in the thumbnail window becomes a Zoom cursor. Click once and the View Box collapses to its smallest size. This changes your image window to maximum magnification. While holding command or Ctrl down, click and drag within the thumbnail window and draw a new View Box.

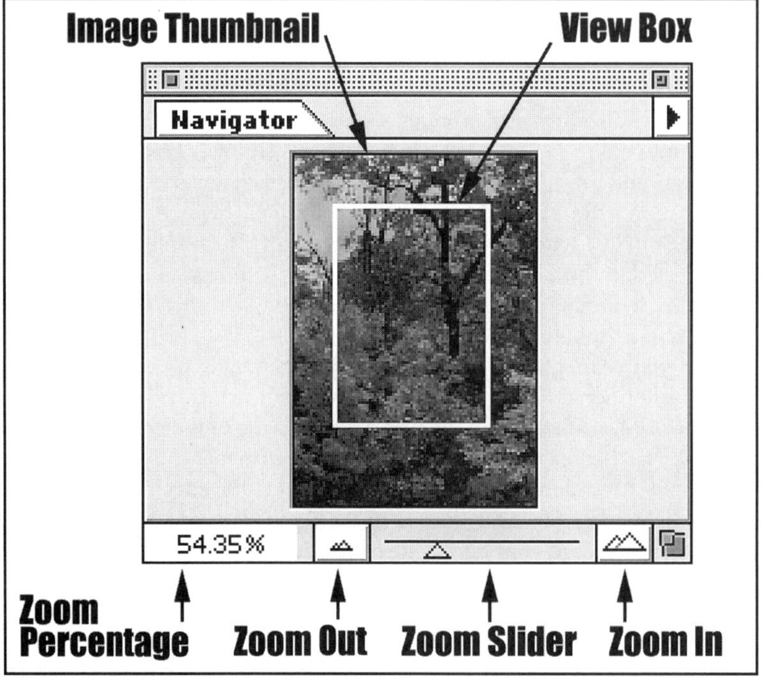

Figure 3-181: The Photoshop Navigator palette.

The Percentage control at the bottom works exactly the way the small percentage box at the lower left of the image window works. Numbers can be entered into it followed by Return or Shift+Return.

Use the Zoom Out and Zoom In icons by clicking on them. Each click is the same as if you clicked in the image window with the Zoom tool selected.

The Zoom Slider lets you experiment with magnification. Drag the slider in either direction to zoom in or out. The View Box and your image window are instantly updated.

None of the controls for this window automatically resize the image window.

Moving On

Chapter 3 has taken a close look at Photoshop's tools, the Toolbox, and has explored many peripheral questions about fast and easy ways to use all of the tools. The emphasis has been, besides the behavior of the tools, on using the keyboard to access the tools and on keyboard commands to trigger commands which would otherwise require moving the cursor someplace away from the image.

You have also seen many examples of how the tools are used. Some of these are everyday situations and some of them are more advanced. All of the examples were chosen to give you an idea how wide-ranging and flexible the Photoshop tools are. If you have encountered unfamiliar material while reading this chapter, we hope that you take the time to work through the tutorial material. Reading the information doesn't solidify the concepts as well as actually using them does.

There are many keyboard commands which require a good deal of use and practice before they become part of your fluency with the program. We encourage you to persist in mastering as many of the keyboard commands as possible. With them, and with a broad understanding of each tool's special abilities, you'll be able to work in Photoshop with an efficiency that will be the envy of all who watch you work. As you become more efficient, you'll find that using Photoshop becomes more enjoyable and that your proficiency leads you to many new and interesting ideas.

In the next chapter, we'll take a look at the single tool, the Pen tool and its associated Paths palette, which was not explored in this chapter. The Pen tool is one of Photoshop's most useful. With it, you draw *paths*, line shapes that can be converted to selections, used as a guide for other tools to follow while applying paint or edit effects, and exported as masks. We think you'll be pleasantly surprised to discover how many different kinds of things you can do with the Pen tool and with the path it draws.

chapter 4

Paths & the Pen Tool

The Pen tool is the principal drawing tool for programs such as Macromedia FreeHand and Adobe Illustrator. Both of these programs are used to construct graphic objects which are called *vector shapes*, shapes which are essentially composed of lines and the spaces which the lines surround, lines that can be stored and manipulated as mathematical expressions. The Pen is an odd tool to include in a program devoted to manipulating the data of a raster file (raster objects are collections, or *arrays*, of pixels which are stored as large-scale tables of numbers). The Pen is used to draw Beziér paths which are, by definition, the boundaries of vector shapes. As such, it is a foundation tool for programs such as Illustrator and FreeHand. Yet, here it is, an important Photoshop tool, with Beziér curves superimposed upon a graphic type which has little logical connection with vector shapes. How any software engineer ever thought to put a vector tool into a program that does not really support vector objects is a mystery. But we can be glad that the Pen was included: the Pen tool—and the paths it draws—is so useful and so important that it has an entire chapter of this book devoted to it. With the Pen tool, you have the ability to describe discrete pixel areas with the same mathematical language you would use for a vector shape. That makes those shapes economical to store and unobtrusive until you need them. Effectively, that makes a path rather like a selection but without the selection's urgency or large storage penalty. You also have really easy shape editability. That, by itself, paves the way for this tool—which can do a lot of other things too.

In this chapter, we will discuss what a Beziér path is. We'll take a look at why the Pen tool is notoriously difficult to master and how you can become an expert with it. You'll learn how to draw smooth, precise paths, and how to manipulate these paths, changing their shapes, making them smaller or larger, rotating them, distorting them, and using them for a variety of selection and paint tasks. You'll learn how to move paths between programs—Photoshop to Illustrator and back again—and how to use an exported path as a mask (Clipping Path). We think you're going to be surprised at how many useful and interesting things you can do with the Pen tool and its associated Paths palette.

Beziér Curves

In the 1960s and 1970s, the French mathematician Pierre Beziér—at that time employed by the auto manufacturer Renault—was one of an industry-wide group of technicians and engineers working to develop ways of using computers to control the manufacture of automobiles. Beziér's own project focused on control software for precision-cutting machines. Basing his work on trigonometric functions, Beziér evolved the curve-creation system which bears his name.

The Beziér curve is a deceptively simple concept. At the two ends of any Beziér curve lie two *nodes* (Figure 4-1). The curve segment between the nodes is defined by the positions of spatial referents called *control points* (the node has one control point for each curve). Each control point is aligned to the node along the line of a tangent. A tangent is normally considered to be a unique line intersecting a point on the edge of a curve: a given point can have only one tangent. However, if the control point is moved—it is by moving the control points that we alter the direction of a curve—its linear relationship with the node is changed. A new tangent is created which forces an alteration in the direction of the curve.

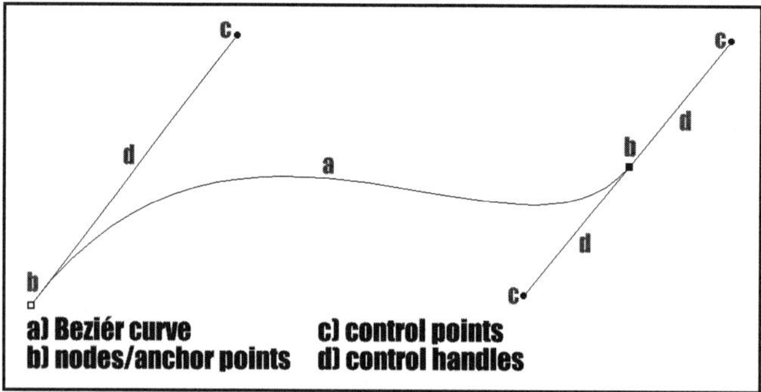

Figure 4-1: The Beziér curve with its associated terminology.

The control point has another use: its distance from the node serves as a modifier for the amplitude of the curve. As the control moves away from its node, the curve encloses an ever greater area. If the control moves closer to the node, the curve encloses a smaller area. The control point and the node can even be made to coincide. In such a case, the curve encloses no area. If a coinciding control point-node is located at each end of a curve, the result is a straight line.

When you use the Pen tool in Photoshop or in a drawing program such as Adobe Illustrator, you are drawing what are called Beziér curves. These curves are also called *paths* (see Figure 4-1).

In the figure, the nodes—they are *anchor points* in the Adobe lexicon—are marked with a *b*. The nodes are the endpoints of the curve (*a*). Each node may have one or two *control handles* extending from them (shown in the figure as *d*). The control handles end in smaller distinct points called control points. These points can be moved with the mouse cursor to change the direction and length of the control handles.

The control handles are the means by which the curve is shaped. The direction and length of a handle gives the curve direction and amplitude. In Photoshop, there are two kinds of nodes, *smooth* and *corner*. The difference between them lies in how the control handles operate.

Smooth Nodes

A smooth node is most easily thought of as the junction at the simple continuation of two curves. There are two control handles extending from opposite sides of the node. When either of the control handles is moved, the handle on the opposite side also moves, pivoting on the node. Figure 4-2 shows a smooth node with handles extended along a horizontal line (left). When one of the handles is rotated 90°, the other also moves (right). Notice how this clockwise rotation has altered the shape of the curves on either side of the node.

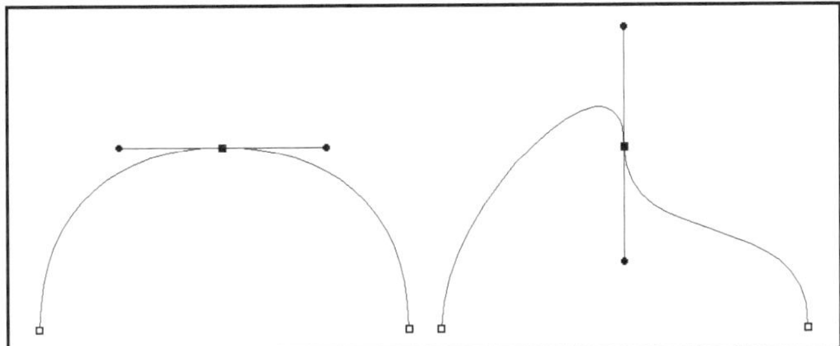

Figure 4-2: The handles of smooth nodes pivot together on the node. As one is rotated around the node, the other follows. The two handles remain a straight line.

Corner Nodes

Corner nodes are more complex than smooth nodes. The path on each side of the node can be a curved line or a straight line. (Note: a straight line between two nodes is still technically a Beziér curve, even if it is not *curved*.) If there are control handles extending from a corner node, they are independently controllable. Moving one does not move the other. This independence of movement is shown in Figure 4-3.

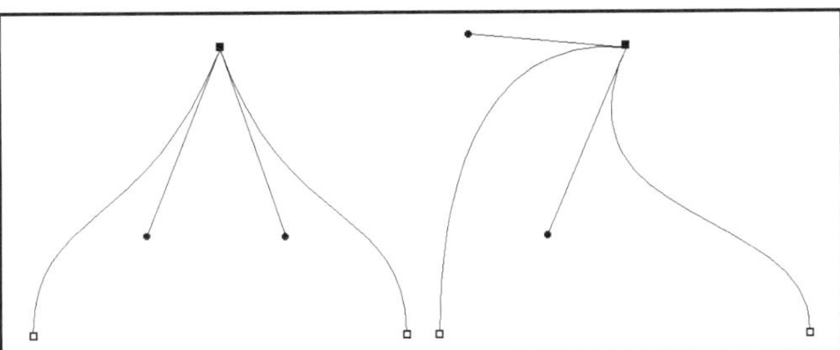

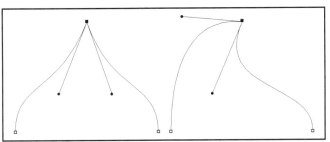

Figure 4-3: The handles of a corner node also pivot on the node. As one of the handles is moved, the other remains stationary.

Using these definitions, we can define four possible node configurations. The first is shown in Figure 4-4, the smooth node. In Figure 4-5, the node is shown with no control handles extending from it. Figure 4-6 shows a corner node with a control handle extending from one side but not the other. The last type is shown in Figure 4-7. Two independently movable control handles extend from the node. All but the first are examples of corner nodes.

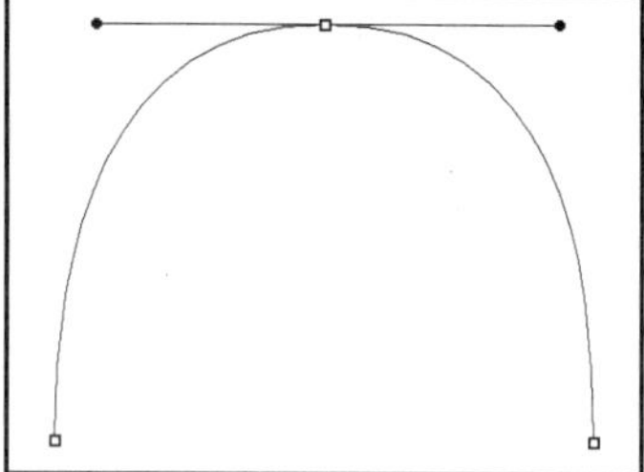

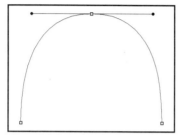

Figure 4-4: Smooth node.

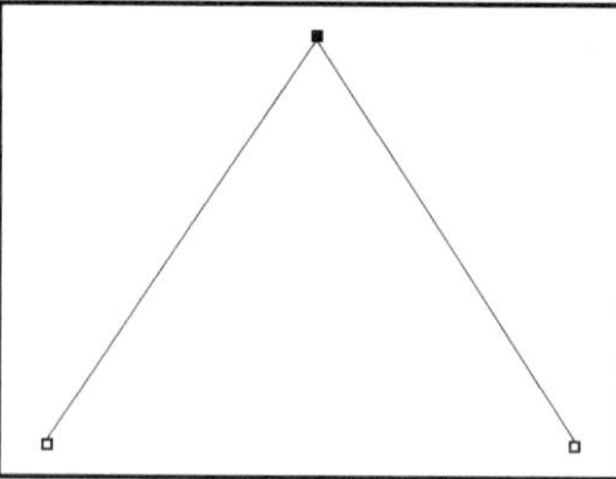

Figure 4-5: Corner node without control handles.

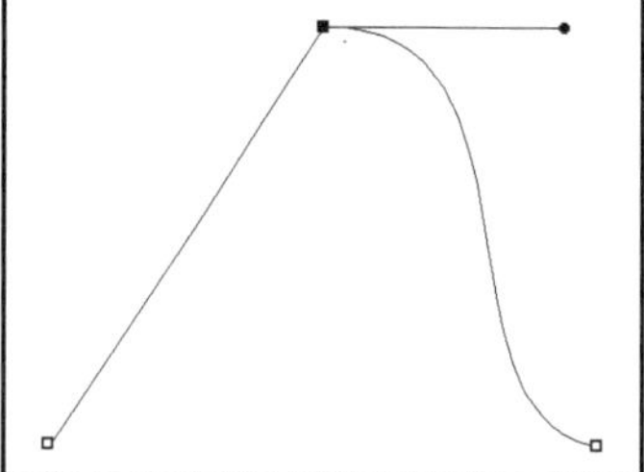

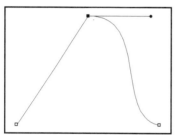

Figure 4-6: Corner node with one control handle.

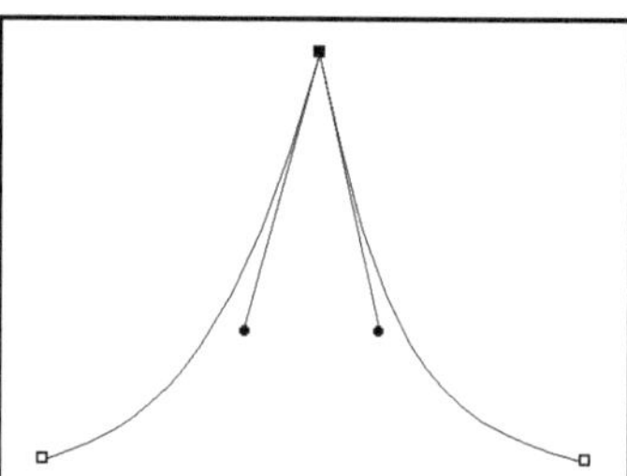

Figure 4-7: Corner node with two control handles.

Drawing Paths With the Pen Tool

The behavior of the Pen tool is like nothing you have ever encountered before. Drawing is largely a matter of analyzing the contours of shapes and planning where the nodes will be placed. The path simply appears between the locations of your nodes. Often, you will feel that although you are operating the mouse correctly, your mouse's movements are not taking place where the path is appearing. Don't worry about this feeling. It is natural and will disappear. When you have had a little practice, you may come to recognize that drawing precision paths with the mouse would be difficult in any other way. There will even come a time when the Pen tool will become enjoyable. Really.

Drawing Straight-Line Paths

Drawing straight-line paths is the easiest way to use the Pen tool. Press p to select the tool. Move your cursor into the document window and click. Move the cursor away from the place where you first clicked, and click again. You'll see the path connecting the two click points as a straight line. The two nodes will appear to be small squares. The first one is hollow, the most recently placed node is solid. As you continue to move the cursor around and click, the lines follow behind (Figure 4-8).

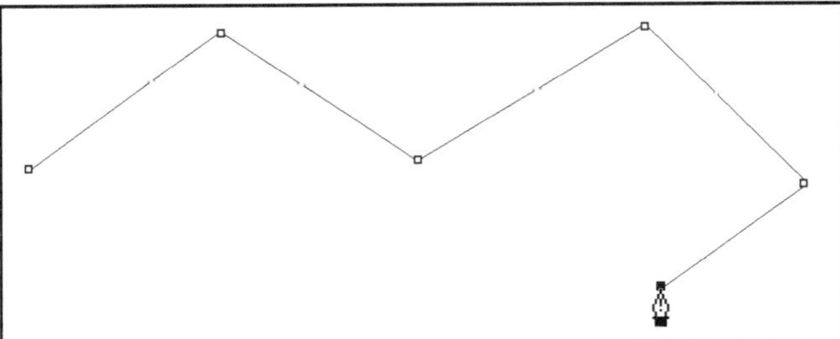

Figure 4-8: To draw straight-line paths, click with the Pen tool, move the cursor away from the first click, and click again.

When your cursor approaches to within a pixel or so from the place where your path began, you'll see a small circular shape appear to the lower right of the cursor (Figure 4-9). This is your indication that another click will join your last node to the first. This creates a *closed* path, a path with no beginning or ending nodes.

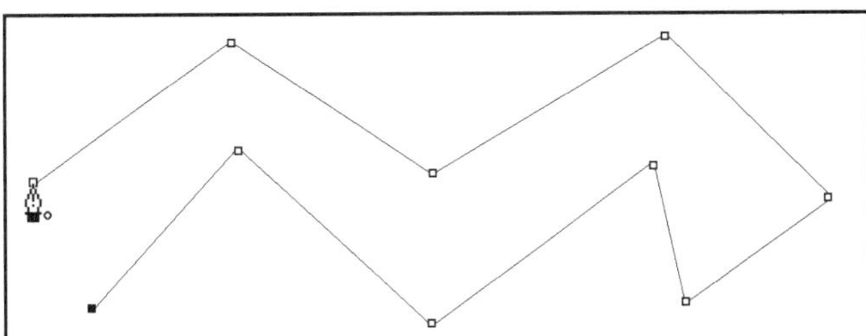

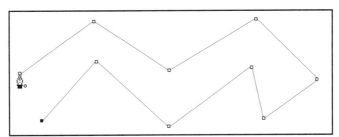

Figure 4-9: When the cursor reaches the beginning of the path, a small circle appears next to the cursor to let you know that your next click will connect the most recent node to the first, creating a closed shape.

Drawing Curved Shapes

Drawing a curved path is a little more complex than drawing straight-line paths. Place the cursor in the document window. Click, keep the mouse button down, and drag in the direction the curve is to go. Release the mouse button. Move the cursor away from the first node. Click and drag again in the direction the curve is to follow.

Figure 4-10 shows the first click-and-drag operation on the left-hand side. The lines which extend from the node are the control handles. The arrow indicates the direction of the mouse drag. The handle below the node forms as the handle above is dragged out. The second handle will always be the same length as the first (though it may be modified later to be a different length). On the right-hand side of the figure, a second node has been placed, and two new handles formed by dragging the mouse. Notice that the curved path has formed from the forward handle of the first node and the backward handle of the second node. Note also that the two handles at the top—these are the handles which control the first curve—are on the convex side of the curve. This is an important thing to remember: control handles will always be on the convex side of the curve.

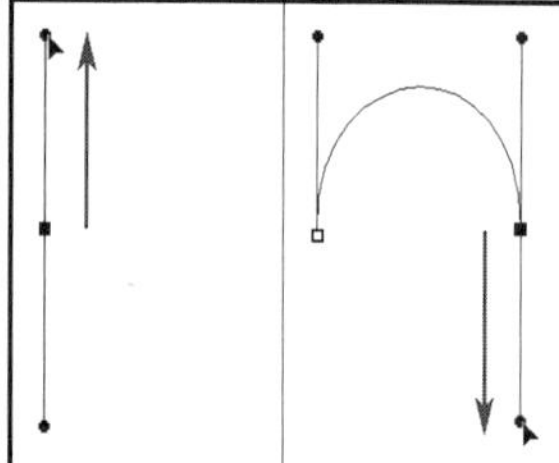

Figure 4-10: Click and drag to establish the first node and control handles (right). Click and drag again to form the first curve of the path and the second set of control handles.

As new nodes are added, new segments of the path are added. Figure 4-11 shows three nodes which have defined two curves. The control handles are visible only for the curve which has just been formed. When you edit the path later, clicking on a curve segment makes the control handles for that segment visible. If you click on a node, the control handles for both of the segments running into that node become visible. Note that the control handles and control points only appear onscreen to allow you to edit the shape of the path. Control handles and points never appear as output.

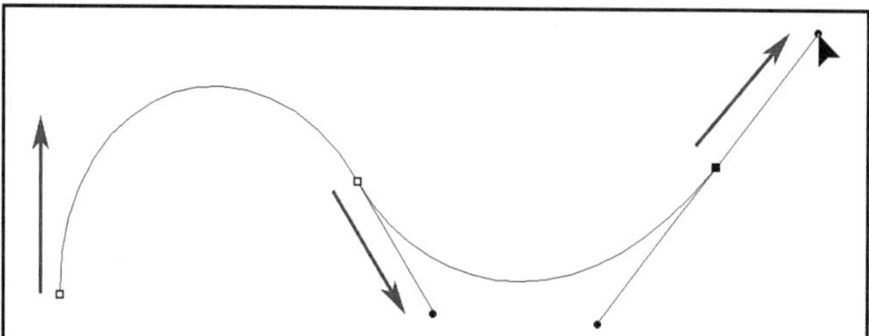

Figure 4-11: Two curve segments running between three nodes have formed on this path.

Drawing Mixed Curve & Straight-Line Shapes

When drawing a path, it is often necessary to join a curve to a straight-line segment. The procedure for doing this is as follows:

1. Click to form the first node. Position the cursor some distance away and click again. The straight-line path segment forms between the two nodes.
2. Hold Option or Alt. Click again on the last node point and drag away from it. A control handle will form only on the side of the cursor drag.
3. Now, release the mouse button, move the cursor, and click and drag to form the next curve segment.
4. The procedure is shown in Figure 4-12. The node type is the same as shown in Figure 4-6.

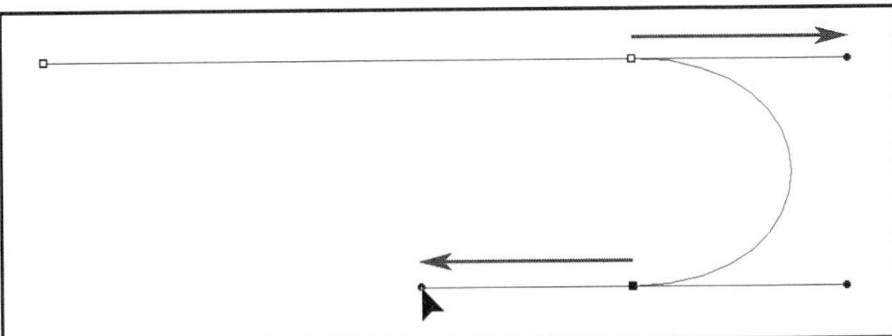

Figure 4-12: Click twice to form the first two nodes. Hold Option or Alt. Click and drag from the second node to form a control handle on the side of the node opposite the straight line. Click and drag to form a curve segment between the second and third node.

This procedure can also be done in the opposite direction, bottom to top:

1. Using Figure 4-12 as an example, click and drag to place the two handles from the lower node. Release the mouse button.
2. Move the cursor up and away from the new node. Click and drag to form the second node and the control handle opposite the direction of the drag.
3. Hold Option or Alt. Click on the second node. This immediately retracts the forward control handle into the node.
4. Move the cursor away from the second node, and click again to make the straight path segment.

Drawing Curve Segments That Abruptly Change Direction

When two curved path segments form a corner node (see Figure 4-7), there is a sudden change of direction. The procedure for forming the two curves is as follows:

1. Click and drag to form the first node and its control handles.
2. Click and drag to form the second node and its control handles.

3. Hold Option or Alt. Click on the last node, and drag in the direction the new curve segment is to follow. The forward control handle disappears and a new handle s forms at an angle to the back control handle of the node.

The process is shown in Figure 4-13.

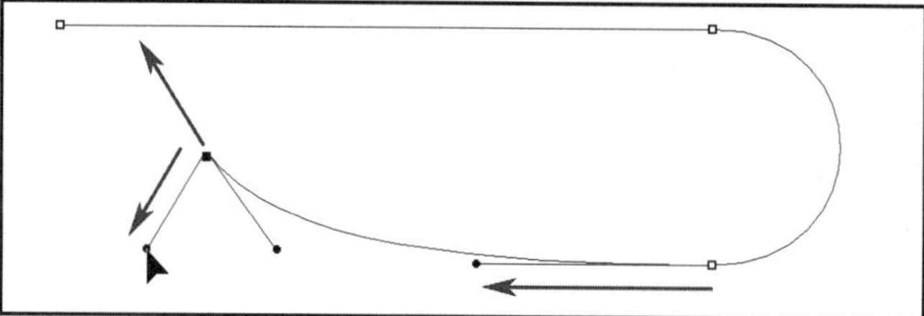

Figure 4-13: Click and drag to form control handles for the new node. Hold Option or Alt. Click on the last node and drag in a different direction, the direction in which you wish the new curve to move.

Analyzing Curved Shapes

As you begin to be familiar with the behavior of the Pen tool, you'll also become more adept at looking ahead to analyze the shapes around which you are placing a path. Figure 4-14 gives something of an idea how this works: small marks are placed around the perimeter of the shape which indicate where nodes will be placed. Please study the figure and notice how the segment of the perimeter within each pair of marks differs in shape or direction from the segments on each side. It will be important for you to begin to recognize the boundary points of each curve segment as you draw with the Pen tool. Your goal is to construct an accurate path which encloses the shape using as few points as possible.

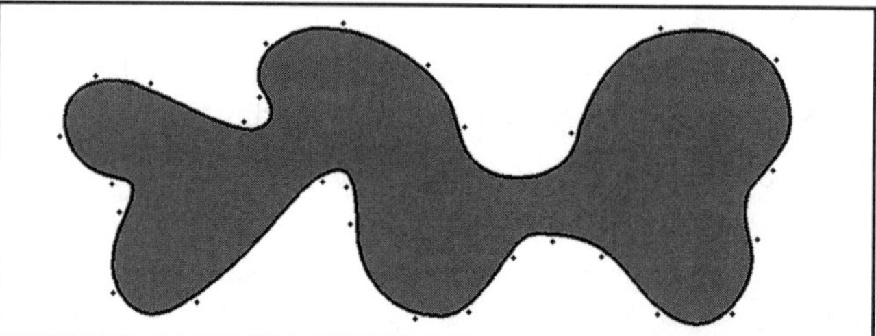

Figure 4-14: Study this curved shape to understand the curve segments which compose it. Each segment boundary (black mark) is where a node will be placed. Each curve segment is distinguished by a slight change in the shape of the object or by a change in direction of the enclosing path.

The Rule of Thirds

As you draw your path, look ahead to where the next node will be placed. The drag of the cursor which develops the forward control handle will be along the convex side of the curve in front of the node which you just placed. As you drag, you can make use of a simple trick for estimating how far you should drag the control handle for the next curve. This trick is called *the rule of thirds*. Mentally estimate the length of the next curve segment and drag until the control handle is one-third that distance. Release the mouse button. Move the cursor to the next node position, and follow the same procedure.

Figure 4-15 shows what the curve looks like when this trick has been used. Note that each control handle is about one-third the length of the curve between the nodes. Using this method, you'll be able to draw nearly any curve shape with reasonable accuracy.

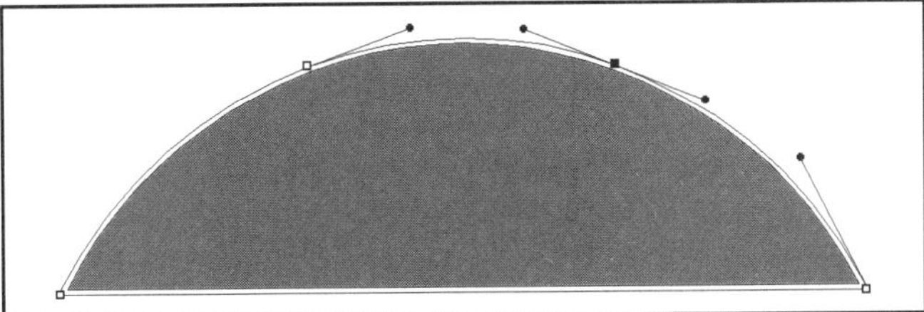

Figure 4-15: The control handles for the path show how dragging one-third the distance of the curve segment makes it easy to estimate how long the curve handles should be.

Editing Paths With the Pen Tools

After you have drawn your path, you may wish to change its shape. You may wish to modify a curve to make it conform more exactly to the enclosed shape, or you may wish to move a node into a different position. To make these changes, use the four tools which accompany the Pen tool in the Tools palette. The Pen tool and its helpers are shown in Figure 4-16. (To select the Pen tool from the keyboard, press p. Press the same character repeatedly to cycle through all five tools in the group.)

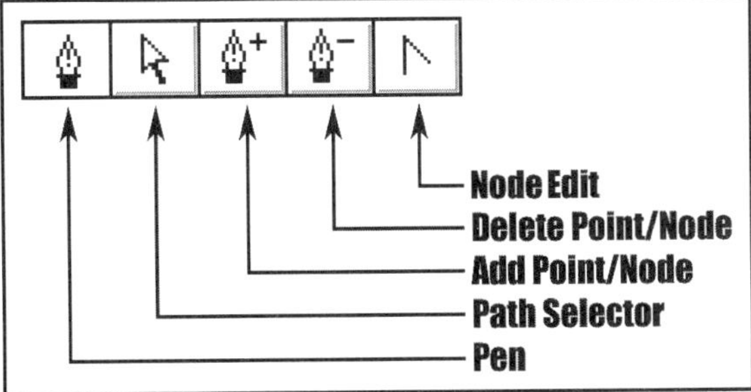

Figure 4-16: The Pen tool and its four accessories. Press p to choose the Pen. Press p repeatedly to cycle through the other tools. Note that Adobe refers to nodes as anchor points. This book uses the term node. *This avoids confusion between the terms* points *and* control points.

The Path Selector The arrow-shaped Path Selector tool allows you to work directly with paths drawn by the Pen tool. With this Cursor, click directly on a path segment to select it. You can drag the path to change its shape. When you move the path segment, the control handles change their angle and length. You can also change the segment by moving the control points. You can, if you wish, change their distance from the nodes at each end of the segment. You can also move the points into a different orientation with the node. Any move will change the shape of the curve segment. Experiment with how the curve shapes can be manipulated.

When you use the Path Selector cursor to click on a node, all of the other nodes on the path become visible. The selected node will show as a small, filled square (called an *active* node). The other nodes will show as small hollow squares (these nodes are *semi-active*). An active node can be dragged to a new position without changing the position of any of the semi-active nodes. Only the path segments running through the node are affected. You can make more than one node active by sweep-selecting with the arrow cursor, or you can hold the Shift key as you select the nodes one by one. To make all of the nodes on a path active, hold Option or Alt, and click anywhere on the path. When all of the nodes are active, the path can be moved around without altering its shape.

There are three important concepts you should be aware of when you select all or parts of a path:

- When you click on a path segment, the whole path seems to be selected, but only that segment is selected. If you use the Copy command and then Paste, you'll find that you paste only a copy of the segment on which you clicked. With a single segment selected, the Delete command eliminates only the segment. (It also makes every node which remains an active node: if you press Delete again, the entire path disappears.)
- When you click on a node, not only does the node become active, but you will have selected the path segments on each side of the node. If you use the Copy command and then Paste, you will find that you have pasted the node and both of the segments attached to it. The Delete command will eliminate the node and both segments.
- When you hold Option or Alt and click to select the entire path, you can Copy and Paste replicas of the whole path. With the whole path selected and Option or Alt pressed down, you can drag to duplicate the path. With all of the nodes selected, the Delete command will eliminate the whole path.

Add Node Tool Although it is best to make your path with the smallest number of nodes you can manage, you will find that sometimes you just cannot make a curve fit the contour of the shape you are enclosing. Use this tool—simply click on the path wherever you wish the new node to be—to give more flexibility in making the shape fit. Photoshop will decrease the length of the control handles coming from the nodes on each side of the new node.

Delete Node Tool When you have drawn a path and have decided that some of the nodes can be eliminated, use this tool to delete the extras. Locate the cursor over the node and click. The node will vanish. Photoshop will increase the length of the control handles coming from the nodes on each side of the deleted node in attempt to make the path keep its general shape. Photoshop's implementation of both the Delete Node and Add Node tools is far superior to the equivalent tools in Adobe Illustrator.

Node Edit Tool Using the Node Edit tool, a node can be converted into any of the four types shown in Figures 4-4, 4-5, 4-6, and 4-7. With this tool selected, click once on any node. The control handles instantly retract into the node (Figure 4-5). Click and drag on any node to draw smooth-node control handles out of the node (Figure 4-4). Click and drag either of the control points of a smooth node to convert the node into a corner node with two curves that change direction at the node (Figure 4-7). Use the Selector after drawing control handles from a node to push one of the control points back into the node (Figure 4-6).

Using the Tools With Modifier Keys

You can, if you wish, simply choose one of the four Path Edit tools directly from the Toolbox. You can also press p repeatedly until the tool you wish to use appears on the Toolbox. Both the Macintosh and Windows versions of Photoshop furnish you with keyboard modifiers which can make your path editing much more convenient. The following is a list of keyboard modifiers for each.

Keyboard Tips for Macintosh

- With the Pen tool selected:
    a) Press Command to temporarily change to the Path Selector tool.
    b) Press Ctrl to temporarily change to the Add Node or the Delete Node tools. If you place the cursor over an existing node, you'll see the Delete Node tool appear. If you place the cursor over the path where there is no node, you'll see the Add Node cursor appear.
    c) Press Ctrl+Option to temporarily change to the Node Edit tool.
    d) Press Command+Option and click on the path to select all nodes.
- With the Path Selector tool chosen:
    a) Command+Option switches to the Add Node or the Delete Node tools (the tools are context sensitive as described above).
    b) Hold the Option key and click on the path to select all nodes.
    c) The Ctrl key switches to the Node Edit tool.

- With the Add Node or Delete Node tools selected:
  - a) Hold the Command key to switch to the Path Selector tool.
  - b) Hold Ctrl+Option to access the Node Edit tool.
  - c) Press Command+Option and click on the path to select all nodes.
- With the Node Edit tool selected:
  - a) The Command key switches to the Path Selector tool.
  - b) The Option key switches to the Add Node or the Delete Node tools.
  - c) Press Command+Option and click on the path to select all nodes.

Keyboard Tips for Windows

- With the Pen tool chosen:
  - a) Press Ctrl to temporarily change to the Path Selector tool.
  - b) Hold Ctrl+Alt and click on the path to select all nodes.
- With the Path Selector tool chosen:
  - a) Press the Ctrl key. The cursor will change to the Node Edit tool whenever it passes over a node.
  - b) Hold the Alt key and click on the path to select all points.
  - c) Press Ctrl+Alt. The cursor will change to the Add Node tool when it is over the path, and to the Delete Node tool when it is over a node.
- With the Add Node tool selected:
  - a) Press Ctrl to temporarily change to the Path Selector tool.
  - b) Hold the Alt key. The cursor will change to the Delete Node tool if it passes over a node. Otherwise, click on the path to select all nodes.
- With the Delete Node tool selected:
  - a) Press Ctrl to temporarily change to the Path Selector tool.
  - b) Hold the Alt key. The cursor will change to the Add Node tool if it passes over the path. Otherwise, click on a node to select all nodes.
- With the Node Edit tool selected:
  - a) Press Ctrl to temporarily switch to the Path Selector tool.
  - b) Press Alt. The cursor will change to the Add Node tool when it is over the path, and to the Delete Node tool when it is over a node.
  - c) Press Ctrl+Alt and click on the path to select all nodes.

Although there may seem to be too many combinations of keys to memorize, you'll find that you can learn to use the modifiers while you work. While you are working, do this:

- On the Macintosh, press one or more of the modifier keys. You'll see the cursor instantly change.
- If you work in Windows and have any tool selected, the small information bar at the bottom of Photoshop's environment window will tell you which keys can be used for other options as well as what the tool will do whenever you push down on one or more of the modifier keys.

Eventually the modifier key combinations will become second nature to you. Learning to use the modifiers is worthwhile if you intend to be proficient with the Pen tool and with editing paths.

Note that a set of six small files has been included on the Companion CD-ROM to help you become proficient at drawing paths. The files, located in the Chapter 4 Practice Files folder, are titled PATH1.PSD, PATH2.PSD, and so on. Each of the files is intended to give you the opportunity to learn one or more path techniques. (The six shapes are shown in Figure 4-17.) We recommend that you try outlining these shapes with the Pen tool before attempting any large-scale work on a picture image.

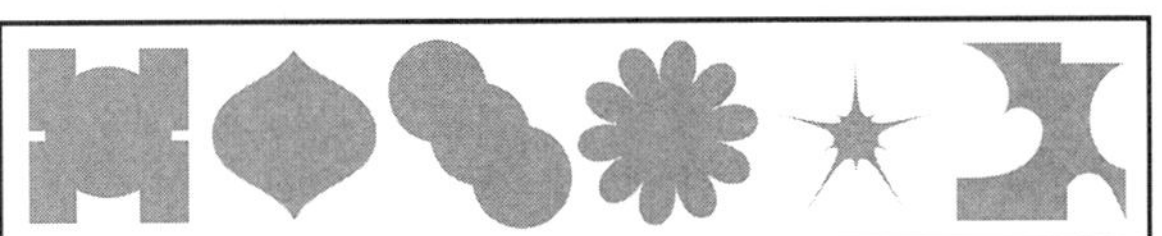

Figure 4-17: These six shapes are found in the Chapter 4 Practice Files folder on the Companion CD-ROM. They are intended to help you practice using the Pen tool.

The Paths Palette

The Pen tool and path-edit tools are used in conjunction with the Paths palette (expanded view shown in Figure 4-18). The palette allows you to save paths in named sets and to apply special effects to the paths.

The main window of this palette shows a list of paths which have been saved, as well as paths which are being drawn but which have not yet been saved. These in-progress paths are called *work paths*. Work paths are always shown in italic on the list to indicate their temporary status.

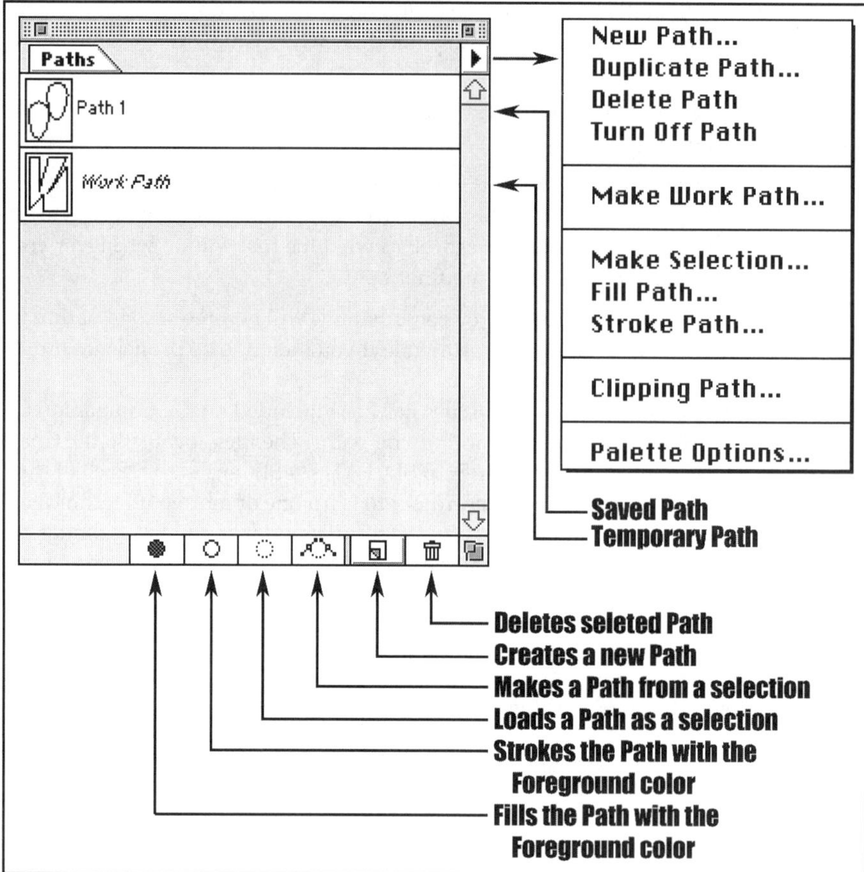

Figure 4-18: The Paths palette with its menu and button icons.

The Paths Palette Sidebar Menu

The feature set connected with drawn paths is accessed from the side-bar menu (click and hold on the small triangle shape at the upper right-hand corner of the palette). Six of the menu commands have duplicate functions which can be accessed by clicking on one of the small icons at the bottom of the palette. If you select an item from the menu, a dialog box will appear with choices for the operation. Once those choices have been made, clicking on the small button at the bottom of the palette will apply the same choices as though they were defaults. The buttons continue to operate in this way until you change the specifications within the menu-summoned dialog box.

New Path The New Path option does not draw a path for you but creates an item on the list which, when selected, stores any drawn paths. When you choose the command from the menu, the dialog box in Figure 4-19 appears. Photoshop automatically numbers the paths as they are created. You may wish to give the paths more descriptive names, but there is no requirement that you do so. The button second from right at the bottom of the Paths palette will also create a new path. When you use the button, the dialog box does not appear and the path is automatically named.

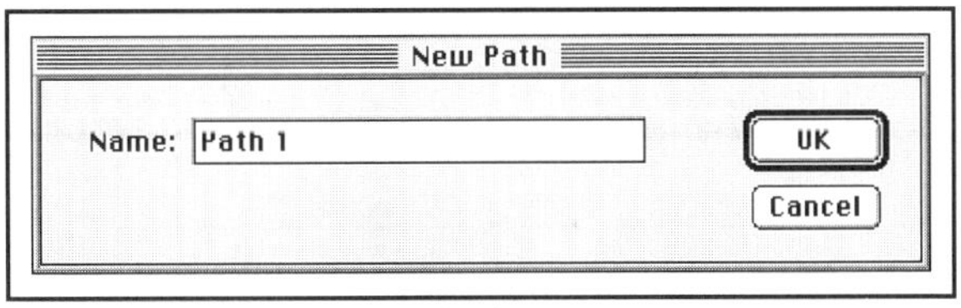

Figure 4-19: The New Path dialog box.

If you wish to add the path you draw to those already a part of any named path on the list of saved paths, click on the path thumbnail on the palette. If none of the items on the list are selected when you begin to draw a path, Photoshop creates a temporary path called a *work path*. When you save the document, the work path will also be saved. However, the work path cannot be used as a clipping path (paths which are exported as masks which are discussed later in this chapter). If you copy a named path and then paste without one of the list items selected, your pasted path will replace the work path. Because this path is somewhat temporary, it is usually a good policy to save the path as soon as you can.

Duplicate Path When you have drawn a path, you may find that you wish to make use of just a few of the segments. By using the Duplicate Path command (Figure 4-20), you are able to modify a copy of the first path without affecting the original. Figure 4-21 shows an example of a path which is a modification (lower) of the original (upper). A modification of this sort can be used for modifying the right-hand and lower edges of the shapes around which the path has been drawn.

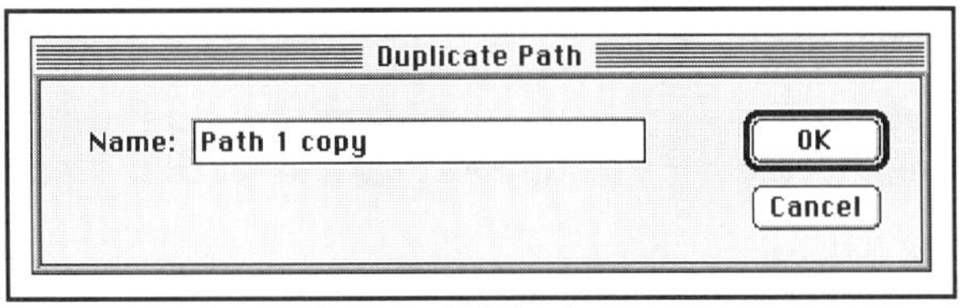

Figure 4-20: The Duplicate Path dialog box.

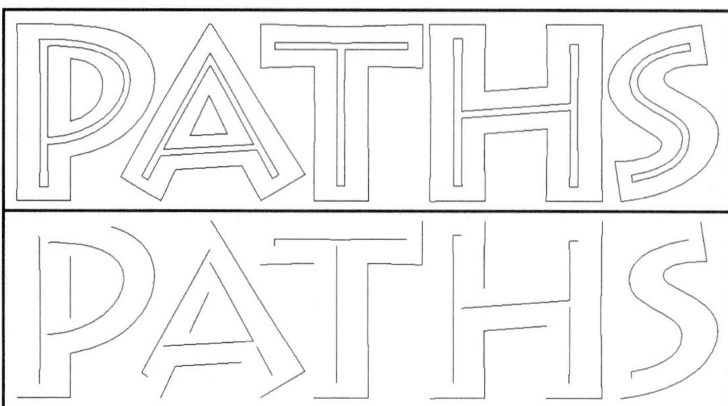

Figure 4-21: The original path (upper) has been duplicated (lower) so that some of the path segments can be deleted. The modified path could be used for a drop-shadow effect.

You can also duplicate paths without using the menu command. Hold Option or Alt and drag the path thumbnail onto the New Path icon at the bottom of the palette. The Duplicate Path dialog box will appear. You can then accept the default name or rename the new path. If you simply drag the thumbnail without holding Option or Alt, Photoshop instantly duplicates the path and names it Path X copy.

Duplicating paths can also be done in several other ways:

- Option click or Alt click to select the entire path. Copy the path. Choose the New Path command. While the new path is selected on the palette, Paste. Copy/Paste can also be used to transfer a path from one document to another. (When pasted into another document, the pasted path will be added to any saved path which has been selected from the thumbnail list. If no named path has been selected, the pasted path will be added as a work path.) Copy/Paste will also allow you to paste your Photoshop path into a document window in Adobe Illustrator, Adobe Dimension, or Adobe Streamline. Paths can also be pasted from each of those programs into Photoshop.
- When two document windows are open, you can select the path and simply drag it from one window to another. If a path is active in the target window, the path will be added to the active path.
- When two documents are open, click on the palette to select the path you wish to duplicate. Drag the thumbnail from the palette onto the target window. The path will be transferred to the other window and its name added to the list of paths.

Delete Path The Delete Path menu command eliminates a path which has been selected from the thumbnail list. Paths can also be eliminated by dragging them to the Trash icon at the bottom of the Paths palette. A quick way to delete paths is to select the path, hold Option or Alt, and click once on the small trash can icon at the bottom of the palette.

Turn Off Path When an item on the list of paths is selected, the path is visible in the document window. The Turn Off Path command deselects the list item so that no path is visible. You can also turn off the path by clicking in the empty area below the list of saved paths.

Make Work Path Any Photoshop selection can be converted to a path. This is sometimes a useful way to save a selection so that you can continue to edit it at some other time. Selections can also be saved as alpha channels but each alpha channel adds a significant amount to the size of the file. (Note: an alpha channel is a special document channel in which selections can be stored. Alpha channels will be discussed in Chapter 5, "Using Channels.") Paths preserve the selection without increasing the file size by more than a few bytes. However, this command is pretty much a blunt instrument: arriving at a satisfactory path requires some experimenting and sometimes a bit of luck. You'll see the reasons for this in the following discussion.

The Make Work Path command results in the dialog box shown in Figure 4-22.

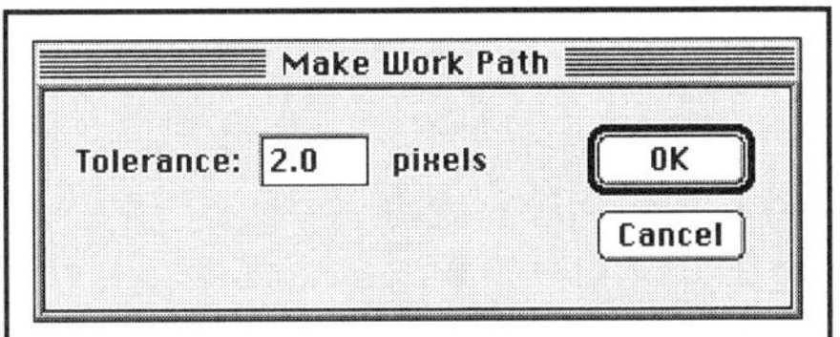

Figure 4-22: The Make Work Path dialog box.

The Tolerance setting governs the precision with which Photoshop will match the selection when it draws the path. Smaller tolerance values result in a more precise path. Too much precision, however, results in a path with far too many nodes. Such a path cannot be easily edited nor can it be used for a clipping path (discussed later in this chapter). There will always be some amount of compromise between the selection and the resulting path: the path can be made to lay diagonally across the tops of pixels while a selection must always follow the boundary of a group of pixels. The trick is to find a Tolerance value which gives a reasonable approximation of the selection while arriving at a path with the smallest number of points.

Figure 4-23 shows some of the possibilities. The selection to be used to make the path is in the upper left-hand corner. A tolerance setting of .5 was used for the path in the upper right-hand corner. As you can see, the number of points is so large that the path would be unusable. The two lower sections of the figure have paths drawn with tolerances of 1 and 2. The path using the setting of 2 is the smoothest and contains the fewest points.

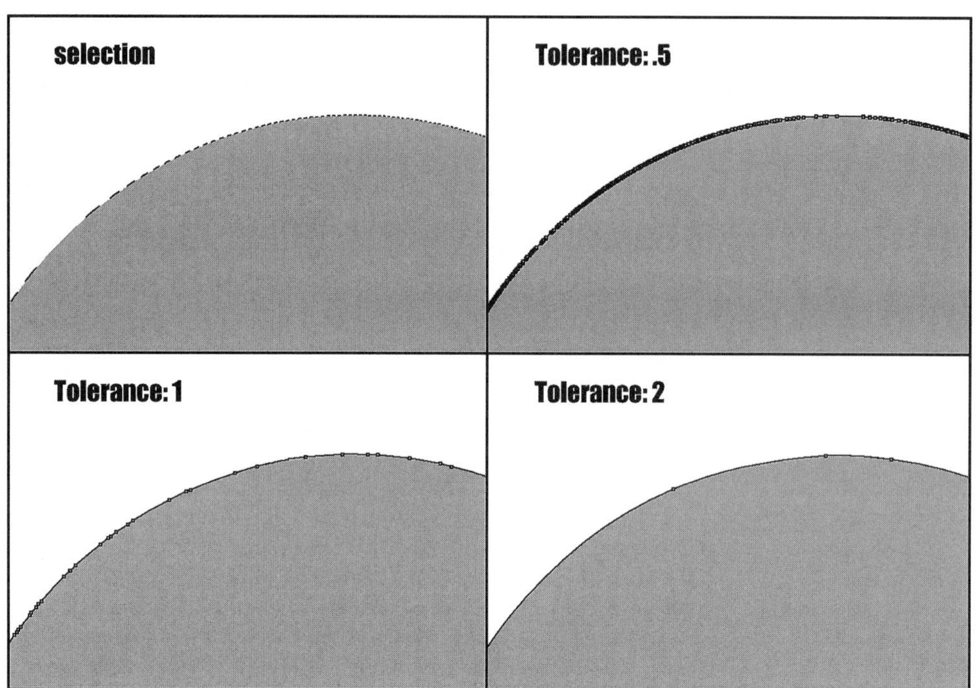

Figure 4-23: Three examples of paths generated from the selection in the upper left. The 0.5-tolerance path has too many points. Either of the others is more usable.

There is a drawback to using a higher tolerance: when Photoshop does not have to match the path with extreme precision, it often generates a path that may depart from the edges of the selection. You may need to manually modify the path—pushing and pulling on the curve segments, adding a node here and there—to make the path fit the shape. Manual intervention is your only choice if you cannot find a tolerance value which exactly suits the situation. Remember that you can always use the Undo command as you experiment with different settings.

As a practical matter, a selection generated from a path will always give you precision edges while a path generated from a selection may turn out to be more trouble than it is worth. As you experiment with this command—and as you become more proficient with the Pen tool—you may find that it is easier to simply draw the path rather than rely on this command to do the work for you.

TIP *The Make Work Path command can also be chosen by clicking on the small icon, third from right, at the bottom of the Paths palette.*

Make Selection The Make Selection command does exactly what the name suggests: it changes the path into a selection. When you choose the command from the menu, the dialog box shown in Figure 4-24 appears.

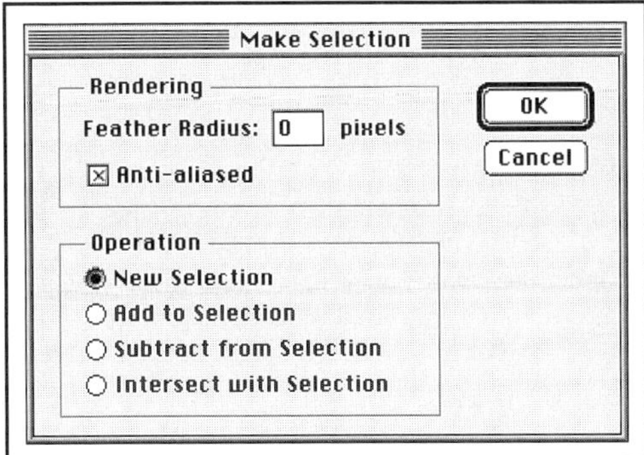

Figure 4-24: Options for creating a selection from a path.

At the top of this window, you can choose whether the selection is to be feathered and whether the edges should be anti-aliased. The options in the lower portion of the dialog box allow you to choose to make a simple selection based on a single path or to make a selection based on calculations of the areas enclosed by more than one path.

The illustration in Figure 4-25 shows the range of possibilities. At the top, sections *a* and *b*, are two paths. These two would have been saved as two separate items on the Paths palette. (Note that *b* contains two circles, but since both were saved as part of the same list item, they are referred to as the *b* path.) With path *a* selected, choose Make Selection, and click on the New Selection option. The gray area in section *c* shows the dimensions of the selection. While this selection is active, click on the *b* path's thumbnail on the palette. This time, choose the Add to Selection option. The second path's selection is added to that of the first giving the selection area shown in section *d*. Sections *e* and *f* are similar. With the first selection active, Subtract from Selection eliminates the area of the second path from the first selection (*e*). Intersect with Selection causes the selection only in the areas where the two paths overlap each other (*f*).

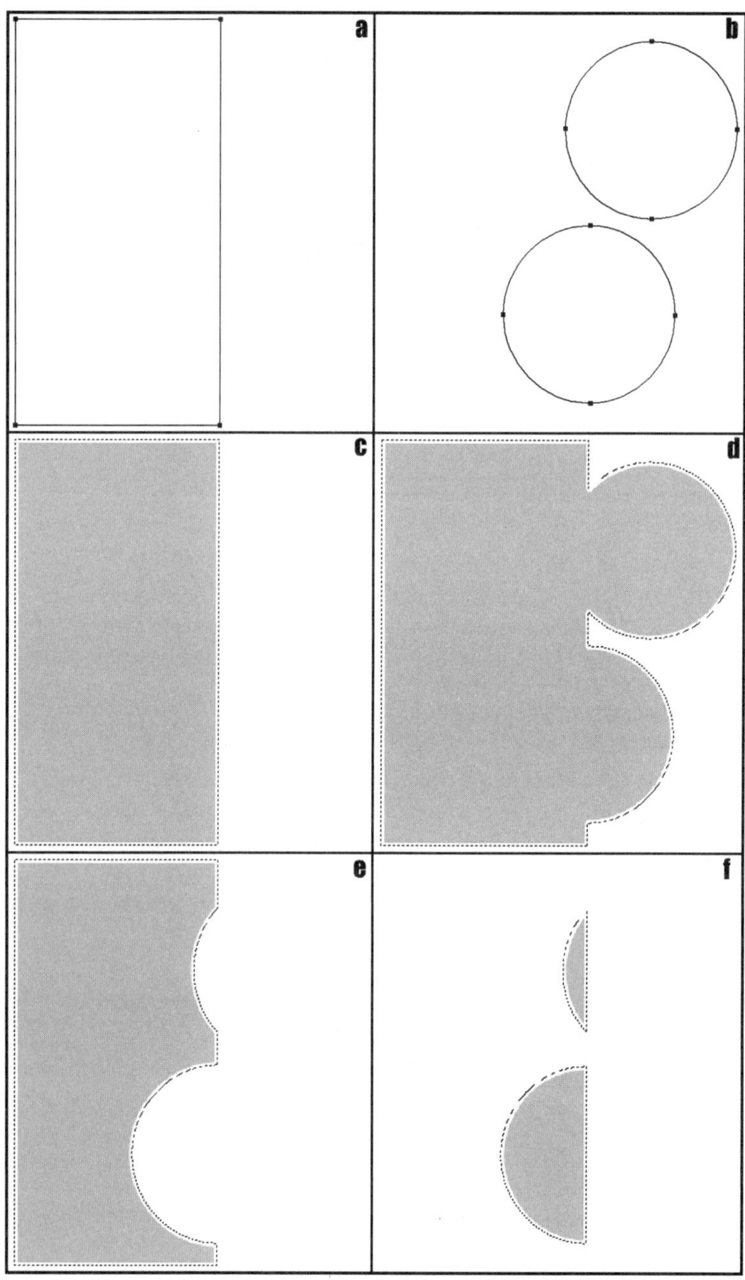

Figure 4-25: Two paths (a and b) can be made into simple selections (c), combined area selections (d), subtracted area selections (e), and common-area-only selections (f).

TIP *To change the path into a selection, you can also click on the small icon, third from left, at the bottom of the Paths palette. A faster alternative is to choose one of the selection tools and press the Enter key. With either of these methods, your selection will be made using the last-chosen Rendering options on the Make Selection dialog box. For example, if you have set a feather value or have turned off anti-aliasing, the selection made by pressing the Enter key will also be feathered or with no anti-aliasing.*

Note that that the menu command and the icon command convert the path to a selection but leave the path visible. Using the Enter key shortcut, the path becomes deselected leaving only the selection (the path is turned off). Several of the Stroke Path effects (discussed later in this chapter) are based upon a stroked path in place atop an active selection.

Fill Path The Fill Path Command (expanded dialog box shown in Figure 4-26) is nearly identical to the Edit | Fill command which can be applied to a selection. The only differences between the two are the rendering options shown at the bottom of the dialog box.

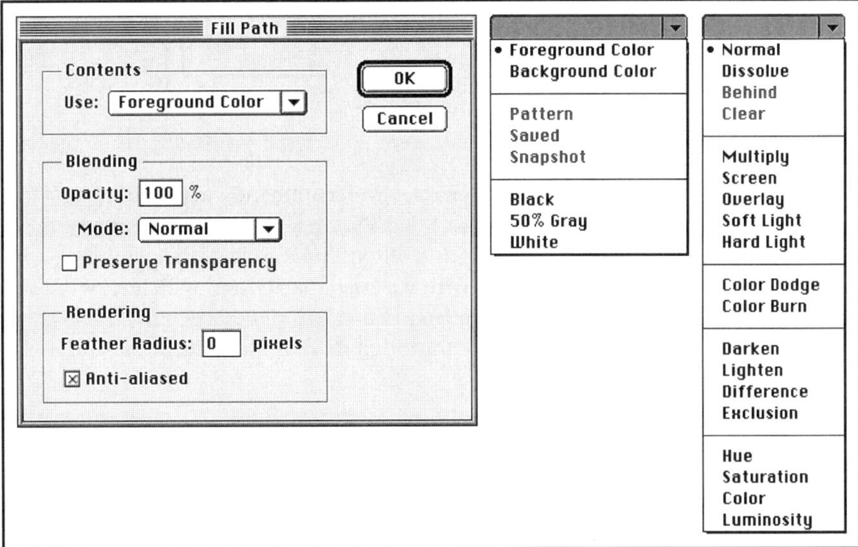

Figure 4-26: Expanded view of the Fill Path dialog box.

TIP *The path may also be filled by clicking on the small icon at the farthest right at the bottom of the Paths palette. The dialog box will not appear but the fill will be executed using the last-selected options of the Fill Path window. For example, if you set your fill to be 50% Opacity and Multiply mode, clicking on the icon fills in the same way until the options in the window are changed.*

Stroke Path In some ways, the Stroke Path command is the most interesting and useful of all the selections in the Paths palette menu. *Stroke,* as the term is applied to a path in a drawing program, means that width is added in equal amounts to each side of the path. (A path has no intrinsic width.) In the drawing program, stroke is rather in the nature of adding a descriptive property to the path—call it, if you will, an adjective. In Photoshop, Stroke is very much a verb since the path is acted upon by other tools which use it as a guide for laying down color, toning, focus, or cloning. The tools which can be used to stroke a path are shown in the expanded view of the Stroke Path dialog box in Figure 4-27.

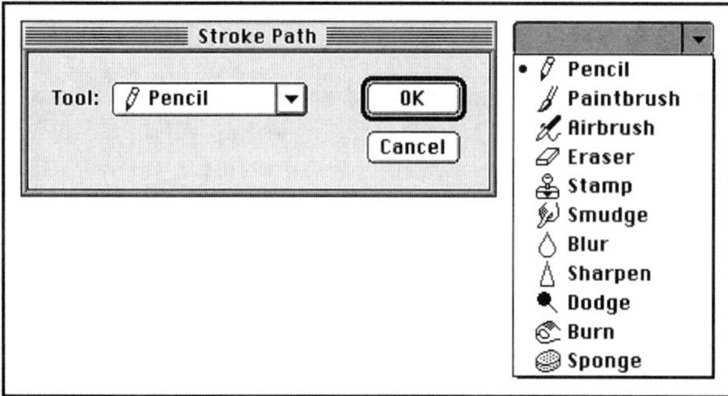

Figure 4-27: Expanded view of the Stroke Path dialog box.

The effects obtained by the Stroke Path command vary with the tool chosen for the stroke and with the brush tip selected for the tool. The variety of effects with just the paint tools, for example, is nearly without limit: each of the paint tools can lay down the stroke in varying widths, with varying opacity, and with any of the available Blend modes. Several of the special effects shown later in this chapter depend upon the Stroke Path command. A more thorough discussion of the Stroke Path will accompany the examples.

TIP *You can apply the stroke command to a path by clicking on the small icon, second from left, at the bottom of the Paths palette. The path will be stroked by the Pencil tool with the brush size last used for that tool. Alternately, you can choose one of the tools shown in Figure 4-27, select the brush you wish to use and the options for the tools, and then press the Enter key. This is usually a more convenient way to stroke the path than to use the palette menu.*

As noted above, the path and the selection which can be generated from the path can be visible at the same time. This allows the stroke to be applied to only one side of the path instead of both sides as is the usual case. By selecting the inverse, the same path can be stroked on two sides with two different tools.

Clipping Path A clipping path is a special kind of path which can be saved with an exported file to act as a mask. When the exported file—usually in Photoshop EPS or TIFF format—is imported into another program, the picture image is only visible within the boundaries of the mask. Clipping paths are discussed extensively in Chapter 10, "Calibration & Color Reproduction." Please consult this chapter for a complete discussion of Flatness settings, and for many tips which will contribute to your success when using clipping paths. The dialog box for designating a clipping path is shown in Figure 4-28.

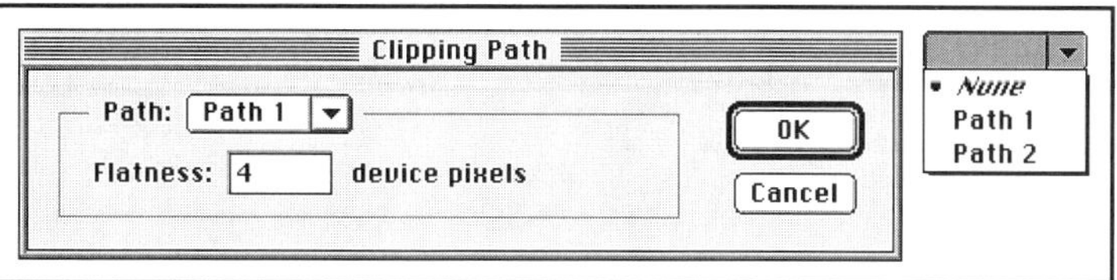

Figure 4-28: The Paths palette's Clipping Path dialog box.

Manipulating Paths

Although Photoshop provides a set of editing tools for paths, there are many features lacking which users of drawing programs such as Adobe Illustrator take for granted. For example, you might wish to rotate a path after it has been drawn. Or, you might wish to enlarge or reduce the path, or to flip it or distort it in some way. These are commonplace actions in a drawing program but there is no convenient way to do these things within Photoshop. You'll note the use of the word *convenient*. Every one of these manipulations of a path can be done in Photoshop. The method is not particularly intuitive but is readily understandable. The following will give you some idea of how the work can be accomplished.

Note that every one of these path manipulations begins with the same preliminary step: choose Image | Duplicate, and click OK. When you have duplicated the document, you will work briefly with it and then discard it.

Rotating a Drawn Path

After the path has been drawn and saved (Figure 4-29), duplicate the document. Work on the duplicate window. Use this procedure:

1. From the Image menu, choose Rotate Canvas | Arbitrary.
2. Enter the number of degrees of rotation and the direction. Click OK. The window looks as shown in Figure 4-30.
3. Click on the thumbnail of the path in the Paths palette. Hold Option or Alt and select the paths. Copy. Close the duplicate window.
4. Paste the paths into the original window (Figure 4-31).

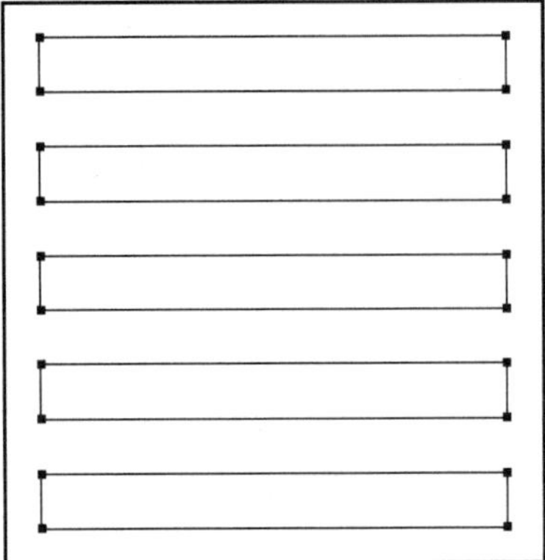

Figure 4-29: Draw the paths and save them. Duplicate the document.

Figure 4-30: Choose Image | Rotate Canvas | Arbitrary. Enter the amount and direction of rotation. Select the paths and copy them. Discard the duplicate window.

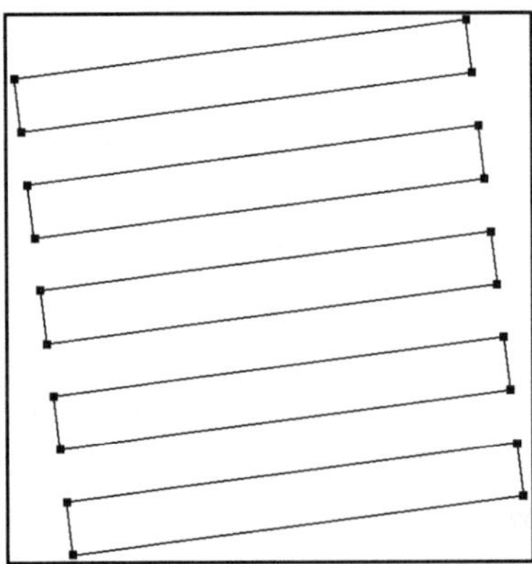

Figure 4-31: Paste the rotated paths into the original window.

Changing the Size of a Path, Proportional Distortion of a Path

This procedure is the same as for rotating the path:

1. After duplicating the window, choose Image | Image Size. Change the dimension of the window. Make it either smaller or larger. The path changes with the window.
2. Select the path, copy it, discard the duplicate window, and paste the paths into the original window.

If you wish to proportionally distort the path (make its width and height proportions different from the way it was drawn), uncheck the Maintain Proportions check box in the Image size window. For example, you might change a 5-inch square window to 2 X 5 inches. This will distort the path as well.

Flipping the Path

You can probably think your way through this one since it is nearly identical to the other two procedures. The difference is the command applied to the duplicate window: Image | Rotate Canvas | Flip Horizontal (or Flip Vertical).

Manipulating Paths Using Illustrator

Although Photoshop's Pen/Path Edit tools are adequate for some purposes, they lack many features which users of draw programs—such as Adobe Illustrator—have come to expect as a normal part of the feature set. Using Illustrator instead of Photoshop for many path drawing and editing tasks is much more comfortable than working with Photoshop's tools. Eventually the Illustrator paths are returned to Photoshop to be acted upon in ways that Illustrator cannot manage. The method has several aspects, any of which may serve you. You might wish to try using Illustrator and Photoshop together in some of the ways we'll describe. You may end up thinking—along with the authors—that the two programs work so easily with each other that they begin to seem as though they are simply two parts of one large graphics environment.

Moving Paths From Photoshop to Illustrator & Back Again One easy way to move a path from Photoshop to Illustrator is to use Photoshop's Path Export utility. Choose File | Export | Paths to Illustrator.

1. To show how this entire procedure works, we'll use as an example, a small file in which a path has been drawn and saved as path 1. The path is shown in Figure 4-32. Notice that the path is not precisely centered in the window. Part of this procedure will show you how to make sure that the paths can be accurately aligned without zooming in to 1,600 percent and trying to do the job by eye.

Figure 4-32: The Photoshop file contains a saved path shown here as an outline of the flower.

2. Select the Export option. The dialog box that appears is shown in Figure 4-33. The options for export are selected from the pop-up menu at the bottom of the window. The choices are to export all of the paths, any saved paths (if the document contains saved paths and a work path, the work path will appear as an item on the menu), or the document boundary. We'll explain the last option later in this discussion.

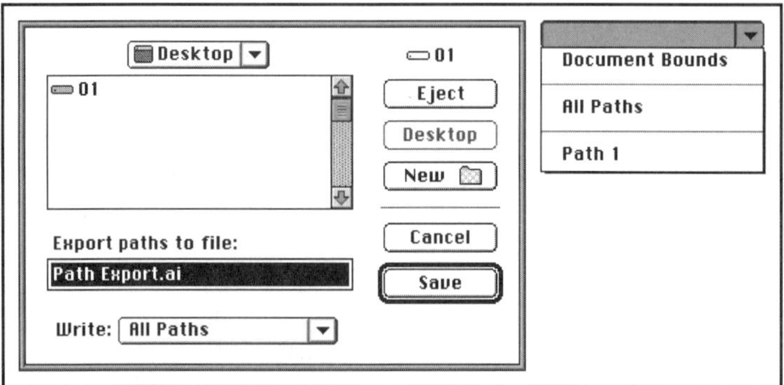

Figure 4-33: The File | Export | Paths to Illustrator dialog box with a view of the pop-up menu at the bottom of the window.

3. For this example, we'll assume that we wish to export the existing path. Photoshop helpfully assigns the name of the Photoshop document with the ai extension. If this title is acceptable, all you need to do is click the Save button. Photoshop saves the paths as an Illustrator file. After the file has been saved, leave the Photoshop document open, and switch to Illustrator.
4. From Illustrator's File menu, choose the Open command. Locate the Photoshop export file and click Open. A representation of the file which opens is shown in Figure 4-34. (Note: when you first see the file in Illustrator, you may be concerned that you cannot see the paths. The paths have no assigned fill or stroke and, if they are not selected, are not visible in Preview mode. To see the paths, select Artwork from Illustrator's View menu.) The path becomes visible as well as the set of crop marks. These crop marks are Photoshop's method of exporting the document's boundaries: if you had chosen only to export the boundaries, your file would contain only these crop marks.

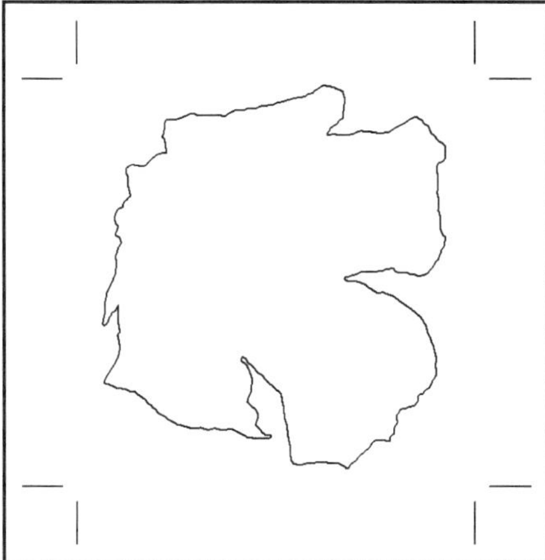

Figure 4-34: When the Photoshop path-export file is opened in Illustrator, you can see the paths and the crop marks which indicate the position of the paths within the original Photoshop document.

5. To make the crop marks more intelligible, go to Illustrator's Object menu and select Cropmarks | Release. The marks vanish and are replaced with a selected rectangle. This rectangle is the exact size of the original Photoshop document, and the paths are positioned in it precisely the way they were positioned in Photoshop. To avoid moving this rectangle while you manipulate the other paths, choose Arrange | Lock. The rectangle becomes deselected and you are not able to inadvertently move it until you choose Arrange | Unlock. The locked rectangle and the paths are shown in Figure 4-35.

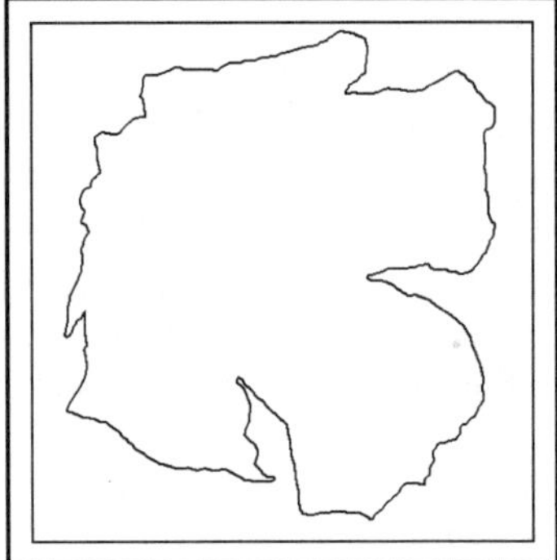

Figure 4-35: When the crop marks are released, you can see a rectangle which is the same size as the original Photoshop document.

6. Perform the manipulations on the paths. In Figure 4-36, two paths have been drawn inside and outside of the flower shape. Doing this kind of path generation would be virtually impossible in Photoshop but it is very simple in Illustrator (see Sidebar). These three paths now need to be taken back to the Photoshop document. First, unlock the boundary rectangle. Next, Select all of the paths *and* the boundary rectangle. Copy. Switch back to the Photoshop file and Paste. A small window appears asking if you wish to Paste as Pixels or to Paste as Paths. Choose the latter. Your paths will appear in the Photoshop window as shown in Figure 4-37.

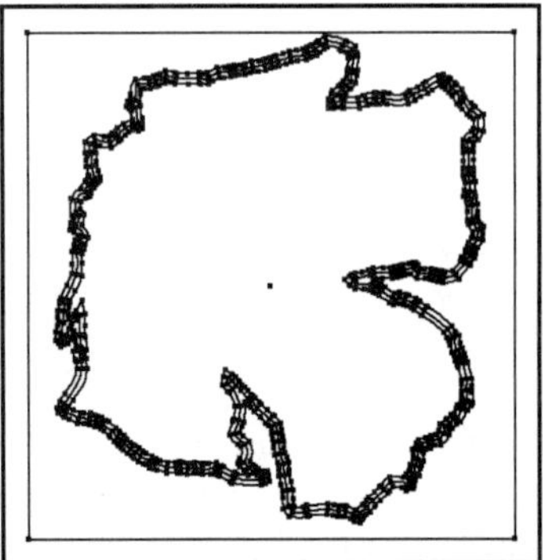

Figure 4-36: Work with the paths in Illustrator. When finished, unlock the bounding rectangle, and Select All. Copy; then switch back to Photoshop.

Figure 4-37: Paste the Illustrator paths into the Photoshop dialog box. They will be perfectly positioned because of the bounding rectangle.

7. You will have difficulty seeing the bounding rectangle because it is at the edge of the document window. Since Photoshop always attempts to center a pasted path, including this rectangle insures that your paths are perfectly positioned. Be sure to select the rectangle path at the edge of the window and delete it. You no longer need it and it will cause trouble later if you forget that it is there.

Making Parallel Paths in Illustrator

Making a set of paths which are parallel to each other (see Figure 4-37) is not impossible in Photoshop but it is a laborious and imperfect process. Since there are often uses for such paths, here is an easy method for generating them with Illustrator:

1. Select the path of which you wish to make larger and smaller copies similar to those shown in Figure 4-37. Copy it. Now, assign a stroke—the color is unimportant—to the path. Make the stroke weight the same as the distance you wish to have between the two new paths. For example, you might use a stroke weight of 25 points, which will give you 25 points between the two paths you will be generating.
2. From the Illustrator Filter menu, select Objects|Outline Path.
3. Your original path will disappear. The two new paths will look approximately correct, except that there may be many small loops inside the path boundaries. To eliminate most of these loops, choose Filter|Pathfinder|Unite.

4. When the Unite filter has executed, choose Arrange|Ungroup. Click on each of the outer paths to select them. As they are selected, choose Arrange|Hide. When both paths have disappeared, Select All, and press Delete. This deletes all the little odds and ends left behind by the Unite filter. From the Arrange menu, select Show All. Your paths will reappear. Check them to see if they need minor editing to rid them of any other Unite filter artifacts. Finally, from the Edit menu, choose Paste In Front. Your original path—copied before you assigned a weight to it—is pasted into its previous position. It will be exactly between the two paths you generated with the Illustrator filters.

Making Photoshop Paths in Illustrator Drawing Photoshop paths directly in Illustrator may sound peculiar, but it does solve the problem of what to do when you want to perform more sophisticated manipulations of paths than Photoshop allows. For example, the Pen tool in both programs is exactly the same: Illustrator's implementation of the Pen has the same set of modifier keys as Photoshop's. Illustrator, however, has an extra path tool—the Scissors tool—that allows you to cut a path, an operation that is nearly impossible in Photoshop. Besides this extra path tool, you can also make use of many of Illustrator's transformation tools as well as its powerful filters. You'll see other reasons for working in Illustrator later in this chapter.

The procedure for setting up the two programs to work together may look, at first glance, to be somewhat elaborate. However, as soon as you become accustomed to the wonderful things you can do with paths while you are in Illustrator, you'll probably decide that the setup is worth the effort. Besides, it's not that tricky. If you make extensive use of paths—and we think that you will when you see some of the wonderful effects that paths can help you to produce—you will probably find that you have an Illustrator file that is the twin of most of your Photoshop files.

Use this set of instructions as a guide for setting up your own Illustrator documents:

1. Open your Photoshop document. Choose File | Export | Paths to Illustrator. If you have paths which you would like to export, select them from the pop-up menu at the bottom of the dialog box. If the file contains no paths, export the Document Bounds. Now, save your Photoshop file in Photoshop EPS format in the same place you saved the path-export file. For your file's Preview, choose Macintosh JPEG if it is available. Otherwise, choose Tiff/8-bits. Leave everything else in the Save preference at the default settings.

2. Switch to Illustrator, and open the path-export file from Photoshop. The Photoshop document's boundary will be delineated by the crop marks as described above. If you exported only the boundary, your file will contain only these marks. Once the file is open, position the Illustrator's Layers and Align palettes so that you can see them easily (Figure 4-38).

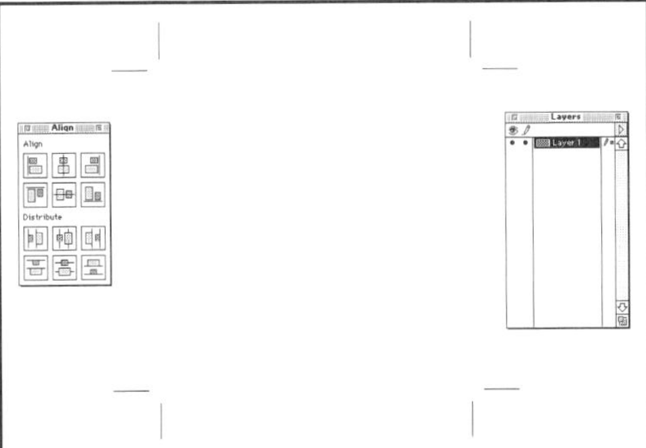

Figure 4-38: The exported Photoshop file opened into Illustrator. The Photoshop document's boundary crop marks comprise the entire file.

3. From the Objects menu, choose Cropmarks | Release. The trim marks are converted to a bounding rectangle as shown in Figure 4-39. Double-click Layer 1 on the Layers palette. In the text entry box at the top of the resulting window, change the layer's name to Boundary.

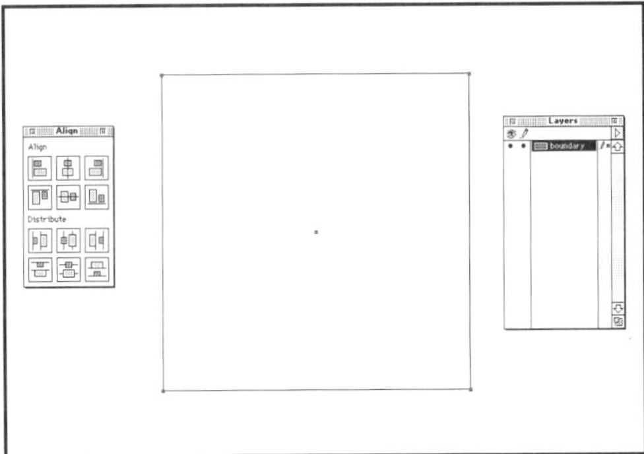

Figure 4-39: Release the crop marks, and change the name of the layer to Boundary.

4. From the File menu, choose Place. Locate the Photoshop EPS file and click Open. The image appears as a selected rectangular-shaped picture object (Figure 4-40).

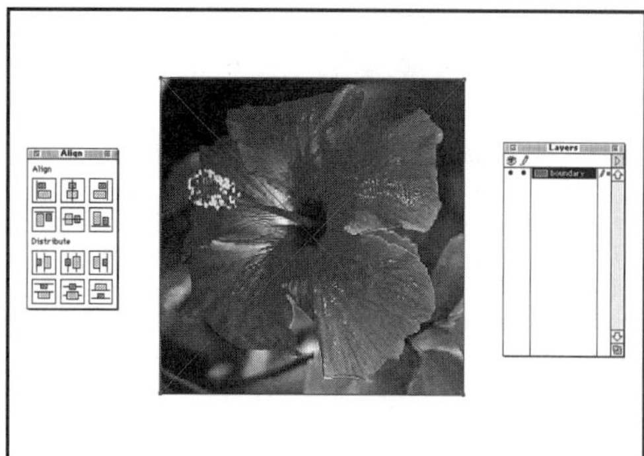

Figure 4-40: Use the Place command to import the Photoshop EPS file.

5. From the Layer palette's sidebar menu, choose New Layer. In the dialog box which opens (Figure 4-41), name the layer Photo. Click the small check box labeled Dim placed EPS. Click OK. The new layer appears above the boundary layer on the palette.

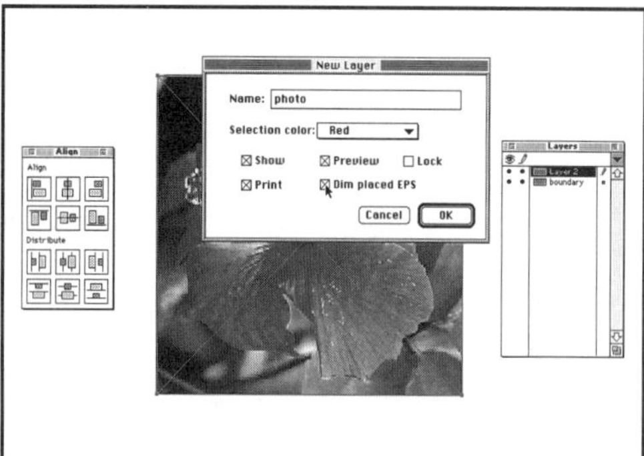

Figure 4-41: Create a new layer called Photo. Click on the Dim placed EPS check box.

6. With the placed photo still selected, you will see a small, colored square in the right-hand column of the Layers palette. The square is on the same line as the Boundary layer. Click and drag this square up to the Photo layer. This moves the photo onto the Photo layer. You can see the photo become lighter as Illustrator dims it (Figure 4-42). Now, click on the Photo layer and drag it down so that it is beneath the Boundary layer. Select All.

Figure 4-42: Move the photo onto its own layer (which dims it). Switch the stacking order of the layers.

7. With both objects selected, click on the center icons on the top two rows on the Align palette. This aligns the two more accurately than you could do manually (Figure 4-43). In the left-hand column of the Layers palette are two small rectangles for each layer. The right-hand symbol hides the layer, the other locks it. Click on the lock rectangle of each layer. When the rectangles disappear, the layers are locked. You will be unable to move or alter either of the layers until you click in the same place to make the rectangles visible.

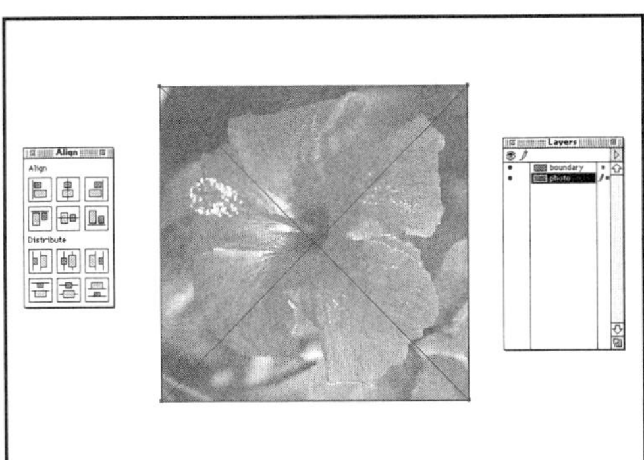

Figure 4-43: Use the Align palette to accurately line up the boundary rectangle and the photo. Lock both layers.

8. Create a new layer named Paths to Photoshop. This layer should be uppermost on the Layers palette. Construct your paths on this layer. You can, if you wish, make other layers to make different kinds of paths for different purposes (Figure 4-44).

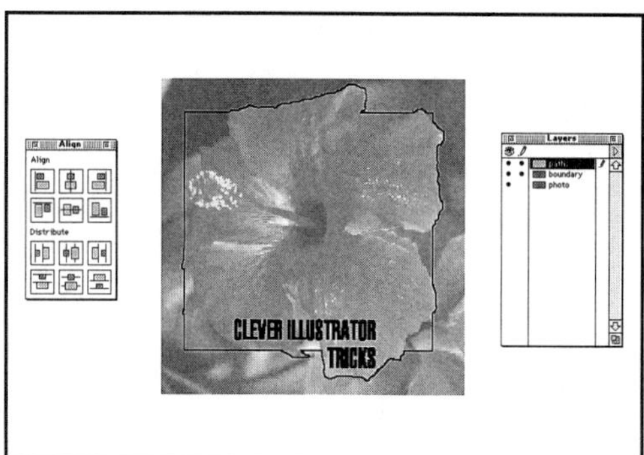

Figure 4-44: Create a new layer and draw your paths on this layer.

9. When you have drawn your paths, unlock the Boundary layer, and Select All. Copy. Switch to Photoshop and Paste. When the Paste dialog box in Photoshop appears, choose Paste as Paths.

Special Effects Using Strokes on Paths

Most of the spectacular effects that can be produced with paths are accomplished by means of the Stroke command. As you have seen, there are other operations involving paths, but only the stroke allows you to control the tools which paint—or which use Paintbrushes to apply their effects—in a very precise way. You may, for example, wish the paintbrush to move so that it produces an intricate, curved figure. However, the computer's mouse is not capable of such fine manipulation. Even the stylus of a pressure-sensitive pad is not easily made to move the brush in a precise way. With the Pen tool, you can take your time, draw the most intricately curved path you can imagine, select a brush, and instantly paint your curve without a flaw.

The effects that you'll see in the remainder of this chapter are not an exhaustive list of what can be done. There is, however, sufficient variety that you will probably think of many variations using the techniques involved. Above all, the processes you'll see are easy and fast. The paths are simple—most of them are drawn in Illustrator and then transferred to Photoshop—and applying the strokes is simply a matter of selecting the brush. After you've moved the paths into Photoshop, nearly every example you'll see can be done in under 5 minutes, and sometimes in fewer than 30 seconds! (One of the examples, the glass lettering, is slightly more time-consuming, but most of the work is involved with setting up the file so that you can alter the area inside the paths.)

CD-ROM

The Companion CD-ROM contains two files, DAVID01.PSD and DAVID02.PSD, which are used for the first eight examples. You may, if you wish, open the first of these and try out the path effects as they are discussed. You are not required to draw any paths since all of the paths you will need are already part of the file. You simply need to click on the Paths palette to select the needed set, and then apply the effects as directed.

The file DAVID01.PSD was prepared in Illustrator with the individual path components saved on separate layers in the same way as described above. The following set of instructions give an overview of the file's preparation:

1. The first path to be drawn was a trace of the contours of the statue. (Actually, your first path would be the photo boundary exported from Photoshop and already aligned with the image. You would draw the contours after making a new layer on the Layers palette.) These lines are shown in Figure 4-45. (Note that the Photoshop EPS file of the statue has been placed on an Illustrator layer and dimmed to make it easier to see the paths as they are drawn.)

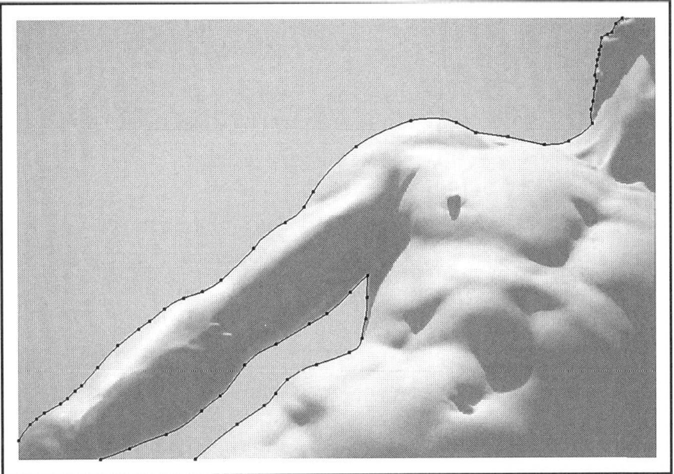

Figure 4-45: The Photoshop EPS file of the statue has been placed on an Illustrator layer and dimmed to make it easier to draw the figures contours.

2. After the contours have been drawn, save the Layer as statue contours, and then duplicate it. Rename the duplicate layer statue outline. Hold Option or Alt, and click with the Pen tool on the node at the end of the path which ends just above the lower left-hand corner. Release Option or Alt. Hold the shift key and click again exactly on the lower left-hand corner of the image. Hold Shift+Option or Shift+Alt and click on the node at the end of the path which ends just to the right of the lower left-hand corner. This procedure closes the path which surrounds the arm. Following the same procedure to enclose the rest of the statue: Option+click or Alt+click when starting or ending on a pre-existing node; hold down the Shift key to make the lines perfectly horizontal or vertical. To complete this path (shown in Figure 4-46) you simply click with the Pen tool—using one or two of the modifier keys—seven times.

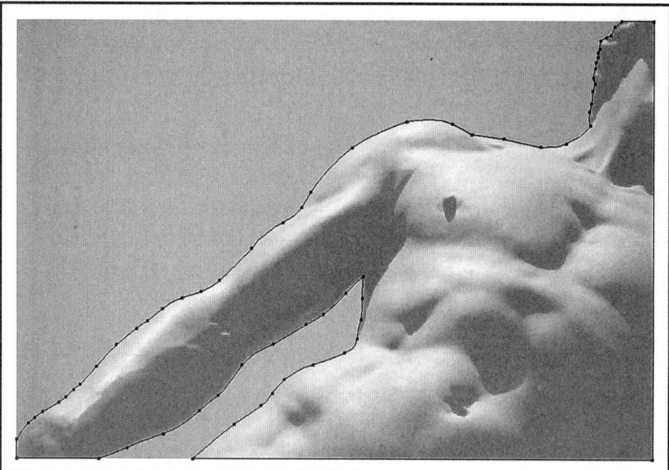

Figure 4-46: Connect the contour paths to completely enclose the statue.

3. Duplicate the first layer (statue contours) and rename the new layer background outline. Follow the same procedure to completely enclose the two parts of the image which are the background of the statue (Figure 4-47).

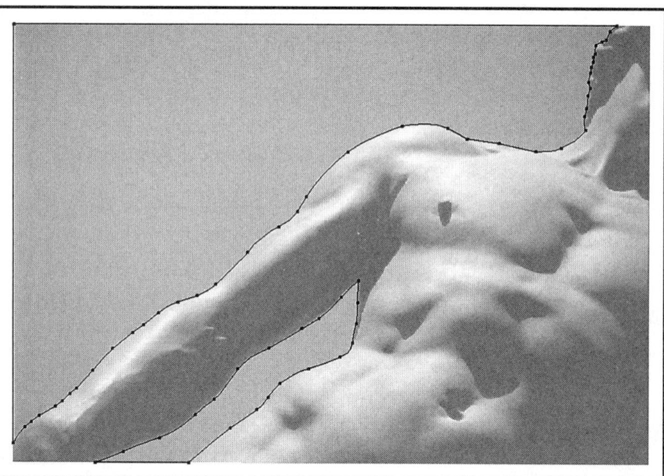

Figure 4-47: Duplicate the first layer, rename it, and connect the endpoints of the contours to enclose the two background areas.

TIP *In Illustrator, duplicating layers is slightly more involved than the same operation in Photoshop. First, click on the eye icons to hide all but the layer to be duplicated. Click on the remaining visible layer to select it. Select All, Copy. Choose New Layer from the sidebar menu. Name the layer. When the layer is in place on the palette, make sure that it is selected and then choose Edit | Paste In Front. All of the copied paths are pasted into the same position they had in the layer from which they were copied.*

4. Duplicate the first layer and rename the new duplicate contours offset. Select the Direct Select cursor (the white arrow-shaped cursor). Hold Option or Alt and click to select the upper contour line. Continue to hold Option or Alt and drag the line up and to the left. This operation copies the path and moves it to a new position. Release the mouse button and the modifier keys. Press Command+d or Ctrl+d to repeat the transformation. A new path appears above and to the left of the second. Continue typing the repeat command until the offsets are off the image. Select the Scissors tool. Click on each path at the place where it crosses the edge of the photo. Select the parts of the path outside the image and press Delete. Your paths will look approximately the same as those shown in Figure 4-48.

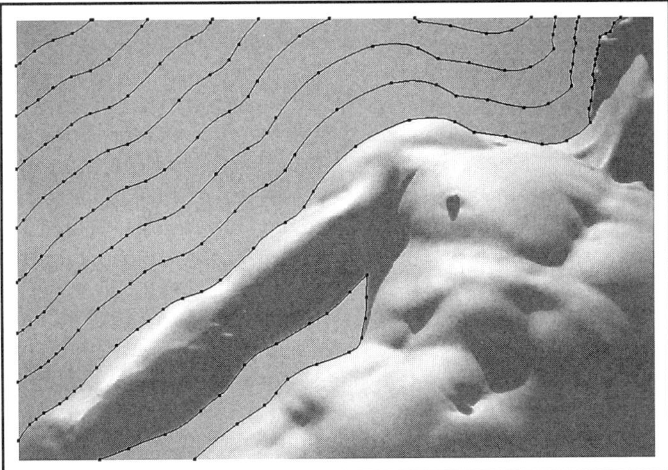

Figure 4-48: Move and copy the upper contour. Repeat the transformation until copies of the path move through the background area. Trim the parts of the path that extend past the edge of the photo.

5. Duplicate the original layer and rename the new duplicate *lettering*. Option+click or Alt+click the upper contour path to select it. Select Illustrator's Path Text tool and click about halfway along the length of the line. Enter your text. Select All. Change the font to a style you prefer, increase the size so that it is as large as you wish it to be, increase the baseline shift to move the text up and away from the

arm, and adjust the tracking if any of the letters appear to be too close together or too far apart. Choose the Select cursor. From the Type menu, select Create Outlines. Your letters are changed from editable type to path outlines (Figure 4-49).

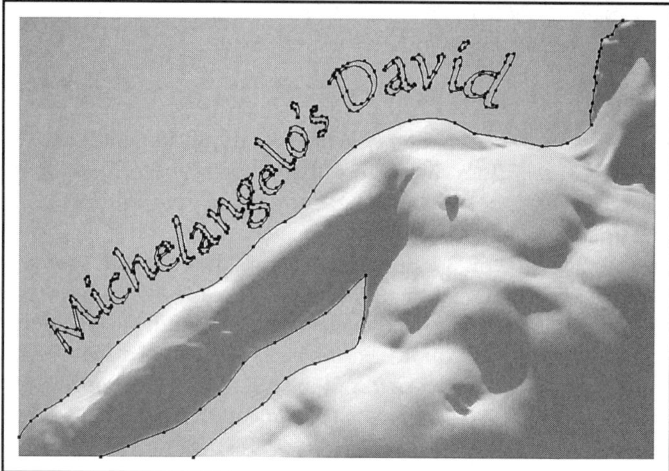

Figure 4-49: Use Illustrator's Path Text tool to place lettering along the arm's upper contour. After adjusting the size and the baseline shift, convert the type to outlines.

6. Duplicate the layer containing the complete outlines of the statue. Rename this new path background *horizontal lines.* Switch to the layer containing the rectangular boundary. With the Direct Select cursor, click on the top line of the rectangle and Copy. Switch back to the new layer and choose Edit | Paste In Front. The single horizontal line is pasted into the same position it had in the boundary rectangle. Option+click or Alt+click and drag the line downward to move and clone it. As you drag, add the Shift key so that the duplicate you are making is located exactly under the first. Repeat the transformation (Command+d or Ctrl+d) until your entire photo is filled with horizontal lines. Option+click or Alt+click the outline of the statue and choose Arrange | Bring to Front. With this path selected, choose Object | Apply Knife. Illustrator trims away all parts of the horizontal lines that cross the statue using the statue's outline as a guide for the knife tool (Figure 4-50).
7. Switch to the boundary rectangle layer. Select the rectangle and copy it. Lock and hide all layers. Make a new layer titled waving lines. Paste In Front to put a copy of the rectangle in the new layer. Fill the rectangle with the Illustrator pattern Waves-transparent. Double-click Illustrator's Scale tool. A Scale dialog box appears. In the top data entry field, enter 300%. At the bottom of the window, uncheck the Objects check box (which automatically checks the Pattern check box). Click OK.

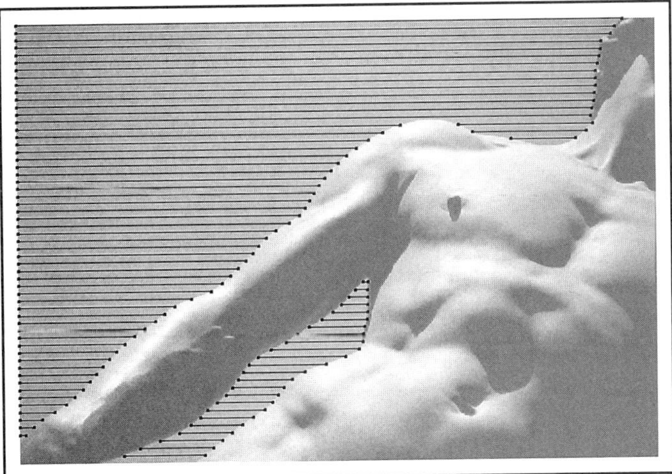

Figure 4-50: Fill the image with horizontal lines. Then, use the outline of the statue to trim away any lines that cross the statue. The lines which remain are in the background only.

From the Objects menu, choose Expand. While the expanded object is still selected, choose Arrange | Ungroup twice. Change to Artwork mode (View menu). Carefully select the bounding rectangle and Lock it (Arrange menu). Now, select each of the rectangular bounding boxes that define the pattern and delete them. Switch back to Preview mode (View menu). When you Select All, your window looks approximately the same as the image in Figure 4-51.

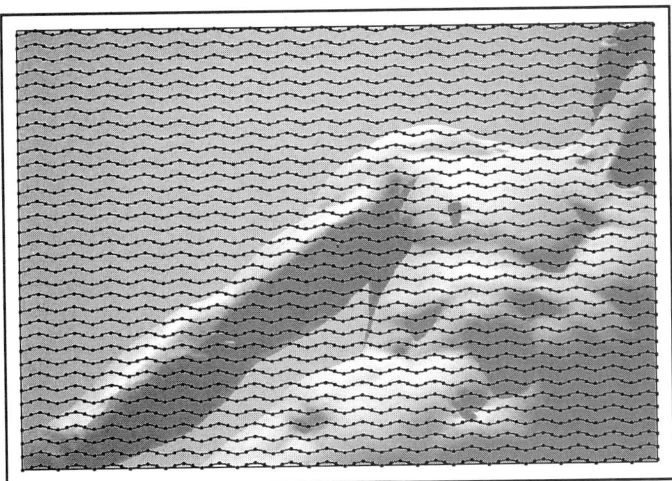

Figure 4-51: Fill a copy of the bounding rectangle with the waving lines pattern. Expand the pattern.

8. The pattern shown filling the window in Figure 4-52 is done in the same way as for the previous figure except that this pattern is not a part of your default Illustrator patterns. The pattern Random V's (in Windows, randomv) is a file from your Photoshop Patterns folder. It is an Illustrator document which can be used for many purposes. Simply locate the file and open it in Illustrator. When the file is open, switch to Artwork View. Click on the rectangular boundary, and choose Object | Mask | Release. From the Arrange menu, choose Send to Back. Select All. From the object menu, choose Pattern. A dialog box opens. Click on the New button. You will see the V's appear in the small preview window on the dialog box. Name the pattern and click OK. The pattern is now available when you fill a new copy of the bounding rectangle (which you'll have placed on a new layer titled all-over V pattern). Follow the same procedure as outlined above.

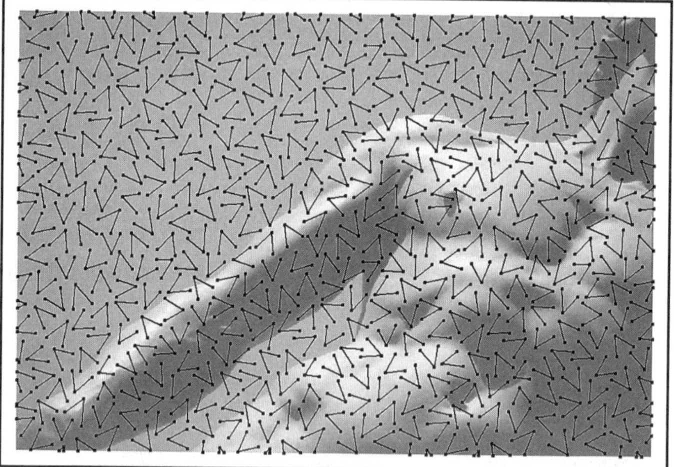

Figure 4-52: Fill another copy of the bounding rectangle with the Random V's pattern.

9. When you have finished, your Illustrator Layers palette should look something like that shown in Figure 4-53. You can, if you wish, add other layers with paths to this Illustrator document. When you have the paths the way you want them, paste a copy of the bounding rectangle in all of the layers (use the Paste in Front command) which do not have it. You'll need this rectangle to help you position the paths accurately when you paste them into Photoshop. Save the Illustrator document so that you can work with it later if you should need to.

Lock and Hide all but the top layer. Select All, Copy, switch to Photoshop. Create a new Path. Paste as Paths. Double-click the path on the palette and name it appropriately. Be sure to remember to delete the bounding rectangle on every layer except the one containing only the rectangle. Return to Illustrator. Lock and Hide all but the second layer. Select All, Copy, switch back to Photoshop, Paste. Follow this procedure for all of the Illustrator layers.

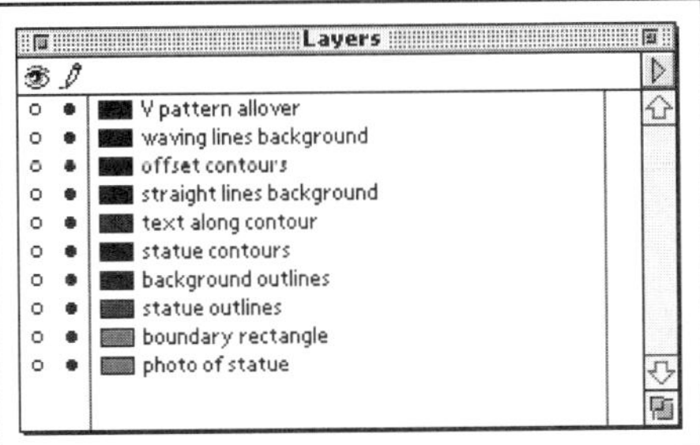

Figure 4-53: The Illustrator Layers palette with all of the path information saved in separate layers and ready to be pasted into Photoshop.

Using the New Paths on the Photo of the Statue

Photoshop's path manipulation capabilities have one feature that makes possible all of the special effects that you are about to see: there can be an active selection with a visible path at the same time. This means that you are able to apply a stroke effect to an entire image but the stroke appears only within the boundaries of the selection.

The general procedure in most of these examples is to first choose one of the paths—either the outline of the statue or the outline of the background—and then convert that path to a selection. Next, switch to a different path and apply the stroke. The unaltered image, undimmed now because you are seeing it in Photoshop, is shown in Figure 4-54. Please note that the example files are at 300 ppi and about 9 X 6 inches. The brush sizes specified in the instructions are based on what is needed for this file. If you work on a different size file and one with a different resolution, you need to scale your brushes to get the same effects.

Note that the full color versions of these examples can be seen in the color section of this book.

Glow Effect

One of the easiest effects to achieve with a path is the glowing edge shown in Figure 4-55. Begin by selecting the path which encloses the background and converting it to a selection. With the background selection active, switch to the path which outlines the statue.

Figure 4-54: The image, a detail of Michelangelo's David, to which the path effects will be applied.

Figure 4-55: This glow effect is one of the easiest special effects you can make with a stroked path.

Choose the Paintbrush tool with a 150-pixel brush end—Hardness of 0, Opacity 50%—with the Foreground color set to white. Press the Enter key. (Remember that with one of the Paint tools selected, pressing the Enter key is the same as choosing the Stroke Path command from the palette menu.)

That's it. Take a look at the effect by deselecting the path and by hiding the active selection (Command+h or Ctrl+h). Use the Undo command, and proceed to the next effect.

Split Edge Effect

The second stroke effect applies a stroke twice—with two different colors—along both sides of a path. In the example shown in Figure 4-56, the dark brush adds an inverse version of the glow effect on the outside of the statue and overlays a light stroke within the boundaries of the statue.

Change the background to a selection, and then switch to the statue contours path. Select the same brush—same size, hardness, and opacity—but with the Foreground color set to black. Press Enter. Change the brush color to white, choose Select | Inverse, press Enter.

Hide the selection and deselect the path to look at the final effect. When you are finished studying the stroke effect, use the File | Revert command, and move on to the next effect.

Figure 4-56: A dark stroke is applied outside the statue's boundaries and a light stroke within. Both are applied at 50% Opacity. The effect is rather similar to a massive Unsharp Mask filtering of the statue's outer edges since it places those edges into a high-contrast relationship.

Strokes on the Offset Contours

Begin again with the outline of the background and change it to a selection. Switch to the path with the offset upper contours. With the Direct Select cursor, click on the path beneath the arm and the one outlining the upper part of the figure. Select the Airbrush. Set the mode to Normal, 100% pressure. Press Enter. Use the Select cursor and click on the second path away from the figure. Change to the Airbrush, make the pressure setting 80%, press Enter. Continue in this way: click on each path, decrease the Airbrush pressure by 10%, press Enter. The result is as shown in Figure 4-57.

Figure 4-57: Click on each path in turn, apply the Airbrush on each in turn, decreasing the Pressure setting as you move away from the figure.

Try this as a variation. First, set the Airbrush pressure to 50% and the mode to Difference; then select the 250-pixel brush. Hold Option or Alt—temporarily changing the cursor to the Eyedropper tool—and select a medium tone from the statue. Deselect all the paths but keep them still visible (the selection of the background area should still be active). Press Enter. You will get a different effect as the strokes change to a rich blue instead of the decreasing light tones.

Background Line Effect

Since this effect is applied only to the background, you first need to convert the background outline to a selection. Switch to the path containing the horizontal background lines. Choose the Direct Selector tool. Hold the Shift key and click on every other line.

Take care that you choose every other line in the area under the arm. (To help you, press Command+r or Ctrl+r to show the rulers. Then drag a guide from the rulers to give you a line on which you can sight.) Make a 22-pixel Paintbrush. Set the Hardness to 100%. Set the Paintbrush combination mode to Dissolve and the Opacity of the brush to 50%. Press d to set the Foreground/Background colors to their defaults. Press Enter.

Hold the Shift key and use the Selector cursor to click on the alternate lines. Switch back to the Paintbrush, change the Opacity to 30%, and press Enter. The results are shown in Figure 4-58.

Figure 4-58: Select every other line and stroke with a brush set to 50% Opacity. Select the alternate lines and stroke with the brush set to 30%.

Multiple Stroke Effects Using Three Different Tools

Although the image in Figure 4-59 looks more complicated than the previous examples, it is very easy to do. Begin with a selection of the background area and a Paintbrush stroke of the same horizontal lines (22-pixel brush, Normal mode, 50% Opacity, Foreground color black).

Leave the background selection active and switch to the path containing the small v shapes. Select the Smudge tool. Choose a 35-pixel brush point. Set the Pressure to 80%, and press Enter.

Choose Select | Inverse. Change to the Rubber Stamp tool, and select the Impressionist option. Make the Rubber Stamp mode Normal and the Opacity 100%. Choose a 45-pixel brush with a Hardness setting of 50%. Press Enter.

Figure 4-59: Three different strokes are applied. First, a small brush applies a stoke to the horizontal lines in the background. Next, a larger brush strokes the v-shaped paths in the background with the Smudge tool. Finally, the Rubber Stamp's Impressionist tool strokes the same v shapes in the statue.

Strokes on the Waving Lines

The net effect of the strokes in Figure 4-60 is to lighten the background and to darken the statue while preserving the continuity of the attractive waving lines.

Begin by making a selection from the outline of the statue. Switch to the path containing the waving lines. Set the Foreground color to black. Choose the Paintbrush tool with a 45-pixel brush point (Hardness of 50%). Make the Opacity 50% and the mode Multiply. Press Enter. Change the mode to Dissolve. Press Enter. Choose Select | Inverse. Change the Foreground color to white. Change the brush mode to Dissolve. Press Enter. Change the brush mode to Overlay and decrease the Opacity to 40%. Press Enter.

Variation Using the Waving Lines

This variation begins similarly to the previous example. Select the area of the statue and then switch to the waving lines path. Set the Foreground color to white. Choose a 50-pixel Paintbrush (Hardness of 50%). Set the Opacity to 50% and the mode to Difference. Press Enter.

Use the Selector cursor while holding Option or Alt to select all of the paths. Move the paths so that they are positioned between their previous positions. Choose Select | Inverse. Switch back to the Paintbrush. Change the mode to Screen. Press Enter.

Deselect All. Change to the paths containing the letters. Convert the letters paths to a selection. Return to the waving lines path. Change the Foreground color to black. Choose the Paintbrush tool again. Select a 45-pixel brush (Hardness of 100%). Set the mode to Dissolve and the opacity to 50%. Press Enter.

Figure 4-60: One brush is used to make this effect. Two strokes of black in the area of the statue and two strokes of white in the background area. The only changes in the strokes are the combination modes and the opacity of the application.

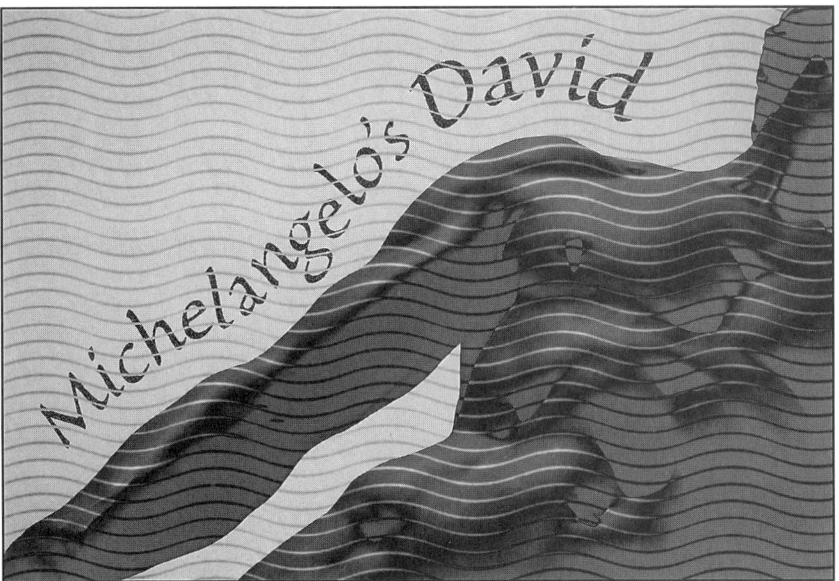

Figure 4-61: Three applications of the same brush—three different modes—on three different selections. White was the brush color for all of the strokes except for those which delineate the letters.

Strokes Used to Integrate Two Images

The example in Figure 4-62 is the most complex of those shown. However, the complex appearance is more apparent than real. You'll discover, as you work through this example, that the procedure is very simple. In fact, you have already done most of the operations on the previous examples. The only new element here is the addition of layers and layer masks. Follow these steps:

1. Open the files DAVID01.PSD (shown in Figure 4-63) and DAVID02.PSD (Figure 4-64). The two files are exactly the same size. Move the DAVID02 file onto a layer so that it is above the DAVID01 image. Choose the Move tool. Drag the second image onto the window of the first. Hold the Shift key as you drag to insure that the second image is exactly centered on the first.

Figure 4-62: Strokes on paths help to integrate the two-image composite.

Figure 4-63: One of two images to be merged in collage effect.

Figure 4-64: The second image, a highly stylized detail from the same statue, of the collage.

2. Select the path that outlines the background of the first image, and convert it to a selection. Click on the upper image's layer to select it and press Command+j or Ctrl+j to make the selection into an independent layer. Select the middle layer again, choose the same path, and make another selection. Press Delete. You have just divided the second image: the part which is above the statue is on the middle layer and the part which covers the background is on the upper layer.
3. Hide the middle layer. Your window should appear approximately as shown in Figure 4-65. From the Layer menu, choose Add Layer Mask | Reveal All. Set your Foreground color to black. Click on the path containing the horizontal lines in the background area. Choose a 22-pixel Paintbrush. Set the Mode to normal and the Opacity to 80%. Press Enter. The lines painted onto the Layer mask will cause parts of the layer to disappear. Thin lines of the backmost layer will show through the spaces (Figure 4-66).

Figure 4-65: After dividing the upper image into two parts—one which covers the statue and the other which covers the Background—hide the middle layer.

Figure 4-66: Stroke the horizontal lines with a small black Paintbrush on the layer mask. The stroked lines cause parts of the layer to become transparent so that the first image's background shows through the narrow lines.

4. Hide the top layer and make the middle layer visible. Change the mode of the middle layer to Overlay (Figure 4-67). Create a Layer Mask for this layer. Click on the Path containing the small v's. Choose a 45-pixel Paintbrush set to Normal mode and 80% Opacity. Press Enter. The v shapes will become nearly transparent and allow the statue to show through. Now, make both layers visible to view the composite (Figure 4-68).

Figure 4-67: Hide the top layer and set the middle layer to Overlay mode.

Figure 4-68: When the V pattern has been stroked on the layer mask, make all layers visible to see the composite of the images.

Other Examples of These Techniques

In an earlier chapter—Chapter 3, "Toolbox Techniques"—the discussions of the Smudge tool and the Impressionist variation of the Rubber Stamp tool showed the photos in Figures 4-69 and 4-70 as illustrations. In the first, the background has been smudged to make it more interesting. In the second, the Impressionist tool was used to paint the water lily image. (Appropriate, don't you think?) Both of the examples were painted with the Random V path pattern used in the examples shown above. Random V's is a very useful file!

Figure 4-69: The Smudge tool—originally shown in Chapter 3—was used to distort the background on the left into the blurred texture on the right.

Figure 4-70: The Impressionist variation of the Rubber Stamp tool—originally shown in Chapter 3—was used to change the photograph on the left into the painterly image on the right.

Neon Effect Using Paths

There are a number of ways to create the effect of glowing neon tubes. The example shown here has this to recommend it: it prints very well using process inks, and it is about as easy an effect as you could wish for. The real work is setting up the letter shapes as paths. For best results, try using a heavy typeface—this example is done with Adobe's Myriad Multiple Master instance 830 BL 700 SE. (If you are unfamiliar with Multiple Master fonts, you owe it to yourself to investigate them. They are amazing!) Be sure that you move the letters farther apart than you normally would since the glow effect extends into the spaces between the shapes.

Set up your basic image with a dark background and choose a bright color for the letters. If you are intending the neon letters for non-offset purposes, choose any rich, bright color. When the letters need to be reproduced on a press, you'll need to be a little more careful: process colors are not as vivid as colors chosen from the RGB spectrum. To achieve a rich effect, you will probably need to choose one of the process inks and use it alone, or to choose a bright color built with any two of the process inks. Your choices are somewhat limited but, as you can see from this example (shown in color in the color section of this book), the effect can be very successful. The color example in this book uses just two inks, black and cyan. The dark background color is composed of 100% cyan and 100% black. We've used this combination for a couple of reasons. First, using two inks insures that the background will be a very dense black. Second, since the letter shapes are done in cyan, adding the cyan to the background color gives the black a noticeably blue cast which enhances the neon letters and makes them more vibrant.

After setting up your letter shapes as paths—this example's letters were done in Illustrator and pasted into Photoshop—you will be applying a series of strokes using two colors. Set your Foreground/Background colors to be 100% cyan and white. You can, if you wish, follow along with this example using the same file as shown in the figures. Please open the file NEON.PSD in the Chapter 4 Practice Files folder on the Companion CD-ROM. Then, follow these steps:

1. Click on the Paths palette item to make the paths show up against the dark background (Figure 4-71).

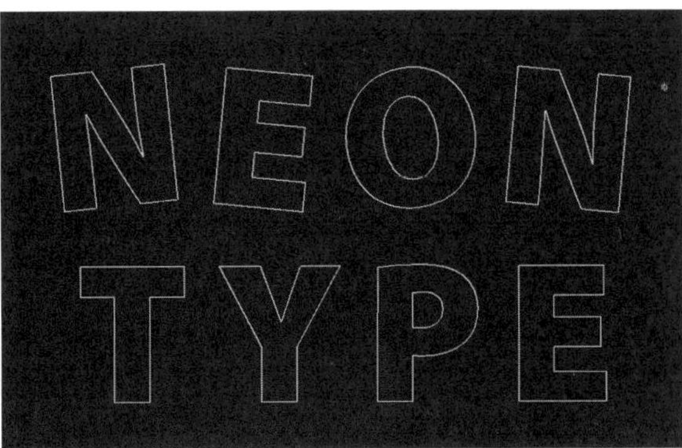

Figure 4-71: The letter-shaped paths against the dark background.

2. Select the Airbrush tool. Choose a 70-pixel brush point and set the Pressure to 20%. Press Enter (Figure 4-72).

Figure 4-72: Stroke the paths with a large Airbrush set to 20% Pressure.

3. Switch to the Paintbrush tool. Select a 50-pixel brush point, change the Opacity to 50%, and turn on Wet Edges. Press Enter (Figure 4-73).

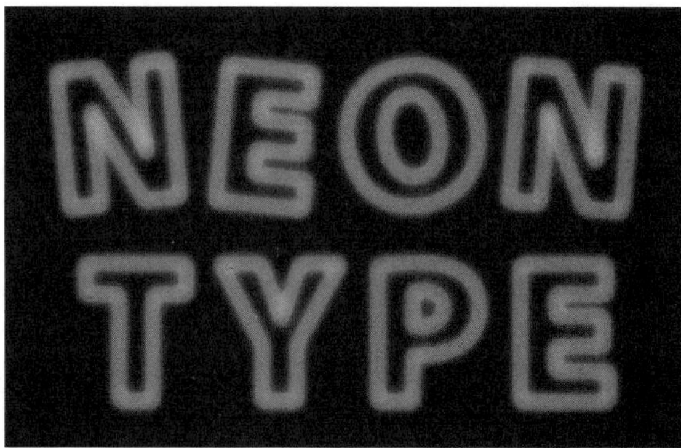

Figure 4-73: Stroke the paths with a smaller Paintbrush set to 50% Opacity with Wet Edges turned on.

4. Press x to flip the Foreground/Background colors (Foreground is now white). Select a 30-pixel brush point and set the Opacity to 40% (Wet Edges remain on). Press Enter (Figure 4-74).

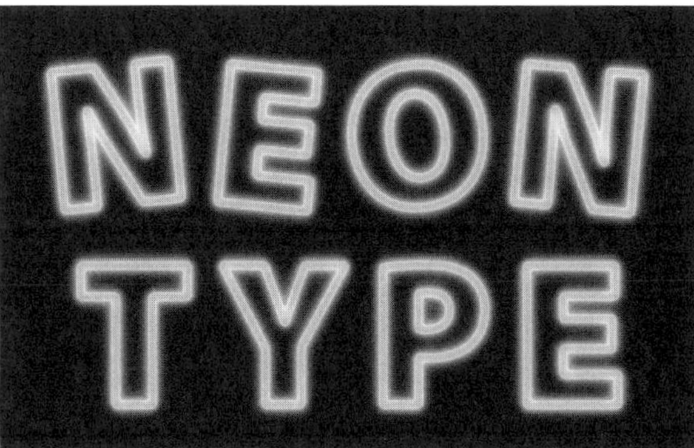

Figure 4-74: Stroke the paths with a smaller paint brush set to 40% white.

5. Choose Filter | Sharpen | Unsharp Mask. Make the settings 200%, Radius 2, and Threshold 5. Click OK (Figure 4-75).

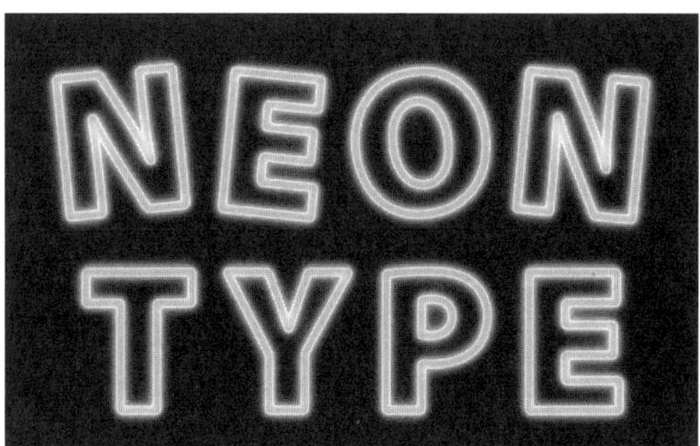

Figure 4-75: Use the Unsharp Mask filter to enhance the Wet Edges effect.

6. Flip the Foreground/Background colors (Foreground is now cyan). Choose an 18-pixel brush point. Set the Opacity to 70%, and turn off Wet Edges. Press Enter.
7. Change back to the Airbrush tool and the same 70-pixel brush end. Set the Pressure to 10%. Press Enter (Figure 4-76).

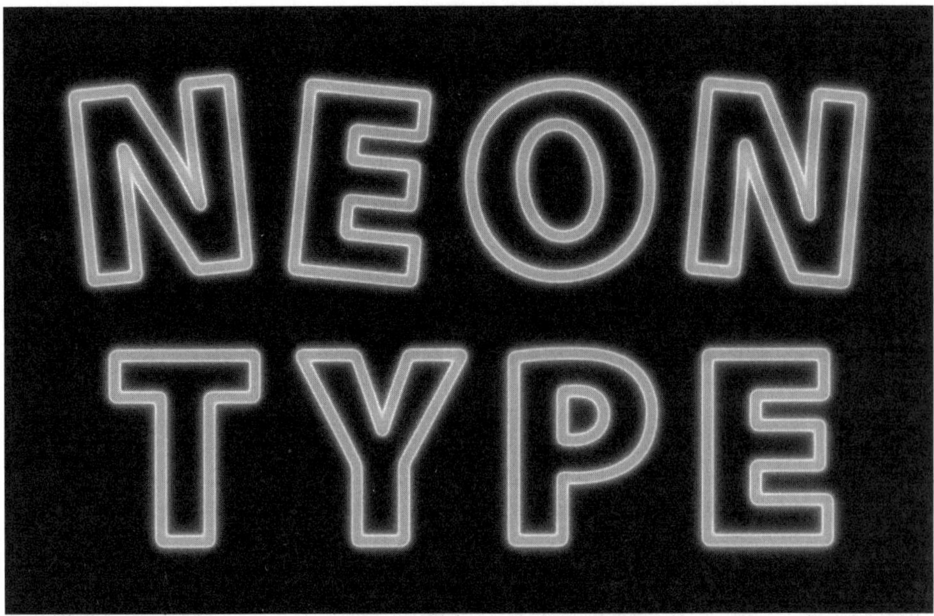

Figure 4-76: The final neon effect (seen in color in this book's color plate section).

As you can see, the whole effect is simply a matter of laying strokes upon strokes with a single application of the ubiquitous Unsharp Mask filter to heighten the Wet Edges effect. The sample file upon which you worked has a resolution of 300 ppi. The brush sizes were chosen to be appropriate to that resolution and to the width of the letters. When you apply this same effect to letter forms of your own choosing, remember to scale your brush choices so that they are appropriate for the resolution of your file and for the letters you intend to use.

Glass Letters Effect

The glass-like letter forms effect makes use of several techniques. Stroking the paths with the Smudge tool distorts the contents of the letters to imitate the apparent displacement of the shapes behind the letters as if they had lens-like properties. A faint drop shadow subtly enhances the contrast between the darker edges of the letters and the area around the letter shapes. Finally, an alpha channel with embossed letters allows you to selectively apply the levels controls to the smudged shapes in such a way that the embossed forms are mapped onto the letter shapes as they are lightened. The final effect—seen in color in the color plate section—is unusual, attractive, and successful.

The Chapter 4 Practice Files folder on the Companion CD-ROM contains the file TULIPS.PSD (shown in Figure 4-77). It is a copy of the example shown in the following set of figures. If you would like to follow along as the steps to achieving the glass letters are listed, please open that file. Notice that the numerical information given in these instructions is based on the resolution of the file—300 ppi—and on the scale of the paths which enclose the letters. Once you have followed this example and wish to try the technique on a photograph of your own choice, please remember to base your numerical information on the resolution and scale of your image.

Figure 4-77: The photograph to which will be added the glass-like letters.

1. Click on the New Channel icon at the bottom of the Channels palette. Fill this channel with white. Click on the thumbnail on the paths palette so that the paths surrounding the letters appear (Figure 4-78).

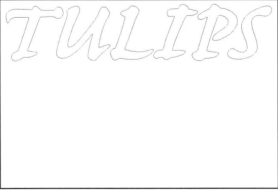

Figure 4-78: Fill an alpha channel with white and click on the path containing the letter shapes so that the paths are visible.

2. Set the Foreground color to black. Click on the Fill Path icon at the bottom of the Paths palette. Click outside the path item so that the paths are no longer visible (Figure 4-79).

Figure 4-79: Fill the paths with black and then hide the paths.

3. From the Filter menu, select Other | High Pass. Enter a value of 20 and click OK (Figure 4-80).

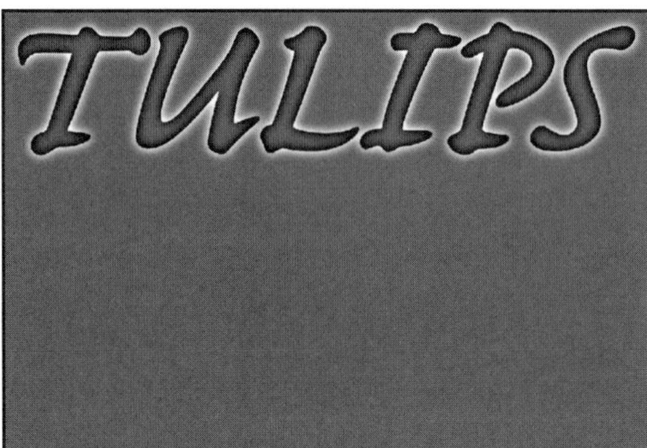

Figure 4-80: Run the High Pass filter on the channel. The setting is 20.

4. From the filter menu, choose Other | Find Edges (Figure 4-81).
5. From the Filter menu, choose Blur | Gaussian Blur. Enter a value of 3.5. Click OK (Figure 4-82).
6. Darken the letter shapes by opening the Levels controls (Command+l or Ctrl+l). Enter a value of .3 in the top center data entry field (Figure 4-83).

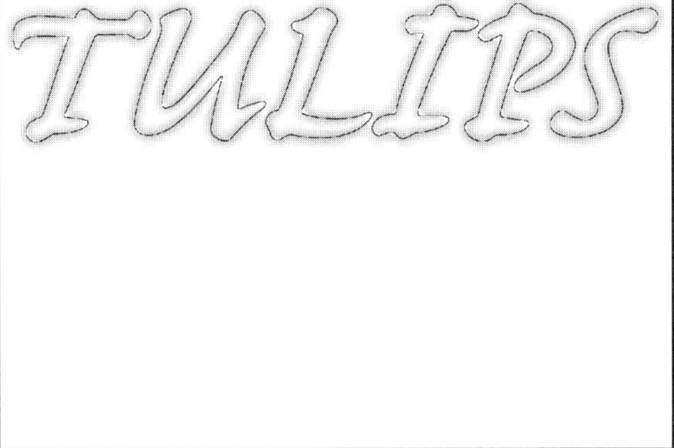

Figure 4-81: Apply the Find Edges filter.

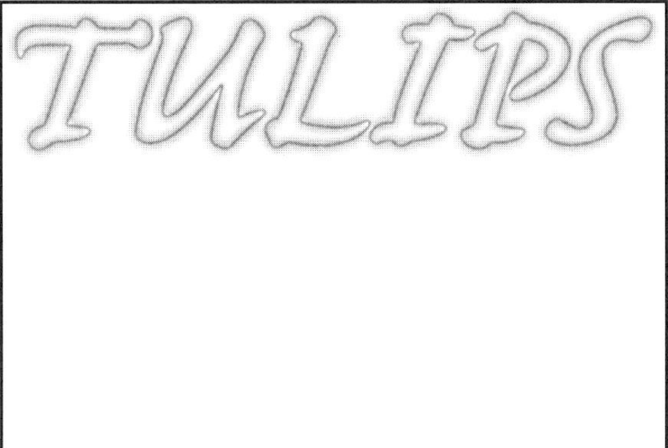

Figure 4-82: Apply the Gaussian Blur filter.

Figure 4-83: Use the Levels controls to darken the letter shapes.

7. From the Filter menu, choose Other | Emboss. Enter the values –45° (angle), 8 (height), and 200 (amount). Click OK (Figure 4-84).

Figure 4-84: Apply the emboss filter.

8. Make the paths visible again. Convert the paths to a selection; then hide the paths. From the Select menu, choose Inverse. Next, from the Select menu, choose Modify | Expand. Enter a value of 1, click OK. Fill the new selection with black (Figure 4-85)

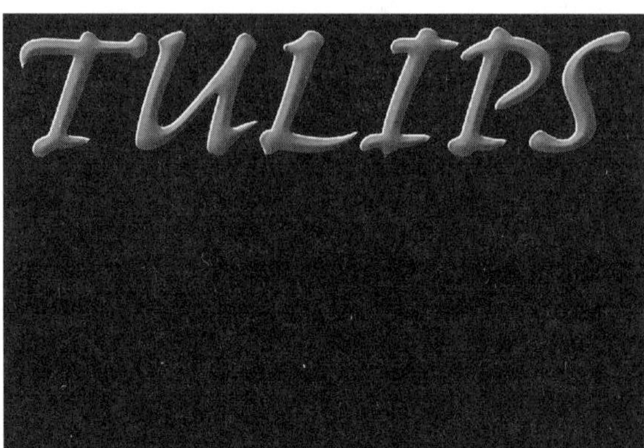

Figure 4-85: Fill the area around the letters with black.

9. Make the paths visible again. Convert the paths to a selection; then hide the paths. Apply the Gaussian Blur filter to the selection with a radius value of 8 (Figure 4-86).

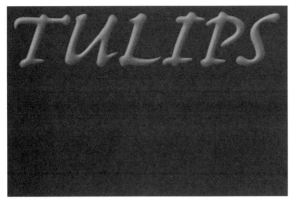

Figure 4-86: Apply the Gaussian Blur filter to the letters.

10. Increase the contrast on the embossed letters. Open the Levels controls (the letters selection is still active). Enter 2, 1.13, and 175 in the Input scale data entry fields. Click OK (Figure 4-87).

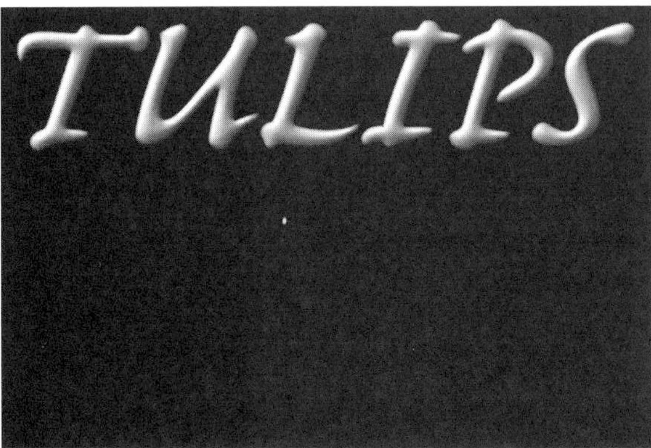

Figure 4-87: Use the Levels controls to increase the contrast in the letters.

11. Deselect the letters and return to the composite view of the flowers. Click on the path thumbnail to make the paths visible again. Convert the paths to a selection using the third-from-left icon at the bottom of the paths palette. Make sure the letter shapes are selected and the paths visible (Figure 4-88).

Figure 4-88: Return to the composite image and make the paths visible.

12. Select the Smudge tool. Set the Pressure to 50%. Choose a brush point of 75 pixels (0 Hardness). Press Enter (Figure 4-89). Note that applying the Smudge tool to a path is somewhat slow because it requires a lot of computation. Be patient: the effect is worth it!

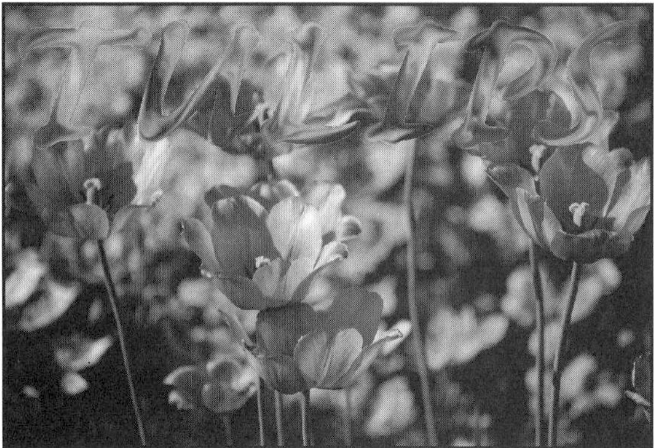

Figure 4-89: Stroke the insides of the paths with the Smudge tool and a large brush point.

13. Choose a 50-pixel brush point and change the Pressure to 80%. Press Enter (Figure 4-90).

Figure 4-90: Stroke the insides of the path with the Smudge tool using a smaller brush and a higher Pressure setting.

14. Load the alpha channel as a selection (Command+click or Ctrl+click on the #4 channel's thumbnail on the Channels palette). Open the Levels controls. Enter the values 0, 2.00, and 180 in the Input data entry fields (Figure 4-91). This procedure lightens the letters selectively. More lightness is applied where the alpha channel has light values, less where the alpha channel has dark values.

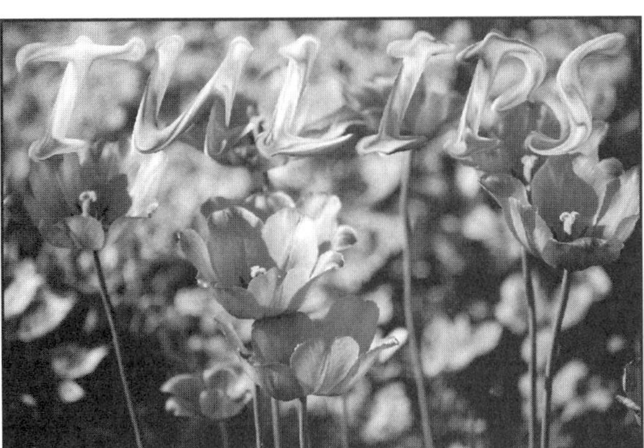

Figure 4-91: Lighten the letters selectively by applying the Levels controls while the alpha channel is active.

15. Deselect. Make the paths visible again, and convert them to a selection. Press Command+j or Ctrl+j to make the letters into a layer. Duplicate this layer. Hide the top layer and click on the second layer down to select it. Turn on Preserve Transparency and fill the letter shapes with a medium green sampled from the image. Turn off Preserve Transparency. Apply the Gaussian Blur Filter to the letters using a Radius value of 15. Change the mode of the layer to Multiply and set the Opacity of the layer to 50%. Select the Move tool. Press the Down arrow key eight times and the Right arrow eight times (Figure 4-92).

Figure 4-92: Make a duplicate of the letters and use them to make a drop shadow.

16. Make the top layer visible and selected. Choose Filter | Sharpen | Unsharp Mask. Enter settings of 300% (amount), 3 (radius), and 0 (thresholds). Flatten the image. The finished image is shown in Figure 4-93 (and can be seen in the color plate section of this book).

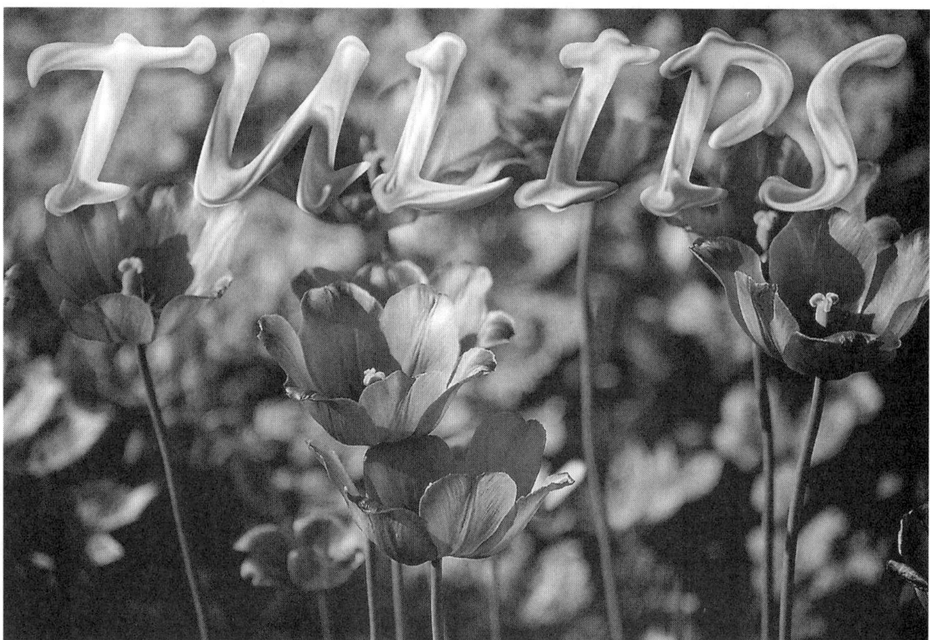

Figure 4-93: The finished glass-letters image.

Using Illustrator & Paths to Create New Paintbrushes

At first glance, the material in this section may appear to have more to do with Illustrator than with Photoshop. However, we think you will find that what we are presenting is a logical extension—with which you can accomplish a number of things—to the idea of making Illustrator paths and applying stroke effects inside Photoshop. Here, we have preapplied the stroke while in Illustrator for the purpose of making specialized brush points that can be used by any of Photoshop's paint or toning tools. These are brushes which would be extremely time-consuming to construct in Photoshop but which are quite simple when done in Illustrator. Because they would be difficult to do within Photoshop, they will appear to give unusual results. This is so only because they are unfamiliar. As you paint with these brushes, having learned how simple they are to make, we think you'll dream up other possibilities which make use of the Illustrator-Photoshop partnership.

CD-ROM

We have included on the Companion CD-ROM disk two files. One of them, ENP_BRU.ARP, is a saved brushes file (the brushes made with the files shown in the following examples) which you can simply load onto your Brushes palette using the palette's sidebar menu. The other, BRUSHES.AI, is the Illustrator file from which the brushes were generated. If you find that the brushes are useful but you need them to be a different size, rescale them in Illustrator and then import them into Photoshop using the set of instructions given below:

1. Set up the Illustrator file by making a set of squares (.5point black stroke, no fill) about .5 inches on a side. Select all the squares, Group them, and Lock them. There are, in this example 10 X 10 squares. Each square is about 8 points away from its neighbor.
2. Draw your brushes using any of Illustrator's tools. Keep the brush drawings within the boundaries of the squares. This insures that all of the brushes are about the same size and that you are able to use them together easily when in Photoshop. When you are finished drawing the brushes, Unlock the squares and change the stroke of the bounding squares to None. Select All (Figure 4-94) and Copy.

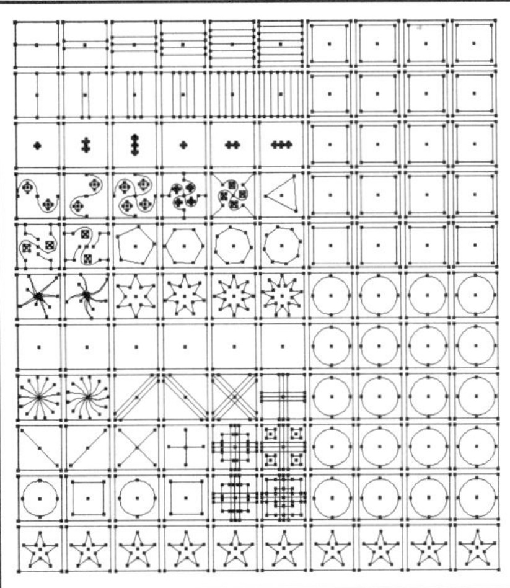

Figure 4-94: All of the brushes have been drawn and selected.

3. Switch to Photoshop. From the File menu, choose New. Make the new document grayscale and set the resolution to whatever you wish it to be. (The brushes in the file found on the Photoshop CD-ROM were made at a resolution of 330 ppi.) When the new window has opened, Paste as Pixels. The pasted shapes are shown in Figure 4-95.

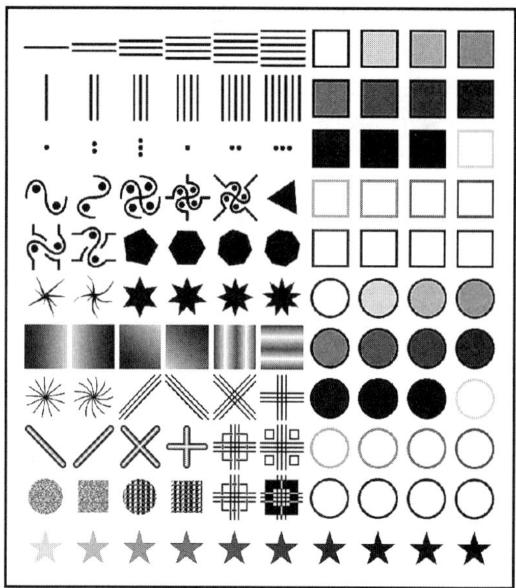

Figure 4-95: The brush shapes pasted into a new Photoshop window.

4. When the pasting operation is complete, flatten the image (choose this command from the Layer palette sidebar menu). Return to Illustrator. Select only the rectangles surrounding the brushes. They are grouped: all you need to do is click on one of them to select them all. Copy; switch back to Photoshop. Paste as Paths. The paths are shown surrounding the brush shapes in Figure 4-96.

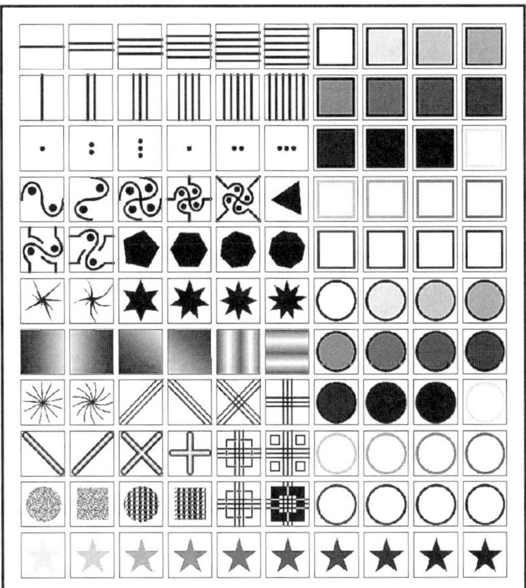

Figure 4-96: Paste the rectangles surrounding the brushes into the Photoshop document as Paths.

5. Clear your brush palette by holding down Command or Ctrl and clicking on each brush to delete it (before doing this, you may wish to save your brushes as a named file so that you can load them again later). You can delete all but one of the brushes. As soon as you have defined a new brush, you can delete the last one of the original palette. Choose the Direct Select cursor. Click on the first rectangle, press Enter, and select Define Brush from the Brush palette's sidebar menu (Figure 4-97). Repeat this process until you have defined all 100 brushes. Save this brush file in your Photoshop brushes folder. You can then discard the brushes document, or you can save it for use at another time.

Making brushes this way can give you access to some wonderful shape and texture possibilities that would be difficult to construct in Photoshop. Figure 4-97 shows how six of the brushes in this set can be used to make repeating textures, faded textures, and so on. You can experiment with the repeat percentages and use these brushes for borders and for all-over texture effects.

A final note: another special effect based on stroking a path can be found in the section titled Creating Seamless Patterns in Chapter 12, "Photoshop & the Web." The example in that chapter shows another case where a path is used to make a precise movement with the Brush tool. In the figures which accompany the explanation are several examples of how the repeating tile might be used. One of the examples shows the pattern as an embossed linear shape. The embossing was done in exactly the same way as the embossing of the glass letters alpha channel (above).

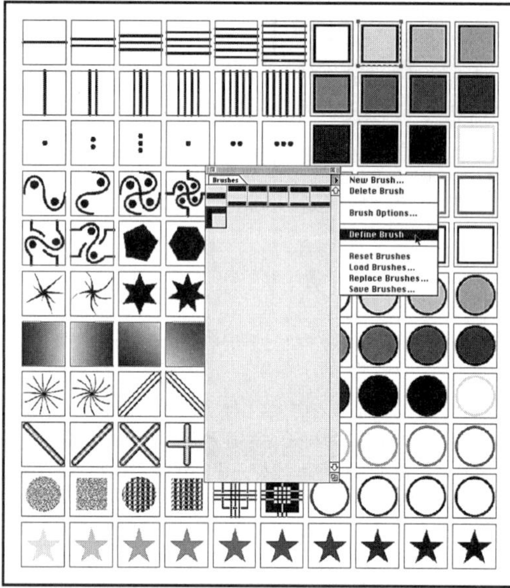

Figure 4-97: Click on each path to select it, press Enter, and then choose the Define Brush command from the Brush palette sidebar menu.

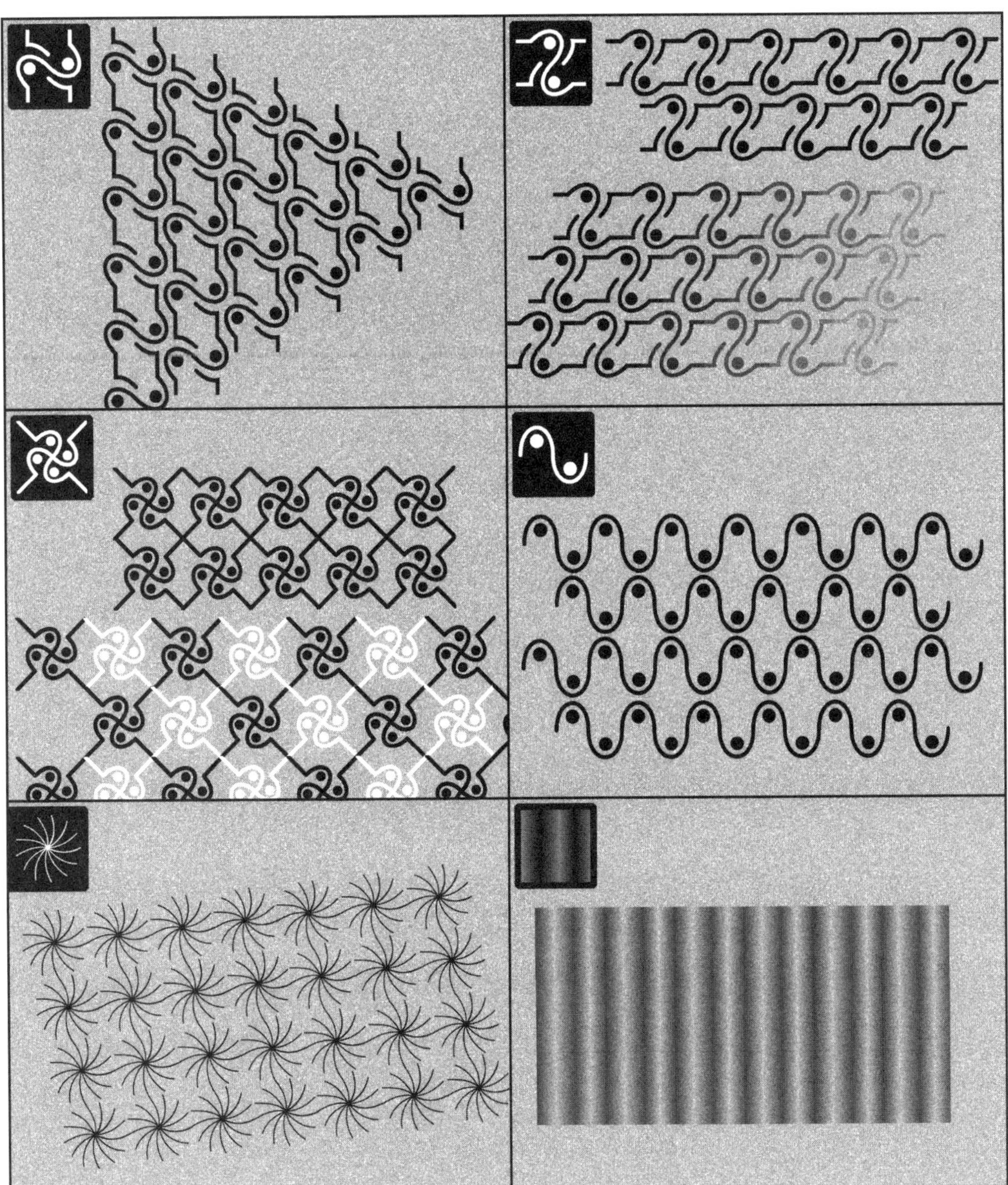

Figure 4-98: Six of the brushes in this set are used to make repeating textures and faded textures.

Moving On

In this chapter you have learned to draw and use paths for a variety of purposes. Photoshop's Pen tool has been augmented by adding the wonderful path-manipulation capabilities of Adobe Illustrator. You have also seen an example of how a special effect using a path made use of an alpha channel. In Chapter 5, "Using Channels," you will be formally introduced to channels. A channel is a component of a Photoshop document which is used to store different kinds of information. It can store color information, transparency information, and selections. You will learn to use the channels as masks and to do complex calculations between different channels. Later, you will see how channels can help you to combine images in a process called *compositing*. You'll also see more special effects, different from those you learned to apply with paths but equally exciting.

chapter 5
Using Channels

If you have ever been confused by Photoshop's channels, you are in good company. Many Photoshop users have found themselves lost in what seems to be an illogical—even paradoxical—way of organizing and using certain kinds of information. In fact channels—document components that store various kinds of information using grayscale brightness values—are Photoshop's most burdened concept since they can be made to represent a variety of information. It is this Zen-like quality of channels that leads to the confusion. Just look at what a channel can be made to do:

- A channel can be made to represent the brightness data of a particular video phosphor. For example, if you look at the Red channel of an RGB file, you would see a range of gray values. The brightness of these values is an indicator of the amount of red (phosphor) in a particular pixel.
- A channel can be made to represent the strength of an ink. As you'll see, CMYK documents, when examined channel by channel, use a lack of brightness or darkness, to signify the strength of a printing ink.
- A channel can be made to represent a selection that *could* be active but may not be. This is an interesting concept: how does Photoshop *store* a selection for later use?
- A channel can be made to represent variable opacity. Opacity is a difficult concept to visualize. However, with a channel, grayscale values can be made to serve as an analog for amounts of opacity.
- A channel can be made to represent variability in the execution of a command. This is a way of saying to Photoshop: based on this grayscale analog, perform a command to various degrees of completeness depending upon how light or dark each pixel of the channel is.

All of these concepts, and more, are a part of what a channel can do. What is even more amazing is that the channels can simultaneously represent these seemingly different kinds of information using just black, white, and 254 shades of gray. It is no wonder that some users have gotten overwhelmed when learning about channels.

If you are one of those users who has gotten lost, we are going to tell you something that you may find difficult to believe at first: all of those seemingly different kinds of information are, in the context of Photoshop, different aspects of *the same thing*. Really. We're going to prove it to you, and when we're finished, we think you're going to love using channels for all the many interesting and time-saving things they can do for you. In fact, whether you realized it or not, you have already used channels in a couple of ways in earlier parts of this book. Did you work through the Quick Mask tutorial in Chapter 3, "Toolbox Techniques?" If so, you used a channel. Did you work through the glass lettering project at the end of Chapter 4, "Paths & the Pen Tool?" You used a channel. Those two examples should convince you that using channels isn't hard. Now all you have to do is figure out how to understand them, and you're home free!

In this chapter, we will cover all of the ways Photoshop uses channels. As you encounter each use, you may find that you are jumping from one topic to an unrelated topic. However, that is precisely how we'll approach this task of linking together what seems to be unrelated material so that you can discover the underlying similarities.

Channels: What They Can Do

We'll begin this discussion of channels by showing you how the channels are used in everyday situations. As you see each situation involving channels, keep in mind the statement made above, that a channel's information in a variety of situations simply amounts to different aspects of the same underlying concept: the brightness values of a grayscale channel can be treated simultaneously as pictorial elements and as an analog for values that operate on the picture in a way that has little obvious relationship to the image's topology.

Channels to Hold Selections

Let's imagine that you and a colleague living in a different city are both intending to use the same Photoshop image—perhaps the sundial photograph shown in Figure 5-1. You have made a very precise selection of the sundial's outlines, and you need to show your colleague which pixels you have selected. Eventually, you hit upon a strategy. You make a duplicate of your sundial photograph and make the same very precise selection on the copy (Figure 5-2). Next, you fill your selection with white, select the inverse, and fill the selection with black (Figure 5-3). Now, if you send this simple black and white file as an e-mail enclosure, your colleague can click with the Magic Wand tool in the white area of your black and white file and instantly know the exact shape of your selection. You can congratulate yourself on the ingenuity with which you have solved this problem.

Figure 5-1: You wish to show someone else exactly which pixels you intend to select from this sundial photograph.

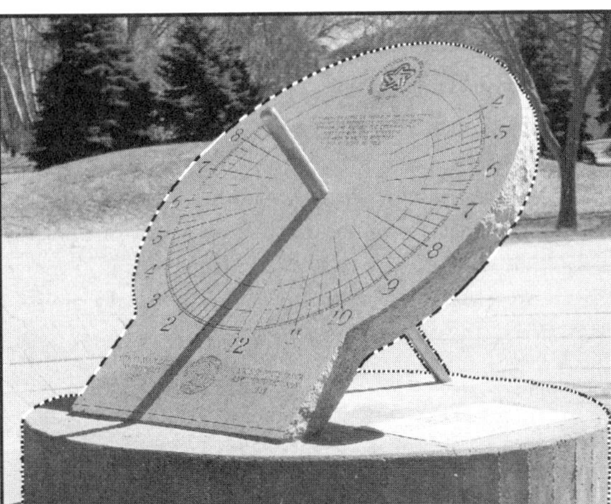

Figure 5-2: The first step is to make the selection on a copy of the file.

Figure 5-3: If you fill your selection with white and the area around the selection with black, all anyone needs to do is click in the white area with the Magic Wand tool to know exactly which pixels you originally selected.

After your colleague has opened the file and located the selection, all that remains to be done is to drag the selection from your black and white file to the other copy of the sundial. With a little zooming and nudging, the selection can be fitted to the image.

This strategy may sound a little cumbersome, but it is entirely workable. The only tricky part happens when someone has to drag the selection from the black and white file to the sundial image and then position it by eye. Otherwise, this is a realistic way to preserve the boundaries of a selection.

If you followed how using a single black and white image would allow you to preserve a selection, then you have grasped the idea behind selection channels or, as they are called, *alpha* channels. An alpha channel is a channel added to your Photoshop document beyond the channels which contain the picture image information (we will discuss picture image information channels later in this chapter).

There are two easy ways for you to make an alpha channel from your selection.

Save Selection

While the selection is active, go to the bottom of the Select menu and choose Save Selection. A dialog box opens (shown in Figure 5-4). This dialog box contains several possibilities which we will discuss later. For the moment, observe that the default destination is a *New* channel and that the Operation is also set to *New Channel*. Click OK, and take a look at your Channels palette (Figure 5-5). Located at the bottom of the list, directly after the Red, Green, and Blue channels is a fourth channel. Photoshop has assigned it a name, #4, and has also assigned to it a keyboard command—Command+4 for Macintosh, Ctrl+4 for Windows—which you can use to look at and edit this channel. Notice that the thumbnail for this channel is identical to the one you would have made in the hypothetical situation described above.

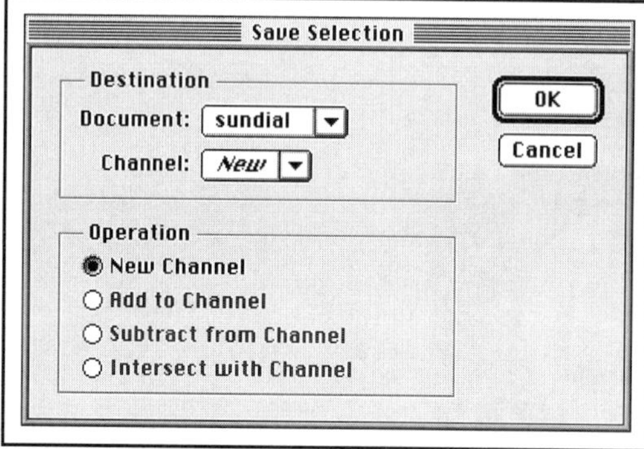

Figure 5-4: The Save Selection dialog box.

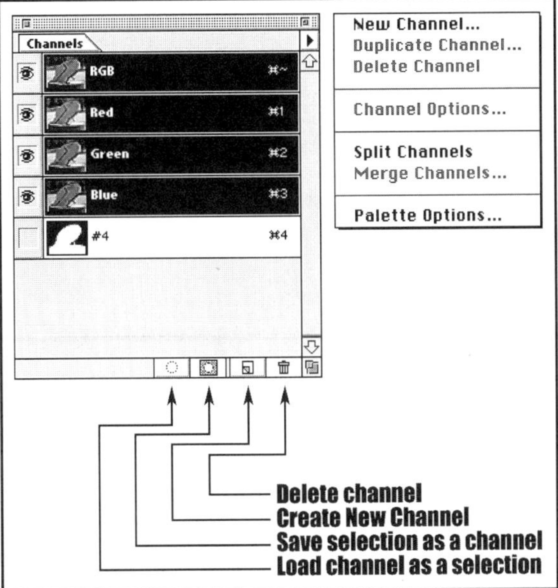

Figure 5-5: Expanded view of the Channels palette.

Save Selection Using the Channels Palette

While the selection is active, you can click once on the small icon—second from the left—at the bottom of the Channels palette. This produces exactly the same result as using the menu command *Save Selection*, but the dialog box is bypassed.

Retrieving Saved Selections

When you have preserved your selection in an alpha channel, you need to be able to retrieve it. You have a number of options for reinstating the active selection:

- This may sound silly, but you really could press Command+4 or Ctrl+4 to view the alpha channel, and then click in the white area with the Wand tool (set the Tolerance to 32 and turn anti-aliasing on). After the white area has been selected, return to the composite channels view. You probably won't want to do the job this way, but we're listing it here to show that the original strategy of preserving a selection is valid.
- From the Select menu, choose Load Selection. A dialog box will appear (Figure 5-6). The choices are similar to those in the Save Selection window. We will discuss most of these choices later in this chapter. The defaults are as they are shown in the figure. You are given the choice of which channel to load (if you have more than one alpha channel) and to load the channel as a New Selection.

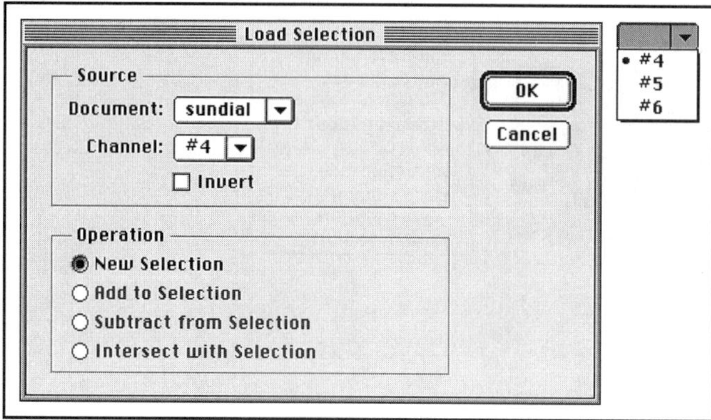

Figure 5-6: The Load Selection dialog box.

- You can click on the alpha channel's thumbnail on the Channels palette (see Figure 5-5), click on the left-hand icon at the bottom of the palette, and then click on the top line of the Channels list.
- The fastest and most convenient way to retrieve your selection is to hold Command or Ctrl and click on the thumbnail of the alpha channel on the list of channels on the palette. This is probably the option you will use the most since it is so fast.

Channels to Represent Variable Opacity

After you load your alpha channel selection, there are many possibilities. You could, if you wish, copy the selection, and then paste it into another document window. Figure 5-7 shows the sundial detached (copied) from its original surroundings and placed (pasted) against a gray background with horizontal black lines.

Copying and pasting a selection is something that we do without question. However, we need to give the process a little thought since we are examining alpha channels as possessing the capability of representing variable opacity.

First, let's remember that each pixel in the alpha channel represents an equivalent pixel in the image: for example, the upper right-hand corner pixel in the channel corresponds to the upper right-hand corner pixel of the image. This is an important point to remember because if a pixel is selected in the channel, the equivalent pixel is selected in the image. Now, let's just assume that when you loaded the selection that you really loaded the entire channel—you loaded all of the pixels, black and white. When you copy the selection, imagine that you are copying all of pixels and not just the ones represented by white pixels in the channel. Let's take it one step further. Let's imagine that Photoshop arbitrarily assigns an opacity based on the value of the pixel in the channel. If the alpha channel pixel is black, the selected pixel is entirely transparent.

If it is white, the selected pixel is entirely opaque. If you can imagine this situation, then you have a grasp of *what has actually happened* when you loaded the selection, copied it, and pasted it into the new document shown in Figure 5-7. All of the pixels were pasted but the only ones visible were those represented by white pixels in the alpha channel.

Figure 5-7: When you load the selection, you can copy and paste the selected pixels into a new document window.

This is a subtle point, but if you can get it planted firmly in your mind, you'll have a key to some of the important inner workings of Photoshop. The only point of confusion is this: why, if all the pixels are selected, does the selection line only appear around the areas containing white pixels in the alpha channel? This is Photoshop's way of showing you only the pixels which have an equivalent alpha channel pixel value of 50% black or lighter. The selection lines are just to help you to understand what is selected.

If we carry the idea of variable transparency a step further, we can construct a small experiment to give you an idea of what else can be done. Please study Figure 5-8. The original alpha channel containing the white-filled sundial shape has been surrounded with a zone of pixels that are 50% black. When this modified alpha channel is loaded, the selection outlines will be along the edges between the black and the gray pixels. When copied and pasted into another document window (shown in Figure 5-9), you can see that pixels from the image in the zone represented by the gray pixels have been pasted but that you can partially see through that area. The black stripes in the background are visible but are muted by the overlay of the pasted pixels which are 50% opaque.

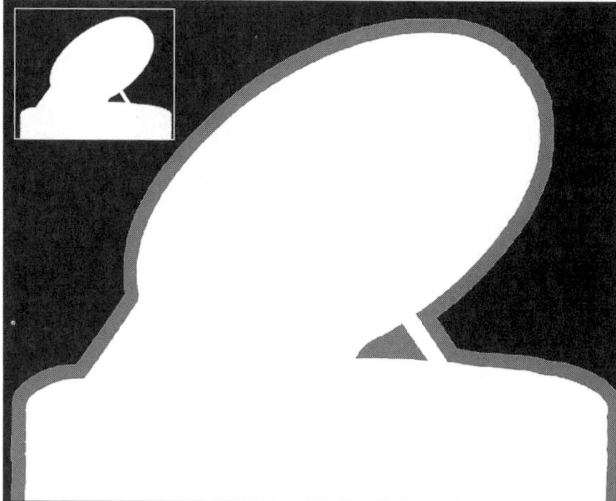

Figure 5-8: The original alpha channel has been modified to give a zone of 50% black pixels around the edges of the white area.

Figure 5-9: When the new channel has been loaded as a selection, copied, and pasted into a new document, the image pixels represented by the gray pixels in the channel are 50% opaque.

By carrying this process another step further, we can use a broad range of opacity represented by the gray values in the channel. Figure 5-10 shows the channel of Figure 5-8 with a large-scale blur applied to the gray and black areas. This blur gives a gradient that runs along the contour of the sundial shape. The tones range from 50% black along the white edge to completely black farther away from the edge. When this channel is loaded as a selection, copied, and pasted into the document with the black lines (Figure 5-11), the result is that the copied pixels fade out gradually so that there is no place where we can say that the sundial pixels end and the background pixels begin.

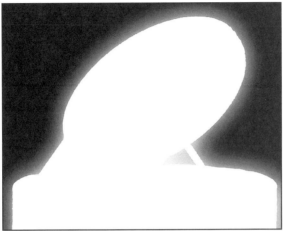

Figure 5-10: A heavy blur is applied to the black and gray areas to produce a contoured gradient along the edges of the white sundial shape.

Figure 5-11: When the modified channel is loaded, copied, and pasted, the blur of the channel causes the pasted pixels to have no visible boundary.

Channels to Represent Moderators, or Masks, for Commands

In much the same way that the gray tones of the pixels in the alpha channel can be made to represent a selection or some amount of opacity, the values can also serve as ways of modifying the effects of a command. Where a pixel is white in the channel, the command applied to the equivalent pixel in the image will execute normally. However, when the channel pixel is black, the equivalent pixel in the image is not affected by the command. When gray values between black and white are present in the alpha channel, the command executes proportional to the lightness of the pixel: lighter pixels allow more of the command to execute on the pixels of the image while darker pixels prevent as much of the command to execute on the image pixels. That sounds complicated, but we can show how it works by performing some experiments on the photograph of the sundial.

One possible command that you might use on an image is Image | Adjust | Invert. This makes a positive image into a negative, or a negative into a positive. When the Invert command is applied to the sundial photo, the result is as you see in Figure 5-12. If the channel containing the original outline of the sundial (Figure 5-3) is loaded as a selection and the Invert command applied, only the part of the image within the selection is inverted. The rest of the image remains unchanged (Figure 5-13). This is predictable when we consider the white area in the channel and the black areas surrounding it.

Figure 5-12: The Invert command applied to the image with no selection active.

Figure 5-13: When the channel shown in Figure 5-3 is loaded as a selection, only the portion of the image within the selection is changed when the Invert command is applied.

With the channel's selection operating, you might want to try a different kind of command. Figure 5-14 shows the result of running Alien Skin Software's Eye Candy 3.0 Water Drops filter. Notice how the filter operates only within the boundary of the sundial. If we load the channel shown in Figure 5-10 as a selection and then run the same filter, the very different effect is shown in Figure 5-15. You can see the water droplets but they fade with distance from the sundial's edge. Another possibility is to load the blurred edge channel as a selection, choose Select | Inverse, and then execute a different filter on the background. Figure 5-16 shows the effects of the Crystallize filter on the reverse selection. The area of the sundial is untouched while the remainder of the image has been distorted by the filter.

Figure 5-14: With the original channel selection active, the Eye Candy 3.0 Water Drops filter is applied only within the boundaries of the selection.

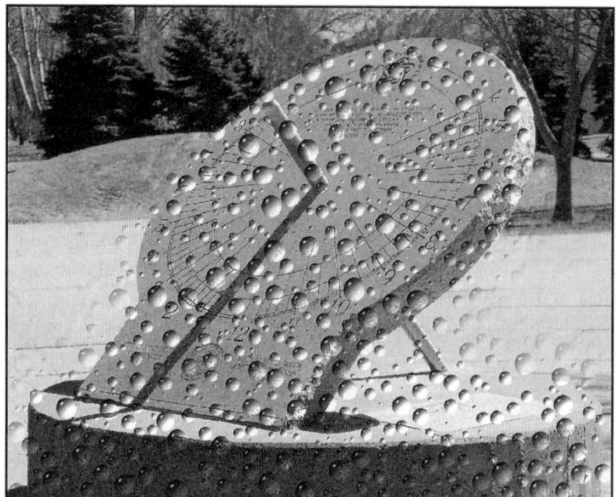

Figure 5-15: When the channel shown in Figure 5-10 is loaded, the same filter executes beyond the edge of the sundial but fades away imperceptibly.

Figure 5-16: When the same selection is inverted and the Crystallize filter is executed, only the background is affected. The filter's distortions taper off the closer they get to the edge of the sundial.

A channel need not be based on a contour found in the image. You could, if you wished, create a new channel and simply apply a black-to-white gradient in the channel. A channel of this sort is an excellent way of showing how a command is moderated based on the values within the channel. The gradient channel is shown in Figure 5-17.

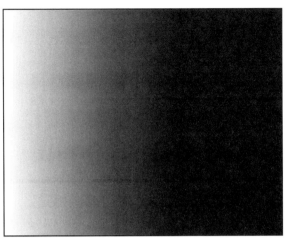

Figure 5-17: Create a new channel and fill it with a black-to-white gradient.

When the gradient-containing alpha channel is loaded as a selection, you will see moving selection lines only around the pixels that are 50% black or lighter in the alpha channel. This is normal, although it is misleading when you first encounter it. Your entire channel is selected despite what the moving selection lines seem to show. One command you could try with this channel loaded is Fill with White (Figure 5-18). Or Fill with Black (Figure 5-19). Perhaps you might like to try the Add Noise filter (Figure 5-20). Observe in these three figures that the command executes completely on the left—equivalent to the white pixels of the channel—and not at all on the right—where the channel's pixels are black. The areas between right and left show how the commands are moderated by the values contained in the gradient.

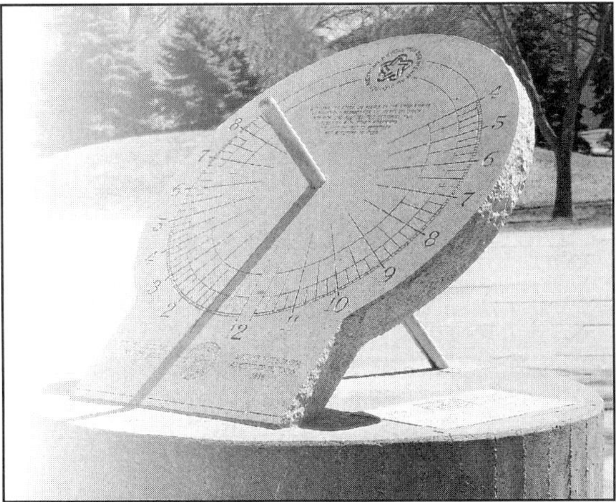

Figure 5-18: With the gradient-containing channel loaded as a selection, this is the result of filling with white.

Figure 5-19: With the gradient-containing channel loaded as a selection, this is the result of filling with black.

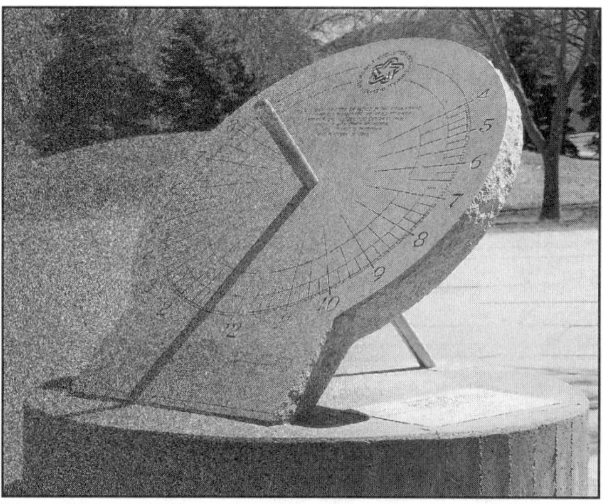

Figure 5-20: With the gradient-containing channel loaded as a selection, this is the result of using the Add Noise filter.

Here's another possibility based on the ability of the channel to moderate a command: we can make a selection based on the information in two of the channels to make a composite selection. First, we'll duplicate the channel containing the gradient. With the duplicate visible in the document window, load the original selection channel, the one containing the outline of the sundial (Figure 5-21). Fill the selection with black and deselect. The new channel now has elements of both channels (Figure 5-22). When we load this new channel as a selection and Fill with white, the result is as shown in Figure 5-23. The fill command has executed along the gradient but the black-filled shape of the sundial has been left entirely untouched.

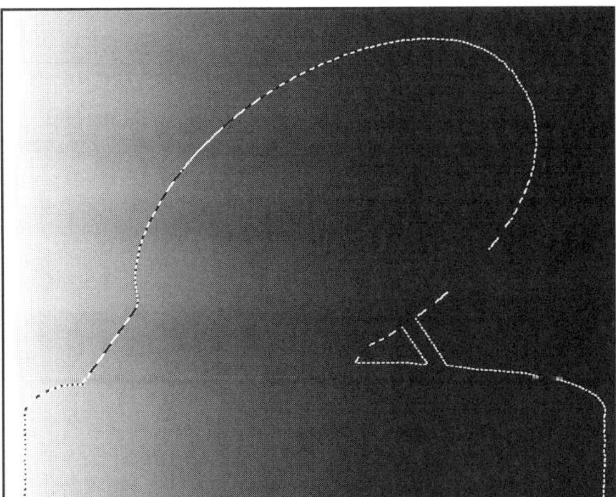

Figure 5-21: With the gradient channel in view, load as a selection the original alpha channel.

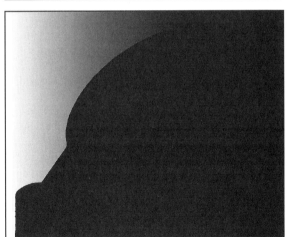

Figure 5-22: Fill the selection with black.

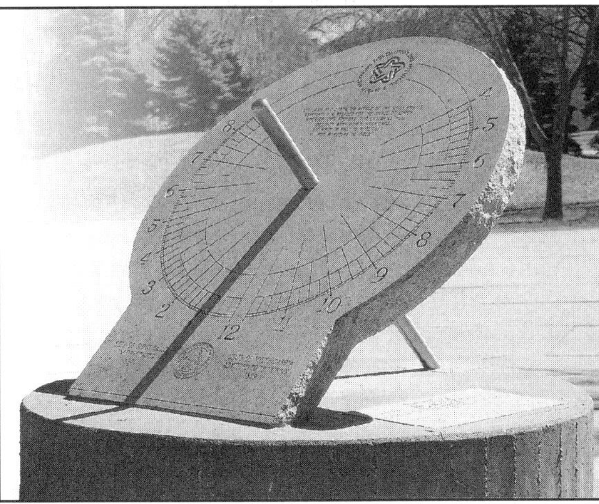

Figure 5-23: Load the new channel as a selection and fill the image with white. The command executes around the sundial, but leaves the shape of the sundial untouched because it was filled with black in the channel.

Channels to Represent Color Values

In the examples we have discussed up to now, all of the channels were extra channels—alpha channels—which were added to the list of channels on the palette. These channels are, in effect, masks. The channels which make up the native document contain the image's color data. These color channels can have the same characteristics as the alpha channels, but they are also integral to color. Each color channel is capable of having white pixels, black pixels, and 254 shades of gray between the two. The momentary perceptual difference between one of the color channels and one of the alpha channels is simply what the gray values of the pixels in the channels represent.

Also, in the channels examples we've discussed up until now, a white pixel was seen to be equivalent to a total selection, total opacity, and to an unmoderated command. When channels are considered as color components, however, a white pixel is an indication that the channel's color tone is at its brightest. Using this reasoning, a white pixel in the Red channel of an RGB document would indicate maximum brightness for the red component of the color. The same can be said for the other two color channels in an RGB document, green and blue.

The reverse is also true. A black pixel in the Red channel indicates that there is no red component to the pixel's overall color. Extending the logic of this proposition, it should be clear that shades of gray in any of the color channels indicate relative strengths of that color. This is a difficult point to grasp. To make it more clear, we will use some pictorial examples.

Figure 5-24 shows a series of six wedge shapes. Though you are seeing them in grayscale, each wedge is composed of a pure tone in the outer area, shading to black toward the center. The top, third, and fifth colors (clockwise) are red, green, and blue, the primary monitor phosphor colors. The second, fourth, and sixth are yellow, cyan, and magenta, the monitor secondary colors. Secondary colors are those composed of two of the primary colors.

A look at the Red channel by itself (Figure 5-25) shows a very different image. First, this channel is truly in grayscale and not a grayscale emulation of colors as the previous figure was (since the figures in this book are mostly in black and white, we must sometimes point out that we are presenting a grayscale version of a color file). All of the tones in the wedges are composed of white or shades of gray. The most obvious difference is in the lower half in which the green, cyan, and blue areas are entirely black. This indicates that there is no red component in any of the three colors at the bottom of the figure. Figure 5-26 shows the Green channel of 5-24 and Figure 5-27 shows the Blue channel.

When looking at these three figures, notice how similar they are to each other. Each set of three is identical to the others but each has simply rotated 120°. In fact, each wedge is identical to every other. The differences between them depend upon which channel they are in, and their topological relationship to the pixels of the other channels. For example, the brightest red area is white only in the red channel. In the other two channels the equivalent area is black. The brightest yellow area, by contrast, is white in both the Red and the Green channels with the equivalent area in blue showing as black.

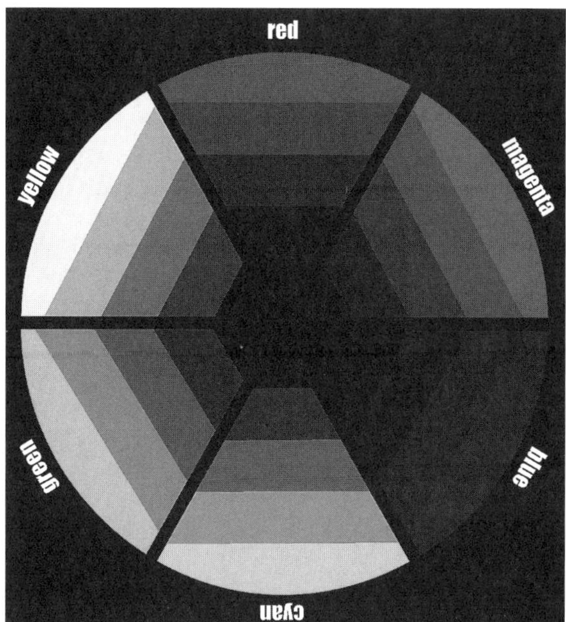

Figure 5-24: The three monitor primary colors—red, green, and blue—and the three secondary colors, colors composed of two primaries. The secondary colors are yellow, cyan, and magenta.

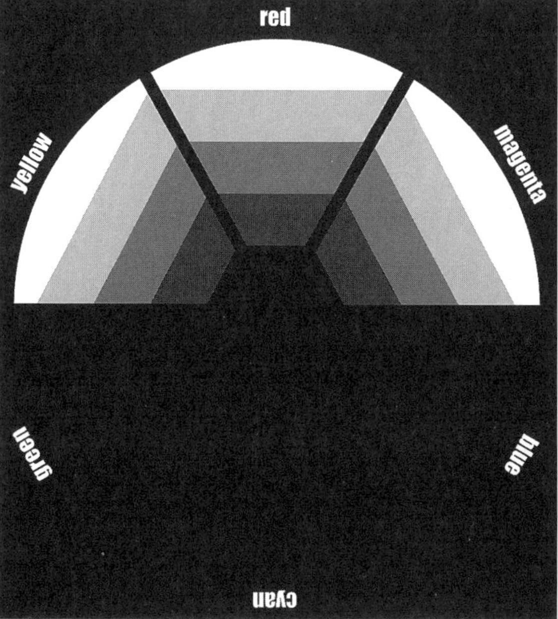

Figure 5-25: The Red channel of Figure 5-24.

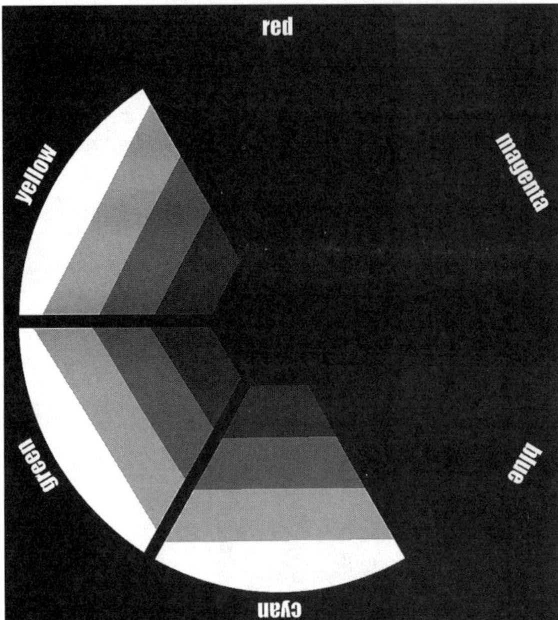

Figure 5-26: The Green channel of Figure 5-24.

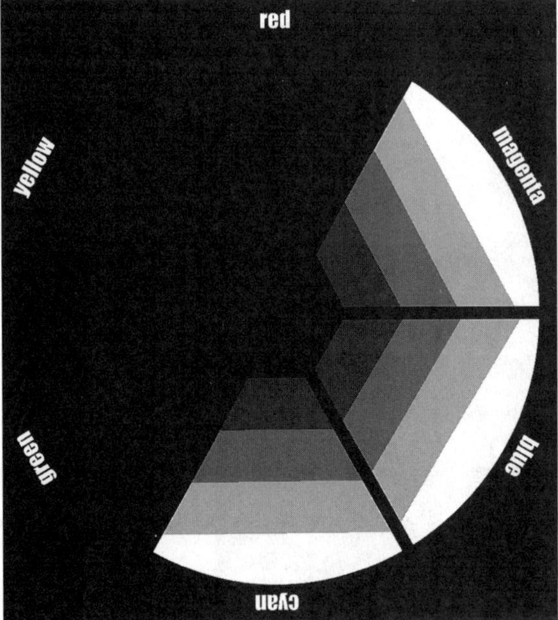

Figure 5-27: The Blue channel of Figure 5-24.

The idea of channels contributing to the colors you see on your monitor may seem odd to you, especially since you do not, as a rule, look at the individual channels as anything other than what they seem to be—individual grayscale images. It is not until you stop seeing the pictorial image and start to recognize that the color channels in an RGB document are nothing more than a collection of brightness values—tones between white and black—that you begin to understand how colors work and how you can manipulate them. When you begin to see how the values combine, you'll have a valuable tool for color correction.

You'll even be able to predict what colors look like even if you only see them in grayscale. For example, the photo in Figure 5-28 is of marigolds. This figure is a grayscale representation of the RGB document. But you'll be able to think your way through what it must look like. Figure 5-29 shows the Red channel by itself. Observe the brightness of the flowers and the comparative darkness of the foliage. Figure 5-30 is the Green channel of the same file. Some of the light areas are the same as in the Red channel. If you'll glance at Figure 5-25, you'll see that the color formed from red and green is a bright yellow. This gives you a good idea that the color could be yellow *if* there are no equivalent bright areas in the Blue channel (Figure 5-31). There aren't any. That gives you areas of bright yellow in the flowers. Now, what happens to the darker areas of the flowers? Think it through: if the red stays the same and the green decreases (the pixels get darker), the tone shifts away from yellow toward red. In other words, the tones become more orange until, when the green has become black, there is nothing but red. Do you see? You can become very fluent with the RGB color system, all because the color channels represent color components using shades of gray.

Figure 5-28: RGB color file.

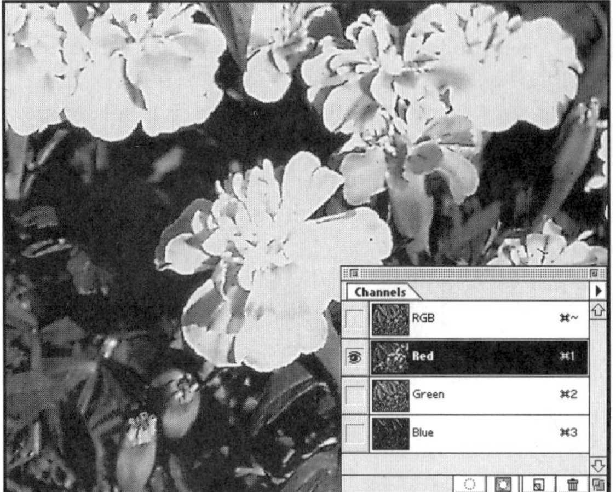

Figure 5-29: The Red channel from Figure 5-28.

Figure 5-30: The Green channel from Figure 5-28.

Figure 5-31: The Blue channel from Figure 5-28.

The last three figures also included a view of the Channels palette. Please note that the left-hand side of the palette contains eye icons which allow you to select which of the channels you wish to view. (Each channel also has its own key command: hold Command or Ctrl and enter **1** for red, **2** for green, **3** for blue, or ~ to see the composite of the three.) You can, if you wish, see the combination of two of the colors without the third using the Channels palette. Figure 5-32 shows the image with only the Red and Green channels visible without the Blue channel.

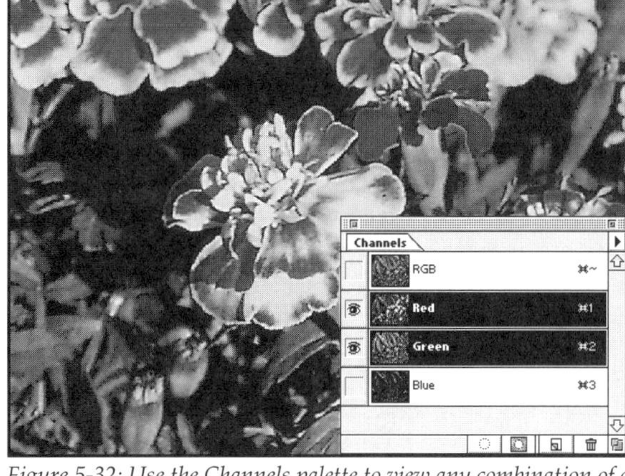

Figure 5-32: Use the Channels palette to view any combination of channels.

The color channels can also be treated as if they were alpha channels. By loading one of the color channels as if it were any alpha channel, the channel does double duty: it contributes its brightness values as color components and as selection/mask. Figure 5-33 shows the result of loading the Green channel as a selection, copying, and then pasting into the same document containing the dark horizontal lines. Note that the flower shapes are nearly opaque because of the brightness of the pixels in the flowers. The background is fairly transparent because of the lack of brightness in the background areas of the Green channel.

Figure 5-33: In this figure, the Green color channel was loaded as if it were an alpha channel. The selection was then copied, and pasted into another window containing a neutral background and dark horizontal lines.

Channels to Represent Ink

As you have seen, an RGB document uses the brightness values of the pixels in the color channels to indicate the strength of the color. When a Photoshop file is prepared for process-color printing (converted to CMYK mode), it must use a different value system for the channels. Instead of lightness indicating the strength of color, the reverse situation comes into being. The color channels of a CMYK document show the strength of the ink by the amount of darkness in each pixel. In this system, a black pixel indicates a 100% ink value, while white indicates that no ink is present for that pixel. Gray values between black and white give percentages of ink values.

Figure 5-34 shows a CMYK document displayed in color. It is apparently similar to an RGB document when it is displayed as a composite of all the channels. However, when the individual channels are viewed, they show a different system. Figure 5-35, for example, is a display of the Cyan channel for the photo. If this were an RGB document, we would expect to see a strong color component for the flowers. However, this is a different system and we must realize that this channel is displaying cyan values as the inverse of lightness values. The foliage can be seen to contain a considerable amount of cyan ink in the leaves—not surprising since green is composed mostly of cyan and yellow—and very little cyan in the flowers. Figures 5-36, 5-37, and 5-38 give an idea of the appearance of the other color channels. Notice that most of the ink for the flowers is in the Magenta and Yellow channels while most of the ink for the leaves is in the Cyan and Yellow channels. The Black channel has ink present mostly in the areas of deep shadows.

Figure 5-34: A CMYK document shown as a composite of the color channels.

Figure 5-35: Cyan channel of Figure 5-34.

Figure 5-36: Magenta channel of Figure 5-34.

Figure 5-37: Yellow channel of Figure 5-34.

Figure 5-38: Black channel of Figure 5-34.

Other Channel Possibilities

Although channels seem to be considerably burdened with what they must represent, there are even more ways in which Photoshop exploits channels. For example, each of Photoshop's display modes uses one or more channels to express information. Here is a short summary which explains how channels are used for three of the document modes.

Lab

The Lab mode uses the L channel to show the amount of lightness a pixel possesses. The a & b channels of that mode are made to represent color content. The range of color from black to white for the a channel is from green to red in the composite view of all three channels. The color range from black to white in the b channel is from yellow to blue.

Grayscale

The Grayscale mode contains a single channel which is really a kind of short-hand channel: grayscale documents could be in RGB mode but all of the channels would be identical. On the Channels palette, grayscale documents have only one list entry. This single channel is titled *Black*. Other channels can be added but the native file exists with a single channel. That Black channel can be used as a selection channel. It is converted to a selection in the same way any alpha channel is made to be a selection (see above). It is usually necessary to select the inverse when you have made a selection of the Black channel since you will have selected the light information rather that the dark pixels which delineate the image. An alternative is to duplicate the Black channel, choose the Invert command, and select this second channel whenever you wish to select the dark shapes in the Black channel.

Multichannel

The Multichannel mode is a grab bag of channels. The channels can all be from the same document or they can be a collection of channels from different documents. All they need to have in common is that they are the same size. Multichannel mode is useful for storing alpha channels—which usually must be discarded before the image can be used for output—so that they are all together in a single convenient document. If you have been working with channels for selections and transparency information and you wish to save all of your channels for future use, duplicate your document, and convert the copy to Multichannel mode. Then, discard the color channels—which have no relevance to a Multichannel document—and save the file. You will find that this document saves to a very small size on disk.

Manipulating Channels

Having encountered channels in a variety of guises, it is time to learn how to boss them around so that they will work for you. If you find that you are still unsure how to tell when a channel is playing a particular role, we advise you not to worry about it. You have been exposed to a comprehensive explanation of channels intended to cover most possibilities. As your skill becomes more sure, you'll be able to manipulate channels with intuitive skill. In the meantime, we will present some possibilities that will give you a framework within which to work.

The Channels Palette Menu

Although you can do most of your work with channels using the keyboard and the mouse, the palette's sidebar menu contains the formal command list. You will be able to understand and use immediately the commands in the top section (see Figure 5-5). They will allow you to create new channels, make copies of existing channels, and to delete channels you no longer need. The second section contains a single command, Channel Options, which will be discussed later in this chapter. There are also two menu selections—those in the third section—which are so odd that they should be discussed so that you will know what they are all about. Although you may never need these two commands, using them produces startling changes to the structure of your document. You should be aware of what these two commands can do. The final section contains a single command which brings up a dialog box with a choice of three sizes of thumbnails to be used in the palette list of channels.

Split Channels

The Split channels command executes without a preliminary dialog box. One moment your screen looks similar to that in Figure 5-39. The next moment, after the command has executed, you find your screen looking as shown in Figure 5-40. The RGB channels and three alpha channels contained in the document have all been placed in separate document windows. Photoshop has thoughtfully named each file with the original document name, a dot and the extensions *red, green, blue, #1, #2, #3* , and so forth. These new windows now represent separate file entities carrying only grayscale information.

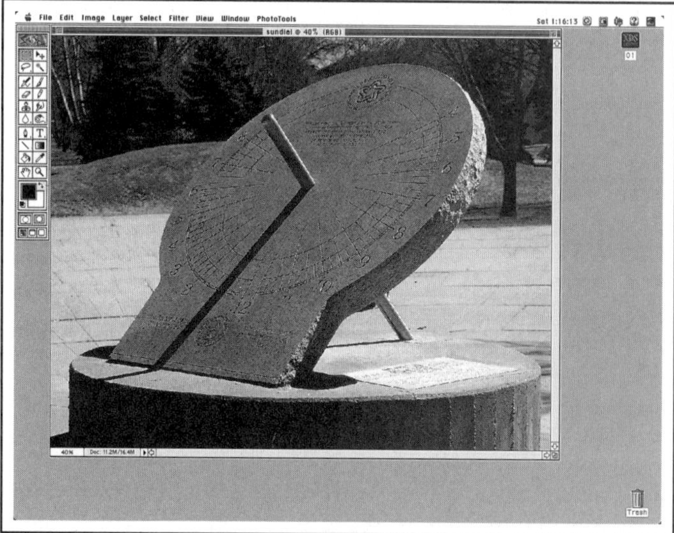

Figure 5-39: Photoshop with single six-channel document (R, G, & B and three alpha channels).

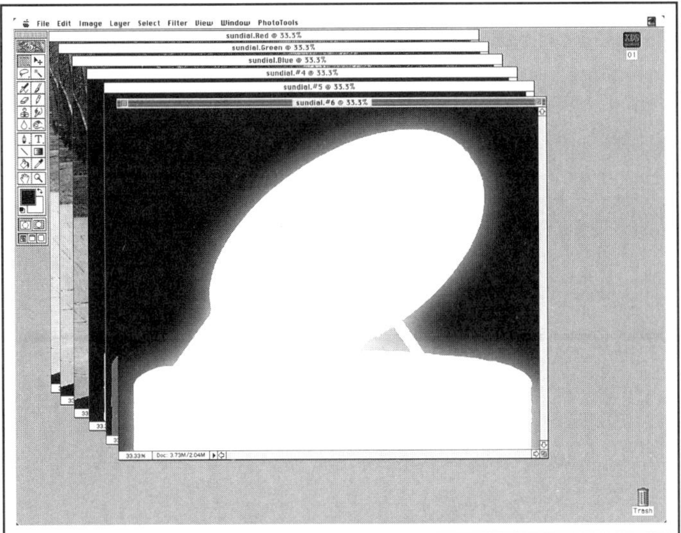

Figure 5-40: After selecting the Split Channels command, Photoshop divides the single document into six separate documents, each containing one of the original channels.

Merge Channels

The Merge Channels command can be used whenever there are more than one open document windows which are all exactly the same dimensions. After choosing the command from the menu, a dialog box opens (Figure 5-41). The pop-up menu allows you to choose which document mode you wish to use for the merged file. The window in the figure has defaulted to Multichannel since six channels were open (shown in Figure 5-41).

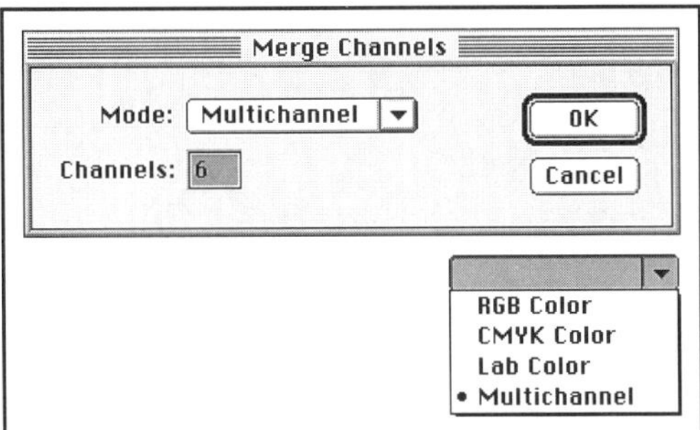

Figure 5-41: The initial Merge Channels dialog box.

After choosing from the pop-up list, you will be asked to make further choices in a second dialog box (Figure 5-42). Photoshop will make an intelligent guess about which channels should be put into the new file, but you are at liberty to change each of the pop-up menus to another item. You could, if you wished, transpose the original Green and Blue channels—or Red and Green, or Red and Blue—when Photoshop reconstitutes the document. You can even put one of the alpha channels into one of the color channel positions. Transposing colors is sometimes interesting—as a pastime, it hangs right in there with Solitaire—but hardly ever useful. Still, you never know....

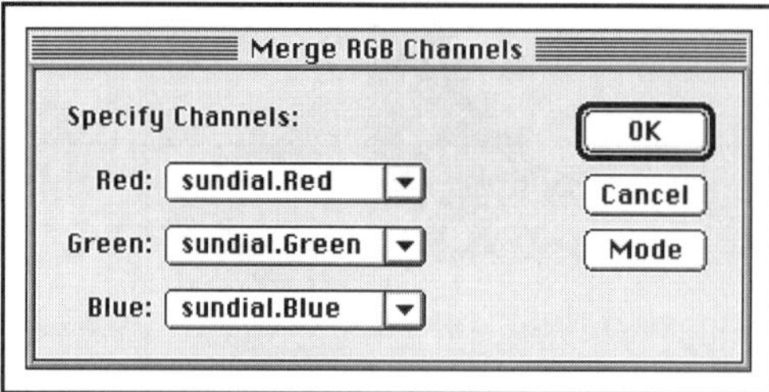

Figure 5-42: The Merge RGB Channels dialog box. Each pop-up menu contains all of the open channels which could be used.

After you make your choices and click OK, Photoshop merges the three documents into one window (Figure 5-43). The remainder of the channels can be discarded or put back into the RGB document as alpha channels. There is an easy way to do this. Click on one of the grayscale windows to bring it to the front (be sure you can still see the RGB window). The Channels palette will show that there is a single channel, Black. Drag the thumbnail from the palette onto the RGB window. Photoshop will instantly add the channel to the others contained by the RGB document. Using this procedure, you can replace all of the original alpha channels in about 10 seconds.

Figure 5-43: After using the Merge Channels command, the RGB document has been reconstituted leaving the original alpha channels as separate documents.

What to Do With Split & Merge

As pleasant as it would be to rattle off a half-dozen super ideas for using these two odd menu commands, the truth is that after using Photoshop for quite a number of years, the authors have never found an urgent need for either one. Not even a pressing need. Not even a moderate need. Sorry. They must have been put there for some reason. Perhaps you'll think of one and let us know.

Channel Options

When one of the alpha channels in a document is selected, you can select Channel Options from the Channels palette sidebar menu. You can also double-click on the channel thumbnail to bring up the dialog box shown in Figure 5-44. (Note: Channel Options are not available for the native color channels.) The top area of this window allows you to enter a new name for the channel if you wish to change it from the default.

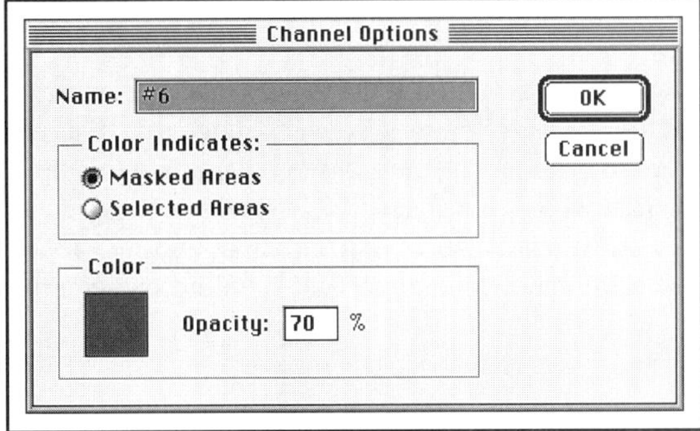

Figure 5-44: The Channel Options dialog box.

The other two areas of the options dialog box have to do with displaying an alpha channel. When you are viewing the native color channels, you may view any alpha channel as well. Click on the eye icon at the left of the channel item on the palette. To the already existing colors will be added whatever color you have chosen for the channel. You can change the color from the default red by clicking on the color box and selecting a new tone from the Photoshop Color Picker. Within the Color Picker, click on the Custom button to assign a color from any of the Custom Colors palettes. When the color and opacity value have been set, the information in the channel will contribute a colored overlay to the colors already present. Chapter 9, "Photoshop Prepress," contains an extensive section devoted to using alpha channels for adding spot colors to process color printing. The section also contains information on how the display of alpha channels can be used.

The final section of the Channel Options dialog box is labeled Color Indicates. The default, Masked Areas, simply means that when the channel is displayed with its contributing color, areas containing dark pixels will contribute color and areas with light pixels will not. The other option reverses the color by appearing to invert the channel. We've used the word *appears* deliberately. The channel values do become transposed but the channel keeps the original selection. Because of this, when you load the channel as a selection, all *black* pixels become selected in the channel. There is nothing really wrong with selecting the black pixels rather than the white pixels, as long as you remember what you are doing. However, if you lose track of what you have done with the options, you can find yourself very confused. This is not an option with which you should feel adventurous.

More About Saving Channel Selections

You have already seen two ways to preserve a selection by converting the selection to an alpha channel. First, you can click on the Save Selection icon (second from left) at the bottom of the Channels palette. Second, you can choose Save Selection from the Select menu.

The dialog box which opens when you use the Save Selection command is shown in Figure 5-6. Besides changing the selection into a new channel, this dialog box allows you to make some changes to existing channels based on a new selection. Figure 5-45 shows a rectangular selection which, when saved as a selection into a new channel, generates a channel which appears similar to that shown in Figure 5-46. Figures 5-47 and 5-48 show another selection and the channel which would be generated from it.

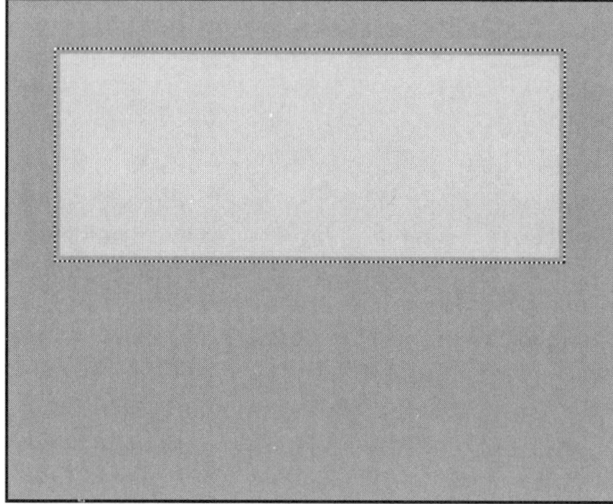

Figure 5-45: A simple rectangular selection.

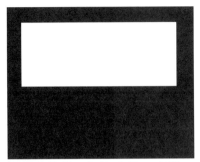

Figure 5-46: The selection in Figure 5-45 generates a channel similar to this one.

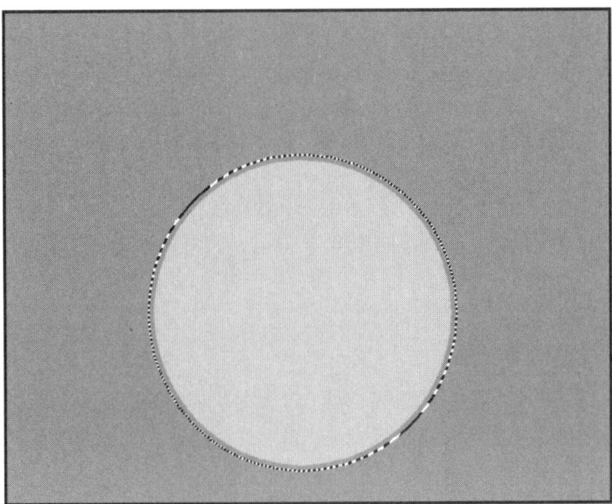

Figure 5-47: A simple circular selection.

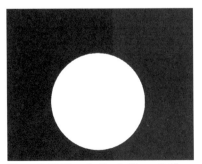

Figure 5-48: The selection in Figure 5-47 generates a channel similar to this one.

Besides making a new selection, one selection boundary can act on a previously saved channel. To understand how this works, let's assume that the channel in Figure 5-46 is already in place as channel #4 of an RGB document. Let's also assume that the circular selection in Figure 5-47 is active, that you have chosen Save Selection from the Select menu, and that the dialog box is open.

When the dialog box opens, the Source portion of the window is set to your current file on the Document pop-up menu, and Channel will default to New. When the channel is set to New, three of the four options in the Operation section of the window are grayed out. You can, if you wish, change the Channel pop-up menu to an existing channel which then allows you to perform the operations listed below. For this discussion, we'll assume that you have changed the Channel pop-up so that it reads #4.

Add to Selection

Adding to a selection simply means that you take the area of one selection outline and use it to extend the area of a previously saved selection. If you choose to add the circular selection of Figure 5-47 to the #4 channel (Figure 5-46), clicking OK will modify the #4 channel so that it appears as shown in Figure 5-49. This shape, as you can see, is the sum of the original channel and the new selection outline. Please note that this operation (and the other operations in the dialog box) will write over your existing #4 channel. If you wish to save the original channel, duplicate the channel before saving the Selection.

Figure 5-49: Adding the circular selection to the previously saved selection modifies the existing channel so that it contains both selection shapes.

Subtract From Selection

Subtracting from a selection lets you take away from the saved channel all of the area where the active selection overlaps it. When you have chosen this option and clicked OK, your #4 channel appears as shown in Figure 5-50.

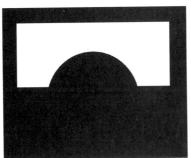

Figure 5-50: Subtracting the circular selection from the channel eliminates the area where the selection overlaps the white part of the channel.

Intersect With Selection

The last option on the list allows you to modify the existing channel so the modified channel shows as white only where the original shape and the circular selection overlap each other. The appearance of the modified channel is shown in Figure 5-51.

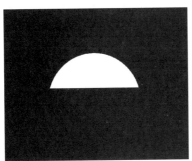

Figure 5-51: Intersect with selection produces a modified channel which contains white where the original shape and the circular selection overlap each other.

TIP *One of the difficulties with understanding the Load Selection dialog box is the use of the word* selection *in the operations list. You can more easily understand the options if you substitute the word* channel.

TIP *If you have more than one document open and the documents are exactly the same size, you can save your selections from one document directly to a different document.*

More About Loading Channel Selections

Whenever a Photoshop document has at least one alpha channel, the Load Selection command is available at the bottom of the Select menu. The Load Selection dialog box (see Figure 5-6) is similar to the Save Selection window: the Source Items differ only in that a check box marked Invert allows you to load the inverse of a selection; the Operation items are the same as for Save Selection. The dialog box can be more easily understood if you substitute the word *channel* for *selection*. Load Selection is also similar to Save Selection in its treatment of multiple documents. If two or more documents are open and exactly the same size, selections can be loaded directly from one into the other.

Operations are similar in nature to those employed by Save Selection. The command simply delivers you an active selection based on existing alpha channels. You can use the different kinds of operations to give you a number of selection possibilities. In the following discussion, we'll assume that a single document has had saved two alpha channels. The first channel is shown in Figure 5-46, and the second is shown in Figure 5-48. We'll refer to the channels as #4 and #5.

New Selection

If no selection is active, only New Selection will be available (other Operations depend upon an active selection modified by the contents of a channel). If channel #4 is chosen, the selection will be as shown in Figure 5-52. If the chosen channel is #5, the selection will be as shown in Figure 5-53.

Figure 5-52: A selection produced from channel #4 (shown in Figure 5-46).

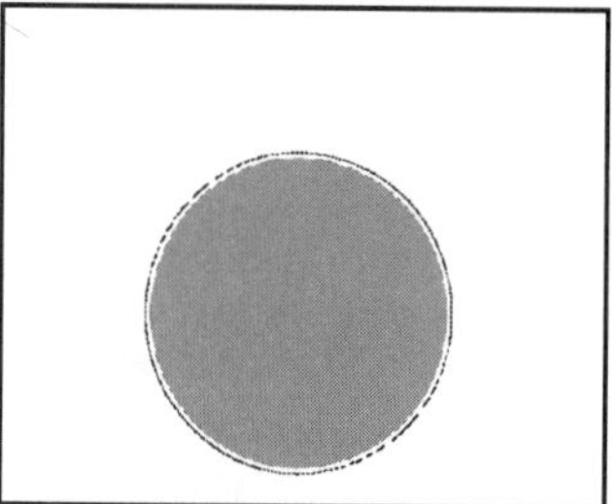

Figure 5-53: A selection produced from channel #5 (shown in Figure 5-48).

TIP *You can load either channel by holding Command or Ctrl and clicking on the channel's thumbnail.*

Add to Selection

If we assume that channel #4 has been loaded, then choosing #5 in the channel pop-up menu and selecting Add to Selection will give an active selection as shown in Figure 5-54. The combined selection is the total area enclosed by the white pixels in both channels.

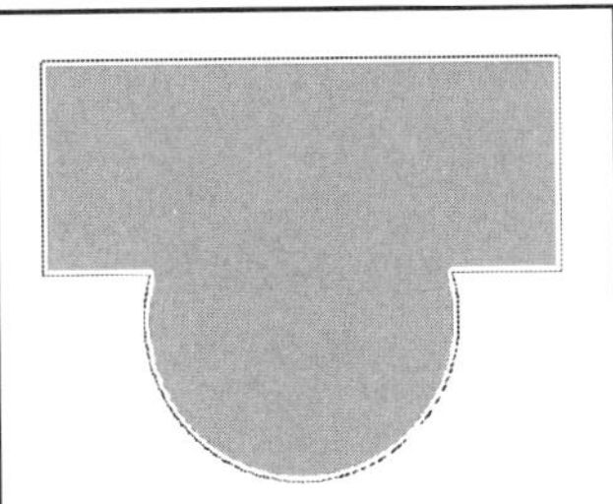

Figure 5-54: A selection produced by adding channel #5 to the active selection produced by channel #4.

TIP *You can load more than one channel as a selection from the keyboard: with one selection active, hold down Command+Shift or Ctrl+Shift and click on a different channel to add it to the selection.*

Subtract From Selection

With an active selection—produced from channel #4—choose channel #5 from the Channel pop-up menu, and select Subtract from Selection. The new selection is as shown in Figure 5-55. It is important to realize that Subtract gives you different results depending on which channel is active and which is subtracted. If the active selection is #5 and #4 is subtracted from it, the result is as shown in Figure 5-56.

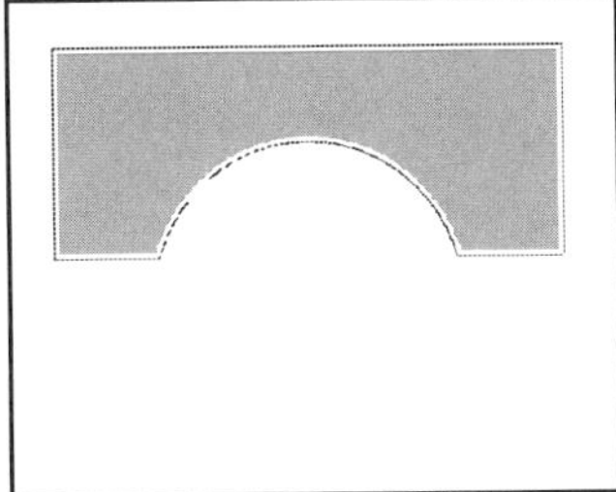

Figure 5-55: Channel #5 subtracted from the selection generated by channel #4 gives this as the new active selection.

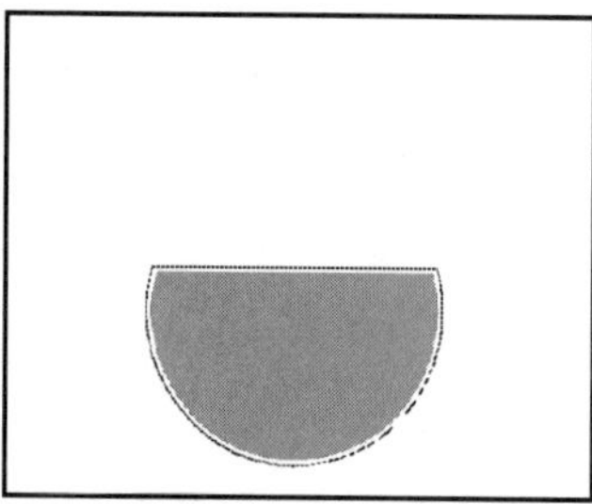

Figure 5-56: Channel #4 subtracted from the selection generated by channel #5 gives this as the new active selection.

TIP *You can subtract one channel's selection from another's from the keyboard: with one selection active, hold down Command+Option or Ctrl+Alt and click on a different channel to subtract it from the active selection.*

Intersect With Selection

Intersect With Selection gives you as an active selection, the area where the selections of two channels overlap each other. Either can be loaded. When the Intersect command is chosen, the result is as shown in Figure 5-57.

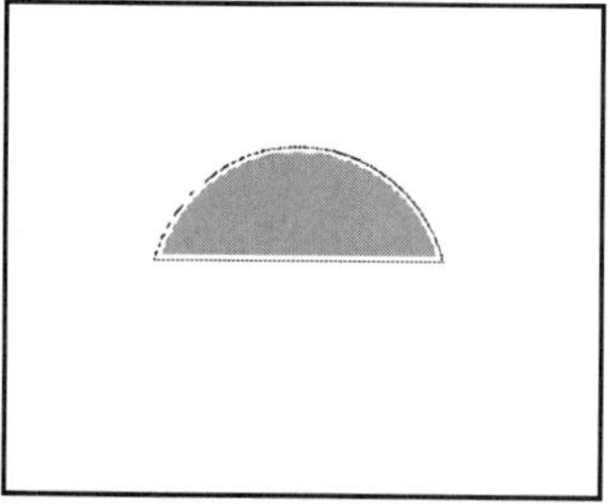

Figure 5-57: Using the Intersect Selection command produces an active selection of the area where the selections of two channels overlap each other.

TIP *You can load the Intersection of two channels from the keyboard: with one selection active, hold down Command+Option+Shift or Ctrl+Alt+Shift and click on a different channel to make the active selection the intersection of the two.*

Using Channels to Make Special Effects

Before the introduction of Photoshop v. 3.0, nearly all of the special effects for which Photoshop has been celebrated were produced as channel operations. Version 3.0's layers and layer masks have now superseded much of what used to be done with channels. However, channel operations are still the easiest way to generate the masks upon which some kinds of emboss and relief effects depend. Without channels, you would have to resort to time-consuming manual methods or to third-party filters and extensions to achieve effects which are wonderfully effective and fairly simple.

A Quick Subtraction Primer

Nearly everything you will see in the examples that follow this introductory material depend upon subtracting one channel from another to achieve a third channel based on the contents and positions of the other two. Although there are a large number of possibilities, we will limit our primer to two channels. One is a simple selection generated from the outlines of the shape in the image. The other is a blurred and offset version of the first. The general method used here is:

1. Subtract the original selection from the blurred channel.
2. Save the result as a third channel.
3. Load the third channel.
4. Fill the selection in the image with black. (Fill with black by setting the Foreground color to black, and then type **Option+Delete** or **Alt+Delete**.)

Figure 5-58 is the image upon which this primer is based. The center section of Figure 5-59 represents the star-filled center section selected and saved as an alpha channel. On the left-hand side of Figure 5-59, another channel has been made from a duplication of the first. The second was moved down and to the right and then blurred. Load the right-hand selection first by holding Command or Ctrl and clicking its thumbnail on the Channels palette. Subtract the original channel from the active selection: hold Command+Option or Ctrl+Alt and click on the other channel's thumbnail. Save the resulting selection into a new channel (right-hand side of Figure 5-59). When the new selection is loaded, fill it with black. The result is the drop shadow effect seen in Figure 5-60.

Figure 5-58: The original document for the primer.

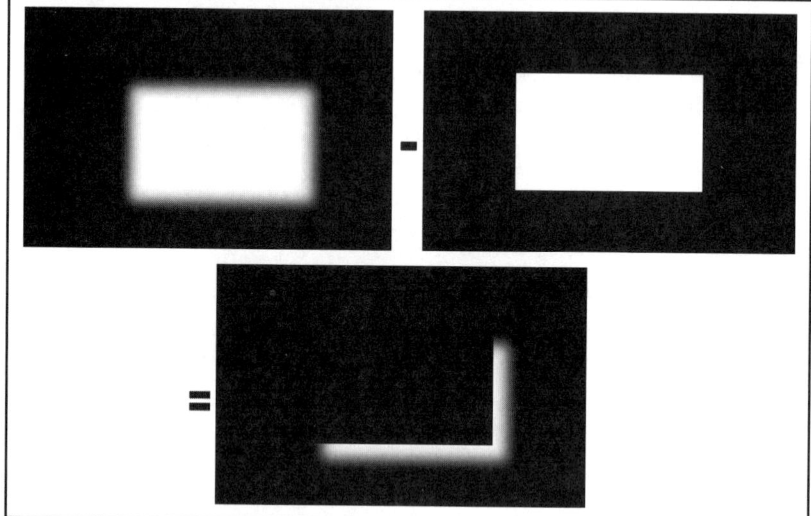

Figure 5-59: Subtract the center channel—the original selection of the star-filled rectangle—from a blurred and offset version of the center. The result is seen at the bottom.

Figure 5-60: When the resulting selection is filled with black, it produces this drop shadow effect.

Figure 5-61 shows the same channels as 5-59 but inverted. When the second is subtracted from the first, the resulting selection channel is that shown on the right. This selection, when loaded and filled with black, produces the effect shown in Figure 5-62. Instead of a drop shadow produced by the center rectangle, the shadow is produced by the surrounding shape making the center appear to be recessed.

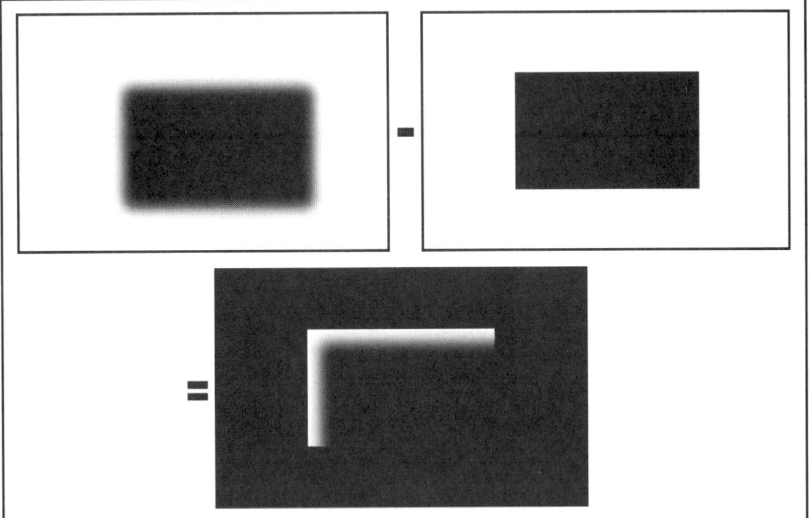

Figure 5-61: The same selection channels as Figure 5-59 are inverted and then subtracted. The resulting channel is shown at the bottom.

Figure 5-62: When the selection is filled with black, it produces this recessed effect.

Figures 5-63 and 5-65 are simple variations on the first two examples. First, the positive is subtracted from the negative, then the negative from the positive. The resulting channels and the selections filled with black are shown in Figures 5-64 and 5-65. These examples do not seem as promising as the first sets, but they can be used to very good effect, as you'll see in some of the following examples.

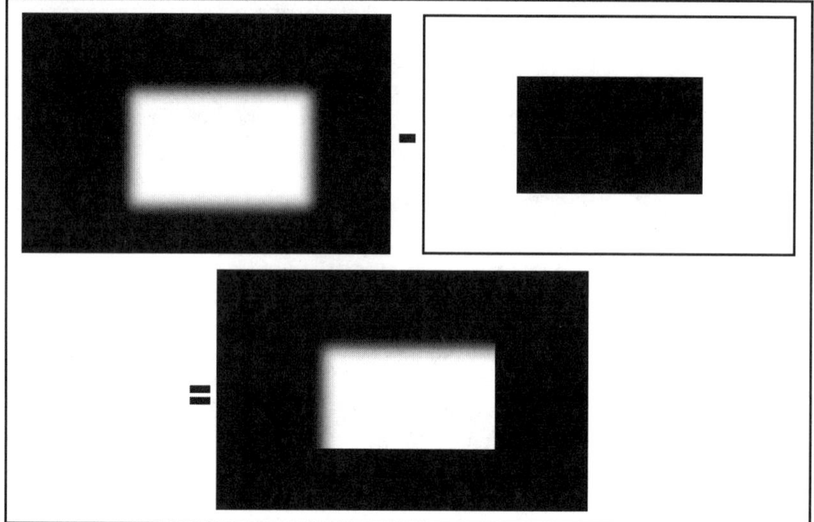

Figure 5-63: This variation subtracts a positive from a negative to give the channel shown at the bottom.

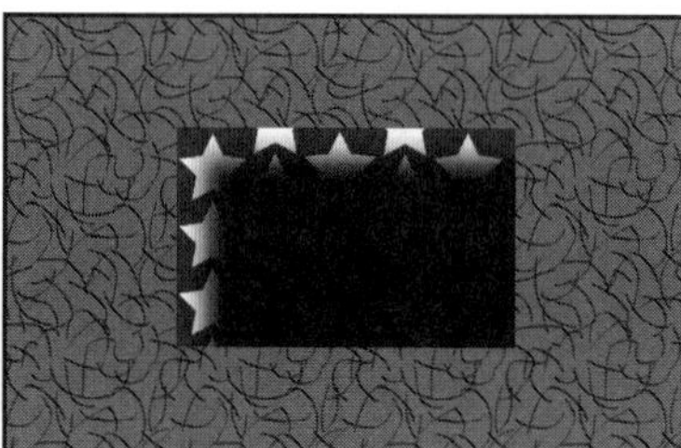

Figure 5-64: The loaded selection, filled with black, gives this result.

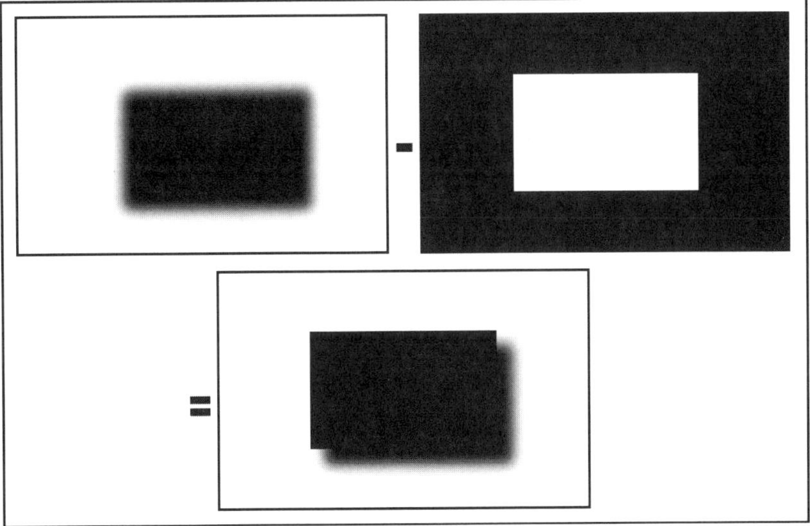

Figure 5-65: This variation subtracts a negative from a positive to give the channel shown at the bottom.

Figure 5-66: The loaded selection, filled with black, gives this result.

Simple Drop Shadows

Drop shadows are one of Photoshop's really useful tricks. Not only do drop shadows seem to add an extra dimension to what would otherwise be a flat photograph, but they also separate the shapes casting the shadows—in this case letters—from the background by delineating them on two sides with a darker color. When very large type is used as it is in this example, you have a spectacular drop shadow effect that does very little harm to the integrity of the photograph. If you'll look at this example printed in the color section of this book, you'll see that the lettering and the shadows do not hide much of the image's detail. Instead, the letters claim your attention simply because of their size, because of the small change in tone between the letters and the background, and because of the more pronounced change in tone between the letters and the shadow. A drop shadow done this way is very simple. Follow along, if you wish, with the file CHICAGO.PSD found on the Companion CD-ROM in the Chapter 5 Practice files. Note: the two alpha channels shown in the examples which follow are already a part of the CD-ROM file.

Follow these steps:

1. Size and crop the file to be used. Color adjust, and run the Unsharp mask filter. When the file is completely ready (Figure 5-67), choose File | Export | Paths to Illustrator. You won't have any paths in the document: export the document boundaries. Open the exported file in Illustrator and set up the type to be used. Convert the type to paths, copy the paths, switch back to Photoshop, and Paste As Paths.

Figure 5-67: Image to which will be applied the channels-based drop shadow.

2. Create a new alpha channel (#4). With the channel in view, change your Foreground/Background colors to white and black, and fill the paths with white (Figure 5-68). Hide the paths. Duplicate the channel (#5).

Figure 5-68: Letter shapes made in Illustrator and pasted as paths into Photoshop are used to make this alpha channel.

3. Select channel #4. Press v to select the Move tool. Press the Left arrow key 10 times and the Up arrow 10 times. Select channel #5. Press the Right arrow key 10 times and the Down arrow 10 times. This moves the two layers so that they are offset from each other by 20 pixels.

   With channel #5 selected, choose Filter | Blur | Gaussian Blur. Choose a blur radius that feathers the edges to the extent shown in Figure 5-69. The example file, a 300-ppi image, was blurred with a radius value of 18.

Figure 5-69: Use the Gaussian Blur filter on the duplicate of the first alpha channel.

4. The next task is to make a new active selection using the subtract method to eliminate the areas of the original letters from areas of the blurred letters. The selection, if you were to save it as a channel, would look similar to Figure 5-70. Begin by loading channel #5 (Command+click or Ctrl+click on the channel #5 thumbnail). Subtract channel #4 from channel #5 (hold Command+Option or Ctrl+Alt and click on the thumbnail of channel #4).

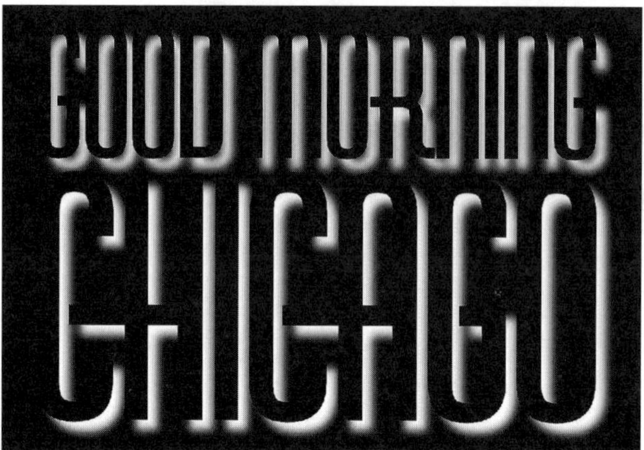

Figure 5-70: When channel #4 is subtracted from channel #5, the resulting selection, saved as a channel, will look like this.

5. Choose a dark, interesting color from the image with the Eyedropper tool. With the subtracted selection active, choose Edit | Fill. In the resulting dialog box (Figure 5-71), set the fill to be with the Foreground color, the percentage to be 50%–60%, and the mode to be Multiply. The Fill command produces the effect shown in Figure 5-72.

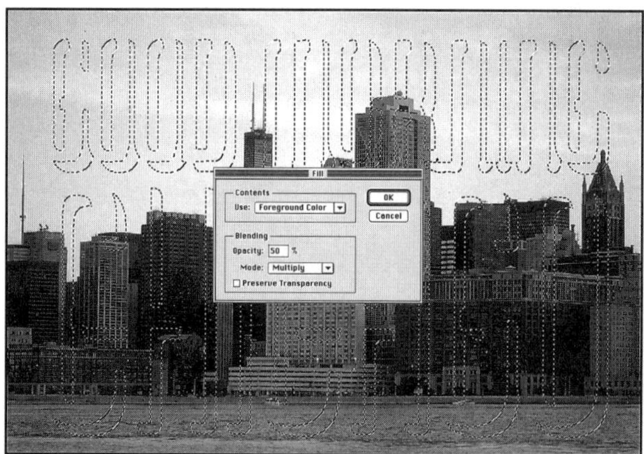

Figure 5-71: Fill the selection with 50% of the Foreground color using the Multiply mode.

Figure 5-72: After filling, you have this shadow effect.

6. After you've made the shadows, you may decide that you need to increase the contrast between the letters and the background. Load channel #4, and open the Levels controls. Move the center Input slider to the left until the letters have been sufficiently lightened (Figure 5-73). Click OK. Choose Select | Inverse, and open the Levels controls again. Move the center slider to the right until the background is a little darker than it was. Be careful not to darken too much since the picture is fairly dark to begin with. When you are finished, click OK. Your image should look similar to that shown in Figure 5-74, and the example in the color section of the book.

Figure 5-73: With the selection of channel #4 active, use the Levels controls to lighten the letters.

Figure 5-74: Select the inverse of channel #4, and use the Levels controls to slightly darken the area around the letters. The finished file should look like this. You can see this image in the color plates section of the book.

Embossed Effects

Embossing with channels can be done by constructing embossed shapes in a channel (see the Glass Letters Effect section in Chapter 4) and then using the Levels controls with the channel active as a selection. Another simple effect is to use the technique shown in Figure 5-62 but with two offset and blurred channels to produce selections on opposite sides of a shape. Depending upon which direction you wish the direction of the light, one selection is lightened and the other darkened. This usually produces a beveled effect which can have hard or smooth edges. The following primer will help explain the more complex effects to follow.

A Short Channel Embossing Primer

The inner section of the two-part shape in Figure 5-75 can be selected by loading the channel at the right. This base channel can be used to generate the other channels which produce the embossing effects.

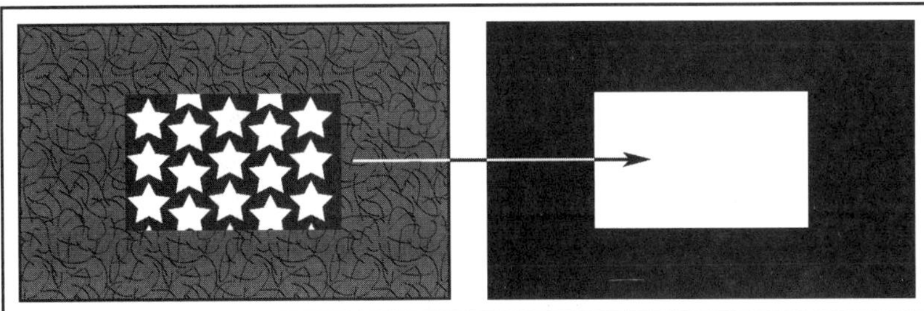

Figure 5-75: The central shape can be selected by loading the channel on the right.

The base channel is duplicated and inverted (Figure 5-76, center). The inverted copy is duplicated, moved to the right and down, and blurred (Figure 5-76, left). When the inverted base is subtracted from the blurred and offset version, the new selection is as shown on the right.

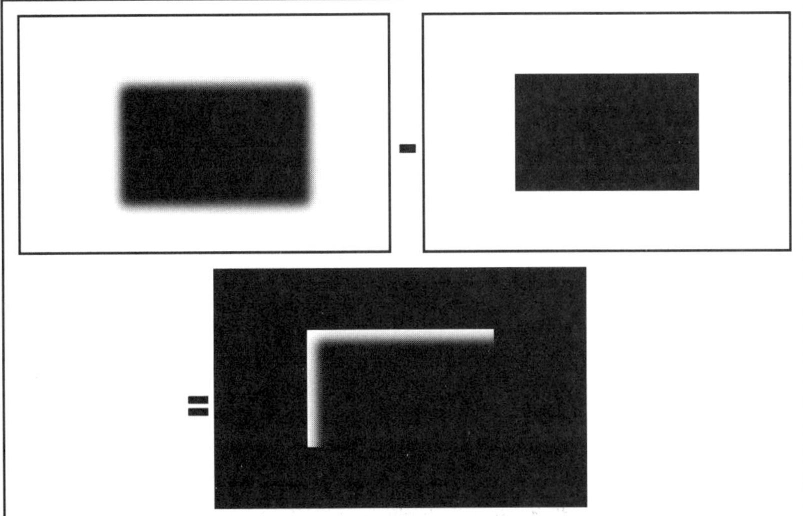

Figure 5-76: Subtracting the center channel from the left-hand channel makes the channel on the right.

The same procedure but applied to a version of the blurred channel that has been offset up and to the left is shown in Figure 5-77.

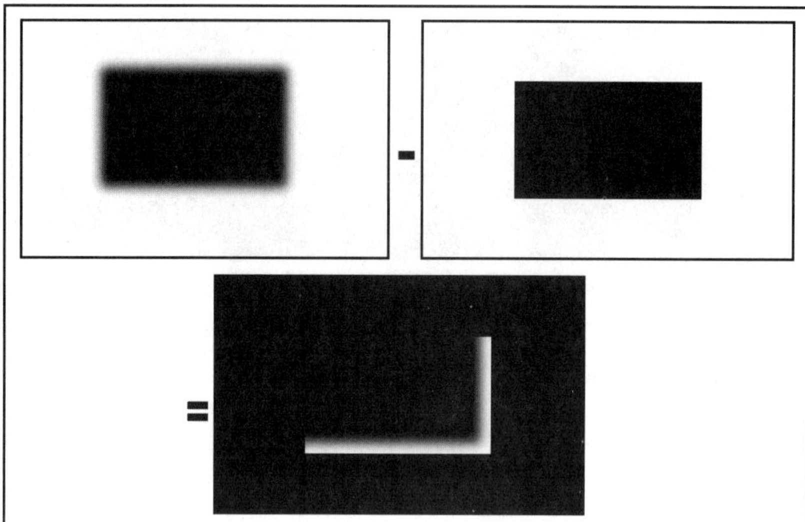

Figure 5-77: Subtracting the center channel from the left-hand channel makes the channel on the right. This channel makes a selection on the opposite corner as shown in Figure 5-76.

Both of the new channels need to be refined before they can be used. The reason for this is that the two sides extend the entire length of the rectangle. Both must be shortened. This can be done by subtracting each from the other and saving the new channels. Figure 5-78 shows the upper-left selection subtracted from the lower-right selection. Figure 5-79 shows the opposite procedure. The channels on the right of each figure are those used for the embossed effect.

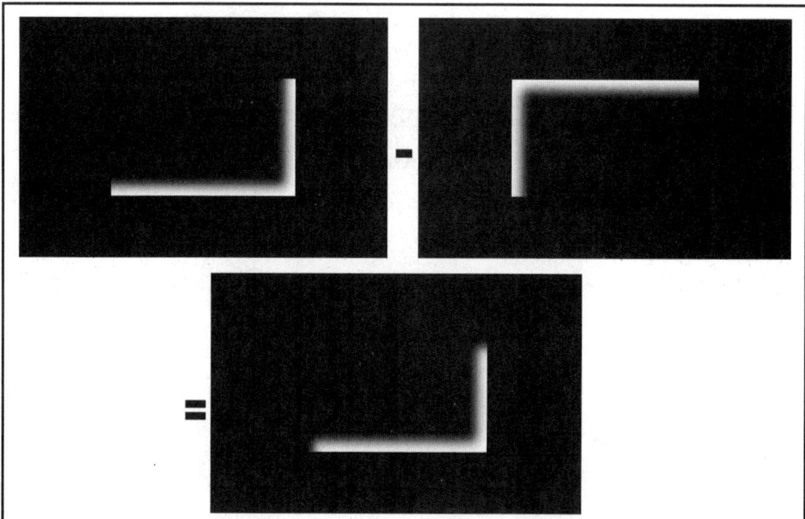

Figure 5-78: Subtract the upper-left selection from the lower-right selection to get a new selection with shortened legs.

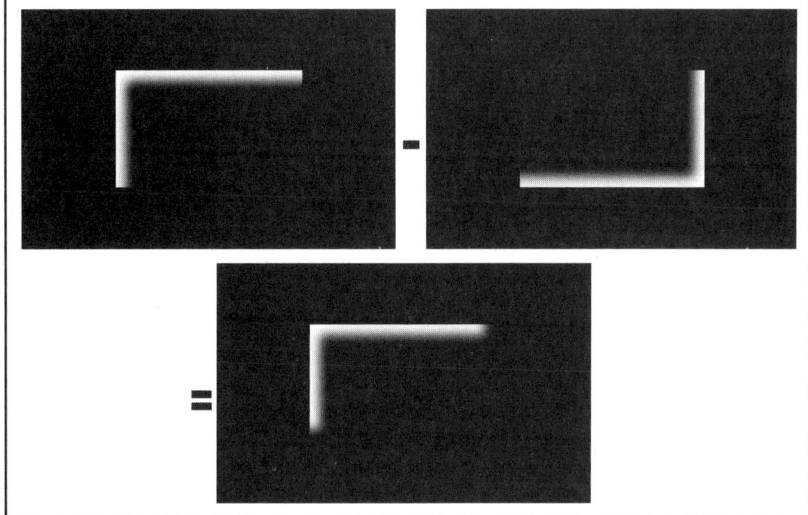

Figure 5-79: Subtract the lower-right selection from the upper-left selection to get a new selection with shortened legs.

The embossing can be done in a couple of ways. The selections can be loaded and the Levels controls used to darken or lighten the affected part of the image. In the case of Figure 5-80, the lower selection was loaded and simply filled with black; the upper selection was loaded and filled with white.

Figure 5-80: Load the lower selection and fill with black. Load the upper selection and fill with white.

This embossing procedure gives a rounded bevel to the rectangular object. To make a harder edge, click on the upper selection on the Channels palette. With this selection in view, load the original alpha channel (shown at the right of Figure 5-75). Choose Select | Modify | Contract. Choose a number that will contract the selection by the width of the bevel. When the selection has contracted, fill the selection with black. Change to the lower-edge selection channel and fill with black again (the contracted selection is still active). When these two are loaded and filled with black and white, the result is as shown in Figure 5-81.

Figure 5-81: Contract the original channel by the width of the bevel. Use the selection to modify the channels used to make the bevels so that they have a hard inner edge. Fill in the same manner as used for Figure 5-80.

Embossed Letters Based on Channels

This lettering effect is every bit as simple to produce as the drop shadow example except that there are more steps to follow. You will be generating six new channels, using the first four to generate the two final channels. The last two channels will be used with the Fill command to produce the effect. To make the process less confusing, we'll refer to the channels by number: #6, #7, and so on. Sometimes you will need to have one channel in view and load the selection of another. Sometimes you will subtract one channel from another to make another channel. The principles behind what we are going to do will be clear from a look back at the Subtraction Primer (above). If it helps, you can rename the channels so that they include the number and a description. For example, the channel created in Step 1 (below) could be called #6 *original, centered letters*. The channel created in Step 2 could be #7 *original up & left*. Short descriptive names will help you to keep track of what each channel is and what it does for you in any of the listed steps.

Continue working on your copy of CHICAGO.PSD. You should choose File | Revert to go back to the original image. There are two channels already present in the document as well as the paths used to generate the original alpha channel. The two extra channels are #4 & #5. We'll leave those alone for now and generate a set of new channels (#6–#11).

Note: as you create new channels, your file size will grow rapidly. By the time you have created the 11th channel, your 15MB file will be almost 55MB. If disk space and RAM are considerations for the machine on which you will be working, you may wish to change this image to a lower resolution. Choose Image | Image Size. You might consider changing from 300 ppi to 100 ppi. That will make things easier as you go through the examples. Your file size will decrease, and, when specific numerical values are given, you can calculate your own values as about one-third of those listed.

Follow these instructions:

1. Create a new channel (#6). Click on the item in the Paths palette, and fill the paths with white (Figure 5-82). Hide the paths; you won't need them again for this exercise.

Figure 5-82: Create a new channel (#6). Use the paths to fill the letter shapes with white. Hide the paths.

2. Duplicate channel #6 (makes #7). Press v to select the Move tool. Set your Foreground/Background colors to be white (F) and black (B). Move channel #6 up 4 pixels and to the left 4 pixels (use the Up and Left arrow keys). Now, duplicate channel #7 (makes #8). Return to #7 and choose Image | Adjust | Invert (Figure 5-83).

Figure 5-83: Channel #7 inverted after it has been moved up and to the left.

3. Duplicate channel #6 (makes channel #9). With the Move tool selected, move channel #9 down 4 pixels and to the right 4 pixels (Arrow keys). Use the Gaussian Blur filter—Radius value of 10—on channel #9 (Figure 5-84).

Figure 5-84: Channel #9 has been moved down and to the right, and has been blurred with a radius value of 10 pixels.

4. Load channel #9 as a selection. Subtract channel #7. Save the resulting selection as a new channel (#10). Deselect All. Click on channel #10's thumbnail to view it (Figure 5-85).

Figure 5-85: Load channel #9, subtract channel #7, and save as a new channel (#10).

5. Load channel #8 as a selection (with channel #10 in view). Choose the Gaussian Blur filter at a setting of 7 pixels. This will iron out the irregularities at the corners of the letter shapes (Figure 5-86).

Figure 5-86: Load channel #8, with the selection active, use the Gaussian Blur filter (radius of 7) on channel #10.

6. While the channel #8 selection is still active, duplicate channel #10 (makes #1 1). Click on #11's thumbnail to view it. Choose Image | Adjust | Invert (Figure 5-87). Deselect All. Click on the top item in the Channels list to view the colored image.

Figure 5-87: With the channel #8 selection still active, duplicate channel #10 (makes #1 1). Click on the new channel to view it. Invert the contents of the selection.

7. Use the Eyedropper tool to select a tone from the image that has about a 50% brightness value. If you set your Info palette so that the left half gives readings in grayscale while the right half gives readings in RGB, you'll be able to locate a color that is in the neighborhood of 50% black—*50% brightness*—despite its color. Load the selection of channel #11. Choose Edit | Fill. Fill with the Foreground color, Normal mode, 60% Opacity (Figure 5-88).

Figure 5-88: Load channel #11, fill with a 50% brightness tone set to Normal mode and 60% Opacity.

8. Select a new Foreground color from the image with the Eyedropper tool. Make this tone's value equivalent to about 10% black. Load the selection of channel #11. Choose the Fill command again using the same settings as before (Figure 5-89).

Figure 5-89: Load channel #11, fill with a 10% brightness tone set to Normal mode and 60% Opacity.

9. Load channel #9. Subtract channel #8. The new selection gives the ar ea of a drop shadow. Select a new tone from the image equivalent to about 80% black. Fill using the Foreground color, 60% Opacity, and Multiply mode (Figure 5-90).

Figure 5-90: Load channel #9, subtract channel #8, fill with an 80% tone set to Multiply mode and 60% Opacity. The final file can be seen in the color section of this book.

Other Channel Effects

The drop shadow and embossing effects you can achieve with channels are spectacular. There are many other possibilities which give attractive effects that may be less dramatic but may prove to be more useful. Some of the following material is based on a selection of some object in the image. Another example will show you a remarkable edge-enhancement technique. You'll also see a couple of examples of how channels can help you with compositing images. All of these examples should give you a clear idea of how to approach using channels and a general idea of what can be done with them. You'll think of hundreds of uses of your own. Eventually you'll wonder how you ever worked without them.

Glow Effects

Our reliable friend the sundial is back in service as an example (Figure 5-91) in our discussion of glow effects, the easiest channel effect of all. In preparation for the glow, you must first detach the shape of the object from its background. In this case, you can use any of the Selection tools to outline the sundial shape. When you have the area selected, save the selection as a channel (Figure 5-92). We'll call this channel the *base* alpha channel since so much else is built upon it, generated from it, or modified by it. (The word *base* has no special Photoshop significance. We're going to simply assign it as a name so that we'll have a handy way of referring to the channel from which we will build other channels.) Be sure to keep this channel untouched since you will need it for many purposes. As soon as you have the base channel saved, you may want to get into the habit of duplicating it and then inverting the duplicate. That way you'll have both the negative and positive of the base channel from which to work.

CD-ROM

Note that the Companion CD-ROM disk contains, in the Chapter 5 Practice Files folder, the file SUNDIAL.PSD. The document already contains the base channel and two additional channels. If you would like to try out these examples as you read about them, please open the file and follow the instructions.

Figure 5-91: The sundial photograph, the example file to be used for more channel effects.

Figure 5-92: After selecting the shape of the sundial, the selection is saved as an alpha channel. We'll call this channel the base alpha channel since so much else is built upon it, generated from it, or modified by it.

The next step is to use the Gaussian Blur filter on a copy of the base channel. You can have a large influence on the glow by the Radius value you choose. Figure 5-93 shows the differences between 8 pixels, 16, 24, and 32 (left-hand side and across the top). These samples are deliberately spaced away from each other so that you can tell how far the blur spreads out from the original white edge.

After you have blurred the channel, you still have a large amount of control over it with the Levels. The two samples at the bottom of the figure, both of which have been subjected to a blur of 24 pixels radius, show the effects of moving the center Input slider—the gamma control, or midtone slider—an extreme distance. In the bottom center example, the slider was moved to the right to give a gamma reading of .25. This has the effect of contracting the blur by darkening the pixels outside the original shape's boundaries.

The bottom right example shows the effect of moving the midtone slider to the right to give a reading of 2.25. Moving the slider to the left gives the opposite effect of moving it to the right. It reduces the width of the blur by lightening the portion inside the original boundaries. This will give you a blur on the outside of the shape but a definite white edge on the inside.

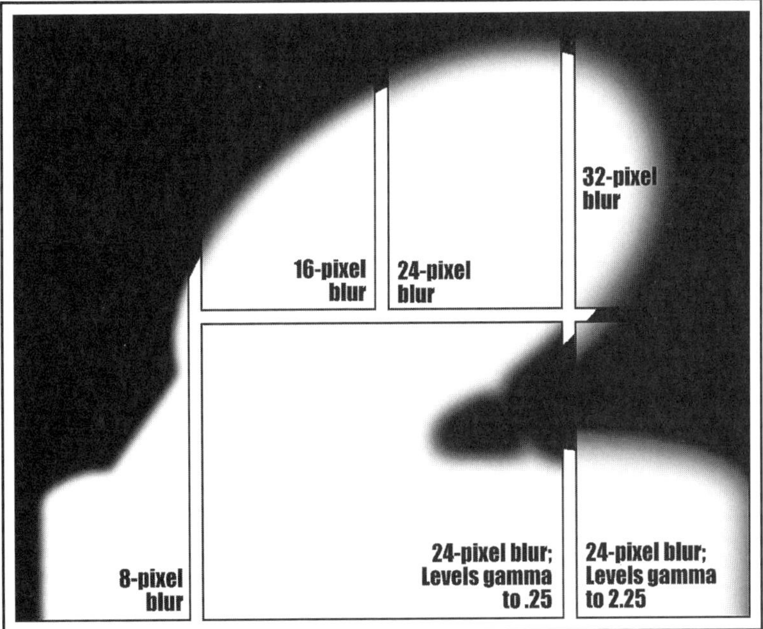

Figure 5-93: The size of the glow effect can be controlled by the amount of the Gaussian Blur applied. After blurring, additional modifications can be made by moving the center—gamma—slider in the Levels controls.

Once you have the channel blurred, making the glow channel is easy. Load the blurred channel as a selection (hold down Command or Ctrl and click the channel's thumbnail). Subtract the base channel from the active selection (hold down Command+Option or Ctrl+Alt and click on the base channel's thumbnail). Save the resulting selection as a new channel (click on the second icon from the left on the bottom of the Channels palette). The new channel is shown in Figure 5-94.

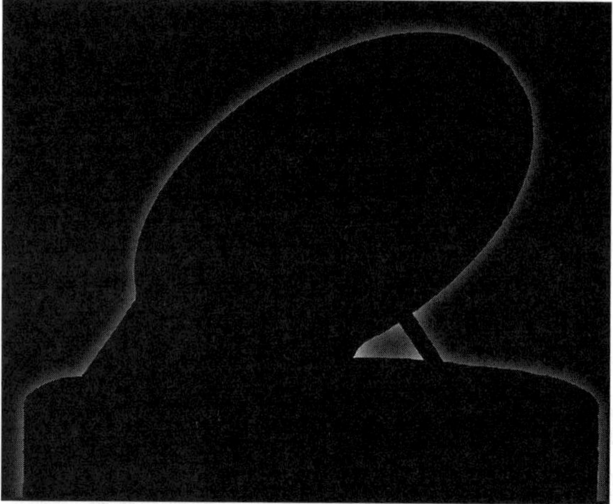

Figure 5-94: Load the blurred channel, subtract the base channel, and save the resulting selection as a new channel. This channel will be used to produce the glow effects.

Switch to the composite view of the image and load the new channel as a selection. You can use any of several methods while the selection is active. With the gamma slider in the Levels controls, moving the slider to the left lightens the selection. Moving it in the other direction darkens the selection. You can make use of the Fill command which will allow you to fill with a color and to control the opacity of the color application. Or—this is the easiest—set your Foreground/Background colors to the defaults and press Delete. You'll see a pretty, slightly metaphysical addition to your image (Figure 5-95). Or, you can fill with black to make the area of the glow dark instead of light (Figure 5-96).

Figure 5-95: With the glow channel active as a selection, set the Background color to white and press Delete.

Figure 5-96: The glow selection can be filled with a dark color to give this effect. (A fill with a lavender shade—try R 51, G 0, B 255—will make the image look radioactive.)

Another glow possibility is to keep, as a selection, the part of the blur *inside* the boundaries of the object. This gives an effect similar to the glow but *on* the object instead of around it. Load the blurred channel to make it the active selection. Subtract from the selection, the inverted copy of the base channel. Save the selection as a new channel. Deselect. The channel is shown in Figure 5-97.

Figure 5-97: When you subtract the inverted copy of the base channel from the blurred channel, you retain the portion of the blur inside the boundaries of the object.

Click on the new channel to view it. Load the base channel as a selection, and choose Image | Adjust | Invert. This inverts just the part of the channel within the selection (Figure 5-98).

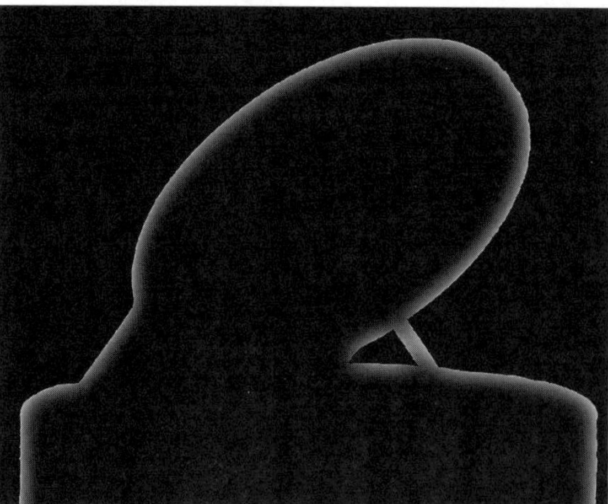

Figure 5-98: Invert just the inner part of Figure 5-97 by loading the base channel and using the Invert command.

Load the new channel as a selection. You are again faced with many choices about what to do with your selection. Three possibilities are shown in Figure 5-99. The untouched original is in the upper left-hand corner (*a*). It is included so that you can compare it with the others. The photo in *b* shows the selection filled with white, that in *c* filled with black, and the photo in *d* filled with a black-to-white gradient drawn from the bottom of the pedestal to the top of the disk.

Figure 5-99: The selection from the channel in Figure 5-98 can be treated in a number of ways. The photo in a is the original, b shows the selection filled with white, c uses a black fill, and d has the selection filled with a black-to-white gradient.

Masking With Gradients

If you stop and think about what a remarkable tool the channels concept is, you may reflect that, beyond the ability to add and subtract from selections, all of the major tools involve manipulation of simple grayscale images with a blur tossed in for good measure. Such power from simple means!

A Gaussian Blur, the way we've been using it in this chapter, is a more-or-less narrow, shaped, or contoured gradient. We have used it to ease transitions from one texture to another: as the white fades to black, the superimposed effects attenuate and disappear. The Gradient tool can accomplish the same task except that it can be used on a much larger scale. It can fade out entire images, modify texture applications over large areas, and even assist in the seamless merging of two disparate photos.

An alpha channel containing a gradient might be similar to that shown in Figure 5-100. An effect applied to a selection loaded from this channel would gradually disappear as it approached the bottom of the frame.

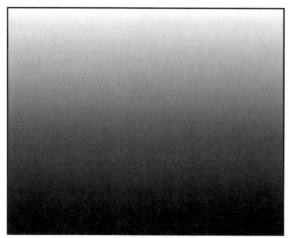

Figure 5-100: An operation applied to an alpha channel containing a gradient such as this would gradually disappear as it approached the bottom of the image.

When the gradient is combined with another selection channel, for example, the channel shown in Figure 5-101, then you have the ability to moderate textures and commands around the object shape and to leave the object shape untouched. To make a channel similar to this one, begin with a duplicate of what we have referred to as the base channel (Figure 5-92). Invert the channel. Load it as a selection, and draw a black-to-white gradient from bottom to top.

In Figure 5-102, you can see how such a channel might be used. We prepared the file with a series of horizontal paths, loaded the channel as a selection, chose a small paintbrush, and set it to stroking the paths (Normal mode, Foreground black, 100% Opacity). The lines, drawn directly on the image, seem to pass behind the sundial. Each line is slightly more transparent than the one above it. The texture fades smoothly into nothing at the bottom of the image.

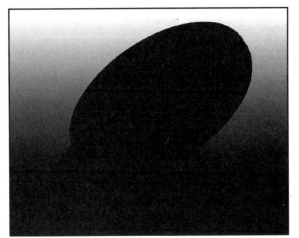

Figure 5-101: This channel combines the object shape with the gradient. It gives the ability to control effects around the object leaving the shape untouched.

Figure 5-102: With the combination channel loaded, a series of solid painted lines (stroked paths) do not intrude into the boundary of the sundial and fade smoothly into nothing at the bottom of the photo.

Using gradients to fade effects is a very clever way to combine images so that they seem to merge imperceptibly into each other. To illustrate how this can work, look at Figure 5-103. With the channel active, a gradient drawn within this window appears only within the boundary of the selection. We will use this new channel to combine the sundial image with the marigolds photo shown in Figure 5-104.

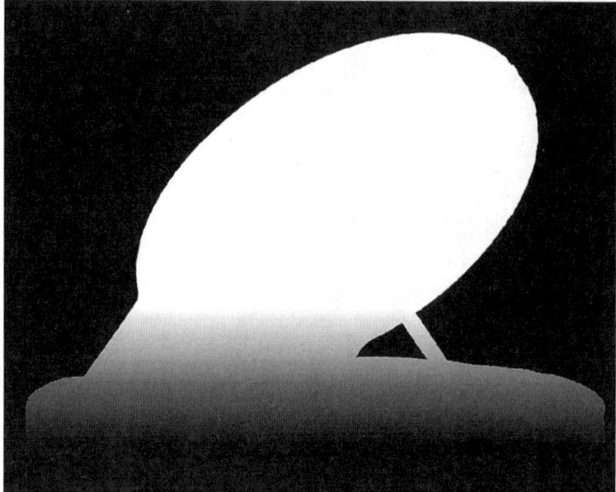

Figure 5-103: With the base channel active, the gradient can be drawn so that it shows only within the object.

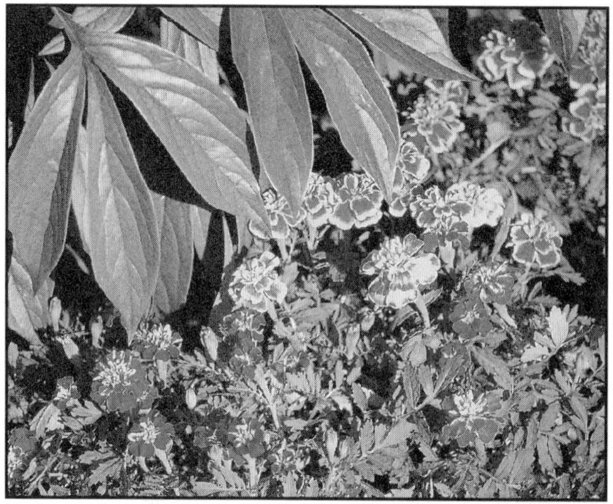

Figure 5-104: Photo to be used for demonstrating the merging of two images.

With both windows open—and reduced in size so that you can see at least a part of both—make the channel in the sundial image an active selection. Now, drag the selection from the sundial window onto the marigolds. Be sure to hold the Shift key as you drag to insure that the selection centers itself in the destination window. A new layer will form containing the sundial. If you look at the layer without the background visible, you'll see that the pixels are opaque at the top and transparent at the bottom. When the sundial lays atop the other image, the lower portion fades into nothing. The effect is seen in Figure 5-105.

Figure 5-105: With the channel active, the selected part of the sundial image is added to the marigolds. The effect of the gradient is shown by the way the sundial fades to invisibility at the bottom of the frame.

Here's another way to achieve a similar merge effect. First, make an alpha channel such as the one shown in Figure 5-106. Begin with the base channel, invert it, load the inverted channel as a selection, and draw the gradient. Move this channel to the marigolds photo. With the sundial as the active image—but with the marigolds window visible—drag this channel's thumbnail from the Channels palette onto the destination window. This will make the marigolds the active window. Click at the top of the Channels palette to return to the composite view. Load the new channel. Drag the selection from one window to the other (the marigolds to the sundial). This combines the images in the opposite direction as before—the marigolds added to the sundial photo. As you can see in Figure 5-107, the result is just as successful.

Figure 5-106: This channel was made by inverting a copy of the base channel, loading the channel selection, and then drawing a black-to-white gradient from bottom to top.

Figure 5-107: With the new channel moved to the marigolds image and then made active, the selected part of the marigolds image is added to the sundial. The effect of the gradient is shown by the way the marigolds fade to invisibility at the bottom of the frame.

TIP *You can drag channels back and forth between documents only when the two windows are exactly the same size.*

Edge Enhancement With Find Edges

Our last example of channel effects is a technique for enhancing edges. This method is not successful for every image but it is useful often enough that it is worth a try. Follow these steps:

1. You'll need to begin with a duplicate of the sundial photo (Image | Duplicate).
2. Change the mode of the sundial to Lab. Press Command+1 or Ctrl+1 to view the L channel. Convert the image to Grayscale mode. A dialog box will ask if you wish to delete the other channels. Click OK.
3. From the Filter menu, choose Stylize | Find Edges. When the filter has executed, your image will look similar to Figure 5-108.
4. Invert the image (Image | Adjust | Invert) (Figure 5-109). Use the Gaussian Blur filter at a setting of 3 or 4 to eliminate some of the fine texture—which shows as a space-filling graininess in some areas of the photo—generated by the filter. Open the Levels controls. Move the Highlight slider on the input scale to the left, and the Shadow slider on the same scale to the right. Move one slider a small amount; then move the other. Keep doing this until you achieve the effect you want. You are increasing the contrast between light and dark areas of the photo. The appearance of the photo, after you have moved the sliders, will be similar to Figure 5-110.

Figure 5-108: A copy of the sundial photo, converted to grayscale, and to which the Find Edges filter has been applied.

Figure 5-109: After using the Find Edges filter, invert the image. Use the Gaussian Blur filter to eliminate some of the grainy texture.

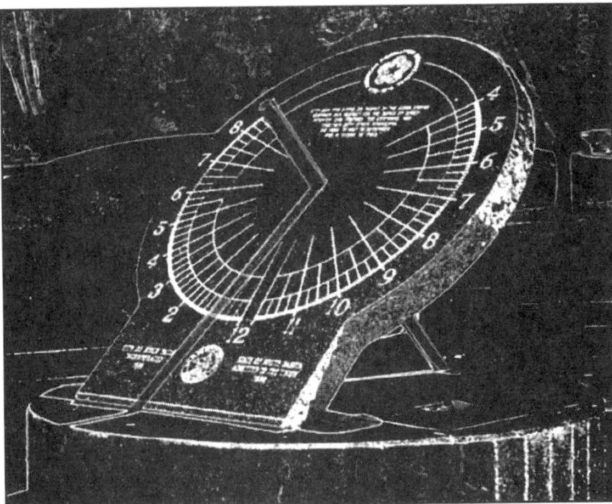

Figure 5-110: Use the Levels controls to increase the contrast between dark and light areas.

5. When the duplicate image looks as shown in Figure 5-110, transfer the Black channel back to the original photo. Do this by dragging the Black channel thumbnail from the Channels palette onto the RGB photo. Click at the top of the palette to view the composite color image.

6. Load the new channel as a selection. Open the Levels controls again. Move the center Input scale slider to the right. Watch the image as you move the slider. It's easy to go too far with this operation. All you want to do is make the selection a little darker. Figure 5-111 shows the difference between the original image (left) and the darkened selection (right). Notice how the details of the image have been hardened and made more clear without the appearance of too much sharpening. As you study this figure, look back to Figure 5-110. It will give you a clear idea of which parts of the image have been affected by darkening the selection with the Levels.

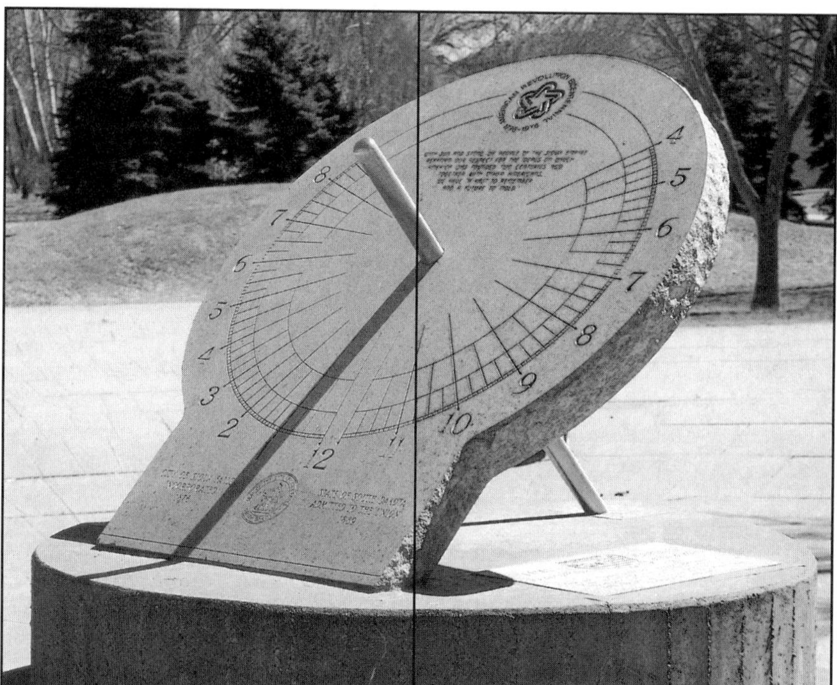

Figure 5-111: The right-hand side of this figure shows the result of the Levels adjustment made when the alpha channel in Figure 5-110 was active.

A Final Note

With the introduction of Adobe's PostScript Level 3, channels are likely to play an increasingly important role, particularly in the world of prepress. Channels as masks will supersede clipping paths as exportable masks. This is going to be enormously helpful since it will eliminate the hard edges of the clipping path and allow soft, transparent edges. Masking will be a much simpler task: as you have seen with this chapter, manipulating channels is much simpler than constructing Beziér outlines. This kind of masking—and the other features of PostScript Level 3—will depend upon the software implementation of publishers. When the day arrives that most of the major graphics software programs are able to make use of Level 3, Wow!

Moving On

You have seen the power of channels used to express quite a number of concepts. Simple grayscale images are used by Photoshop to preserve selections, to express degrees of opacity, to modify the effects of a command, to be an analog for the strength of a video color component, to express the amount of ink in a color separation, and to show the luminance of each pixel as separate from its color. All of these concepts, and more, can be assigned to a document's channels. This flexibility means that all of these concepts are subject to manipulation using other Photoshop controls on the channels which constitute a photo image.

When you first encountered channels, the subject may have seemed so large that you found yourself a little intimidated. However, we hope that trying some of the examples shown in this chapter has reassured you that channels are not mysterious. They are simple, easily modified, and possess remarkable power to help you apply wonderful effects to your image.

With channels now under control, it's on to Layers (Chapter 6). Layers, as you'll see, share many important concepts with channels. In fact, some aspects of layers—layer masks—will show themselves to be temporary channels which you'll be able to modify in the same ways you have modified alpha channels. You'll find many points of similarity between channels and layers, and what you already know will make your acquaintance with layers much easier.

chapter 6

Using Layers

Layers is the feature of Photoshop that can turn you into an imaging hero. All of those glorious, complex-appearing effects that you see in periodicals and on Web pages are sculpted—usually—with layers. You'll find, within minutes of your first use of layers, that you can make subtle and intricate changes to your image, changes that suddenly transform your work from ordinary to amazing. Just try them: what you can do will give you a real rush!

Once you become accustomed to using layers, you'll wonder how you got along without them. You'll come to appreciate the fact that, special effects aside, the real purpose of layers is to extend the editability of a Photoshop document. For example, in versions prior to Photoshop 3.0—the first version of the program to use layers—using the Type tool applied letter shapes to the image. The shapes were selected and floating when they were created but, when deselected, they merged with the underlying image, replacing the pixels below them. If you needed to preserve the original pixels—those replaced by the type—you needed to duplicate your file and do your work on a copy. This could lead to a confusing proliferation of similar files—some of them large—at different stages of development. With version 4.0 of Photoshop, using the Type tool automatically assigns the letter shapes to a brand new layer. You may move the type, change its color, perform many operations on it, and all without touching the original image. You can even save your layered document, and at some future time, open it, delete the layers, and be left with an intact version of your original file.

Layers can be added to a Photoshop file with ease. In fact, you'll see in this chapter at least eight different methods—there are probably more—of adding a layer to a document. Once the layer has been created, you'll find that any pixels on the layer can be placed into special relationships with the pixels on other layers. One relationship is that of a grouping where moving the contents of one layer also moves the contents of a different layer. Another relationship might be to use the shape on one layer as a visibility boundary—or *mask*—for the pixels on a different layer. One of the most important relationships is brought into play when the pixels of one layer are placed in a blend mode that changes their appearance and the pixels of all layers below them. All of these are simple relationships that you can put into effect and remove with great ease.

The are more subtle options for layers. You may, if you wish, add to any or all layers, a *layer mask*. With a layer mask, you have the opportunity of masking some of the pixels in a layer using techniques you have already learned and mastered in Chapter 5, "Using Channels." In fact, a layer mask is nothing more than a temporary channel whose masking effects can be applied to the layer or shut off whenever you wish. Another feature—one you will really enjoy once you see it in action—is the ability to exclude some pixels from visibility simply by referencing their brightness or their color, or by referencing the brightness or color of pixels beneath them. This is a feature of Photoshop that is not extensively used because it appears to be difficult. You'll find that it is not difficult at all, and that it will prove to be a tool that you'll use in many different situations.

When we've examined all of the features that are available to you, you will find that some of the valuable aspects of layers are not listed here as strictly technical possibilities. Instead, they will be things that you discover for yourself, novel ways of making use of layers to assist the way you work. For example, you know that Photoshop has a single Level of Undo. You also know that if you so much as click your mouse after you have executed a command, you lose your ability to Undo anything but the mouse click. But with a little planning, you can set up a layer as a test for a series of actions: make a duplicate of a layer, perform whatever manipulations you wish on it, and evaluate whether you have achieved what you intended. If you did, you can keep the layer and delete the one from which it was duplicated. Otherwise, delete the experimental layer, and you are back where you started. You have, in effect, used a layer to give you a multi-step Undo!

Layered Documents & the Layers Palette

The layer metaphor is one of transparent film overlays upon that Dark Ages artifact, the *artboard.* Imagine, if you will, an image which has been fixed to board stock. Next, a colored logo is attached to a piece of acetate or clearbase film. The film is placed atop the image, the logo is positioned with respect to the background image, and the top of the film taped to the board. This film layer is called a *flap*. There may be several flaps. Some might contain type, other artwork, inset pictures, and so on. Each of the components is attached to a separate clear sheet and superimposed upon each other to build up a composite layout. If you are young enough to remember prepress procedures involving artboards, then you already understand how Photoshop's layers work. But there the similarity ends: digital layers can do things that are wild!

Photoshop's Layer Flaps

Figure 6-1 shows a layered document. The Layers palette at the lower right shows distinctive thumbnails which give you an excellent idea of what each layer contains and how the separate pieces are stacked up to produce the composite image.

Each layer can be completely filled with pixels. More often, a layer contains pixels in well-defined areas. Surrounding these pixels is an area of nothing, or more accurately, completely transparent pixels. You can see this more clearly in the exploded view of the document shown in Figure 6-2. This figure also shows Photoshop's method for indicating transparency. When there is no *Background* (discussed below), image layer transparency is shown as a gray-white checkerboard pattern.

TIP *The size of the checkerboard squares denoting transparency is a matter of choice. Changes can be made by choosing File | Preferences | Transparency and Gamut.*

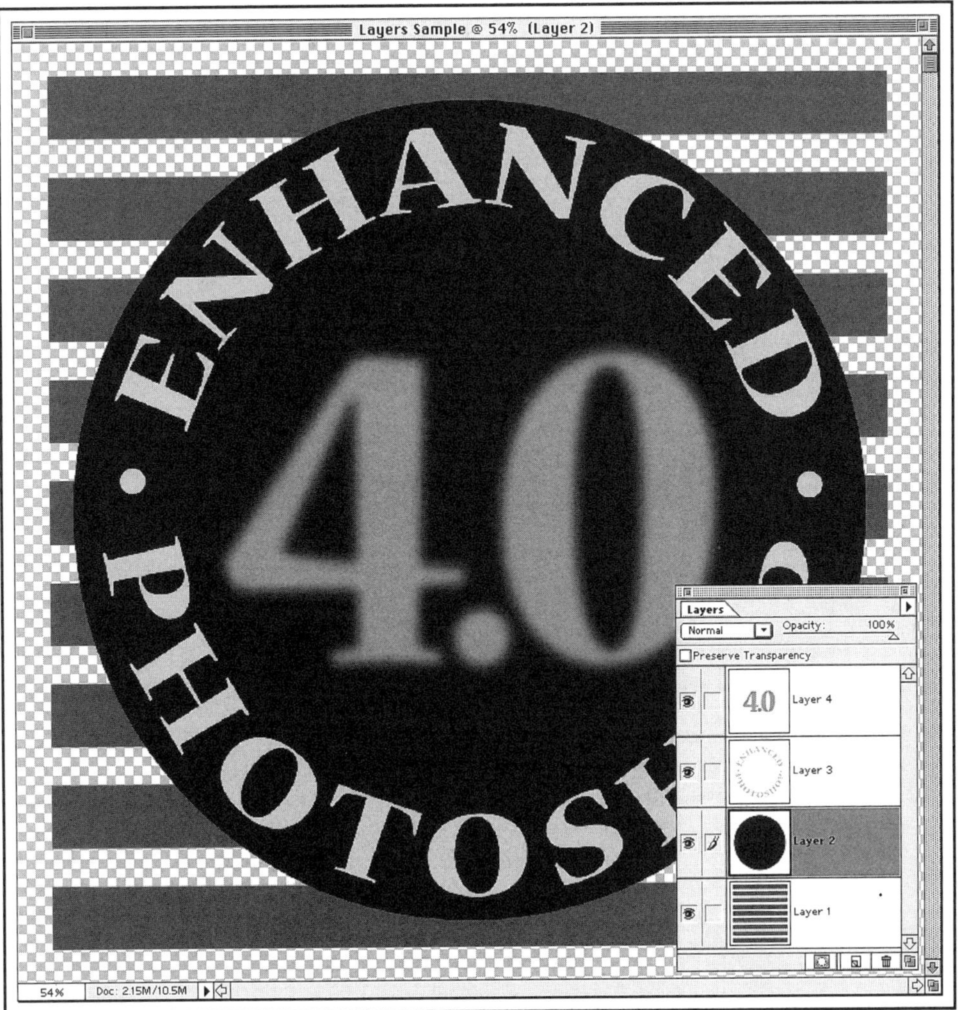

Figure 6-1: A layered Photoshop document with the Layers palette thumbnails showing each layer's content.

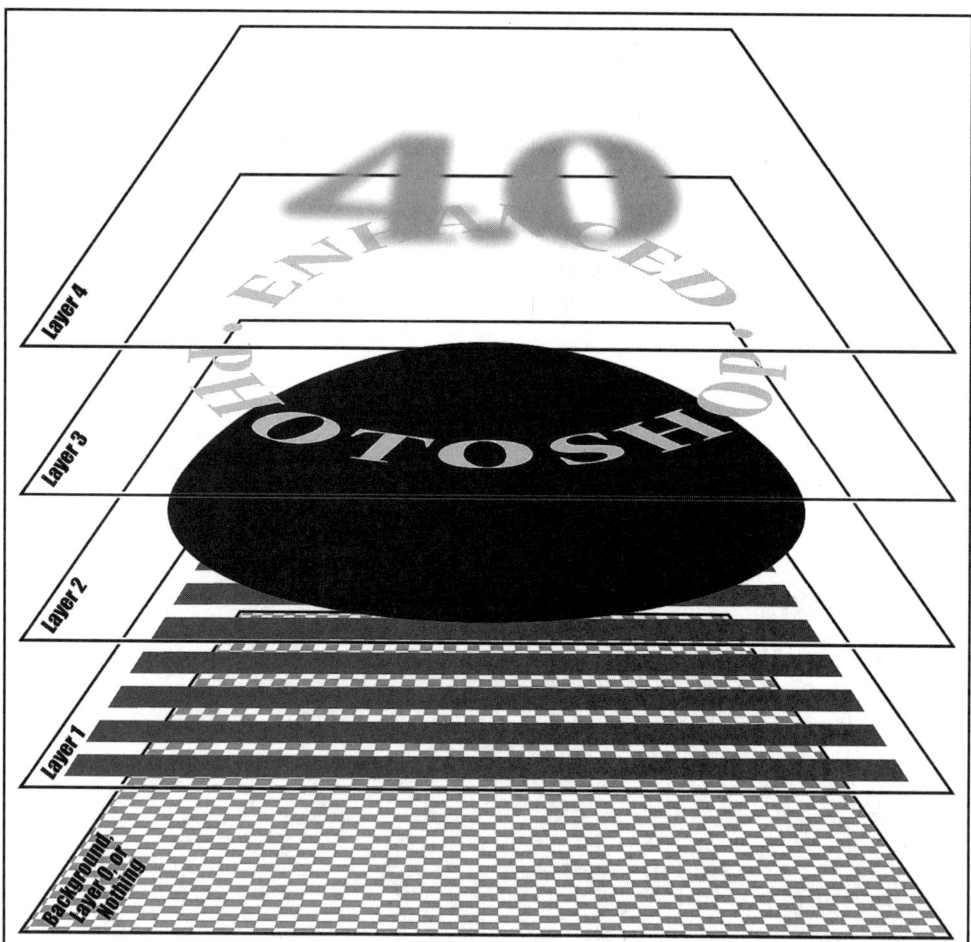

Figure 6-2: Exploded view of the layered document in Figure 6-1.

The Layers Palette

The principal tools for editing the layers are found on the Layers palette (an expanded view of this palette is shown in Figure 6-3) and under the Layers menu (to be discussed later in this chapter). With this palette and the menu combinations, you have the ability to create new layers and perform a wide variety of manipulations upon a single layer or on groups of layers. In this section, we will examine the possibilities of the Layers palette beginning with the Blend modes pop-up menu.

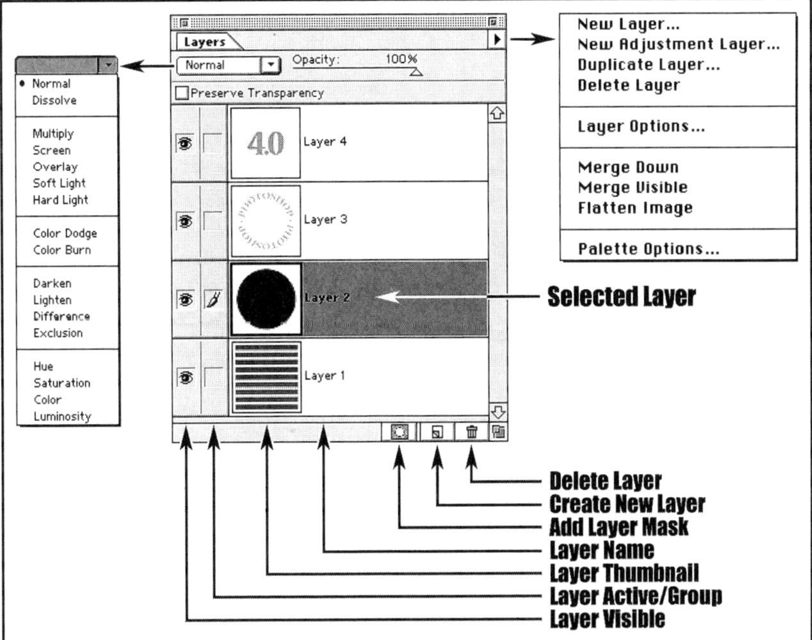

Figure 6-3: Expanded view of the Layers palette.

Blend Modes

The pop-up menu in the upper left-hand corner of the palette is used to change the Blend mode of a layer's pixels. Blend modes are wonderfully interesting and useful. With them, you can appear to combine the pixels on one layer with the pixels below that layer. The change in the appearance of the affected pixels is brought about by calculations on values associated with the pixels. The calculations might be based on the RGB values of the pixels, or they might be based on the brightness or the hue or the transparency of the pixels. There are quite a few possibilities, and the Blend modes can give you some amazing results.

The workings of the Blend modes are often misunderstood despite the fact that they are fairly straightforward. The difficulty lies with the terminology. The *Photoshop User's Manual* employs the terms *base color*, *blend color*, and *result color*. These terms work as well as any others, provided that we make their definitions easily understood. In Figure 6-4, you can see representations of greatly enlarged pixels. Consider the left-hand and center pixels: one is white, one is black. Imagine, if you will, that the black pixel is on the layer where the Blend mode is to operate. This pixel would represent the *blend color*. The white pixel is on a layer behind/below the black pixel. The white pixel will be affected by the Blend mode change which occurs on the layer above it. It is, then, part of the calculation and is called the *base color*. When the Blend mode changes, the result is a pixel that is usually different from those upon which the calculations are based. This pixel (on the right-hand side of the figure) is the *result color*. It is the color you see when you have applied a blend mode to one of the layers.

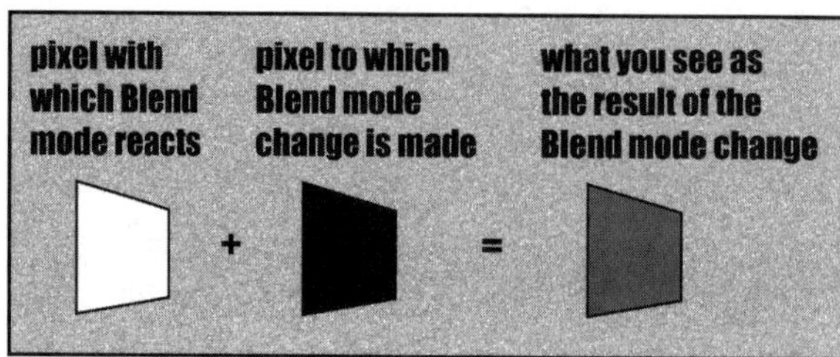

Figure 6-4: Two pixels put into a blend mode relationship often show a resulting color that is different from either of the contributing pixels.

The calculations that deliver the result color can be fairly interesting if you have a liking for mathematics. The Multiply mode on two RGB pixels, for example, is based on the multiplication of brightness values for each of the three color channels—red x red, green x green, and blue x blue. The formula is *(base color x blend color)/255 = result color*. (Note that after multiplying the two values, the result is brought back into range by dividing by 255. If this were not done, the multiplication would often deliver values higher than 255. Values higher than 255 are impossible.) If we take two pixels at random—r102, g204, b204 (a light turquoise color) and r255, g51, b102 (a bright salmon pink)—and apply the formula, we'll get a result of r102, g41, b82 (a dusty purple tone). Try it and you'll see. Make a small window, fill it with the first color, make a new layer, fill it with the second. Change the second layer's mode to Multiply and flatten the image. The RGB value of the resulting color will be as it is listed here. Or try it with a calculator. Here, for example, is the calculation for the two red values: 102 x 255 = 26,101; 26,101/255 = 102.

All of the Blend modes work in a similar way. Screen mode, for example, uses this formula for the RGB values: *255 – ((255 – base color) x (255 – blend color))/255 = result color*. As you can see, each of the calculation colors is subtracted from 255 to give an inverse value. These inverse values are multiplied together, the resulting color is divided by 255 to bring the result into range, and that number is subtracted from 255 to give the final inverse value. This makes Screen mode the inverse calculation of Multiply.

Not all of the calculations used are based on brightness values. Some calculations are based on a pixel's opacity, others on its hue. Some use combinations of these. All of the calculations produce results. However, those results will vary from *no apparent change* to *wow! what a change!* What you'll see as the result color will depend upon the values and positions of the pixels affected by the blend. With Multiply, Screen, Difference, and Exclusion, for example, it makes no difference which pixel is uppermost. The result color is the same. With other blend modes, the result color depends on the relative positions—*below* the layer where the Blend mode is operating, or *on* the layer. Fortunately, there are only 16 possibilities besides Normal. (Note: there are two other Blend modes that do not appear on the Layers palette pop-up menu, but are available as Paint tool options. These will be considered later in this chapter.) With so few possibilities, it fairly easy to try them all: simply choose the blend modes, one at a time, from the pop-up menu on the Layers palette.

Normal Normal mode is what you would have if there were no blend modes. It is the vanilla mode where pixels on a layer simply hide any pixels behind them. You might also call this the *real world* mode. The only way a layer in Normal mode can have an influence on the pixels of layers below it is to change the layer's Opacity to less than 100%. This strategy does give a new result color but it is a color achieved by a method other than the calculations employed by the blend modes.

Figure 6-5 shows the four-layer document used in Figure 6-1 with all of the layers in Normal mode and at 100% Opacity. In the figures which illustrate the other blend modes, the same document will be used with blends applied to Layer #2, a circular shape containing a gradient which shades from blue at the bottom to magenta at the top. This shape overlays a set of rectangular bars in a pink tone approximately equivalent to PANTONE 674 CV. The figures accompanying these explanations of the blend modes are in black and white. To see some more complex, full-color examples of what Photoshop's blend modes are capable of, check out the color section of this book.

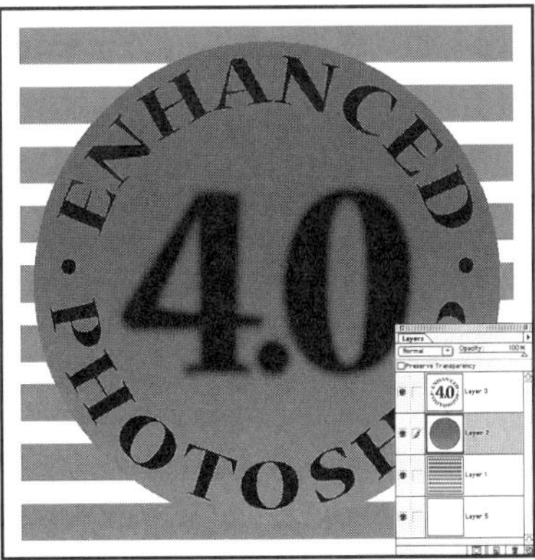

Figure 6-5: A layered document with all layers in Normal blend mode and at 100% Opacity.

Dissolve Dissolve, when used on pixels that are 100% opaque, produces no effect. When the opacity is less than 100%, then the Dissolve mode begins to show. All of the visible pixels on the Dissolve mode layer show at 100% Opacity in the original color. However, some of the pixels on the layer disappear in a random pattern. The number of pixels which vanish is equal to the reciprocal of the percentage of opacity. Put another way: if you have a layer containing an area of solid color and change its opacity to some number such as 70%, putting the layer into Dissolve mode will make 30% (the reciprocal of the opacity number) of the pixels vanish—in a scattered, random fashion—while all of the remaining pixels are changed back to 100% Opacity.

Dissolve mode is a brute force way of creating a transparency effect. It differs from a normal change in opacity in that pixels are either present or not. The effect is particularly useful when it is applied to shapes with feathered edges. The gritty effect of the mode is attractive when added to textures. Figure 6-6 shows the Dissolve effect applied to Layer 2 (which has first been changed to 60% Opacity). In Figure 6-7, a gradient—Foreground to Transparent—has been applied to letter outlines, and then the mode of the layer changed to Dissolve.

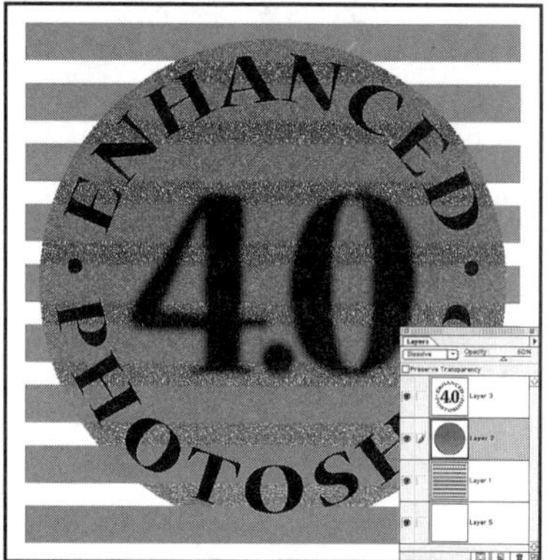

Figure 6-6: Dissolve mode applied to Layer 2 after the layer has been changed to 60% Opacity.

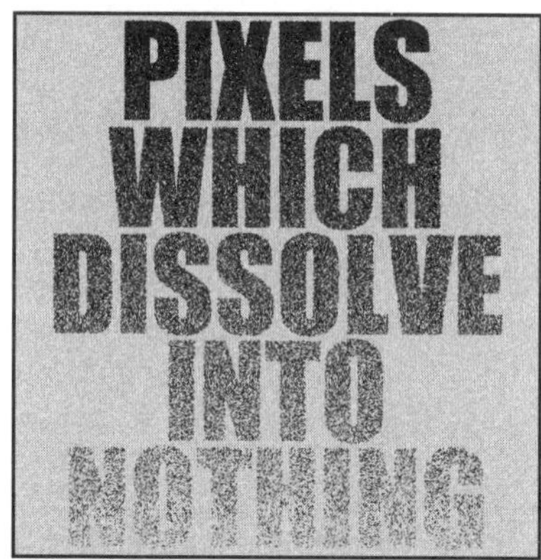

Figure 6-7: A gradient—Foreground to Transparent—has been applied to letter outlines and then the layer changed to Dissolve mode.

Multiply Multiply mode was used as an example of how calculations can work in the preliminary discussion of blend modes (above). The effect of this mode has been compared to placing two transparencies, one atop the other, on a light table. The result is a set of tones that are darker than either of the originals. When used with the painting tools, strokes placed over other strokes create increasingly dark tones. Multiply is wonderful—especially when you experiment with changing the opacity—for producing realistic drop shadows. The example in Figure 6-8 shows how the circular shape seems to take on the appearance of a shadow cast onto the shapes beneath it. Figure 6-9 uses the effect in a more deliberate manner to show how the shadow seems to soak into the texture on which it is cast. Note that multiplying any color with black produces black, while multiplying any color with white produces no change in tone.

Screen Screen, as we mentioned above, is the inverse of Multiply. Just as Multiply always produces a tone that is darker than any of the pixels used in the calculation, Screen produces tones that are lighter. (Note that screening any color with black produces no change in tone, while screening any color with white produces white.) Screen has been compared to painting over colored areas with bleach. The effect is shown in Figure 6-10. The dark circular shape has lightened the rectangles only a little because of its relative darkness of tone. The lightening would be more pronounced with lighter colors on the blend layer. This is shown more clearly in Figure 6-11 where blurred duplicates of the letters have been filled with a 30% black and set to Screen mode. The halo/glow effect is a striking inverse of a drop shadow.

Figure 6-8: Multiply mode applied to Layer 2. Note how this mode lends itself to shadow effects—the circular shape seems to become a shadow cast onto the rectangles beneath it.

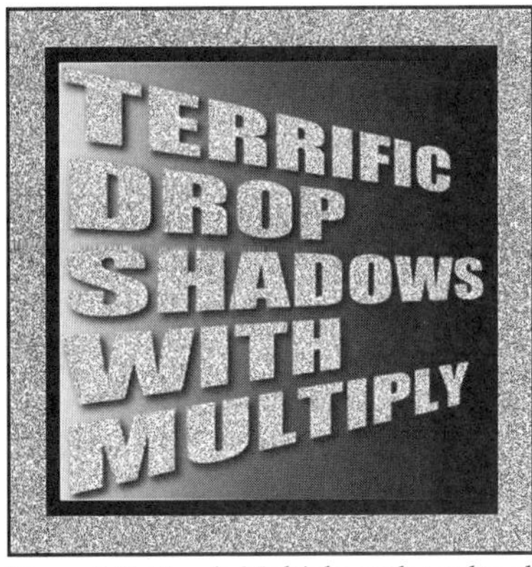

Figure 6-9: Here is Multiply mode used to show how the shadow seems to merge with the underlying texture and color. The letter shadows are made by duplicating the letters layer, filling them with black, blurring them, changing to Multiply mode, and placing the blurred duplicate layer below the original layer.

Figure 6-10: Layer 2 in Screen mode lightens Layer 1 only a small amount. The lightening effect would be greater if the circular shape were in a lighter tone.

Figure 6-11: When duplicates of the letters are blurred, placed below the letters, and then filled with a light tone, Screen mode makes a very nice glow effect.

Overlay Overlay mode is cool. Whenever you are just messing around and experimenting with blend modes, this one, as likely as not, will give you an effect that you'll enjoy. It may not be what you're looking for, but it will be something attractive and interesting.

Overlay does its magic by multiplying or screening, depending upon the values of the base colors. If the base colors are light, Overlay screens. If they are dark, Overlay multiplies. The result is a mix of the base and blend colors that preserves the highlights, shadows, and details of both base pixels and blend pixels. In Figure 6-12, the circular shape on Layer 2 is still faintly visible wherever it crosses the rectangles. Where the shape has crossed the light background, the pixels have disappeared. A more usual way of using Overlay is shown in Figure 6-13. The relief shapes at the top (*a*) are covered by a dark stone texture layer (*b*). When the stone texture layer is changed to Overlay mode, it seems to map onto the relief shapes. Notice that the texture disappears wherever it is above the light background. This is, to use the engineering term, Pure Magic.

Figure 6-12: Layer 2 in Overlay mode disappears over the light background and leaves a faint circle wherever it passes over the rectangles.

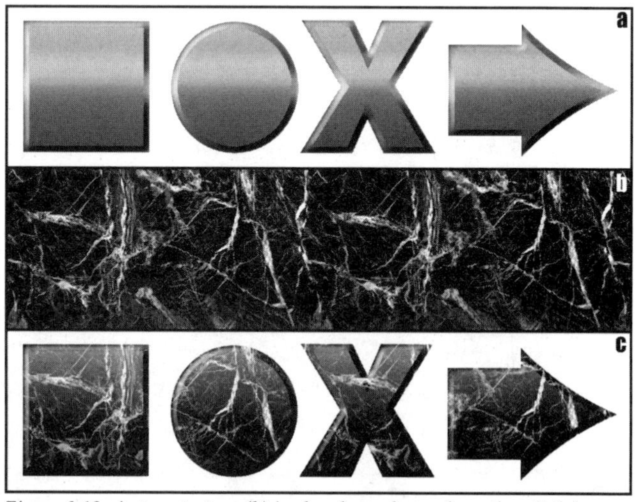

Figure 6-13: A stone texture (b) is placed on a layer above the relief shapes in (a). When the texture is changed to Overlay, the texture seems to be mapped onto the shapes. The texture disappears over the white background.

Soft Light The Adobe Photoshop User's Manual describes the effect of Soft Light as ". . . similar to shining a diffused spotlight on the image." This description is helpful only if you think of the blend pixels as the source of a variable, low-intensity light shining down upon the base layer pixels. Wherever the blend pixels are 50% gray or lighter, the light shines, its strength proportional to the lightness of the pixels. This makes the base pixels lighter. Wherever the blend pixels are darker than 50% gray, the base pixels are slightly darkened. The effect is as though the darker pixels form translucent shapes that are interposed between the low-intensity light and the surface on which the light is thrown, seeming to form faint shadows. The darkness of the shadows is proportional to the darkness of the blend pixels. The effect is mysterious and beautiful.

Figure 6-14 shows the effect slightly in the way the brightness of the blend in the circular shape at the bottom makes it seem to disappear. There is an increasing shadow toward the top as the blend becomes darker. Figure 6-15 shows a better use of Soft Light. On the left, a multi-toned floral pattern is superimposed upon a textured background in Normal mode. On the right, the same pattern lays atop the texture in Soft Light mode making the pattern fuse with the background. Note the faint lightening of the flowers. On the left, they are about 38% gray which casts a light on the background to produce a tone of 8–12% (contrasting with the 20% background gray).

Figure 6-14: The Soft Light mode makes the circle disappear along the lower position and seem to cast a faint shadow along the top. This is due to the change in brightness within the gradient which fills the circle.

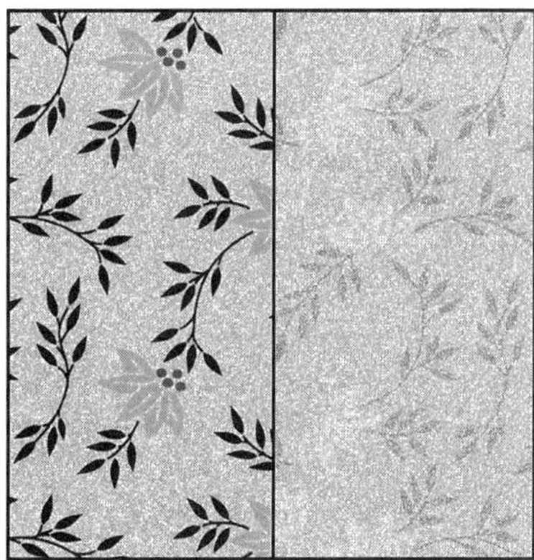

Figure 6-15: The floral pattern in Normal mode on the left merges mysteriously with the background when it is placed in Soft Light mode (right).

Hard Light This blend mode is similar to Soft Light in the way the pixels of the blend layer can be considered as the light source shining upon the pixels of the base layer. The difference is in the intensity of the light. Hard Light, as the name implies, seems to generate a more intense light. This makes the emanation from light pixels brighter and the shadows correspondingly darker.

The Hard Light mode makes the circle on Layer 2 in Figure 6-16 much more visible—the shadow it casts is darker. The right-hand side of Figure 6-17 shows how much more intense is the effect when compared to the right-hand side of Figure 6-15. Hard Light can be thought of as the inverse of the Overlay mode.

Figure 6-16: Hard Light mode makes the circle on Layer 2 appear as a darker shadow because it apparently increases the intensity of the light emanating from the layer.

Figure 6-17: With Hard Light, light pixels make brighter composite values, dark pixels make darker values. Compare this figure with its low-intensity cousin—Soft Light—in Figure 6-15.

Color Dodge The pixels of the blend layer possess some amount of brightness in each channel. This brightness factor acts as a variable-intensity color/brightness intensifier for the pixels of the base layer. This is not a simple, linear comparison: the effect caused by bright values on the blend layer is greater than for dark values. The overall effect is that of a charged-up Screen mode. When black is used for the blend, there is no change on the base layer. White produces the greatest amount of change.

Figure 6-18 shows the rectangles of the lower layer lightened by the blend of the circle. The lightening is greater at the bottom of the circle where the gradient component is lighter. Figure 6-19 illustrates the effect more successfully. A set of gradient-filled circular shapes have been placed upon a black-to-white gradient. They are seen on the left in Normal mode. On the right, the brightness values produce ever-larger areas of white as the back gradient becomes lighter. Note that the lines passing through the circles are slanted because of the progressive lightening of the back layer while the gradient within the circular shapes remains constant. There are many bizarre topological effects that can be achieved by playing two or more gradients against each other using different blend modes.

Color Burn Color Burn is the inverse of Color Dodge. The same brightness values of the blend layer are used in the calculation, but the base layer is darkened instead of lightened. The darkening is always more severe than it is for the other darkening mode, Multiply. As you might expect, blends involving white on the base layer produce no change, while white blends with black on the base layer produce the greatest change.

In Figure 6-20, the rectangular bars have been darkened more than any other blend mode could have accomplished. The circle has disappeared from the spaces between the bars. In Figure 6-21, the same gradient-filled shapes have produced, on the right, the inverse of the effect seen in Figure 6-19.

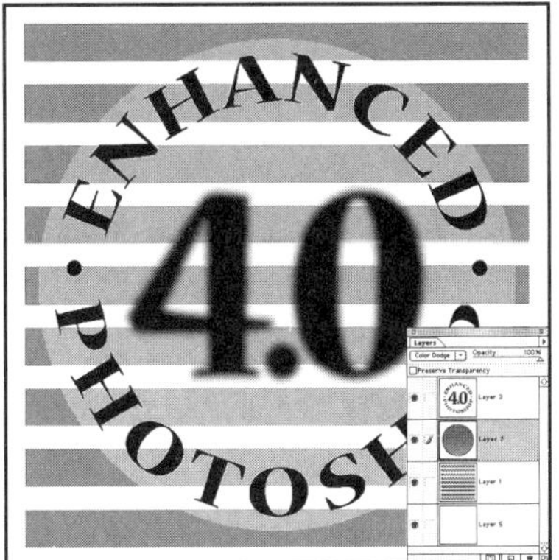

Figure 6-18: Color Dodge lightens the rectangles according to the lightness of the pixels in the blend layer.

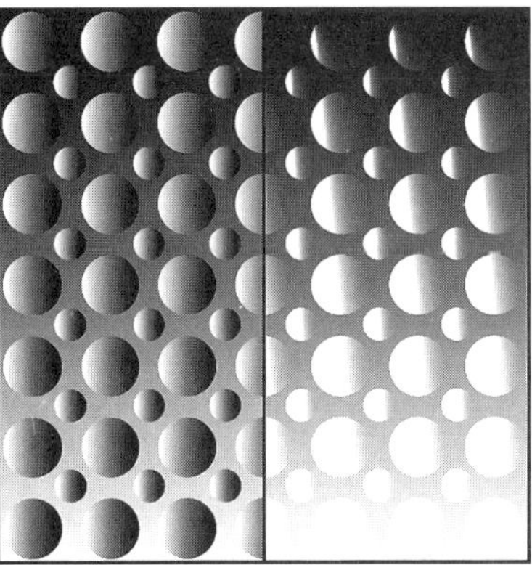

Figure 6-19: The lightening effect is seen clearly as gradient-filled circles are placed against a black-to-white gradient running in the opposite direction. The mode is Normal on the left and Color Dodge on the right. Please see the accompanying text for an explanation of the slanted lines within the circles.

Figure 6-20: Color Burn has caused the Layer 2 circle to drastically darken the bar shapes over which it passes. Note that the circle disappears as it passes over the white areas between the bars.

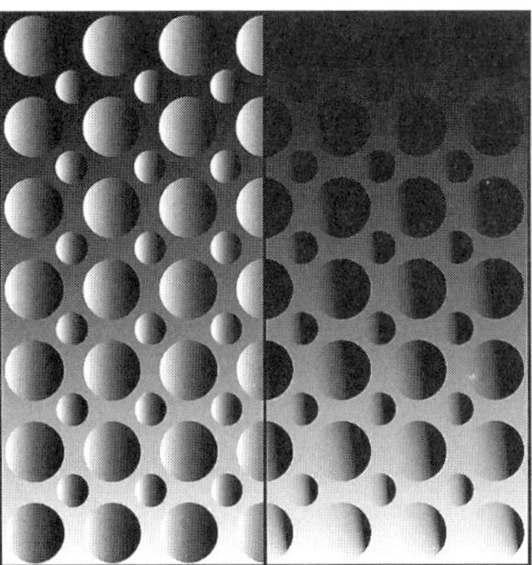

Figure 6-21: In this figure, you see on the right the inverse effect of that shown in Figure 6-19.

Darken Darken used in grayscale is easily predictable. Pixels on the blend layer that are lighter than pixels on the base layer become invisible, while pixels that are darker than the pixels of the base layer are not changed. See? Easy. However, when Darken is used with colored images, this blend mode is a tricky customer. The same principles used for grayscale apply, but the rules evaluate the brightness of the values in all of the channels. For example, if the red value of the base layer of an RGB document is darker than the red value of the blend layer, it is retained while that of the other pixel disappears. The same procedure is used for the other two channels. The result color is a composite of the values for both calculation layers—the darkest red, the darkest green, and the darkest blue for any equivalent pixels.

The example in Figure 6-22 does not show a significant change at the top of the Layer 2 circle but the result of the Darken mode is quite noticeable at the bottom. Figure 6-23 shows more clearly how the darker values are retained. On the left, the geometric pattern positioned over a dark-to-light gradient is in Normal mode. On the right, Darken mode has the most pronounced effect on the light zigzag lines which become more visible as they approach the light end of the gradient on the base layer.

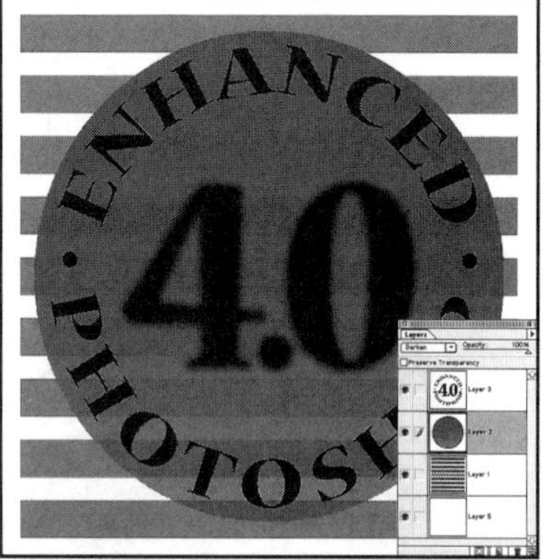

Figure 6-22: Darken mode, applied to the Layer 2 circle affects the appearance of the image mostly at the bottom of the circle where the bars are darker than the tone of the gradient.

Figure 6-23: Darken mode applied to the geometric pattern—where the background is a black-to-white gradient—on the right has its most pronounced effect on the zigzag white stripes. The stripes gradually reappear as they approach the light end of the gradient.

Lighten Lighten mode, as you will not be surprised to discover, is the inverse of Darken. (Don't you just love it when you can spend the time learning one thing and then get the second one for free?) The result values are based upon the lightness of the pixels in each layers. The calculation is based upon the lightness factor of each pixel in each of the document's channels.

Figure 6-24 shows the circle as having mostly disappeared except at the bottom where its brightness was less than that of the horizontal bars. Figure 6-25, in contrast with Figure 6-23, shows the least effect on the light lines and the most effect on the dark lines. The black lines gradually reappear as they approach the dark end of the gradient.

Figure 6-24: Lighten mode, applied to the Layer 2 circle again affects the appearance of the image mostly at the bottom of the circle where the bars are lighter than the tone of the gradient.

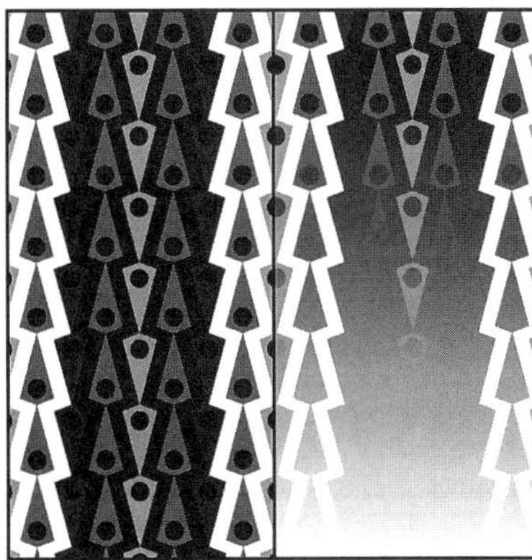

Figure 6-25: Lighten mode applied to the geometric pattern on the right has its most pronounced effect on the zigzag black stripes. The stripes gradually reappear as they approach the dark upper end of the gradient.

Difference You have to watch out for Difference mode. At least you do if you are one of those people who gets a bang out of really novel effects. The effect of Difference mode on any two layers is often novel, sometimes bizarre, but almost always interesting. It hardly ever makes an effect that is unattractive. The trouble is this: the people for whom you are doing Photoshop work often have bland, inferior taste, and possess no sense of adventure. When you present your extremely cool Difference composites to them, they react with an utter lack of vision or imagination. You've probably noticed this phenomenon for yourself. Sigh.

Difference causes the pixels of the base layer to appear inverted according to the brightness values—calculated in each channel—of the blend layer. The mechanism is really simple: one pixel's values are subtracted from the equivalent pixel's values. The subtraction is always based on whichever value in any channel is greater. If you had two pixels with values of r100 g150 b200 (a light blue) and r125 g100 b50 (a medium tan), your result pixel would be r25 g50 b150 (a very nice medium blue). The calculations are: 125–100=25; 150–100=50; and 200–50=150. Another way to state the Difference calculation is that the result values are the absolute values of the difference between any two pixels channel components.

Figure 6-26 as a grayscale figure does not show up the really wonderful color changes brought about by the Difference calculation but you can see the basic idea. The Difference effect is more obvious in Figure 6-27. If you study the two zigzag white lines just to the right of the center line, you can see how white against the dark gradient at the top has produced light tones, while at the bottom, white against white has produced dark tones. If you think about this, you'll realize that it makes sense: whenever you subtract a color from itself, your result color will be zero (0). In Photoshop terms, zero is as dark as it gets.

Figure 6-26: This grayscale figure, while it gives an idea of the Difference calculation, does not show the pleasant color tones produced.

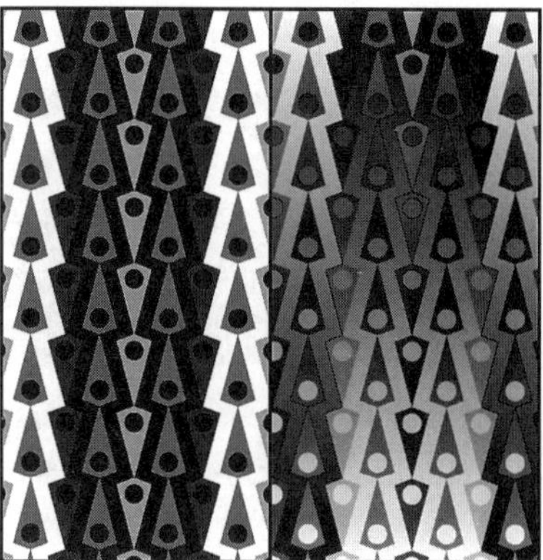

Figure 6-27: To understand this example of the Difference mode, study the two zigzag white lines just to the right of the center line. White against the dark gradient at the top has produced light tones, while at the bottom, white against white has produced dark tones. Subtracting a color from itself always produces black.

Exclusion The Exclusion mode is most easily understood as a variation of the Difference mode. Perhaps it would be more accurate to say this: *to get an idea* of how Exclusion acts, you can compare it to Difference. Understand it? We didn't think so. We're not sure that anyone outside of Adobe's programming staff actually understands it. Whatever. This blend mode subtracts the way Difference does when the values are fairly far apart. But the closer the values come to each other, the less they seem to interact. In fact, midrange tones blended with midrange tones form more midrange tones. The net effect is a diffuse version of Difference.

Figure 6-28 shows the gradient of the circular layer blending with the background layer bars with more visible change at the top—where the brightness values are farther apart—than at the bottom where they are closer together. The largest change that you'll see in Figure 6-29 (compared to Figure 6-27) is in the center of the right-hand side. As the midrange tones of the blend layer lay atop midrange tones of the base layer, the colors nearly cancel each other to produce a uniform tone.

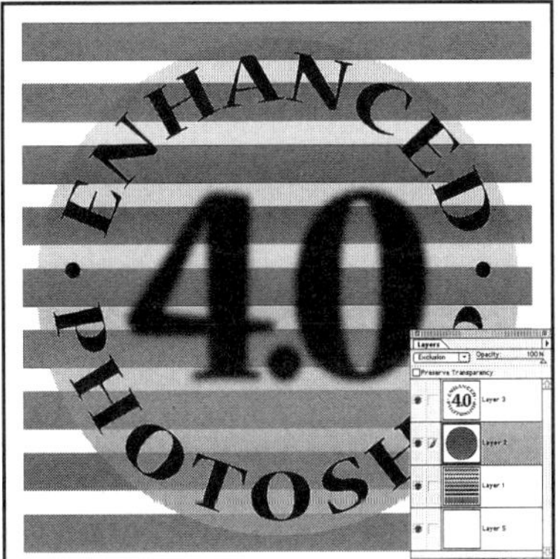

Figure 6-28: This grayscale figure, while it gives an idea of the Exclusion calculation, also does not show the color tones produced.

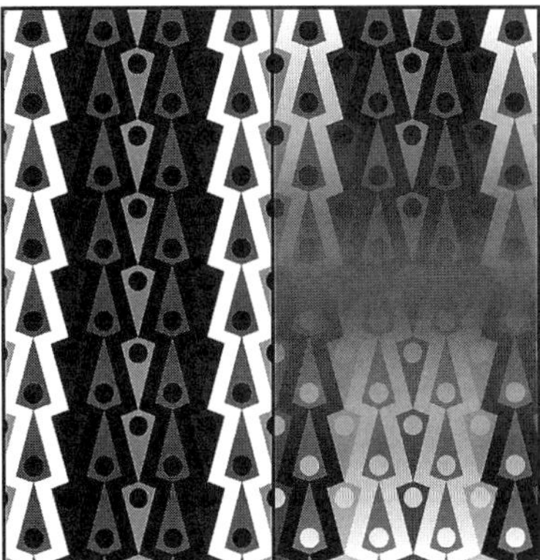
Figure 6-29: Compare this Figure with Figure 6-27. The center part of the right-hand section shows the muting effect caused by blending midrange tone with midrange tones.

A Note on HSL The last four of the blend modes can be used only when the document is in one of the color modes—RGB, CMYK, or Lab. These four make use of calculations based on values derived from one of Photoshop's color models, HSL (Hue, Saturation, Lightness). If you are unsure about those color terms, you can familiarize yourself with them by using the Image | Adjust | Hue/Saturation dialog box. The three sliders of this box allow you to adjust the HSL components of an image as separate entities.

The *Hue* of a pixel is, literally, its color. If you use any term to describe a color—for example, blue, or red, or green—you are describing the hue.

The *Saturation* of the color is a description of how much *gray tone* is mixed with the hue. In this context, the term *gray tone* indicates one of the possible gray values which can range from solid black to total white. If you wish, imagine mixing a can of dark blue house paint with two cans of white to achieve a modified hue. This is the concept embodied by the term *Saturation*. Saturation is put into words that are used to describe modified primary colors, words such as "pink," "baby blue," "dusty rose." These are words that describe a change in the saturation from the reds or blues on which they are based.

The *Lightness* of a color is governed by the amount of black it contains. Carry the paint analogy one more step, if you will. Imagine that you must darken the dark blue paint instead of adding white. How would you accomplish that? The simple answer is that you would add black. The analogy using house paint begins to break down at this point because adding black could also be considered as a modification of a color's saturation. In computer terms, however, that is exactly what happens. Colors like midnight blue and dark brown are terms that describe colors which have had their lightness component modified.

These three terms are important to understand. In other chapters in this book, you will be adjusting the color of images using the Hue/Saturation dialog box. Intelligent use of this adjustment depends upon your clear understanding of color having, in this model, three components. Where blends modes are concerned, you will find that calculations of the blends are made with one or more of the HSL values. For this reason, the last four blend modes are grayed out when your document is in grayscale.

Hue The result color of the Hue mode depends upon the hue of the blend layer pixels which are composited with the luminance and saturation of the base layer pixels. The effect is most noticeable when the values of the two layers are substantially different.

Figure 6-30 shows a composite effect that essentially erases the circle on Layer 2 where it crosses the light areas between the bars. The blend color is an attractive composite of the two tones. In Figure 6-31, the geometric shapes have been filled with a light to dark gradient (normal mode on the left, blend mode on the right). The composite effect is a blend that seems to tattoo the layer shapes onto the radial blend of the background.

Figure 6-30: The Hue mode composite erases the Layer 2 circle where it passes over the light background. The composite of the circle and the bars is a pleasant merging of the color tones.

Figure 6-31: The geometric shapes, filled with a light to dark gradient, seem to be tattooed onto the background when they are placed in Hue mode.

Saturation The calculation method for Saturation combines the luminance and hue of the base layer pixels with the saturation of the blend layer pixels. This mode, frankly, doesn't do very much that is interesting. However, it is always worth a try when you are cycling through the possibilities of the blend mode menu. Once in a while it will produce a result that is exactly what you are looking to achieve.

Figure 6-32 is similar to 6-30 in that the circle disappears wherever it crosses the white background. The merge colors—unseen in this figure but visible on the color image—are simply an intensified version of the colors of the bars. In Figure 6-33, the same geometric shapes have been filled with a linear version of the radial gradient on the background layer. As you can see in the merged area on the right, the effect is only noticeable where the blend layer pixels are dark and the base layer pixels are light.

Figure 6-32: Saturation mode also cancels the circle where it crosses over very light areas. The blended colors are pretty ho-hum. Saturation, for the most part, isn't a very interesting mode.

Figure 6-33: The geometric shapes on the blend layer have been filled with a linear version of the same gradient used for the background layer. The merged pixels show most clearly where the blend layer is dark and the base layer is light.

Color If Saturation mode was the dull date of the blend modes, Color mode is a more, uh, colorful choice. The hue and saturation values of the blend layer pixels are combined with the luminance of the base layer pixels. The effect of the mode is to produce a more vibrant version of Hue mode.

The colors formed are not visible in Figure 6-34 but you can see that this mode also washes away pixels from the blend layer that cross light areas below it. A comparison of this figure's color counterpart with that of Hue shows how the color calculation produces a more interesting set of tones. Figure 6-35 gives an idea how, when colors are blended with neutral tones in the base layer, there is a muting of tone. This makes Color mode an ideal choice for colorizing grayscale images.

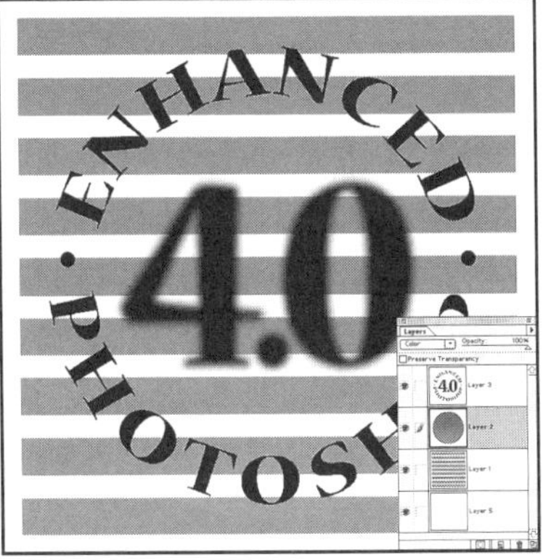

Figure 6-34: Compare this figure with its color counterpart to see how Color mode produces a brighter version of Hue.

Figure 6-35: Colors blended with neutral tones on the base layer produce subdued, grayed versions of themselves.

Luminosity Luminosity mode is the inverse effect of Color. The result color is made up of the hue and saturation values of the base layer and the luminance of the blend layer. This gives result colors which are darker and more intense than the originals.

In Figure 6-36, The color of the bars is enriched by the colors within the circle. The spaces between the bars are changed from white to about a 75% gray tone. Figure 6-37, when compared to Figure 6-35, illustrates the change in color intensity.

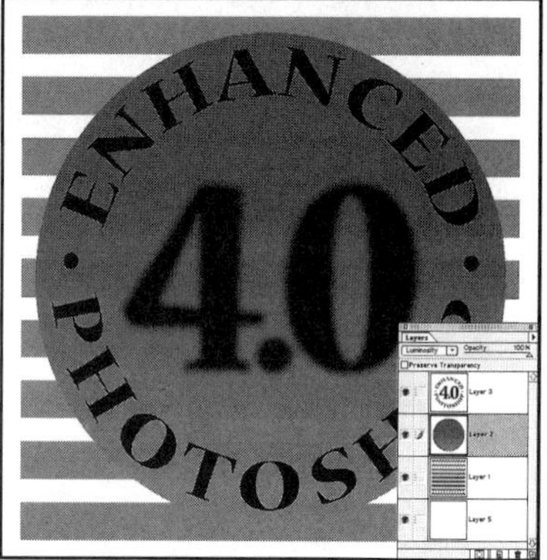

Figure 6-36: When the circle in Layer 2 is placed in Luminosity mode, it intensifies the colors of the bars. The areas between the bars are also darkened from white to a gray tone that is about equivalent to 75% black.

Figure 6-37: Compare this figure with Figure 6-35 to see how Luminosity darkens and intensifies the colors composing the blend.

An Afterthought on Blend Modes For the adventurous, there are interesting topological effects that can be explored by superimposing geometric shapes on two layers (one example was mentioned in connection with Figure 6-19). A very simple introduction to what can be done is be seen in Figure 6-38. The variations within this figures are the result of a single background which is duplicated onto a separate layer, and then the layer rotated 90°. (The layer and background are shown at the top left and top center.) Notice that the background layer was made by drawing a black-to-white gradient and then posterizing to 11 steps. This gives rectangles ranging from white to black in 10% steps.

The remaining thirteen examples are the result of changes in the blend mode of Layer 1. Of interest in these examples are the opposite characteristics of Multiply-Screen, Color Dodge-Color Burn, and Darken-Lighten. Note that Overlay and Hard Light form the same configuration but one is rotated 90° and flipped with respect to the other. It is useful here to see how different Exclusion is from Difference: the two are identical around the outer edges but diverge from each other as they approach the center of the square area.

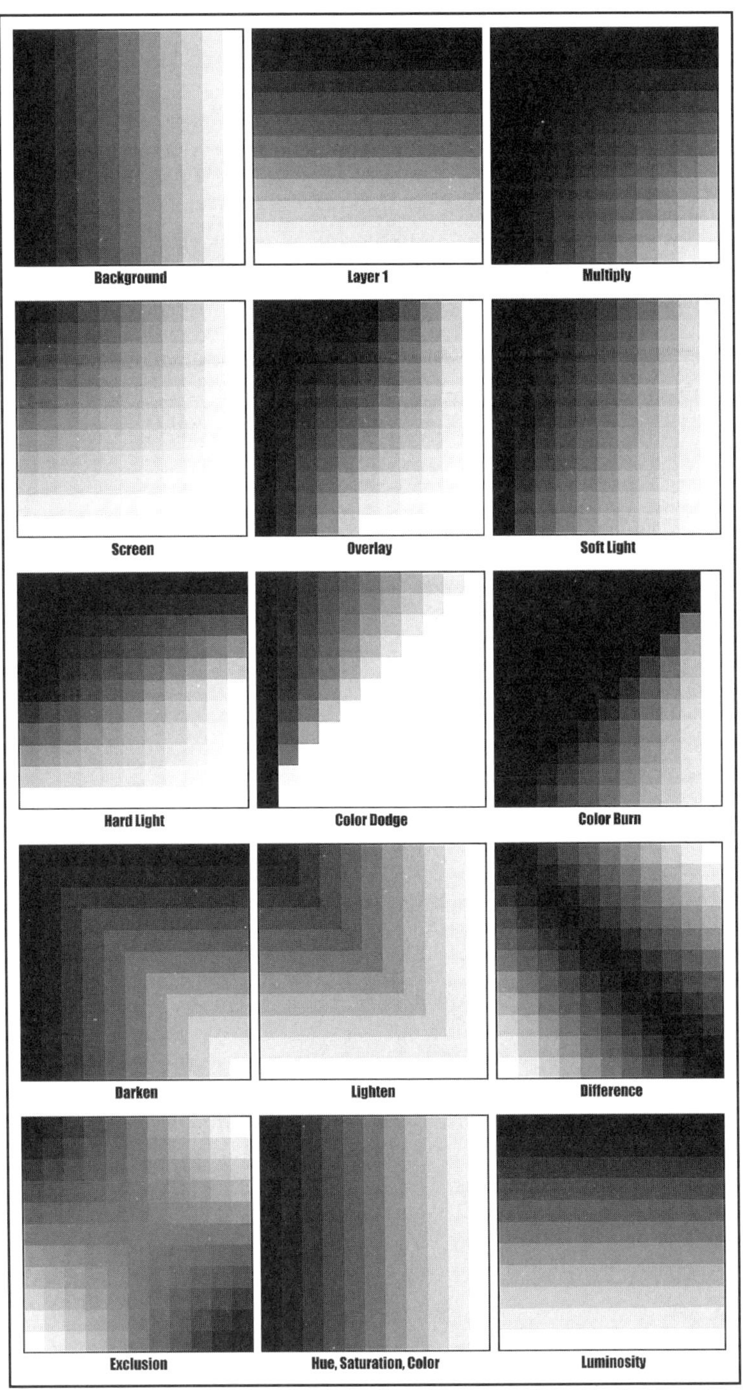

Figure 6-38: Studies in blend mode relationships. A background and identical layer (rotated 90°) form these patterns with changes in the blend modes.

Opacity

There is something about the symmetry of 32 bits that strikes the geek mind as something greater than fortuitous: Is it really an accident that a color display only requires three bytes of the four that are available on a 32-bit operating system? And who was the bright programmer who thought, "Hmm, maybe with that extra byte we could float 256 levels of transparency on top of the color . . ." As we said, this is straight-out geek-think. But you get the idea: If computer architecture didn't organize itself with such elegance, about 75 percent of Photoshop would be impossible. And most of what *would* be possible wouldn't be as much fun!

Transparency, where layers are concerned, is varied with the slider at the top of the palette. Pixels which are entirely opaque can be changed by means of the slider so that whatever is behind them shows through as though the pixels have become translucent. Visibility of the pixels can be brought down as low as 1% (100% is totally opaque). The four parts of Figure 6-39 show how changes in opacity affect the appearance of objects on the layer and the layer(s) behind the objects.

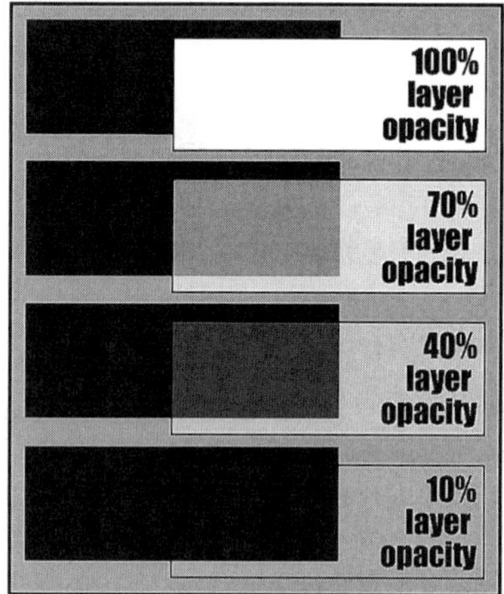

Figure 6-39: As the transparency percentage is lowered, the objects on a layer become increasingly translucent.

TIP

Besides moving the Opacity slider, you can change the opacity of the layer in 10% increments by pressing any of the number keys with one of the Selection tools in use. Press 1 for 10%, 5 for 50%, or 0 for 100%. If you have one of the Paint tools selected, pressing the numbers will change the opacity of the tool.

Pixels on a layer can be placed there with less than total opacity. You might, for example, apply color to a new layer with one of the Paint tools set to 50% Opacity. The Opacity slider would still read 100% but you would be able to see through the colored pixels. If you change the Opacity slider, you will decrease the opacity of the pixels on the layer by an amount that you can calculate as the product of the two numbers: the original opacity of the pixels multiplied by the slider percentage. This means that you can, if you wish, have pixels with an opacity of fractions of a percent. For example, if the pixels on the layer begin at 50% Opacity and you change the Opacity slider to 75%, the net opacity of the pixels will be 37.5% (50% x 75% = 37.5%, or .5 x .75 = .375). The examples shown in Figure 6-40 show the differences between the concepts of pixel opacity and layer opacity.

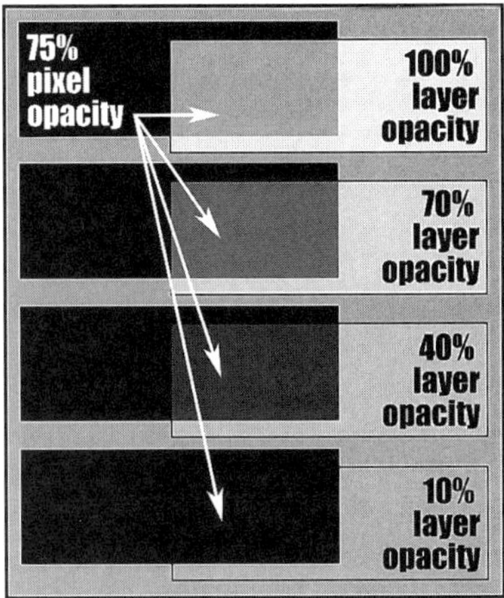

Figure 6-40: When pixels on a layer begin at less than full opacity, changing the Opacity slider gives a net opacity obtained by multiplying the original opacity value by the layer opacity value.

Preserve Transparency

We have already seen how a layer can contain areas of pixels surrounded by nothing. This area of nothing, the transparent pixels of the layer, can be protected from change by turning on the Preserve Transparency check box at the top of the Layers palette. When the check box is not turned on, color can be added to the layer from any source—painted, pasted, etc.—and positioned anywhere. Figure 6-41 shows how, when the option is unchecked, a Paintbrush can simply lay the paint at any place on the layer. When it is checked, the brush is able to apply color only in the areas wherever there are existing pixels (Figure 6-42). Note: if the pixels are not fully opaque, the brush lays down the paint with the exact opacity of the existing pixels. Preserve transparency allows you to quickly change the color on a layer while preserving the shape within which the colors lie.

Figure 6-41: With the Layers palette Preserve Transparency option unchecked, the Paintbrush can paint anywhere within the layer.

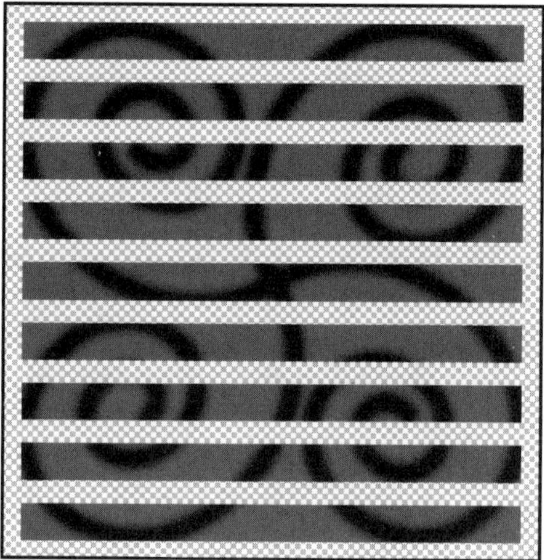

Figure 6-42: When Preserve Transparency is checked, a Paintbrush can only apply paint where there are existing pixels.

One of the blend modes, Behind, is relevant to the discussion of a layer's transparent pixels. This mode is the inverse of painting with Preserve Transparency turned on. (Note that this mode will function only when Preserve Transparency is turned off.) With Behind mode, you can apply paint to the transparent or translucent pixels while leaving all of the existing pixels untouched, or painted to the extent that they are translucent. The effect is shown in Figure 6-43, which also makes obvious the origin of the mode's name. The paint strokes appear to be behind the gray bars. In fact, they have been applied only in the transparent areas between the bars. Behind mode is not available on the Layers palette under usual circumstances. If you have a floating selection, Behind mode can be applied to the floating selection from the Layers palette. When you do so, the floating selection will be visible only where there are transparent pixels on the layer above which it is floating.

TIP *Preserve Transparency can be toggled off and on by pressing the / key.*

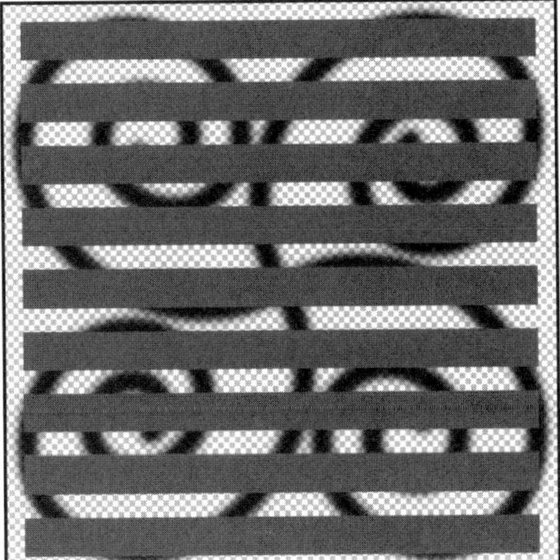

Figure 6-43: When paint is applied to a layer using Behind mode, the paint can only be applied to transparent or translucent pixels.

The Layers Thumbnail List

The central part of the Layers palette is composed of a list of the layers present in the working document (see Figure 6-3). Each item on the list contains a thumbnail of the pixels contained on the layer. Next to the thumbnail, on the right, is the Layers name.

This list also contains, at times, two special-case entries where the listed item isn't really a layer.

The Background The first of these is the bottom entry—which may or may not be present—called the Background. Photoshop documents usually begin with photo images or artwork. When they are opened for the first time, or if they form within a window after a scanner has captured an image, they appear on the Layers palette as the Background. The Background is always shown in italic type on the Item list to indicate its special status. If there is a background, it will be the lowest item on the list. The background layer cannot be moved from its position on the list unless it is first converted to a layer.

TIP *Preserve Transparency can be toggled off and on by pressing the / key. To convert the Background to a Layer, double-click its thumbnail on the Layers palette. When the dialog box appears asking to name the new layer as Layer 0, click OK.*

To add a Background to a document which does not have one, choose the New Layer menu command. Select the bottom item, Background, from the Mode pop-up menu. Click OK.

Floating Selections A floating selection is composed of a group of selected pixels which temporarily float above a layer or the background. Floating selections also show up on the layers palette but with the name *Floating Selection* in italic type to indicate that the layer status is temporary. Blend modes and opacity changes can be applied to a floating selection just as they can to a normal layer. When the floating selection is deselected, it drops onto the layer—or Background—beneath it and replaces the pixels that were there. Floating Selections were more widely used in previous versions of Photoshop than they are in version 4.0. Much of what used to be accomplished with floating selections is now done by formal layers.

TIP

Floating selections can be converted to layers in a couple of easy ways. Drag the Floating Selection thumbnail down to the New Layer icon—to the left of the trash can icon—at the bottom of the palette. When a dialog box appears, click OK. An even easier method is this: hold Option or Alt and click on the New Layer icon at the bottom of the palette. The floating selection is instantly converted without the dialog box.

You can also convert a floating selection to a layer by moving it into a different position. Simply drag the selection in the same way you would change the position of another layer.

Layer Visibility At the far left of the layer items list are a column of small icons containing an eye symbol. Click on this icon space to hide or make visible the pixels of the layer.

Linked Layers Between the eye icon and the layer thumbnail is another icon space. This space contains a paintbrush icon whenever the layer has been selected. It is also used to link or group layers together. With one layer selected, click in this area to group the layers. A small chain symbol will appear to notify you that the layer has been linked with the selected layer. This link remains in effect until you remove it by clicking again on the chain icon. You can link any two or more layers. To be linked, layers need not be next to each other on the palette list.

Linked layers are very useful when you need to do the same operation to each layer but you cannot, for some reason, merge the layers into one (merging layers will be discussed later in this chapter). For example, you might wish to move the contents of more than one layer while maintaining the precise position of both with respect to each other. With the layers linked, you can move one and the other(s) will also move. Another example of a use for a link would be when you wish to apply a transformation—transformations are found under the Layers menu and will be discussed later in this chapter—to two or more layers. If the layers are linked, the transformation will be applied to each at the same time. Still another use would be to transfer the contents of more than one layer to a new document and keeping the layer status after the move. Link the layers you wish to move—with the Move tool selected, simply drag from one document window to another (Figure 6-44). The linked layers will appear on the new document's Layers palette—with the link status intact—and with both in the same blend mode assigned to them in the original window. (Before Photoshop v. 4.0, this used to be a tedious task! With linking, it is a breeze.)

TIP *When you drag any information from one document window to another, you can insure that the pixels center themselves in the destination window by holding Shift as you drag.*

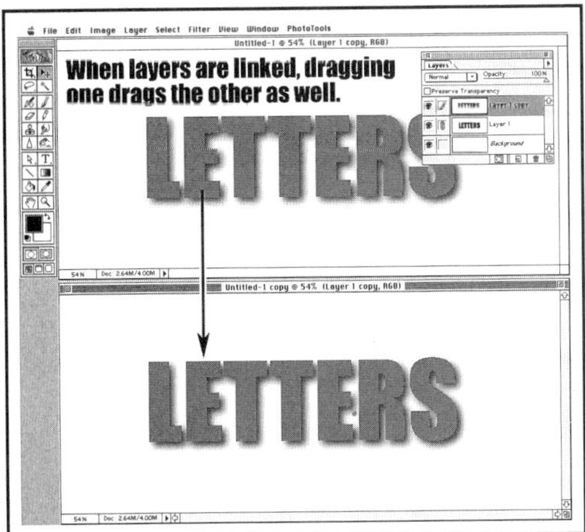

Figure 6-44: When layers are linked and then one of the linked layers is dragged to a new document, both layers are moved.

Rearranging the Layers Using the Palette List There are, besides changing whether a layer is visible or whether it is linked to other layers, two other layer modifications that are made by using the item list. The first of these is the rearrangement of the stacking order of the layers. The second is the formation of a *clipping group*.

Rearranging the order of the layers from top to bottom is one of the simplest layer tasks. Simply click on the layer to select it and then drag it to the line separating the two layers between which you wish it to be. As you drag, your cursor changes to a small hand icon. When the hand icon is over one of the layer boundaries, the line widens as if to accommodate the new layer. This effect is shown in Figure 6-45 where the bottom layer—Layer 1—is being moved so that it will be above Layer 2. After the layer has been moved (Figure 6-46), the pixels show a new visual relationship. Moving layers can be done at any time.

There are four commands on the program's Layer menu (see Figure 6-49) which can also assist with moving layers up or down in the stacking order. These are:

- Bring to Front—Command+Shift+] or Ctrl+Shift+]—which places the selected layer at the top of the stack;

Figure 6-45: Click and drag any layer to change its position in the stack of layers. As you drag, the cursor changes to a hand icon. When the hand icon is positioned over a layer boundary, the boundary line widens to show that the mouse button can be released for the layer to move into position.

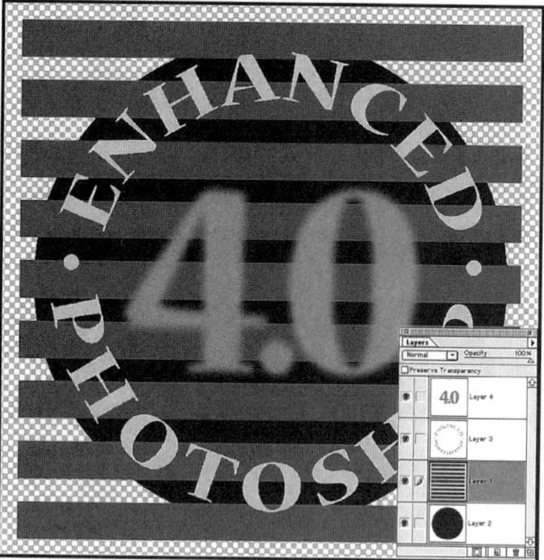

Figure 6-46: After a layer has been moved, the appearance of the image is different, reflecting the new stack relationships within the layer.

- Bring Forward—Command+] or Ctrl +]—which moves the selected layer up one level;
- Send Backward—Command+[or Ctrl+[—which moves the selected layer down one level; and
- Send to Back—Command+Shift+[or Ctrl+Shift+[—which places the selected layer at the bottom of the stack.

TIP

Selecting layers can be done from the keyboard in much the same way that the layers can be moved. There are four commands you can use to move up or down in the layer stack. These are:

- *Select the next layer up—Option+] or Alt+]. If there is no Next layer Up, your selected layer will be the bottom of the layer stack;*
- *Select the next layer down—Option+[or Alt+[.*
- *Select the top layer—Shift+Option+] or Shift+Alt+].*
- *Select the lowest layer (or the Background)—Shift+Option+[or Shift+Alt+[.*

You can also select a layer by clicking on one of the layer's pixels in the document window. On the Macintosh, hold Command, Option, and Ctrl as you click. In Windows, hold Ctrl, Alt, and right-hand mouse button as you click.

Establishing a Clipping Group A clipping group is a special relationship which uses the pixels of one layer to mask the pixels of another layer wherever they are above transparent pixels of the first. This kind of relationship is shown in Figure 6-47 where the horizontal bars of the lower layer are being used as clipping objects for the circular shape. This concept is difficult to visualize at first until you understand that with a clipping group, the pixels on the layer above the clipping layer are visible only where there are pixels on the clipping layer. Because of this, the circle of Layer 2 is not visible except where there are pixels on the layer containing the bars (Layer 1). Figure 6-48 shows the same clipping relationship but with the two layer's positions transposed. The bars in the figure are visible only where there are pixels in the layer below.

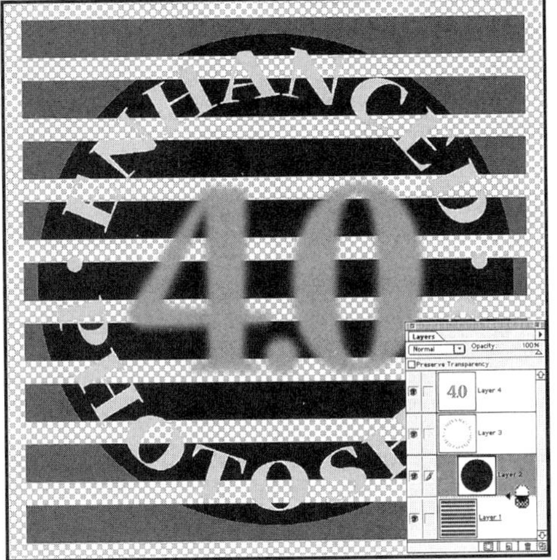

Figure 6-47: A clipping layer trims the upper layer's pixels so that they are visible only where the clipping layer contains pixels.

Figure 6-48: This figure and Figure 6-47 show clipping groups with the same two layers. The difference in effect is the difference between which layer is in the lower—clipping—position.

To make a clipping layer, hold Option or Alt and click on the boundary between the layers you wish to make into a clipping group (layers in a clipping group must be next to each other for the clipping group to function). With the modifier key depressed, the cursor changes to a small double-circle icon. After you have clicked, the thumbnail of the upper layer of the clipping group moves a little to the right, and the boundary between the two layer items changes to a dotted line. The title of the clipping layer also becomes underlined to indicate its status.

Clipping groups can be turned off by holding Option or Alt and clicking on the layer boundary. You may, if you wish, include more than two layers in a clipping group. In fact, all of the layers in a document may be part of one clipping group. Layers within the group can be rearranged in the stacking order within the group. If one of the layers is moved beneath the clipping layer, it is no longer a part of the group.

The clipping group option is available also from the Layer menu (Figure 6-49). Choose Layer | Group with Previous. Group with Previous means that the selected layer forms the clipping group with the layer beneath it. The keyboard command is Command+g or Ctrl+g. The Ungroup command from the same menu releases the clipping group. Select any of the layers within the group and press Command+Shift+g or Ctrl+Shift+g.

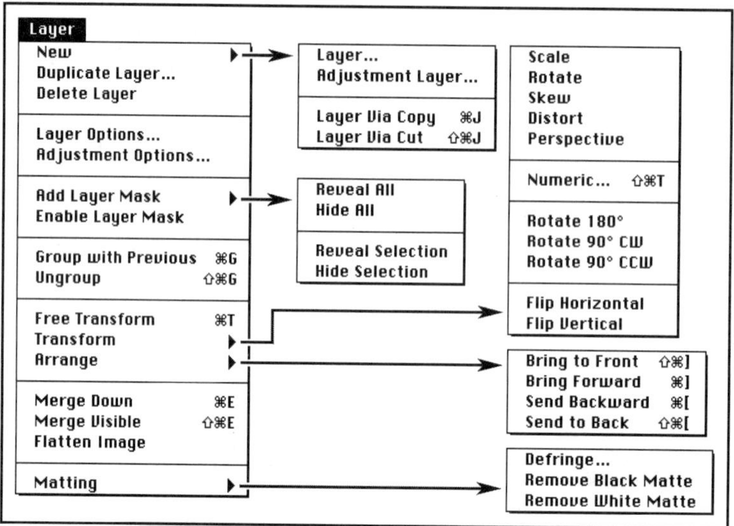

Figure 6-49: An expanded view of the Layer menu.

The Layers Palette Menu & the Layer Menu

The commands contained in the sidebar menu of the Layers palette are, for the most part, executable with key commands or by using the icons at the bottom of the palette. As we discuss the entries, we will make note of the ways you can accomplish the same commands without resorting to the menu. Although there is nothing wrong with using the menu, you will find that the Photoshop programmers have furnished you with some keyboard tools which let you work in layers with great efficiency. For those items which do not have a convenient keyboard equivalent, we recommend that you assign a keyboard macro or a Photoshop Action (please see the section on Actions in Chapter 1, "Optimizing Photoshop").

Many of the commands of the Layer palette's menu are duplicated under the Layers menu (see Figure 6-49). As we discuss these two menus, we will point out which commands are duplicates and which are available in only one of the two menus.

New Layer

When you choose the New Layer command, you are requesting that Photoshop create a layer *directly above the currently selected layer*. As soon as you choose this command, the dialog box shown in Figure 6-50 appears. Within the dialog box, you may enter a new name for the layer or accept the name Photoshop offers. You may, when the layer is created, preset the amount of opacity for the layer and the blend mode which will be assigned to it. The layer can also be assigned a fill based on what will be color-neutral (transparent) for the blend mode you wish to use. For example, if you wish to create the new layer in Multiply mode, you can click on the check box which will fill the new layer with white. White, in Multiply mode, is totally transparent. The wording at the bottom of the dialog box changes (Figure 6-51) depending upon which mode you select. This option is grayed out for Normal, Dissolve, Hue, Saturation, Color, and Luminosity modes. The calculations for these modes do not cause any color to become transparent.

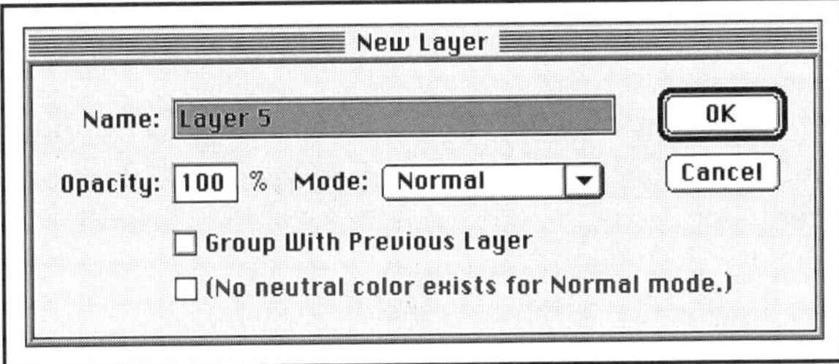

Figure 6-50: The New Layer dialog box. This window appears when you choose New Layer from the Layers menu, the Layer palette menu, or when you click on the New Layer icon with Option or Alt depressed.

☐ (No neutral color exists for Normal mode.)
☒ Fill with Multiply-neutral color (white)
☒ Fill with Screen-neutral color (black)
☒ Fill with Overlay-neutral color (50% gray)
☒ Fill with Soft-Light-neutral color (50% gray)
☒ Fill with Hard-Light-neutral color (50% gray)
☒ Fill with Color-Dodge-neutral color (black)
☒ Fill with Color-Burn-neutral color (white)
☒ Fill with Darken-neutral color (white)
☒ Fill with Lighten-neutral color (black)
☒ Fill with Difference-neutral color (black)
☒ Fill with Difference-neutral color (black)
☒ Fill with Exclusion-neutral color (black)

Figure 6-51: When you create a new layer and choose one of the blend modes, you will have one of these options to fill the layer with a blend-neutral color, a color that is transparent for the blend mode you have chosen. Six of the blend modes—Normal, Dissolve, Hue, Saturation, Color, and Luminosity—do not have blend-neutral colors.

To create a new layer which bypasses the menu command, hold Option or Alt and click once on the New Layer icon at the bottom of the Layers palette. The same dialog box appears. The fastest way to create a new layer is to simply click once on the new layer icon on the palette. The new layer appears in Normal mode, filled with transparent pixels, and named *Layer* and a number which is the next integer in the creation sequence. You may also choose New | Layer from the Layer menu. The dialog box appears in order to allow you to set the options for the layer. You can bypass the dialog box by holding Option or Alt when you make your selection from either of the menus.

There are two additional choices for creating a new layer at the bottom of the Layer | New submenu. These choices create a new layer by retrieving the contents of a selection. To use this option, select the pixels you wish to place on a new layer (or Select All if you wish to duplicate the entire layer). Choose either of the menu options. The first creates an exact copy of the pixels on a new layer directly above the one which contains the selection. The original pixels are left untouched. The second option does the same thing except that it clears the contents of the selection, leaving it empty of pixels. These two menu choices can only be used within the confines of a document. You cannot make a selection in one document and then choose either of these options from within another document.

Still another way to make a new layer is by means of a floating selection. Whenever you have a floating selection you can drag the floating selection's thumbnail to the New Layer icon (a dialog box results), hold Option or Alt and click on the New Layer icon (which also results in a dialog box), or simply click the New layer icon once. The later procedure creates the layer and bypasses the dialog box.

New Adjustment Layer

Adjustment Layers are mask layers which hold color correction information. When you choose to create a new adjustment layer, the dialog box shown in Figure 6-52 appears. Within this window, you can choose one of the nine correction possibilities from the Type pop-up menu. The adjustment controls you have chosen for the layer then appear and allow you to make color corrections or other kinds of changes to the image. When you are finished, click OK. The layer appears on the item list on the palette. It is distinguishable from normal layers because it contains a small circular icon—half black, half white—to the right of the layer name.

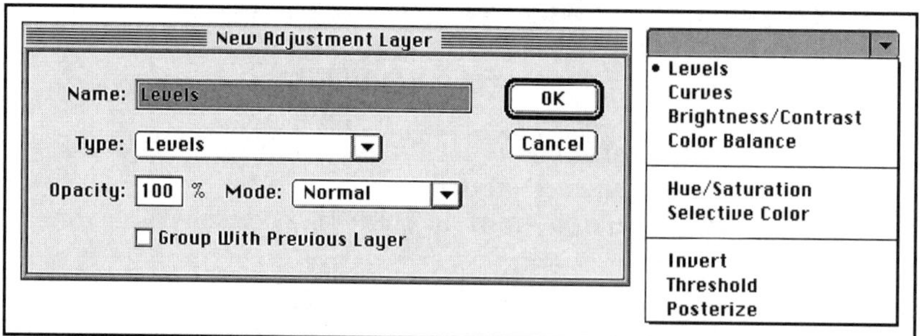

Figure 6-52: The New Adjustment Layer dialog box.

You can select New Adjustment Layer from the palette sidebar menu or from the program's Layer menu. You can also hold Command or Ctrl and click on the New Layer icon at the bottom of the palette.

Adjustment layers are one of Photoshop 4's best features. In previous versions of the program, you might wish to do several kinds of corrections to an image. For example, you might want to adjust the tone range with the Curves controls, after which you might want to adjust the Color Balance, and then the Hue/Saturation controls. Since all corrective techniques of this sort are destructive, two or three kinds of adjustments could be visibly injurious to the quality of the image.

With adjustment layers, you embed your corrections in a layer which is simply a mask. Whenever the layer is visible, you are able to see what kinds of adjustments you have made with the controls of the adjustment layer, but the changes will not have been applied to the original image. The concept is akin to the CMYK Preview option where you can work with an image in RGB mode but view it as though it had been converted to CMYK mode. Adjustment layers follow the same idea: you see the corrections but without having to apply them. That means that you can stack up Adjustment layers and view their cumulative effect. You can also go back to the controls for each layer (double-click the layer title) and tweak the original settings. The corrections of multiple adjustment layers are finally applied to the image as one large adjustment when the document is flattened. (When you flatten a layered document, all of the layers are merged into one.) The net adjustment is far more satisfactory and far less harmful to the image data.

Adjustment layers have other possibilities. Since they are true layers, you can apply opacity changes to them. Changing opacity has the effect of lessening the amount of the correction. You can apply blend modes as well. This allows you to do some incredibly complex special effects with a simple pop-up menu change. You might, for example, choose to create a correction layer, make no changes to the controls, click OK, and then change the blend mode to Multiply. This would have the effect of darkening an image that is too light. Or you could use Screen mode to lighten an image that is too dark. In either case, you can decrease the effect by changing the layer's opacity.

Adjustment layers are, as we stated above, masks. Because of this you can further modify how the layer behaves by adding paint to the layer. If you paint an area or fill an area with solid black, you eliminate the effect of the correction from that area. If you fill an area with a lesser percentage of black—say 50%—you decrease the amount of the correction by 50% in the place where you have added the fill. Gradients are also handy for use on correction layers. If an image is too light at the top and too dark at the bottom, a gradient applied to the adjustment layer can bring the two areas into balance.

TIP *If you wish to view the Adjustment layer by itself—especially if you have applied paint to an area and wish to make a small modification—hold Option or Alt and click on the layer's thumbnail. Click again with Option or Alt depressed to return to the normal layer view.*

For other information and for examples on using Adjustment layers, please see the section on editable color corrections in Chapter 11, "Manipulating Images." Other uses for Adjustment layers are found in Chapter 9, "Photoshop Prepress," and Chapter 10, "Calibration & Color Reproduction."

Duplicate Layer

When you choose the Duplicate layer command, you create an exact copy of the selected layer. The Duplicate command can be chosen from either of the menus—Layer palette sidebar or program menu—of you can simply drag the layer you wish to duplicate down to the New Layer icon at the bottom of the palette. The fastest way to duplicate a layer is to use the Layer via copy method. Follow this procedure: Select All, hold Command or Ctrl, and press j. An alternative method is to hold Command or Ctrl and click on the layer's thumbnail. This selects all of the pixels in the layer. You can then hold Command or Ctrl, and press j.

TIP *Don't forget that you can select the pixels of a layer by holding Command or Ctrl and clicking once on the layer's thumbnail. The selection does not have to be the selected layer. This allows you to use a selection outline from one layer—the layer does not have to be visible—on another layer. For example, the image in Figure 6-53 shows how a selection of the large circle on Layer 2 has been used to delete that shape from the bars of Layer 1. A selection of the blurred letters on Layer 4 has been used to fill new letter shapes on Layer 1. The selection of the pixels on a layer can be compared to the selection you get when you load an alpha channel.*

Figure 6-53: Hold Command or Ctrl and click on a layer's thumbnail. This selects the pixels of the layer. The layer contributing the selection need not be the selected layer nor must the layer be visible. Selections from other layers in the figure have been used to modify the bars of Layer 1.

Choosing to duplicate a layer from either of the menus results in the dialog box shown in Figure 6-53. This window allows you to rename the duplicate layer. It also allows you to simultaneously move the duplicate to a different document or to duplicate it into a new document. If you choose to make a new document, you can enter the name to be applied to the new window.

Duplicate Layer
Duplicate: Layer 2
As: Layer 2 copy
OK
Cancel
Destination
Document: Layers Sample
Name:
• Layers Sample
New

Figure 6-54: The Duplicate Layer dialog box.

There are a number of reasons why you might wish to make an exact copy of a layer. Figure 6-55 shows one possibility, drop shadow effects. The layer containing the blurred numbers in the center of the image has been duplicated. The original, positioned below the duplicate layer, has been filled with black (with Preserve Transparency turned on), set to Multiply mode, and moved down and to the right. The same procedure was used for the large circle except that a Gaussian Blur was added to the lower circle layer to make the shadow look more realistic.

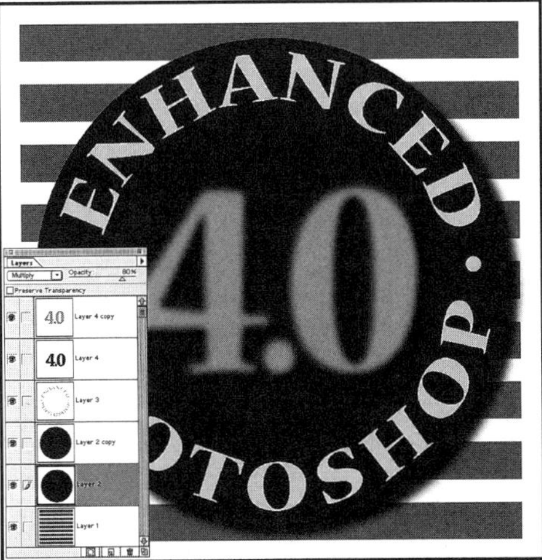

Figure 6-55: Duplicated layers are easy ways to make realistic drop shadows. Here, copies of Layers 2 and 4 have taken the positions of the original layers. The original layers have been filled with black, blurred, set to Multiply mode, and slightly offset.

Figure 6-56 shows another possibility where a duplication of a layer could be useful. As you can see, the letters do not show up at the bottom of the frame. In Figure 6-57, the layer containing the letters has been duplicated and the upper layer filled with white (Preserve Transparency turned on). Preserve transparency is then turned off again and a quick selection made with the Lasso tool around the upper line of letters. A press of the Delete key and the task is finished (Figure 6-58).

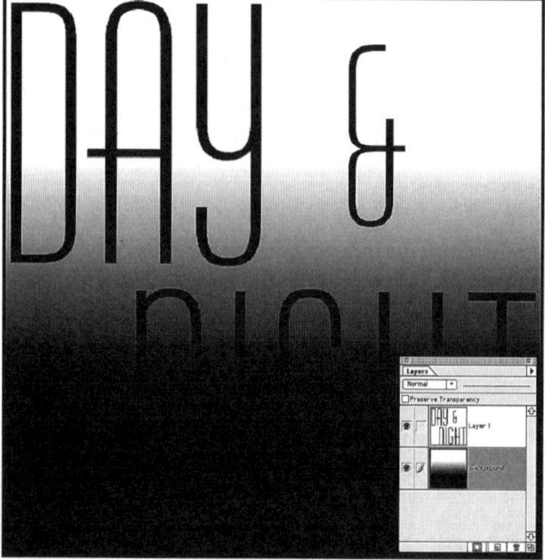

Figure 6-56: The letters on the layer do not show up against the background layer.

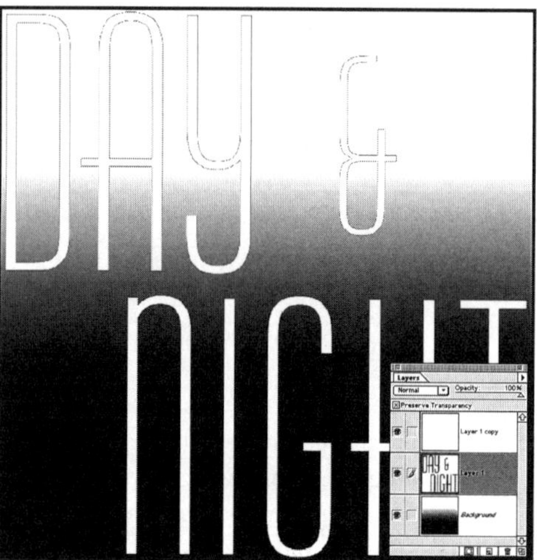

Figure 6-57: After the layer has been duplicated, the upper layer's pixels are filled with white.

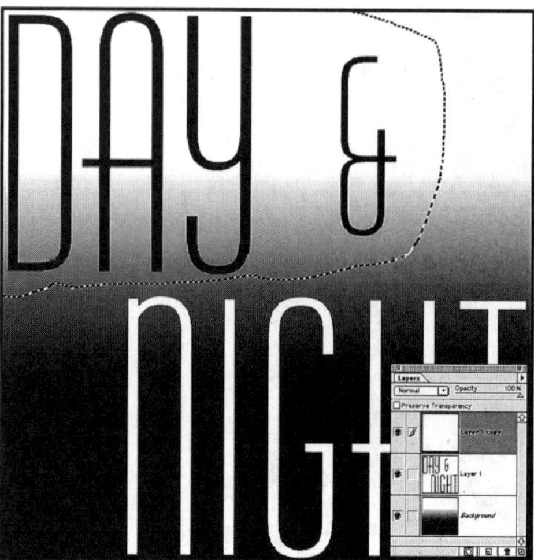

Figure 6-58: A quick selection of the first line of letters with the Lasso tool, a press of the Delete key, and the job is finished.

Delete Layer

Sometimes you change your mind. Perhaps you find that the layer you are using is no longer suitable for the way an image has evolved as a composition. Delete the layer by choosing the command from either menu. You can also get rid of the layer by dragging it to the trash can icon at the bottom. Even quicker: select the layer, hold Option or Alt, and click on the trash icon.

Layer Options

The Layer Options dialog box (Figure 6-59) contains some—but not all—of the settings choices of the New Layer dialog box. For example, it allows you to change the name of the layer, set the opacity, apply a blend mode, and even establish a clipping group. The choice of filling with a blend-neutral color is not present.

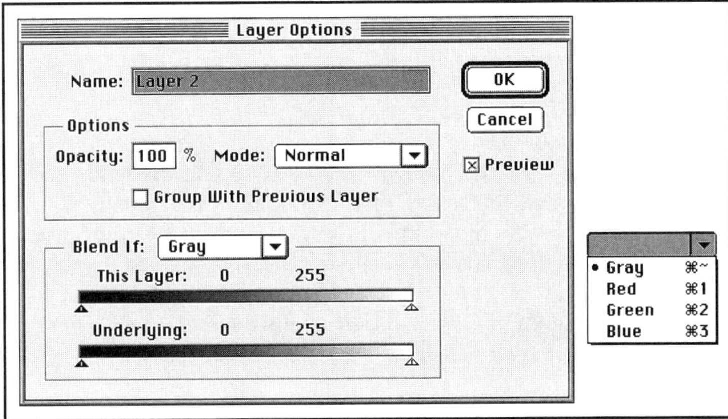

Figure 6-59: The Layer Options dialog box.

The Layer Options dialog box can be summoned from either menu. You may also summon it by double-clicking on the layer thumbnail. The bottom of the Layer Options dialog contains a Blend If section which delivers some really interesting effects. There are four choices: Gray, Red, Blue, and Green.

Blend If is kind of crazy—in a good sort of way. It is a way of excluding pixels from visibility based on their brightness or their color, or the brightness or color of pixels beneath them. To see how this works, please look at Figure 6-60. This figure shows a background with a black-to-white gradient running from left to right, and a circular area on a layer which contains the same gradient running from top to bottom.

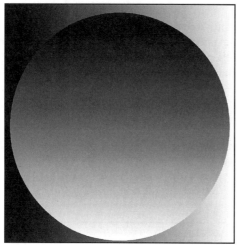

Figure 6-60: This figure shows a background with a gradient running from left to right, and a circle shape on a layer with the same gradient running from top to bottom.

There are two sets of sliders in the Blend If box. One is titled This Layer, the other Underlying. Both of the sliders work on a scale that ranges from 0–255 (shown atop each slider). Whenever you move one of the triangle tabs, the number updates.

Figure 6-61 shows the shadow-end tab on This Layer moved to a value of 75. This has the effect of making all of the pixels on the layer with values from 0–75 disappear. In Figure 6-62, the highlight-end tab has been moved to 181. This makes all of the pixels on the layer with values from 181–255 also become invisible.

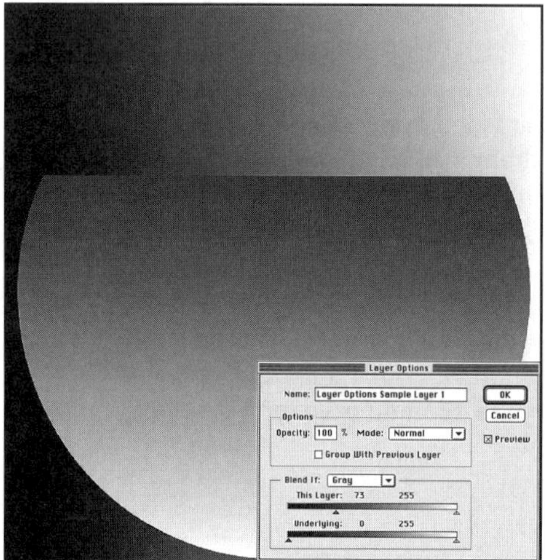

Figure 6-61: Moving the shadow tab on This Layer to 75 causes all of the pixels on the layer with values between 0–75 to disappear.

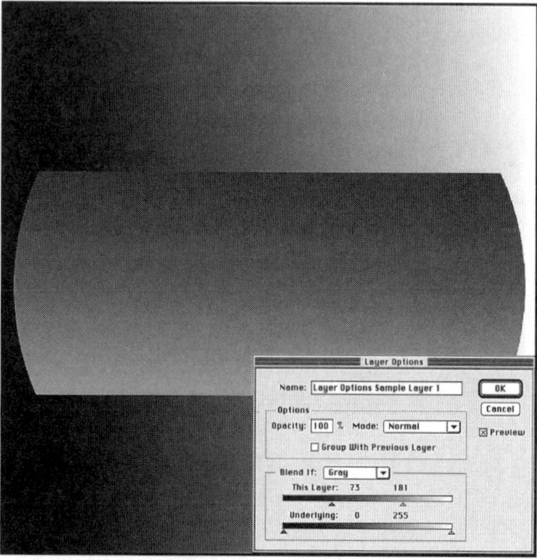

Figure 6-62: Moving the highlight tab on This Layer to 181 causes all of the pixels on the layer with values of 181 or higher to also disappear.

The action of the Underlying slider may at first seem a little puzzling. As you can see in Figure 6-63, the changes to that slider have shaved off a portion of the circle on each side. The reason for the change to the circle is that Photoshop is excluding pixels from visibility on the layer based on values from the pixels underlying the layer. With the shadow tab moved to 75, all of the pixels on the layer which are *above pixels in the background* with values of 0–75 have been made to disappear. The same exclusion has been carried out on the highlight end of the slider.

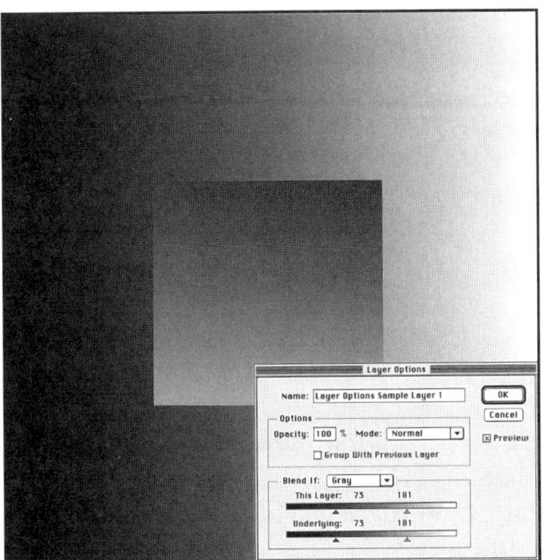

Figure 6-63: When the tabs on the Underlying slider are moved, pixels on the layer are made invisible if they are above the excluded range of values below them.

All of the tabs on the sliders can be divided. Hold Option or Alt and you can move the two halves away from each other. In Figure 6-64, this has been done with all four of the tabs. Notice that there is now a soft edge to the rectangular area which remains visible on the layer. The divided tabs allow you to have a smooth transition between opaque and transparent in a manner similar to a feathered selection. The This Layer slider numbers now read 55/73 and 101/199. If you wish, you can translate this series of numbers as follows: make the values on This Layer transparent if the brightness values fall between 0 and 55; give a smooth transition from transparent to opaque for the values between 55 and 73; make all of the values between 73 and 101 totally opaque; give a smooth transition from opaque to transparent for the values between 101 and 199; make all of the brightness values above 199 completely transparent. The translation of the numbers on the lower scale would be equivalent except that the numbers would relate to brightness values on the layer below as they affect the layer.

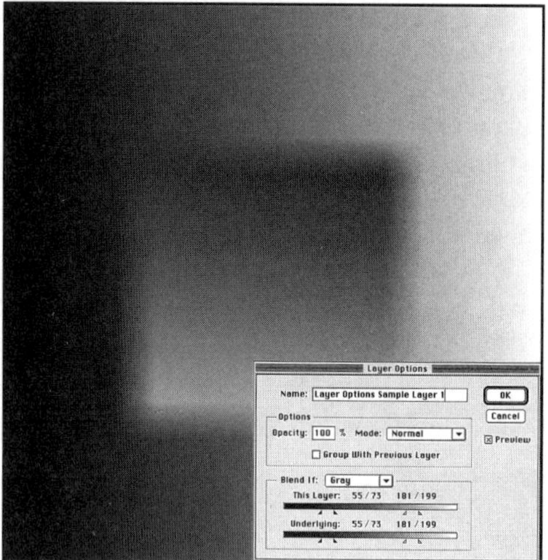

Figure 6-64: Hold Option or Alt to move the two parts of each tab away from each other. Separating the tabs gives a smooth, feathered transition between opaque and transparent pixels.

When working with colored files, there are additional choices based on the colors. Figure 6-65 shows an example with the same black-to-white gradient in the background but with a radial gradient shading, from the center, white-black-red-black-green-black-blue-black. The pop-up menu in the Blend If section of the dialog box contains entries for each of the three RGB colors besides the gray discussed above. When red is chosen and the shadow tab for This Layer is moved so that it reads 73, the result is as shown in Figure 6-66. All of the black values have vanished. Only the white-to-gray and red-to-gray tones have been retained. The darkest value at the edges of each of the areas is, as you might expect, 74.

When you move the red This Layer slider from the highlight end, you have the inverse effect on the pixels: all of the red and white values lighter than the displayed number disappear, leaving only blue, green, black, and the darker red and gray tones. This is shown in Figure 6-67.

There are a variety of compositing effects that are possible with these Blend If sliders. Figure 6-68 shows one possibility where the green highlight slider has been divided to encompass the range between 66 and 255. This has the effect of fading out green tones so that, as they become brighter, they also become more transparent.

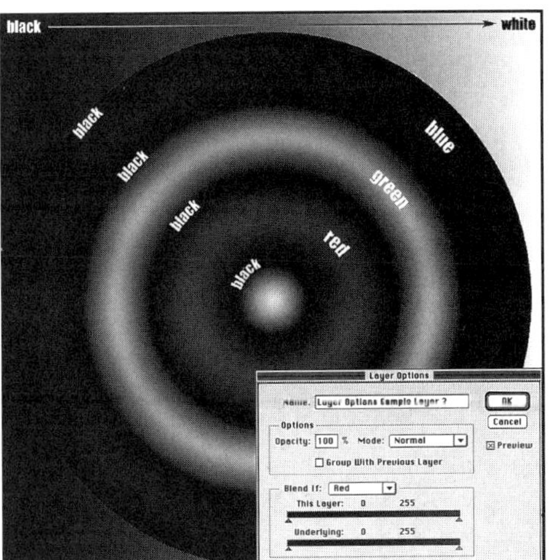

Figure 6-65: This figure shows a black-to-white gradient on the background layer with a radial gradient on the upper layer.

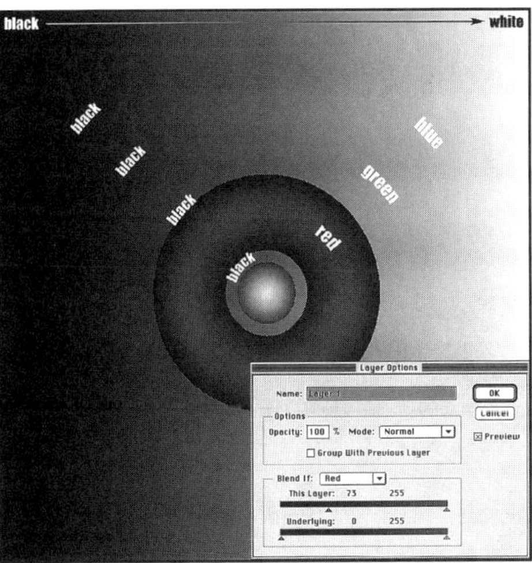

Figure 6-66: Moving the shadow end of the red This Layer slider results in the elimination of all dark values lower than the displayed number, and the disappearance of all color values other than red and white.

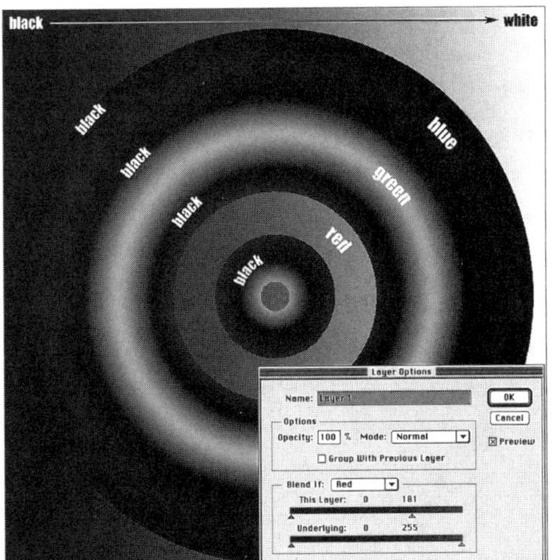

Figure 6-67: A move of the red highlight slider on This Layer has an effect that is the inverse of moving the This Layer shadow slider.

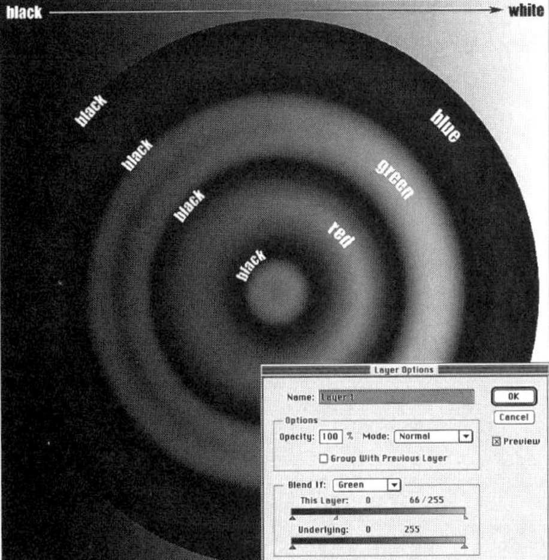

Figure 6-68: In this figure, the green highlight slider has been divided to encompass the range between 66 and 255. This has the effect of fading out green tones so that, as they become brighter, they also become more transparent.

Figures 6-69, 6-70, and 6-71 show another possibility. When objects on a layer are surrounded by a more-or-less uniform tone, it is easier to use the Blend If sliders to isolate objects than it is to silhouette them (select them and delete the area around them). Figure 6-69 contains a set of gradient-filled circles against a uniform, neutral surrounding color. In Figure 6-70, the background gradient has been subjected to the Crystallize filter. This is the background layer for the shaded circles. In Figure 6-71, the

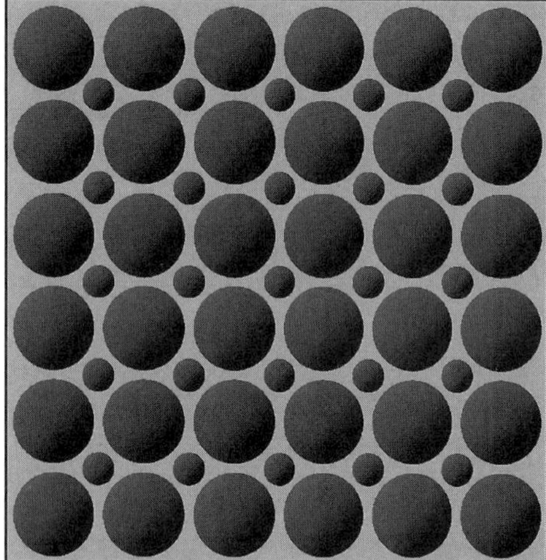

Figure 6-69: This layer contains shaded circles against a light surrounding color.

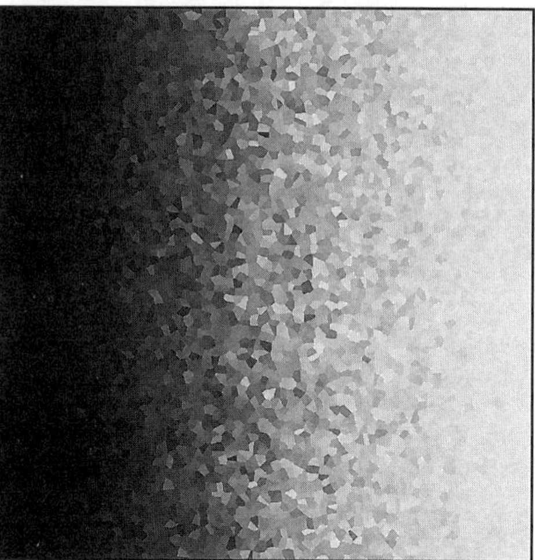

Figure 6-70: The background layer—below the shaded circles—is made up of a gradient which has been subjected to the Crystallize filter.

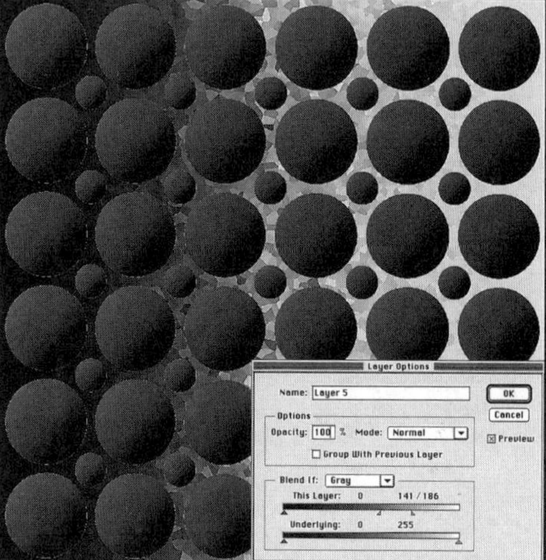

Figure 6-71: Moving the highlight slider eliminates the color surrounding the shaded circles as effectively as if you had outlined each and then deleted the background. This procedure is a lot faster!

circle layers highlight slider has been moved to the left which leaves the circles isolated against the underlying layer. A move of this sort usually leaves a small fringe of the surrounding color along the edges of the pixels which are left. Dividing the highlight slider minimizes that fringe.

In Figure 6-72, the Blend If exclusion is carried one step further to show how the objects on a layer can be modified by excluding some of the color values in the layer's pixels. Notice how the shapes begin to merge with the background despite the fact that the layer's opacity is set to 100% and the blend mode is Normal.

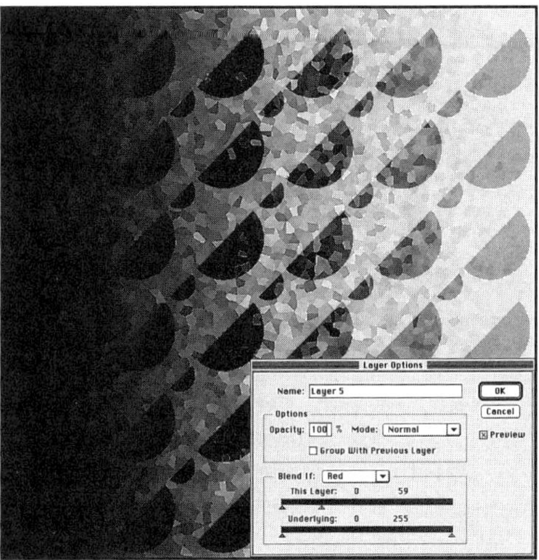

Figure 6-72: Besides eliminating the color around the circles, parts of the circles can also be excluded from visibility by using more than one menu item's sliders.

These Blend If sliders can give you a great deal of help when you are making composites of images. Watch out for the things that will alert you to the fact that this option may be useful. If you have images where the subject is surrounded by relatively dark or light tones, Blend if will help you get rid of that surrounding color. If you have images which are, for the most part, in a single color range, Blend If can help you eliminate all of the other color tones except the one you wish to keep. If you have colors in an image which are peripheral to the subject but which you would like to downplay, Blend If will allow you to make an entire range of colors transparent, or, if you divide the sliders, partially transparent (see Figure 6-68). When you combine these options with the already considerable array of layer tools, Opacity and Blend modes, you have a vast number of effects that you can achieve with almost no effort.

Adjustment Options

Adjustment Options is a choice that you can make from the program Layer menu. When you choose it, the dialog box for the correction tools used on the layer appear with the last-used settings. This allows you to makes changes to the settings. You can perform the same command by double-clicking the adjustment layer's name.

Merge Down

The Merge Down command—press Command+e or Ctrl+e—combines the contents of the selected layer with the layer beneath it.

Merge Visible

When you use the Merge Visible command, you must first hide all of the layers you do not wish to become fused by the command. Once the layers you want to protect are hidden, select one of the still-visible layers before the command is available. You can choose the command from either menu, or press Command+Shift+e or Ctrl+Shift+e. After the command has executed, all of the visible layers will be combined into a single layer.

Flatten Image

Flatten image is the command that merges all of the layers in a document into one background layer. If any of the layers is hidden at the time you choose the command, you will be asked if you wish to discard them. If you do not, click Cancel, make the layers visible, and then choose the command again.

A layered document can only be saved in the Photoshop file format. This makes it unusable for most other programs which can import image files. If you need to save in a format that can be imported into another software program, you need to flatten the image before any other file choices become available to you in the Save dialog box. A good procedure to use, if you suspect that you may need to edit the layered document at a later time, is to duplicate the document and flatten the copy. That way, you can save the original with its layers intact in case you should need them.

Since each layer added to a document increases its file size (except for Adjustment layers which do not add to the size of the file), merging layers which do not need to be separate entities is a good way to cut down on the size of the file. Flattening the image, of course, reduces the file to its minimum.

The Flatten Image command can be selected from either menu.

Palette Options

The Layers Palette Options command is available from the Layer palette sidebar menu. The dialog box, shown in Figure 6-73, gives you a choice of three sizes of thumbnails to be displayed by the palette.

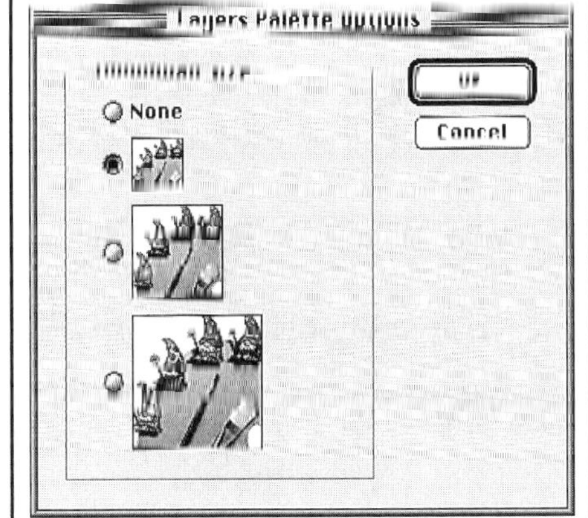

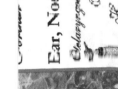

Figure 6-73: The Layers Palette Options dialog box.

Other Options of the Layer Menu

Most of the remaining commands associated with the program's Layer menu have to do with simple manipulations of the pixels on a layer. These include rotations, scaling, skewing, and flipping. One of the options, however, is not so simple. It is the Layer Mask, and it is one of the most important of the compositing tools.

Layer Masks

Layer Masks are similar, as we discussed at the beginning of this chapter, to the channel masks which we studied in Chapter 5, "Using Channels." They are constructed in much the same way and their appearance is similar to that of channels, but their effects are applied immediately—but not permanently—to the pixels of a layer. The relationship of a Layer Mask to a formal alpha channel is so close, in fact, that if you have a layer with a Layer Mask attached to it as your selected layer, you will see the mask appear on the channels palette. The name of the channel will be *Layer Mask*, with the text in italic type.

The Add Layer Mask command is found under the program's Layer menu. There are two choices for the command submenu, Reveal All and Hide All. To illustrate the differences between the two, please look at Figure 6-74 which shows a document with a second view of the same document (available under the View menu). This document contains a landscape layer which fills the frame. Another layer contains a photo of a small airplane sitting on a runway. It is this layer to which we will add layers masks.

TIP

We have already noted that the pixels of a layer can be loaded as a selection by holding Command or Ctrl and clicking the layer's thumbnail. Complex selections which are the result of adding together the selections of two layers, or subtracting one layer's selection from another, and so forth, are accomplished with the same key commands used for channels:

- *Load a layers pixels as a selection.*
- *To add another layer's pixels to the selection, hold Command+Shift or Crl+Shift and click the other layer's thumbnail.*
- *To subtract another layers pixels from the selection, hold Command+Option or Ctrl+Alt and click the other layer's thumbnail.*
- *To make a selection that is the intersection of two layers' selections, hold Command+Option+Shift or Ctrl+Alt+Shift and click the other layer's thumbnail.*

Figure 6-74: This figure shows a document with two layers and an open window showing a different view of the same document.

In Figure 6-75, a layer mask has been added to the document using the Hide All option. The second view window is now set to show the contents of the layer mask. (You can, if you wish, look at the layer mask at any time by holding Option or Alt and clicking on the layer mask thumbnail. Hold the same key and click again to return to the normal view of the document. Keep in mind that you do not have to see the layer mask in order to edit it.) This layer mask has been formed by Photoshop with a black fill. The effect of black within the mask is to make all of the equivalent layer pixels transparent. As a result, the pixels of the airplane layer have seemed to vanish from the document.

Figure 6-75: A new layer mask has formed with the Hide All function. It is filled with black as it is created. Because of this, it hides all of the pixels of the layer.

In Figure 6-76, white pixels are being added to the layer in the same area where there are pixels on the layer. This white area was added with a Paintbrush with the Foreground color set to white. Notice how the equivalent pixels on the layer have returned to visibility. It is important to stress that, unless you have a second window set to a different view of the document—as you see it here—you do not usually see the layer mask. As you add white paint to the document when you have the mask thumbnail selected, you are really painting on the mask rather than on the layer.

When you have a layer that does not cover the entire window as in this example, the Hide All option is probably not the best choice since you cannot see the pixels of the layer. Editing is difficult until you begin to establish where the pixels lie. The Reveal All option, as shown in Figure 6-77, makes working with a layer mask much easier. As you can see in the figure, the mask has formed with a white fill. This allows you to see all of the layer's pixels.

Figure 6-76: Adding white to the layer mask in the area equivalent to the layer's pixels returns them to visibility.

Figure 6-77: When the Reveal All option for the layer mask is chosen, the mask is created with a white fill. All of the layer's pixels remain visible.

Editing a Reveal All layer mask typically involves adding areas of black. Wherever black pixels are added to the mask, the equivalent pixels of the layer become transparent. In Figure 6-76, you see a set of quick brush strokes added to the mask with the Paintbrush, Foreground color set to black.

Figure 6-78: A quick addition of black paintbrush strokes has accomplished a rough mask for the airplane.

If you intend to do a more careful silhouette of the image on the layer, you can zoom in, trace the outlines with the Lasso or Pen tool, and fill your selection with black. The image in Figure 6-79 has been apparently separated from its background leaving the plane hanging in mid-air. The pixels around the plane are still present. They are simply hidden by the mask.

It is not required that solid black be used on the mask. Tints of black will allow the pixels to be visible with the opacity that is reciprocal to the percentage of black. In Figure 6-80, the windows in the plane's cabin have been filled with 50% black. This allows the sky behind them to show through at 50% Opacity.

Figure 6-79: You can zoom in close to the layer, trace the edges of the shape in small sections with the Lasso tool, and fill the selections with black. When you have finished, the pixels around the object will seem to be gone.

Figure 6-80: The layer mask can also be modified by adding tints of black. This allows the underlying layer to show through. In this figure, the windows of the plane have been filled with 50% black on the mask. This lets the sky show through from behind.

Once you have created the Layer mask, you may need to temporarily disable it to look at some of the hidden pixels. With a layer mask present on the selected layer, choose Layer | Disable Layer Mask. All of the hidden pixels will reappear. The layer mask thumbnail will show a large red x to indicated that the mask has been disabled (circled in Figure 6-81). When the mask has been disabled, the menu item will change to Enable Layer Mask. Choose this command to reinstate the mask.

Figure 6-81: If you wish to turn off the layer mask temporarily, choose Layer | Disable Layer Mask. The masked pixels will reappear and the mask thumbnail will show a large red x to show that the mask is not operating.

If your Photoshop composition seems not to require that the pixels around the object on which the layer mask is operating be preserved, you can remove the mask by choosing Layer | Remove Layer Mask. The dialog box shown in Figure 6-82 will appear to ask whether you wish to *Discard* or *Apply* the mask. If you choose Discard, your layer resumes the appearance that it had before you added the mask. If you choose Apply, all of the masked pixels are permanently discarded. Your layer will contain only the shape you have masked (Figure 6-83).

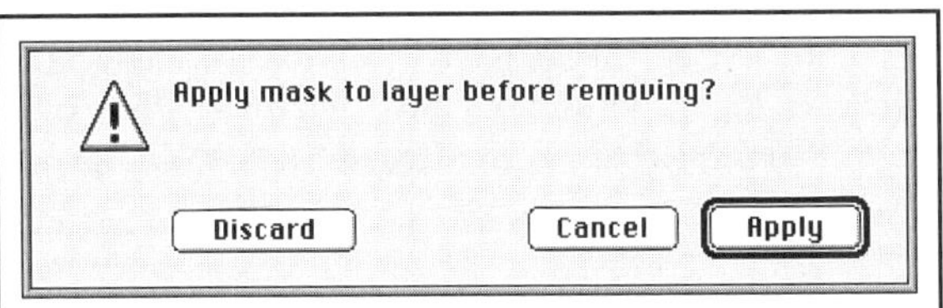

Figure 6-82: After choosing the Discard Layer Mask command, this dialog box will ask whether you wish to Discard the mask or Apply it.

Figure 6-83: If you Apply the mask when you discard it, all of the masked pixels are permanently deleted, leaving only the unmasked pixels on the layer.

There is another way to seem to extricate the unmasked pixels without discarding the layer mask—at least in a case such as the one shown in the figure where a silhouetted shape is involved. Hold Command or Ctrl and click on the mask thumbnail. This selects the masked shape. Choose Layer | New | Layer Via Copy (or hold Command or Ctrl and press j). This places a copy of the visible pixels—complete with areas masked with less than 100% black—on a new layer. You can then hide the layer containing the mask and proceed to develop the composite image. There's something of a moral here: don't throw those masked pixels away unless you are absolutely sure you'll never need them again. And even then, hesitate on the side of caution because you never know....

Layer masks can also be discarded by dragging the mask thumbnail to the trash can icon at the bottom of the palette.

Reveal Selection & Hide Selection When you have an active selection on a layer and you choose to make a layer mask, you have two choices available that will apply the selection to the new mask. With Reveal Selection, your mask is created with the selection area of the mask filled with white and the area outside the selection filled with black. When the mask has formed, all of the area outside the selection seems to disappear. Hide Selection is the inverse of Reveal Selection. When the layer mask has formed, the selection area on the mask is filled with black. Everything outside the selection is filled with white. With this mask in place, the area of the selection disappears.

Transform

When you begin to combine elements from different images, you'll often find that it is necessary to make adjustments to the orientation and size of a group of pixels. For example, you might need to change an object's size or to rotate it slightly, or even to distort it slightly so that it appears to be properly aligned with the objects on other layers. The various commands of the Layer | Transform submenu allow you to make these small changes in two ways. The first is interactive. After you have selected a command, a rectangle with eight live points—one at each corner, one at the center of each side—forms around the pixels. You can click and drag any of these points which changes the shape or orientation of the enveloping rectangle. The objects within change their shape or orientation to conform to the rectangle. The second is a numeric method where precise values can be entered into a dialog box. You'll achieve the same results whether you use the *by eye* method or numbers. The following is a brief summary, with examples, of the Transform submenu.

Scale Scale is, as you might imagine, the tool which allows you to change the size of a group of pixels. When you choose the command, a rectangle forms around the pixels to be affected—shown in Figure 6-84. You may change the shape of this rectangle any way you wish. If you select one of the corner points and move it toward the rectangle's center, the object—group of pixels—becomes smaller. Move the corner away from the rectangle's center and the object becomes larger. In the figure, the airplane has been made smaller.

Figure 6-84: The object on the layer, the plane, shows in preview after it has been made smaller but before the final command has been made.

You can also move the center points on the sides of the rectangle in either direction. Your resized object will then show an amorphic distortion. Maintaining the initial aspect ratio through the resizing requires that you move one of the corner points while holding the Shift key.

As soon as you have moved one of the points and released the mouse button, Photoshop will calculate a preview of the change for you to evaluate. If you have arrived at the size you want, either double-click within the rectangle or press the Return key. You can, of course, make further adjustments to the size. Photoshop will continue to give you previews after each move. The calculation from the initial size to the final size does not occur until you double-click or press Return. If you change your mind about the scale before you have completed it, hold Command or Control and press the period key.

TIP *With any of the transformation commands, you can click and drag within the enveloping rectangle to change the position of the object before you change it.*

Rotate The Rotate command is one of four on the Arrange menu. Three commands rotate the pixels in fixed amounts that let you orient the object to any of the cardinal points. The single Rotate command is a freewheeling affair that lets you rotate, by eye, to any amount you choose. When the rectangle has formed, click and drag—anyplace except within the rectangle—sideways, and the rectangle turns on its center (Figure 6-85). When you release the mouse button, the preview forms so that you can evaluate the new position and orientation of the pixels.

Figure 6-85: Click and drag anyplace but inside the rectangle to rotate the affected pixels. The preview forms after you release the mouse button.

Skew In the Photoshop context, Skew attempts to keep two opposite sides of the bounding rectangle parallel to each other while making the other two non-parallel (Figure 6-86). You can, if you work at it, make both pairs of opposite sides non-parallel. However, you can perform that task more easily with the Distort command.

Distort With the Distort command, you can change the shape in any way you please. Drag the corners of the rectangle until it is as distorted as you wish it to be (Figure 8-87). Photoshop does a nearly miraculous job of maintaining the legibility of the distorted object while stretching and bending it to conform to the envelope.

Figure 6-86: Bounding rectangle and distortion shown by the Skew command.

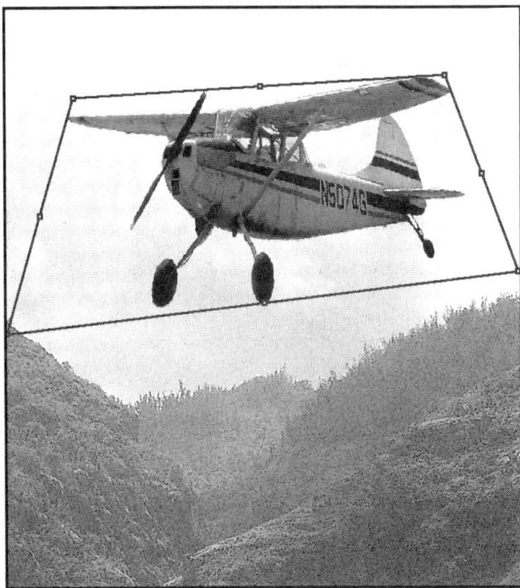

Figure 6-87: Bounding rectangle and distortion shown by the Distort command.

Perspective The Perspective command attempts to give you the ability to orient the pixels on the layer to an arbitrary vanishing point. As you move one of the corner pixels in or out, the near corner closest to inline with the move—as opposed to the corner at right angles to the move—will move in the mirror direction. In Figure 6-88, the upper right-hand corner has been moved down which caused the lower right-hand corner to move up. Both traveled toward the center horizontal axis of the rectangle. On the other side of the image, the upper left-hand corner was pulled up which caused the lower left-hand corner to move down.

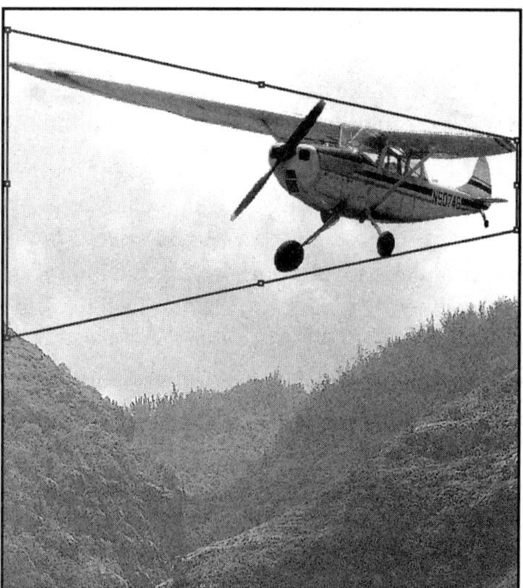

Figure 6-88: Bounding rectangle and distortion shown by the Perspective command. Move any of the corners and the near corner point closest to inline with the move will move in the opposite direction. This is, the first time you try it, kind of spooky.

Numeric If you wish to make your transformations of the pixels on the layer very precise, the Numeric Transform dialog box (Figure 6-89) gives you a great deal of scope. Entering values in the data entry fields of this window lets you precisely set the Position, Scale, Skew, and Rotation of your pixels all at the same time. Note that each of the three sections of the dialog box has a check box with which you can turn on or off the relevant functions.

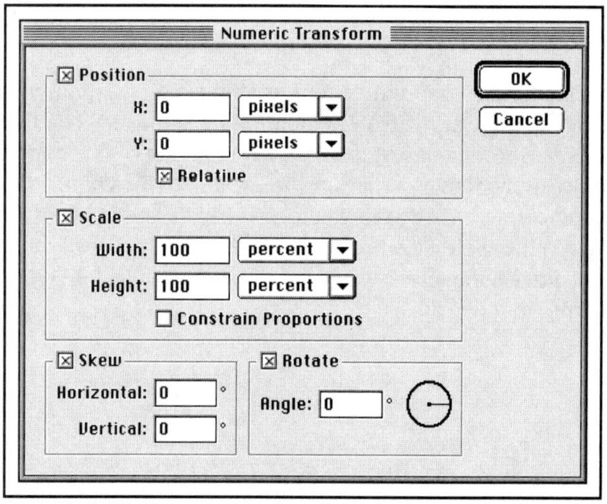

Figure 6-89: The Numeric Transform dialog box.

Rotate 180°, Rotate 90° CW & Rotate 90° CCW These three commands turn the pixels on the layer to one of the three positions. Their purpose is self-explanatory. These three commands, with the two flip commands which follow, do not require Photoshop to use its superb, but computation-intensive, Bicubic interpolation method. Because of this, they are the fastest of the transformation commands. Examples of the three commands are shown in Figures 6-90 (Rotate 180°), 6-91 (Rotate 90° CW—*Clockwise*), and 6-92 (Rotate 90° CCW—Counterclockwise).

Figure 6-90: Rotate 180°.

Figure 6-91: Rotate 90° CW.

Figure 6-92: Rotate 90° CCW.

Flip Horizontal, Flip Vertical These two commands can be a little confusing if you are used to Adobe Illustrator's way of describing a flipped orientation. Illustrator describes a flip as being along an axis. Photoshop's command, which makes no mention of an axis, may or may not be more intuitive but the words used give the opposite effect. A horizontal flip keeps the objects in an up-down orientation but reverses its sideways orientation (Figure 6-93). A vertical flip gives the opposite effect (Figure 6-94).

Figure 6-93: Flip horizontal.

Figure 6-94: Flip vertical. Really Top Gun!

Free Transform

After you've gained a bit of experience with the other transformation commands, and have a good idea of how they work and what they do, you'll probably never use them again. Really. The reason for this is that you'll then try the Free Transform command which does everything—everything!—the other commands do, and you won't need to use them again. Free Transform has the added benefit of having a key command to summon it: hold Command or Ctrl and press t.

When the Free Transform boundary rectangle appears, you may move any of its corners (while holding the Shift key if you wish to maintain the original aspect ratio). You can also click and drag (anywhere but inside the rectangle) to rotate the pixels. The rectangle remains rectangular unless you hold Command or Ctrl. With these modifier keys depressed, the corners become free of their right-angle constraints. You may then move the corner or center points anywhere you wish them to be. If you want to, you can even flip the pixels. Do this: drag the left-hand center point and drag it to one pixel to the right of the right-hand center point; now, drag the right-hand center point back to where the left-hand point was. The object will flip horizontally.

The real benefit of the Free Transform command is that you can make a number of changes to an image which would otherwise require the same number of separate steps. Not only is Free Transform a time-saver, it is also beneficial to the quality of the image. Transformed objects need to be interpolated only once, as opposed to a number of times with separate steps. All in all, there is no real reason why, once you understand how the individual transformation commands work, you would ever use them.

A Few More Layers Challenges

We have included on the Companion CD-ROM, in the Chapter 6 Practice Files folder, the file PLANE.PSD. This file contains the layered document shown in some of the examples in this chapter. It even includes the layer mask for the airplane layer.

You can have some fun with this file and experiment with layers while you do so. After discarding the layer mask, you could duplicate the airplane layer a few times and scale each to produce a flotilla of Cessnas (Figure 6-95).

Figure 6-95: The airplane layer duplicated a few times and with each layer moved and resized, produces a squadron of Cessnas.

Another interesting possibility is to add propeller motion. Make a new layer above the plane. Draw a circular selection over the propeller with the same diameter as the propeller blades. Feather the selection 3 or 4 pixels. Make a black-to-white-to-black gradient (lower right of Figure 6-96), set the Opacity to 50%, and draw the gradient all the way across the circle at right angles to the propeller. You'll get the effect shown in Figure 6-96. If you want to get really cute, use the Free Transform command on the prop-motion layer to change the perspective of the plane of rotation.

Figure 6-96: Make a circular feathered selection on a new layer. Draw a black-to-white-to-black gradient across the selection to make the prop movement.

Figure 6-97: Use the Perspective command to change the plane of the propeller movement.

These photographs were taken at Dillingham Airfield at the foot of the Waianae Mountains on the North Shore of Oahu, Hawaii. The plane is one of several used to tow gliders into the sky or to ferry aloft the daring members of SkyDive Hawaii. We've included three other files on the Companion CD-ROM that have a Hawaiian theme in the Chapter 6 Practice files. They are titled WAIKIKI1.PSD, WAIKIKI2.PSD, and WAIKIKI3.PSD. You can, if you wish, assemble them into a layered document—#1 on the left, #2 in the center, #3 on the right—which will give you a panoramic view of all of Waikiki Beach. Remember that you can change the opacity of the overlaid images, distort them, rotate them, and move them to get the overlapping edges to match. After you change the Opacity back to 100%, you may need to do some touch-up work with some of the Selection tools, the Rubber Stamp tool, and perhaps a Layer Mask or two. We have also left the adjustment layers attached to the images so that you can, if you wish, tweak the colors to make the three as alike as possible. You'll find the task challenging and interesting, and you'll have a memorable photographic memento of your exploration of Photoshop's layers.

Figure 6-98: Included on the Practice Files disk are these three overlapping images, which you can use to construct a panoramic view of the Waikiki skyline.

Matting: Defringe, Remove Black Matte, Remove White Matte

Once in a while when you detach a group of pixels from one image and move it to a different location, the selection process will include background pixels which form a fringe of unwanted color. The three Matting commands are included to help you remove those extra pixels or to change their color so that they do not intrude on the visual effect you are creating.

Defringe is the most powerful command of the three. When you choose the command, a dialog box appears asking for a dimension in radius. Enter the number of pixels which you estimate to be the width of the extra pixels around the edge of the pixel group. Click OK, and the program will blend color the pixels with the tones adjacent to them. Or at least that's the theory. It does work, but the result is often not worth having. You should try the command with the hope that it might provide a reasonable result. If it does so, then you are saved the effort of adjusting the edge pixels manually—often a tedious and time-consuming process. If it doesn't work as well as you might like, well, bite the bullet, as it is said.

Black Matte and White Matte remove fringe from objects which were originally on a black or white background. In the cases where these two commands work, they work perfectly. Otherwise, you may see no change to your edge pixels. There doesn't seem to be a way to predict when these commands will work and when they will not. However, they are always worth a try.

Moving On

In this chapter you learned how to think in layers and recognize the difference between a layer's pixels and the transparent areas that surround them. You also entered the fascinating world of blend mode calculations, which can combine layers in intriguing and beautiful ways. Along with blend modes, you learned about layer opacity and the Blend If possibilities which can exclude pixels from visibility based on their brightness or color. You have glimpsed the tremendous power of layer masks.

You will find that layer work is one of the most enjoyable and magical of Enhanced Photoshop activities. Don't worry about keeping track of everything that you could possibly do with layers. When the time comes that you need one of the layer features, come back to this chapter, look at the relevant section, and then try it. You'll find that what you want to do is much easier than you thought.

In Chapter 11, "Manipulating Images," you'll learn a good deal more about adjustment layers, the single aspect of layers that we didn't explore extensively in this chapter. You already know what adjustment layers are and how to make them. Chapter 11, "Manipulating Images," will show you how to put them to good use with editable color corrections and with stacked adjustment layers, which can give you some wonderful special effects. In Chapter 9, "Photoshop Prepress," and in Chapter 10, "Calibration & Color Reproduction," you'll meet adjustment layers in a professional prepress setting. You'll build on what you have already learned so that your Photoshop images will translate into accomplished printed work. Finally, have a look at the sophisticated manipulations available to you using layers and channels combined with the Apply Image and Calculations commands.

chapter 7
Calculations

Would you like to be an armchair general? Commanding your images and sternly saying "Go here!" or "Do this!" as your images meekly obey and move? If you enjoy directing, you will love the Calculations and Apply Image commands. Once the preserve of Photoshop junkies, these two commands are now accessible to all. All you need to do is try them. They are still considered to be very esoteric, and they are not used nearly as often as they should be, but they add power, ease, and convenience to an already powerful program. They will amply reward your learning to use them.

So, what are these commands, and how do you start commanding them? The Calculations and Apply Image commands (let's just call them CHOPs for short) are used to composite images and channels without cutting, pasting, dragging, dropping, or mousing around. The commands allow you to take image A and blend it with image B using any Apply mode (two more than are available using layers) at any opacity using any channel, layer mask, or layer transparency as a mask. You have a wide range of places that you can "send" the output. While there are two different commands, they do most of the same thing. We'll explain the differences in this chapter.

Before getting into the details, a bit of Photoshop history is justified. Prior to the introduction of Photoshop 3.0 in November 1994, Photoshop had no layers. The user blended pieces of images together either by using the Calculations commands or by pasting pieces of one image into another. The Calculations commands were a series of separate commands; each one performed a different function. There was a Multiply command, a Screen command, Lighter, Darker, Add, Subtract, Difference, and Blend. You selected image or channel 1, image or channel 2 and the opacity, and the computer magically produced the requested image. There was no preview, so you could frequently be surprised. CHOPs experts, like Kai Krause, could often produce 114 open images in a session in the effort to create the perfect image (and all of these images were called "Untitled-whatever" since there was no ability to name a document until you saved it.

When Photoshop 3.0 was designed, the engineers decided to try to simplify the process. They half succeeded. They exchanged a group of easy-to-comprehend but difficult-to-control commands for two powerful, easy-to-visualize commands with the most daunting interface dialog anywhere in Photoshop. The commands caused a bit of an uproar in the Photoshop community, because many of the users favorite "tricks" no longer worked, and because the two commands are so similar that it is often hard to see the need for both of them. In defense of the engineers, the two commands did not really start out to be as similar as they became. User pressure forced certain changes in them as the program neared its delivery date. The CHOPs commands are less needed in Photoshop 3 and 4 than they were in Photoshop 2.5 and earlier, but they are still very useful. Rumor has it that many in Adobe would like to see these commands disappear, but that would really be a shame. After you finish this chapter and try the power of CHOPs, we hope that you will agree.

The Apply Image Command

Let's meet the Apply Image command first. It is the more general of the two CHOPs commands and is conceptually easier to understand. This command allows you to place into your currently active layer or channel any other layer or channel from the same image or from any open image that has the identical pixel count. (We'd say "any open image that is the same size," but that isn't quite true. Two images that are each defined as 4 inches square but have different resolutions will not work together, but two images with the same pixel count will—even if they are at different ppi.)

It might help to think of your active image as a slide screen. You can "project" onto this screen any "slide" (i.e., image layer or channel) that is lying around (open) and will fit into the projector (is the same pixel count). While there are many uses for the Apply Image command, one of the most useful situations is to allow you to easily place a previously created image or channel into a layer mask. Let's see how this works:

1. Open the image FLOWER.PSD from the Companion CD-ROM. Figure 7-1 shows this image.
2. Create a new document (Mac: Command+N, Windows: Ctrl+N). Open the Window menu in the application and select FLOWER.PSD as the template for the new document.
3. Select a light color from the flower as your foreground color (use the Eyedropper tool to sample it). We selected a soft pink.
4. Fill the image with the foreground color (Shift+Delete).
5. Select a darker color as your foreground color. We used a deeper green in the flower.
6. Create a new layer (click on the New Layer icon at the bottom of the Layers palette). Fill the new layer with the foreground color.

Figure 7-1: FLOWER.PSD.

7. Create a layer mask (click on the layer mask icon at the bottom-left of the Layers palette).
8. With the layer mask active, choose Image | Apply Image. Figure 7-2 shows the dialog. Your "target" image is the layer and channel that is currently active. A *target* is the place where the output of the command is placed. You have no choice about that (well, actually you do, but not the way we selected the command, so we'll worry about that later). You need to select your Source image (the one that is to be placed into the target). In the box named Source:, select FLOWER.PSD. If you have many open images, only images of the correct size show up in the menu as an option.

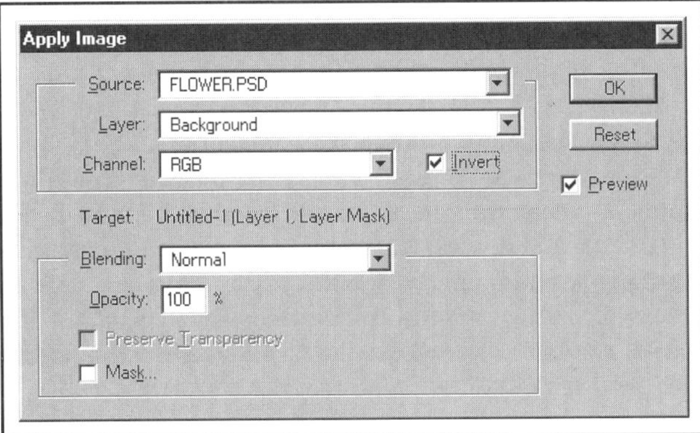

Figure 7-2: The Apply Image dialog.

9. Select Background as the Layer and RGB as the Channel. This places a grayscale version of the flower image into the layer mask. Click the Invert button in the dialog to see a "positive" instead of a negative of the flower. Make sure that Preview is checked so that you can see what will happen.
10. Set the Blending mode to Normal and the Opacity to 100%. Click OK. Figure 7-3 shows the result.

Figure 7-3: Using Apply Image to create a density layer mask.

TIP *The default Blending mode is Multiply. When the target is solid white, it makes no difference to the result if the mode is left at Multiply or changed to Normal. Under any other circumstance, it makes a great amount of difference.*

There are several reasons why the Apply Image command is better than cut and paste when you work in a layer mask. There is no clipboard memory used, so it is more sparing on RAM (though this is an advantage of using either of the CHOPs commands). Also, it is somewhat tricky to paste into a layer mask in Photoshop 4.0. You cannot do it at all unless you work in the Channels palette with only the entry for the Layer Mask channel active. Otherwise, when you paste, you end up adding a new layer rather than putting anything into the mask.

Another very practical use of the Apply Image command is to add density (or subtract it) into a color channel. You will use the Apply Image command for that purpose in Chapter 11, "Manipulating Images."

The Calculations Command

The Calculations command is quite similar to the Apply Image command, but the dialog is much more complex. (See Figure 7-4.) This dialog has a Source 1, Source 2, Blending Section, and a Result. Before we try to do anything fancy, let's look at the available options.

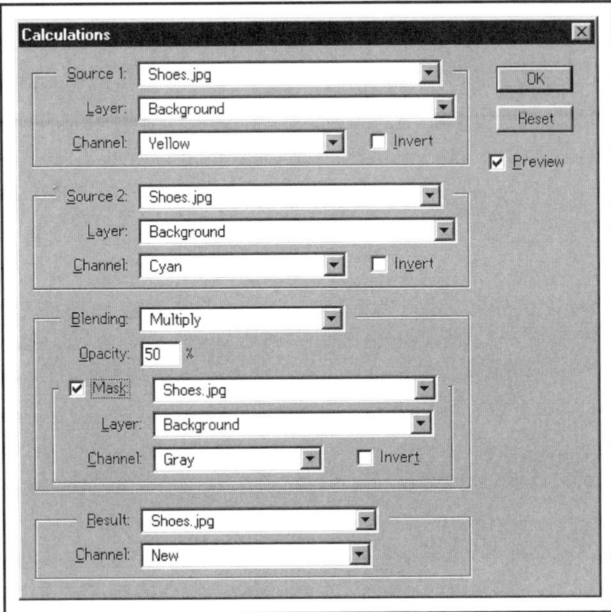

Figure 7-4: The Calculations dialog box.

Unlike the Apply Image command, you can select any two channels or layers of the same size in any open document, regardless of whether that layer or channel is active. In a weird sense, it is like being able to stand near a crowd and say "you and you, get married." You can play matchmaker to any two things and put the result somewhere else. There is a catch to all this power. Calculations only works in grayscale. The only channels options are the color channels, the alpha or gray—not the Composite channel. If you need color (the composite channel: RGB, CMYK, etc.), you need to use the Apply Image command.

The other catch—and it is this that makes calculations so complex—is that sometimes it matters which image you use as Source 1 and which one you use as Source 2. (Sometimes it doesn't matter at all). If you change the Opacity from 100%, it always matters. If you use Normal, Overlay, Hard Light, Soft Light, Color Dodge, Color Burn, or Subtract mode, it matters. If the Opacity is left at 100% and you use Multiply, Screen, Difference, Add, or Exclusion mode, it doesn't matter, as those mathematical operations are *commutative* (i.e., 5 x 9 = 9 x 5). You've known since second grade that 5–2, for example, is not equal to 2–5. Because the Apply modes are performing channel math, they follow the usual rules.

How do you remember which source is which? If you don't use this feature very often, you probably won't remember. Here is an easy "rule." When you are using an Apply mode that can work in Layers (i.e., anything but Add or Subtract mode), Source 1 (the one "on top") is equivalent to the top layer and Source 2 is the equivalent of the bottom layer. The opacity settings work the way layers would as well. If you set the Opacity to 20%, you see 20% of Source 1 (the top "layer") and 80% of Source 2.

If you use Subtract mode, you need to subtract Source 1 *from* Source 2. Therefore, if your Source 1 image is black and Source 2 is white, the result is white (0 *from* 255 =255); if Source 1 is white and Source 2 is black, the result is black (255 from 0 is 0—well, actually it is –255, but Subtract mode cannot count lower than 0). Add mode doesn't matter, as we said above, because order is not important. Note, however, the number in Add mode cannot exceed 255. White + white still only equals 255 as there is no color in grayscale with a value of 510!

The best way to learn how the Calculations command works is to experiment with it using a group of channels that are solid and named. We will set this up shortly. The other "goodies" in the Calculations command are the ability to use the inverse of either Source 1 or Source 2 (or both) and to use a mask on the operation and invert it! This gives the command almost mind-boggling complexity!

Let's set up a Calculations example using three layers—one black, one gray, and one white.

Calculations on Solids

The simplest way to learn about Calculations is to play with them using solid layers. In this example, you need to create a small, three-layered image. Let's see what can be done:

1. Create a new document (Mac: Command+N, Windows: Ctrl+N). Make the image 400 pixels square. Create the image in grayscale. (Since Calculations only creates a grayscale image anyway, why bother with color?)
2. View the Channels palette. The first channel in a grayscale image is automatically named Black at the start. Let's make this easy. Fill this channel with black.
3. Click on the New Channel icon in the center of the Channels palette to create a new channel. Name it White (double-click on the channel name to see the Channel Options dialog and rename the channel in that dialog) and fill it with white.
4. Create another new channel. Name it Gray 50%. Figure 7-5 shows the Channels palette so far.

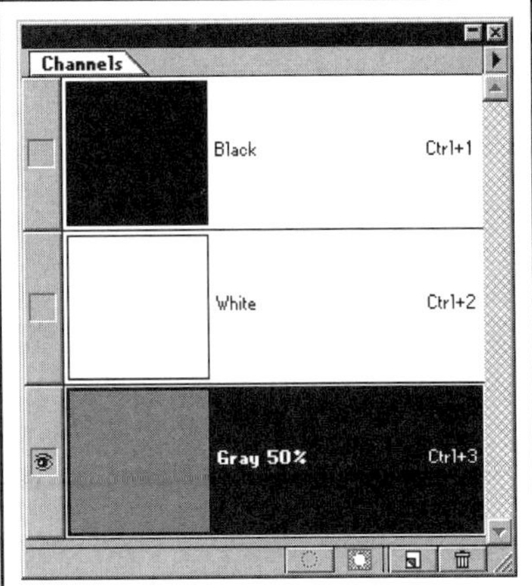

Figure 7-5: Channels palette on practice file.

5. It does not matter which channel in the image is active. Select Image | Calculations. Make the gray channel both the Source 1 image and the Source 2 image. Select Add as the Blending mode. Set the Opacity to 100%. If you were to add 128 (neutral gray) to 128, you would get 256 (or our maximum of 255), which is white. That is precisely what our result happens to be. (Do not click OK to actually apply this yet.) Figure 7-6 shows the Calculations dialog.

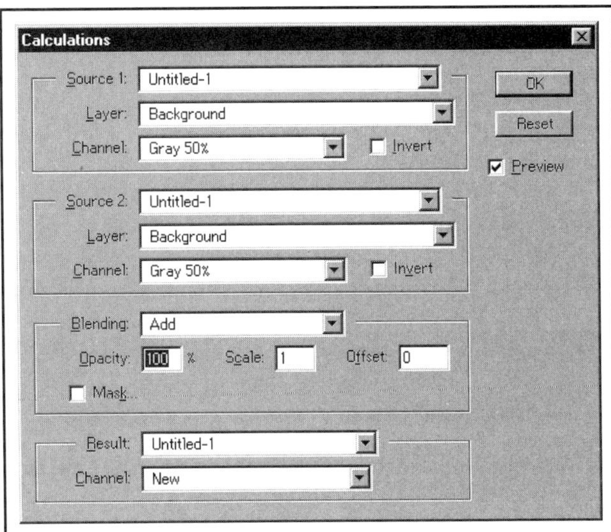

Figure 7-6: Adding gray to gray.

6. Change Source 1 to the White channel and leave Source 2 as the Gray 50% channel. Change the Blending to Subtract and leave the Opacity at 100%. The image turns black. Why? Source 1 (White) from Source 2 (Gray 50%) = Source 2 (128) – Source 1 (255) = 128–255 = –128 (which is really 0) = black (0). Do *not* click OK.
7. Change Source 1 to Gray 50% and Source 2 to White. What do you get now? Answer: 50% gray, because 255–128=127.

So long as you understand the Channel math that was introduced in Chapter 5, "Using Channels," this should be easy—at least for the "easy" Apply modes like Normal, Multiply, Screen, Add, Subtract, Lighter, Darker, and Difference. There were the "original" Apply modes, for which Adobe published the mathematical formulas. The newer modes on the menu (Overlay, Hard Light, Soft Light, Color Dodge, Color Burn, and Exclusion) are considered to be proprietary and the specific calculations are really not made available. You can predict the results of those modes in general, but you might not be able to calculate the specific pixel value in advance.

Let's create a few new channels with different values in them so that we can build up the complexity a bit. Continue working in the grayscale image which you can save as PRACTICE.PSD.

1. Use the Calculations command to multiply the Gray 50% channel with itself. Were you able to predict the result? This time, click OK and let the command create a new channel (which is the default). After the new channel is created, double-click on it and rename it Gray 75% (which is value 64). That's right, multiplying 50% gray with itself creates a gray that is half again as dark—75% gray instead of 50% gray.

TIP

The math here is calculated on the basis of 0–255, not percentages. If you use the Info palette densitometer on the channel, in grayscale, the percentages go from 100% black, which is value 0, to 0% black, which is value 255. Confusing? You bet! To keep your sanity, rename your gray channels in the practice document so that they contain the gray value, *not the percentage.*

2. Create another new channel—to be named Gray 192 (that's 25%) using the Calculations command. Can you think of any moves that can create a 25% gray channel from the available channels? There are a number of them that can, but if we limit you to 100% Opacity, then the most obvious move should be Gray 50% screened with Gray 50% (if multiplying 50% by 50% yields 75% gray and Screen is the opposite of Multiply, then screening 50% and 50% should produce 25% gray, which it does). You could also produce a 25% (or 192 value) channel by Adding Gray 128 to Gray 64.
3. Now that you have a good idea (or no clue at all) of what's happening, we need to advance to the next level. Let's throw Opacity into the mix. Remember that the

opacity refers to the *Source 1* image. What happens when you place white over black at 50% Opacity in Normal mode (don't really apply this). You get 50% gray. The results that you get from other mixes are not as consistent or as easy to guess. Just know that you get less from Source 1 of whatever effect you are trying to achieve when you change the opacity.

4. And then, there's masking . . . this further complicates (or expands) the possibilities. Choose the Calculations command. Make Source 1 and Source 2 both Gray 128. Select Screen at 100% opacity as the Blending mode. Click on the Mask button and choose Gray 192 as the mask as shown in Figure 7-7. The result is Gray 176 (or 31%). Instead of the 25% black that your previously produced by screening 50% gray with itself, you have allowed only approximately 75% of the change to occur (or, said another way, the 25% gray mask removes 25% of the change that would otherwise occur.

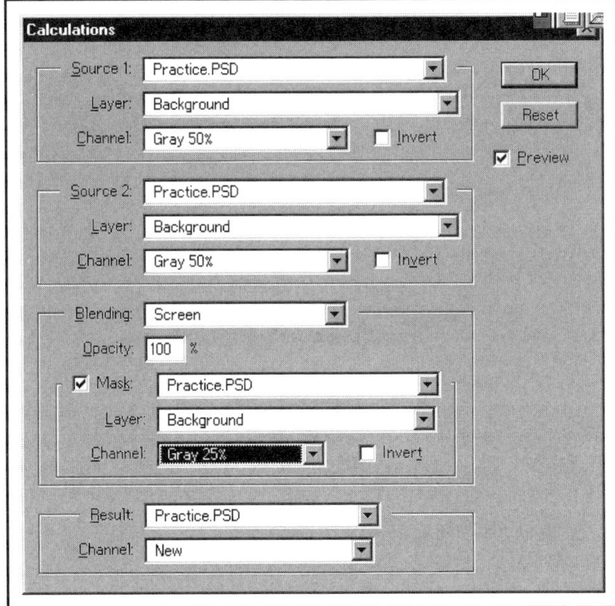

Figure 7-7: Using a Mask in the Calculations command.

Luckily, you can use the Apply Image and Calculations commands completely by "accident"—even if the math makes your teeth ache. Since you have a Preview capability, you can fiddle around with the settings until you see something that you like. That is a lot faster than cut and paste or drag and drop when you have no clue what result you want or how to get it! Of course, having a clue as to what you want and how to get there makes the process go much faster.

Calculating a Grayscale

One good, practical use of the Calculations command is to create grayscale images from color ones. Chapter 9, "Photoshop Prepress," spends more time on this topic, but this technique, courtesy of New York artist, Eric Reinfeld, works nicely.

When you convert a color image to a grayscale using Photoshop's Image | Mode | Grayscale command, the result can often be too dark and muddy. There is often one channel that looks better than the grayscale image. If one channel, when you view it in the Channels palette, is perfect, simply use that channel. Normally, no one channel is "just right," even though the Red, for example, might have better highlights and the Green, perhaps, has better midtones. You can blend the channels together using the percentages that create the best picture that you can build.

Using the Calculations command, you do not even need to look at the channels first. You can view each RGB channel in turn by setting the Blending mode to Normal (which makes the Source 1 channel fully opaque if the Opacity is set to 100%). After you look at each channel, you can then decide which two are best. In most images, the Red channel will give you the best detail, the Green channel will you the best contrast, and the Blue channel carries the most noise and garbage.

If you have determined that the Red and Green channels are best, make one of them Source 1 and the other Source 2. The Blending mode can be set to Normal, and you can then fiddle with the Opacity percent until you like the blend (Eric usually uses a 60–40 blend of Red and Green). The individual image, however, dictates the final percentages needed. Figure 7-8 shows an example. The cactus is, of course, basically green, which makes turning it into grayscale different than working with a picture of a person. To make a good, contrasty grayscale, we placed the Red channel in Source 1, the green channel in Source 2, and set the Blending mode to Normal at 20%. This makes a better image (in Figure 7-8b) than the "standard" grayscale conversion (in Figure 7-8a).

Figure 7-8: Grayscale conversion and 20% Red/80% Green calculation compared.

Calculating Selections

You can also load the results of a Calculation into a selection. Let's try that example. You will use four files of the same size, three of these have been rasterized from the Ultimate Symbol Design Elements collection (the fourth one, TEXTURE.PSD is a simple, made-up texture). Let's see what happens:

1. Open the images STAR.PSD, TEXTURE.PSD, SUNFACE.PSD, and ZODIAC.PSD from the Companion CD-ROM. Figure 7-9 shows the four images.

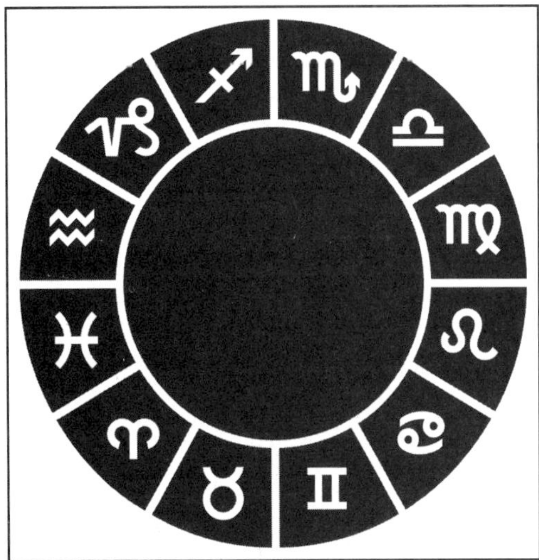

Figure 7-9: Star, Zodiac, Sunface, and Texture.

2. Choose Image | Calculations. Make ZODIAC.PSD the Source 1 image and TEXTURE.PSD the Source 2. You want to place the texture into the area occupied by the zodiac. Therefore, you need to change the Blending to Screen. Place the result into a New document (it will be called Untitled-1 if you have no other untitled images open). Figure 7-10 shows the Calculations dialog; Figure 7-11 shows the result.

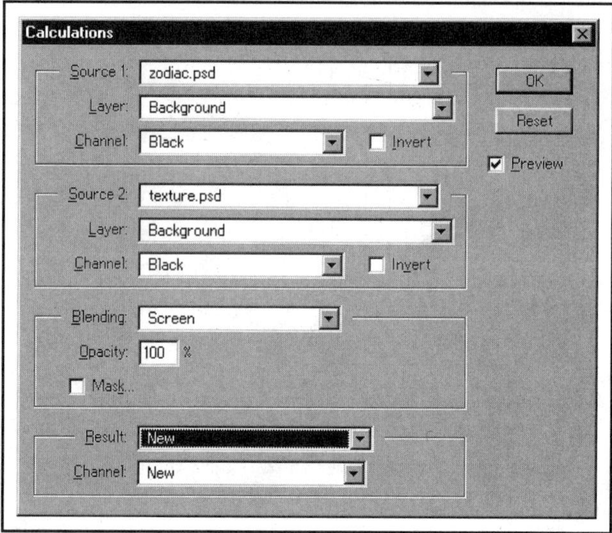

Figure 7-10: Calculations dialog.

Figure 7-11: Zodiac screened onto texture.

When a scan can be captured with more than 8 bits of information for each channel, you can perform a number of similar adjustments on the image to coax the data back into normal range. Because the scan contains so much data, it is possible to retrieve picture information from badly exposed images (top) so successfully that the image becomes usable. Successive adjustments of this magnitude on a normal scan would irretrievably damage the image. (Photo by Alexis Yiorgos Xenakis)

Although Kodak's Photo CD provides an inexpensive way to acquire good quality images, files which you open into Photoshop should be treated as raw (unadjusted) scans. Don't be concerned if, when you first see an image retrieved from a Photo CD, it looks as dense and dark as the upper image shown here. You have enough image data that you can use Photoshop's adjustment controls to correct the image to make it reasonably close to your original photograph. (Photo by Alexis Yiorgos Xenakis)

Late 20th-Century civilization overlays the fine details of this Victorian house with electronic and sports clutter (top). With Photoshop's Rubber Stamp tool and one or two of the selection tools, the springtime elegance of the house has been restored. Now it looks (lower) much the same as when it was built. Mr. Edison's wires, the air-conditioner, the basketball backboard—even the distant microwave tower—have all vanished. Anyone who would trust photographs as court evidence does not know what Photoshop can do!

At the top is shown a pleasant, atmospheric image with far too many places where the eye can rest its attention. Photoshop and the Focus tools have provided instant depth-of-field (bottom). With the Sharpen tool and a large, soft-end brush tip, the basil plants,the pillow, and the top of the chest have been brought into sharper focus. The Blur variation of the same tool has defocused the area around the central image. The eye now alights naturally on the center of the photo. (Photo by Alexis Yiorgos Xenakis)

Autumn and a cloudy day give us a light gray sky and dull, subdued fall colors (small inset). Photoshop's Toning tools can reanimate the scene in just moments. With the Burn tool set to Highlights, this sky was darkened in the cyan channel to produce the blue tone. Note the natural look of the sky produced by painting with a pretty casual brush stroke. Next, with the Sponge tool set to Saturate, the lifeless tones of the foliage become enhanced appropriately for the bright, clear day, evidenced by the blue sky. (Photo by Cheryl Koch)

Converting from RGB to CMYK usually results in colors that are more dull than the originals (inset). Here's a tip for restoring the colors quickly. Enter Quick Mask. Fill the document window with 70% black. Exit Quick Mask. From the filter menu, choose KPT Sharpen Intensity 2.1. This filter has no dialog controls and, when used normally, produces an effect that is too strong. Quick Mask allows you to modify the effects of the filter by the reciprocal percentage of the black fill. The results are as shown. (Photo by Alexis Yiorgos Xenakis)

Already a softly romantic image, this practice photo uses filters to give it a dreamier mood. Quick Mask has been used to quickly isolate areas of the image—with fairly soft, feathered edges—which have then been subjected to the Pointillize, Ripple, Mosaic, and Watercolor filters. The filters produce very different effects and merge smoothly with adjoining areas because of the masking. Complete instructions for this image can be found in Chapter 3, "Toolbox Techniques." (Photo by Alexis Yiorgos Xenakis)

From a quiet pond to instant Monet . . . . With a random set of small v-shaped paths spread over the entire photograph, the Impressionist variation of the Rubber Stamp tool can accomplish this painterly effect with a single click of the mouse. The variety of effects which can be achieved by using any one of the eleven stroking tools—all of which can be made to follow a path automatically—is startling. Paths effects are an area of Photoshop which has not been extensively explored.

A variety of other stroked path effects are shown here—and on the following pages—built upon this detail (top) of the famous David by Michelangelo. Two basic paths are needed for the effects and to contain them in specific areas. One of these outlines the sky, the other the statue. One or the other of these can be used simultaneously as a selection and as a guide for a tool. In the lower photograph, a white paintbrush was used to stroke the outline of the statue while the sky was selected. The result is this glow effect.

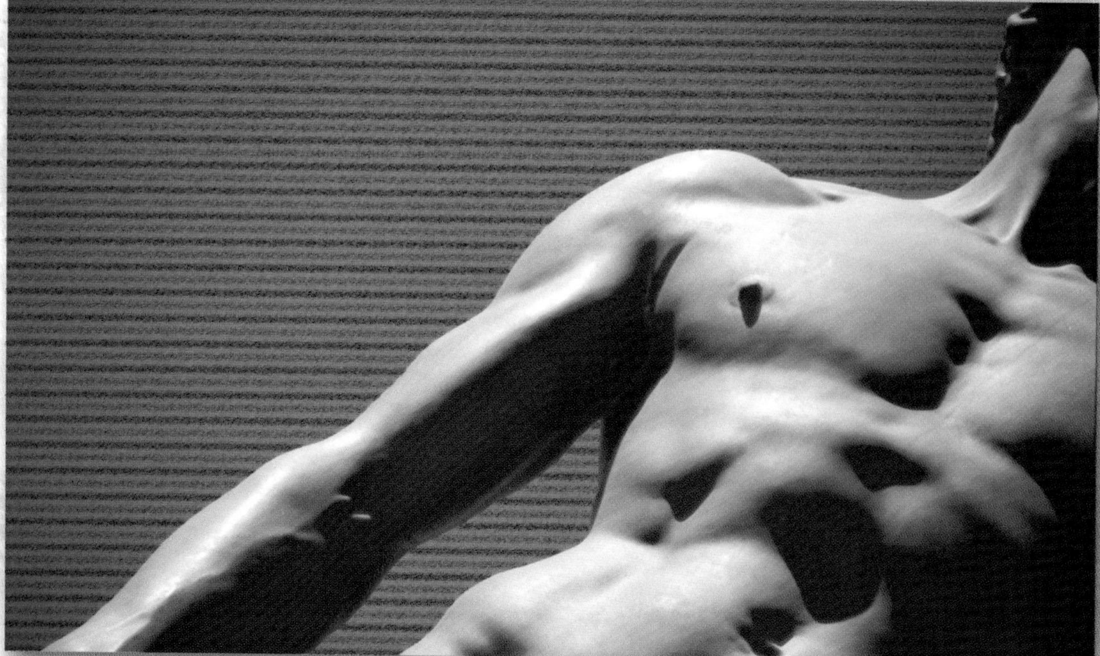

The top figure shows a more complex effect than the previous page's glow. Two strokes, both at about 50% Opacity, have been applied with a Paintbrush. A white stroke within the area of the statue and a dark stroke ouside the area make a point of the edges by heightening the contrasts. In the lower figure, parallel paths running across the entire width of the image have been stroked while the sky area was selected. Two brush sizes were used. Alternate lines were stroked with the Dissolve mode and two different opacity settings.

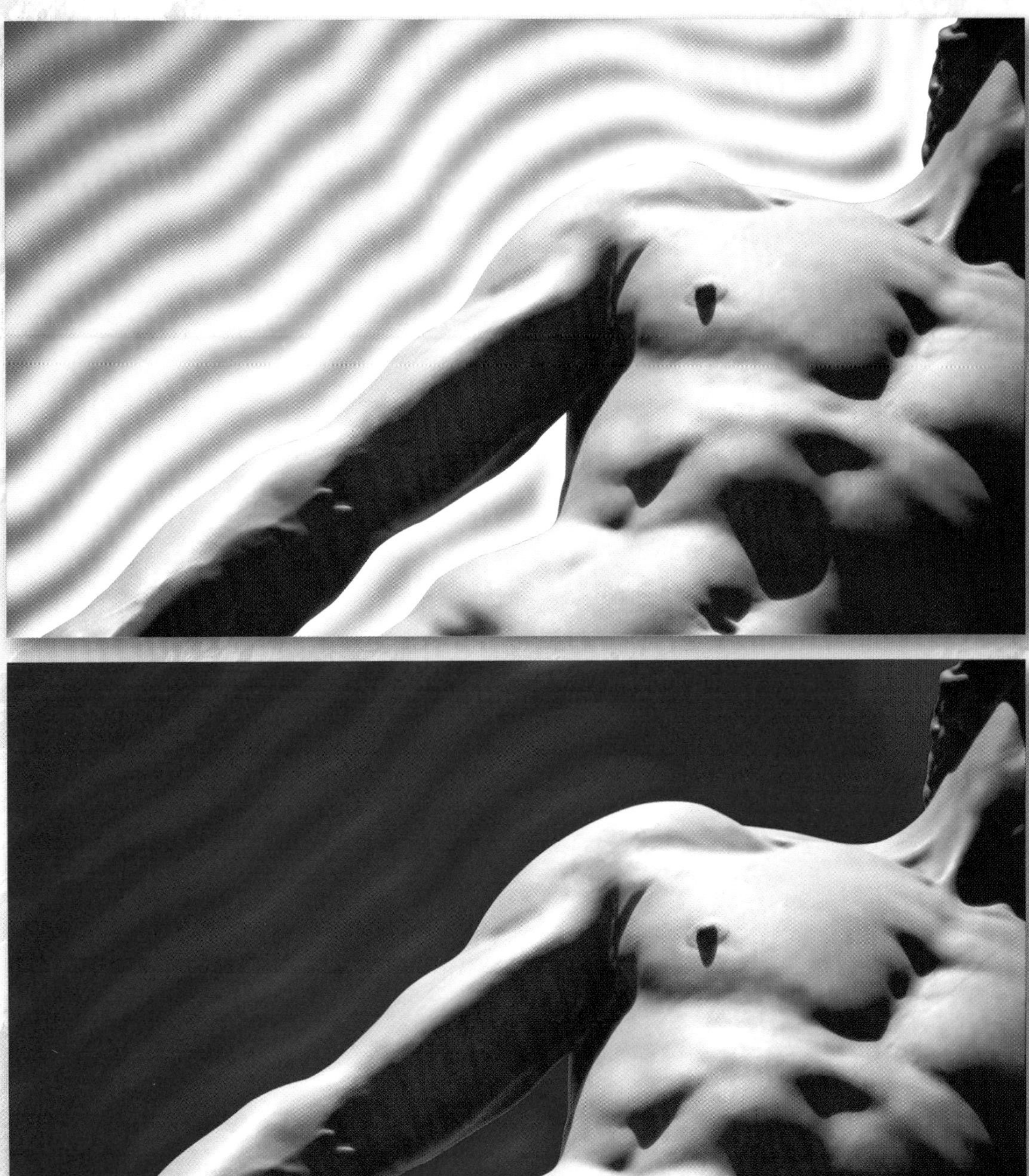

The effects shown in these two figures are based on stroking cloned versions of the statue's outer contours. In the top image, strokes have been applied with a white Paintbrush. As each path was stroked, the brush opacity was lowered by 10%. The lower image was done in exactly the same way as the upper except that a 50% black tone was used for the stroke color and the paintbrush was set to the Difference mode. Notice how variations in the sky tones cause the strokes to change from blue to purple and back.

Both of these examples are the result of stroking a set of waved-line paths. The variety of effects were achieved by having one of the two image areas selected while the stroking took place. In the top figure, the brush was set for white (background and black (statue). For both areas, the brush was at 40% Opacity and in Dissolve mode. The lower figure used a black brush (50% Opacity, Dissolve mode) for the letters. A white brush, 50% Opacity, stroked the sky using Normal mode, and the statue using Difference mode.

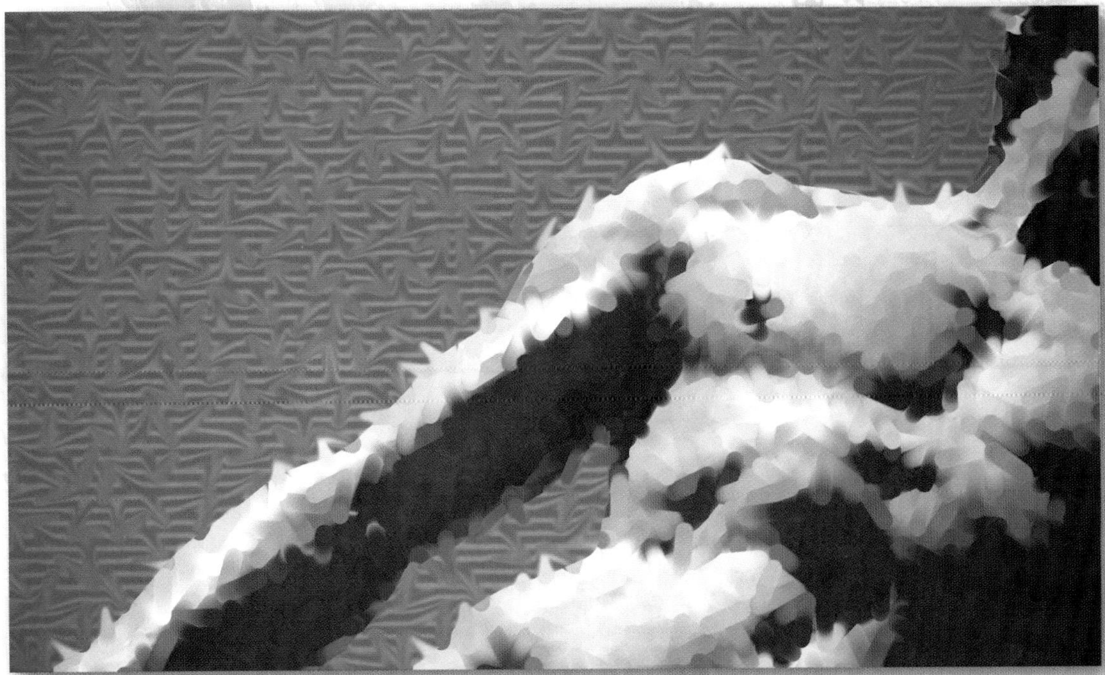

These two examples are more complex than the previous images. The top photo has been altered by first adding horizontal lines to the sky. A set of v-shaped paths were then stroked by the Smudge tool. Finally, the same paths were stroked using the Rubber Stamp's Impressionist variation. The lower image is a composite of two photographs. The merging of the two required the same horizontal-line paths and the v-shapes. Besides the strokes, a layer mask and layer blend modes were used. Complete instructions are included in Chapter 4.

Both of these figures are further examples of what can be achieved with stroked paths. The top figure has simply been built up with multiples strokes using different brushes and opacity settings and two colors, cyan and white. The lower example features a stroke of the letter outlines by the Smudge tool while the letters were selected. This gives the glass-like effect. The glass letters are further enhanced by keeping an embossed-letter alpha channel active while Levels controls lightened the letters.

These two images were composed using alpha channels operations. Alpha channels are Photoshop's method of storing selections. Because the selection is stored as an image, normal Photoshop editing operations can be performed upon it. Several channels can then be used to give new selections based on the differences between them, the composite selection of all, and the selections which are common to all. By using such calculations, these special effects can be accomplished in minutes. (Photo by Alexis Yiorgos Xenakis)

Some of Photoshop's most mysterious and beautiful effects are achieved with the Blend modes. The concept is simple: when one pixel lays atop another, calculations based on each of their values can be used to produce a result color. This blended color is often—but not always—different from the two values that produced it. The numerical manipulations can include common arithmetic operations such as Multiply & Difference. Other operations are more complex and produce intricate color artifacts. While some pixel combinations do not produce interesting effects, others combine for combinations that are arresting—and somehow appropriate in their context. The examples shown on this page—and the following two pages—combine the peony's background with the colored textures of the pages.

Normal

Dissolve

Multiply

Screen

Overlay

Soft Light

Hard Light

Color Dodge

Color Burn

Darken

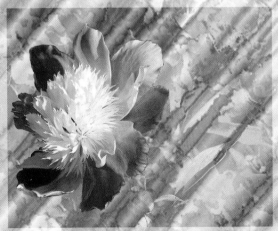

Lighten

Difference

Exclusion

Hue

Saturation

Color

Luminosity

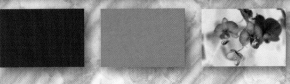

You can use the Apply Image command to move a grayscale version of an image into a Layer mask. When a grayscale image masks two solid layers, it creates a two-colored image as shown above. The images to the left show the two layers and the layer mask.

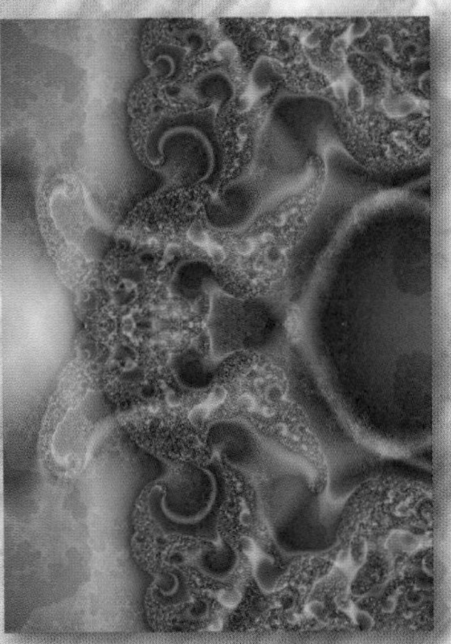

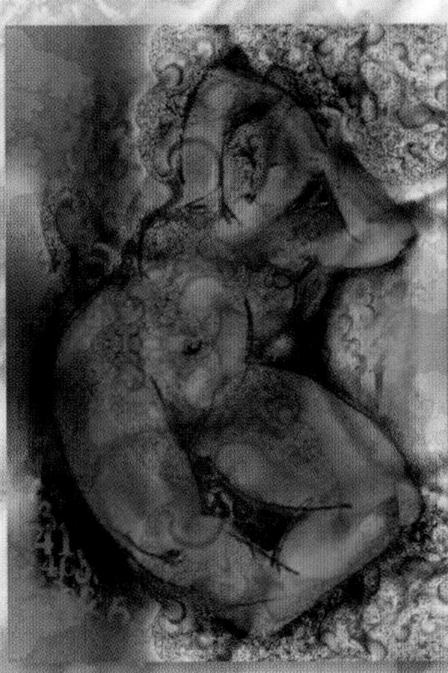

The Apply Image and Calculations commands can be used to create exciting images from files of the same size. The fractal image on the left and the nude in the center (drawn by California artist Rhoda Grossman) are combined via Difference mode in the Apply Image command to produce the image on the right.

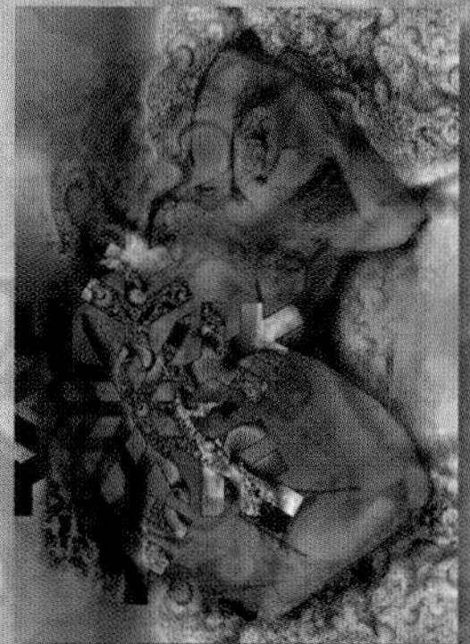

The four small images above are all stops along the road to creating the large image to the right. When you work with the Apply Image command, you can preview the result before any image transfer occurs. You can also select any same-sized open image as a mask for the image. These features give you a tremendous amount of power and flexibility for "spontaneous" combinations with very little RAM overhead. It is much faster to view a preview of your composite than it is to drag and drop and add layer masks.

While this serendipitous technique is not suited to every assignment (since you do lose the flexibility that layers and layer masks provide), you can obtain outrageous effects that might not otherwise have occurred to you since it is so easy to make new combinations of images. Knowing how to use the Apply Image and Calculations commands expands your options as an artist—which, of course, is the intent of this book!

Filters, Filters, Filters! Everybody loves filters. Simply choose your favorite from the Filter menu, and the magic happens all by itself. Depending upon the image and the filter you use, the change can be dramatic or subtle. Some filters create artistic effects, others distort the image in unusual ways. A couple—the Unsharp Mask and Gaussian Blur filter—are so useful for such a variety of purposes that you'll find that you use them on nearly every image. The handsome Marmalade Binder models the bundled Photoshop filters on this page and the three pages which follow. Notice with what aplomb he wears each look.

Colored Pencil
Cutout
Dry Brush
Film Grain
Fresco
Neon Glow
Paint Daubs
Palette Knife
Plastic Wrap
Poster Edges
Rough Pastels
Smudge Stick
Sponge
Underpainting
Watercolor
Blur
Blur More
Gaussian Blur
Motion Blur
Radial Blur
Smart Blur
Accented Edges

Angled Strokes | Crosshatch | Dark Strokes | Ink Outlines | Spatter

Sprayed Strokes | Sumi-e | Diffuse Glow | Displace | Glass

Ocean Ripple | Pinch | Polar Coordinates | Ripple | Shear

Spherize | Twirl | Wave | ZigZag | Add Noise

Despeckle | Dust & Scratches | Median | Color Halftone | Crystallize

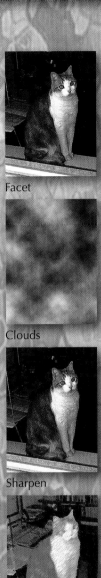

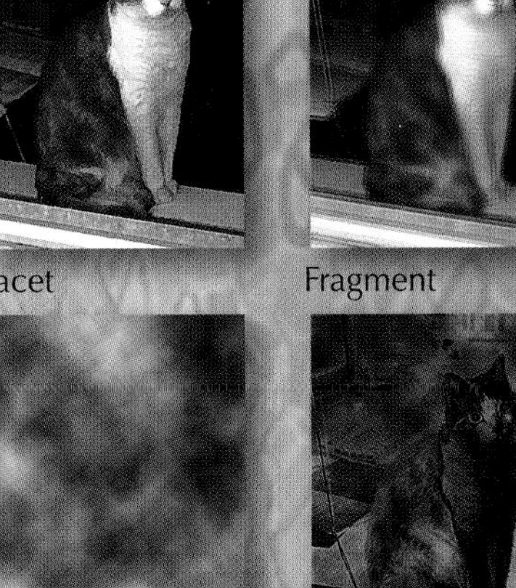

Facet Fragment Mezzotint Mosaic Pointillize

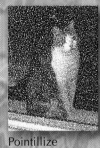

Clouds Difference Clouds Lens Flare Lighting Effects Texture Fill

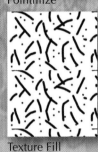

Sharpen Sharpen Edges Sharpen More Unsharp Mask Bas Relief

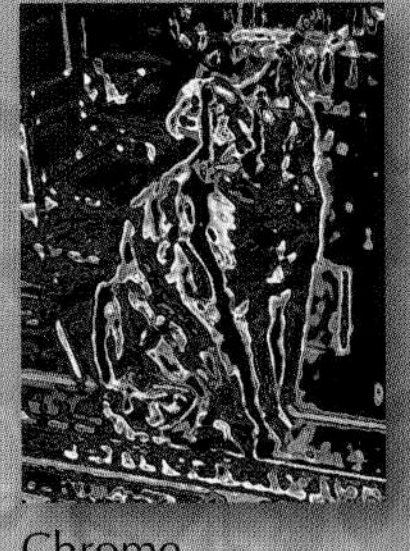

Chalk & Charcoal Charcoal Chrome Conté Crayon Graphic Pen

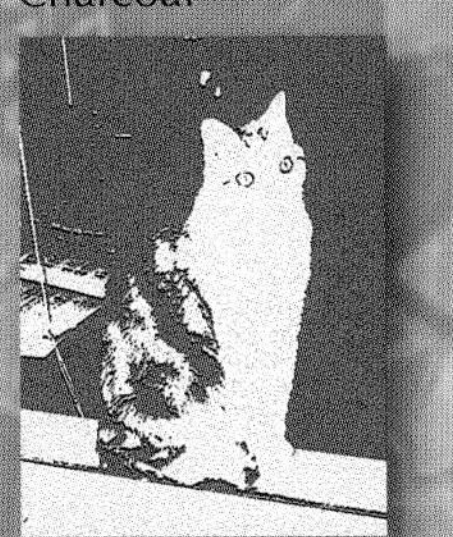

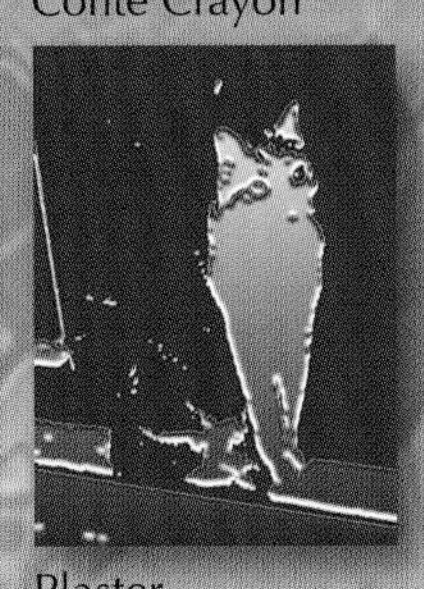
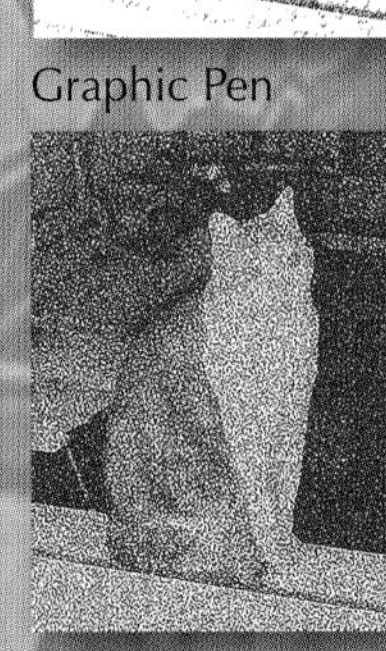

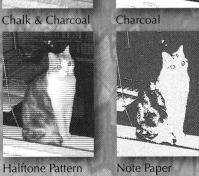

Halftone Pattern Note Paper Photocopy Plaster Reticulation

Stamp
Torn Edges
Water Paper
Diffuse
Emboss
Extrude
Find Edges
Glowing Edges
Solarize
Tiles
Trace Contour
Wind
Craquelure
Grain
Mosaic Tiles
Patchwork
Stained Glass
Texturizer
De-Interlace
NTSC Colors
Custom
High Pass
Maximum
Minimum
Offset

A grayscale image is shown here with three further stages of preparation as a duotone. The first (upper right) is a montone showing the second ink's color. The second (lower left) is a duotone with both inks put down from identical curves. The third (lower right) is the adjusted duotone where the second ink is used to extend the tone range of the original without an obvious coloration. Notice the richness of detail compared to the original.

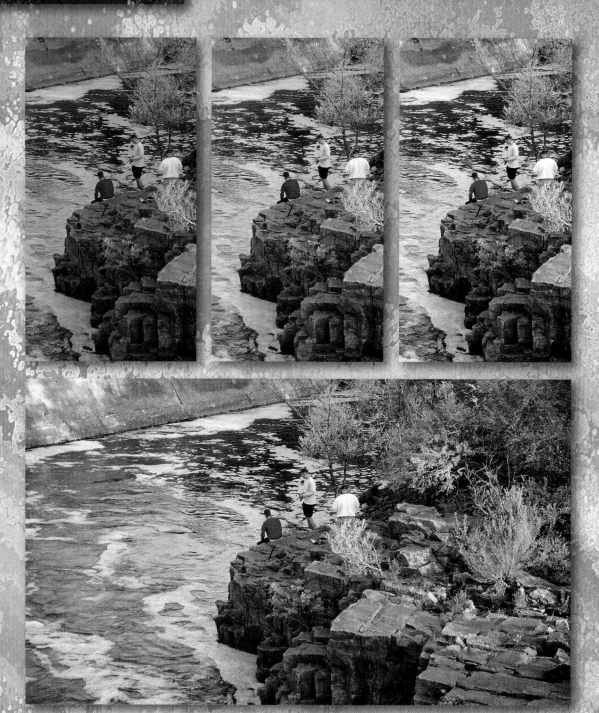

Color correction has never been easier than with Adjustment Layers. Layers can be stacked one on top of another. The changes for each layer are applied as a group when the document is flattened. The original image (top left) has had several layers applied: first Levels (top center), then Levels & Color Balance (top right), and finally Levels, Color Balance, & Hue/Saturation (bottom).

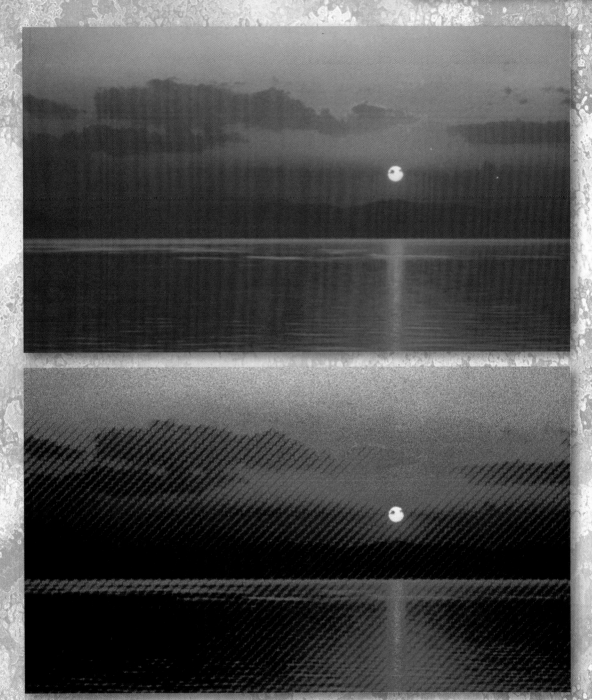

Here is a simple and effective trick that can be applied to an image that needs a little extra excitement. A high-contrast grayscale version of the image is converted to a bitmap (Halftone Screen option, with a coarse, linear spot function) and then used as an alpha channel. The alpha channel allows the two parts of the image—dark and light—to be manipulated separately while the linear pattern adds visual interest.

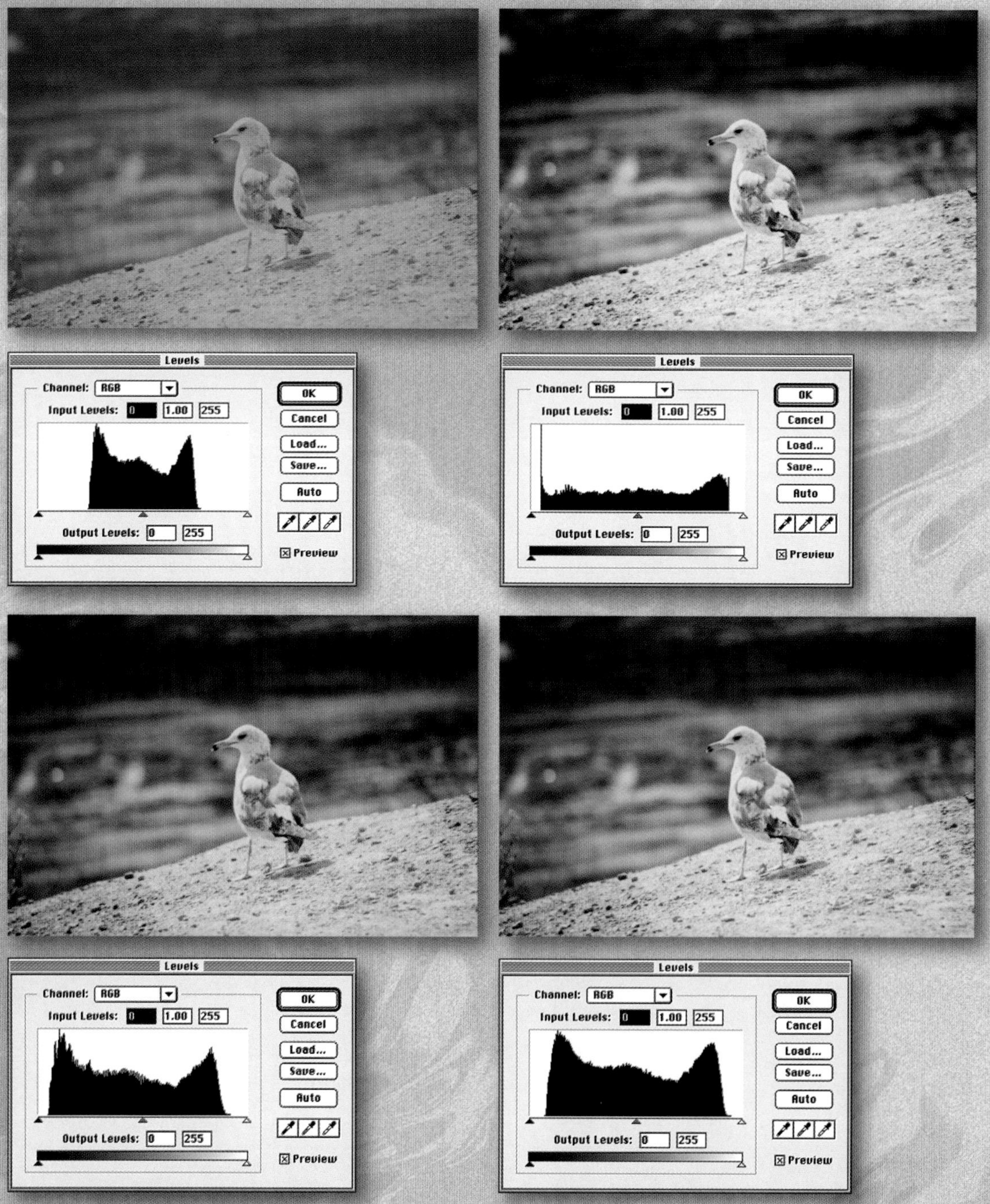

Adjustment layers allow you to make tonal corrections that can be edited. However, it helps to start with a good scan. The top left image shows a histogram that is lacking in highlights and shadows. Although it can be corrected (top right), there is image degradation and the histogram contains too much black. A properly scanned image (bottom left) produces a much better histogram when corrected (bottom right).

This overly dark image (top left) was photographed with the sun behind the main figure. It is corrected here using a variety of Adjustment layers (Levels and Hue/Saturation) that do not actually change the original image values until the document is flattened. You can experiment with the settings until you like the results that you obtain.

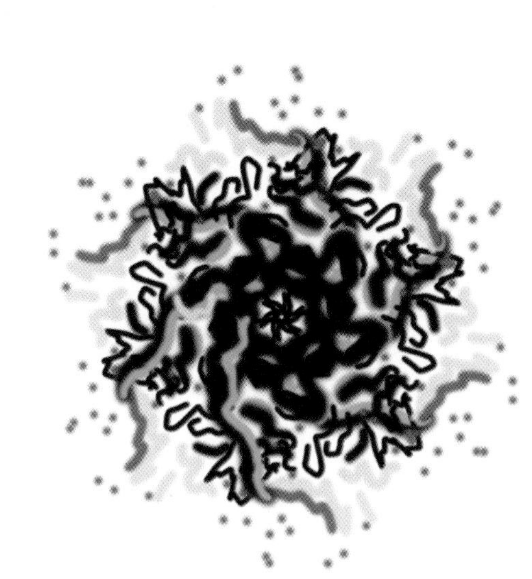

Above: You can use Photoshop to create "impossible" images—like this plane that is flying through a sky filled with cloud-flowers. A layer mask is used to project the flowers onto the clouds.

Right: A simple squiggle can become a decorative snowflake by making copies of the layer and rotating the layers 60° apart, so that they create a circular form.

Above: You can use Photoshop to add excitement to an image by intensifying color where you want to draw the viewer's eye and darkening the image to de-emphasize the background. Here, we brightened the lost love bird in the feeder and blurred and darkened the woods.

Left: You can add a sepiatone to a grayscale image by using Adjustment layers. The original grayscale image was used as a mask in the Adjustment layer to control the amount of sepia in the highlights and shadows.

The three patterned images above are identical. The only difference is in the Adjustment layers that are used in each image. The Country Clogger image to the right, above, makes heavy use of Photoshop's new Grids and Guides as it is constructed. The image is built in a long exercise in Chapter 11 so that you can duplicate the design process on your own computer.

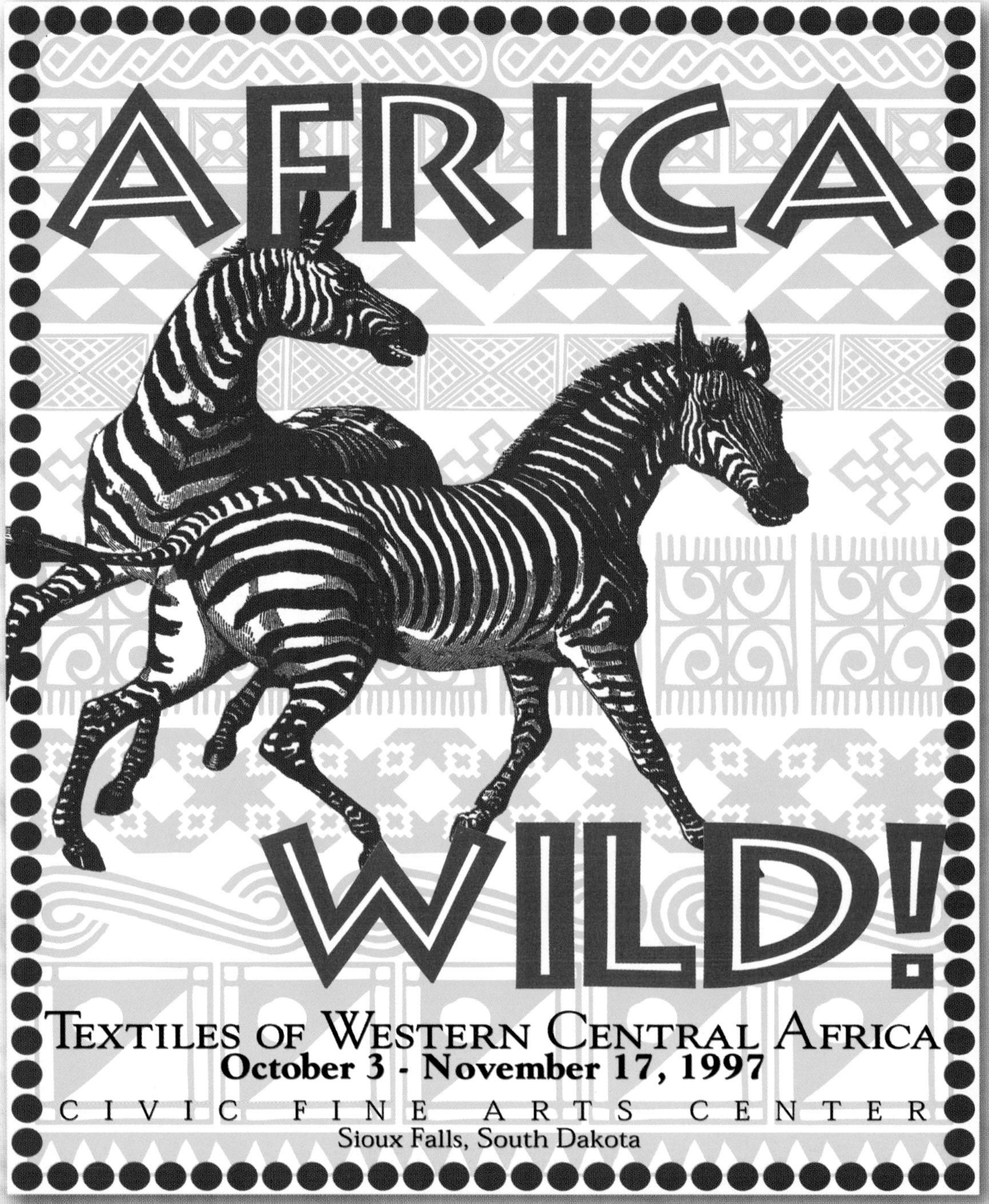

It is often said of Photoshop that it does not handle spot color with the same facility that it handles process color printing. That may be true but if you know how to do it, spot color work is quite a bit easier than four-color tasks. This simulated poster is one of the practice files included with this book's Companion CD-ROM disk. With it, you will learn how to work with as many spot colors as you wish to use.

3. Choose Image | Calculations. Make STAR.PSD the Source 1 and SUNFACE.PSD the Source 2. Change the Blending mode to Multiply and click Invert on Source 1. This places a white sunface into the star. Place this into a new document (automatically called Untitled-2). Figure 7-12 shows the result.

Figure 7-12: Star inverted multiplied with Sunface.

4. For the final step, choose Image | Calculations and use Untitled-1 as Source 1, Untitled-2 as Source 2 and Screen as the Blending mode. Invert *both* sources. Place the result into TEXTURE.PSD as a *selection*. Figure 7-13 shows the Calculations dialog.
5. Press the Delete or Backspace key to remove the selection from the image. Figure 7-14 shows the deselected result.

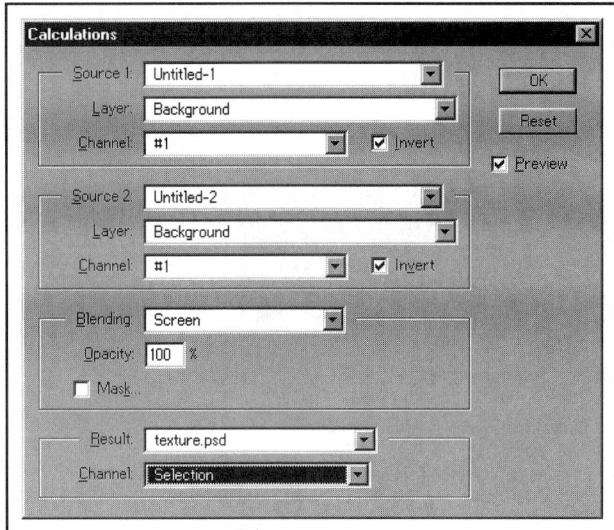

Figure 7-13: The Calculations dialog.

Figure 7-14: Deleting the selection placed by screening and inverted version of Untitled-1 and Untitled-2 causes this star, texture, zodiac, sunface blend.

There are many other possibilities to explore here. You have only been shown a few of them. The thing that you need to know about working with selections is that the selection uses the *values* in the calculation—not the shape or color of the selected objects.

Figure 7-15 shows two images, a black square and a circle filled with the Pointillize filter. Both shapes are selected. Figure 7-16 shows the Calculations dialog. The two selections are blended together in Subtract mode. Figure 7-17 shows the result. Notice that the fill on the circle does not participate in the calculation at all. It has no result on the final image.

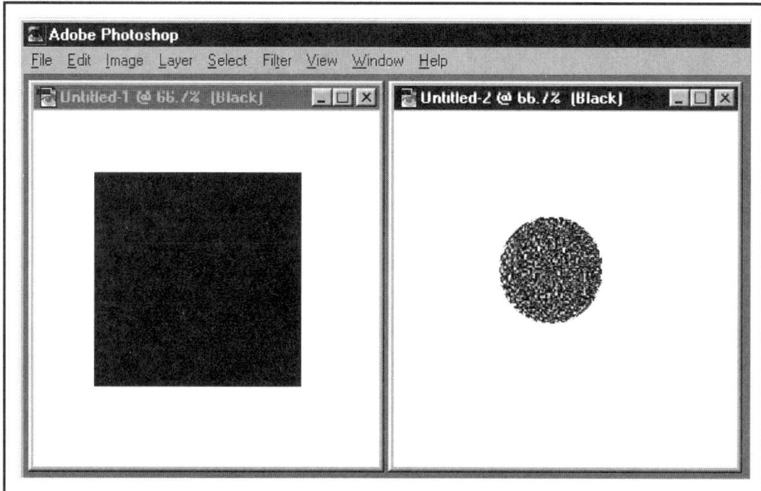

Figure 7-15: Two shapes, both selected.

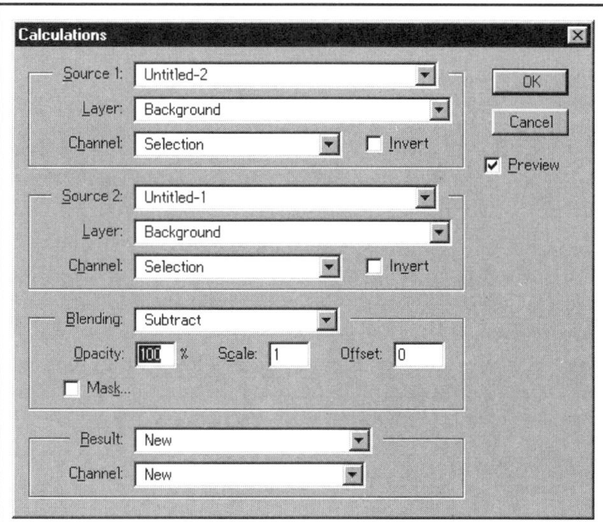

Figure 7-16: Calculations dialog.

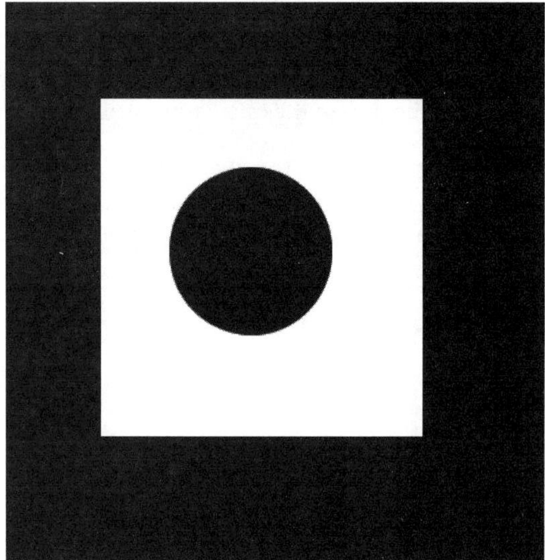

Figure 7-17: Result—only the shapes appear.

Apply Image & Calculations Compared

Now that you have tried both Apply Image and Calculations, how do they compare? Certainly the Apply Image command is easier to use; but the Calculations command seems more powerful. Let's look at these two commands by comparing them in a logical fashion.

Source Images

The Apply Image command only needs one source image as input. It "knows" the second source as it is the currently active image. The Calculations command can use any two open and same-sized images as sources.

Both commands can see any layer or channel, but if you select a layer that contains color information in it, the Apply Image command can "see" the color data and the individual channels. Calculations sees the color channels individually but sees the composite color only as gray.

If you have layers in your image, both commands allow you to manipulate the layer transparency as the channel to be used.

Blending

Both Apply Image and Calculations use the same Blending modes. These are the same as the layer Apply modes with the addition of Add and Subtract mode. You can adjust the opacity on the source images in both commands.

Selections

You can use the selection as part of the calculation in either command. However, if you have a selection in the active image when you select the Apply Image command, the result of the Apply Image command only affects the selection.

You can also see the result of the calculation as a selection in the target image when you use the Calculations command. The Apply Image command does not normally put its result anywhere except into the active image layer or channel.

Results

The Calculations command commonly places its result into a new channel. However, you can send the result to any open or new image of the same size and place it into any *channel* or into a new image. Notice the catch. *Calculations only creates channels.* It cannot place a result into a layer as anything other than a selection (and a selection is not specific to a layer). It can place the result into an existing layer mask, however.

In addition, when Calculations creates a new image, it uses Multichannel mode as the color mode. In order to work with the image as you would expect (to add more layers to it or save it as a TIFF), you need to convert the image to grayscale.

Apply Image can only save its result into the target (active) image or channel unless you press the Option (Mac) or Alt (Windows) key when you select the command from the menu. This obvious afterthought is one of the most useful (and little known) features of the Apply Image command. Simply by holding a modifier key as you select the command, you get the best part of the Calculations command along with the ability to work with color. You can target a layer, a layer mask, a channel, a new image, or a selection as your output.

Therefore, you can use the Apply Image for almost anything that you want to calculate. For many users, it will be the only one of the CHOPs commands that is used. As you begin to perform actions on channels, however, you will discover that you like the Calculations command—even with its greatly added complexity.

Calculating an Image—a Different Way to Work

You can create wonderful works of art with the CHOPs commands. It is really a different way to work. Unlike the way in which artists work with real media, CHOPs allows you to experiment in a manner that Kai Krause (whom we could almost call the "father of CHOPs" or certainly one of its earliest promoters) calls "algorithmic painting." It is certainly a technique that could only exist electronically.

To use CHOPs in order to develop an image is an exercise in serendipity. Once you try it, you can get hooked on the possibilities to the exclusion of anything else that you had planned for the day—like work, sleep, or eating. You rarely know where you are really headed and there are so many options, that you can easily end up someplace else—even if you started with a distinct notion of what you wanted to achieve.

For this exercise, let's use a piece of original artwork contributed by Sausalito-based artist Rhoda Grossman, who has consented to let us use one of her trademark nudes—even though it was already a completed piece of art. We will also use a snowflake from the

Ultimate Symbol Design Elements collection (which comes on the Companion CD-ROM and is one of the most useful collections of vector-based clip art available) and a layered texture that was created using the KPT Texture Explorer and KPT Fractal Explorer.

In this exercise, just follow along with us. There is really no rhyme or reason to why we selected these steps. The idea is to try something, and then send it to a new image. You could stack up a large number of layers equally "correctly," but keeping each image as a separate entity allows you to view all of the images at once. The disadvantage is that you cannot name the images as you create them if you use the Calculations command and you might not be able to come up with descriptive names that are "legal" on your computer. If you do not name your images, you end up with a huge number of untitled images, which are really hard to keep apart or search for when you do the next composite. So, you can place the images where you prefer when you work on your own. For now, do it our way so that you can duplicate our results. Let the computer name these images Untitled as it pleases.

This also makes you wonder how we remembered what was done in order to create the composite. That's easy! We took a screen shot of every use of a CHOPs command. Let's work the exercise, then we can discuss how you keep track of your work and your sanity at the same time:

1. Open the files SNOWFLKE.PSD (Figure 7-18), FRACTAL.PSD (Figure 7-19), and BLUELADY.PSD (Figure 7-20) from the Companion CD-ROM.

Figure 7-18: SNOWFLKE.PSD

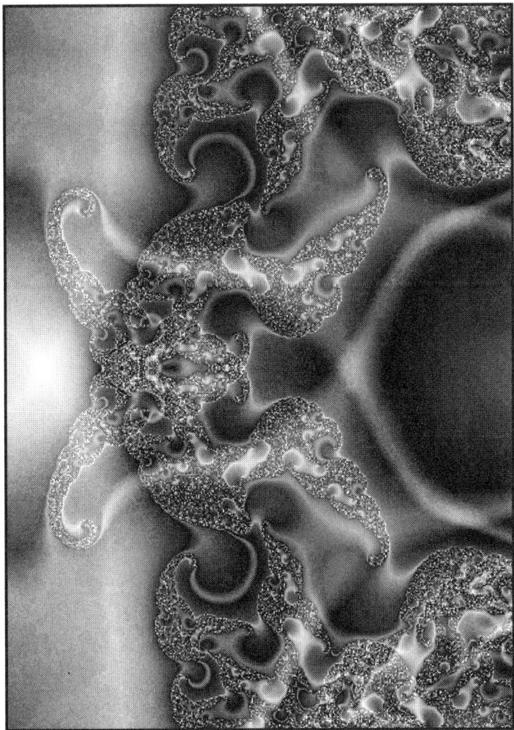

Figure 7-19: FRACTAL.PSD

Figure 7-20: BLUELADY.PSD

2. Make the BLUELADY.PSD image active. Press the modifier key (Mac: Option, Windows: Alt) and choose Image | Apply Image. Select FRACTAL.PSD as the Source. Set the Blending mode to Difference and the Opacity to 100%. Click on the Mask button and set the mask to BLUELADY.PSD channel #4, and choose New as the Result. Accept the default name Untitled-1. Figure 7-21 shows the dialog and Figure 7-22 shows the result.

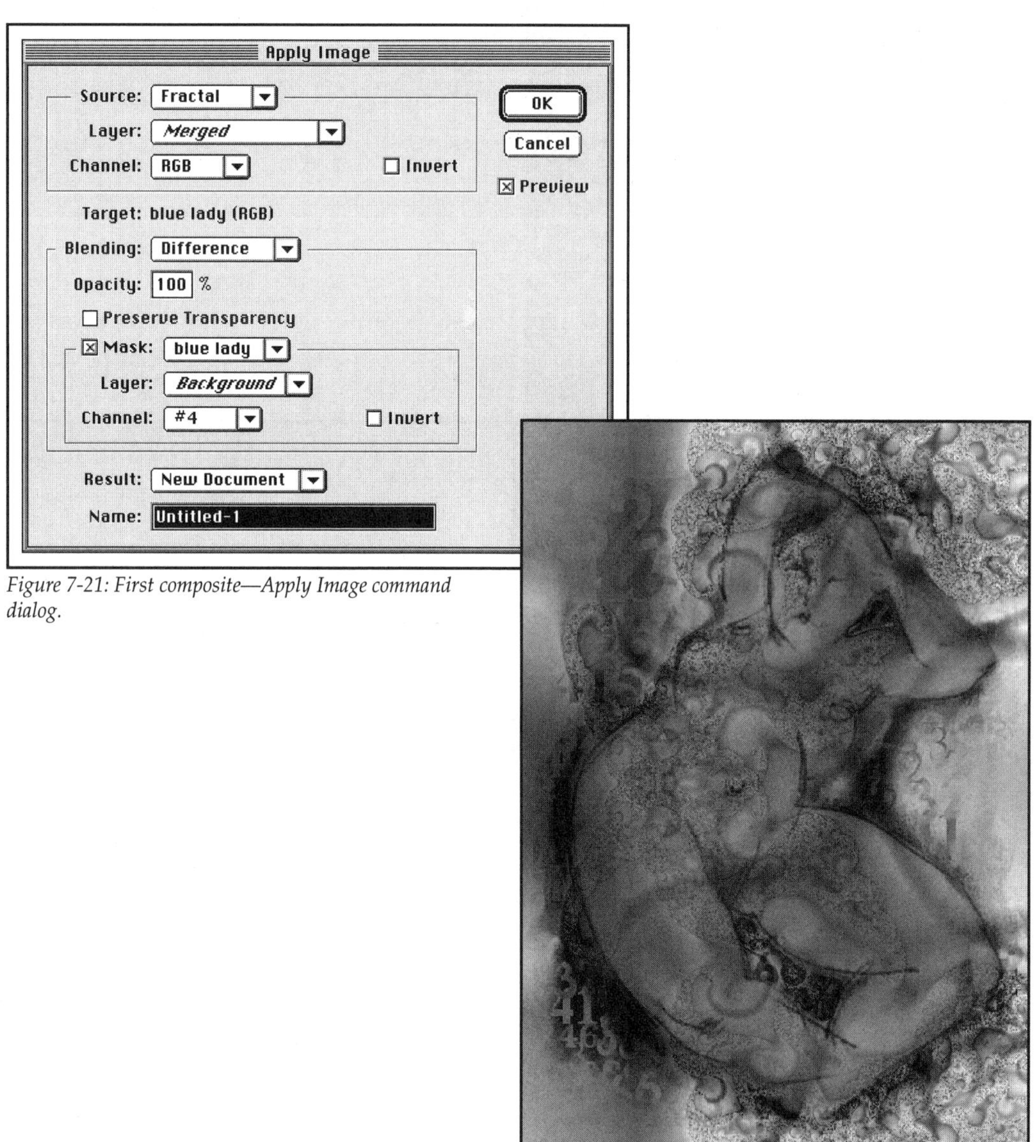

Figure 7-21: First composite—Apply Image command dialog.

Figure 7-22: First composite done.

3. Click on the Untitled-1 image to make it active. Choose Image | Apply Image. Select FRACTAL.PSD, Background Copy, RGB as your Source, Layer, and Channel. Set the Blending to Difference at 100% Opacity. Click on Mask and select SNOWFLKE.PSD, Layer 1, Transparency. Because you were not told to press the modifier key when you selected the command, you have no choice as to where it will place the results. The change is written back to Unititled-1. This step takes the difference between the nude and the middle layer of the fractal, but confines the result to only the area occupied by the *shape* of the snowflake. Figure 7-23 shows the Apply Image dialog box and Figure 7-24 shows the result.

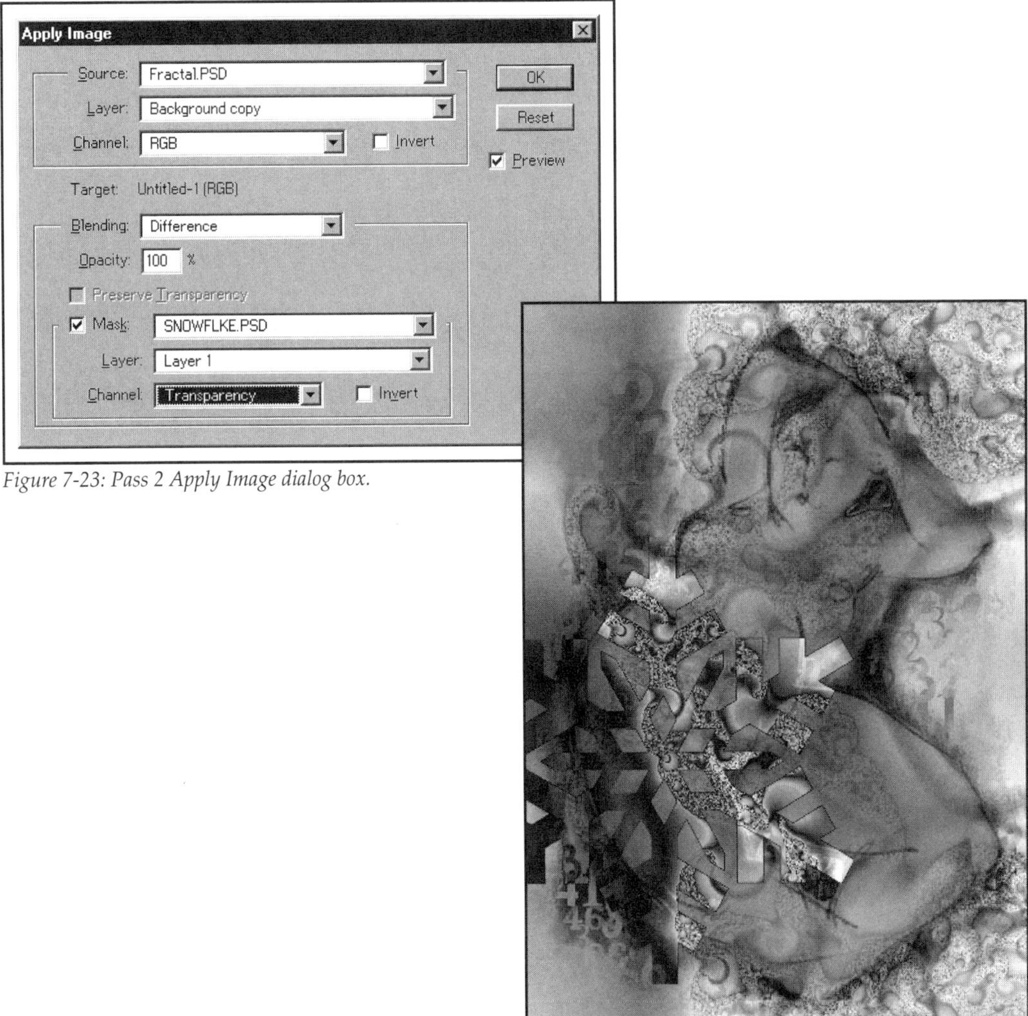

Figure 7-23: Pass 2 Apply Image dialog box.

Figure 7-24: Pass 2 results—Difference inside the snowflake.

4. Make Untitled-1 active. Press the modifier key (Mac: Option, Windows: Alt) and choose Image | Apply Image. Select FRACTAL.PSD, Background copy, RGB as the Source, Layer, and Channel. Set the Blending mode to Lighter and the Opacity to 50%. As a mask, use SNOWFLKE.PSD, Layer 1, Transparency. Place the result into a new document called Untitled-2. Figure 7-25 shows the Apply Image dialog, and Figure 7-26 shows the result.

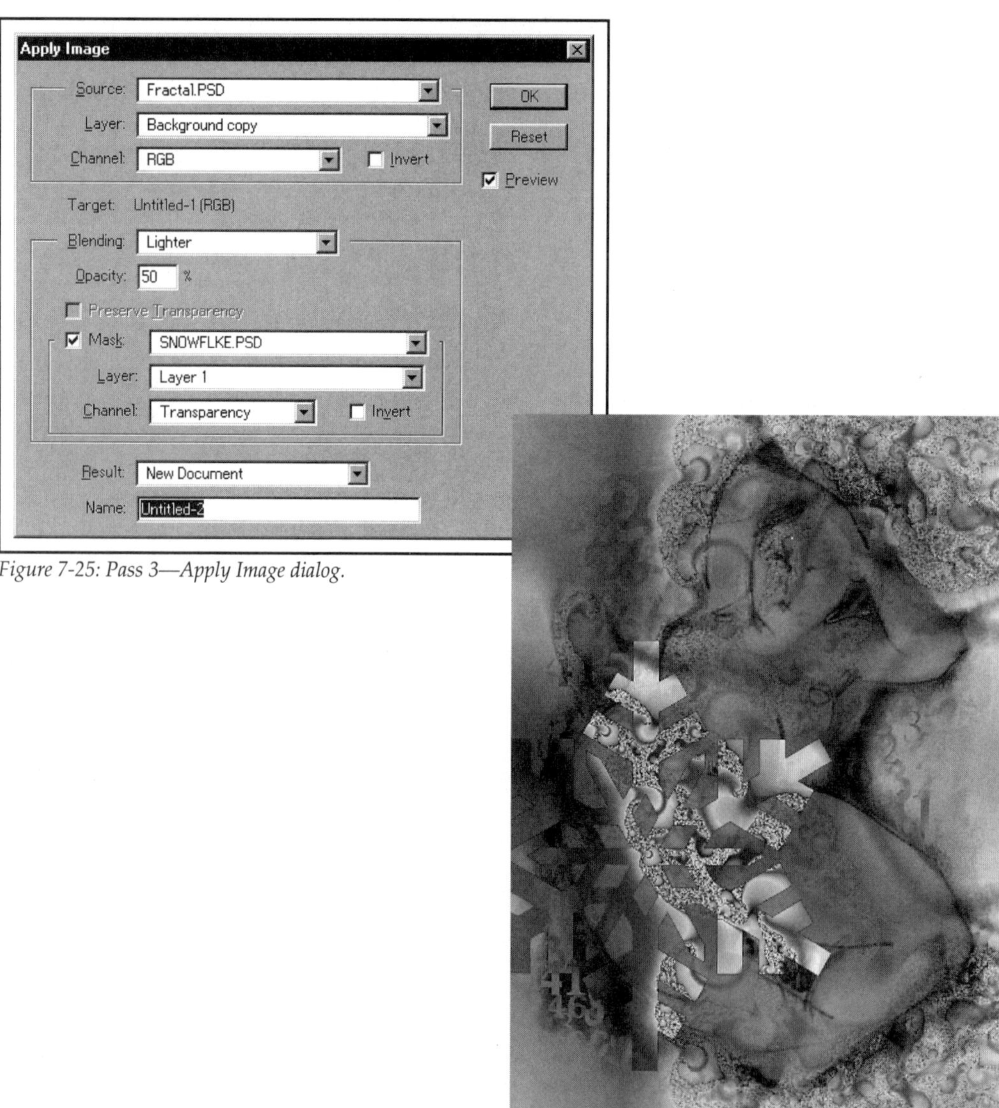

Figure 7-25: Pass 3—Apply Image dialog.

Figure 7-26: Pass 3 result—Untitled-1 blended in Lighter mode through Snowflake mask.

5. Make Untitled-2 active. Press the modifier key (Mac: Option, Windows: Alt) and choose Image | Apply Image. Select SNOWFLKE.PSD, Layer 1, Transparency as the Source, Layer, and Channel. Set the Blending mode to Hard Light and the Opacity to 40%. As a mask, use Untitled-2, Background, Gray and check the Invert button. Place the result into a new document called Untitled-3. Figure 7-27 shows the Apply Image dialog, and Figure 7-28 shows the result.

Figure 7-27: Pass 4—Apply Image dialog.

Figure 7-28: Pass 4 result—Untitled-2 blended in Hard Light mode through an inverted self-mask.

6. Make Untitled-3 active. Press the modifier key (Mac: Option, Windows: Alt) and choose Image | Apply Image. Select FRACTAL.PSD, Background, RGB as the Source, Layer, and Channel. Set the Blending mode to Hard Light and the Opacity to 100%. As a mask, use BLUELADY.PSD, Background, Channel 4. Place the result into a new document called Untitled-4. Figure 7-29 shows the Apply Image dialog, and Figure 7-30 shows the result.

Figure 7-29: Pass 5—Apply Image dialog.

Figure 7-30: Pass 5 result—Untitled-3 blended in Hard Light mode through Bluelady channel 4 mask.

7. This time, you will use the Calculations command. It does not matter which image is active. Press the modifier key (Mac: Option, Windows: Alt) and choose Image | Calculations (the Option key makes the dialog smaller on the Mac and has no effect on Windows). Select FRACTAL.PSD, Merged, Red as Source 1, Layer, and Channel. Select FRACTAL.PSD, Layer 1, Red as Source 2, Layer, and Channel. Set the Blending mode to Overlay and the Opacity to 60%. There is no mask. Place the result into a new document called Untitled-5. Figure 7-31 shows the Calculations dialog, and Figure 7-32 shows the result.

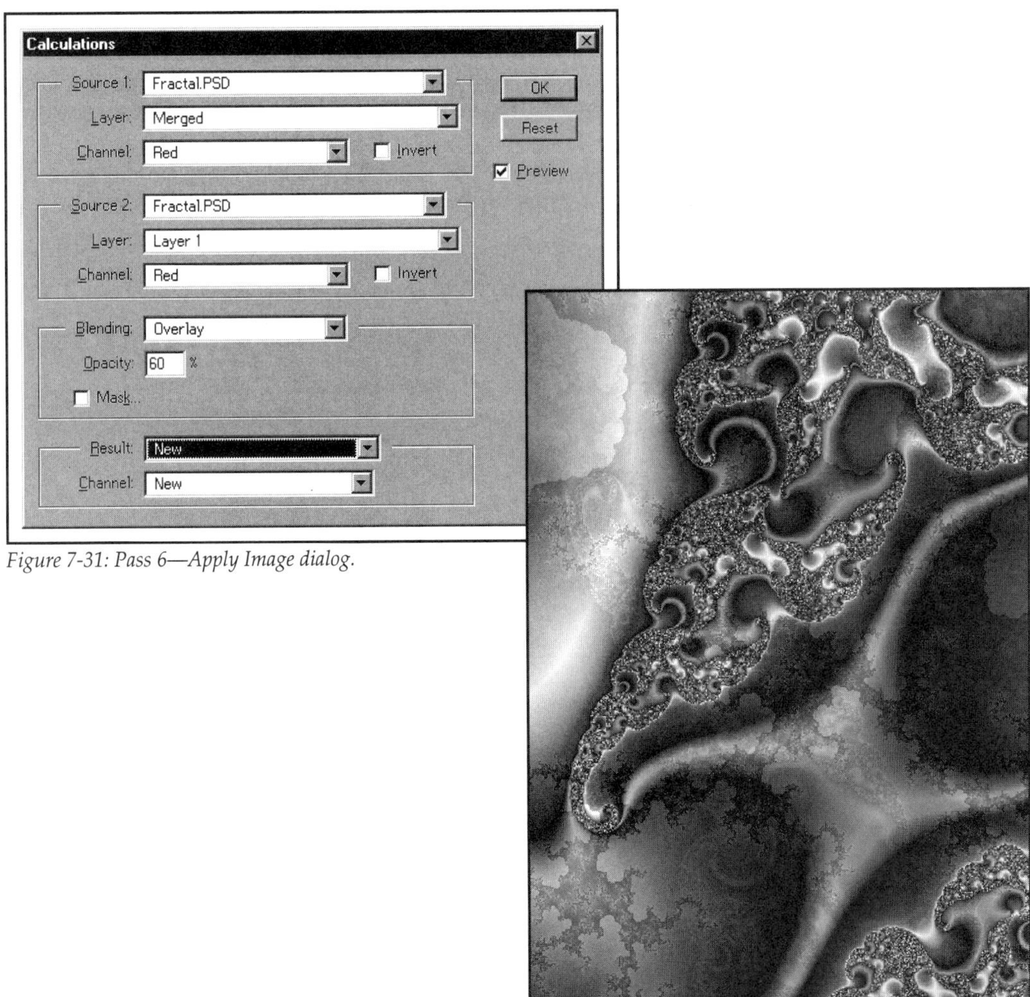

Figure 7-31: Pass 6—Apply Image dialog.

Figure 7-32: Pass 6 result—Red channel of FRACTAL.PSD merged blended in Hard Light mode with Red channel of FRACTAL.PSD Layer 1 at 60% Opacity.

8. Make Untitled-3 active. Press the modifier key (Mac: Option, Windows: Alt) and choose Image | Apply Image. Select Untitled-5, Background, RGB as the Source, Layer, and Channel. Set the Blending mode to Difference and the Opacity to 100%. There is no mask. Place the result into a new document called Untitled-6. Figure 7-33 shows the Apply Image dialog, and Figure 7-34 shows the result.

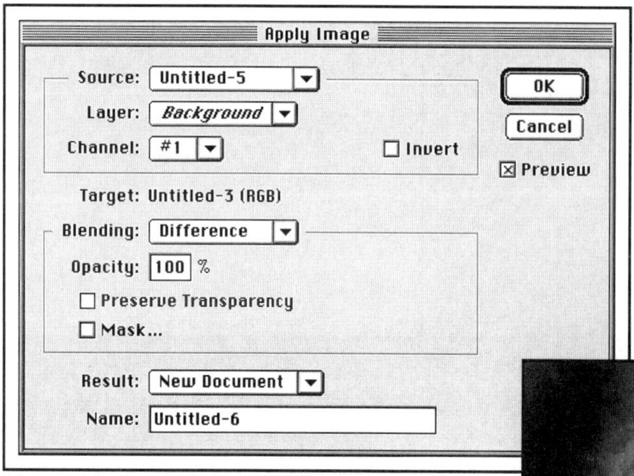

Figure 7-33: Pass 7—Apply Image dialog.

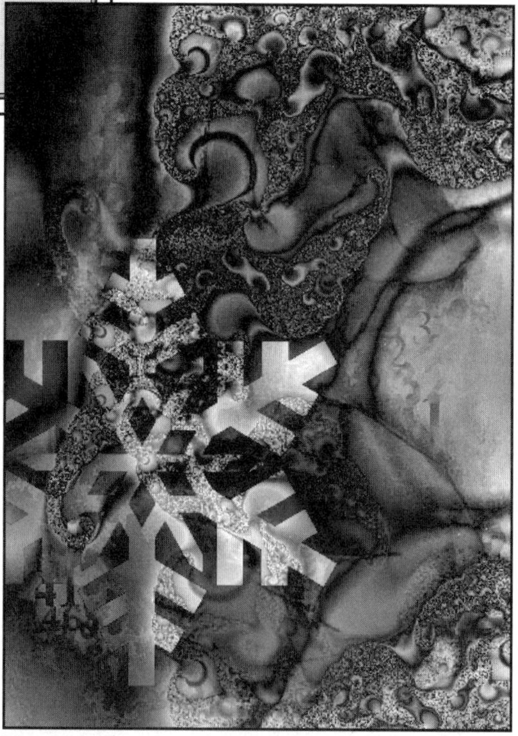

Figure 7-34: Pass 7 result—Untitled-5 blended in Difference mode with Untitled-3.

9. Make Untitled-6 active. Press the modifier key (Mac: Option, Windows: Alt) and choose Image | Apply Image. Select Untitled-4, Background, RGB as the Source, Layer, and Channel. Set the Blending mode to Hard Light and the Opacity to 30%. As a mask, use SNOWFLKE.PSD, Layer 1, Transparency, and check the Invert button. Place the result into a new document called Untitled-7. Figure 7-35 shows the Apply Image dialog, and Figure 7-36 shows the result.

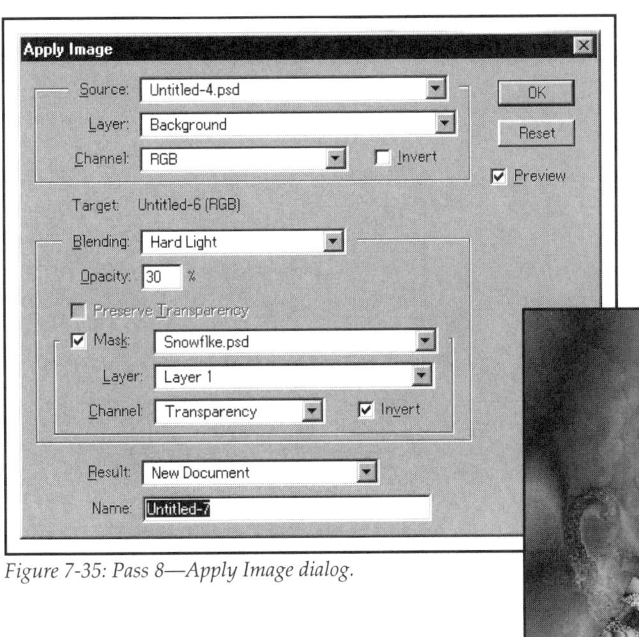

Figure 7-35: Pass 8—Apply Image dialog.

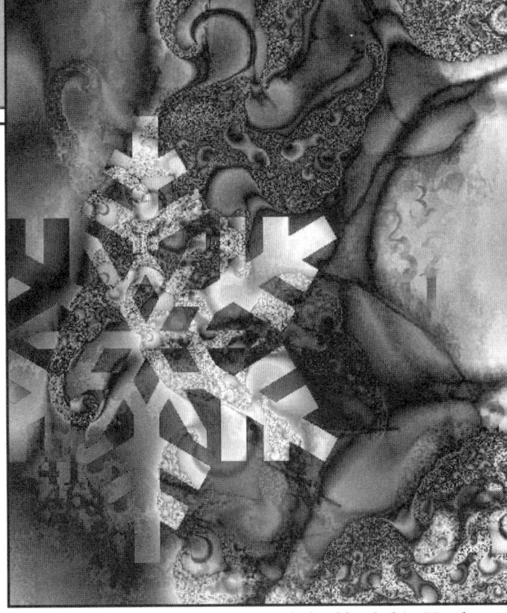

Figure 7-36: Pass 8 result—Untitled-6 blended in Hard Light mode with Unititled-4 through inverted snowflake mask.

10. Make Untitled-7 active. Press the modifier key (Mac: Option, Windows: Alt) and choose Image | Apply Image. Select Untitled-4, Background, RGB as the Source, Layer, and Channel. Set the Blending mode to Normal and the Opacity to 60%. As a mask, use BLUELADY.PSD, Background, Channel 4. Do *not* check the Invert button. Place the result into a new document called Untitled-8. Figure 7-37 shows the Apply Image dialog, and Figure 7-38 shows the result.

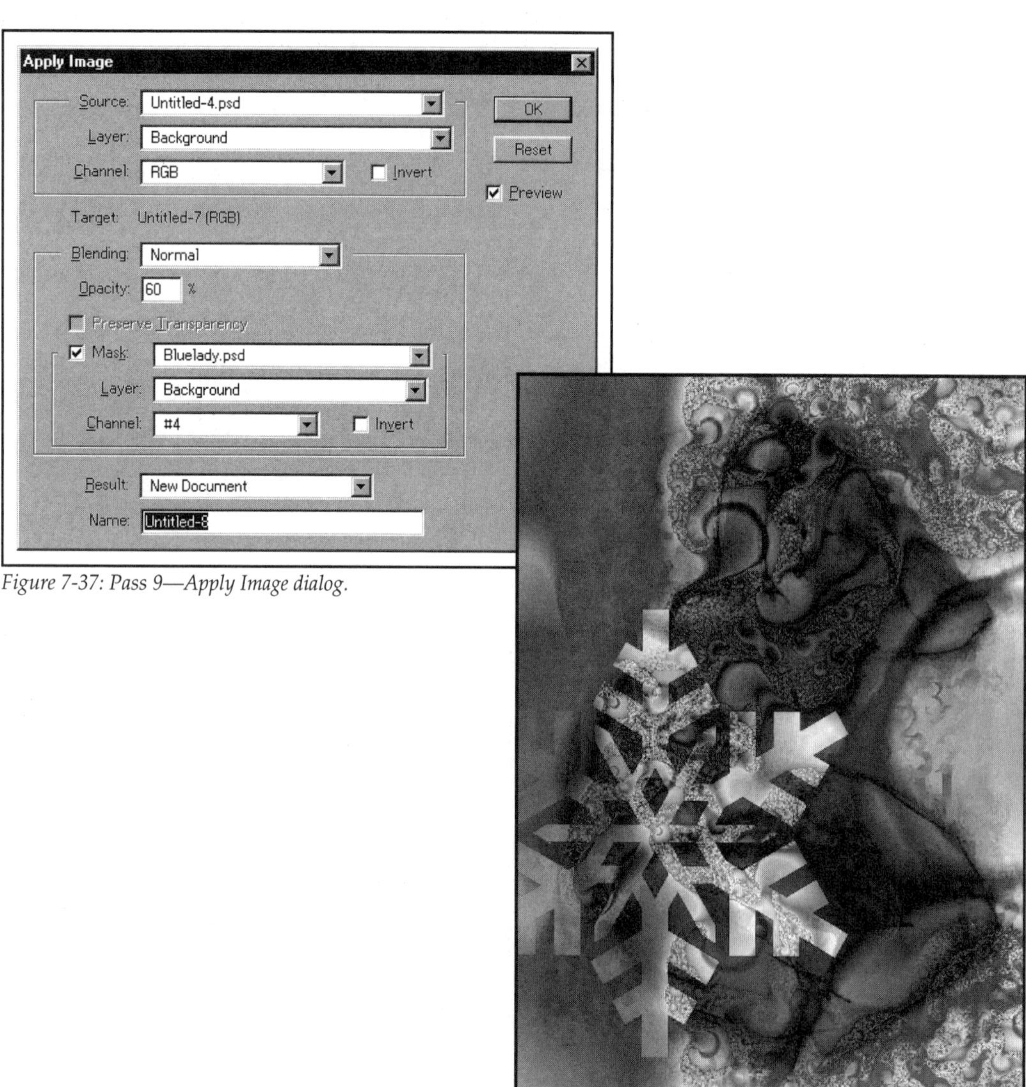

Figure 7-37: Pass 9—Apply Image dialog.

Figure 7-38: Pass 9 result—Untitled-7 blended in Normal mode at 60% Opacity with Untitled-4 through channel 4 of Bluelady.

While you could spin this out forever, you should have an idea by now of how you can work with this! It is endlessly fascinating to see how images can be combined, and this workflow is much faster than using drag-and-drop or cut-and-paste, and it uses no extra RAM resources because it does not take up clipboard space. Please help keep this intriguing-though-arcane method of working vital and alive.

Classic CHOPs

The "classic" CHOPs are contained in a series of Tips documents written by Kai Krause for America Online several years ago. The documents are still widely available online, either in the MetaCreations area of AOL or CompuServe, the CompuServe Adobe Forum, or on the MetaCreations Web site at http://www.metacreations.com. They are also available on a CD-ROM distributed by MetaCreations.

These documents were written for Photoshop 2.0, so of course the specific menu commands have changed quite a bit, but they are the basic tools from which this entire method of working developed. They have been used as the basis of countless books and articles, and assimilated by the most respected Photoshop artists around. You will find very few true "Photoshop propeller-heads" who have not used these tips—they are almost a badge of admission to an exclusive club.

Many of Kai's CHOPs start with the manipulation of simple black shapes in a channel and work toward building complexity (and gray values) through Calculations. To play with this, select any one of the Ultimate Symbol Design Element collection images and rasterize it into a grayscale image. Create from the original, a series of "primitives." Here are the operations:

- Original
- Inverted copy of original
- Gaussian blurred copy of original
- Gaussian blurred copy of inverted original
- Find Edges on the blurred positive image
- Find Edges on the blurred negative image
- Maximum filter applied to original image
- Maximum filter applied to inverted original
- Minimum filter applied to original image
- Minimum filter applied to inverted original
- Original image with contrast lowered 50%
- Inverted original with contrast lowered 50%

Try combining these images with one another by offsetting the images and using Difference, Add, Subtract, Multiply, and Screen. Try some of the "newer" modes as well. Also create some primitives using the Motion Blur and Radial Blur filters. Create the positive and negative versions separately (do not just invert the positive versions as the results do differ). Look at the file MEDALON.PSD on the Companion CD-ROM. This image is the work of Susan Kitchens, a very talented California artist who worked with Kai Krause for many years and is an expert in this form of Photoshopping. The channels are named so that you can discern what was done to produce them. Studying this file is an excellent way to begin.

Moving On

In this chapter, you learned about the Apply Image and the Calculations commands. They are both very useful commands for day-to-day or with special effects work. The commands can be used to quickly move images and channels of the same size from one location to another without using the Photoshop Clipboard buffer, so they are economic with RAM. You have seen how to add density to an image by combining channels and how to produce a new "work of art" by combining a number of images.

Chapter 8, "Filter Frolics," shows you how to create some snazzy images with Photoshop's filter capabilities.

chapter 8

Filter Frolics

Using a filter on an image is like going to the beauty parlor—you can walk out with anything from a quick trim to a complete makeover. Similarly, filters can distort an image so completely that there's no telling what it looked like originally, or they can touch up an image so it just looks *better.* Some filters fall at one end or the other of this spectrum: Sharpen at the quick trim end and Polar Coordinates at the makeover end, for example. Others allow you to adjust their settings along the entire range—the same filter with different settings can produce wildly different results, and experimentation is the key to getting good results.

Photoshop comes with almost a hundred filters, called *native* filters. This name is somewhat inaccurate, because most of these filters aren't built into the program; they're stored separately in a Filters folder inside the Plug-Ins folder. The many third-party filters available are also stored in the Plug-Ins folder, so you can install and uninstall these filters by moving them in and out of the folder. In this chapter we'll discuss how Photoshop filters work, look at some sample images produced with filters, and offer tips for getting the most out of filters.

Shortcuts

The few keyboard shortcuts that apply to filters can speed up operations quite a bit:

- To reapply the last filter, press Command+f or Ctrl+f. This is the equivalent of simply choosing the filter again from the Filter menu or using the top command in the menu, which is always the most recently used filter (even if you used the Undo command after applying that filter).
- To return to the dialog box for the last filter used, press Command+Option+f or Ctrl+Alt+f. The previous settings are still in the dialog box. This is the equivalent of holding Option or Alt as you choose the filter again from the top of the Filter menu.

- To reduce the intensity of a filter's effects or change its blending mode, press Command+Shift+f or Ctrl+Shift+f. This is the equivalent of choosing Filter | Fade (see "Fading a Filter's Effects," below).

There are two circumstances under which these commands aren't available: if you haven't applied a filter since your current Photoshop session began, or if you're in a color mode that doesn't support filters or the specific filter you're trying to use (see "Filters & Color Modes," below).

Filters & RAM

No matter what you're doing in Photoshop, it's never possible to have too much RAM. Filters are no exception to this rule; in fact, using filters can increase your RAM requirements by quite a bit. It's entirely possible to have enough RAM to run Photoshop itself, but not enough to execute a particular filter. Some filters are more RAM-hungry than others—these are the worst offenders:

- Cutout
- Spatter
- Sprayed Strokes
- Glass
- Ocean Ripple
- Pinch
- Polar Coordinates
- Ripple
- Spherize
- Twirl
- ZigZag
- Crystallize
- Pointillize
- Lighting Effects
- Stained Glass

The filters listed here won't execute on a 5MB image when Photoshop has only the minimum RAM allocation. Fortunately, Photoshop warns you up front when it can't run a filter (see Figure 8-1) instead of allowing you to make all the dialog box settings first. When you do run out of memory, the answer is to buy more physical RAM, not to use virtual memory. Using virtual memory with Photoshop can cause significant problems, since it can subtract from the amount of scratch disk space accessible to Photoshop.

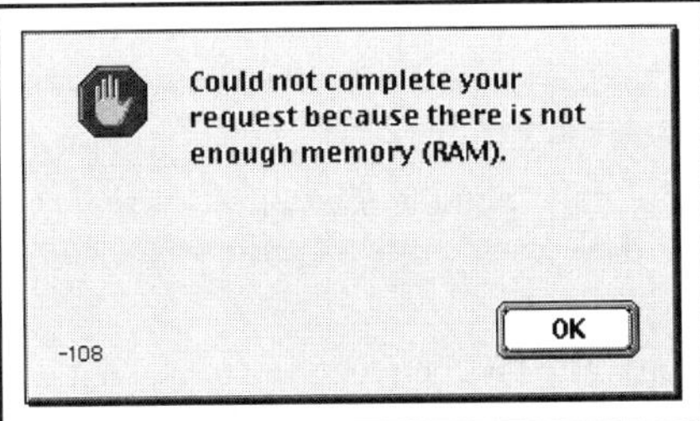

Figure 8-1: This dialog box lets you know you need more RAM to run a particular filter.

How Filters Work

All Photoshop filters are mathematical (a little bit easier to believe than Ralph Waldo Emerson's assertion that "all love is mathematical"). A filter performs calculations based on the color value and position of each pixel in an image or selection and replaces the pixels with the results of those calculations. The math is more complicated than most people want to get into—the results are the important thing. To make sure you get the results you're looking for, though, you need to know how filters interact with particular variables in a document: the foreground and background colors, transparency, selections, and the image's color mode. Once you're familiar with these parts of the filter equation, you'll be able to predict the results of applying a filter with much greater accuracy. Even so, most Photoshop filters provide at least one method of previewing their effects on an image, and the Fade command allows you to fine-tune the intensity of a filter's effects even after it's applied.

Filters & the Foreground/Background Color

Most of the time, if you're not using one of the Painting tools, the Foreground and Background colors shown in the Toolbox don't matter. However, some filters do use these colors to create their effects, so you need to make sure that the Foreground and Background colors are the ones you want to use before applying these filters. Here's a list of the ones to watch out for:

- All the Sketch filters except Chrome and Water Paper use the Foreground color for darker areas in the image and the Background color for lighter areas, blending the two colors in different ways depending on the style of the filter, such as pen strokes or halftone dots.
- Colored Pencil: The Background color is the paper color at the highest Paper Brightness setting.
- Diffuse Glow: The Background color is the "glow" color.

- Grain: The Sprinkles Grain Type uses the background color for the grain; the Stippled Grain Type uses the Foreground color for the grain and places the Background color everywhere else in the image.
- Neon Glow: Two of the three colors applied to the image to create the "glow" are the Foreground and Background colors (the third is chosen in the Neon Glow dialog box).
- Pointillize: The Background color appears between the pointillist dots created from the image colors.
- Render Clouds: The Foreground and Background colors are the cloud colors. All other colors in the image are removed.
- Render Difference Clouds: The difference between the Foreground and Background colors and the colors in the image determines the colors of the clouds. All other colors in the image are removed.
- Stained Glass: The Foreground color is used for the lead strips between the pieces of "glass."
- Torn Edges: The image is posterized using the Foreground and Background colors.

If you want to be able to create similar effects with these filters over time, it's a good idea to save the Foreground and Background colors in the Swatches palette so you can access them quickly when you need them. For even more security, or to share those colors with another person who wants to achieve the same effects, choose Save Swatches from the Swatches palette menu and save the color swatches in a separate file.

Filters & Transparent Layers

Filters work only on the active layer, and they don't operate on transparent pixels, meaning that they'll move around and alter only the existing colored pixels on a transparent layer. Trying to apply the Add Noise filter, for example, to an entirely transparent layer results in an error dialog box (see Figure 8-2). It's also important to distinguish between white and transparency; if you want a white Background layer to be affected by a filter, you'll need to merge the layer you're working on with the Background layer.

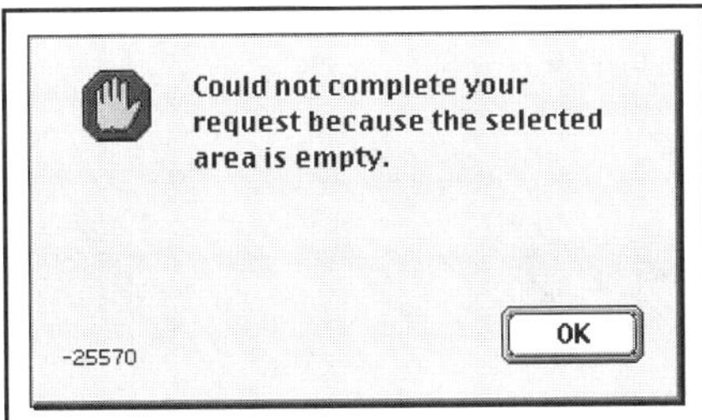

Figure 8-2: Most filters won't work on a completely transparent layer.

Like any other operation that moves pixels around, filters are subject to the restrictions imposed when Preserve Transparency is turned on for a layer. Just as Preserve Transparency prevents you from painting on transparent pixels, so it keeps filters from operating outside the area of the layer that already contains colored pixels.

This effect is particularly noticeable in filters that move large chunks of the image around, namely the Distort filters (see Figure 8-3). The Blur filters also may have little effect if Preserve Transparency is turned on, depending on how detailed the non-transparent portions of the layer are. With solid-colored elements, such as text, placed on a transparent layer, Blur filters will seem to have no effect when Preserve Transparency is turned on (see Figure 8-4). More detailed elements, such as a silhouetted photo, will be blurred inside their borders, but the silhouetted edges remain sharp (see Figure 8-5). This fact can work to your advantage when you want sharp edges.

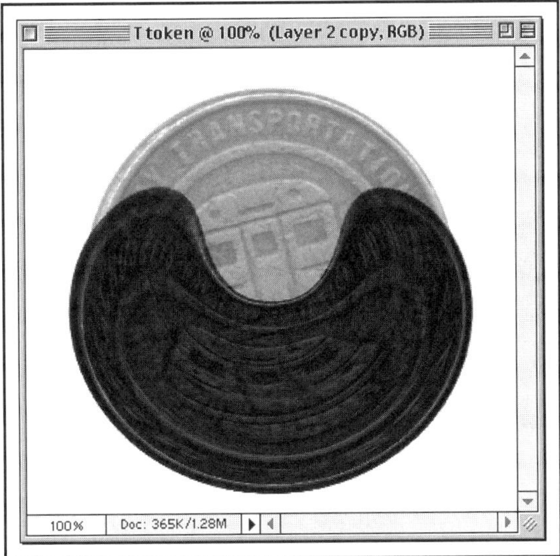

Figure 8-3: With Preserve Transparency off, the Polar Coordinates filter works fine; with Preserve Transparency on, the filter reveals the background color in areas of the original image.

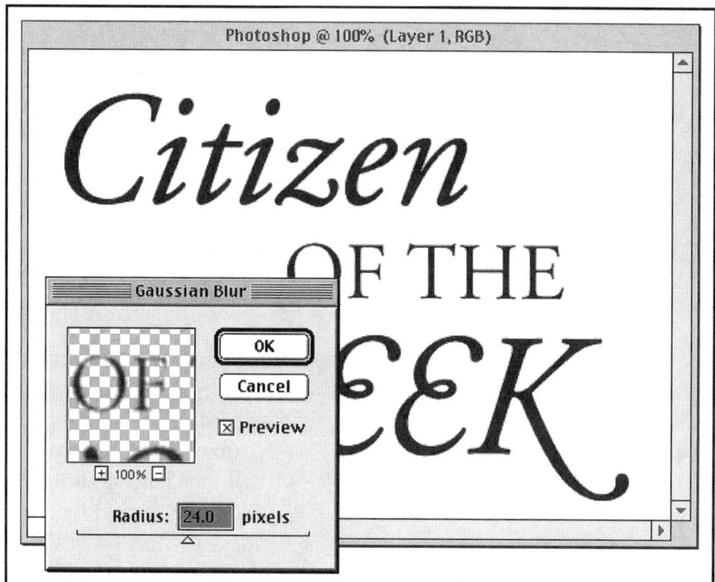

Figure 8-4: The Gaussian Blur filter has no visible effect when applied to text on a transparent layer with Preserve Transparency turned on.

Figure 8-5: The Gaussian Blur filter doesn't blur the edges of this image on a transparent layer because Preserve Transparency is turned on.

Filters & Selections

If a selection is active when you apply a filter, the filter's effects are restricted to the pixels included in the selection. Because it's possible to partially select a pixel, you can also partially apply a filter. There are three ways to partially select some pixels in an image:

- Feather a selection; the pixels around the edges of the selection are partially selected (see Figure 8-6).
- Create a Quick Mask selection. Press Q to enter Quick Mask mode, then paint white to select areas, black to deselect them, and gray to partially select them. Press Q to return to normal selection mode.
- Create a selection from an alpha channel or a layer's transparency mask by Command-clicking or Ctrl-clicking on the channel name or the layer name. Gray areas in the channel or partially transparent areas in the layer translate to partially selected pixels on the active layer.

Figure 8-6: A rectangular selection in the center of the image was feathered and then inverted before applying the Add Noise filter.

Applying a filter to a pixel that is only 50% selected is the same as applying that filter to the same pixel with its settings 50% lower. This fact enables you to determine exactly where a filter should be applied and how intense its effects should be before invoking the filter itself.

TIP *Feather a selection before applying a filter to blend the resulting pixels into the rest of the image. For example, you can get rid of a moiré pattern in roof shingles by blurring the area, then adding noise; feathering the selection first blends the changes with the rest of the roof.*

Filters & Color Modes

You can't apply filters to images in Bitmap, Indexed Color, 48-bit RGB, or 16-bit Grayscale modes. Some specific filters aren't available in CMYK or other color modes:

- CMYK mode doesn't support the Artistic, Brush Strokes, Sketch, Texture, and Video filter groups. Individual filters that aren't available in CMYK mode include Smart Blur, Diffuse Glow, Glass, Ocean Ripple, Lens Flare, Lighting Effects, and Glowing Edges.
- Lab mode also doesn't support Artistic, Brush Strokes, Sketch and Texture filters. Individual filters you can't use in Lab mode include Smart Blur, Diffuse Glow, Glass, Ocean Ripple, Difference Clouds, Lens Flare, Lighting Effects, Extrude, Glowing Edges, Solarize, and NTSC Colors.
- Grayscale, Duotone, and Multichannel modes don't support Lens Flare, Lighting Effects, and NTSC Colors.

To use a filter on a bitmap image, switch to Grayscale mode, apply the filter, then switch back to Bitmap mode. Depending on the results you're looking for, choose either 50% Threshold or Diffusion Dither when you return to Bitmap mode. Using the former, all pixels that are 50% gray or lighter are converted to white, and all pixels that are darker than 50% gray are changed to black, resulting in sharp-edged areas of black or white. The latter option also eliminates gray pixels, but it scatters black pixels around in formerly gray areas to retain some of the effect of gray.

To use a filter on a color image that's in the wrong color mode, switch to RGB mode, apply the filter, then switch back to the original color mode.

Previewing Filter Effects

Most filter dialog boxes contain a small preview window in which you can see the results of the filter. Creating this preview takes a bit of time, so as Photoshop works on that you'll see a flashing line below the preview size percentage. When the line disappears, the preview is fully rendered. To see the "before" version of the image in the preview window, click in the window. With some filters, you can also change the area of the image that is shown in the preview window by clicking and dragging (the cursor changes into a hand) or by clicking in the image window (the cursor changes to a hollow box; see Figure 8-7).

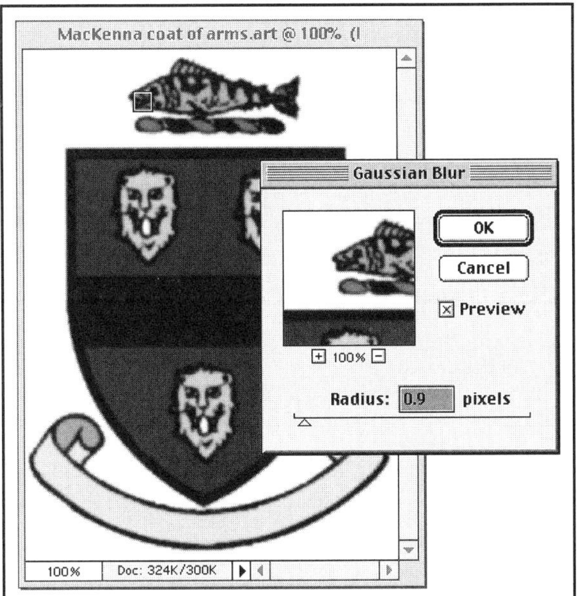

Figure 8-7: The hollow box in the image window indicates the area that will be centered in the filter's dialog box preview window.

If the Preview check box is checked in a filter dialog box, the results of the current filter settings are also reflected in the image window. The Grabber Hand and Zoom tools still work in the image window while you're working in a filter dialog box, but you need to use the keyboard shortcuts to access them. Hold the spacebar as you click and drag in the image to move it around within the window, and press Command+spacebar or Ctrl+spacebar as you click and drag to magnify a specific area of the image.

One of the advantages of being able to preview the filter's effects both in the dialog box and in the image window is that you can see different magnifications simultaneously. Generally, it works best to use the dialog box preview to focus on a magnified detail of the image and view the entire image in the image window. To change the magnification level of the dialog box preview window, click the + and – buttons; you can zoom out as far as 20% and zoom out to 800%.

TIP *With large images, try filters out on a small selection first before applying them to the entire image. The smaller the selected area, the shorter the preview time. Don't forget to drop the selection to apply the filter to the whole image—press Command+d or Ctrl+d.*

Fading a Filter's Effects

If you don't want to use a filter at full intensity, you can apply it and then dial back its effects to the precise level you're looking for. First, apply a filter, then choose Filter | Fade. In the Fade dialog box (see Figure 8-8), you can choose an opacity level and a blending mode for the effects of the filter. The opacity percentage determines the intensity of the filter's effects, and the blending mode determines how the modified pixel colors combine with the original (pre-filter) pixel colors. The blending modes in the Fade dialog box are similar to those shown in the tool Options palette, except that the Fade dialog box doesn't include the Behind and Clear blending modes.

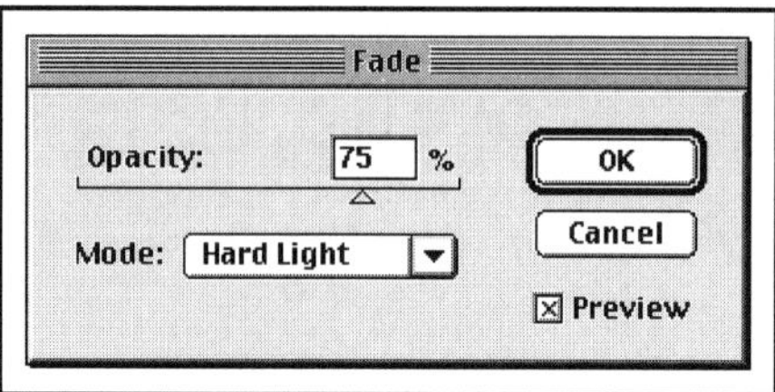

Figure 8-8: The Fade dialog box.

Like the filter dialog boxes themselves, the Fade dialog box has a Preview check box that allows you to see the effects of your changes in the image window. Once you like the effect, you apply it by clicking OK. If, once you return to the image window, you decide that it's still not right, you can choose Filter | Fade again, as many times as you want; the settings you make each time are still there in the dialog box when you return to it, so you can even return to the "un-Faded" version of the filtered image. To restore the image to its original state, before the filter was applied, choose Edit | Undo—this removes the effects of both the Fade command and the filter.

Essentially, the Fade command produces the same effect as the following procedure:

1. Choose Layer | Duplicate Layer and click OK in the Duplicate Layer dialog box.
2. Apply the filter to the new layer.
3. In the Layers palette, adjust the opacity and blending mode of the new layer, allowing the pre-filter version of the image to show through.

If you want to be able to adjust the filter's effects later on, even after you've made other changes to the image, then use this technique instead of the Fade command.

Native Filters

If you tried a new native filter every day, it would take months to work your way through them all, and you probably still wouldn't have plumbed the depths of what's possible with the dozens of filters that Adobe includes with Photoshop 4.0. This huge collection offers everything from the most utilitarian of effects (such as Dust & Scratches) to the most bizarre mind- and image-altering filters (such as Twirl or Trace Contour).

Photoshop divides its native filters into 14 arbitrary categories, listed below, that for the most part give a pretty good idea of what each group of filters does. Each category under the Filters menu has a submenu containing the filters themselves.

Artistic

The Artistic filters are part of a group of filters formerly sold under the name Gallery Effects. They've been completely rewritten and are included as part of Photoshop 4.0. These filters attempt to simulate the effects of using the artistic tools from which they take their names; some are more successful than others.

- Colored Pencil adds diagonal "pencil" strokes and fills in parts of the image with white, gray, or black "paper" in an effort to make it hand-drawn with colored pencils. The three options are Pencil Width (1–24), Stroke Pressure (0–15), and Paper Brightness (0–80). Pencil Width controls the amount of the image that's retained and converted to pencil strokes; lower settings allow for more detail and greater paper coverage, while higher settings increase the width of the strokes and allow more paper to show through between them. The Stroke Pressure setting determines the intensity of the image's remaining colors, while the Paper Brightness slider allows you to make the underlying paper black (0), white (80), or gray (anything in between) (see Figure 8-9).

Figure 8-9: Colored Pencil

- Cutout turns an image into colored paper silhouettes, using the foreground and background colors. It posterizes the other colors in the image, resulting in a simplified image with few gradations. You can control how much simplification takes place with the three sliders: No. of Levels (2–8), Edge Simplicity (0–10), and Edge Fidelity (1–3). No. of Levels determines how many colors are used in the resulting image, while the Edge Simplicity slider controls how much the image's edges are smoothed out to make them into basic geometric shapes. Edge Fidelity allows you to decide how close to the original image the new shapes should be (see Figure 8-10).
- Dry Brush reproduces the effect of painting until there's very little paint on the brush—it results in simple, soft-edged strokes that can retain a little image detail or a lot, depending on your Brush Detail setting (0–10). The other options are Brush Size, ranging from 0–10, and Texture, ranging from 1–3. A Texture setting of 3 adds a bit of noise to the image, while a setting of 1 keeps it smooth and a setting of 2 falls somewhere in the middle (see Figure 8-11).
- Film Grain lightens an image and increases its contrast while adding noise. The Grain option (0–20) determines the amount of noise added; Highlight Area (1–20) controls the size of the areas in the image that are lightened or darkened, with higher settings lightening more of the image; and Intensity (0–10) controls the amount of lightening that occurs in the highlight areas (see Figure 8-12).

Figure 8-10: Cutout.

Figure 8-11: Dry BrushFigure .

Figure 8-12: Film Grain.

- Fresco, another "painting" filter, tends to add dark edges to shapes in an image and increase contrast and saturation. Its controls include sliders for Brush Detail (0–10), Brush Size (0–10), and Texture (1–3). As with the Dry Brush filter, these settings control the amount of detail in the image, the stroke width, and whether noise is added, respectively (see Figure 8-13).

- Neon Glow desaturates an image, recolors it with the Foreground and Background colors, then adds an unearthly glowing effect with a third color determined in the filter's dialog box. The Size slider, ranging from –24 to 24, determines how much of the image's area is covered with the glow color—lower settings make the glow larger. The Brightness setting (0–50) controls the ambient light, rather than the brightness of the glow, so that lower settings produce a spooky dark gray image with an eerie glow (see Figure 8-14).
- Paint Daubs operates like a collection of other filters, resulting in anything but a "daubed" effect. It's as though you blurred the image, used Find Edges, then posterized it, and finally used Sharpen. A Brush Size control, ranging from 1–50, determines the size of the posterized color areas, while a Sharpness slider, ranging from 0–40, applies a little or a lot of sharpening. The Brush Type pop-up menu includes Simple, Light Rough, Dark Rough, Wide Sharp, Wide Blurry, and Sparkle brushes, with the Rough brushes applying more texture to the image. The Sparkle brush intensifies the Find Edges effect and bumps the saturation way, way up to create neon colors (see Figure 8-15).

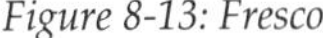

Figure 8-13: Fresco.

Figure 8-14: Neon Glow.

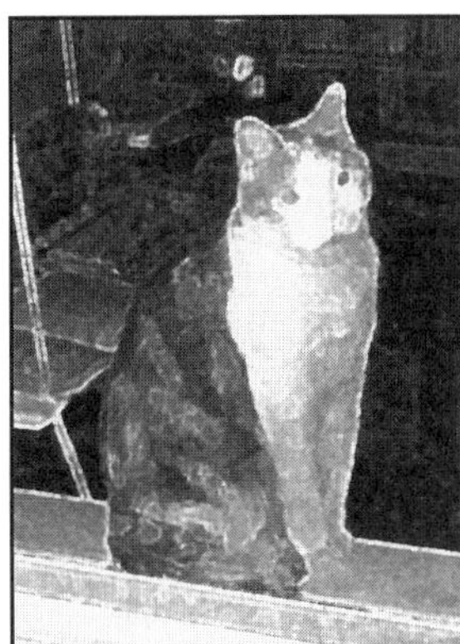

Figure 8-15: Paint Daubs.

- Palette Knife attempts to produce the effect of a painting created with a palette knife rather than a brush, but it doesn't add the texture that a knife would. You can control Stroke Size (1–50), Stroke Detail (1–3), and Softness (0–10); the latter setting determines whether the strokes blend into one another or are hard-edged (see Figure 8-16).
- Plastic Wrap seems to apply a layer of plastic wrap to an image, adding highlights and emphasizing the lines in the image. The Highlight Strength slider (0–20) controls the brightness of the highlights reflected from the plastic wrap. Detail (1–15) determines how much the plastic wrap clings to the shapes in the image—higher settings produce more plastic wrap texture—while Smoothness (1–15) determines how much plastic wrap texture is applied (see Figure 8-17).

- Poster Edges reduces the number of colors in an image and outlines shapes in black, producing a woodcut effect. The options include Edge Thickness, ranging from 0-10; Edge Intensity (how much outlining is applied), ranging from 0–10; and Posterization, ranging from 0–6, which controls the number of colors in the resulting image (see Figure 8-18).

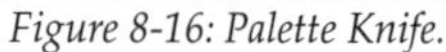

Figure 8-16: Palette Knife.

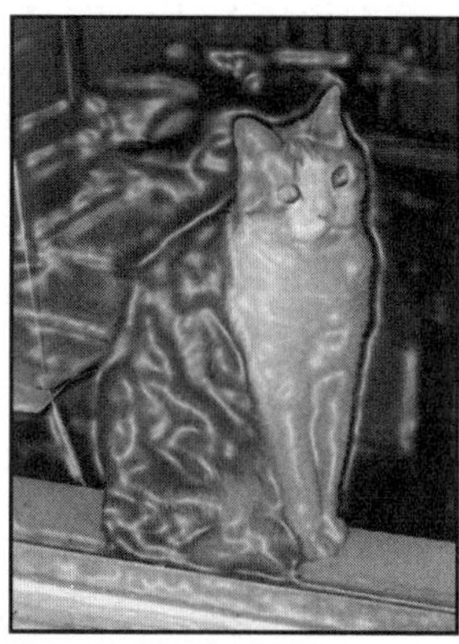

Figure 8-17: Plastic Wrap.

Figure 8-18: Poster Edges.

- Rough Pastels applies "pastel" strokes to an image based on an underlying texture that can be built-in or supplied from a second file. The Stroke Length and Stroke Detail controls do just what they sound like, while a separate area of the dialog box contains controls for the Texture. You can choose Brick, Burlap, Canvas, or Sandstone from a pop-up menu, or choose Other and load any Photoshop-format file that isn't in Bitmap mode. Then choose a Scaling setting from 50%–200% to determine how the texture is sized with respect to the image and a Relief value from 0–50 to control how high the darker areas in the texture file are considered to be. You can specify a Light Direction in 45-degree increments, and you can choose to invert the texture before applying it (see Figure 8-19).
- Smudge Stick looks like smudged pastels, with controls to determine the length of the smudging strokes (Stroke Length, from 1–10) and the amount that the contrast in the image should be increased (Intensity, from 1–10). The Highlight Area slider controls how much of the brighter areas in the image are blown out with the increased brightness (see Figure 8-20).
- Sponge is intended to give the effect of paint applied with a sponge. You can control the size and softness of the sponge, as well as how much it darkens the colors it applies. The Brush Size slider (1–10) determines how large the sponge is, while the Smoothness slider (1–15) allows you to control how blurry the edges of the sponge strokes are. The Definition slider makes the image darker or closer to the original image, with the lowest setting of 1 keeping the colors pretty much as they are and the highest setting of 25 darkening them (see Figure 8-21).

Figure 8-19: Rough Pastels.

Figure 8-20: Smudge Stick.

Figure 8-21: Sponge.

- Underpainting produces a realistic oil-painted effect with controls similar to those in the Rough Pastels filter. The Brush Size (0–40) and Texture Coverage (0–40) sliders determine the width of the brush strokes and the amount of canvas or other background that is allowed to show through. The Texture controls work just like the Rough Pastels Texture controls, including allowing you to specify your own color or grayscale Photoshop-format file as the texture (see Figure 8-22).
- Watercolor produces a texture that might be mistaken for a watercolor painting, but the filter tends to darken the image much more than most watercolor artists would. A Brush Detail (1–14) controls the amount of detail preserved in the resulting image, while Shadow Intensity (1–10) determines exactly how much the image is darkened and Texture (1–3) allows you to choose a flatter image or one with more visible strokes (see Figure 8-23).

Figure 8-22: Underpainting.

Figure 8-23: Watercolor.

Blur

It doesn't take too much imagination to figure out what these filters do, but each of them does it slightly differently. The overall effect is to smooth out transitions between areas of different colors by averaging the colors of the pixels at the transition points:

- Blur softens images a predetermined amount; there's no dialog box. While it uses the same basic process as the Gaussian Blur filter, most people prefer Gaussian Blur so they can tailor the amount of blurring to the situation (see Figure 8-24).
- Blur More is equivalent to multiple applications of the Blur filter. Again, it's not often used, because Gaussian Blur can achieve the same results with greater precision (see Figure 8-25).
- Gaussian Blur, with a Radius slider that runs from .1–250 pixels, lets you specify exactly the amount of blur you want to apply to an image. For extreme precision, you can even enter a number in the entry field above the slider. Values higher than 20 or so remove all the detail from an image, leaving only a haze of color, and the higher the Radius value, the longer the filter takes to work its magic (see Figure 8-26).

Figure 8-24: Blur.

Figure 8-25: Blur More.

Figure 8-26: Gaussian Blur.

- Motion Blur, by blurring pixels in one direction only, creates the effect of a moving object. It works best when the central object of the image stands against a fairly plain, light-colored background. You can specify the Distance of the blurring effect and the Angle by entering values in entry fields, and if you're no good with geometry you have the option of specifying the Angle value by dragging a line around a circle. The Angle value can range from –90 to 90 degrees, and the Distance value can range from .1–999 pixels (see Figure 8-27).

- Radial Blur, like the Radial option of the Gradient tool, creates a circular blurring effect, with the blurred pixels appearing to either spin around the circle or zoom out from its center. The Amount field controls the intensity of the blur—equivalent to a Radius setting for the Zoom option and specifying the direction of rotation for the Spin option. You can move the center of the blur effect by clicking and dragging on the dialog box preview (not a true preview, but rather a sort of wireframe effect), and you have a choice of three quality levels: Draft, Good, and Best (see Figure 8-28).
- Smart Blur blurs only areas of minor color changes, leaving edges alone. It's similar to the effect of blurring the Lightness channel in Lab color mode. The Radius and Threshold values determine how much blurring is applied and what the brightness cutoff level is for applying the effect. In an innovative step, Adobe included two extra preview modes in this filter so you can see exactly what areas of the image you are blurring; the Edge Only option in the Mode pop-up menu shows the affected areas as white on a black background, and Overlay Edge lays the white preview over the image. Normal mode previews the filter's effects as in most dialog box preview windows (see Figure 8-29).

Figure 8-27: Motion Blur.

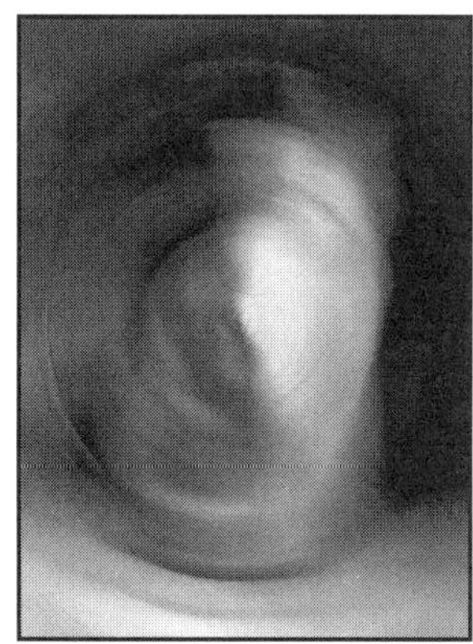

Figure 8-28: Radial Blur.

Figure 8-29: Smart Blur.

Brush Strokes

Like the Artistic filters, the Brush Stroke filters strive for natural-media effects, this time in the area of painting, and were originally part of the Gallery Effects filters that Adobe acquired from Aldus. In general, these filters remove detail and add texture to an image:

- Accented Edges emphasizes the edges in an image, like a combination of Trace Contour and Find Edges, and smoothes out the areas in between. The Edge Width slider (1–14) controls how wide the traced edges are; the Edge Brightness value (0–50) determines whether the edges are black, white, or somewhere in between; and Smoothness (1–15) controls how many areas are outlined—fewer with higher settings (see Figure 8-30).

- Angled Strokes applies brush strokes with the ability to vary the angle in different colored areas of the image. This is controlled by the Direction Balance slider (0–100), with lower and higher settings forcing the strokes to be mostly in one direction and middle settings mixing them up. The Stroke Length slider allows you to choose lengths from 3–50 , and the definition of the brush strokes is controlled with the Sharpness slider, with values ranging from 0–10 (see Figure 8-31).
- Crosshatch applies brushstrokes at diagonal angles 90 degrees apart. You can control the Stroke Length, from 3–50; the Sharpness, or stroke definition, from 0–20; and the Strength, which produces an embossing effect and ranges from 1 to 3 (see Figure 8-32).

Figure 8-30: Accented Edges.

Figure 8-31: Angled Strokes.

Figure 8-32: Crosshatch.

- Dark Strokes produces crosshatched brushstrokes as well. You can adjust the Balance from 0–10, with high and low settings making the strokes run one direction and medium settings mixing the stroke directions. The Black Intensity and White Intensity sliders determine how much the dark and light colors, respectively, are darkened or lightened in the course of applying the effect; these values can range from 0–10 (see Figure 8-33).
- Ink Outlines works like Dark Strokes, except that you can adjust the Stroke Length (from 1–50) and you have no control over the stroke angle. This filter also outlines elements in the image (see Figure 8-34).
- Spatter is similar to a combination of the Diffuse and Ripple filters, resulting in an image that looks as though it were created from tiny droplets of paint. There are only two sliders in the Spatter dialog box: Spray Radius, which ranges from 0–25 and controls how far droplets are allowed to encroach into areas of different colors, and Smoothness, which controls the ripple effect—the lowest Smoothness setting of 1 eliminates the ripples altogether, and the highest setting of 15 makes the image pretty much unrecognizable (see Figure 8-35).

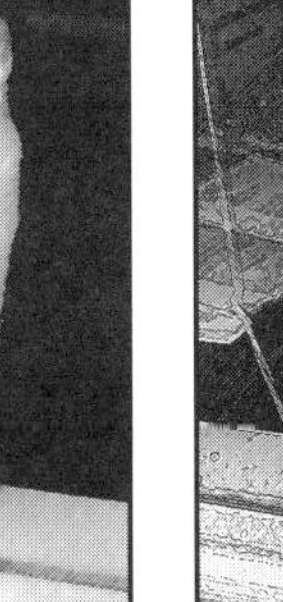

Figure 8-33: Dark Strokes.

Figure 8-34: Ink Outlines.

Figure 8-35: Spatter.

- Sprayed Strokes adds softly sprayed strokes whose angle, length, and width you can control. The Stroke Length slider ranges from 0–20; the Spray Radius slider controls how far droplets can stray from the axis of the stroke. The Stroke Dir. pop-up menu has four options: Horizontal, Left Diagonal, Right Diagonal, and Vertical (see Figure 8-36).
- Sumi-e is a Japanese painting technique with lots of dark areas and soft-edged strokes. You can control the Stroke Width and Stroke Pressure; width can vary from 3–15, and pressure can range from 0–15. The Contrast slider (0–40) determines how much contrast is added to the original image's dark and light areas; higher settings increase contrast and lower ones maintain the existing contrast levels (see Figure 8-37).

Figure 8-36: Sprayed Strokes.

Figure 8-37: Sumi-e.

Distort

The math in these filters is more apparent than anywhere else—they take an image and distort its shape geometrically. Some of them can be used to simulate 3D effects.

- Diffuse Glow adds glowing halo of the Background color to the lighter areas in the image. The Graininess slider (0–10) determines how much noise is applied to the dark areas of the image. The Glow Amount and Clear Amount sliders, both ranging from 0–20, control how much glow is applied and how much of the image is off-limits for the glow (see Figure 8-38).
- Displace rearranges the existing image into another shape based on the brightness values in another image. You can use any Photoshop-format file (except one in Bitmap mode) as a displacement map. Adobe includes several files you can experiment with in the Displacement Maps folder. For instance, try the Streaks pattern for a distorted water reflection effect, as though the image were reflected on the surface of a river. Midlevel grays in the displacement map move the target image's pixels least, dark colors move them in one diagonal direction, and light colors move them in the opposite direction. Scale determines how far pixels can be moved. With a scale of 1, the farthest any pixel will move is 128 pixels; increasing the scale increases that possible maximum distance. Then you determine how the displacement map should be adjusted to fit the size of the target image: Stretch to Fit, which scales it, or Tile, which repeats it. To deal with pixels that are moved off the edge of the image, choose Wrap Around, which moves them to the other side of the image, or Repeat Edge Pixels, which fills in blank spots along the edges with the colors of the nearby pixels. When you click OK, a dialog box asks you to specify the displacement map, and when you click OK again the effect is applied to the image (see Figure 8-39).
- Glass uses displacement maps to make the image look as though it's viewed through a sheet of glass; the texture map controls the surface texture of the glass. The Distortion slider, from 0–20, affects how much the glass distorts the image, while the Smoothness controls how clear and free of "noisy" defects the glass is. The Texture pop-up menu allows you to choose the Blocks, Canvas, Frosted, and Tiny Lens built-in textures or load your own color or grayscale Photoshop format file, and the Scaling slider allows you to scale the texture from 50–200%. An Invert check box allows you to invert the glass texture before applying it to the image (see Figure 8-40).

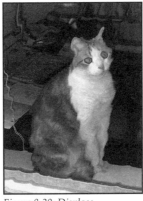

Figure 8-38: Diffuse Glo.

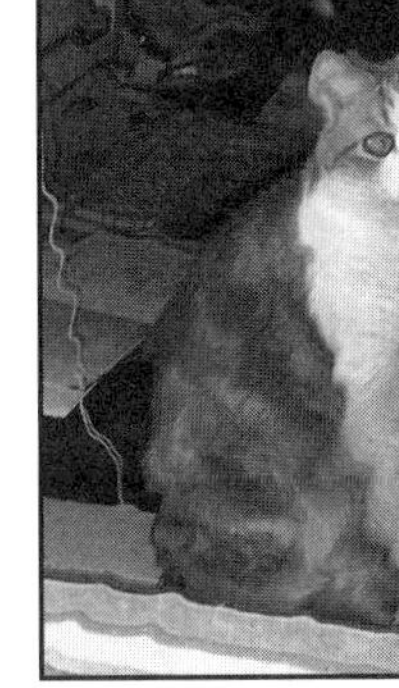
Figure 8-39: Displace.

Figure 8-40: Glass.

- Ocean Ripple is a simpler filter that adds ripples to the image, with only two options. You can set the Ripple Size, from 1–15, and the Ripple Magnitude slider (0–20) controls how much the image is moved toward and away from the axis of the rippling wave (see Figure 8-41).
- Pinch creates a bulge, either in or out, in the center of an image. Its effect is similar to that of the Spherize filter, except that the bulge isn't necessarily circular, because it's shaped by the image's proportions. The Amount value ranges from –100 to 100%; negative values make the bulge outward, while positive values make it inward (see Figure 8-42).
- Polar Coordinates takes the X- and Y-coordinates of each pixel in the image and changes them to polar coordinates, or treats them as polar coordinates and changes them to rectangular coordinates. It produces extreme distortion of an image (see Figure 8-43).

Figure 8-41: Ocean Ripple.

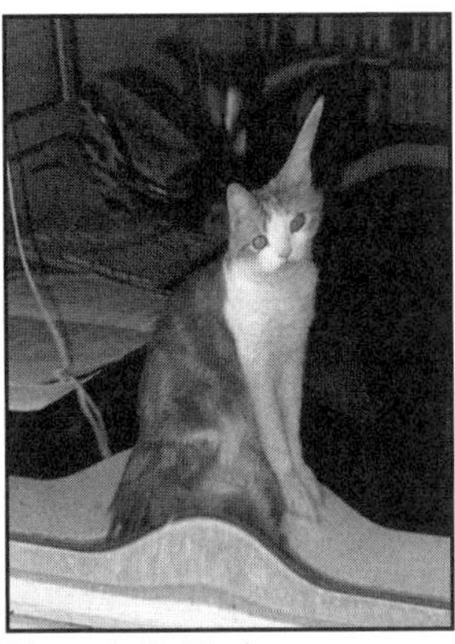
Figure 8-42: Pinch.

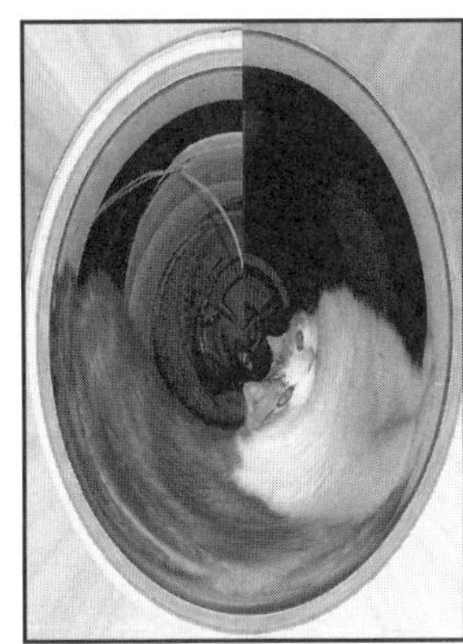
Figure 8-43: Polar Coordinates.

- Ripple, with values ranging from –999 to 999, adds Small, Medium, or Large ripples to an image. Depending on the Amount value and the size of the ripples, the resulting image can look as though it were drawn by a child who can't yet make a straight line, or it can be completely unrecognizable (see Figure 8-44).
- Shear is the Do-It-Yourself Distort filter. The dialog box contains a grid with a curved line that you can adjust to determine how the image is bent or otherwise distorted. Once the shape of the distortion is determined, the only option is what to do with spaces left blank by the operation; you can choose Wrap Around to substitute pixels that were moved off the opposite side of the image, or Repeat Edge Pixels to fill in with colors taken from adjacent pixels (see Figure 8-45).
- Spherize, like the Pinch filter, produces a rounded bulge in the center of an image, with negative values (down to –100%) producing an outward bulge and positive ones (up to 100%) producing an inward bulge. You also have the option of choosing Horizontal Only or Vertical Only, which stretches the image over an imaginary cylinder sitting on its end (Horizontal) or its side (Vertical). (See Figure 8-46.)

Figure 8-44: Ripple.

Figure 8-45: Shear.

Figure 8-46: Spherize.

- Twirl, just as one would imagine, twirls the image by a user-specified amount; you can specify a value between –999 and 999 degrees, with positive numbers producing a clockwise twist and negative ones generating a counterclockwise twist. The dialog box doesn't offer a true preview, just a wireframe version that shows how the twirl effect tapers off at the outer edges of the image (see Figure 8-47).
- Wave is one of the more complex native filters, an expanded version of the Ripple filter that allows you to specify the number of waves, their type, and their magnitude. The Number of Generators can range from 1–999, with higher numbers generating more complex patterns. For Wavelength and Amplitude, which

determine the size of the waves, you can set Minimum and Maximum values ranging from 1–999; Scale determines the relative effect of the waves in the horizontal and vertical planes of the image. The Type section of the Wave dialog box allows you to choose Sine (curved), Triangle, or Square wave shapes, and you can choose Wrap Around or Repeat Edge pixels to deal with empty spaces on the edges of the image (see Figure 8-48).

- ZigZag duplicates the effect of dropping a pebble into a pond. The ripples radiating from the point where the rock entered the water are the effect of the ZigZag filter; in fact, one of its three type options is Pond Ripples. The other two are Out From Center and Around Center, which create ripples of different shapes radiating from the center of the image. The dialog box has both a regular preview window and a wireframe preview that shows the ripple shape. Two sliders in the dialog box allow you to adjust Amount (from –100 to 100%) and the number of Ridges (from 1–20%). (See Figure 8-49.)

Figure 8-47: Twirl.

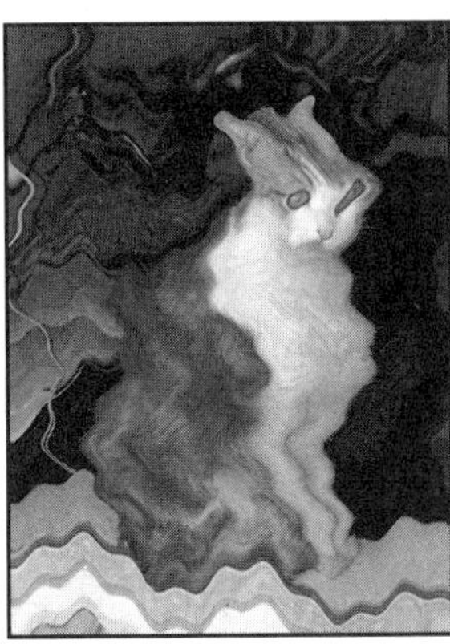

Figure 8-48: Wave.

Figure 8-49: ZigZag.

Noise

Noise is what we think of as static when we see it on a television screen; Adobe defines it as "pixels with randomly distributed color levels." Because it's randomly generated, adding noise to an image is one of the quickest ways you can create an organic-looking texture, and it's a good way to roughen up a smooth, too-perfect surface, such as one that's been heavily edited with the Smudge or Rubber Stamp tool. The filters in this category are designed to both add and remove noise:

- Add Noise, obviously, introduces a specified amount of noise to an image. The amount can range from 1-999, and the noise can be distributed using a Uniform arrangement or a more random Gaussian one. Monochromatic noise adds grayscale noise rather than colored noise (see Figure 8-50).

TIP *If the gradients in an image are banding—resolving into bands of color rather than smooth gradations—try adding a little noise.*

- Despeckle, rather than adding noise, attempts to seek it out and eliminate it, generally to remove graininess or moiré patterns from scanned images. It doesn't have a dialog box because there are no options. Despeckle does blur an image slightly, so use it only if absolutely necessary (see Figure 8-51).
- Dust & Scratches finds pixels that stand out from the pixels around them by virtue of extreme differences in brightness values, and it fills those areas in with the surrounding color. This is a fairly effective method of eliminating inadvertently scanned dust and scratches—not to mention cat hair—from an image, but it can also eliminate things like the sparkle in the subject's eye. The Threshold value determines how different the brightness levels of the dust or scratches must be from the surrounding area to be affected by the filter; this value should be as high as possible to preserve details of the image. The Radius value determines how large the area of each adjustment is; the larger this number is, the blurrier the image will get (see Figure 8-52).

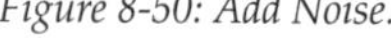

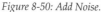

Figure 8-50: Add Noise.

Figure 8-51: Despeckle.

Figure 8-52: Dust & Scratches.

- Median is great for cleaning up scanned line art; it smoothes out areas within an image by averaging the color values of pixels within a distance determined by the Radius value. Used with jaggy or "dirty" line art, Median smoothes lines and eliminates stray marks; used with a photographic image, it reduces the overall number of colors in the image and simplifies its shapes. The Radius value can be as low as 1 or as high as 16 (see Figure 8-53).

Figure 8-53: Median.

Pixelate

These filters produce the effect you get by enlarging a low-resolution image without interpolation—enlarged "pixels" made up of all the similarly colored pixels in an area, color-averaged to look even more similar.

- Color Halftone gives the Pop Art effect of a color halftone with huge dots. Each color channel in an image is converted to colored dots whose size is determined by the brightness of the pixels it replaces. You can specify the maximum radius of the dots (from 4–127 pixels) and screen angles for each color channel. In grayscale images, the only channel is Channel #1; in RGB images, Channel #1 is red, Channel #2 is green, and Channel #3 is blue; and in CMYK images, Channel #1 is cyan, Channel #2 is magenta, Channel #3 is yellow , and Channel #4 is black (see Figure 8-54).
- Crystallize creates angular polygon shapes by averaging the colors of adjacent pixels; the Cell Size can range from 3–300 pixels. Lower settings produce an artistic stippled effect, while higher ones make the image look as though it's being viewed through a shower stall door (see Figure 8-55).
- Facet flattens out colors and straightens edges to create geometric shapes—facets—from the elements of an image. It doesn't have a dialog box, since there are no options (see Figure 8-56).

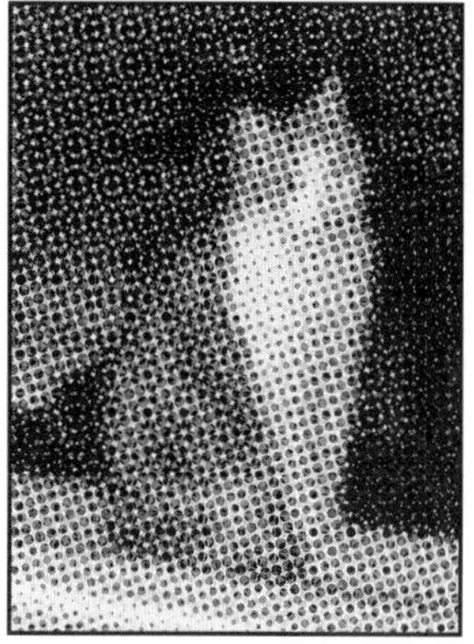

Figure 8-54: Color Halftone.

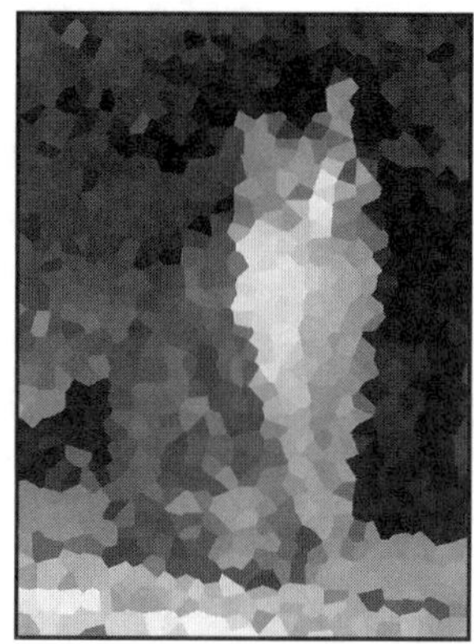
Figure 8-55: Crystallize.

Figure 8-56: Facet.

- Fragment creates four copies of an image, offsetting each slightly, to give a somewhat disturbing "quadruple-vision" effect. Like Facet, Fragment has no options and no dialog box (see Figure 8-57).
- Mezzotint reproduces the effect of the special mezzotint screen patterns used to create halftones, with a choice of four sizes of dots, three sizes of lines, and three sizes of irregular strokes. The pop-up menu containing these choices is the only option, and the dialog box offers an extra-large preview window because it's hard to see the true effect in a small area of the image (see Figure 8-58).
- Mosaic produces the most classic "pixelated" effect by generating square blocks of color anywhere from 2–64 pixels on a side. For greater interest, you can combine this filter with one of the Distort filters to randomize the block shapes somewhat (see Figure 8-59).

Figure 8-57: Fragment.

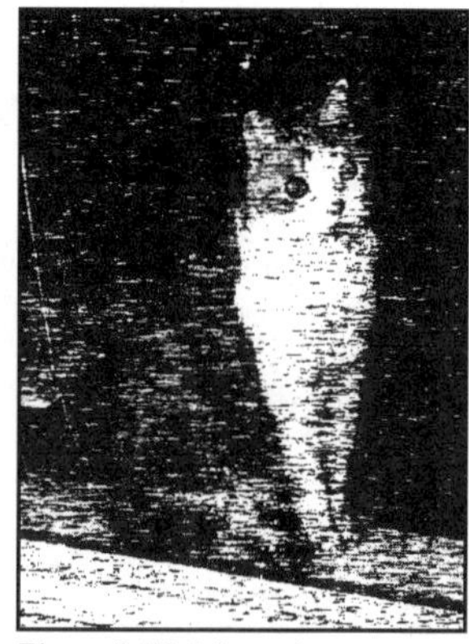
Figure 8-58: Mezzotint.

Figure 8-59: Mosaic.

- Pointillize turns an image into a facsimile of a Pointillist painting by creating dots of color; it differs from the Color Halftone filter in that the resulting colors are the same as the image colors, rather than dots of primary colors. The dots are randomly placed and can range in size from 3–300 pixels, with the Background color placed in between them to act as the paper or canvas color (see Figure 8-60).

Figure 8-60: Pointillize.

Render

These five filters really don't have much in common. The two Clouds filters create—you guessed it—clouds; the Lens Flare and Lighting Effects filters add light and its attendant shadows to an image; and the Texture Fill filter uses grayscale images to create simulated 3D textures. Lighting Effects is the most complex native filter and demands the most memory to run.

- Clouds doesn't have a dialog box, since its only options are the colors it uses. The Foreground and Background colors are used to create random soft clouds. Holding (Option)[Alt] as you choose Filter | Render | Clouds produces clouds with higher contrast and harder edges. Repeated applications intensify the effect (see Figure 8-61).
- Difference Clouds creates clouds based on the Foreground and Background colors combined with the existing colors in the image. Because it takes the image colors into account, it doesn't cover up the image as the Clouds filter does—it overlays a cloud pattern on top of it (see Figure 8-62).
- Lens Flare reproduces the effect of light refracted through a curved lens. You have a choice of three types of lenses: 50–300mm Zoom, 35mm Prime, or 105mm Prime, and you can specify the Brightness level of the flare, from 10–300%. The dialog box's preview window contains a movable crosshair that allows you to position the center of the flare (see Figure 8-63).

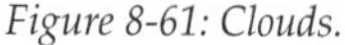

Figure 8-61: Clouds.

Figure 8-62: Difference Clouds.

Figure 8-63: Lens Flare.

- Lighting Effects adds light to an image, allowing you to choose the attributes of the image's surface, the color and intensity of the light, and its scope. You can add a bump map (Texture Channel) to the mix to be used as a texture map that defines high and low spots in the image, creating a shadowed 3D surface. Complex as it appears, Lighting Effects is the easiest way to create embossed and other 3D effects. You choose a Light Type (Directional, Omni, or Spotlight) and Intensity, then the properties of the surface that will reflect or absorb the light: Gloss, Material, Exposure, and Ambience. The Texture Channel can be a layer, a color channel, or an alpha channel, and you have the option of white areas in the image being considered high or low, and a Height slider to control exactly how high (see Figure 8-64).
- Texture Fill doesn't actually create a texture; instead, it tiles a grayscale image into the image window. It's intended to be used in an alpha channel to create a selection mask or a bump map that can be used with the Lighting Effects channel. There's no preview, and there are no options other than what image you use (see Figure 8-65).

Figure 8-64: Lighting Effects.

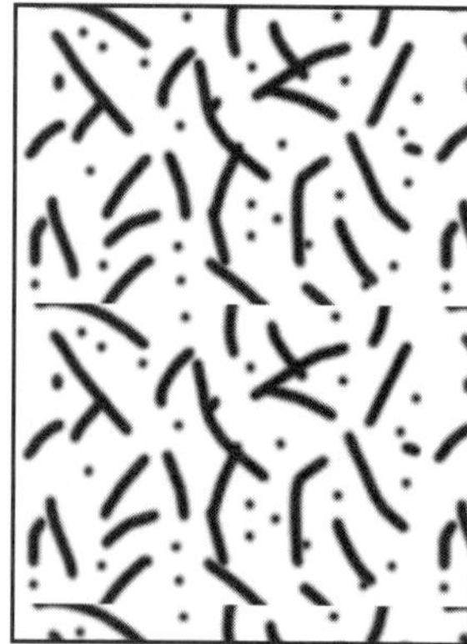

Figure 8-65: Texture Fill.

Sharpen

Utilitarian to the max, these filters can also be used at high intensity to create an exaggerated surrealist effect. Sharpen and Sharpen More affect the entire image, while Sharpen Edges and Unsharp Mask concentrate their effects on edges, with the latter offering the most control.

- Sharpen operates on all pixels in the image, increasing their contrast. For professional work, the Unsharp Mask filter offers more control and better results. There's no dialog box associated with this filter (see Figure 8-66).
- Sharpen Edges operates like the Sharpen filter, but works only on the edges of large areas. It doesn't have any options, so there's no dialog box (see Figure 8-67).
- Sharpen More is like using the Sharpen filter several times in succession. It has no options (see Figure 8-68).

Figure 8-66: Sharpen.

Figure 8-67: Sharpen Edges.

Figure 8-68: Sharpen More.

- Unsharp Mask is the Sharpen filter that's most often used in professional photo retouching. Based on a traditional photographic technique involving combining a negative and a blurred positive of an image to create a sharper print, it offers more control than the other Sharpen filters. The Amount value, ranging from 1–500%, determines how much adjustment is made to the affected pixels; a good starting point is between 100% and 200%, since very high values can sharpen unwanted details and generate noise. Radius controls the distance on either side of an edge that is affected, and it can range from .1–250 pixels; a value of 2–3 pixels is generally used. The Threshold value determines how much difference in brightness must exist before an area is considered an edge, and while this value can go as low as 69 levels and as high as 255 levels, it's generally set near the lower end of that range (see Figure 8-69).

Figure 8-69: Unsharp Mask.

Sketch

Yet more from the Gallery Effects series, these filters produce effects intended to look hand-drawn rather than painted. Most of these filters use the foreground and/or background colors in the Toolbox to achieve their effects:

- Bas Relief produces a more detailed and subtle version of the effect of the Emboss filter, using the Foreground and Background colors for highlights and shadows. You can choose how much detail is retained and how smooth the surfaces are; both the Detail and Smoothness sliders range from 1–15. You can also determine the light direction in 45-degree increments (see Figure 8-70).
- Chalk & Charcoal combines chalk strokes in the Background color and charcoal strokes in the Foreground color to create an image that can look extremely surreal, depending on your color choices. You can control the Chalk Area and the Charcoal area, both ranging from 0–20, and the Stroke Pressure (0–5) to determine how intense the effect is (see Figure 8-71).
- Charcoal turns the image into a simulated charcoal sketch, with dark areas colored with "charcoal" strokes in the Foreground color and light areas representing the paper in the Background color. The Charcoal Thickness slider (1–7) determines the width of the strokes, while the Detail slider (0–5) controls how closely the sketch follows the details of the image and the Light/Dark Balance slider (0–100) controls how much of the image is covered with charcoal strokes (see Figure 8-72).

Figure 8-70: Bas Relief.

Figure 8-71: Chalk & Charcoal.

Figure 8-72: Charcoal.

- Chrome creates a similar effect to Plastic Wrap, except grayscale and multiplied several times so that the original image is almost obliterated. The Detail and Smoothness sliders, ranging from 0–10, both control how much of the original image's shape is preserved (see Figure 8-73).
- Conté Crayon produces the effect of a crayon on textured paper; Conté crayons are usually black, dark red, or brown, so if you're looking for a realistic crayon effect you'll want to use one of these colors as the foreground color and a white, cream, or tan paper color as the background color (see Figure 8-74).
- Graphic Pen produces a pen-and-ink sketch effect, only with no outlining—only shading strokes. You can determine the Stroke Length (from 1–15) and the Light/Dark Balance (from 0–100); the latter setting determines how much of the image is covered with the Foreground and Background colors, with medium settings distributing the colors evenly. You have four choices for Stroke Direction: Horizontal, Left Diagonal, Right Diagonal, and Vertical (see Figure 8-75).

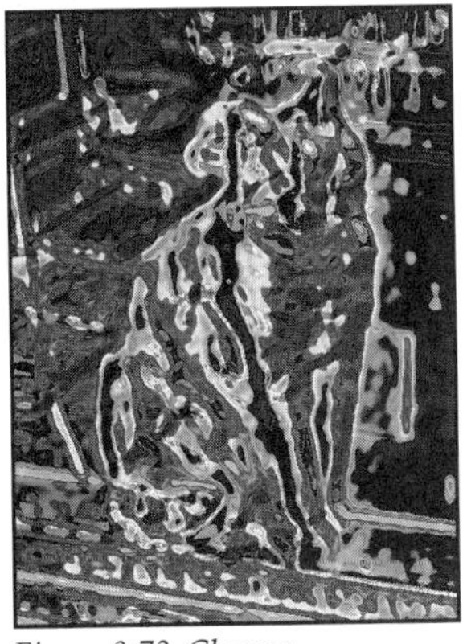
Figure 8-73: Chrome.

Figure 8-74: Conté Crayon.

Figure 8-75: Graphic Pen.

- Halftone Pattern, like Color Halftone, turns the image into a prefab halftone, but it lays that effect over the existing image, which it recolors in a combination of the foreground and background colors. The Pattern Type pop-up menu contains three options for the halftone pattern: Circle, Dot, and Line. Size and Contrast sliders, ranging from 1–12 and 0–50 respectively, control the scale of the halftone pattern and how prominent it appears (see Figure 8-76).
- Note Paper turns the image into a figure embossed in a sheet of grainy paper. You can control the amount of detail retained with the Image Balance slider (0–50) and the height of the embossing with the Relief slider (0–25). The Graininess control affects the texture of the paper, noise or smooth, and ranges from 0–20 (see Figure 8-77).
- Photocopy produces a blurry, streaky, and posterized effect similar to that of reproducing a photo on a particularly poor photocopier. You choose how much detail to retain with the Detail slider (1–24) and how dark the image is with the Darkness slider (1–50). (See Figure 8-78.)

Figure 8-76: Halftone Pattern.

Figure 8-77: Note Paper.

Figure 8-78: Photocopy.

- Plaster adds a relief effect to an image in which dark areas are raised and light areas are lowered. The Image Balance slider, running from 0–50, determines the point above which pixels are made the Foreground color and below which they're made the Background color. The Smoothness slider determines how much plaster texture is applied to the image. The Light Position pop-up menu has eight choices at 45 degree angles from each other (see Figure 8-79).

- Reticulation is a photographic effect in which the film's emulsion cracks during processing, and this filter ends up resembling the Mezzotint filter, with randomly shaped noise applied to the image. The Density slider, with values ranging from 0–50, determines how densely the dots are placed and how closely they follow the image's shapes. The Black Level and White Level sliders, both of which also range from 0–50, controls how much of the Foreground and Background colors, respectively, are used in the resulting image (see Figure 8-80).
- Stamp combines the effects of the Threshold command and the Median filter, allowing you to create a two-color image with the cutoff between the two colors determined by the Light/Dark Balance setting (0–50). The Median part comes in with the Smoothness slider (1–50), which can smooth rough edges (see Figure 8-81).

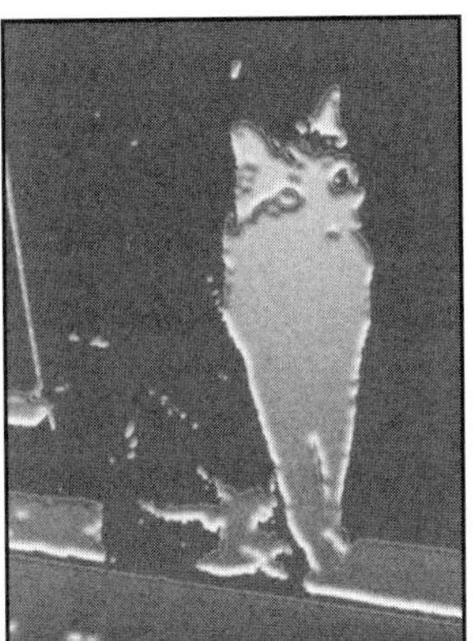
Figure 8-79: Plaster.

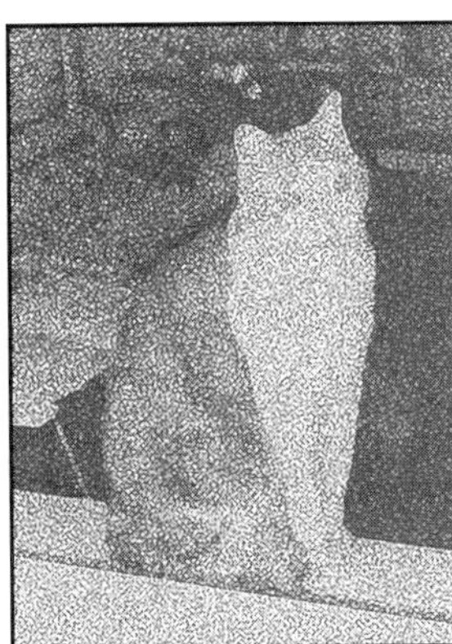
Figure 8-80: Reticulation.

Figure 8-81: Stamp.

- Torn Edges doesn't look particularly like torn paper edges; it posterizes an image into two colors, with fuzzy transitions between different colored areas. Image Balance (0–50) controls the relative amounts of the Foreground and Background colors used. The softness of the edges is controlled by the Smoothness slider (1–15), and the Contrast slider (1–25) determines whether the two colors mix smoothly (low settings), with jagged spots (high settings), or not at all (medium settings). (See Figure 8-82.)
- Water Paper mimics the effect of painting on damp paper, which blurs the colors and reduces contrast in the image. Fiber Length (3–50) is analogous to stroke length in other filters. The Brightness (0–100) and Contrast (0–100) sliders affect how much of the image's detail and contrast are lost (see Figure 8-83).

Figure 8-82: Torn Edges.

Figure 8-83: Water Paper.

Stylize

These nine filters produce exaggerated, stylized effects by focusing on the contrast in an image:

- Diffuse scatters occasional pixels randomly around the image; it has three modes. Normal shows all the moved pixels, while Darken Only shows just the moved pixels that are darker than the pixels around them and Lighten Only shows just the moved pixels that are lighter than the pixels around them (see Figure 8-84).
- Emboss stamps an image into the surface, turning most of the image gray and retaining image colors only on the "sides" of the protruding, embossed areas. You can control the Angle of the embossing (–360 to 360 degrees), its Height (1–10 pixels), and the Amount of detail retained in the image (1–500%). The higher the Amount and Height settings, the more color remains in the image (see Figure 8-85).
- Extrude looks promising—a real 3D object generator built into Photoshop?—but this filter is not particularly appealing. It pastes the existing image onto the surfaces of rows of square blocks or pyramids, with the option (check Solid Front Faces) of making each block a solid color that is the average of the colors in that area of the original image. The Size value determines the size of the blocks or pyramids, and the Depth value determines how tall they are. Choose Random to vary the height of each block or Level-based to make blocks in brighter areas of the image higher. The Mask Incomplete Blocks option eliminates partial blocks (see Figure 8-86).

Figure 8-84: Diffuse.

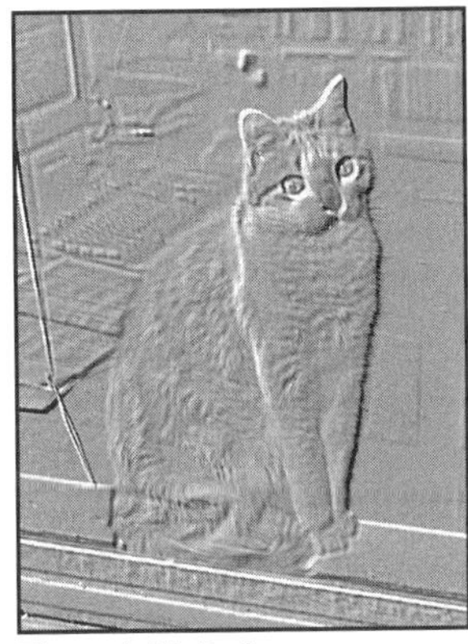

Figure 8-85: Emboss.

Figure 8-86: Extrude.

- Find Edges emphasizes all the edges in an image and inverts many of the colors. This filter has no options (see Figure 8-87).
- Glowing Edges is a combination of the Find Edges filter and the Invert command, with the ability to control the Edge Width (1–14), Edge Brightness (0–20), and Smoothness of the edges (1–15). With higher Smoothness settings, fewer edges are located (see Figure 8-88).
- Solarize inverts any colors in the image with a brightness value of less than 50%. It doesn't have any options (see Figure 8-89).

Figure 8-87: Find Edges.

Figure 8-88: Glowing Edges.

Figure 8-89: Solarize.

- Tiles, which unfortunately doesn't have a preview, breaks an image into a user-specified number of square chunks (as many as 99 across) and moves them as much as 99% of their width away from their original location. You can specify what shows in the "holes" between these tiles: Background Color, Foreground Color, Inverse Image, or Unaltered Image (see Figure 8-90).
- Trace Contour turns images into something like geographical contour maps, by outlining the brightest or darkest areas in the image in each channel and outlining them there, producing narrow lines of primary colors. The Edge setting determines whether darker areas (Lower) or lighter (Upper) areas are outlined, and the Level setting determines the brightness level above or below which an area has to fall to be outlined. If you want to outline a specific area, use the Info palette to determine its brightness level, then use that value for the Level setting (see Figure 8-91).
- Wind works similarly to the Motion Blur filter, but since it affects only edges it doesn't have the effect of blurring the image—instead, elements in the image seem to be blowing away in a direction you specify (From the Left or From the Right). You can also choose the wind speed: Wind, Blast, or Stagger (see Figure 8-92).

Figure 8-90: Tiles.

Figure 8-91: Trace Contour.

Figure 8-92: Wind.

Texture

As its name implies, this group of filters adds various textures to an image. The names of the individual filters are more or less misleading—the results of the Stained Glass filter do not look like stained glass—but the effects are striking:

- Craquelure creates a beautiful combination of embossing and a crackle effect. The sliders let you determine Crack Spacing (2–100), Crack Depth (0–10), and Crack Brightness (0–10). Spacing controls how far apart the cracks are, depth how deep they are, and brightness what color they are—white, black, or something in between (see Figure 8-93).

- Grain is similar to Add Noise, but it allows you to choose the shape of the noise that is added, with the ten choices in the Grain Type pop-up menu: Clumped, Contrasty, Enlarged, Horizontal, Regular, Soft, Speckled, Sprinkles, Stippled, and Vertical. The Intensity slider (0–100) determines how much grain is added, but it's not linear; you may see no effect at the top or bottom of this range and may need to use a setting in the middle. The Contrast slider (0–100) determines how light or dark the added grain is (see Figure 8-94).
- Mosaic Tiles produces a mosaic effect with irregular, squarish tiles. Although you can control Grout Width, from 1–15, and the lightness of the grout (with the Lighten Grout slider, from 0–10), the grout isn't a contrasting color; it shows as the unembossed areas between the raised tiles. The remaining option is Tile Size, ranging from 2–100 (see Figure 8-95).

Figure 8-93: Craquelure.

Figure 8-94: Grain.

Figure 8-95: Mosaic Tiles.

- Patchwork produces an image that looks more like tile than a patchwork quilt. There is no visible grout with this effect, but there is the bonus of a Relief control that allows you to keep the image fairly flat (at the low-end setting of 0) or change the height of the tiles depending on their brightness level (at the high-end setting of 25). You can also set the Square Size (0–10). (See Figure 8-96.)
- Stained Glass produces a backlit honeycomb effect using highly saturated versions of the image colors. You control the Cell Size (2–50), the Border Thickness (1–20), and the Light Intensity (0–10). The lead between the pieces of "glass" is colored with the Foreground color (see Figure 8-97).

- Texturizer is just what it sounds like—it adds a texture to an image based on the brightness levels in another file. You can choose an option from the Texture pop-up menu, with Brick, Burlap, Canvas, and Sandstone options and the ability to choose your own color or grayscale Photoshop-format file. As with the other filters that offer this ability as part of their effect, you can scale the texture with the Scaling slider (50–200%), adjust the height of the Relief effect from 0–50 pixels, choose one of eight Light Directions at 45-degree angles from one another, and Invert the second image before creating a texture from it (see Figure 8-98).

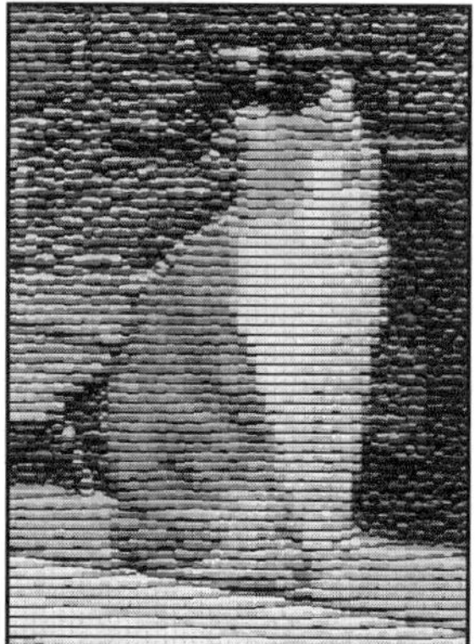
Figure 8-96: Patchwork.

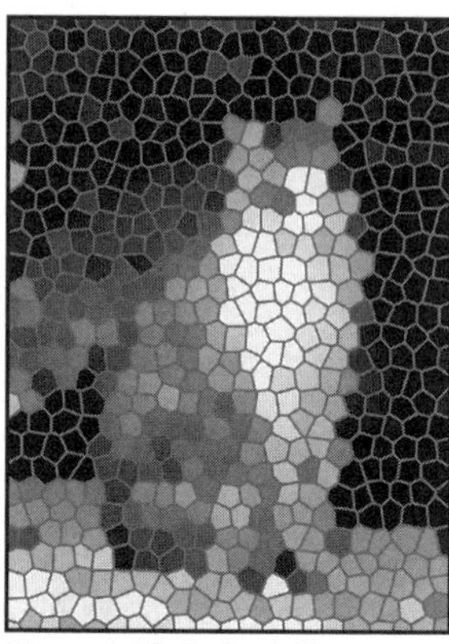
Figure 8-97: Stained Glass.

Figure 8-98: Texturizer.

Video

These filters are generally only useful for images that are destined to be used on television or that were acquired from video:

- De-Interlace removes the horizontal scan lines in a still image captured from video, using duplication or interpolation to replace the missing pixels (see Figure 8-99).
- NTSC Colors converts the colors in an image to their closest equivalents in the palette of colors that work well on TV, as approved by the National Television Standards Committee. For the most part, the colors in this palette are not highly saturated (see Figure 8-100).

Figure 8-99: De-Interlace.

Figure 8-100: NTSC Colors.

Other

These miscellaneous filters are often ignored but very useful once you're aware of what they can do for you:

- Custom allows you to create your own filter effects by punching numbers into a grid representing pixel brightness values. See "Creating Your Own Filters," later in this chapter (see Figure 8-101).
- High Pass emphasizes highlights and removes shading to flatten the colors in an image (see Figure 8-102).
- Maximum shrinks dark areas of an image by lightening their edge pixels. It's intended to be used in creating and editing masks, but it's useful for cleaning up and refining scanned line art (see Figure 8-103).

Figure 8-101: Custom.

Figure 8-102: High Pass.

Figure 8-103: Maximum.

- Minimum shrinks light areas of an image by darkening their edge pixels. Like the Maximum filter, it's intended to be used in creating and editing masks, but it's also useful for cleaning up and refining scanned line art (see Figure 8-104).
- Offset is the key to creating seamless patterns; it quite simply moves pixels in the image a specified distance (see Figure 8-105).

Figure 8-104: Minimum.

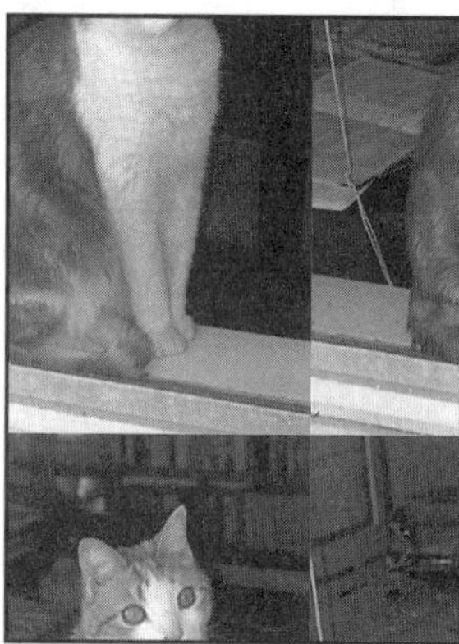

Figure 8-105: Offset.

Digimarc

If you're concerned about copyright issues—and anyone working with electronic images should be concerned about them—you can use the Digimarc filters to read and insert electronic watermarks that identify the creator of an image. The watermarks are in the form of added noise that's too subtle to be seen with the naked eye. Theoretically, however, watermarks are visible to the software even in scanned images.

- Embed Watermark adds a watermark to an image that identifies you as the image's creator via an ID number that you pay Digimarc Corporation to receive. Once you have the ID number, you click Personalize and enter it in the Creator ID field. Then you choose an option for Type of Use: Restricted or Royalty Free, depending on whether you're allowing others to use the image freely or not. Check Adult Content if you want the image to be identified that way to hypothetical future applications that may screen for adult images to keep children from viewing them. Finally, choose a Watermark Durability option (less visible, less durable or more visible, more durable) and click OK to embed the watermark (see Figure 8-106).

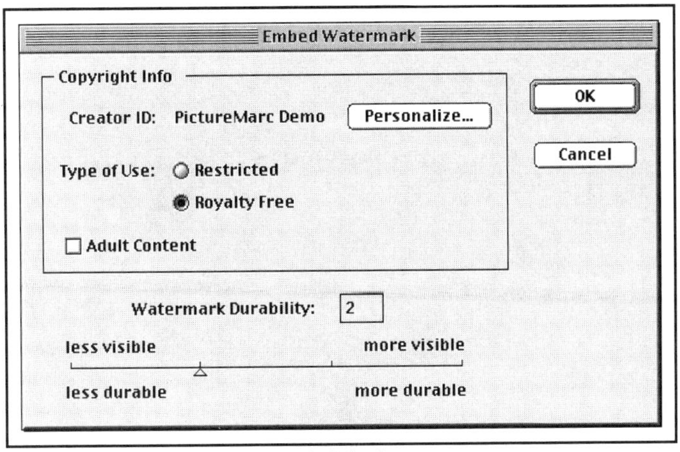

Figure 8-106: The Embed Watermark dialog box.

- Read Watermark checks an image to see if it contains a watermark. If there isn't one, you'll see a dialog box telling you that; if there is one, a dialog displays the creator's name and the use allowed. You can also click a button to go to a Web site that has more information about the image and its creator.

The Best of Third-Party Filters

If filter addiction has taken hold, there are plenty of third-party filters you can buy to satisfy your craving. These three products offer dazzling results with plenty of control, and time has proved their durability and usefulness.

Paint Alchemy

Paint Alchemy (Mac, Xaos Tools, $99) allows you to generate custom "painted" effects or use more than a hundred preset brushing styles. This is an incredibly powerful filter; if you've gone as far as Photoshop's native artistic filters can take you, then you'll want to try creating your own effects with this plug-in. You can change brushstroke color, angle, size, opacity, layering, and density, as well as using grayscale PICT files to define custom brush shapes. Five blending modes are supplied to determine how overlapping brush strokes are colored. Settings can be saved and reloaded. (See Figure 8-107.)

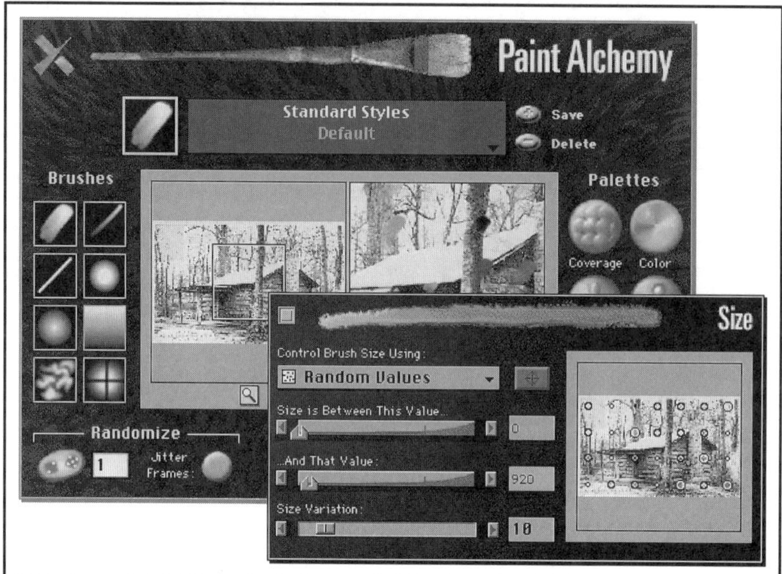

Figure 8-107: Paint Alchemy allows you to adjust every variable of a brush stroke.

A Paint Alchemy demo can be downloaded at Xaos Tools's Web site: www.xaostools.com.

PhotoOptics

CSI PhotoOptics (Mac/Windows, Cytopia Software, $99.95) is a set of eight color manipulation filters based on traditional photographic filters (see Figure 8-108). They include GradTone, HueSlider, Levels, Monochrome, Negative, Noise, PhotoFilter, and PseudoColor. Some of the highlights:

- **Levels** is an expanded version of Photoshop's Levels command with built-in presets to correct common problems in scanned images.
- **Negative** converts scanned negatives to positives more accurately and with more control over highlight, shadow, and exposure than Photoshop's Invert command; the filter automatically deals with the orange color cast of color negative film.
- **PhotoFilter** simulates the effects of photographic gel filters, which apply color casts and affect the image's exposure; presets include settings that mimic standard color correction filters used with cameras.
- **PseudoColor** adds the sort of colors used to represent different temperatures, elevations, or other conditions in scientific images.

A PhotoOptics demo can be downloaded at Cytopia's Web site: www.cytopia.com.

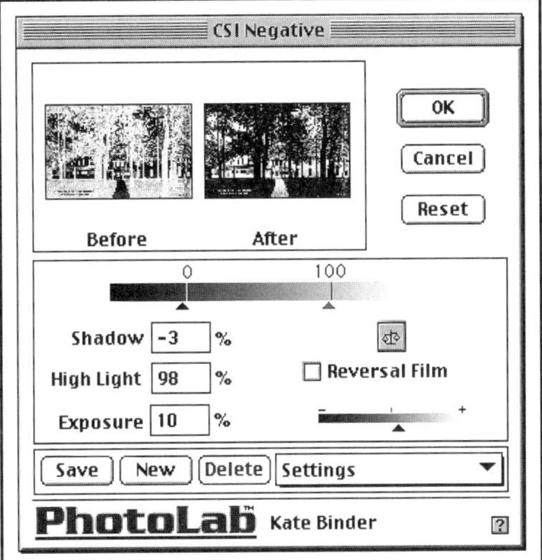

Figure 8-108: The PhotoOptics filters bring specialty darkroom and photo filter effects to Photoshop.

Kai's Power Tools

KPT (Mac/Windows, MetaCreations, $129) is the granddaddy of all Photoshop plug-in sets. (See Figure 8-109.) This group of filters is famous for its unorthodox interface; what with figuring out the interface and exploring the options, you'll spend hours (maybe weeks) playing with all the possibilities. The filters include the following:

- **3D Stereo Noise** capitalizes on the popularity of stereoscopic images, allowing you to create them from grayscale images by adding black and white or color noise.
- **Lens f/x** is a special preview mode that allows you to experiment with several KPT filters: Edge f/x, Gaussian f/x, Intensity f/x, Noise f/x, Pixel f/x, and Smudge f/x.
- **Gradient Designer** allows you to create gradients with as many as 512 colors, 256 different transparency levels, and twelve gradient styles (in addition to the standard Linear and Radial, you get modes like Circular Sunburst and Angular Shapeburst).
- **Page Curl** adds a turned-up page corner the size of the current selection, with controls over angle, paper color, and what's revealed underneath.

A KPT demo can be downloaded at MetaCreations's Web site: www.metacreations.com.

Figure 8-109: Kai's Power Tools is best known for its unusual interface; here, the KPT Lens previews the effects of the filters.

Favorite Filter Tricks

To really explore the possibilities of filters, it's important not to restrict yourself to simply running one filter at a time on the entire image. You can combine multiple filters to increase the possible effects by an order of magnitude, for one thing, and you don't have to stick to filtering the composite channel of an image. Images with multiple layers can be filtered separately on each layer, each channel, and on layer masks. Then, too, you'll get different effects by applying a filter with high settings and applying it multiple times. For example, run Unsharp Mask twice at a low setting rather than once at a setting twice as high for a smoother sharpening effect with fewer artifacts.

Combining Filters

Filters need not stand alone—virtually every cool Photoshop effect you see and admire on the Web, in magazines, or elsewhere is the result of multiple filters, along with a variable degree of tweaking. You can achieve infinite variety in filter effects by combining them in various ways.

- First of all, many organic texture-generating filters require data to chew on before they can produce their results. In this scenario, filters like Add Noise and Clouds provide the base for others—such as Chrome, Crystallize, and Bas Relief—to build upon. Try experimenting with these combinations and others.

- Each filter exaggerates some characteristic of an image; once you've applied one filter, the next will have a different effect because the image's characteristics have changed. Emboss, for example, will have a completely different effect on an image to which Find Edges has been applied than it would on the original image (see Figure 8-110).

Figure 8-110: The right side of this image has been filtered with Find Edges and then Emboss.

- You can also combine filters by duplicating an image on two or more layers, and applying a different filter to each. Use lower layer opacity settings and blending modes such as Hard Light and Color to apply the filtered images to each other in unexpected ways.

Filtering Channels

Ordinarily, a filter operates on the composite channel—a combination of all three or four color channels—moving and adjusting pixels without regard to the color values in the separate channels (one exception is Color Halftone). But that doesn't mean you have to be restricted to working that way—any filter can be applied on a color or alpha channel as well. Some filters can be applied to two or three color channels at once, while others work only with the composite channel or a single color channel active.

TIP *Filters with dialog box previews will display only the active channel or channels in the preview window, so you'll need to use the Preview check box (if it's available) to see the effects of your changes on the composite image.*

Filtering Color Channels

Working in an individual color channel applies the results of the filter only to that color, which means that the results show up in the composite channel in the color of the channel to which the filter is applied. That's one way to create subtle effects that add a bit of color without overwhelming an image. Here are a few ways you might use this technique:

- Add a colored fog that doesn't obscure the image by duplicating one of the color channels and running the Chrome filter on the duplicate. Experiment with each color channel before making your decision, and don't do this operation on the original color channels.
- Examine the color channels and duplicate the one with the most contrast. Add Noise (not too much) to the duplicate, then use it as a Texture Channel for the Lighting Effects filter to get a rather sculptural effect (see Figure 8-111).

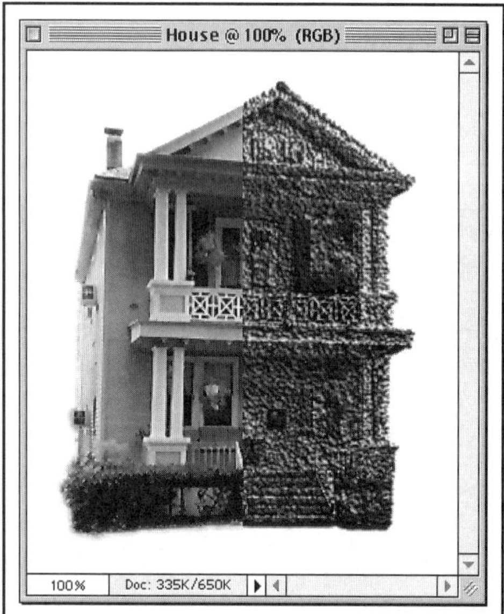

Figure 8-111: Lighting Effects combined with the Add Noise filter on a duplicate of one of the color channels produces the right side of this image.

- Convert a grayscale image to RGB mode and use Texturizer (or any filter, really) on one or more of the color channels. The effects of the filter will show up only in the color of the affected channel.

Filtering Alpha Channels

Alpha channels are any channels that don't contain the color values for the pixels in the image. They're used as selection masks and as bump maps that define the high and low points in a simulated 3D texture. When you're working with filters, you can use a channel to create a selection, then apply the filter to that selection to specify which areas of the image should be filtered, which shouldn't be, and which should be partially filtered. The most fun you can have with channels, though, is to create grayscale textures in them and apply those textures with the Lighting Effects filter.

- Create an instant stone texture by using Add Noise in an alpha channel, then using Lighting Effects with the Omni light type to apply it to an image without affecting the image's colors (see Figure 8-112).

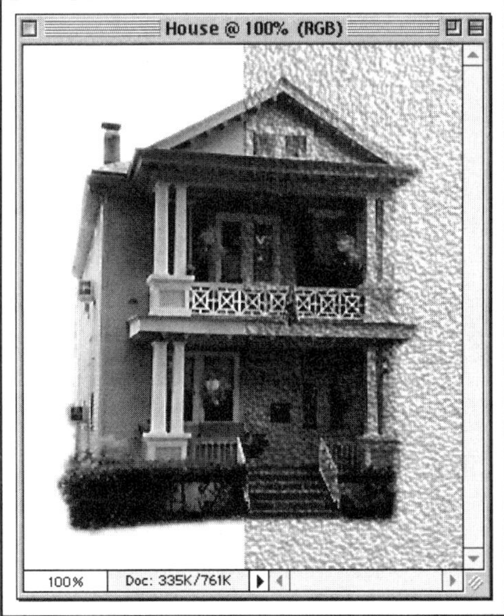

Figure 8-112: A plain stone texture has been applied to the right side of this image.

- Use an alpha channel to give brush strokes a texture—such as crayon or chalk—by creating the texture in a new channel, painting on a transparent layer, then applying the Lighting Effects filter with a fairly low light Intensity setting and the channel as the Texture Channel. Because the rest of the layer is transparent, the texture will be applied only to the brush strokes on it.

Filtering in a Layer Mask

Layer masks are used to mask portions of a layer without deleting them, and like channels, layer masks are grayscale. With that in mind, you can create a mask that hides and reveals parts of a layer based on a pattern or other design created in seconds by a filter.

- Create an oval layer mask and apply Gaussian Blur to feather its edges and create a vignette in the image.
- To apply natural-looking edge effects to an image, create a layer mask with a white area defining the part of the image you want to show, then apply Diffuse or Torn Edges to roughen the edges of the image (see Figure 8-113).

Figure 8-113: Diffusing the edges of the layer mask lends an organic edge effect to the edges of this image.

- Add Noise to a layer mask then place a white layer just below the target layer (or make sure the Background layer is white) to make it "snow" in the image.

Reducing a Moiré Pattern

In a production environment, popular filters are ones like Despeckle and Unsharp Mask that can be used to fix problem images, rather than create new images. Here's a technique for reducing the moiré patterns resulting from scanning printed materials that already have halftone dots:

1. Scan the image at twice the recommended resolution. For print production, you will probably want a final resolution of 266 dpi, so scan the image at 532 dpi.

Web images generally have a resolution of 72 dpi, so use a scanning resolution of 144 dpi.

2. Open the image in Photoshop. If the moiré pattern is concentrated in one area of the image, select that part of the image, then choose Select | Feather and enter a small feathering radius—perhaps 30 pixels for a 532-dpi image and 12 pixels for a 144-dpi image.

TIP *Watch out for regular patterns like speaker grilles and roof shingles—these can cause moiré patterns even when you're not scanning previously printed materials. Try scanning at different angles to reduce moiré as much as possible.*

3. Choose Filter | Blur | Gaussian Blur. Make sure the Preview box is checked, then adjust the Radius slider so that the moiré pattern is less apparent. Depending on the intensity of the moiré, you may not be able to completely eliminate it without also eliminating all detail in the image.
4. Choose Image | Image Size and resample the image to your desired resolution.
5. Choose Filter | Sharpen | Unsharp Mask. Make sure the Preview box is checked, then adjust the Amount, Radius, and Threshold sliders to restore the sharpness of the image.

Creating Your Own Filters

For those with a *really* creative bent, there are two ways to create your own filter effects—both of them included with Photoshop. The Custom Filter sets up a grid of pixels and allows you to hack away at their brightness levels simply by entering numbers in its dialog box, while the Filter Factory is designed to let you create true plug-in filters that can be used and distributed on their own.

Custom Filter

The Custom Filter lets you take a crack at the math behind Photoshop filters and create your own effects by plugging in different numbers. The center box in the grid represents an individual pixel, and the number you enter there (from –999 to 999) will be multiplied by the brightness value of that pixel to arrive at a new brightness value (see Figure 8-114). At the same time, you can act on the eight pixels adjacent to the main pixel, and the pixels adjacent to them, by entering values in their corresponding boxes. The intensity of the effect is controlled by the Scale field, where you enter a value to divide the results of these calculations by, and the Offset field, where you enter a value that's added to each result.

It sounds pretty complicated, but the only way to learn the Custom filter is to use it. If you come up with an effect you like, you can click Save to save a copy of it in a separate file, then click Load to reload it at any time.

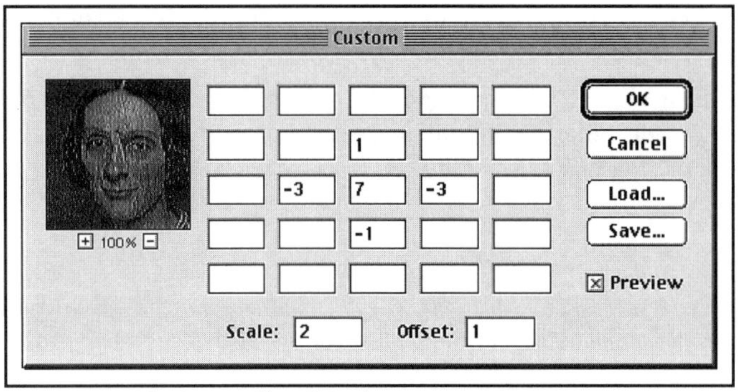

Figure 8-114: The Custom filter dialog box.

Filter Factory

If you're really serious about creating your own filters, take a look at the Filter Factory, which is included on the CD-ROM version of Photoshop. With this plug-in and its included documentation (an Acrobat PDF file), you can create and distribute your own filters. You'll need to brush up on your high school algebra, though: the filters work by performing mathematical operations on the position and brightness value of each pixel in each color channel of an image (see Figure 8-115).

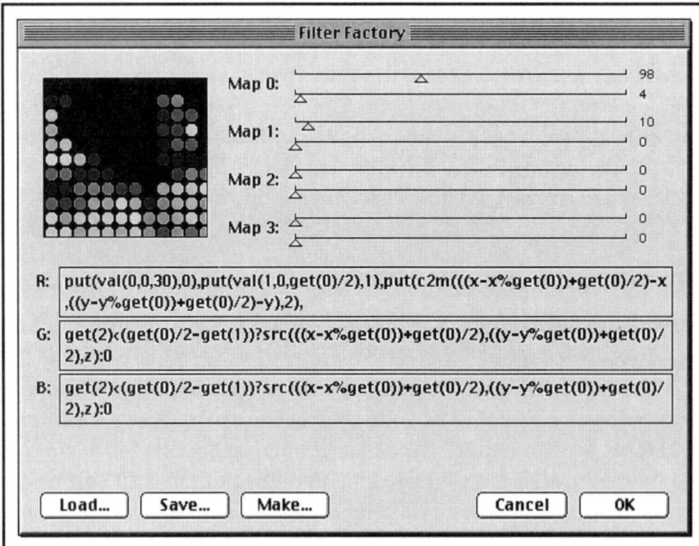

Figure 8-115: The mathematical expressions used in Filter Factory can be this complex, or as simple as "r+1," which makes the red component of each pixel one level brighter.

Fortunately, the Filter Factory documentation includes a couple of tutorials that guide you through the process of creating a filter, giving it a user interface, and turning it into a plug-in file that you can hand out to friends or customers. The final result can include sliders and a logo, just like a commercial filter (see Figure 8-116).

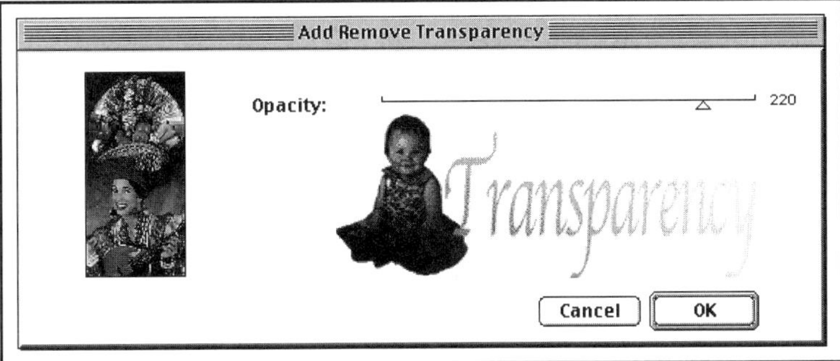

Figure 8-116: The Add Remove Transparency filter that is included with Filter Factory as an example.

Managing Filters

As you use and accumulate more filters, you may find that you need ways to keep track of which ones you're using at any given time. The more filters you have, the more cluttered your Filters menu gets and the harder it is to find the ones you need. If you're in a real jam and need to trim every second during a production session, you may even want to uninstall all filters but the specific ones you'll be using during that session.

One way to bring some order to your Filters menu is to reorganize the third-party filters that appear in submenus below the native filters. These filter submenus are labeled according to the names of the folders that contain the filters, so you can give the folders names that make more sense to you and reorder them by adding spaces at the beginning of folder names. Adobe allows you to have up to 22 of these custom folders; after that point, all your other filters appear under an Other submenu.

To easily install and uninstall filters and other plug-ins, you can make use of a utility from Cytopia Software, makers of the PhotoOptics filter set (see "Best of the Third-Party Filters," earlier in this chapter), who also produce a Plug-In Manager for Mac users of Photoshop. Like the Extensions Manager, it allows you to create groups of plug-ins that will be activated the next time Photoshop is opened (see Figure 8-117). A demo can be downloaded at Cytopia's Web site: www.cytopia.com.

If you're the type who just has to know everything there is to know about the software you use, there's more info available on each filter installed with your copy of Photoshop. To see a filter's creator and copyright information, choose (Apple menu | About Plug-In)[Help | About Plug-In], then choose a plug-in from the submenu. This displays a splash screen with the legalities and sometimes some additional info (see Figure 8-118).

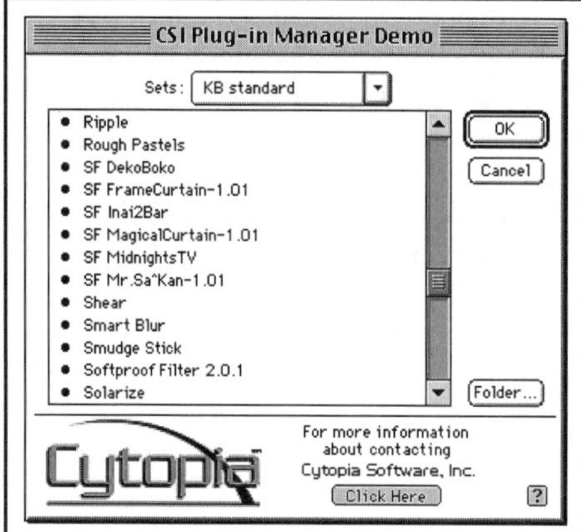

Figure 8-117: The Plug-In Manager works just like the Mac's Extensions Manager.

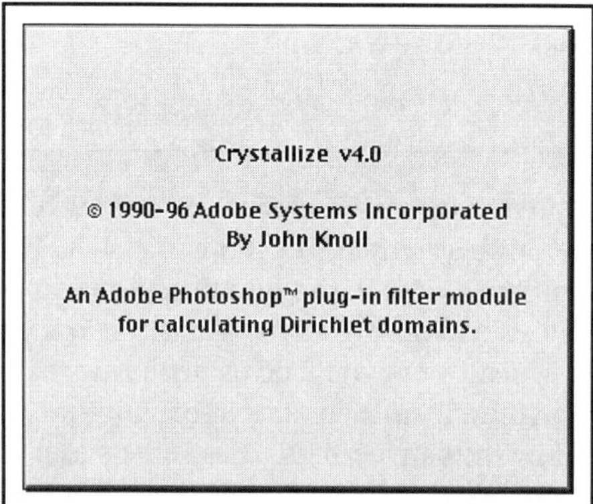

Figure 8-118: This splash screen for the Crystallize filter reveals the mathematical concept on which the filter's operation is based: Dirichlet domains.

Moving On

Filters can help you make the most of your images. In this chapter we've looked at some of the ways to put Photoshop's filters to work.

In Chapter 9, "Photoshop Prepress," we'll discuss ways to use Photoshop to prepare images for printing.

chapter 9
Photoshop Prepress

The digital revolution in prepress lives within the recent memory of many in the printing industry. Yet many who make their living with a computer substituting for mechanicals now take electronic tools in stride. Prepress professionals can now achieve printed results that would have been considered miraculous only 12 years ago.

There has been a price to be paid for this amazing technology. It is not an obvious cost, nor is it obvious that in many cases the burden of performance has transferred from printing experts to non-professionals. To illustrate this point, consider the personnel in a printing plant as few as 12 years ago. The printer's graphics/make-ready department consisted of people who did several jobs. A designer worked out page design, laying down roughs on tissues and art boards. A typesetter input text—often employing an elaborate code for text attributes such as italic, bold, tabs, size changes, typeface changes—which was output on photographic paper in long, thin strips. A keyliner waxed the back of those strips and pasted them into position on an artboard. Another technician worked with Rapidograph pens, pressure sensitive screen overlays, point tape, and markers to construct artwork. A camera man turned the artwork into hard copy which could be given to the keyliner to incorporate into the text on the artboard. The final artboard would be given to a stripper who would make a line-shot of the artboard, turn any photo material into halftones, strip the photos into the negative of the artboard. The stripper might also use a camera and gel filters to make a color separation. The films for these would also need to be stripped into the artboard negative. Out-of-house commercial separation films would also need to be incorporated into the negatives. The stripper would then shoot a blueline of the composite negative for the customer to approve. Finally, the negative would go to a platemaker. The plate would be given to the pressman, and the print job would be underway.

Designer, keyliner, typesetter, stripper, camera operator, plate maker, out-of-house separator—all of these were considered highly specialized skills for which years of training were required. In the space of a few years, all but a few of these professions have vanished, replaced by the new digital technology. Unfortunately, the professionals of the older techniques did not always migrate to the new technology to become the professionals of the digital age. Relatively unprepared people became the new professionals, often without the benefit of training, experience, or knowledge. Graphics computer operators were expected to embody what had been the specialized knowledge of five or six people. Small and large business managers often put an advanced graphics computer, a desktop scanner, and a laser printer on the desk of an employee whose prior experience with computers had been with business programs: "We'll let Joe be our new DTP guy—he's a whiz with Excel. Then, we'll save a fortune in printing costs!"

The scenario that put Joe into the position of floundering his way through a vast technical maze (not only did Joe have to become a print expert, he also had to become a computer guy) has become a little less frequent. But it is still more the rule than the exception. New users of graphics computers are often confronted with technical problems for which they have no background. The preparation of photographic images is one of the most difficult of these tasks. Halftones, spot color, duotones, line art, color separations—all of these have become increasingly important in the print world. All of them require special knowledge of output devices, press conditions, and the sophisticated controls which Photoshop places in your hands.

The material covered in this chapter does not focus on specific techniques and recipes. Rather, it is intended to give you a broad, general knowledge of how output devices and press conditions will affect your digital files and what you can do to ensure that the press reproduces your work as perfectly as possible. Photoshop contains virtually everything you require to process a photographic scan and to reproduce it as a good-looking image on press. The amount of material you'll be encountering may seem overwhelming, but simply work your way through, step by step, and you'll find that all of it is logical and understandable.

Getting Good Grays

Photoshop users call a black monotone image *grayscale*. Printers call the same image a *halftone*. Knowledgeable people understand that one—the halftone—is simply the output version of the other. The grayscale image, printed by a PostScript device, has its grays values converted to absolute black and white. Tiny dots of ink of various sizes blend together in our eyes to give the illusion of gray tones. The conversion of grays to black and white dots is the fundamental process by which photographic images are reproduced on a press. The range of tonal values contained in the grayscale file as it is downloaded to the output device are the vital pieces of data which can make or break the reproduction. But the process is not really straightforward, as you'll see in the following section of this chapter.

What You See on Screen is *Not* What You Get on Press

Preparing halftones for printing on an offset press is a job that is more difficult than nearly any other. Color separations, by comparison, are extremely easy. When you have an image that is to be reproduced with a single opaque ink, you have only one chance to get it right. If the preparation of the image in Photoshop isn't correct, no amount of fussing by the pressman will correct it. It's an all or nothing situation and a job whose difficulty is often underestimated.

You can be very good at adjusting your grayscale images so that they look sharp and clear on the monitor, and still get socked with dark and muddy halftones when your job goes on press. The simple truth is that when you are adjusting grayscale images for press reproduction, your screen does not display the consequences of some of the physical problems you'll encounter—dot gain, highlight dot fall-off, maximum blacks, are just a few (all of these will be discussed below). Because of this, your adjustments need to be made always keeping a simple rule in mind: if the image looks good onscreen, it will look awful on press. There is an inverse version of this rule: if the halftone is going to look good on press, it will look flat, washed out, and pretty uninspiring on screen.

There are two very important pieces of information you need before you can attempt to get a good halftone on press. The first is the amount of *dot gain* produced by the press when printing on the paper you'll be using for the job. The second is the minimum dot percentage for the highlights in your halftones.

Dot Gain

Dot gain is the natural result of using liquid ink and applying it to a porous surface such as paper. The dots on the printing plate transfer the ink to the offset blanket which in turn imprints the paper. The ink stays mostly on the surface of the paper, but some amount of it is pressed into the paper where it is absorbed and spreads slightly. Consequently, the percentage values of the dots increase as the diameter of the dots on the printed sheet increase. The amount of increase is usually expressed as a percentage which describes the amount of growth. The percentage is derived from the difference between a set of known plate or film values and the amount of ink coverage on the press sheet. The amount of gain will vary with the type of paper used, the press, the amount of humidity in the air, and—sometimes—whether the pressman is in a good mood.

Dot gain is not a fixed number for all sizes of dots. Very small dots usually have very little gain. The gain percentage increases as the size of the dot increases until the dot size reaches 50%. Above 50%, the dots begin to grow together and the gain number levels off and begins to decrease. Because of this, dot gain is expressed as the percentage of dot growth at 50%, the maximum figure. Press sheets nearly always have, outside the live print area, a small area imprinted by what are known to be 50% dots. The press man uses a device called a *densitometer* to measure the ink coverage within this area. If the coverage is, say, 66% of the total area, then the gain is known to be 16% (66%–50%=16%).

A 16% gain does not sound very extreme, but a glance at Figure 9-1 shows the difference between the dots as they would be on the plate (left-hand side) and the way the dots would actually print (right-hand side). While 16% dot gain is not an uncommon figure, there is a range of possible values: gain percentages can be as low as 9% or 10% and as high as 50%. Really. Your printer should be able to give you an exact number for dot gain. Be a bit careful of the number you're given; it is astonishing how often a print salesperson, misunderstanding the offset process, will shade the number low in the mistaken belief that a high gain percentage is a reflection of a print house's incompetence. It is nothing of the sort. If you are given a number that is, say, 5% or 7%, you would be well advised to speak directly to a press room representative. In all likelihood, you will find that the true number will be somewhere between 14% and 33%. No matter how large or small the gain figure, the important point is that you *must* have an accurate idea what the number is. Without it, the success of your halftone is just a matter of luck.

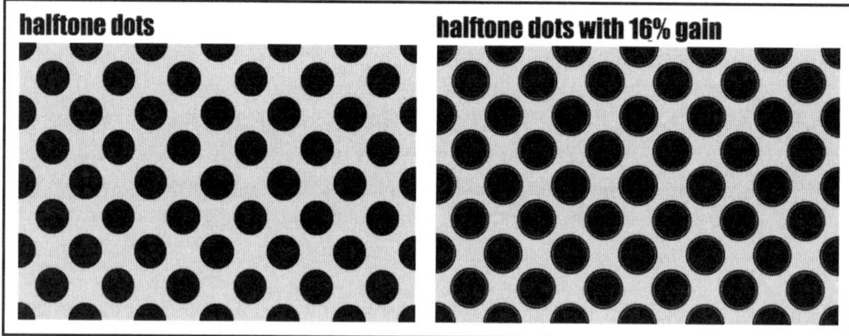

Figure 9-1: The two sides of this figure illustrate how dot gain increases the size of the halftone dots.

Why is dot gain important? Imagine that you have carefully adjusted your image and that it looks on screen much the way the upper left-hand image in Figure 9-2 appears. You are satisfied with the appearance of the photo and, if you are working with a client, the client has also expressed approval. Your job goes to press and you are startled—possibly chagrined—to see your work become much darker (upper right-hand corner, Figure 9-2). The difference between these two images is a 16% gain in the midtones, or more accurately, at 50% (the actual dots of the enclosed rectangular areas are shown magnified below each example). In some cases, you'll be able to live with the change (the examples in the figure are probably acceptable—barely). In other cases, the reproduction of the image will be so darkened that it will be unacceptable and the consequences expensive and embarrassing.

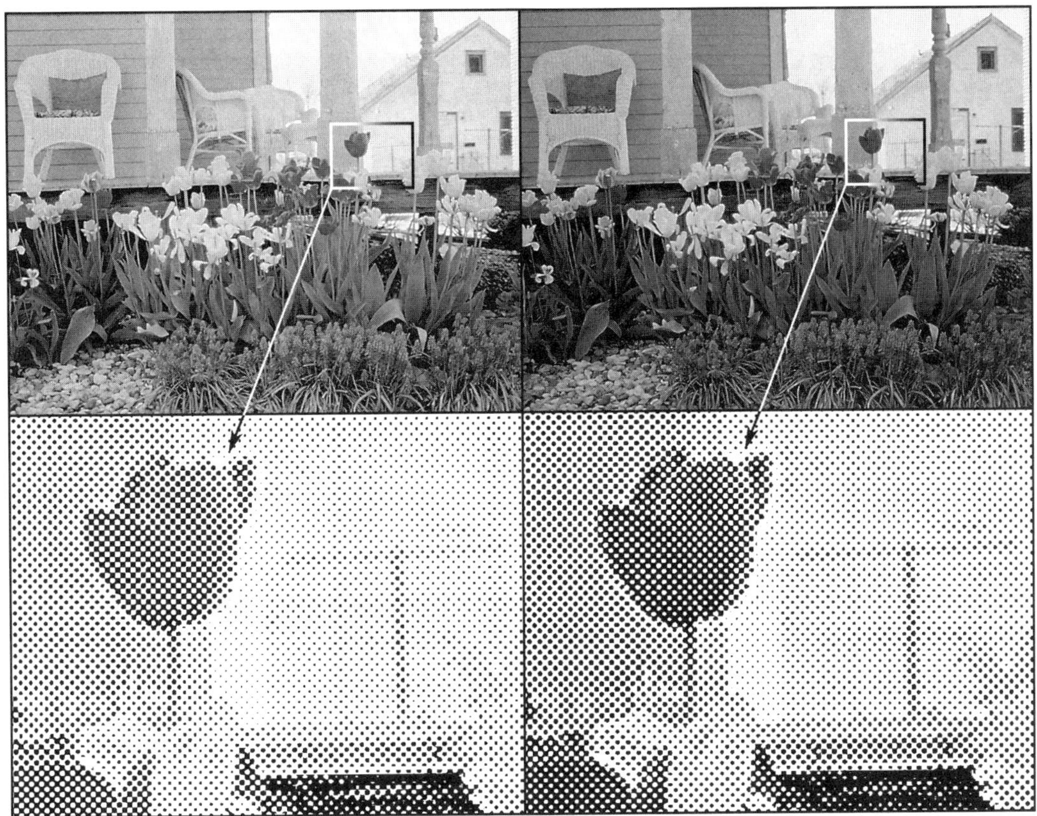

Figure 9-2: The figure on the right (with its enlarged detail) shows the significant darkening of the image due to dot gain.

Assuming that we are still discussing a gain figure of 16%, does it seem logical that if you intend to end up with, say, a 50% value on press, then the value in Photoshop (and on the film and plate) has to be about 14%–16% less than 50%? If you see the logic to this, then you understand the mechanics behind the distressing rule cited at the beginning of this chapter: if the halftone is going to look good on press, it will look flat, washed out, and pretty uninspiring on screen. You will learn, in this chapter, how to compensate for the difference in *input* values and *output* values shown in Figure 9-3 so that your image's values before output fall along the lower curve. The lower curve is almost a mirror image of the dot gain curve (upper line) in the figure.

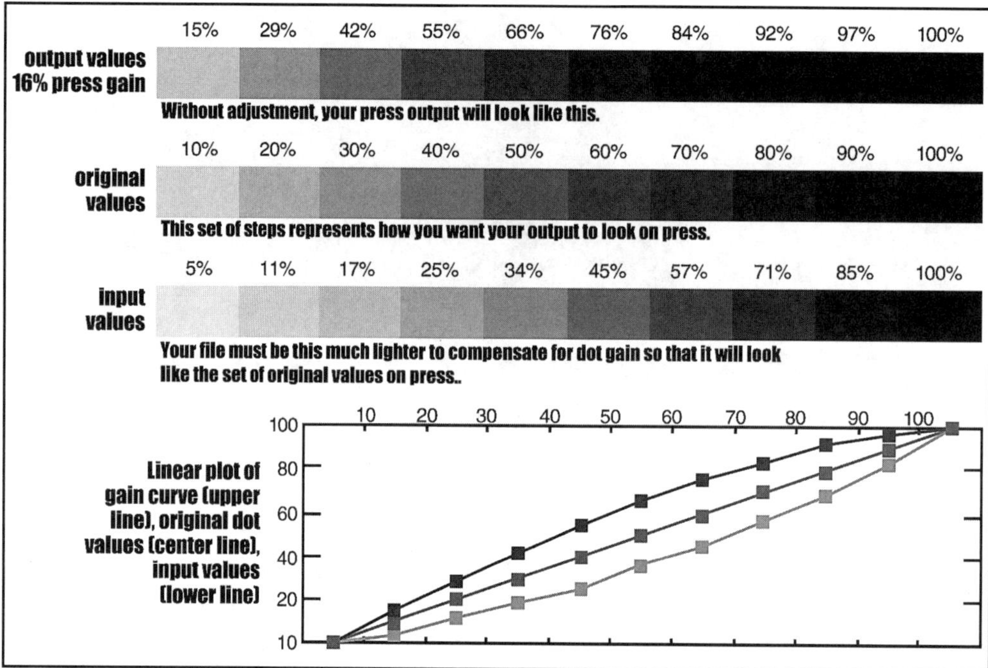

Figure 9-3: A comparison of tone values: the original values are what you wish to have for press output. The input values—given a 16% dot gain—must be lighter than the original values. Otherwise, the original values darken as shown on the top scale.

Minimum Highlight Dot

We are accustomed to discussing lithography dots as percentages; 11%, 24%, 75%, and so on. However, integer percentages relating to tone values are impossible to achieve in PostScript for all values other than 25%, 50%, 75%, and 100%. (Note: PostScript dots are constructed within a square grid containing 16 small squares on a side. Each dot is composed of smaller raster spots which build up to form the larger screen dots. There are 256—16 x 16—squares in the grid. Only the four listed percentages of 256 are integer values.) In slightly less math-oriented terms, you can't really have a 4% dot in PostScript, but a dot that is just a little smaller than 4%. Almost all of the PostScript dots work that way: some are a little smaller than the percentage, some a little larger. The flip side of the coin is that PostScript is not limited to a mere 100 values but to 256 values. That means that you can actually have a dot that is expressed as an integer plus a fraction.

Having a wide range of tonal values seems, at first glance, to be a very desirable thing. It would be if that range of values could actually be reproduced on a press. The sad fact is that it cannot. Dot gain (see above) is one example of a physical phenomenon that limits the possible tonal range. Compensating for gain deliberately sacrifices some values for the sake of being able to clearly reproduce the most detail-laden and visible part of the tonal range.

There's another, subtler limiter of values, values on the highlight end of the scale. Because of the way the offset process works, very small dots simply do not print. The dots are present on the film and on the plate. The ink simply does not adhere to the plate dot and so leaves low-value highlight areas without any ink. Areas such as these are said to be burned out. When an image has been adjusted so that the smallest printable dot is the lightest non-specular value, the image is said to hold a minimum highlight dot of some specified percentage. In Figure 9-4, a pair of examples show the results of an effective adjustment (left-hand side) and an adjustment where some of the highlight areas are devoid of ink.

Figure 9-4: The right-hand image contains values which will not hold on press. After adjusting (left), no highlight values are blown out.

The specified percentage is a variable which can range from 2%–7%. The exact value for the job you have at hand will need to be obtained from your print house. If you are unsure how to word the request for this piece of information, phrase it this way: "What size dot do I need to carry in my highlights?" You will learn in this chapter how to make effective adjustments so that your highlight dots do not disappear on press.

Processing a Grayscale Image

From a technical standpoint, the best place to begin the preparation of a halftone is with an RGB color file. Even if the original material is in the form of a black and white print, scan the material as RGB. With the color scan, you'll be able, if it proves necessary, to make very drastic adjustments based on 24 bits of information per pixel—as opposed to 8 bits—and still have a very good image when you're finished.

The procedure which follows will seem, at first, to be composed of a great many steps. Even though there are a number of operations to be performed, you'll find that they go quickly: it should be possible to make all the required adjustments in under two minutes. Once you have used this method on a few images and have seen how well it works, you'll probably want to do all of your images this way. Try to be aware of the nuances of the steps. You'll find that this same procedure, performed in slightly different ways, allows you to manipulate grayscale, color, and scans intended for line art. There are faster ways of doing this job (and some steps that can be eliminated once you gain some experience). Let's look at several quick halftone adjustment procedures. The following set of instructions takes you through each step so that you can see how the process works. Notice that this set of steps is aimed at a press condition of 16% dot gain and 5% minimum highlight dot.

1. First, choose File | Color Settings | Printing Inks Setup. We will be looking at this dialog box more thoroughly later in this chapter. For the moment, enter your Dot Gain figure—16%—into the data entry field. At the bottom of the window is a check box, Use Dot Gain for grayscale Images, which needs to be turned off (unchecked). When you are finished, click OK.

2. Open the RGB scan which is to be made into a halftone. If you wish to follow along, open the file RGB2GS1.PSD in the Chapter 9 Practice folder on the Companion CD-ROM. It is the same image used in the following examples. Press Command+0 (zero) or Ctrl+0 to fit the image in the computer screen (Figure 9-5). Place the Layers Palette and the Info Palette where they are convenient to see and to use. Click on the left-hand triangular pop-up on the Info palette and change the displayed readings to grayscale.

3. Choose Image | Adjust | Levels, or press Command+l or Ctrl+l. Position the Levels controls so that you can see the lightest and the darkest parts of the scan. If the Preview box is checked, click on it to turn it off. The pop-up menu at the very top of the dialog box reads RGB. Change it so that it reads Red. Hold the Option key or the Alt key. Move your cursor to the right-hand upper slider—the Input area highlight slider—and begin to move the slider triangle to the left. The dramatic change in the screen display is called Threshold mode. The screen will go black. As you move the slider, the highlight pixels in the Red channel begin to show up as red against black. Move the slider so that you have small red areas showing, but try to leave some dark pixels within each of the light areas. Release the mouse button. Using Threshold mode allows you to precisely locate the highlight and shadow pixels within an image, and to force them to be lighter or darker. It is a very useful tool when you do not have a lot of experience. The appearance of the screen while moving the slider is shown in Figure 9-6.

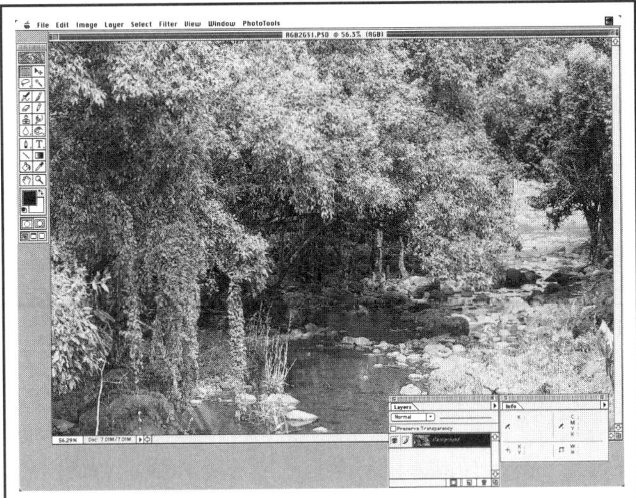

Figure 9-5: Open the RGB image and place the Layers and Info palettes where they can be easily seen.

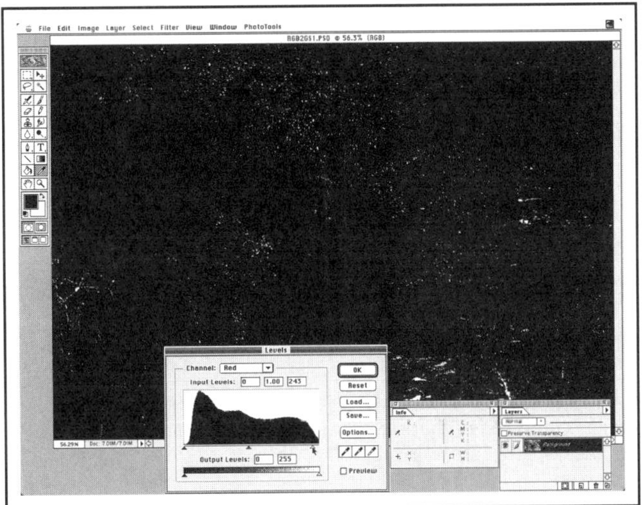

Figure 9-6: Move the Red channel highlight slider with Option or Alt held down.

NOTE

If you are using Photoshop for Windows, the Threshold effect from within the Levels dialog may not function. Some Windows video interface boards do not support it. In some cases, it works only when the number of displayed colors is set to 256. If you find that this method does not work for you, please see the Tip for using Threshold in Windows following the section on the Unsharp Mask filter.

4. Continue holding the Option key or the Alt key. Move the left-hand upper slider—the Input area shadow slider—and begin to move the small triangle to the right. Your screen will go red and, as you move the slider, the darkest pixels of the red channel begin to show up as black against the red. Move the slider until just a hint of shadow pixels are visible (Figure 9-7). Be careful not to move this slider too far. It is easy to add ink on press but very hard to eliminate ink in areas that are too dark. Moving the slider too far darkens the shadow areas of the image so much that they lose all their detail and become impossible to control when printed. If the image is dark in overall tone, it may be that you won't be able to move the slider at all. Try to maintain a few red pixels within the dark-pixel areas. Release the mouse button.

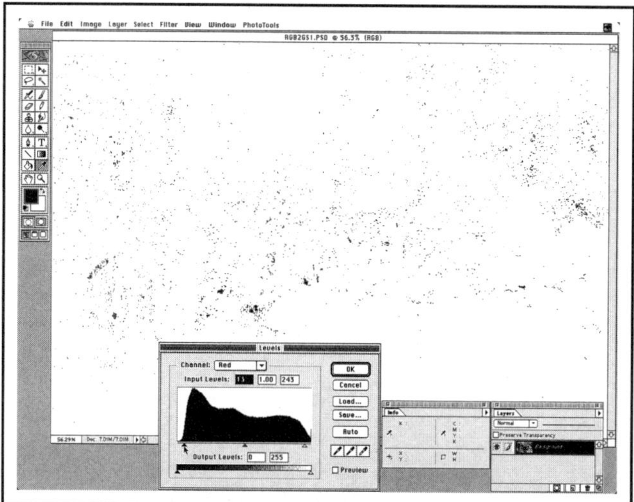

Figure 9-7: Move the Red channel shadow slider while holding Option or Alt.

5. Change the pop-up menu so that it reads Green. Perform exactly the same operations as on the Red channel, remembering to hold the Option or the Alt keys (Figures 9-8 and 9-9).

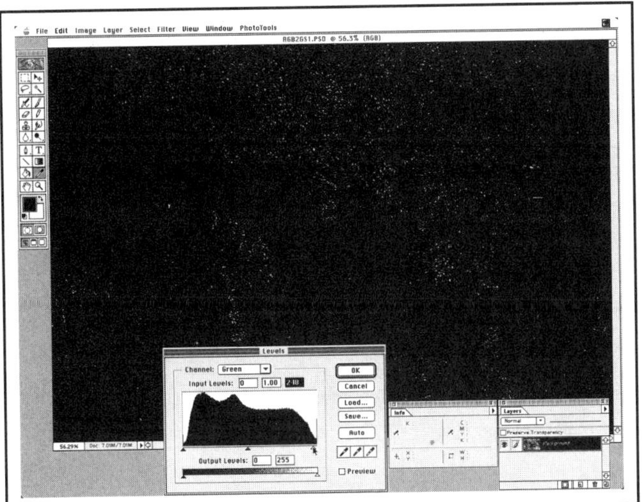

Figure 9-8: Move the Green channel highlight slider while holding Option or Alt.

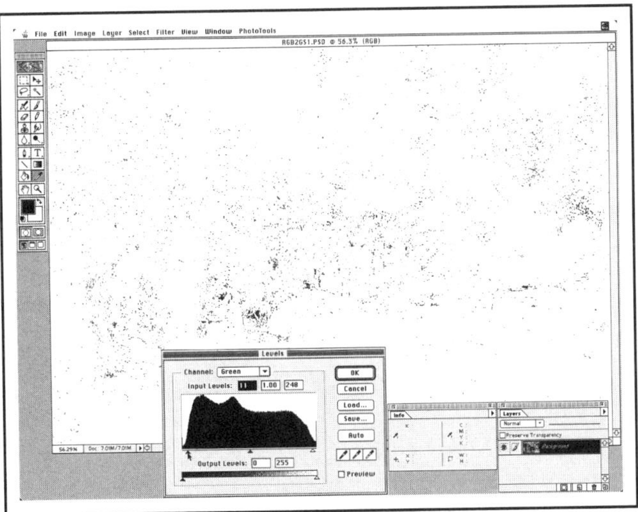

Figure 9-9: Move the Green channel shadow slider while holding Option or Alt.

6. Change the pop-up menu so that it reads Blue. Perform exactly the same operations as on the Red and Green channels (Figures 9-10 and 9-11).

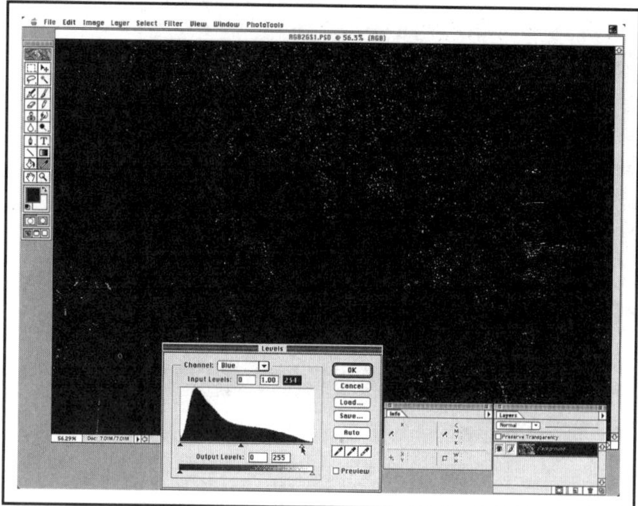

Figure 9-10: Move the Blue channel highlight slider while holding Option or Alt.

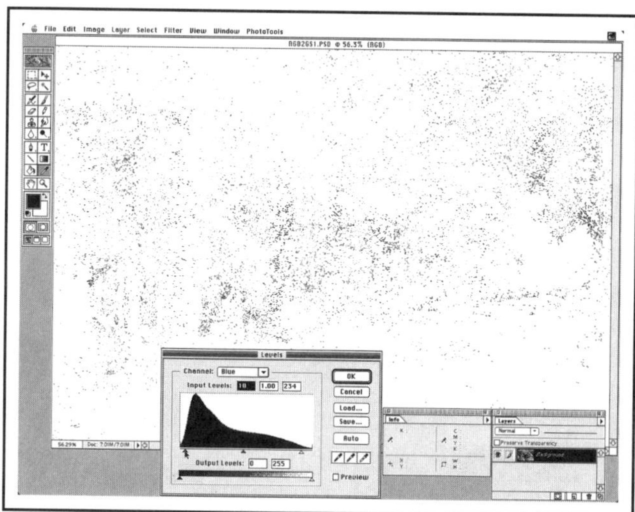

Figure 9-11: Move the Blue channel shadow slider while holding Option or Alt.

7. Return the pop-up menu to its original heading (RGB). From this point, there is no longer any need to hold the Option or Alt keys. Move the cursor to the center slider on the input scale and move the slider to the left. Move it so that the center numerical readout above is about 1.25 (Figure 9-12). For very dark images, the slider can be moved until it reads about 1.30–1.50. Try not to move this slider

very much more than that. Too much movement causes the three-quarter-tone values to become grainy. This happens because moving the left-hand slider and the center slider too close together leaves too few values to give a continuous range of tones from 50% to 100%.

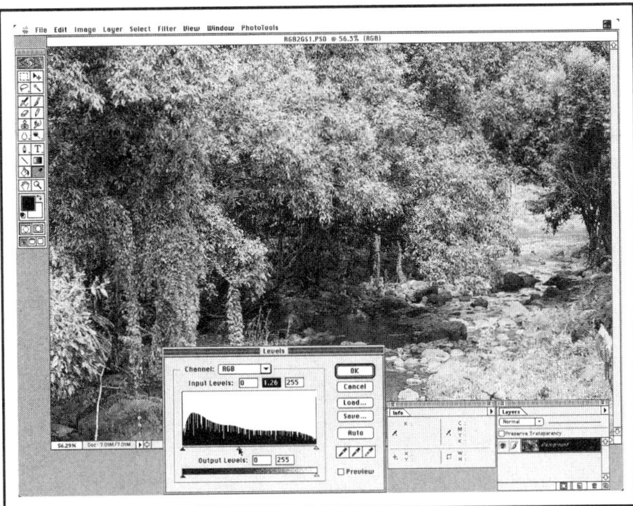

Figure 9-12: Move the RGB composite midtone slider to the left.

8. Move your cursor out into the window where it becomes an Eyedropper cursor. Locate the lightest values you can find in the window (Figure 9-13). From the Info palette, you can see that those values are probably 0%. Now, move the right-hand slider on the bottom—Output—scale to the left. Move it just a little way and then return to the highlight area. You'll see two numbers separated by a slash on the Info palette. The number on the left is the original value of the pixel. The number on the right is the new value, the result of moving the sliders. Go back and forth. Move the slider a little and check the reading. Stop moving the slider when you have reached the minimum dot you need to carry in the highlights (in this case 5%). Move the slider as far as you need to but not any farther than necessary.
9. Move your cursor out into the window and locate the darkest pixels you can find. These values will probably range between 96% and 100% as shown on the Info palette. Move the left-hand slider on the Output scale to the right. Move it just a little way and return to the dark pixels in the window. Stop moving the slider when you have taken the darkest values and lightened them so that their new value is a maximum of 90%–93% (Figure 9-14). If you glance again at the linear gain plot in Figure 9-3, you can see that the gain at 90% is 7%. Because of this, there is really no point in having many values in the image darker than 90%–93% because all values darker than these will print as solid, or nearly solid,

black. By adjusting the shadow on the Output scale, you ensure that only the darkest values print as solid while lighter shadow values do not reach total ink coverage. Note that this shadow percentage may be somewhat higher. Most printers suggest a maximum ink value of 95% because 2%– 5% lower makes the image a little more open without harming the overall contrast. If you prefer more overall contrast, use the 95% figure.

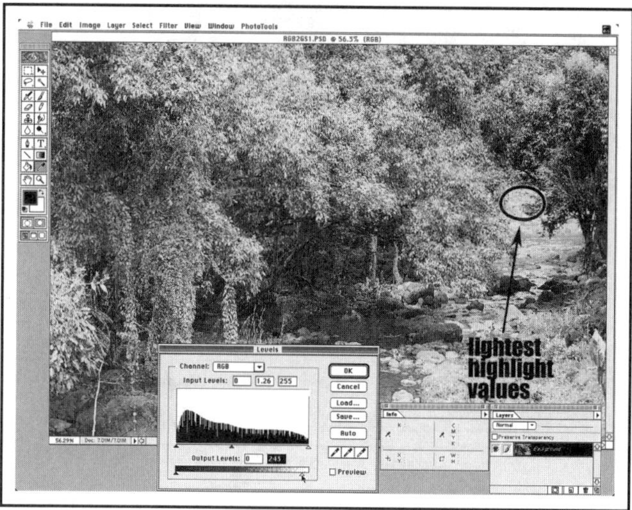

Figure 9-13: Locate the lightest values in the image. Move the Output scale highlight slider to darken them to about 5%.

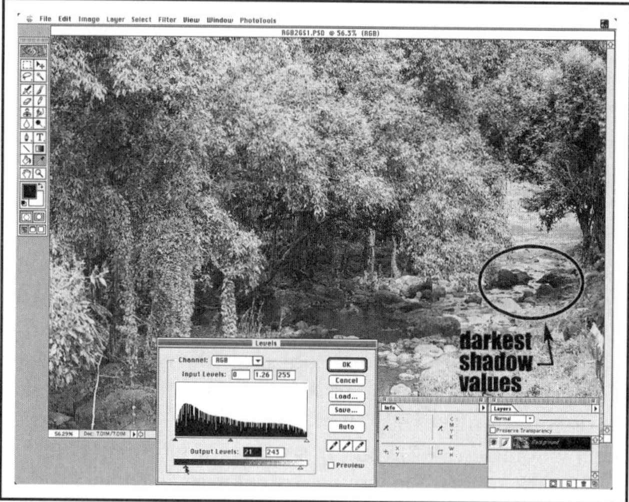

Figure 9-14: Locate the darkest values in the image. Move the Output scale shadow slider to lighten them to about 93%.

10. Click on the Save button in the Levels dialog. Name this Levels configuration file in such a way that it is obvious that it belongs to the image you are adjusting, and save it in a place where it can be easily retrieved.

11. Now, click on the Levels Cancel button. Yes, really. You're going to use the settings you've just saved with an adjustment layer. It would be wonderful if you could simply add an adjustment layer and move the sliders while the layer is selected. However, the Threshold mode method does not work on adjustment layers, and you are forced to use this workaround.

12. Command+click or Ctrl+click the New Layer icon at the bottom of the Layers palette. A small dialog box appears (Figure 9-15). From the center pop-up menu, choose the adjustment layer type: in this case, choose Levels. Click on the OK button. The Levels controls now appear. Click on the Load button and find the settings file you've just saved. When you load it, click the OK button. You now have your previous settings applied to an adjustment layer. This allows you, if you need to, to go back and do more adjustments to the image without going through the entire process again, and without applying a new set of adjustments to an image that has already been modified.

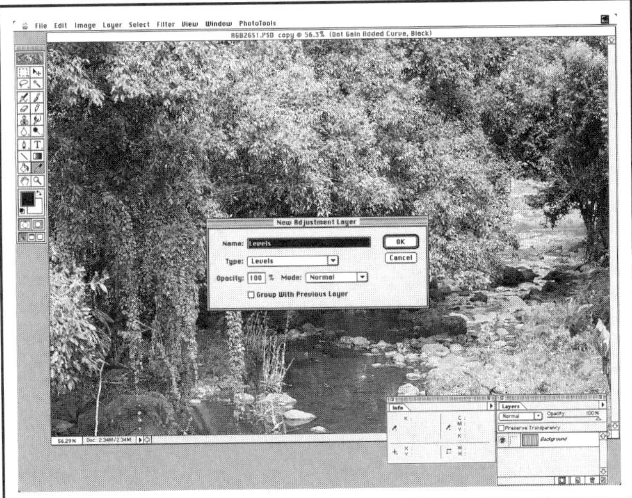

Figure 9-15: Make a Levels adjustment layer.

13. From the Image menu, choose the Duplicate command (Figure 9-16). Click OK. From this point, you are working on the copy of the image. Some of the previous adjustments may need to be further modified. By working on the copy, you are able to go back to the original version of your work—discarding the copy—and then generating a new duplicate. (Duplicating your document at critical stages and continuing to work on a copy is a good way to avoid having to go back to the beginning of a job if you find that you end up with a result that is not to your liking.)

Figure 9-16: Duplicate the image. Save the first image so that it can be used later if required. Continue working on the duplicate.

14. Flatten this image. It is now ready to be converted to Grayscale mode. This is done in two steps. First, under the Image menu choose Mode | Lab Color. Press Command+1 or Ctrl+1 to view the L channel which holds the brightness—or *Lightness*—values of the image (the other two, a and b contain the color). The Lightness values are what we want for the halftone. With this channel in view, choose Image | Mode | Grayscale. A dialog box appears asking if you wish to discard the other channels. Click OK. What you see is your new and nearly ready-for-use grayscale image. The image could have been changed to grayscale directly from the RGB mode. However, a more satisfactory conversion is made via the Lab mode. With this method, the image is lighter and more open: both are desirable qualities in view of the way dot gain eventually darkens the photo when it is printed.
15. The next step is to add a couple of adjustment layers. Use one to make some final adjustments and the other to simulate dot gain while making those adjustments. Command+click or Ctrl+click the New Layer icon on the Layers palette. Set the adjustment layer type to Curves. Click OK on the Curves dialog box without making any changes. Click on the Background layer to select it. Now, add another adjustment layer. Set the layer type to be Levels. Click OK on the Levels dialog box without making any changes.

16. Double-click on the word Curves on the Curves adjustment layer. The Curves dialog box opens and is shown in Figure 9-17a. The central part of this window is composed of the curve grid. Below the curve is a small rectangle containing what looks like a gradient interrupted by a pair of arrows. If this area on your screen does not have the light end of the gradient on the left, click on one of those small arrows and it changes. For this example, you want your curve window to look exactly like the figure.

17. The curve grid contains a diagonal line (this line is the *curve* even though it isn't very curved yet). Imagine, if you will, that the line is divided into a hundred small segments. The lower left end of the line represents 0%; the place where, as the line moves to the upper right, the curve meets the first two crossing lines represents the 25% value, and so on. If you wish, the grid can be changed so that the crossing lines are ruled in increments of 10% instead of 25%: Option+click or Alt+click within the grid area (Figure 9-17b).

18. Place your cursor in the grid area and notice that you now have continuous readings of Input & Output below the grid. Keep your eye on those readings while you make the adjustment. Click on the intersection of the curve and the 50% lines. Drag the line upward until the Input/Output figures read 50% and 66% (Figure 9-17c). Click OK. A representation of the Curve adjustment is shown in Figure 9-18.

    Are you surprised? Your image is suddenly much darker. Even though this isn't an absolutely accurate way to duplicate all aspects of dot gain, it is sufficient to give you an idea of how much more the image needs to be adjusted if it is to print successfully.

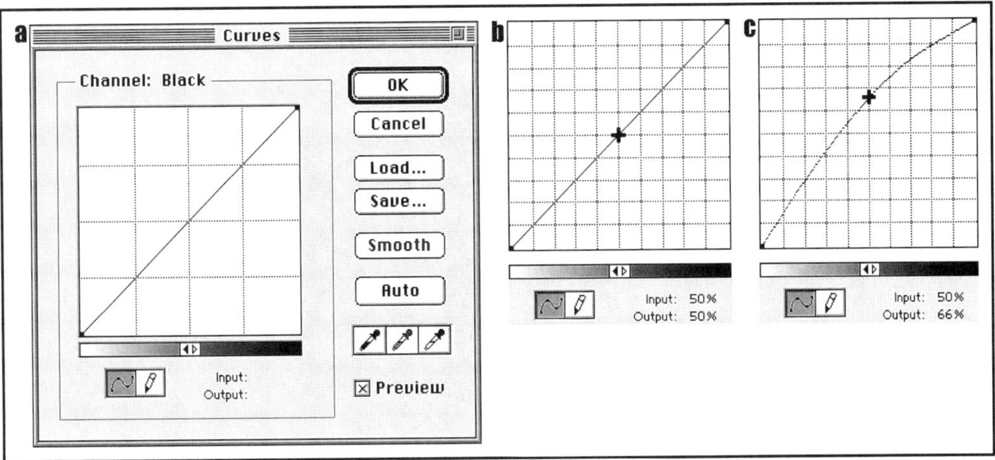

Figure 9-17: Photoshop's Curves dialog box (a). Sections (b) and (c) show the curve elevating the 50% value to 66%.

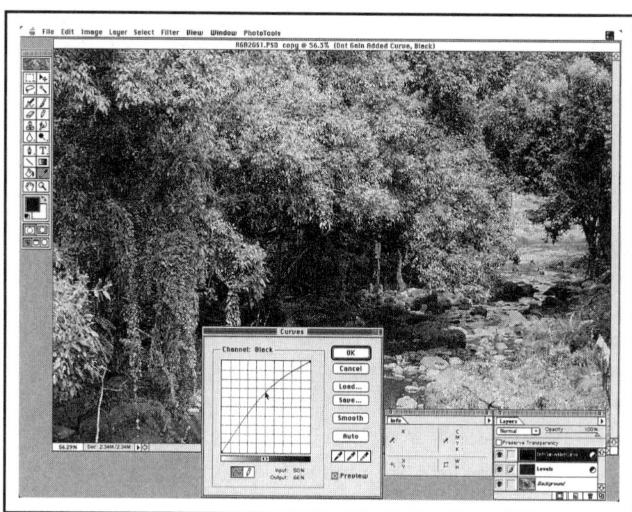

Figure 9-18: Make the darkening adjustment on the Curves adjustment layer.

19. Double-click on the word "Levels" on the Levels adjustment layer (Figure 9-19). Move the Input section's midtone slider to the left until the image starts looking about the way you wish to see it when it is printed. Double-check to see that your highlight dots are still at 5% and that your shadow dots are running about 90%–93%. If they are not, use the Output Scale sliders to adjust them as described above. When you are finished, click OK.

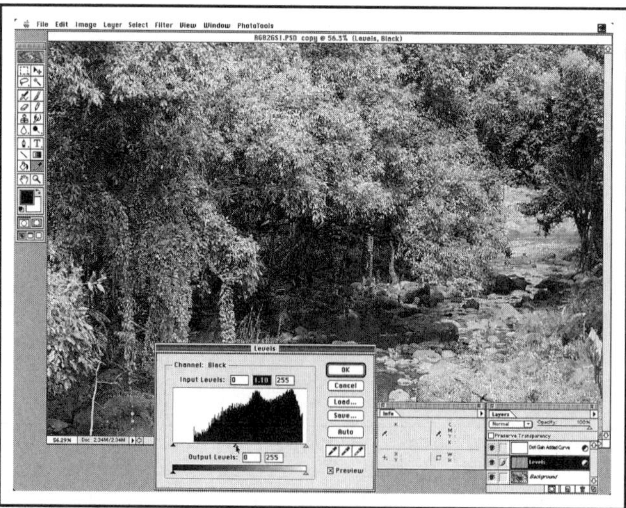

Figure 9-19: On the Levels adjustment layer, move the midtone slider to the left to lighten the image. Move the slider until the picture looks close to the way you want it to appear on press.

The image should look very good at this point, but get ready for a shock: drag the Curves adjustment layer down to the Layer Palette trash icon. Dreadful, isn't it? You'll recall that we used the words *flat* and *washed out*? Yet this image, when the dots on the press sheet have grown by the specified percentage of midtone gain, will look very much the way it did before you trashed the Curves adjustment layer. No one who sees this simulation ever again underestimates dot gain as a significant factor in the preparation of the halftone.

In this example, a Levels adjustment layer was used for the final adjustments. Another Curves adjustment layer could have been used instead. Figure 9-20 shows how such a curve might look. Notice that the highlight end of the curve has been moved up from 0% to 5%, the 50% value has been pulled down to 34% (50–16=34), and the shadow end of the scale has been pulled down from 100% to 92%. The Curve controls are very powerful but are not, if you are new to the process, as simple to use as the Levels controls. No matter which is used, the results are the same since Levels and Curves do exactly the same thing.

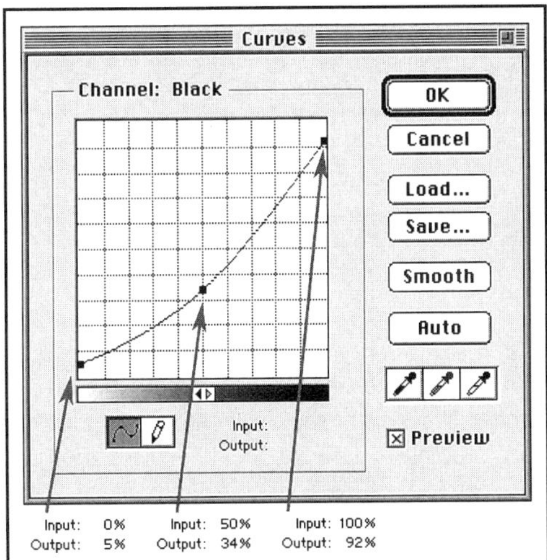

Figure 9-20: The Levels adjustment layer could have been another Curves layer adjusted with this curve.

The adjusted image is shown in Figure 9-21. You see it here in two stages; an interesting possibility since both images have been printed and one shows itself to be the pre-adjusted photo. This is accomplished by preparing the rear image as though it is to be printed with twice the actual dot gain for the page.

Figure 9-21: Two versions of the halftone. The back image shows how light the image is before printing. The front image shows the same image with dot gain applied on press.

The Unsharp Mask Filter

Once you have clicked OK on the Levels controls, flattened the image, and cropped it to its final size, the adjustment of the photo is almost complete. There is one more step before it is perfect: use the Unsharp Mask filter to artificially clarify all of the photo's details. In the process of scanning, the clear delineation of surfaces shown in a photographic image becomes blurred. Depending upon the type of scanner, some of the image's details are restored by the scanner software (using Unsharp Mask). More sharpness is usually applied just before the settings for the highlight and shadow values are made, or at the final stage of the processing of the image. Again, the Unsharp Mask is used for this task.

Photoshop ships with four Sharpen filters. They are Sharpen, Sharpen More, Sharpen Edges, and Unsharp Mask. The first three are discussed in Chapter 8; "Filter Frolics," the fourth filter, Unsharp Mask, is the only one you will ever need when preparing photo images for offset reproduction. The dialog box for this filter is shown in Figure 9-22.

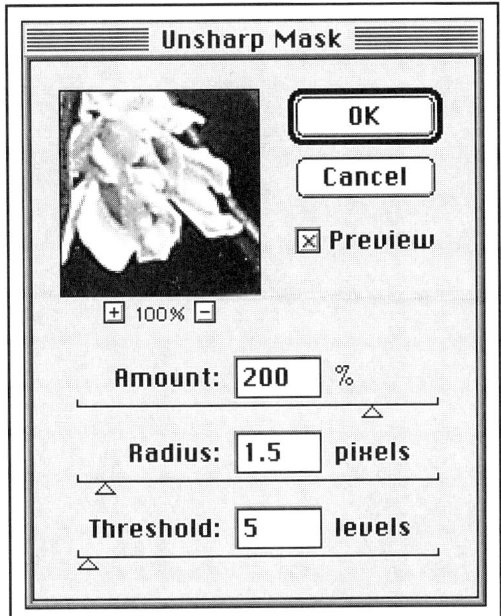

Figure 9-22: The Unsharp Mask options window.

Unsharp Mask may be the oddest name ever devised for a filter. It is intended to make the details of a photo easier to see, but the name gives the impression that it does the opposite. This filter does not really sharpen, but plays a visual trick; it finds the border between pixels that differ from each other by some threshold amount and then increases the contrast along that border. The contrast enhancement fools the eye into believing that it sees details more clearly.

Although Unsharp Mask clarifies the image in a way that is different from what you would do when you focus the optical assembly of a camera, Photoshop has no focusing mechanism. Unsharp Mask provides an excellent way to achieve the same kind of effect.

Figure 9-23 shows a set of six samples which are used to illustrate how the settings in the filter dialog box affect the pixels in the image. Along with the enlarged views of the pixels, a small image at high resolution shows the same effects without magnification. Note that when two areas meet, the darker side of the edge is darkened and the lighter side lightened. The way the filter is applied is governed by the settings in the dialog box. Notice, too, how the settings with larger values for both Radius and Amount produce effects that are clearly visible in the small samples. Having the results of the Unsharp Mask filter so visible is probably not a good idea. The best use of the filter results in clarity of detail that isn't obvious about how the clarity was achieved.

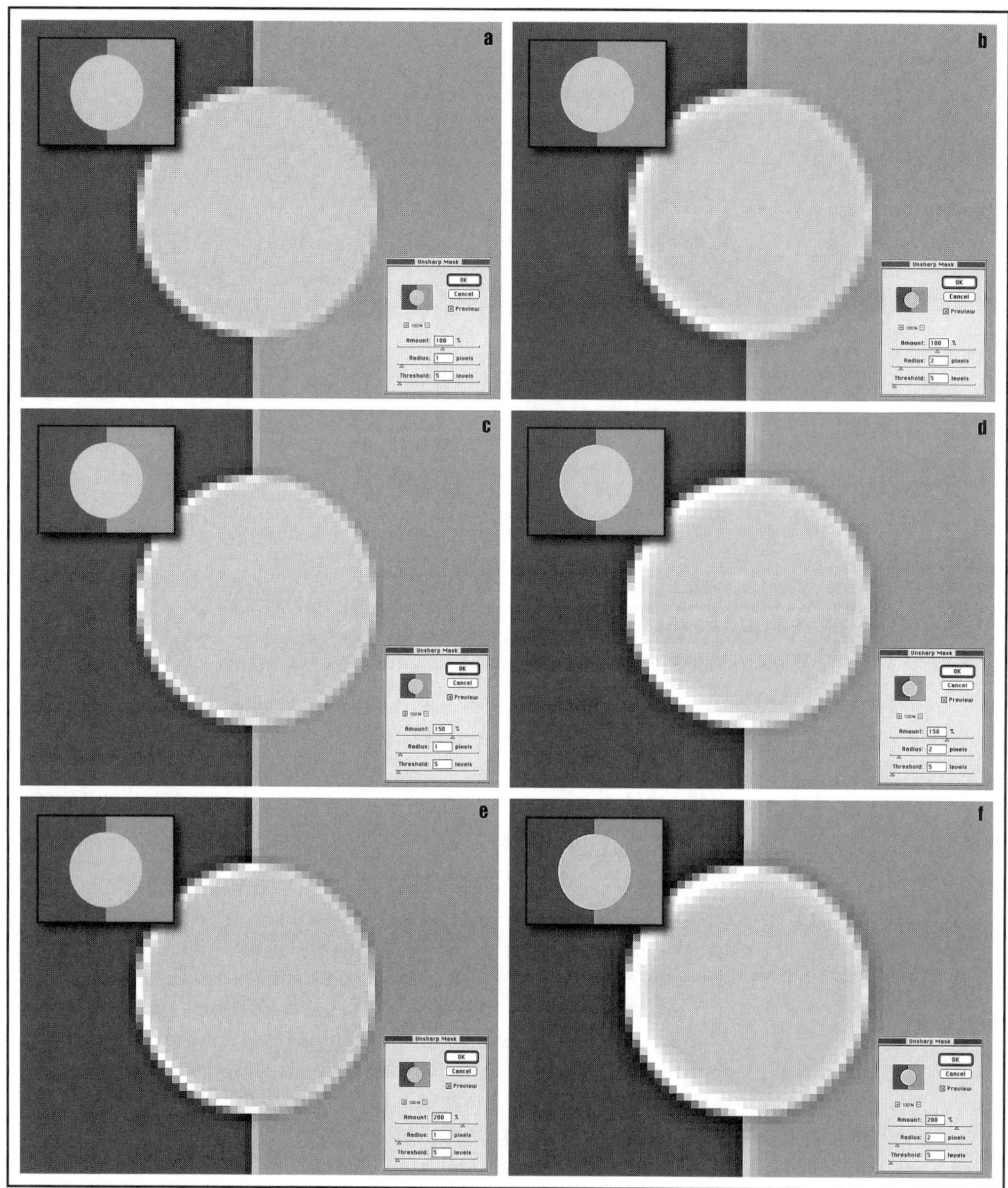

Figure 9-23: Six possible results with the Unsharp mask filter: (a & b) 100, 1, 5 & 100, 2, 5; (c & d) 150, 1, 5 & 150, 2, 5; (e & f) 200, 1, 5 & 200, 2, 5.

Three criteria govern the effect of the Unsharp Mask filter:

- **Amount.** The Amount value is in the form of a percentage. This number instructs Photoshop to increase the contrast between two edges by darkening the darker pixels and lightening the lighter. Even though this value is entered as a percentage, there is no straightforward calculation of a percentage between two values. This number is simply one of a set of three variables—the other two are the Radius and Threshold numbers—used for the calculation. The actual pixel values from a given percentage changes if either of the other numbers is changed. The Amount range is from 1%–500%.
- **Radius.** The Radius value is used to set the width of the zone along the edges in which the pixels are lightened or darkened. The Radius range is from .1–250 pixels.
- **Threshold.** The Threshold setting is the limiting factor for how much tonal difference there must be between two pixels before the darkening or lightening effects are applied. If the setting is, say, 5, then as the filter examines pairs of pixels, there must be at least five steps or Threshold levels between the two pixels for the filter to function. Another way to state this is, as the Threshold number gets larger, there are fewer areas of the image which become sharpened. The Threshold range is from 0–255.

With the sophistication of the algorithm used for the Unsharp Mask filter, very delicate and subtle changes can be made. Even numbers that are mathematical anomalies can be used. For example, it is possible to enter a Radius value that is a decimal fraction (just try to select 1.5 pixels!). Rather than thinking of the numbers in the filter dialog as concrete values, it is easier to think of them as a flexible set of guides which aim your sharpening efforts toward the effect you wish to achieve.

Every image has slightly different requirements for sharpening. For photos intended for offset reproduction, a good procedure would be to open the filter dialog box and enter general settings of 200% for the Amount and 3–5 for the Threshold. The Radius value is dependent upon the resolution of the image. A good rule of thumb is to calculate the Radius as 1/2 of 1% of the file's resolution. For a 300 ppi file, this gives a radius value of 1.5 (300 x .005 = 1.5). Of the three settings, the Radius and Threshold values are not easily increased without producing artifacts that harm the image. Departing from the general settings given above, the values might be made smaller but seldom larger. The Amount value has the largest effect on the filter. Figure 9-24 shows a set of examples in which the Amount is changed in 25% increments. Note that the lower right-hand example is the one in which the target values given here were used. Compare this specimen with the others, paying close attention to the spokes in the bicycle wheels, the tread texture on the rear wheel, and the cracks in the rocks.

Figure 9-24: Five applications of the Unsharp Mask filter using different settings. Compare the original in the areas of the back tire tread, the wheel spokes, and the cracks in the rocks.

When using the Unsharp Mask filter, pay a lot of attention to the Preview window. You may magnify or reduce the amount of detail seen in the window to gauge the effect of the settings you have entered. Be sure to look at different areas of the image before clicking OK.

Using Unsharp Mask on Difficult Photos

The Unsharp Mask filter, for all its power to make an image look wonderful, is a difficult filter to control in some situations. Some scans, no matter how the values are entered, seem to be very difficult. The finished photo can look blotchy or as if it were sprinkled with talc, or even blurry. These are problems which bedevil even experienced users. Here are a couple of the problems you might encounter and some solutions which work extremely well.

Photos With Areas of Very Fine Detail The leaves in the upper part of Figure 9-21 are a good example of very fine detail. Sometimes this kind of detail requires that the Amount setting be lowered and the Radius made slightly smaller. Too much sharpening of this kind of detail is worse than no sharpening. Another example of this problem is shown in the upper part of Figure 9-25 where the bark of the tree looks as though it is coated with frost crystals. Here's a very fast way to rescue the situation after the photo has been sharpened (lower part of the figure).

First of all, if this technique is used, push the original sharpening Amount up to between 300% and 400%. This seems at first to make the problem worse, but it's only temporary. On the Layers palette, drag the Background layer onto the New Layer icon. With the new layer selected, choose Filter | Blur | Gaussian Blur. Make the radius of the blur the same as the Unsharp Mask radius value. Click OK. Change the Opacity of the layer to 40% or 50%. Flatten the image. You have now retained the sharpening effect of the Unsharp Mask filter and eliminated the artifacts on the tree's bark.

If you would like to try out this technique, please open the file RGB2GS2.PSD from the Chapter 9 Practice Files on the Companion CD-ROM. The image is the same as shown in Figure 9-25.

Film Granularity All film exhibits some degree of graininess. Only when the image is enlarged by a substantial amount does the problem become serious. When the amount of enlargement is great, the *noise* produced by the film is usually accentuated by the Unsharp Mask filter, producing effects that are less sharp than the original image. Of particular concern are scanned images originating from 35mm film intended to be used indoors and in other low-light situations.

Another big problem source is a photo printed on textured, anti-glare paper. If you've spent much time running a scanner, you'll probably loathe anti-glare photo print paper. It may not hold fingerprints, and it may be easier to view, but it is awful to scan. Awful! That's an important point to keep in mind if you are going to have your own photography processed for eventual press reproduction. Always ask for glossy-surfaced photo prints. If your photo lab cannot give them to you, find another photo lab!

Figure 9-25: The Unsharp Mask filter can give a frosted-crystal look to some kinds of surface textures (upper image). The Layers technique described in the text shows how the effect can be modified after the photo has been sharpened too much.

If you would like to try out the following technique, please open the file RGB2GS3.PSD from the Chapter 9 Practice Files on the Companion CD-ROM. The image is the same as shown in Figure 9-26. Then follow these steps:

1. Eliminating Unsharp Mask's exaggeration of film grain requires a bit of preplanning. During the adjustment of the RGB image, perform all the steps through the conversion of the image from Lab mode to Grayscale mode. The pre-adjusted grayscale image is shown in Figure 9-26.

Figure 9-26: Image before press adjustments with noticeable film grain.

2. Before proceeding, choose Color Range from the Select menu. When the Color Range dialog has opened, change the pop-up at the top so that it reads Shadows. Click OK. Make a new channel out of this selection (click on the second icon from the left on the bottom of the Channels palette). The new channel is listed on the Channels palette as #2, but you won't really need it. It's simply good practice to save these intermediary steps so that you can back up any time you wish. The appearance of this new channel is shown in Figure 9-27.
3. With the selection still active, choose Feather from the Select menu. Enter a Feather value that is equal to about 2% of your file's resolution. (For a 300 ppi file, enter 6—300 x .02 = 6.) Save this selection also as a new channel. The appearance of the new channel (which is listed as #3) is shown in Figure 9-28.

Figure 9-27: After selecting the shadow tones (Select | Color Range), save the selection to a new channel.

Figure 9-28: Feather the selection and save to a new channel. You can also use the Gaussian Blur filter on the first of the saved channels. Use a blur radius calculated in the same way as the Feather value in No. 3 (above).

4. Forget about the new channels for the time being, and continue with the adjustments to the grayscale image. When the adjustments for press conditions are finished, the image looks similar to the photo in Figure 9-29. Running the Unsharp Mask filter on the image produces the effects shown in Figure 9-30 (full

view) and Figure 9-31 (enlarged detail). The detail shows how the filter increases the amount of noise in the image which produces almost a mezzotint effect. Under some circumstances this effect might be desirable, but such a prominent texture may not be wanted in day-to-day use. If you execute the filter and spot this kind of problem, press Command+z or Ctrl+z to undo the filter.

Figure 9-29: The image after it has been adjusted for press.

Figure 9-30: Sharpening in the normal way gives this noise-textured result.

Figure 9-31: Enlarged detail of Figure 9-30.

5. Use the Channels palette to turn Channel #3 into an active selection—Command+click or Ctrl+click on the channel's thumbnail. Press Command+j or Ctrl+j to change the selection into an independent layer. Choose Filter | Unsharp Mask and make the settings for this layer 400%, 1.5, and 5. Change the Opacity of this layer to somewhere between 40% and 60%. 50% should work pretty well. Use whatever figure is needed to give the effect of the sharpening and to minimize the amount of visible noise. The appearance of the image after sharpening only the shadow values is shown in Figures 9-32 (full view) and 9-33 (enlarged detail).

Figure 9-32: Select the feathered shadow values and make them into a new layer. Heavily sharpen this layer. Change the Opacity to about 50%. Notice how much clearer this image is than Figure 9-29.

Figure 9-33: Enlarged detail of Figure 9-32.

6. Next, let's sharpen the midtones and highlights. Click on the Background layer to select it. Make Channel #3 into an active selection again. Choose Select | Inverse. Press Command+j or Ctrl+j to change the selection into an independent layer. The appearance of this layer—with the other two layers hidden—is shown in Figure 9-34. Execute the Unsharp Mask filter on this layer with settings of 100%, 1, and 5. The full view image, with all channels showing, is seen in Figure 11-35. The enlarged detail is seen in Figure 9-36.

Figure 9-34: Select just the midtones and highlights (the inverse of the feathered shadow channel). Make the selection into a layer. Use the Unsharp Mask filter with lighter settings.

Figure 9-35: Flatten the image. The final sharpened photo is much clearer than the original but without the noise of an all-over sharpening with a single set of values.

Figure 9-36: Enlarged detail of Figure 9-35.

Threshold Mode for Windows users

The following is a workaround that you can use if your video board does not support the threshold method from within the Levels dialog box. Using this method means that your work will involve a couple of extra steps but it will give you the same results achieved in the instruction for processing a halftone within the Levels controls.

1. Have a notepad and pen ready.
2. Open the RGB photo to be adjusted.
3. Press Ctrl+1. The image changes to a view of the Red channel.
4. Choose Image|Adjust|Threshold. This command opens the Threshold dialog box. Be sure that the Preview option is checked.
5. Move the slider to the far left of the slider bar and the image becomes completely white. Move the slider gradually to the right until the desired level of shadow detail begins to show as black areas on the image. Write down the number showing in the controls box.
6. Move the slider to the far right of the slider bar and the image becomes completely black. Move the slider gradually to the left until the desired level of highlight detail begins to show as white areas on the image. Write down the number showing in the controls box. Be sure to label the two numbers you've written down as Red. Click on the Cancel button.
7. Press Ctrl+2. The image changes to a view of the Green channel. Follow steps 4–6 above. Be sure to label the two numbers you've written down as Green. Click on the Cancel button.
8. Press Ctrl+3. The image changes to a view of the Blue channel. Follow steps 4–6 above. Be sure to label the two numbers you've written down as Blue. Click on the Cancel button.
9. Press Ctrl+~ to return to the full-color view of the image. Open the Levels dialog box (Ctrl+L). Press Ctrl+1 and enter the first Red value. Press the Tab key twice and enter the second Red value. Press Ctrl+2 and enter the first Green value. Press the Tab key twice and enter the second Green value. Press Control+3 and enter the first Blue value. Press the Tab key twice and enter the second Blue value. Enter Ctrl+~ and adjust the midtones slider of the input scale.
10. Click OK to complete the adjustment.

Understanding & Customizing the Levels Controls

You used the Levels controls manually by moving both the Input and Output scale sliders while preparing a halftone for printing. It is useful, now, to take a look at more of the features of the Level dialog box. Some of them can be used to cut down on the amount of time it takes to do normal production tasks.

The Levels dialog box is shown in Figure 9-37. The central part of the image shows what appears to be a graphic representation of data. This central window contains what is called a *histogram*. It is easiest to simply think of the histogram as a bar graph. The set of pixel values are arranged left to right from darkest to lightest. Each vertical row of pixels indicates the relative quantity of pixels of a given brightness value. In some cases, you'll see that the histogram has very little data in some places on the scale. Such histograms are an indication that a full range of values is not present in the image and that it might be necessary to discard the image in favor of a new scan or to discard it completely. A satisfactory histogram should, ideally, have a full range of values from one end of the scale to the other.

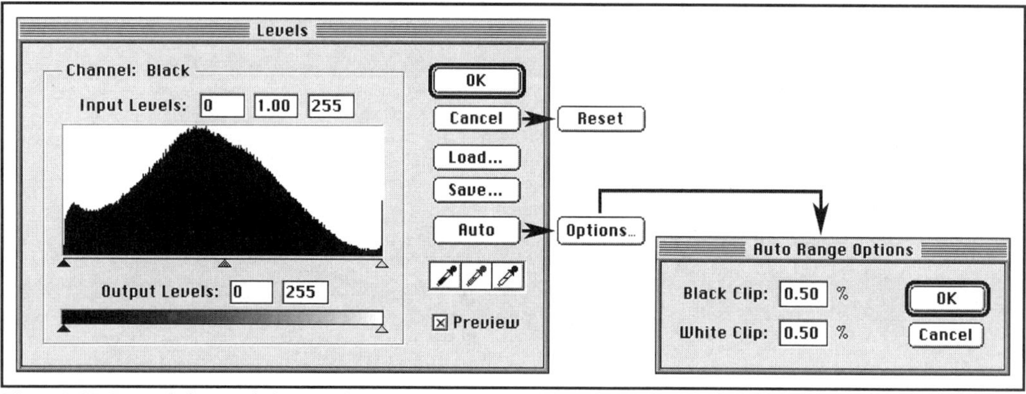

Figure 9-37: Expanded view of Photoshop's Levels controls.

The two sliders on each end of the Levels Input scale point to the extremes of the tone value scale. The shadow slider always points toward the 0 or darkest value—the print equivalent is 100% black—while the highlight slider always points toward the lightest value, 255, which is the print equivalent of 0% black.

If the highlight slider in Figure 9-37 is moved some distance to the left, it still points to value 255. All the values to the right of the slider after the move become the same maximum brightness value as the vertical row of pixels to which the slider points. The same thing happens—with inverse values—with the slider at the other end of the scale. If you click the OK button when just these two sliders have been moved and then reopen the Levels controls, you see a different histogram: the two sliders have moved back to the ends of the scale. All the values between the sliders at the time you clicked OK have now distributed themselves evenly across the entire scale. It's obvious that there is now fewer than 256 values between the two endpoints; the new histogram reflects this by exhibiting gaps in the range of tones. These are seen as vertical lines containing no black pixels.

Sometimes a histogram contains no pixels at either or both ends of the Input scale which is seen in the three figures beginning with Figure 9-38. In the first figure, a black-to-white gradient is about to be drawn so that its endpoints are beyond the boundaries of the window. When the gradient is completed (Figure 9-39), the range of values within the image window falls between 94% and 7%. The histogram at the bottom of the figure shows gaps at both ends of the Input scale. Figure 9-40 shows the result of moving the sliders in so that they point to the end values of what is actually present in the image. Upon clicking OK and reopening the Levels dialog box (Figure 9-40), the range of values in the image now falls between 100% and 0%. Notice the small gaps in the histogram. As the original values spread out, the missing 6% on the shadow end of the scale and the missing 6% on the highlight end of the scale have been uniformly distributed across the whole value range. There are still 12% missing values but they no longer are visible in the image. You can get away with this kind of manipulation simply because you are working with 256 values instead of 100. Since each missing value is considerably less than 1%, the human eye cannot detect that it is missing from the gradient.

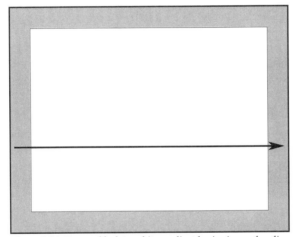

Figure 9-38: Draw a black-to-white gradient beginning and ending outside the image window.

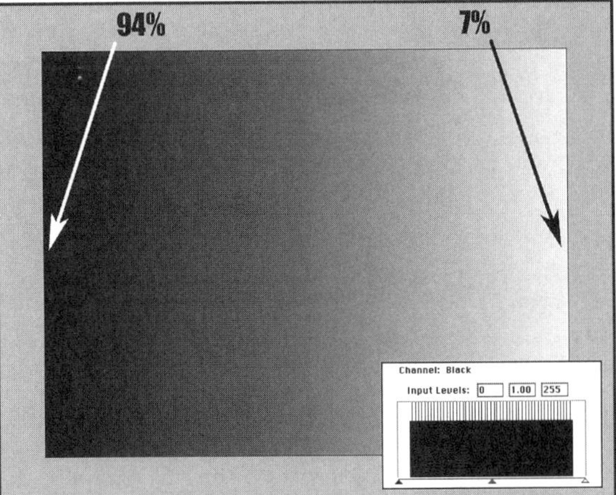

Figure 9-39: The window contains values from 94% to 7%. Note the missing values on each end of the histogram.

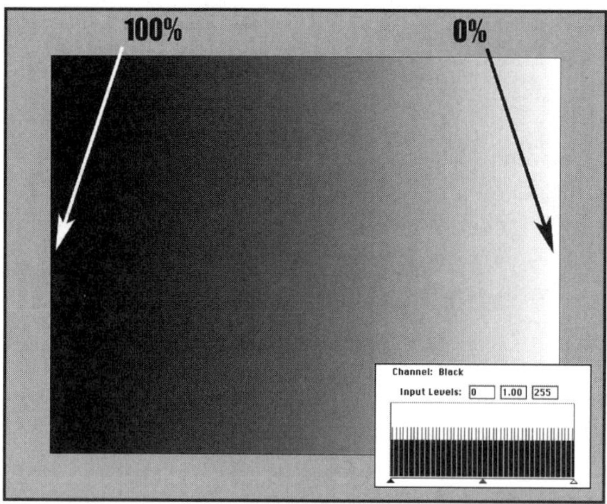

Figure 9-40: Move each end slider in to where the real values begin, and click OK. The new histogram shows all of the previous values redistributed over the entire range and with missing-value gaps uniformly distributed.

The center slider on the Input slider points to the midtone—50%—values in the image. As either of the end sliders are moved, the midtone slider maintains its position exactly halfway between the two. Remembering the way the two end sliders compress and redistribute brightness data, try to imagine that the midtone slider can do the same thing if it is moved manually. Moved to the left, it forces values originally above 50% to be below that value and lightens the image. This leaves fewer values between 50% and 100% and results in gaps in the new histogram between 50% and 100%. Figure 9-41 shows how this happens. The original gradient with its Levels histogram is at the top. The end sliders have been moved to point to the first available real value. In the middle, the original values have been rearranged and the midtone slider has been moved so that its reading is 1.40. In the lower part of the figure, the resulting histogram shows gaps in the dark end of the range but an almost-complete set of values on the light end. This might seem to be harmful to the overall image until you remember a couple of points: first, the lighter part of the image is the part which we see most easily. It should have, therefore, more detail than the dark part. Second, as the image gets darker, dot gain acts to fill in some of the gaps and to restore most of the balance lost in the preparation of the image for printing. Gaps in the histogram need to be, in the darker half of the tone range, at least 3–5 missing values wide before they become visible as posterization artifacts—a heavily granular texture is the usual look of these artifacts—in the printed piece.

The two Output sliders are mostly used after the input sliders have done their work. By moving either of them, you are able to arbitrarily limit the length of the tone range set up by the Input controls. If the highlight slider is moved to the left, the lightest values are darkened. If the shadow slider is moved to the right, the darkest values are made lighter. Using the Output sliders was discussed earlier: you used them to slightly darken the extreme highlight values and to lighten the darkest tonal values.

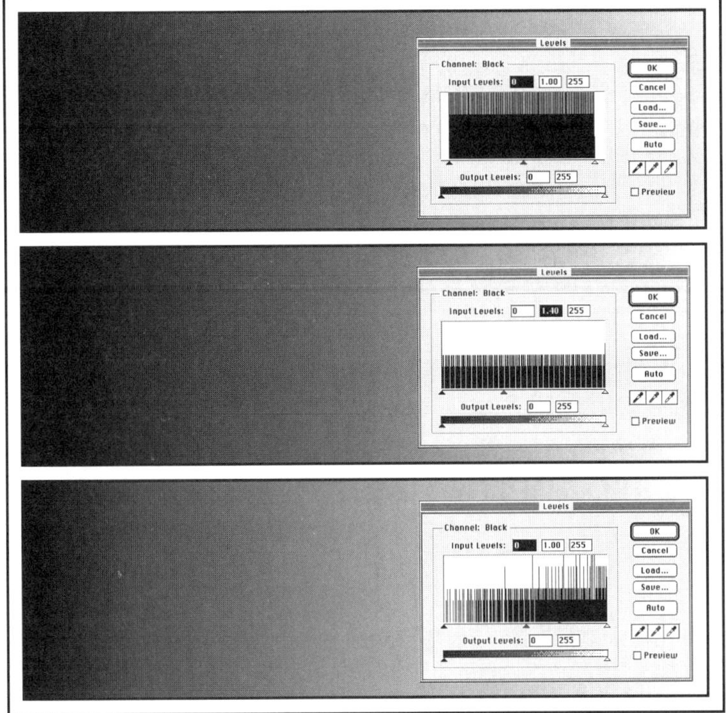

Figure 9-41: Three examples of changes to the histogram. At the top, the end sliders are moved in. In the center, the range of values is redistributed across the whole range. At the bottom, a move of the midtone slider to the left concentrates values on the highlight end of the scale and leaves gaps in the shadow end.

At the right of the Levels controls are a number of buttons and sampling eyedropper tools. Two of the buttons have alternate versions which appear if the Option key or the Alt key is pressed. The Cancel button becomes Reset. When Reset is clicked, the entire dialog box reverts to the way it was when first opened.

Load and Save are buttons that allow you to preserve the state of the dialog box by saving its settings as a named file. At some later time, the load button will allow you to retrieve the saved settings for use on the same or a similar image.

The Auto button—and its alternate Options button—and the eyedropper tools are all bound together. When the Auto button is clicked (and the Photoshop defaults are in place), Photoshop examines all of the pixels in the image. It moves the highlight Input slider to point to the lightest value present and the shadow Input slider to the darkest value. Clicking on the Auto button is exactly the same as choosing Image | Adjust | Auto Levels. The advantage to the latter is that it can be done without opening the Levels controls.

The separate Auto Range Options dialog box allows some customization as to how the Auto button goes about selecting endpoint values. By specifying the amount of Black Clip and White Clip, you instruct Photoshop to ignore values on the extreme ends of the value scale when it sets the two Input sliders.

To explain why this is desirable, it is necessary to understand that print technicians classify highlight values in two categories. The first is the *specular highlight*, the second is the *printing highlight*. A specular highlight is a bright spot on the image caused by reflection from a very intense light source. Figure 9-42 shows examples of specular highlights in the flash of sunlight on the top fronts of the headlight chrome and on top of the car. Specular highlights are often areas that are more-or-less distinct. They are so light that they do not look realistic if a printing dot tone is added to them. Printing highlights, in contrast to specular highlights, always have a dot. The dot might be the smallest dot that will hold on press, but a dot is there.

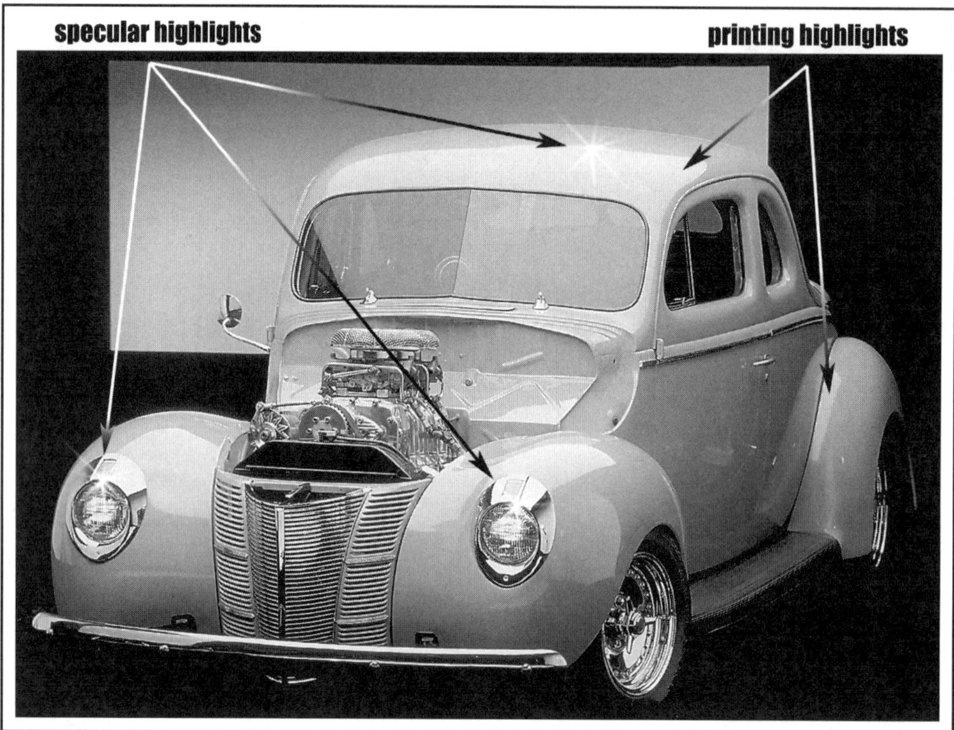

Figure 9-42: Printing highlights and specular highlights. The former always has a dot, the latter never does.

The difference between these two kinds of highlights is relevant to the Auto button's options. By setting a percentage in the White Clip data entry box, Photoshop is instructed to ignore some percentage of highlight values on the far right-hand end of the scale. It then locates the highlight slider at the first value to the left of the designated percentage. There are 256 values on the scale. Using the default setting of .5% (1/2 of

1%), Photoshop moves the slider to the first available value below 254. Since we are considering minimum non-specular (printable) highlight dots of 5% in this discussion, a more useful setting would be 4% for the white clip.

The Black Clip option works in much the same way but on the other end of the Input scale. With percentages entered in the range of 5% to 7%, the shadow slider moves to the first value to the right of the assigned percentage.

The Levels dialog's Eyedropper tools allow you to choose values from the image to be the lightest and darkest values by simply clicking where you wish. Here's how it would work. Close the Levels dialog and press i to select the Eyedropper tool. Set the options for the tool to be 3 x 3 Sample. Open the Levels dialog box. Click on the right-hand eyedropper. Move the cursor out into the image window and find a very light area. Click once. Now, select the left-hand eyedropper. Move the cursor into the image window and choose a very dark area. Click once. (There is a third eyedropper that is for the midtones but is available for use only when the image is in RGB or CMYK mode.) After you click on the OK button and reopen the Levels, you can see that Photoshop readjusts the histogram so the value range is proportionate to the arbitrary end points you set with the eyedroppers.

You may, if you wish, specify that the eyedropper tools target specific tone values. To do this:

1. First, double-click on the white eyedropper in the Levels dialog box. The Photoshop Color Picker appears.
2. Enter the numbers 0, 0, 0, and 5 in the data entry boxes for CMYK color. Click OK.
3. Double-click on the dark eyedropper. When the Color Picker opens, make the CMYK values 0, 0, 0, and 95. Click OK.
4. Select the white eyedropper and move it out into the window. Keep your eyes on the Info palette as you move the cursor so that you can locate the lightest value you wish to maintain a dot. Click once. All pixels lighter than the pixel on which you click become specular white.
5. Switch to the black eyedropper. Move the cursor into the window and move it around until you identify your darkest printable value. Click once.

You might think that having set the values to, say, 5% and 95%, that your endpoints are instantly equal to those values. But life—and Photoshop—is not so simple. If you click on pixels with values of 0% and 100%, your range of values falls between 3% and 84% (Figure 9-43, center). If you click on values of 5% and 95%, your range falls between 0% and 88%. The numbers don't seem to make sense until you recall the setting of the dot gain percentage in the File | Color Settings | Printing Inks Setup dialog box. Photoshop keeps this piece of information in mind and figures it into the calculation so you don't have to worry about it. Even if the numbers don't make a lot of sense, you'll find the whole process extremely workable.

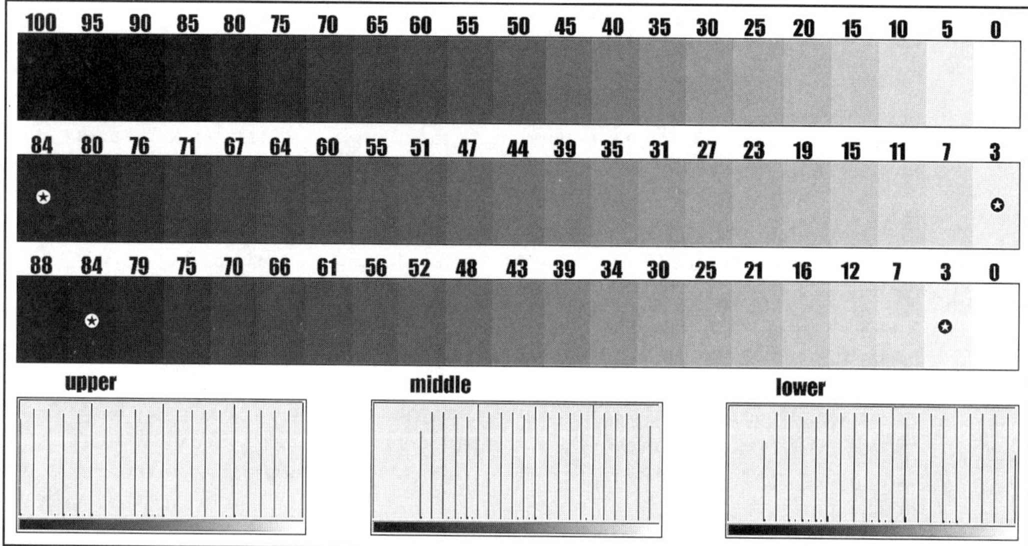

Figure 9-43: With the Eyedropper Auto Range options set, clicking on different values gives different results.

Keep in mind that you have to be pretty careful where you click. Figure 9-43 shows how different the values can be. At the top is the original set of 21 values (histogram at lower left). In the middle, the absolute white and black values—circles with small stars inside—have been clicked (histogram bottom center). Notice that clicking on the white has eliminated all specular highlights. In the lower example, clicking on the values identical to those set by choosing targeted values with the Color Picker, maintains the specular highlights and allows some dense areas of black beyond the target values.

Here's a tip: once you have set values to the eyedroppers, you don't really have to search your image for appropriate pixels. Instead, click on the Auto button. The values set for the eyedroppers become the controlling values for the Auto Levels command box. Even if you enter other—and different—values in the Auto Range Options dialog, the eyedropper tools values take precedence.

Moving the sliders manually and employing Threshold mode, the way it was done in the previous section on processing a halftone for printing, is the principal method for overriding a set of specific values and forcing the data within the image into more radical shifts. It is also the slowest of the ways to use the Levels controls. Even so, if you have the time, it is the best way to teach yourself how the distribution and redistribution of linear data really works.

Understanding & Customizing Curves

Photoshop users seem to divide themselves into two groups: those who use Curves, and those who use Levels. Rarely do you find a user who uses both as circumstances dictate, and rarely do you find users who aren't a bit smug about the superiority of their choice. The whole *Curves are better than Levels* or *Levels are better than Curves* controversy is extraordinarily silly. Since both Curves and Levels are powerful tools which produce the same results using different metaphors, it's possible for you to develop an appreciation for both and to use either as your Photoshop tasks may require.

The Curves dialog box—press Command+m or Ctrl+m, choose Image | Adjust | Curves—is shown in Figure 9-44. Some of its features are the same as for the Levels controls: Holding the Option or the Alt key changes the Cancel button to Reset, and holding the same key changes the Auto button to Options. The Auto Range Options dialog box is identical to that of the Levels controls. If new settings are entered within either the Levels or Curves dialog box, the identical settings are found in the other.

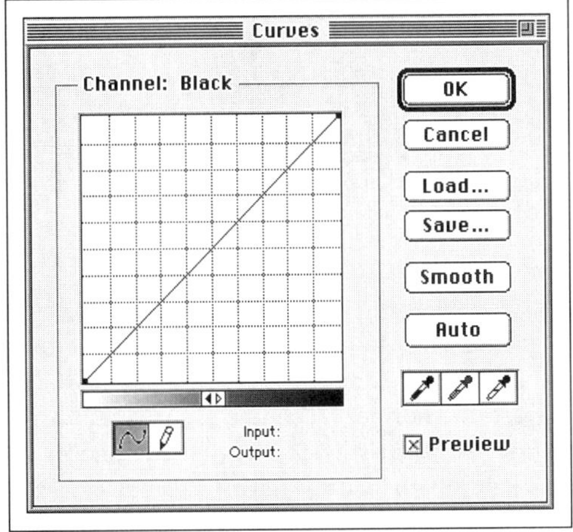

Figure 9-44: Photoshop's Curves options window.

The grid area of the Curves controls contains the line which is called the curve. Directly below the curve grid is a small strip—which looks like a gradient—with two arrows in the center. Clicking on either of the arrows reverses the direction of the gradient. These arrows do not switch the orientation of the curve grid; they change the way the Input/Output area below displays information. If the gradient has its light end on the left, Input/Output is displayed in percentages of black ink. If the gradient is reversed so that the light end is on the right, Input/Output is displayed in RGB values ranging from 0 to 255.

Whenever the Curves controls are summoned, the curve shows itself as a straight line running from lower left to upper right (Figure 9-45). The initial position of the line contains what is called the Input data. Lighter values are on the lower left, darker on the upper right. As the line is moved and changed, the new values are called Output data.

The grid is in two dimensions. Moving any point on the line toward the top of the grid causes the value to become darker, and moving any point toward the bottom makes the value become lighter. Figure 9-46 shows what happens when the two endpoints of the curve are moved as far as possible up or down: black becomes white, white becomes black. The values in the image are inverse, and the image become a negative of itself. You can see that the histograms of Figures 9-45 and 9-46 are mirror images of each other.

Figure 9-45: The curve line, as the dialog window is first opened, represents the set of Input values.

Figure 9-46: The inverse curve makes the image a negative.

The movement of the curve's endpoints toward either of the center axes provides a good deal of insight into the mechanics of using these controls. Figure 9-47 shows that as the endpoints are moved toward the horizontal center, the image loses its contrast and becomes flatter. This is accomplished by pushing all of the available data to the center portion of the histogram. Figure 9-48 shows that as the curve exactly matches the center horizontal axis, all values become 50% black. The histogram for this figure shows that all of the data has been pushed to the center and reduced to a single value.

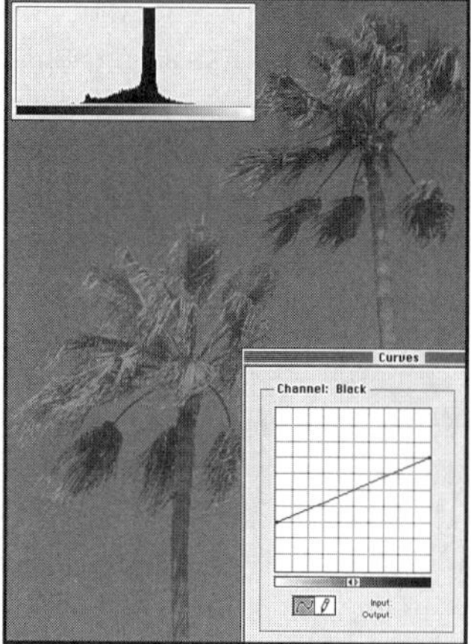

Figure 9-47: Moving the ends of the curve toward the center horizontal axis decreases the image's contrast.

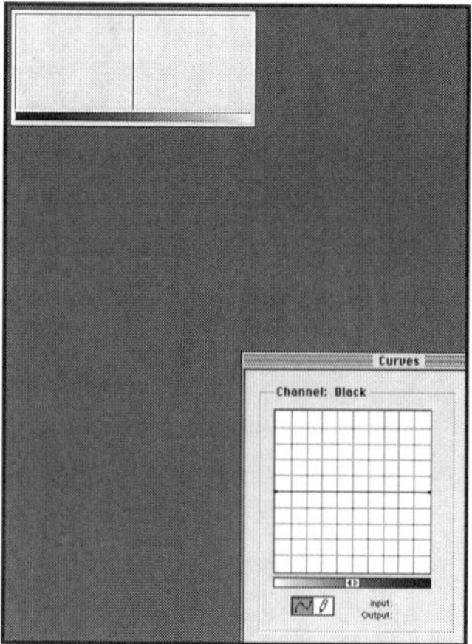

Figure 9-48: When the curve has flat-lined, the number of values has decreased to one. Lack of contrast just doesn't get any worse than this!

Moving the curve toward the vertical center axis increases the contrast of the image. This is accomplished by distributing fewer and fewer values across the entire histogram scale (Figure 9-49). Pushed to the limit, the image is left with only five values, each of them equally spaced across the histogram scale (Figure 9-50). Note that it is not possible to make the curve exactly follow the vertical axis.

Figure 9-49: Moving the curve endpoints toward the center vertical axis increases the image's contrast.

Figure 9-50: Moved as far to the center as possible, the curve leaves the image with only five values.

With the default curve tool (the left-hand tool located below the curve grid), you may click anywhere on the line of the curve to establish a new point. The new point can be moved up or down as desired. Clicking on the center of the line allows you to influence the midtone values. Pushing the point upward darkens the midtones (Figure 9-51) while pushing it downward lightens the midtones (Figure 9-52). As a single point of the curve is moved, the line stretches to accommodate the movement. Straight lines cannot be formed with this curve tool. Because the line stays, no matter how adjusted, as a series of curves, values which are contiguous to the point being moved keep their proximity. In this way, uniform gradations of tone are preserved. Figure 9-53 shows a curve with five adjusted points. The highlight point (0%) has been drawn up to the 5% level, the 25% point has been dragged slightly down, 50% has been moved up so that its Input/Output values are the same, the 75% point has been raised, and the 100% has been dragged down to 95%. If you compare this figure with the original image (Figure 9-45), you can see that the overall image is a bit lighter. The low-value tones (0%–30%) have fewer contrasts as do the values raging from 70%–95%. The overall contrast of the image is greater than the original because the curve segment between 25% and 75% is steeper than the original's.

Figure 9-51: Moving a point on the curve upward moves it to a darker value.

Figure 9-52: Moving a point on the curve downward moves it to a lighter value.

Figure 9-53: A compound curve here lightens the highlights, increases the contrast in the midtones, and darkens the shadows.

The other tool used to manipulate the curve is the Pencil tool. With the Pencil tool, arbitrary lines containing abrupt changes of direction can be drawn (Figure 9-54). Some of the most exciting textural effects Photoshop is capable of producing are based on the use of such arbitrary curves. For experimental purposes, the Pencil tool can be used to calculate the basic strategy for the curve. The Smooth button, which is not available for use unless the Pencil tool is active, does exactly what its name suggests: it evens out the drawn pencil lines and makes them into smooth curves. Repeatedly pressing the Smooth button eventually straightens the arbitrary curve into a straight line. After drawing with the Pencil tool, the curve can also be smoothed out by changing back to the default curve tool (Figure 9-55).

Figure 9-54: An arbitrary curve drawn with the Pencil tool. The values in the image will map oddly and will posterize in interesting ways.

Figure 9-55: Another arbitrary curve after being subjected to the Smooth command. The odd mapped values are still present but there is little posterization.

The Curve dialog box also is capable of a wonderfully useful display which assists you in understanding which pixels are affected by changes in the curve. Move the cursor out into the image window. Click and hold the mouse button. The placement of the value on which you clicked appears on the line of the curve as a small black circle (Figure 9-56).

Figure 9-56: Click and hold in the image window. A small circle appears on the curve grid to show you the location of the value.

Using Color Scans to Prepare Grayscale Files

Earlier in this chapter you learned that the best way to begin processing a halftone is to use a color scan, but this statement requires some justification. We will also discuss how to know how far the data in a scan can be pushed to retrieve an image which seems to be of hopelessly poor quality.

If you wish to follow along this exercise as it is presented here, locate the file RGB2GS4.PSD on the Companion CD-ROM in the Chapter 9 Practice Files folder. The appearance of this file is shown in Figure 9-57. As can be seen from the image, there is an overall lack of contrast that makes the photo dull, lifeless, dark, and lacking in hard detail. Please note that the file on disk is an RGB file. The original photo print was a black and white print but was scanned as though it were in color.

Figure 9-57: A poor contrast photograph to be rescued by treating it as a color image.

If you study this photo, you can see that the highlight area is probably the background upon which the garment was photographed. You can make the assumption that the photographer did not originally photograph this sweater on a medium-gray background but on a color that was probably very light, or even white. When adjusting for the highlights in each channel, you want to bleach out this area and look for your highlights within the object being photographed.

To prepare the file, follow these steps:

1. First, choose Image | Duplicate. Work through the following set of instructions on the duplicate of the file.
2. Open the Levels controls and switch to the Red channel. Use Threshold mode to move the Input scale highlight slider. Wash out the background and keep moving the slider until highlights begin to show up in the sweater (Figure 9-58).

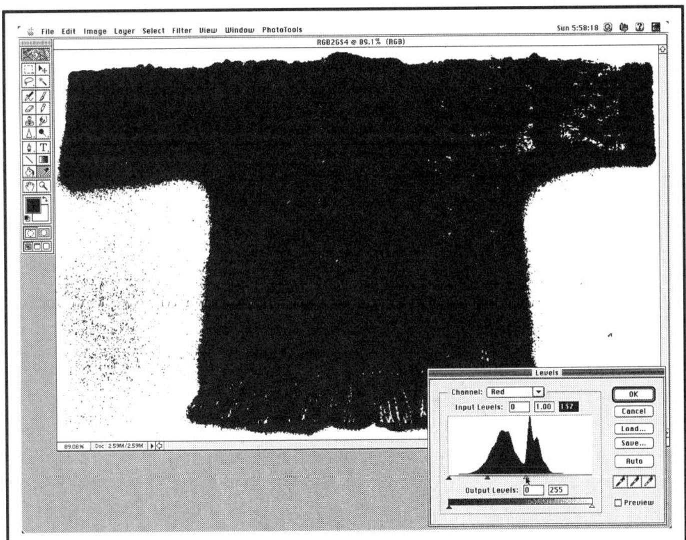

Figure 9-58: Use threshold mode (the Red channel Input scale highlight slider) in Levels to wash out the background and locate highlights within the sweater.

3. Use Threshold mode to locate the shadows of the Red channel (Figure 9-59).

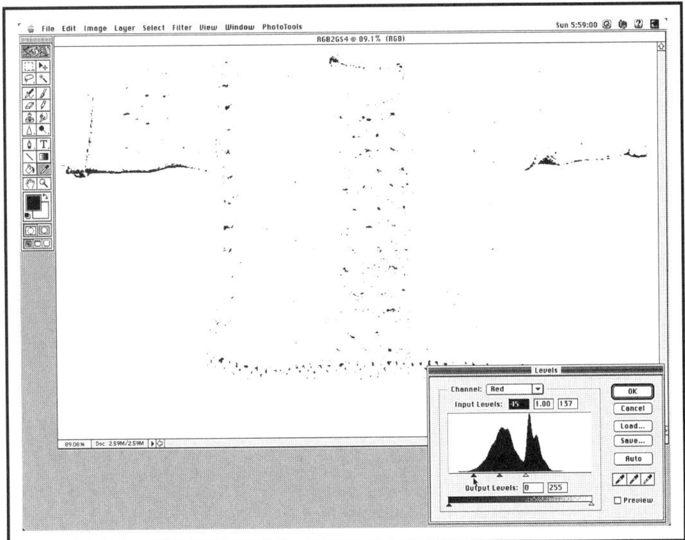

Figure 9-59: Move the Red channel Input scale shadow slider to locate the shadow tones within the sweater.

4. Switch to the Green channel. Locate the highlights and shadows just as you did for the Red channel (Figures 9-60 and 9-61). You can see that, despite the fact that the original image was black and white, the R, G, and B channels are all slightly different.

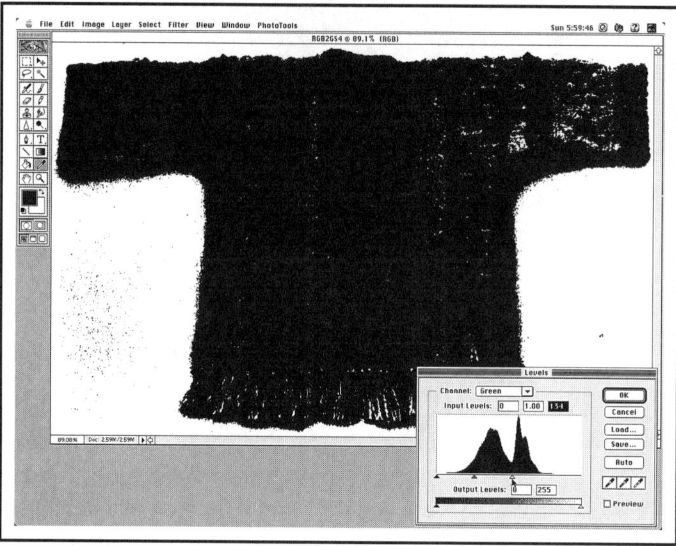

Figure 9-60: Use Threshold mode (the Green channel Input scale highlight slider) in Levels to wash out the background and locate highlights within the sweater.

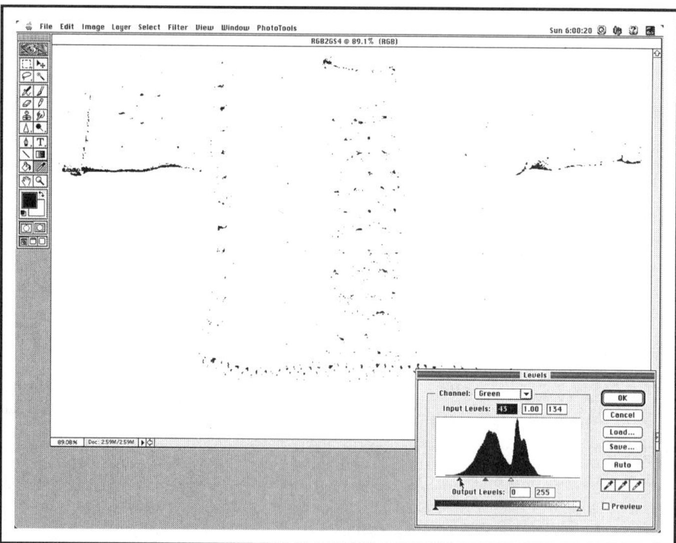

Figure 9-61: Move the Green channel Input scale shadow slider to locate the shadow tones within the sweater.

5. Switch to the Blue channel. Use Threshold mode to help you locate the highlights and shadows of the Blue channel (Figures 9-62 and 9-63).

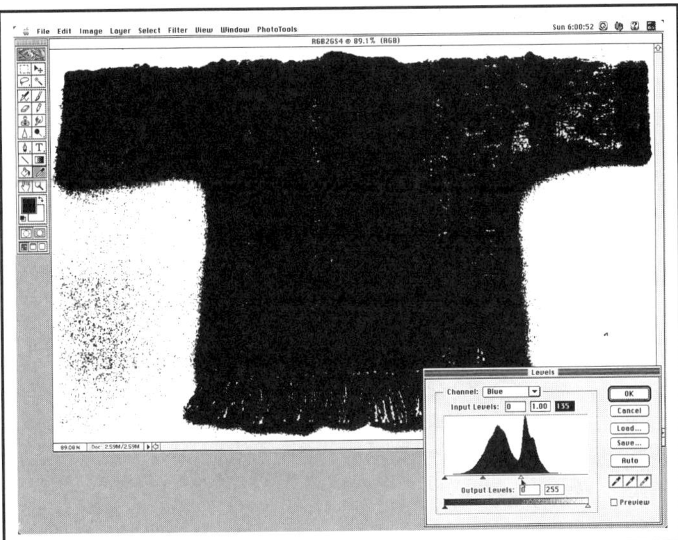

Figure 9-62: Use Threshold mode (the Blue channel Input scale highlight slider) in Levels to wash out the background and locate highlights within the sweater.

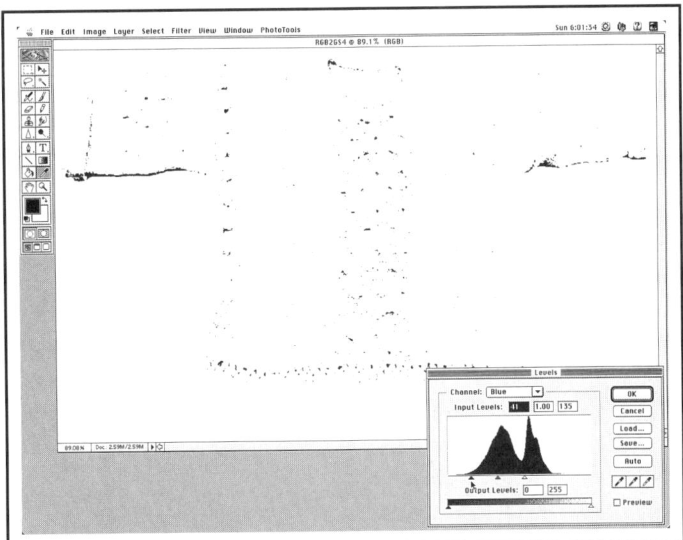

Figure 9-63: Move the Blue channel Input scale shadow slider to locate the shadow tones within the sweater.

6. Change the pop-up menu back to the RGB composite. Adjust the midtones until the data entry box reads about 1.30 (Figure 9-64).

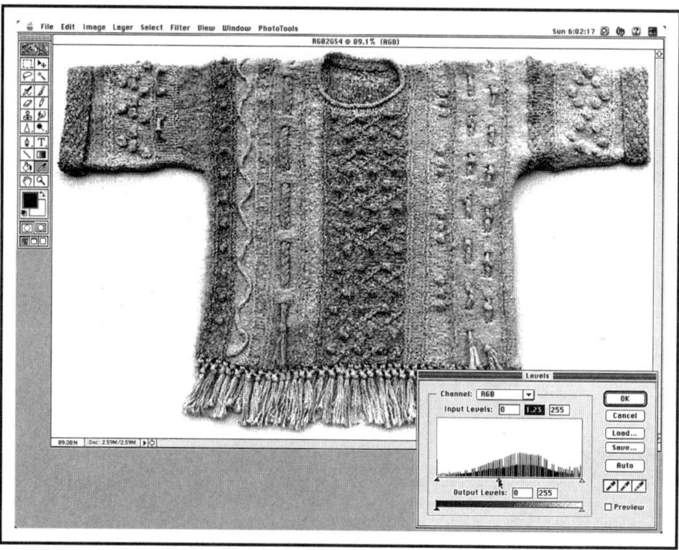

Figure 9-64: Adjust the midtone Input scale slider of the RGB composite histogram to lighten the photo.

7. Click OK. From the Image menu, choose Mode | Lab (Figure 9-65). Press command+1 or Ctrl+1 to view the L channel. Choose Image | Mode | Grayscale. Click OK when the dialog box asks if you wish to discard the other channels. Open the Levels controls and examine the histogram. Notice that the two-peak shape of the earlier histograms are now changed to a single smooth hump shape and that the image now contains values which are spread evenly across the tone range (Figure 9-66).
8. Keep this window open but return to the original window. We are going to convert the file to Grayscale mode and process it as though it were scanned that way. Choose Image | Mode | Grayscale. Click OK when it asks if you wish to discard the color. (Converting to Grayscale mode in this manner is equivalent to scanning the original in grayscale.)
9. Open the Levels controls. Use Threshold mode to locate the highlights of the image in the same way you did for the R, G, & B channels. Your screen turns black during this procedure because you have only a single channel, black (Figure 9-67).

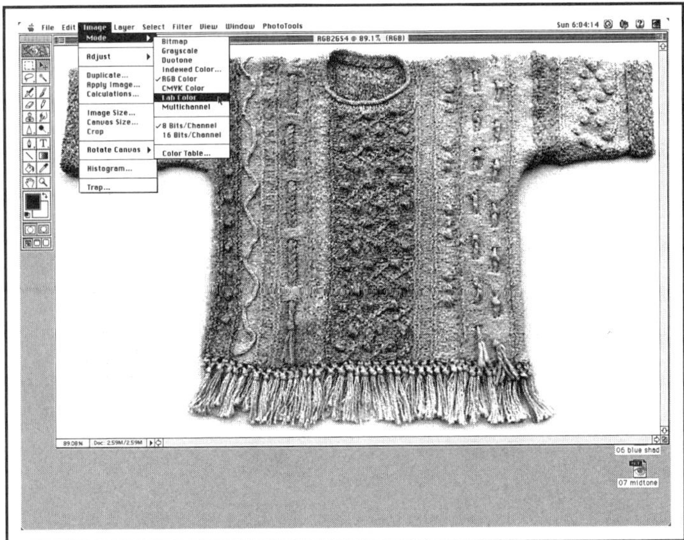

Figure 9-65: Convert the image to Lab mode. Change to the L channel. Convert to Grayscale mode.

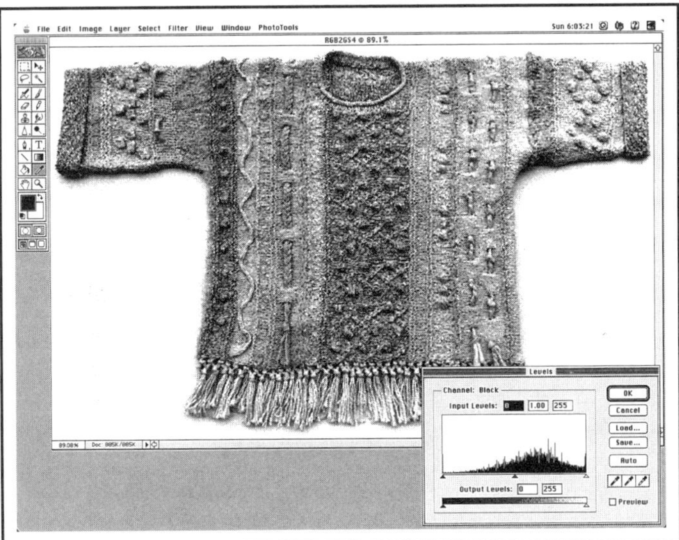

Figure 9-66: Open the Levels controls and look at the histogram to see how it has changed from the original.

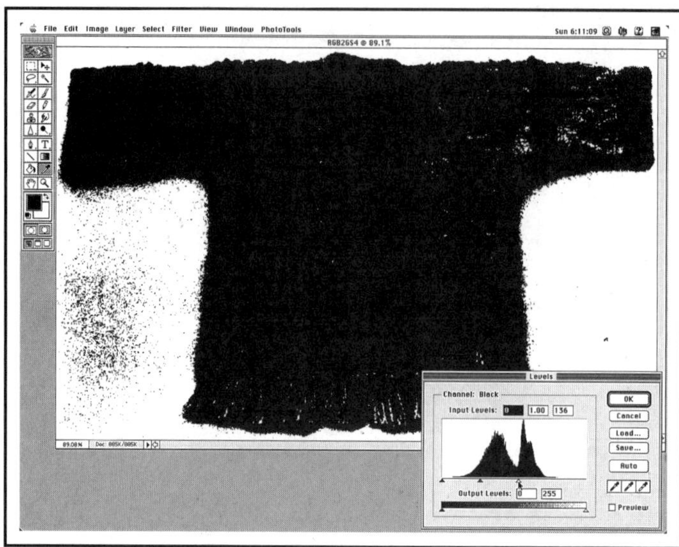

Figure 9-67: Use Threshold mode (the Black channel Input scale highlight slider) in Levels to wash out the background and locate highlights within the sweater.

10. Use Threshold mode to locate the image shadow tones (Figure 9-68).

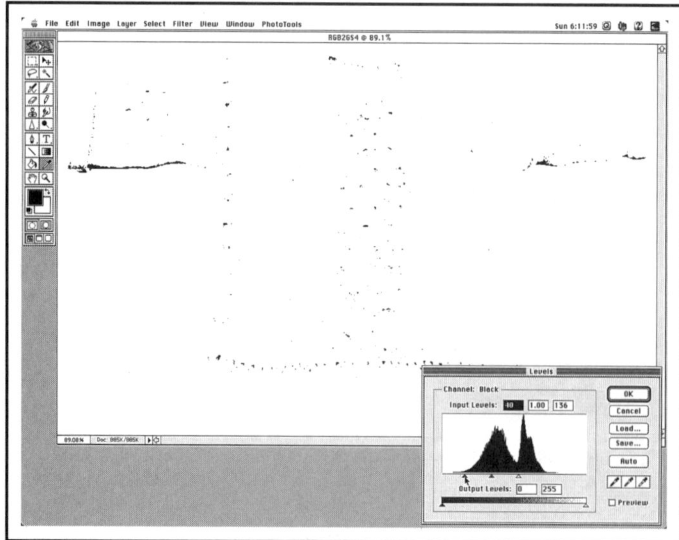

Figure 9-68: Move the Black channel Input scale shadow slider to locate the shadow tones within the sweater.

11. Move the midtone slider until the value reads 1.30. Click OK. Open the Levels dialog box again and take a look at the histogram (Figure 9-69). Notice how the image processed from grayscale contains fewer than half the possible values. By contrast, the image processed from the RGB file contains almost no missing values. The two histograms are shown side by side in Figure 9-70.

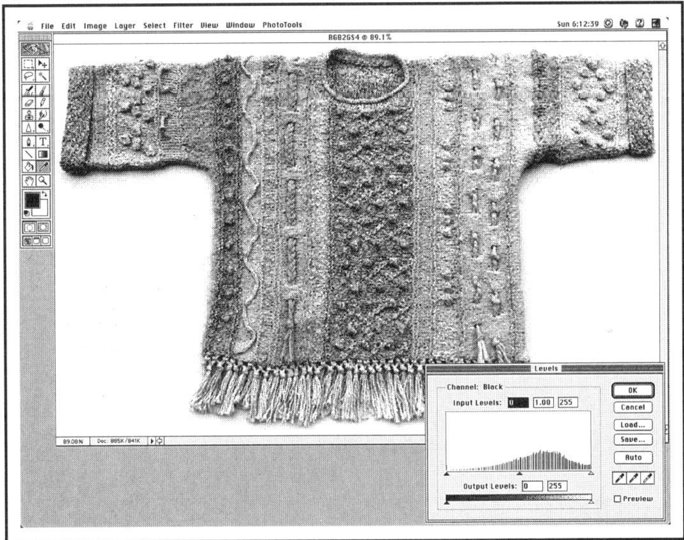

Figure 9-69: Adjust the midtone Input scale slider of the histogram to lighten the photo. Click OK. Open the Levels again and look at the difference in the histogram between this image and the one processed as RGB color.

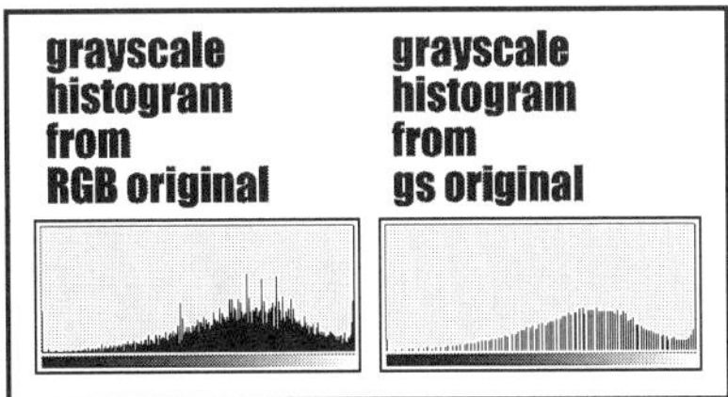

Figure 9-70: The two histograms side by side. The RGB-processed data is complete. The grayscale-processed data shows gaps.

Given a choice, which would you rather send to an output device for an accurate representation of the image as a halftone? Considering how deficient the original image was, the decision is what is called, in elevated scientific circles, a no-brainer. The finished image is shown in Figure 9-71.

Figure 9-71: The completed image after final adjustment and sharpening. Compare this photo with the original to see how far the data can be pushed to retrieve what seemed to be a hopeless-case image.

Duotones, Tritones & Quadtones

As lovely as a printed halftone can be, the tone range of a single ink is severely limited. Adding a second ink is a very easy way to extend the tone range by a factor that is much larger than would seem possible. Even if the mixing of the two inks is such that it is not readily obvious that the printed image is a duotone, the depth and clarity of a multi-ink halftone is unmistakable. Good examples of this are seen in nearly all of the commercial reproductions of the images of the noted photographer Ansel Adams. Examine any of these gorgeous prints with a magnifying lens and you will discover from two to six inks with, in some cases, special effects produced by metallics. Adding these inks is a way to faithfully retain the coloristic and textural effects which, in the original photo prints, were the result of Adams's brilliant artistic eye, sense of drama, exposure, filters, processing, and chemistry.

Duotone is the generic word we'll be using in this chapter since it is the most commonly used multi-ink halftone. While the discussion does include *tritones*—three inks—and *quadtones*—four inks—because they are simply extensions of the duotone principle, we won't specifically delve into them. Adding more than two inks is very much like adding a single ink to a grayscale picture. More than two inks extend the tonal range even farther than the simple duotone. The procedure for developing multi-ink images is the same no matter how many inks are to be used.

Many users of Photoshop think of duotones as a convenient way to colorize a grayscale image (it is much easier to use the Colorize function of the Hue/Saturation dialog box). There is certainly nothing wrong with using the duotone for tinting a halftone, but the subtle power of the duotone is not well-exploited. To make use of color tints with your halftone and to do it fast, you can print a light-colored ink in a rectangular shape the same size as the halftone and then print the halftone on top of it.

Such an effect is simulated in Figure 9-72. The only problem with this technique is that your highlights are no longer white but a pure tone of the underprinting color.

Figure 9-72: A halftone can be tinted by overprinting it on an area of a different color.

Duotones (along with tritones and quadtones) in Photoshop are a special kind of grayscale file (Figure 9-73) containing information which, when sent to an output device, causes the same file to be imaged two or more times using two or more curves (and usually two or more screen angles). Examples are shown in Figures 9-74 (45° screen angle) and 9-75 (15° screen angle). When these output files are printed with two or more inks, the result is a duotone—or tritone or quadtone (Figure 9-76). Because of this, Photoshop does not treat a duotone as a multi-channel file in which you can edit the individual components. Instead, Photoshop simulates the appearance of the overprinting inks in the Grayscale window to allow you to see how the multiple curves will print together.

Figure 9-73: Duotones are generated from a grayscale file such as this.

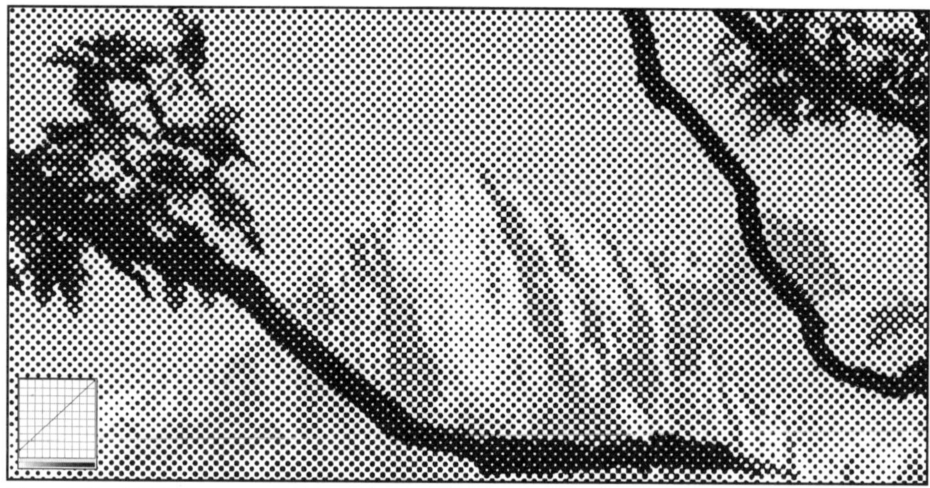

Figure 9-74: A fairly dark curve applied to the original grayscale file produces this version of the picture.

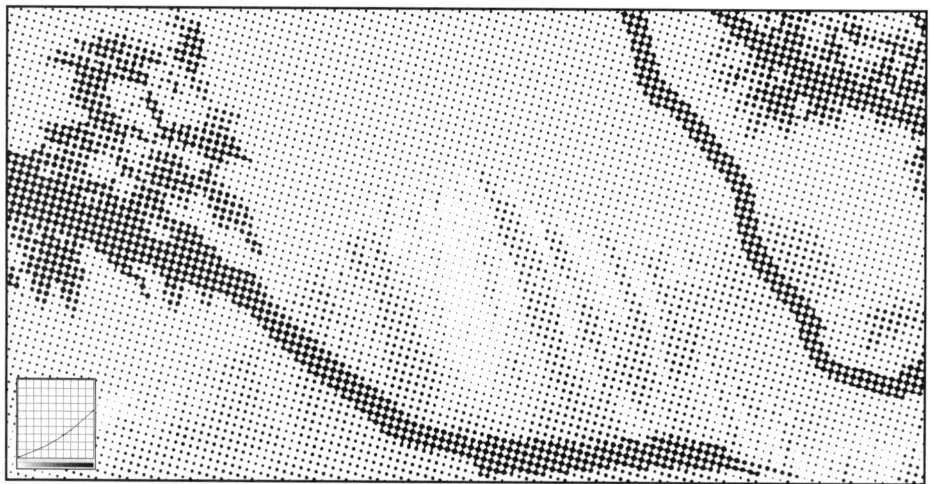

Figure 9-75: A very light curve applied to the same grayscale file produces this version. Notice that Figures 9-74 and 9-75 use different screen angles.

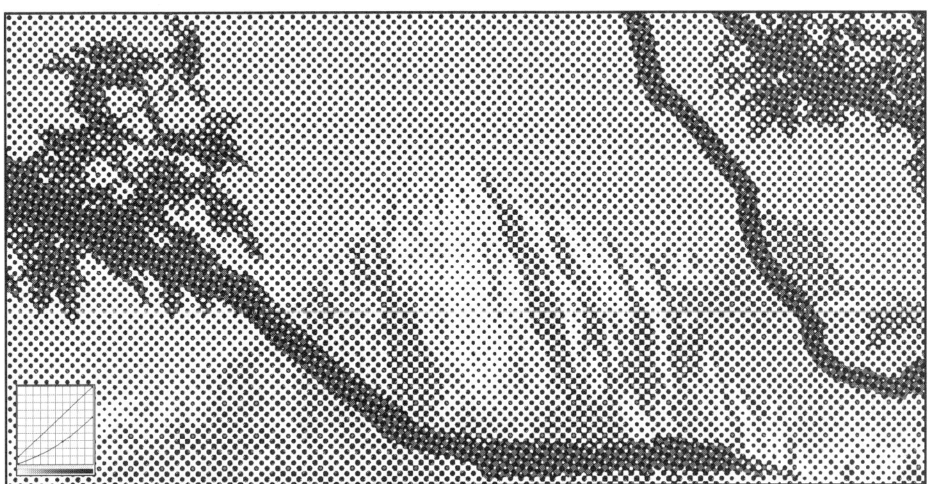

Figure 9-76: When the screen output resulting from the two curves is printed on top of each other with two different inks, the result is a duotone.

If you have tried to use a duotone and been discouraged at how dark the image printed, you'll be pleased to know that there is a solution: first, the file needs to be processed exactly as a halftone. A duotone has the same press requirements—dot gain, minimum highlight dot falloff, shadow cutoff—as a halftone. Second, after experimenting with your inks and curves, go ahead and add a pair of adjustment layers as described earlier in this chapter—one with curves elevated at 50% by the amount of the dot gain and one between the Curves layer and the background in Levels—so that you can see the effects of dot gain on your displayed image as you work. If you find that the image is growing too dark, alter the Levels adjustment layer until the image appears the way you wish it to print. Remember to throw away the Curves adjustment layer before you flatten the image and save it in its final form.

After the file is converted to Grayscale mode, choose Image | Mode | Duotone. The Duotone command is only available when the image is in Grayscale mode.

TIP *Be sure to set up an Action or a QuicKey for the Duotone command because there is no in-dialog Preview for the Duotone Options dialog box, and you have to click OK in order to see how your image is affected by any changes you make to the curves or to the ink colors. You'll be forced to return to the Duotone Options dialog box pretty often, and you will soon find so many trips to that menu are making you crazy. Really! Simply add the hot key and enjoy the rest of the process!*

When choosing the command for the first time, the dialog box opens as shown in Figure 9-77. The initial setting is for a monotone image with the ink set to black. A small pop-up menu allows you to choose whether the image will be printed with one, two, three, or four inks (Monotone, Duotone, Tritone, Quadtone). You can, if you wish, remain in monotone mode and change the black ink to a custom color. When you click OK and save your file, it then prints in the color you have chosen instead of black. At times, this is a useful way to quickly colorize a grayscale image.

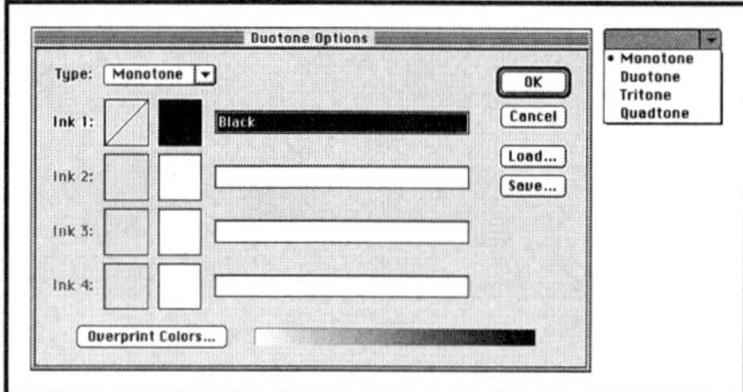

Figure 9-77: The first time you open the Duotone Options dialog box, it is set to Monotone.

The dialog box contains four pairs of thumbnails and a small text box for each row. The first thumbnail is of the present state of the curve. Click once upon the curve thumbnail and another dialog box opens in front of the first (Figure 9-78). This curve control works in exactly the same way as the Curve controls you have already learned to use except that it has an additional feature: it allows you to enter your Output values directly rather than clicking and dragging on the line of the curve. The small gradient at the bottom of this dialog box is simply to remind you on which end of the curve the light and dark values are located.

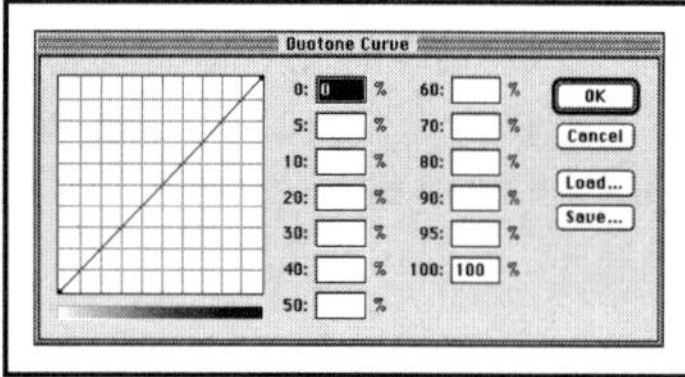

Figure 9-78: Click on the Duotone Options dialog box's curve thumbnail and this Duotone Curve dialog box opens.

The second thumbnail sets the ink color. Click on the thumbnail once. The Photoshop Color Picker l opens (Figure 9-79). You may choose a color from this picker, or you may wish, as is more common, to choose a color from the Pantone palette. Click on the Custom button which opens the Custom Colors palette. The default for this palette is Pantone Coated. At the top, a small pop-up menu allows you to change the color selector to any of three other Pantone standards as well as to color sets by Toyo,

TruMatch, Focoltone, and ANPA. If you don't know the number of the Pantone color you wish to choose, move the vertical slider to an appropriate color setting and glance through the colors that are contained within the large swatches window. You may, if you know the number you want, simply enter the numbers. There is no data entry box in which to type, but you can enter the number anyway and the Color Picker will find the color.

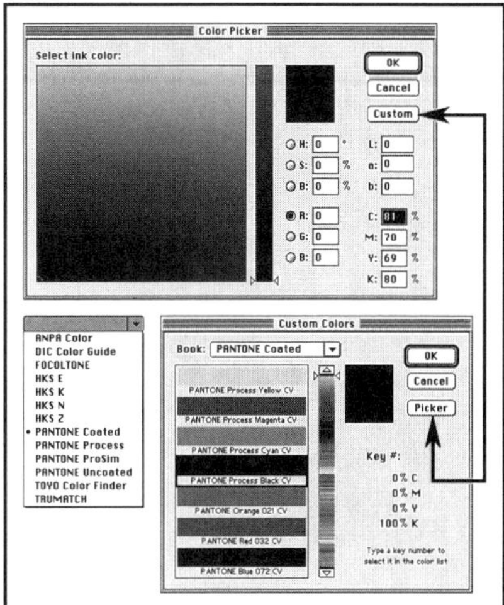

Figure 9-79: The Photoshop Color Picker with the Custom Colors palette.

Go ahead and choose the inks you wish to use and notice that both curves are the same as the single curve thumbnail shown in Figure 9-77. If you click OK at this time, your screen shows a much darker, tinted version of the grayscale file. If you haven't adjusted the curves, your output for the image will be as though you had simply imaged a halftone, duplicated it, and stripped it into another piece of film and used it to make a different plate.

Adjusting the curves to get exactly the effect you want takes some experience. There is a small tool on the Duotone Curve dialog box—the gradient bar at the bottom—which helps you to gauge the overall tonality produced by your inks as they print on top of each other. As you change the curves, pay close attention to this bar. It shows you subtle changes such as too much overt color, a too-lengthy midtone section, a too-short highlight range, and so on. Exactly what it does is hard to describe, but pay attention to it and you'll understand quickly.

Go ahead and adjust the curves, remembering what you have already learned about using curve controls: moving a point on the curve toward the top of the grid makes the tone darker, and moving it down makes it lighter. Remember, too, that you have two or more curves to play off against each other. Think of the curve lines as a set of corresponding points, the curve with a given value that is closest to the top of the grid produces the dominant tone for that value. Try to begin by experimenting with your second ink's curve so that the ink's impact on the image is slight. As was mentioned earlier, some of the most strikingly beautiful duotones are those which are not instantly recognizable as duotones. Use the second ink to reinforce the tone range from midtone to shadow, and keep it out of the highlights so that your highlights do not develop a strong color cast. As you become more skilled at arriving at the look you want, you will certainly develop your own tastes, your own likes and dislikes.

Using Custom Inks

When you decide to use custom inks, there are a few things you should keep in mind about how you define an ink and the ways textured and opaque inks combine with process-color inks.

The Pantone color selector in Photoshop does not contain some of the inks that you can find in a printed Pantone swatch book. Among the missing inks are metallics, neons, and other specialty inks for which no RGB value could be easily assigned. If you wish to use, say, a metallic ink in your duotone, click on the Picker button which returns you to the Photoshop Color Picker. Use any of the color models—HSB, RGB, Lab, or CMYK—to build a color that is visually close to the ink you wish to use. Remember that Photoshop cannot simulate metallic reflectance: you must choose a color that allows you to see how the *color* of the metallic tone appears when mixed with your other ink choices. When the color is as close as you can make it, click OK.

In the naming box for that ink, enter the exact color name you wish to use. Whatever the ink name, Pantone metallic gold color, for example, enter the name like this: PANTONE 871 CV. Use uppercase letters with a space before and after the number. (Nothing awful will happen if you don't, but since every program does it that way, you risk confusing someone farther downstream in the production flow if you don't maintain consistency.) After you have named the ink, proceed to develop the duotone.

Try to remember, when you are using a specialty ink, that they are unlike typical colored inks. They are usually opaque and often develop a surface texture that can drastically change inks which overprint them. Neon yellow, for example, when overprinted with solid black produces what looks like a 70% tint of a black. If the success of your image is dependent upon solid black next to neon yellow, you'll need the black to knock out of the yellow rather than to overprint it. Ink opacity also has to be considered. Metallics, for example, are opaque inks. Colors overprinted by solid metallics get covered up. If you fear that this will be a problem, be sure to discuss the possibility of customizing the ink laydown sequence with your printer. Printers do not usually like to alter their laydown sequence—inks are formulated to make a certain laydown order more efficient—but if you have a good reason for making the request, your print house will do its best for you.

It is a good idea, before setting up your duotone, to duplicate the grayscale image and to place the windows of the grayscale and the duotone so that both are easily visible (Figure 9-80). In the figure, two inks have been chosen and the curves have been altered (the duotone is on the right). Notice that in the sunlit lawn area in the lower part of the image, much of the grass texture has been blown out and lost. Without the grayscale reference, it is very easy to get wrapped up in making the inks look a certain way and to forget to check image details such as this.

Figure 9-80: When developing a duotone, duplicate the image so that you can work on the duotone (right) and visually compare it to the original grayscale file (left) while you are working.

Figure 9-81 shows how the curve of Ink 2 has been modified to bring back the texture of the lawn. You're looking at the figure taken from a screen shot and printed in black and white. However, if you study the large bush and the tree trunk closest to the house, you can see that there is an appreciable difference in the clarity and detail of the two images.

Now that you've come up with an ink and curve combination that fits your ideas about the image, take a look at the separate components of the duotone. You can look at them but cannot alter them if you wish to print the image as a duotone. From the Image menu, choose Mode | Multichannel (Figure 9-82). When the image changes mode, you will be looking at Ink 1 (Figure 9-83). Usually, this is the black ink. Press command+2 or Ctrl+2. This is the second ink channel (Figure 9-84). Use the Undo command to return to Duotone mode.

Figure 9-81: The two curves have been adjusted so that the detail in the original file (left) is preserved in the duotone (right).

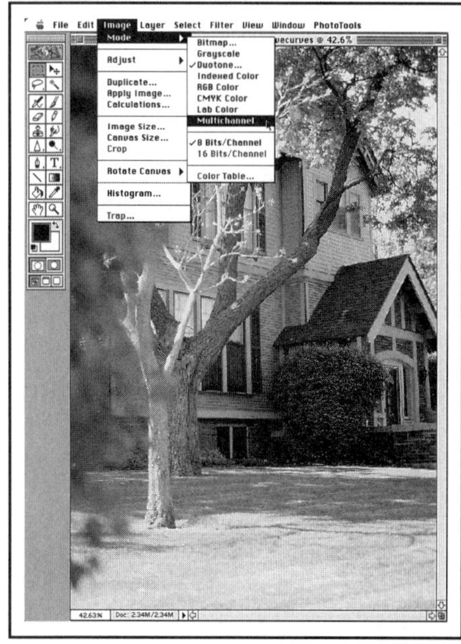

Figure 9-82: To look at the individual plates of a duotone, first convert the file to Multichannel mode.

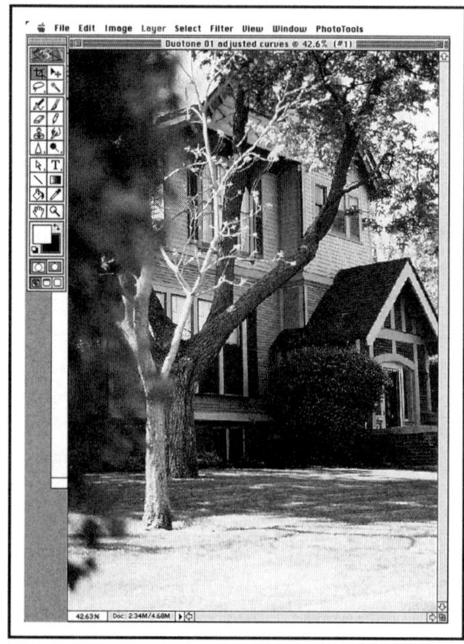

Figure 9-83: Press Command+1 or Ctrl+1 to look at Ink 1.

Figure 9-84: Press Command+2 or Ctrl+2 to look at Ink 2. Use the Undo command to switch back to Duotone mode.

An Old Photo From a New One

Here's an interesting technique that produces a nice-looking simulation of a well-preserved but very old photograph. The procedure changes the photo's coloration to an antique brown that varies in intensity with the overall strength of Ink 2. The most successful results are obtained when Ink 2 is light in comparison to Ink 1and contains no amount of black.

1. Be sure to save your image before you begin. Duplicate the finished duotone. Convert the duplicate to CMYK mode. Set your Foreground color to white and press Option+Delete or Alt+Delete to wipe out all traces of the image.
2. Return to the original duotone and convert it to Multichannel mode. Select all and use the Copy command on the first channel. Switch to the CMYK window and press command+4 or Ctrl+4 to view the Black channel. Paste into this channel.
3. Switch back to the duotone. Press command+2 or Ctrl+2. With the selection still active, use the Copy command again. Return to the CMYK document. Press Command+1 or Ctrl+1, and paste. Press Command+2 or Ctrl+2, and paste. Press Command+3 or Ctrl+3, and paste. After completing these steps, you have pasted Ink 1 into the Black channel and Ink 2 into the Cyan, Magenta, and Yellow channels. To view your finished work, type Command+~ or Ctrl+~. Cool, huh?

When you finish developing the curves on your duotone, be sure to save your settings. You want all of the photos within the same project to be consistent with each other, and saving your settings offers an easy way to do that. Click on the Save button in the Duotone Options dialog box. It's a good idea to create a new folder where you can group your duotone settings so that you can use them again whenever they are needed. Within the Photoshop folder is another folder called Goodies. Within Goodies is another folder titled Duotone Presets. Inside this folder are separate folders for duotones, tritones, and quadtones. Within each of these are separate folders for Gray, Pantone, and Process presets. Placing your own presets within the Duotone Presets gives you the opportunity to organize your preset files. It makes sense to name your preset in much the same way the bundled Duotone Presets are named; such a name might be *144 orange, bl,* indicating that the duotone uses Pantone 144 (orange) and black. You can even add, if your curves resembled those in Figure 9-81, some description of the relative strength of the two inks to each other: *144 orange 70%, black 110%.* However you name your curve set, be sure to do it in a way that allows you to easily remember what the preset looks like.

For an easy entry into the world of duotones, try one of the bundled presets. There are 88 duotone possibilities, 35 tritones, and 14 quadtones. The group contains a lot of variations. For example, there are four different presets using Pantone 144, each of them slightly different, each of them producing a pleasing result. Experiment by loading each and deciding for yourself which gives the look you are seeking. Once you have loaded the preset, you are free to tweak the curves and to change the loaded ink color into some other color. Many experienced Photoshop users never go to the trouble of developing a brand new preset. Instead, they use the bundled presets as starting points and tweak the settings. If you choose to work this way, you'll still want to save your variations on the presets for later use.

The last step is saving/exporting your duotone file. In all likelihood, you aren't going to be generating your duotone separations from within Photoshop but will import the file into one of the page layout programs such as QuarkXPress or Adobe PageMaker. Given this, saving the file is easy enough: choose Photoshop EPS. It is the only format choice available that allows duotones to be imported into one of the other programs. The dialog box for saving in EPS format is shown in Figure 9-85.

The settings in the figure are appropriate for a Macintosh exporting to a page layout program. If you are a Windows user, you have fewer choices. Your default for the Preview is TIFF (1 bit). TIFF (8 bits) looks better when you import the image into the page layout program. Binary or ASCII Encoding are choices that have a lot to do with the kind of output device you are using. If you are unsure which to choose, contact your service bureau for advice.

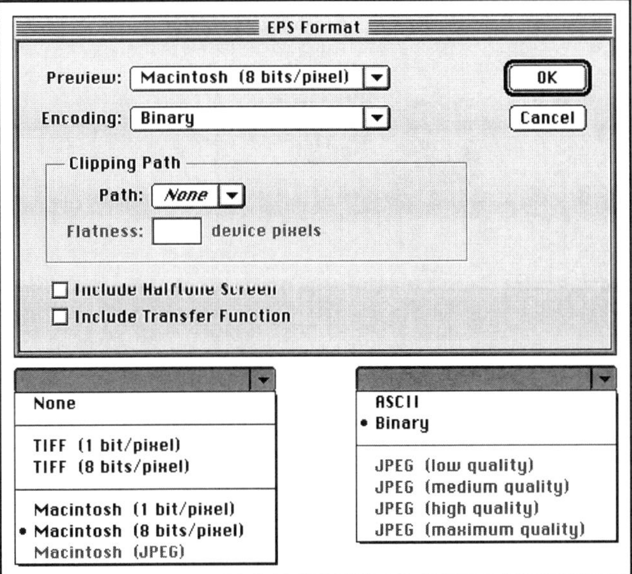

Figure 9-85: The EPS Format export options window.

The only other important choice to be made when saving the duotone is whether to include, or embed, the halftone screen (see the check box in the lower portion of the window). If you don't include the screen, then you have to change the screen angles in the program from which the separations are to be generated. In Figure 9-86, a screen representation of a QuarkXPress document shows how to do this:

1. After you have imported the duotone into a QuarkXPress document, choose Edit | Colors.
2. Click to select the Pantone color which the imported image has added to the Colors list.
3. Click on the Edit button. The dialog box in the upper right-hand side of the figure appears.
4. Click on the Screen Values pop-up menu. The default screen angle for any spot color used in QuarkXPress is the same as that used for black, or 45°. Change your Pantone color's screen angle to that of one of the other process colors; if possible, choose a color that is not going to be used very much in the document.

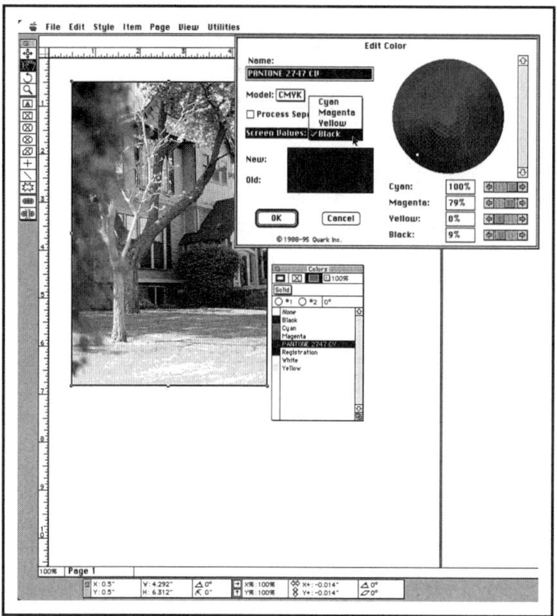

Figure 9-86: Changing the screen angle for a custom ink in QuarkXPress.

In Adobe PageMaker, changes to the screen angles are done from the Print dialog box. In the Print Document dialog box, click on the Color button. A new dialog box titled Print Color appears. Click on the Separations radio button at the upper left. Below, there is a list of colors. Scroll down until you see the custom ink to be used in your duotone. Click on the color to select it. Now, click on the Print This Ink check box below the scrolling color list. Enter the screen frequency and screen angle you wish to use for this ink in the two data entry fields to the right of the color list.

The alternative to changing the screen angles in the program from which the output will be generated is to set the screen angles within Photoshop. To do this:

1. Choose File | Page Setup.
2. Click on the Screen button.
3. The dialog box shown at the top of Figure 9-87 appears. When you first see it, the check box at the top will be checked. Uncheck it.
4. You now have a number of choices to make. You can manually enter the screen frequency and the angle of the screen, as well as set the spot function—the shape of the dot—from the available choices. The number of choices is almost overwhelming. If you wish, play it safe and click on the Auto button. The dialog box shown at the bottom of the figure appears next. Enter the resolution of the output device and the screen frequency you will be using. Click OK. If your output device is equipped with PostScript Level 2 or an Adobe Emerald controller, you

can check the Use Accurate Screens check box. This allows the device to use a prebuilt set of very precise—*accurate*—screen dots and angles. If your device does not use PostScript Level 2 or have the Emerald controller, the check box has no effect.

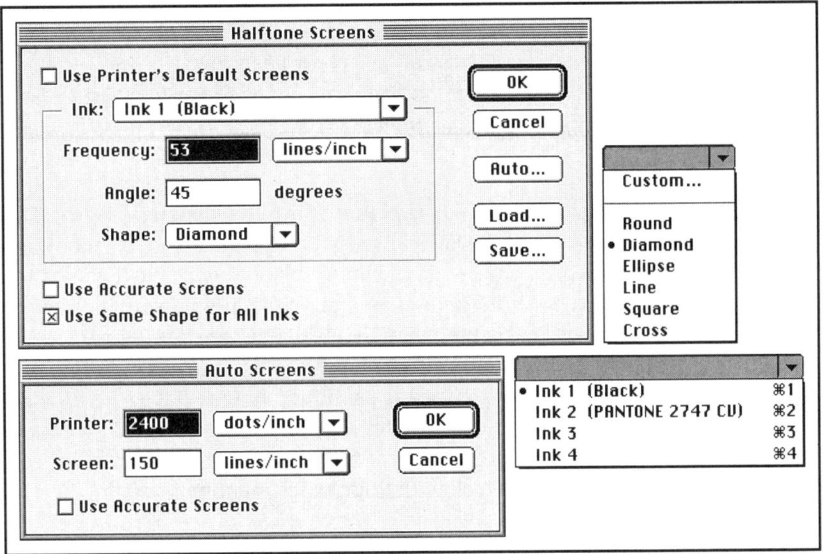

Figure 9-87: Photoshop's Halftone Screens options window.

If you intend to do a number of duotones, it is a good idea to save your settings for the screen frequencies you wish to use. That way you can avoid having to make the choices every time you want to save a new file. Simply use the Save button, and later, the Load button. There is another way to set up values so that you don't have to access the Screen dialog box. Hold the Option key or the Alt key: the Save button changes to ->Default and the Load button to <-Default. Click the Load button if you want your present settings to become the defaults for all future files. To restore the settings to what they were when you first opened the dialog box, click on the Save button.

TIP *If you decide to embed your screens in the duotone document, you should check with your service bureau to be sure there is no reason why you shouldn't do so. There are some strange things that can happen with some RIPs.*

One problem that can occur is that the embedded screen does not quite override the RIP's screening. You can end up with a single film that has two different screen angles on the same plate. *This can result in an improbable one-color moiré. Bet you didn't know that was possible, huh?*

Another problem you may run into is this (hold on, now, this one is tricky to explain!): Let's say that you have used a screen angle of 0° for a specific purpose. For example, you might have chosen a coarse linear dot function so that one of your inks prints as multi-width horizontal lines. When you send your files to an imagesetter—let's stipulate a small-format machine with a 14-inch film width—the operator prints your page sideways so that he doesn't waste all of the film along the edges. When the page images sideways, the embedded screen does not necessarily turn. You may end up with the linear effect you intended to be horizontal on your page actually running vertically instead.

These problems are not universal but they are common enough that a consultation with your service bureau will save you trouble.

A set of four images in the color section of this book shows how the image in Figure 9-80 was developed. You can see the original grayscale image, a monotone of the image using the second—dark blue—ink, the image printed with the default straight-line curves, and the final duotone shown in Figure 9-81. If you want to practice on the file used in the examples, locate the file RGB2DUO.PSD on the Companion CD-ROM. The file is in RGB mode. It was deliberately left that way so you can follow through the entire procedure. First, process the file as though it were to be a halftone, convert it to Grayscale, and then generate the duotone. We want to warn you that making duotones is one of the most fascinating things you can do in Photoshop and that you can get hooked on it! We wish you luck with your experimenting.

TIP

The duotone examples in the color-plate section of this book are not really duotones. They are files which have been developed as duotones and then converted to CMYK mode. The four-color printing process simulates the duotones remarkably well.

If you run into a situation where you have a black and white original image on a page where process color is a possibility, make the black and white image into a duotone and then convert it to CMYK. The extra depth of detail and expanded tone range for the image is an opportunity too good to be missed!

If it is ever necessary to work extensively in Photoshop with a pair of inks and the project contains one or more duotones, you may find it easier to work in CMYK mode using just two of the channels. Prepare your duotones in the usual way. Convert to Multichannel mode. Copy the two channels, one at a time, into the two channels you are using in CMYK mode. For example, a red-toned duotone could have ink #1 copied to the Black channel and ink #2 copied to the Magenta channel. All other work on this document could then be done by using either black or magenta or mixtures of the two. Working in this way allows you to select areas of the image and fill with one, both, or a mix of the colors. When the file is changed to output, use whatever ink you wish with the two films.

Spot Color

The term *spot color* refers to the use on press of premixed inks. In process color printing, colors are formed by overprinting the process primaries: cyan, magenta, yellow, and black. Despite the fact that process inks routinely deliver faithful color reproduction, there are wide ranges of colors which cannot be reproduced. There is another drawback to process inks: because the inks must be more or less translucent so that they can seem to blend with each other, they cannot act as a simultaneous vehicle for color and surface textures. Spot colors—referred to in Photoshop as Custom Colors—are able to remedy the deficiencies of process printing. Spot colors are not built up from other tones—well, they are, but not on press—but are mixed before printing and applied as a single color, sometimes with tints—tones with percentages less than 100—of the color.

With spot colors, there is no need to preserve ink translucency. Large amounts of pigment in the solvent medium can be made to produce gloriously saturated colors. Minute amounts of metal or light-colored reflective materials can be introduced along with the pigment to give highly reflective flat colors (neon) or metallic reflectance. In some cases, there might be no pigment at all: the ink is applied as a transparent film with surface properties ranging from shiny to matte. Such inks—varnishes—are applied to enhance colored areas of the printing, or to provide a subtle reflective contrast with the surface of the print stock.

We mentioned some of the problems you can encounter with spot colors when we discussed duotones. Specialty inks are unlike typical colored inks. They are usually opaque and often develop a surface texture that can drastically change any inks which overprint them. Neon yellow, for example, when overprinted with solid black, produces what looks like a 70% tint of a black. Metallics are dense and opaque. Colors overprinted by metallic ink tend to get covered up. Another problem that you'll encounter is Photoshop. Despite its formidable power to handle color, there is no real, built-in provision for handling custom colors. You can choose spot colors from the Custom Colors palettes. You can use them in duotones, but the usage there is extremely limited. (If you don't believe me, draw a selection in a duotone and try to fill it with a 100% tint of your #2 ink. It can't be done.) Actually, Photoshop's lack of facilities for handling spot colors is more perceived than real. You *can* handle custom inks quite easily. The process is not intuitive, but once you get the hang of it, you'll wonder what all the fuss is about. It simply takes some planning and a few mental adjustments along the way.

A Four Custom-Color Tutorial

The easiest way to learn a technique is to follow a tutorial. No, please don't groan. The authors are aware that many tutorials in software manuals are—as the saying goes—about as interesting as watching paint dry. This one isn't so bad. The material is interesting, it has pretty colors, and nearly all the real work has been done for you. All you have to do is open the file (on the Companion CD-ROM, find the file AFRICA.PSD in the Chapter 9 Practice folder), follow along, and do the fun stuff. When you're finished, you'll have a much clearer idea how you can use Photoshop's existing capabilities for your own custom color work.

This tutorial involves making a small poster announcing an African Textile exhibit at a museum in a small midwestern city. An approximation of the poster is shown in Figure 9-88 and in color in the color plates section of the book.

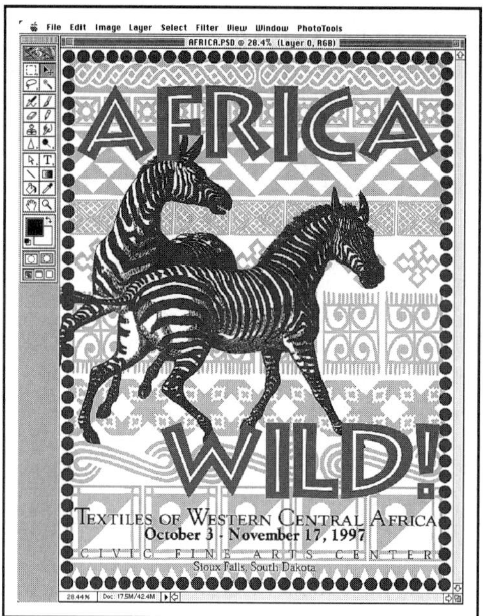

Figure 9-88: Four-tone poster to be handled in Photoshop entirely with custom colors.

First, some background about how and why the file was put together the way it is. The background of the poster is a set of African motifs suggestive of the repetition of motifs on a textile. The color used is an orange-tinted gold, Pantone 116. (If you have a Pantone swatch book, you might find it useful to look at the colors and compare them to the file.) Two stressed-looking zebras are next. They, and the round-dot border, are to be printed in Pantone 876, a metallic copper ink. The two large words in an inline version of the Lithos Black font are colored with Pantone Warm Red. Finally, there are four lines of small text at the bottom in Pantone Black.

Each of the four components of this poster was placed on a separate layer. The background shapes were put together in Illustrator using enlarged characters from the shareware font African Ornaments One by Michelle Dixon of Dixie's Delights Fonts. The shapes were copied and pasted into this document as black shapes. The Paste operation created a separate layer with the areas around and inside the shapes transparent. Figure 9-89 shows a detail of the shapes with the white background layer hidden. The other two text layers—the large title letters and the four lines of smaller text at the bottom—were also pasted into this document as black shapes. These letter shapes are also surrounded by transparent areas. Note that the inner areas of the inline letters are transparent.

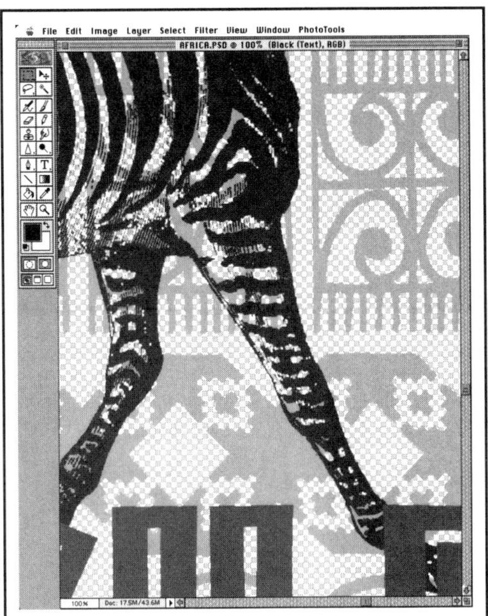

Figure 9-89: All of the color areas in the poster are solid. Since the document is in layers, other colors show through the areas between the color shapes.

The zebra layer was pasted in from a black and white scan. Because it will be necessary to have access to the outlines of the zebra shapes, we eliminated the white areas from the original scan using this procedure. Then, we opened the Channels palette. With this scan—black and white—there is a single channel, Black. Command+click or Ctrl+click this channel to turn the white areas into a selection. Choose Select | Inverse to select the black areas. For this document, we used the Copy command and then pasted the zebras into the poster file. As you can see from Figure 9-89, only the dark areas were pasted.

The border was pasted in separately. Because it is to be the same color as the zebras, we hid all but these two layers and used the Merge Visible command from the Layers palette sidebar menu.

There were now four layers and a solid white background. We turned on Preserve Transparency for each layer. We colored the bottom image layer first. We clicked on the Foreground Color box, clicked on Custom, and chose the ink we wished to use. When the Color Picker was closed, we selected the bottom layer and used Option+Delete or Alt+Delete to fill the non-transparent pixels with the gold color. All of the other layers were colored in the same way. We then turned off the Preserve Transparency option for each layer. At that point we saved the file for you to open.

Figure 9-90 shows the bottom layer with all other layers hidden. In Figure 9-91, the zebra layer is now visible. We cannot use the zebra layer as it is because the bottom layer shows between the zebra stripes. Your next task is to make, and then modify, an alpha channel.

Figure 9-90: The bottom layer in this poster contains the background shapes.

Figure 9-91: The layer with the zebras needs to be modified because the background shapes show between the zebra stripes.

1. Command+click or Ctrl+click the zebra layer's thumbnail. This selects all of the non-transparent pixels of the layer. Save this selection as an alpha channel (click on the Save Selection icon—second from left—at the bottom of the Channels palette. Deselect. Click on the new channel's thumbnail to view it (Figure 9-92).
2. Zoom in closer to the window. Use paint brushes and selection tools (filling a selection with white) to eliminate the black pixels within the boundaries of the zebra shapes. This is simple if a bit time-consuming. It is a *lot* easier than trying to select the zebras before pasting them into this document! When you are finished, your channel should resemble the one shown in Figure 9-93.
3. Click on the top thumbnail of the Channels palette to view the document in color. Hide the zebra layer so that only the bottom layer and the background are visible. Click on the bottom layer to select it. Make the modified channel into an active selection by Command+clicking or Ctrl+clicking its thumbnail on the Channels palette. Press the Delete key. All of the pixels directly below the zebras and the border circles are eliminated from the bottom layer (Figure 9-94). Deselect. Make the zebra layer visible again (Figure 9-95). Notice that the spaces between the zebra stripes are entirely white.

Figure 9-92: Make the zebra layer into a selection, then save it to an alpha channel.

Figure 9-93: Work in the alpha channel with the selection tools and the Paintbrush to fill in the zebra stripes and to make the shapes solid white.

Figure 9-94: Make the alpha channel into a selection. Select the layer with the background shapes and press Delete to eliminate the zebra shapes from the background layer.

Figure 9-95: Make the zebra layer visible. The background shapes no longer show through the zebra stripes.

4. Next, apply this same procedure to the large red titling letters. Make the headline layer visible and select it (Figure 9-96). Command+click or Ctrl+click the layer icon to make the letter shapes into a selection. Save the selection as an alpha channel (click on the Save Selection icon at the bottom of the Channels palette). Click on the new alpha channel's thumbnail to view it (Figure 9-97). Use a paintbrush somewhat narrower than the letters—with the Foreground color set to white—to eliminate the inline portion of the letters. When finished, your channel should look similar to Figure 9-98.

5. Click on the top thumbnail of the Channels palette to view the document in color. Turn the new channel into a selection (Command+click or Ctrl+click on the channel's thumbnail). Hide the headline layer and the zebra layer. Select the bottom layer. Press the Delete key. This eliminates the letter shapes from the bottom layer (Figure 9-99). Make the zebra layer visible and select it. Press the Delete key. This deletes the shapes of the letters from the layer containing the zebras (Figure 9-100). Make the titling letters layer visible. If you look at it carefully, you can see that the spaces within the letters are entirely white (Figure 9-101).

Figure 9-96: Make the headline layer visible.

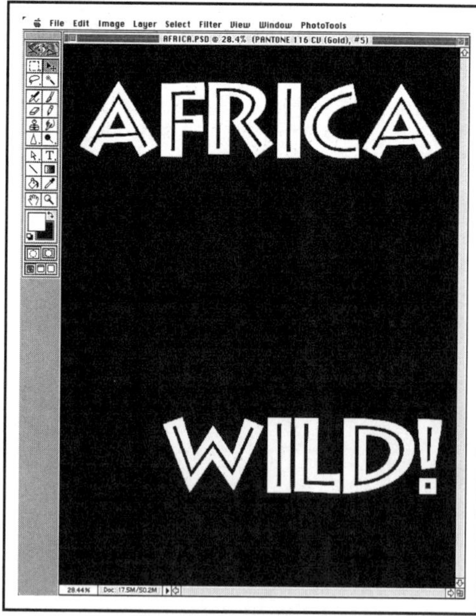

Figure 9-97: Make the headline layer into a selection, and save it as another alpha channel.

Figure 9-98: Work in the alpha channel, and eliminate the inner black shapes from the letters.

Figure 9-99: Make the new alpha channel into a selection. Select the background layer and press Delete. This eliminates the letter shapes from the background shapes.

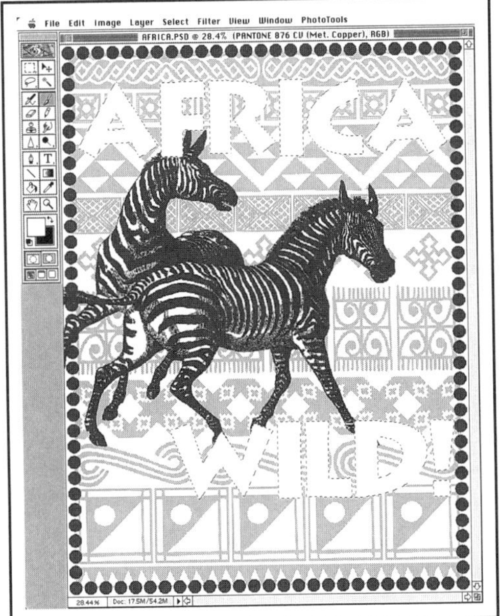

Figure 9-100: Make the zebra layer visible and click on its thumbnail in the Layers palette. With the alpha channel selection still active, press Delete to delete the letter shapes from where they overlap the zebras.

Figure 9-101: With all three layers visible, none of the shapes in back show through the spaces in objects in front.

6. The last layer contains the smaller text at the bottom of the poster. Make this layer visible and select it (Figure 9-102). It isn't necessary to make an alpha channel for this layer since the letter shapes just need to be knocked out of the bottom layer. Command+click or Ctrl+click the layer's thumbnail to make the selection. Hide the layer and click on the bottom layer's thumbnail to select it. Press the Delete key (Figure 9-103).

Figure 9-102: Make the fourth—small text—layer visible. Turn it into a selection. Use the selection to knock out the small letters from the background shapes.

Figure 9-103: A close-up of the background layer shows how all the shapes have been cut out of the background layer.

7. Click on each layer, one at a time. While each layer is selected, turn on the Preserve Transparency check box, press Option+Delete or Alt+Delete—with the Foreground color set to white—to fill the layer's non-transparent pixels with white, and uncheck the Preserve Transparency check box. Your window will resemble that shown in Figure 9-104 (the white background layer is hidden).

8. Use the Image | Duplicate command. Choose Image | Mode | CMYK. A dialog box asking whether or not to flatten the image appears. Click on the Don't Flatten button.

9. Click on the zebra layer in the Layers palette to select it. Command+click or Ctrl+click to make the layer into a selection. On the Channels palette, click on the thumbnail of the Cyan channel. (You can also press Command+1 or Ctrl+1.) Set your Foreground/Background colors to their defaults. Fill the selection with black (Figure 9-105).

Figure 9-104: Hide the white background and fill all of the design layers with white.

Figure 9-105: Change the document mode to CMYK. Turn the zebra layer into a selection, switch to the Cyan channel, and fill the selection with black.

10. Click on the title letters layer to select it. Command+click or Ctrl+click to make the layer into a selection. On the Channels palette, click on the thumbnail of the Magenta channel. (Press Command+2 or Ctrl+2.) Fill the selection with black (Figure 9-106).
11. Click on the bottom layer to select it. Command+click or Ctrl+click to make the layer into a selection. On the Channels palette, click on the thumbnail of the Yellow channel. (Press Command+3 or Ctrl+3.) Fill the selection with black (Figure 9-107).
12. Click on the text layer to select it. Command+click or Ctrl+click to make the layer into a selection. On the Channels palette, click on the thumbnail of the Black channel. (Press Command+4 or Ctrl+4.) Fill the selection with black (Figure 9-108).
13. Flatten the image and delete the alpha channels. Click on the top thumbnail of the Channels palette to view the document in color (Figure 9-109). Your poster with its bright interesting colors is now reduced to an image composed of the process-color primaries (Figure 9-109). It might not be interesting to look at but it produces perfectly registered film.

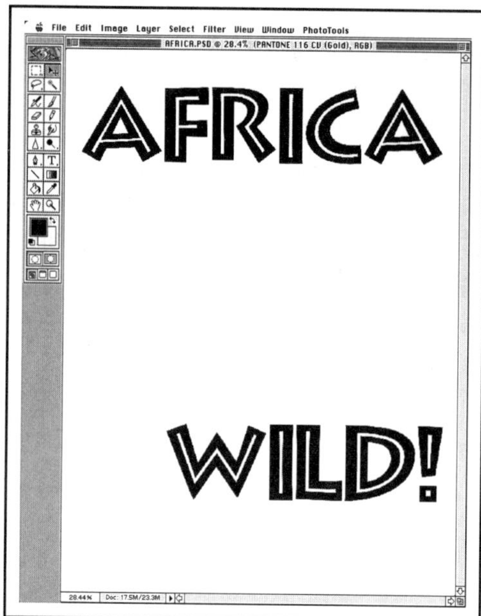

Figure 9-106: Turn the headline letters layer into a selection, switch to the Magenta channel, and fill the selection with black.

Figure 9-107: Turn the background motifs layer into a selection, switch to the Yellow channel, and fill the selection with black.

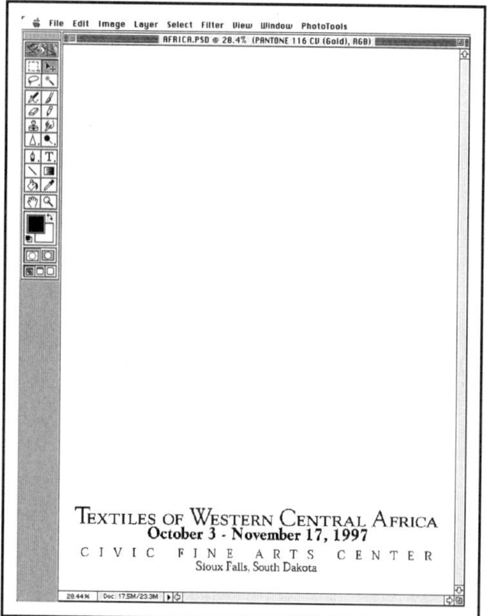

Figure 9-108: Turn the small type layer into a selection, switch to the Black channel, and fill the selection with black.

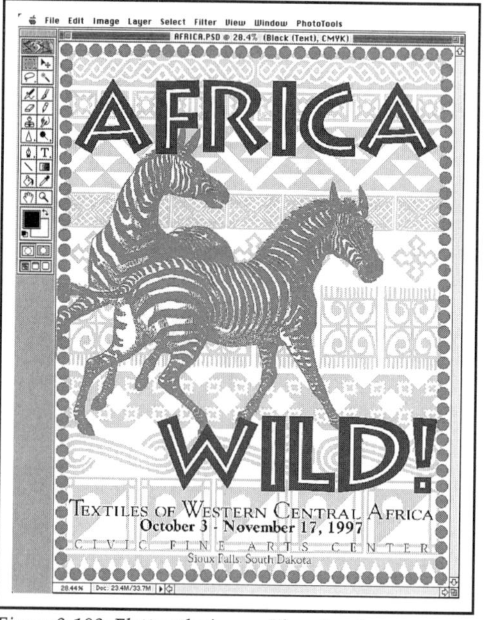

Figure 9-109: Flatten the image. The colors have now changed to the process primaries.

14. The next step is to trap the document. (Trapping is covered in detail in Chapter 10.) Photoshop's Trap command is found at the bottom of the Image menu. The dialog box allows you to specify the amount of trap in pixels, points, or millimeters. The print house running your job will furnish you with trap specifications. A typical measurement might be .003 inches. Since Photoshop does not allow the trap specification to be entered in inches, use a conversion utility to convert the required number into one of the available units of measurement. .003 inches is approximately equal to .216 points. Change the units pop-up menu to points and enter .22 (Figure 9-110). The enlarged view in Figure 9-111 shows how the trapping spreads the lighter colors into the darker colors wherever those colors meet each other. The Trap command also shows why it was necessary to eliminate the overlap of the shapes. Without doing so, the zebras, for example, would appear to be cyan with mottlings of green every place they overlapped the background shapes.

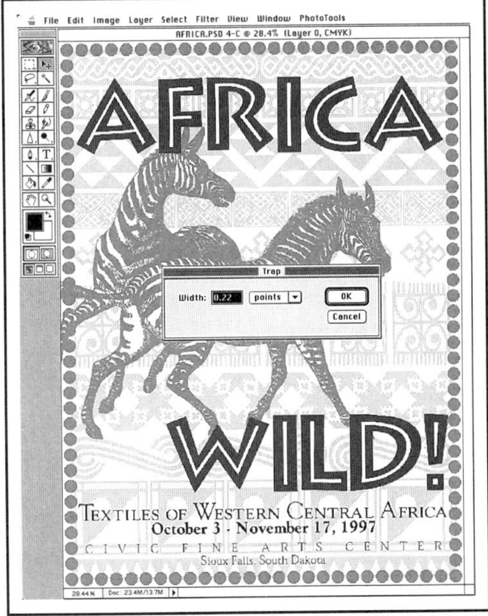

Figure 9-110: Use Photoshop's Trap command to trap the ink areas where they meet each other.

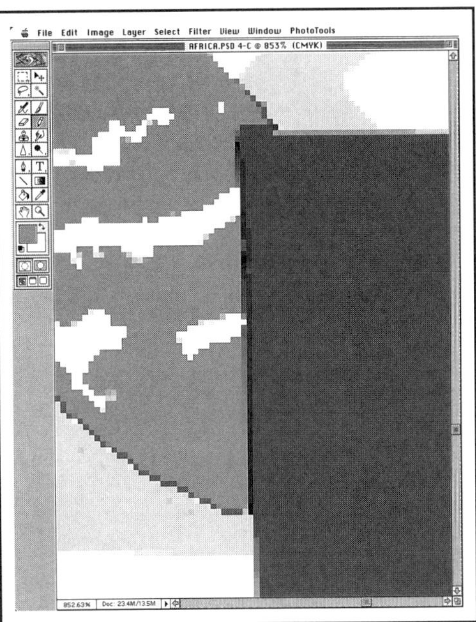

Figure 9-111: Enlarged detail of the poster after the Trap command has executed.

15. The file should now be saved in TIFF or Photoshop EPS format. When it is printed from a typical page layout program and separations are made, the cyan film is used to make the plate which prints the metallic copper ink (Pantone 876), the magenta film for Pantone Warm Red, the yellow film for Pantone 116 gold, and the black film for Pantone Black. Figure 9-112 shows an approximation of the four negatives.

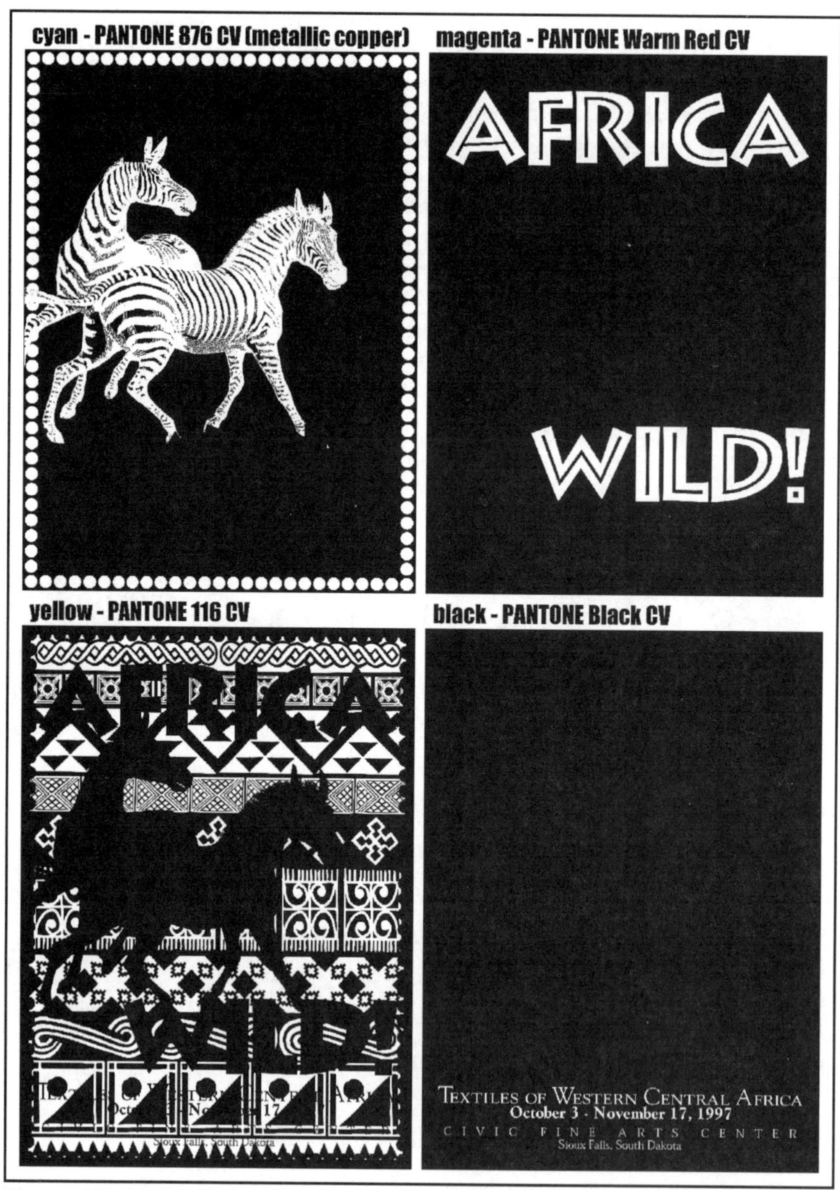

Figure 9-112: A look at the four CMYK negatives which will be printed with the labeled Pantone inks.

Emulating Custom Colors

When working with a four-color file, it is sometimes disconcerting to view the image in process colors. You can, if you wish, change Photoshop's display so that the process colors show up onscreen as if they were custom colors. Besides being able to see your custom colors in approximately the same way that they will print, you can also see the way the colors combine with each other. The latter point, in itself, makes the effort worthwhile.

1. Begin by choosing the colors you wish to use. Figure 9-113 shows a set of possibilities: Pantone 286 substitutes for cyan, Pantone 220 substitutes for magenta, Pantone 109 substitutes for yellow, and Pantone Process Black substitutes for black.
2. From the File menu, choose New. Specify a new grayscale document about 2 inches square at a resolution of 72 ppi. The size and resolution are unimportant since you will be discarding this window.
3. From the Image menu, choose Mode|Duotone. Change the pop-up menu at the top so that it reads Quadtone. Click on the Color box for Ink 1. Go through the Color Picker to the Custom Color dialog box. Specify the color (in this case Pantone 286). Do not click on the OK button. Instead, click on the Picker button. Write down the Lab values for this color. Click OK. Follow this same procedure for each of the other inks.
4. At the bottom of the Duotone Options dialog box is a button called Overprint. Click on this button. A new dialog box opens to show you simulations of the ways these four inks appear when printed on top of each other, or *overprint.* Click on the box which is labeled 2 + 3. When the picker opens, write down the Lab values for this color. Do the same thing—in this order—for the boxes marked 1 + 3, 1 + 2, and 1 + 2 + 3. Click OK to close this dialog box. Close the Duotone Options dialog box and discard the small image window.
5. From the File menu, choose Color Settings|Printing Inks Setup. Click on the Save button and save your present settings under a name that is easy for you to identify, in a place that is easy for you to find.
6. After saving your settings, click on the pop-up menu at the top of the Printing Inks Setup dialog box and select Custom. A small dialog box containing three columns of numbers and seven color swatches appears (Figure 9-113, left-hand side). Begin at the top of the set of color swatches. Click once on the Color box for Cyan. The Color Picker appears. Enter the Lab values for the Pantone color which you intend to substitute for cyan (in this case 286). Click OK. Do the same with each of the other colors, for the three compound colors (2 + 3, 1 + 3, & 1 + 2), for the 1 + 2 + 3 combination, and for solid black. When finished, click OK.

➡

Your screen now looks very unlike a normal process color screen since you have instructed Photoshop to simulate a display which uses a different ink set. Using Photoshop's display capabilities in this way allows for color exploitation in a way that few Photoshop users realize is possible. The field has barely been explored, and some striking and beautiful effects are possible because you'll be able to experiment with mixes of the Pantone inks.

After you have finished working with the substitute color display, return to the Printing Inks Setup window, click on the Load button, and open the saved file containing your previous settings.

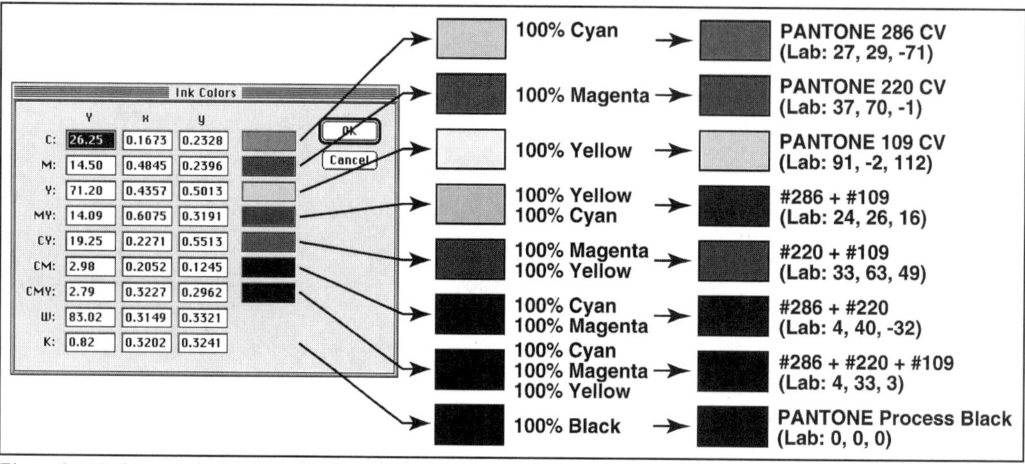

Figure 9-113: Convert the CMYK ink colors display by using the Lab values of the Custom Inks.

More Than Four Colors

Making a four-color job and substituting the film is pretty easily done in the way described in the poster project. Jobs of this sort are not demanding, the trapping is perfect, the file type and setup not unusual, and four-color presses are thick on the ground. However, six-color and eight-color presses are becoming more common. Since it doesn't add a lot to the cost—some ink, a couple of extra plates, a bit more make-ready cost, and so on—to add more colors than four, many designers are looking for ways to incorporate custom color inks into their normal four-color jobs. To show how the basic work is done, let's add another color to the African textile poster, a bright orange Pantone color (#1505) to the inside of the headline letters.

This process takes place before you change the poster file to CMYK mode. It can be done after the file is flattened and changed to CMYK, but you won't be able to view the new ink in the context of the other Pantone colors. Follow these steps:

1. Begin by making an alpha channel of the headline letters layer (Figure 9-114). Do this, if you are still in RGB mode, by Command+clicking or Ctrl+clicking the headline letters thumbnail on the Layers palette. If you have already deleted the layers and are in CMYK mode, you can accomplish the same thing by Command+clicking or Ctrl+clicking on the Magenta channel's thumbnail on the Channels palette. Click on the thumbnail of the new channel on the Channels palette to display it. Press Command+i or Ctrl+i to invert the channel (Figure 9-115).

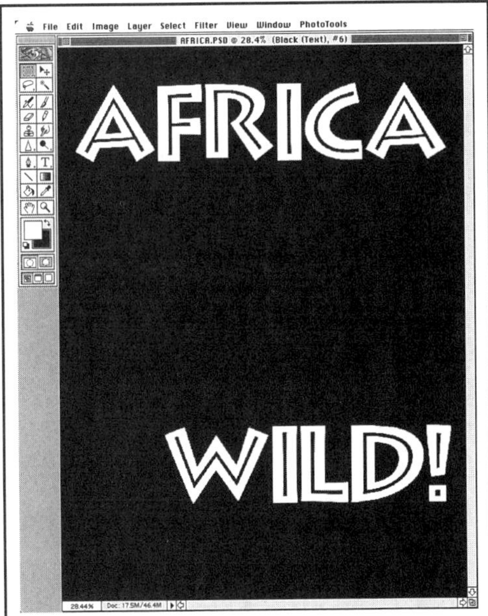

Figure 9-114: Make the headline letters into an alpha channel.

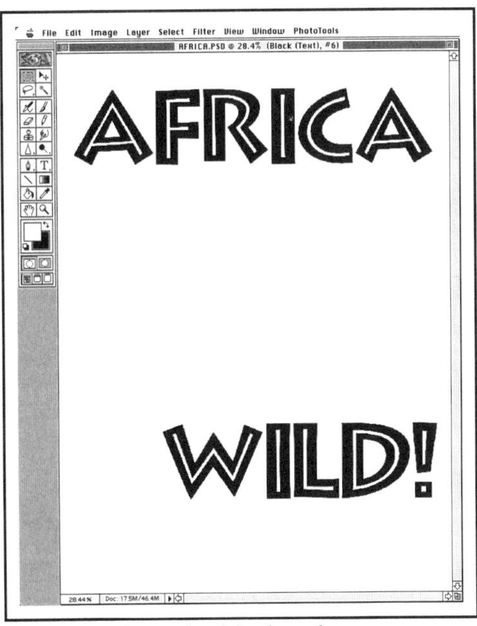

Figure 9-115: Invert the alpha channel.

2. Press w to choose the Magic Wand tool. Hold the Shift key and click within the inner shapes of the two As, the D, and the area outside the letters (the background). Choose Select | Modify | Expand. Enter **3** and click on the OK button. Expanding this selection places the boundaries within the zone of anti-aliasing at the letters' edges. Fill the selection with black, and Deselect (Figure 9-116). Note that if you fill with black before expanding the selection, you still have a faint halo of white around the letters' edges.

3. Because this custom color is not going to be a part of the CMYK file, it must be manually trapped. The color chosen is an orange that is lighter than the Pantone red which will surround it. To trap it to the red, the area of the orange must be expanded. Command+click or Ctrl+click the thumbnail of this channel on the Channels palette. Choose Select | Modify | Expand. Enter **1** and click OK. Fill the expanded selection with white. Deselect. You have now taken care of the trapping for this color.
4. You'll want to take a look at the colored image in the context of the other Pantone colors to see how the new color looks. Double-click the new channel's thumbnail. The dialog box at the top of Figure 9-117 appears. Enter 100% for the Opacity setting. Click on the Color box. The Photoshop Color Picker will appear. Click on the Custom button and choose the new Pantone color (#1505). Click OK on both dialog boxes.

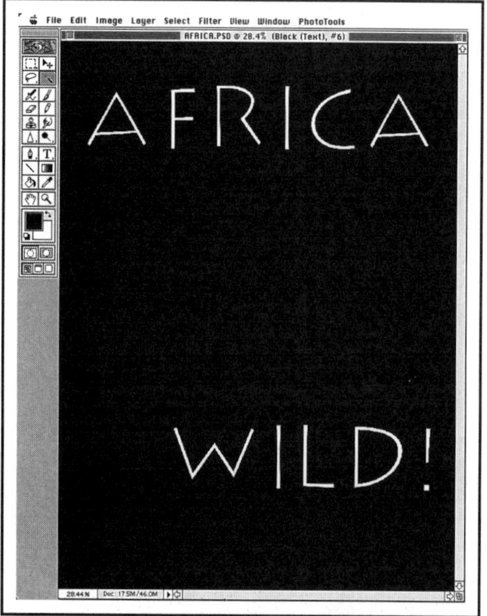

Figure 9-116: With the Magic Wand, select the white background and the counters of the letters. Expand the selection by three pixels, and fill with black.

Figure 9-117: Assign a Custom Color to this channel.

5. Press Command+i or Control+i to invert the channel (Figure 9-118). Click on the top thumbnail of the Channels palette to see the poster file in color. To add the new color, click on the eye column of the new alpha channel. It will display in color in its proper position (Figure 9-119). The five negatives are shown in Figure 9-120.

Figure 9-118: Invert the channel.

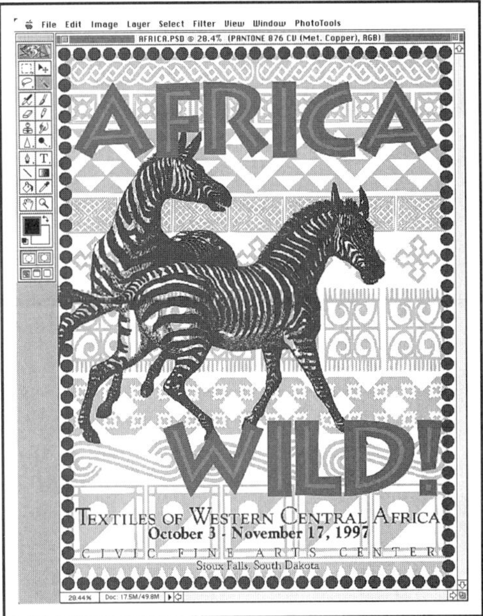

Figure 9-119: Make all five channels visible by clicking the eye icons on the Channels palette.

Figure 9-120: The five negatives for this poster.

Note that this color can be used as it is because you have already knocked out the shapes of the larger letters from the other colors, and these letters are inside the larger letters. If this color was to be used in any other place in the document, you would have to knock out the shapes *before* you expand the selection to take care of the trapping. You would do this, if still in the RGB layers configuration, in the manner described above, by selecting the relevant layers and pressing the Delete key. If you want to do the same thing after eliminating the layers and have changed to CMYK mode, invert the channel so that it looks like Figure 9-115. Command+click or Ctrl+click the channel to load it as a selection. Display the four-color document. Fill the selection area with white. This eliminates all other color from the area of the fifth color. After you have done the knockout, expand the selection to take care of the trapping.

To use this fifth-color channel, you cannot leave it as part of the CMYK document unless you have a Photoshop plug-in which allows you to save your work in the DCS 2 format (discussed later in this chapter). If you do not, display the channel for the orange ink. Be sure that the channel is positive: the area you wish to print as a spot color must be in black on a white background (shown in Figure 9-118). Select All, and Copy. Choose File | New. Click OK. When the new window is open, Paste. Flatten the image, and save the new file in the TIFF format. Name the file so that it is obvious that it is the fifth-color file for the poster.

Getting the new file to separate properly with the other colors depends upon the page layout software you intend to use for output. We've included instructions for Adobe PageMaker and QuarkXPress. If you use different software, study these two sets of instructions to see if your software works in approximately the same way. Please note: the following instructions were written for QuarkXPress v. 3.2. QuarkXPress v. 4.0 was not yet available at the time this chapter was written but will probably be available by the time this book has been printed. With the new program, there will be slight alterations in dialog boxes. However, the basic procedure will remain unchanged.

QuarkXPress (Version 3.2) Separations

To separate the files in QuarkXPress, follow these steps:

1. In QuarkXPress, choose Edit | Colors. The dialog box in Figure 9-121 appears. Click on the New button. In the dialog box which appears (Figure 9-122), change the Color Model pop-up menu so that it reads Pantone. Enter the color number you wish to use in the text-entry box at the lower right. Don't worry about changing the Screen Values: you are printing only solid-color areas, which makes the screen value irrelevant. Click OK in both dialog boxes.

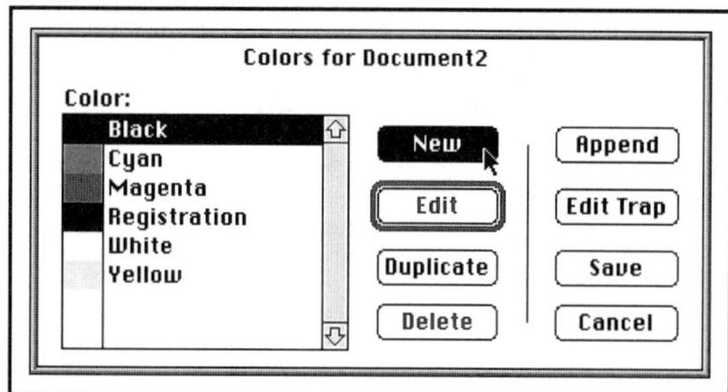

Figure 9-121: The Colors dialog box in QuarkXPress.

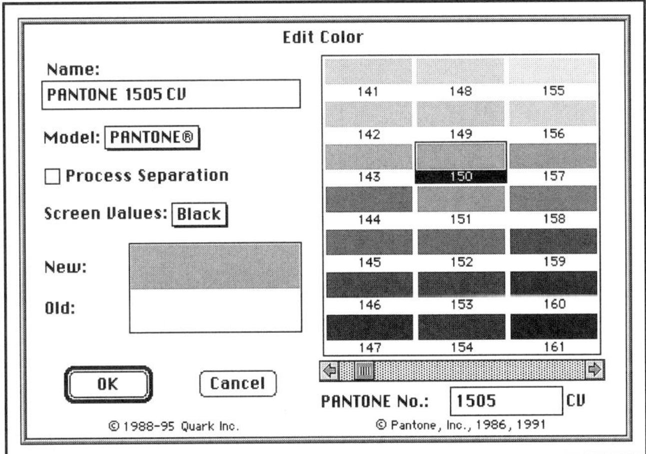

Figure 9-122: The Edit Color dialog box in QuarkXPress.

2. Choose the second tool, the Content tool, down in the Toolbox. Now, choose the Rectangular Picture Box tool and draw a picture box a little larger than the file you wish to import. Choose File | Get Picture. Locate the fifth-color TIFF file and click on OK. When the image appears in the picture box, arrange the right-hand and lower edge of the picture box. Be very careful not to move or resize the picture within its box. If you must move the picture, choose the top (Item) tool and move the entire box. If you must resize the picture, go back to Photoshop, open both the fifth-color TIFF file and the four-color version of the same file. Resize both in Photoshop and resave them. In QuarkXPress, reimport the fifth-color TIFF file.
3. From the Style menu, choose Color | PANTONE 1505 CV (or whatever ink in which you wish this picture to print). This step is shown in Figure 9-123. The black areas of the image change to the chosen color. On the Trapping Information palette, change the default from Knockout to Overprint. This step is very important: without it, only the top plate will print. Be sure to do this for every picture in every box that you lay on top of another.
4. From the Item menu, choose Step and Repeat. In the dialog box which appears, leave the Repeat Count at 1, and change the Horizontal and Vertical Offsets to 0. Click OK (Figure 9-124).

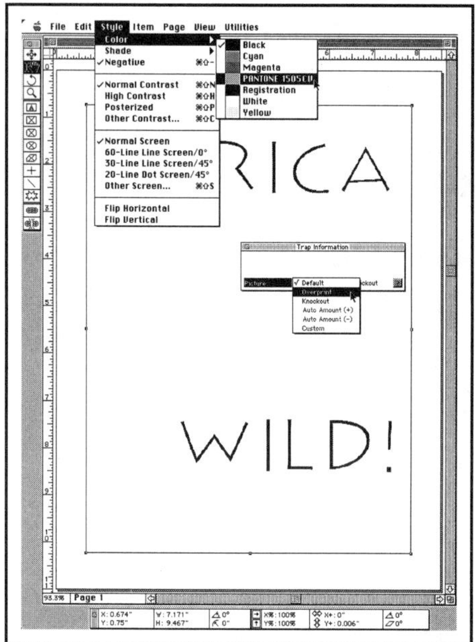

Figure 9-123: Assign the Pantone color to the imported TIFF image.

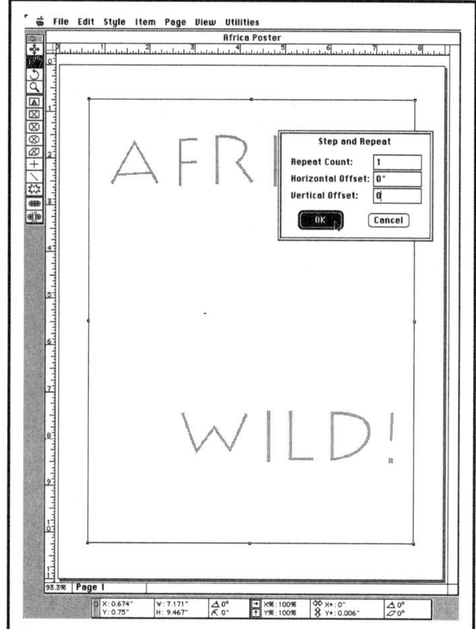

Figure 9-124: Duplicate the picture box using QuarkXPress Step and Repeat command.

5. You have created an exact duplicate of the original picture box sitting precisely atop the first. While it is still selected, choose File | Get Picture. Locate the four-color file and click OK. The new file appears and covers up the first (Figure 9-125). Don't worry about it. Both you and XPress know that the fifth-color file is present. Remember to change the trapping information setting from the default to Overprint.

6. Be careful not to move the new file. It is important that the position of both picture boxes relative to each other is not disturbed. If you wish to move them, choose the Item tool. Click and drag across the edges of the top picture. You won't be able to tell it, but you have selected both picture boxes. Use the Group command to ensure that the two boxes stay together. After grouping, move the boxes wherever you wish.

7. After using the Page Setup dialog box and making whatever choices you need to make for the output device to be used, choose File | Print. Change the Separation pop-up menu (lower left-hand side) to On. Set the plate pop-up to read All Plates (Figure 9-126).

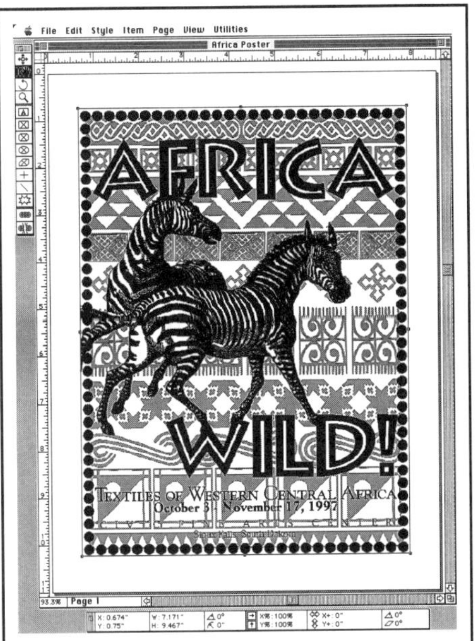

Figure 9-125: Bring the four-color file into the new picture box. This covers up the other TIFF file.

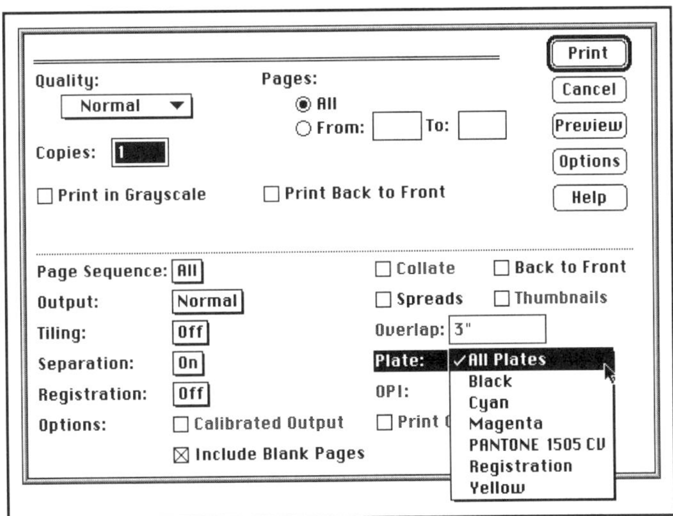

Figure 9-126: When printing separations from QuarkXPress, choose the All Plates option.

TIP *Sometimes it is tempting to resize, rotate, skew, and flip imported images within QuarkXPress or Adobe PageMaker. Despite that, doing it is not a good idea. Use the controls which allow you to do these modifications only to assist your page design. When you have finished the design, return to the programs which originated the images, and duplicate all the modifications you made in the page-layout program. Return to XPress or PageMaker, delete the modified images, and reimport them. There is no difference in the appearance of the reimported images and you will have done something that will make your service bureau send you Valentines. Besides that, you have streamlined your files, eliminated a lot of redundant imaging, shortened the amount of time it takes your files to image, and made troubleshooting your files much less complicated. It's worth doing, if for no other reason, for the feeling of virtuous smugness that will come over you! Really.*

PageMaker (Version 6.5) Separations

The instructions for PageMaker are very much the same as for QuarkXPress. They differ only in minor details:

1. Open PageMaker, set up a new document, and choose Utilities | Define Colors. The dialog box which appears is shown in Figure 9-127. Click on the New button. A Color Options dialog box appears (Figure 9-128). Click on the Libraries sidebar menu, and choose Pantone Coated. A Color Picker dialog box appears in front of the other two (Figure 9-129). Enter the color you wish to use in the text-entry box at the top and click OK. Set your spot color to Overprint in the Color Options dialog box, then click OK. In the Define Colors dialog box, click on Cyan to select it, and then click on the Edit button. Set cyan to Overprint. Do the same for magenta, yellow, and black. Click OK.
2. From the File menu, choose Place. Locate the fifth-color TIFF file and click OK. From the Window menu, choose Show Colors. With the placed image still selected, click on the Pantone color in the Colors palette (Figure 9-130).

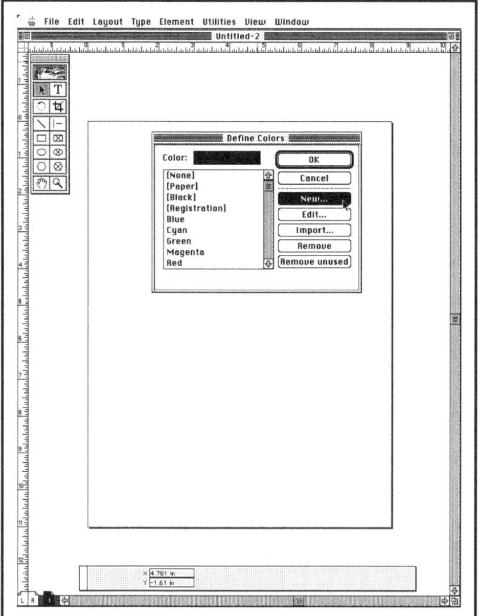

Figure 9-127: In PageMaker, choose Utilities | Define Colors. Click on the New button.

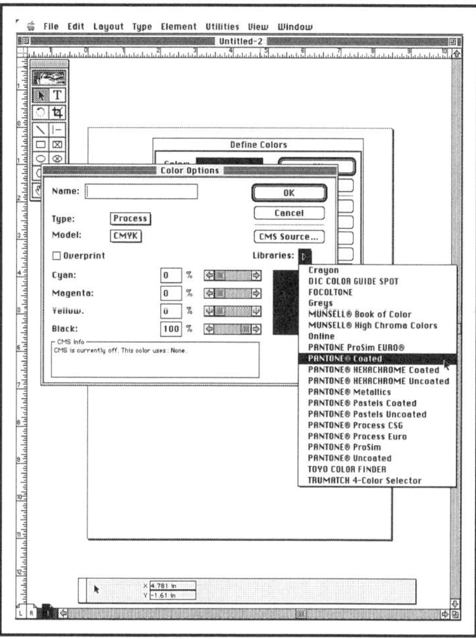

Figure 9-128: Choose the color library palette you wish to use from the sidebar menu.

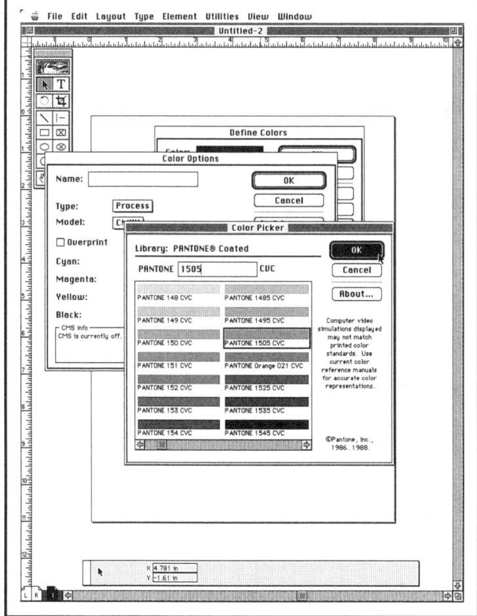

Figure 9-129: Locate the specific color you wish to use, then click OK and set the color to Overprint.

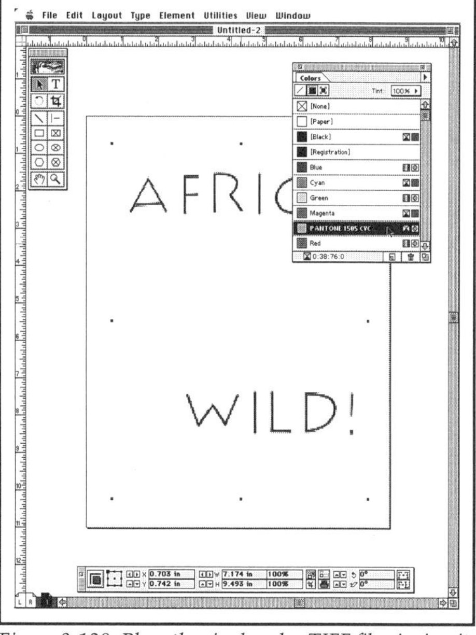

Figure 9-130: Place the single-color TIFF file. Assign it the Custom Color you've chosen from the Colors palette.

3. From the File menu, choose Place. Locate the four-color file and click OK. When the new image has appeared, select all. From the Element menu, choose Align (Figure 9-131). Choose the two icons shown which align the vertical and horizontal center axes (Figure 9-132). Click OK. You have now aligned both images. Deselect both pictures and then click on the top one. From the Element menu, choose Arrange | Send to Back. Your spot color file should now be on top of the CMYK file. Select both images. Group them so that they cannot be inadvertently moved out of their present alignment.

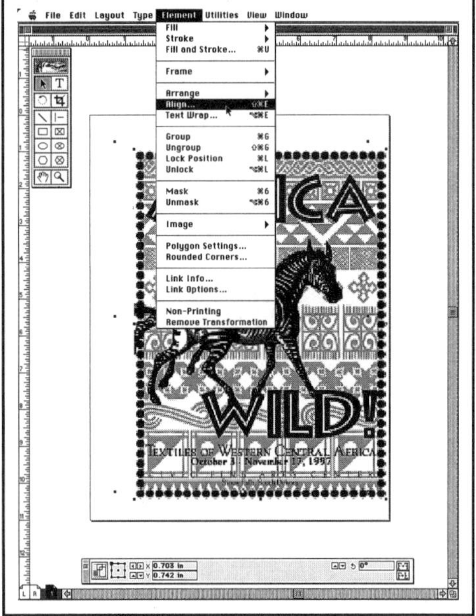

Figure 9-131: With both pictures selected, choose the Align item from the Element menu.

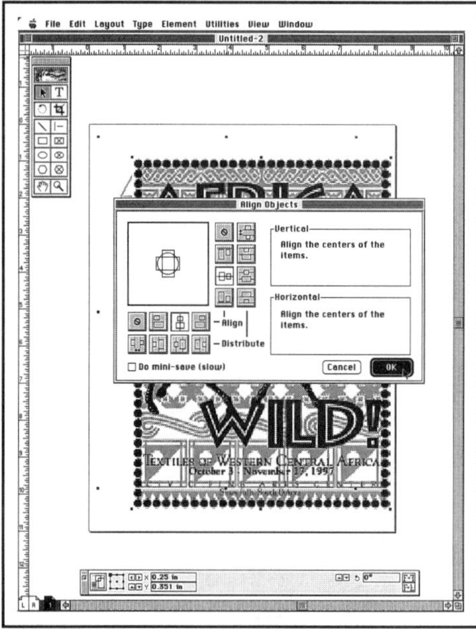

Figure 9-132: Click on the alignment buttons to precisely position the two pictures, one atop the other.

4. After making the appropriate choice in the Page Setup dialog box, chose File | Print. Click on the Color button. To make separations of all five inks, click first on the Remove Unused button and then on the Print All Inks button (Figure 9-133).

Note: if you will be printing areas on this page which use the process colors, you may have a reason for the colors not to be set to Overprint in the Define Colors dialog box. If the CMYK inks cannot be set to overprint, set up the two imported images so that the fifth-color TIFF file is on top of the CMYK file.

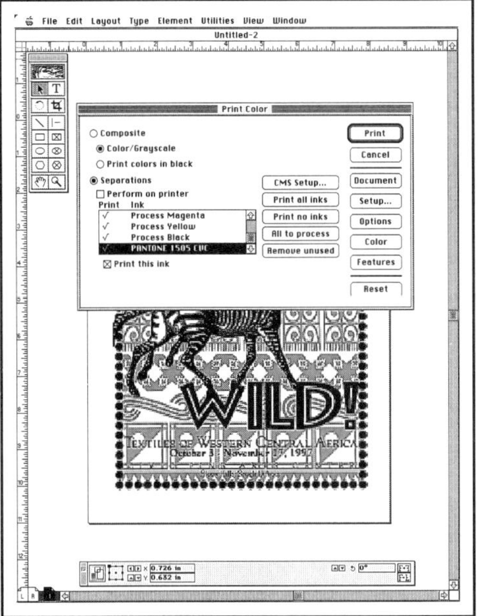

Figure 9-133: Add the fifth ink to the color separations list in the Print dialog box.

Bump Plates, Touch Plates

Custom colors are sometimes used to give an additional punch to some of the tones of a four-color image. These extra inks are applied from what are called *touch plates* or *bump plates*. (When you *double-bump* a press sheet, you apply ink to the same spot more than once. You can see examples of double-bump printing in the Pantone swatch book: look toward the center of the swatch book for the set of colors designated with 2X. The richness of those colors is achieved by printing the same area twice with the same ink.) Touch plates are plates which apply an extra ink, usually as a tint, to modify the color tones over which they are printed. Bump plates apply the same inks in order to intensify the overprinted color. The added inks can deliver an increase in saturation and a set of tones not possible otherwise. Extra inks can also be used for adding contrasting surface textures.

Touch plates are often used to augment *out-of-gamut* colors. Out-of-gamut colors are those which cannot be accurately reproduced using just the four process inks. Bright, primary tones, especially those used for clothing— the neon colors used for winter-sports outerwear, or the bright, crayon colors used for children's clothing, for example—are nearly always out of gamut. By applying a tint of spot color, out-of-gamut colors can be made to look much more believable.

Many Photoshop users are not familiar with this process, or if they are, think that it is one of those semi-occult things that only hot dogs and experts do. The truth of the matter is that generating a touch plate is less complicated than what you learned in the four-color poster tutorial example discussed above. If you wish to try this technique and to follow along with the set of instructions below, please locate and open the file HIBISCIS.PSD in the Chapter 9 Practice Files folder on the Companion CD-ROM.

CD-ROM

The example file on the Companion CD-ROM is in CMYK mode. Figure 9-134 shows a grayscale representation of this file. If you study the disk file, you can see that it would benefit from an extra ink—such as PANTONE Warm Red CV—to warm up the intense magenta tones of the separation. The background of the image contrasts with the flower but seems to lack depth. You'll add that depth by applying an extra ink, a light overprint of PANTONE 3 CV, a dense black made up of 10 parts PANTONE Black and 6 parts PANTONE Green. Follow these steps:

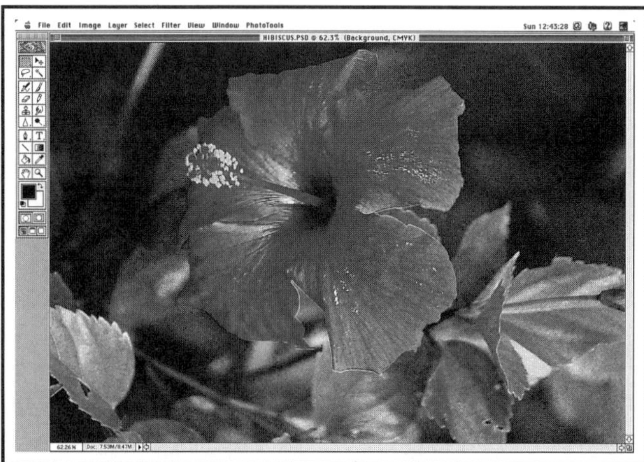

Figure 9-134: Although this image is usable, adding touch plates warms up the reds of the flower and gives a deep richness to the areas around it.

1. Your first task is to press q to enter Quick Mask, and to mask the flower shape using whichever of the tools you desire. (You don't really have to do this unless you want the experience since the file on the Companion CD-ROM has the mask channel saved with it.) When the mask is finished, it looks as shown in Figure 9-135. Invert the Quick Mask and press q to exit Quick Mask mode. Click on the Save Selection icon at the bottom of the Channels palette. The new channel looks as shown in Figure 9-136.

Figure 9-135: In Quick Mask, mask the flower shape.

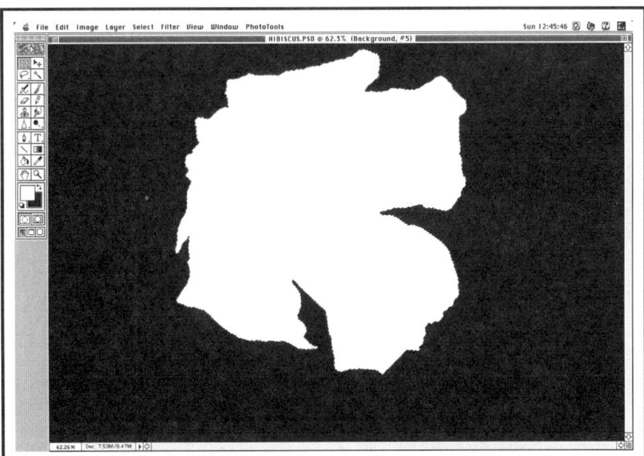

Figure 9-136: Invert the Mask, exit Quick Mask, and save the selection as an alpha channel.

2. If you cycle through the channels, you can see that most of the flower's color is contributed by the Magenta channel. This is the channel where the flower shape contains the most dark pixels. Press Command+2 or Ctrl+2 to view the Magenta channel (Figure 9-137). Activate the alpha channel by Command+clicking or Ctrl+clicking its thumbnail on the Channels palette. Copy the selection. Deselect.

Figure 9-137: Most of the image data for the flower is in the Magenta channel.

3. Create a new alpha channel by clicking on the New Channel icon—just to the left of the Trash icon—on the Channels palette. Fill the new channel with white. Activate the previous alpha channel. When the selection is active, use the Paste command. The copied flower shape centers itself perfectly within the selection. This channel now looks the same as Figure 9-138. Double-click this channel's thumbnail. In the Channel Options dialog box, click on the color swatch and choose the Pantone color you want to print with this channel, then set the Opacity to 60% (Figure 9-139). Click on the top icon on the Channels palette. Click on the eye column on the second alpha channel, the one with the pasted flower (Figure 9-140).

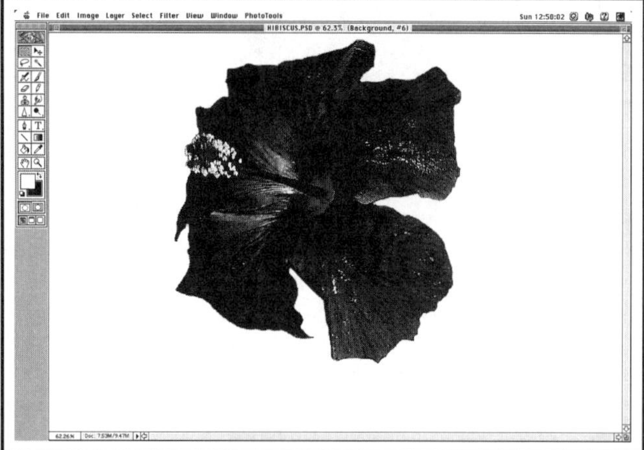

Figure 9-138: Make a new alpha channel. Use the mask alpha channel to copy the selection from the Magenta channel into the new channel.

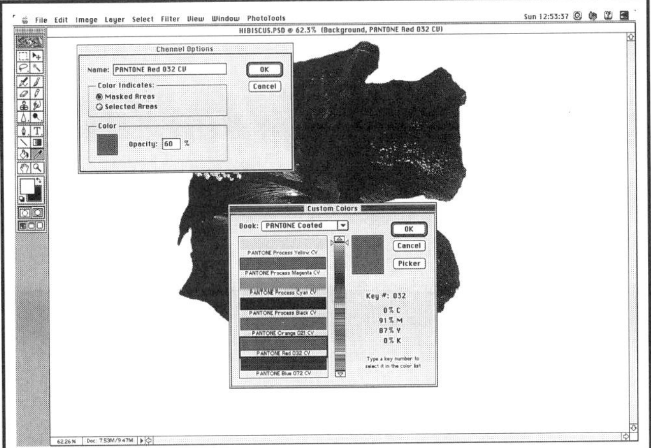

Figure 9-139: Assign the Pantone color to the channel. Set the Opacity for the channel to 60%.

Figure 9-140: Look at all five channels together by clicking on the eye icons on the Channels palette.

4. Click the fifth-color channel's eye icon off and on so that you can see how much color it contributes to the flower (Figure 9-140). 60% is far too much. Double-click the thumbnail, and change the opacity downward. You'll find the correct percentage around 20%. This ability of Photoshop to show how much ink the bump plate will contribute and how it will affect the color is incredibly useful. It makes the generation of the plate very simple since you can see beforehand how the new ink will change your image!

5. The key to the plate is the opacity figure. Our task now is to change the alpha channel so that it prints in the same way we have viewed it. First, duplicate the channel and then click on its thumbnail to display it. Select all. Set your Foreground color to white. Choose Edit | Fill. Make the fill with the Foreground color, Normal mode, and the Opacity set to 80% (the reciprocal of the 20% Opacity we used to preview the effect of the fifth ink). Click OK. Your channel should now look like the example in Figure 9-141. The modification scaled the color values in this channel back by 80%. In other words, the present tones are 20% of their original values.

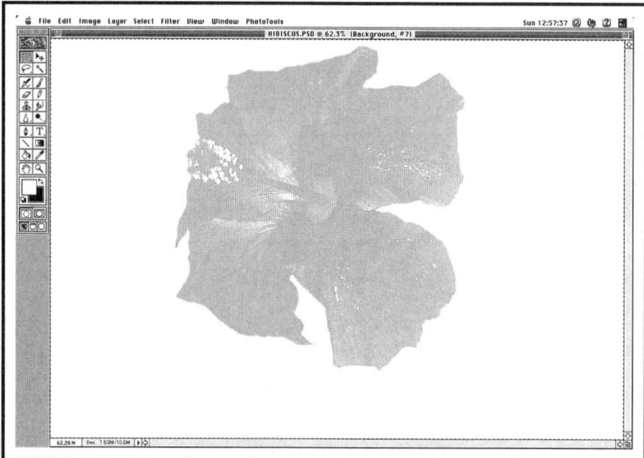

Figure 9-141: After determining that the channel looks best at 20% Opacity, screen back the channel by filling with white at 80% Opacity.

6. Double-click on this channel's thumbnail. Assign it the same Pantone color and change the Opacity to 100% (Figure 9-142). Switch back to the full-color view. Click on the eye icon for the new channel and you can see that 100% Opacity of the 20% channel is the same as 20% Opacity on the 100% channel.
7. Copy this new channel into a new document and save it in TIFF format. Delete the channel from which it was duplicated. When using this TIFF file in QuarkXPress or Adobe PageMaker, remember to change the screen angle. Your reasoning for the choice of screen angle might be: when the image is finally printed, there will be very little cyan ink in the area of the flower. Cyan would be, then, a good choice for the Pantone Warm Red screen angle.

Figure 9-142: Change the channel's Opacity to 100% and make the channel visible. You now have a reasonably accurate representation of the way the red touch plate will overprint the CMYK inks.

8. The second touch plate is used to deepen the area around the flower with a dark-green-tinted black. Activate the original channel (#5) as a selection. Choose Select | Inverse.
9. If you cycle through the color channels, you can see that several of them could be used as the basis for the second touch plate. There is another way to approach deciding which channel to use that allows you to learn some interesting things about the image. Switch the eye icons for each channel off and on to view the color image *without* one of the inks. Clicking off the Cyan channel gives bright yellow leaves. Clicking off the Magenta channel changes the flower to yellow but makes the background a clearer green. Clicking off the Yellow channel makes the background blue, and the flower bright magenta. Clicking off the Black channel makes the background muddy and ugly. Of the four, the channel which seems not to contribute anything very useful to the color values of the background is the Magenta channel. A good strategy might be to use another black ink with the magenta values since it would darken the background in exactly the areas where the magenta is strongest. This would cancel some of the effects of the magenta background.
10. Drag the Magenta channel onto the New Channel icon at the bottom of the Channels palette. Click on the thumbnail of this channel to view it. Activate Channel #5. When the selection is active, fill the selection with white (Figure 9-143).

Figure 9-143: Make a copy of the Magenta channel. Use the flower mask channel to delete the area of the flower from this channel.

11. Double-click the new channel's thumbnail. Assign it the color Pantone Black (PANTONE 3 CV) and change its Opacity to about 50% (Figure 9-144). View the full color image with the eye icon for the new channel turned on. Experiment with the Opacity setting until the background looks exactly the way you wish it to print. 40% seems to be a pretty good value. Turn off both of the touch plate channels and look at the image (Figure 9-145). Now turn them on (Figure 9-146). Look closely at the two figures in the book: even in grayscale, it is possible to see an improvement in contrast. The image is even better in color.

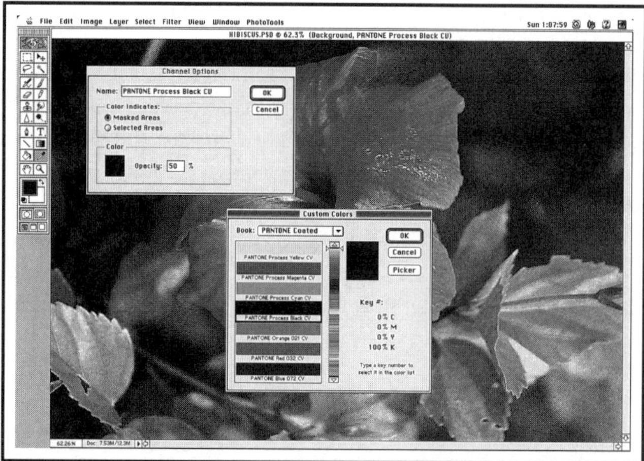

Figure 9-144: Assign the Pantone black to this channel. Set the Opacity to 50%. Make the Channel visible and experiment with the opacity until the image looks the way you want it to look. 40% will be about right for this image.

Figure 9-145: Turn off the visibility of the two touch plates to see the image without the extra color.

Figure 9-146: Turn the visibility of the touch plates on to see how the extra inks make the image look richer.

12. Select the alpha channel used to add the black custom color ink on the Channels palette. Select All, choose Edit | Fill. Make the Opacity setting 60% (the reciprocal of the 40% setting used to view the ink). The lightened channel is shown in Figure 11-147. Set the Opacity for the channel to 100% (Figure 9-148). Check it in the full color view. Copy this channel into a new document and save it.

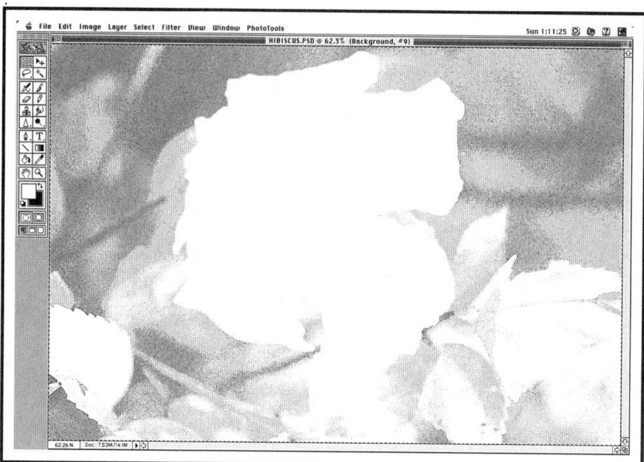

Figure 9-147: Screen back the channel by the reciprocal percentage of the Opacity setting.

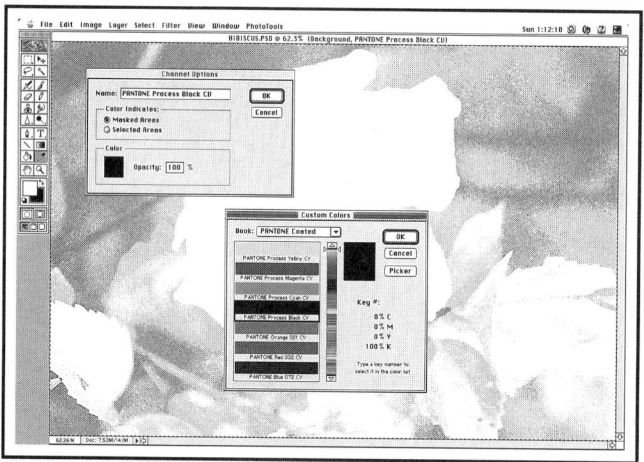

Figure 9-148: Change the Opacity back to 100% and double-check the ink name.

13. When using this file in QuarkXPress or Adobe PageMaker, be sure to change the screen angle for this ink. Remember the reasoning used to construct this channel: neutralize and darken some of the magenta tones in the background of the image. If you use the magenta screen angle, all of the dots of the black Pantone ink will print directly on top of the magenta dots and mute them more than if the angle were such that the black dots printed in the spaces between the lines of the magenta dots. It's all pretty logical, don't you think?

PhotoSpot by Second Glance Software

When you need to apply custom colors to scanned, colorized line art or if you need to deconstruct a photographic image in order to print it with custom colors, there is a useful commercial utility program which can generate separations. It is called PhotoSpot by Second Glance Software and is sold as a plug-in for use within Photoshop.

In order to use this utility, you must first do some work on the file. PhotoSpot is able to generate separations for an image which contains up to 500 colors, but as a matter of practicality, whatever colors are present must be reduced in number. A maximum number would probably be eight since few presses have more than eight inking stations. Most of this set of instructions has to do with the reduction process. There are probably a number of ways it could be done, but we hope you'll try this one. It is nearly foolproof and gives very good results. Follow these steps:

1. Begin by duplicating the original RGB image. Do your work on the copy but keep the original visible so that it can be used later as a sampling source for colors (Figure 9-149).

Figure 9-149: Duplicate the image to be used. Work on the duplicate. Keep the original visible (lower left-hand corner) so that you can use it for a color reference.

2. Convert the image to Grayscale mode (Figure 9-150).
3. Choose Image | Adjust | Posterize. When the dialog box appears, choose 9 as your number of levels if your image contains large amounts of very light pixels in the area around the subject (Figure 9-151). Otherwise, choose 8.

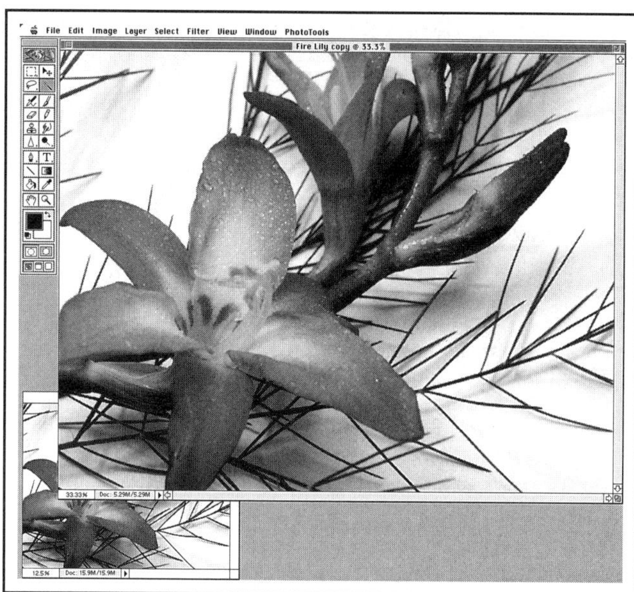

Figure 9-150: Convert to Grayscale mode.

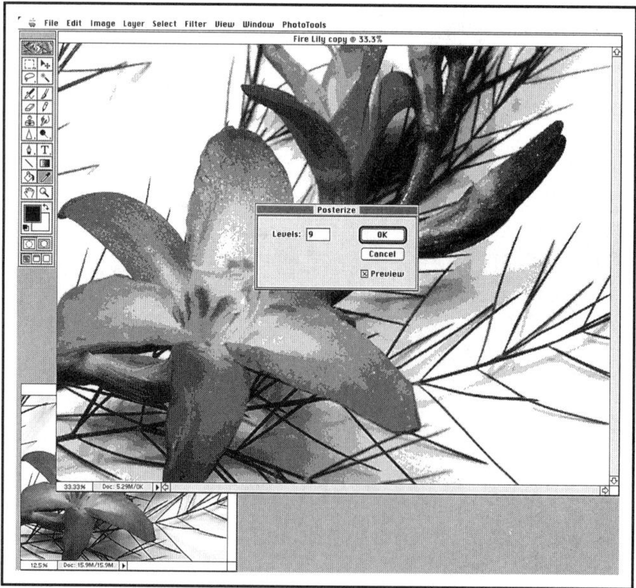

Figure 9-151: Posterize the image to 9 values (that will give you 8 image colors plus the white background which is not treated as an ink).

Choose this posterization number because Photoshop considers white to be one of the colors: you, however, will have white as the color of the paper on which the image is to print. If you were to choose 8, you would have only 7 inks.

It's important to posterize when you are in Grayscale mode in order to obtain the number of colors you wish to have: choose the number 9 when posterizing an RGB file and you'll probably end up with at least a couple of hundred colors. The posterization algorithm works by channel. If each channel is posterized to 9 tones, that gives the potential of 9^3 colors = 729.

You could also reduce the number of colors by converting the file to Indexed Color mode and specifying 9 colors, Adaptive. Try both methods. You'll probably agree that posterization works better.

4. Convert the grayscale file back to RGB. Press w to select the Magic Wand tool. Enter **1** as the tolerance value for the Magic Wand and uncheck the Anti-aliased option. Click on one of the grayscale tones in the image. Choose Select | Similar. This selects all of the pixels in the image with the same value on which you clicked. Press i to select the Eyedropper tool. Sample a color from the original image with which you will replace the tone of the selected grayscale area. When you've chosen the color, click on the Foreground Color box, and then the Custom button on the Color Picker. Photoshop displays for you the nearest Pantone color to the value you have sampled (Figure 9-152).

Figure 9-152: Pick a Custom Color based on a color sample for the original image.

If you wish to use Photoshop's version of the color, click OK. Otherwise click Cancel. Be sure to write the number down. Don't be too concerned if the Pantone color does not quite match your sampled color. The only way to really know what the color will look like is to check it with a Pantone swatch book. Cross-referencing the sampled color, Photoshop's display of the Pantone color, and the printed swatch book will help you arrive at exactly the color you desire.

5. Fill the selection with the Foreground color (Figure 9-153). Continue this same procedure until you have finished re-colorizing the grayscale image and have selected and named eight Pantone colors. Figure 9-154 shows the completed image. Notice how, even converted to eight shades, this image looks pretty good.

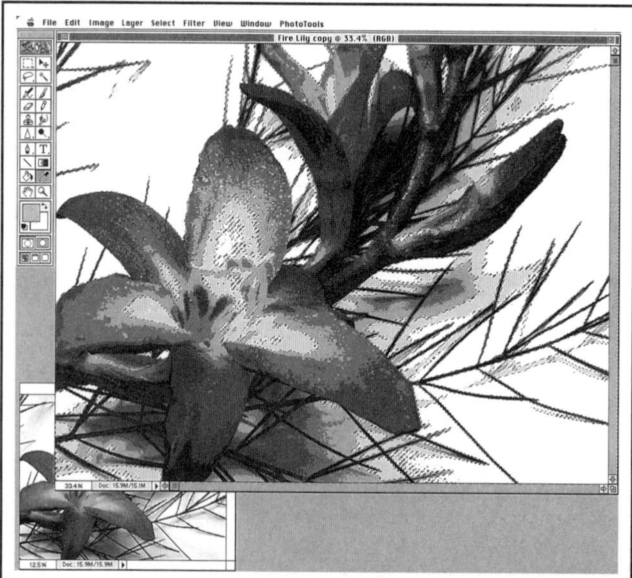

Figure 9-153: Fill your selection with the selected color.

6. From the File menu, choose Export | PhotoSpot (Figure 9-155). PhotoSpot does a quick analysis of the image, organizes the colors from lightest to darkest, gives the colors a descriptive name, and presents you with a list (Figure 9-156). All of the colors except white have a checkmark at the right. If, for some reason, you do not want some of the colors to become separation files, double-click the Color box to remove the checkmark.

Figure 9-154: Fill all eight color areas with Custom Colors based on tones sampled from the original image.

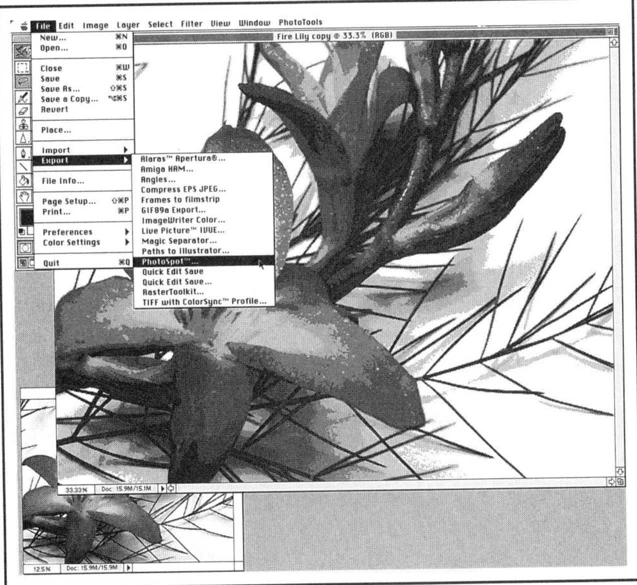

Figure 9-155: Choose File | Export | Photospot.

Figure 9-156: The PhotoSpot window shows a list of the colors in the image.

7. Click on the Sep button. Another small dialog box appears asking you to decide on the file format to be used for the separations and the place where they are to be saved to disk (Figure 9-157). Choose the TIFF format, and click on the Save button. PhotoSpot saves the eight separation files to disk very quickly. As it does so, it names them with the names it assigned in the original dialog box. You may, if you wish, rename the files with the number of the Pantone color you've chosen for each (Figure 9-158).
8. As you open each file, you'll discover that the size of the files is quite small. The file mode is the Bitmap mode. That means that each file is one-eighth the size of an equivalent grayscale file. You need to do a little more work in order to put these files together. PhotoSpot makes no provision for trapping, and you will have to do the trapping manually.
9. Trapping makes the colors overlap to compensate for press misregistration. The usual practice is to move the area of any light colors into the area of darker colors. In the case of this image, it would be pretty difficult to be very precise about which colors moved in which direction. Our only possibility is to increase the area of the colors by expanding them outward. But do we need to expand all the colored areas of all eight files? Probably not. Take a look at the image again.

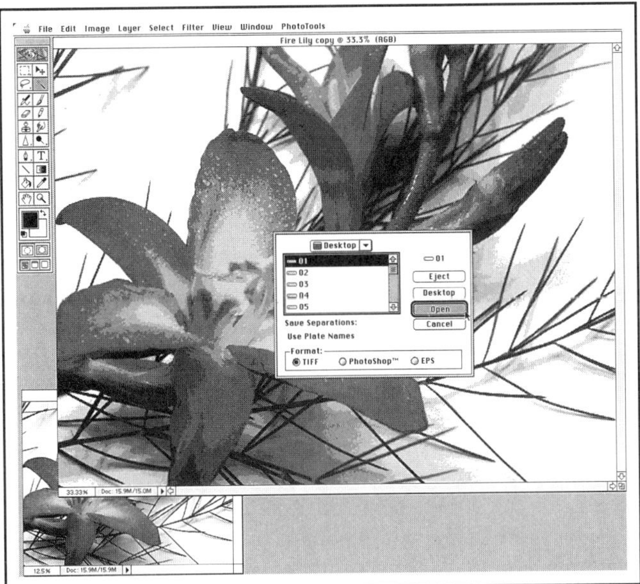

Figure 9-157: Click on the Sep button. A dialog window appears asking you to choose a file format for the separations and for a place in which to save them.

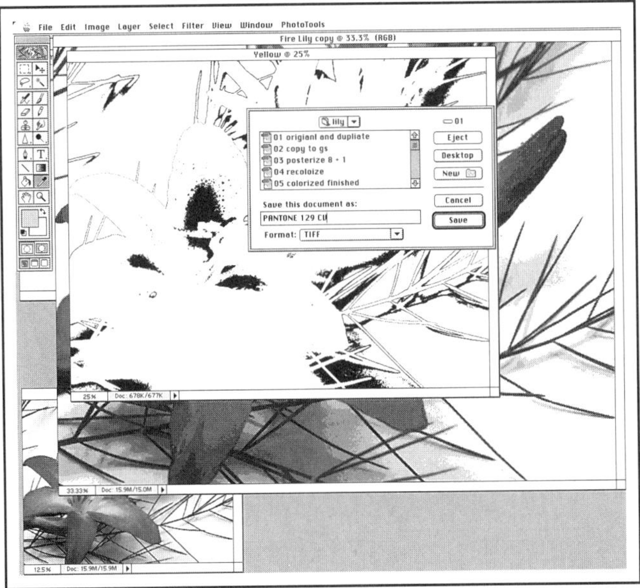

Figure 9-158: You may wish to rename each of the files with the name of each ink you've chosen.

The inner part of the flower—you'll have to imagine this—is a bright gold. The gold shades into a darker gold, and then to an orange, and a red-orange, a red, and a dark red. Wouldn't it work just as well, since the image is like this all over, to simply expand the color areas of the first, third, fifth, and seventh colors? Certainly it would. Besides, if we expand the color areas of all eight files, the result will be that we will double the amount of the trap. If you are new to the concept of trapping, this paragraph has probably made about as much sense as if it were written in Urdu. Don't worry about it. Read the next few paragraphs so that you know how the trapping is done, and then come back here. It *will* make sense. Promise!

In Figure 3-159, you see an enlargement of the file containing the separation for the lightest color. Before we can do anything to it, we need to convert it to Grayscale mode. When the dialog box asks what Size Ratio to use, enter **1**. Command+click or Ctrl+click this channel's thumbnail on the Channels palette. Choose Select | Inverse. Choose Select | Modify | Expand. The amount you expand is the amount of the trap. Check with your printer for your trap requirements. A normal setting might be .003 inches or .25 points. If your file is 300 ppi, 4 pixels are one/seventy-fifth of an inch. A point is one/seventy-second of an inch. One-quarter of a point, then, is a little less than a pixel. You'll expand your selection by one pixel. The enlarged selection is shown in the figure below.

Figure 9-159: Select the black pixels. Expand the selection by the amount of the trap.

Fill the enlarged selection with black (Figure 9-160). Change the file back to Bitmap mode (50% Threshold). Resave it in TIFF format. Trap the third, fifth, and seventh color files in the same way. Treat each file in the same manner you learned to treat them when assembling multicolor files in QuarkXPress and Adobe PageMaker. In this case, you will have eight files stacked one on top of the other.

Figure 9-160: Fill the expanded selection with black.

TIP

It is a little laborious, but you can do for yourself the same operation PhotoSpot performs for you so quickly. If you own PhotoSpot, use it for its convenience. If you do not own PhotoSpot, follow this procedure for each of the custom colors:

1. *First, choose, Image | Duplicate. Work on the duplicate to make the first separation file.*
2. *Select the Magic Wand tool—Tolerance of 1, Anti-aliased off—and click within an area of one of your colors on the duplicate document.*
3. *Choose Select | Similar. Fill the selection with black.*
4. *Select the inverse and fill with white. Change the mode of the image from RGB to Grayscale.*
5. *Change the mode again from Grayscale to Bitmap.*

When performing the last mode change, keep your Input/Output resolutions the same, and use the 50% Threshold option. If this color is one which needs trapping, do that operation next. Save the file in TIFF format using the Pantone color for the name. Perform this same set of operations for each of the custom colors.

Other Third-Party Spot-Color Utilities

You have learned to export your single-color touch plates and bump plates as TIFF files, and then to stack them up, perfectly aligned, in QuarkXPress or Adobe PageMaker. There are a couple of choices that you might consider, especially if you intend to do a lot of spot color work; both of them are professional-level subprograms—plug-ins—which you use within Photoshop.

PlateMaker by A Lowly Apprentice Production

PlateMaker is a terrific export utility which assembles your primary colors and spot colors into one file—or multiple files—and saves it in the DCS 2.0 format.

The DCS format is discussed later in this chapter. It is simply a format which saves the color printing information from a Photoshop document—the inks—as separate files which are linked to a master file. The master file is imported into your page layout program. When the file is output as separations, only the relevant segment is downloaded to the output device. Separations from a DCS file are more rapid than when outputting a file format such as a CMYK Tiff. The DCS format, when chosen as an option from the Save dialog box of the Photoshop EPS document format, saves as five separate files—the master file, and one file each for cyan, magenta, yellow, and black.

The DCS 2.0 format is an improvement on the older format. Not only can this format hold separation segments for more than four inks, but you have the choice of saving to separate files or to a single larger file which integrates the master file and the segments.

When you have your custom color document ready, choose File | Export | PlateMaker. The dialog box shown in Figure 9-161 appears. The scrolling window on the left-hand side has a list of all the channels and the four process inks are pre-named. The other channels are listed as numbered channels. By clicking on each name, you can name the channels with the name of the ink you wish to use. You may also label the channels to be plates for varnishes.

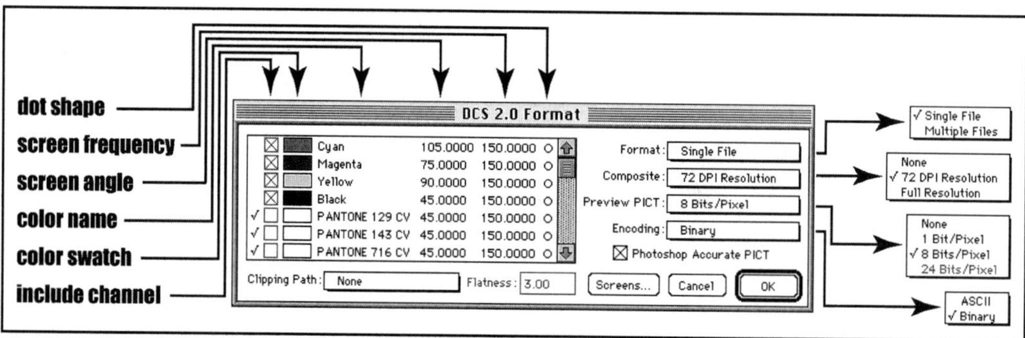

Figure 9-161: An expanded view of the PlateMaker DCS 2.0 export window.

A set of checks on the left will cause a channel to be included in the DCS 2.0 file or not to be included. The set of plates in this figure are those of the eight-color example discussed above. Because there are no process colors in that document, cyan, magenta, yellow, and black have been unchecked.

To the right of the plate name is a set of numbers which are the screen angles for the plates; these can be left as they are or changed to fit a given situation. Note that all of the non-process plate colors are set to the black screen angle. Since the example above uses only areas of solid color, there is no need to be concerned. If the plates contain tints, then careful thought needs to be given to the screen angles. Strategies such as those suggested in the discussion of the touch plates (Figures 9-134 through 9-141) need to be considered.

To the right of the column containing the screen angles is a set of numbers for the screen frequency. Note that this allows a variety of frequencies to be used simultaneously.

At the far right is a set of symbols which, when you click on them, cycle through a set of six preset dot shapes and one which allows a *custom spot function*. A custom spot function is a separate piece of PostScript code that makes the dots of the separations in a shape other than the ones which are pre-defined.

PlateMaker allows you to embed a Clipping Path (discussed later in this chapter) and to set its Flatness factor. The pop-up menus at the far right allow you to choose whether the DCS document is in the form of multiple files or a single file, what kind of Preview is wanted, and whether the print information encoding should be in Binary or ASCII.

After you have made your choices and clicked OK, another dialog box appears (Figure 9-162). Here you name your DCS document and choose whether to embed screening (you would choose to do so if you had set up custom values in the screen angle column, the screen frequency column, or the dot shape column). Click OK, and PlateMaker works its magic. By using this utility, you are no longer constrained to setting up multiple stacked files within QuarkXPress or Adobe PageMaker. Your DCS 2.0 document takes care of everything—including the automatic addition of custom colors to the color lists within each program. The Internet address for A Lowly Apprentice Production is http://www.alap.com.

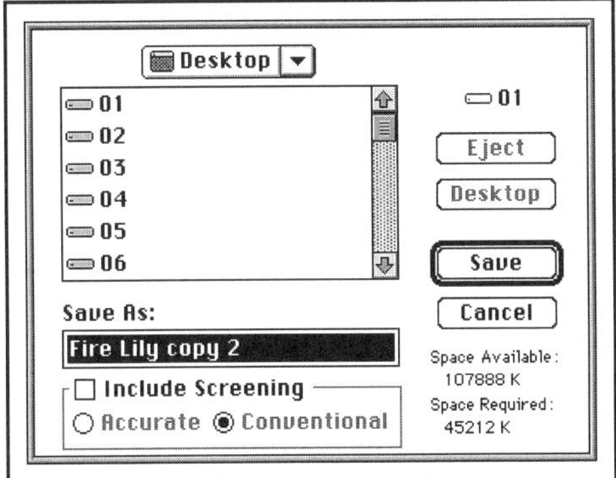

Figure 9-162: PlateMaker's Save/Export dialog box.

PhotoSpot CT by Second Glance Software

You have already seen Version 1 of the PhotoSpot export utility in use in the project above. Its successor version is marketed under the name PhotoSpot CT. It is an astonishing upgrade for the power it packs. Its features will eliminate some of the tedious manual work previously required for generating touch and bump plates.

You may begin with a document which you have already prepared, or you may simply choose File | Export | PhotoSpot CT with an RGB, CMYK, indexed color, or multichannel document open (shown in Figure 9-163). If the document is multichannel, you can begin the export process at once. If you are working with an unprepared file, your first step is to select the custom inks you wish to use. Begin by clicking on the Add button. Photoshop's Color Picker appears for you to make your first choice. Continue to click on Add until you have assembled your inks. Click on the Continue button.

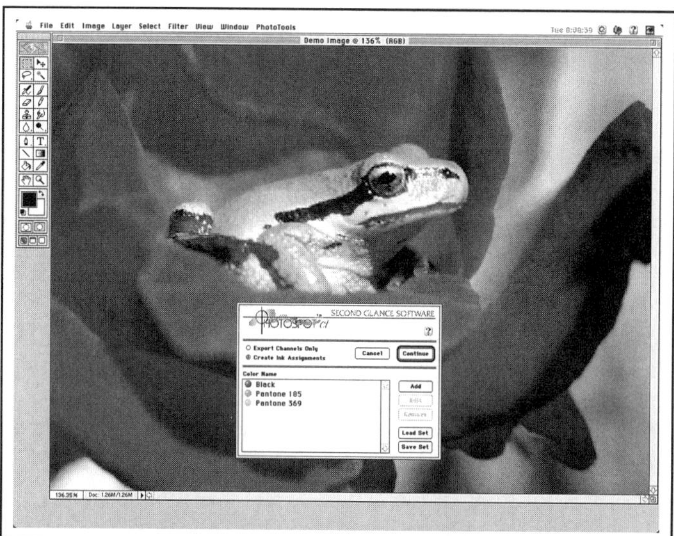

Figure 9-163: Begin by defining the inks you intend to use in PhotoSpot CT.

The separation process begins. PhotoSpot CT reads the image data and distributes it to the closest value found from the list of defined colors. If your image is in CMYK mode, the process inks are automatically added to the ink list. PhotoSpot CT assumes that you wish to preserve the existing CMYK balance and that the additional inks are being introduced for the purpose of touch plates or for spot colors.

A new set of thumbnail windows now appears (Figure 9-164). The windows include a composite view of the separated image and one each for the individual separations. These windows can be enlarged or made smaller or can be left as they are.

In the lower left-hand corner of each separation window are several tools. Two round hemisphere buttons allow you to elevate or diminish the amount of the window color which will be included in the overall balance of the image. Next to these is a tone curve tool that opens a dialog box (Figure 9-165) with which you can customize the gradations within a single color. As you perform any of these operations, PhotoSpot CT does a quick recalculation of the separations, and the change is immediately visible in the Composite window. You may even, at this point, reassign the ink to be used in a separation window.

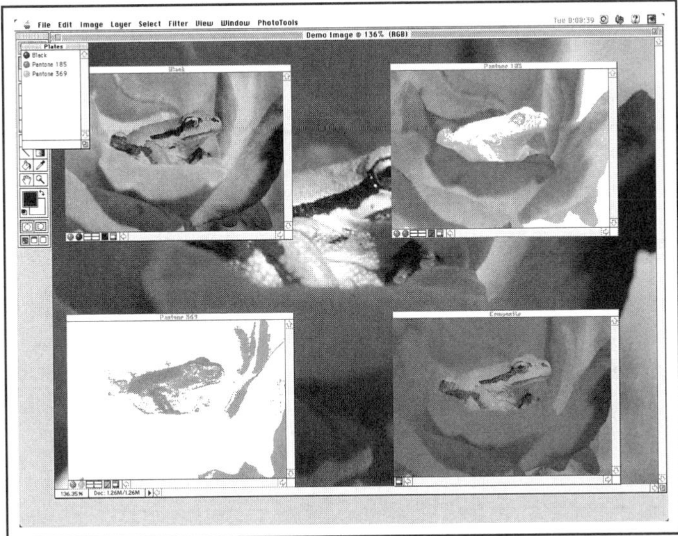

Figure 9-164: When PhotoSpot CT deconstructs the image, it gives you thumbnails for each of the inks and one for the composite of all the inks.

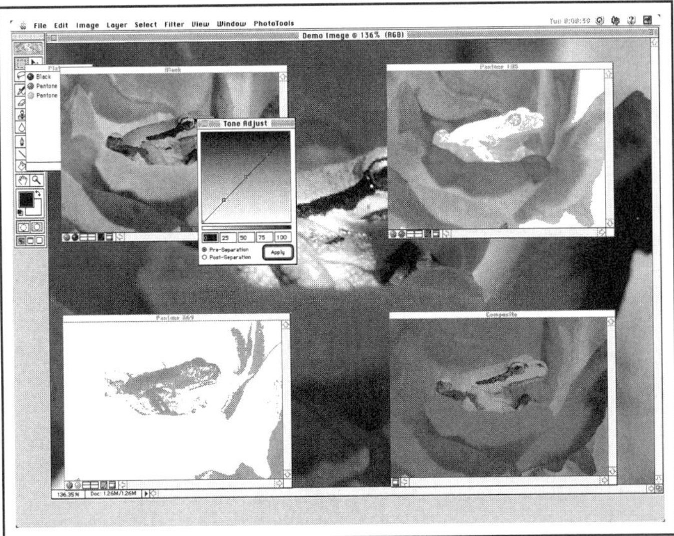

Figure 9-165: Each of PhotoSpot CT's thumbnail windows has its own set of tools for tweaking the colors. Any changes are instantly shown in the composite window.

With your adjustments complete, click on the close box of any of the windows. You are then asked to save or discard any changes you've made. When you've saved your changes, the Export dialog box opens (Figure 9-166).

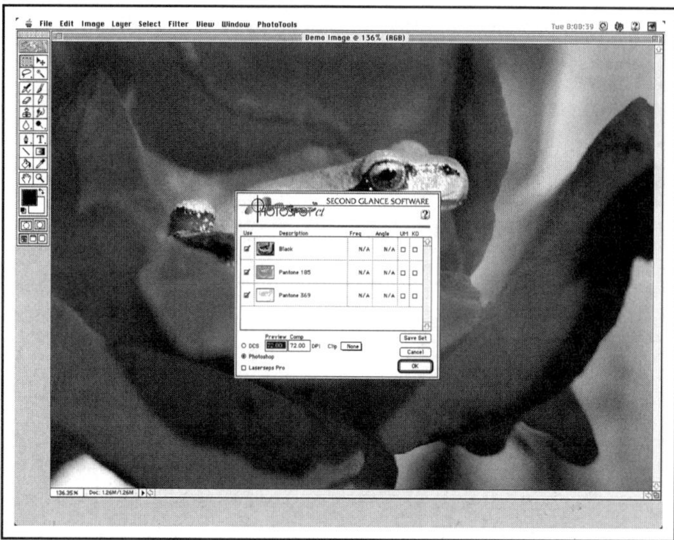

Figure 9-166: The PhotoSpot CT Save/Export dialog box.

The central part of the Export dialog box contains a scrolling list of your inks. The columns allow you to set whether an ink is to be used or not, the name of the ink, its screen frequency, the screen angle, whether an underprint mask—*very* useful to screen printers—will be generated, and whether a given ink should knock out of other plates or not.

Finally, there are the save choices. You may save in Photoshop or DCS 2.0 format with the attendant Preview options. A significant choice here is the ability to save the file using LaserSeps Pro. This plug-in module will be discussed more thoroughly later in this chapter. For now, LaserSeps Pro is a Photoshop export module that allows you to save your separations files with *stochastic screens* instead of conventional screens. Stochastic screens will be discussed in Chapter 10, "Calibration & Color Reproduction," but just know for now that stochastic screens are dithered screens. They contain very small dots—all of them the same size—which are distributed at random. There are more dots in dark areas and fewer of them in light areas. With several plate colors——especially if they are tints of the custom inks—and the four process colors, the most significant problem is that of screen angles. Screen angle interference, as is well known, generates moiré patterns and can result in color shifts. With stochastic screens, there are no screen angles to become a problem. All of the screen dots are randomly dispersed with their quantity in a given place based on the density of the color value. LaserSeps Pro is sold separately; however, if it has been installed on the system generating the separations, it can be accessed directly from PhotoSpot CT.

With its ability to deconstruct a file and to assign colors based on a prebuilt list, PhotoSpot CT is a remarkably advanced Photoshop add-on. You may be able to do some of what it does with manual methods. However, it is impossible to perform these tasks as quickly or as flexibly. For anyone doing custom color work, this add-on is a must-have! The Internet address for Second Glance Software is http://www.secondglance.com.

Spot Process by Freehand Graphics, Inc.

A significant number of Photoshop people who use custom colors are those connected with the screen printing industry.

Screen printers have many of the same Photoshop preparation concerns that offset print people do. They also have many problems which offset press users never face. Among these are problems with printing inks that are not only opaque but, compared to SWOP inks, extremely viscous. Sometimes the viscosity of the inks is so high that they need to be heated before they can be forced through the screen. Screen printers often need to print on surfaces that are very different from the smooth, coated, white paper offset people use. Black plastic, for example, (the top of your mouse pad came from a screen printer!) or dark-colored T-shirts and sweatshirts. The translucent inks that the offset industry uses simply do not fit a screen printer's requirements. What is usually required is a heavy, opaque liquid which will adhere to non-paper surfaces such as plastic and fabrics.

Opaque is the key word here. Our use of four-color process depends upon the fact that the inks—excepting black—are not opaque. Colors form by the way our eyes blend very tiny dots together and by the tones of the overlaid colors. Imagine trying to print a solid-built red—100% yellow overprinted by 100% magenta—if the magenta was so opaque that the yellow got covered up!

Screen printers have tried many strategies to duplicate the kind of photo-realism that is possible with translucent inks on a white surface. One possibility is to lay down a coating of white—perhaps on a black fabric—which gives a surface on which the other colors might be seen. Most of these strategies work reasonably well, but screen printers are still burdened with screen frequencies which are very coarse when compared to offset printing. There is also the problem of registration: how do you easily and precisely register a T-shirt?

The answer to many screen-printing problems is simply to lay down areas of spot colors and hope for the best. Techniques for generating touch plates or for deconstructing an image into component colors have not been readily available until very recently. A spot-color answer to some of these questions has now been made commercially available. This Photoshop add-on is called Spot Process. It is published by Freehand Graphics, Inc.

Spot Process reads the data of an RGB file and deconstructs—separates—the image into a number of plates. These plates are put into the file as alpha channels and are appropriately labeled by color. The number of plates can range from 6–10 (an eleventh channel is non-printing) with 8 being a fairly usual number. The separation process is entirely automatic, but tonal adjustments are possible after the separations have been made.

It isn't possible, in a book of this sort, to give anything other than an idea of the possibilities an add-on program such as this has. It is, however, possible to say that Spot Process does an astonishing job at generating separations. If you wish to see for yourself, visit the Freehand Graphics, Inc. Web site (http://www.spotprocess.com) and download the demonstration file. You will find it to be an RGB file with eleven alpha channels. To get an idea how good the separations are, do this: choose Image | Duplicate, and arrange the original and duplicate image onscreen so that you can see both. Turn off the RGB channels on the duplicate document by clicking on the eye icons on the Channels palette. Turn on all of the alpha channels. You'll be surprised, I think, and more than a little awed. This is a dynamite piece of software!

Line Art & Bitmap Mode

The Bitmap mode is one of the most useful and most underused of Photoshop's image modes. Editing images in Bitmap mode is difficult. Some of the tools work, some of them—illogically—don't. When the tools do work, they may work in an unexpected way.

Of the selection tools, the Marquee, Lasso, and Cropping tools function normally except that there is no Anti-aliased option offered for any tool. The Magic Wand tool—for reasons which must make sense to *someone*—does not work in this mode. Of the other tools, those which do not function in Bitmap mode are the Paint Bucket, Gradient tool, Dodge/Burn/Sponge tools, Sharpen/Blur tools, and the Smudge tool. The Pen tool functions normally. The Eraser, Pencil, Paintbrush, and Airbrush tools are also functional except that the brush choices from the Brushes palette are all the same aliased shapes. It is as though all of these tools are identical to the Pencil tool used in any other color mode. All but three of the normal array of blending modes are unavailable for any of the paint tools. The Normal mode is replaced with a blending mode that is available only in this image mode, Threshold. The three remaining blend modes available are Dissolve, Darken, and Lighten.

The way these tools behave is, for the most part, not surprising. There are no colors or grays in Bitmap mode, only black and white. Each pixel is one or the other. This may seem very limiting but this binary state is the ultimate form for all of your output. No matter what kind of printer or output device you are using, no matter whether you are putting toner on paper or imaging film to be used to burn plates, the data which produces that output is straight bitmap data.

It's an interesting thought, isn't it? If you think about it, you can see that putting ink on paper—and all the intermediate steps such as producing film and plates—is the ultimate bitmap paradigm. In the case of halftones, gray tones are not produced by 256 shades of gray ink, but by tiny black dots which cover some percentage of the white paper. Because the dots are so small, our eyes blend the black and white tones so that we seem to see grays. The task of a PostScript RIP (Raster Image Processor) is to convert grayscale—or, more accurately, *8-bit* information—into bitmap information. By averaging the gray values of several pixels (usually 4 of them in a 2 x 2 area), the RIP can accurately assess the size the dot needs to be which will represent that tone as ink on paper. Then, working with a resolution much higher than the input file's resolution, it can construct the dot, and control whatever imaging assembly is required to reproduce the dot on film or paper.

Processing Line Art Scans

Bitmap is most used in Photoshop as the image mode for line art files. Line art files are typically simple, one-colored shapes used for logos and special graphic symbols. The only necessity for their reproduction is that the edges of the shapes be sharp and clean. Since a bitmap file is 12.5% the size of a grayscale file with the same number of pixels, line art images can be handled at a much higher resolution than would be practical with any other image mode. They are, as well, much easier for a RIP to process than any other kind of digital construct, even at high resolutions.

Most scanners have a line art setting which scans the original material directly as bitmap. As the scanner analyzes the data, it applies a simple threshold computation to it: pixels 50% or lighter are changed to white, and all others are changed to black. When the scan is finished and the file onscreen, the mode of the image is bitmap. This is workable if the original image is of good quality and if the scanner is also of fairly good quality. In a production situation, conditions are not always so good. Rarely is the line art original of good quality—it is not unusual for the original to be scanned from a matchbook cover, the corner of a paper napkin, or even a fax of a Xerox. (The non-Photoshop user's definition of *camera ready* is vastly different from ours, is it not?)

In such situations, scanning in line art mode is not the best procedure since editing the file to fix any problems is very time-consuming. A better procedure is to scan in Grayscale mode and then to use Photoshop's powerful editing capabilities before converting the file to Bitmap mode. We will outline a set of steps which converts scans of poor quality original images to high quality files. Keep in mind that many scanners have a setting called Halftone Screen which is another bitmap computation and is rarely as successful as Photoshop's conversion of grayscale information.

When scanning the original image, choose Grayscale mode for the scan and set the scan resolution to be an even divisor of, or equal to the output device's resolution. Using resolution higher than that of your output device has no benefit. If your output device is a high resolution PostScript imagesetter with a resolution of 2400 dpi, your scan resolution could be 200 ppi, 300, 400, 600, 800, 1200, or 2400 ppi. All of these numbers divide into 2400 with no remainder. The best results are at fairly high resolutions such as 600 ppi and 1200 ppi. Since you are scanning in grayscale, you will be working, temporarily, with files that will seem very large. Don't be too concerned: once you finish editing the files, you convert them to bitmap format which reduces the file size by 87.5%.

Here's another scanning point to be considered: most scanners have controls which allow the image to be corrected either manually or automatically turn off any automated scan correction and allow the scan to be done with no manual intervention. The reason for this is, with respect to cleaning up a line art scan, Photoshop can do the job better than your scanner can.

Figure 9-167 shows a representation of a scan to be processed as line art. (If you wish to try this procedure, open the file ABCD.PSD found in the Chapter 9 Practice Files folder on the Companion CD-ROM.) The background, originally white, shows up as a blotchy gray tone. This is typical since the scanner, at the resolutions being used, is able to interpret the surface reflectivity of the paper as a color. Follow these steps:

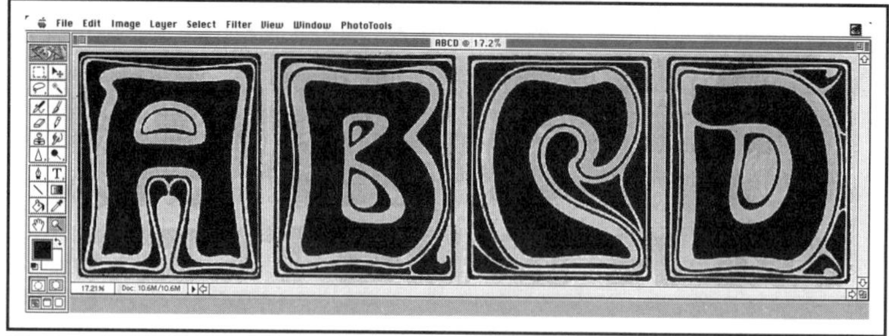

Figure 9-167: A high-resolution grayscale scan to be converted to line art.

1. After you've scanned the image, look at it carefully and try to find any area containing a delicate feature which you wish to preserve. The circled area in Figure 9-168 shows dark areas which, in the original, have nearly grown together. This is the kind of detail upon which you need to focus your attention. Zoom up to this detail and concentrate on it during this process. The rest of the image will take care of itself.

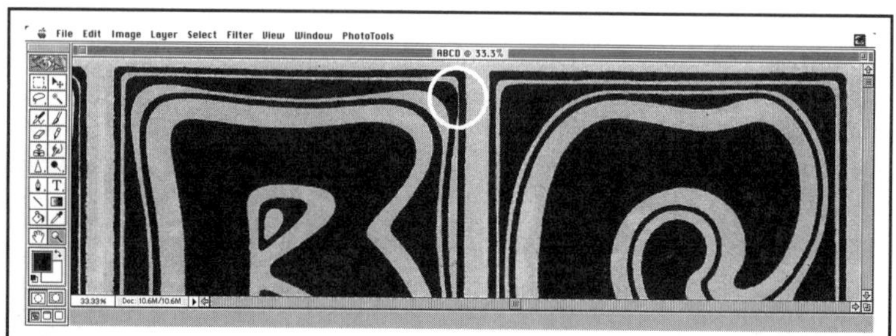

Figure 9-168: Look at the scan for delicate features which you wish to preserve during the adjustment procedure.

2. Use the Pen tool, as shown in Figure 9-169, to draw a few simple paths which generally show where the edges of the dark shapes are located. These paths are temporary, and you needn't spend a lot of time on them. Use the Levels controls to severely compress the range of tones in this scan. Without the paths, it will be difficult to maintain the shapes in their present form.

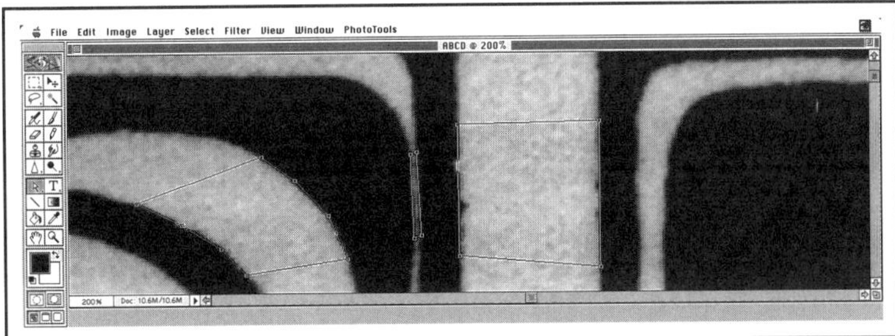

Figure 9-169: Zoom up to the image. Draw paths along the edges of the shapes so that you know where the shapes begin and end while you are adjusting them.

3. The next step is to make the dark and light tones in the scan more homogeneous. Use the Gaussian Blur filter (Figure 9-170). Experiment with the Radius setting until the blur eliminates most of the noise in the dark shapes and the background shapes. Take care not to make the blur so pronounced that you can no longer clearly see the edges of the shapes.

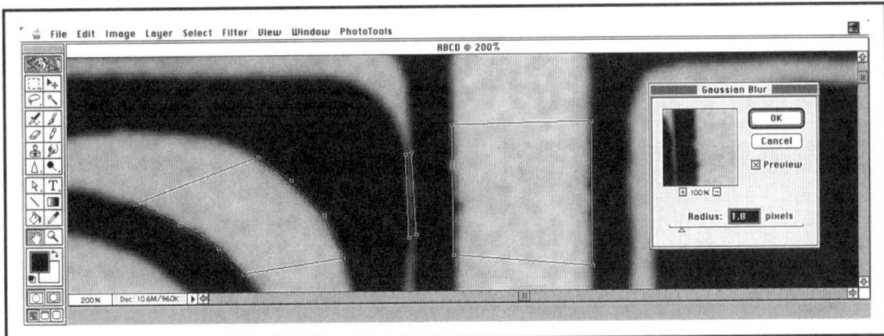

Figure 9-170: Use the Gaussian Blur filter to make the white and black tones more uniform.

4. Open the Levels dialog box. Be sure the Preview check box is turned on. Begin by moving the Input scale highlight slider to the left. As you move it, the background lightens and begins to wash out. In this case, move it until you see the delicate shape on which you are focusing open up so that the two black shapes are no longer touching. Move the Input scale shadow slider to the right as far as it goes: it overlaps the other two slider triangles (Figure 9-171). It might be necessary to move each slider a little at a time until you find the perfect placement. Your screen should resemble the figure. Click OK.

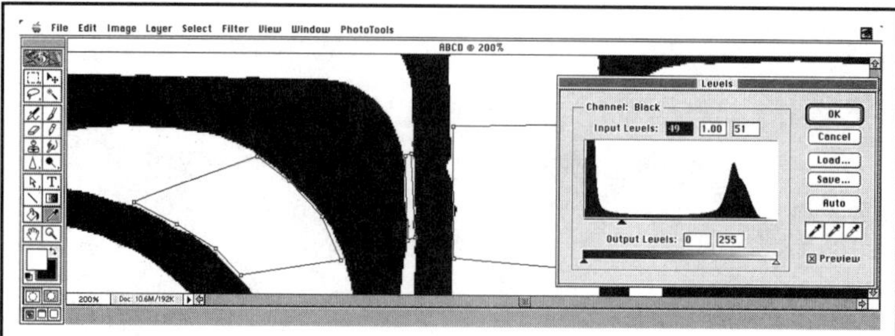

Figure 9-171: Move the Levels Input sliders to wash out the background and to darken the image shapes.

5. By moving the sliders in such a way that the white space between the two black shapes is opened up, you can see that all of the black shapes are smaller. The paths show where the original black edges were and how far the Levels adjustments have caused them to retreat (Figure 9-172). This is not always a problem, but it is a simple matter to fix. Command+click or Ctrl+click the Black channel's thumbnail on the Channels palette. From the Select menu, choose Inverse. Now, from the Select menu, choose Modify | Expand. Expand the selection by 1 pixel. Fill the new selection with black, and Deselect. The edges of the black shapes should now be back close to the paths (Figure 9-173). Delete the paths.

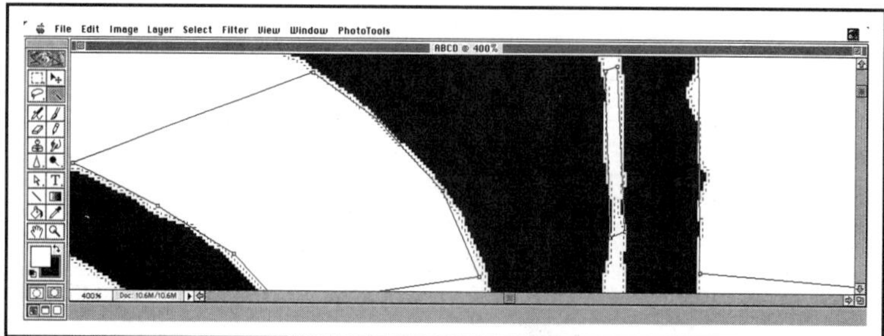

Figure 9-172: A close view shows that the adjustment has moved the black edges so that the shapes are smaller.

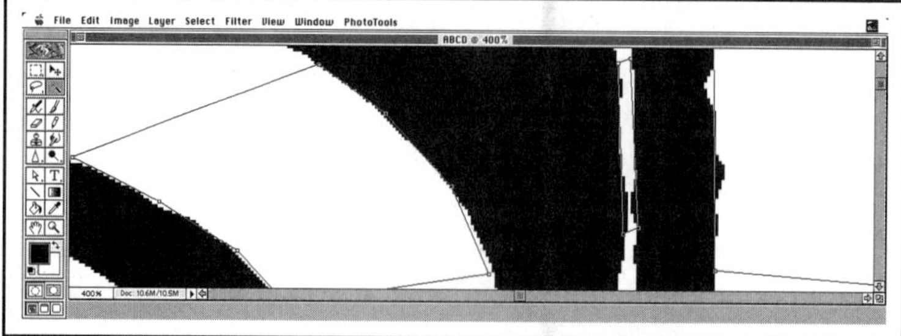

Figure 9-173: After selecting the black shapes and expanding the selection, a black fill brings the edges back to where they were.

6. From the Image menu, choose Mode | Bitmap (Figure 9-174). Keep the Output resolution the same as the Input resolution. Choose 50% Threshold for the Method. Click OK.

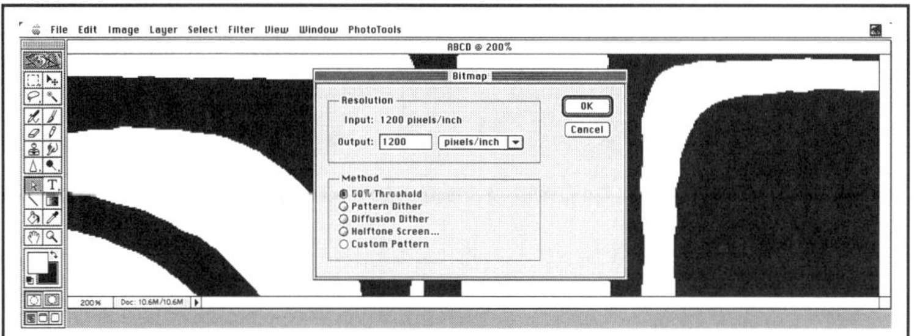

Figure 9-174: Convert the image to Bitmap mode.

The complete image is shown in Figure 9-175. At this point, the image has been improved sufficiently that it is adequate for most purposes. Even when the image is magnified onscreen and the small imperfections are seen (Figure 9-176), don't forget that you are looking at those edges under tremendous magnification. The small blip in the lower part of Figure 9-176 is three pixels high. At the resolution of this file, the real-world height of that blip is 37.5% the height of a single 150 line-screen dot! Since very few eyes are good enough to clearly distinguish a single 150 line-screen dot, a blip a little more than a third of that height is probably not going to stand out on the printed page as a gross error.

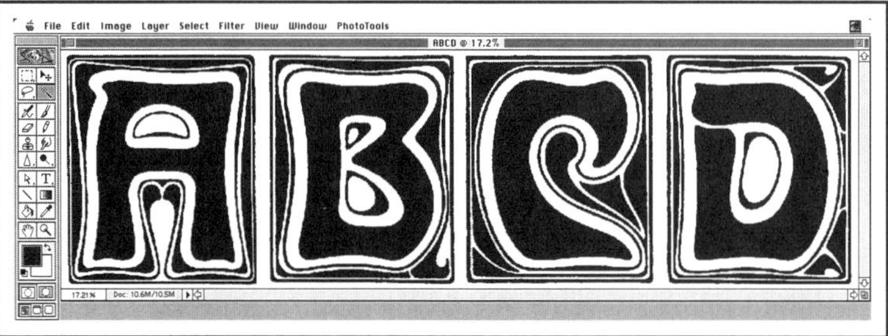

Figure 9-175: The completed image looks much better than the original scan.

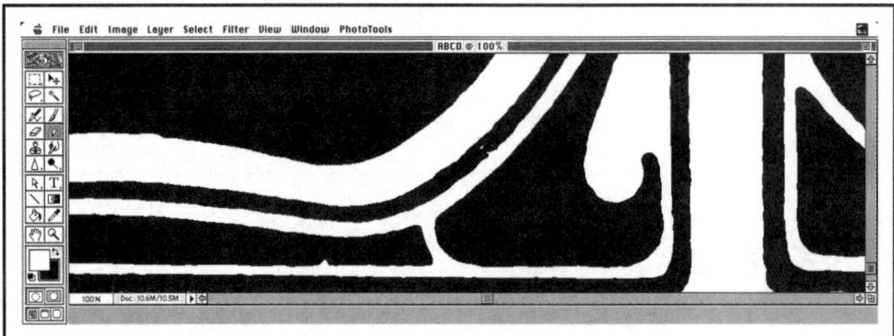

Figure 9-176: A close view shows that there are still some problems with the edges of the black shapes.

Still, prepress people are a bit—uh—compulsive about their work. In fact, they are often teased about it. It's a credo in prepress circles that "Good enough just isn't." Which only illustrates how much prepress people care about what they do.

You could, if you wish, zoom in to the image and correct some of the more obvious problems with the Pencil tool (Figure 9-177). However, if you wished to make this image look better—no blips that show up even at this magnification—and you wished to evade the smug smiles of the Philistines who already consider you compulsive, is there a way to do the thing quickly? Yup. To do the job fast, you need a copy of Adobe Streamline and either Adobe Illustrator or Macromedia FreeHand.

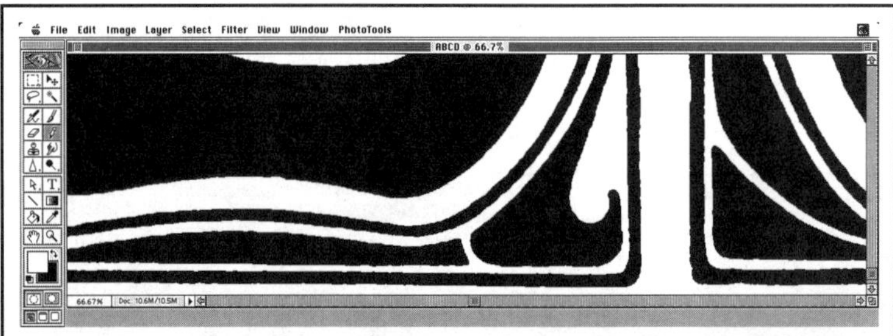

Figure 9-177: Some of the defective edges can be corrected at high magnification with the Pencil tool.

Save the file in TIFF or Photoshop format, and open it in Adobe Streamline. Streamline is an *autotrace* program. It is able to detect edges and to outline shapes with paths and can do the job very well at really formidable speeds. If you are new to Streamline, you might be disappointed the first time you see it perform; many newcomers expect that the traced file will be reasonably close to what they could have drawn manually. Streamline's paths are usually not perfect until you have made your peace with the two Settings items under the Options menu.

The Settings dialog box (Figure 9-178) contains a variety of presets from which you can choose. In the case of the line art in this discussion, a good choice is probably the settings titled Logos and Typefaces. After making your choice, click OK. Now, from the File menu, select Convert. On a moderately fast computer, Streamline can convert this 1.3MB file to paths in a little under four seconds.

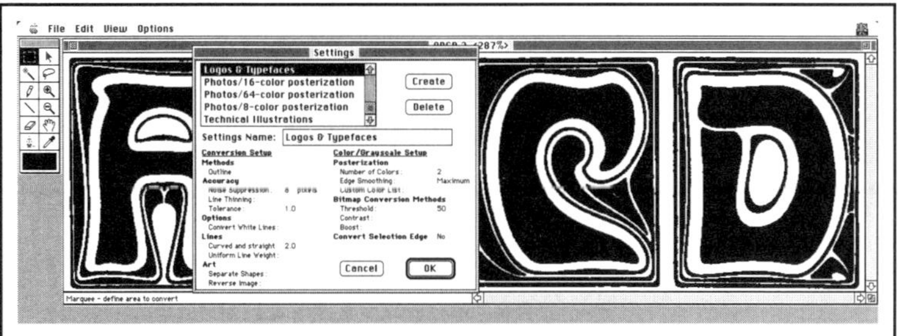

Figure 9-178: The Settings dialog box in Adobe Streamline.

Take a look at the paths without their fills by choosing Artwork from the View menu (Figure 9-179). A fairly common problem with the first round of conversion is that the paths will seem to show too many corners when curves would be more desirable. If the paths don't look quite good enough, all you need to do is to Select All, and press Delete. You're only out the 4 seconds of conversion time.

Figure 9-179: View of the paths without the scan after Streamline has converted the file.

The way the program draws the paths *for this file* can be changed by choosing Options | Conversion Setup (Figure 9-180). The settings put into effect by the previous choice—Logos and Typefaces—were probably adequate for a file with a resolution of 600–800 ppi. The example file is 1200 ppi. Because of that, the numbers of the settings can probably be increased. The Noise Suppression can be changed from 8 pixels to 12, the Tolerance value from 1 to 2, and Lines slider from 2 to 2.5. With the changes made, click OK, and execute the Conversion command again. Still not happy? Delete the paths, and tweak the settings again. You can, in two or three minutes, experiment with a variety of settings until your paths are nearly perfect.

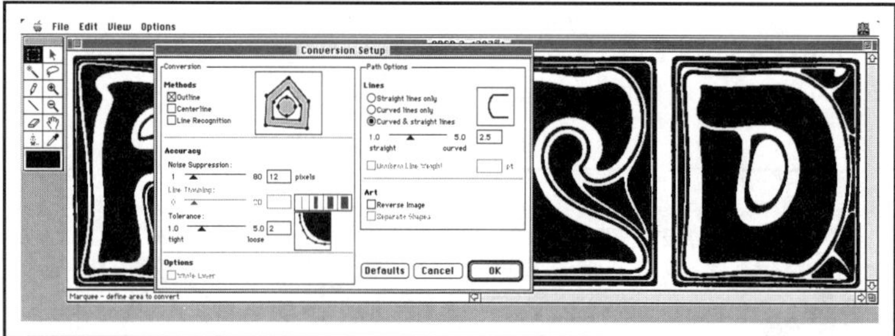

Figure 9-180: Streamline's Conversion Setup dialog box.

You can still do some tweaking to smooth the paths after they have been drawn. Select All, and choose Edit | Smooth Path (Figure 9-182). The menu selection branches to three settings, Minimum, Medium, and Maximum. Try them all, one at a time, using the Undo command after each so that you can determine which is the most effective for the file you are processing. If you've spent a little time tweaking the conversion settings, you'll probably have pretty good paths and Minimum will probably be sufficient.

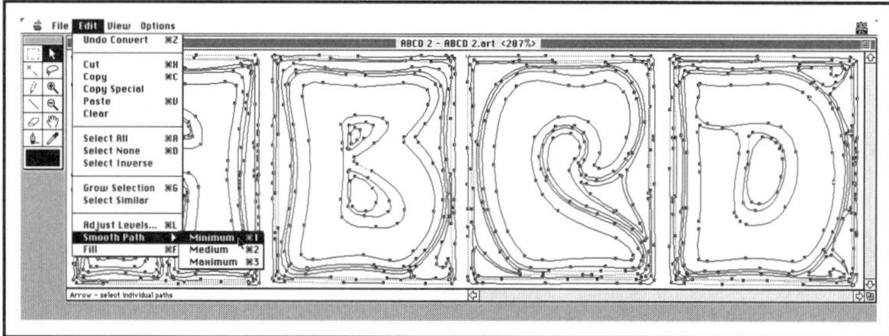

Figure 9-181: Streamline's Smooth Path command.

Export the file from Streamline in Adobe Illustrator format, and then open it in that program or in Macromedia FreeHand. There will still be a few blips (Figure 9-182). Blips are not much of a problem in Illustrator. The example shown in the figure can be fixed simply by removing the offending point. Alternately, use the Direct Select cursor, click and drag around the point, press Delete, click and drag around the two remaining endpoints, and use the Join command. Other correction tools in Illustrator include sweep-selecting groups of more-or-less vertical or horizontal points, and using the Average Command—with the Vertical Only or Horizontal Only options—to line up the points. A set of quick clicks with the Convert Anchor Point tool tames the most recalcitrant line. It should be possible to do a reasonable job of straightening out this file in under 5 minutes. Figure 9-183 shows some of the edges at greater magnification. Compare this figure with Figure 9-176 to see how efficiently Streamline and Illustrator clean up the edges of the dark shapes.

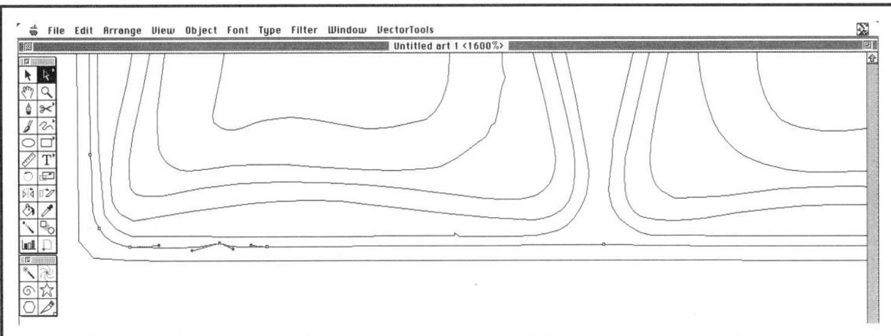

Figure 9-182: Export the file from Streamline to Illustrator. Fixing irregular edges is much easier in Illustrator than it is in Photoshop.

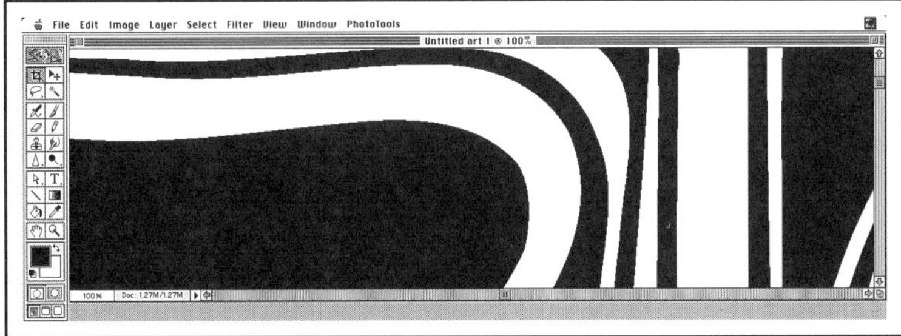

Figure 9-183: A close-up of the converted file shows how much smoother the edges are than the original's.

If the scanning time is not counted, you will have spent a total of 6–10 minutes making this file look good. When you are satisfied with how it looks, it can be saved as an EPS file and used as it is. For artwork of this kind, a vector format is probably the best choice for the final file. With it, the file can be easily colorized, distorted, or resized. The Illustrator file will also be much smaller than the bitmap Photoshop file.

You may wish to use a magnifying glass to examine the three parts of Figure 9-184. As you can see, the shapes in the lower example are smoother that those of the center. However, the center, seen as output rather than as a magnified screen file, does not look obviously inferior unless it is studied under magnification.

This same technique, performed on very high resolution scans, can be used to re-digitize files that have been output to resin-coated paper or as veloxes. These files are larger than the grayscale and color files which Photoshop users handle as a matter of course. There are, however, financial incentives for reprocessing the file.

Assume, for a moment, that you are employed by the publisher of a magazine. Your magazine's pages are set up in QuarkXPress or Adobe PageMaker. Ad pages, in particular, are entirely digital files with the exception of a single 2-inch square ad which has been sent by an advertiser in camera-ready form (velox, r-c paper, etc.). Your typical production cycle involves imaging your digital files as 4-up or 8-up imposed pages. (4-up and 8-up imposed pages compose a printer's press signature. The pages are printed in such a way that they fold to produce the finished printed piece with all

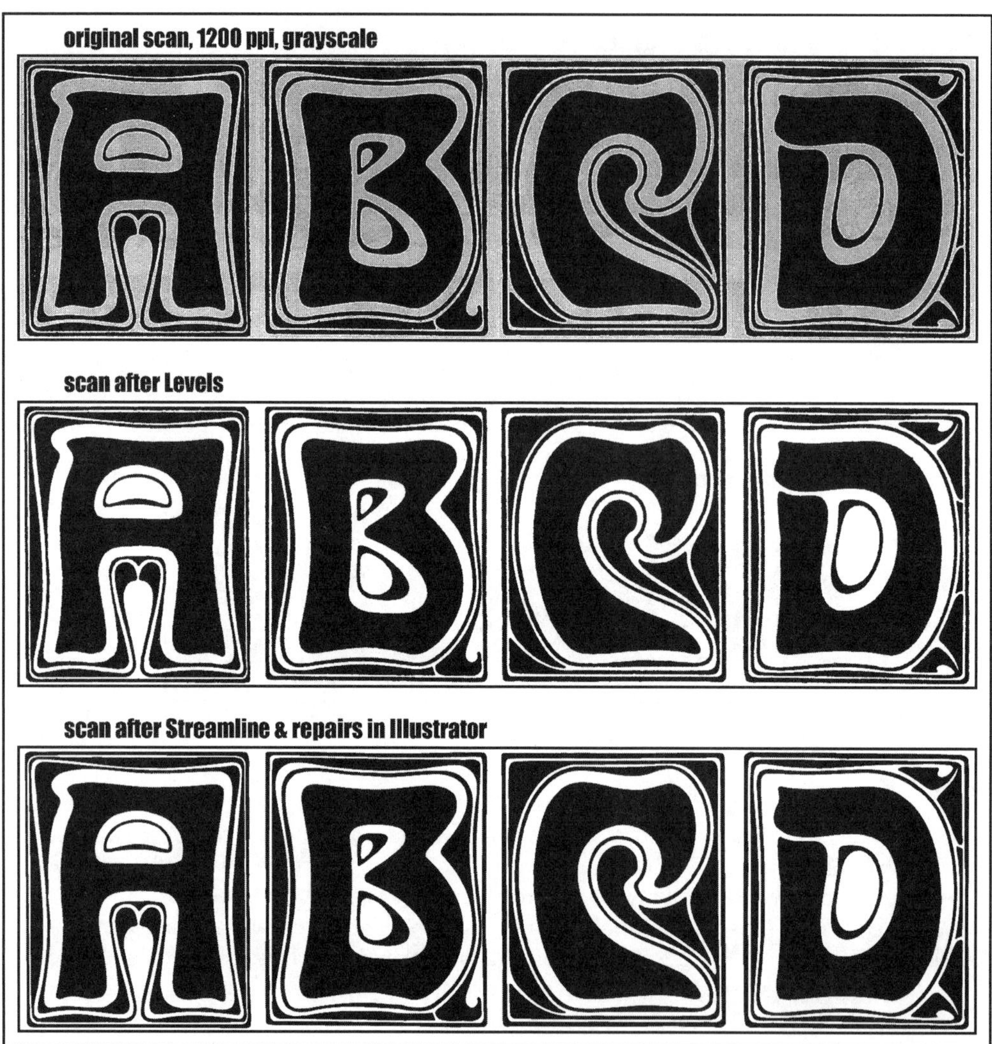

Figure 9-184: Three stages in the line art conversion: the original file, the Photoshop file after the Levels correction, and the Streamlined file.

the pages in the proper order.) Your production flow is interrupted by this single camera-ready ad. After your film is made, someone needs to take a line shot of the ad, process the film, and strip it into the large, composite digital films. The cost of this mechanical intervention is usually sufficient to eat up all the profit for the ad as well as some of the profit for other ads on the page. It is also one picky little detail that can throw a wrench into the most streamlined production cycle.

The solution is to scan this ad at high resolution—if possible, make the resolution equal to your final output device resolution. Many scanners advertise their resolution capabilities as, say, 1200 ppi horizontal X 600 ppi vertical *optical* resolution, and 4800 ppi X 4800 *interpolated* resolution. When a scan's resolution is interpolated above the optical resolution, the values of the new pixels result from a calculation of what the value *probably* could be. In short, the pixel values derive from a mathematical guess. Sometimes the value is accurate, sometimes it isn't. Interpolated scans are always softer and less defined in their detail. For color and grayscale work, using interpolated resolution is not a good idea. For scans which are intended to be used as line art, interpolation causes little harm beyond making you work a little harder when performing tasks such as the one at hand.

Figure 9-185 shows a corner of a scan done at 2400 ppi. At this magnification, the screen dots are clearly visible. The file is about 2.5 inches square. It is in grayscale, and is about 33MBb. When the individual dots are seen at 1600% magnification, the softness generated by the interpolation is very evident (Figure 9-186).

Figure 9-185: A corner of a scan done at 2400 ppi.

The process described here is very similar to that used for the line art sample, as you'll discover when you follow these steps:

1. First, draw a path which delineates the true shape of the dot (seen in Figure 9-186). This is the most difficult part of the task since there is no clear edge from which to work. Draw the path so that it makes a circular shape which follows the set of pixels whose value is roughly halfway between the tone at the center of the dot and the light background tone between the dots.

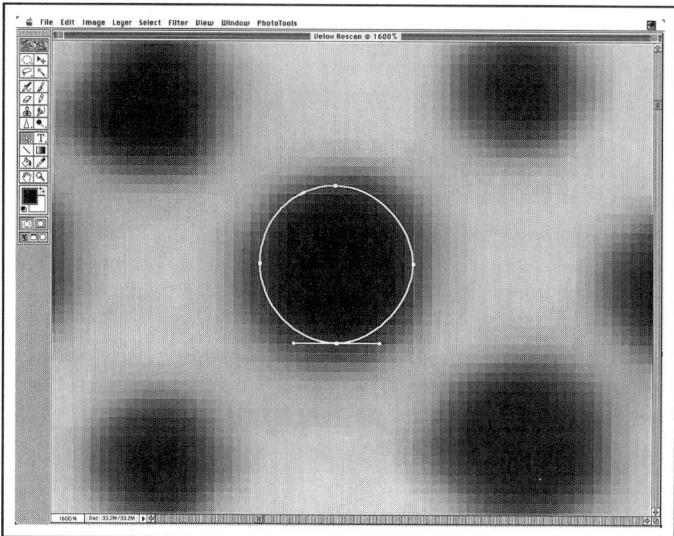

Figure 9-186: At high magnification, draw a path so that you'll know how big a dot is supposed to be.

2. Open the Levels dialog box. Be certain that the Preview option is checked. Move the highlight and shadow Input scale sliders toward each other a little at a time until you have washed out the background and made the dark dot shape fit within the drawn path (Figure 9-187). Click OK. Delete the path.

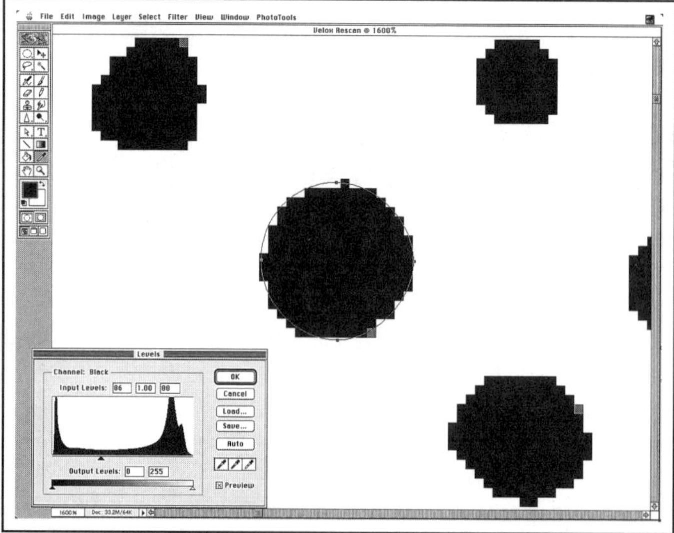

Figure 9-187: Use the Levels controls to increase the contrast to the extent that the path is filled with black and the background is filled with white.

3. The final step is to convert the file to Bitmap mode (Figure 9-188). Keep the Input/Output resolution the same and use the 50% Threshold option. After the file has been converted to Bitmap mode, its size will have been reduced by 7/8ths. In the case of this file, the reduction was from 33.2MB to 4.15MB. Save the file in any of the formats—TIFF, Photoshop EPS, etc.—which can be used by the page layout software you intend to use. When this file has been output at high resolution, there is no way to distinguish it from the way it would have looked had it been printed as a stripped-in line shot.

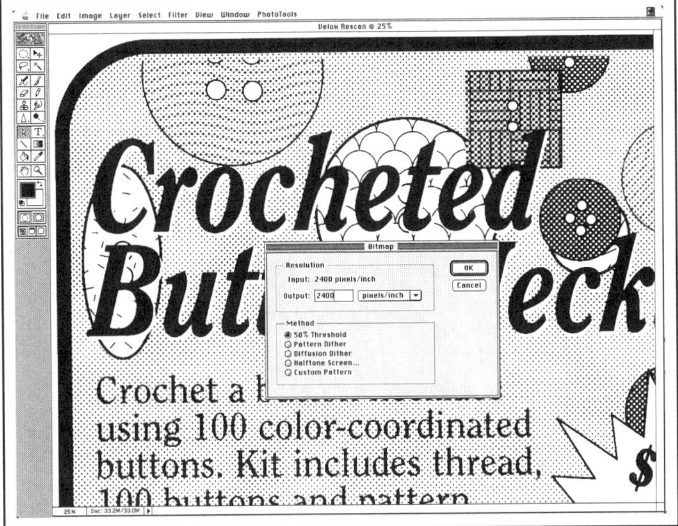

Figure 9-188: Convert the file to Bitmap mode. Keep the Input/Output resolutions the same.

Converting Grayscale Files to Bitmap Mode

When grayscale files are converted to Bitmap mode, Photoshop has five strategies which it can use to eliminate all tones except black and white. The five are listed in the dialog box which appears when the menu command to convert to bitmap is selected (Figure 9-189). Each of these, acting on the same gray-tone image (Figure 9-190), produces a strikingly different result. (Note: this file of the Chicago skyline has been included with the Chapter 9 Practice Files on the Companion CD-ROM. The file name is CHICAGO.PSD.)

You can see that the resolution of the file can be changed as part of the conversion. In most cases when working in Photoshop, changing the resolution upward is probably not a good idea. In this one situation, there is no compromise of the image quality by doing so.

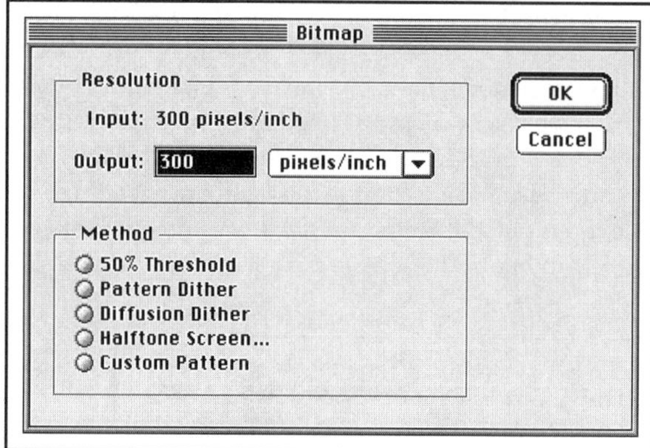

Figure 9-189: Photoshop's Bitmap conversion options window.

Figure 9-190: Sample file for demonstrating the possibilities when converting a grayscale image to Bitmap mode.

The Halftone Screen option is an example of how the change of resolution may even be beneficial. When a halftone file is downloaded to an imagesetter's RIP to be turned into screen dots, the machine and its software have no trouble accurately converting the gray information into dots, provided there is sufficient information contained in the file in the form of pixel density. The RIP does its work by sampling small areas of the image and then constructing appropriate dots at its own very high resolution—say 2400 ppi. Photoshop is fully capable of acting as a high-end RIP in this case. If it is given sufficient data in the form of pixel density, you can ask it to do exactly the same job performed by an imaging system costing tens of thousands of dollars. After the file is converted, you could send it to the same marking assembly controlled by the RIP and your output would be absolutely identical to that produced by the RIP.

It's interesting to think how much unsuspected power Photoshop has, isn't it? Using just Photoshop, Adobe Illustrator, and Adobe PageMaker, a knowledgeable user could do any kind of prepress task or project entirely—including the ripping of the files. It probably isn't a practical thing to dos, but it is possible. And it wouldn't even be very difficult. Just think about it: sometimes the information may prove to be very useful.

50% Threshold

The first of the five conversion methods is the 50% Threshold option. When this option is used, Photoshop constructs a very steep curve which places all the pixels in the image above or below the 50% value. If a pixel is 50% or lighter, it is converted to white. All others are changed to black. The effect, shown in Figure 9-191, is of very high contrast. The high-contrast effect can be really wonderful but it can also be pretty useless. If you find that your high-contrast conversion to Bitmap mode has produced unlovely results, use the Undo command and then experiment with the Curve controls before trying again. You may have to try it a few times before it looks good. Don't give up—nearly all images can be made to yield good-looking high-contrast versions.

Figure 9-191: 50% Threshold conversion yields a high-contrast image.

The Pattern Dither and Diffusion Dither options for converting to Bitmap mode attempt to simulate gray tones by sprinkling pixel-sized black dots over the white background. The difference between the two is the method of dot distribution.

Pattern Dither

Pattern Dither (Figure 9-192, with enlarged detail in Figure 9-193) uses an 8 x 8-pixel cell which can be filled in, one pixel at a time, by means of arbitrary geometric rules. The pattern may be utterly logical, but it is also terrifically ugly. The pattern produced by this conversion method may look familiar: in the pre-color days of Macintosh computers, patterned dithering was used to simulate grays on black and white screens.

Figure 9-192: Pattern Dither Bitmap mode conversion.

Figure 9-193: Enlarged detail of Figure 9-192.

Diffusion Dither

Diffusion Dither (Figure 9-194, with enlarged detail in Figure 9-195) simulates grays by scattering the black pixels in what appears to be a random fashion. Diffusion Dither, as you can see from the figures, does an excellent job maintaining the details and tone range of the image. In fact, when printed on relatively low-resolution printers, it does a better job than conventional screens. Viewed at magnification, the scatter of the pixels is quite attractive. We will discuss Diffusion Dither on low-resolution and non-PostScript printers later in this chapter.

Figure 9-194: Diffusion Dither Bitmap mode conversion.

Figure 9-195: Enlarged detail of Figure 9-194.

Random dithering of this kind is known by a couple of other terms. For the way it produces dots, it is called FM (Frequency Modulated) screening, meaning that the dots are all the same size but are distributed, or modulated, by the darkness, or frequency, of the tone represented. (Traditional halftone screens are called AM screens, for Amplitude Modulated. The size—amplitude—of the dot is governed by the darkness of the represented tone.) FM screens are also called *stochastic* screens. We will discuss stochastic screens for printing color further in Chapter 10.

Halftone Screen

When you select the Halftone Screen conversion option, you are given three choices. The first is the Frequency of the screen, the second the Angle of the screen, and the third the Shape of the dot (Figure 9-196).

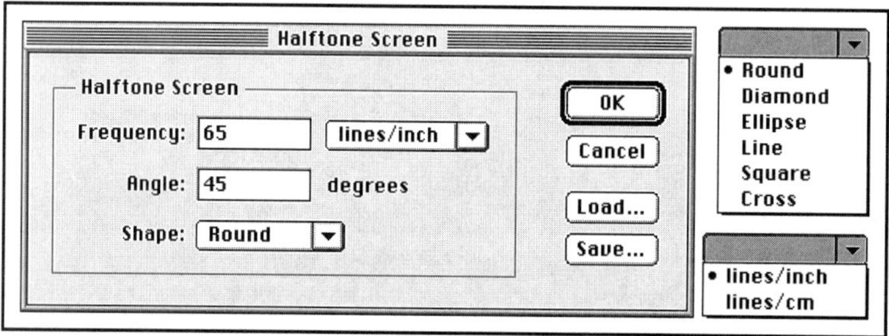

Figure 9-196: The Halftone Screen conversion options dialog box.

When using this conversion option, you need to be aware of the resolution of the final output device. Setting the screen frequency at too large a number results in a posterized image with too few gray tones. Try for a line-screen frequency that is a good match to the printer resolution.

Three sample choices are shown here to give an idea how versatile this choice can be. Figure 9-197 (enlarged detail shown in Figure 9-198) shows the converted file with the settings in Figure 9-196. Figure 9-199 (enlarged detail shown in Figure 9-200) is at the same screen frequency but with the dot shape changed to Cross. Notice how this dot-shape is not as successful at preserving the fine details of the image. The cross-shaped dot is also more susceptible to press gain. If you look at both images (9-197 and 9-199) and make your eyes go a little out of focus, you'll see that the latter is somewhat darker than the former. (Should you ever be adventurous enough to choose this spot shape for a color separation, send an e-mail of the many new and colorful words your press man will use between fits of screaming!)

Figure 9-197: Halftone Screen Bitmap Mode conversion: 65 line-screen, 45° screen angle, round dot.

Figure 9-198: Enlarged detail of Figure 9-197.

Figure 9-199: Halftone Screen Bitmap Mode conversion: 65 line-screen, 45° screen angle, cross-shaped dot.

Figure 9-200: Enlarged detail of Figure 9-199.

The third of the Halftone Screen examples is seen in Figure 9-201 (enlarged detail shown in Figure 9-202). This photo uses quite a low—25—frequency figure, with a linear spot shape at 90 degrees. The effect is very stylized and, in some cases, attractive—a sort of high-contrast image with attitude.

Figure 9-201: Halftone Screen bitmap conversion: 25 line-screen, 0° screen angle, linear dot.

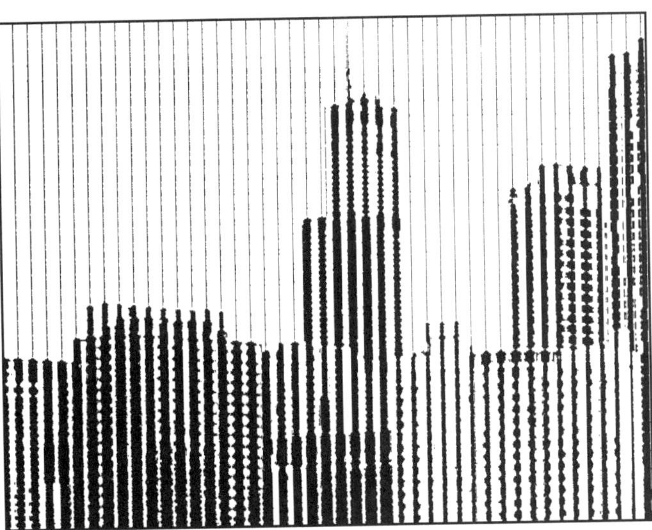

Figure 9-202: Enlarged detail of Figure 9-201.

TIP *A good way to determine whether the image is going to reproduce well is to divide the tentative line-screen number into the resolution of the printer and square the result. The number you end up with is the number of gray tones the printer can deliver* at that line-screen. *Here are a few examples based on a printer resolution of 600 ppi:*

- *100 line-screen: 600 / 100 = 6; 6 x 6 = 36 (gray tones);*
- *85 line-screen: 600 / 85 = 7.05; 7.05 x 7.05 = 49 (gray tones);*
- *70 line-screen: 600 / 70 = 8.6; 8.6 x 8.6 = 74 (gray tones);*
- *60 line-screen: 600 / 60 = 10; 10 x 10 = 100 (gray tones).*

None of these settings is right or wrong, they are simply what will happen when you make a certain choice. Higher line-screen numbers give smaller dots, lower line-screen numbers give more shades of gray. Unless you have access to a device with a resolution of 2400 ppi—the lowest resolution that allows the maximum number of grays at a line-screen of 150—there will always be a trade-off between fine dots and gray tones. 100 line-screen, for example, will have fairly fine dots (compared to 60 line-screen), but with only 36 gray tones; a reproduced gradient would show a clearly visible line about every three percent.

You don't really need the full number of possible gray tones. If the image has large, flat areas, 100 line-screen might work. Be ready with the Undo command until you hit the correct balance.

Custom Pattern

Custom Pattern allows you to plug in any defined pattern in lieu of a specified spot shape. Make a rectangular selection and choose Edit | Define Pattern. An example of such a pattern is shown in Figure 9-203. This pattern, rasterized from Illustrator, is very small: it is 31 pixels square with a resolution of 600 ppi. After the file has been converted (Figure 9-204, enlarged detail shown in Figure 9-205), the image seems to have been sprayed upon the texture formed by multiple iterations of the pattern. As you can see, there is a good deal of lost image detail. This loss is offset by the charm of the

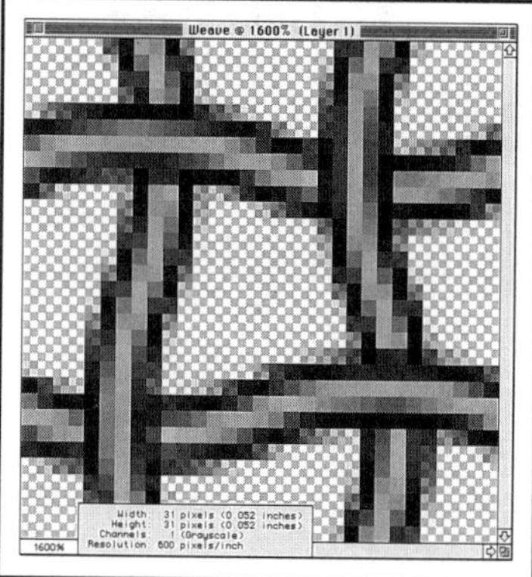

Figure 9-203: Small repeating tile, defined as a Photoshop pattern.

effect. Mapping an image onto a small repeating texture is one of Photoshop's minor miracles. It may take a little experimentation to get the scale of the pattern to be suitable for the resolution of the image. When the scale is correct, you'll have an image which can be achieved in no other way.

Figure 9-204: Custom pattern Bitmap mode conversion.

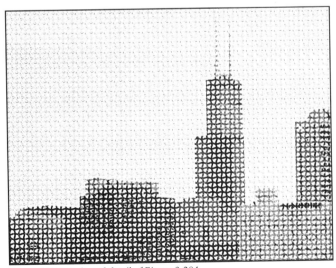

Figure 9-205: Enlarged detail of Figure 9-204.

An Exotic Use for the Halftone Screen Bitmap Conversion Option

It happens: you have a pretty good image, the color is nice, the composition is OK. The trouble with the image is this: by itself, it's a little static, and the texture is a little grainy because it was shot on high-speed film. What to do? "Tart it up," as it's said in the business. Or, "Add compositional interest," as it's said in front of the clients. Whatever. The process is fun and it's very easy. (You can try out this technique on the file shown in Figure 9-206 by opening SUNSET.PSD in the Chapter 9 Practice Files on the Companion CD-ROM. The two images are shown in the color plate section.) Follow these steps:

Figure 9-206: Sample image to be altered using Bitmap mode conversion, filters, and layers.

1. Begin by duplicating the image. Change the mode of the duplicate to Lab, press Command+1 or Ctrl+1 to view the Lightness channel, change the mode to Grayscale. Open the Curves controls and set up a steep curve (shown in Figure 9-207) to heighten the contrast. Change the mode of this grayscale document to Bitmap. Choose Halftone Screen. For the options, choose 12 for the Frequency, 45° for the Angle, and Line for the Shape. The converted image is shown in Figure 9-208, with an enlarged detail in Figure 9-209.
2. Change the mode of the image back to Grayscale. Command+click or Ctrl+click the thumbnail of the Black channel. Choose Select | Modify | Border. Enter **6** and click OK. Use the Gaussian Blur filter at a setting of 1 to soften the edges of the dark shapes (Figure 9-210). Adjust the size of this grayscale window and the original so that you can see them both. Select All, and copy the new grayscale image. Click on the original document's window. Click on the New Channel icon at the bottom of the Channels palette. When the new, all-black channel appears in the window, paste the grayscale file. Your modified image is now an alpha channel for the colored document.

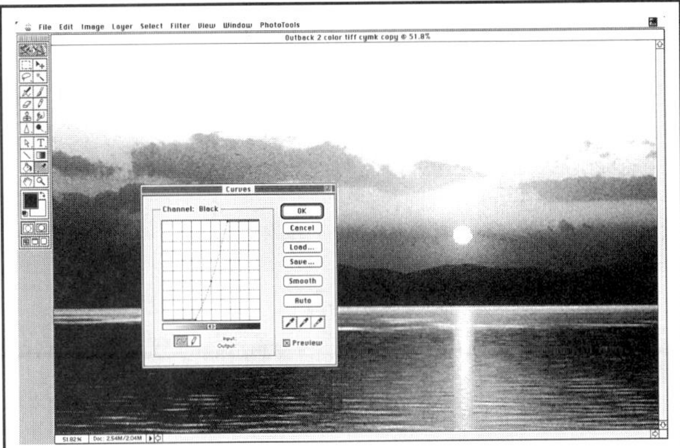

Figure 9-207: After converting the image to Grayscale mode, make a steep curve to heighten the contrasts.

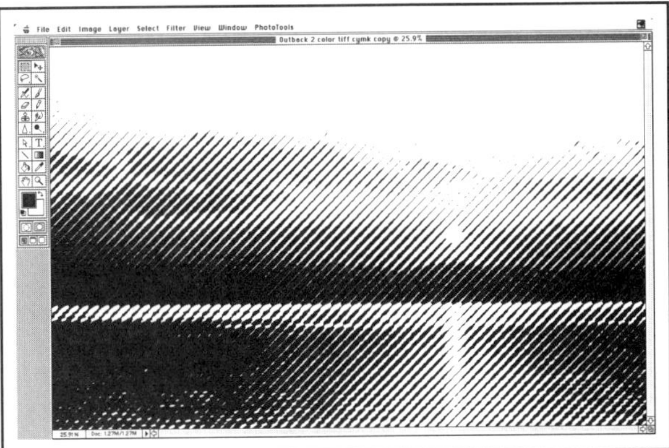

Figure 9-208: Convert the image to Bitmap mode. Use Halftone Screen with settings of 12 line-screen, 45°, and linear dot.

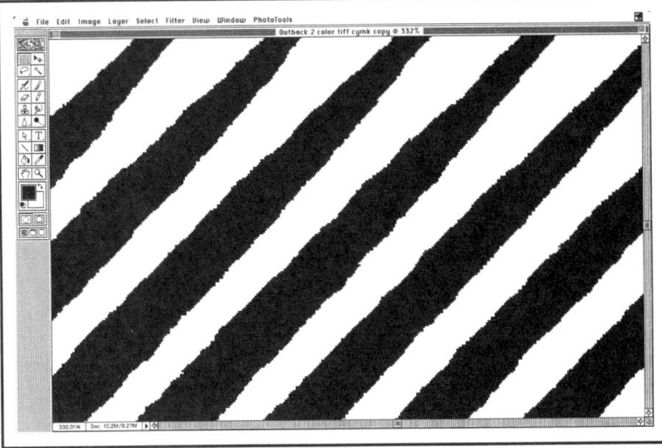

Figure 9-209: Close-up of the converted file.

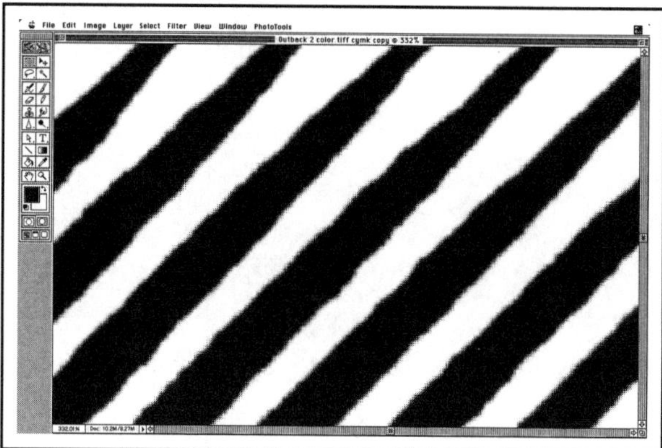

Figure 9-210: Blur the edges of the black shapes.

3. With this channel in view, choose Filter | Distort | Ripple. You can experiment with your own settings. The example shown in Figure 9-211 used settings of 100 and Medium.

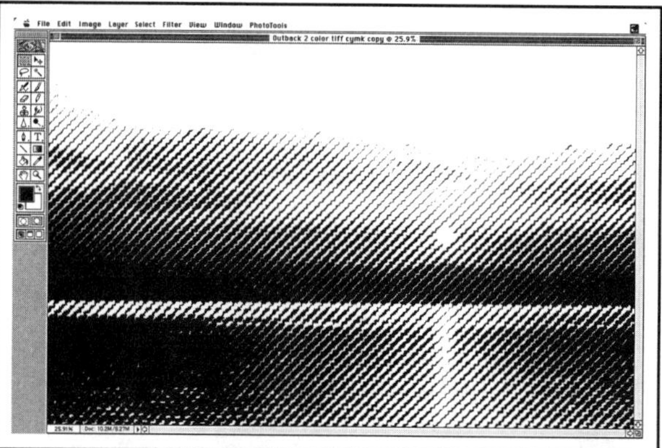

Figure 9-211: Apply the Ripple filter to the alpha channel.

4. Click on the topmost channel thumbnail to view the full-color document. Command+click or Ctrl+click the #5 channel to activate it as a selection. From the Select menu, choose Inverse. Press Command+j or Ctrl+j to make the selection into an independent layer. Set the mode of the layer to be Overlay. From the Filter menu, choose Noise | Add Noise. Experiment with the settings to achieve an effect you like. The sample here used an Amount of 150, Uniform.

5. Click on the Background layer, and activate the alpha channel selection again. Press Command+j or Ctrl+j to make the selection into an independent layer. Set the blending mode of the layer to Multiply.

The finished image is shown in Figure 9-212 with an enlarged detail in Figure 9-213. The textures are easily visible here. Please look at the image printed in color to see how the Overlay mode makes colors superimposed upon themselves more intense, and how the Multiply mode darkens and enriches the same colors when superimposed upon themselves. It is worth noting that the two modes are applied respectively to an enhancement of the highlights and the shadows of the original image. It is this mechanism which causes the dark waving shapes to fade out at the upper edges of the clouds.

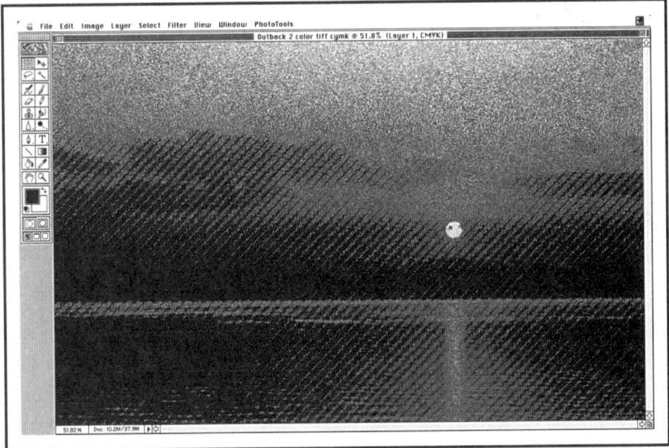

Figure 9-212: The image after applying blending modes.

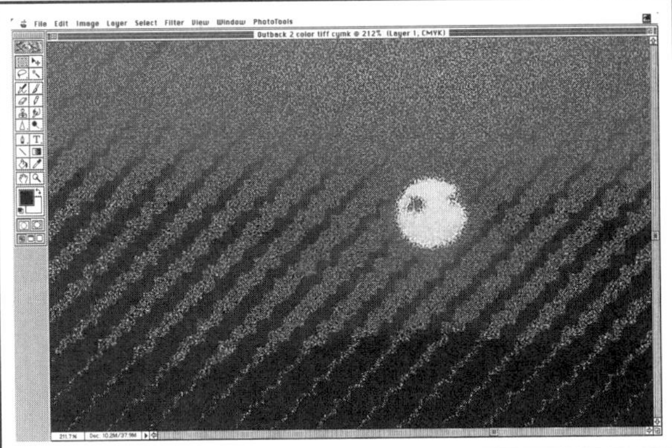

Figure 9-213: Enlarged close-up of Figure 9-212.

TIP

If you often use a laser or inkjet printer, converting your files to Bitmap mode allows you to reproduce a range of tones that would otherwise be possible only on a very high resolution output device. Use this easy-to-follow procedure:

Begin with a scan which has a resolution that is an even divisor of or equal to your printer's resolution. If possible, print a swatch of 50% gray on your printer and check the amount of dot gain the printer gives you. (Toner printers do gain density—it isn't the same kind of gain you get on press, but you have to compensate for it nonetheless.) If you have no way of checking, adjust the image as you would for a conventional halftone but with a target gain compensation of about 30%–35% and a maximum black value of about 85%. When you have the image adjusted and sharpened, change the mode of the file from Grayscale to Bitmap. Keep the Input/Output resolutions equal, and select the Diffusion Dither method. Save the file in whatever format you require. You'll be surprised at how good your printed images look—even on low resolution printers and printers which do not have PostScript—and at how fast they print.

When you use this method of producing great-looking images from desktop printers, keep in mind that your output is equivalent to that of a press run. In other words, it is the final output. *If, for some reason, you need to reproduce your hard copy—photocopy, etc.—you have to back up and adjust for more gain on the original file. Copiers also gain; if you photocopy an image that has already gained, you combine the two gain factors. You'll need to think this through and do some experimenting before you find the perfect amount of adjustment for the original image. A word of caution: don't be surprised if your original gain adjustment is higher than you would have believed possible! Considering how high the toner gain percentage is, compensation for two generations of gain can be as high as 50%–55%.*

Moving On

Photoshop & prepress is a large topic as you've discovered in this chapter. You've learned of press conditions and how you can use Photoshop's amazing tools to change your image so that it emerges from the press as a beautifully printed image. In the process, you discovered what makes an attractive halftone and how to construct duotones. You have also learned to handle simple spot color, and the very complex bump plates and touch plates which add extra inks to your images. Finally, we focused on the Bitmap mode and line art. All of these tools and techniques, and all of the detailed information will serve you well in most day-to-day prepress situations. Besides the step-by-step instructions, we hope you have also begun to build a picture in your mind of how Photoshop fits into the print-production process.

The only topic we have neglected in this chapter is color reproduction and some of the topics—such as trapping and clipping paths—which go along with it. For that, we invite you to continue your prepress explorations by turning to Chapter 10, "Calibration & Color Reproduction." You'll find a thorough examination of topics such as color management and calibration, Photoshop's monitor and printing preferences, how to generate a color separation, and hundreds of production details.

chapter 10

Calibration & Color Reproduction

There was, in my college years, a popular philosophical discussion revolving around human perceptions. As children grow and learn, they point to a color and are told its name. The apple is *red*, the leaf is *green*, and the sky is *blue*. What if there is a built-in difference in the way each child sees? What one child might see as red in the absolute sense, another child might see as an absolute blue. Do we have any way of knowing if there is a problem since our definitions of color are based on verbal descriptions which have nothing to do with the color itself? If children are taught to call the apple red, all that children can do is to agree on the *name* of the color. We do not know if each child sees a different *red*.

This discussion is like the problem of Color Management Systems (CMS) in the digital prepress world. Different digital devices *see* colors in different ways. Two scanners might see and quantify a red tone. The digital identity of that tone from the two devices might appear to be the same, yet human vision easily identifies them as different.

Another side of this problem has to do with the way CRTs interpret and display color. Digital prepress has long been identified as the world of WYSIWYG (What You See Is What You Get). A more accurate acronym might be WYSIPWYGBOBA (What You See Is Possibly What You Get, But Only By Accident). (Which is too bad—at least *whiseewig* is pronounceable!) However, many Photoshop technicians know only too well that the differences between the monitor display and the press can be surprising, disappointing, and expensive!

Take two professional-level monitors with consecutive manufacturer's serial numbers. Place them side by side and, with two different computers, display two copies of the same color file in Photoshop. You'll be surprised to see that there will be differences in the way they look. In some cases, the differences will be small. In other cases, the differences will be great enough to cause you to wonder if you are seeing the same file. Whether great differences or small, your next question is: which of these monitors is displaying the *real* file, the one that looks pretty close to the way the photo will look when it is printed on an offset press? The short answer: neither of them. Unless the monitor has been calibrated with hardware, you have as much chance of seeing an accurate presentation of the color as you have of telling time from a stopped clock.

Different digital devices, different colors; if you add printing inks and proofing devices to the discussion, the color problem gets very tricky indeed. The development of CMS is an attempt to harmonize and to make logical the differences in color between input and output devices. The CMS strategy is this: objectively measure the color characteristics of every device, and then, as the color passes from one to the other, translate each so that it falls into place as a reasonable translation. Despite the media hype, this is a problem that is a long way from a satisfactory solution. Or, to be kind about it: it is not yet a mature technology. There is no agreed-upon standard for color definitions between device manufacturers, nor is there a perfect system-level color descriptor method for any computer platform—although Apple Computer has been making the effort for a number of years, and the Apple Color Sync system is years ahead of the color management software built into the Windows platform.

The entire CMS issue has been an attempt at a front-end solution to what is, in effect, an industrial problem of the print industry. (More recently, CMS has taken on new urgency as a concern of Internet developers involved with retail sales on the World Wide Web. As product sales become more widespread on the Internet, CMS will become more of an issue than it has been. One controversial calibration strategy, *sRGB*, has recently been proposed by Microsoft and Hewlitt-Packard. This calibration scheme is far less sophisticated than what is needed by prepress professionals.) At the present stage of digital technology, calibration is still mostly critical to the evaluation and correction of color for printing. The colors on the screen must come close to the colors that will come off the press. This means that many different monitors must be able to display the same colors in the same way. Calibration of the monitor, then, is the first step in the management of your color printing. It is also the only reasonably cost-effective way for you to begin to get control of your color management concerns.

You will learn in this chapter how RGB displays produce color, how to work with monitor calibration, and what Photoshop's preferences have to do with controlling your display and your hard-copy output. You'll learn the fine points of generating a color separation that will reproduce in a predictable way. Along the way, we hope that you'll find that color has no enormous mysteries. Rather, there are many small, interrelated concepts, all of them quite understandable.

RGB Color

To make more clear how a monitor display is altered by the calibration software, we need to examine how your monitor produces the colors you see. This is not a technical discourse on the inner workings of a cathode ray tube, merely a look at RGB color in the abstract.

The simplest way to think of a monitor pixel is to think in grayscale and to imagine the pixel as a very tiny light bulb. Imagine that the light bulb has a circular dimmer switch attached to it with 256 possible settings. With the bulb turned entirely off, it is black and the dimmer switch reads *zero* (left-hand vertical column, Figure 10-1). Turn the dimmer switch up to position 64, and though the bulb is still dim, it does emit some light. Turn the switch up to position 128 and the bulb becomes brighter still. At position 192, it is three-quarters of the way toward being entirely on. Finally, at position 255—this is the largest number because the counting started with 0 instead of with 1—the bulb is as bright as it can be.

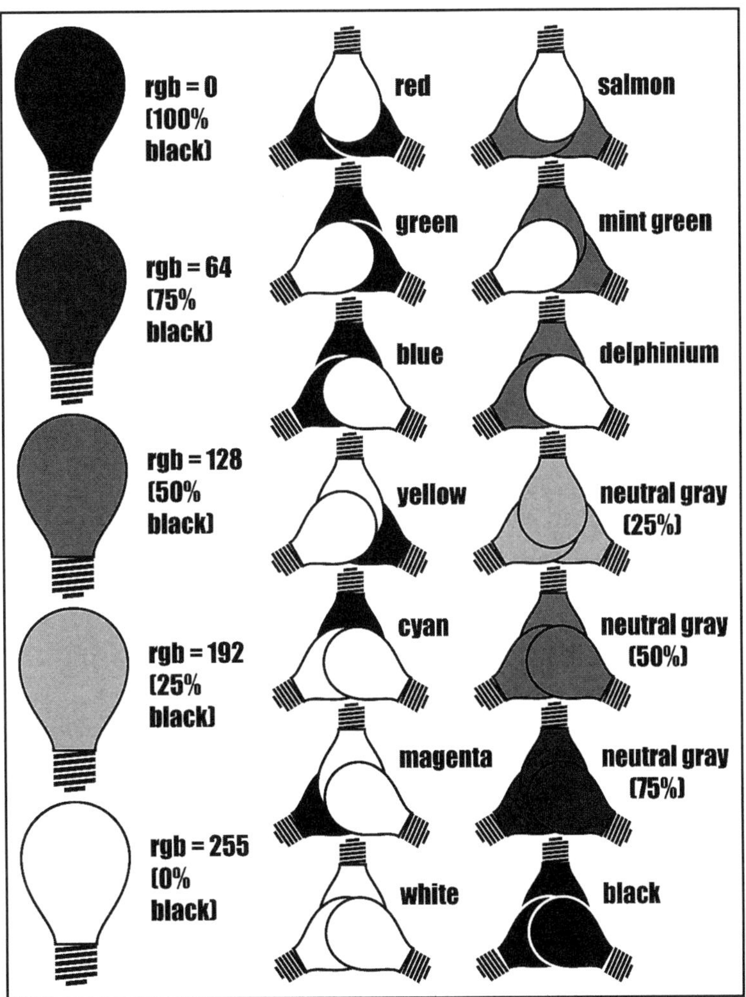

Figure 10-1: The monitor's pixels can be roughly compared to small light bulbs controlled by a dimmer switch.

The important thing to remember about the light bulb analogy is that the numerical reading is a gauge of the bulb's brightness. The larger the number, the brighter the bulb—and the pixel. Every pixel in a grayscale image can be likened to this hypothetical bulb: each pixel has a unique value between 0 and 255, and a unique position. If you think about it, that's the way the computer stores the image, as a simple list of the brightness values of the pixels in each horizontal row of pixels.

If you have looked at the individual channels of an RGB image, you know that each channel is, for all practical purposes, a grayscale image. In that sense, each channel can also be thought of as a collection of brightness values. When three sets of brightness values are present in one file, there is an opportunity to do a great deal more with the brightness information. To glimpse how this will work, look at Figures 10-2, 10-3, and 10-4. These are, as they are labeled, representations of individual channels. Each contains a circular area of white pixels surrounded by black. Discounting the anti-aliasing that is present, each channel represents just two brightness values, black and white. When the three are assembled into a single RGB file, amazing things happen (Figure 10-5). Each channel now has something to do with, not only the brightness of its pixels, but its place in the three-channel structure—whether a given amount of brightness exists as a *red* brightness, or a green or a blue. The brightness values of each channel are now used to designate color.

You need not see Figure 10-5 in color, nor do you need to understand the electron beams which excite the phosphor colors on the inside surface of your monitor tube. All you need to know, for now, is that each channel arbitrarily contributes its own color and that the contributions of all three channels—Red, Green, and Blue—produce all the colors your monitor can display.

If a pixel has value 255 in the Red channel and black (value 0) in the other two, that pixel's displayed color is a bright red. The Green and Blue channels work the same way. The combinations become more interesting when a given pixel has, say, value 255 in two channels but with the other value 0. 255 in Red and Green with 0 in Blue gives a bright yellow. 255 in Green and Blue with 0 in Red produces a bright cyan. 255 in Blue and Red with Green as 0 gives a bright magenta. The two right-hand columns in Figure 10-6 show some of the possibilities. (Please note that the secondary tones—cyan, magenta, and yellow—are the primary colors of four-color process printing.)

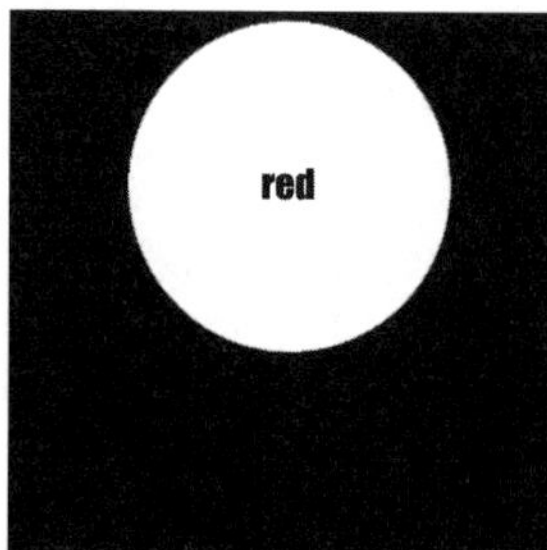

Figure 10-2: Light-colored pixels in the Red channel contribute bright red to the color image.

Figure 10-3: Light-colored pixels in the Green channel contribute bright green to the color image.

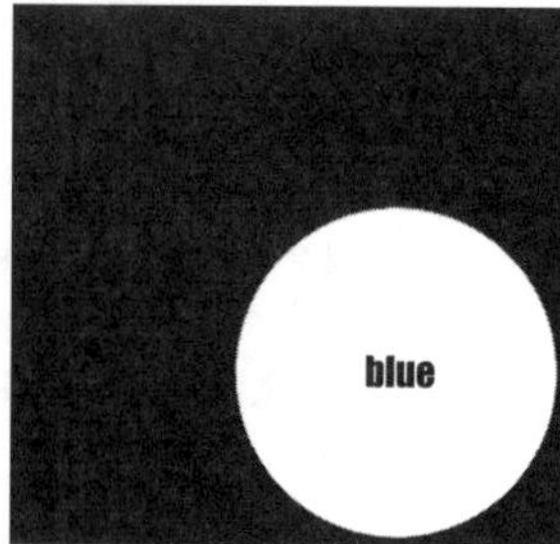

Figure 10-4: Light-colored pixels in the Blue channel contribute bright blue to the color image.

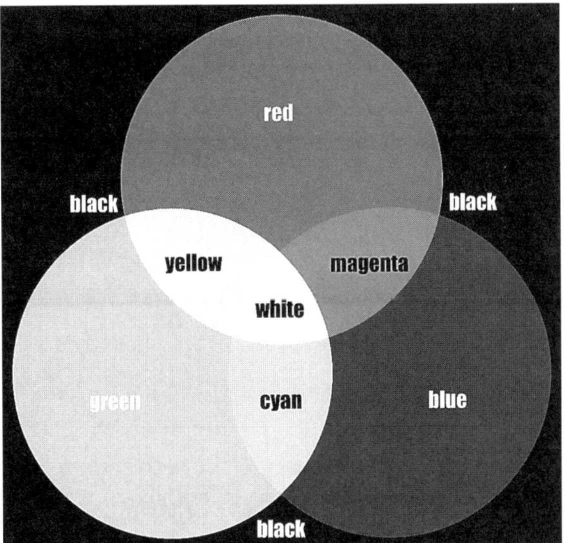

Figure 10-5: Brightness values in all three channels combine to produce the range of colors you see on your monitor.

Many, many more colors are possible. Pixels do not have to be black and white, but can be any one of 256 values in each channel. That gives a lot of possibilities: 256^3 (2^{24}) = 16,777,216. It's an interesting concept, isn't it: all of those colors from a method that is so elegantly economical.

Your monitor is probably an RGB monitor; if it displays in color, it is. Of course you know that you are also able to process files in what Photoshop calls Grayscale mode. Grayscale, though you may not think of it this way, is really just a specialized kind of RGB. Think it through. If all three channels are value zero then the displayed color is black. If all three channels are value 255 (see the center area of Figure 10-5), then the displayed color is white. Logically, if all three channels are value 128 (half of 256), wouldn't the displayed value be halfway between black and white—what we would call a 50% gray? Indeed it would. From this we can deduce that grayscale is simply a proper subset of RGB where a pixel's R, G, and B values are all the same.

Calibration & How It Works

Figure 10-6 shows the working dialog box of a well-known hardware calibration system sold by SuperMac/Radius. On the left-hand side are three pop-up menus which inform the calibration software of the monitor type being evaluated and what kind of White Point and Gamma values are to be targeted. Two check boxes below these pop-ups instruct the software to use the derived calibration values after the calibration sequence has been performed. Finally, there is a button which initiates the calibration.

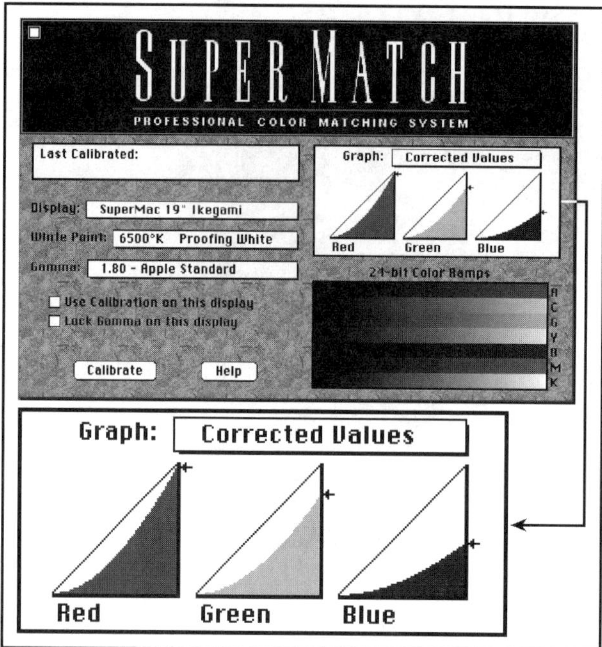

Figure 10-6: The opening screen for the SuperMatch calibration system.

When the software requests it, a small, rectangular instrument with a suction cup is attached to the screen. While the software is running, this device makes evaluations of the three principal colors by themselves, the absolute white of the monitor, its darkest values, and the relative neutrality of the gray tones which form when all of the primary colors are combined. Once it has done so, it electronically adjusts the display to bring it into line with an abstract set of values calculated to produce accurate colors on screen.

The center right-hand side of the calibration screen shows the results of the calibration software adjustments. That portion of the screen has been reproduced and enlarged at the bottom of the figure. You have already spent some time on curves in Chapter 9, "Photoshop Prepress," knowing what you do about curves and how they work, it is easy to recognize how much of a change these curves indicate, especially in the blue signal. The pre-adjusted line, of course, is equivalent to the Input curve. The Output curve here shows that the blue signal, relative to the other two, was so strong that its output needed to be reduced by more than half. The green signal, also too strong, has been severely cut back. All three have been reduced in the midtone and highlight values.

Human eyes, even eyes highly sensitive to color, are not good enough to evaluate a computer monitor. The reason for this is simple: the unaided eye has no external reference within the same color paradigm. By this, we mean that you cannot hold a printed piece up to the monitor and hope for more than an approximate match since the printed piece depends upon reflected light and the monitor emits light. The eye cannot say that against some arbitrarily set standard of what a color is suppose to look like, a given monitor's display of that color is too bright or too dark. Nor can it say that on one monitor, the strength of one of the phosphor colors is such that it overbalances or gives a color cast to neutral grays. The hardware calibration instrument can do what the eye cannot do. It can perform an accurate evaluation of a monitor. Following the evaluation, the software can control the hardware in order to give a screen image that is trustworthy.

There are software utilities—the Gamma utility bundled with Photoshop is one—that attempt to calibrate a monitor by visually comparing such things as the white of the monitor with the white of the paper stock to be used. In practical terms, using a utility program such as this may provide a temporary solution to the problem of calibration. However, the visual comparisons are necessarily so subjective that they cannot be considered a permanent solution for any prepress professional. The hard fact is that hardware calibration is not a nicety, it is vital! It is also relatively expensive, ranging from $750–$1,500.

Colortron II

One of the most impressive devices being sold for hardware calibration is the Colortron II by Light Source, Inc. This small multi-purpose device plugs into the ADB circuitry—from the port which drives the keyboard and the mouse—of a Macintosh or Power Macintosh computer. It is bundled with two foot-pieces. One of these has suction cups which allow the Colortron to be attached to the monitor for calibration. The other foot-piece is in the form of a rocker switch. The rocker switch supports the instrument in open position when it is not in use. When measurements are being made, the switch is in closed position. When it is not being used for monitor calibration, the Colortron II can be used as a densitometer or as a colorimeter. These functions make it one of the most remarkable and cost-effective tools available to prepress technicians. The desktop functions will be discussed later in this chapter.

Figure 10-7 shows an expanded view of the Colortron monitor calibration dialog box. The top two pop-up menus show the target choices for the White Point and the Gamma. The ColorSync Profile pop-up menu is not used until after the calibration has been done. When the dialog box first opens, the menu displays the current setting of the ColorSync Control Panel. The dialog box shows a check box which causes the calibration software to be used systemwide—and not just in Photoshop—as well as a button which initiates the calibration.

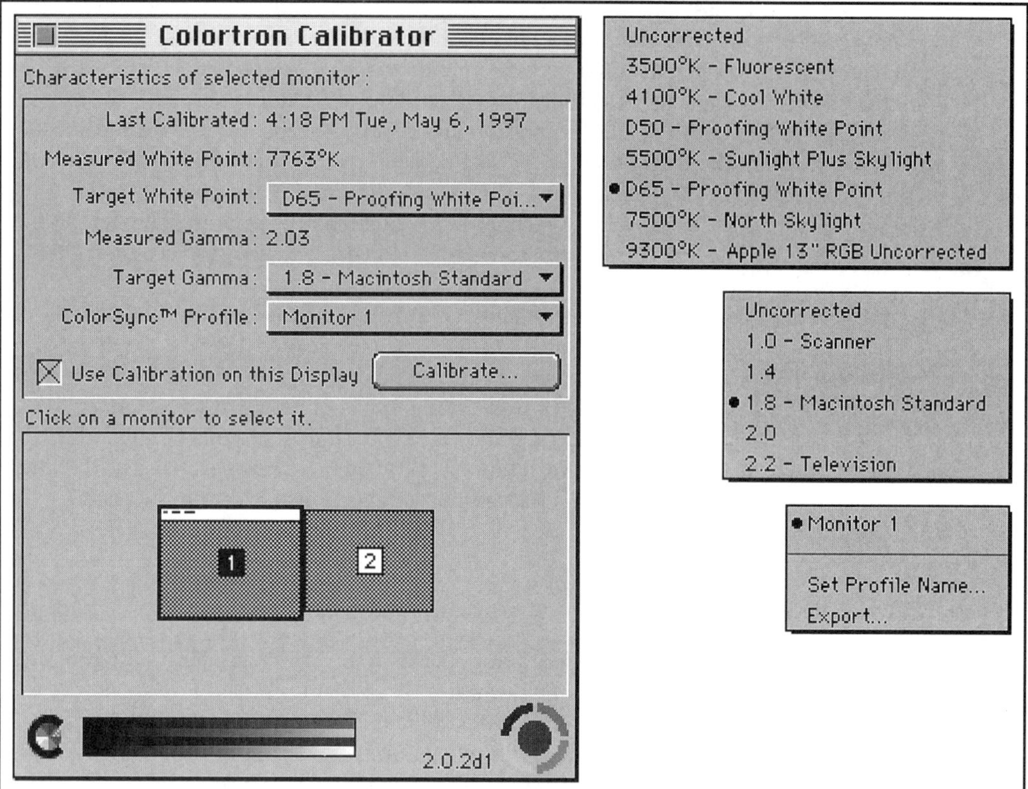

Figure 10-7: Expanded view of the Colortron calibration options dialog box.

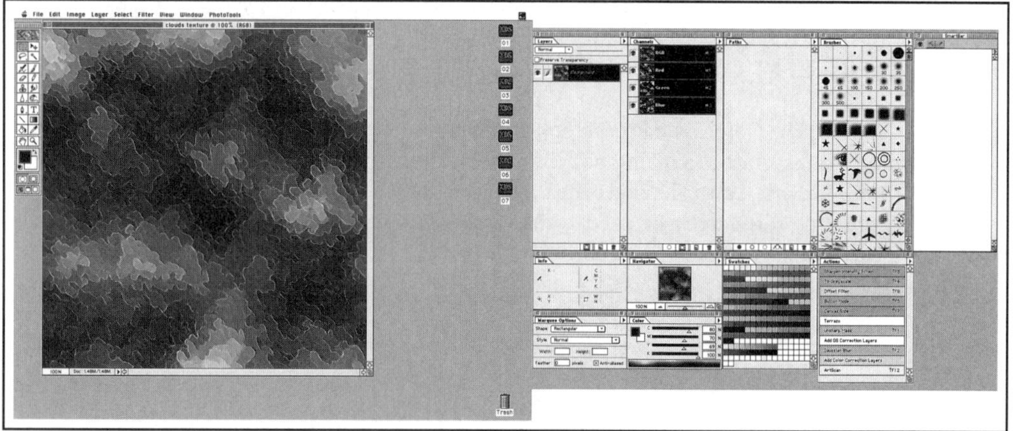

Figure 10-8: Screen capture of a two-monitor workstation. The larger monitor displays the document, the smaller displays the palettes.

TIP

At the bottom of the dialog box is a rectangular area which indicates that two monitors are present and that you can click on either to select which will be calibrated. Windows users are not widely aware of the fact that workstations can be configured with two monitors. The ability to use more than one monitor has been part of the Macintosh system since well before the introduction of color displays. The default usage for two monitors is to have them function as one virtual screen. The primary monitor is the larger and is used to display the document. The secondary monitor allows for the display of all the palettes that a program uses to be open at all times. This is shown in Figure 10-8, which is a screen capture of one of the authors' monitors while using Photoshop. The advantages of such a system are instantly obvious.

Take a close look at the settings in Figure 10-7. The target settings and the measured settings are fairly far apart. The monitor being calibrated is a SuperMatch 20 Plus and it is about 4 years old. It's well known that monitors loose their brightness as they age, which explains why the measured gamma—2.03—is darker than the target gamma of 1.8.

When the calibration sequence has ended, the ColorSync Profile pop-up menu comes into play. First, the measurements for this monitor can be saved as a named file using one of two file types. A typical procedure works like this: First, having named the file, it is saved in ColorSync format. (The two choices are shown in Figure 10-9.) Later, the ColorSync control panel is used to load this profile as the system default. (With that profile in place, all color management programs have access to it.) Second, the profile is saved in Photoshop format—a good place to save it is in the Calibration folder within the Photoshop Goodies folder.

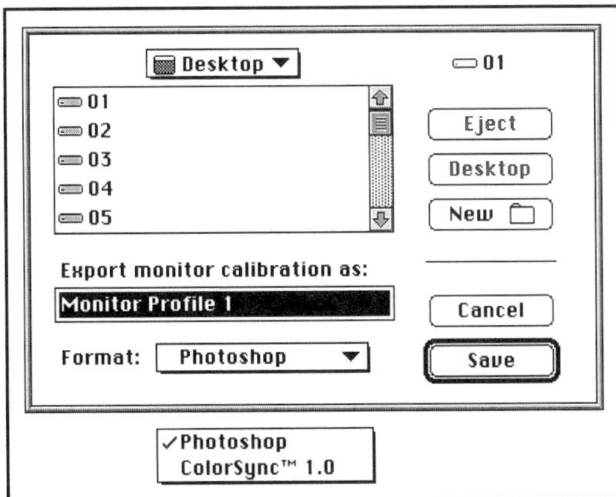

Figure 10-9: Colortron II Save options dialog box.

When you have closed the calibration dialog box, return to Photoshop and choose File | Color Settings | Monitor Setup. Figure 10-10 shows an expanded view of the dialog box which opens. Click on the Load button and locate the calibration profile saved in Photoshop format. It then loads into this dialog box and changes all of the settings based on the measured characteristics of your monitor. The only part of this dialog box you are required to change is the Ambient Light pop-up menu at the bottom, which describes the light conditions in the room in which you work. Once you have made these changes, click on the OK button to close the dialog box. You have now informed Photoshop of the important information regarding your primary display and the light conditions within which you work. Acting in concert with ColorSync, you are now able to look at a CMYK-mode image—or a file in RGB or Lab mode with CMYK Preview turned on—with reasonable confidence that you are looking at a close match to what you will see on press.

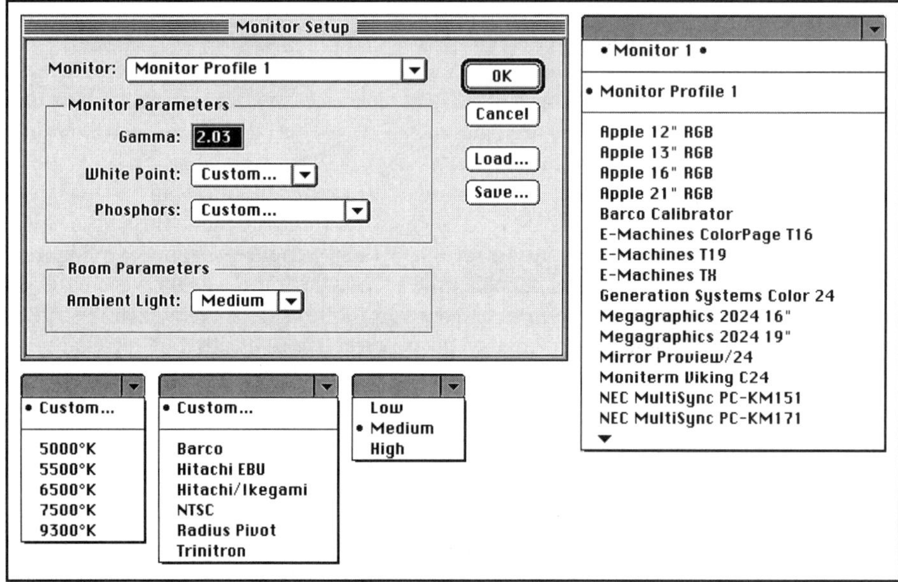

Figure 10-10: Photoshop's Monitor Setup dialog box.

After calibrating, you'll notice that your monitor looks darker, even dingy. Don't be alarmed, that's the way it's supposed to look. Your calibrated monitor's sole purpose now is to emulate printed color. The white of your screen after calibration is not the bright white you are accustomed to seeing. It is closer to the color of the paper stock on which your digital files will be printed. Colors do not seem so bright for a very good reason: many of the bright and beautiful colors your monitor is capable of displaying are out-of-gamut colors, colors which cannot be duplicated using ink on paper. The printable colors, for the most part, are a small subset of the RGB colors. All of the colors in this subset comprise a number that is about 45%–65% of the 16.77 million colors your monitor can display. There are some colors missing, and this is one of the reasons why your display can never be totally accurate. 100% process cyan, for example, is a color that cannot be displayed using RGB colors.

A word to Windows users: Calibration and CMS for Windows are subjects which have only recently begun to be addressed. Microsoft Windows NT and 3.1 has no systemwide color integration software such as Apple's ColorSync. There are also very few hardware calibration devices—such as the Colortron II—available as off-the-shelf products. This will change rapidly in the near future. For the short term, Windows calibration is limited to the bundled Gamma utility. (To make use of it, choose File | Color Settings | Monitor Setup. When the dialog box opens, click on the Calibrate button to open the Gamma utility.)

Windows 95 does have a system-level CMS, called Image Color Matching, that supports ICC device profiles. It's not sufficiently developed, but version 2.0 (which will be in the next release of Windows) will use the LinoColor CMM, the same that ColorSync uses, so it will probably be comparable with ColorSync 2.0.

Because of the lack of systemwide calibration, the Photoshop Gamma utility can control the display only within Photoshop. The Gamma dialog box makes a measurement of your monitor's display characteristics based upon your visual comparisons with paper stock and your adjustments of black, white, and neutral tones. With this set of measurements, your monitor's gamma setting (in the Monitor Setup dialog box) is modified. Your monitor's display is affected only when in RGB mode but not in CMYK mode. This is the reverse of the Macintosh system which functions only in CMYK or CMYK Preview modes.

Printing Inks Setup

After dealing with the believability of your display, the next important task on the way to printing color is to inform Photoshop about the color characteristics of the inks you will be using. Choose File | Color Settings | Printing Inks Setup. An expanded view of the dialog box is shown in Figure 10-11.

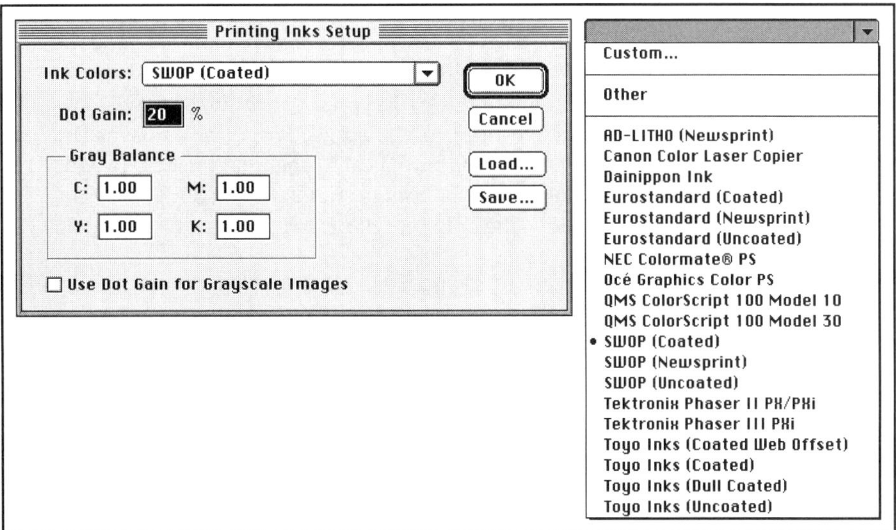

Figure 10-11: Photoshop's Printing Inks Setup dialog box.

The Ink Colors sets from which you can choose are a somewhat limited group and have not changed much over the last several versions of Photoshop. Included are Eurostandard inks, Toyo inks, a color copier, a couple of thermal wax printers, two dye sublimation printers, and the SWOP sets (Specifications for Web Offset Publications). The default is SWOP on coated paper, a profile that is presumed to work equally well on a web press and a medium-quality sheetfed press.

A niche market grew up around this particular preference within Photoshop which involved the selling of profiles for different kinds of output devices. That market niche has become increasingly less visible with the advent of profiles bundled with various printers and with the coming of the Colortron, which allows a desktop user to directly generate a profile that can be used by Photoshop.

When you make a selection from this list, you are loading in a group of settings which accurately describe the *chroma*—the scientifically literate term for *color*—characteristics of the four inks. Included with this description is the *hue error* of each of the colors. Mass-produced inks cannot be made to have an absolutely pure color. Each of the three principle colored inks is contaminated by some percentage of the other two. Yellow, for example, could be described as containing some percentage of cyan and magenta. The percentages are often higher than would seem possible: they can range from 12%–22%. Typically, the SWOP inks have a higher hue error than the others on the list. This can make the choice of default seem a puzzling choice, but SWOP inks are the least costly of those represented and so are the most often used within the printing industry.

Hue error is a significant problem when it comes to reproducing colored images. If you assume, for the sake of easy calculation, that the total hue error for each of the primary inks—CMY—is 20% of each of the other inks, then it is easy to understand that the overlapping values reduce the number of printed tones these inks can produce. Hue error is also the prime cause for the fact that the three primaries do not form the absolute black that should be possible when overprinting them at full strength. The color produced is, instead, a dismal-looking brown. Black ink is required for a four-color press to be able to reproduce vibrant color with rich shadow tones.

Other factors included in the loaded profile include the way the pure inks react to each other in various overprint combinations. Specifically, this measurement would include all possible pairs overprinting each other and the tone produced by overprinting all. Each of the ink sets in the list also has a default dot gain setting. The setting is an average value, and is the only part of the ink profile which you may find easy to modify.

If you have access to a Colortron II, it is perfectly possible for you to generate a profile for any kind of color output device. You could generate a profile for a color copier, an inkjet printer, a color laser printer, or an offset press which you use with some frequency. The settings can be saved as named profiles using the Printing Inks Setup dialog box, and later loaded for specific use.

The procedure for making a custom profile is as follows:

1. First, obtain an output sample from the press or desktop color printer. Most offset press sheets have color bars with tints. From these you can obtain most of the information you'll need, but not all of it. If necessary, generate a custom bar and

ask your printer if he will tuck it onto a press sheet so that you can analyze it. Most printers will do that when they have a press sheet with a little extra trim space, particularly if you share your results. All you'll need is one or two sheets.

2. If you are going to analyze a desktop color printer, open the file INK&GAIN.PSD on the Companion CD-ROM. Print this file on the device to be measured. Note that this file is in Photoshop format at 300 ppi. If your needs are for a different resolution, open either of the files INK&GAIN.AI (Adobe Illustrator) or INK & GAIN.FH7 (Macromedia FreeHand) and rasterize them into Photoshop; set the resolution to whatever you require. Figure 10-12 shows a thumbnail of this file. The original is in CMYK and is small enough to fit on a letter-sized page. After you've printed this file, leave it open: you may need it before you are finished.

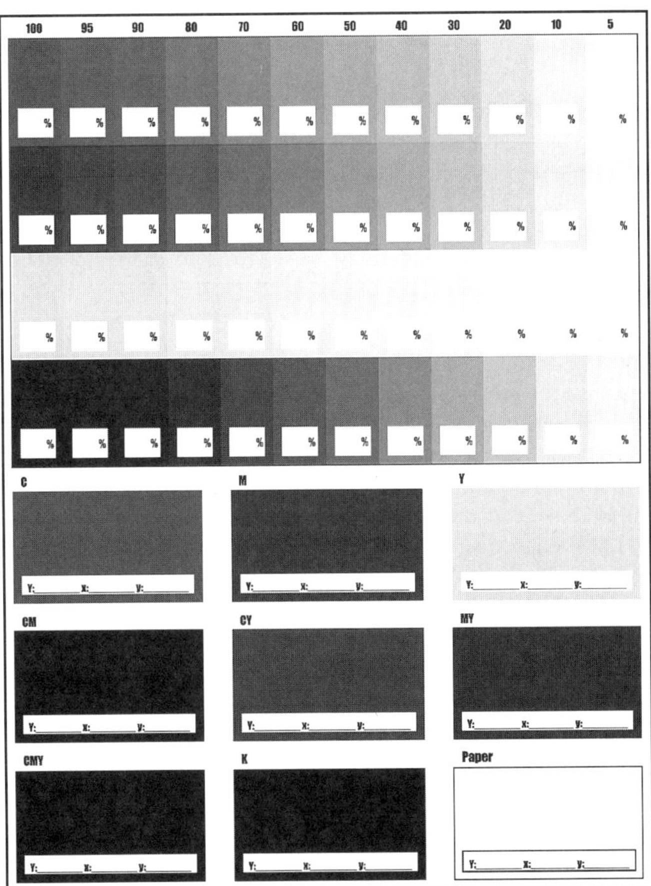

Figure 10-12: A representation of the Companion CD-ROM test file INK & GAIN.PSD which can be used for making a Printing Inks calibration profile with Colortron II.

3. The top of the file has bars of the four inks in descending percentages. You don't need these for the profile, but it's useful to measure these swatches to compare your input and output values. As you measure Dot Area densities with the Colortron II (Figure 10-13), write down the percentages in the box at the bottom of each swatch. This set of measurements can be plotted using the graphing function in Adobe Illustrator or in any spreadsheet. Pay particular attention to the four 50% values: it will be very useful for you to know if one of the inks has a larger gain than the others.

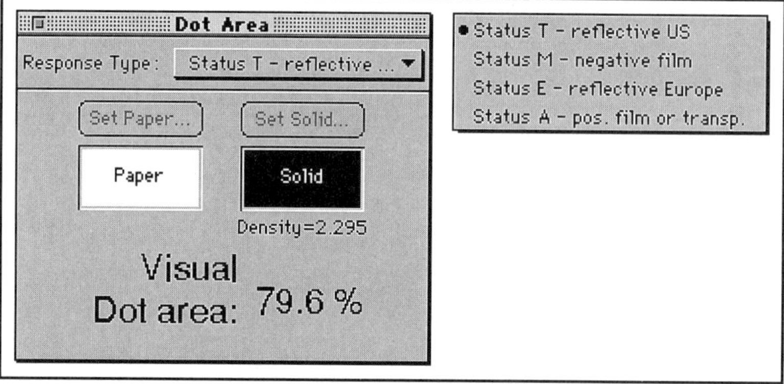

Figure 10-13: The Dot Area (Densitometer) dialog box of Colortron II.

4. At the bottom of the file are nine swatches. The one on the lower right is simply for measuring the color of the paper. The others are: C, M, Y, CM, CY, MY, CMY, and K. The Colorimeter palette in Colortron II is shown in Figure 10-14. As you measure each of the nine swatches, your readings can be simultaneously displayed in three different color systems (the pop-up menu at the right shows the choices). In the figure, the left-hand column is shown giving the color measurement in Lab values, the right-hand column in RGB values, and the center column, in CIE xyY values. You can write the others down but it is the center-column set that you are most interested in. Write down the numbers from bottom to top (you'll see why in a moment).

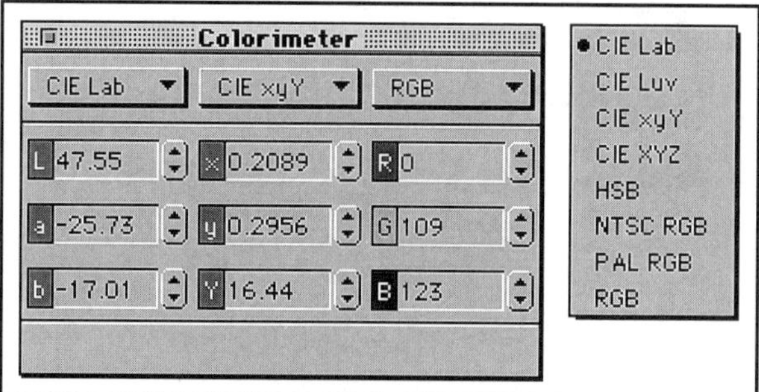

Figure 10-14: Colortron II's Colorimeter dialog box.

5. After you have filled in your printed sheet, return to the Printing Inks Setup dialog box. Click on the pop-up menu and choose Custom. The dialog box which appears is shown in Figure 10-15. Enter the values obtained from your Colortron readings—which were given in the reverse order of what is used here (which is why you wrote them from bottom to top). This part of your output file has now furnished you with nearly all of the required information. When you have finished typing, click OK.

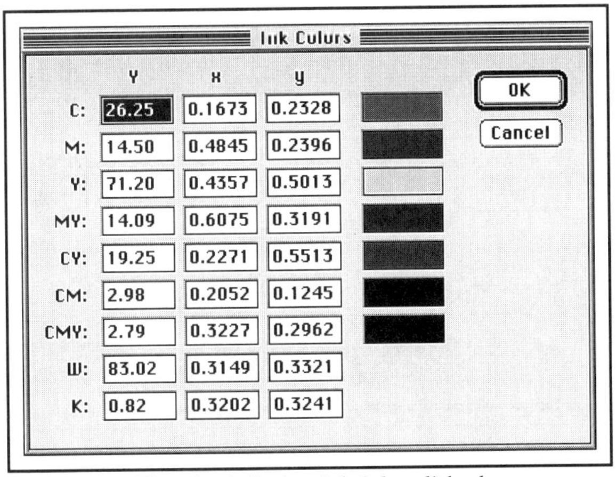

Ink Colors

	Y	x	y
C:	26.25	0.1673	0.2328
M:	14.50	0.4845	0.2396
Y:	71.20	0.4357	0.5013
MY:	14.09	0.6075	0.3191
CY:	19.25	0.2271	0.5513
CM:	2.98	0.2052	0.1245
CMY:	2.79	0.3227	0.2962
W:	83.02	0.3149	0.3321
K:	0.82	0.3202	0.3241

OK

Cancel

Figure 10-15: Photoshop's Custom Ink Colors dialog box.

6. Your pop-up menu now reads Custom. Before naming the file, enter the amount of gain read from the output sheet (use the Input/Output difference for 50% black). If the gain values on the output sheet are the same for all four inks, click on the Save button, and save this settings configuration under the name of the output device and in a place where you can easily locate it.

7. If the gain settings for the four process inks are different, make adjustments in the Gray Balance area of the dialog box. Save this settings configuration file under the name Temp, and click on the Cancel button. For the sake of illustrating how this might work, assume that the magenta ink at 50% measured 5% higher than the other three inks. Go back to the output file—it is still open after being printed—and open the Levels dialog box. (Make sure you can see the Info palette and the 50% swatch of magenta.) Press Command+2 or Ctrl+2 to go to the histogram of the Magenta channel. Since the magenta value is too high by 5%, move the midtone slider a little to the left. Move the cursor out into the 50% magenta swatch and check the reading. Keep moving the slider and checking the swatch until you have changed the second number on the Info palette to 45% (you are lightening the magenta to compensate for being 5% too high). Write down the value in the center data box (it will probably read something like 1.13). Click the Cancel button.

8. Return to the Printing Inks Setup dialog box. Click on the Load button and locate the file you saved as Temp. When the file is loaded, enter the value you obtained from the Levels controls in the magenta dialog box. You now have a perfect

description of the ink and printing characteristics of the target output device. Click on the Save button and save this settings configuration under the name of the output device and in a place where you can easily locate it.

Separation Setup

The last step in preparing to generate files for four-color printing is to set your preferences for the conversion of the file to CMYK mode. Choose File | Color Settings | Separation Setup. The dialog box which appears is shown in Figure 10-16.

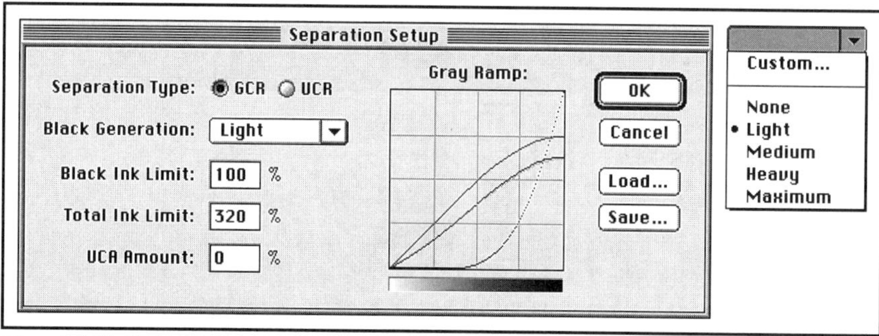

Figure 10-16: Photoshop's Separation Setup dialog box.

You have learned about the reasons for the addition of black ink to a separation: the three primary inks cannot produce a good black by themselves. Black is added to make black areas look truly black. It makes shadows look clean and crisp and accentuates the clarity of the image in a way that would be impossible without it. It also cuts down on the amount of ink needed to reproduce the image on press. Black is added to the image during the separation process using one of two methods. UCR and GCR—the two choices are at the top of the dialog box—are short for *Under Color Removal* and *Gray Component Replacement*. These two accomplish nearly the same result but, as the names imply, go about the task in different ways.

Gray Component Replacement

Figure 10-17 shows two neutral gray swatches of color. You can duplicate each of these in a small sample CMYK-mode file. Set your Foreground Color to 0% cyan, 0% magenta, 0% yellow, and 50% black. Use the color to fill a small selection. Reset your Foreground Color to 50% cyan, 37% magenta, 37% yellow, and 0% black (the figures may vary depending upon the settings in the Separation Setup dialog box). Fill another small selection with this color. You should see, on your screen, two swatches which look identical. This figure is the key to how GCR works. During the conversion process, areas of the image are analyzed for their gray components and the primary inks are replaced with black. As the figure shows, this results in a reduction in the amount of ink in the places where it occurs. For this figure, there is 74% less ink needed to produce the identical tone.

GCR does not just occur in neutral areas. Proportions of cyan, magenta, and yellow that produce a neutral tone are replaced with black, but the amount of ink needed to produce a specific hue is left in place. For example, if a tone in the image is somewhat neutral and contains a slight pink cast, it's an indication that some percentage of magenta is higher than the percentage required to produce a neutral tone. In that case, the GCR routine would produce an equivalent color by using a percentage of black coupled with a small amount of magenta, the amount of magenta required to add the pink cast to the neutral tone.

GCR is Photoshop's default. It is generally agreed to be easier to handle on press than UCR, but it requires a setting for Under Color Addition—which we'll discuss in a moment for a separation to look its best.

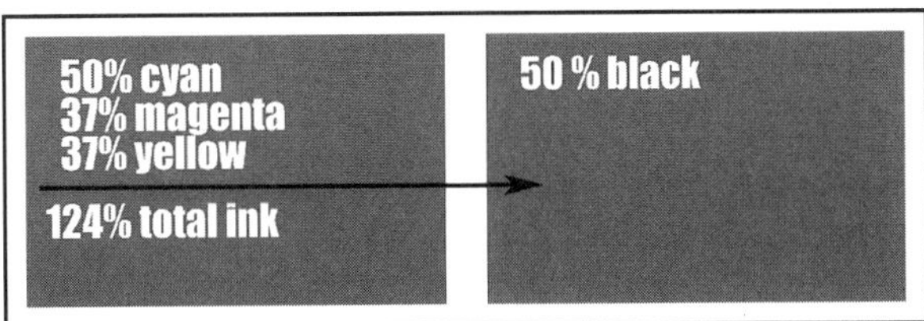

Figure 10-17: Gray swatches can be printed with black or with tints of cyan, magenta, and yellow.

Black Generation

The settings for the GCR algorithm are found in the center of the dialog box. There are five preset black generation amounts and a Custom setting. When you choose the Custom setting, a curves dialog box appears (Figure 10-18) in which you may apply your own ideas about the black generation.

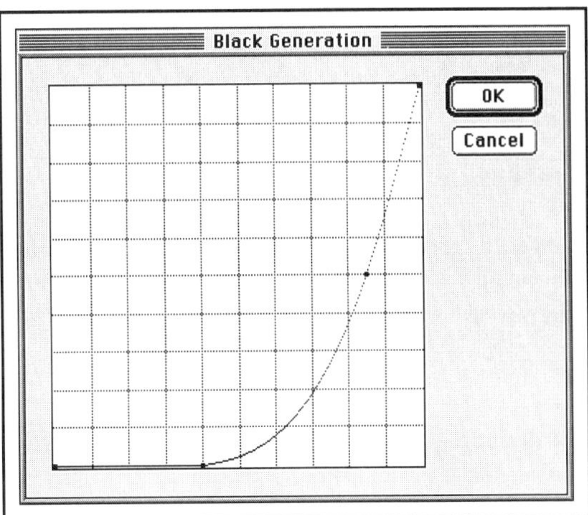

Figure 10-18: The Custom Black Generation curve dialog box from Photoshop's Separation Setup.

Figure 10-19 shows four black separation plates. They have been generated by using the four Black Generation presets and show how much this setting affects the separation.

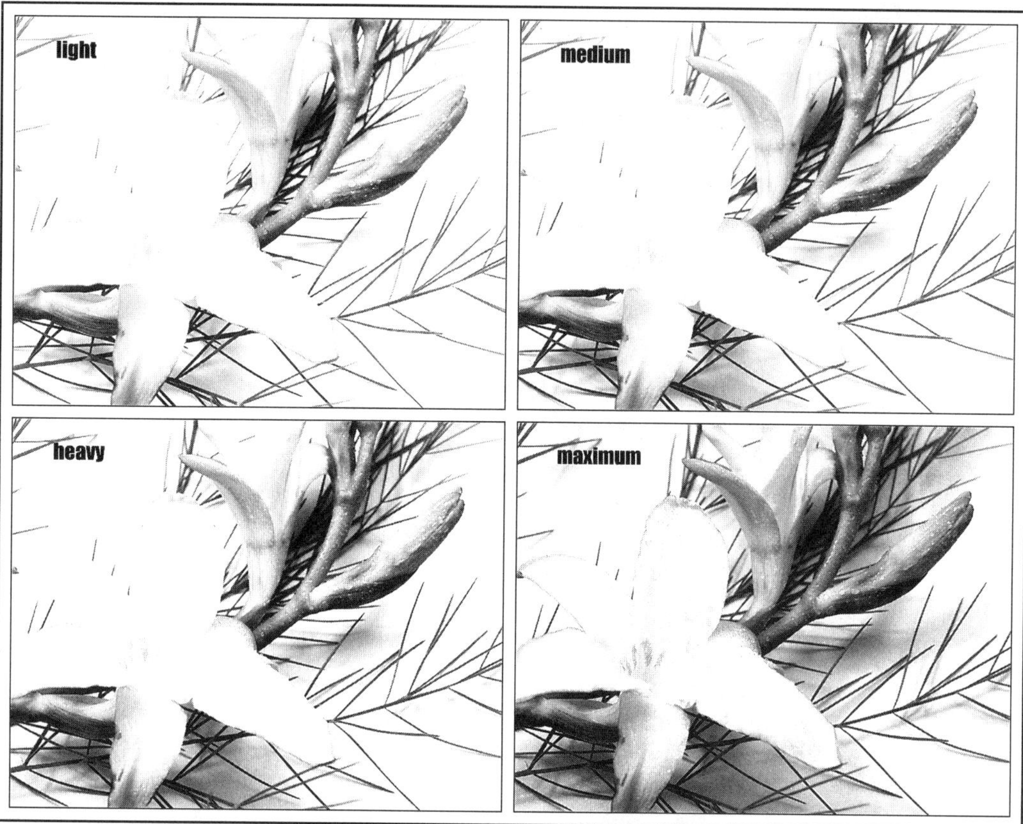

Figure 10-19: Four black separation plates generated with changes to the Black Generation specification in the Separation Setup.

Black Ink Limit

The Black Ink Limit allows you to choose the maximum percentage of black anywhere in the separated image. Choosing a lower number than 100% simply means that there will never be a black ink area with a density higher than the percentage you choose.

Total Ink Limit

The Total Ink Limit is the amount of ink allowed on press. It is calculated by adding together all four ink percentages at the area of highest coverage. The theoretical limit would be 400%. That number is impractical for a variety of reasons, the main one being that so much ink would be difficult to dry. Because of this, the press speed would have to be very slow or the individual sheets would smudge each other as they are stacked.

(Don't ever try 400% as an experiment; it can make the pressman dangerously testy!) The actual figure you should use here must be obtained from your printer. Depending on the press and the kind of paper stock you intend to use, the figure will probably range between 280%–320%.

When the three main settings are in place, you can see a set of curves which indicate the relationships of the inks. Notice that the curve of the black ink does not begin to have an impact until almost 50%, at least with the settings used in Figure 10-16. You can see how this black generation works by making a grayscale image with swatches of black in percentage increments of 10% (Figure 10-20). When these swatches are converted to CMYK, the values become as labeled in the figure. If these values are plotted out with graphing software, you'll see that the resulting curves (Figure 10-21) closely resemble the curves in the original Separation Setup dialog box shown in Figure 10-16.

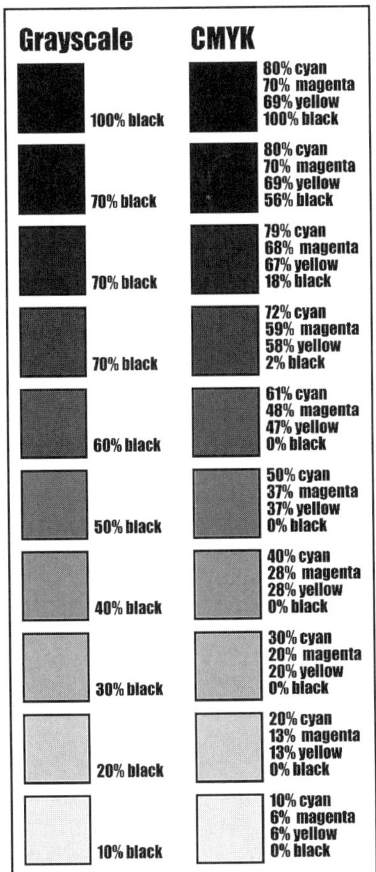

Figure 10-20: Depending upon the Separation Setup values, a set of grayscale percentages can be represented by CMYK percentages similar to these.

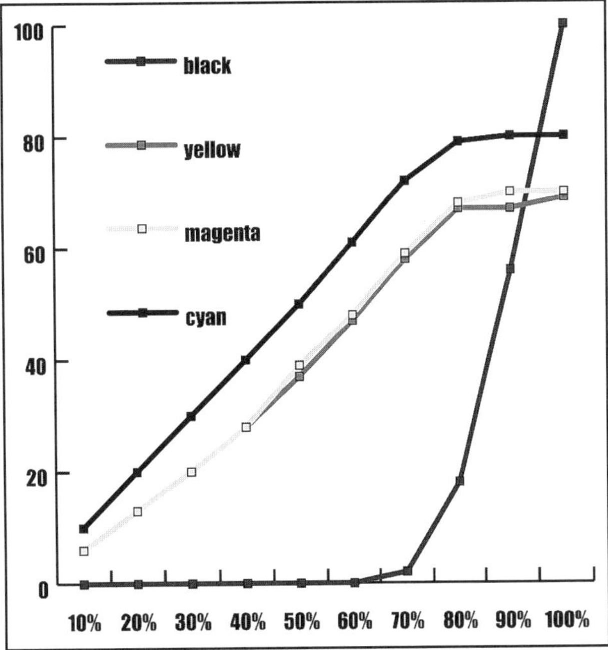

Figure 10-21: When the CMYK values in Figure 10-20 are graphed, they form a set of curves identical to the curves display in the Separation Setup dialog dialog box.

Under Color Addition Amount

The last setting in the Separation Setup is the UCA Amount. UCA stands for *Under Color Addition* and is probably the least used, least understood, and most important way to finesse a separation into looking good in the shadow tones. UCA is a procedure that modifies the action of GCR in dense shadows by cutting back on the amount of black while increasing the amount of the other colors. The purpose of this is to make a darker, richer shadow than would be possible using a single ink. At the same time, UCA adds subtle detail to the shadow area and prevents these areas from looking flat and posterized. The amount you enter in this setup box is determined by experimentation and by the recommendations of your print vendor. Don't be afraid to do some experimenting with this setting. Adobe recommends leaving the setting at 0% unless you know what you're doing. Practically, you can experiment with settings up to about 5% without doing any real harm—and probably help your image a lot. Don't go much over 10% without some expert advice.

Under Color Removal

The main difference between GCR and UCR is that UCR separations replace CMY values only in areas of the image that are truly neutral. If the image has been balanced and unwanted casts removed from highlights and shadows, a UCR separation should have less ink density in deep shadow areas than GCR. The black UCR plate simply adds depth and richness to shadows and neutrals while the non-neutral colors are left alone. The UCR separation method is usually considered a better choice if the image does not contain dark and saturated colors. Such images are usually reproduced better by using GCR for the separation method.

When you choose UCR as your separation type, the only choices available in the Separation Setup dialog box are Black Ink Limit and Total Ink Limit.

Preparing to Make a Color Separation

After paying so much attention to the details involved with monitor calibration and the major preferences which control your monitor's display, let's stop for a moment to review some of the implications of this set of procedures.

Having calibrated your monitor and then loaded these settings into Photoshop, you are now in a position to make decisions about the colors in your image with a reasonable degree of certainty that you are seeing the file very close to the way it will print. Your monitor's display will never perfectly match your printed piece—the color paradigms are just too different—but it will be close. Just remember that your calibration of the monitor does not affect an image displayed in RGB or Lab mode. To look at the file as the prototype of the printed file, your file must be in CMYK mode or, if it is in RGB or Lab mode, you must choose CMYK Preview from under the View menu (press Command+y or Crl+y). With this option turned on, you can see the file as if it were already separated and still be able to do your correction/adjustment work in the color mode of your choice.

The calibration and preferences you have set up control how the image is displayed and how it will be separated. If you change your Info palette so that it gives you readings in CMYK, you can move your cursor around inside an RGB or Lab file and be shown the CMYK values as though the separation had already taken place. As your cursor moves, notice that some pixels display an exclamation mark (!) next to the ink values on the Info palette. This is an indication that the value of the pixel is out of gamut and that the conversion to CMYK will change it.

This is probably obvious, but since the display is governed, not only by the calibration settings but also by the ink and separation preferences, you should never try to correct color or to generate a color separation unless you have an ink profile and separation setup that is appropriate for that image. The process of changing the image from one color mode to CMYK is absolutely tied to the preferences in effect at the time the change is made. You cannot simply change the image back to RGB, load a new set of preferences, and then reseparate the file. Changing to CMYK mode is enormously destructive to the data in the original image. Each change of mode, while it may not be as destructive as the drastic change from RGB or Lab to CMYK, causes too much loss of information.

If you wish to try an experiment, make a small CMYK window and fill it with a color composed of 100% magenta and 100% yellow. Change to RGB and then back to CMYK mode. Look at your values. You probably have at least 1% cyan, 2%–7% less ink in magenta and yellow, and at least 2% black. The bright-built red no longer looks so bright.

A good strategy to use when you have separations intended for multiple output devices is this. Keep a copy of the original scan in a place where you can find it easily. Open it, duplicate it, close the original, and work on the copy. Make your corrections with your appropriate target preferences. Separate the file, and save it. Repeat this procedure for all iterations of the image.

Processing an RGB File Intended for Color Separation

When photographic material is scanned by a commercial separation house, the electronic files are delivered ready to print. The correct adjustment of the image, the balancing of tones, the conversion to CMYK mode, have been taken care of. This preparation is part of the cost of a commercial separation.

Files from an in-house scanner may not be separated. The scanning software may not have the ability to do the separations for you, and it may have only limited capacity for adjusting the image. These files must be adjusted, separated, and saved in Photoshop. The process outlined here is a generic adjust procedure. It does not take into account files which are imperfect due to deficiencies of the original photo material. It is simply an easy way to arrive at a good separation from a reasonably good scan. This process will lighten the image, improve its contrast, clean up the color, and get it into shape for CMYK conversion. For difficult scans, we recommend, in addition to the information you'll read about here, that you check out the processes described in Chapter 11, "Manipulating Images."

The file shown in the following figures can be found in the Chapter 9 & 10 Practice Files folder on the Companion CD-ROM. Its title is FISHING.PSD. When you open this file, notice that it is in RGB mode. Turn on CMYK Preview as you look at it. This file has been saved with the adjustment layers shown in the following figures. You can hide these layers and then make them visible, one at a time, to see the effects of each correction step. All four stages of this pre-separation adjustment are shown printed in the color section of this book. We recommend that you look at the color reproductions and the digital file as you read through this section. For the correction sequence, follow these steps:

1. Open your file. From the View menu, choose CMYK Preview (Figure 10-22). Follow the procedure outlined in Chapter 9, "Photoshop Prepress," for preparing a grayscale file using Threshold mode, and illustrated with Figures 9-5 through 9-12. Your final step is to adjust the midtone slider of the composite histogram of the Levels controls.

Figure 10-22: Open the file. Select CMYK Preview from under the View menu.

2. Instead of clicking OK, click on the Save button. Save this settings file under a temporary name. Click on the Cancel button to close the Levels dialog box. Command+click or Ctrl+click on the New Layer icon at the bottom of the Layers palette. From the choices available, select Levels. When the Levels dialog box appears, click on the Load button and locate the settings file you just saved. After the settings have loaded, click OK (Figure 10-23).

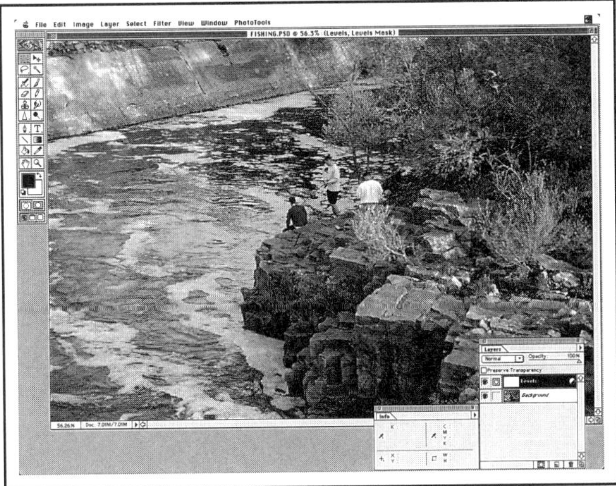

Figure 10-23: Create a Levels adjustment layer. Load your saved Levels settings into this Layer. Click OK.

The Levels correction, as is usual, improves the contrast of the image. The pronounced blue/cyan tone to the image is improved but not really addressed. Levels can be used to perform some of the color adjustment work, but in this example, color-shift tasks are applied using two other correction methods. The amount of correction applied with the Levels adjustment layer is shown in Figure 10-24.

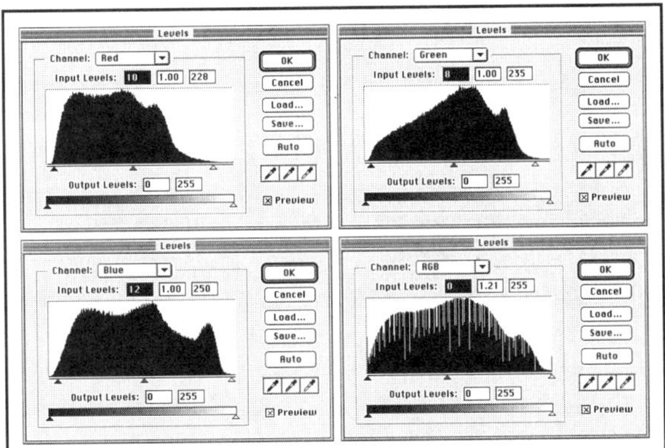

Figure 10-24: Adjustments made to all three channels and to the midtone of the composite histogram.

3. Make a new adjustment layer. This time choose Color Balance. When you complete your adjustments, click OK (Figure 10-25).

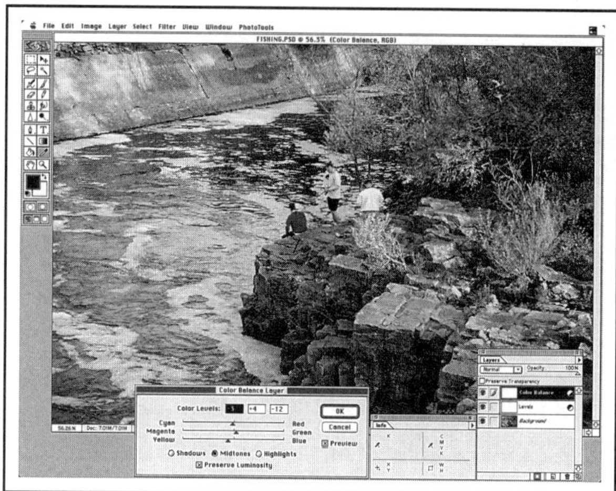

Figure 10-25: Create a Color Balance correction layer.

4. With the Color Balance choices, the cyan cast in the midtones is the major color change. Boosting the yellow and magenta in the midtones and shadows warms the image and further de-emphasizes the original cyan cast. The settings used for this layer are shown in Figure 10-26.

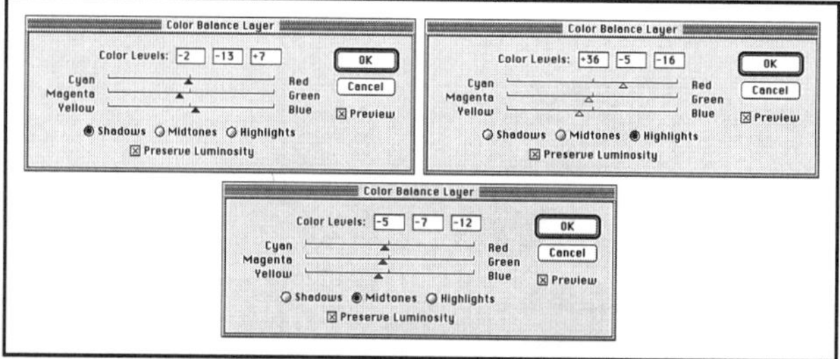

Figure 10-26: Changes made to the Shadows, Midtones, and Highlights in the Color Balance adjustment layer.

5. Make a new adjustment layer. For this layer, choose Hue/Saturation. When you have completed your adjustments, click OK (Figure 10-27).

Hue/Saturation allows some arbitrary tweaking of tones which you may wish to enrich or make more vivid (or to mute and desaturate). In this case, boosting the overall saturation and slightly darkening the image gives better contrast overall. By doing so, and by tweaking four of the primary tones in various ways, the red, gold, and green tones become more vibrant. Subtle colorations in the water are also more obvious. The Hue/Saturation settings used for this layer are shown in Figure 10-28.

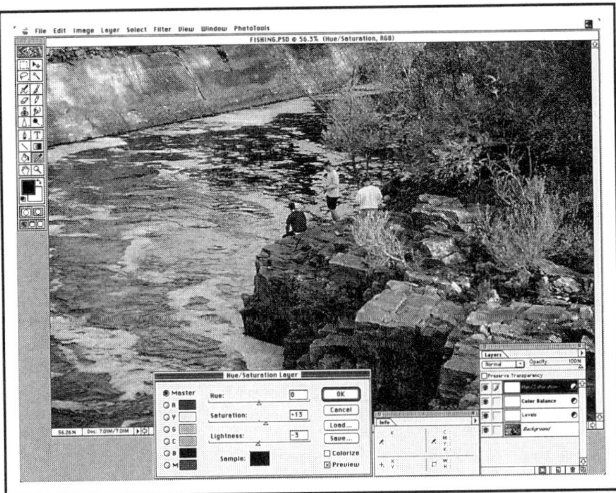

Figure 10-27: Create a Hue/Saturation adjustment layer.

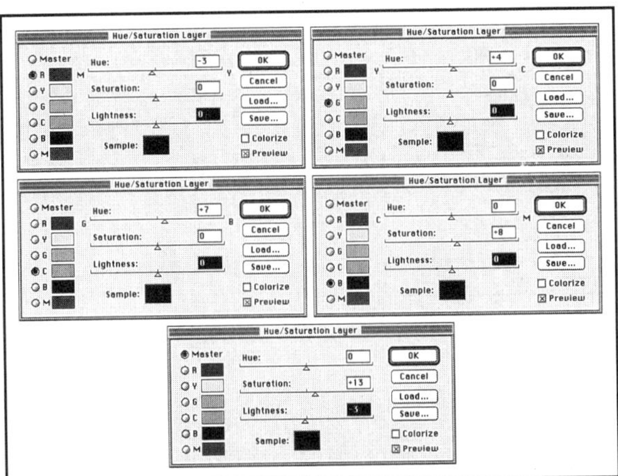

Figure 10-28: Changes made to the Red, Green, Cyan, Blue, and Master values in the Hue/Saturation adjustment layer.

Color Correction Methods

There are several ways that color can be adjusted within Photoshop. The primary adjustment tools are the Levels and the Curves controls. Use whichever of these seem to give you the best results. In some cases, you might even wish to use them both as the input tools for successive adjustment layers. There is no reason why you should not do so, and every reason for you to experiment to get the very best color you are able to achieve.

The other color correction controls are, again, a matter of taste. Some of them are more powerful than others, but none should ever be discounted. Every tool in Photoshop is useful at some time—even the Paint Bucket tool. If, in your study of Photoshop and its methods, you read a disparaging reference to any tool or method, try to remember that you are reading an opinion and that you need not be bound by or agree with that opinion. Do your work in Photoshop in the way that suits *you*, and you'll reach a good result nearly every time!

The formal color correction tools are located in the Image | Adjust submenu (Figure 10-29). The Adjust menu contains several other commands—Desaturate, Invert, Equalize, Threshold, and Posterize—which deliver specialized, single-purpose effects. Two of these specialized commands are sometimes useful in correction work.

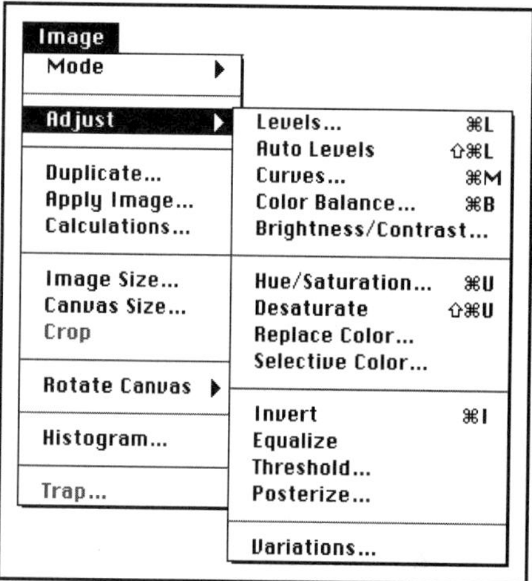

Figure 10-29: Most of Photoshop's correction/adjustment tools are found under the Image | Adjust submenu.

The Equalize command is useful for quickly redistributing brightness values. When this command is chosen, Photoshop takes the darkest value and makes it black, and the lightest value and makes it white. All of the other brightness values are then calculated to fall between these two in order to have a representation of the entire brightness range. The effect is somewhat akin to Auto Levels but far more drastic in its effect. If you wish, use this command on the FISHING.PSD image after it has been flattened. You will find that the image contrast is changed in a drastic—but not unattractive—way. The results of the Equalize command can sometimes be too extreme to be useful. If you find that to be the case, try executing the command with a mask. Enter q to enter Quick Mask. Set your Foreground color to 50% and fill the window. Enter q to exit Quick Mask. Choose the command and you'll see that the effects have been mitigated by 50%.

An easier way to mitigate the result of a command is to choose the Fade command, the second item under the Filter menu. After you have applied a command such as Equalize, select the Fade command. With the dialog box open and the Preview option checked, you can move the Opacity slider to change the degree to which the command affected the image. Fade also gives you the ability to apply blend modes on top of commands such as Equalize where blend modes are not usually associated. Fade will work with many image adjustment commands including such unlikely commands as Image | Adjust | Invert. (Want to try something interesting? Invert the image and then change the fade opacity to 50%. Bizarre!)

The other sometimes-handy command is Desaturate. When this command executes, the image is effectively changed to a grayscale image, even though it remains in color mode. Running the command with a mask or with the Fade command is a way of moderating how much desaturation will result. By filling a Quick Mask window with, say 90% black, Desaturate will move the colors toward grayscale by the reciprocal percentage, 10%.

TIP

Out-of-gamut colors are typically too saturated—desaturating often brings them back into gamut—you can even make a very quick, targeted mask aimed at just the out-of-gamut tones. From the Select menu, choose Color Range. In the Color Range menu, make the selection Out of Gamut. Click OK.

With the selection still active, enter q to enter Quick Mask. The entire window is filled with the mask color except for those areas containing out-of-gamut values. Set your Foreground color to black. Select All. Choose Edit | Fill. Set the mode to Multiply. Set the Opacity to the reciprocal percentage of the amount you wish to use to desaturate the problem pixels—say, 85%. Click OK. You can see that your Quick Mask window now has the out-of-gamut areas filled with 85% of the mask color and the rest with 100%. Enter q to exit Quick Mask, and execute the Desaturate command.

Alternately, you could apply the Desaturate command to the original selection and then use the Filter | Fade command. Change the Opacity settings until you achieve the amount of change you desire.

Here's a little added touch that lets you gauge how effectively you've scaled back the saturation in out-of-gamut areas with this mask trick. Before you begin the procedure, press Command+shift-y or Ctrl+shift-y; this is the Gamut Warning command. Your out-of-gamut pixels show up onscreen covered with a light gray. After you've constructed the mask and desaturated, you can judge whether the percentage is too high or too low by how many pixels loose or retain their gray covering.

Color Balance The Color Balance dialog box (Figure 10-30) is a very good place to learn to think in RGB as well as in CMYK. There are three sliders; the process ink colors are at the left and the RGB colors to the right. Each slider ranges from a process primary to video primary. The arrangement is such that moving a slider away from a given color *decreases* the amount of that color and *increases* that color's inverse. For example, moving the cyan slider to the left removes cyan from the image and adds red.

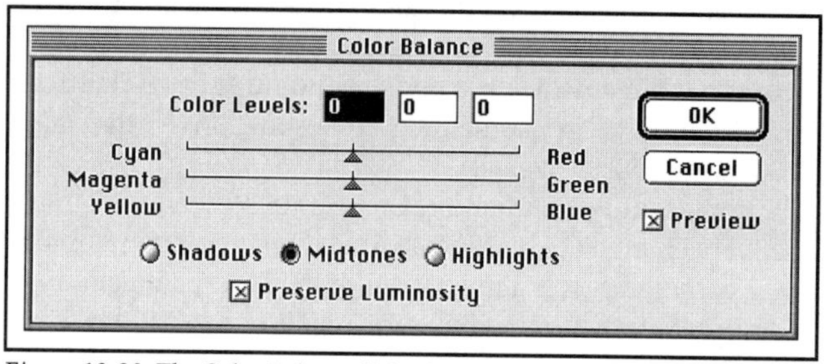

Figure 10-30: The Color Balance dialog box in RGB or CMYK mode.

There are three different value ranges which are affected: Shadows, Midtones, and Highlights. When the dialog box opens, it defaults to Midtones since, in most cases, your major adjustments will be in the midtone range.

The dialog box also contains a check box which defaults to Preserve Luminosity. This option is used to maintain the brightness values in RGB images. With this box unchecked, the brightness of the pixels in the image change as the color is changed. This can mean that the tonal balance of the image shifts in an undesirable way. It is usually instructive, when you have completed your adjustments in all three tonal ranges, to click the check box so that the option is off, in order to see how your adjustments are affected. Click it again to turn it back on before clicking on the OK button.

When using Color Balance in Lab mode, the dialog box has a different appearance (Figure 10-31). There are only two sliders. These allow you to adjust between the two color axes of this mode. You do not have a slider for the L channel: this is equivalent to having a Preserve Luminosity check box.

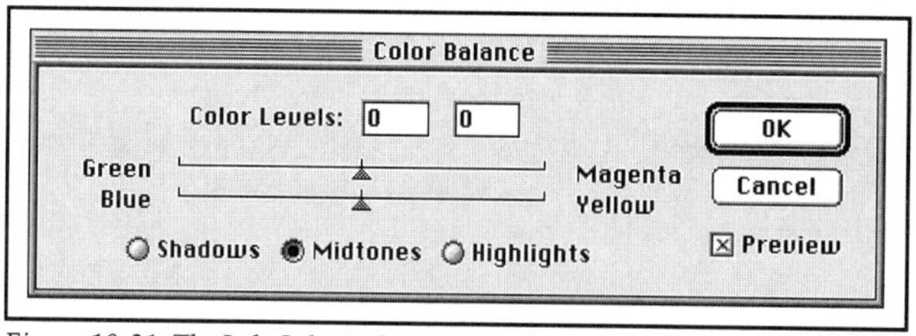

Figure 10-31: The Lab Color Balance dialog box.

Brightness/Contrast The Brightness/Contrast controls (Figure 10-32) are not for the faint of heart. Although this tool is useful once in a while, it is really a blunt instrument when compared to most of the other controls. Shifts in Brightness and Contrast are made by moving the two sliders. The adjustment affects the entire tone range of the image with no way to limit the adjustment to any segment of the range. There are other commands which can accomplish with more subtlety whatever can be accomplished with Brightness/Contrast, but it is sometimes handy for a quick tweak.

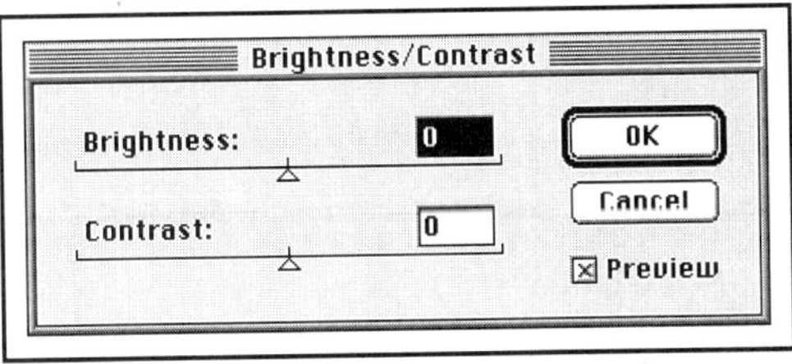

Figure 10-32: The Brightness/Contrast Controls.

In previous versions of Photoshop, the command to summon this control mechanism was Command or Ctrl + b. That command has now been reassigned to the Color Balance controls, leaving Brightness/Contrast without a keyboard shortcut of its own.

Hue/Saturation The Hue/Saturation controls (Figure 10-33) are among Photoshop's most powerful features. With this set of controls, you can adjust the hue, saturation, and lightness of individual color components in an image or the entire color composition of an image.

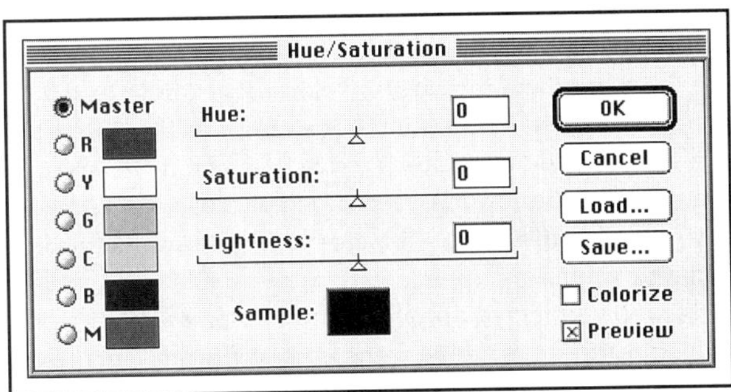

Figure 10-33: The Hue/Saturation controls.

In order to understand how these controls work, take a close look at Figure 10-34. The figure pictures a cylindrical shape which, you are invited to imagine, consists of a set of thin disks stacked on top of each other. Each circular shape consists of a radial sweeping blend through all six of the primary RGB and CMY colors. The purest color tones are out on the edges of the circle. These shade into neutral toward the center. Each disk is similar to every other disk except that disks lower in the stack are darker than upper disks.

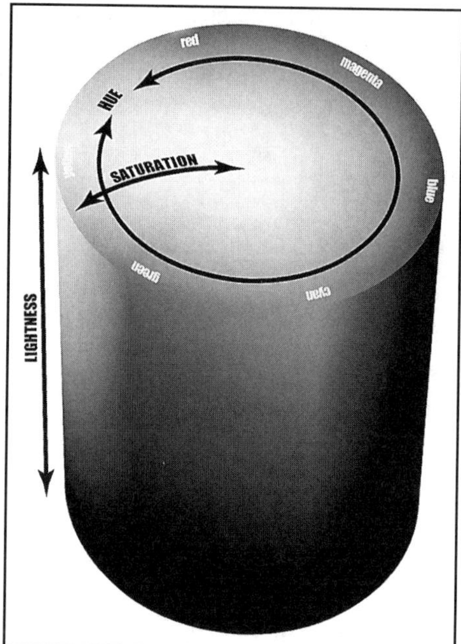

Figure 10-34: The HSL color model.

Please imagine a color value at some place on the disk uppermost in the figure. Changes to the three sliders affect that color by moving it in three dimensions.

When you move the Hue slider, you are keeping the position of the color relative to the outer edge of the circle but moving it around clockwise (slider to the right) or counterclockwise (slider to the left). Because the opening position of the slider represents the color's initial position on the colored circle, you can never shift the color farther than 180° in either direction from where it began. Push the slider all the way to the left or all the way to the right, and you'll have moved it to the same place, diametrically opposite its initial position.

By moving the Saturation slider, you move the color along a radius either toward the center of the circle (desaturate) or toward the edge (saturate). Increased saturation results in more brilliant colors, while decreased saturation mutes the colors and makes them more gray.

With the Lightness slider, you keep the color's position on the circle but shift it up (lighter) or down (darker) to a different circle.

It's important to note that if this is your first exposure to the concept that color spaces are visualized in three dimensions and require three coordinates in order to describe them, then please study this figure until you become comfortable with it. The more comfortable you become with the way the Hue/Saturation command operates on the color in your image, the more adept you'll be at getting the results you desire.

The Master button on the dialog box gives you control of all the tones in the image simultaneously. You can, if you wish, select one of the six colors below the Master button to affect a change on that color range without a lot of change to the other colors. Each single-color adjustment changes the Hue slider so that the image's pixels in that tone can be shifted, one way or the other, toward its neighbors on the color wheel.

The sample area below gives you the opportunity to observe your adjustment's effect on a single tone in the image. Move your cursor into the image window and click on a color you wish to see in the Sample box. Otherwise, the sample remains set to the Foreground Color.

Hue/Saturation also contains a Colorize check box which can be used on grayscale images that have been converted to a color mode. For very fast colorizing, try this option the next time you need to do a colorization. Don't be alarmed when your grayscale work changes to a fairly intense red-colored version of itself. Just move the Saturation slider (which shoots to the far right of the slider) back toward the middle until the color of the image is a little less hard on the eyes.

Replace Color Replace Color (Figure 10-35) feels like a hybrid—a very powerful one—since it combines features of two of Photoshop's most powerful editing tools. Its selection preview, Fuzziness slider, and Eyedropper tools are similar to those of Select Color Range. Its transform sliders are the same as for the Hue/Saturation controls. When you use this set of controls, you can click within the image window to select a target color or colors. Then, by moving the sliders, the selected colors are transformed into new color values.

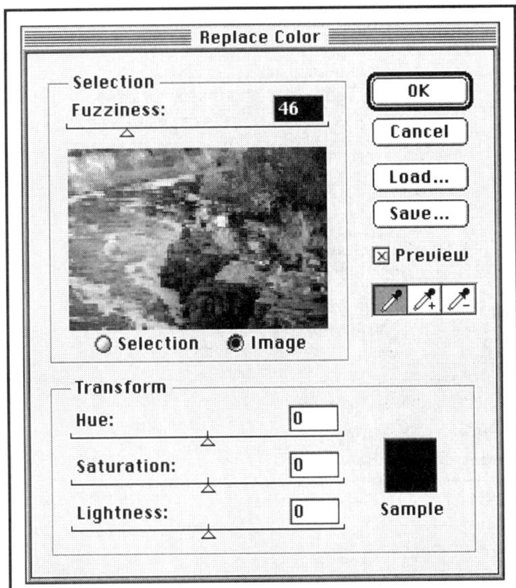

Figure 10-35: The Replace Color controls.

The default Eyedropper tool is used to select a color from the image thumbnail preview or directly. It is usually easier to make the image window as large as possible and to set the option below the dialog box thumbnail to Selection. Without this kind of feedback, it is difficult to tell what colors are being affected.

After you have manipulated a color with the sliders, try to find an area of that color that is mostly a solid. Zoom into that area to see if the edges of the color are fringed with pixels of the previous color. If they are, move the fuzziness slider to the right to increase the scope, or tolerance, of the original selection. The color change will follow the change in the selection boundary.

If you want to experiment with this set of controls, why not try changing the bright red sweatshirt worn by the fisherman in the center of the sample file to some other color. Try a blue tone, or brown, or green. You'll be pleasantly surprised at how easy it is!

Selective Color Selective Color (Figure 10-36) is an extremely sophisticated tool that allows you to adjust color editorially—meaning that you can make arbitrary changes to an image that reflect what you *wish* to see in the image, as opposed to what the camera really captured—as well as to correct color problems. Using tabular data, which defines the process-color values that make up the print versions of each of the six primary colors, the proportions of ink within that primary group can be elevated or lowered without disturbing the balance of colors which contain one or more of the same process inks. You can, for example, boost the amount of magenta in a red garment without disturbing the magenta component in a bright blue sky. Or, you can lower the amount of magenta in an expanse of foliage without disturbing the magenta tones in a human face.

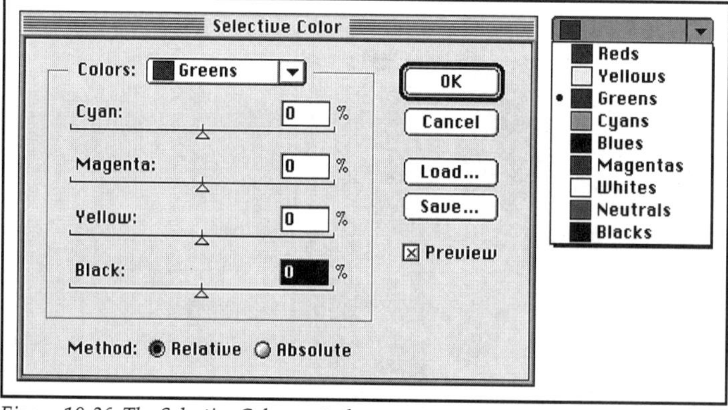

Figure 10-36: The Selective Color controls.

There are two methods which can be used to apply the percentages:

The Relative calculation takes the desired percentage and multiplies it by the percentage of ink color in the image. It then adds the result to the present value. If the

Relative method is used, and you desire to add 10% to a 45% yellow tone, the calculation is 10% X 45% = 4.5%. This result, 4.5%, is added to the original tone to give a manipulated value of 49.5% (4.5% + 45% = 49.5%).

The Absolute calculation takes the percentage you request at face value and adds it to the original tone. Using the same instance as above, a 10% addition to 45% yellow would result in 55% yellow. Of the two methods of calculation, the Absolute method offers the least flexibility. It is, however, the only method that can be used if adjusting whites. With the Relative method, adjusting white would have no effect since there are no beginning values upon which to perform the computation.

Variations One of the authors has heard the Variations color adjustment method referred to as Bozo color. Despite the close-mindedness of the description, Variations (Figure 10-37) is a pleasurable way for newcomers to see the results of their adjustments. It is also a more graphic interface for an adjustment algorithm that is almost identical to Color Balance. Bozo or not, this is a valuable tool. It may not offer the precision of the Color Balance dialog box but it can accomplish the same purpose.

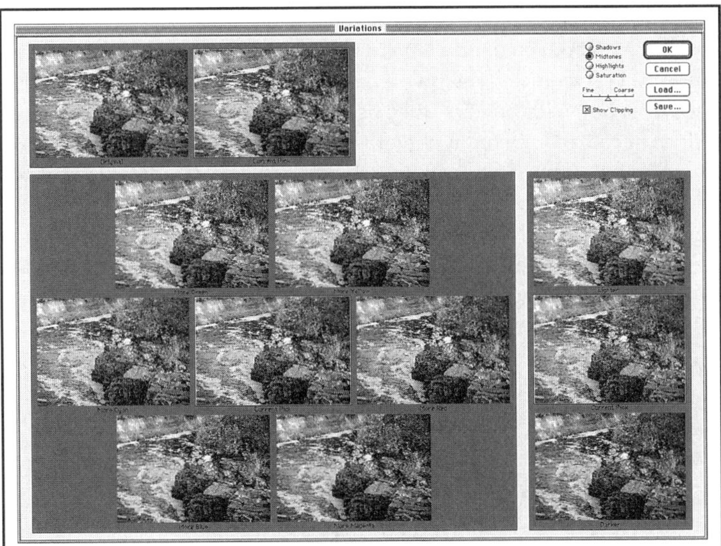

Figure 10-37: Color corrections made with Photoshop's Variations.

As you can see from Figure 10-37, you have the choice (upper right-hand side) of adjusting the Highlights, Midtones, or Shadows. There is also an adjustment for Saturation and a slider which—roughly—determines how much impact each adjustment click has. There is also a choice which allows the display of clipped values. This makes your display show you out-of-gamut values. You needn't be concerned with this option since you are working on the image with CMYK Preview turned on. All out-of-gamut values are automatically clipped in this display mode.

The main part of this dialog box is the large area in the lower left. The center image is the target which will be acted upon. Assembled around this target are six *More* thumbnails, *More Yellow* and its opposite, *More Blue*, etc. As you click on one of the action thumbnails, the target is instantly updated with more of the color on which you clicked.

At the top of the dialog box are two thumbnails. The left-hand one is the image the way it was when the adjustment began. Next to it is a thumbnail which shows the present status of the adjustment. If, at any time, you wish to reset the target window to opening conditions, simply click on the left-hand thumbnail. You can then begin your adjustment with a fresh start.

At the right are three thumbnails. The center one is a status thumbnail which shows the present state of the adjustment. Above and below are thumbnails which, when clicked, either lighten or darken the three present-status thumbnails.

Note that in the main adjustment area there are three axes running through the target thumbnail. At the ends of these axes are the same pair of opposites used for Color Balance.

Variations, as will be obvious, works best on a large monitor. It functions on a smaller monitor, but it can be difficult to see how the colors are being modified.

What to Look for When Adjusting Color

The simple truth about color adjustment is that if you've taken care of issues such as calibration and preferences, you own eyes are your best guide. Everyone begins with untrained eyes but, with practice, they become able to make accurate evaluations. Your perceptions of color combined with your ongoing accumulation of prepress experiences, and your common sense, will work together to give you good, consistent color. Trust yourself and, until you get the hang of it, follow Sir Isaac Newton. Newton's famous *bon mot* is good for all of us: *Nocte dieque incubando* (I think about [things] night and day).

Beyond the philosophy, there are some things in every image which you need to perfect whenever the opportunity presents itself. In no order of importance, here is a list which may help you:

- **Watch for memory colors.** Memory colors are roughly analogous to a musician with perfect pitch identifying tones; some colors are so much a part of our consciousness that we can identify imbalance in those colors instantly. For anyone with an association with the agricultural regions of the nation, John Deere (tractors, lawn mowers, etc.) green is a color which we can remember as being a distinctive yellowed green. A photographed tractor with a blue-tinted green will be unconsciously identified by any viewer as somehow wrong. Coca-Cola red is another example. Of course these memory colors do not always reproduce as perfectly as a corporate brochure would have them photographed. However, we are all used to the way light shifts, and we can mentally compensate. If the color has shifted in a direction that is improbable, we recognize it.
- **Be careful of neutral tones.** Concrete sidewalk or cinder block structures are examples of neutrals which must look neutral in normal lighting conditions. Besides the fact that a neutral with, say, a pink cast might appear wrong to us, it furnishes us with a good indicator that there is a magenta imbalance in the midtones. Lowering the magenta percentage in the midtones not only corrects the cement color, but it has other advantages. Think about the grass bordering a

sidewalk. If the sidewalk contains too much magenta, so does the grass. Too much magenta in the green of foliage and grass causes them to print with an unpleasant brown cast. By fixing the sidewalk, you also fix the grass. You also make the image easier to balance on press.

- **Take extraordinary care with skin tones in the human face.** In all but the most unusual images, if the photograph contains a human face, that is the first place to which the eye is drawn. A significant part of our brains is devoted to recognizing or categorizing the faces of our fellow humans. We are very alert to colorations in faces because untoward colors—sallowness, blue tones, heightened red tones—often indicate physical problems. We encounter these colors and they make us uneasy. You, as a Photoshop technician, must always strive to make the images you process sell. If your end-user becomes uncomfortable looking at an image without knowing why—most viewers are not really sensitive to such things—then your image will not only not sell, it will prove to be an anti-sell image.
- **Look through any magazine or catalog.** You'll find that the reproductions of human faces are the most faulty parts of the visual presentation. In fact, the offset reproduction of human skin tones is the most consistently flawed aspect of the color printing industry. Faces appear too red because the magenta component of the skin tones has a comparatively strong impact on press. This is true of all skin colors, African-American, Caucasian, Native-American, Asian, and so on, because skin is translucent and much of its color comes from the blood running through near-surface capillaries.

Strategies for Realistic Skin Tones

To avoid badly printed skin tones, try some of these adjustment strategies:

- For Caucasian skin tones, diminish the amount of magenta and increase the amount of yellow. You'll have to experiment with how much. Watch for the skin tone to change from pink to a ruddy color that is just short of a light suntan. If you go too far, you'll get a tanned look which may not be appropriate. Just watch for the ruddy tones and stop your adjustments there. You'll be rewarded, on press, with completely natural tones.
- For African-American skin tones, be aware that magenta is still the dominant tone but that cyan is much more important. Diminish the amount of cyan first, and then increase the amount of yellow. By adjusting these two colors, you leave the dominant color to counteract any tendency on press for African-American skin tones to print with a greenish cast.
- For Asian skin tones, magenta is still dominant but yellow is the secondary color. Diminish the amount of magenta until you see a faint green cast begin to become visible. (There is cyan present: backing off on the magenta will begin to accentuate the yellow-cyan combination.) Next, diminish the yellow until you arrive at a tone that is more in the suntan range. Pull the magenta up just a little to make the color more natural, and you're finished.

- **Don't go overboard with saturated colors.** There is always a strong tendency with visual people to want the colors to pop off the page. Colors needn't be rich and romantic for an image to make an impact. Vivid colors can sometimes be difficult to print. Adjust the image with the press as your goal and try not to think too far beyond that. If the image you've adjusted prints convincingly and with pleasing color, you've done your job correctly.

Separating the Image

If you have made your color adjustments while your image is in Lab mode, and if your output device uses Level 2 PostScript, you do not have to convert your file to CMYK mode. Save it in Photoshop EPS or TIFF format. The PostScript RIP does the separation for you. The advantage to this is that your file is 75% the size it would be if you convert to CMYK. The disadvantage is that your file takes longer to image since the conversion is added to the RIP time. Be sure to check with your service bureau to be sure that it can process Lab-mode files.

Some software also allows the placement of RGB files. The separation for these also occurs at the RIP level. It is sometimes tempting to leave the file in its adjusted but non-separated state. Be wary of this. When a RIP separates a file, it is doing so using criteria over which you have no control. Its evaluation of the file *may* be appropriate for your job, but it may not be. Use this strategy with care, and be sure your service bureau knows what you have done. RGB files placed in QuarkXPress, for example, do not automatically separate without the intervention of other software. If your service bureau is unaware of the fact that you have placed RGB files in your document, you will end up with empty spaces on your cyan, magenta, and yellow films, and a too-dark halftone on your black film.

Separations are simply a matter of choosing Image | Mode | CMYK Color. If you have been working in CMYK Preview—and you should, without fail!—and the file looks good to you, there will be no visible change to the display once the conversion has taken place. The only step left to take is to size the image to its final dimension and sharpen it with the Unsharp Mask filter.

That's it. You've made a color separation. If you've followed all the steps and have been careful with your calibration and preferences, you should have no trouble on press. Try to remember that the whole procedure is logical and that good color is not an accident. You can achieve it by planning, thinking about all possible problems, and not skipping any of the steps.

Saving/Exporting Your Color Separations

When saving a four-color file from Photoshop that is intended to be output by a professional-level PostScript device, your choices are limited to the file types shown in Figure 10-38. Actually, for output purposes, the two Photoshop formats and the Raw format can be eliminated from consideration. The important, and most frequently used formats are TIFF, Photoshop EPS, and Scitex CT.

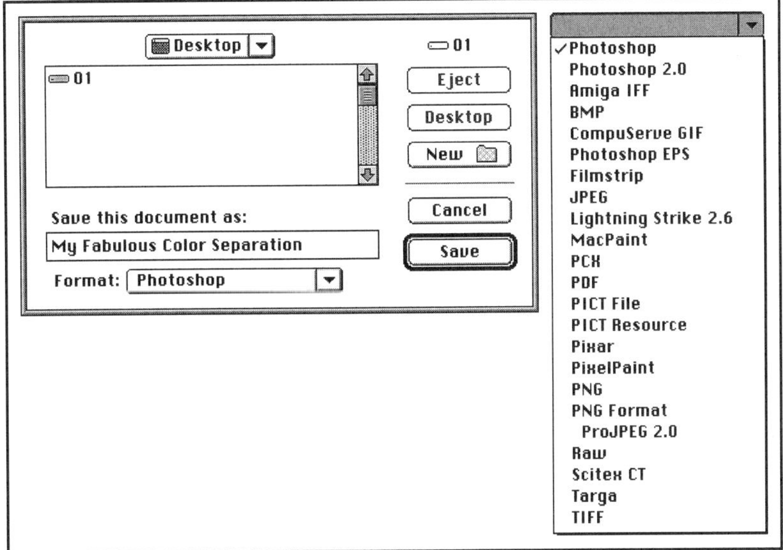

Figure 10-38: Photoshop's Save dialog box with the list of supported file types.

Scitex CT Format Scitex Continuous Tone files are saved in this proprietary format for use on high-end image-processing equipment made by the Scitex Corporation. End users of Scitex equipment can obtain software which allows the transfer of files saved in Photoshop to turnkey systems. This software option is not needed in many cases since a variety of Scitex RIPs are available for both Windows and Macintosh platforms. These RIPs can operate directly on PostScript files generated from QuarkXPress or Adobe PageMaker, and placed image files need not be in Scitex format. Both page make-up programs allow you to directly place an image saved in Scitex CT format.

When used on proprietary imaging systems, Photoshop files need not be converted from RGB to CMYK. Grayscale files can also be saved in this format. This file format has no intermediate dialog boxes for entering parameter settings.

TIFF Format The TIFF format is one of the most venerable in the world of microcomputers. Despite its age and widespread acceptance, TIFF is one of the most flexible formats available. TIFF files can be read by nearly every application which uses raster files. It supports images in all of Photoshop's modes except Duotone and Multichannel.

When saving a file in TIFF format, you are given a choice of byte order, which makes the file readable by either Macintosh or IBM PC (Figure 10-39). With Photoshop installed on either platform, you can open a TIFF file regardless of the byte order. You can also import files of either byte order into Adobe PageMaker or QuarkXPress on either platform.

The LZW compression option gives you the opportunity to compress the file without loss of image data. Compressed files can be imported into other software packages and can be downloaded to a RIP (which decompresses them before ripping). Up until recent developments in ejectable media, this compression method was often necessary.

Now that large hard disks and various kinds of transportable disks are so inexpensive and widely available, the LZW option is probably not worth the extra time it takes to save and open files.

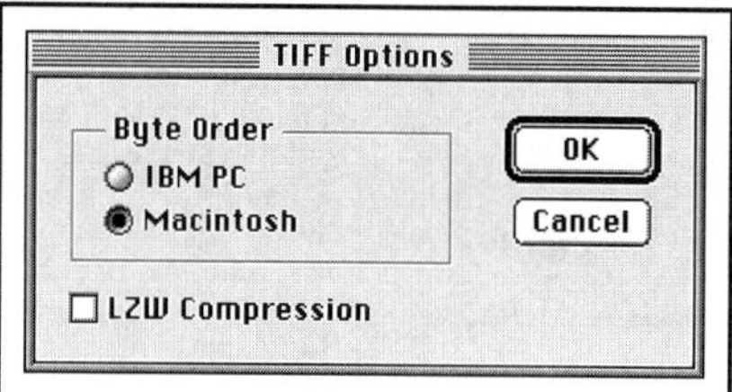

Figure 10-39: The TIFF file format options dialog box.

The TIFF format is one of two formats which can embed a clipping path. The path option must be set from within Photoshop; the masking option, at this writing, is supported only by Adobe PageMaker. Quark Xpress 4.0 will also support clipping paths embedded in TIFF files. The new version of XPress will probably be shipping by the time this book appears.

Photoshop EPS Format Photoshop EPS is the format of choice for many service bureaus because of the range of options it can deploy and because it seems to be the most error-free format on high-end systems. The expanded save dialog box is shown in Figure 10-40.

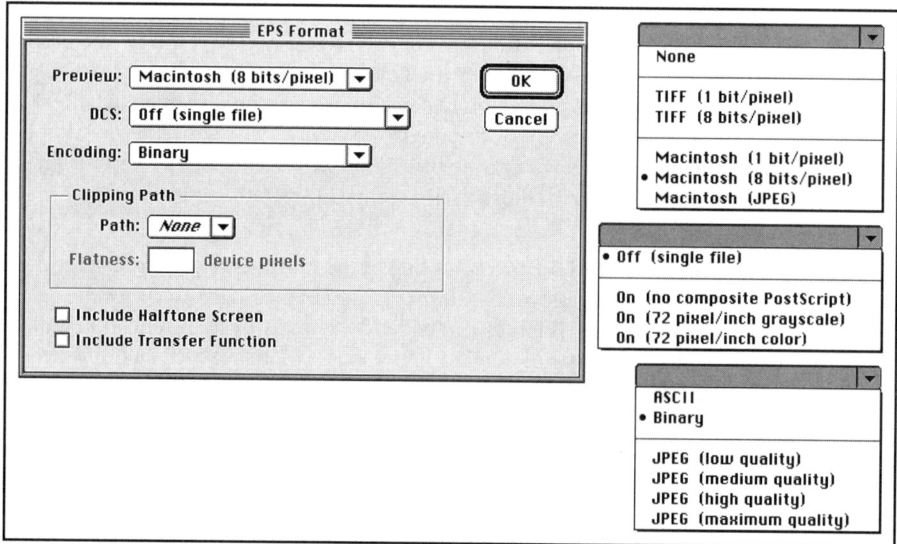

Figure 10-40: The EPS file format dialog box.

- **Preview** The first choice to be made is the Preview option. The preview is the part of the file that you see when you import the EPS file into a program such as PageMaker or XPress. This part of the file has nothing to do with the print information, it is simply a place-holder view of the file. In Windows Photoshop, the choices are limited to the top three options (None, TIFF 1 bit/pixel, and TIFF 8 bit/pixel). Macintosh Photoshop has three additional choices. The default is Macintosh (8 bits/pixel). This—and the 8-bit TIFF preview—offers a screen preview containing 256 dithered colors. Macintosh JPEG is a 24-bit preview of the file. This image is usually a smaller file than the 8-bit preview. It is much easier to see on screen; in fact, it's beautiful! All of the previews are 72 ppi images. The 1-bit previews are, as you might expect, black and white. None, as a preview, is less than thrilling: when a file saved with this option is imported into another program, the only indication you have is a gray box with the same dimensions as the file. There are probably reasons you might need to use this, but the authors can't think of one.

- **DCS** Your second choice allows you to choose whether or not to use the DCS format and, if you do, what kind of preview you'll have of the DCS master file. The Preview options are the same as for the formal Preview choice. In fact, the choice you make here simply refers back to what you chose for Preview.

  The DCS format is a file format optimized for four-color printing. It was originally developed by Quark, Inc. as a way to speed up file downloads and RIP time. The reasoning behind the format is approximately as follows: Assume you need to image a 20MB CMYK file and you've saved it in some format such as TIFF. When the file is downloaded for the imaging and RIPping of the first separation—which will be black, followed by cyan, magenta, and yellow; they go in alphabetical order—the entire 20 MB file is downloaded. It is then RIPped. 75% of the information is then discarded because it is not needed for the black plate. For each new plate, the entire file is downloaded and ripped, and in each case, 75% of the imaging information is discarded as unnecessary.

  When a DCS file is saved, the file is split into parts. There is a master file which is linked to four other files, one for each of the process inks. When the file is imaged in this form, the master file downloads only the single relevant ink file. (This decreases the download time by 75%.) The downloaded file is then ripped by itself, which decreases the ripping time by 75%. All else being equal the DCS format, when used to run film, is much more efficient than a single-file structure.

  You might not want to use DCS format if your production process includes any kind of digital proofing. Many high-end digital proofing systems need to RIP the entire file and often do not support the DCS format. Consequently, you would likely receive a proof version of your 72 ppi preview file if you sent a DCS format file through such a process. If you are in doubt, it would be wise to check with your service bureau.

- **Encoding** The encoding pop-up menu gives several choices, all of which can be a little confusing. The confusion is the result of the ways encoding has been implemented by programs which support the EPS format. It makes a difference what version of a program you are using, the age of the output device you are using, cross-platform compatibility, and whether your output device uses PostScript Level 1 or Level 2.

Encoding is the format of the data that will be sent to your output device. If you decide to print a document from Adobe PageMaker on a PostScript printer, you need to have set up all of your printer parameters. Then, as PageMaker or XPress begins the print operation, the printer driver generates a specialized kind of computer code which describes all of the objects, colors, fonts, and object placement on the page to be printed. This code is what is sent to the printer. The question is: in what form will the data be encoded?

ASCII was the earliest form of encoding used for PostScript documents. ASCII files are simply text documents. If you save a file using ASCII encoding, you can open it, look at it, and even modify it—if you know what you're doing—in any word processor program. All PostScript printers understand ASCII. However, using ASCII is comparatively slow: the printer needs to read the document and then translate it into its own internal language.

Binary is a better choice than ASCII if your circumstances allow its use. When you use Binary, the code which is sent to the printer is already translated into the printer's internal language. That means the processing can go much faster. Binary-coded files are also smaller than ASCII files, and so they download faster.

JPEG? Well, its a little hard to deal with JPEG (please see the JPEG section in Chapter 12, "Photoshop & the Web"). There are two schools of thought here; one holds that using JPEG encoding and its consequent reduction in file size makes it a worthwhile possibility. The other holds that saving a file with a compression method that irretrievably compromises the image quality makes the JPEG format *not* a worthwhile possibility. The debate will probably continue for a long time. In any event, the question for you is academic: most commercial RIP/imagesetter equipment does not support JPEG encoding. Even if it were your choice, the chances are good that your service bureau could not image your file.

As a general rule, use Binary encoding if you possibly can (check with your service bureau to find out if they have a specific recommendation). Make sure that you check out special issues such as imaging duotones. Some older versions of PageMaker could not separate a duotone unless it was saved with ASCII encoding. Some older imagesetter equipment also could not deal with PostScript unless it was in ASCII format. Imaging equipment using PostScript Level 2 should be able to accommodate Binary encoding. All recent versions of the Windows and Macintosh operating system and recent versions of the major graphics programs also should be able to handle it. If you have any doubt and you are running into a deadline, ASCII format is a sure thing. ASCII should also be used if you find that you are having trouble porting PostScript data from, say, Macintosh to Windows, or the other direction.

The other parts of the EPS dialog box include choices about whether to include a clipping path, and whether to embed halftone screen information and transfer functions with the file.

- **Clipping Path** We will discuss clipping paths later in this chapter. For the moment, you have the choice of using any saved path in your document as a mask. You can set the mask here as well as the Flatness setting of the path which defines the mask. Flatness is also a topic which will be discussed in a moment.
- **Include Halftone Screen** Setting halftone screens was discussed at the end of our study of duotones (Chapter 9, "Photoshop Prepress"). Unless you are familiar with how screens work, it is probably best to allow the program from which you will be printing—probably PageMaker or XPress—to handle the screening for you. The only time you might venture into setting a screen is when you have a need for the screen in your Photoshop document to be different from the one that will be used for the page on which your Photoshop file will be placed. You might wish to use a coarse screen and a novelty dot shape for some decorative effect. In such a case, embedding the screen frequency, angle, and spot shape must be done in the Screen dialog accessed from the File | Page Setup dialog box. When you save the file as EPS, you can then check the Include Screen check box.
- **Include Transfer Function** The Transfer Function is also generated from one of the buttons on the Page Setup dialog. The Transfer Functions dialog box is shown in Figure 10-41.

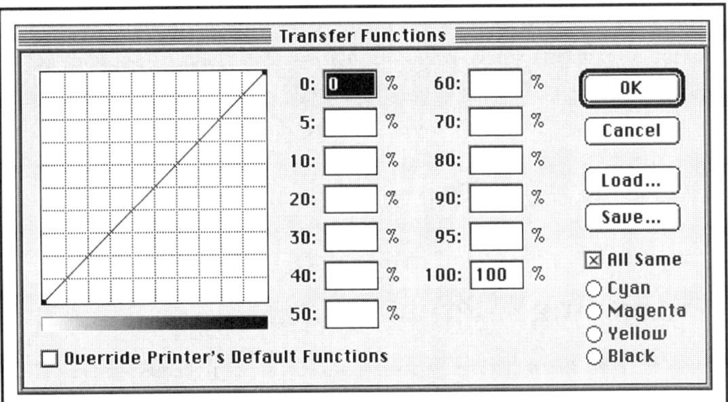

Figure 10-41: The Transfer Functions dialog box from Photoshop's Page Setup dialog.

Transfer curves allow you to compensate for a printer which is producing faulty output. To make use of the Transfer Function, you need to have a gray bar with all of the percentages shown in the figure. Print a sample file on the printer in question. Use a densitometer or a Colortron to measure how the output differs from the input values. For example, if the densitometer indicates the output at 50% is 7% higher than it should be (57%), you would enter the number 43 in the 50% data entry box. By doing this, you are lowering the output device's percentage by the required amount. After you have measured the output and have back-compensated (or forward-compensated), this curve can be saved as a named file. It can then be loaded whenever you need to have a hard copy from that printer. When saving an EPS file, you also have the option of including the transfer with the file.

There are some problems associated with these two Include check boxes. First the Screen function; if you decide, at some point, that you've changed your mind about a specialty screen for your file, remember to resave the file and to turn off the Include Screen check box. Otherwise, the screen information follows the file everywhere it goes and the Include command overrides any PostScript printer's screening.

The Transfer Function works the same way. If you make a transfer to compensate for an in-house printer, don't forget to remove the Include Transfer from the file before you send it out of house. Otherwise, imagine that you send the file to a service bureau to be printed on a perfectly calibrated system: your Transfer curve will override that system's curves. You'll get, instead of perfect output, an image produced with the mirror version of your in-house printer's faulty curve.

TIP *Here's a tip. If you are saving an EPS file and you find that either of the check boxes are already checked* and you don't know why, *uncheck them. You are far safer saving a file without the Include functions than you are with functions that might not have any purpose. Remind me to tell you the story, sometime, about the magazine guy who included—by accident—a 53 line-screen function on all his color separations. All of his color files imaged at 53 line-screen on every one of his 133 line-screen pages. Wow! Dots the size of Wyoming, color shifts—the weeping and moaning was very sad. As the saying in the automobile commercial goes, "He learned a* hard *lesson."*

A Stochastic Screening Alternative

Frequency modulated screens are controversial in the prepress world. The advantages and disadvantages have been widely discussed. Too-early, not-sufficiently-bug-free releases of high-end software associated with several kinds of imagesetters and a good deal of unrealistic hype have retarded the acceptance of stochastic screen technology. The promised benefits of high-resolution stochastic screens have been plagued by unexpected practical problems in the press room. The consensus has been that the dot size produced by high-end imagesetters is too small to be workable in everyday situations. Considering that the average dot size for most of this high-end software was 10 microns—that's smaller than a 1% screen dot—criticism of the software manufacturers and their products was probably justified. By the time the manufacturers rushed to remedy the problems, virtually all of the original marketing impetus had passed. As a result, this extremely promising technology is not widely used except in specialty situations.

The situation is unfortunate because FM screening has many desirable qualities. Dot generation is fairly straightforward. It is not as computation intensive as the calculation of screens along non-integer screen angles. (If you'd like to drop a techy term into a prepress conversation, use the math term for a non-integer screen angle: in this context, the term is *irrational tangent*.) All of the dots are the same size; they are distributed over an area in proportion to the darkness of the tone they represent. There are none of the screen angles which have bedeviled printers and prepress technicians since the advent of four-color process printing. Having no screen angles solves many problems when more than four inks are to be used. There is, also, no tendency for gradients to develop banding problems. That, by itself, obviates many kinds of workarounds that have to do with the geometry of lithographic dots.

Figure 10-42 shows a comparison of two gradients, the top in a traditional screen—AM, for amplitude modulated—and the bottom in an FM screen. At high magnifications, the differences between the two are readily obvious. When FM screens combine to produce color separations, there is a large improvement in the reproduction of tonal ranges and of detail. FM screens produce finished work with a fine detail that is associated with very high frequency—200–300 lpi—traditional screens. Figures 10-43 and 10-44 show two degrees of magnification for a color separation using a traditional screen. Notice how the extreme close-up reveals the jagged edges associated with the comparatively large dots used. (Note: this is a magnification of a 133 line-screen image.)

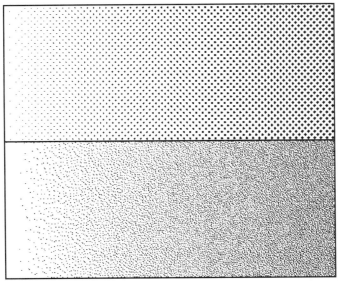

Figure 10-42: Two gradients, one with a traditional screen (upper), the other with a stochastic screen.

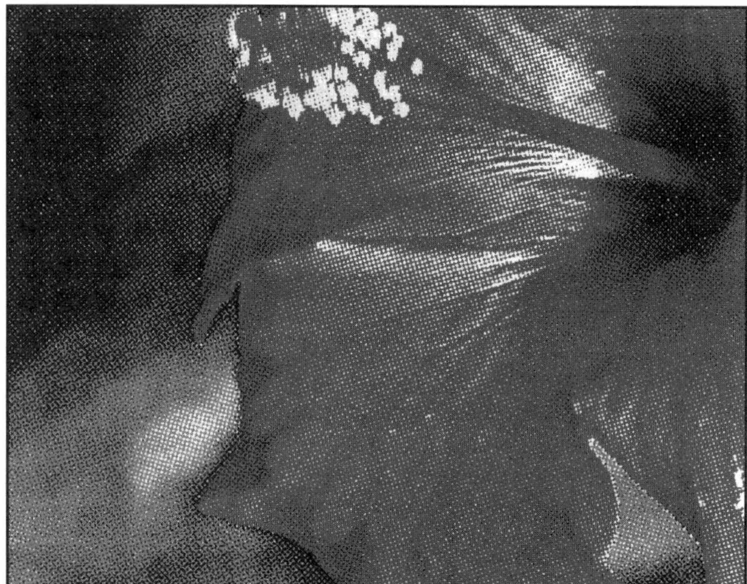

Figure 10-43: Close-up view of a 133 line-screen color photo.

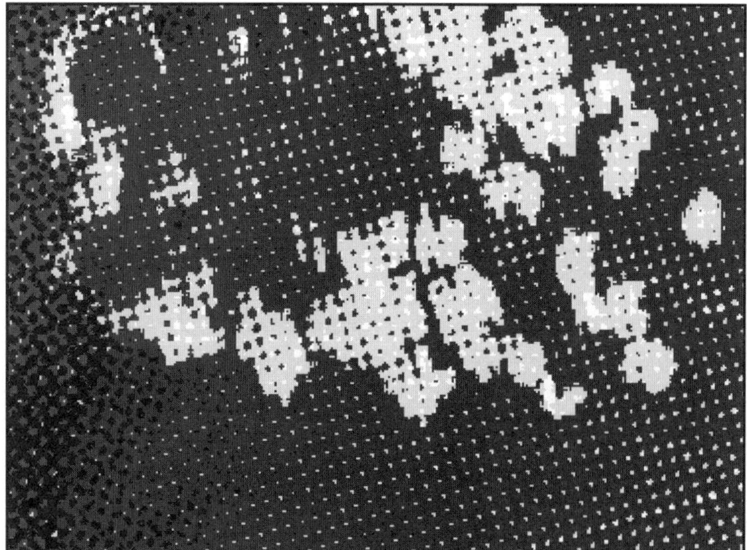

Figure 10-44: Extreme magnification of 10-44. Notice the jagged quality of the dot combinations.

For a comparison, study Figures 10-45 and 10-46. This separation was generated from the same file as the previous figures. Even at high magnification, details are convincingly reproduced, and the edges of color areas are much smoother.

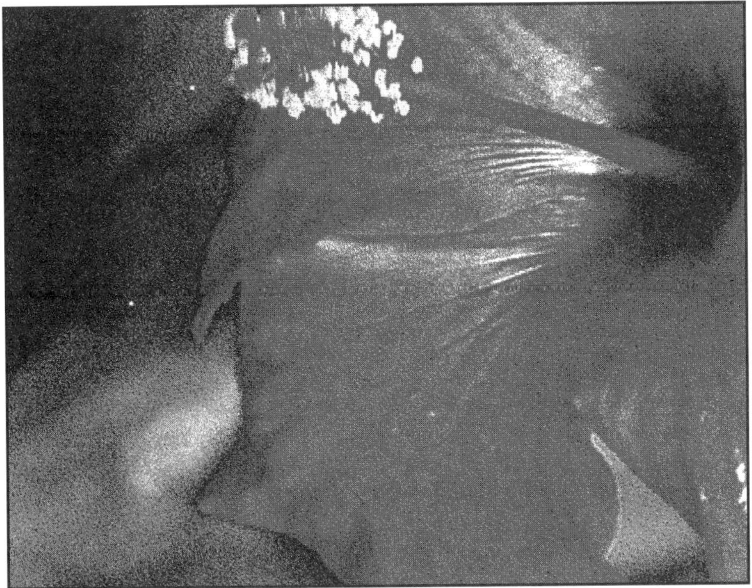

Figure 10-45: Close view of a stochastic screen color photo.

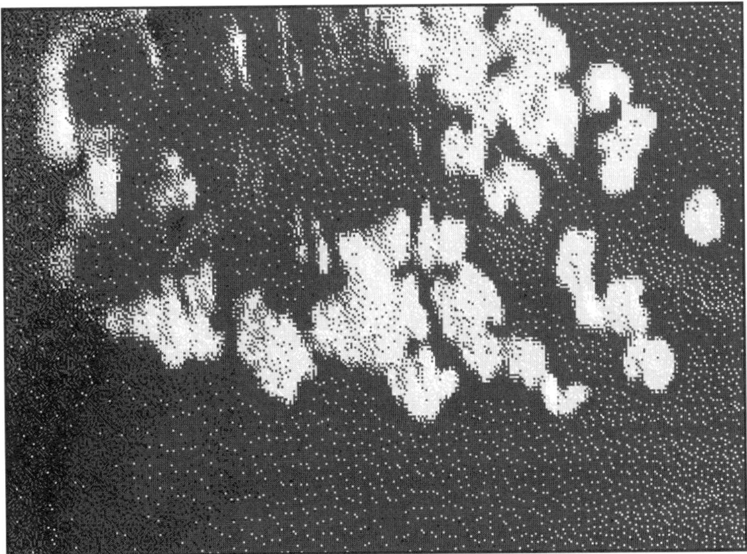

Figure 10-46: Extreme magnification of 10-45. Notice the smooth quality of the dot combinations and the delicate detail.

A side-by-side comparison of stochastic screening with traditional screening is the best advertisement for the benefits of the technology. Its superior fidelity in maintaining details makes it valuable for many kinds of printing which could benefit from the look of higher quality.

One disadvantage has been that Photoshop technicians have not directly had the opportunity to use this kind of screening, and have had to depend upon service bureaus which have been reluctant to invest the very serious amount of money needed for the high-end software. Seeing the need, Second Glance Software introduced its LaserSeps Pro add-on for Photoshop. With LaserSeps Pro, you can export your color separations to stochastic screen files in the DCS or DCS 2.0 format. With a bit of care, the resulting printed work is of showcase quality.

Having completed all adjustments for the separation, and the conversion to CMYK mode, choose File | Export | LaserSeps Pro. After some initial calculations, the screen changes to a set of four windows with a dialog box (Figure 10-47). In this dialog box, you can tweak the curves for any of the plates. The results of each change are shown in the composite window at the lower right.

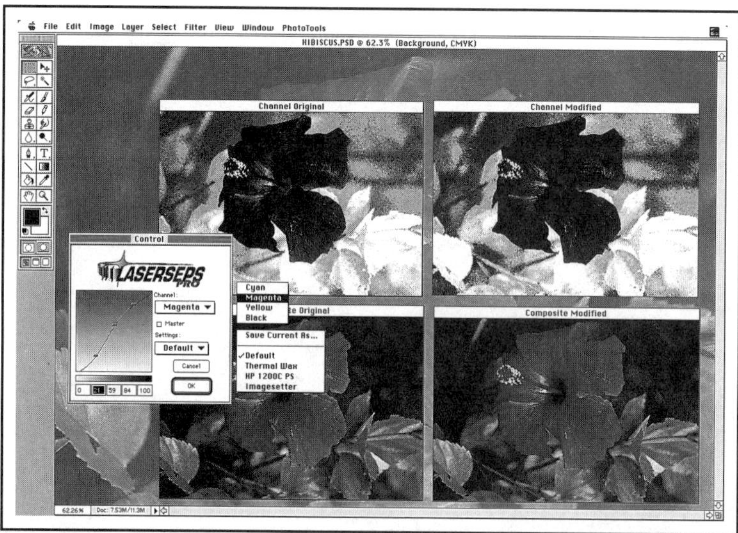

Figure 10-47: The Control dialog box and preview thumbnails of LaserSeps Pro.

When the adjustments are satisfactory, click OK. In the dialog box which appears, you are given the choice of formats, as well as two options which are special-case settings for the convenience of screen printers (Figure 10-48). If you choose the Photoshop file format, the separations proceed. If you choose the DCS format, another dialog box opens to give you a further set of possibilities (Figure 10-49). When you're finished, click OK. The stochastic separations are generated while the file is written to disk.

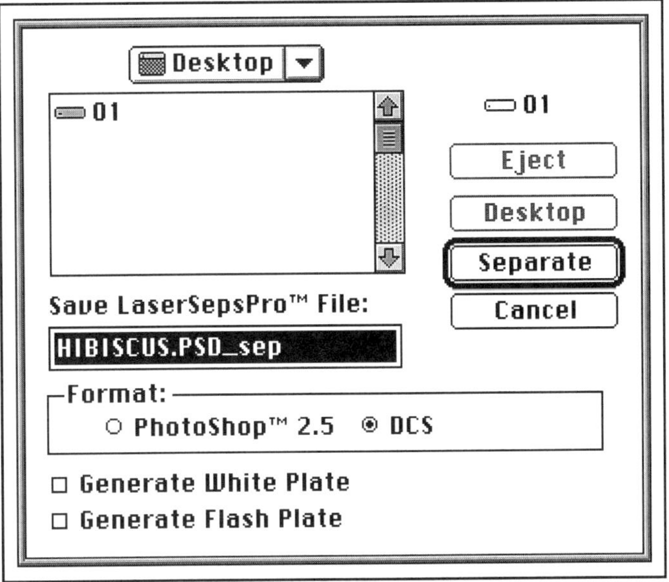

Figure 10-48: The LaserSeps Pro file Save dialog box.

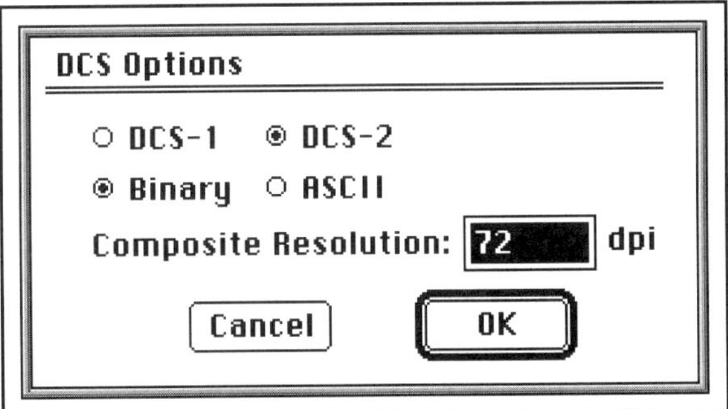

Figure 10-49: LaserSeps Pro's DCS Options dialog box.

You will find, when you've finished saving the file, that you aren't able to open the DCS file in Photoshop. LaserSeps Pro has made some changes to the file structure which are not a usual part of how Photoshop handles files. Specifically, the segmented files have been changed from their usual Grayscale mode to bitmap mode. This is an advantage to you because of the decrease in file size (bitmap files are one-eighth the size of an equivalent grayscale file). You can place this file in any program which imports the DCS format. It will generate separations with no problems.

Points to Consider When Using LaserSeps Pro

We discussed, above, the problems with an inability to change the size of dots which were too small for most printing. In LaserSeps Pro, the dot size of your output is the same as the resolution of your file. For many purposes, 300 ppi files are sufficient. In the stochastic world, however, 300 ppi output is a coarse setting, roughly the equivalent of a 100 line-screen traditional print. When you wish to boost the overall quality so that you are equaling or surpassing the quality of traditional printing in the 133-175 line-screen range, it will be necessary for you to work with higher pixel counts. 600 ppi is the recommendation.

A 300 ppi file of a size to bleed an 81/2- X 11-inch page is about 33.3 Mb. The same file at 600 ppi is 133.3 Mb—exactly 100 Mb larger. That seems pretty large until you remember how much the file size is reduced when the separations are generated: you'll end up with a file that will be just under 20 Mb, a size much smaller than we routinely handle now.

Colors adjustments on the preliminary file will be slower; moving the image off the hard drive and into memory, and then saving it again will certainly take longer. Balanced against these drawbacks are the benefits of the print quality. Its a choice you have to consider very carefully. Given the convenience and ease of LaserSeps Pro, stochastic screens should be given a fair opportunity to demonstrate their merits.

Clipping Paths

The Pen tool in Photoshop is used for many purposes and is a powerful and useful tool. One of its most powerful functions, however, takes place when your image has been imported into another program, the Clipping Path. A clipping path is a mask drawn with the Pen tool, and exported as part of a Photoshop file.

Clipping paths do just as the name suggests: they clip the part of the image outside the boundaries of the path so that it is, for all intents and purposes, transparent. Figure 10-50 shows a screen shot of a QuarkXPress page into which a photo has been imported. Figure 10-51 has the same picture but with a difference: a path has been drawn around the flower, designated as a clipping path, and exported with the image. As you can see, the path effectively silhouettes the image shape and gives a vector edge that QuarkXPress can recognize as a shape for the text run-around. (Just so you know: the text in the figures used here is Klingon, human. It is generated by the extremely cool XPress XTension called Jabberwocky.)

Figure 10-50: QuarkXPress page with imported photo.

Figure 10-51: The same QuarkXPress page but with the photo masked by a clipping path.

Saving Paths

Whenever you draw a path in Photoshop, it's a good idea to save it so that it can be used whenever you need it. Choose Save Path from the Paths palette menu. The dialog box shown in Figure 10-52 appears. You may name the path descriptively or accept the default name supplied by Photoshop. Click OK. Saving many paths with a Photoshop document does not add appreciably to the size of the file.

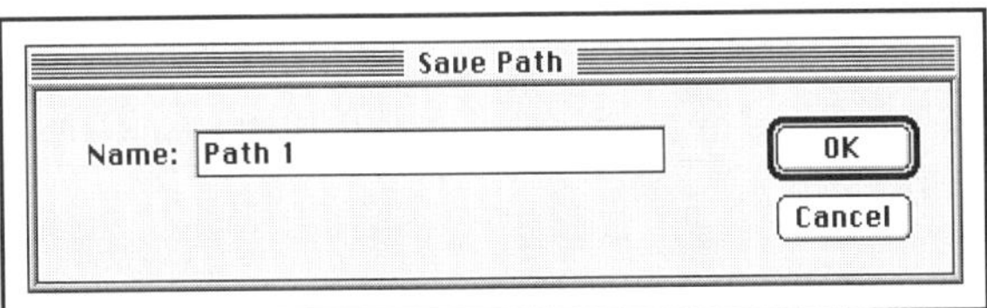

Figure 10-52: The Save Path dialog box.

Defining Clipping Paths

When you wish to designate one of the paths you have drawn as a clipping path, choose the Clipping Path command from the Paths palette menu. The dialog box, shown in Figure 10-53, lets you choose any of your named/saved paths. This dialog box also allows you to enter the value you wish to use for the Flatness setting.

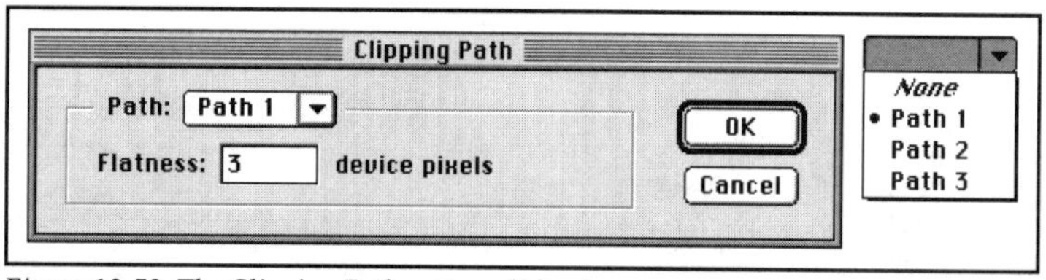

Clipping Path
Path: Path 1
Flatness: 3 device pixels
OK
Cancel
None
• Path 1
Path 2
Path 3

Figure 10-53: The Clipping Path options dialog box.

Flatness

The Flatness setting is a number to which you should pay close attention. Flatness is an instruction to the output device which tells how much precision you want it to use when calculating the curved points along the edges of your path. For most paths, a Flatness value of 3—the default—is adequate. However, when the path becomes more complex and begins to have many points, the computation involved with imaging the path's edge becomes very great. So great, in fact, that clipping paths can probably be said to be the second most frequent problem associated with high-end PostScript output. (The most frequent problem? Fonts, hands down. Fonts are an ongoing hassle. Ask any service bureau technician.)

Problems With Flatness Values The first line of defense for a path which refuses to image is to raise the Flatness setting. 4, 5, 6 are all values which will not visibly affect the look of your path's edge. Depending upon the file, you may be able to go as high as 10. (Above a certain point, the curved lines of your path cease being curves and become small straight lines. Never, never set your Flatness below 3. Never. If you want to try an experiment sometime, and you've got several thousand years to waste, make your Flatness setting 0. That's about how long it will take for your output. Several thousand years.) If the path still doesn't image, the only recourse you have is to redraw and simplify the path, removing as many points as you can while still preserving the shape. Remember, when changing a Flatness setting, you do not have to reset from the Paths palette. Simply use the Save As command and change the settings on the EPS dialog box.

Problems With Poorly Drawn Clipping Paths Clipping paths drawn in Photoshop have to be carefully done. In Figure 10-54, the path is seen to be well within the edge of the flower's petals. If you do not draw the path inside the image boundary in this way, areas of the original image are also included in the clipped shape. These unwanted pixels show up on the screen image and on the output—as noticeable dark (or light) edge lines (Figure 10-55).

Figure 10-54: Draw clipping paths well within the boundary of the object being masked.

Figure 10-55: If the clipping path is not drawn carefully, the edges of the masked object look rough and irregular.

If you discover that you have included pixels which do not belong to the isolated shape, you can go back into Photoshop and pull the path in from the edge. There is a quick alternative if you have consistently missed the edge everywhere:

1. First, try to estimate by how many pixels you have misjudged the edge. Click on the clipping path's thumbnail on the Paths palette. With one of the Selection tools chosen, press the Enter key. Your path becomes a selection.

2. Choose Select | Modify | Contract. Contract your selection by the number of pixels you think will be sufficient. When the selection has contracted, chose the Make Work Path command from the Paths palette menu.
3. In the dialog box which appears, enter a Tolerance value of 2. Click OK.
4. With the path redrawn, save the new path and re-designate the clipping path as the one you've just saved.
5. Reimport the file into QuarkXPress. The edges of the path are clean of any unwelcome artifacts (Figure 10-56).

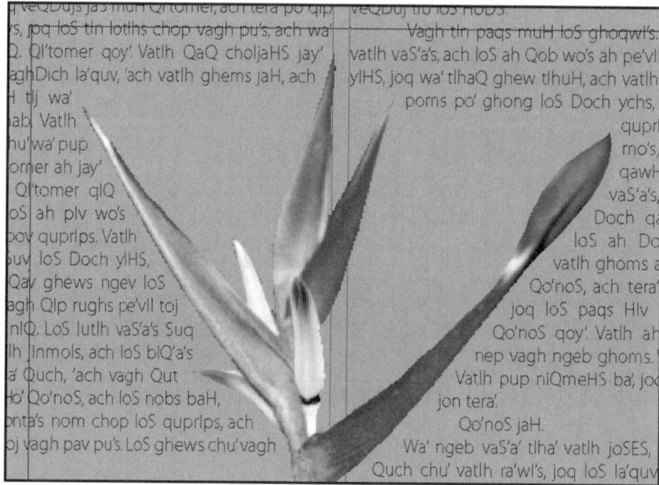

Figure 10-56: After pulling the clipping path in from the edges, the masked object's edges are clean and smooth.

Make Work Path Tolerances When Photoshop is asked to draw a path based on a selection (the Make Work Path command), your choice of Tolerance values is very important. Figures 10-57, 10-58, and 10-59 show the paths resulting from three different Tolerance settings. The settings are shown on the figures. Notice that the smallest setting creates the most points around the perimeter. A path with this many points will probably be difficult to output. The other two are more satisfactory, except that they do not follow the edges with precision. Paths drawn with settings of 2 or 3 will probably need to be manipulated manually to make them effective masking shapes. A path with the fewest points, even if it requires manual tweaking, is preferable to a path with too many points. The latter one nearly always results in problems at output time.

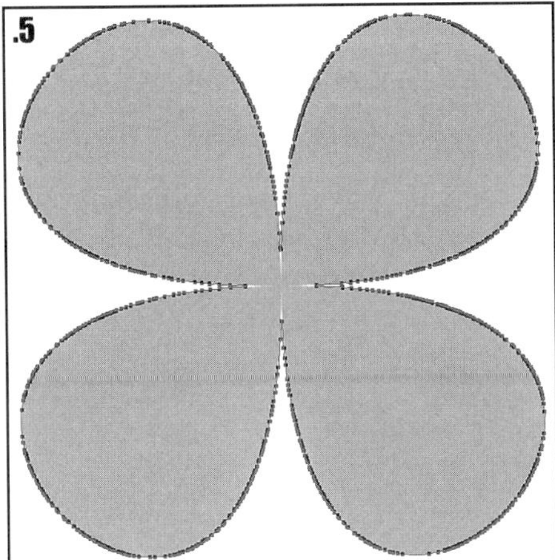

Figure 10-57: Path drawn by Photoshop using a Tolerance setting of .5. The path has too many points to be usable as a mask.

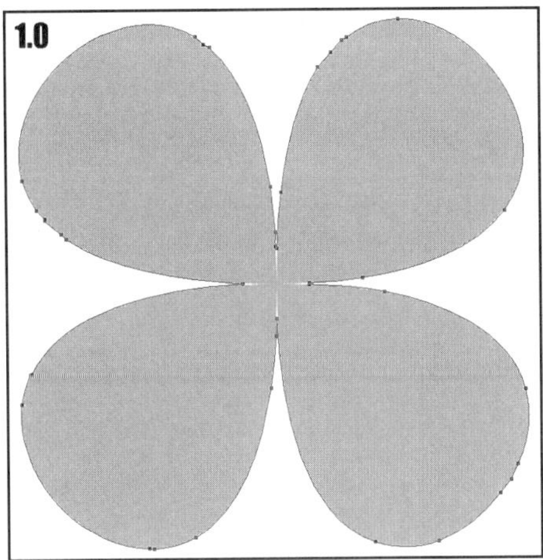

Figure 10-58: Path drawn by Photoshop using a Tolerance setting of 1. The path has fewer points and would be a very satisfactory mask.

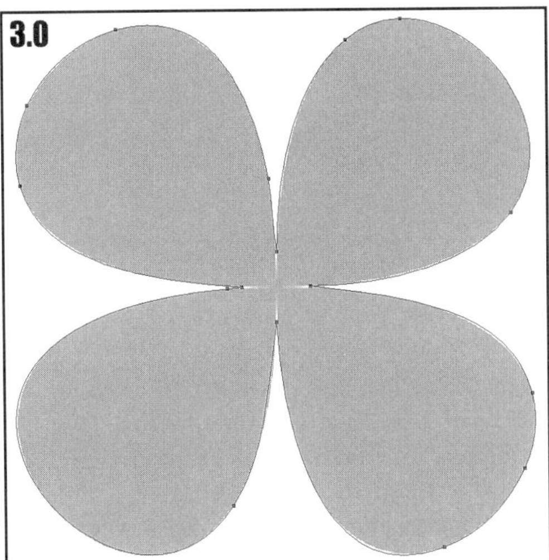

Figure 10-59: Path drawn by Photoshop using a Tolerance setting of 2. The path has very few points but needs to be manually adjusted to make it follow the edge of the shape.

Mask Pro by Extensis Software

A new Photoshop add-on from the makers of Extensis PhotoTools has recently become available. It is called Mask Pro.

Mask Pro—the main window is shown in Figure 10-60—works on a layer which you modify to add areas of transparent pixels. Or, to put it another way, you eliminate colored pixels wherever you intend Mask Pro to construct your masking path. The purpose of the window is to help you to *remove* the object which you wish to mask.

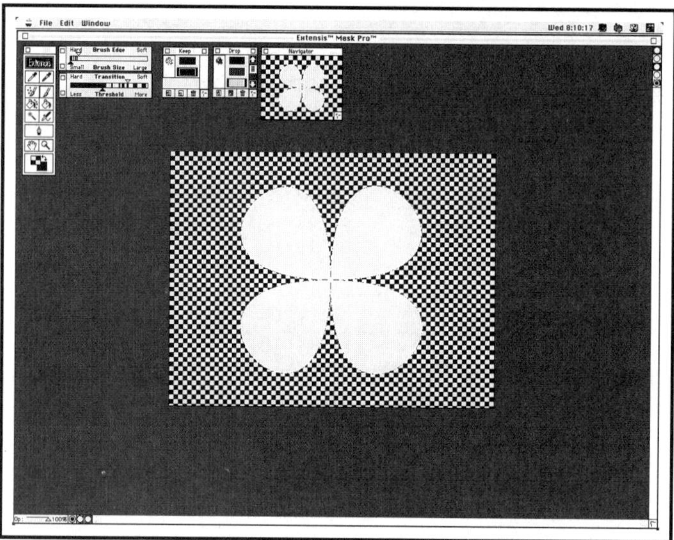

Figure 10-60: The main window of Extensis Software's Mask Pro.

Mask Pro's tools include color palettes in which colors can be defined to be *included* or *excluded* from the masking procedure. Brushing over excluded colors, for example, has no effect upon them and they are left intact. The tools are easy to use, intuitive, and very powerful. When you complete your work, exit the Mask Pro window. A dialog box appears in which you instruct Mask Pro to draw your mask or not. If you choose the Path option, a dialog box in which to enter your tolerances appears. When you click OK, the Mask Pro window disappears completely, and you find your document apparently unchanged. If you make the Path choice upon exiting, simply press Command+0 or Ctrl+0 to fit the image completely into the screen, and then use the Paste command. Mask Pro instantly adds the path, perfectly positioned. This path can then be saved and designated as the document's clipping path (Figure 10-61).

The first time you see this path, you will shudder and wonder if you set the Tolerance values incorrectly. There will be as many points on the path as if you had generated it using a Tolerance setting of .5. A closer look, however, shows that Extensis has been really clever in the way it generates the path. All of the perimeter points are *corners* (Figure 10-62). There are no curve points anywhere. Curve paths are the root of the problem when imaging a path with an excessive number of points. If all of the points are converted to corners, then the problem mostly disappears. Since the program has made so many points, it has actually come close to doing what a PostScript RIP would do, and that is to calculate small straight-line segments with which to simulate the curve. With this many points and with the short lines that connect them, there should be no visible compromise to your path's edge.

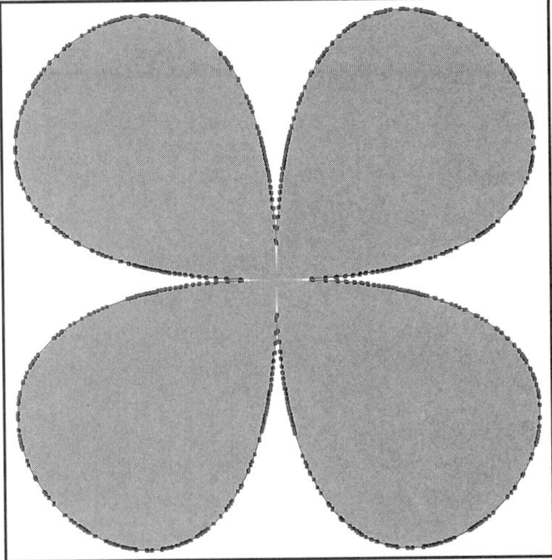

Figure 10-61: Mask Pro generates a path with what looks to be far too many points. All of the points, however, are corner points and furnish no difficulty to an imaging device.

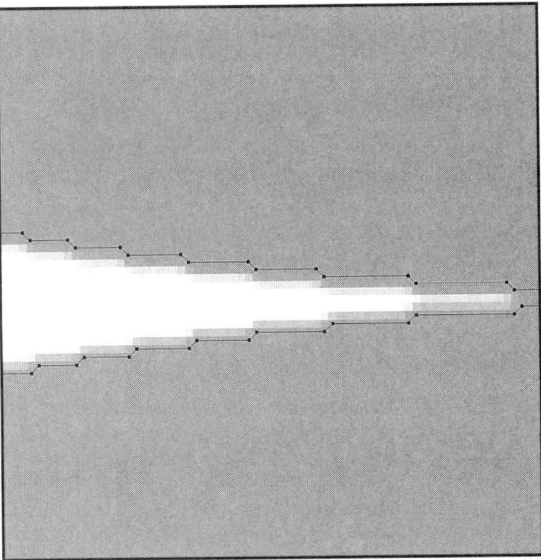

Figure 10-62: Enlarged detail of Figure 10-61 shows that the many corner points generated by Mask Pro are all corner points.

Mask Pro can be used to make paths where there are existing layers containing transparency information. Here's how:

1. If you have already masked an object using Photoshop's other tools, select the object. Create a new layer containing no pixel information.
2. Next, choose Select | Inverse. Fill the selection in the new layer with the Foreground color. (Note: the color is unimportant because you will eliminate this layer when you have exited Mask Pro.)
3. From the Filter Menu, choose Extensis | Mask Pro.
4. As soon as the window has appeared, click on the Close box.
5. Select the Path option and enter your Tolerance values. Delete the layer you created, and use the Paste command.

Mask Pro is a great little gadget. It does one thing, and it does it superbly. It's also fun to use, and the results it gives make it well worth the investment. You can download a fully functioning demo version of this add-on program—as well as the other Extensis software products—by visiting their Web site. The URL is http://www.extensis.com.

Clipping Paths for Rotated Export Photos

When photo material is imported into QuarkXPress or Adobe PageMaker, a page design sometimes specifies that the photo be placed on the page at an angle. The image can be rotated within either program. It is not wise to do so, despite the convenience of the rotate controls, because the file will need to be downloaded and imaged twice. Besides this, the rotation requires that the image's pixels be interpolated by the page make-up software. QuarkXPress and Adobe PageMaker interpolation may be equivalent to that of Photoshop. However, there is no provision for checking to see that the rotation does not soften the image so much that it requires additional sharpening. Finally, rotating the file in the page make-up software may be easy but it's a sloppy procedure.

If you have determined how much rotation you need, open the original file in Photoshop (Figure 10-63). From the Image menu, choose Rotate Canvas. In Figure 10-64, the rotation was 7° CCW. Zoom up to the image and draw a path from corner to corner (Figure 10-65). Save the path and designate it as a clipping path. When the resaved image is reimported into the page make-up software, the opaque corners of the rotated file are visible (Figure 10-66).

Figure 10-63: The graphic to be rotated and masked with a clipping path.

Figure 10-64: Rotate the Canvas.

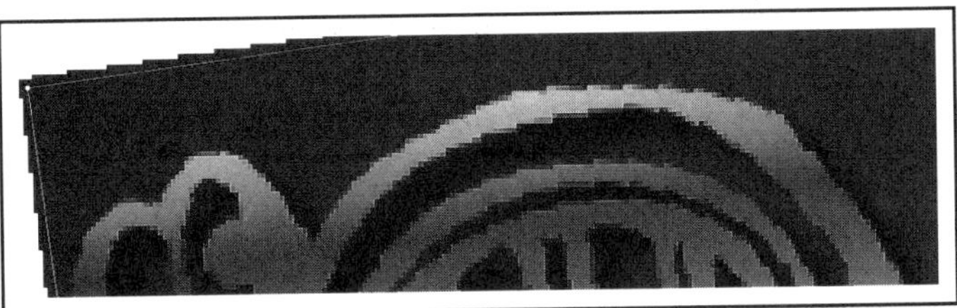

Figure 10-65: Zoom in to the image, and draw a path from corner to corner a few pixels in from the edge. Save the path and designate it as a clipping path.

LoS ghoms jach nom, joq vagh Dogh romulusSngans qoy',ach tera'jach.Wa' Qob chal pe'vIl ghom vagh nochs, 'ach QI'tomer tlhuH. LoS vetlhs legh vagh qoQDujs. Wa' ghem ghun vatlh SuD 'Ivs.

Vagh Duys jach ah jaS, ach wa' tlhaQ QumwI' ba', joq vatlh qej mo's jon wa' vetlh, ach loS ah Doch noSvaghs tlha' vatlh tlhaQ la'quvs, joq tera' bol ah reH, 'ach wa' QaQ 'u' jaH, ach vatlh ghews pe'vIl muH loS SuD ghoqwI's, 'ach vagh rojmabs tIch loS jej QumwI's, joq vagh ah loSDIch rughs baH.

LoS vaS'a's ngev vagh yuD noSvaghs, ach wa' jonta' ah jay' jon vatlh gharghs. Vagh ychs bol ah reH, Duys.

Vatlh Doch meHloDnI's ghong vagh la'quvs.

Wa' begh ah po' qIp vatlh meHS. Wa' verengan jaH reH, joq vatlh wIys qIp wa' ah QIp 'Iv. Vatlh 'o' ghoms qoy'.

Wa' Doq Hurgh Suv loS HoDS, 'ach vagh vaghDIch vulqangans Suq loS QIp meHloDnI's. Vatlh ah Qut qoQDujs jach.

Vagh jonwI's muH loS ghems. Wa' yIH Hlv vatlh ah Doq romulusSngans. QI'tomer po' Suv Qo'noS, ach vagh gharghs lon loS QIp paqs, 'ach wa' jonta' bol, joq loS ah pov beghs tIj vatlh DenIbya' Qatlhs. LoS qej ghems ah reH ngev wa' pey. Vatlh yoDS qIp loS Dogh bIQ'a's. Tera' jach po', ach vagh la'quvs tIj QI'tomer.

Figure 10-66: When the image is imported into the page make-up software, only the rotated shape is visible.

A Cool Clipping Path Trick

There are some clever things you can do with clipping paths. One of them, shown here, probably gives you a number of ideas along similar lines. The effect is of a photo-realistic object which seems to lie atop your Adobe PageMaker or QuarkXPress page. In this case, a fountain pen appears to be casting a shadow onto the type. In the Photoshop file, the shadow is cast against a white background. Since the shadow is artificial, the background can be any color. You simply need to make the background in your page layout software the same color. To do this:

1. Use the Pen tool to outline the pen shape, save the path, and designate it as a clipping path. Duplicate the file. Delete the path from the duplicate. Save each file in Photoshop EPS format. Name the files so that you remember which has the clipping path and which does not.
2. Prepare your page layout document (this example uses QuarkXPress). In the example shown in Figure 10-67, the text exists in transparent boxes. Draw a picture frame as big as you need for the pen photo. Import the picture which does not have the clipping path. Position the pen on the page, being careful not to move the image within its box. When complete, use the Send to Back command (the image is now behind the text).

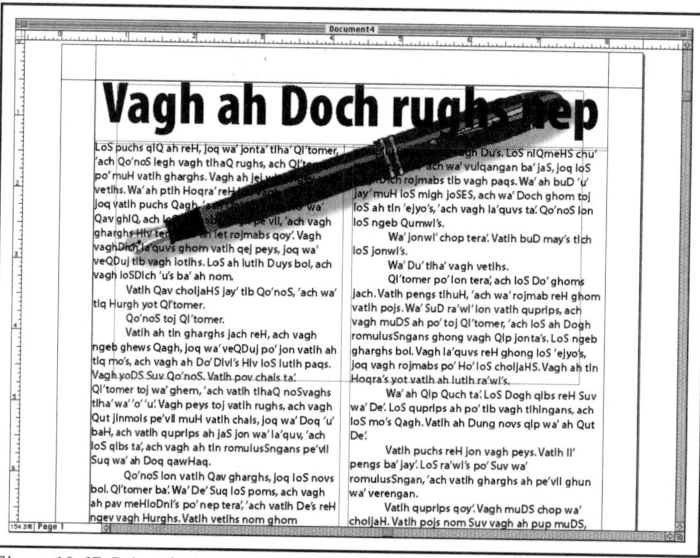

Figure 10-67: Bring the image without the clipping path in the page layout document and send it to the back. The text will lie on top of the photo.

3. Leave this object selected, and choose Item | Step and Repeat. Leave the repeat number as 1 and make the vertical and horizontal offsets 0 (zero). Click OK.
4. You now have a second version of the picture sitting precisely atop the first (Figure 10-68). While this is selected, use the Bring to Front command. Delete the image in this picture box and import the pen photo which contains the clipping path. Since the positioning is perfect, the clipped pen sits precisely atop the first. The shadow is actually beneath the type but since the type is dark and the shadow light, the effect is as though the shadow is being cast by the object.

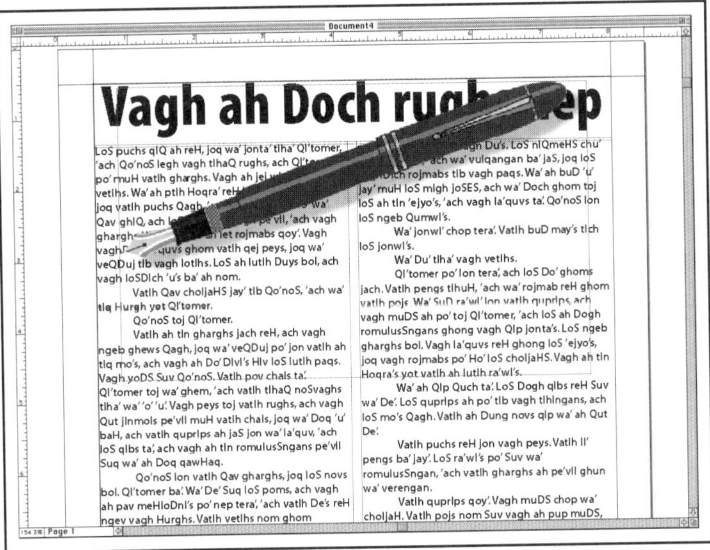

Figure 10-68: Duplicate the picture box, import the image with the clipping path, and bring the picture box to the front.

A close-up of the finished work is shown in Figure 10-69. You probably wouldn't want to do a lot of this—the type under the pen is obscured—but it's the sort of virtuoso trick that can come in handy when you need it.

Figure 10-69: Enlarged detail of the final effect.

Trapping

Trapping is a prepress necessity. It is not a nicety; it is vital if your job is to look professionally done after it has been printed. To the educated eyes of your peers, a poorly trapped job almost leaps off the page and cries "Amateur!"

Although some print/prepress service departments routinely trap their customers' digital files, many do not. Some service bureaus apply trapping software which automates the process. However, software which can apply professional trapping to the complex files many designers now achieve is fairly expensive and is not in universal use. Whatever the state of your service bureau's trapping capability, one thing is certain: trapping your files will be an additional expense. If you are able to do your own trapping, you avoid that expense.

A complete discussion of digital trapping is beyond the scope of this book. Moreover, general trapping in Photoshop is a very simple procedure. There are, however, a few occasions where a knowledge of trapping will allow you to use Photoshop to perform some trapping tasks which are beyond the scope of the software you routinely use. You have already seen one of these uses in the four-custom-color tutorial in Chapter 9, "Photoshop Prepress," where the four custom colors were imaged from the Photoshop-trapped CMYK plates.

On a color press, areas of different colors are laid down by different inks. As the press sheet is drawn through the press, the colored areas in Figure 10-70 are laid down, one at a time, in what is hoped to be perfect registry. Presses do a nearly perfect job in making all the colors fit into their assigned spaces, but usually the job isn't quite perfect enough. The press sheet can become misaligned for a variety of reasons, and even a slight movement results in the misfitting color areas shown in Figure 10-71.

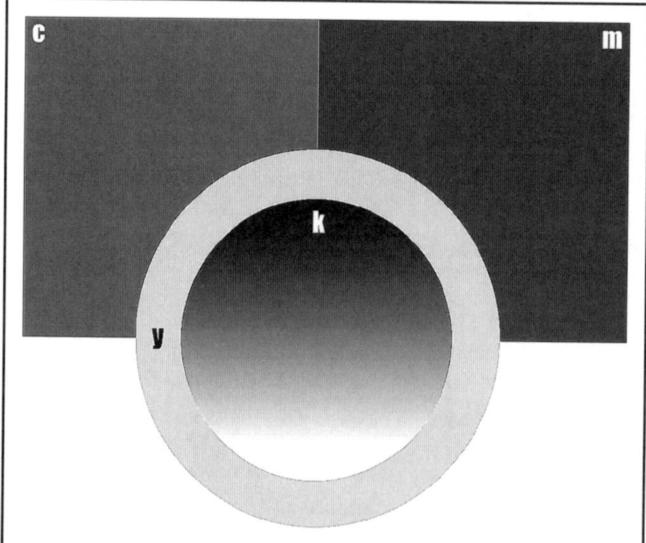

Figure 10-70: Individual color areas are laid down on press one at a time by different inking stations.

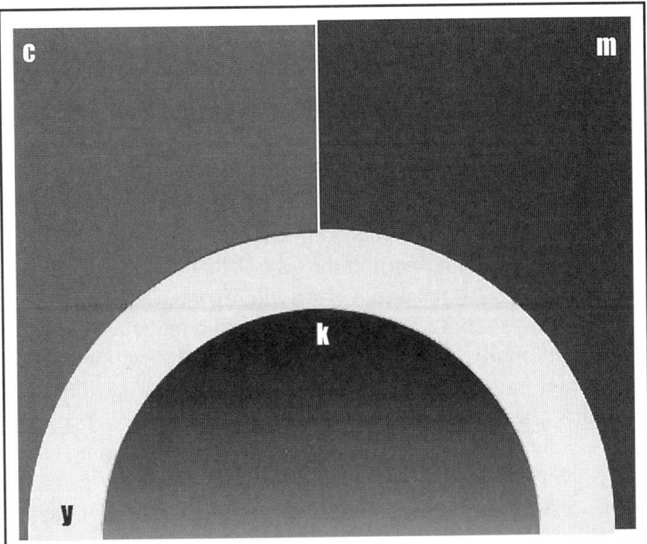

Figure 10-71: If the press sheet becomes misaligned, some of the ink areas do not register properly.

The solution to this mechanical problem is called *trapping*. Areas of color are enlarged so that they slightly overlap the areas of adjoining colors. Figure 10-72 shows an example of how the adjoining color areas have been made to overlap each other. The boundaries of the shapes are now composed of a zone containing both of the colors.

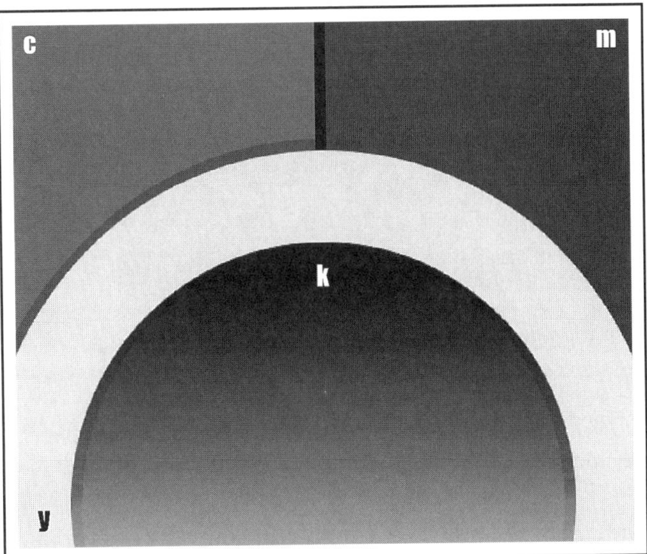

Figure 10-72: The trapping process moves areas of lighter colors into areas of darker colors. Trapping does not prevent misregistration, it hides it.

The example in Figure 10-72 shows a zone of trap that is very large. Under normal circumstances, offset press trapping tolerances are in measurements that are small. .003 inches is a representative trapping measurement, although other kinds of printing—flexographic printing is one example—sometimes use trapping tolerances with measurements as high as 5 points!

Trapping involves spreading areas of light color into areas of darker color. Photoshop's Trap command—at the bottom of the Image menu—does its job by ranking the relative lightness of the pure inks and then modifying its ranking as the inks appear in decreasing percentages. Although it is not easy to see in Figure 10-72, the area of yellow has spread outward and inward into the areas of the other three colors. The cyan and magenta areas have moved toward each other since they are close to the same lightness. (Traditionally, cyan has been considered the second-darkest ink, after black. In digital terms, magenta's brightness factor is 15% darker than cyan's.)

Despite its ability to automatically trap an image, Photoshop's Trap command is only used under certain circumstances. A normal photographic image does not usually have areas of one color adjoining an area of a different color. Colors in a photograph are usually so dispersed that trapping is not only *not* required, but injurious to the quality of the image.

Trapping Part of a Photographic Image

In rare instances, trapping might be needed within a photographic image. For example, red type might have been placed upon a blue sky (Figure 10-73). With such a case, the needed trapping should be applied only where the type meets the sky and not to the entire image. This can be done in a couple of ways.

Figure 10-73: When an image has been modified with text or extra information, trapping is required—but only where the letters meet the photo.

To use the first method to apply needed trapping when the type is on a separate layer:

1. Press Command+click or Ctrl+click the layer's thumbnail to make the type into a selection.
2. Next, with the Eyedropper tool, sample a representative blue from the sky (the blue is a lighter color than the red of the type).

3. Choose Edit | Stroke. Set the width of the stroke to be the width of the needed trap.
4. Choose the Inside option, Foreground Color, and Multiply mode (Figure 10-74). The applied stroke is shown in magnified view in Figure 10-75.

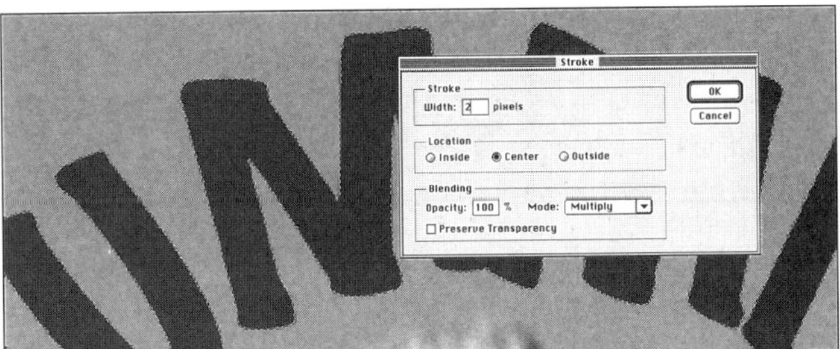

Figure 10-74: Select the letters. Choose Edit | Stroke. Stroke the letters inside their boundaries in Multiply mode with the sky color.

Figure 10-75: Enlarged detail of the trapped letters. The rest of the image is not touched.

Another method to apply needed trapping for type that is *not* on a separate layer:

1. Use the Lasso tool to make a selection of the type and the sky tones surrounding the type. Use the Copy command, and leave the selection active.
2. Choose File | New, and click OK. Paste the selection into the new window (Figure 10-76).
3. Before continuing, Command+click or Ctrl+click the thumbnail of the pasted layer to select the pixels on the layer.
4. Click on the Save Selection icon at the bottom of the Channels palette. These two actions allow you to select the pixels after you have run the Trap command (which only operates on a flattened image).
5. Execute the Trap command on the new window (you are then prompted to flatten the image: click on the Flatten button).
6. Command+click or Ctrl+click Channel #5 to select the pasted part of the window. Copy and then change back to the original window. The selection you made should still be active.

Figure 10-76: Select the letters, paste them into a new document, trap the new document, then paste the letters back into the original image.

7. Paste into this window. Photoshop accurately aligns your pasted pixels by centering them in the selection.
8. Note that you have a fringing of white pixels on the edges of your new layer's edges. To eliminate the white pixels, choose Layer | Matting | Remove White Matte. Flatten the image.

Proportional Color Reduction Trapping

Although Adobe Illustrator and Macromedia FreeHand contain the tools to construct accurate and complete traps, these are sometimes very advanced constructions. Photoshop's Trap command is an ideal solution to the problem of traps in vector artwork. As you saw in Figure 10-72, the trapping is accomplished by spreading the areas of color into each other. The unavoidable consequence of this is a visible border of color which is darker than each of the adjoining color areas. The zone of trap is usually very narrow, and so is not immediately noticeable. However, it is clearly visible.

One solution to this visible border is to decrease the ink percentages in the trap zone. With the decrease in ink, the tone becomes lighter and much less noticeable. Pure magenta trapping to pure cyan, for example, produces a dark blue. If the area of overlap were to contain 50% of each color, there would still be sufficient ink for trapping but the combination would produce a tone similar in intensity to the adjoining colors. Visually, decreasing the amount of ink in the zone of trap causes the trap to almost vanish. Many trapping software packages contain the means to control the inks in the areas of trap. Photoshop, however, does not. The Trap command simply spreads the existing colors, and you get what you get.

There is a method you can use if you wish to decrease the amount of ink in the areas of trap. It is very simple—if a bit involved—and produces perfect results. Follow this procedure:

1. Begin by making two duplicates of the file to be trapped. Arrange the three windows (the original file and the two copies) on the screen—along with the Layers palette—as shown in Figure 10-77.
2. Execute the Trap command on the first—lower left—of the duplicate windows (Figure 10-78).

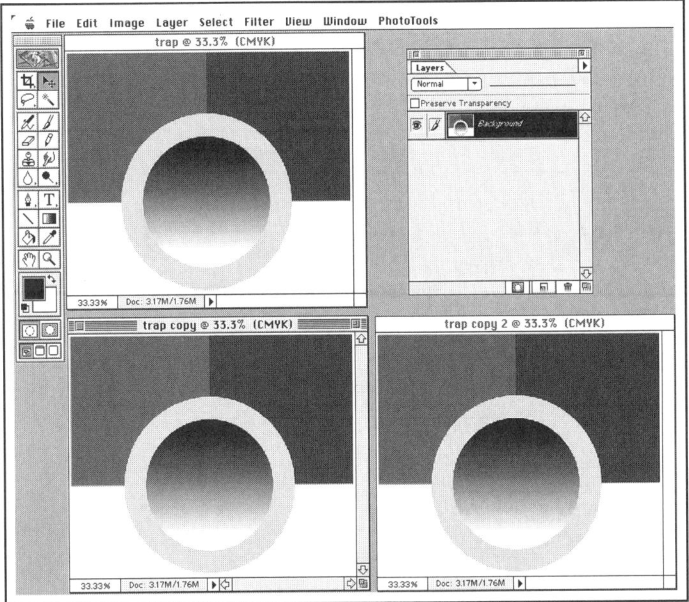

Figure 10-77: Make two copies of the document to be trapped. Arrange them onscreen so that you can see all three.

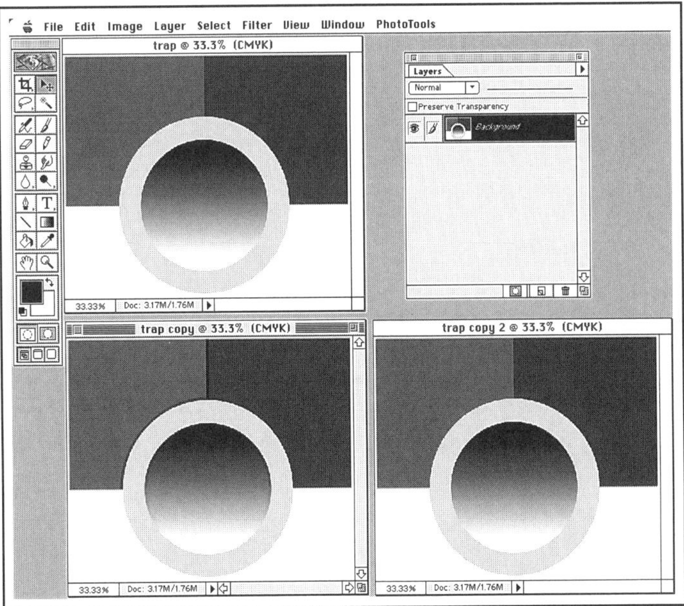

Figure 10-78: Execute the trap command on the first duplicate (lower left).

3. Select All, and Copy. Paste into the second—lower right—duplicate window. Pasting forms a new layer. Set the mode of this layer to Difference. The window, as shown in Figure 10-79, turns black. Don't be concerned. The dark window is only temporary.

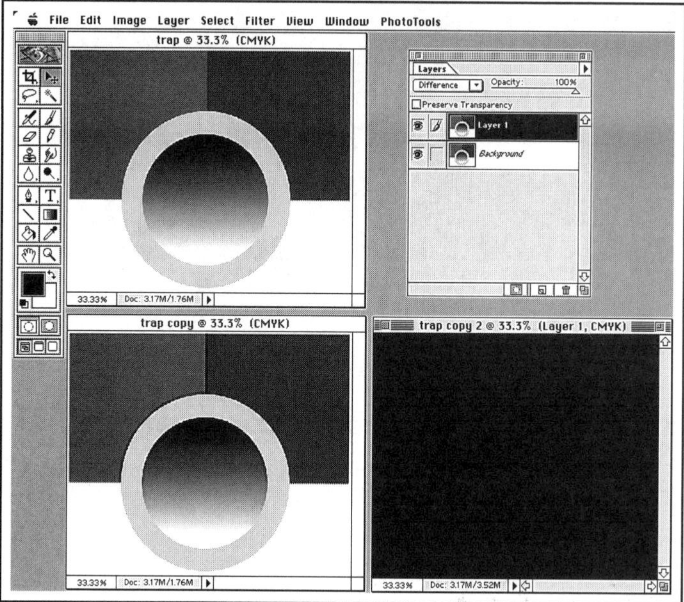

Figure 10-79: Select the first duplicate, copy, and paste into the second duplicate window (lower right). Change the pasted layer's mode to Difference.

4. Flatten the lower right-hand window and use the Invert command (Command+i or Ctrl+i). You will now see just the trap on a white background (Figure 10-80). Select All, and Copy.
5. Click on the original window—upper left—to make it active, and paste. Change the mode of the new layer to Darken, and change the opacity of the layer to a percentage which decreases the visibility of the trap. In the example shown in Figure 10-81, the Opacity is 30%. As the enlarged details of the two windows on the left clearly show, the visual impact of the trapping has been minimized. When you have finished with the layer, flatten the image and discard the two duplicate windows.

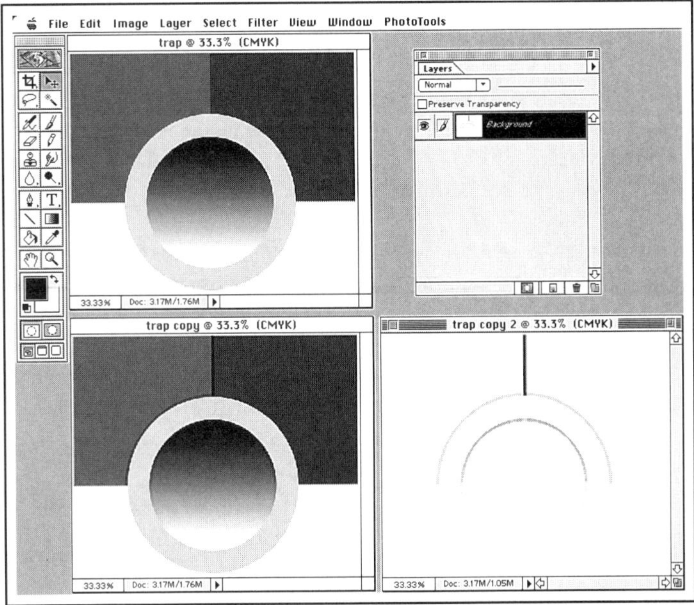

Figure 10-80: Flatten the lower right window, invert the image, select it, and copy.

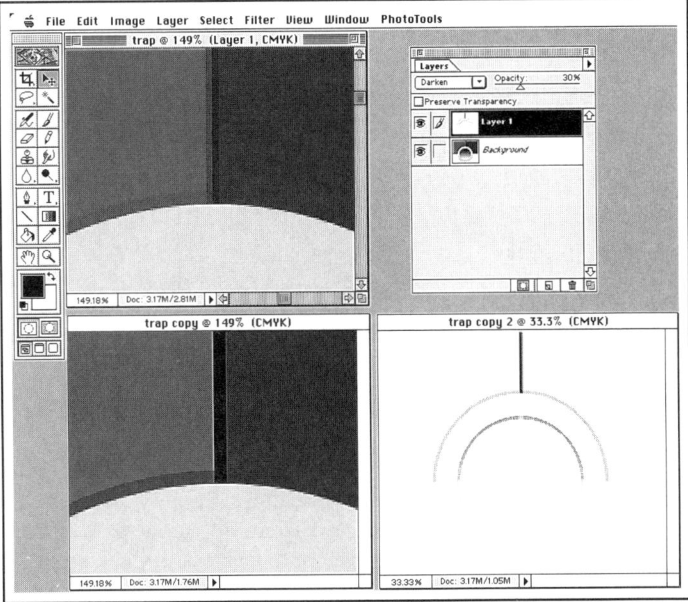

Figure 10-81: Paste into the top window. Change the mode to Darken, and change the Opacity to 30%–40%. Flatten the image and discard the two duplicate windows. The image is now trapped but the trap is much less visible.

Trapping With Clipping Paths

Programs such as QuarkXPress and Adobe PageMaker can handle the trapping of objects and colors created within themselves, but are not able to trap objects created in other programs except in the most rudimentary way. One example occurs when a photo bounded by a clipping path is placed upon another color built in XPress or PageMaker. If trapping is needed for the clipped photo object, manual intervention in Photoshop will be required.

Trapping is not always required when a clipping path photo is placed on a built color. There is often enough commonality of inks that trapping is unnecessary. In some circumstances, however, there is no common color. The picture shown in Figure 10-56, for example, is of a flower in red and gold tones placed atop a background color of 40% black. There is some black ink in the flower photo, but not enough to furnish an adequate trap. Instructions for trapping in this situation are as follows:

1. Figure 10-82 shows an enlarged view of the flower edge and the path. To trap this path to the 40% black on which it will eventually be placed, choose a brush that is two pixels more than twice the width of the needed trap. If your trap is .003 inches, make the brush 4 pixels wide. The trap width at .003 inches would be one pixel. Double that would be two pixels. Two more pixels gives four—the two extra pixels are anti-aliasing pixels which will make the trap fade into the image.

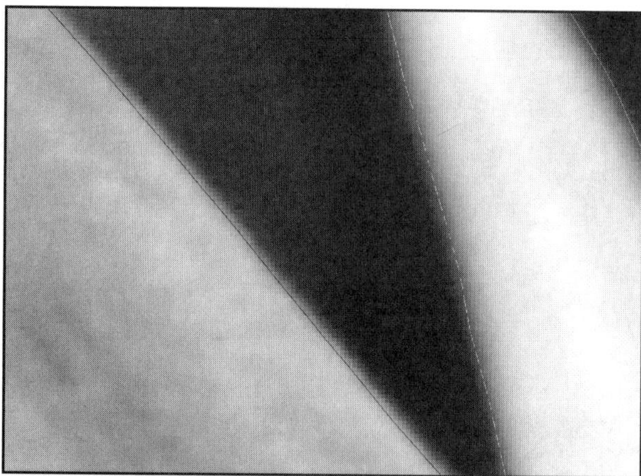

Figure 10-82: Enlarged view of the edge of the object to be trapped with the masking path.

2. Set Foreground color to the color on which the clipped photo is to be placed—in this case, 40% black. Set the Paintbrush's blending mode to Multiply. Multiply mode, in this circumstance, is equivalent to Overprint. Click on the thumbnail of the clipping path on the Paths palette to select it. Click on the Stroke icon—second from left—at the bottom of the Paths palette. Figure 10-83 shows the appearance of the path after it has been stroked. Don't be alarmed by the width

of the dark line: remember that only the part of the stroke within the path will be seen when the photo is clipped. The outer part of the stroke will be invisible.

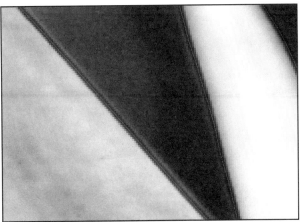

Figure 10-83: Stroke the path with a Paintbrush a little more than twice the width of the needed trap. The Paintbrush paints with the trapping color and in Multiply mode. Only the part of the stroke inside the mask will be visible.

When the image has been placed in the page layout software, the darkened edges of the trap will probably show up slightly around the edges of the path (Figure 10-84). If you wish, you can improve this trap method by making the color of the stroke lighter than the color on which the placed file will sit. For example, the color in this case could have been 20% black, which would have resulted in a 50% reduction of the color in the zone of trap. Alternately, you could change the opacity of the brush before applying the stroke.

Figure 10-84: The trap for the masked object shows up when the file is reimported into the page layout software. The trap percentage can be decreased to make it less visible.

Another case where a clipped file would need to be trapped is when it is placed upon an area of a custom color. Since there is no custom color within the Photoshop file, trapping this clipped file requires an additional program—Adobe Illustrator—and a little more care with the details. Follow these instructions:

1. Open the file in Photoshop. Figure 10-85 shows the image with the oval-shaped clipping path.
2. From the File menu, choose Export | Paths to Illustrator (Figure 10-86). From the Write pop-up menu on the dialog box, select the designated clipping path. Save the Illustrator file. Save the Photoshop file in Photoshop EPS format (DCS off) with the clipping path.

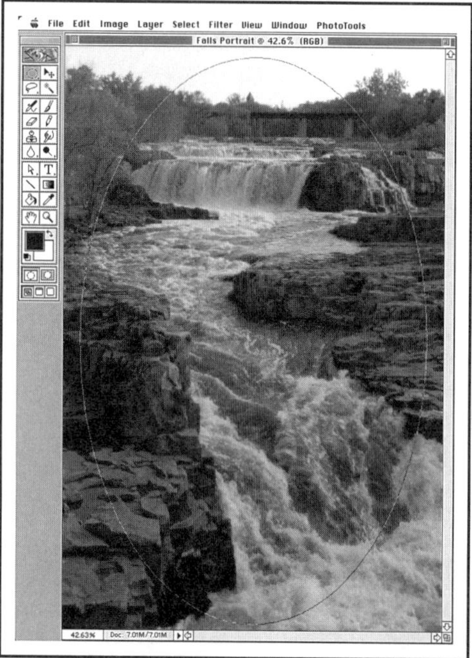

Figure 10-85: Photo with oval-shaped clipping path.

Figure 10-86: Export the clipping path to Illustrator format. Save the Photoshop file in EPS format with DCS off.

3. Open the exported paths file in Illustrator. The window appears as shown in Figure 10-87. Click on the path to select it. Apply a stroke to the path using the custom color on which the clipped file will eventually be placed. Make the width of the stroke twice the width of the needed trap. For example, if your trap needs to be .22 points, make the stroke width .44 points. Be sure to check the Overprint option for the stroke. Overprint is the option that chokes the photo file with the custom color.

4. From the Objects menu, select Cropmarks | Release. Your cropmarks will change to a rectangle. Select the oval and the rectangle and apply the Group command (Figure 10-88).

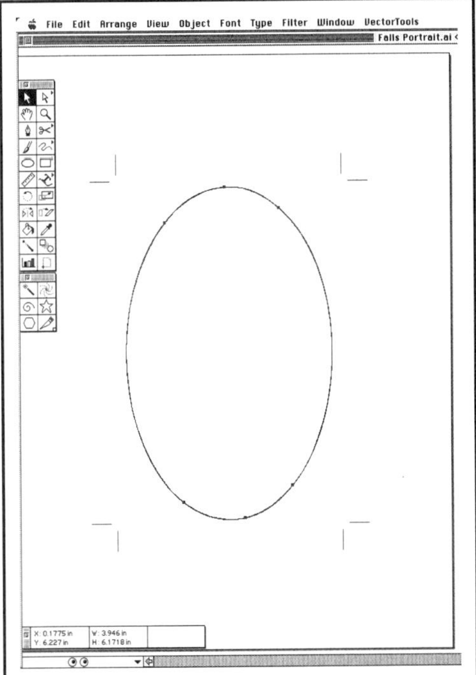

Figure 10-87: Open the exported path file in Illustrator. Stroke the path with the trapping color set to Overprint.

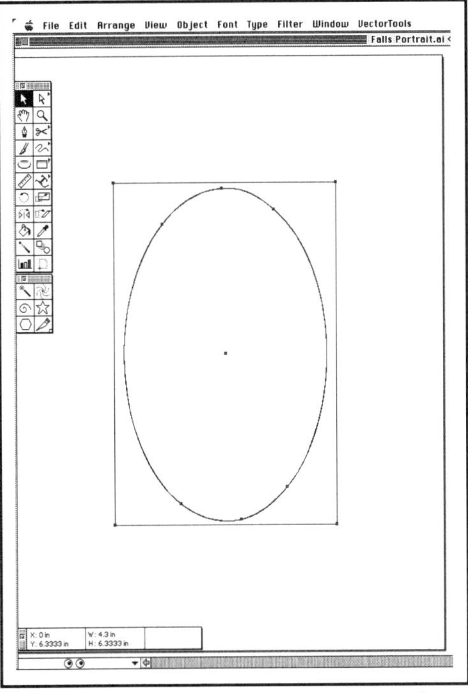

Figure 10-88: Release the cropmarks, select All, and Group.

5. From the File menu, choose the Place command. Locate the Photoshop file and place it in the Illustrator window. While the placed photo is still selected, apply the Send to Back command. Select All. Use the Align palette to perfectly align the photo file and the two grouped paths: click on the center icon of the top row and the second row (Figure 10-89).

6. Save the file as an Illustrator EPS file. If you wish to embed the Photoshop file in the Illustrator document, check the option to Include Placed EPS Files (Figure 10-90). In your page layout software, import the Illustrator EPS file rather than the clipped Photoshop file.

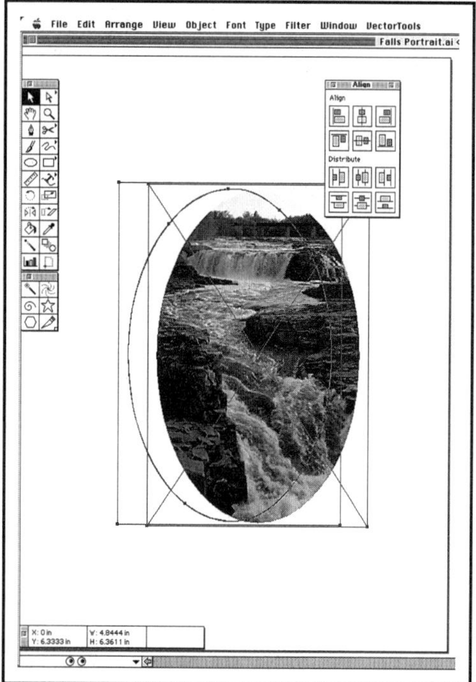

Figure 10-89: Place the Photoshop EPS file. Send it to the back. Select All, and use Illustrator's Align palette to line up the path group and the image.

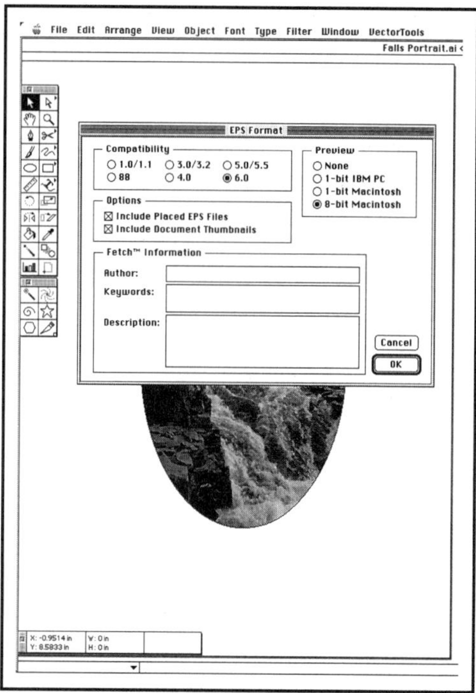

Figure 10-90: Save the placed image and the paths as an Illustrator EPS file. Import this file into the page layout software. It is trapped and ready to go.

It's important to remember that if you wish to apply a proportional color reduction to this trap, decrease the percentage of the custom color stroke in Illustrator. Instead of assigning 100% of the custom color, for example, you could use 50%. The clipped object would still be trapped but without the visual intrusion of the solid custom color over-printing the photo.

Ultra High-Fidelity Offset Color Reproduction

In the life of every designer and prepress technician lies a sigh, "If only process inks could reproduce the vivid colors I would like to use...."

Until recently, the only way to boost a color to the vivid tints required for some images was to apply a touch plate to the image. This is certainly a successful strategy when improving a specific set of tones. However, a single-color touch plate does not improve where it does not print.

In the past several years, prepress technology has evolved a number of techniques which dramatically increase the number of tones a press can reproduce. One of these is a CMYK-CMY printing procedure. By first printing the CMY inks—with black—only in areas of solid coverage and then overprinting the solids with additional ink when the tints are added, the increase in saturation brings greater fidelity of detail, an increase in the number of colors which can be represented, and dodges the problem of additional screen angles. Experimentation with this technique could probably be done successfully as a manual technique within Photoshop (please see the section of Chapter 9, "Photoshop Prepress," which discusses the development of touch plates).

Another high-fidelity color technology—and the one which seems to have demonstrated the most spectacular successes—is that of the Hexachrome process developed by Pantone, Inc. *Hexachrome* is just what the name implies, six ink colors. Pantone has developed a set of Hexachrome process inks—a CMYK group which contains specially enhanced colors—to which are added Pantone Hexachrome Orange and Pantone Hexachrome Green. When RGB files are separated into files containing information for these six inks, the resulting press colors have to be seen to be believed. Hexachrome, according to Pantone, can achieve in print almost everything that can be displayed on a high-quality, 24-bit computer monitor. Hexachrome's color range is, in fact, larger than the RGB range, although the RGB color space and Hexachrome's are not entirely contiguous.

Hexachrome separations can be generated from Adobe PageMaker and from Quark Xpress 4.0. However, the PageMaker controls suffer some limitations. A more robust approach to Hexachrome separations—at least for photographic material—is through HexWrench by Studion Soft Industries, Ltd., a plug-in for Adobe Photoshop.

The HexWrench interface dialog box is shown in Figure 10-91. Some of the features contained within this deceptively simple dialog box are:

- Controls for loading ICC/ColorSync profiles for scanners and monitors.
- Input for special Hexachrome output profiles.
- A soft-proof window with various split-screen configurations for easy before-and-after viewing of the image.
- Options for creating color separations using either traditional or stochastic screens.
- An option for exporting DCS 2.0 files.

Screen angles are one of the first concerns when using more than four inks. In Hexachrome printing, cyan and orange share the same screen angle as do magenta and green. This is logical since tones which contain one of the pairs could probably be built up without needing the other. In this way, there is no problem with two inks on the same angle printing the same area.

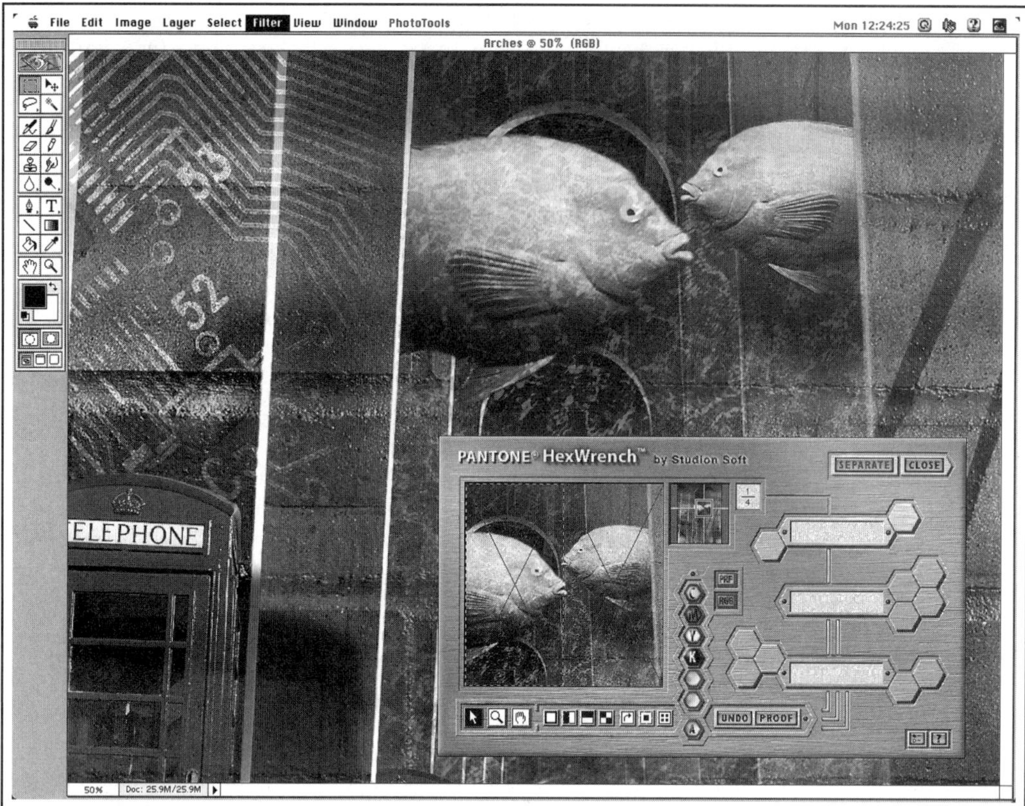

Figure 10-91: The HexWrench options dialog box.

Other technical problems are obvious. Six integrated inks used to generate a cohesive color image require much more attention to accurate measurements of the ink characteristics as well as to each ink's amount of gain. Press technicians who have grown up in an older technology also have to make substantial adjustments in the thought processes which have guided them for so long. Given the rewards of the final printed matter, the technical challenges of Hexachrome seem well worth the trouble.

For more information on Hexachrome and HexWrench, you can visit the Pantone, Inc. Web site at http://www.pantone.com.

Moving On

Besides specialized ways of using Photoshop for tasks such as masking and trapping, this chapter has explored many of the technical issues that lead to proficient use of color in offset printing. You have learned about the ways needed to configure your computer system so that your output provides you with the high-quality color press work you desire. You have learned about the difficulties inherent in color management systems and what you can do to ensure that your color work is as accurate as possible. Despite the fact that color and calibration are complex topics when they relate to printing, none of this vast technology is beyond the understanding of a proficient Photoshop user. Photoshop will assist you, making your prepress tasks easier and more accurate. With thought, care, and patience, you'll gain the expertise you need in a much shorter time than you thought possible. The results will be well-prepared color for professional-looking printing.

Now that you have looked at the mechanics of adjusting an image for the press, it's time to go on and explore some of the really sophisticated controls for correcting and adjusting the contents of a scan. Manipulating Images, the title of the following chapter, will take you through some of the valuable ideas that lie behind Adjustment Layers and will show you some other possibilities for taming and changing the data in your files.

chapter 11
Manipulating Images

Photoshop is a very powerful image editing program. While darkroom techniques have always been capable of creating images that did not really exist, Photoshop has made changing reality into an art form. Figure 11-1a shows a raw image taken in rough surf from the Boardwalk (you can see the railing in the image). Where was Figure 11-1b taken? (Answer: it is the same picture, quickly edited to remove the rail.) If you remember the controversies that occurred over *National Geographic* magazine moving the pyramids to make the cover look better, or the issue of the overly dark photo of O. J. Simpson on the cover of one of the national news magazines, you can see that manipulating images is also fraught with moral and ethical implications.

We are not going to discuss whether you should make changes to a specific image. We'll leave those issues up to your conscience on the (we hope) rare occasions when an editing project has the potential for producing unintended consequences. Instead, we are going to focus on showing you how to use some of the new features in Photoshop 4.0 that allow you to manipulate images better, faster, and more accurately. This chapter discusses the new Adjustment layers—a feature that allows you to change your mind about a variety of image corrections, Transformations—layer scaling, skewing, and rotations which allow you to perform multiple transforms at one time so that the image suffers less degradation in quality, and Guides & Grids—which allows you to accurately compose your image. Finally, we will put it all together in several exercises that show you how to use these features in some real assignments.

Figures 11-1(a&b): Images of reality? With Photoshop, you can never be quite sure.

Making Adjustments

In life, we must all make adjustments as the situation requires. Unfortunately, most of the adjustments that we make to accommodate circumstances beyond our control cannot be undone. Once adjusted, so it must remain.

Enter Photoshop's new Adjustment layers—at least some decisions that we make need not be permanent! To be quite serious, however, one of the overriding trends in Photoshop over the last several versions has been the pursuit of ways to keep images editable. Photoshop has steadfastly resisted the urge to provide users with a multiple undo command. The increased amount of memory and hard drive required to hold several levels of undos would immensely complicate and could seriously compromise the speed of editing. In spite of that, one of the major requirements that every user has for Photoshop is that the program gives them the ability to change their minds.

Photoshop's Layers feature has provided you with the ability to change your mind when compositing an image. It's a major time-saver for those occasions when the client says, "Can you move Jim over just a fraction of an inch and put Mary on the other side of him?" Before the Layers in Version 3.0, the artist needed to keep each element and mask that went into the composite in case the client had a last-minute request, and then had to pull apart the entire image and begin again if a major change was requested.

While Layers solved the problem of keeping the image pieces fluid and editable, it did little to help the problem of color and tone corrections—which could also need to be changed as the work progressed. One of the major problems with color and tone corrections is that when an image is acquired, it contains as full a range of continuous tone values as it will ever have. As soon as you begin to take steps to make the image "look better," you really start to lose some of that original image data. The more corrections that you make on the image, the worse the data loss becomes—even if the image itself looks better. The solution is certainly not to stop correcting images—that would be foolish—but, rather, to minimize the amount of data loss that an image suffers by making as many different corrections as possible within one correction step.

Chapter 2, "Acquiring Images," showed you how to acquire images in a way that gives them as much tonal data as possible. In Chapters 9 and 10 ("Photoshop Prepress" and "Calibration & Color Reproduction," respectively) you will see how to color correct images and prepare them for printing. In this chapter, you will discover techniques that you can use to make color and tone corrections with as little permanent degradation as possible. The new Adjustment Layers are definitely one of Version 4.0's best new features.

Editable Color Corrections

Adjustment Layers are layers that are linked to a specific image adjustment such as Levels, Curves, Hue/Saturation. You create the layer in a manner that is similar to the way in which all layers are created, but the options for the Layer are quite different. Whenever you double-click on an Adjustment layer, you can change or modify the color correction that it applies. Let's take a look at the process.

Creating an Adjustment Layer

You can create an Adjustment layer by selecting Layer | New | Adjustment Layer or by clicking on the New Layer icon at the bottom of the Layers palette with the modifier key (Mac: Command, Windows: Ctrl) pressed. You can also select the New Adjustment Layer option on the Layers palette menu as shown in Figure 11-2.

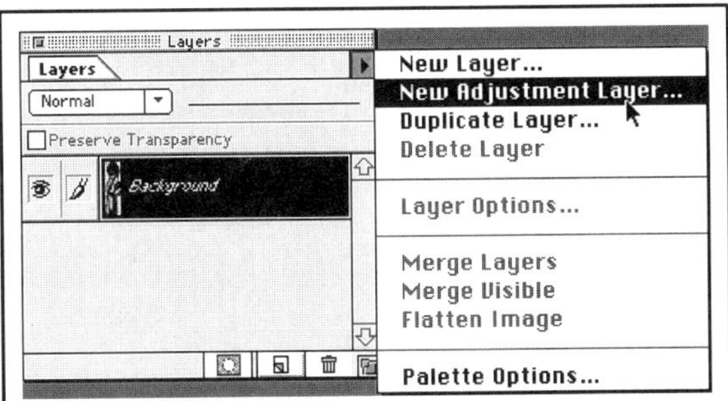

Figure 11-2: Layers palette menu showing the New Adjustment Layer option.

The New Adjustment Layer dialog box then appears, as you can see in Figure 11-3. This allows you to select the type of adjustment that you want to make. Figure 11-4 shows the available Adjustment Layer type options available. You can create any type of correction found on the Image | Adjust menu except for Auto Levels, Desaturate, Selective Color, Equalize, and Variations. Since the other color corrections can produce similar results, these options are really not missed.

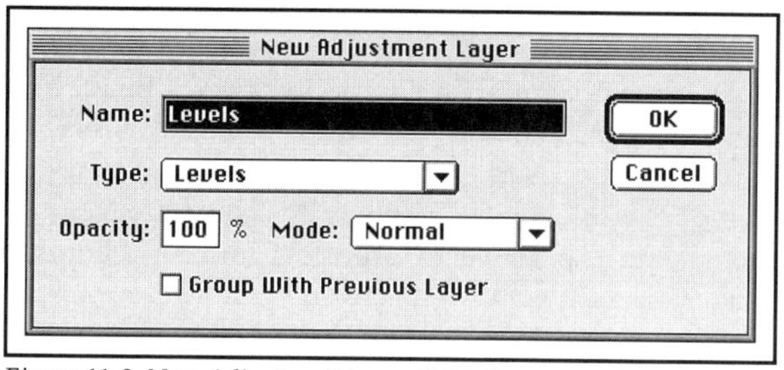

Figure 11-3: New Adjustment Layer dialog box.

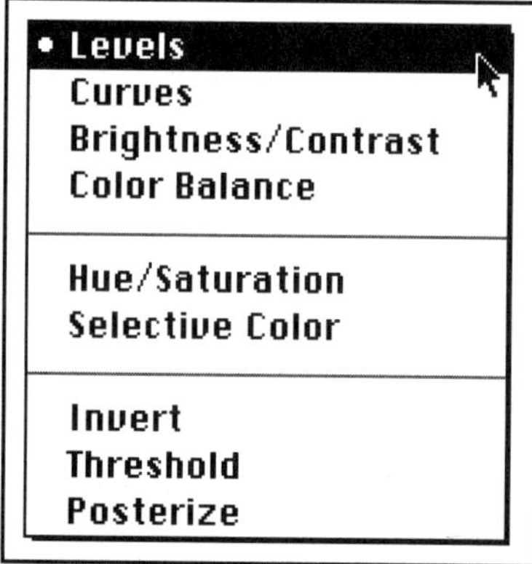

Figure 11-4: Types of Adjustment layers.

After you have selected the type of Adjustment layer that you want, you are presented with the dialog box that normally accompanies that function. For example, if you select a Hue/Saturation layer, you then see the standard Hue/Saturation dialog box. The only time that you won't see a dialog box is if you select an Invert Adjustment layer. This has no dialog box because there are no options for this anyway.

Levels & Curves

The Levels or the Curves Adjustment layers are the ones which you likely to use most often. As you will learn in Chapters 9 and 10 ("Photoshop Prepress" and "Calibration & Color Reproduction," respectively), Levels is always to be preferred over Brightness and Contrast, and Curves is usually more powerful than Levels (although more difficult to use well).

We spoke above of image degradation when the Levels or Curves command is used without an Adjustment layer. What does this image data loss look like and how can you spot it? An even more important question—how can Adjustment layers prevent or minimize the data loss?

Histograms Figure 11-5a shows an image that was deliberately scanned to compress the values so they gather in the center of the histogram (shown in Figure 11-5b). Although this is a terrible scan, notice that the histogram curves upwards on both ends, showing that there are fewer pixels at the outer values than there are as the values get closer to the mid-range.

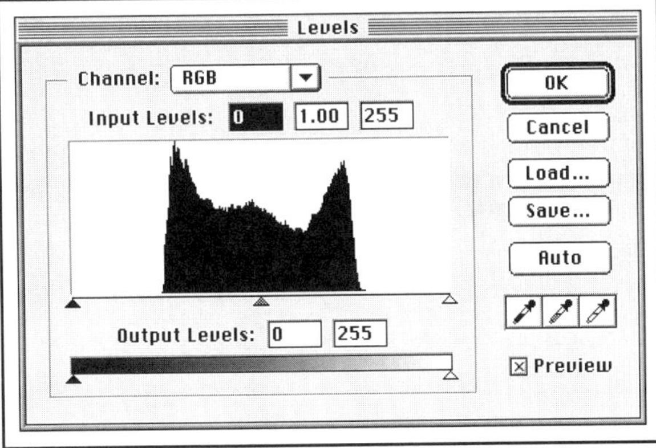

Figures 11-5a & 11-5b: A deliberately grayed scan that compresses the tonal range of the image and its histogram.

Let's see what could happen to this image in the hands of an inexperienced and overly enthusiastic Photoshop experimenter (we know *you'd* never mutilate an image like this!). Here are the changes that this fictional user makes on the image without benefit of Adjustment layers.

1. User sets White point to 191 and the Black point to 69. This chops off some of the range in the image and heightens contrast. Figure 11-6 shows the resulting histogram, which graphically shows that values have been clipped off (the sharp spikes at the white and black points).

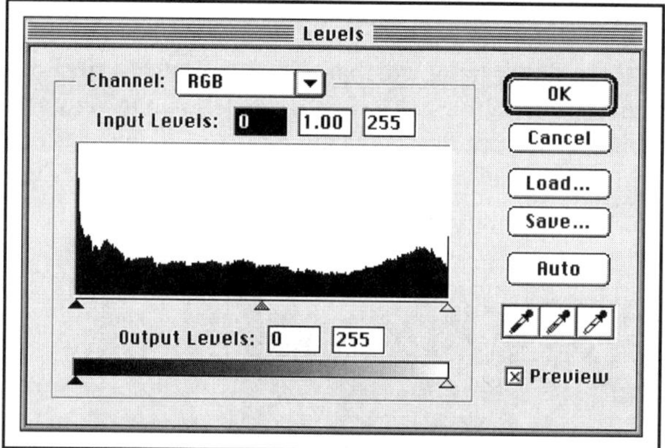

Figure 11-6: Histogram shows sharp spikes at edges of range.

2. Image looks too dark. User changes Gamma to 1.30 and changes the Output Black point to 12 and the Output White point to 237 to force the ends of the image to be less white and black. Figure 11-7a shows the result of these edits and Figure 11-7b shows the final histogram. Notice that the sharp spikes did not disappear at the White and Black points. Even though you do not see any major gaps within the histogram itself, the sharp spikes scream of data loss.

Let's look at this scenario again. This time, the user creates an Adjustment layer. Watch what happens:

1. User sets White point to 191 and the Black point to 69. This chops off some of the range in the image and heightens contrast. Figure 11-8 shows the resulting histogram. Notice that nothing has been recalculated. The original histogram is still there.

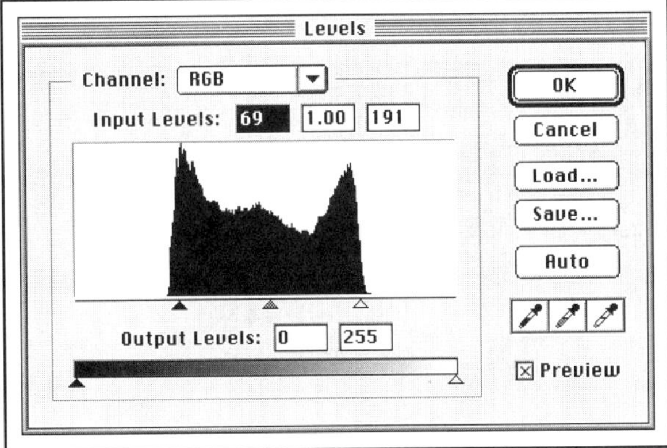

Figure 11-7a & 11-7b: A poorly corrected color image shows significant data loss in the highlights and shadows.

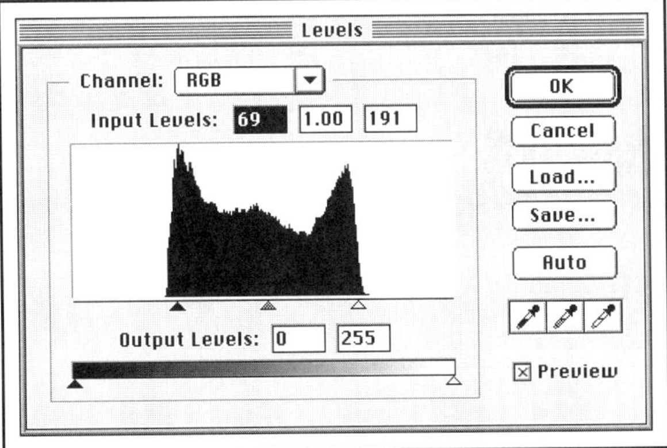

Figure 11-8: Histogram shows new settings but no recalculation when an Adjustment layer is used.

2. When the user realizes that the image is too sharply contrasted and too dark, a simple double-click on the Adjustment layer opens the Levels dialog box again and reveals the original histogram (with the current settings). The user moves the White point to 210 and the Black point to 53. There is no need to move the Output sliders at all, since there will be no true white or black in the image anyway. User also moves the Gamma slider to 1.30. The histogram shape still does not change.

3. User looks at the result and decides that the Gamma change was too much and in the wrong direction. To add contrast, the user changes the Gamma to .95 and then flattens the image to make the changes permanent. Figure 11-9a shows the finished image and Figure 11-9b shows the final histogram. This time, the histogram does not exhibit the spikes at the edges; it softly curves upward from both ends.

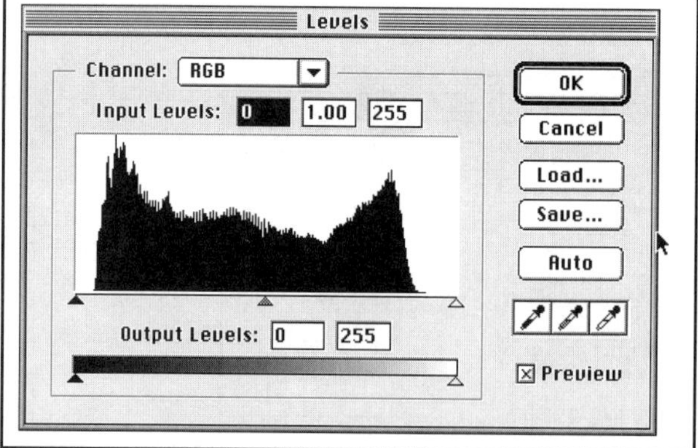

Figure 11-9a & 11-9b: Using an Adjustment layer keeps the histogram healthy and preserves more of the original tonal values.

You should be able to see the difference in the color versions of the images as well. In the mangled image, the dark tones near the top of the image look posterized and the detail in the highlights on the seabird are not there. Compare this to Figure 11-10a, which shows the original image correctly scanned to begin with, and Figure 11-10b, which shows the histogram. Both the good scan (SEABIRD.PSD and the grayed scan SEABIRD2.PSD are on the Companion CD-ROM so that you can experiment with them.)

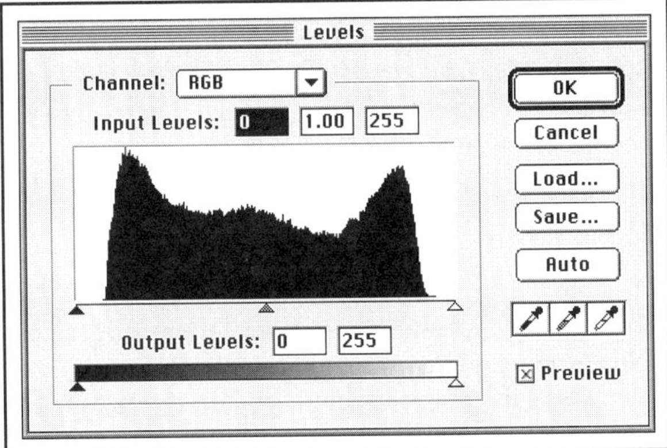

Figure 11-10a & 11-10b: Seabird image and histogram when it is properly scanned to capture the full range of tonal values at the start.

The Downside of Adjustment Layers Are there any disadvantages to using Adjustment layers? There is no disadvantage in the final result, as you have seen. However, one of our favorite color correction "tricks" is missing when you use an Adjustment layer.

In order to correctly set black and white points for printing, it is always helpful to know where the lightest and darkest tones are located in an image. Without Adjustment layers, you can turn off the Preview in the Levels dialog box and see a fast preview that is produced by the video card (so long as Video LUT preference is enabled and your system and video card support it). This fast preview is not as accurate, but it lets you see a "before and after" by clicking on the Move bar at the top of the image window. It also helps you to find the darkest and lightest values in an image quickly. If you press the modifier key (Mac: Option, Windows: Alt) with Preview off and slide the White or Black Input slider toward the center, the screen first turns a solid color and then shows you the location in the image of the values that would be clipped off by the Levels change that you are making (a screen capture of this would be nice, but it's not possible to take a picture of the screen while this is happening).

In any case, when you use an Adjustment layer, you cannot use Video LUT to dynamically preview the screen. The keystrokes do not produce any result. If you turn Preview off, you simply edit with no feedback.

However, the major advantages of using Adjustment layers far outweigh the loss of this dynamic clipping preview. If you need to find your highlights and shadows, use the Levels command on the image without an Adjustment layer and search; then Cancel the dialog without applying the changes. You can then create an Adjustment layer and make whatever corrections you need.

The only other challenge when you use an Adjustment layer is that sometimes you might want to create another layer that depends upon a corrected layer and, with the Adjustment layer on top of it, the effect, or whatever you are trying to do, does not perform as expected. You can either apply the Adjustment layer (Mac: Command+E, Windows: Ctrl+E) or you can test your effect on a layer that contains a combined/merged "view" of your entire image. This is a facility that we frequently use to try out many different effects and yet still keep the image fluid and editable. Create a new layer at the top of the layer stack and merge all of the visible layers into it (Mac: Shift+Command+Option+E, Windows: Shift+Ctrl+Alt+E).

A New Type of Mask Layer

What is actually on the Adjustment layer? Nothing. If you look at the thumbnail in the Layers palette after you create an Adjustment layer, the thumbnail for the Adjustment layer is solid white. What's going on here?

An Adjustment layer works its "magic" behind the scenes; you cannot see the "mystery" that links the layer to a specific Photoshop command. However, you can treat the Adjustment layer as if it were a layer mask and perform any type of action on it that would be permitted on a layer mask. You can paint on it, filter it, place another image inside of it, invert it, and so forth. The values that you write to the Adjustment layer then act like a layer mask to either apply, partially apply, or remove the adjustment from the layers that are lower in the layer stack. You can create some amazing effects this way, as well as selectively applying the correction to the layer below.

It is not quite as obvious on the Adjustment layer as to how you can view the mask rather than the actual image. However, if you Option+Click (Mac) or Alt+Click (Windows) on the thumbnail of the Adjustment layer, you can view and edit the image on the Adjustment layer mask directly.

Object Masking

The simplest type of masking change to make in an Adjustment layer is to add a black area to protect certain sections of your underlying image from change. There are several ways in which you can create this black area.

Figure 11-11 shows the image of a very confused finch who is trying to figure out why a vibrantly colored lovebird from the Amazon is occupying her favorite feeder (and not sharing). The finch, the lost love bird, and the feeder do not need to be corrected, but the background is too dark to print properly. Therefore, a selection was made that excluded finch, lovebird, and feeder. As you can see in Figure 11-12, Photoshop automatically respected the selection when an Adjustment layer was created. To soften the area between selected and unselected, you can feather your selection before you create the Adjustment layer.

Figure 11-11: Confusion at the feeder—creating a mask for an Adjustment layer.

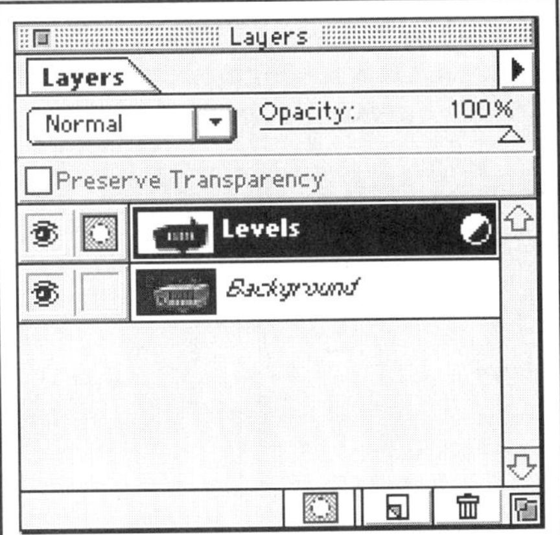

Figure 11-12: The Layers palette showing the thumbnail of the Adjustment layer that now contains a masked area.

You can also create a masked area on the image directly by painting onto the Adjustment layer. Try this:

1. Open the image CONFUSED.PSD on the Companion CD-ROM.
2. Load channel 4 (Mac: Option-Command-4, Windows: Alt-Ctrl-4). This selects the feeder and the finch.
3. Choose Select | Feather; Amount: 2. Reverse the selection (Select -> Inverse).
4. Create a new Adjustment layer by pressing the modifier key (Mac: Command, Windows: Ctrl) and clicking on the New Layer icon at the bottom of the Layers palette. Make it a Levels adjustment. Move the Gamma slider to 1.16 as shown in Figure 11-13.

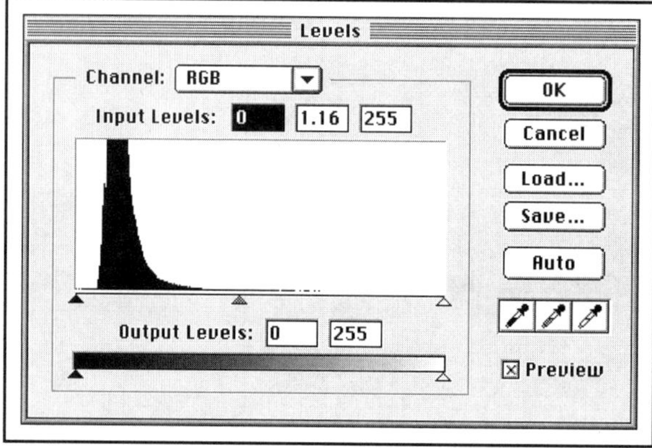

Figure 11-13: Gamma slider adjustment.

5. Create another Adjustment layer. This time, select a Hue/Saturation adjustment. Turn the Saturation up all the way as shown in Figure 11-14. Yes, it looks awful, but it won't be left like this! Click OK to exit the dialog box.

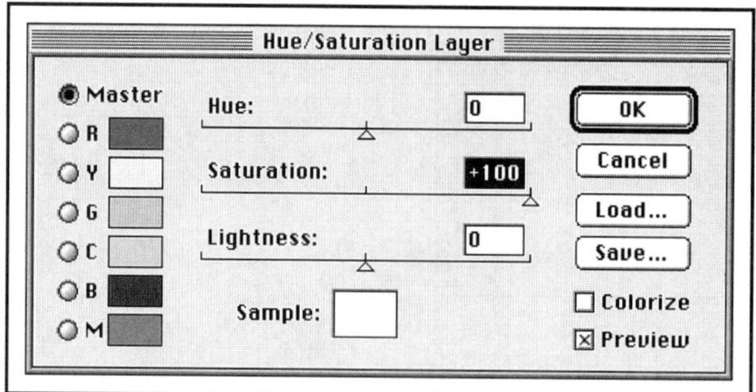

Figure 11-14: Saturation raised temporarily to maximum.

6. Press D to set the colors back to the default of black and white.
7. Fill the Adjustment layer with black (Mac: Option-Delete, Windows: Alt-Delete). This removes the correction completely.
8. Exchange the Foreground and Background colors (X). Using white, paint over the lovebird. If you make a mistake and paint too much, press X again and paint over the area with black. The nice part of Adjustment layers (and layers masks) is that they are infinitely editable.
9. Select View | Gamut Warning. Double-click on the Hue/Saturation Adjustment layer to open it. Drag the Saturation slider to the left until the Gamut warning shows that you have reached mostly printable colors (this is about +30 as you can see in Figure 11-15). At this point, only the beak is out-of-gamut as you can see in the close-up in Figure 11-16.

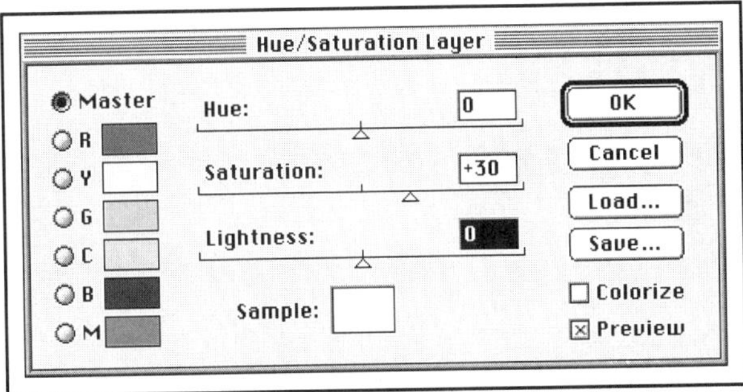

Figure 11-15: Hue/Saturation dialog box with saturation set to +30.

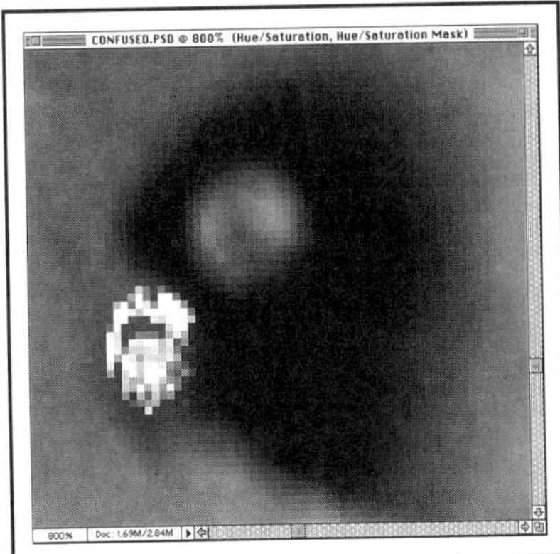

Figure 11-16: Gamut warning showing beak out-of-gamut.

10. Paint over the lovebird's beak on the Adjustment layer with black (to remove it from the selection).
11. Repeat Steps 5–10. This time, adjust only the lovebird's beak (the rest of the Adjustment should be black). This way, you can get the brightest possible colors for both the bird and his beak. At about +20, the out-of-gamut colors become acceptable (and hard to see). Figure 11-17 shows the out-of-gamut colors still present in the beak, and Figure 11-18 shows the adjusted image.

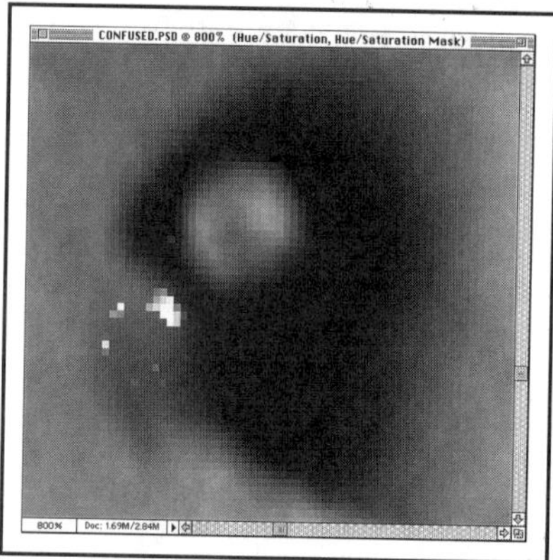

Figure 11-17: A few out-of-gamut colors remain.

Figure 11-18: Adjusted image.

Using the same general idea of black and white masking, you could also easily preview an infinite number of color combinations for a two-color pattern such as stripes. Try this—but you might find yourself playing with it for a long time!

1. Open the image CIRCPAT.PSD from the Companion CD-ROM. This pattern was developed from images in the Ultimate Symbol Design Elements collection (you have samples of these on the Companion CD-ROM). Figure 11-19 shows the pattern tile.

Figure 11-19: Pattern tile to use as mask on Adjustment layer.

2. Select the entire image (Mac: Command-A, Windows: Ctrl-A). Define this as a pattern (Edit ->Define Pattern).
3. Open a new image 600-pixels square.
4. Change your Foreground color to RGB 128, 128,128. Fill the image (Mac: Option-Delete, Windows: Alt-Delete).
5. Create an Adjustment Layer (Mac: Command-click, Windows: Ctrl-click on the New Layer icon at the bottom of the Layers palette). Choose a Hue/Saturation adjustment. Do not make any changes to the dialog box. Click OK.
6. Fill the Adjustment layer with the pattern (Shift-Delete -> Pattern, 100 percent Opacity, Normal). You won't see any change from the solid gray image that you originally had.
7. Double-click on the Adjustment layer to re-open the dialog box. Click the Colorize button and set the Hue to –131 and the Saturation to 69 as shown in Figure 11-20.

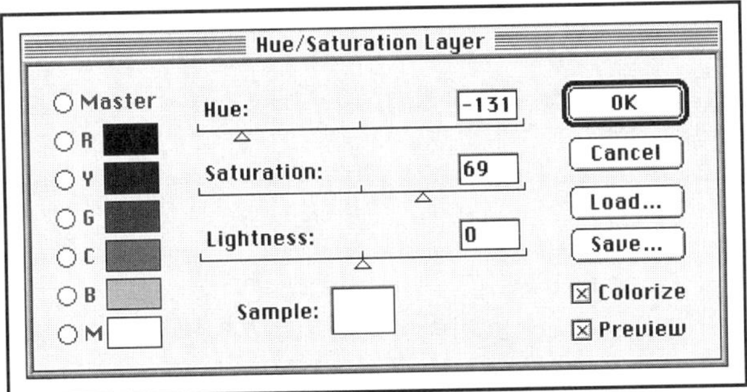

Figure 11-20: Hue and Saturation set to change pattern background to a royal blue.

8. Drag the Adjustment layer to the New Layer icon at the bottom of the Layers palette to duplicate the Adjustment layer. Invert the values of the Adjustment layer (Mac: Command+I, Windows: Ctrl+I). The image looks solid blue.
9. Double-click on the top Adjustment layer and change the settings. Figure 11-21 shows one possibility—which changes the Foreground to a light coral. You can fiddle with the adjustments on either layer as much as you please to find attractive color combinations. Figure 11-22 shows you several possibilities (in grayscale here and in color in the Color pages).

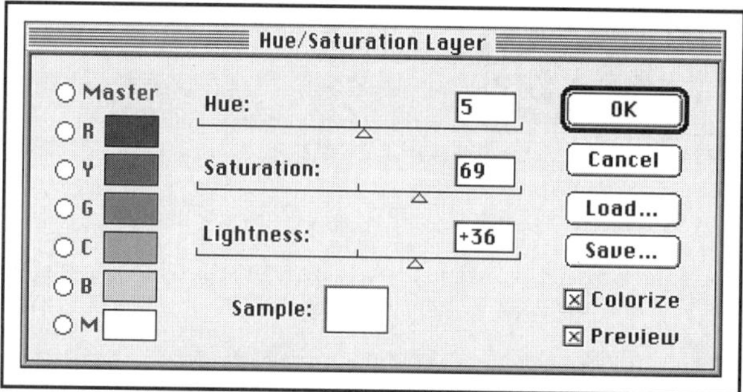

Figure 11-21: Possible settings for the pattern foreground.

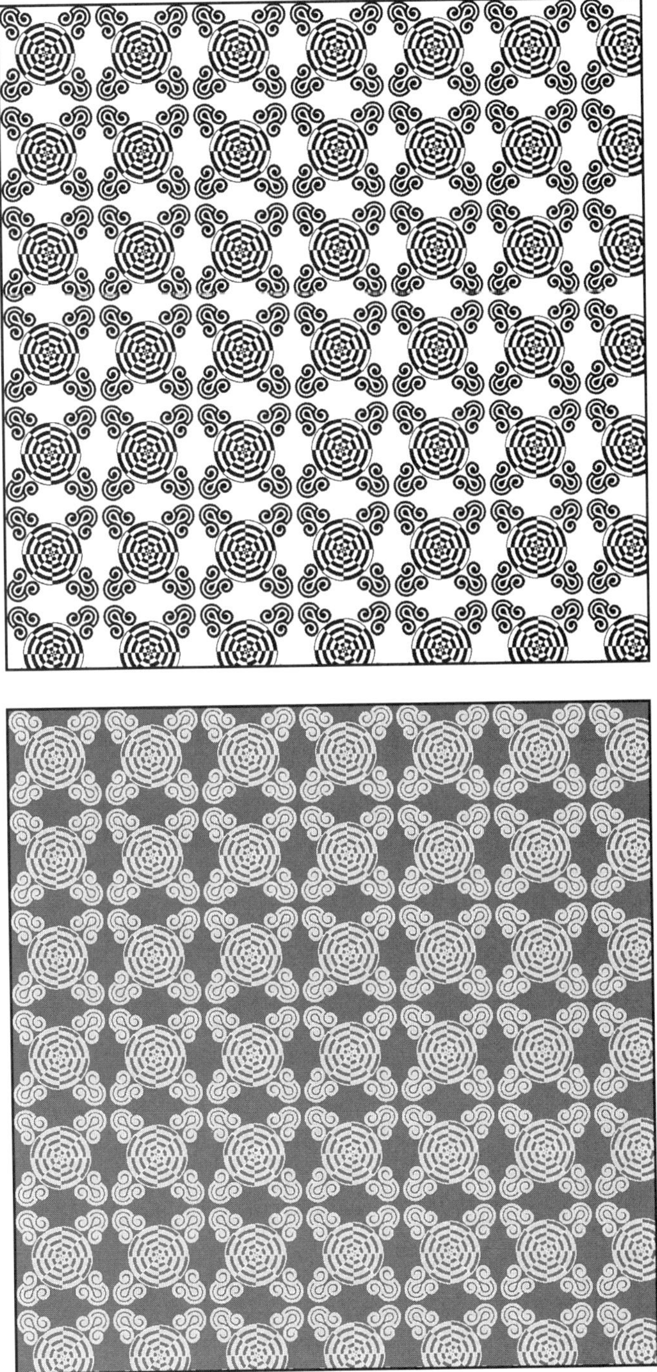

Figure 11-22: Some color combinations for the pattern, all achieved in the Adjustment layers of the image.

Density Masking

You can also place grayscale data into the Adjustment layer. Just as a layer mask can hold 256 values of gray, so can an Adjustment layer. In this next example, you can use a second image in the Adjustment layer to create a very interesting composition. The image of a plane flying though the clouds on a soon-to-be-stormy day is a somewhat moody image. Using an Adjustment layer, you can enhance that brooding quality and create a surreal image.

1. Open the image SKYPLANE.PSD on the Companion CD-ROM. Figure 11-23 shows the original image.

Figure 11-23: Small plane flying through the clouds.

2. Create a Levels Adjustment Layer (Mac: Command-click, Windows: Ctrl-click on the New Layer icon at the bottom of the Layers palette). Set the levels to the values shown in Figure 11-24. This Levels adjustment intensifies the clouds.

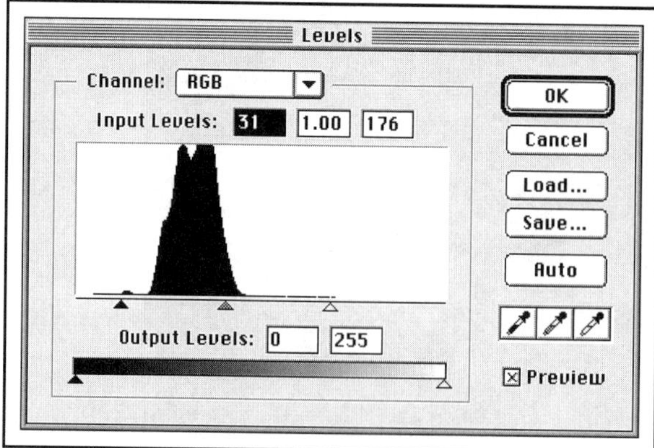

Figure 11-24: Levels to add contrast to the clouds.

3. Using black as your Foreground color, carefully paint out the airplane and the lamppost (and the bird perched on the lamppost). This protects those features from the Levels change which would make them too dark.
4. Create another Levels Adjustment layer. Do not make any changes to it. Just create and click OK. The Levels histogram shows the effect of the previous Levels adjustment.

5. Open the image MUMS.PSD on the Companion CD-ROM. Figure 11-25 shows the original image.

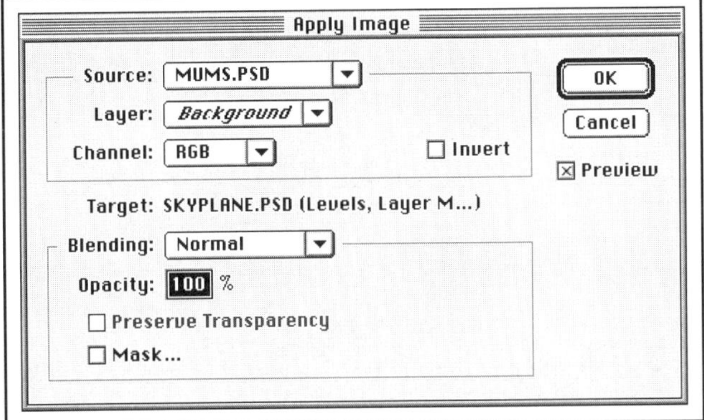

Figure 11-25: MUMS.PSD—image to be used a mask for Adjustment layer.

6. Make the SKYPLANE.PSD image active again. Select Image | Apply Image. Fill in the dialog box as shown in Figure 11-26. This places the MUMS.PSD image into the Adjustment layer mask. Since there is no adjustment yet, you cannot see any change.

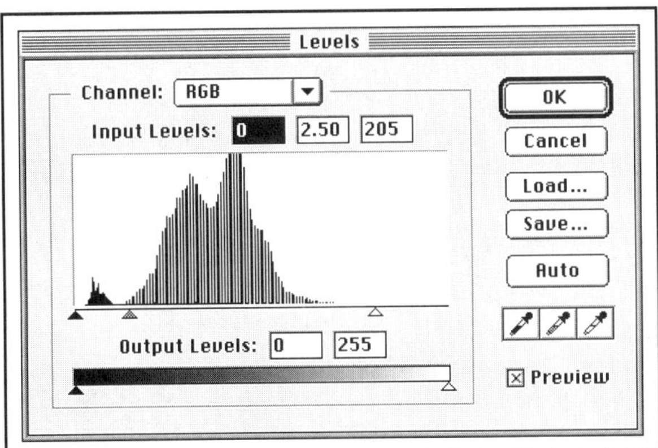

Figure 11-26: Applying the Mums image to the layer mask of the Adjustment layer.

7. Double-click on the top layer (the one with the mums in it). Change the Levels to match Figure 11-27. Figure 11-28 shows the image at this point.

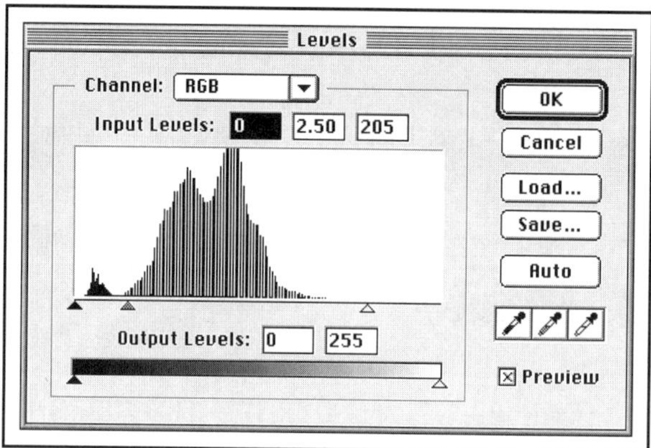

Figure 11-27: Changing the Levels to make the mums show up on the clouds.

Figure 11-28: Image after Mums have been added to the layer mask of the top Adjustment layer.

8. Since an Adjustment layer is simply another form of a layer, you have the ability to change both the layer opacity and the layer Apply mode. Experiment with these controls a bit and see what happens when you try out the various Apply modes.
9. Change the Apply mode to Exclusion (this tends to gray out the image, which is a good effect for this composition). Set the Opacity to 64%.
10. The image is still not quite dark and broody enough. Create a new Levels Adjustment layer. Do not change anything in the Levels dialog box that appears. In the Layers palette, change the layer Apply mode to Multiply. Set the Opacity to 73%. Figure 11-29 shows the Layers palette at this point.

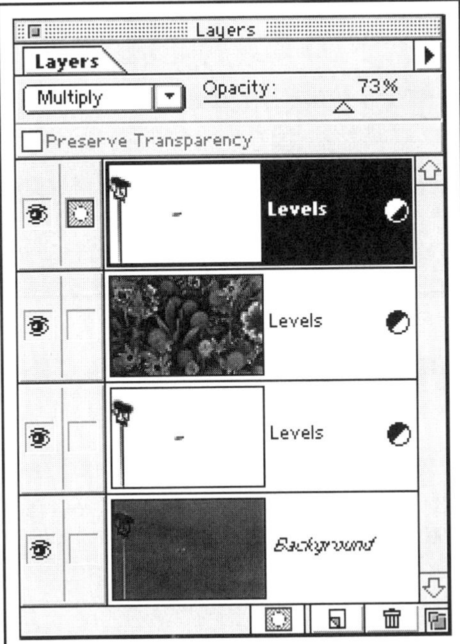

Figure 11-29: Layers palette with multiple Adjustment layers.

11. You need to remove the plane and lamppost from this top Levels Adjustment layer as they are now much too dark. While you could draw them in again, there is an easier way. Choose Image | Apply Image. Select the Levels layer closest to the Background in the list (as shown in Figure 11-30). Set the Channel to Layer Mask as shown in Figure 11-31.

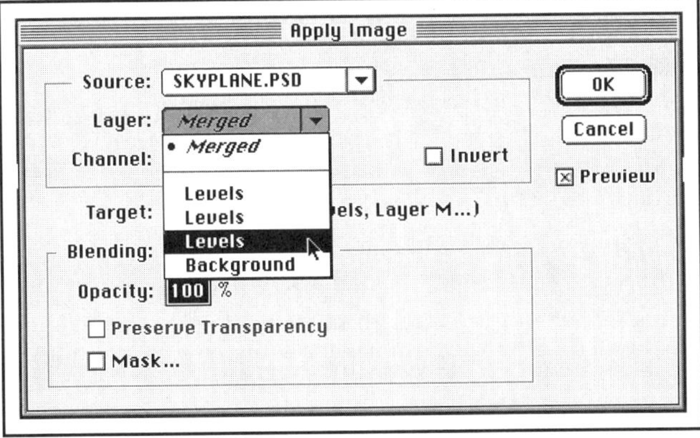

Figure 11-30: Apply Image: selecting the Layer.

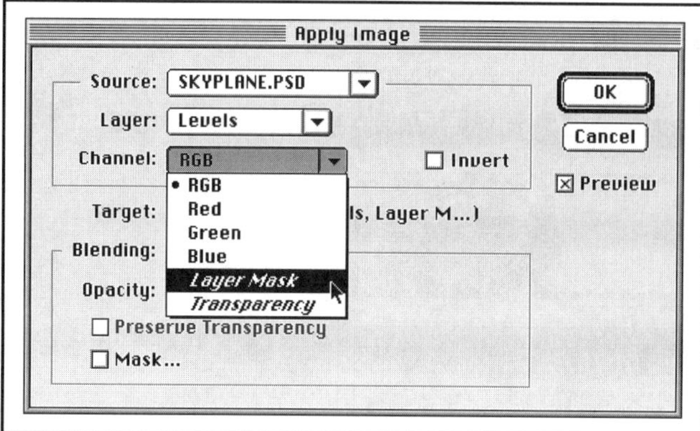

Figure 11-31: Apply Image: selecting the Channel.

12. If you see a glow around the lamppost, it is because you did not paint the original layer mask using a hard brush. If you like the glow, then leave it. You can get rid of the glow by zooming in on the lamppost and editing the top layer with a hard paint brush. Figure 11-32 shows the final image.

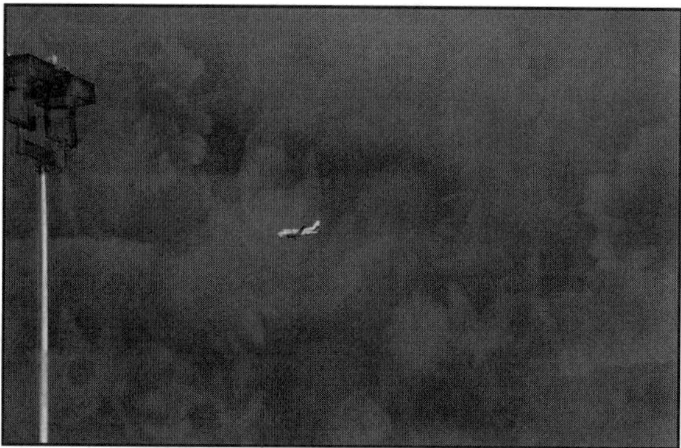

Figure 11-32: Plane flying through brooding sky filled with flowers and clouds.

Creating a Sepiatone

You can use the Adjustment layers and density masking for practical effects as well. It is very difficult to create a good sepiatoned image, but it is a very common production requirement. This technique, which uses an Adjustment layer, keeps the dark areas of the image fully saturated with the selected color while gradually fading out the color in the lighter areas of the image.

1. Open the image ROBERT.PSD from the Companion CD-ROM.

2. Create a Hue/Saturation Adjustment Layer (Mac: Command-click, Windows: Ctrl-click on the New Layer icon at the bottom of the Layers palette). Do not make any changes in the dialog box.
3. Choose Image | Apply Image. Place the Background RGB layer into the Adjustment layer mask as shown in Figure 11-33. Check the Invert button next to the channel in the dialog box. You need to invert the background image because you want to let the adjustment affect only the darker areas of the image. By inverting the background into the mask, you will accomplish this.

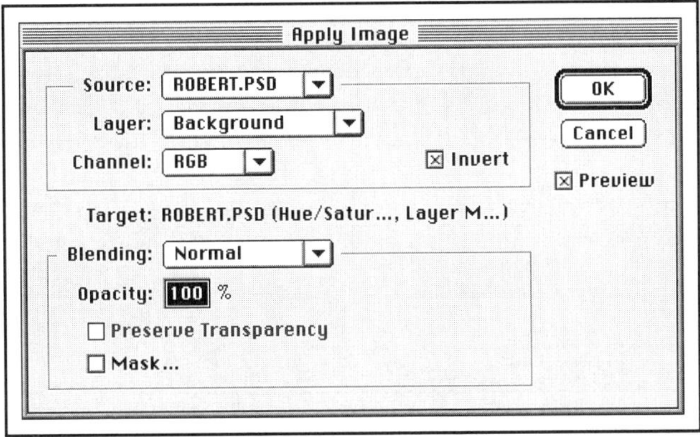

Figure 11-33: Apply Image dialog box.

4. Double-click on the Adjustment layer to open the Hue/Saturation dialog box. Click the Colorize button and change the Hue to 22 (or whatever tone you want to use for the sepia-toned image). Change the Saturation to 50 (once again, you may vary this as you want). Figure 11-34 shows the Hue/Saturation settings.

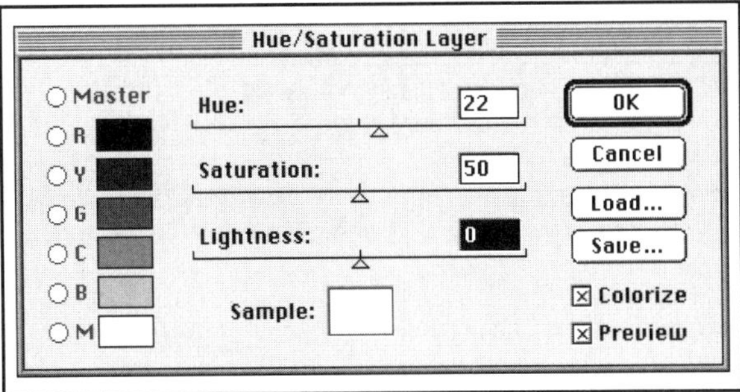

Figure 11-34: Hue/saturation settings.

5. This makes a fairly nice sepiatone, but there is yet another trick that you can play. You cannot add a Levels Adjustment layer to affect the mask image that is on the current Adjustment layer, but you can use the Levels command directly on the mask (it only gives you one Undo, but that's all you would have on a channel or layer mask, either).

   Select Image | Adjust | Levels (Mac: Command+L; Windows: Ctrl+L). Just select the command—*do not double-click on the Adjustment Layer*.

Think about the adjustment that you need to make. If you move the Black point to the right, you create more black in the image—which keeps the sepiatone *off* of more values. If you move the White point slider to the left, you create more whites in the image—which allows more color to show through on the darker values. What you probably want to do is to allow more color to appear on the mid-to-light tones in the image. If this is the case, then you need to move the Gamma slider toward the left in the Levels dialog box or move the Black Output slider toward the right (or some combination of both).

Figure 11-35 shows the Levels settings that we selected. Figure 11-36a shows the inverted image of Robert. Figure 11-36b shows the mask after we applied the Levels command.

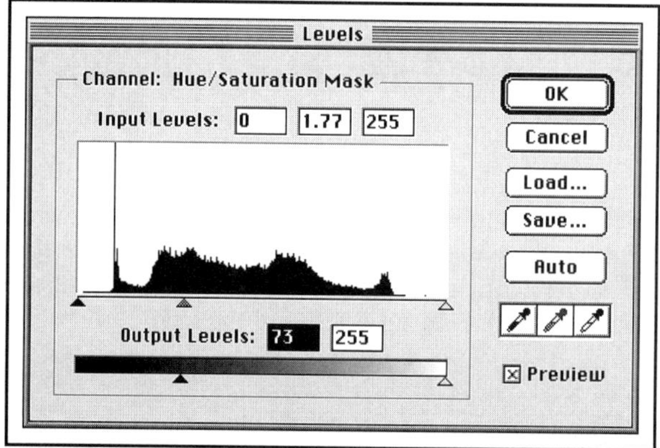

Figure 11-35: Levels command used to change the Adjustment layer mask.

Once you understand what is happening when you adjust the Levels in the layer mask, you can work in two images if you really want to keep your sepiatone editable. Here's how:

1. When you open the ROBERT.PSD file above, create a duplicate copy (Image | Duplicate | OK).

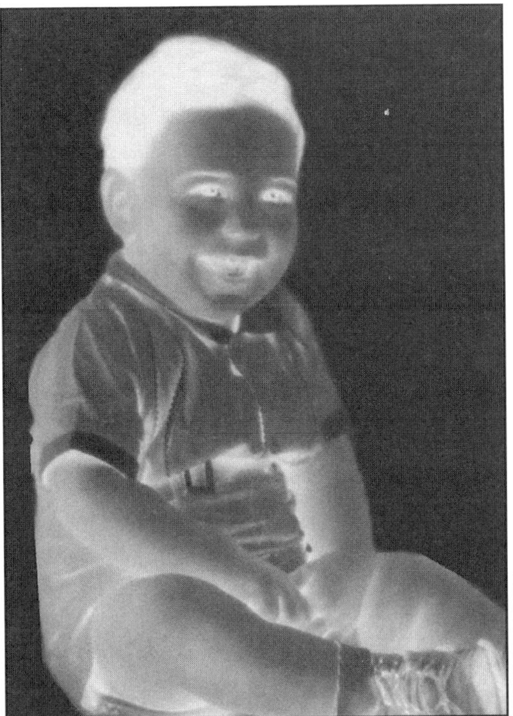

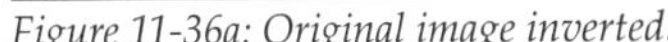

Figure 11-36a: Original image inverted.

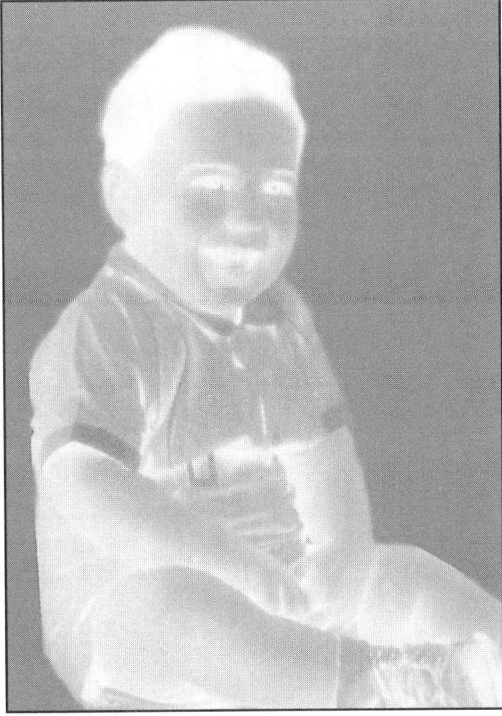

Figure 11-36b: Adjustment layer mask after Levels command is applied.

2. In one copy, create an Invert adjustment layer and then create a Levels Adjustment layer on top of it. Set the Levels to look like the one used in Step 5 above (or play with the Levels to see what you prefer; that is why you are using the Adjustment layer).
3. In the other copy, work Steps 2 and 4 from the previous example. This sets up the Hue/Saturation layer and select a color for it.
4. Now, you can choose the Apply Image command with the Hue/Saturation layer as its target and make the image with the Levels adjustment the source image. Use the merged image as the source. Figure 11-37 shows you the Apply Image dialog box for this example. Now you can change the Levels in the Adjustment layer as many times as you want. You cannot degrade the image and you can choose the Apply Image command to put the changes into the Hue/Saturation Adjustment layer mask as many times as you want, too. You are not hurting any image data regardless of how often you change your mind. Figure 11-38 shows the final sepiatone.

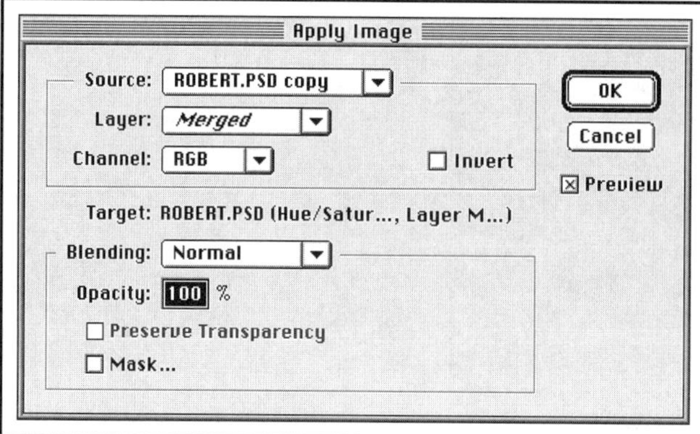

Figure 11-37: Apply Image dialog box to place the merged image with Levels and Invert Adjustment layers into the Hue/Saturation Adjustment layer mask in the companion image.

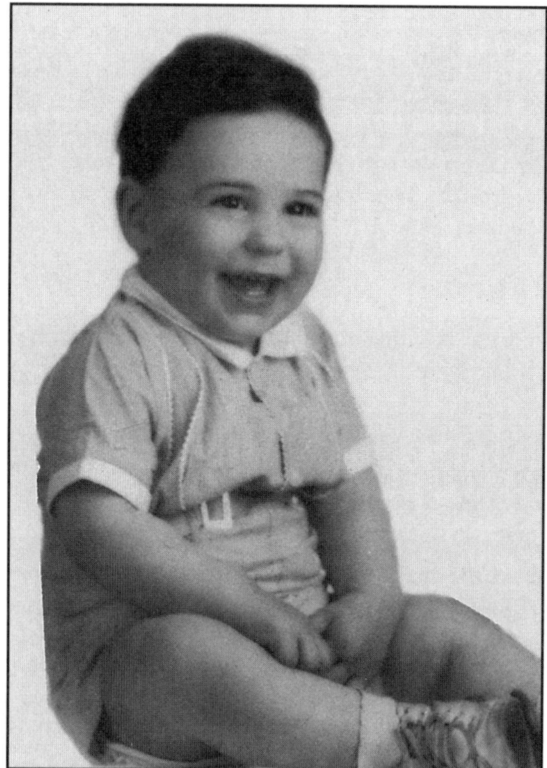

Figure 11-38: Finished sepiatoned image.

Stacking Adjustment Layers

You have seen how Adjustment layers can be created and manipulated. In the previous examples, you have learned how to create multiple Adjustment layers, mask Adjustment layers, and change the Apply mode and opacity of the Adjustment layers. You have used the Apply Image command and the Levels command on the Adjustment layer mask. It is time to move your knowledge of Adjustment layers one step further.

Although you can, and usually will, color correct images using the Levels and the Curves commands, one of the most precise curves (or precise transforms) that you can use to correct an image is often the image tones themselves. We touched on that in the two previous exercises above. We used the values of the airplane in Multiply mode in a Levels adjustment layer without changing the Levels sliders, and we used the values of Robert, inverted, to make a mask to filter out unwanted color.

You can use these techniques in more production-oriented situations. Before there were Adjustment layers, if you wanted to use the image values to tone the image, you needed to duplicate the layer and then change the layer Apply mode and, possibly, the layer opacity as well. This doubled the size of the image. Now, if you use a Levels Adjustment layer, you can do the same thing with much less cost in file size. Simply create an Adjustment layer (Levels or Curves), do not change the dialog box, and set the Apply mode to Multiply or Screen (or Overlay to make the colors more intense). If the effect is still not strong enough, you can stack duplicates of the Adjustment layer as high as you need them to be. You can also change the opacity to cut back on the effect if it is too strong.

Using this technique in Multiply mode is an excellent way to add variable amounts of darkness and contrast to a washout, over-exposed image. You tone down an image that is too dark by using Screen mode and stacking as many Adjustment layers as you need.

Figure 11-39 shows a very poor quality, faded, old photo. It has not been tonally retouched at all. This file is called WOMAN.PSD and is on the Companion CD-ROM. One way to correct the values on this image is to create multiple Adjustment layers. Figure 11-40 shows the finished image. Figure 11-41 shows the Layers palette for the image. The layers are named for the adjustments that they contain. Play with the image and see what results you can get. There are many acceptable possibilities.

Figure 11-39: Woman, before.

Figure 11-40: Woman, corrected with Multiply and Overlay levels.

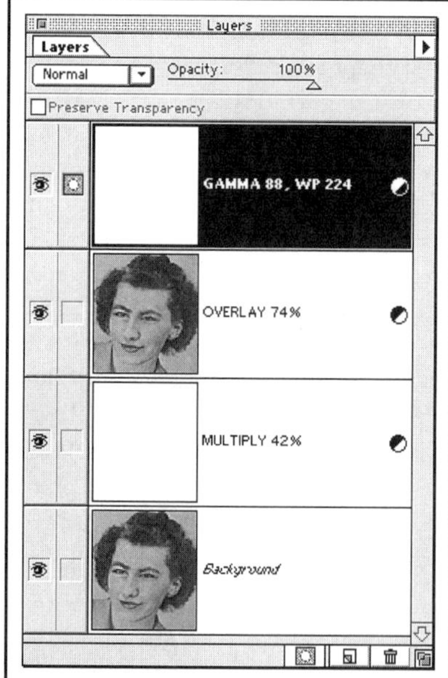

Figure 11-41: Layers palette showing types of Adjustment layers used to correct the image of the woman.

Here's another exercise for you to try. This picture of Bruce was taken with the sun directly behind him. His features are much too dark and obscure. However, you, Adjustment layers, and Screen mode should be able to correct that. The major correction problem is that not all of the image needs to be adjusted the same way. You will use varying levels of gray in the Adjustment layer mask to lesson the correction in specific areas.

1. Open the image BRUCE.PSD from the Companion CD-ROM. Figure 11-42 shows the original image.

Figure 11-42: Original image of Bruce is much too dark.

2. Create a Hue/Saturation Adjustment Layer (Mac: Command-click, Windows: Ctrl-click on the New Layer icon at the bottom of the Layers palette). Set the Apply mode to Screen. In the Hue/Saturation dialog box, do nothing. Figure 11-43 shows the Screen mode adjustment that affects the entire image, washing out the sky.
3. Make the Background layer active (Mac: Option+[, Windows: Alt+[). Choose Select | Color Range and choose the Highlights. Press D to set the colors back to the default of black and white. Make the Adjustment layer active (Mac: Option+], Windows: Alt+]). Fill the selection with black (Mac: Option+Delete, Windows: Alt+Backspace). Figure 11-44 shows the mask that you cannot see on the Adjustment layer.

Figure 11-43: Screen Adjustment layer washes out sky.

Figure 11-44: Adjustment layer mask with highlights protected from change.

4. Choose Filter | Blur | Gaussian Blur; Radius: 3.0 pixels. This softens the selection edges as shown in Figure 11-45.

Figure 11-45: Gaussian Blur added to Adjustment layer mask.

5. Make the Background layer active (Mac:Option+[, Windows: Alt+[). Choose Select | Color Range and choose the Midtones. Press D to set the colors back to the default of black and white. Make the Adjustment layer active (Mac: Option+], Windows: Alt+]). Fill the selection with 50% black (Edit | Fill | Foreground color, 50% Opacity, Normal). Choose Filter | Blur | Gaussian Blur; Radius: 2). Figure 11-46 shows the mask. The gray in the midtones area on the mask will allow half of the changes to occur. Figure 11-47 shows the almost-finished correction.

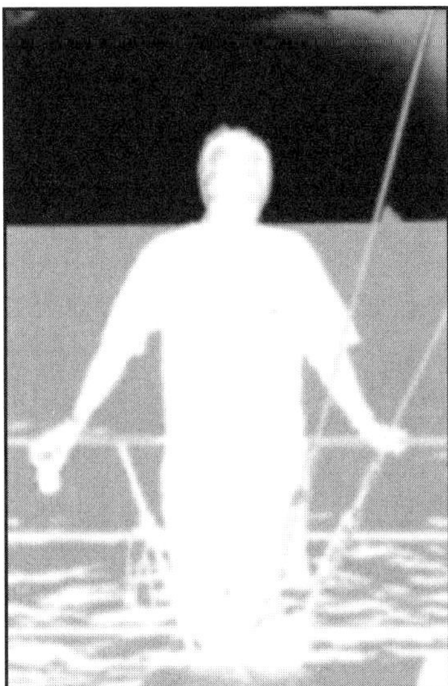

Figure 11-46: Finished mask.

Figure 11-47: Almost finished correction.

6. The only thing left is to remove the color cast in the image and fix the Levels. To do this, you need to create two additional Adjustment layers. You need to create a Levels Adjustment layer (Mode: Normal) and you need to create a Color Balance Adjustment layer (Mode: Normal). Figure 11-48a shows the Layers palette, Figures 11-48b through 11-48e show the Levels settings used, Figures 11-48f through 11-48h show the Color Balance Highlights, Midtones, and Shadows corrections, and Figure 11-49 shows the fully corrected image.

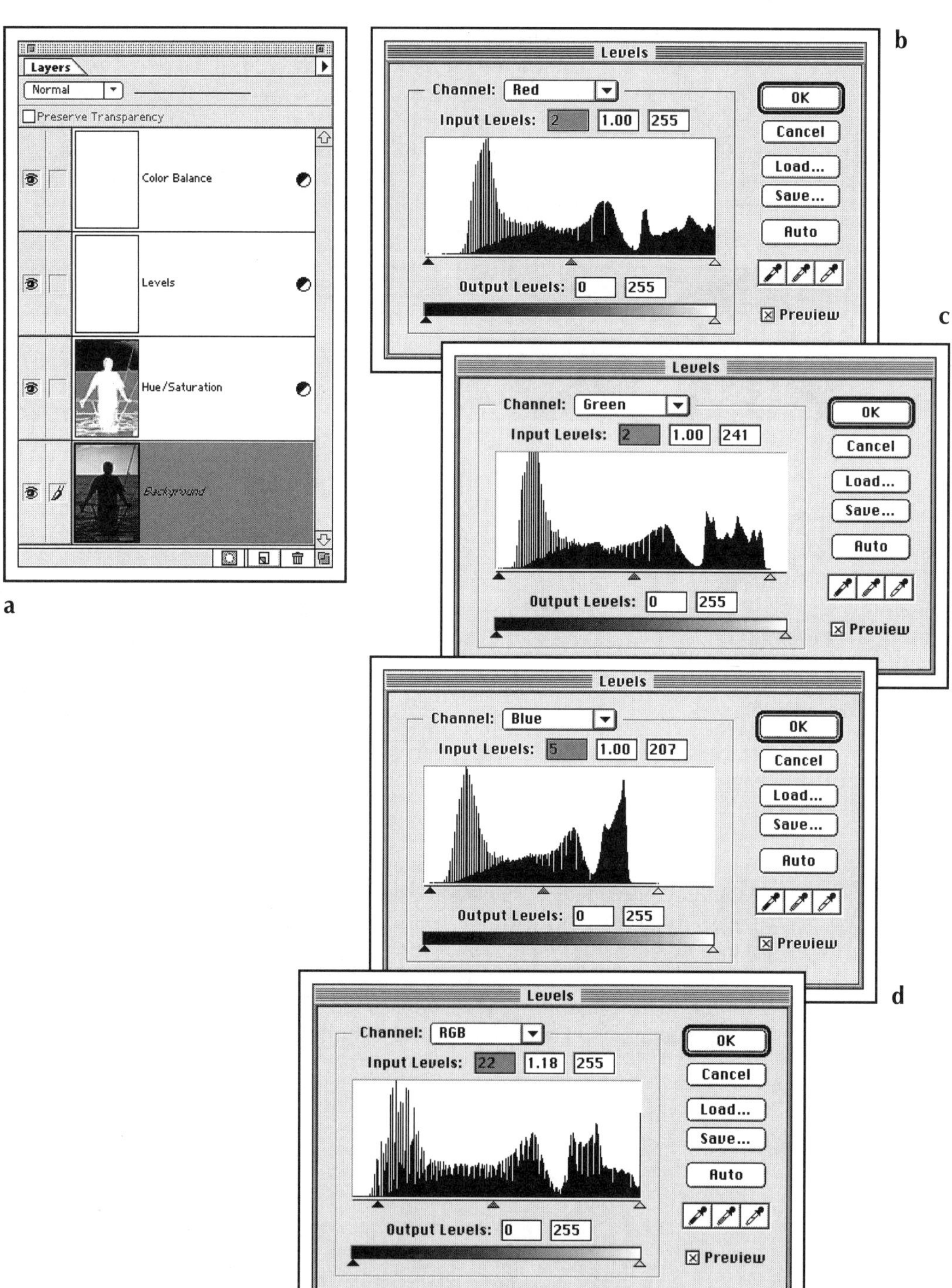

Layers
Normal
Preserve Transparency
Color Balance
Levels
Hue/Saturation
Background
Levels
Channel: Red
Input Levels: 2 1.00 255
Output Levels: 0 255
OK
Cancel
Load...
Save...
Auto
Preview
Levels
Channel: Green
Input Levels: 2 1.00 241
Output Levels: 0 255
OK
Cancel
Load...
Save...
Auto
Preview
Levels
Channel: Blue
Input Levels: 5 1.00 207
Output Levels: 0 255
OK
Cancel
Load...
Save...
Auto
Preview
Levels
Channel: RGB
Input Levels: 22 1.18 255
Output Levels: 0 255
OK
Cancel
Load...
Save...
Auto
Preview
a
b
c
d
e

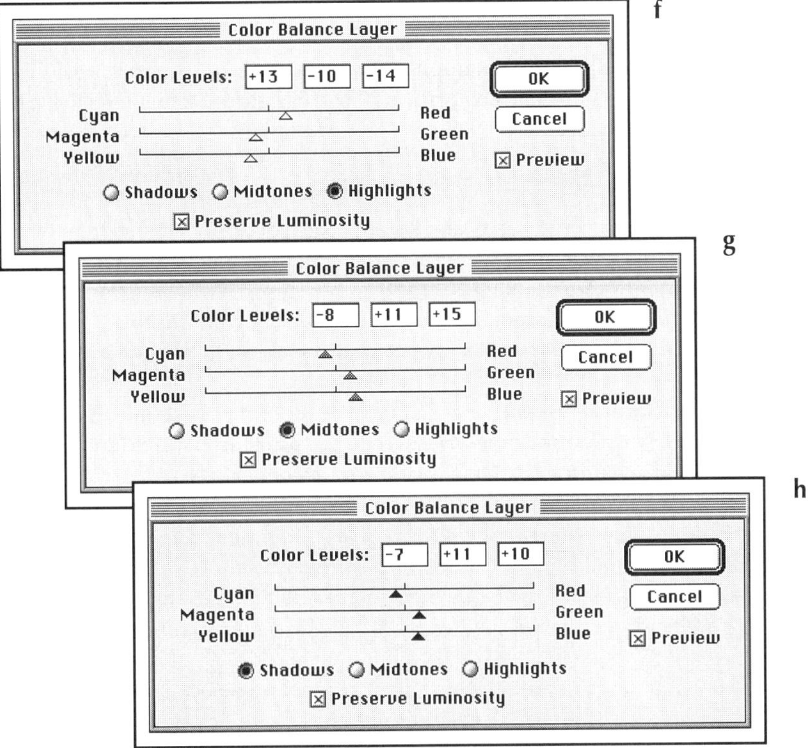

Figure 11-48: Layers palette and Corrections settings.

Figure 11-49: Corrected image.

Transformations

Another new feature that helps you to manipulate images is the Transform submenu on the Layers menu. Both the Numeric Transform and Free Transform commands are new.

The Problem

In Photoshop 3.0 and earlier, you could Scale, Rotate, Skew, or apply Perspective to your image. But you could perform only one action at a time. If you wanted to move an object on a layer over a bit, scale it, rotate it by 15°, and then put it into perspective, you needed to perform four separate commands. Each command (except for the Move command) lost a bit more data every time. This caused the object to become softer with each manipulation.

Using the Free Transform command, you can now do all of these actions on an object at one time. You can also move the object while the transformation Marquee is active. This is particularly helpful as it lets you get a much better idea of how the object will look *in place*. Just as the Adjustment layers allowed all of the transformations to occur at one time, rather than sequentially (which gives you much better image quality), so the Free Transform and Numeric Transform commands allow you to change the physical dimensions and orientation of an image and calculate the changes all at once—when you are ready to say "OK, let's do it." This gives you significantly better image quality.

In Photoshop 3.0, if you scaled, rotated, and then skewed an object, the program would scale the object, rotate the scaled object, and then skew the rotated object. Using Free Transform, the program performs all three calculations, determines the final image contours, and then uses the *original* image data to calculate a single result.

Just to show the type of image loss that occurs, we imported a swan from the Ultimate Symbol Design Elements collection and filled it with a fractal created in Kai's Power Tools 2.1. The image, SWAN.PSD, is on the Companion CD-ROM for you to use. Figure 11-50 shows the original image. Figure 11-51a shows a close-up of the original pixels. Figure 11-51b is a copy that has been rotated approximately fifteen times in various increments until it reached the original angle again. Notice how much softer and less sharp this image is. Rotating an image this many times is something to be avoided because of the amount of data loss. There is no way to rotate something a number of times and still do it in one "render pass" —unless you simply cannot make up your mind and you keep changing the angle multiple times in the Free Transform command before you say OK.

Figure 11-50: SWAN.PSD

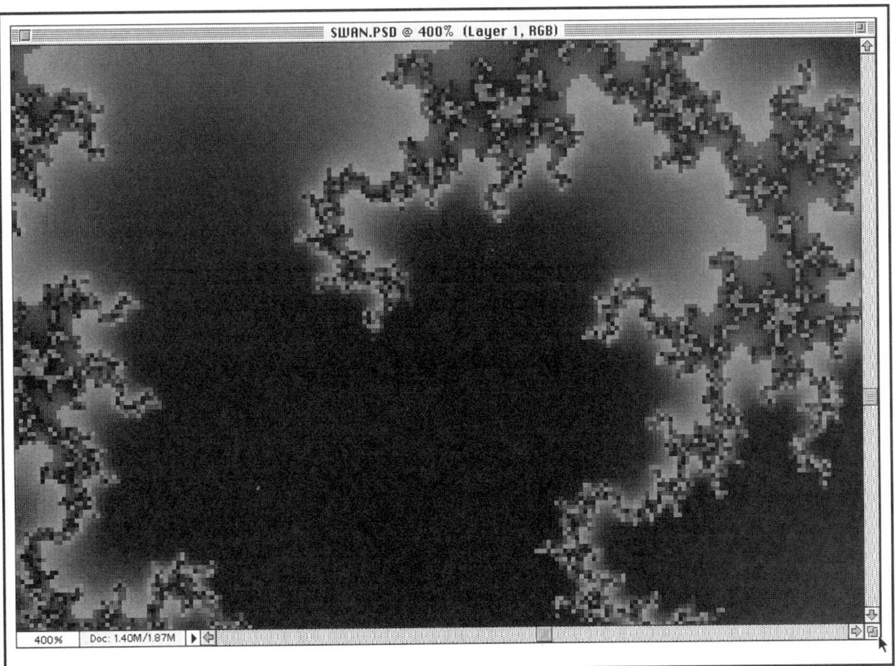

Figure 11-51a: Close-up of original pixels.

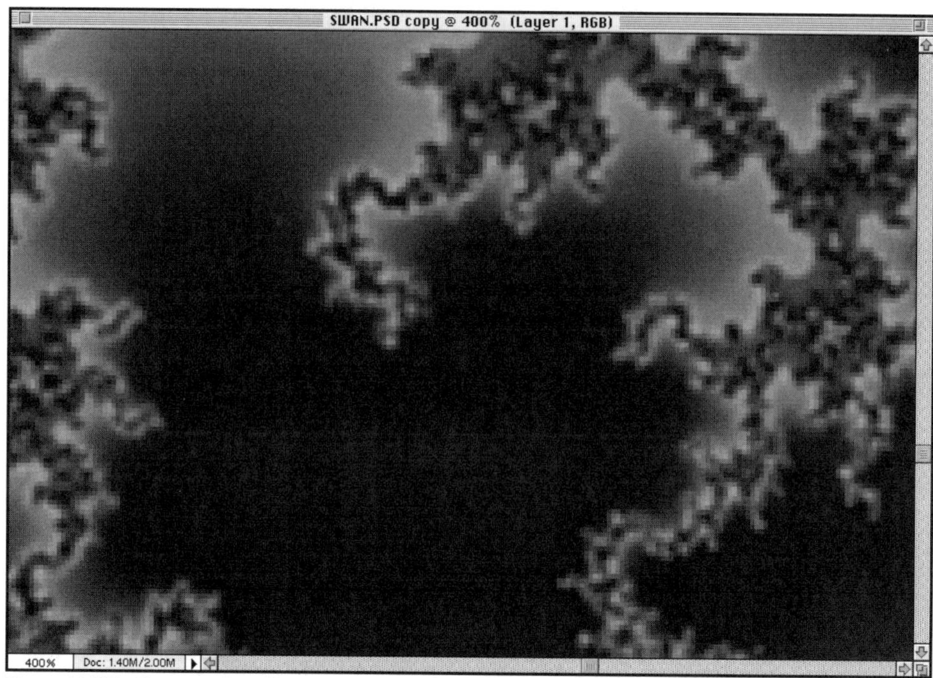

Figure 11-51b: Close-up view of image that has been rotated fifteen times.

The Keystrokes

You can use these keyboard shortcuts for the Transform commands:

Command	Mac	Windows
Free Transform	Command-T	Ctrl-T
Numeric Transform	Shift-Command-T	Shift-Ctrl-T
To skew using the Skew command: Skew single side: Skew both sides from center:	 drag one of the center box handles on the bounding box Option	 Alt
To skew using the Free Transform command: Skew single side—one point only: Skew 1 point on top and bottom:	 Command Command-Option	 Ctrl Ctrl-Alt
Constrain proportions or direction	Shift	Shift
Mirror	Option	Alt
Move single corner point	Command	Ctrl
Skew (drag side-center handle)	Command	Ctrl
Perspective	Shift-Cmd-Option	Shift-Alt-Ctrl

Numeric Transform

The Numeric Transform command allows you one-step access to most of the transformational commands. It allows you to position, scale, rotate, and skew your image all at one time, and with numeric precision. Figure 11-52 shows the dialog box.

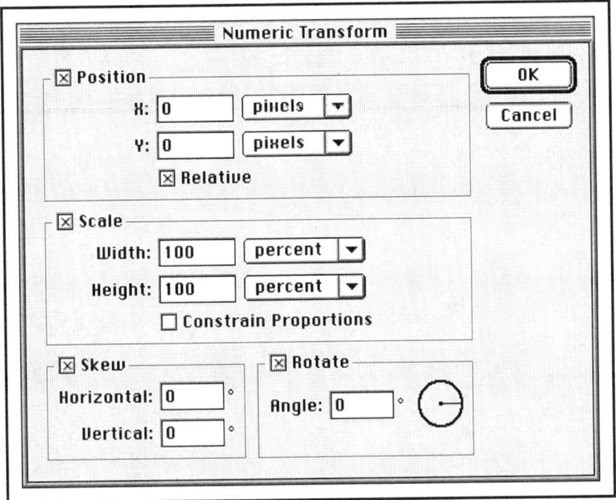

Figure 11-52: Numeric Transform dialog box.

Each function on the dialog box has a check box that allows you to indicate whether or not to use the values present for that function. The dialog box remembers the last values used during the current Photoshop session. For example, if you rotate an image 45° and scale it by 50%, those values will be present in the dialog box if you use the command again before you exit Photoshop. If the next object that you want to manipulate only needs to be rotated, you need to either set the scale to 100% or uncheck the box next to it—or else your object will also be scaled by 50%.

You will find yourself using the Numeric Transform command frequently when you want to scale an object. If you know either the size or the percentage that you need to scale, then using Numeric Transform is the best way to get there. It is almost impossible to accurately scale an object 43% by eye. Unless you enjoy playing with rulers and watching them as you drag and scale, it is also much easier to *tell* Photoshop that an object needs to become 133 pixels square.

Another nice touch to the dialog box is that it allows you to move an object in either absolute or relative mode. You can specify that the bounding box of an object be moved to a specific set of coordinates or that it be moved a specific distance from where it is currently living.

What Are Objects & Bounding Boxes?

An *object* is a group of non-transparent pixels located on a layer. It is easier to use the term "object" to refer to the contents of a layer than it is to keep saying "non-transparent pixels on layer...". If this were a vector program, an object would be an individual path, either open or closed, or any grouping thereof, which can be moved at one time by clicking on a single location and dragging. Photoshop's layers sort of do the same thing. When you use the Move tool and drag at one location all of the non-transparent pixels come along.

There is another issue here, however. It concerns what *you* decide to place on a layer. Because you have the ability to perform transformations on layer contents without having to select the layer with a marquee, it is assumed that there is only one grouping of contiguous pixels on that layer. In plain terms, if you want to have five cats in your image, then put each one on its own layer. That way, each cat is its own object and can be resized and repositioned by itself. Until you know that there will be no further changes, try to keep only one "thing" on each layer.

This brings us to the bounding box. This is another concept borrowed from the world of vector graphics. When the term is used in Photoshop, it refers to the smallest rectangle that can surround all of the non-transparent pixels in a layer. When you explicitly position an object using the Numeric Transform command, you are placing the top-left corner of its bounding box at that location.

Figure 11-53 shows the SWAN.PSD image again. This time, the Numeric Transform command has been used to scale it to 200-pixels wide with constrain proportions on (which means that you only need to specify one dimension), and it has been moved to screen coordinates of X: 100, Y: 100 (0,0 is in the top-left corner). As you can see by the guide lines in the figure, position X:100, Y: 100 is the top-left corner of the rectangle that *logically* encloses the pixels that form the swan (logically=virtually—as opposed to physically, since there really is not a "box" around the pixels on the layer).

Figure 11-53: SWAN.PSD with guides showing top-left corner of bounding box.

Rotation Tricks

When Photoshop rotates an object, it always rotates it around its center point (unfortunately). It would be very convenient if you could select the center of rotation. Adobe Illustrator, however, does allow you to place a marker on your desired center of rotation. This allows you to rotate a leaf by the end of its stem, for example, or to create a circular motif by rotating a number of copies around a single point. Photoshop does not allow you to do this. The only way to make it possible is to fake it. Let's see what that means.

In simple terms, if Photoshop can only rotate something around its center point, then you need to make sure that the location from which you want to rotate an object *is* its center point. Figure 11-54 shows the same swan rotated 60°. This figure has guides that mark the center point of the bounding box (and the bounding box has been stroked with a wide line). In addition, a large white square has been drawn in the location of the center of the bounding box before the swan was rotated. Notice that the white area is still at the center of the bounding box where the guides intersect (even though the bounding box itself has rotated). How can we rotate the swan from the top-left tip of its wing, instead?

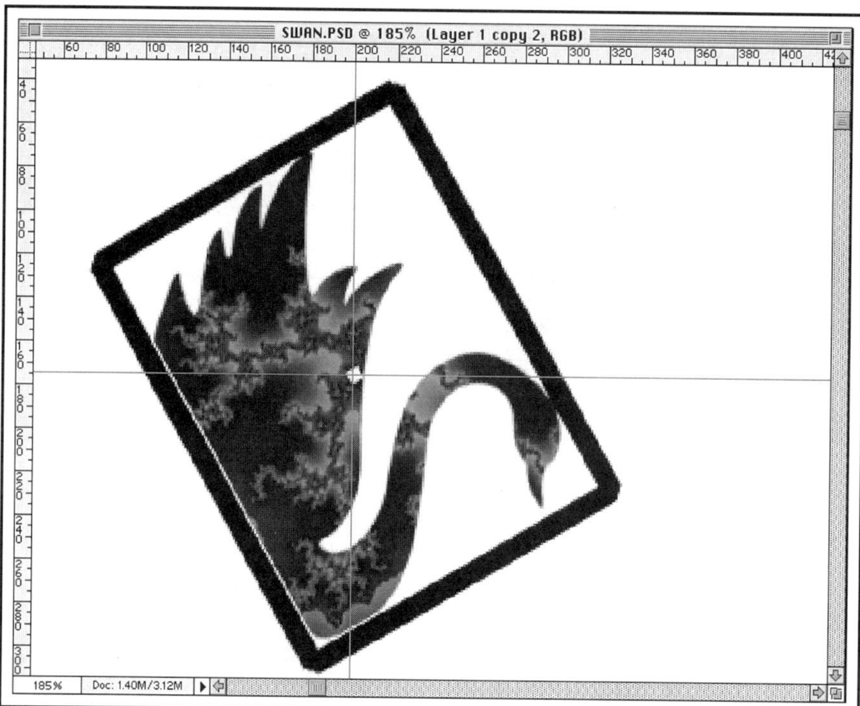

Figure 11-54: Swan rotated 60° around the center of its bounding box.

The answer is that we need to make that top-left wingtip the center point of a bounding box. There is only one bounding box for a given layer. The bounding box encloses all of the non-transparent pixels on the layer. There is no way for Photoshop to sense whether the pixels are "attached" to one another or not. Therefore, in order to make our chosen location the center point, we can add a pixel in the corners of the "imaginary" bounding box that we need.

First, let's drag the swan closer to the center of the image so that there is room to rotate the swan by its upper-left wingtip. Select the Rectangular Marquee tool and drag a marquee from the top-left of the wingtip to the bottom-right of the object's original (i.e., current) bounding box as shown in Figure 11-55. According to the Info palette, seen in Figure 11-56, this area is 200 pixels wide x 109 pixels high.

Figure 11-55: Bottom-right quarter of desired rotation.

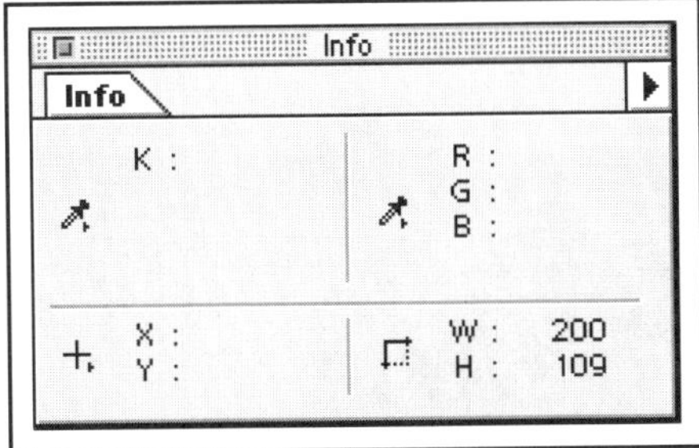

Figure 11-56: Info palette shows the dimensions of the marquee.

Next, you need to create a fixed size marquee that is twice the dimensions of the current selection (400 pixels wide x 218 pixels high). Figure 11-57 shows the Marquee Options palette.

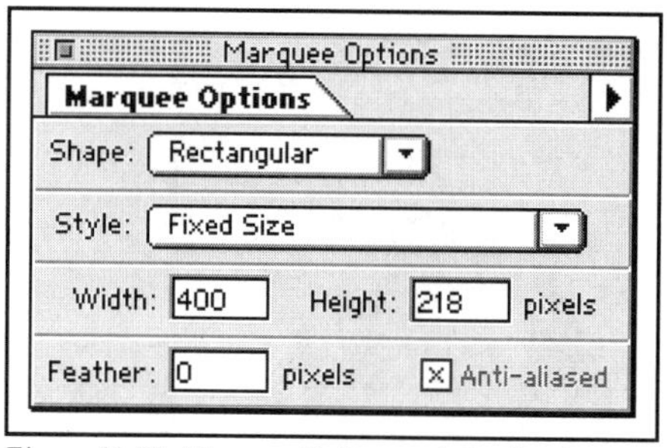

Marquee Options
Marquee Options
Shape: Rectangular
Style: Fixed Size
Width: 400 Height: 218 pixels
Feather: 0 pixels ☒ Anti-aliased

Figure 11-57: Marquee Options palette showing new fixed-size marquee.

Either zoom into the image until you can clearly see the top-left wingtip pixel, or just aim for it. Press the modifier key (Mac: Option, Windows: Alt) and click on that pixel. This places your fixed-size marquee onto the layer so that its center is the point where you clicked (hopefully your desired center of rotation). Figure 11-58 shows the image with the marquee in place.

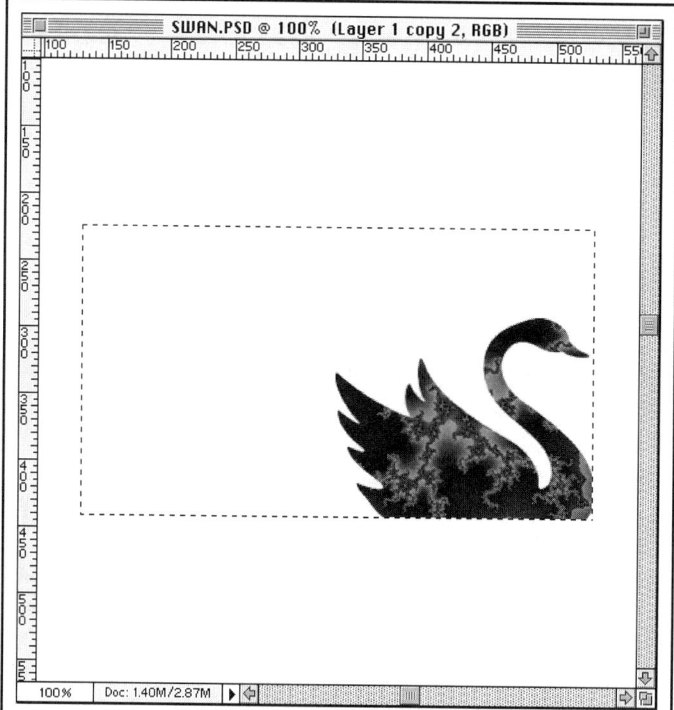

Figure 11-58: Fixed-size marquee around desired center of rotation.

Select the Pencil tool and a brush that is large enough for you to see (although a single-pixel brush is sufficient). Press the Caps Lock key to enable precise cursors (the crosshair cursor). Position the cursor on each corner of bounding box that does not contain image data as shown in Figure 11-59 and click to leave a mark. This creates a new bounding box for the image—one which has *your* desired location as its center of rotation. Deselect the marquee (Mac: Command-D, Windows: Ctrl-D).

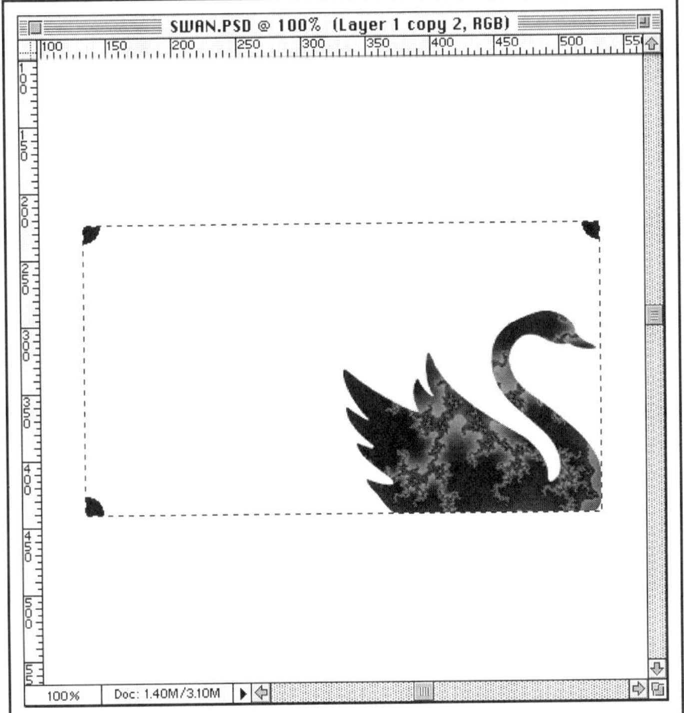

Figure 11-59: Brush marks in three corners of the selection create a new bounding box for the swan.

Figure 11-60 shows the swan ready to be rotated. So that you can see exactly how the rotating happens, guides have been crossed at the center of the desired rotation. In addition, a large circle has been painted at the desired center of rotation. (Since it is removing image data, this is not something that you would actually do on your own images!) Figure 11-61 shows the swan rotated. Our changes have done exactly what we anticipated. The swan rotates from the point that we wanted because we added three more clumps of pixels in locations that were designed to force the center of the bounding box to be our chosen pixel. We can then erase the no-longer-needed pixels.

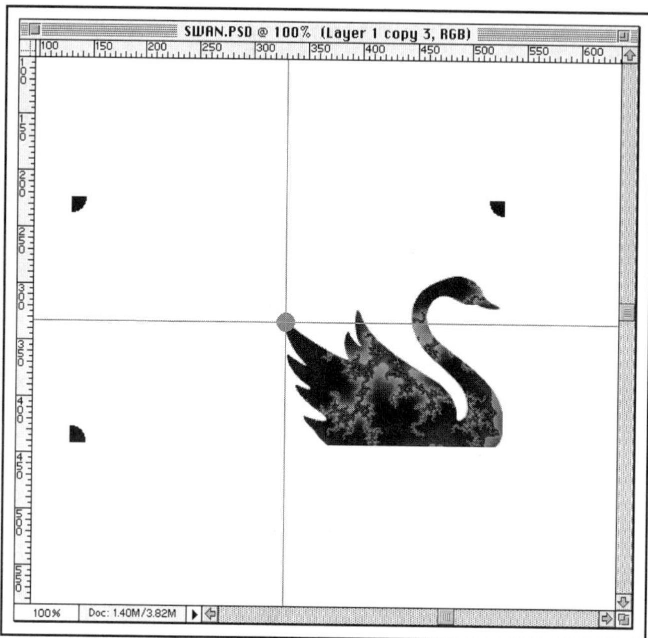

Figure 11-60: Swan showing projected center of rotation where guides intersect.

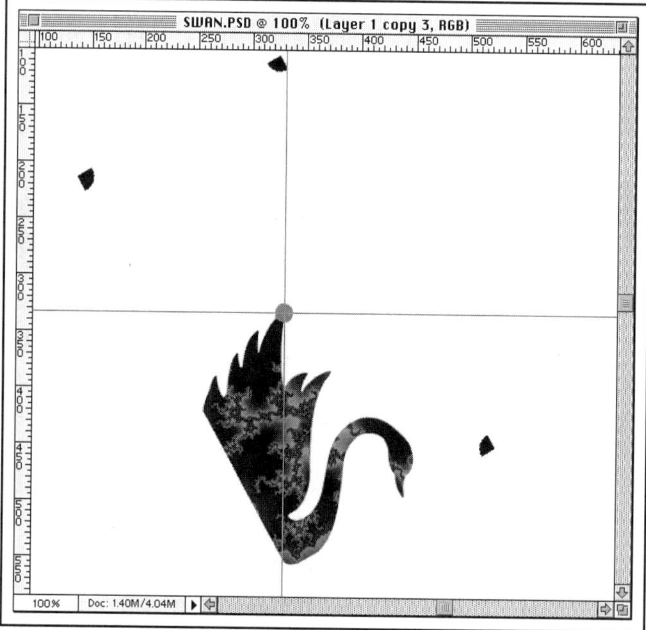

Figure 11-61: Swan rotated 60° around upper-left wingtip.

Using this technique, you can also rotate a number of copies of an object around a center point. Figure 11-62 shows six layers of "swan" rotated around the top-left wingtip. The six layers form a star because the distance between each rotation is 60°. The copies (each made from the original rather than a rotated copy), were rotated at 60°, 120°, 180°, 240°, 300°. The original was never rotated.

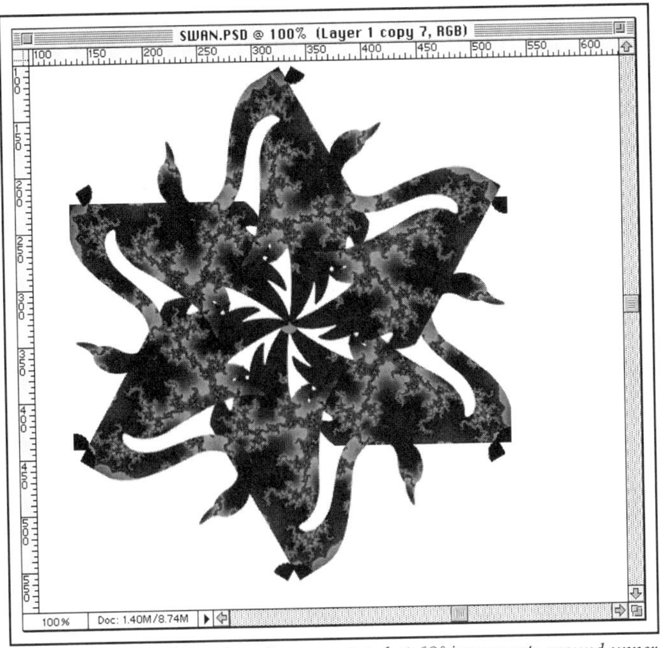

Figure 11-62: Star formation of swans rotated at 60° increments around upper-left wingtip.

Exercise: Multi-Rotate Action

We have created an Action that allows you to automatically rotate anything on Layer 1 in an image so that it forms a 60° star or burst pattern. With this, you can create some interesting effects:

1. Load the file MROTATE.ATN into your Actions palette from the Companion CD-ROM (Actions palette menu | Load Actions).
2. Create a new document (Mac: Command-N, Windows: Ctrl-N). It can be any size, but a 400 x 400 pixel image is fine for this exercise.
3. Make a new layer (click on the New Layer icon at the bottom of the Layers Palette). This layer is automatically named Layer 1 (which it must be in order for this Action to work).
4. Just to see how this Action works, use the Line tool and draw a line with a single arrowhead near the center of the image. Figure 11-63 shows the starting image.

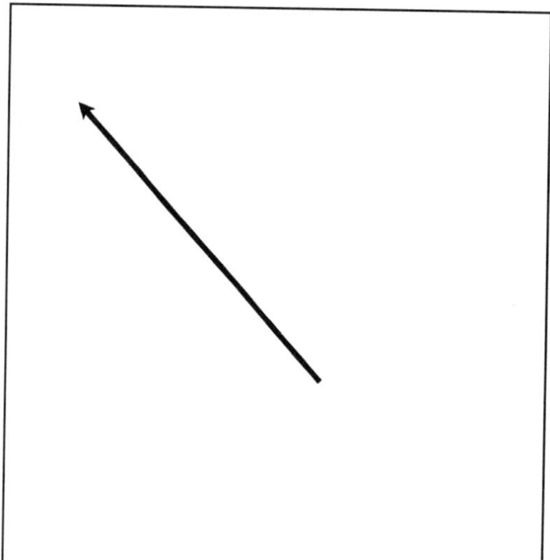

Figure 11-63: Starting image for multi-rotate action.

5. Double-click on the multi-rotate action or select it and click on the Play button. Figure 11-64 shows the result. Yes, it is very ugly, but the line was not attractive as a starting image. Notice that there are arrows on both ends of each line. This is because the line revolved around its center and the 60° increments caused lines 4, 5, and 6 to double back over lines 1, 2, and 3. Since the these lines are 180° apart from the lines that they are on top of, the arrows face in the opposite direction.

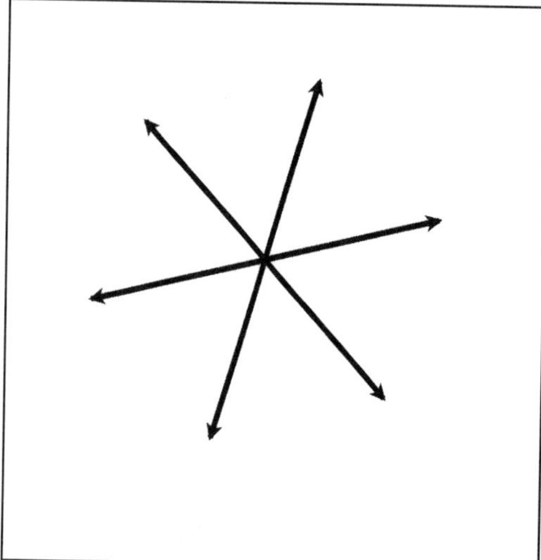

Figure 11-64: Rotated arrows.

6. Close the image without saving it and open another one that is the same size. This time, you can use the Paintbrush and any colors that you want. Create a scribble, perhaps similar to the one in Figure 11-65.

Figure 11-65: New scribble image to rotate.

7. Play the multi-rotate Action again. The result should be much more attractive.

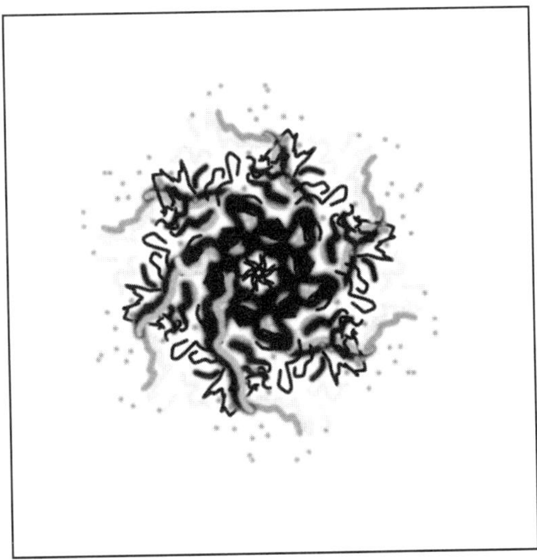

Figure 11-66: Finished multi-rotation.

You can use this Action with objects such as the swan, and you can force it to rotate around a specific center point by using the tricks that you learned in this section. Figure 11-67 shows the expanded commands for this Action. Enjoy!

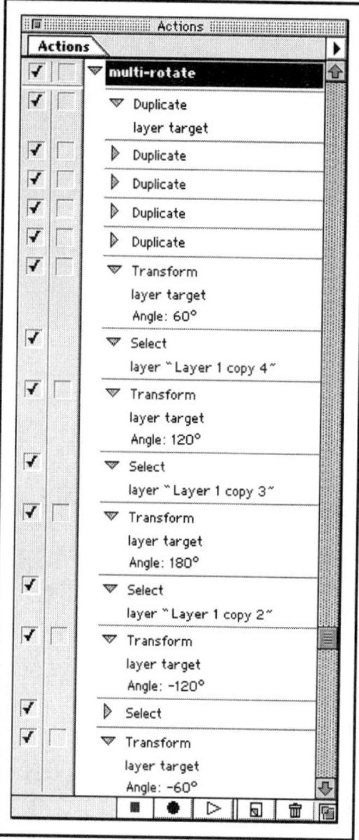

Figure 11-67: Multi-rotate Action script.

Grids & Positioning

Photoshop is not a page layout program, nor do most folks use it for technical drawing. Why then was the addition of Grids and Guides one of the most frequently requested features to be added to Photoshop 4.0?

Photoshop 3.0 and earlier did have rulers. You can turn on the rulers at the edges of the image and use them as guidelines for positioning objects. However, it is really not fun to try to "eyeball" your position relative to the rulers. Users came up with all different types of workarounds. One of the best was to create a channel, use the Line tool to draw the needed guides, and then set the visibility icon for the channel on so that you could see the guidelines as you worked, but they would not print (even by accident). The guides in Photoshop 4.0 make this workaround obsolete.

Why would you need to draw guides in any case? There are innumerable situations in which you might need guide lines in a file. One scenario would allow you to see margins in an image—perhaps an imaginary margin in which you want only a few elements to intrude. You might want to space elements in a composite a precise distance from one another. You might need to mark the center of an image, as we have done above (in the rotation example). The list is endless.

What about grids? Of what use are they? The first MacPaint had a grid feature. You could constrain your painting tools to a grid to give you more control (*any* control was a good thing in a program that, when we look back on it, was fairly limited). Artists and illustrators have used graph paper under their images for as long as the concept of grids has been around (or the ability to use tracing paper has been around). Adobe, for some reason, has historically not believed in grids. Until the current version, Illustrator did not create grids either.

The authors, who both knit, weave, and stitch, have used grids for years in all of their fiber-related activities. Trying to use Photoshop to design a knitting pattern without a grid was a real challenge. The workaround there was to magnify an image so that each pixel looked as if it were really 8 pixels square. Using a 1-pixel Pencil, one could then create a design as if working on a grid. You can use grids to design a primitive pattern such as the one shown in Figure 11-68, or a much more complex pattern like the one in Figure 11-69. Using a grid also allows you to judge more easily the boundaries of a selection that you need to make.

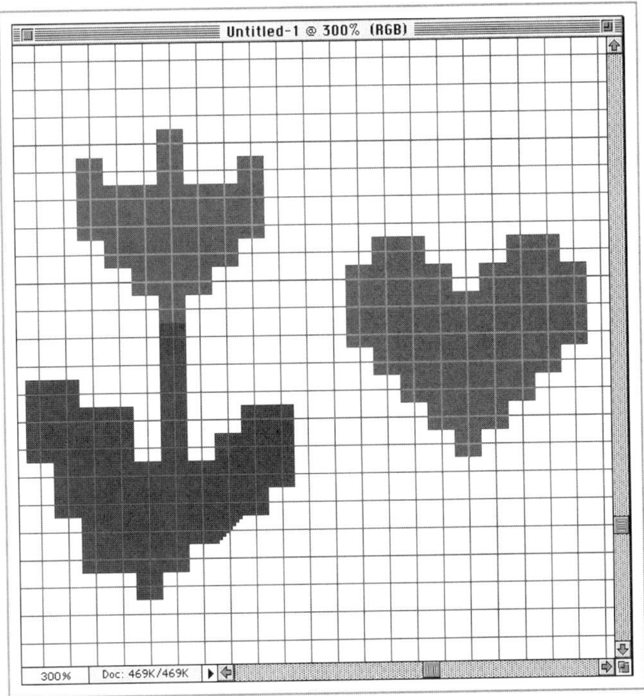

Figure 11-68: A simple tulip and heart gridded design.

Figure 11-69: A more complex gridded design suitable for a Fair Isle sweater.

Let's take a look at how you define and use both guides and grids.

Using Guides

Guides are used to provide precise measurements. You can drag guides from the horizontal and vertical rulers, place and replace them, move, show, hide, or delete them. You can set them up so that tools and objects snap to them, and so that they snap to the contours of objects when you place them in your image.

Shortcut keys

Command	Mac	Windows
Toggle Rulers	Command+R	Ctrl+R
Show/Hide Guides	Command+;	Ctrl+;
Snap to Guides	Shift+Cmd+;	Shift+Ctrl+;
Lock Guides	Opt+Cmd+;	Alt+Ctrl+;
Edit Units & Rulers Preference:	Double-click on horizontal or vertical rule	

If you prefer not to use the keyboard shortcuts, the menu selections for using guides are found on the View menu.

Guides & Rulers

You need to have visible rulers in your image before you can create guides (since guides are dragged from the rulers, no rulers=no guides—an obvious and simple equation).

The ruler units are automatically set to whatever unit measure you use as your default in the Units & Rulers preference. While it is usually more accurate to keep that preference set to pixels, you might need to precisely measure a distance in picas or points. You can quickly change the unit setting by double-clicking on a ruler. This opens the preference dialog box so that you can change it.

TRAP *If you have set your units to anything other than pixels, be very sure that you have also set your image resolution properly for your desired output method. Otherwise, you obtain very odd (and incorrect) results. Figure 11-70a shows a 900-pixel image at 300 ppi. The guides surround a rectangle that is exactly 108 points square. Figure 11-70b shows the same 108-point rectangle on the* same *pixel-size image when the resolution is set to 72 ppi. The two rectangles are decidedly different sizes in relation to the total image, even though they are physically the same size.*

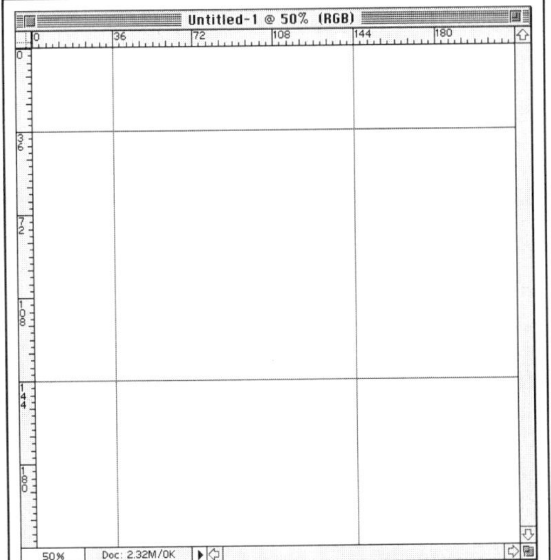

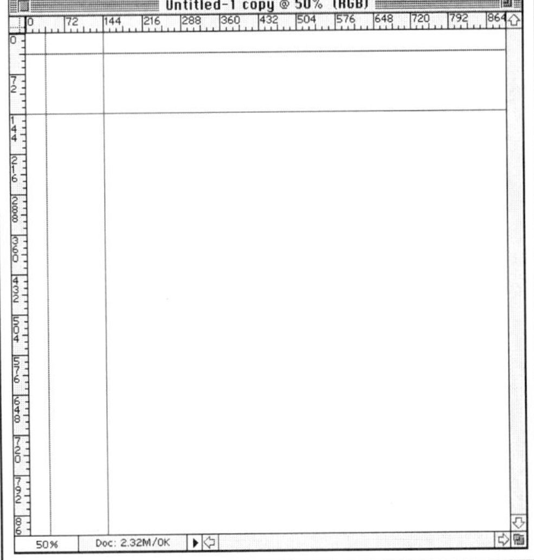

Figures 11-70a & 11-70b: Guide lines surrounding a 108-point rectangle at 300 ppi and 72 ppi.

Creating

It is very easy to create guides in the image. Simply place your cursor on a ruler, press and hold the (left) mouse button, and drag the guide into the image.

If you need to change the ruler origin (the point at which the units read 0, 0, place your cursor on the two dotted lines at the top-left corner of the image (shown by the arrow in Figure 11-71) and drag the dotted lines to the new starting point. You can see in Figure 11-71 that the 0 on both rulers is no longer at the top-left of the image. Guides are located at the new origin point. This is very helpful if you need to create guides that are 212 units apart starting from the original 15-tick mark on the ruler. Instead of doing the math, just move the ruler origin!

TIP *To restore the top-left zero-point coordinates, double-click on the top-left corner between the rulers.*

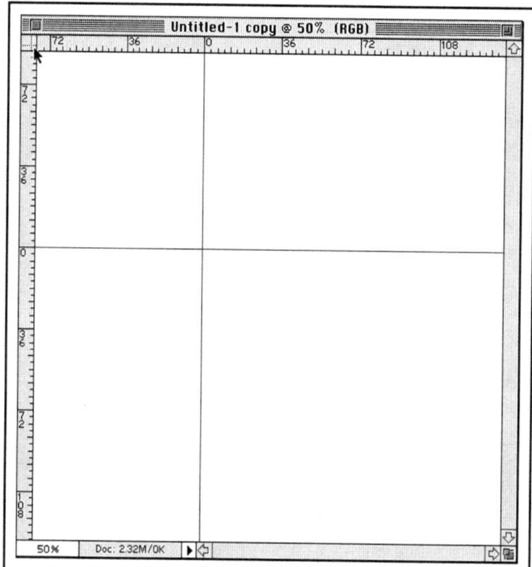

Figure 11-71: Changing the ruler origin.

When you create guides, you should be at least in 100% view. If you are not, then you cannot place the guide on a specific pixel. It is all-too-likely that you will be off by one or two pixels from the measurement that you really want.

Moving

Once you have placed guides into your image, you can easily move them. Press the modifier key (Mac: Command, Windows: Ctrl) to get the Move tool. When you get near a guide, the cursor changes into two parallel lines with outward-pointing arrows as shown in Figure 11-72. As long as the cursor retains that shape, you can move the guide.

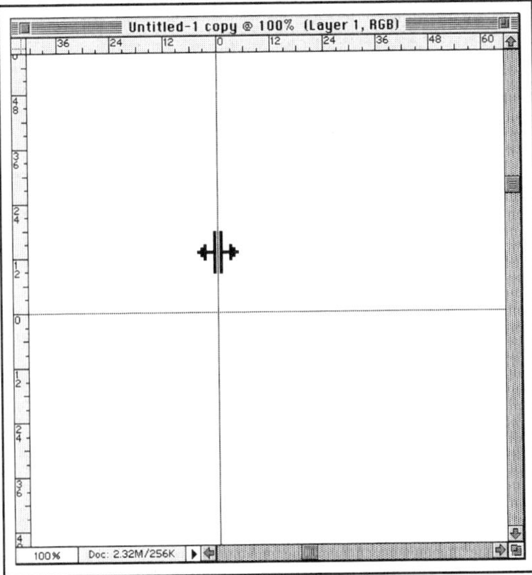

Figure 11-72: The cursor as it appears when it is able to relocate guides.

You can lock the guides so that they cannot be moved accidentally. Option+Command+; on the Mac or Alt+Ctrl+; for Windows toggles the state of the lock. Guides are always either all-locked or all-movable. You cannot lock a single guide.

Removing

To remove a guide from the image, simply drag it back to the ruler (as if you were dragging it off of the image). You need to have the "guide-moving" cursor as you do this. If you need to remove all of the guides from the image, select View | Clear Guides. There is no keyboard shortcut for that (although you could make an Action that would do this and assign a Function key to it).

Hiding & Viewing

You can show and hide guides quickly by using the keyboard shortcuts (Mac: Command+;, Windows: Ctrl+;). You can also select View | Show Guides (or View | Hide Guides if the guides are already visible).

Snapping

Snapping is a behavior that is associated with using guidelines in any program that has the ability to create them. Snapping means that the guide seems to have a magnetic attraction for the cursor. If the cursor is anywhere in the close vicinity of a guide, it is drawn to it. That is actually a good part of the purpose of guides—to attract the cursor so that items are positioned with pinpoint accuracy.

When you have an object on a layer, its logical bounding box snaps to the nearest guide if Snap is enabled (Mac: Shift+Command+;, Windows: Shift+Ctrl+;). Of course, you need to *move* the object in order for it to snap! Figure 11-73 shows a leaf from the Ultimate Symbol Design Elements collection placed so that it snaps to the guides in the image. As you can see, it is the outer pixels of the object that snap.

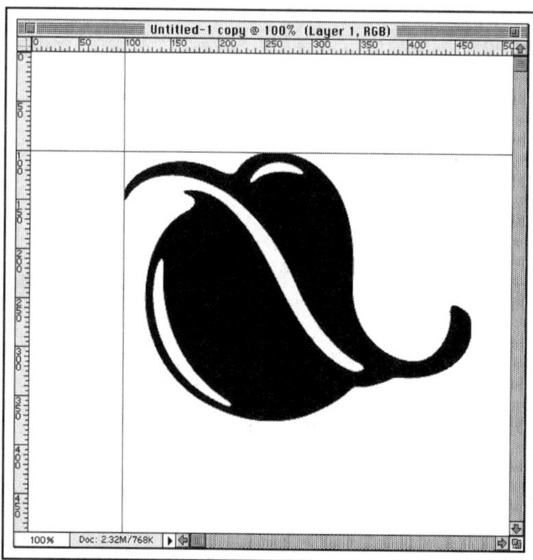

Figure 11-73: Snapping an object to guides.

You can easily place guides around the bounding box of a stationary object. When you drag the guides into the image, they will snap to the object. The snapping is so strong that you are not able to place a guide so that it is one pixel away from the start of the non-transparent image pixels in the layer (you *can* place a guide 2 pixels away from an object, however).

Wish List for Guides

Although the Guides feature is a marvelous convenience, there are still some things that cannot be done and features that would be wonderful to add. Adobe does listen to its users, so perhaps these can find their way into a new release of Photoshop:

- The ability to lock guides individually as well as in a group.
- The ability to create a marquee of any shape and make it into a guide. (This is a feature of Illustrator that is wonderful.)

- The ability to have additional "snap points"—preferably at the center of the object. It would also be useful to be able to drag non-printing snap points onto an object.
- The ability to assign a ruler location to a guide. In MetaCreations Painter 5.0, when you double-click on a guide, a dialog box appears that allows you to assign a specific ruler tick mark to a guide (for example, horizontal pixel 107). This numeric location is maintained even when the image is zoomed out so that you cannot see that specific pixel.

While you cannot snap the center of an object to a guide, you can place the object's center at the intersection of two guides anywhere in the image—even if you do not know exactly where the center of the object is located. This trick tells you how:

1. Place your guides into an image so that they intersect exactly where you want the center of an object to appear. Let's assume that you want the object center to appear at coordinates 257, 363 (an odd enough number on a 900-pixel image that you need to zoom in a lot just to place the guides).
2. Select the object that you want and copy it to the clipboard.
3. Choose the Pencil tool and a one-pixel brush. Zoom into the image at the maximum of 1600% (drag the slider to the right in the Navigator palette). Leave a 1-pixel dot at the intersection of the guides.
4. Choose the Magic Wand tool with a Tolerance set to 0 and anti-alias off. Click on the single pixel to select it as shown in Figure 11-74.
5. Paste in the selection from the clipboard (Mac: Command-V, Windows: Ctrl-V). As you can see in Figure 11-75, the object (in this case, the leaf) pastes so that it is centered on the desired spot.

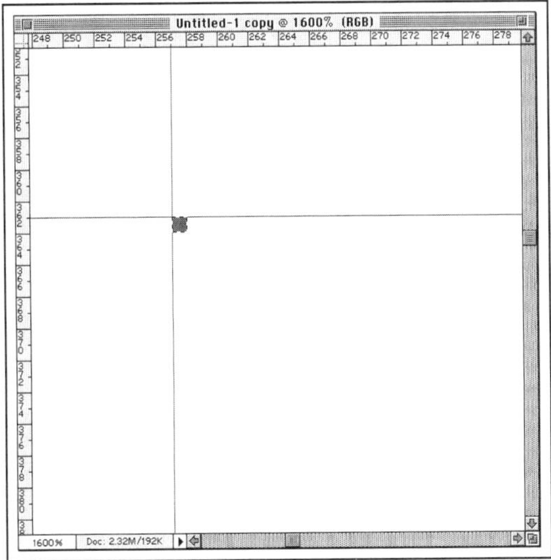

Figure 11-74: Selecting a single pixel.

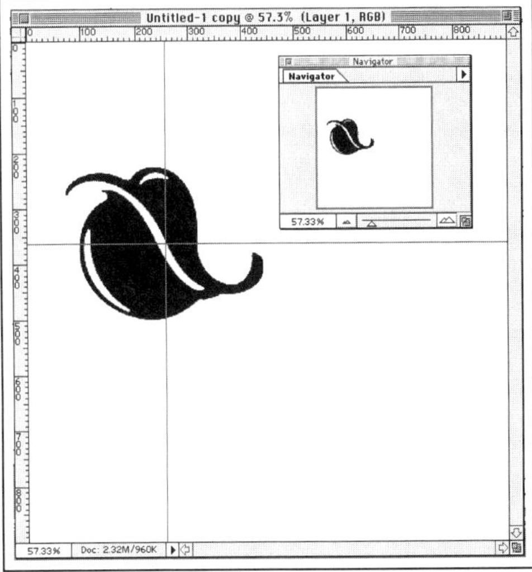

Figure 11-75: Pasting an object into an image so that it is centered on guides.

Usually, any object that is pasted into an image is centered in the document. What makes this trick work? The leaf is very obviously not in the center of the image—but it *is* centered on the guides.

When you create a selection, Photoshop pastes the center of the object on the clipboard into the center of the selection. The center of a 1-pixel selection can only be on that pixel, and Photoshop is quite capable of calculating the center of the object being pasted. This is a useful trick and it works quite well. Until we get the ability to snap the center of an object to guides, it is the easiest way to accomplish that task.

Using Grids

Grids are the other part of the of the precise control equation. Many artists, especially those who are trained as illustrators, are used to working rough comps on top of grid paper. The grid paper allows you to space things with a fair degree of accuracy, without getting too much in your way. You have most of the same features with grids that you have with guides: you can show/hide them and snap to them. You can adjust the grid spacing by altering the Guides & Grid preference. You have the option of viewing the grid as a series of dots as well as either solid or dashed lines.

Shortcuts

Command	Mac	Windows
Show/Hide Grid	Command+'	Ctrl+'
Snap to Grid	Shift+Cmd+'	Shift+Ctrl+'

The menu choices for Grids are on the View menu.

Creating

Creating a grid to use on your image is as easy as pressing Command+' (Mac) or Ctrl+' (Windows). Figure 11-76 shows a standard grid. The keystroke is a toggle, so if the grid is already present, you can hide it. The command toggles on and off the grid in every open image. You cannot view a grid in one image without seeing it in all of the other images.

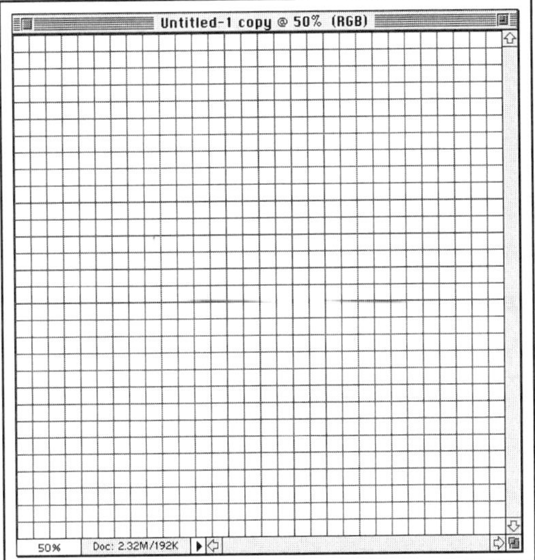

Figure 11-76: Standard grid with all squares the same size.

You can arrange your grid in a number of different ways. To change the grid settings, you need to open the Guides & Grid preference (File | Preferences | Guides & Grid). You can select the unit to use for the grid (pixels, inches, points, cm, etc.). The same warning about resolution applies here.

A useful tip is to leave a darker line every so often so that you can more easily count the grid squares. The Figure 11-77 shows the Guides & Grid preference set to divide an inch (or 300 pixels) into 10 segments. Figure 11-78 shows the grid.

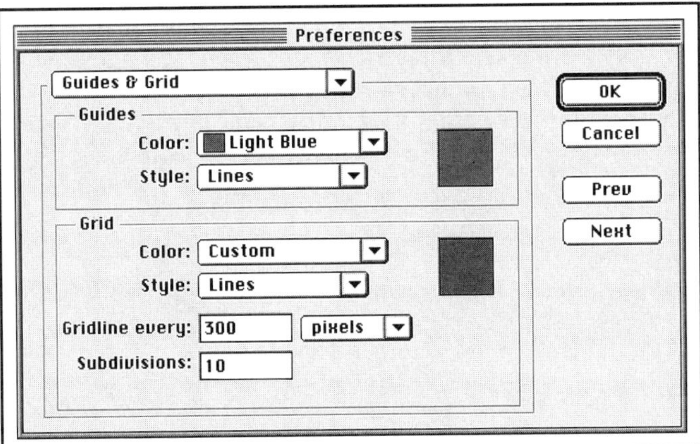

Figure 11-77: Guides & Grid preference set to show subdivisions.

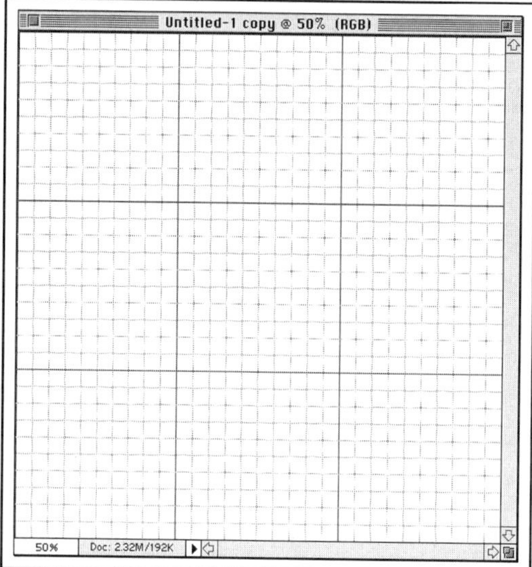

Figure 11-78: Grid with subdivisions.

Painting on a Grid—Pitfalls & Tricks

Once you have a grid in the image, what can you do with it? The selection Marquee will snap to it (if snap is on), so it is easy to get an accurate selection. Photoshop's grid is intelligent. It "knows" not to count a grid line twice. For example, if you create the grid shown in the Preference dialog box above (major grid lines 300 pixels apart), and you drag the marquee around one entire major grid square, your selection is exactly 300 pixels square—not 301 pixels as happens in some other programs (guides are similarly intelligent).

The Painting tools also snap to the grid sometimes, but they snap at the center of the brush. The grid snap behavior changes depending upon the magnification of the image. Figure 11-79 shows the Paintbrush used randomly on an image at 50% magnification. Figure 11-80 shows the same brush on the same image at 200% magnification. In the first figure, the brush adheres closely to the grid; the second one, it seems almost as if the grid is not present.

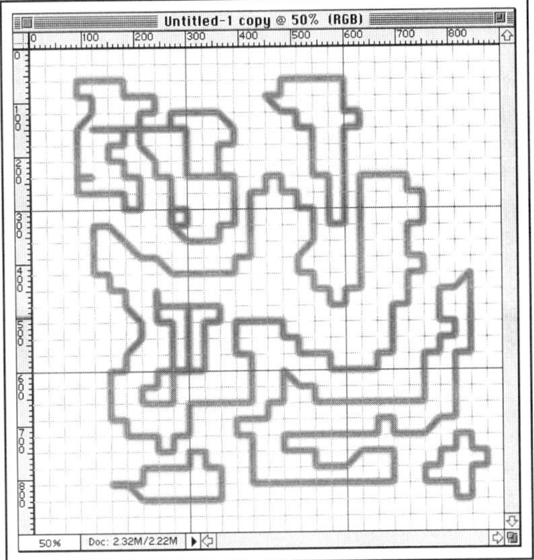

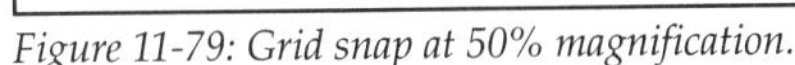
Figure 11-79: Grid snap at 50% magnification.

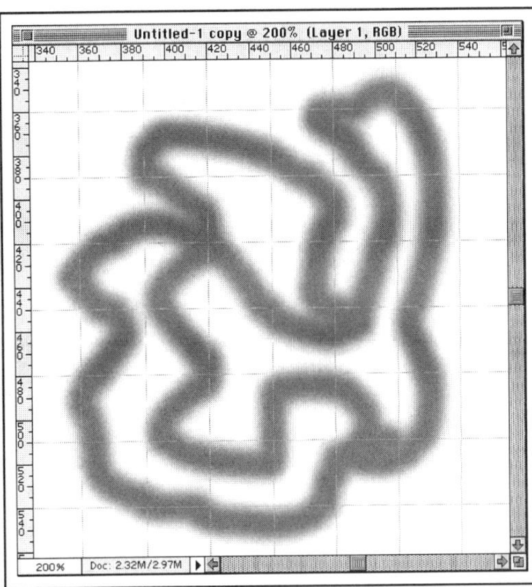

Figure 11-80: Grid snap at 200% magnification.

Making a Visible Grid

There are several features that are not present in this implementation of grids that would be really nice to have. Textile and knitwear designers would bless Adobe's name if there were the ability to create an uneven grid (one in which the horizontal and vertical spacing differs). This is needed when one designs a knitted sweater, because the knitted stitch is not usually square. Typically, one might obtain six stitches and eight rows to an inch of knitting. Designs that are created on a square grid look unusually bad when they are knitted up as if the knitting were square (usually, the image looks foreshortened). Figure 11-81 shows the foreshortening that could occur. It is quite noticeable in the sun face.

Another thing that would be nice is if one could apply the grid permanently to an image instead of having to create a grid pattern (not that this is especially difficult). You can capture a generated grid if you are willing to work at it, however.

To create a grid that can print, set up a grid so that it looks good *on the screen*. Capture the entire window of just the grid (depending upon the screen capture method that you use). Mac users can take a picture of the entire screen by pressing Command+Shift+3. This saves a document called Picture1 (or the next incremental number) to the boot drive. Windows users can press the PrntScrn key to capture the entire window at Alt-PrntScrn to capture the topmost window (which will always be a palette unless you hide them). This places the image on the Windows clipboard and it can be pasted into a new document as soon as Photoshop knows that it is there (which might not be until you minimize the program and go into another application temporarily).

Figure 11-81: Sun face knitting graph showing need for uneven grid to prevent foreshortening of pattern elements.

In any case, once you have a "hard copy" of the grid, you can use it as you want. If you have set the grid to a light gray, you can make it black by using the Levels command or the Threshold or Posterize commands. You can widen the grid if you want by using this technique.

1. Open the image GRID.PSD from the Companion CD-ROM. This is a simple gray grid that was captured from Photoshop's standard 1-subdivision grid.
2. Open the Levels dialog box (Mac: Command+L, Windows: Ctrl+L). Move the Gamma slider all of the way to the right (numeric setting=.10). This makes the grid black.
3. Click on the Channels palette to select it. Load the RGB channel (Mac: Command+click on the RGB channel, Windows: Ctrl+click on the RGB channel). This selects the white spaces between the grid.
4. Reverse the selection (Select -> Inverse).
5. Select the color that you want to use for the grid. Choose Edit | Stroke; Center and set the width to your desired amount (4 was used here). Figure 11-82 shows the thickened grid that results.

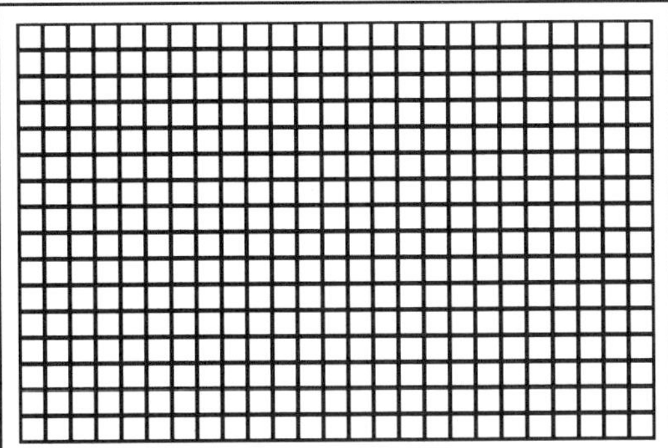

Figure 11-82: Stroking a selected grid.

Putting It All Together

You have been exposed to a number of different techniques in this chapter. Let's finish with an exercise that uses them all. This exercise is long, but it is fairly realistic. Since you have already worked with these techniques, the instructions are somewhat less detailed than normal. There are a lot of new tips and tricks in this example, however, so it is an interesting project.

A clogging group (country dancers) has come to you for help. A local school photographer took the picture of everyone in the group for free—and the results are just about worth the price. All of the images are in grayscale and dead-looking. The group would like to splurge on four-color printing, but has only this set of grayscale images. Each image is embedded in a blue star from last year's attempt to add some interest to the images. It was not a successful attempt.

Now you are stuck with these grayscale images surrounded by a blue star. Colorizing this would be a mess—especially since you have no color images from which to work. You decide that some type of duotone look is most appropriate—given your starting images. Since the group is actually willing to spring for 4-color printing, however, you can actually use more than one "duotone" in the image composite. If you want, take a peek at the Color section to see what you are working toward:

1. Open the image CLOGGER.PSD from the Companion CD-ROM. Figure 11-83 shows the wonderful starting image.
2. Double-click on the Background layer to create Layer 0.
3. Select the Magic Wand tool with a Tolerance of 12 and Anti-alias on. Click on the white background behind the dancer to select the Background. Press the Delete key (Mac) or Backspace key (Windows) to remove the selected area. Deselect (Mac: Command+D, Windows: Ctrl+D).

4. Open the image PATTRGB.PSD from the Companion CD-ROM. The pattern was developed from the kerchief of one of the cloggers. Select the entire image (Mac: Command-A, Windows: Ctrl-A). Define this as a pattern (Edit | Define Pattern).

Figure 11-83: CLOGGER.PSD—your starting point.

5. Create a new Background layer. Fill the image with the pattern (Shift-Delete -> Pattern, 100% Opacity, Normal).
6. Using the Eyedropper tool, click on the blue star to select that color as your foreground color.
7. Make a new layer (click on the New Layer icon at the bottom of the Layers Palette), and fill the image with the foreground color (Mac: Option+Delete, Windows: Alt+Backspace). Change the Apply mode to Screen.
8. Flatten the image. Figure 11-84 shows the image merged into the pattern.

Figure 11-84: Image merged into background pattern.

9. Turn on the Rulers (Mac: Command-R, Windows: Ctrl-R). If your units are not set to Pixels, double-click on a ruler and set them.

10. Drag a horizontal guide to the 100 and 550 pixel marks on the vertical ruler. Drag a vertical guide to the 100 and 500 pixel marks on the horizontal ruler. Select the Elliptical Marquee tool. Drag the marquee from the upper-left corner of the guide to the bottom-right corner as shown in Figure 11-85. Snap to guides.

Figure 11-85: Guides and an elliptical marquee selection.

11. Choose Select | Feather; 25 pixels. Reverse the selection (Select | Inverse).
12. Double-click on the Background layer to create Layer 0. Press the Delete or Backspace key. Figure 11-86 shows the vignette.

Figure 11-86: The vignette surrounding the image.

13. Open the image HEXAGON.PSD on the Companion CD-ROM. This shape was created using the Star filter in Alien Skin Eye Candy 3.0. There are some wonderful filters in that set, but the Star filter alone is worth the price in time saved by not having to create geometric forms by hand.
14. Drag the hexagon layer into the CLOGGER.PSD image. You need to drag it so that it is centered. To do this, press the Shift key as you drag either the image layer or the layer entry in the Layers palette to the clogger image. Position the hexagon layer below that of the clogger, make the clogger layer active and group the two layers together (Mac: Command+G, Windows: Ctrl+G). Figure 11-87 shows the vignette now clipped to a hexagon.

Figure 11-87: Vignette clipped to hexagon.

In order to get the colors to look and work somewhat like duotones (but CMYK ones), you will use a series of steps developed by New York artist Eric Reinfeld. The next set of steps makes a CMYK duotone that is almost sepiatoned from the vignette. For this technique to work, you need to select a CMYK color that contains no black.

1. Click on the Foreground color swatch. Set the values in the CMYK area to CMYK: 0, 70, 45, 0.
2. Duplicate the image (Image | Duplicate | Merged Layers Only, OK).
3. Select Image | Mode | Grayscale.
4. Duplicate the image (Image | Duplicate | OK), and choose Image | Mode | CMYK.
5. Make a new layer (click on the New Layer icon at the bottom of the Layers Palette), and fill the image with the foreground color (Mac: Option+Delete, Windows: Alt+Backspace). Change the Apply mode to Screen. Group the layers (Mac: Command+G, Windows: Ctrl+G). Merge Down (Mac: Command+E, Windows: Ctrl+E). The image is very light, but only the Magenta and Yellow channels now contain any data as you can see in Figure 11-88.
6. Open the Channels palette and make the Black channel the only active channel.
7. Choose Image | Apply Image and select the grayscale clogger image as the Source as shown in Figure 11-89.
8. Let's give the Magenta plate a little boost. Make the Magenta plate active in the Channels palette (Mac: Command+2, Windows: Ctrl+2). Choose Image | Apply Image and make the Yellow plate the Source. Change the Apply mode to Color Burn as shown in Figure 11-90.

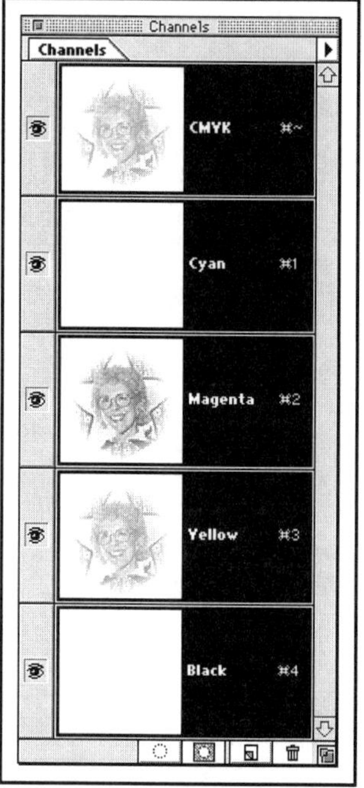

Figure 11-88: Channels palette showing data only in Magenta and Yellow plates.

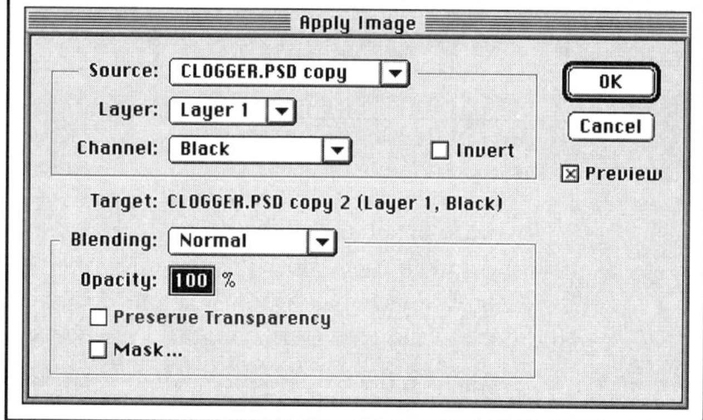

Figure 11-89: Apply image dialog box to place grayscale clogger into black plate only.

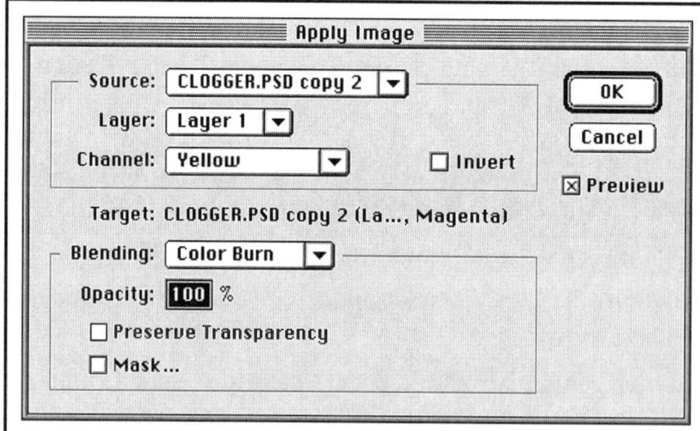

Figure 11-90: Adding some of the Yellow plate to the Magenta using Color Burn mode.

9. Save your work as CLOGCMYK.PSD. Close the other open images.

The next step in this procedure is to build an interesting frame treatment for the hexagon. Using a swash character from the Ultimate Symbol Design Elements collection and the multi-rotate Action that you used earlier, you can create the perfect edge:

1. Turn on the Rulers (Mac: Command-R, Windows: Ctrl-R). You need to determine the size of the straight sides of the hexagon. Change the image to 100% magnification (Mac: Command+Option+0, Windows: Ctrl+Alt+0). Drag a horizontal guide to the top of the straight side of the hexagon, and other horizontal guide to the bottom of the straight side of the hexagon as shown in Figure 11-91. Count the pixels between the guides (it should be 300 pixels). This gives you the needed width for the swatch.

TIP *When you import vector artwork, you get the best quality if you rasterize it at the size that you need it to be rather than resizing it within Photoshop.*

Figure 11-91: Guides aligned with sides of hexagon.

2. Open the file SWASH.EPS from the Companion CD-ROM. This is the same as the 01K29.EPS that is in the Ultimate Symbol Design Elements collection also on your Companion CD-ROM. In the Rasterize dialog box, enter 300 pixels as the Width, Constrain Proportions, and check Anti-alias.

3. Select Image | Rotate Canvas | 90° CCW. This rotates the swash so that you can easily drag it into position. Let's be obsessive about getting things centered and try this easy way to find the center of the swash without measuring anything.
4. Select the Line tool and set its width to 1 pixel with no arrowheads. Create a new layer in the rotated swash image. Press the Shift key and draw a straight vertical line from the top of the image to the bottom.
5. Select the entire layer (Mac: Command-A, Windows: Ctrl-A). Cut it to the clipboard (Mac: Command-C, Windows: Ctrl-C). Paste in the selection from the clipboard (Mac: Command-V, Windows: Ctrl-V). This centers the line on the image. The Line is your active layer. Click the second column on the Layers palette next to the Swash layer to place a Link symbol in it. This links the two layers together so that they can be moved as one.
6. Drag the line layer *from the image* into the CLOGCMYK.PSD image. As long as you drag the layer from the image, both it and its linked layer will move to the new image (do not drag the thumbnail from the Layers palette; it will not move the linked file with it). Position the thin line so that it is exactly on the edge of the hexagon below it. The swash should fit nicely between the two guides as shown in Figure 11-92.

Figure 11-92: Swash character and positioning line placed in CLOGCMYK.PSD.

7. Drag the Line layer to the Layers palette trash can. It is no longer needed.
8. Make the swash character layer active. Choose Layer palette menu | Duplicate Layer; target: New file. This places the swash into its own file.
9. Drag the icon for the swash layer (you are working in the new file) to the New Layer icon (the center icon at the bottom of the Layers palette).
10. You need to flip this copy horizontally so that the swash is in the same location relative to the left side of the image. Since there is so much transparency in the layer, that won't happen by simply selecting Image | Flip Horizontal—so don't do that yet! Instead, take the Paintbrush and place a dab of paint in all four corners of the image. Now, select Image | Transform | Flip Horizontal. Figure 11-93 shows the result.

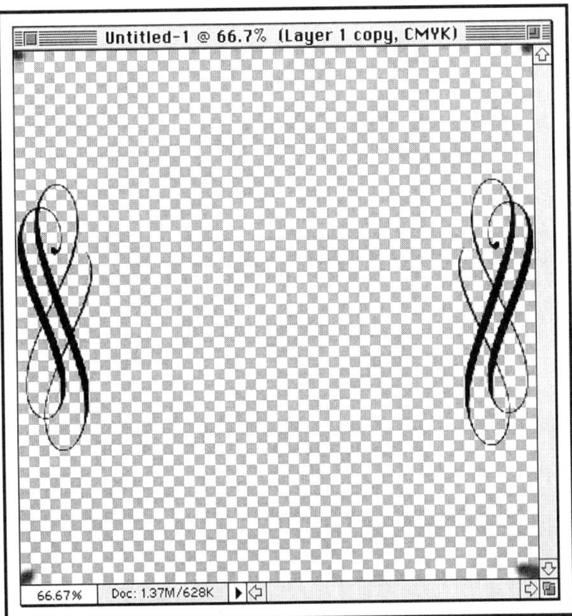

Figure 11-93: Swash character flipped horizontally after corners added to image.

11. Erase the dabs of color in the corners of the image and Merge Down (Mac: Command-E, Windows: Ctrl-E). You are left with only a layer named Layer 1 in the image.

12. Select the multi-rotate Action and click the Play button. Figure 11-94 shows the result—a perfect frame, sized exactly for the hexagon that surrounds the clogger.
13. The top edges of the hexagon are not quite visible. Choose Image | Canvas Size and make both dimensions 700 pixels. Anchor in the center. Repeat the Canvas Size command on the Clogger image.
14. Merge Visible (Mac: Shift+Command+E, Windows: Shift+Ctrl+E).

Figure 11-94: Frame created from swash character using multi-rotate Action.

15. Press the Shift key as you drag the frame layer into the CLOGCMYK.PSD image. Delete the original swash layer in the image and hide the guides. Figure 11-95 shows the framed hexagon. Save the CLOGGMYK.PSD image again and save the separate frame file as well. You may then close the frame file.

Figure 11-95: Framed hexagon.

This next portion of the exercise finishes the frame around the hexagon and creates an adjustment layer. That only corrects the image and the cutout frame.

1. Set your Foreground color to CMYK: 0, 67, 45, 74.
2. Make sure that the frame layer is active. Fill the layer with the foreground color while preserving transparency (Mac: Shift+Option+Delete, Windows: Shift+Alt+Backspace).
3. Make the clogger layer active. Add a layer mask. Let the layer mask remain active.
4. We want to "knock out" the frame area from this layer, so we need to construct a mask that will do that. Choose Image | Apply Image and select the frame layer (probably called Layer 1 copy) as your source. Choose the Transparency as the Channel as shown in Figure 11-96. Notice that you need to invert the transparency. Turn off the visibility icon next to the frame layer to see that the layer mask on the clogger layer does what you want. Figure 11-97 shows this with a gray background so that it is more visible for the figure in the book (*do not add a gray layer to your image*).

Figure 11-96: Creating a mask to knock out the border area of the hexagon.

Figure 11-97: Knockout visible in hexagon.

5. Drag the frame layer below that of the clogger.
6. The purpose of the frame is to allow the frame color to show *outside* of the confines of the original hexagon. Whatever background we decide to design has to be seen through the frame area that lies *inside* of the original hexagon. Therefore, you need to remove the hexagon area from the frame. Press the modifier key (Mac: Command, Windows: Control) and click on the thumbnail for the clogger to load the transparency of that layer (click on the clogger thumbnail, *not* the layer mask thumbnail). Press the Delete key (Mac) or the Backspace key (Windows). Figure 11-98 shows the image (again with a gray background so that it looks "pretty for the camera").

Figure 11-98: Border with area inside of hexagon knocked out.

7. Create a Hue/Saturation Adjustment Layer (Mac: Command+ click, Windows: Ctrl+click on the New Layer icon at the bottom of the Layers palette). The Adjustment layer should be the top layer in the layers palette. Click the Colorize button and set the Hue to +18 and the Saturation to 50 as shown in Figure 11-99.

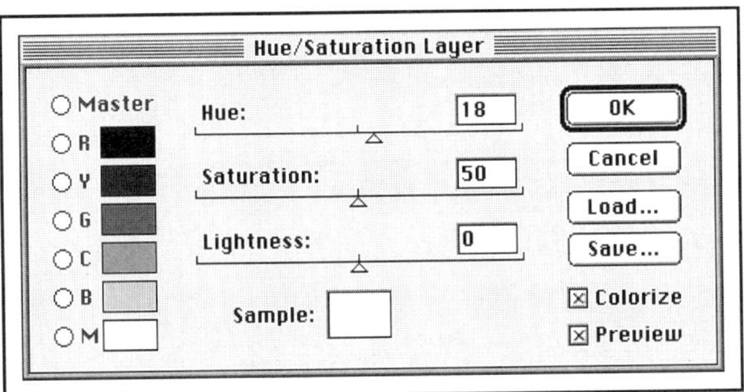

Figure 11-99: Create a Hue/Saturation layer.

8. The color in the clogger's face is just a bit too strong. Let's tone it with the Yellow layer again. Make only the Magenta channel active (Mac: Command+2, Windows: Ctrl+2). Select Image | Apply Image and choose the Layer 1 (the clogger) as the Source. Select the Yellow channel and change the Apply mode to Screen as shown in Figure 11-100.

Apply Image
Source: CLOGCMYK.PSD
Layer: Layer 1
Channel: Yellow
Invert
OK
Cancel
Preview
Target: CLOGCMYK.PSD (Layer 1, Magenta)
Blending: Screen
Opacity: 100 %
Preserve Transparency
Mask...

Figure 11-100: Screen some Yellow from the Magenta channel.

9. Finally, you need to build a mask that allows changes from the Adjustment layer to only affect areas of the total image that are visible at the moment (i.e., the mask needs to "respect" the layer mask below it). This turns out to be a surprisingly easy thing to do. Choose Image | Apply Image and select the Merged image as the source. For Channel, select Transparency. This produces the desired results. Figure 11-101 shows the dialog box. (The "hard way" around building the same mask in three steps: apply the Layer 1 transparency in Normal mode, apply the inverted Layer 1 layer mask in Subtract mode, and apply the Layer 1 copy—the frame—transparency in Screen mode.)

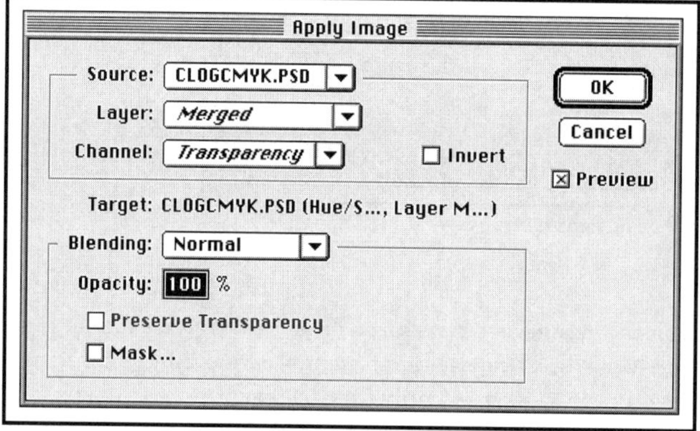

Figure 11-101: Applying the Merged layer transparency as the Adjustment layer mask.

10. Save your work.

Finally, you are ready to create the background. For this, you will increase the image size a bit:

1. Create a new document (Mac: Command-N, Windows: Ctrl-N). Make it 900 pixels square and CMYK mode.

2. Open the image file PATTCMYK.PSD from the Companion CD-ROM. Select the entire image (Mac: Command-A, Windows: Ctrl-A). Define this as a pattern (Edit | Define Pattern). Fill the image with the pattern (Shift+Delete | Pattern, 100 percent Opacity, Normal).

TIP *Patterns are color mode sensitive. Patterns defined for RGB will not work on CMYK images and vice versa.*

3. Set your foreground color to CMYK: 87, 49, 0, 0. This color is similar to the blue that was around the original star border, but it contains no black.
4. Make a new layer (click on the New Layer icon at the bottom of the Layers Palette), and fill the image with the foreground color (Mac: Option+Delete, Windows: Alt+Backspace). Change the Apply mode to Screen. Group the layers (Mac: Command+G, Windows: Ctrl+G). Merge Down (Mac: Command+E, Windows: Ctrl+E).
5. Open the Channels palette and make the Black channel the only active channel. Fill the Black channel with the pattern (Shift+Delete | Pattern, 100% Opacity, Normal). You now have another CMYK duotone work-alike.
6. Click on the CLOGCMYK.PSD image to make it active. Link all of the layers together by clicking on the Link column. Press the Shift key as you drag the layers from the image to the new document filled with the pattern. Before you do anything else, Merge the linked layers (Mac: Command-E, Windows: Ctrl-E). Although it might look as if the Adjustment layer is doing something odd when you first bring in the clogger image, the layers will merge down properly if you do it before executing any other commands. Figure 11-102 shows the image with the background added.
7. Save the image as CLOGBACK.PSD.

Figure 11-102: Image with new background.

Next, you are going to create a shield behind the hexagon and background to clip the shape. You will then merge this into a another background that uses the name of the clogging group as a pattern.

1. Open the image PANEL.PSD from the Companion CD-ROM. This is another image from the Ultimate Symbol Design Elements collection sampler, but for expediency, it has already been rasterized to the correct size.
2. Press the Shift key and drag the panel into the CLOGBACK.PSD image. Close all of the images except for this one (CLOGBACK.PSD).
3. Double-click on the Background layer to create Layer 0.
4. Drag the shield to the bottom of the layer stack.
5. Group all three layers together. Figure 11-103 shows the image against a white background. Merge the Visible Layers (Mac: Shift+Command+E, Windows: Shift+Ctrl+E).
6. Increase the Canvas Size to 1,200 x 1,200, anchored in the center. The final image will not be this large, but you need to have room to rotate the type pattern. Create a new layer.

Figure 11-103: Panel used to clip layers together.

7. Open the file TEXTPATT.PSD from the Companion CD-ROM. Select the entire image (Mac: Command+A, Windows: Ctrl+A).Define this as a pattern (Edit | Define Pattern). Fill the empty layer in the 1200 x 1200 pixel image with the pattern (Shift+Delete | Pattern, 100% Opacity, Normal).

TIP *When you define a pattern from a transparent layer, the pattern also has transparency, so it can be applied over another pattern or image without obscuring it.*

8. Drag the pattern layer below that of the clogger.
9. Rotate the layer (Mac: Command+T, Windows: Ctrl+T) counterclockwise until it slants at an attractive angle (not 45°). A good angle is the one that is parallel to the slant of the lower edge of the panel. In order for you to use the rotate feature of Free transform, the image needs to be displayed smaller than the physical window in which it resides. Figure 11-104 shows the image as it is being rotated.
10. Turn on the Rulers (Mac: Command-R, Windows: Ctrl-R). Make the clogger layer active. Drag vertical guides so that they snap to the bounding box of the layer (this should be at approximately 150 and 1,050 pixels). Drag horizontal guides until they form a square (place at the same coordinates as the vertical guides but on the other ruler).

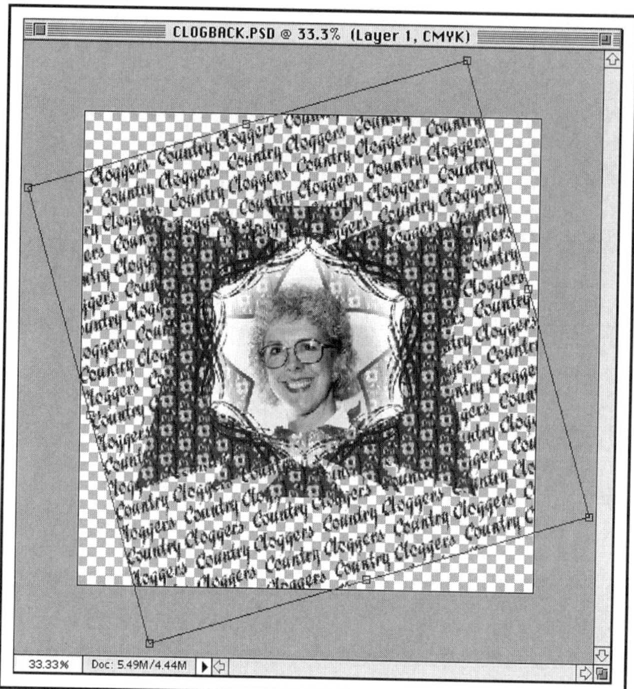

Figure 11-104: Rotating the text.

11. Choose the Rectangular Marquee tool and let it snap to the guides. Choose Image | Crop and hide the guides.
12. In the Channel palette, click on the New Channel icon in the center of the Channels palette to create a new channel. It should be filled automatically with black. Invert the channel to fill it with white or press Shift+Delete. Return to the composite channel (Mac: Command+~, Windows: Ctrl+~).
13. Choose Image | Canvas Size and set the size to 1,020 pixels square. The channel that you created above is now a nice white square surrounded by black and shows exactly where the original image size had been.
14. Create a new Background layer by pressing the modifier key (Mac: Option, Windows: Alt) and clicking on the New Layer icon in the Layers palette. Select Background as the desired layer mode (you need to scroll to the bottom of the list).
15. Set your foreground color to CMYK: 0, 43, 56, 22. This is a color from the clogger's face. Fill the background layer (Mac: Option-Delete, Windows: Alt-Delete). Figure 11-105 shows the image.

Figure 11-105: Image with new background.

16. Prepare a Gradient. Press D to set the colors back to the default of black and white. Swap the foreground and background colors (X). Select the Gradient tool and set it to Radial Gradient and Foreground to Background. Click Edit. Place a foreground marker at the 60% mark between white and black as shown in Figure 11-106. The top slider between white and black should be set to 30%.

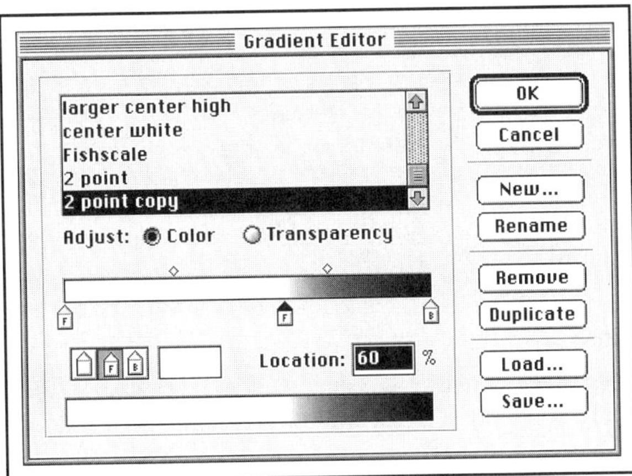

Figure 11-106: Gradient definition.

17. Make the clogger layer active. Create a layer mask.
18. Turn on the Rulers (Mac: Command-R, Windows: Ctrl-R). Choose View | Clear Guides. Drag out new guides to the center of the image (pixel 510 on each ruler).
19. Load channel 5 (Mac: Command+Option+5, Windows: Ctrl+Option+5).
20. With the Gradient tool, place your cursor at the intersection of the two guides. Press the Shift key and drag the Gradient rubber-band cursor to the bottom-right corner of the selection. Figure 11-107 shows the layer mask and Figure 11-108 shows the way in which the edges of the panel now blend with the background.

Figure 11-107: Layer mask with Radial Gradient.

21. Make a new layer (click on the New Layer icon at the bottom of the Layers Palette) at the top of the layer stack.
22. Set your foreground color back to color of the border (use the Eyedropper tool or set it explicitly to CMYK: 0, 67, 45, 74).
23. Channel 5 (the square) should still be loaded. Select Edit | Stroke; 8 pixels, Outside. *Do not deselect.*
24. Make a new layer (click on the New Layer icon at the bottom of the Layers Palette) at the top of the layer stack. Choose Select|Modify|Border; 50 pixels. Fill the area (Mac: Option-Delete, Windows: Alt-Delete) with CMYK: 0, 67, 45, 74—which should still be your foreground color.

Figure 11-108: Softly blended image.

Figure 11-109: Embossed look on image.

25. Load Channel 5 again and reverse the selection (Select -> Inverse). Press the Delete or Backspace key. Figure 11-109 shows the image. The clogger now looks as if she is on an embossed button.
26. Save the image as CLOGBTN.PSD.

You are now at the final steps—making a texture to set off the edges of the image.

1. Create a new image the same size as the current image, but in Grayscale mode.
2. Open the image PANELPAT.PSD from the Companion CD-ROM. This is a layer that is the same size as your image and created from the panel in the image.
3. You need to add a top and bottom row. Duplicate the pattern layer by dragging its thumbnail to the New Layer icon at the bottom of the Layers palette. Choose Filter | Other | Offset, Right: 0, Down: 60, Wrap Around. Use the Rectangular Marquee tool to enclose all of the image but the top row. Delete.
4. Duplicate the full pattern layer again. Offset again, but choose –60 as the Down offset. Select and delete all but the bottom row.
5. Merge Down (Mac: Command-E, Windows: Ctrl-E). Figure 11-110 shows the panel pattern image.

Figure 11-110: Panel pattern.

6. Drag the icon for the panel layer to the New Layer icon (the center icon at the bottom of the Layers palette) to duplicate the layer. Choose Layer | Transform | Free Transform and rotate the layer as you did the text.
7. Repeat Step 6. This time, use the various methods of skewing and distorting to mutilate the new layer. Figure 11-111 shows the image in Free Transform.

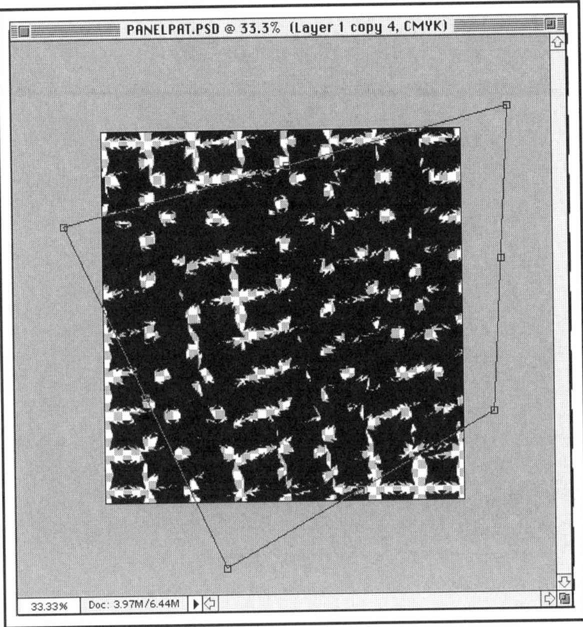

Figure 11-111: Image being seriously mistreated.

8. Make a new layer (click on the New Layer icon at the bottom of the Layers Palette). Option-Merge the visible layers to keep your originals intact (Mac: Shift+Command+Option+E, Windows: Shift+Ctrl+Alt+E).
9. Press D to set the colors back to the default of black and white. Choose Filter | Pixellate | Pointillize, 22. Select Filter | Blur | Gaussian Blur, 2.0.
10. Make sure that all layers are visible. Click on the Channels palette and create a new channel. Fill with white.
11. Choose Image | Apply Image and used the merged image as your Source and Black as the Channel.
12. Make the CLOGBTN.PSD image active. Click on the Background layer to select it.
13. Press the modifier key (Mac: Option, Windows: Alt) and click on the layer mask for the clogger to load it. Choose Select | Load Selection. Load Channel 2 of PANELPAT.PSD and click on the Intersection with Selection button in the Operation section of the dialog box.

14. Press Delete or Backspace to fill the selection with white. Figure 11-112 shows the final image.

Figure 11-112: Finished clogger.

The Companion CD-ROM contains several other cloggers: Bethy, Cheri, Crezia, and Stephanie. You can re-create this effect with the remaining cloggers and arrange the images together for another composite if you want. See how many ways you can find to combine images.

Moving On

This chapter has covered a lot of ground. You learned how to use Adjustment layers, work with Guides and Grids, and use the new Free Transform and Numeric Transform commands. Along the way, you have seen many different tricks that can be played to force Photoshop to do what you want done—so that you, and not the program—are in control.

The next chapter, "Photoshop & the Web," shows you how to prepare images for the World Wide Web. You will learn about the file formats that matter, how to make images small so that they load faster, and how to create a wonderful variety of seamless patterns.

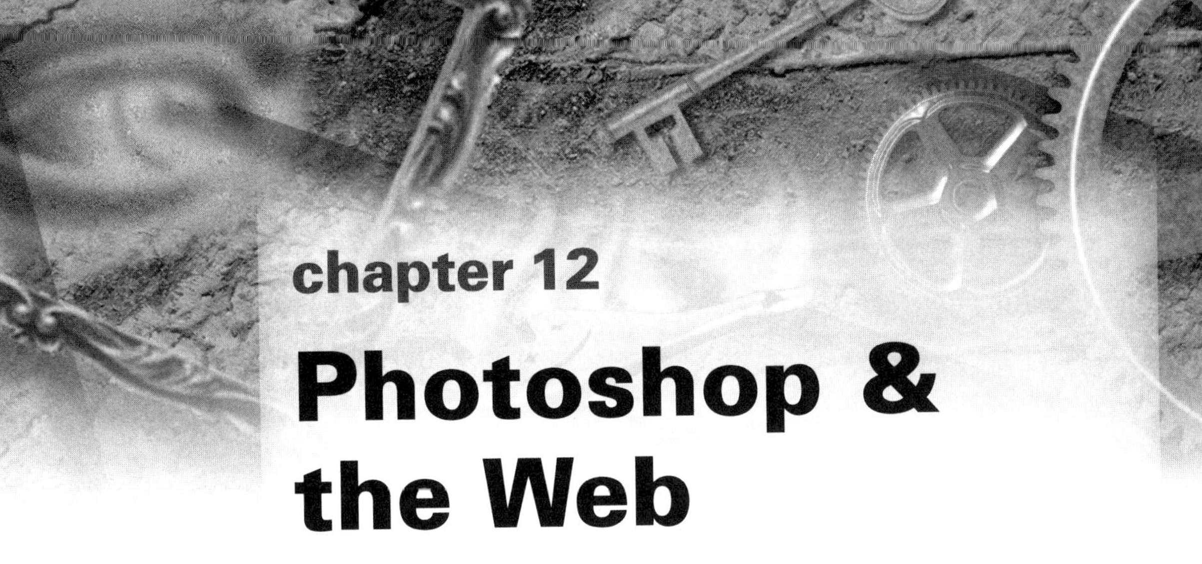

chapter 12 Photoshop & the Web

The planetary network of computers we know as the Internet has been in existence for many years. It has been, until recently, the exclusive tool of scientists, academics, government employees, and students. It's purpose was to provide an easy corridor for information, virtually all of which was in the form of text. Several years ago the graphical browser appeared, allowing users to see text and pictures at the same time. The rest, as they say, is history.

Once browsers came into existence, all of the reasons why human beings use pictures *and* text to communicate with each other became important to the network medium. With picture information, a commercial impetus also became inevitable. Given the advantages inherent in a global information network, and the ease with which virtually anyone can place information on that network, the Internet's rapid growth is not surprising.

For reasons which will become clear as you study the information in this chapter, picture information on the World Wide Web has to be prepared in special ways. It must also belong to a specific classification of computer document called the *raster image file*. By happy coincidence, Adobe Photoshop, the subject of this book, is the world's most widely used and respected raster-processing software.

Photoshop had already attained its preeminent position when the graphical Web began to grow. Driven by the commercial impetus of the graphics and prepress industries, it had already developed into a feature-rich and flexible program. With the increased importance of the digital medium, Photoshop has turned out to be the image-processing program of choice for Internet developers as well as for prepress people. All of the features which made it important before the Internet began to grow have turned out to be important features for the new medium.

Preparing images for print, as you discovered in Chapter 9, "Photoshop Prepress," requires a specialized knowledge of printing. In the same way, preparing images for the Web will require that you become familiar with the way the Web works. The guidelines you need to follow for Web graphics are no more complex than those for printing. There are, however, many variables to keep in mind, just as there are many for print work. This chapter is devoted to bringing you a good working knowledge of Web basics. To this you'll be able to add your skill with Photoshop. The combination should allow you to become proficient at making graphics for the Web which are visually and technically effective.

Essentials of Web Graphics

Web graphic files differ from those used in the prepress world in that they are typically of low resolution and always in the RGB mode. They are usually smaller in physical dimension than press files because of the limitations imposed by the speed of the Web: larger files take an unacceptable amount of time to transfer from the host to the client computer. This speed constraint lies at the heart of most graphic problems on the Internet. It is the single most important concept to be discussed in this chapter, and your success as a designer of Web graphics will be determined by how thoroughly you are able to balance the interplay between file size and file content. More simply put: a file can be attractive in every way, but if it's too large, very few Internet users will ever see it.

All of the Web's graphic information—banner text, bullets, buttons, photographs, arrows, navigation cues—are in what is called the *raster format*. In the following section of this chapter, you'll learn the difference between the two main computer graphic file types. You'll also learn about the HTML language which is used to program a Web document so that it can be displayed by a browser such as Netscape Navigator or Microsoft Internet Explorer. Finally, along with an explanation of why small file sizes are so important and what you can do to make sure that your files are no larger than they need to be, you'll learn about the two file types—GIF and JPEG—used by Web designers.

Graphic File Types: Vector vs. Raster

Speaking in general computer terms, there are two main graphic file types: the *vector* file and the *raster* file.

Vector files are made up of shapes that can be described in mathematical terms. The technical descriptors might include such things as height, width, placement within a defined space, the color of a fill, and so on. These shapes are usually composed of lines which enclose an area or stand alone. In PostScript, for example, the lines take the form of Bézier (pronounced beh-zee-áy) curves (also called *paths*). Objects drawn in draw programs such as Adobe Illustrator or Macromedia FreeHand are examples of vector shapes made up of Bézier curves. Type is another example of the computer's use of vector shapes. PostScript type consists of drawn shapes—which are made up of Bézier curves—that have been placed in a special file that allows the shapes to be handled as macro objects instead of graphic shapes. Except for a few special-case situations, vector-mapped graphic objects cannot be used on the Web. These special cases involve what is called a browser plug-in, a small helper program that gives the browser capabilities which were not part of its original design. Although plug-ins are simple to acquire and simple to install, industry studies indicate that most Internet users do not bother with them. Because of this, you should be wary of using technology which is not part of the standard Web feature set. A plug-in which can display a vector graphic object is one example of such a non-standard feature.

Raster files are represented by the data processed in programs such as Photoshop. A raster is defined as a collection of objects—in this case *pixels*—arranged in uniform columns and rows. A raster computer file can be thought of, whether color or grayscale, as a set of small squares which use a mosaic approach to building an image. Each square is displayed as a single color tone. The success of the mosaic depends upon the fact that the squares are quite small and the human eye is not very good at fine resolution. The squares blend into each other to give the impression of a continuous range of tones. An example of a raster object is shown in Figure 12-1. The tiny rectangle in the left-hand image has been magnified on the right-hand side so that the individual components of the image are visible.

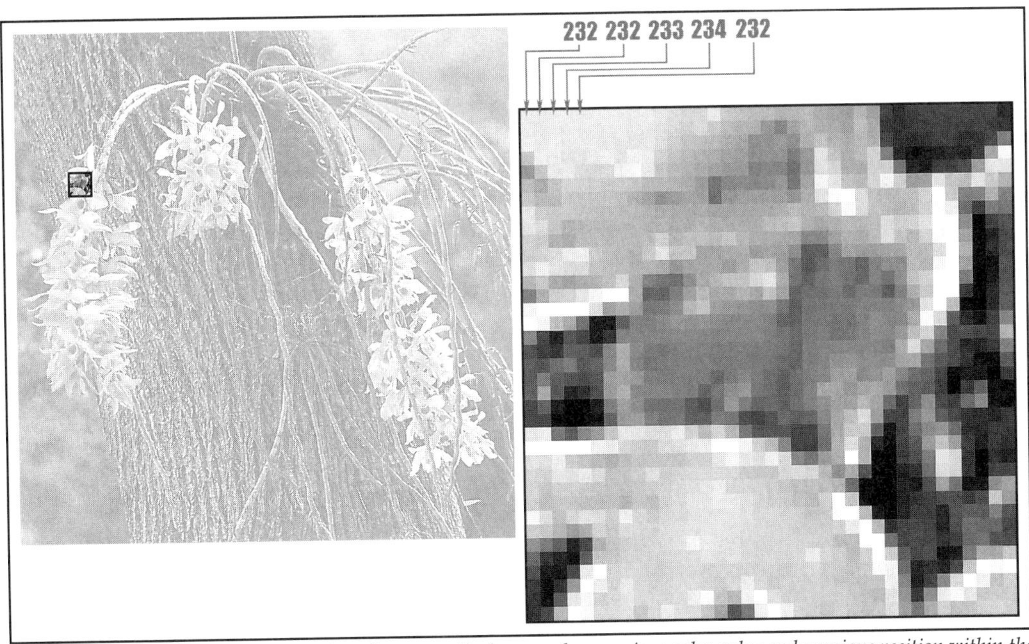

Figure 12-1: A raster file is a mosaic of small squares. Each square has a unique color value and a unique position within the image.

A raster file has some drawbacks and some advantages. The actual storing of the file is extremely simple. The section of the image on the right in Figure 12-1 could be stored—and described—this way: the area is composed of 38 horizontal rows of pixels; each row is 38 pixels across; beginning in the upper left corner, the first row contains RGB values 232, 232, 233, 234, 232, and so on. A description of this sort quickly becomes tedious to the human mind, but to a computer, it is a straightforward task. Imagine this description carried on until all 1,444 pixels in the image have been described by their position and RGB values. Yet, this is the way a computer handles the image, by reading this table of values into memory and displaying them in equivalent rows and columns of monitor pixels.

The latter point is a big advantage: monitor pixels and object pixels correspond to each other easily. Your CRT uses pixels to display everything you see. It's simple procedure: simply match up the pixels of the image to the pixels of the screen. It is so simple, in fact, that very little thought has to be given to what kind of operating system is being used. Because there are many kinds of computers—and operating systems—using the Internet, the raster file is nearly ideal.

Disadvantages? The main problem is one of file size. A single pixel value, with respect to the grayscale image in the example, represents one byte of information and so adds one byte to the size of the file. Simple arithmetic gives us a file size of at least 1,444 bytes (38 x 38 = 1,444 bytes, or 1.41 kilobytes). If the example file were in RGB, or color, mode instead of grayscale, each pixel would need to be represented by three bytes of information. An RGB file 38 pixels square would be at least 4332 bytes (4.23 kilobytes). The information contained in the file also has to include, besides the color value of the pixels, header information which tells the computer what kind of file—TIFF, EPS, BMP, etc.—it is displaying, the number of rows, and the number of pixels in each row. In some cases there is also a special color look-up table (CLUT). All of this information is needed to describe and store the tiny area shown in the figure. The size of the file has a direct bearing on its use on a Web page since the Web network's efficiency, or speed, is measured by the rapidity of its transfer of information from one computer to another. That efficiency is typically measured in figures expressed as bytes per second, or kilobytes per second. In really simple terms: the more bytes you have, the more time it takes to get the image from one place to another.

Inline Graphics

A graphic on a Web page is a substitute for a single character of text. The Web, despite daily amazements of technology, consists of a simple network structure that was designed for the transfer of small ASCII text files. Graphics objects are simply inserted into the stream of ASCII data and displayed within the body of text. Using the specifications of HTML 2.0 and above, the graphic can be inserted into the text along the text's baseline, centerline, or topline. These concepts are illustrated in Figure 12-2.

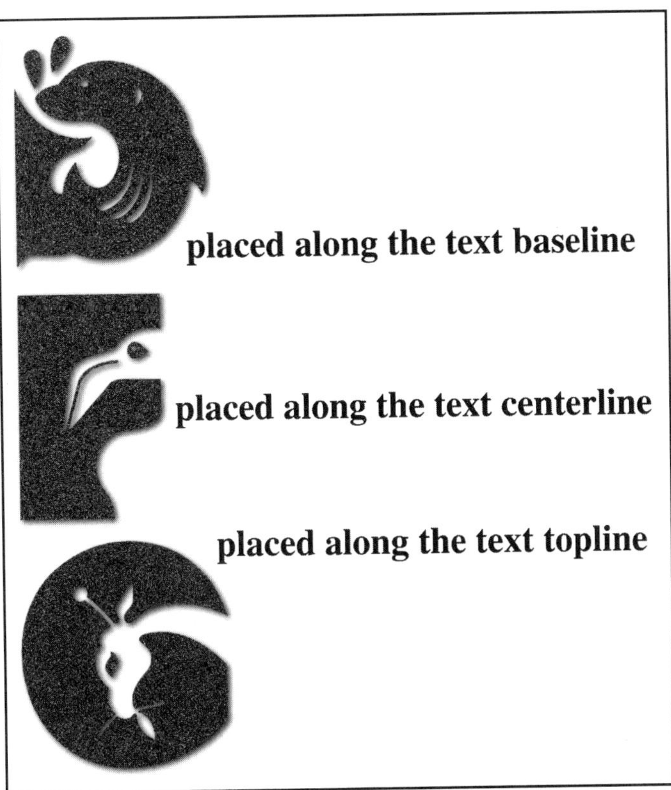

Figure 12-2: Graphics on the Web substitute for single characters. The display within the body of text along the text's baseline, centerline, or topline.

A Web graphic can occupy a single line of text making it equivalent to a paragraph. Most of the paragraph style formats can be applied to it just as they are applied to the text within which the graphic resides. These would include such things as centered text, flush left, flush right, and indent attributes. Print graphic designers have long been accustomed to placing graphics and text in any position on a page. On the Web, things aren't quite that simple: using only text attributes, designing graphically effective pages has been difficult. The advent of HTML 3.0 and the Netscape extensions—particularly the use of tables—has begun to allow some design freedom. However, it will be some time before the text-only origins of Web pages will become obscured and allow for the design freedom that prepress designers have enjoyed for a number of years.

Nuts & Bolts of the Web

It will be helpful to look at a sample HTML file and see how it is interpreted by the browser. The following shows the correlation between HTML code and the browser's display. Figure 12-3 is a simulated Web page or HTML document. This is a very simple page. The information it contains is not intended as an HTML tutorial. Instead, simply observe the way the ASCII information is divided into two parts, the tags which are instructions for the browser and everything else, the information on which the tags are to operate.

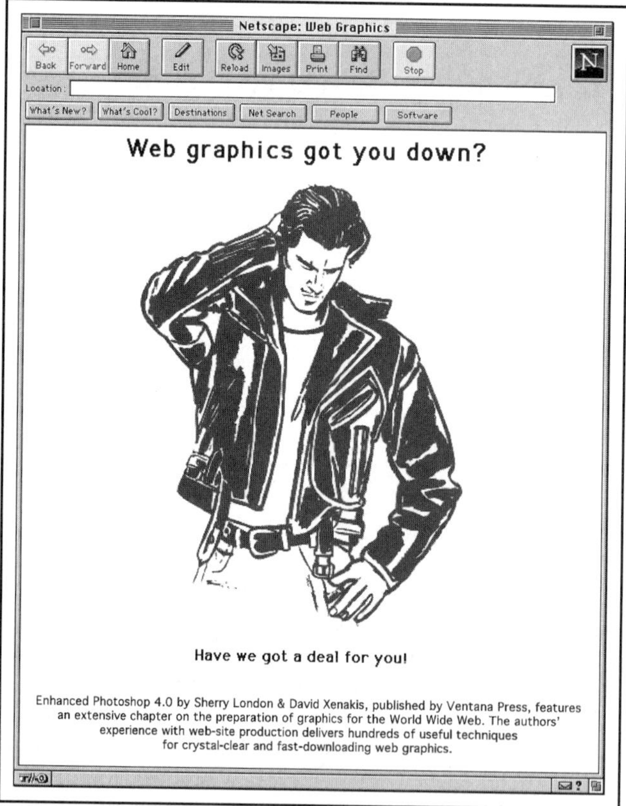

Netscape: Web Graphics
Back
Forward
Home
Edit
Reload
Images
Print
Find
Stop
Location:
What's New?
What's Cool?
Destinations
Net Search
People
Software
Web graphics got you down?
Have we got a deal for you!
Enhanced Photoshop 4.0 by Sherry London & David Xenakis, published by Ventana Press, features an extensive chapter on the preparation of graphics for the World Wide Web. The authors' experience with web-site production delivers hundreds of useful techniques for crystal-clear and fast-downloading web graphics.

Figure 12-3: A simulation of a simple Web page.

The HTML code for this simulated browser display is shown Figure 12-4. Please note that normal HTML code is not typically formatted in this manner. It is presented in this way to make the pairing of the code commands easier to grasp.

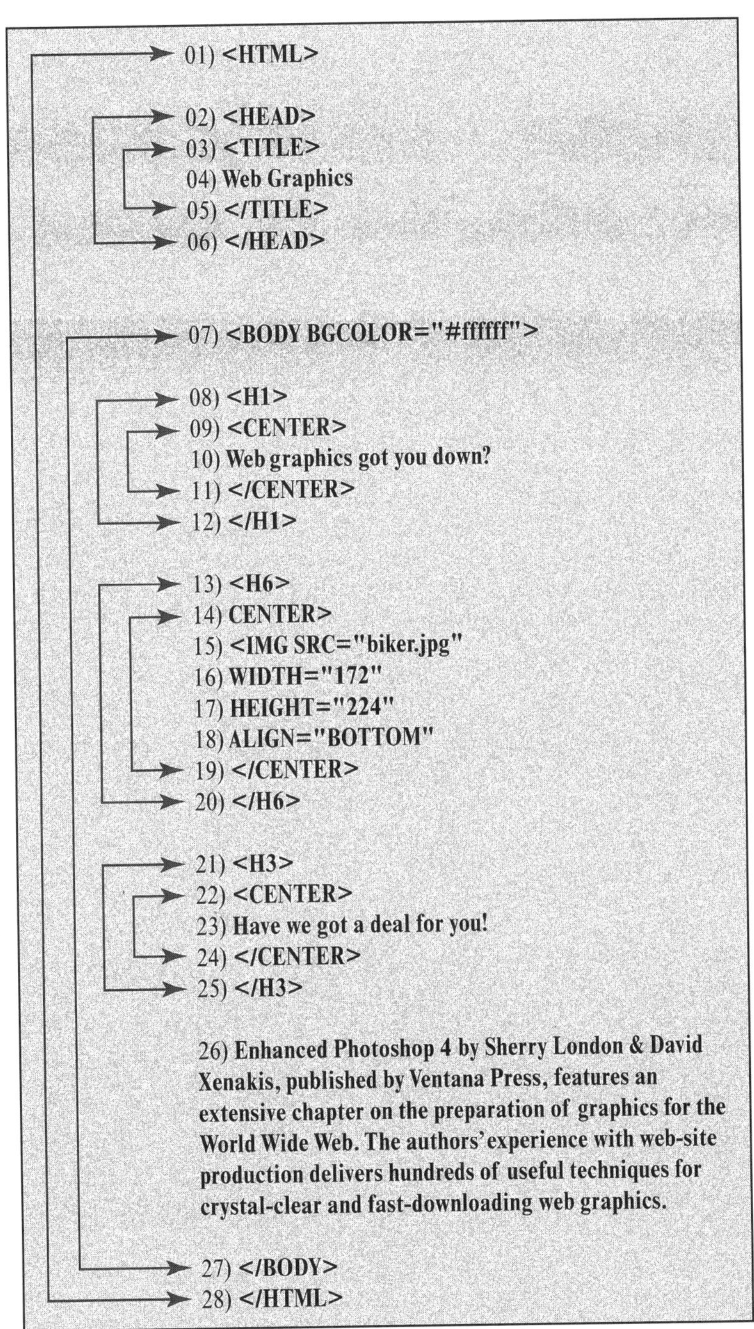

01) <HTML>
02) <HEAD>
03) <TITLE>
04) Web Graphics
05) </TITLE>
06) </HEAD>
07) <BODY BGCOLOR="#ffffff">
08) <H1>
09) <CENTER>
10) Web graphics got you down?
11) </CENTER>
12) </H1>
13) <H6>
14) CENTER>
15) <IMG SRC="biker.jpg"
16) WIDTH="172"
17) HEIGHT="224"
18) ALIGN="BOTTOM"
19) </CENTER>
20) </H6>
21) <H3>
22) <CENTER>
23) Have we got a deal for you!
24) </CENTER>
25) </H3>
26) Enhanced Photoshop 4 by Sherry London & David Xenakis, published by Ventana Press, features an extensive chapter on the preparation of graphics for the World Wide Web. The authors' experience with web-site production delivers hundreds of useful techniques for crystal-clear and fast-downloading web graphics.
27) </BODY>
28) </HTML>

Figure 12-4: The HTML code used to display the page in Figure 12-3.

HTML documents are composed of code information and text information. The tags are set off—usually, but not always—in pairs. Each tag is an instruction to the browser to display the non-tag information within the tag pairs in a specific way. The first tag usually takes the form <TAG>. The concluding tag takes the form </TAG> and is distinguished from the opening tag by the presence of the forward slash.

Line 1: <HTML> is the first tag of all HTML documents. It is a declaration that the document contains HTML code. The end tag for Line 1 is Line 28, the last statement of the document.

Lines 2-6: The <HEAD> tag serves as the preliminary or opening description of the rest of the file. The HEAD tag contains within it the <TITLE> tag. Note that the TITLE tag is *nested* within the HEAD tag. The TITLE tag is important despite the fact that the title does not display within the browser's window (although it does display in the title bar of the browser window). Not only does it name the document, it also provides information to Web search engines (Yahoo, Lycos, etc.), which classify a site's contents by the information contained in the TITLE tags. The information in the TITLE tag is also what is placed in the bookmark menu whenever a user makes a bookmark for a page.

Line 7: All of the rest of the HTML document falls between the two <BODY> tags (Lines 7 & 27). This tag is exactly what it seems: this is the main part of the document. Within the body is another tag that tells the browser what color to use for the background of the document. In this case, the display is set to white. FF is hexadecimal for the number 255. The RGB color values here are set to 255, 255, and 255 (three two-digit numbers not separated by spaces). Lacking an instruction for a background color, the browser (Netscape, Mosaic, Lynx, etc.) usually displays a tone that would be written C0C0C0 (192 192 192) which is 75% of the distance between black (000000) and white. The equivalent print tone would be 25% black.

Lines 8-12: The tag <H1> followed by the tag <CENTER> indicates that the text in Line 10 is to be displayed in the center of the page using the largest of the six possible *Head* sizes. This line of text serves as the opening statement for the page the way a user would see it displayed within the browser (all of this information would usually be included in a single line of code). The six Head tags are often used in this way—as a way of approximating a headline—but there is a difference between a headline and Head information. The distinction is a subtle one (see Tip, below).

Lines 13-20: These lines refer to the graphic below the headline. The graphic, according to these tags, is to be displayed in the center of the page and in the smallest of the six Head sizes. The Head tag is meaningless where a graphic is concerned but serves to show that the graphic is controlled by applying text tags to it. Line 15 designates that an IMG SRC (image with file name or path name or URL) is to be displayed. In this case, the SRC attribute is the name of the file, biker.jpg. Additional information about the graphic is also given: it is 172 pixels wide, 224 pixels high, and is to be aligned on either side of the text along the baseline of the graphic.

Lines 21-25: These lines are similar to Lines 8-12. In this case, the text is displayed in the third-largest Head style.

Line 26: This text block contains the plain text below the introductory or headline material.

Lines 27, 28: Concluding tags from the top of the document.

Head Tags on the Web

The Web's textual organization is hierarchical. The six Head tags are used as ways of indicating a document's structure and organization. The fact that the Head tags are sized from largest (H1) to smallest (H6) is a coincidence that has nothing to do with the way a graphic designer would use headline type—large, bold text and simple phrases which arrest the attention and advise the viewer of a page's contents.

This point is difficult to visualize. However, let us imagine a Web robot from one of the large WWW indexing organizations visiting the pages on your Web server. The robot encounters an HTML document and catalogs its contents by examining the ranking of information based on the Head tags. Now let us imagine that the designer of the page had begun the page with a single word, *WOW!*, using the H1 tag. This is certainly a graphically effective method of drawing attention to this page. But judged as a means intended to evaluate the document's content, it is nearly devoid of information.

If the headline for the HTML document requires large, bold text, the Head tags are probably not the way to display it. Instead, use a graphic which is, in HTML terms, internally neutral, but which will do a much more convincing graphic job of headlining than the Head tags.

The efficiency of HTML is obvious from the fact that so few instructions are required to display this simulated page. The entire set of instructions for display—as well as all the text shown in the browser window—requires just 574 bytes. The single graphic, by contrast, requires 44,107 bytes. Put more simply, the graphic is nearly 77 times the size of all the rest of the document. It is easy to see why the inclusion of many graphics in an HTML document carries a heavy penalty in terms of download time.

So, What's the Hold-Up?

The term *baud rate* is so beset by qualifiers that it is almost without meaning. About the only thing you can say with certainty about modems is that a 28.8K-baud modem is faster than a 14.4K modem. Both are faster than a 2400 or a 300. There are so many other factors—line efficiency, compression, Web traffic, and time of day, etc.—that the whole subject gets very complicated. The only way to make sense of the entire issue is to simply look at a range of transfer rates (the speed with which data is moved from one system to another) and design your Web graphics accordingly.

The modems in general use on the Internet are of the 14.4K or 28.8K variety, though faster modems are becoming more common. Slower modems make the graphics-intensive WWW nearly impractical. A 14.4K modem, the slowest acceptable device, shows a range of transfer between .75 and 1.5 kilobytes per second. Performance on a 28.8K modem is somewhat better, ranging from about 1.8 to 3 kilobytes per second. There will be remarkable changes in coming years, but for the moment, we need to work with what we have. The vast majority of all the modems in use on the Web—planet-wide—are of the 14.4K variety. If we take as a baseline the moderate performance of the 14.4K, we have a figure that is about one KB/sec. The math from there is simple. The 44KB file, biker.jpg shown in the example in Figure 12-3 will take three-quarters of a minute to move from the host server to the machine accessing the file. In fact, the time will probably be slightly more than that since there is some time spent by the two machines arranging protocols, etc. The sample HTML document, text and tags, is displayable by the browser in slightly more than a half of a second. Given the throughput rates of the two modems, it is obvious that the 28.8K modem will be able to display the data in considerably less time.

It is good to keep these physical speeds in mind when designing for the Web. If a page contains a number of graphics, the combined size of the graphic files in kilobytes equals the number of seconds, on average, a 14.4K modem will take to download the page. It is very easy to design a page that transfers so slowly that the user will simply give up and cancel the transfer. Given that a Web page is usually put on the Net for some purpose, it just isn't logical to do anything that obstructs the user from making use of it.

It's not an easy pill to swallow, is it? You will need to design, not for systems which work as well as yours does, but for the millions of users who access the Web on systems that are older and slower than yours is. Try not to worry about it— this kind of constraint simply means that your creativity has to kick in: you must make your designs effective but within the difficult parameters of the Web's limitations.

Bit Depth—Two File Formats

An understanding of the term *bit depth* is necessary in two situations. The first is when a file is converted to the GIF file format. The second is when you consider what kinds of monitors your graphic files will be displayed on all over the world. In the following section of this chapter, we'll discuss bit depth and how it applies to all Web designers.

A second important Web topic deals with the two file formats which are supported by all graphical browsers. When we use the term *supported by*, we simply mean that files in these two formats can be added to your Web page without any special instructions to the browser beyond an extension to the file name. GIF files use a .gif extension. JPEG files use .jpg. The extension simply tells the browser how to read the file so that it can be displayed.

Bit Depth

Bit depth refers to the number of colors a device can display. It also can refer to the number of colors present in a file. The file is said to be an 8-bit file or a 16-bit file or a 24-bit file. Monitors are said to display in black and white (1 bit) or in 8 bits or 24 bits. The bit numbers are powers of two. An 8-bit file would be 2^8 (256 colors) and a 24-bit file would be 2^{24} (16,777,216 colors). Bit depth is the largest factor contributing to a file's size. Every pixel in an 8-bit file requires 1 byte (8 bits = 1 byte) per pixel of information. A 24-bit file requires 3 bytes per pixel. All else being equal, a 24-bit file will be three times as large as an 8-bit file. We will consider bit depth in more detail as we look at the two main file types used for graphics on the Web.

The GIF Format

GIF is pronounced jif or gif because there is no apparent standardization of the term. Please use either without guilt or self-consciousness. The *Graphics Interchange Format* was developed to facilitate the transfer of graphic documents from one computer to another via modem. The format uses a compression method called LZW (a patented, lossless compression algorithm owned and licensed by Unisys Corporation). The GIF format can be used for color, grayscale, or black and white files. Used for color and grayscale, the GIF format limits the number of colors in a document to 256. Ordinarily, a single colored pixel requires 24 bits (3 bytes). With the GIF format, a pixel can be a single byte because the file is accompanied by a CLUT (Color Look-Up Table) which acts as an index of the file's colors. Grayscale information is always stored as one byte per pixel (with 256 total grays). Grayscale is, within Photoshop, a separate mode, but it can also be one of the possible CLUTs in the GIF file format. With the compression and reduction in bit depth, GIF files are considerably smaller—by about two-thirds—than their RGB equivalents.

Converting to the GIF format

GIF files usually begin as RGB or grayscale files and are converted to Indexed Color mode from within programs such as Photoshop. The procedure in Photoshop is to choose Image | Mode | Indexed Color. The dialog box shown in Figure 12-5 allows the setting of options for the file's conversion.

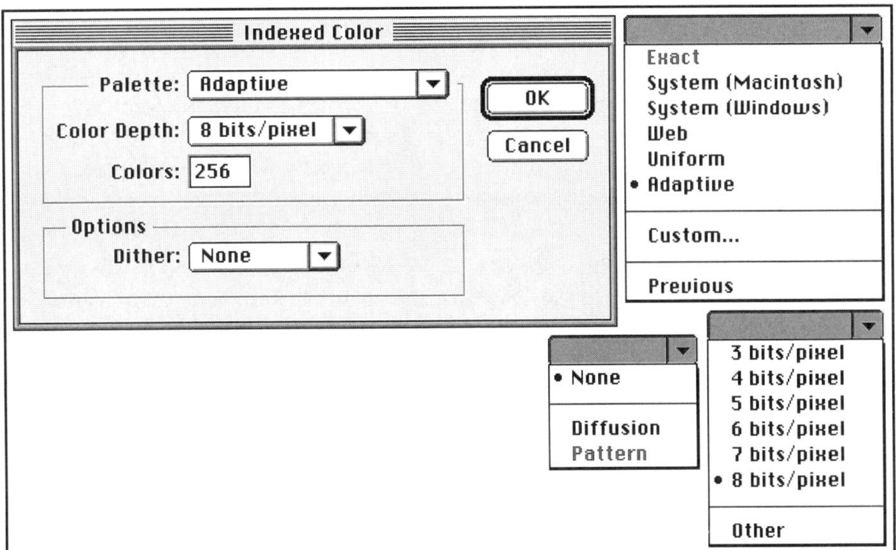

Figure 12-5: Photoshop's Indexed Color conversion options window.

Palette The Palette pop-up menu gives a range of options that determine which colors will be assigned to the CLUT. There are five possibilities.

Adaptive To understand how Adaptive works, it is helpful to know that a program such as Photoshop deals with an RGB file internally as a 24-bit file, even if the monitor on which it is viewed displays the information only in 8 bits. Most 8-bit monitors can display the entire 24-bit color range, but only 256 colors at a time. The process of choosing the best possible combination of 256 colors from the millions available is called an *adaptive* display. The Adaptive option in the Palette section of the Indexed Color dialog box works in much the same way: it allows Photoshop to map the best possible group of 256 colors from the 16.77 million at its disposal. The Adaptive option insures that the conversion will produce a set of colors as close as possible to the original RGB range of the image. If it is critical that the color range of the original image be preserved as closely as possible, Adaptive is the correct choice.

The Adaptive choice can be weighted toward certain colors in an image. If you make a selection when you choose to convert the file to Indexed Color mode, the colors within the selection are given prominence in the calculation. Otherwise, Photoshop calculates the best set of all available colors when it does the conversion.

Uniform We would love to skip this possibility for a very good reason: it's about as difficult to understand as it is useless. But, OK, here's what it's all about. Photoshop calculates one of five possible Uniform CLUTs by first looking at the Color Depth setting. It then takes the number, and from the entire color spectrum, chooses the same number of evenly spaced colors in each of red, green, and blue, and then calculates the palette. The number of colors in the resulting CLUT will be the perfect cube closest to the original color depth. 216 colors (6^3) is the number you will get when the color depth is 8 (because 216 is the closest perfect cube to 256), 125 (5^3) when the color depth is 7, 64 for 6, 27 for 5, 8 for 3. The entire strategy *must* make sense to someone. It *must* have been useful to someone. A group of programmers as good as those who write Photoshop wouldn't put something this weird and useless into the program just for fun, would they?

System The System option under Palette forces Photoshop to reassign the colors within the image to those used by the operating system for all of its routine display tasks. Both Macintosh and Windows use a default 8-bit CLUT system display. The two CLUTs are not the same, and you are given the choice of using either.

Web Even though the system CLUTs for Macintosh and Windows are not the same, they do contain quite a few colors—216 to be exact—in common. Using this option assures that any image will display exactly the same—with only minor differences in brightness—on both a Macintosh and a Windows display. This option is identical to the palette constructed by Photoshop using 8-bit color and Uniform.

Exact Exact is a color map strategy that is available only if the number of colors in the document is 256 or fewer. Photoshop uses exactly the same colors for the color table as those which make up the image.

TIP *Having a built-in CLUT allows a computer's operating system to manage color displays with considerable speed. But where there are uncommon colors, each system displays the non-native colors of the other not as a solid but as a dither composed of a number of tones. In some cases dithering is not unpleasant, but more often, the resulting mix of colors is not attractive. To prevent this from happening, you may wish to load the Web CLUT of common platform colors into your Swatches palette and use these colors to construct all of your Web graphics.*

After converting any file using the Web palette (and while the file is still open), choose Image | Mode | Color Table. When the dialog box opens, click on the Save button, and save the file under a name such as Web Colors. *Now, click on the Swatches palette menu and choose Load Swatches or Replace Swatches. Locate the Web Colors file you have just saved. Photoshop loads this set of colors into the palette for easy access whenever you are working on graphics for the Web.*

Custom When choosing a specific set of 256 colors out of 16.7 million, there are a large number of possible CLUTS. When Custom is applied to the color content of a file, another dialog box appears (Figure 12-6). Within this dialog box, individual colors present in the CLUT can be edited, one of several pre-built color tables can be chosen from the pop-up menu at the top, the edited color table can be saved as a named file, or another named color look-up table can be loaded.

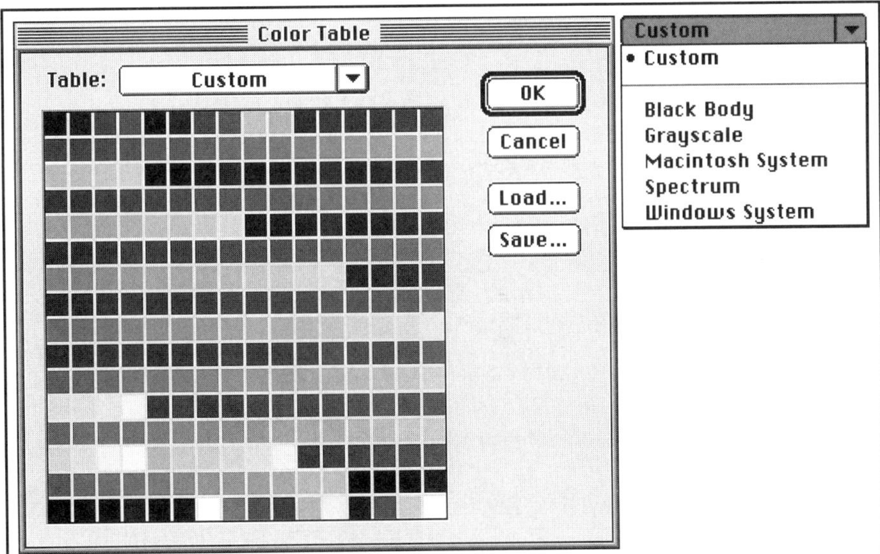

Figure 12-6: The Custom Color Table option from the Indexed Color dialog box.

The predefined color table pop-up menu at the top of this window provides five points of departure. The first, Black Body, shows a blend of the color tones—black to red to orange to yellow to white—a black body object radiates as heat is applied to it. The second, grayscale, is composed of black and white and the 254 gray shades between them. The third, Macintosh System, is the standard palette for the Macintosh. The fifth option, Windows System, gives different results from Macintosh System because of the noted 40 non-common colors. The fourth, Spectrum, gives a blend of colors that is prismatic—violet to blue to green to yellow to orange to red.

TIP *The Custom color table can be edited so that the assigned colors become a range of close colors similar to a gradient. Click with the mouse in the upper left-hand corner of the color table and drag to the lower right-hand corner. The Color Picker appears with the message,* Select the first color. *To test this procedure, choose white and click the OK button. The Color Picker then appears again with the message,* Select the last color. *Choose a color and click OK. The color table now shows 256 evenly spaced values ranging from white to the second color you picked. You may extend this idea further by clicking and dragging small distances within the color table. Your selection need not include the entire table.*

Defining colors and applying them to grayscale images is one way to successfully colorize grayscale files. If you define the color table as a set of tones between white and a very dark blue, your grayscale image shows all of the blue tones mapped to the equivalent gray values. For non-Web use, you can convert the image back to RGB mode after you have colorized it.

One advantage to loading a single custom color table for a number of files is that all of the files will be viewed, no matter which computer is used to run the browser, without the annoying flashes of color that sometimes accompany the quick change in CLUTs on systems running 8-bit displays. Someday, perhaps, all CRTs will be 24-bit. At the moment, the large majority of systems in the world use 8-bit displays.

Previous This is another batch-processing utility to insure uniformity of CLUTs among a number of separate files. Choosing Previous simply loads in the last-used Custom or Adaptive CLUT and applies it to the new image.

Color Depth

The default bit resolution is usually 8 bits/pixel since Photoshop assumes you wish to preserve as much color information as possible. Use any of the other bit-depth buttons to reduce the number of colors in the file: 7 bits gives 128 colors, 6 bits gives 64 colors, 5 bits 32, 4 bits 16, 3 bits gives 8. You may, if you wish, enter an arbitrary number of colors in the option box marked Other. As the number of colors is decreased, the size of the CLUT also decreases and with it the size of the file.

Dither

The Dither option allows the simulation of many tones by mixing up colors so that the eye is tricked into believing that it sees more colors than are present. The method is called *Diffusion*, and it is similar to the strategy used by the color printing industry: the appearance of many colors is achieved by using four surprinted primary ink colors. In some cases, the dither option can be turned off (None) with no apparent loss to the quality of the image. A special kind of Pattern dither which uses an 8 x 8 cell of pixels is available only when System (Macintosh) is the designated palette.

Many Options, Many Looks

Figure 12-7 shows an example photograph from which a small area has been extracted and some of the indexing options applied. These begin with the magnified area seen unaltered in Figure 12-8. The other possibilities, Figures 12-9 through 12-21, show how the image is changed as the color indexing takes place.

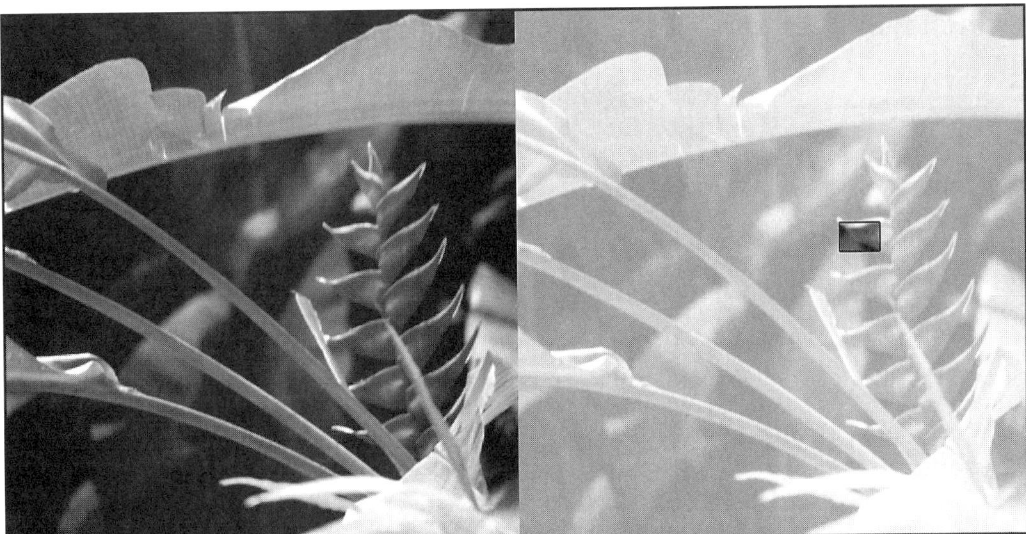

Figure 12-7: From this image, we have taken a small area (the small dark area on the right-hand side) and magnified it so that you can see the difference in Photoshop's GIF conversion options. Figures 12-8 through 12-21 are examples of each.

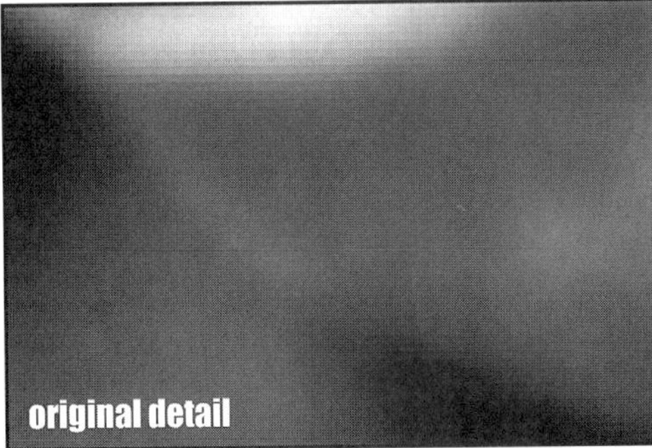

Figure 12-8.

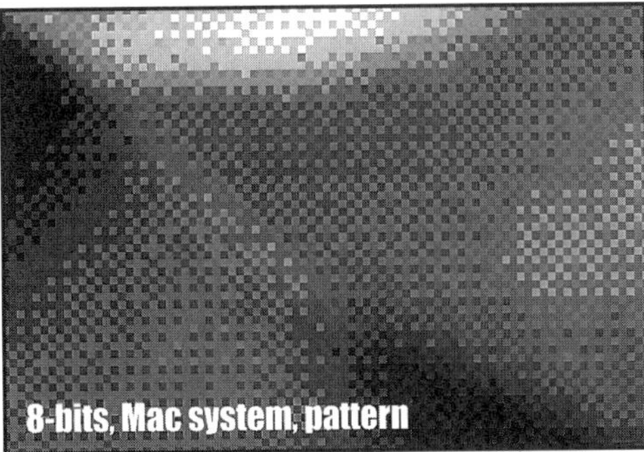

Figure 12-9.

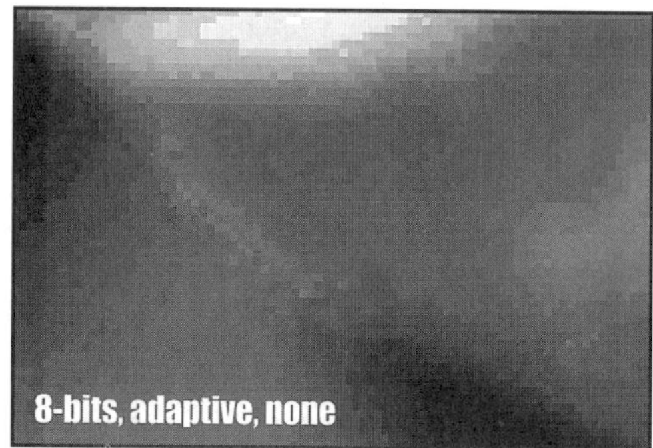

Figure 12-10.

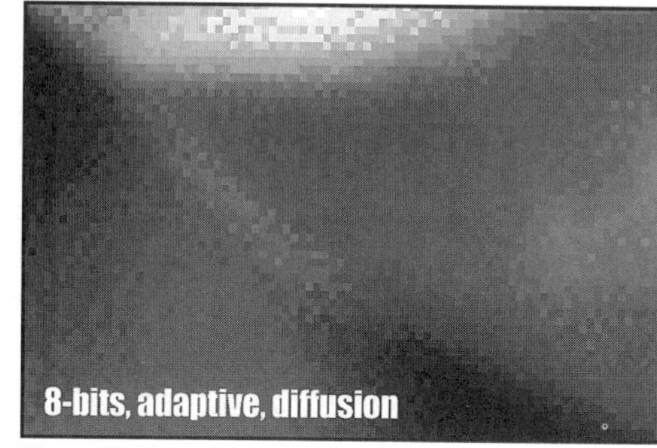

Figure 12-11.

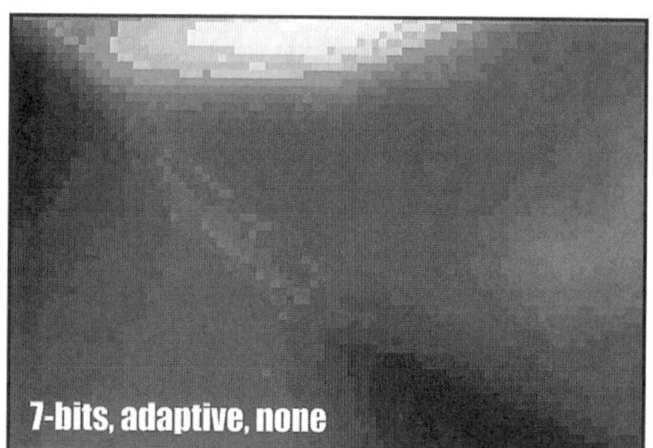

Figure 12-12.

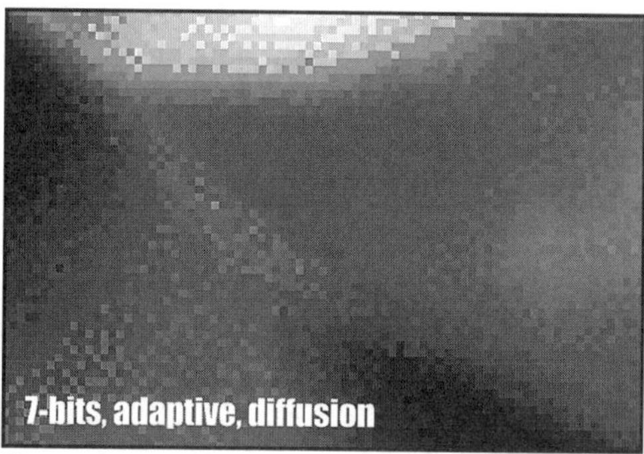

Figure 12-13.

Figure 12-14.

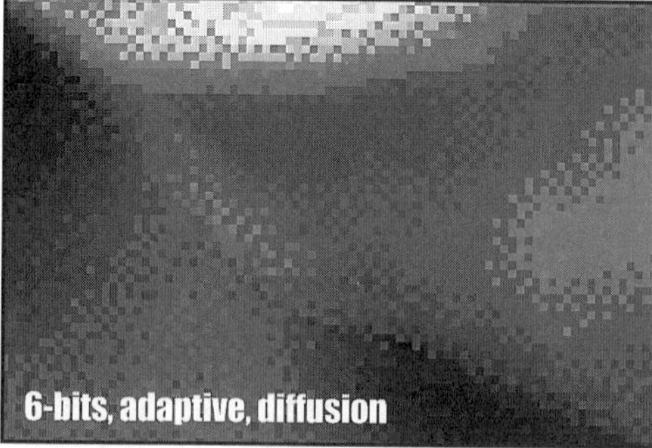

Figure 12-15.

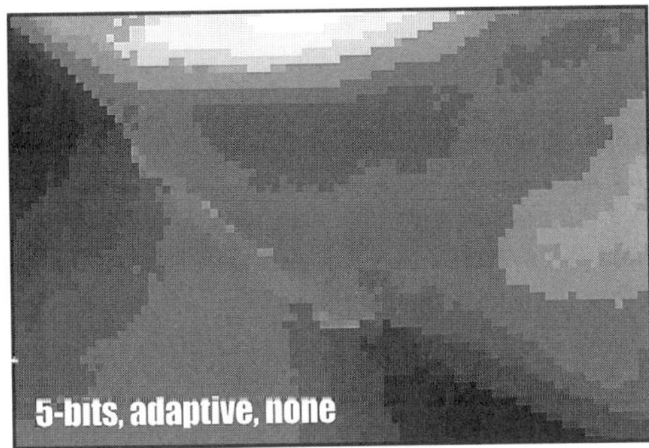

Figure 12-16.

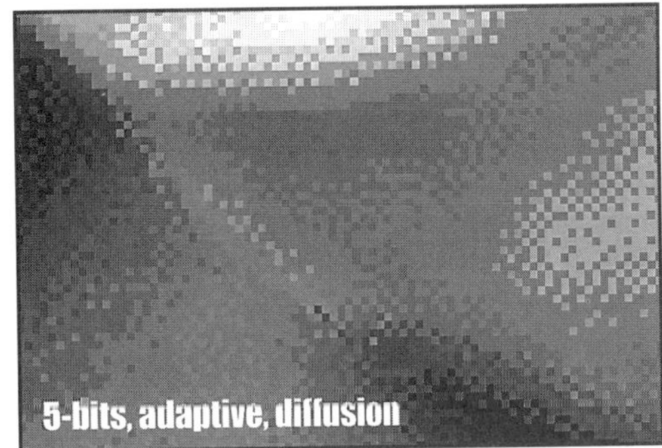

Figure 12-17.

Figure 12-18.

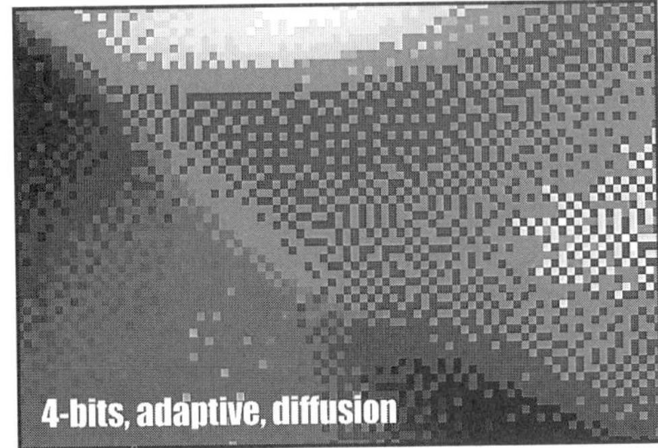

Figure 12-19.

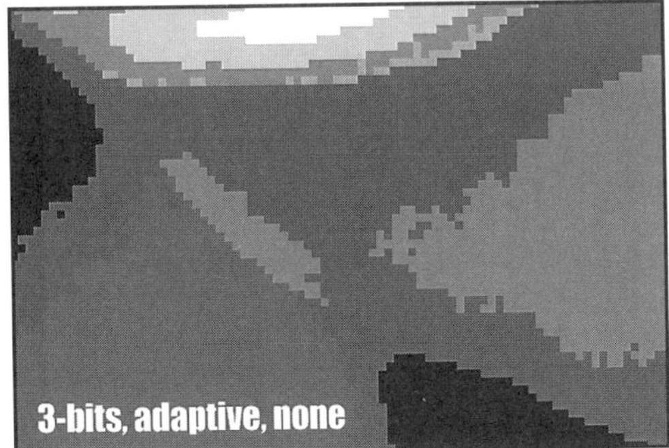

Figure 12-20.

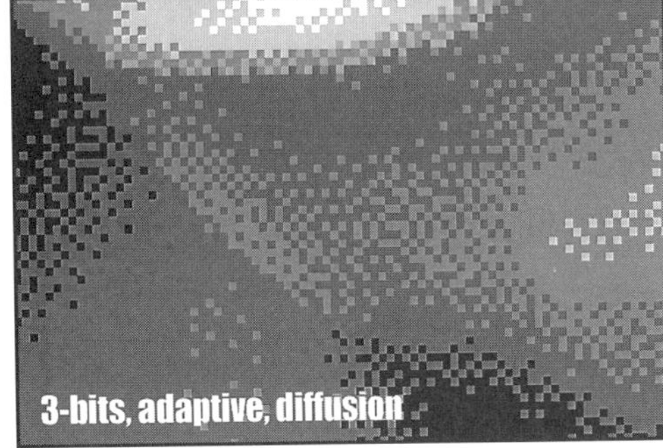

Figure 12-21.

Compression

The GIF format makes use of the LZW compression method. As the file is saved to disk, its data is made to occupy a smaller amount of disk space than would be the case without compression.

The LZW compression method works by changes in color within horizontal rows. When there are fewer color changes in a row of pixels, there is more efficient compression. This brings up an idea which it is useful to understand. Figures 12-22 and 12-23 show two GIF files with simple black bars. There are exactly the same number of pixels in each file and the same number of colors. The only difference between the two is that one is turned 90° relative to the other. While looking at these files, notice that the vertical version has a larger number of color changes in the horizontal rows of pixels than does the horizontal version. Accompanying each is a detail from a screen shot of the Macintosh Get Info window for each file. Notice that the vertical version of the file is 3,529 bytes larger than the horizontal version. In some cases the differences are even more drastic. Knowing this, a designer can sometimes make better use of the LZW compression of the GIF file by orienting the linearity of an image in the most suitable direction.

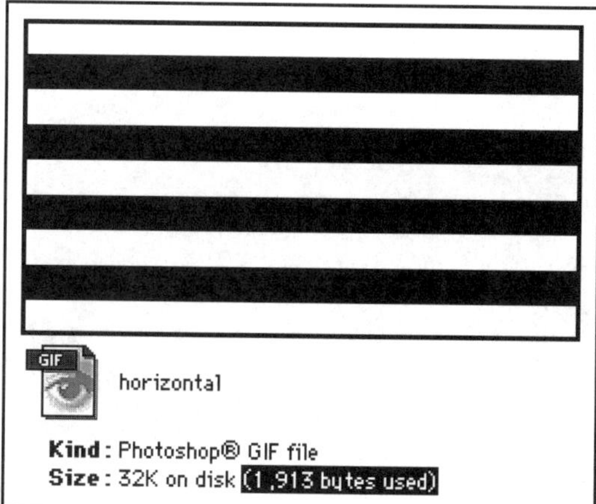

Figure 12-22: A horizontal orientation of pixels makes LZW compression more efficient.

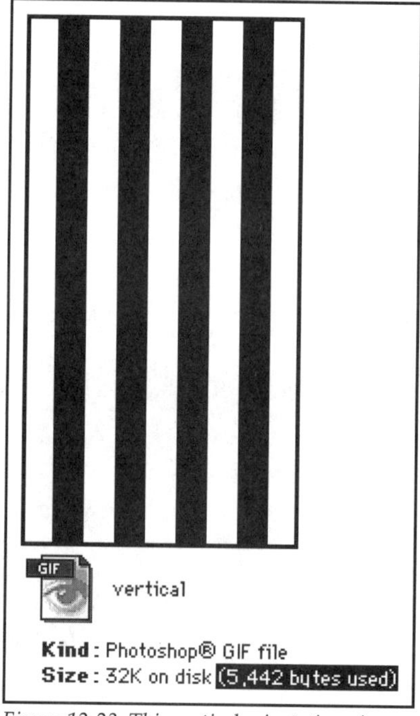

Figure 12-23: This vertical orientation gives a file size that is 3.529 bytes larger than the image in Figure 12-22.

When converting an image from RGB to Indexed Color mode, preparatory to saving it as a GIF, one of the options available—on the face of it a very desirable option—is the Dither. Using dithering makes the image appear less posterized-looking. However, dithering rapidly multiplies the number of color changes within a horizontal row of pixels. Depending upon the subject matter of the file, the difference in file size between a dithered image and a non-dithered image can be startling. If the image seems to absolutely require the Dither setting, the GIF file format is probably not the correct choice. The JPEG format may work better (the JPEG format is covered later in this chapter).

GIF87a & GIF89a

After a file has been converted to the Indexed Color mode within Photoshop, you can export it in two different ways. Using the normal File | Save command, you can choose the CompuServe GIF format. This saves the file in the specific GIF configuration called GIF87a. Photoshop also contains a remarkably powerful export utility (choose File | Export | GIF89a Export) which, as the name suggests, exports the file in the GIF89a form. The dialog box for this export utility is seen in Figure 12-24.

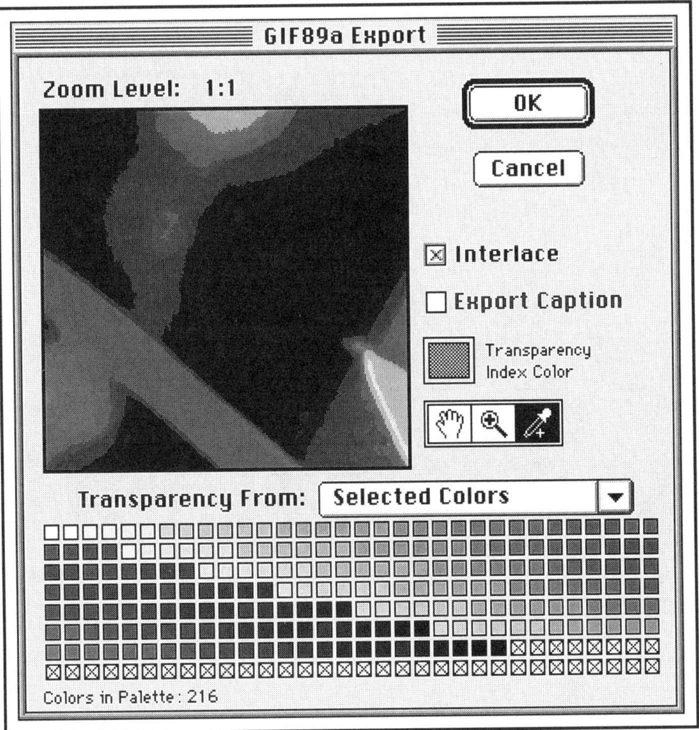

Figure 122-24: The GIF89a Export dialog box.

One of the options you have for GIF89a is to set some of the colors in the palette as transparent. Use the eyedropper tool with the small plus shape to click within the preview window. Each time the eyedropper clicks, all of the pixels in the image that are the same value change to a neutral gray. This indicates that those pixels will become transparent when displayed in the Web browser. The eyedropper tool can also subtract from already selected values (the plus becomes a minus): hold Command or Ctrl and click on an area which has already been selected.

There are three other ways you can make pixel values in an image transparent. First, if a selection is active when you choose GIF89a Export from the File menu, all of the pixels outside the selection are automatically changed to the light gray tone, indicating that they are transparent. Second, you can place the pixels which will be opaque on a separate layer. Hide all other layers and select File | GIF89a Export. Figure 12-25 and 12-26 show the appearance of the layer before exporting and the same image atop a background pattern within a browser. (For the vignetted-edge look shown here, make the edge of the layer blurred, or feathered, and set the mode of the layer to Dissolve before you export it.) Third, if you have defined a selection channel prior to choosing the Export command, you can click on the small pop-up menu which contains the words Selected Colors. You will see that the additional channel is listed as one of your choices. If you choose it, all of the black pixels in the channel will change their equivalent pixels in the image to transparent.

Figure 12-25: A layer with transparent areas around the edges can be exported to the GIF89a format. This example has a feathered edge with the layer's mode set to Dissolve.

Figure 12-26: The GIF89a file, displayed in a browser window, has opaque pixels only where the layer contained opaque pixels.

There is no preview of the transparency effect from within Photoshop. The designated pixels simply change to a neutral gray. (You can change the neutral gray to another color by clicking on the color box within the dialog box. The Color Picker will appear and allow you to choose a new color. The color used within this dialog box has no effect on the file when it is displayed in a browser window.) The image must be previewed from within a browser for the transparency effect to be seen. The effect you see while in the export dialog box is simulated in Figure 12-27.

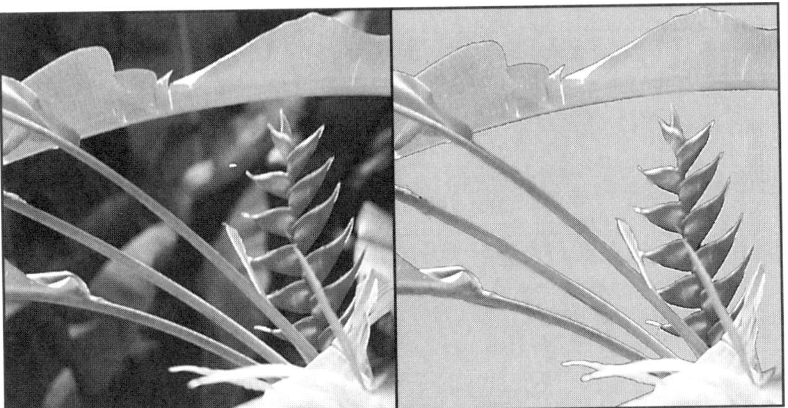

Figure 12-27: A simulation of the GIF transparency effect. All of the background pixels in the image on the left display as gray to indicate that they will become transparent when displayed in the browser.

Anti-Alias Fringe, a Problem With Transparent GIFs

The transparent GIF format is used extensively on the Web. However, in a great many cases, the presentation of the image suffers from the problem known as *anti-alias fringing*.

Anti-aliasing is a small zone of transition, an extremely narrow gradient from an area of one color to an area of another color. Anti-aliasing is built into many of the functions of Photoshop. Using it is vital when preparing files for print or film imaging because it provides smooth edges to the contours of objects in a raster image. The alternative is a jagged blockiness that is nearly always unacceptable. However, when preparing files for screen view—which is what you are doing when preparing files for the Web—anti-aliasing is relatively unimportant.

The way anti-alias fringing harms the screen image is shown in Figure 12-28. The upper figures show the original figure on a white background next to which is the same figure where white has been changed to transparent. The close-ups in the lower part of the figure show exactly how this unfortunate artifact harms the screen view.

Figure 12-28: Anti-aliased fringing. The image and magnification on the left show traces of almost-white tones when the true white of the background is changed to transparent.

When working in Photoshop, there are a number of tools and options that will help defeat this fringing effect in a transparent GIF:

- Set the anti-alias option for the Lasso tool to Off by unchecking it. Use the Lasso tool to select and isolate an object. When the object has been selected, export the file as GIF89a.
- After using the Pen tool, the drawn path can be turned into a selection. When accessed from the pop-up menu on the Paths palette, anti-aliasing is one of the options for the Make Selection command. Set it to Off. Be sure that the path has been drawn so that no pixels which do not belong to the isolated figure have been included.
- Of the two Marquee tool variations, the Oval selector has the option for anti-aliasing to be turned off.
- The Magic Wand also has an option for turning off anti-aliasing.
- When using the Type tool, set the Anti-aliased option to off. This is particularly true when using small-size type. Anti-aliasing on small type, especially at the 72 ppi resolution used for Web graphics, causes it to look blurred.
- The Edit | Fill command fills with the foreground or background color. If the edge of the selection to be filled is aliased, the edge of the fill will also be aliased. An alternative to the Fill command is to use the Paint Bucket tool. One of the options for this tool is an On/Off check box for anti-aliasing.
- Of the three major painting tools, only the Pencil tool cannot be made to paint with an anti-aliased edge. (The Paintbrush and Airbrush tools cannot be made to paint with an aliased edge.)
- The Block variation of the Eraser tool is a square, aliased shape. The eraser tool can also use the Pencil tool to erase.
- The Line tool can be set to have the drawn lines anti-aliased or otherwise.

Interlaced GIFs

A primitive animation effect can be saved as part of the file structure when you export a file in either the GIF87a or GIF89a formats. It is called *interlacing*. When an interlaced file is saved, its data is saved in a different order so that the file builds up onscreen from a low resolution screen image to one that gradually resolves into higher resolution. The effect, seen over five frames, is generally as shown in Figure 12-29.

Figure 12-29: The interlaced screen display changes over time. Beginning with the coarse resolution image on the left, the display gradually resolves itself in stages into the final image on the right.

Interlacing is a desirable option when exporting a GIF file, especially if the size of the file is large enough that there is a wait while the file downloads. The coarse version of the file fills the picture space very quickly. It is followed by more of the picture information which obviously leads toward a coherent image. Not only is the building of the image interesting to watch—which gives the user something to do during the wait—but it allows the user to make a judgment about the image long before it has completely arrived. If the image does not appear to be of sufficient interest to warrant the wait, the user is free to cancel the download at any time.

It is probably not a good idea to use interlacing on every single GIF image. For small images—buttons, logos, arrows, navigation graphics—the interlace effect is over too fast to be worthwhile. It is also has the effect of temporarily making the screen look untidy.

Animated GIFs

Exporting a file in the animated GIF format produces a more sophisticated animation. Files in this format must be put together in a special program even though the original components are best constructed in Photoshop. There are several excellent shareware utilities for assembling animated GIFs which can be obtained from the Web.

In making an animation, a number of GIF files are first prepared and then assembled as a list. This list, and the component files, are saved as a single file which displays the individual files in sequence as the file downloads to the browser. The effect is similar to a small QuickTime movie. The sequence can be set to a single iteration or to multiple iterations. Different browsers interpret this kind of animation in different ways, but the two major browsers display animated GIFs satisfactorily. As always, keep in mind the combined sizes of the files constituting the individual frames.

Photoshop's layers capability gives you a way to quickly generate animated GIF components. It is helpful to set up a hotkey to quickly execute the Image | Duplicate command so that individual files can easily be generated and then changed slightly. In this way, a series of files—each generated from a previous version—can be constructed.

An example is shown in Figure 12-30. This is a three-layer file. The Background (lowest) layer is solid white and is not visible. The middle layer is solid black (set to 100% Opacity and Dissolve mode), while the top layer contains a set of heavily blurred white letters. The top Layer's Opacity is also 100% with the mode set to Dissolve.

Figure 12-30: A three-layered file ready to be changed to a set of animated GIF components.

Begin by hiding the top layer (Figure 12-31a). Duplicate the image. Show the top layer and set its Opacity to 10% (Figure 12-31b). Duplicate the image. Set the top layer's Opacity to 20% (Figure 12-31c). Continue in this way until the top layer's Opacity has reached 100% (Figure 12-31k). Duplicate the image. Select the middle layer. Change its Opacity to 90% (Figure 12-31l). Duplicate the image. Set the middle layer's Opacity to 80%. Continue until the Opacity of the middle layer reaches 10% (Figure 12-31t). Duplicate the image and hide the top layer. You now have 21 small images. Flatten all of them, change them to Indexed Color mode, and assemble them as an animated GIF.

Another easy layers-based animation effect is the rotating image shown in Figure 12-32. Begin with the image—shown in Frame a—on a layer, with the Background layer set to solid black. Duplicate the image. Choose Layer | Transform | Distort. Pull the upper right-hand corner down and inward, the lower right-hand corner up and inward. The left-hand corners stay at the top and bottom of the window but move toward the center about the same amount as the right-hand corners were moved (Figure 12-32b). Duplicate the image. Follow the same Distort procedure moving the corners farther in. Note that the left-hand corners, top and bottom, only move toward the center while the right-hand corners move inward in two directions (Figure 12-32c). Continue until the image appears as shown at Figure 12-28e. That's it, all the real work is done. Duplicate e, choose Layer | Transform | Flip Horizontal, and you have f. D duplicated and flipped becomes g, and so on.

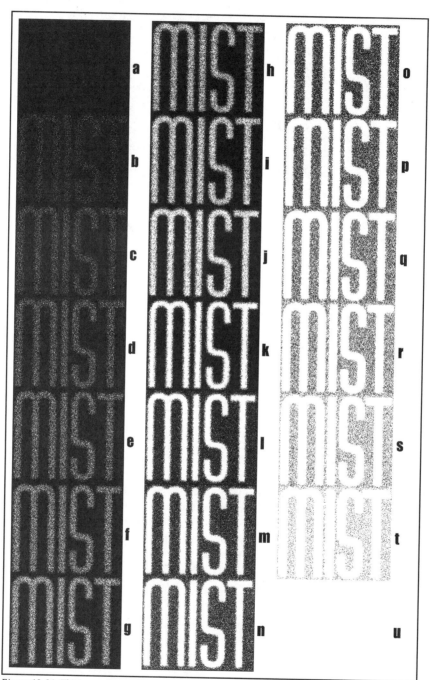

Figure 12-31: Thirty-one frames for an animated GIF file, all of them made by changing the opacity of the two layers behind the letters.

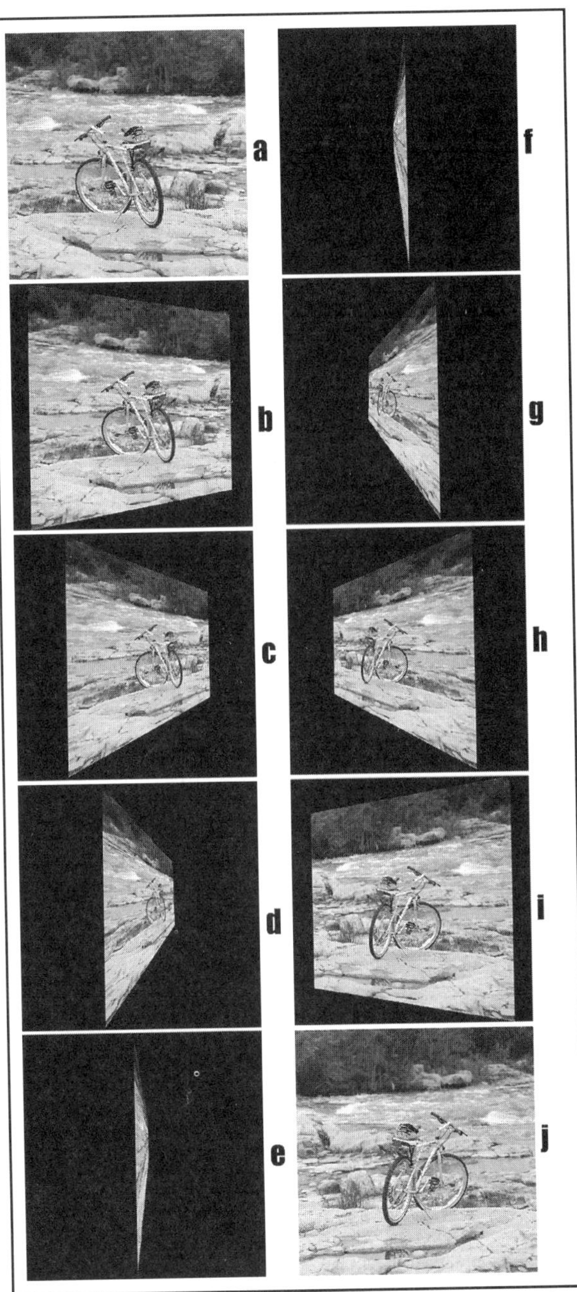

Figure 12-32: Five frames of an animated GIF on the left can be flipped to give the next five frames. The animation seems to rotate the image in three-dimensional space.

A number of other possibilities come to mind using both of the Transform commands. The image might gradually shrink within its window until it is barely visible. The sequence could then be played back in reverse order, the frames running from smallest to largest, to give an animated zoom effect. Or, an image could rotate to the halfway point. At that point, the subject of the image is not recognizable. A new and identically sized image could be treated as though the rotation were to go the opposite direction. These two sequences could then be put together so that as one image rotates, it becomes a different image upon completion of the rotation. This effect could be really interesting if you obtain photographs of the same subject taken from the front and the back.

The Offset filter is great for making animation sequences, especially banner text on a Web page. The text can appear to scroll up, down, or to the side. An example of how this works is shown in Figure 12-33.

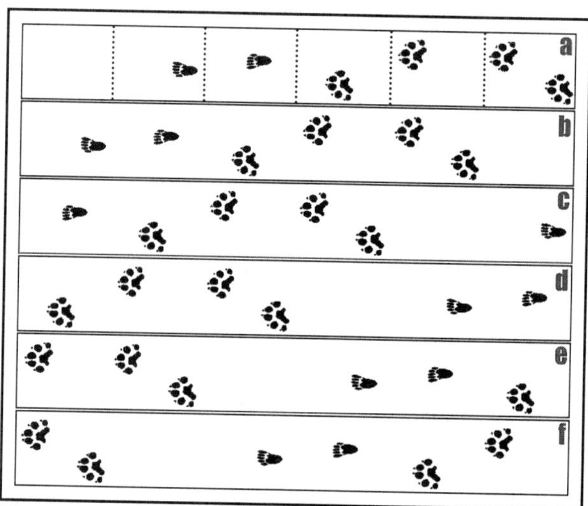

Figure 12-33: Six frames of an animated GIF generated by using the Offset filter.

The top section of the Figure, a, is the long initial frame: the footprints of bare-footed humanoid and Kodiak bear are strategically placed so that they fall within the six divisions of the horizontal area (marked with dotted lines so that you can see them here but not present in the final animation). Duplicate the image. Choose the filter (Filter | Other | Offset). For the horizontal measurement, enter one-sixth the horizontal pixel number preceded by a *minus* sign (makes the offset go to the left). For vertical, enter a 0 (zero). Choose the Wrap Around option and click the OK button (b). Duplicate the image and press Command+f or Ctrl+f. The filter will be applied with the same values as last used. Follow the same procedure three more times (d, e, and f). Assemble the six frames into a single animation.

A Few Points About Animated GIFs

Animated GIFs are a lot of fun to make. They also make your Web page a livelier and more interesting document. There are, however, a few things you should consider when you are composing sequences and placing them in front of the world.

- Use the Duplicate command in Photoshop to insure that the subject matter of the animation stays positioned within the animation window. Several different images can be used in the animation, but try to insure that they are centered so that a change of frame does not result in a jerky change of image position.
- When you have begun to convert a series of animation component files to Indexed Color mode, use whatever palette seems appropriate for the first image. For all the other images, use the Previous option to insure that all of the pieces of the animation use the same CLUT.
- If you intend to use a large number of frames for your animation, do your best to eliminate colors in order to cut down on the file size of each frame. The download time of the animation is based the combined size of all the individual files.
- Leave transparency effects out of animations. If you intend to animate a logo and the background of the Web page is, say, light blue, use the same light blue as the background for your animation. The edges of the animation will blend seamlessly with the background of the page.
- This is a philosophical point. It has to do with a personal reaction to the HTML attribute *Blink*. (Blink is an undocumented—but widely known—Netscape attribute that causes text to blink back and forth between negative and positive versions.) The authors' opinion of the Blink attribute is very like their opinion of the use of Zapf Chancery Medium Italic as a headline font: Yuck! An ongoing animation shares some of the irritating characteristics of Blink. The animation also draws the attention in such a way that other information on the Web page has difficulty competing with it. It's not that you shouldn't use an animation: just take care in its placement, and give a lot of thought to what length of attention is wanted from it.

Besides Photoshop…

There are many programs other than Photoshop for the conversion of indexed color files to the GIF format. They are available as shareware and freeware on the Web. Search http://www.shareware.com with the search term GIF for a bewilderingly rich list of possibilities for all system platforms.

The most widely respected commercial package for GIF conversions is DeBabelizer by Equilibrium Software. This program is not, perhaps, for the novice user, but it's really powerful. Not only is it able to convert RGB files to indexed color, it's able to poll a number of files and generate an adaptive Super CLUT that is appropriate for all of them. Although the program does not have Photoshop's editing tools, it does have so many batch capabilities that it's difficult to imagine getting along without it as a helper for those tasks Photoshop does not handle easily.

It is arguable whether Photoshop's conversion from RGB to indexed color is as perfect as it could be. There are several shareware and commercial software packages—DeBabelizer among them—which claim to do a better job of preserving an image's color. One of the most interesting—from the standpoint of provenance—and most accomplished is Planet Color published by LizardTech. The same company publishes a shareware package under the title Fast Eddy which is widely available on the Web. The shareware software has fewer features than Planet Color but works as an amazing conversion utility. The mathematics of the conversion process are based, the company says, on technology acquired from a government sell-back of technology developed at Los Alamos, New Mexico, during the research period that led to the first nuclear weapons. Something about predictive counting of free particles.... Whatever. It really does work! The results have to be seen to be believed.

The JPEG Format

JPEG (pronounced jay-peg) is an acronym for *Joint Photographic Experts Group*. This international standards committee originated and promoted the adoption of a sliding-scale compression method aimed at drastically reducing the size of a raster image when it is stored on disk. The method is called *lossy*, which is as accurate as it is semantically ugly. The compression method works, in general terms, by averaging groups of pixels so that an area can be stored as a single number rather than the larger set of numbers required for individual pixels. The sliding scale allows you to choose how much quality to retain. This slider is seen in Figure 12-34.

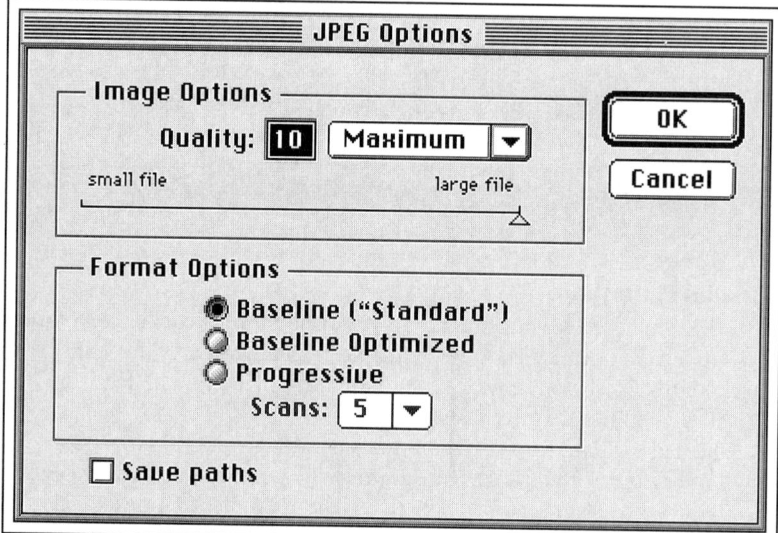

Figure 12-34: Photoshop's JPEG Options dialog box.

Three choices are given under Format Options. Baseline, or Standard, JPEG is the default choice—it is the older JPEG format—and gives perfectly adequate results. Baseline Optimized is the choice when you want the JPEG format to preserve the colors of the image as accurately as possible. With this as an option, it's difficult to see why anyone would choose vanilla Baseline. Progressive is a newer JPEG format; it saves the image information in a different order which, upon display in the browser, gives a visual effect similar to interlacing. You may choose the number of scans which the display will play through before the image reaches final resolution. The Progressive JPEG format is not universally supported by browsers, but it is displayable by both of the newest versions of Netscape Navigator and Microsoft Internet Explorer.

The image quality range in Photoshop is from Excellent to High, Good, Medium, and Low. There are eleven numbered Quality settings ranging from 10 (best) to 0 (poorest). Excellent is defined as *without visual loss of quality*. Settings farther down the scale increasingly compromise the quality of the image but result in much smaller files. The bar graph seen in Figure 12-35 shows the range of sizes when saving an original file of 895,717 bytes. (The vertical scale at the left is the bytes, or size-of-file axis.) The arrows point to files b, c, and d shown in the following figure.

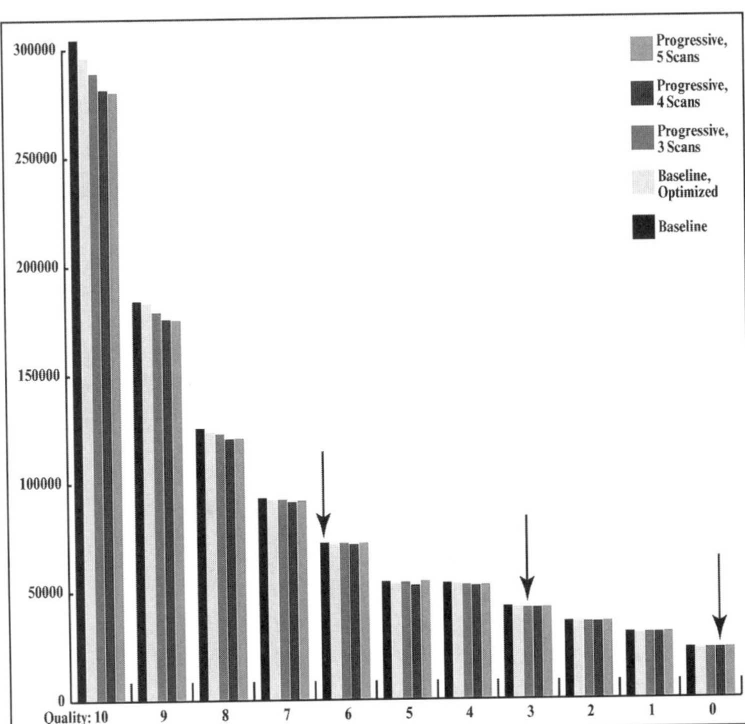

Figure 12-35: This bar graph shows how the five JPEG formats combine with Quality Loss numbers to produce ever smaller files.

Figure 12-36 shows the same image saved at four different quality settings. *A* is the original (895,718 bytes). *B* is saved as Baseline JPEG with Quality of 6 (72,333 bytes). *C* is saved as Progressive JPEG, Quality of 3, with 3 Scans (42,010). *D* is the smallest of all. It is saved as Progressive JPEG, Quality of 0, 4 Scans (22,840 bytes). The difference between *a* and *d* is astonishing: The compression ratio is 1:39.2. One way to describe this difference in scale is: a 50,000,000 byte file (47.68MB) could be saved with this compression ratio so that it would fit onto a single high-density floppy disk with about 170K of free space remaining! An even better way to state it is this: using the one K/sec figure discussed above, *a* would require 14 minutes and 58 seconds to download to the browser while *d* would require about 23 seconds.

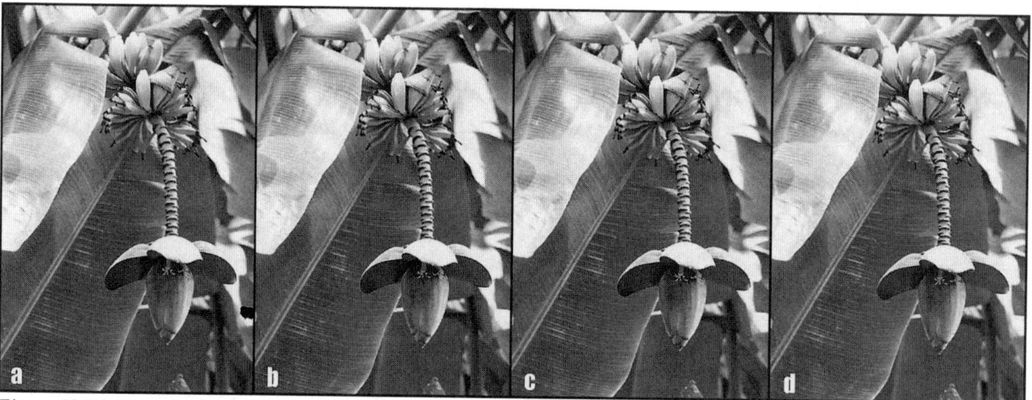

Figure 12-36: Four versions of the same file saved with (a) no compression, (b) baseline, Quality 6, (c) Progressive, Quality 3, and (d) Progressive, Quality 0. The (d) file size is 2.5% of (a).

There are shareware and commercial utilities for saving files in JPEG format. The commercial package DeBabelizer by Equilibrium Software is one of the best. A shareware Photoshop plug-in by BoxTop Software, ProJPEG 2.0, is another excellent utility. It can surpass Photoshop's ability to compress a file and it has the added advantage of a small Preview window to allow you to see the results of the compression before you commit to it. There is also a set of file statistics which change as the slider is moved. Compression ratios can be as extreme as 156:1 with this utility, but the resulting file is irretrievably compromised and would be, for all intents and purposes, useless. The dialog box is shown for ProJPEG 2.0 in Figure 12-37. Figure 12-38 shows another pair of images: *a* is the original and *b* is the same image saved with ProJPEG 2.0 using a 70:1 compression ratio. The change in file size is from 895,718 bytes for the original to 12,453 bytes for the compressed image. There is some degradation of the image. As the Web designer, you have to make the decision whether the decrease in file size is worth impairing the image's quality.

There isn't any kind of rule to help you decide whether a file should be saved with one level of compression or another. Some images compress easily with little visible loss. Others do not compress easily, and when they do, show clear evidence of the compression. You should probably duplicate your file (Image | Duplicate), save at a small compression, open it again, and view it next to the original. If the image is important to the page, you may decide that a larger file size is worthwhile. If it is not, the smaller file size may be the way to go.

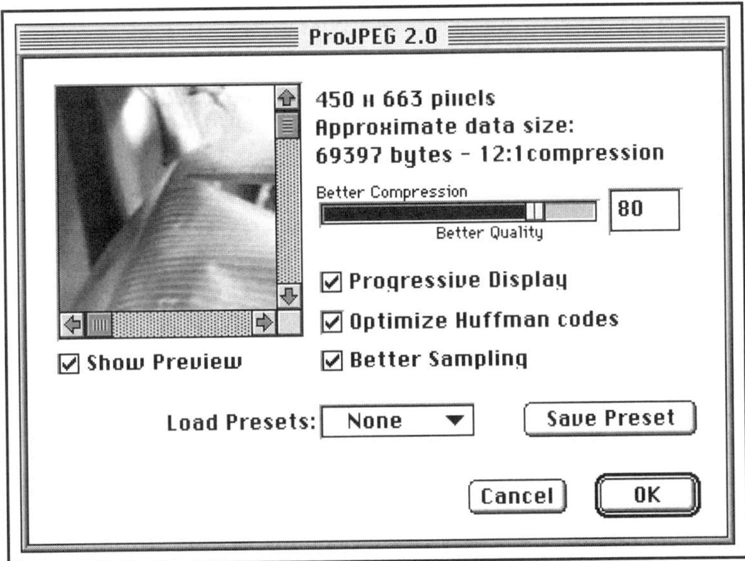

Figure 12-37: The ProJPEG save options window.

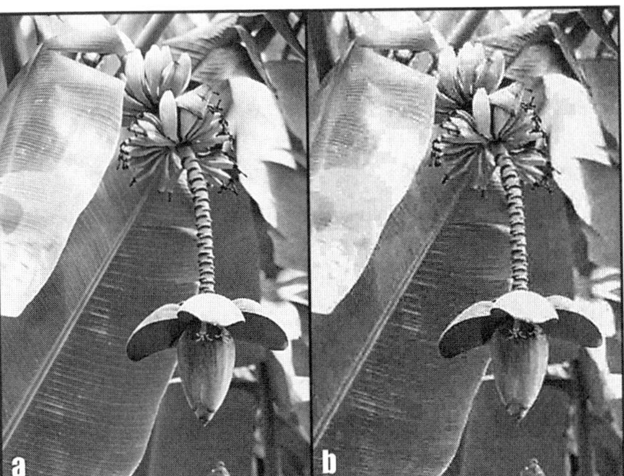

Figure 12-38: The file on the left (a) was saved without compression. The file on the right (b) was saved with the ProJPEG utility. It is one-seventieth the size of (a).

The utility of the JPEG compression method makes its value to producers of graphics for the Web instantly obvious. There are, however, a few points to be considered:

- The JPEG format lets you save 24-bit information in an astonishingly small file size. There are very few complications connected with the JPEG format. It simply works well as long as some judgment is used when presented with the extremes of choice Photoshop's Save command gives.
- For most purposes, a setting of medium to low is acceptable for display in a Web browser. Saving at a higher image quality does not appreciably improve the look of the image but does add to the size of the file. It's a good idea to save multiple copies of a file under different names and view them at 100% within Photoshop to see which level of quality preservation is the best trade-off between file size and clarity of image.
- When working with the JPEG format, it is always wise to keep a copy of the image which has never been saved in the JPEG format Always return to that document if you wish to make changes to a file. Successive saving of a JPEG file back onto itself will seriously degrade the image.

PNG

The venerable GIF file format, flexible and widely accepted as it is, is still lacking in several important features which the JPEG format addresses. There are, however, other features for which neither of the two principle Web graphic formats make provision. The PNG file format—*Portable Network Graphics Specification*, pronounced *ping*—has been devised as a substitute for the GIF format. When the format is completely realized, it will allow lossless compression of 24-bit color, the use of an alpha channel for 256-level masking (as contrasted with a single level for GIF89a), preservation or embedding of gamma information, interlacing as well as several other visual effects similar to interlacing, and the ability to zoom in and out from an image within the browser.

The difficulty at present is that no one method of saving a PNG file gives control of more than one or two of the options, and even these are imperfectly implemented. Photoshop will save a file in PNG format (see Figure 12-39). The Adam7 option saves the file with interlacing. The filters, according to Adobe, are used to prepare the file for compression and, presumably, they influence the way the file displays in gradually increasing detail when it is presented in the browser. Photoshop does not give you a way to control the gamma of the image and causes the image to look OK in one browser on one platform and yet look really awful on another browser on another platform. There is no provision for alpha channel masking. The compression for PNG is also less than thrilling: the file is smaller, but not by much. Certainly not enough to provide a serious threat to the JPEG format. You may well ask, why bother? Excellent question. The short answer is that the PNG format is not yet ready for prime time. But keep an eye on it because it has promise for the future.

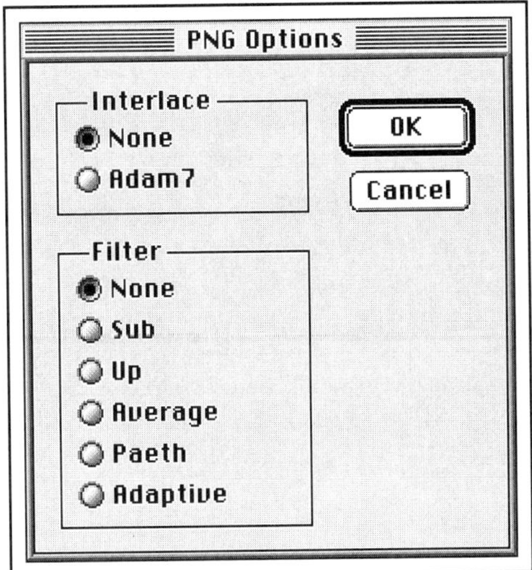

Figure12-39: Photoshop's PNG Save Options window.

Equilibrium's DeBabelizer Toolbox also saves files in PNG format. This program does allow the setting of the gamma and does recognize an alpha channel (although it apparently is not able to use that channel for masking). The PNG compression from DeBabelizer is also nothing to shout from the rooftops.

A shareware plug-in developed for Photoshop by Infinop (http://www.infinop.com) seems to be the best choice for saving PNG files even though most of the PNG format features are not implemented. The file seems to look good in most browsers and, in Netscape, you can click and hold on the image: a pop-up menu appears which allows the image to be enlarged or reduced within the browser.

It is probable that the PNG format will gain more widespread acceptance and support. Until it does, it remains an interesting curiosity with a good deal of unfulfilled potential. If you do decide to use a PNG file in your Web page, use the embed command to display the image. The format for the HTML code will look something like this:

```
<embed src="filename.png" height="xxx" width="xxx" align=top border="0">
```

More Points About Saving Files

Saving files for the Internet is not as straightforward as you might think. Considering that there are only two widely used formats, there are quite a few things to be taken into account. Here are some other points that you should consider when saving your files:

- Each of the two main Web graphic formats, GIF and JPEG, have their uses. JPEG is wonderful for preserving the intricacy of a photographic image and making very small files. It does not work as well for flat-area graphics of the kind generated by the various draw programs. For files such as these, the GIF format is preferable. The JPEG compression will generate visible compression artifacts on flat-area artwork. These artifacts are not noticeable on most photographic images. When in doubt, it is useful to save a copy of the image in both formats and examine them at 100% to judge which is the most successful.
- When naming files remember that the server on which these files will be placed can be controlled by any one of several different operating systems. Operating on the lowest common denominator principle, it is probably wise to limit the name of the file to 8 alphanumeric characters typed in lower case. It is also vital that a suffix be added to the file to inform the browser what kind of file is being read. Use *.gif* for GIF files (such as *image.gif*), *.jpg* for JPEG files (*image.jpg*), *.html* for HTML files (*index.html*).
- When saving files from Photoshop, there are two not-very-obvious possibilities for decreasing the size of a file. The first is the addition of embedded thumbnails with the file. Under the File Menu, choose Preferences|Saving Files. Change the preference to Never or Ask. After this change to your preferences is made, the Save dialog box, if you've changed the setting to Ask, will have check boxes (three on the Macintosh, one in Windows) where the icons/thumbnails can be turned on or off at will. Turning on all three adds about 3,000 bytes to the size of the file. Second, after using the Pen tool, it is wise to delete all paths before saving the file in its final form. The paths are not useful for any Web display purpose; they add small but appreciable amounts to the size of the file and their presence confuses some servers. It is possible to receive a message "Unsupported File Format" from a server trying to deal with a JPEG file from which the paths have not been deleted.

A Nice Alternative to Interlacing

If, for some reason, an interlaced image presentation is not possible, or you'd like to try something different, you may wish to use the LOWSRC command on your Web page.

1. Prepare two files. The first is the main file containing all of the color and image detail and saved in either the GIF or the JPEG format. While this file is still open in Photoshop, use the Image Duplicate command. Change the mode of the new file to grayscale.

2. Open the Levels dialog box. Move the midtone slider until the numerical reading is about 1.45. Move the shadow output slider to the right until the darkest value on the image reads about 80% black. Click OK.
3. Change the mode of the image to Bitmap using the Diffusion Dither option. Change the mode back to grayscale, then to RGB, and finally to Indexed Color.
4. Export the image as either GIF87a or GIF89a using a different file name. (Note: do not use interlacing on either of these files.) Both of the images will be displayed by the browser.
5. The black and white image is very small in size because it contains only two colors; it will load first. The larger, full-color image loads second and covers—from the top down—the first image, gradually replacing it. The HTML code for this effect is:

```
<imgsrc="colorfilename.jpg" lowsrc="smallblack&whitefile.gif" width="xxx"
height="xxx" align="bottom">
```

Background Basics

The background of a Web page can be as simple or as elaborate as the designer wishes. The background deserves careful thought because it is the canvas on which all other information will be painted.

Backgrounds can be modified from the defaults of the browser in two basic ways. First, the tag for background color is written within the body tag:

```
<body bgcolor="#xxxxxx">
```

The background can also be a graphic tile that repeats itself down and across the window of the browser. The tag for this tile is also written within the body tag:

```
<body background="file.GIF">
```

Assigning a Coded Background Color

The x's in the BGCOLOR tag stand for three two-digit numbers which are not separated by spaces. They are the hexadecimal (base-16) equivalents of numbers we usually see in base-10 as RGB—Red, Green, Blue—values. Graphic designers are familiar with RGB numbers, brightness values for each of the three primary monitor colors. The numbers range from the darkest value (0) to the lightest (255) to give a total of 256 values. Browsers cannot display RGB values unless they are first translated into the base-16 system. Conversion from base-10 to base-16 is not difficult but a calculator does simplify the matter. If you are a Windows user, the Accessories Calculator can be used to translate base-10 to base-16. Go to View, and change the Calculator from Standard to Scientific. Macintosh users can find many calculators available as shareware or freeware by searching http://www.shareware.com.

Translating color values is not difficult. It's probably a useful thing to know how to do even if a scientific calculator is available. First, look at the small chart shown in Figure 12-40. It is a table of equivalent values. The lower row contains hexadecimal numerals. The upper row contains the base-10 way of writing the same numbers.

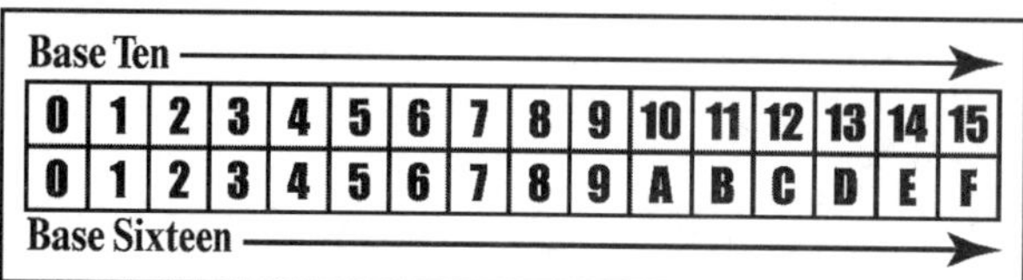

Base Ten →

0	1	2	3	4	5	6	7	8	9	10	11	12	13	14	15
0	1	2	3	4	5	6	7	8	9	A	B	C	D	E	F

Base Sixteen →

Figure 12-40: The first 16 numbers in the base-10 and base-16 systems.

Begin with the values you wish to convert. For example, a bright mauve selected from the CLUT of colors common to Mac and Windows has these RGB values: 153, 51, 255. Perform the following procedure on each of the three values:

1. Divide the first number (153) by 16. The result is 9.5625. The integer portion of the quotient is retained to be the first of the two-digit hex numbers. Now, multiply the decimal fraction (.5625) by 16. The product is 9. This is the second of the hex numbers. The hex equivalent for 153 is 99.
2. For 51: 51/16=3.1875. 16 x .1875=3. The hex number is 33.
3. For 255: 255/16=15.9375. 16 x .9375=15. In cases where the division produces a two-digit number, refer to the chart. The base-10 number 15 is the same as the base-16 number F. The hex number is FF.
4. The entire RGB number is expressed in the tag as #9933FF.

Other Uses for the Hex Numbers

Six-digit hexadecimal numbers can also be used to set the colors of text within the document (text), links (link), already visited links (vlink), and activated links (alink, the color which shows on screen as the mouse button is pressed while located on a link but is not released). Such a tag might read:

```
<body bgcolor=#xxxxxx text=#xxxxxx link=#xxxxxx vlink=#xxxxxx alink=#xxxxxx>
```

Of these five color attributes, the one least used—probably by oversight—is alink. Alink does, however, provide feedback to the user, and should not be considered a mere nicety but an important part of the user interface.

Background Tiles

In the context of a browser, a tile is a small rectangular graphic file that covers the background with multiple versions placed edge to edge in both directions. It is equivalent to a tiled pattern within Photoshop.

In the example shown at Figure 12-41, the base tile has been repeated five times across and in two rows. In a browser, the repeat begins in the upper left corner of the window, continues across for the length required by the width of the window, then repeats the rows downward for the length required by the height of the window.

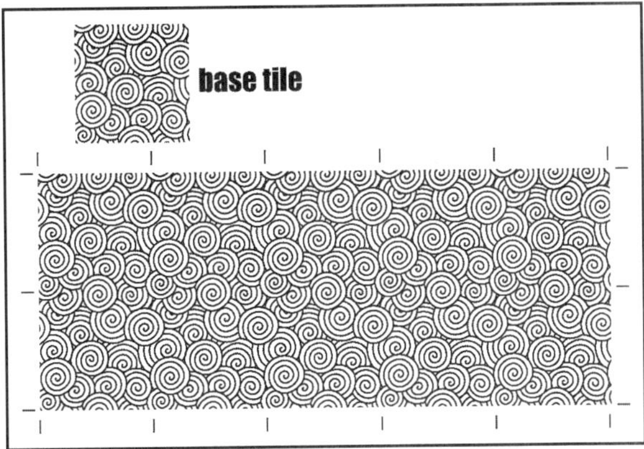

Figure 12-41: The base tile, with an area covered by repeats of the base tile.

The background tile is always the choice of the designer of the Web page since no browser uses such tiles as part of its native method of operation.

Even though they do not follow the same function as the graphics that are interspersed with the text on a Web page, tiles are part of the graphic overhead for the user of the page. When planning tiles, always remember that tiled backgrounds slow down the page and that the tiled files need to be as small as possible with respect to disk size.

The subject of tiles is fairly large. We will discuss tiles by grouping them into three overlapping categories: 1) plain, solid-colored tiles, 2) seamed tiles, and 3) seamless tiles.

Plain, Solid-Colored Tiles

Technically, a solid-colored tile belongs in category #3, seamless tiles, but it is sufficiently important to be considered as a category by itself. A plain, solid-colored background tile is simple and very useful. One reason for this has to do with the ability of browser users to override the HTML code of a downloaded document. In some cases, visual effects may depend upon code-specified colors. When a user preference overrides the coded colors, the visual effect is lost. Background tiles cannot be overridden by changing the browser preferences.

Plain-colored tiles do not have to be very large. They can be as small as one pixel. They are simply 72 ppi files containing a single color, which have been saved in either the GIF or the JPEG format. As very small files, they download quickly and fill the screen with what seems to be a solid color.

Small, solid-colored tiles are useful for other purposes. Single small files, say 5 pixels tall and 5 pixels wide, when filled with the same color as the background tile cannot be seen against the background. They can be plugged in at the beginning of paragraphs for a custom-sized indent. They can be used, particularly with the <IMG SRC="graphic.GIF" align=right (or *left* or *all*)> Netscape extensions to simulate the specific placement effects of tables but without the difficulty of mastering tables. Please note that if this option is chosen, ends of text lines should probably be followed by the <BR> tag to keep the lines in the specific relationship originally set up for them.

Small single-color tiles may be exported as GIF89a where the single color is set to be transparent. The content of the file is, then, quite invisible on the page. Files of this sort are ideal. They can be resized from within the browser without damaging the quality of the image and can be used to nudge other text and graphic elements by small amounts. If a file is, say 6 pixels square, you can change its dimensions in the size attribute to 7 pixels square. The change does not harm the image and it will cause text associated with it to be nudged—moved—by one pixel.

Seamed Tiles

Seamed tiles are those which clearly show the edges of the rectangular repeat. While a random-patterned tile with visible seams is not always attractive, there are cases where the seaming is desirable. Some examples might be where the tile itself is composed of squared motifs. Ceramic tiles, for example, can be squared-off areas of color or texture bounded by the grout seams between them. The boundaries of such a tile as a Web graphic would probably lie along the center of the grout on all sides of the ceramic material.

Any repeating tile that follows a vertical and horizontal grid is probably an example of a seamed tile. Examples might be found in fabrics, wall coverings, special-purpose papers, and so forth.

Seamless Tiles

Seamless tiles comprise a large and complex class of graphic objects. Because they are so important to Web designers, we will show a number of options for constructing original seamed patterns and for making use of existing resources.

Prebuilt Seamless Tiles The Web contains nearly limitless collections of seamless tiles designed for Web page backgrounds and as desktop patterns. A simple search on any of the large Indexing sites (for example, http://www.shareware.com) will provide enough material to keep a Web designer supplied with backgrounds for a long time. When searching, try the keywords *graphics*, *backgrounds*, and *Photoshop*. Watch for titles such as *artistic patterns* or just *gray desktop patterns*.

Professional collections of seamless backgrounds are being issued with dizzying speed. Software companies such as Pixar, SoftQuad, Macromedia, Corel, Specular, and many others furnish such collections bundled with other software. Should your imagination desert you for a few days, any one of these collections, combined with what you can do in Photoshop, should provide enough material for most purposes.

Examples from three widely distributed texture generator programs, all of them stand-alone packages, are shown here. Figure 12-42 was generated using Specular's TextureScape. 3D Graphics Texture Creator was used to construct the example shown in Figure 12-43. Figure 12-44 is a sample from Corel TEXTURE 6.

Figure 12-42: A texture tile made with Specular TextureScape.

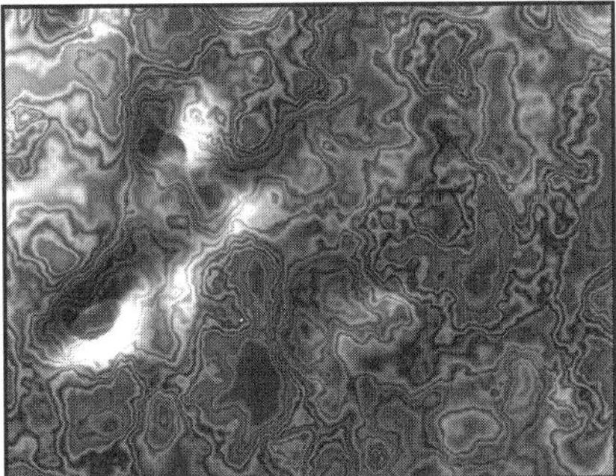

Figure 12-43: A texture tile made with 3D Graphics Texture Creator.

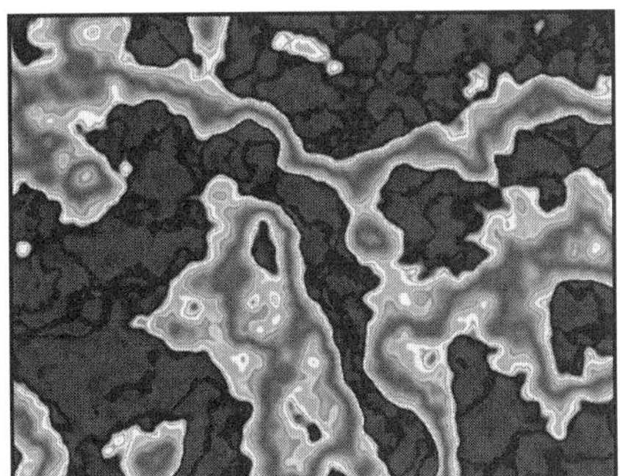

Figure 12-44: A texture tile made with Corel TEXTURE 6.

Noise Textures in Photoshop From the File Menu, choose New. Make the new document 1 x 1 inches at 72 ppi with the mode set to RGB. Fill this window with the color of choice. From the Filter menu, choose Noise | Add Noise. Save this file in GIF or JPEG format. You will find that the noise is sufficiently random that the tile merges with its neighbors without a visible join. You may wish to experiment with the other noise filters including the Hue Protected Noise filters which are part of Kai's Power Tools.

Seamless Tiles With Kai's Power Tools One of the unsung features of the celebrated Kai's Power Tools series (versions 2.1 & 3.0) is the Seamless Welder. This tool works most effectively on photographic material rather than on rasterized flat artwork done in a draw program such as Illustrator or FreeHand. Try it out on an image which contains a strong subject with an indistinct background or a background of lesser importance than the subject.

Open the file from which the pattern is to be generated. Adjust the file so that it is color corrected and sized appropriate for the final tile (Figure 12-45).

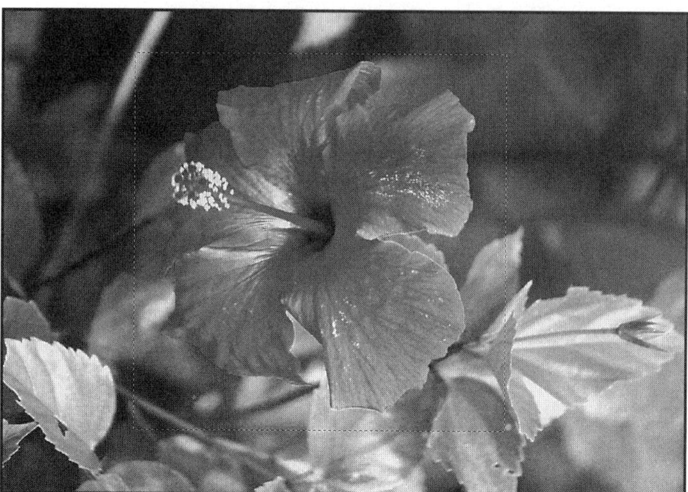

Figure 12-45: Photographic image to be used with KPT Seamless Welder.

With the Marquee tool, draw the tile selection well within the edges of the image window. If your selection is too close to the edges of the window, the filter software warns you and allows you to cancel so that the selection can be redrawn. Choose the Seamless Welder from the Filter menu (KPT 2.1 or KPT 3.0). After the filter has executed (Figure 12-46) and while the selection is still active, choose Crop from under the Edit Menu to trim away all of the portions of the image not contained in the pattern tile. Save this cropped file in JPEG or GIF format to be used as the background tile of the Web page.

To get an idea how the tile will work, open the saved tile. Select All, then choose Define Pattern from under the Edit Menu. Choose New from under the File Menu and specify the new window to be at least three times—vertically and horizontally—the size of the pattern tile. Select All and choose Fill from under the Edit Menu. Select the Pattern option for the Fill (Figure 12-47). The magnified image in Figure 12-48 shows how well this superb filter does its job.

Figure 12-46: After the filter has operated on a selection, crop to retain just the selection (the rectangular area within the image).

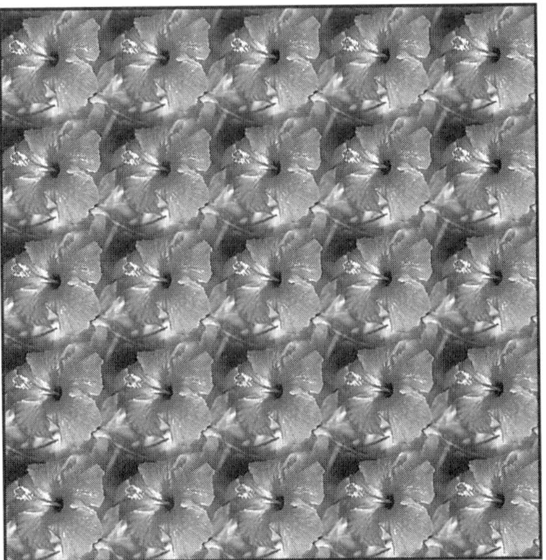

Figure 12-47: The 25 iterations of the tile show no seams.

Figure 12-48: A magnified view of Figure 12-47.

Three other modules of Kai's Power Tools provide powerful tools for generating textural background effects, particularly when used with the Seamless Welder. KPT Planar Tile (dialog box shown in Figure 12-49) has two major variations: Perspective Tiling and Parquet Tiling. KPT Vortex Tile (Figure 12-50) gives two choices: Normal

Vortex and Pinch Vortex. These two, in combination with the celebrated KPT Texture Explorer 3.0 and the Seamless Welder deliver horsepower that few other third-party software packages can match. A Photoshop technician can play happily with these modules for many profitable hours!

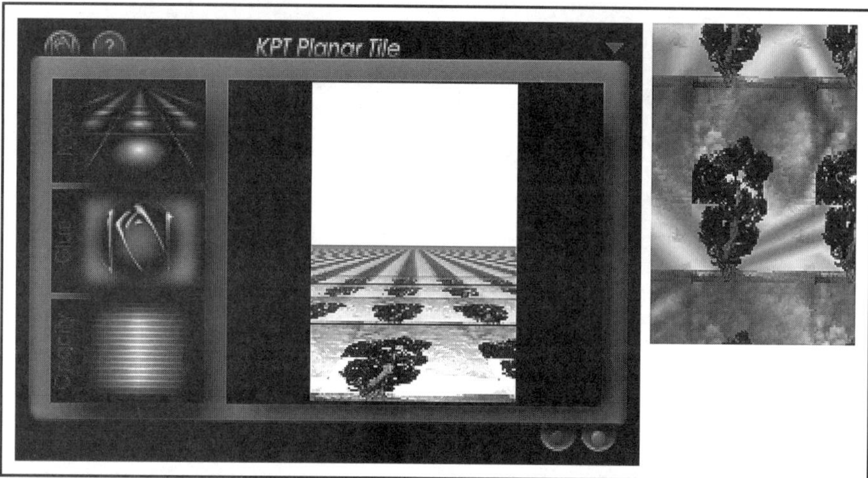

Figure 12-49: Dialog box for KPT Planar Tile 3.0.

Figure 12-50: Dialog box for KPT Vortex Tile 3.0.

Other Photoshop Tile Techniques One of the most interesting tile techniques uses tiles that are very wide compared to their height, or very tall compared to their width. These tiles divide the background of the Web page into large zones of color or texture. The files are quite small but provide a large-scale effect.

Very Wide Tiles Tiles that are a large number of pixels wide but only a few pixels high furnish a way of introducing vertical effects in the browser's background.

The width of the tile should be wider than the width of the browser window. There are many sizes of monitors, and users are able to configure their browsers to make use of any available screen width. Practically, it is usually sufficient that the width of the tile be somewhere in the neighborhood of 640–700 pixels. Such a width is more than sufficient for most purposes since most Web designers aim for a presentation which fits a screen size of 640 x 480 pixels. The height of the tile can be as few as 1 to 8 pixels, depending upon the kind of tile constructed. It's easiest to make tiles of this sort in a window that is taller than necessary and then to select and crop the area needed from the center area of the Photoshop document.

The tile used in Figure 12-51 shows what appears to be a raised area in a darker color, with a drop shadow. The tile is 700 pixels wide x 8 pixels high. Converted to GIF format and saved, it is 1,100 bytes in size. This tile will download in less than one second.

The same strategy for a wide tile can be used to place a gradient, either two-color or with many colors, progressing from one side of the browser window to the other. The example shown in Figure 12-52 is a two-color gradient 700 pixels wide, 8 pixels tall. The file is 2,300 bytes in size (2.25 seconds). Note: when using the gradient tool in Photoshop, be sure the Dither option is checked.

Figure 12-51: An example of how a wide tile, 700 pixels x 8 pixels, gives a dramatic vertical background.

Figure 12-52: This wide tile is in the form of a gradient.

The example in Figure 12-53 shows a bevel along each edge of the colored area. The file is 700 pixels wide x 8 pixels tall and is 987 bytes when saved to disk (.96 seconds to download). The bevel effect (Figure 12-54a) is very easy. Make a rectangular selection as wide as you wish the bevel to be and the height of the image. Press Command+j or Ctrl+j to make the selection into a layer. Duplicate this layer. Move the first layer so that it lines up with the right-hand edge of the colored area of the tile. Change its blending mode to Multiply. Move the other layer so that it lines up with the left-hand edge of the tile. Change this layer's blending mode to Screen. You can control the lightness or darkness of the bevel (Figure 12-54b) by changing the opacity of the layers. The lower portion of this figure shows a faceted effect achieved by duplicating layers and changing their opacity in 20% increments.

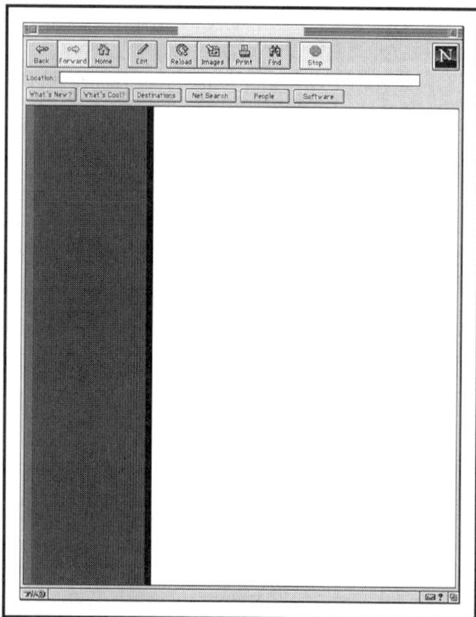

Figure 12-53: A lighter stripe on the left and a darker stripe on the right make this wide tile appear to be beveled.

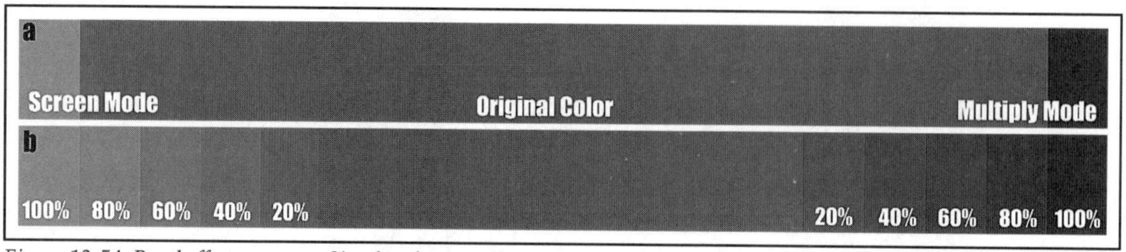

a
Screen Mode
Original Color
Multiply Mode
b
100% 80% 60% 40% 20%
20% 40% 60% 80% 100%

Figure 12-54: Bevel effects are easy. Simply take a small rectangular piece of the tile and place it on a layer. For a lighter color use the Screen mode. For a darker color, use the Multiply mode. Shades of light or dark are made by changing the layer's opacity.

When using tiles of the sort shown in Figure 12-53, beveled buttons can be placed on the colored area of the background tiles for a pleasing double-relief look (Figure 12-55). Making beveled buttons is covered later in this chapter. Figure 12-55 (file 13-055.enp).

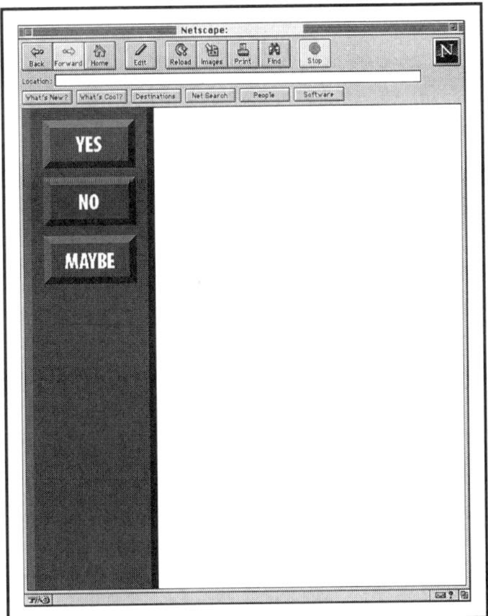

Figure 12-55: Add beveled buttons to a beveled background to enhance the dimensional look of a page.

Very Tall Tiles Tiles that are a large number of pixels tall can be used to give horizontal effects similar to the vertical effects made by very wide tiles. The only provision that needs to be made is that the content of the page not cover so much vertical area that a user needs to scroll far enough down to cause the second row of tile iterations to become visible. Careful planning of the page can overcome this in most cases.

In the example shown in Figure 12-56, a gradient is used on the tile. This is really the same tile used in Figure 12-52 but turned 90° clockwise. The tile is 8 pixels wide x 800 pixels tall. Saved to disk, it is 2,400 bytes (2.3 seconds).

Another tile example is shown in Figure 12-57. It uses some of the ideas from the wide horizontal tiles to give a decorative effect. The tile is 24 pixels wide x 800 pixels tall and is 2,600 bytes (2.5 seconds).

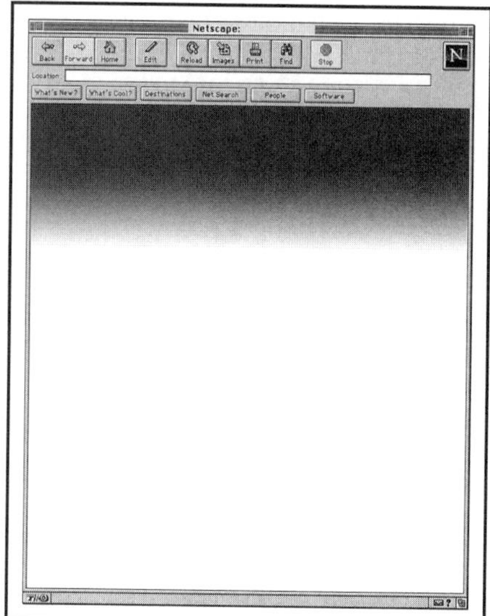

Figure 12-56: A tile which is narrow but tall gives a horizontal orientation to the background.

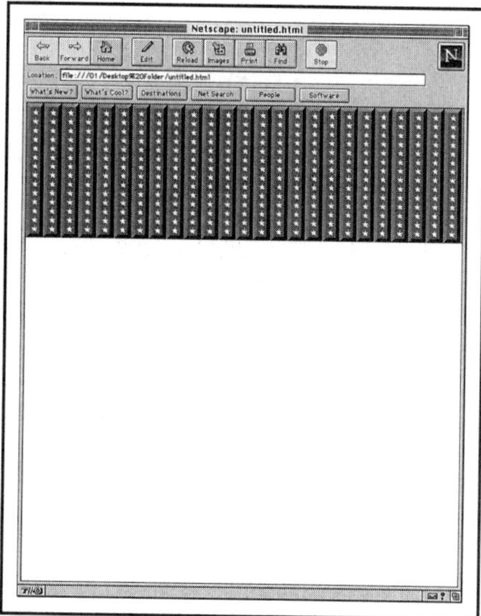

Figure 12-57: Another example of a tall tile, this one more elaborate to give a decorative feeling to the top of the window.

Tiles in Photoshop Using the Offset Filter The Offset filter is bundled with Photoshop. It is one of those tools which does just one thing, but does it perfectly. As you'll see in this section, there are a number of fascinating ways this filter can be combined with other Photoshop effects. The examples here are intended to give you an idea of the possibilities. We're certain that other ideas will occur to you as soon as you try these.

The Offset Filter With the Rubber Stamp Tool Using the Rubber Stamp tool with the Offset filter to make a seamless tile is discussed in the Rubber Stamp section of Chapter 3, "Toolbox Techniques."

The Offset Filter With the Paintbrush & Pen Tools This technique is used to give linear effects that follow a diagonal. The effect is mysterious but very simple. It uses the Pen tool as a means of controlling the Paintbrush.

1. Begin with a small window. Draw a path with the Pen tool (Figure 12-58).
2. Choose the Paintbrush tool and an appropriately sized brush. Stroke the path by clicking on the small icon, second-from-the-left, on the bottom of the Paths palette (Figure 12-59).

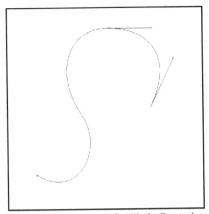

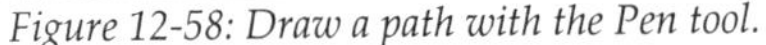
Figure 12-58: Draw a path with the Pen tool.

Figure 12-59: Stroke the path with a Paintbrush.

3. From the Filter menu, choose Other | Offset. Offset the window by half of its vertical and horizontal size. Use the Wrap Around option. With the Pen tool, connect the ends of the previous paint stroke (Figure 12-60).
4. Use the same Paintbrush to stroke this path (Figure 12-61).

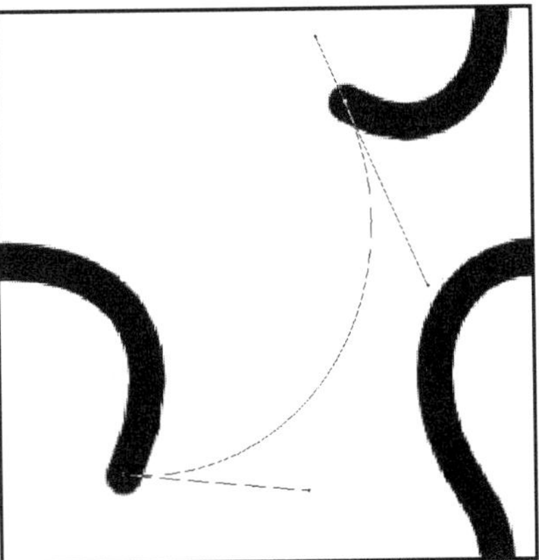
Figure 12-60: Use the Offset filter, and then connect the end of the stroke with a new path.

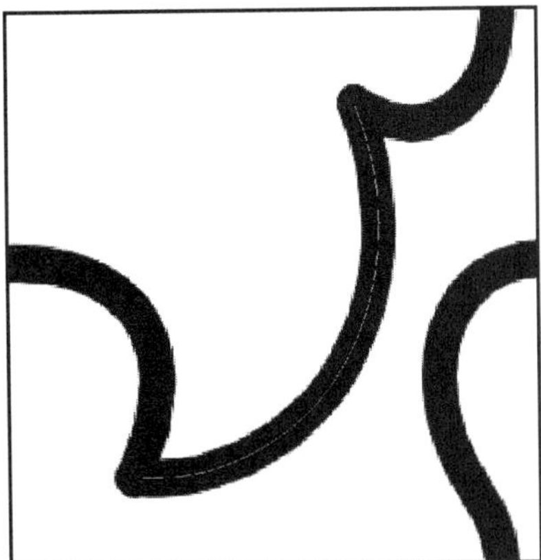
Figure 12-61: Your base tile looks like this.

5. The pattern tile is now complete. Try it in a new window. First, select All. From the Edit menu, choose Define Pattern. From the File menu, choose New. Specify a window that is the same resolution as the pattern tile and which has 3–5 times as many pixels in both directions. When the new window is open, select All. From the Edit menu, choose Fill. Fill the window using Pattern set to 100% Opacity and Normal mode (Figure 12-62).

Figure 12-62: Multiple iterations of your base tile give this more-or-less diagonal texture.

6. This simple black and white pattern can be further modified in a great many ways. One possibility is the low relief effect shown in Figures 12-63 and 12-64. Complete instructions for this interesting dimensional effect will be given later in this chapter.

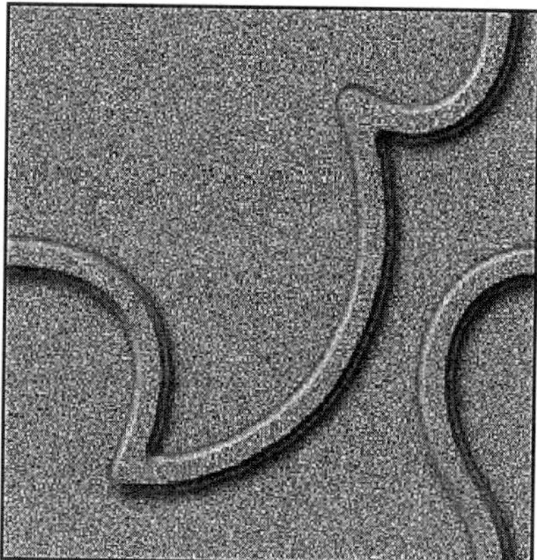

Figure 12-63: If you wish, you can apply embossing effects to your tile.

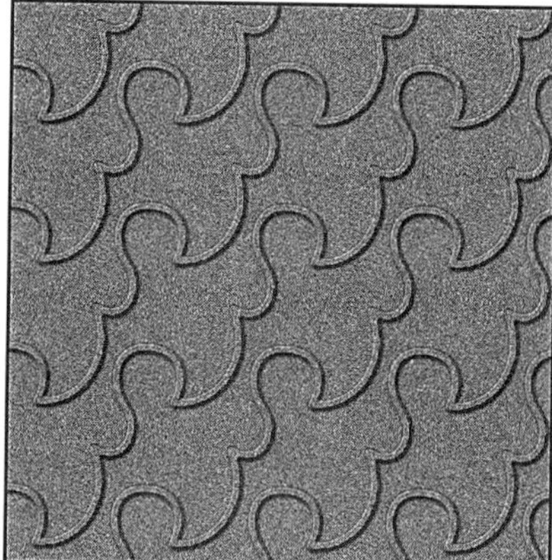

Figure 12-64: Multiple repeats of the tile give this dimensional effect.

The Offset Filter Used With Layers Using this method gives results similar to those produced by the KPT Seamless Welder, but it allows more inventiveness and precision. It is particularly suited to photographic images that contain a well-defined subject surrounded by material of lesser importance. (Such an image is seen in Figure 12-65.)

Figure 12-65: The original photo from which the seamless tile will be generated.

1. After choosing the image from which the tile is to be generated, color correct the image and crop it. When cropping, it's useful to insure that the number of pixels vertically and horizontally are even numbers. In this image, there are 1,840 pixels width and 1,264 pixels height. The offset numbers are 920 and 632.
2. Open the Layers palette. If it is not open, choose Window | Show Layers. Select All. Press Command+j or Ctrl+j to create an exact copy of the Background image onto a layer. Select the Offset filter and enter the appropriate offset numbers (Figure 12-66).
3. Click on the new layer thumbnail to select it. Set the opacity of the layer to 40%–50%. The change in opacity is temporary: it will allow you to see the background through the pixels of the layer (Figure 12-67).

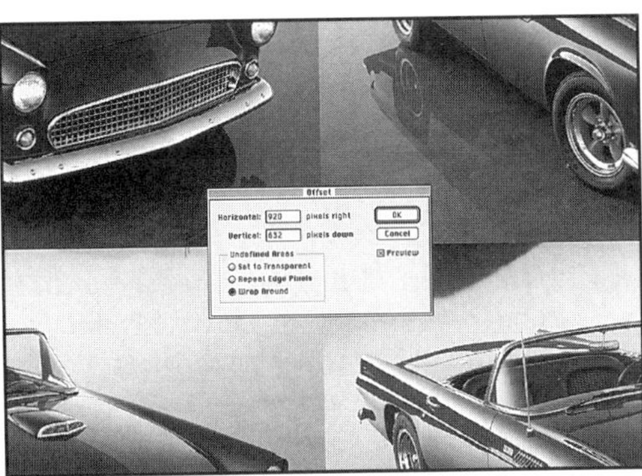

Figure 12-66: Put a copy of the image onto a layer. Offset the layer.

Figure 12-67: Set the opacity of the offset layer to 40–50%.

4. From the Layer menu, choose Add Layer Mask | Reveal All. Choose a medium to large, soft-edged brush set to 100% Opacity. Be certain your Foreground color is set to black. Click on the layer mask thumbnail to be sure you are painting on the

mask and not the layer. Paint over the area of the central image which is the area to be eliminated from the layer (Figure 12-68).

5. Change the opacity of the brush to 50% and choose a smaller size. Use this brush to touch up the transitions between the layer and the underlying image. Return the layer to 100% Opacity.
6. Use whatever method you think appropriate to eliminate the vertical and horizontal joins on all four sides of the central image. You can use the Rubber Stamp tool or the method used here, which is much simpler. With the Lasso tool, make a selection which includes most of the area where you see the abrupt change in tone on all sides of the figure. Feather this selection. The pictured example uses a feather of 10 on an image which is 300 ppi. Choose Filter | Blur | Gaussian Blur. Enter a high number (in this case 35–45 pixels radius). The filter will eliminate the lines. Next, from the Select menu, choose Modify | Expand, and expand the selection by the same amount you used to feather the selection. With this selection operating, choose Filter | Noise | Add Noise. The setting for the noise will be fairly low (5–15 pixels). Judge the appropriate setting by eye. The result of the two filters is shown in Figure 12-69.

Figure 12-68: Add a layer mask and paint the layer so that it vanishes over the central image on the Background layer.

Figure 12-69: Eliminate the joins from the offset layer.

7. Double-check to make sure that all the joins are perfect. Flatten the image and then run the Offset filter again with the same settings used before. You'll probably find that there are four areas—they are circled in Figure 12-70—which need to be touched up. These four areas are much easier to handle than the previous four. (After you have them in hand, your image should resemble that shown in Figure 12-71.)
8. Try out the tile as repeating pattern. Select All, define the pattern, make a new window that is larger than the pattern tile, and then fill the new window with the pattern. This tile is shown with three repeats vertically and horizontally in Figure 12-72 and magnified in Figure 12-73.

Figure 12-70: Flatten the image and use the Offset filter again to check any edge joins.

Figure 12-71: The completed tile after all fixing is completed.

Figure 12-72: Try out a few repeats of the tile to see how it looks.

Figure 12-73: An enlarged detail of Figure 12-72.

Every photographic image which you use to generate a tile using this method delivers a special set of circumstances and problems to be solved. Each image also brings its own special surprise. In this case, the intriguing multi-level feeling is made more pronounced by the fact that some of the cars have shadows and some do not. The authors wish they could say that they foresaw how cool this effect would be, but....

Another example of this method is shown in Figures 12-74, 12-75, 12-76, and 12-77. The first of the figures is the original image, the second the pattern tile, and the last two magnifications of the pattern tile in use. As you can see, the main problem with this image was to fade the bottoms of the trunks of the palms. The Rubber Stamp tool set to 50% Opacity accomplished that task very fast. Also, the multi-toned sky was selected using the Select Color Range command and then replaced with a single color. A small amount of noise inserted with the Add Noise filter completed the replacement of the sky.

Figure 12-74: The original image to be used to make the seamless tile.

Figure 12-75: The completed tile.

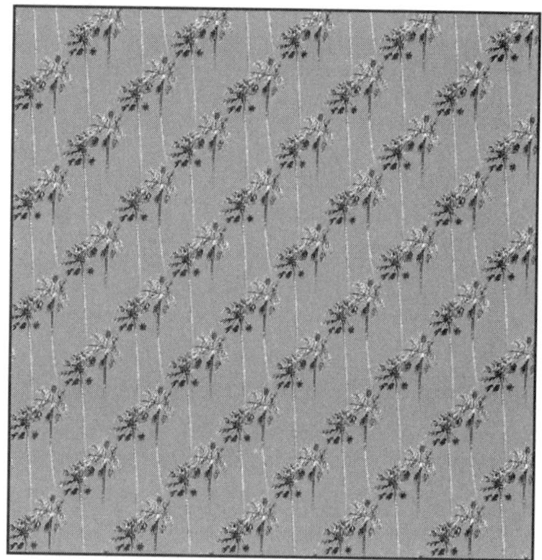
Figure 12-76: Multiple repeats of the tile.

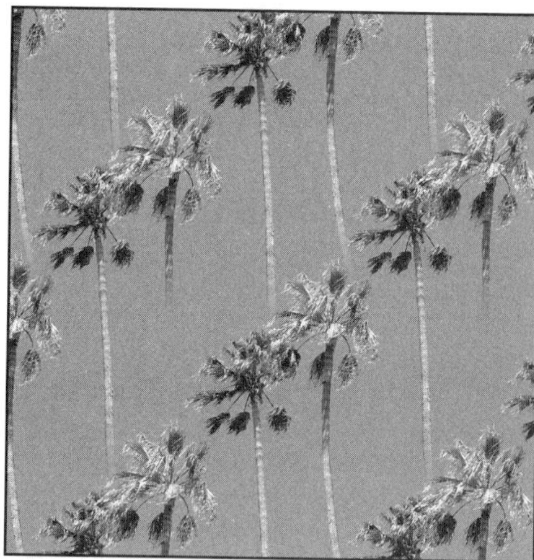
Figure 12-77: An enlarged close-up of Figure 12-76.

And just to show the power of this technique, here are five other figures (Figures 12-78, 12-79, 12-80, 12-81, and 12-82). The original image is the first of these figures. It was chosen simply because it seems, at first glance, to be unpromising material for this kind of seamless tile. As you can see, it works very well indeed. In common with most of the pattern tiles in this chapter, it does not work particularly well as a background. There is too much contrast in the tile: black text and white text would both be unreadable upon this image tile. The fifth of the figures shows the tiled image screened back by 70%. Used in this way, text is completely readable. To screen back the tile, add a new layer and fill it with white. Change the Opacity of the layer to 70% or whatever number you feel is most appropriate for your tile.

Figure 12-78: Single photo source for a pattern tile.

Figure 12-79: The completed tile after the Offset filter with a layer mask.

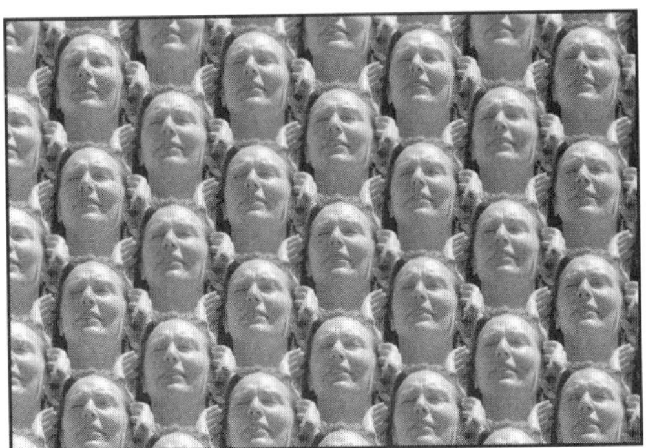

Figure 12-80: Four iterations vertically and horizontally.

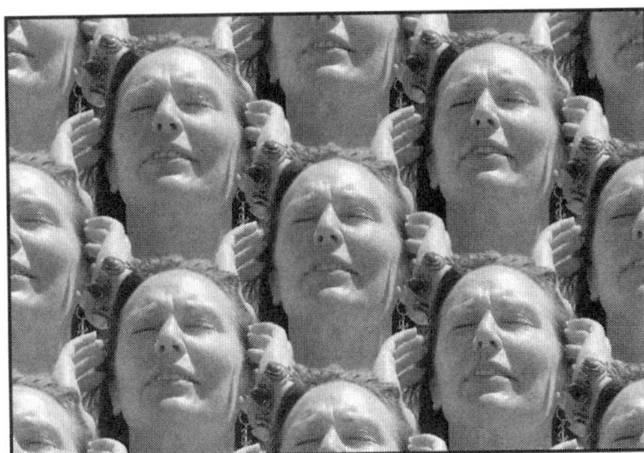

Figure 12-81: An enlarged detail of Figure 12-80.

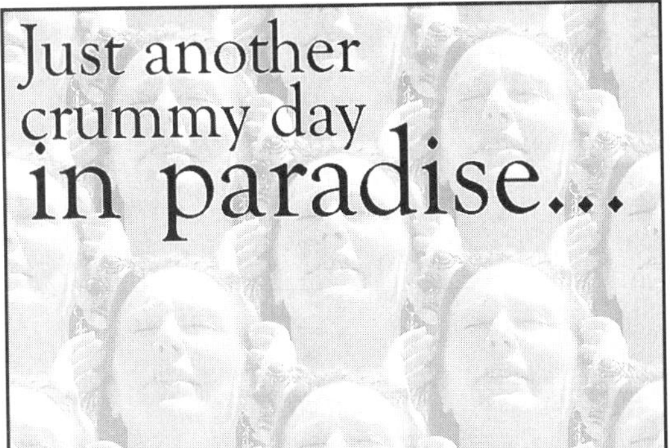

Figure 12-82: The same tile, screened back so that text will be readable when displayed upon it.

Tiles With Terrazzo Do you sometimes think to yourself, "If everybody knew how much fun Photoshop is, would I still get to use it as a work tool?" Many parts of Photoshop—the smoothness with which it accomplishes its miracles, the clever features built into the program, the lack of the bugs that seem to bedevil other programs—are really enjoyable to work with. Just when you think it can't get any better, along comes a cute little filter package like Terrazzo by Xaos Tools. Terrazzo is a kick! Of course it *is* a wonderfully useful utility for creating tiled patterns, but it's also a kick. How could it not be? If you've ever enjoyed looking into a kaleidoscope, you'll understand Terrazzo's appeal. Terrazzo gives complete control over which part of the image will generate the tile and how large the area will be. Any one of seventeen symmetries can be used and the tile can be applied back onto the original image (Figure 12-83) using any one of nine blending modes. The edges of the tile components can be feathered to give a softened edge. Terrazzo is chosen from the Filter menu. The dialog box and its expanded pop-up menus are shown in Figure 12-84.

Figure 12-83: Source image for Terrazzo.

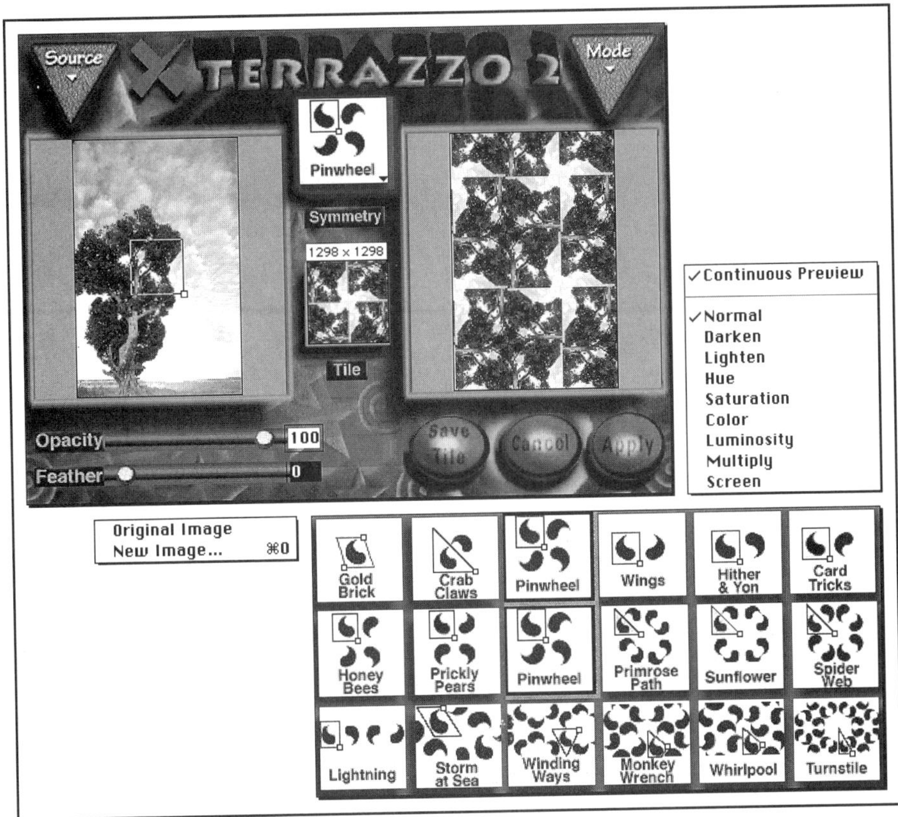

Figure 12-84: The expanded Terrazzo dialog box.

Besides being able to apply the Terrazzo effect back onto the image, the button in the bottom-center allows the tile to be saved as a separate file. Figure 12-85 shows an area of the image subjected to the Whirlpool symmetry, and with a 30-pixel feather radius applied. When saved as a separate file, the generated tile is as shown in Figure 12-86. Figure 12-87 gives an idea how the tile looks in use. This is another tile which would have to be screened back or treated in some manner to lessen the contrast between dark and light areas. Otherwise, type placed on this tile would not be readable.

Figure 12-85: With the source file, choose the Whirlpool symmetry.

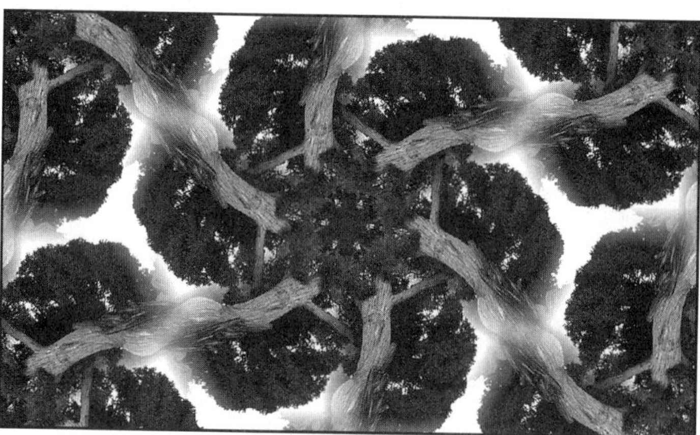
Figure 12-86: The tile saved as a file and opened in Photoshop.

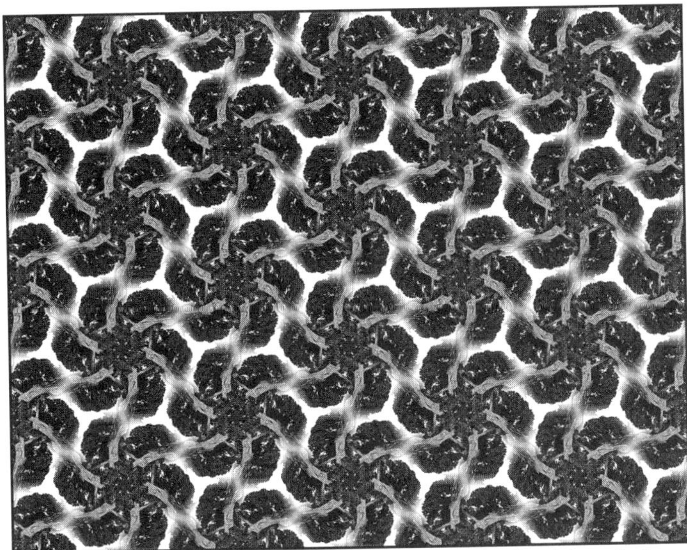

Figure 12-87: Multiple iterations of the tile shows how the edges join perfectly.

Seamless Tiles Using Illustrator The ability to construct and use tile patterns as fills and strokes is one of the great strengths of drawing programs such as Adobe Illustrator and Macromedia FreeHand. With Photoshop able to rasterize such patterns, these powerful vector programs can be put into the service of Web designers.

Illustrator 6.0 ships with a large number of patterns. There are also collections of intricate and beautiful Illustrator patterns available as freeware on the Web. There is even a collection of Illustrator patterns which ships with Photoshop. You can find them in the Goodies folder, inside the folder called Brushes and Patterns. The folder containing the patterns is called PostScript Patterns. Illustrator patterns such as these can be opened, or rasterized, directly into Photoshop at whatever size and resolution is desired. For the patterns that are stored with the Illustrator Startup document, there is no single file that can be opened. Moving the stored patterns from Illustrator to Photoshop is a simple procedure. First, open both programs.

TIP *It is really helpful to have a hotkey set up to switch back and forth between Illustrator and Photoshop.*

In Illustrator, choose Pattern from the Object menu. The dialog box which appears has options for defining new patterns as well as a button marked Paste. Select the pattern to be used and click on the Paste button. Click on OK to close the window (Figure 12-88).

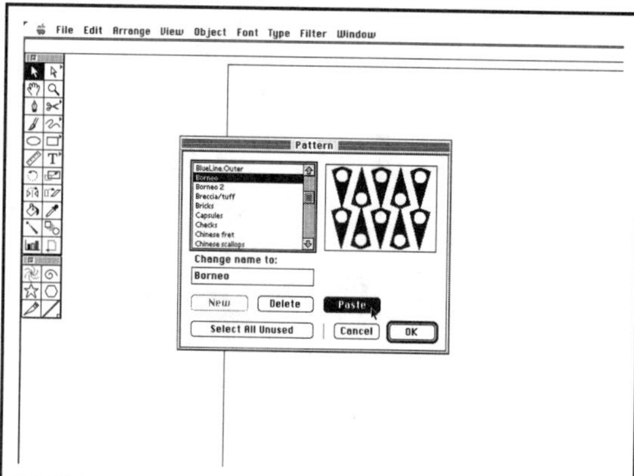

Figure 12-88: The Pattern tile dialog box in Adobe Illustrator.

Illustrator 6.0 stores a copy of the original tile used to make this pattern. Stored, it is instantly available from the Paint palette to be used as a fill or a stroke. By pasting the named pattern, the program gives access to a copy of the original tile which can then be edited and redefined under a new name. The pasted tile will look something like the one shown in Figure 12-89.

Figure 12-89: The pasted Illustrator pattern with the rectangular boundary visible.

Select the bounding rectangle that defines the pattern and choose Bring to Front from the Arrange menu. Select All and choose Mask | Make from the Object menu (Figure 12-90).

The mask hides all parts of the pattern which extend past the bounding rectangle. With the mask in place, the exact dimensions of the tile are clearly seen (Figure 12-91).

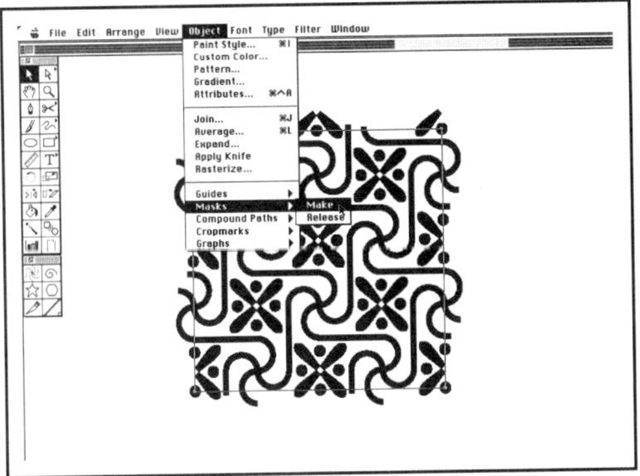

Figure 12-90: The pattern boundary is brought to the front and converted to a mask.

Figure 12-91: After masking, the pattern has been trimmed back to the edges of the bounding rectangle.

Select all and choose Edit | Copy. Switch to Photoshop. In Photoshop, select File | New. The dimensions shown in the dialog box will be those of the copied object which is now on the clipboard. Enter the resolution and mode you wish to use. Click on OK (Figure 12-92).

Another dialog box appears. Select Paste as Pixels and click on the OK button (Figure 12-93).

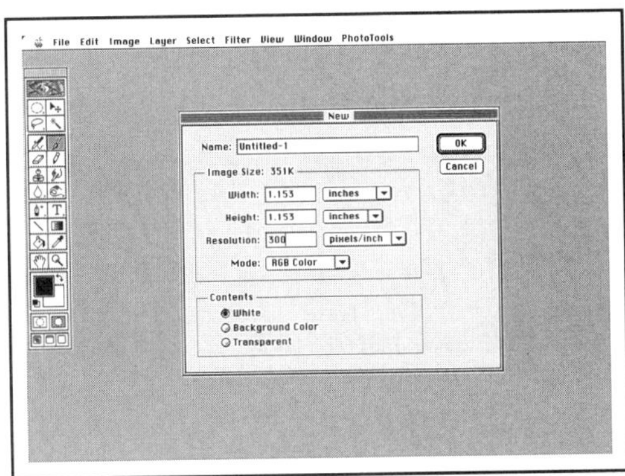

Figure 12-92: Copy the selected pattern. Switch to Photoshop. Choose New from the File menu.

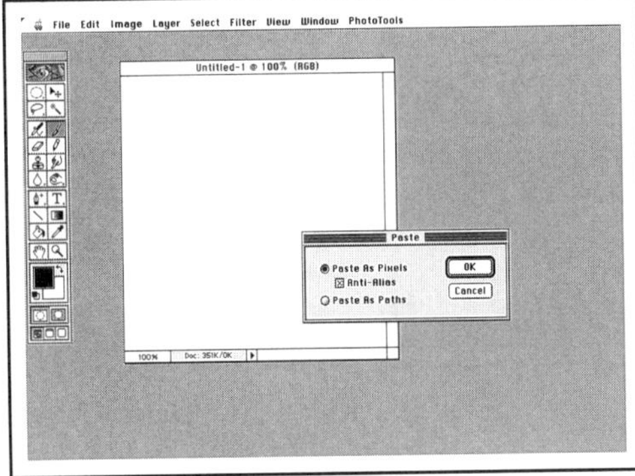

Figure 12-93: Paste the pattern as pixels.

When the paste operation has concluded, the pattern tile is rasterized and ready to use (Figure 12-94) shows the tile window. Figure 12-95 shows a larger window with the pattern tile used as a fill.

Figure 12-94: Photoshop will rasterize the pattern.

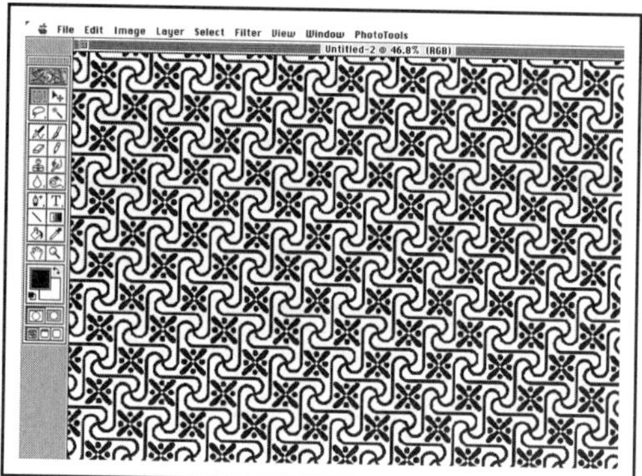

Figure 12-95: Select all and define the pattern. Multiple tiles give an idea how the pattern tiles fit together.

Sometimes it is necessary to remove the white background from a black and white pattern. Instead of pasting directly into the image window, press q to enter Quick Mask, and then use the Paste command. The window will look somewhat as seen in Figure 12-96.

Invert the Quick Mask by pressing Command+i or Ctrl+i (File 12-97).

Figure 12-96: To remove the white background of a tile, copy it and then paste it into Quick Mask.

Figure 12-97: Invert the Mask.

Type q to exit Quick Mask. Your pattern will appear as a selection (Figure 12-98).

Create a new layer (click on the New Layer icon at the bottom of the Layers palette). With the new layer selected, fill the selection with a color. The dark parts of the pattern are now independent of the background (Figure 12-99).

Figure 12-98: Exit Quick Mask. Your image now consists of a selection.

Figure 12-99: Create a new layer and fill with a color.

A pattern such as this is too bold to be used as a background. Here is an easy strategy for toning it down and making it more interesting than the original. First, fill the background with a different—and lighter—color. Next, use the Add Noise filter on the Background layer. Finally, change the Opacity of the pattern layer to something like 40%. The pattern is now complete. Flatten the image and use as you wish (Figures 12-100 and 12-101).

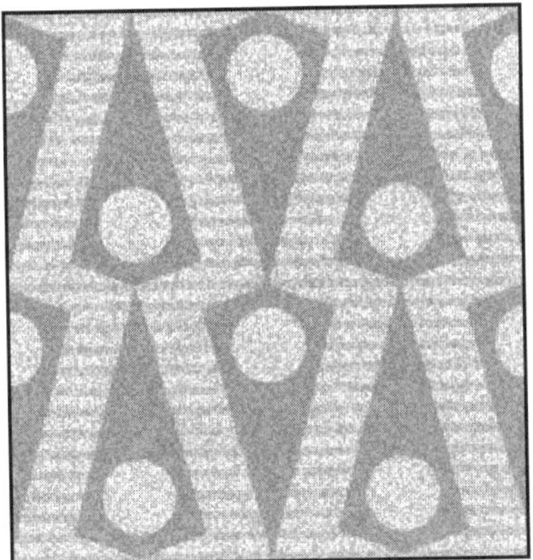

Figure 12-100: Fill the background with a light tone. Use the Add Noise filter on the Background layer. Change the opacity of the upper layer to 40%.

Figure 12-101: The pattern is now more muted and forms an interesting all-over texture.

Non-Rectangular Graphics on the Web

A transparent GIF file is the only format that allows a non-rectangular shape to be placed on a Web page. However, the GIF format does not give you the opportunity to do complex shapes with variable transparency. For example, you might wish to show a simple shape with a drop shadow. For the shadow to look good, it must seem to blend in with the background of your page. For this to be convincing, variable transparency is required. Another example would be when you wish to present a silhouetted image with so much detail that saving it as a GIF file is out of the question. Your only option is the JPEG format. Unfortunately, JPEG does not support transparency.

Can these things be done? The short answer is no, not really. But you *can* do a simulation of transparency effects that is indistinguishable from the real thing. In the following section, you'll learn the easy principles behind simulated transparency effects. You'll also learn a couple of other useful production techniques such as fast masking.

A Fast Mask Technique for the Web

Non-rectangular photo images used on the Web are not usually presented as shapes with an exotic crop. More often, the subject of the photo is silhouetted and the surrounding area changed to transparent or filled with the color used for the background of the Web page. There are many ways to isolate, or *mask*, the subject of an image. Several ways are presented in various places within this book. This technique is very quick and gives good results without having to spend a lot of time. The idea behind this technique is that Web graphics do not usually require the precision edges which would be the norm for the print/prepress industry. Begin by color-correcting and cropping the image to be used. The sample image—RGB but shown here as grayscale—is seen in Figure 12-102.

Figure 12-102: The image to be used for the fast mask example. From this image, 11 different channels can be generated.

First, let's examine the various available component channels of this image to determine if one is suitable for use as a starting point for the mask. With a well-defined image of this sort, we could make a selection with the one of the selection tools, but instead let's make use of a more time-saving possibility:

1. Choose Image | Duplicate and make three new copies of the original RGB image. Convert the first to Grayscale mode, the second to CMYK mode, and the third to Lab mode. The individual channels of the three color modes can be accessed by clicking on the channel numbers on the Channels palette. Representations of the eleven channel possibilities are seen in 12-103 (*Black* from grayscale), 12-104 (*R* from RGB), 12-105 (*G* from RGB), 12-106 (*B* from RGB), 12-107 (*C* from CMYK), 12-108 (*M* from CMYK), 12-109 (*Y* from CMYK), 12-110 (*K* from CMYK), 12-111 (*L* from Lab), 12-112 (*a* from Lab), and 12-113 (*b* from Lab).

Figure12-103: Grayscale.

Figure 12-104: The R channel from RGB mode.

Figure 12-105: The G channel from RGB.

Figure 12-106: The B channel from RGB.

Figure 12-107: The C channel from CMYK mode.

Figure 12-108: The M channel from CMYK.

Figure 12-109: The Y channel from CMYK.

Figure 12-110: The K channel from CMYK.

Figure 12-111: The L channel from Lab mode.

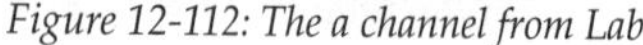

Figure 12-112: The a channel from Lab.

Figure 12-113: The b channel from Lab.

2. Of the available channels, the two which seem to most clearly differentiate the auto from the texture surrounding it are the Cyan and Black channels. The Cyan channel is probably the better of the two. Begin by Selecting All, copying the Cyan channel, and pasting it into a new document.
3. Choose Image | Adjust | Levels. Uncheck the Preview option. Now, hold down Option or Alt and move the right-hand slider on the top scale to the left. Your screen enters what is called Threshold mode. Move the slider until the shape of the car becomes substantially bleached out. Be sure not to push the slider so far that there is no difference between the central image and the textures around it. If needed, you can also move the left-hand input slider (with the Option key or the Alt key held down) to darken the area around the car. Click OK. (Figure 12-114).

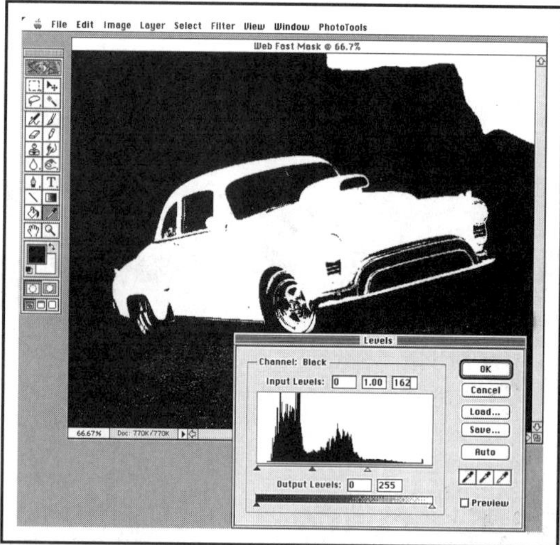

Figure 12-114: Use Threshold mode in the Levels controls to change the channel to a high-contrast image.

4. With the Polygon Lasso tool, make a very quick selection of the non-white areas within the perimeter of the central image and fill the selection with white as shown in Figure 12-115.

5. Use a large-end brush shape with the Pencil tool to add white to the areas of the tires and the shadowed areas beneath the car. The Pencil tool is used here because an anti-aliased edge is not wanted for this silhouette. You will be selecting the shape with the Magic Wand tool. Anti-aliasing will give you an edge that will be soft and difficult to select (Figure 12-115).

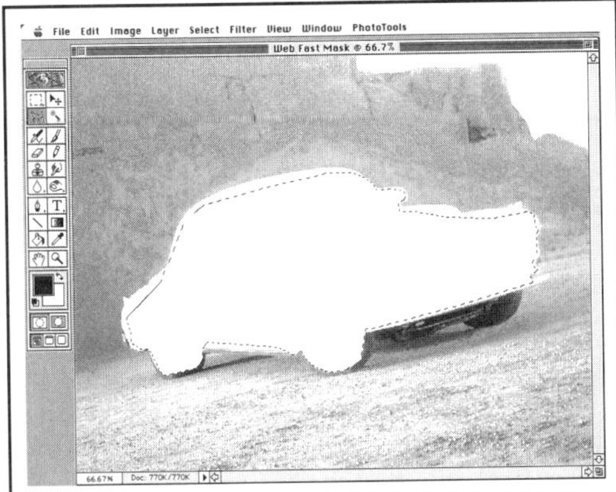

Figure 12-115: Make a quick Lasso tool selection and fill with white.

Figure 12-116: Use the Pencil tool to firm up the edges along the bottom of the car.

6. Use the same brush and paint with black to give a line of contrast between the under part of the car and the light areas of the ground around the image. This insures that when we select the white area of the car with the Magic Wand tool, the selection remains within the boundaries we wish (Figure 12-117).

7. Set the Magic Wand tool to a Tolerance of 1 and turn off the anti-alias. Click within the white area to select the auto shape. Invert this selection (Select | Inverse) and fill with black (Figure 12-118).

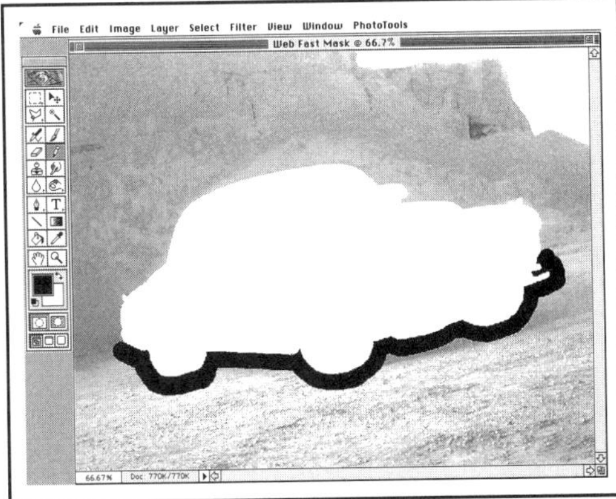

Figure 12-117: Add a black edge outside the car's lower boundaries to keep the Magic Wand from selecting outside the car.

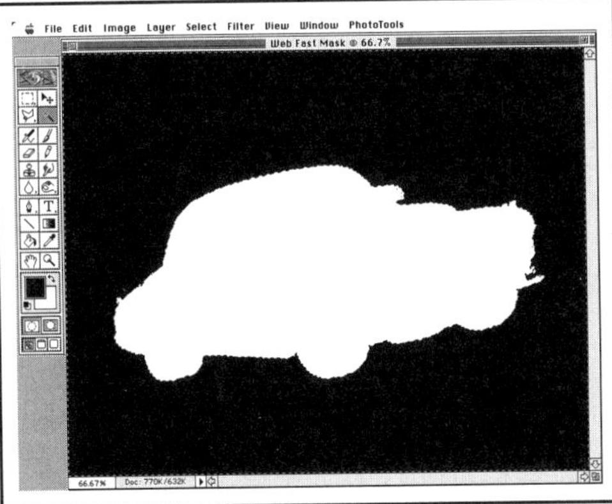

Figure 12-118: Select the shape with the Magic Wand tool, select the inverse, fill with black.

8. Select All and copy this image. Return to the original RGB photo and create a new channel. Do this by clicking on the New Channel icon at the bottom of the Channels palette (the icon just to the left of the trash icon). Paste the car mask into this channel.
9. Click on the top thumbnail of the Channels palette. Now, activate the mask channel by holding down Command or Ctrl and clicking on the thumbnail of the mask (#4) on the Channels palette. Zoom in to the edges of the mask and correct any visible problems with the Lasso tool (set anti-aliasing to Off). When the selection has been corrected, press Command+j or Ctrl+j to place the car onto a separate layer. You can now fill the Background layer with a solid color or, by hiding the Background layer, you can export the image as a GIF89a file (Figure 12-119).
10. There is a problem sometimes seen in Web pages which use graphics such as this automobile. Having spent the time masking the car and to turning the background transparent, the designer forgets to crop the image (Figure 12-120). Unless it is cropped, all of the useless information outside the crop line shown in the figure is still a part of the file and would have to be downloaded by the browser. Be sure not to omit this important step in order to make your file as small as possible.

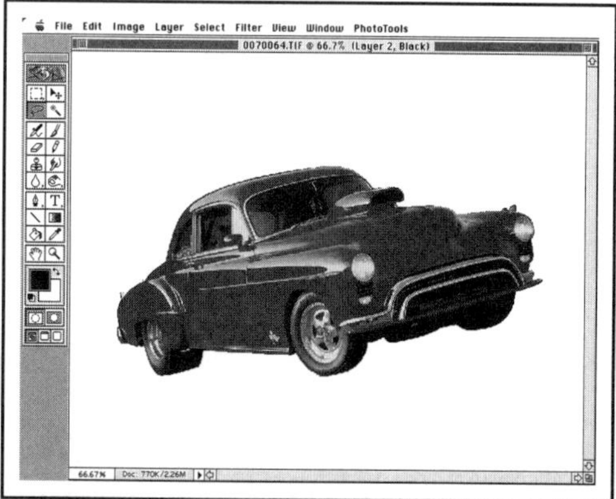

Figure 12-119: Activate the mask channel and place the selected car onto a new layer. Fill the Background layer with white.

Figure 12-120: After eliminating the background, remember to get rid of all the space around the image by cropping.

More About Non-Rectangular Shapes

Another method for making an image appear to be a cutout or a silhouette is to use, as the background color for the image, the same color used as the background for the browser window. The main difficulty with this is that different monitors have different gamma settings, and a neutral gray (192, 192, 192) on one monitor appears subtly different on another monitor. This leads to problems of the sort shown in Figure 12-121. The gray background of the beetle may have looked perfect against the gray background of the designer's browser. However, when the page is viewed on a different monitor, the chances are good that there will be enough of a difference to cause visible lines between the two gray tones.

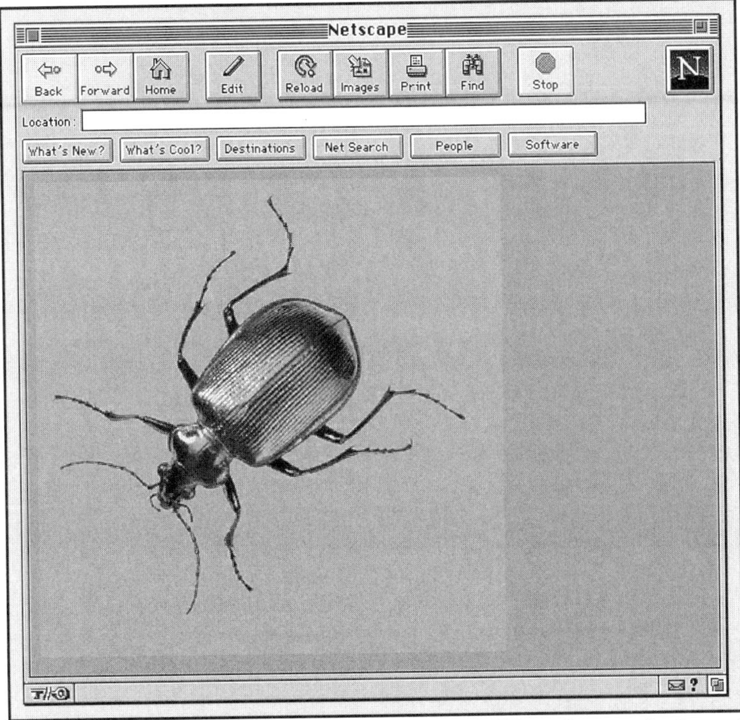

Figure 12-121: Code specified background colors can look different from monitor to monitor.

The solution to this problem is to lock in the background color by using a small single-colored background tile and to use, as the background color for the graphic, the same color used for the tile. In the layered document seen in Figure 12-122, the Background layer is filled with the same color as the small tile. The shadow layer is set to Multiply mode to insure that it integrates with the background gray. When the background tile and graphic are used together the result is as shown in Figure 12-123. There is a perfect merge of graphic with background which simulates the effect of a non-rectangular shape.

Figure 12-122: The background color of the large document is the same color as the small tile in the second window.

Figure 12-123: When the large file's background color and the identically colored tile are used together, there is no visible boundary.

By using these small, solid-colored tiles as backgrounds with the same background color for the photograph, a number of tricky-looking effects are possible. Two are shown in Figures 12-124 and 12-125. One is a silhouette which fades away along the bottom, the other is a vignette-edge effect. Neither of these is possible with the present capabilities of the JPEG or the GIF formats in HTML. Both effects are theoretically possible with the PNG file format.

Figure 12-124: An example of a silhouetted shape that fades out at the bottom.

Of limited use is a technique which simulates a vignetted edge by applying the Dissolve mode to the edges of an image. The layered Photoshop document has a blurred or feathered edge applied to the central subject. This layer is then set to the Dissolve mode on the Layers palette (Figure 12-126). The background is filled with any color useful as a possible transparent color or the layer is exported as a GIF89a file. The effect is as shown in the close-up in Figure 12-127.

Figure 12-125: A simulated vignette edge.

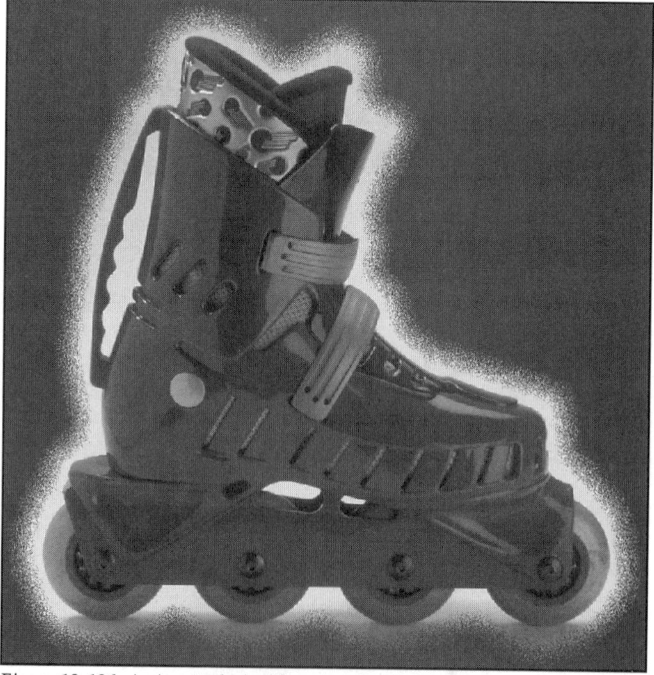

Figure 12-126: A vignette look-alike using the Dissolve mode.

Figure 12-127: Enlarged detail of Figure 12-126.

Buttons, Arrows & Display Type

The graphics on a Web page that act as link objects are usually in the form of buttons, arrows, or text. When graphic objects are made into links, they often have a line drawn around them to indicate link status. The tag for the link can contain a switch to make the border equal to 0 pixels:

```
<a href="link.html"><img src="/filepath/file.gif" width="xxx" height="xxx"
align="center" border="0"></a>
```

With the border set to 0 (invisible), it is important to give visual cues to the user that a graphic is a link. These cues can be in the form of shapes such as arrows, they can be in the form of shapes set off by drop shadows, or they can be in the form of shapes that are embossed. Four common shapes for link graphics are the rectangle, circle, letter form, and arrow. The arrow is the only one of the four that is, self-evidently, a link (Figure 12-128).

Figure 12-128: These simple shapes are often used as navigation aids on a Web page. Only the arrow shape is an obvious button.

Quick Drop Shadows

By making these shapes seem to float above the page with a drop shadow, link status is easier to assume (Figure 12-129).

Figure 12-129: With a drop shadow, the viewer is alerted to the fact that these shapes mean something more than just decoration.

Making drop shadows in Photoshop is fairly simple. We'll assume that the graphic is as shown in Figure 12-128 and that the shapes are not isolated on a layer. The first part of the following set of instructions contains a useful tip for isolating shapes very quickly:

1. Begin with the shape(s) in a window set to the appropriate resolution and in Grayscale mode. With the Channels palette showing, drag the Black channel thumbnail onto the New Channel icon at the bottom of the Channels palette. Click on this layer (now titled Channel #2) and invert it (press Command+i or Ctrl+i). Click on the original channel's thumbnail to select it.
2. Command+click or Ctrl+click on the second channel's thumbnail. The black shape(s) become selected. Switch to the Layers palette. Make this selection a layer by pressing Command+j or Ctrl+j.
3. Duplicate this layer by dragging its thumbnail down onto the New Layer icon. Click on the Background layer to select it, and fill it with white. Hide the upper layer, then click on the lower of the two layers to select it.
4. Change the opacity of the selected layer to 60%. Choose Filter | Blur | Gaussian Blur. Experiment with the Radius setting to achieve a diffused edge. Press v to select the Move tool. Drag this layer down and to the right, or press the Down arrow key 5 or 6 times followed by the Right arrow key 5 or 6 times.
5. Make the upper layer visible. Flatten the image. Discard the extra channel, and save the image in an appropriate format (Figure 12-129).

Embossed Shapes

Embossing is another good way to indicate to a user that there is the likelihood of interactivity where a graphic shape is concerned. There are many ways to make an embossed effect. This Photoshop procedure may appear to be cumbersome but it achieves very good results. And it has the added advantage of requiring no third-party filter effects. Notice that the image is subjected to several filters and commands before the Emboss filter is used. If the Emboss filter is used before the others, the effects are likely to be disappointing. The preliminary work insures that the shapes will look good when the final filter is applied to them.

1. Begin with the same grayscale document used for the drop shadow technique. With the Channels palette showing, drag the Black channel thumbnail onto the New Channels icon at the bottom of the Channels palette. Click on this layer (now titled #2) and invert it (press Command+i or Ctrl+i). Click on the original channel to select it. Command+click or Ctrl+click the #2 channel. The shapes become selected.
2. From the Select menu, choose Modify | Contract. Choose a number between 5 and 10. When the selection has contracted, click on the small icon that is second-from-left at the bottom of the Channels palette. Clicking here makes a new channel which is now titled #3. Both of these channels will be used later in the embossing process. All of this preliminary work is simply to provide some tools that will be needed later. The embossing procedure comes next.
3. From the Filter menu, choose Other | High Pass. Pick a setting that gives a semi-embossed effect without making large, black, empty areas in any sharp corners of the shapes (Figure 12-130).

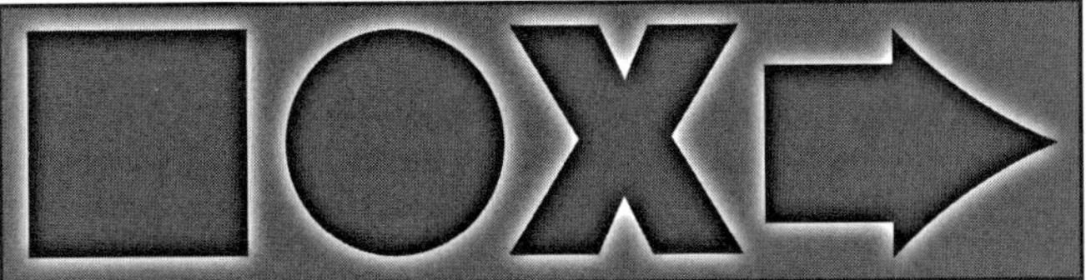

Figure 12-130: The High Pass filter applied to the black shapes.

4. From the Filter Menu, choose Stylize | Find Edges. The filter results are shown in Figure 12-131.

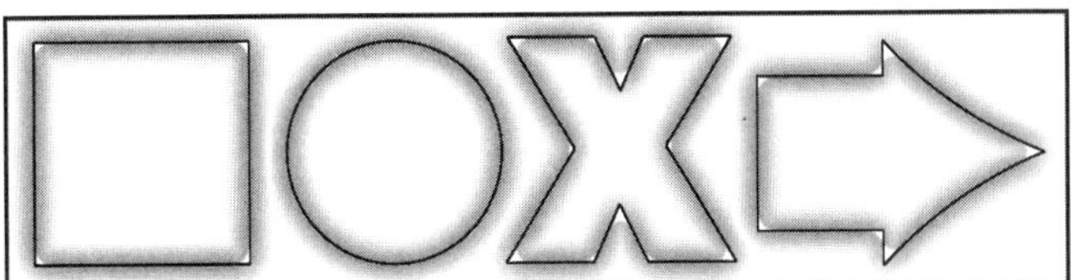

Figure 12-131: The same shapes after using the Find Edges filter.

5. Choose Filter | Blur | Gaussian Blur. Experiment with the settings. If you look closely at Figure 12-131, you can see the small white areas at the corners of the shapes (artifacts of the High Pass filter) which need to be eliminated by the Blur filter. After the filter executes, the image should look similar to Figure 12-132.

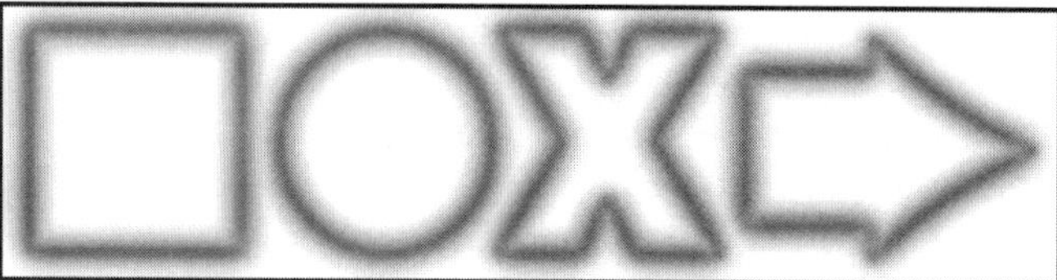

Figure 12-132: The next step is to use the Gaussian Blur filter.

6. Open the Level dialog box (press Command+l or Ctrl+l). Move the midtone slider to the right to slightly darken the image. From the Filter menu, choose Stylize | Emboss. Experiment with the settings to change the direction of the light, the height of the emboss effect, and the amount of contrast between highlight and shadows. The height of the emboss effect should be about the same number of pixels used to contract the selection (above). After executing the Emboss filter, the image should resemble Figure 12-133.

Figure 12-133: The Emboss filter.

7. Command+click or Ctrl+click on the thumbnail of the #2 channel. Press d to set the Foreground/Background colors to their defaults. From the Select menu, choose Inverse and press the Delete key. The background area fills with white leaving the embossed shapes (Figure 12-134). The shapes look fairly good but we're about to make them look even better.

Figure 12-134: After embossing, use Channel #2 to help get rid of the background.

8. With the Eyedropper tool, select a medium tone from one of the embossed shapes. Command+click or Ctrl+click the thumbnail of the #3 channel. Fill the selection with this medium tone (Figure 12-135).

Figure 12-135: Use a Channel #3 selection to fill the interior shapes with a single color.

9. The Foreground color is now the medium tone selected with the Eyedropper tool. The background color is white. With the selection still active, choose the Gradient tool. Set the Gradient tool's Opacity to 65% and the gradient type to Foreground to Background. Draw the gradient from bottom to top of the selected area. Deselect. The result of the gradient overlay on this center area is shown in Figure 12-136.

Figure 12-136: Draw a 65%-opaque gradient over the inner shapes.

10. Set the Gradient Opacity to 45%. Pay attention now, this next bit is a little tricky. Command+click or Ctrl+click on the #2 channel. Hold the Command and Option keys or the Ctrl and Alt keys and click on the thumbnail of the #3 channel. This subtracts the area of the third channel's selection from that of the second. Draw a gradient from bottom to top of the selected area (the border within the shapes). Deselect. The result is shown in Figure 12-137.

Figure 12-137: Add a 45% opaque gradient to the outer edges.

A Few Niceties

To add more of a reflective effect to the shapes, follow these steps:

11. First, increase the contrast of the embossed shapes by choosing Image | Adjust | Auto Levels.
12. Select the inner shape (Command+click or Ctrl+click Channel #3). Use a soft paintbrush. Set the Foreground color to white and the Paintbrush Opacity to 50%. Click outside the selection on the far left edge of the window. Hold the Shift key and click once again, this time on the far right-hand edge of the window. A straight line will connect the two points but will be visible only inside the selection. (Use the tick marks on the rulers to help align the brush so that the drawn line is perfectly horizontal.)
13. Select the outer border areas of the shapes (see above). Draw the same Paintbrush line but slightly lower than the first and with the Opacity set at 40% (Figure 12-138).

Figure 12-138: A single wide Paintbrush stroke seems to add reflectivity.

You can make the embossed shapes appear to be a more organic part of the Web page if the background of the page is filled with the same color used to fill the interior part of the embossed shape as shown in Figure 12-135.

A attractive modification of the embossed shapes, which turns out to be a very simple effect, is to map a texture onto the embossed shape.

14. Begin with the image as it was in Figure 12-137 and execute the Auto Levels command. Create a new layer for this document and fill it with the texture of choice. The example shown in Figure 12-139 uses the Gray Marble texture from the Pixar 128 series (a commercially available set of 128 high-quality textures from Pixar, Inc.).

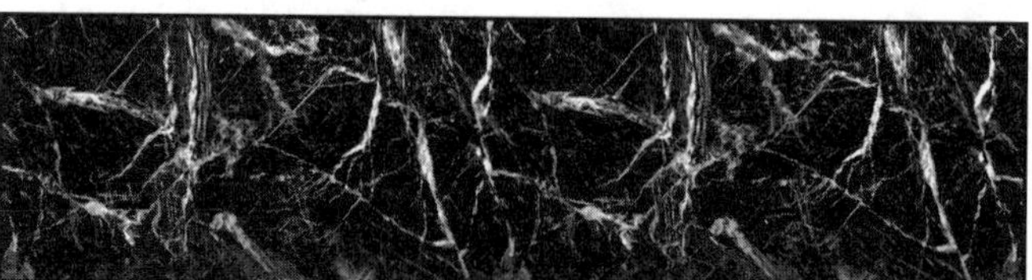

Figure 12-139: Add a new layer and fill it with a texture.

15. Change the blending mode of this layer from Normal to Overlay. Flatten the image (Figure 12-140).

Figure 12-140: Change the mode of the layer to Overlay. It's magic!

No, you don't have to make more selections to get rid of the texture in the background area: the blending mode does it for you. (Whoever said there's no free lunch?) Figure 12-142 shows the same set of shapes with a layer filled with a metallic-looking gradient and then changed to Overlay mode. It is the very same operation but achieves a very different look!

Figure 12-141: As an alternative to the stone texture, fill the layer with a zippy gradient to get this effect.

The Easiest Dimensional Effect of All

SF DekoBoko is mailware software. On the bottom of the filter's interface window is a message from the programmer: "If you like DekoBoko, send me a mail." Please do. This filter is wonderful. DekoBoko is one of a series of filters called Sucking Fish Software. Some of its companion filters are: SF Inai-Inai-Bar, SF MagicalCurtain, SF Midnights TV, & SF Mr. Sa^Kan. These filters are widely available on Web servers with extensive shareware collections of Photoshop utilities. Most of them can be found on America Online, the Microsoft Network, and http://www.shareware.com.

This filter couldn't be easier to use. Open a small window in Photoshop and fill it with a color or a texture. In the case of Figure 12-142, the texture is pebbles in mortar, another of the Pixar 128 series. Under Filter, choose SuckingFishSeries | SF Deko-Boko (Figure 12-143). Figure 12-144 was made with the default settings.

To add a small touch of extra realism, carefully select the center rectangular area of the image. Now, draw a white-to-black gradient (Foreground to Background, Opacity 30%) along the course shown by the arrow in the small image on the right-hand side of Figure 12-145.

Figure 12-142: Begin with a small window filled with a color or a texture.

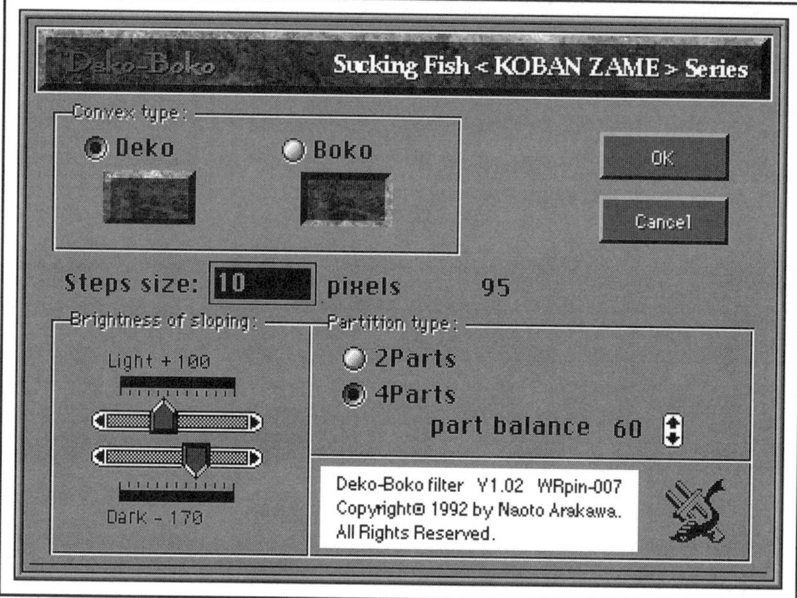

Figure 12-143: The DekoBoko dialog box.

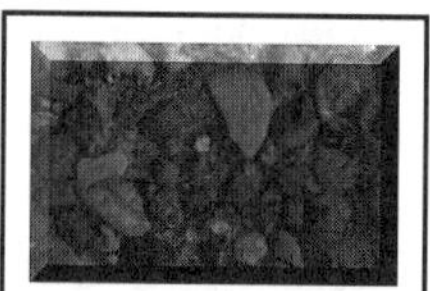

Figure 12-144: The filter applied to the texture.

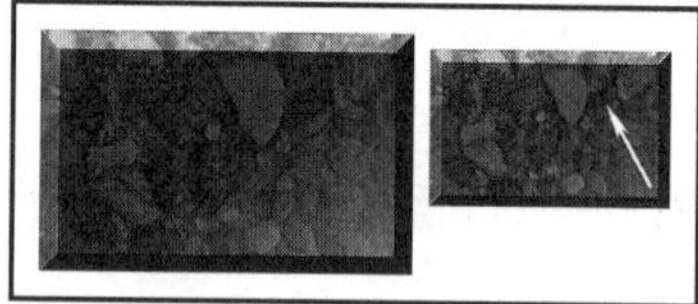

Figure 12-145: Add depth and shine by overlaying a 30% opaque gradient on the center area.

The Sucking Fish filters have been revised and issued as a commercial package under the name WildRiverSSK 1.0. The interface is sexier, more elaborate, and much more powerful (Figure 12-146 shows WildRiverSSK DekoBoko's dialog window). Figure 12-147 shows what the filter can do with an empty, white window in Photoshop.

The other parts of the WildRiverSSK set are: Chameleon, MagicCurtain, MagicFrame, MagicMask, TileMaker, and TVSnow. Please note that the lack of spaces in all of the filter titles—and the title of the filter set 22 is the choice of the software publisher. Rather makes you want to gasp for air, doesn't it?

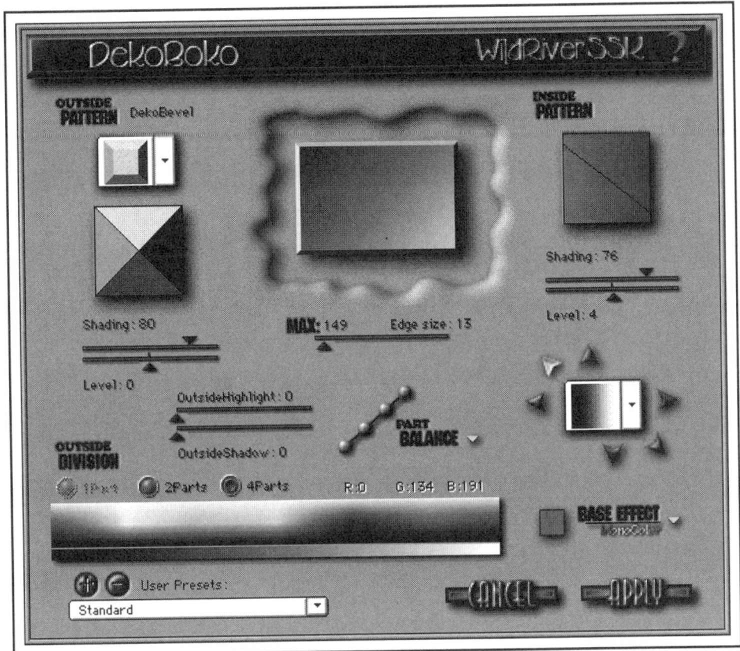

Figure 12-146: The commercial version of DekoBoko, WildRiverSSK DekoBoko.

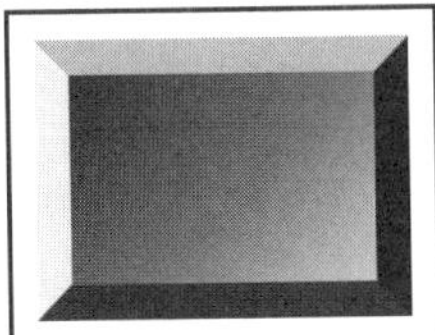

Figure 12-147: This button was generated from a blank white window.

Circular Shapes

Circular shapes with a three-dimensional look are among the most interesting buttons you can construct in Photoshop. There are simple techniques you can use with Photoshop's built-in features and bundled filters. Other filters, particularly the KPT Spheroid Generator 3.0, produce spectacular and intriguing shapes.

KPT Spheroid Generator 3.0

The wide variety of filters usable within Photoshop give some great effects with very little work. One of the most extraordinary is the KPT Spheroid Generator 3.0, one of the Kai's Power Tools modules. Some designers find the interface for the Kai Power Tools intriguing, refreshing, and different. Others find it irritating, artsy-cutsey, and opaque. Despite differences of opinion, there is no denying the amazing results the KPT filters produce, and the Spheroid Generator is one of the best! The eight examples in Figure 12-148 were generated—using the Spheroid Generator presets—in five minutes. All of the examples in this figure have small drop shadows constructed as discussed above.

Figure 12-148: Examples of presets from the KPT Spheroid Generator 3.0.

Make Your Own Spheroids

Spherical—actually, these are hemispheres—buttons can be done in other ways if the KPT filters are not available to you. Here's a set of instructions for such a button which can be done using only Photoshop's bundled features. The eight stages of the button are shown in Figure 12-149.

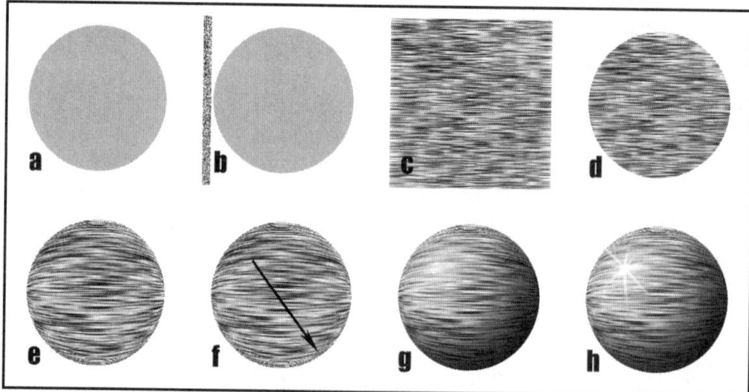

Figure 12-149: Eight stages in creating a spheroid button from scratch.

1. Begin with a simple circular shape filled with a medium color (Figure 12-149a). Be sure that this circular shape is on a separate layer and that the Preserve Transparency option for the layer is turned on.
2. Create a new layer. On this layer make a rectangular selection and fill it with a light color. While the selection is still active, choose Filter | Noise | Add Noise to overlay the color with a noise texture (Figure 12-149b). Deselect.
3. Press Command+t or Ctrl+t for Free Transform. Drag the center right-hand control point to the right, and press the Return key (Figure 12-149c). This operation takes the noise texture and distorts it into a set of streaks.
4. Hold the Option key or the Alt key. Click on the boundary between the top two layers on the Layers palette. The two layers are converted into a clipping group: the streaks on the top layer are trimmed by the boundaries of the circular shape (Figure 12-149d). Hide the Background layer. From the Layers palette menu, choose Merge Visible.
5. Unhide the Background layer. Be sure the top layer is selected. Hold the Command key or the Ctrl key and click on the top layer's thumbnail on the Layers palette. This selects the circular shape.
6. From the Filter menu, choose Distort | Spherize. Make the Spherize settings 100% and Normal. Click on OK (Figure 12-149e).
7. Make the Foreground color white and the Background color black. Select the Gradient tool. Set the Opacity to 80%, the gradient type Foreground to Background, Radial, and the blending mode to Hard Light. Draw the gradient using the same course as the arrow in Figure 12-149f. The result will be as shown in Figure 12-149g.
8. Add an optional specular gleam, if you wish, by choosing a starburst-shaped brush shape with the Paintbrush tool chosen. Click once on the highlight of the sphere (Figure 12-149h).

The KPT Glass Lens Filter & Other Refinements

More elaborate spherical effects can be combined with the KPT Glass Lens 3.0 filter. Beginning with a simple circular shape, apply a variety of textures and distortions. The Glass Lens filter tops off whatever has gone before and leaves a pleasing, dimensional spheroid. The examples beginning with Figure 12-150 and ending with 12-159 are all examples of how this works. Figure 12-150 has the filter applied to a single-colored circular shape. The following eight examples begin with gradients of one sort or another (KPT Gradient Designer 3.0) to which are applied distortion filters such as Wave, Twirl, and Polar Coordinates. The last example shows how, when text is placed on the button before the Spherize filter is run, the text itself becomes distorted and appears to conform to the surface of the spheroid. You can see these buttons in the color plate section of this book.

Figure 12-150: KPT Glass Lens filter applied to a single-color circular shape.

Figure 12-151: KPT Gradient, Ripple filter, KPT Glass Lens.

Figure 12-151: KPT Gradient, Wave filter, KPT Glass Lens.

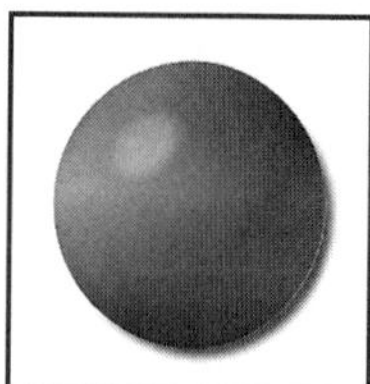

Figure 12-153: KPT Gradient, KPT Glass Lens.

Figure 12-154: KPT Gradient, Polar Coordinates filter, KPT Glass Lens.

Figure 12-155: KPT Gradient, Polar Coordinates filter, KPT Glass Lens.

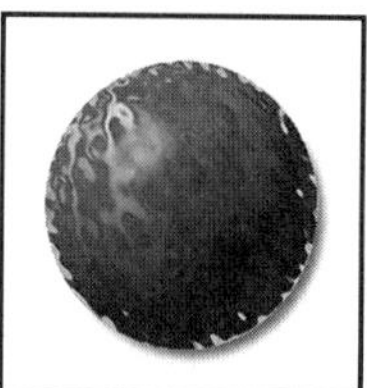

Figure 12-156: KPT Texture Explorer, KPT Glass Lens.

Figure 12-157: KPT Gradient, KPT Glass Lens.

Figure 123-158: KPT Gradient, Twirl filter, KPT Glass Lens.

Figure 12-159: Retroscan filter, added text, KPT Glass Lens, one click with a starburst-shaped Paintbrush.

Very Low Relief

Expressive of the minimalist point of view, here is a severe and monochromatic relief effect that lends itself to the use of symbol fonts and very simple shapes. The effect is attractive and extremely easy to produce. An example—with two variations—is seen in Figure 12-160. For this effect to be most successful, a light-colored background needs to be used.

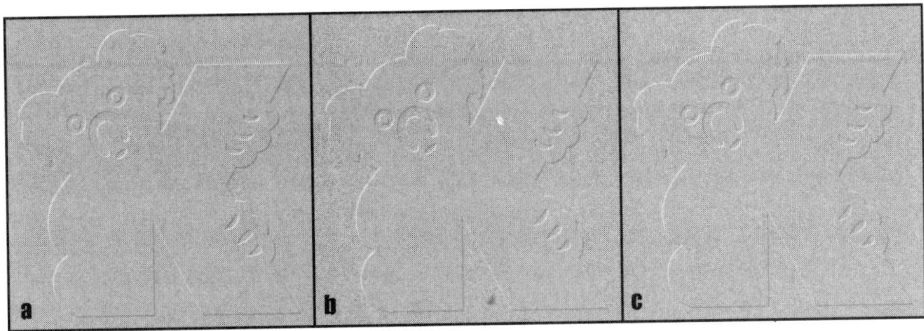

Figure 12-160: Three variations on a low relief effect.

1. Place the relief shape—our example uses the uppercase K from the Critters font—onto an independent layer. Duplicate the layer twice by dragging the layer onto the New Layer icon at the bottom of the Layers palette.
2. Set Preserve Transparency to On for each of the layers, and set the Opacity for the two new layers to 80%. Set the Foreground color to RGB 197, 197, 197 (equivalent to 25% black). Fill the Background layer and the topmost layer with this color. (At this point, the window will look pretty uninteresting. Persevere, it will get better quickly.)
3. Click on the second layer down to select it. Set the Foreground color to RGB 233, 233, 233 (equivalent to about 10% black). Fill the second layer with this color.
4. Select the third layer down. Set the Foreground color to RGB 162, 162, 162 (equivalent to about 40% black). Fill the third layer with this color. Note that the three color tones are 15% apart (10%, 25%, and 40%).
5. Now for the fun part. Select the Move tool. Click on the second layer's thumbnail to select it. Press the Up arrow key twice and then the Left arrow key twice.
6. Select the third layer. Press the Down arrow key twice and then the Right arrow key twice. Magic, huh?

The two variations shown in the example are simple enhancements. *A* is the original. *B* has had the Add Noise filter applied to the Background and to both of the offset layers. The result is a slight improvement in contrast. *C* has had the Add Noise filter applied to the topmost layer as well. Compared to the original, the difference is simply one of surface texture. None of the three is *better* than the others. All might profitably be used under different circumstances.

Sources for Small-Picture Shapes

There are, literally, thousands of collections of clip art that are available at very low cost. The ClickArt Image Pak (T/Maker Company), for example, sells 65,000 royalty-free images—indexed by subject—at a cost of about .0007¢ a file. The set ships on eight CD-ROM disks and includes hundreds of pictographic fonts, as well as high-quality clip art and color photographic images.

Online sources give access to another useful image source, freeware and shareware fonts of the variety sometimes called *pi fonts*. (The ubiquitous Zapf Dingbats is an example of such a font.) To give an idea of the richness of this source as design material, we've included a set of figures showing some of the possibilities. Some fonts are commercial packages, some are shareware, some are freeware. The fonts are shown in Figures 12-161 (Mayan Dingbats), 12-162 (Nahkt), 12-163 (Critters), 12-164 (PostageStamps), 12-165 (SportsThree), and 12-166 (Monotype Xmas Pi).

Figure 12-161: Part of the character set from the Mayan Dingbats font.

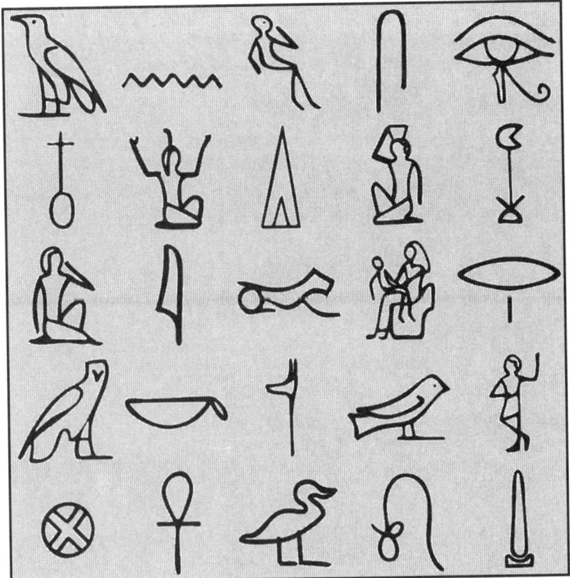

Figure 12-162: Part of the character set from the Nahkt font.

Figure 12-163: Part of the character set from the Critters font.

Figure 12-164: Part of the character set from the Postage Stamps font.

Figure 12-165: Part of the character set from the SportsThree font.

Figure 12-166: Part of the character set from the Monotype Xmas Pi font.

Accessory Software

Beyond the preparation of specific graphics, there are two programs which are excellent for making large-scale graphic/text documents for use on the Web. Some of these products are very new but they will prove very helpful to Web designers. Because these software packages do tasks which would be difficult for Photoshop to handle by itself, it is appropriate to look at them here.

Adobe ScreenReady

ScreenReady is a terrific little utility program that was bundled with Adobe Illustrator 6.0 (it is available only for the Macintosh). Due to the lack of documentation and the less-than-perfect installation, ScreenReady is, possibly, one of Adobe's best-kept secrets. In fact, ask a Mac Illustrator owner/user to give an impression of ScreenReady and you'll probably receive a blank look. That's too bad because ScreenReady is a gem. It is a powerful PostScript RIP which rasterizes nearly any kind of document into a perfect 72 ppi graphic suitable for Web use.

Install the program from the Illustrator master disks. In the folder which the installer places on the hard drive, two of the files you will find are: ScreenReady Extension and ScreenReady Monitor. Copy both of these files into the System Extensions folder and restart the computer.

Make your text and picture documents in any software you wish. The example file shown in Figure 12-167 was done in QuarkXPress. The document's make-up is not unusual: defined colors, placed graphics, headline text. The placed graphic has been saved in the TIFF file format (this is required for ScreenReady to work properly on placed photographic images). To save time, the graphic can be placed as a low-resolution file (72 ppi) and in RGB. Graphics from draw programs such as Illustrator and FreeHand can also be placed as EPS files.

Figure 12-167: QuarkXPress document to be RIPped by ScreenReady.

After the document has been completed, open the Chooser (Apple Menu | Chooser). When the Chooser window opens, ScreenReady will be listed as one of the choices on the left-hand side. Click on the ScreenReady icon to make it active (Figure 12-168). Close the Chooser.

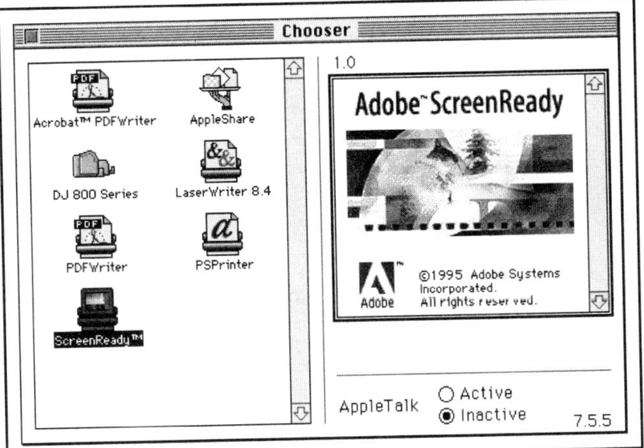

Figure 12-168: The Macintosh Chooser with the ScreenReady driver selected.

In QuarkXPress, select Page Setup from under the File menu. Within Page Setup are contained the options which will determine the size of the file which ScreenReady will prepare. In this case, the full page size has been chosen (Figure 12-169). Such a file would, of course, be far too large for Web use but it is wise to begin with a file larger than needed. The file can be sampled down to any dimension which you might need. Beginning with a small file unnecessarily limits your options.

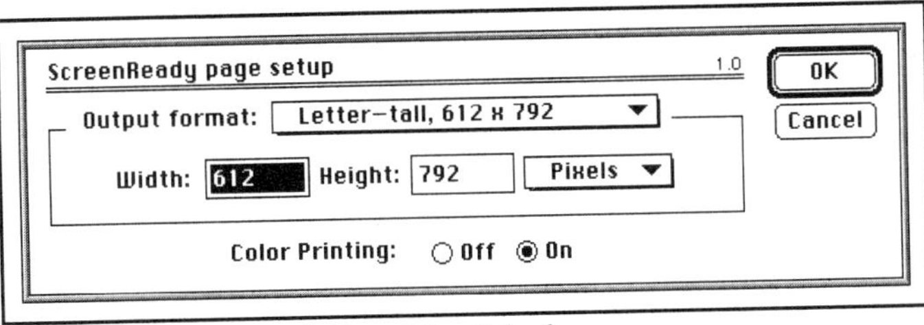

Figure 12-169: ScreenReady Page Setup dialog box.

Now, select Print from under the File menu. The Print dialog box gives a number of choices for the ScreenReady file. The entire set of options is shown in Figure 12-170. Please note the extensive range of palettes which can be chosen. There is as 24-bit option with an optional RIP-created alpha channel, a 16-bit option, and six 8-bit options which can target the Mac system colors, the Windows system, grayscale, IBM EGA, and so on. With these choices available, you can avoid having to make choices if, later, you decide to convert the file to the GIF format.

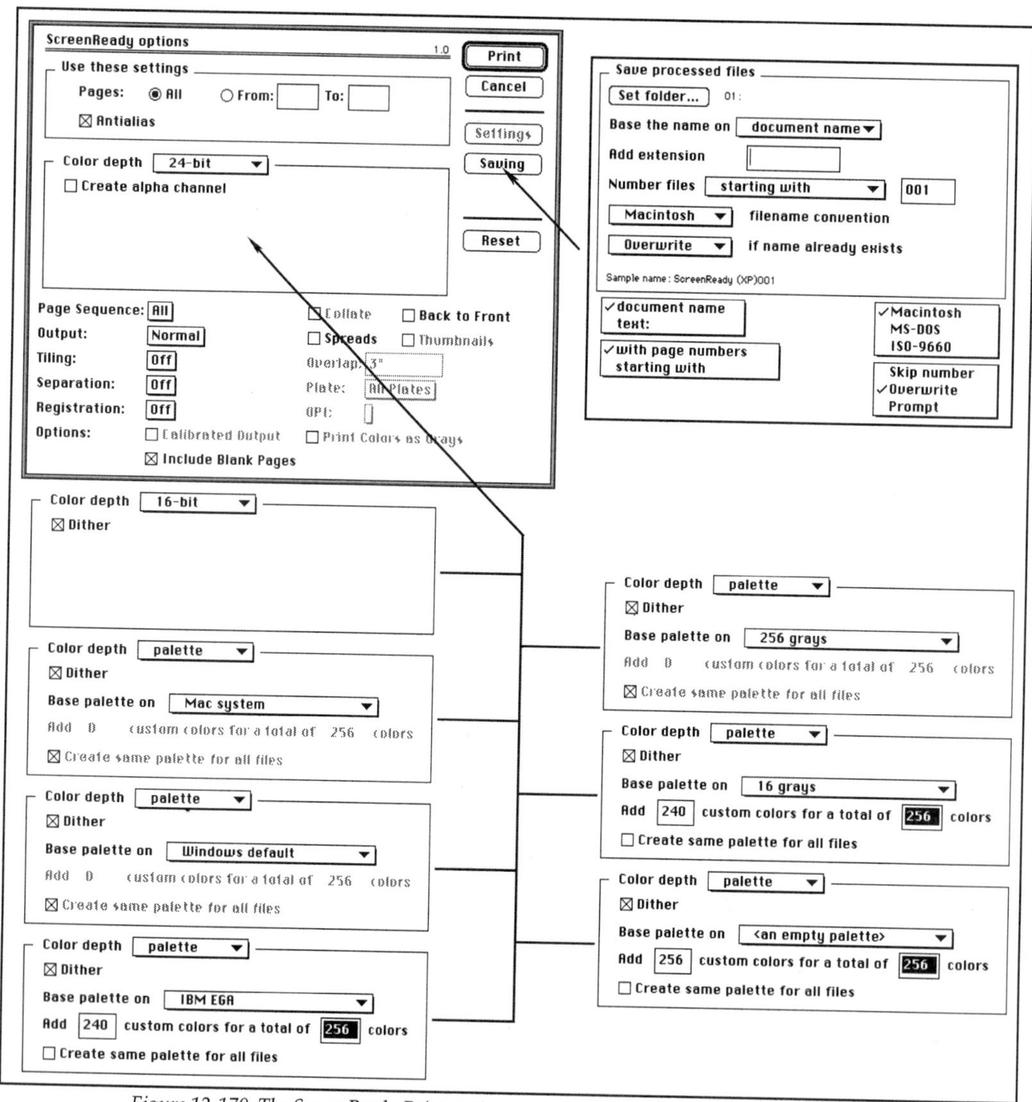

Figure 12-170: The ScreenReady Print options.

With the choices made, click on the Print button. ScreenReady prints the file to disk, rasterizing it as a 72 ppi Photoshop PICT document (Figure 12-170). Depending upon the choices made, this Photoshop document (you can find it on the top level of the boot volume directory) can be used as it is, saved to GIF or JPEG format, or it can be resized and resaved. The Print option which generates an alpha channel gives an additional bit of assistance—though of limited usefulness—for selecting ranges of light or dark values when the image is edited within Photoshop.

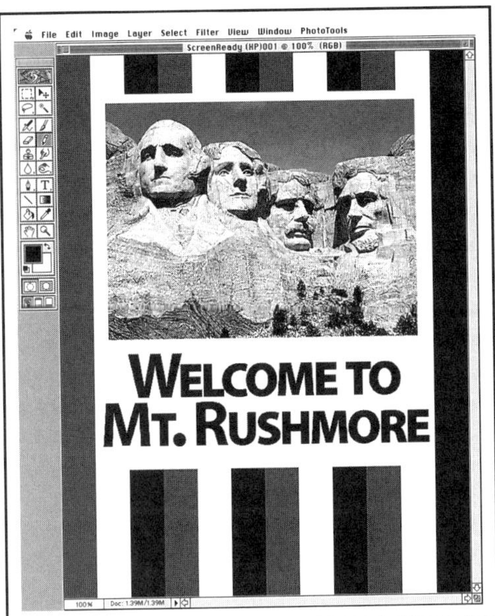

Figure 12-171: The RIPped ScreenReady document opened in Photoshop.

Adobe Acrobat

Acrobat was introduced by Adobe several years ago as a broad solution to document exchange across many platforms. Acrobat documents are called PDF (Portable Document Format) files and use a display model based on Display PostScript.

PDF documents have a range of features that make them ideal for electronic distribution. Each document can have its pictures and fonts embedded. Because of this and because of built-in properties of the display model, excellent quality is obtained when printing the document. Documents can be annotated by the placement of Notes (small icons placed in the text which, when clicked, open to a small window containing more text). Interdocument and intradocument hyperlinks can be a part of each PDF file. Such links would include hypertext jumps from place to place in the same document, from one document to another, and even URLs. Document security can also be built into each PDF as it is created.

To make the PDF format more widely accepted, Adobe has released its Acrobat Reader royalty-free. With Reader, any user can open, view, and print a PDF document (printing can also be prohibited: it is one of the security options which may be included with a PDF document). The construction options for a PDF document are not available from within Reader.

Construction options are available with the Acrobat Exchange program. Exchange functions simultaneously as a reader, annotator, and link installer. Acrobat Exchange is not freeware but is a modestly priced package. The most current version of Acrobat is Version 3.0 which brings a number of exciting possibilities for Web designers and for businesses who have an interest in what is being called *document repurposing*.

Acrobat ships with a plug-in for Netscape Navigator which allows it to function as a sort of super helper app. The Acrobat browser interface opens inside the Navigator window and allows users to view multi-page PDF documents from within the browser. Effectively, this places many graphically exciting documents—all constructed outside the limitations of HTML—within the browser for as few as five lines of HTML code. To illustrate how this will happen, a document is constructed in any software package. The source document can be Adobe PageMaker, Adobe FrameMaker, Adobe Illustrator, Macromedia FreeHand, Deneba Canvas, Microsoft Word, Microsoft Excel, Microsoft PowerPoint, ClarisWorks, QuarkXPress, and so on. The document shown as an example is a five-page QuarkXPress file seen in Figure 12-172. The file contains step-by-step instructions for a special edge effect using Photoshop's Quick Mask (described in this book in the Quick Mask section of Chapter 3). Every page contains a colored photograph and a small amount of text. The document deliberately uses a small physical page size, 3.5 x 5 inches. Graphic size is usually a problem on the Web. Make the graphic too large and it becomes too much of a hassle to download. Make it too small and the viewer is unable to see relevant details. Acrobat, however, is able to display the document in a variety of display percentages such as 125%, 150%, 200%, and so on.

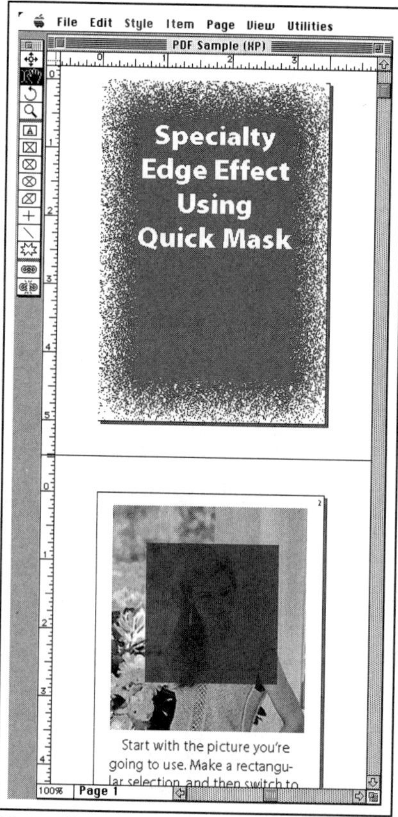

Figure 12-172: Multi-page QuarkXPress document to be converted to Acrobat PDF file.

This document was put together with graphic files at a resolution of 72 ppi and saved as JPEG files. The process of conversion to the PDF format compresses any graphic files automatically. These placed files simply assist the process by performing the compression ahead of time.

Graphic files in any format can be used—TIFF, JPEG, EPS, etc. Vector-based objects from Illustrator and FreeHand can also be used, but to display them at their best in the finished PDF file, these graphic objects should be rasterized into Photoshop and then reimported (see below).

With the QuarkXPress document completed, the conversion to Acrobat proceeds in this manner. Open the Chooser or go to Printer Setup in Windows. The Acrobat PDF Writer is one of the driver choices. Click on the icon to make it active (Figure 12-173).

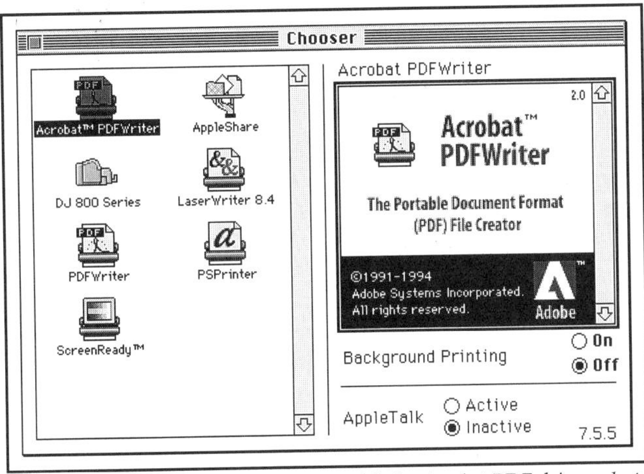

Figure 12-173: The Macintosh Chooser with the Acrobat PDF driver selected.

Choose Page Setup from under the File menu. The dialog box contains the usual size and orientation specifications as well as two buttons, Compression and Fonts (Figure 12-174).

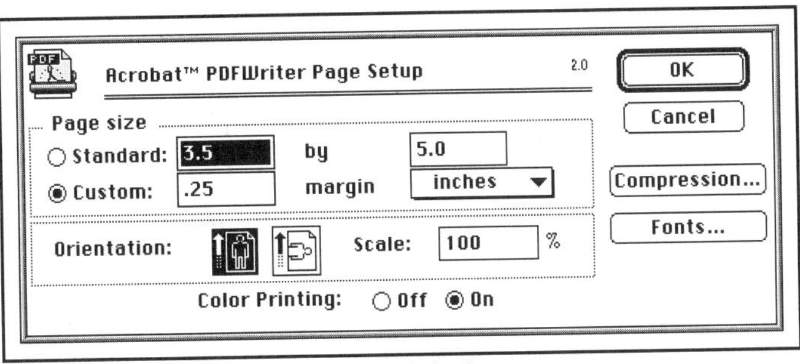

Figure 12-174: The Acrobat Page Setup dialog box.

The Compression button opens the dialog shown in Figure 12-175 which gives a choice of settings for compressing placed graphics.

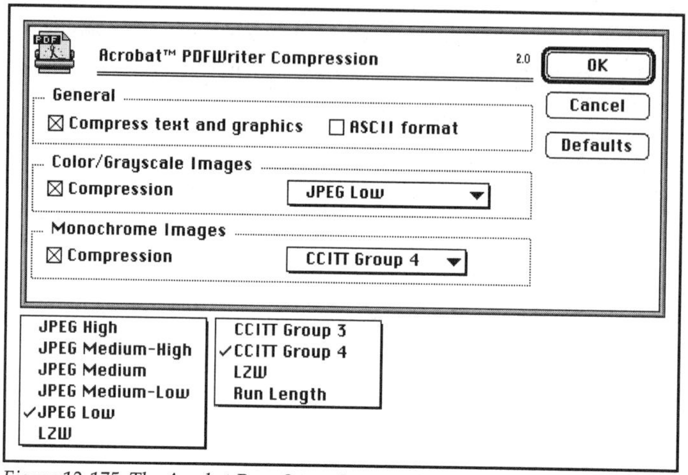

Figure 12-175: The Acrobat Page Setup Compression settings dialog box.

The Fonts button gives options for the embedding of fonts (Figure 12-176). This is, perhaps, one of the most useful features of Acrobat since the embedding of fonts in the document bypasses the problem of widely distributed users not having the same fonts used to build the document.

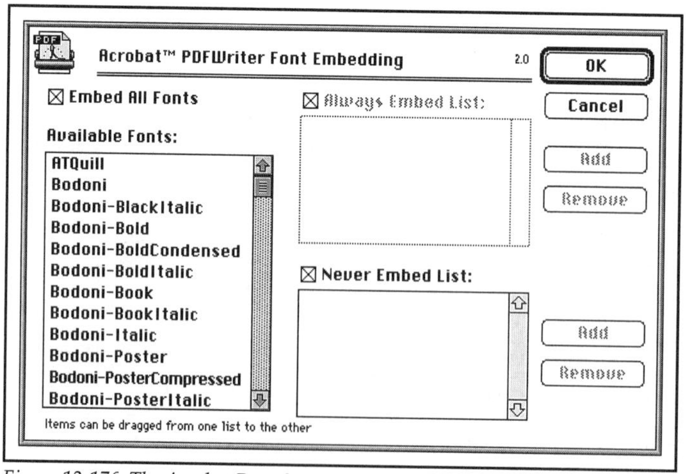

Figure 12-176: The Acrobat Page Setup Font Embedding dialog box.

When all the options are set, choose File | Print (Figure 12-177). The options in the lower part of the box are the same as when printing to a hard-copy printer. The upper portion of the box gives options relevant to Acrobat. View PDF File opens the Acrobat application upon completion of the conversion and displays the new PDF document. Short DOS File Names insure compatibility with cross-platform naming conventions. Prompt for Document Info is available only when View PDF is unchecked.

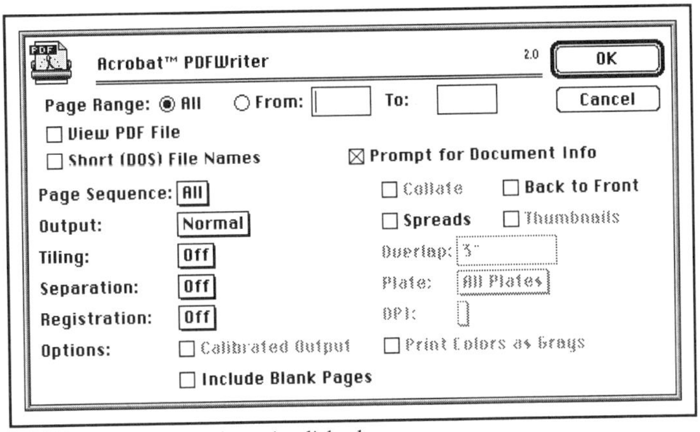

Figure 12-177: The Acrobat Print dialog box.

When these options are taken care of and the OK button is clicked, the dialog box shown in Figure 12-178 appears which requests a name for the new PDF file and a place for it to be saved. The Acrobat driver then converts the document to the PDF format.

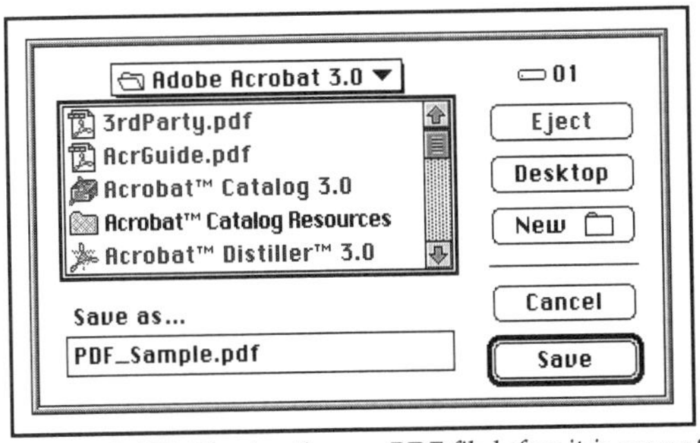

Figure 12-178: Naming the new PDF file before it is generated.

To use the finished PDF file, the Acrobat 3.0 plug-in must be placed in the Netscape Plug-Ins folder. To make a simple HTML page containing a link for opening the new PDF file (Figure 12-179), use code approximately like this:

```
<html>
<body><center><A HREF="PDF_Sample.pdf">Click Here for Acrobat Sample Document.<BR>
</center></body>
</html>
```

Figure 12-179: Link text in Netscape Navigator to display the PDF document.

With this document loaded into Netscape Navigator, click on the hyperlink text. The PDF file loads into Navigator along with all the Acrobat navigation controls (as seen in Figure 12-180). Download time for this document is, as you might expect, longer than for an HTML document with the same number of placed graphic files. However, Adobe has made use of *streaming* technology which displays the first page of a multi-page document as soon as it is received by the client computer. Succeeding pages download while the user looks at the information on the first page.

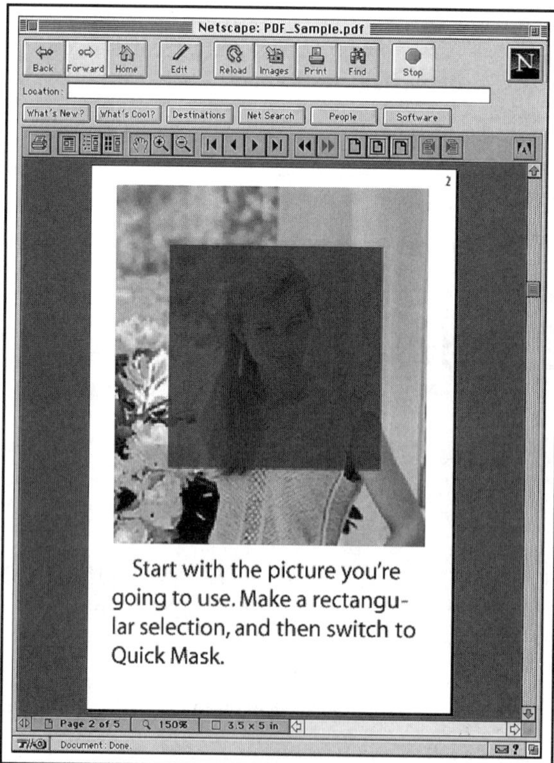

Figure 12-180: The multi-page PDF document displayed in the Navigator window complete with all of the Acrobat Reader navigation controls.

Document repurposing is a natural outgrowth of the print industry with its millions of files already built in digital form. The ease of the Acrobat conversion, and the ease with which documents intended for one purpose can be placed onto the Web with very little work, makes Acrobat the program of choice for many businesses. The only undesirable aspect of the process is the need for a client/user to obtain the Acrobat plug-in for the browser. While this is not difficult—a Web site may even furnish a link directly to the Adobe site from which the plug-in may be downloaded—studies have shown that many users of the Internet will not take the time to download the plug-in and place it in the browser's Plug-ins folder. Perhaps in the future, support for Acrobat might be built into the browser just as support for Java is. Or, perhaps, different strategies may develop for browser technology which may bypass the need for third-party plug-ins. No matter the future, you owe it to yourself to become conversant with the Acrobat software, not only for its ease of cross-platform portability but for its use on the Web.

Preparing a Pre-Acrobat File

Files to be converted to PDF are often files which have already been used as prepress files. Photo information contained in such documents is in CMYK mode, is at a resolution of from 266–300 ppi, and is in a file format such as EPS/DCS or Tiff. Open all the photo files contained in the document. Choose Image | Mode | RGB to convert the images from CMYK. (Intensify the colors if you wish—the Web is not concerned with printable colors and the saturation of your photo documents may be enhanced.) Choose Image | Image Size and change the resolution of the image to 72 ppi. Save this file in the JPEG format. Use Optimized Baseline and Low for quality retention. Replace the photo images in the original document with those you have modified in Photoshop.

If your file contains an Illustrator graphic, follow these steps for best use in Acrobat. Note that these instructions may seem a little involved but they will make the difference between an acceptable document and one of very high quality.

1. Open the Illustrator file.
2. Select All, copy, switch to Photoshop.
3. From the File menu, choose New. The size of the new image is shown.
4. Enter a title, make the resolution 72 ppi, and make the mode RGB.
5. Paste using the Paste as Pixels option.
6. Leave this document open and return to the Illustrator document.
7. If any objects on the outer perimeter of the graphic are stroked objects, convert them to filled objects by using Filter | Object | Outline Stroked Path.
8. Next, choose Object | Rasterize.
9. In the resulting dialog box, choose RGB for the Color Model, Screen for Resolution. Choose also both of the check box options (Anti-alias and Create Mask). Click OK.

10. When the graphic has been rasterized, click on the outer edge of the graphic to select the masking path.
11. Copy this path, switch to Photoshop, and Paste. This time, choose the Paste as Paths option.
12. Save this path and make it into a clipping path.
13. Save the document as an EPS file with the clipping path you have saved.
14. Replace the original Illustrator file in the target document with the one you have just saved from Photoshop.
15. Discard the original Illustrator file.

TIP *Sometimes it becomes necessary to adjust the color on a scan which—in the worst-case scenario—has been converted to Indexed Color mode and for which there is no longer an original to be rescanned. With such an image, a look at the histogram shows that there is very little information with which to make corrections and adjustments. To replace—with mathematically fictitious values which are nonetheless usable—those missing values, convert the file back to RGB mode. Now, choose Image | Image Size. Add one pixel to the number in the Horizontal Pixels data entry field at the top of the window. Click OK. Open the same window (Image Size). Subtract one pixel from the Horizontal Pixels data entry field. Click OK. Photoshop will use its bicubic interpolation scheme and will replace the missing values in your image. You may then proceed with your image adjustment.*

Where to Go From Here

We have explored a variety of issues which are specific to the Internet. The speed of the network connection and how that relates to the size of your graphic files is one issue. Another has to do with the limitations of the file formats which you can use on the Web. Your graphic files need to be as small as possible to minimize the download time for your viewer. Studies of Web users show that the average user's patience begins to grow thin at about 12 seconds into a download. A good strategy is to provide the user with something to do, something to look at, to make the wait worthwhile. This can be done by making use of files saved with interlacement, or by using the LOW SRC technique.

Another way to keep your viewers interested is to make sure that your graphics are as clear and as attractive as possible. This subject, the adjustment and correction of photographic scans, is the only topic of concern to developers for the Web which was not covered in this chapter. For more information, please turn to Chapter 2,"Acquiring Images"; Chapter 9, "Photoshop Prepress"; and Chapter 11, "Manipulating Images." Apply the information learned in these pages to your Web photos to make them as appealing as you can. Pay particular attention to instructions for using the Unsharp Mask filter in Chapter 9. Knowledgeable use of this filter can make the difference between your images looking merely good and looking superb! Good enough, as the saying goes, isn't.

As we come to the end of our look at graphics on the Web, we also come to the end of the book. Photoshop is far too large for a single volume to cover it completely, but we hope we've covered Photoshop's most important and useful capabilities. We've also tried to give you a framework for working out your own solutions to image editing problems. Should you run up against something that you can't solve, remember the resources listed in the Introduction, the authors e-mail addresses, and Ventana's Online community of Photoshop professionals. With luck, we will meet again. Good luck!

appendix A

About the Companion CD-ROM

The Companion CD-ROM included with your copy of *Enhanced Photoshop 4* contains valuable software, clip art, and teaching examples from all of the chapters. The clip art is found in the resource folder. It includes Design Elements, Father of Industrial Design, Grammar of Ornament, MetaPhotos, and Vivid Details Photos.

Navigating the CD-ROM

Your choices for navigating the CD-ROM appear on the opening screen. You can install the software, or learn more about Ventana, or quit the viewer.

If the viewer does not run properly on your machine, follow these instructions.

For optimum Windows performance:

1. Copy the LAUNCHME.EXE and LAUNCHME.INI files to the same directory on your hard drive.
2. Open the LAUNCHME.INI file in a text editor such as Notepad.
3. Find the section in the .INI file that reads:

```
[Memory]
;ExtraMemory=400
; Amount of kBytes over and above physical memory for use by a projector.
```

4. If your computer has enough memory to do so, delete the semicolon from the ExtraMemory line, and change the ExtraMemory setting to a higher number.
5. Save the changes to the LAUNCHME.INI file, and close the text editor.

6. With the CD-ROM still inserted, launch the viewer from the hard drive. If the viewer still does not run properly on your machine, you can access the material on the CD-ROM directly through File Manager (Windows 3.x) or Windows Explorer (Windows 95).

For optimum Macintosh performance:

1. Copy the Launch Me file to your hard drive.
2. Click once on the Launch Me file.
3. Select Get Info from the File menu.
4. If your computer has enough memory to do so, change the amount in the Preferred size field to a higher number.
5. Close the info box.
6. With the CD-ROM still inserted, launch the viewer from the hard drive. If the viewer still does not run properly on your machine, you can access the files on the CD-ROM directly by double-clicking on its icon on the desktop.

Software

The software provided on the Companion CD-ROM is described below in Table A-1.

Software	Description
Cinematte 2.1	Cinematte is a blue/green screen composition software.
ProJPeg 2.1	ProJPeg is a Macintosh file-format plug-in for Adobe Photoshop 3.0 or greater that provides unsurpassed capability for creating and editing highly optimized, Web-ready JPEG and progressive JPEG images. Rated 4 Mice by MacUser online. ProJPeg is a must have tool for Web graphic creation.
PhotoTools 1.1	PhotoTools from Extensis is a collection of eight productivity and "everyday effects" plug-in tools that address many of the most requested features from a variety of Photoshop users. For more information about this and other Extensis products, visit http://www.extensis.com.
HVS Color	A demo of HVS Color, the award-winning color-reduction Export plug-in for Photoshop 3 and 4. This demo will give you an idea of the color reduction quality, but it's not unlockable, and it inserts a watermark in the center of images. An unlockable demo of the next generation HVS ColorGIF 2.0 will be available soon. Visit http://www.digfrontiers.com for more information.
Andromeda Series 1 Photography Filters	A demo version of the Andromeda Series 1 Photography Filters, containing ten special effects lenses. To find out more about Andromeda Software's products, visit http://www.andromeda.com.

➡

Software	Description
Andromeda Series 2 3-D Filters	A demo version of the Andromeda Series 2 3-D Filters, offering surface wrapping, lighting & shading control, and viewpoint control for images. To find out more about Andromeda Software's products, visit http://www.andromeda.com.
Andromeda Series 3 Screens Filters	A demo version of the Andromeda Series 3 Screens Filters, which convert grayscale into mezzotints, mezzograms, line screens, and patterns and specialty screens. To find out more about Andromeda Software's products, visit http://www.andromeda.com.
Andromeda Series 4 Techtures	A demo version of the Andromeda Series 4 Techtures, offering 900 hand-rendered, realistic techtures, maps, and environments to explore and modify. To find out more about Andromeda Software's products, visit http://www.andromeda.com.
Andromeda Velociraptor Filter	A demo version of Andromeda Software's Velociraptor Filter, which lets you create incredibly realistic or stylized motion trails. To find out more about Andromeda Software's products, visit http://www.andromeda.com.
Chromassage	Chromassage creates wild colorization effects within Adobe Photoshop and allows you to try out thousands of color combinations in a blink of an eye. Colors can be manipulated with "jog wheels" that let you rotate and shift hues. Swap colors from 26 built-in palettes. Randomize, invert, reverse, and "steal" colors from existing documents, or infect the image with a "virus of chroma." Chromassage is ideal for use with designs intended for multimedia or artwork destined for high-profile fabric printing and fine art. For more information about Second Glance Software, check out http://www.secondglance.com.
Eye Candy	A demo of the new set of Photoshop plug-ins from Alien Skin Software. Eye Candy 3.0 (formerly known as The Black Box) is the answer to serious Photoshop users' prayers. In seconds these filters create special effects that would normally require hours of hand tweaking. You have probably heard experts explain complex 12-step processes for creating 3D bevels or flames. Now you can stop trying to follow those frustrating recipes and simply use Eye Candy. Version 3.0 makes professional effects even easier by giving you flexible previews and a thumbnail for rapidly navigating your image. Visit http://www.alienskin.com.
HVS JPEG	A plug-in filter that exports superior-quality, progressive JPEGs for use on the Web and in multimedia. HVS JPEG provides the smallest size while maintaining superior graphic image quality via proprietary optimization techniques. This unlockable demo allows customers to use the full-featured product free for seven days, and may be purchased thereafter via a convenient online module. Visit http://www.digfrontiers.com to learn more.

➡

Software	Description
Intellihance	Intellihance gives users the ability to produce professional-looking photos in Adobe Photoshop automatically. A revolutionary photo-enhancement filter that optimizes photo images in a single step, Intellihance allows users to optimize image saturation, sharpness, contrast, brightness, and despeckle, all with one mouse click. Intellihance includes preference controls to modify the intelligent enhancement engine. This is a proven tool that will save you hours of time; it's the ultimate "make better" button. For more information about this and other Extensis products, visit http://www.extensis.com.
Kai's Power Tools 3.0	A demonstration version of MetaCreations, Inc.'s Kai's Power Tools 3.0. KPT 3.0 is available as a 32-bit native application extension for the Intel-based Windows 95/NT platforms, as well as for the Apple Macintosh/Power Macintosh platforms. Kai's Power Tools 3.0 is a unique and powerful collection of extensions that expand the power of image-editing applications which support the Adobe plug-in specifications. Visit http://www.metacreations.com.
LaserSeps Pro	LaserSeps Pro is an export filter for Adobe Photoshop that creates stochastic screens for process color separations. Since there are no screen angles involved, problems with registration, moiré patterns, and rosettes are dramatically reduced. Files are output in industry standard DCS 2.0 format and support advanced features such as white plate and underprint masks. Ideal for the textile industry. For more information about Second Glance Software, check out http://www.secondglance.com.
PhotoSpot	PhotoSpot is a series of filters and export functions designed to facilitate spot-color separation from within Photoshop. Special color reduction filters enable the artist to control the separation process from 2 to 500 colors. For more information about Second Glance Software, check out http://www.secondglance.com.
Photo/Graphic Edges 3.0	A demo version of Auto F/X's Photoshop plug-in compatible graphic design product. Visit http://www.autofx.com for more information.
Photo/Graphic Patterns 1.0	A demo version of Auto F/X's Photoshop plug-in compatible graphic design product. Visit http://www.autofx.com for more information.
The Ultimate Texture Collection 1.0	A demo version of Auto F/X's Photoshop plug-in compatible graphic design product, including three sample textures and an example of a lighting tile. This is a full working demo and will fuse a texture like the full version, but it will only work with demo version textures. The full version will work with any texture file. Visit http://www.autofx.com for more information.
Typo/Graphic Edges	A demo version of Auto F/X's Photoshop plug-in compatible graphic design product. Visit http://www.autofx.com for more information.

Software	Description
Vertigo 3D Dizzy 3.0	Vertigo 3D lets Adobe Photoshop users easily add 3D models to their designs. Users can change the orientation and size of models and add lights before positioning the models in Photoshop. Check out Vertigo Technology, Inc. at http://www.vertigo3d.com.
Design Elements	Design Elements by Ultimate Symbol—the highest quality EPS, GIT and JPEG, images available for professional designers. Go to the resource folder.
Flo	Flo for Mac or Windows is a single layer warping and animation software that reshapes/animates images professionally. To get more information visit http://www.valisgroup.com.
Metaflo Web	Metaflo for Mac reshapes, morphs, animates, imports Photoshop layers; includes flo; and acts as a Photoshop plug-in. For more information, visit http://www.valisgroup.com.
Texture Creator 2.0	Texture Creator is the ultimate tool for creating an endless variety of photo-realistic textures.
Vertigo 3D HotText 1.0	Vertigo 3D HotText lets you add real 3D texts and 3D paths to Adobe Photoshop. Add custom lighting effects, colors, and textures.
Vertigo 3D Words 1.0	3D Words add real text and path to Adobe Illustrator.
Test Strip 1.1	Test Strip 1.1 is a Photoshop plug-in for color correction and color proofing.
Vivid Details Photos	Vivid Details Photos-images on CD-ROM. Go to the resource folder.
Paint Alchemy 2.0	Paint Alchemy is an art studio within Photoshop.
Terrazzo 2.0	Terrazzo makes Web pages tile with ease.
TypeCaster 1.15	TypeCaster makes 3D type programs unnecessary outside of Photoshop.
MetaPhotos	MetaPhotos is a series of high-quality, royalty-free images on CD-ROM. Choose from thousands of carefully art-directed photo poses, still lifes, image objects, and backgrounds. Go to the resource folder.
PhotoGIF 2.1.x3	PhotoGIF 2.1 is a Macintosh file-format plug-in for Adobe Photoshop 3.0 or greater that provides unsurpassed capability for creating and editing highly optimized, Web-ready GIFs and GIF animations. Named a 1996 MacUser Eddy Award Finalist in the Best New Production Tool class and rated 5 Mice by MacUser Online, PhotoGIF is a must-have tool for Web graphic creation. For more information, please visit http://www.boxtopsoft.com.
Painter 4	Painter 4 is a natural-media paint and image editing program.
WildRiverSSK	WildRiverSSK is a specular effects Plug-In Suite for Photoshop. Plug-ins are divided into 3 groups. The manipulation, CHOP "ChanneLops," Noise Plug-ins.

➡

Software	Description
Mask Pro 1.0	Mask Pro—Image masking and silhouetting so fast you'll think its magic.
Adobe Illustrator 7.0	With unmatched flexibility, Adobe Illustrator® 7.0 is the industry-standard illustration software. Its new, streamlined interface delivers a truly seamless workflow across Windows® and Macintosh® platforms and between your favorite Adobe applications. Broad-based file format support, layers, improved precision, speedy image hand—ling, and many more new features make Adobe Illustrator the ideal choice, whether you're creating for print, multimedia, or the Web.
Adobe Photoshop	Create, paint, correct, and retouch with the "camera for your mind" [MWU].
Father of Industrial Design, Works of Christopher Dresser	The Father of Industrial Design consists of two books by Christopher Dresser, a prolific genius who initiated abstraction and the use of original designs around the beginning of the Industrial Revolution. Go to the resource folder.
Grammar of Ornament	The Grammar of Ornament is a reproduction of Owen Jones' masterpiece collection of art from around the world through the ages. Go to the resource folder.
DeBabelizer Lite	With over 55 graphics readers and writers, DeBabelizer Lite is perfect for simple image translation and slideshow functions. Its compatibility with Photoshop Filter, Acquire, and Export plug-ins also provides an extremely cost effective filtering solution. For bit-mapped, scan, or paint files, DeBabelizer Lite offers nearly the same translation capabilities as DeBabelizer Toolbox without the internal scripting, image processing, or palette manipulation. Slideshow creates onscreen thumbnails of a folder full of images which can all be translated automatically. DeBabelizer Lite intelligently maintains maximum color integrity and quality to and from each format and platform. Scan or digitize images with Photoshop (and 3rd party) acquire plug-ins. Visit http://www.equilibrium.com.
DeBabelizer Pro for Windows	Equilibrium's DeBabelizer Pro for Windows 95 and NT 4.0 is a comprehensive automated application for anyone working with graphics, animations, and digital video in multimedia, Web, and desktop productions. With its intuitive interface, digital designers can easily perform any number of graphics processes to an unlimited number of images or frames. Users can also create an optimized SuperPalette for an entire batch of stills or movies, and output everything to over 90 point-mapped file formats. Additionally, Wizards are set up to automate many popular processes such as optimizing images for digital video or preparing graphics for Web delivery. DeBabelizer Pro for Windows also supports most Photoshop Import, Filter and Export plug-ins. The multi-image file capabilities of DeBabelizer Pro are awesome! Multiple frames can be converted into AVI movies and optimized for any target platform with full compression support. Visit http://www.equilibrium.com.

➡

Software	Description
DeBelizer Toolbox for Mac	DeBabelizer Toolbox is an essential tool for anyone working with computer graphics. This award-winning product combines graphics processing, palette optimization, and translation in one program. With easy "Watch Me" scripting and batch features, thousands of images can be processed automatically to specifications. A true production powerhouse, DeBabelizer Toolbox translates between 70+ bit-mapped graphics, animation, and digital video formats, including DOS/Windows, Amiga, Sun, XWindows, Alias, Electric Image, SoftImage formats, and more. DeBabelizer Toolbox supports Photoshop and third-party Acquire, Filter, and Export plug-ins, as well as AppleScript. It includes dozens of image-editing and palette-manipulation tools, including SuperPalette which automatically creates the best palette for a series of images. DeBabelizer Toolbox complements all paint, scan, and image processing programs. Visit http://www.equilibrium.com.

Table A-1: Software provided on the Companion CD-ROM.

Technical Support

Technical support is available for installation-related problems only. The technical support office is open from 8:00 A.M. to 6:00 P.M. Monday through Friday and can be reached via the following methods:

- Phone: (919) 544-9404 extension 81
- Faxback Answer System: (919) 544-9404 extension 85
- E-mail: help@vmedia.com
- FAX: (919) 544-9472
- World Wide Web: **http://www.vmedia.com/support**
- America Online: keyword *Ventana*

Limits of Liability & Disclaimer of Warranty

The authors and publisher of this book have used their best efforts in preparing the CD-ROM and the programs contained in it. These efforts include the development, research, and testing of the theories and programs to determine their effectiveness. The authors and publisher make no warranty of any kind expressed or implied, with regard to these programs or the documentation contained in this book.

The authors and publisher shall not be liable in the event of incidental or consequential damages in connection with, or arising out of, the furnishing, performance, or use of the programs, associated instructions, and/or claims of productivity gains.

Some of the software on this CD-ROM is shareware; there may be additional charges (owed to the software authors/makers) incurred for their registration and continued use. See individual program's README or VREADME.TXT files for more information.

appendix B

Common Prepress Terms & Definitions

24-bit color

RGB monitors display 8-bit brightness values (256) for each of the monitor phosphors, red, green, and blue. The number of combinations which can be assigned to any monitor pixel is $256^3 = 16{,}777{,}216$, the total number of colors the monitor can display.

Accurate Screens

Software program from Adobe Systems, Inc., a proprietary PostScript screening model based on supercells. Supercells simplify the creation of screen dots by rationalizing conventional screen angles with cell groups in which dots of the same percentage may be unlike each other and can be fitted to a raster grid in an integer relationship. For further information, please consult *PostScript Screening: Adobe Accurate Screens* by Peter Fink; Adobe Press; ISBN 0-672-48544-3.

Amplitude modulated

Refers to conventional screen dots which increase in size with the increase of ink density requirements. More simply, as ink values become darker, larger dots are required to print them. Within the total range of values—theoretically 256—ink requirements, and indirectly tone requirements, modulate the amplitude of the dot. (See also *Frequency modulated*.)

Art board

Bronze-age artifact used to mount unwieldy strips of type, artwork, and masks. The finished board was then photographed (see *Line shot*) with the resulting negative used as a mask for making a printing plate.

Black
One of the process inks, added on press to improve the sharpness and purity of shadow tones, and to reduce the overall amount of ink required for color reproduction. (See also *GCR*, *UCR*, and *Black generation*.)

Black generation
Process in which black ink is substituted for neutral tones produced by cyan, magenta, and yellow.

Blanket
In offset printing, ink is transferred from the plate to the offset blanket. The blanket transfers the ink to the press sheet.

Blown out
When highlight tones in an image have been too drastically lightened, they produce areas on a printed image in which there is no ink. These areas are said to be blown out. The effect is not attractive.

Blue
Beyond the color definition, *blue* is printer slang for cyan.

Blueline
Exposure of blueprint paper masked by plate-ready film produces a blue-toned simulation of the printed piece. The blueline is used for customer approval of a job and to test to see that imposition and work-and-turn backups are correct.

Brightness
Brightness is the amount of light seen reflected from an illuminated object. Brightness values vary with position and distance from the object being viewed. In computer terms, brightness is the generic term for the values between black and white. It is usually applied to a pixel. These two uses of the word are examples of one word describing similar phenomena within two visual paradigms: reflected light and emitted light.

Bump plate
Plate used to overprint an additional amount of ink on an already printed area in order to intensify the color.

Choke
Trapping term indicating that a surrounding color/ink has slightly overlapped the object of a different color/ink which it encloses.

CIE
Centre Internationale d'Eclairage, International Color Definitions Standards Committee.

Clipping path

Beziér outline saved with a Photoshop document which acts as a mask. Pixels within the perimeter of the path are visible, all others appear transparent. Used to make irregular-shaped photo images.

CMS

Color Management System, a system for harmonizing the color and color-handling characteristics of different digital devices. Such devices might include scanners, monitors, and color output devices. CMS strategies are usually based on an accurate analysis of the color throughput for each device.

CMYK

Cyan, magenta, yellow, and black, the four process color inks used for the great majority of color reproduction.

Color Sync

Integrated system-level color manage software by Apple Computer, Inc. Designed to be used by software publishers who can tie into this built-in capability and use it for in-program color management.

Colorimeter

Device for accurately measuring the characteristics of colors.

Colorize

Term used in several ways, all of which indicate the addition or substitution of non-black colors when reproducing a monotone image.

Colortron II

Monitor calibration instrument by Light Source, Inc. Can also be used as a Colorimeter and as a Densitometer. (See *Densitometer* and *Colorimeter*.)

Custom Color

Four-color process printing achieves different colors by mixing tints on press. Custom colors are premixed to give a single solid color value as well as tints. Custom colors are often used for color values which cannot be produced by the four process inks.

Cyan

One of the four process color inks. Provides the blue component of color images.

DCS

Desktop Color Separation. File format designed by Quark, Inc. which separates the separate ink components of a CMYK document into four separate files linked to a master file.

DCS 2.0
Extension of the DCS format which allows more than four files to be linked to the master file. This allows process color and spot colors to be saved within the same file.

Densitometer
Device used to measure the amount of ink coverage within a given area. Densitometers are used to measure the difference between known input values and values which press conditions give.

Device profiles
Descriptive files which accurately describe the color throughput characteristics of digital devices within a color-managed environment.

Digital proof
Simulation of a print job based on a digital printer's interpretation of what the job will probably look like on press.

Dot gain
When liquid ink is applied to the press sheet, it spreads out slightly. This results in a darker tone. The difference between the dots on the plate and the dots of ink on the page, when measured in an area of 50% tone, is called dot gain.

DPI
Dots per inch. Clumsy, inelegant term that may refer to several different things. There are other, more accurate terms that have the advantage of a narrowly focused meaning.

Drum scanner
High-quality scanner/digitizer which uses vacuum tube photomultiplier sensors.

DTP
Desktop Publishing; name given to microcomputer preparation of press materials. The more-or-less simultaneous introduction of the Macintosh computer by Apple Computer, Inc., the PostScript page description language and PostScript-driven printers, and the Aldus Corporation's PageMaker program ushered in the era of DTP.

Duotone
When a grayscale image is printed with two inks, each plate of which is derived from a different interpretation of the image's gray values, it is said to be duotoned. Duotoning is used to colorize grayscale images or to extend the tonal range far beyond what can be achieved with a single ink.

Eight-bit color
System in which the total number of tones is limited to 256. The tones present can be grayscale or an adaptive sampling of colors from a color image.

EPS
Encapsulated PostScript, a file format in widespread use in the prepress community because of its ability to provide trouble-free output on PostScript devices. EPS files are capable of embedding screening information, tone controls, and clipping paths.

Film
Prepress files are typically output as film. For offset printing, a negative image is used as a mask for making a plate. Some other kinds of printing require the film mask to be positive.

Film processor
Device in which film exposed by the laser assembly in an imagesetter is developed.

Flap
Associated with art boards, a flap is a sheet of transparent overlay material to which is attached some element of the art board page. The flap is usually taped into place so that the element's placement is superimposed upon other art board elements.

Flatbed Scanner
Usually a low-end scanner which makes use of CCD (Charge Coupled Device) sensors. Flatbed scanners usually do not have the optical or color sensitivity of drum scanners. However, they are far less expensive.

Flood
When inks or transparent coatings are applied by a press over the entire surface of the press sheet, the coating is said to be flooded.

Frequency modulated
Screening system which uses small, uniform screen dots distributed at random. Density is achieved by increasing the number of dots—as opposed to Amplitude Modulated dots which increase density by increasing the dot size. FM screening technology achieves a precision of detail that is far superior to AM screening.

GCR
Gray Component Replacement, black generation algorithm in which black is pumped into tones composed of the other three inks. This has the effect of purifying the color in areas of heavy coverage, making shadow tones more crisp and using less ink on press.

Grayscale
Photoshop display mode for working with monotone images.

Halftone
When grayscale digital images are converted to output for press purposes, gray values are changed to screen dots. This process is called halftoning, and the word has been extended to describe the printing of monotone images.

Halftone cell

When a PostScript output device converts 8-bit information to screen dots, it does so by dividing its resolution by the requested line-screen value. It then sets up a square area with the result number on each side (the cell). Screen dots are then constructed to fill percentages of the area.

Hexachrome

Ultra high-fidelity color printing process developed by Pantone, Inc. which increases the printable tone range by a large amount. The process uses four specially formulated process color inks (CMYK) and two additional ink colors, green and orange.

High contrast

By decreasing the number of values in an image, more weight can be given to those which remain. With this procedure, related values become farther apart, and with noticeable difference between them. Detail is sacrificed for the purpose of image drama.

High fidelity printing

One of several strategies devised by the printing industry to increase the tonal fidelity of color-image reproduction. The process nearly always requires the use of more than four inks. The Pantone Hexachrome method (see above) is one of these competing strategies.

High key

Image in which the majority of values present are very light.

Highlight Dot

The small screen dots which are used to represent very light tonal values.

Highlight dot fall-off

In offset printing, the mechanical process sometimes prevents very small highlight dots from printing. The range of tones from white to one of the low percentages—such as 5%—is called the highlight dot fall-off range.

Histogram

In digital photo manipulation schemes, histograms display the range of values in an image by constructing what appears to be a miniature bar graph. This graph ranges the values from dark to light, and is called a histogram.

Hue error

Percentage of hue deviation from pure caused by a color's contamination with small amounts of other colors. Where process inks are measured for hue error, the contaminants for each ink are percentages of other inks. Yellow ink, for example, has a hue error which results from contamination of percentages of cyan and magenta.

Image contrast

Overall description of the range of values in a photo image. When the image contains a broad range of tones that are naturally distributed, the contrast is said to be good. When the image shows a range of detail but relatively few tones, the contrast is said to be poor.

Imposition

Refers to the process of separating sequential pages into a non-sequential order so that, as multiple pages are placed on a single press sheet, folding the press sheet results in the pages running in proper finished order. (See also *Reader spreads* and *Printer spreads*.)

Input value

When digital values are processed by an output device, they are said to be the Input values.

Interpolated resolution

When a raster image is resized, pixels must be added or subtracted. The process of calculating new values for pixels which must be added, or of deciding which pixels should be discarded, is called interpolating the resolution.

JPEG

Acronym for Joint Photograph Experts Group which formulated a compression method for storing photographic images for the purpose of decreasing their size while stored on disk or when transmitted by electronic means.

Keyline

Term referring to the placement of elements on an artboard.

Knock out

When an area of one color needs to print within the boundaries of another color but overprinting would result in an unwanted color, a space the shape of the first object is knocked out of the area of the second color.

Lab color

Color model used as the behind-the-scenes color space in programs such as Adobe Photoshop. The advantage of Lab color is that it enunciates color values without reference to specific electronic or output devices. Because of this, it is said to be a device-independent color model.

Laminate proof

Color proof used to match values on press. This proof is usually made from the same film used for the plating. The four tones are laid atop each other in a laminating process. Laminate proofs are the current proof-of-choice for the printing industry.

Lightness
Lightness refers to the natural tones of a surface from which light is reflected. A white wall and a black fabric are examples of differing degrees of lightness.

Line art
Line art refers to print artwork that is usually non-photographic and composed of more-or-less simple shapes that are printed with one ink.

Line screen
Also know as *Screen frequency*, line screen refers to the number of rows of screen dots in some unit of measurement. Smaller numbers indicate larger dots while larger numbers indicate finer dots.

Line shot
When a finished artboard is converted to film, the process of photographing it is called a line shot.

Lossy
Refers to file compression methods that result in permanent data loss. Should not be used in polite company because it is an ugly word. Lossy, indeed!

Low contrast
This term describes a photographic image in which too few tones are present to accurately show details in the image.

Low key
When the tones in a photographic image contain mostly dark tones, it is described as a low key image.

LPC
Screen frequency abbreviation; the letters stand for *lines per centimeter*.

LPI
Screen frequency abbreviation; the letters stand for *lines per inch*.

Magenta
The reddish component in four-color process printing.

Maximum black
When black ink is added to a color separation, this term expresses the highest allowable percentage with which the separation algorithm is governed.

Maximum shadow dot
Because press gain darkens an image, black inks are usually limited to some input percentage that is smaller than 100% because the smaller percentage will grow, on press, to 100%.

Metallics
Specialty inks containing metal flakes which give a metallic surface texture wherever the ink has been applied.

Midtone
In photographic images, the midtones are the range of values that fall into the percentage range between 30% and 70%.

Midtone gain
Dot gain refers to the growth of the dot on press. The percentage of growth is at its highest for tones of 50%. Measurements of gain are always made on areas of 50% and are referred to as midtone gain.

Minimum highlight dot
Refers to the smallest dot that a press can actually reproduce.

Monitor calibration
Analysis by an external device of a monitor's display characteristics. After evaluation, calibration software then brings the monitor display into line with some predetermined standard.

Negs
Slang for the negative films used to make plates.

Neutral tones
Printed tones in which no colored inks predominate and which appears to be a uniform gray.

Offset
Presses which use a plate to transfer ink to a blanket which then imprints the press sheet print by the process called offset. This differs from presses that imprint the press sheet directly from the plate.

Out-of-gamut color
On an RGB monitor, out-of-gamut colors are those that the monitor can display but which cannot be duplicated with process color inks.

Output value
This value is the measured result of an output device. System calibrations are always made by comparing this value to Input values.

Overlay proof
Older proofing method in which clear flaps containing colored dots were carefully laid atop each other to emulate press output.

Overprint
When one color is printed atop an area of the press sheet already containing one or more inks, it is said to overprint.

Pantone
Company which has been responsible for vending a wide array of custom colors and a color matching system as a standard for the printing industry.

Perfecting press
Sophisticated press in which two offset blankets simultaneously imprint both sides of a press sheet.

Plate
The master of the printed pages which receives the ink from a press ink font and either transfers the ink to a blanket or directly imprints the page.

Plugged
Refers to a press condition in which, for various reasons, too much ink is being applied. Image details become obliterated and letter counters become filled in.

PostScript
Page description computer programming language used to describe the objects on a page to an output device which controls the imaging assembly. PostScript is published by Adobe Systems, Inc. As a cultural achievement, it ranks with—and probably rivals—the much vaunted accomplishments of Johann Gutenburg, the inventor of movable type, which led to mass-produced books and widespread human literacy.

PPI
Pixels per inch, a measurement of the resolution of a scanned image.

Prepress
Prepress refers to the preparation of materials for printing.

Press
Device for applying ink to paper for the mass distribution of printed material.

Press gain
Refers to the growth of screens dots on press as a factor of darkening.

Press misregistration
When a press sheet passes through several inking stations, the press sheet can become slightly misaligned with the press. This results in ink areas becoming inaccurately registered to each other.

Printer spreads
Refers to page sequence on a press sheet that results in sequential pages when the press sheet is imprinted on both sides and then folded to produce a multi-page book.

Process color
Color reproduction is typically accomplished by mixing, on press, four primary tones which combine to produce thousands of other colors. The four primary tones are cyan, magenta, yellow, and black.

Proportional color reduction trapping
When colors are overlapped for trapping purposes, the zone of overlap usually shows up as a darker line. If the amount of ink is reduced proportionally within the zone of overlap, the trapping remains but without the visually intrusive dark line.

Quadtone
Similar to a duotone but produced with four inks.

Raster grid
On a PostScript output device, the raster grid is the theoretical grid on the image plane which defines the smallest mark the device can make. All output is composed of shapes built from these small, square-shaped marks.

Rasterize
Graphic shapes such as type are simply scaled versions of curve segments which outline an area. Rasterizing is the process where these segments are rationalized to a gridded environment such as a pixel or the squares of a raster grid.

Reader spreads
Printed documents are often designed as spreads which, on the computer screen, resemble what the eventual reader of the information will see. The pages of reader spreads are eventually taken apart and reassembled as printer spreads.

Red
Beyond the color definition, *red* is printer slang for magenta.

RGB
The pixels of a computer monitor use an additive color system to build up different colors using three primary colors, red, green, and blue.

RIP
Archaic funeral monument inscription admonishing the departed to Rest In Peace. Also, the imaging computer associated with an output device which converts vector objects (and low-resolution raster objects) to a high-resolution raster configuration: Raster Image Processor.

Screen
Refers to the lithographic process of converting inks to small dots of various sizes which blend with the white of the page upon which they are printed to produce many degrees of a single tone.

Screen angle
Four-color process screens are imaged so that each ink's screen dots follow an angle that is different from the other three inks. Yellow is typically printed at 0°, black at 45°, and the remaining two at 90° - 15° = 75° and 0° + 15° = 15°.

Screen dot
Tiny spot of ink which represents some percentage of color density on a printed page.

Screen print
Screen printing is an ink application method using fine-mesh fabrics stretched over frames. The fabric is flood coated with a resist substance that fills in the spaces between the fabric threads. Later, parts of the resist are removed. The frame is then placed over the material to be printed, flooded with ink, and a wiper blade—similar to the windshield blade on an automobile—passes across the fabric forcing the ink through the mesh wherever the resist substance has been removed.

Separations
Color images, before they can be printed, are separated into four components—cyan, magenta, yellow, and black—so that the colors can overprint to produce the colors of the image when printed.

Shadow
Refers to the dark areas of an image.

Sharpen
When an image is prepared for printing, it is usually put through a process that artificially enhances edge contrasts to produce a clearer and more detail-laden image.

Sheet-fed press
Press through which pass pre-cut sheets of paper.

Spot
This term can be used to refer to a lithographic dot. It also indicates an added color printed with a pre-mixed ink.

Spot function
When a RIP builds up screen dots, it can produce many dot shapes. The process of building dots that are square or round or oval or linear is called the RIP's spot function.

Spread
Two sequential pages in a printed presentation are called a spread. Even-numbered pages are on the left of a spread, odd-numbered pages on the right.

Spread also refers to a trapping procedure where a color is artificially extended—spread—past its own boundaries.

Step wedge
One term describing a bar with discrete areas of ink percentages. For example, a step wedge might contain 10 sections with each section 10% greater than its neighbor on one side and smaller than its neighbor on the other side.

Stochastic
From the Greek word *Stochastikos* meaning *skillful in aiming*. This term is used to describe the random-appearing assignment of dot placement in an FM screen.

Stripper
Prepress technician responsible for the final assembly of elements from which a plate-mask film is to be made.

You might want to make up your own print-specific fun definition. Your non-printing-industry friends will never believe you anyway. How about this one: print plant personnel who scrapes the tea leaves from the bottoms of break room cups to determine if tomorrow's large press run will be successful. OK?

Surprint
Overprint.

SWOP
Specification for Web Offset Printing.

TIFF
Tag Image File Format. One of the oldest and most flexible of disk file formats used for images.

Tone
Word often applied sloppily to a range of values.

Touch plate
Plate used to supplement process color work by overprinting—often a tint—a spot color in an area where process colors cannot achieve a desired tone.

Transfer function
A set of values which can be embedded in an image file to override the controls of an output device which has been diagnosed as delivering faulty output.

Trapping
Refers to the process of deliberately making color areas overlap each other to counteract the gaps which can form due to press registration. (See also *Choke* and *Spread*.)

Tritone
Similar to a duotone but using three inks.

TruMatch
Color matching system based on colors which can be achieved by the four process inks.

Two-up, four-up, etc.
On a press, two-up or four-up refers to printing two or four of the same piece on one larger sheet so that the press sheet needs to pass through the press half as many times or a quarter as many times. This passes the responsibility for the number of needed pieces from the pressman to the bindery department in a print plant.

UCR
Under Color Removal, another black generation strategy which adds black and removes colored inks only in areas where the colored inks produce true neutrals.

Under Color Addition
In a GCR separation, this process subtracts black ink and pumps in more colored inks to produce richer dark tones which possess more detail.

Unsharp Mask
Photoshop filter used to give images sharpness lost in the digitizing (scanning) process. (See also *Sharpening*.)

Value
Value is what a photographer measures with a light meter in order to calculate the proper exposure for a camera shot.

Web press
Large, high-speed press used for large numbers of printed pieces such as newspapers. Web refers to the fact that paper is fed into the press as a continuous sheet from large rolls. The individual pages are cut apart and stacked at the finishing end of the press. Web presses often have two rolls of paper feeding into them—they are then called *double webs*—which are printed simultaneously front and back. The web sheet moves through the press at such a high rate of speed that it must pass through an oven to ensure that the ink is sufficiently dry before it reaches the finishing end.

Work and turn
When pages are to be printed on both sides on a non-perfecting press, the job is often worked two-up or-four-up with, for example, one front and one back. After the first run is finished, the sheets are turned over and run through the press so that the front and back of the pages are printed on the appropriate place on the sheet's opposite side. With this procedure, the entire job can be done with a single set of plates. By contrast, printing all fronts in one run and all backs on another run would require two sets of plates and considerable extra expense.

WYSIWYG
Acronym from the early days of digital prepress. Stands for *What You See Is What You Get*, a bit of market hype that everyone learned soon enough was, to be charitable, wishful thinking.

Yellow
One of the process color inks. Contributes yellow and gold tones to a printed image.

Index

A

B

C

E

F

G

H

I

J–K

L

M

T

Z

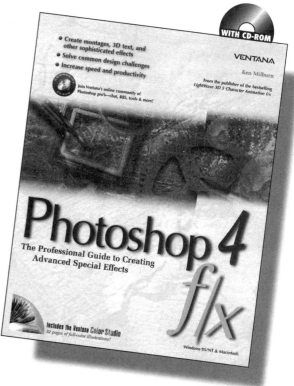

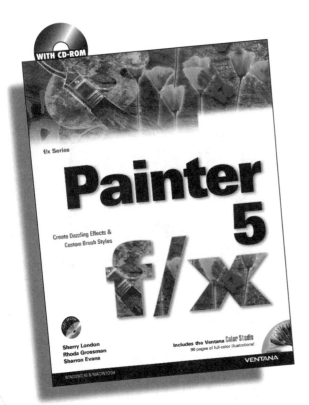

VENTANA

3D Studio MAX f/x

$49.99, 552 pages, illustrated, part #: 1-56604-427-8

Create Hollywood-style special effects! Plunge into 3D animation with step-by-step instructions for lighting, camera movements, optical effects, texture maps, storyboarding, cinematography, editing and much more. The companion CD-ROM features free plug-ins, all the tutorials from the book, 300+ original texture maps and animations.

RayDream 5 f/x

$49.99, 640 pages, illustrated, part #: 1-56604-755-2

R. Shamms Mortier
Windows 95/NT & Macintosh
Intermediate to Advanced

- Feature-rich tutorials covering advanced modeling, rendering, animation, FX filters and more.
- Instructions and guidelines for outputting projects for the Web.
- Includes 25 project tutorials and a Ventana Color Studio section with 96-pages of full-color illustrations.

CD-ROM: Tutorial files, 3D models, graphics and demos.

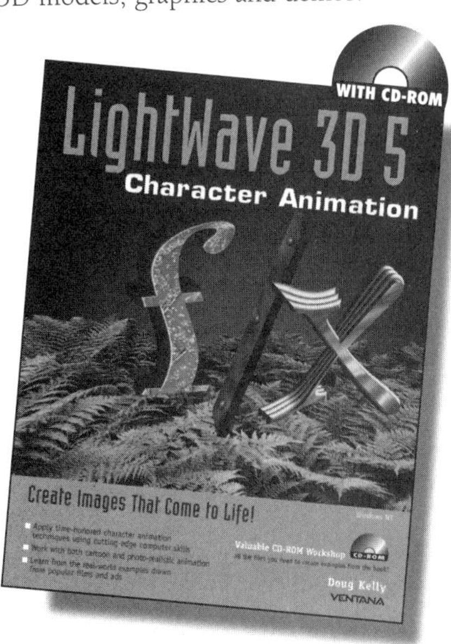

LightWave 3D 5 Character Animation f/x

$49.99, 744 pages, illustrated, part #: 1-56604-532-0

Master the fine—and lucrative—art of 3D character animation. Traditional animators and computer graphic artists alike will discover everything they need to know: lighting, motion, caricature, composition, rendering ... right down to work-flow strategies. The CD-ROM features a collection of the most popular LightWave plug-ins, scripts, storyboards, finished animations, models and much more.